WORKING A DEMOC

Extracts from Reviews

'Another monumental work of reference and subtle interpretation to follow Austin's classic work on the making of the Indian Constitution... he traces the working of the constitution in the turmoil of Indian political life. But this is no dry 'constitutional history. A "must" for libraries, and for serious students of the subcontinent.'
—Judith Brown, Beit Professor of Commonwealth History, Oxford University

'... a book that deserves to rank among the half dozen or so most outstanding publications on the affairs of India written over the last two or three decades.'
—K. M. de Silva, Executive Director of the International Centre for Ethnic Studies, Sri Lanka

'Granville Austin in this splendid study has succeeded, as no one else has.... Austin demonstrates, through a sure command of political and cultural history, how the constitution has made possible an open society, with a lively free press, a judiciary that has maintained its independence, and an electoral system that is equal to those of the established democracies of the West.'
—Ainslie T. Embree, Columbia University

'An enchanting narrative... it gives masterly guidance for the common man, the lawyer, the politician and the academic.'
—*Deccan Herald*

'This giant of a book holds lessons for many of the political conundrums of our age.'
—*The Hindu*

'The book is a treasure trove of knowledge.'
—*The Tribune*

'Granville Austin's study is as much about the course of India's political development as it is about the working of its constitution. ... Very few can match his industry, integrity and talent for delivering candid censure in measured words.'
—*Frontline*

WORKING A DEMOCRATIC CONSTITUTION

A History of the Indian Experience

Granville Austin

OXFORD
UNIVERSITY PRESS

OXFORD
UNIVERSITY PRESS

Oxford University Press is a department of the University of Oxford.
It furthers the University's objective of excellence in research, scholarship,
and education by publishing worldwide. Oxford is a registered trademark of
Oxford University Press in the UK and in certain other countries

Published in India by
Oxford University Press
YMCA Library Building, 1 Jai Singh Road, New Delhi 110001, India

© Granville Austin 1999

The moral rights of the author have been asserted

First Edition published in 1999
Oxford India Paperbacks 2003

ISBN-13: 978-0-19-565610-7
ISBN-10: 0-19-565610-5

Typeset by Eleven Arts, Keshav Puram, Delhi 110 035
Printed in India by Replika Press Pvt. Ltd.

To
N M A
Research Colleague
Relentless Editor
Forbearing Wife

ACKNOWLEDGEMENTS

These well could consume the number of pages defaced here. For nearly everyone involved over the ten years spent researching and writing this book has been helpful. Many have been extraordinarily generous with time, information, and counsel. Some have assisted me in access to private papers. All have given me moral support—not a negligible contribution as the months passed by. With pleasure, I could dedicate a paragraph to each of them. That *would* be a book in itself. But I shall hope that each of the individuals and institutions named will appreciate the extent and the warmth of my gratitude to them.

Institutions

The Warden and Fellows of St Antony's College, Oxford, who awarded me a research fellowship, and where in the sixties I wrote the *Cornerstone* book.

The Ford Foundation, which provided generous financial support, and particularly to R. Sudarshan, Gordon Conway, David Arnold, and Gowher Rizvi.

The American Institute of Indian Studies for generous financial and administrative support, especially to Surinder Suri there.

The Rockfeller Foundation for its award of a residency at the Villa Serbelloni, where I tackled the conclusion to the book.

The Woodrow Wilson International Center for Scholars, for a year to write, and especially to Charles Blitzer and Mary Brown Bullock.

The Fulbright Program for financial support for completing my research.

The Nehru Memorial Museum and Library for unlimited kindness, research assistance and collegial support; especially there to Ravinder Kumar, Hari Dev Sharma (extra-especially), Ms Satinder Kaur, Mr N. C. Mahajan, Ms Usha Gururaj, D. S. Routela, and Moti Ram, and the indefatigable photocopiers—A. K. Avasthi, U. C. Mandal, and D. C. Goswami.

The Parliament Library for unfailing willingness to help, especially to sometime Lok Sabha Secretary General Subhash Kashyap, G. C. Malhotra, Mrs Prem Wadhwa, Mrs Sarojbala, and R. L. Shali.

The Indian Law Institute Library for guidance through the intricacies of law reports, and sometimes of the law—especially the librarian, Pramod Singh.

The Law Commission, especially its wise and long-time member-secretary, P. M. Bakshi.

The Centre for Policy Research for collegiality and guidance (many of whose fellows are mentioned below) and the ever-helpful librarian, Kamal Jit Kumar.

The India International Centre, which is not only the most civilized hostelry in India, under the management of Lalit Joshi and the overall direction of sometime director Eric Gonsalves and its present director, N. N. Vohra, but which also possesses a good library.

The National Institute of Panjab Studies, especially to Mohinder Singh and Ms Kaur.

The Indian Institute Library in Oxford, and especially there to Elizabeth Krishna.

The Institute of Current World Affairs, which years ago supported my first venture into India and the resulting *Cornerstone* book—especially Richard Nolte. And to the late Francis Carnell, who at Oxford shepherded me through that book.

Individuals

These are divided into several groups, beginning with those friends, colleagues, and mentors who risked their reputations by supporting my applications to various institutions for funding to support research and writing. In no particular order, they are: Ainslie Embree, W. H. Morris-Jones, Soli Sorabjee, Howard Wriggins, Kingsley DeSilva, Stanley Kochanek, and Phillips Talbot.

Equally daring individuals read the typescript and gave me their comments and advice. At the top of this list goes Thomas P. Thornton, who suffered through every page and whose critique may be credited with many of whatever virtues the book may have. Howard Wriggins read two portions of the book and made trenchant comments. In India, more than a dozen friends—all active or retired judges, lawyers, civil servants, politicians, academics, and journalists—read and advised me about one or more segments of the draft. One senior advocate read the entire typescript, keeping an eye open for errors in my account of the law, court cases, and so on. I hope that I have made all the corrections necessary. To these individuals, I am exceedingly grateful. They know who they are and how thankful to them I am. But I do not name them to avoid their being thought guilty by association.

I thank the following persons for their permissions to see collections of private papers in the Nehru Library that otherwise would not have been open to me: V. N. Gadgil for access to his father N. V. Gadgil's papers; N. Balakrishnan for access to the All India Congress Committee papers; V. S. Patil for access to his father S. K. Patil's papers; K. S. Ramanujan for access to his father K. Santhanam's papers; S. D. Deshmukh for access to his brother C. D. Deshmukh's papers; S. R. Jahagirdar for access to her father P. B. Gajendragadkar's papers; and Gopal Gandhi for access to C. Rajagopalachari's papers. In each case, access also is attributable to Hari Dev Sharma's invaluable assistance.

Sumi Krishna and A. N. Kaul helped me with research.

Then there have been the friendly associates, friendly colleagues, and just plain friends who in one way or another, or in several ways, have sustained me—and my research colleague and stern editor, NMA—through the years. Some of them go back to my first visit to India in 1960. P. H. Vaishnav qualifies as a godfather of this enterprise, and he knows why. Others include—and they all could go into a category of the extraordinarily kind and helpful—in no order whatsoever: Monu and Chanchal Sarkar, Rupa Janson and Sheelu Uttam Singh, Reka and Inder Malhotra, Sarojini and Pran Chopra, Bapsy and Fali Nariman, Smita and Anil Divan, Soli Sorabjee, Zena Sorabjee, K. K. Venugopal, Ajit Bhattacharjea, Monika, Naqeen, and Habib Tanvir, Shanta and S. Guhan, Premila and Nirmal Mukarji, L. M. Singhvi, B. N. Tandon, P. B. Venkatasubramanian, Francine Frankel and Douglas Verney, Bashir Ahmad, Esha and André Béteille, Ashis Banerjee, Rajni Kothari, Elizabeth and Gopal Krishna, Chandra and Kingsley DeSilva, Swarna and Ashoke Desai, Dhirubhai Sheth, P. N. Dhar, Usha and Rajmohan Gandhi, S. Gopal, P. N. Haksar, Karkee and Abid Hussain, Alice Jacob, Agnese and Gowher Rizvi, Colonel and Mrs K. L. Kapur, Indira and Prem Kathpalia, Prem Kirpal, Sumi Krishna, William Roger Louis, John Lall, Harji Malik, Nayantara Sahgal and Nirmal Mangat Rai, Surjeet, Jasjit, and Gurbir Mansingh, Ajit Mozoomdar, B. R. Nanda, Ashis Nandy, Giri Deshingkar, Sharada Nayak, Pawan and Mool Chand Sharma, A. G. Noorani, V. A. Pai Panandiker, Suzanne and Loyd Rudolph, S. P. Sathe, V. Ramachandran, Sharda and Yashpal Sachdev, Feroza and H. M. Seervai, Leila and Prem Nath Seth, L. P. Singh, Naresh Chandra, Salima Tyabji, T. K. Viswanathan, Bharat Wariawala, M. Ravindran, G. R. S. Rao, H. C. L. Merillat, Evelyn and Neville Maxwell, Thomasson Jannuzi, Nasreen and Matin Zuberi, Ramu and Ashoke Katakam, Robert Hardgrave, Judith Brown, and Marc Galanter.

Finally, my thanks for the energy, skill, and kindness of Anita Roy, my first editor at Oxford University Press in New Delhi, and Ajitha G. S. my second editor, and Jyoti Dhar.

'Gandhi's Talisman'

I will give you a talisman. Whenever you are in doubt or when the self becomes too much with you, apply the following test:

Recall the face of the poorest and weakest man whom you have seen and ask yourself if the step you contemplate is going to be of any use to him. Will he gain anything by it? Will it restore him to control over his own life and destiny? In other words, will it lead to Swaraj for the hungry and spiritually starving millions?

Then you will find your doubts and yourself melting away.

As displayed in Gandhi Smriti,
Birla House, New Delhi

CONTENTS

ABBREVIATIONS

The first time these items are used in the footnotes, which is where they are most used, they are given their full names. The abbreviation then follows in parenthesis. This combination is repeated occasionaliy throughout for the convenience of the forgetful. For the reader who may dip into the book and be confronted by an abbreviation, having not met it when it was introduced, the following list is offered.

AICC   . . . All-India Congress Committee
AR   . . . *Asian Recorder* (a press digest)
AIR   . . . *The All India Reporter* (law reports)
ARC   . . . Administrative Reforms Commission
BJP   . . . Bharatiya Janata Party
CAD   . . . *Constituent Assembly Debates*
CFSA   . . . Congress Forum for Socialist Action
CPI   . . . Communist Party of India
CPM   . . . Communist Party of India (Marxist)
CPP   . . . Congress Parliamentary Party
ICPS   . . . Institute of Constitutional and Parliamentary Studies
INC   . . . Indian National Congress
JCPS   . . . *Journal of Constitutional and Parliamentary Studies*
JILI   . . . *Journal of the Indian Law Institute*
JPI   . . . *Journal of Parliamentary Information*
JPP   . . . Janata Parliamentary Party
NAI   . . . National Archives of India
NLTCM   . . . *Jawaharlal Nehru Letters to Chief Ministers*
NMML   . . . Nehru Memorial Museum and Library
PCC   . . . Provincial/Pradesh Congress Committee
PMA   . . . Parliament Museum and Archives
PSP   . . . Praja Socialist Party
SCC   . . . *Supreme Court Cases*
SCR   . . . *Supreme Court Reports*
SSP   . . . Samyukta Socialist Party
SP   . . . Socialist Party

INTRODUCTION

This is a history of the working of the Indian Constitution from 1950 to 1985, written for Indians and non-Indians—both the well informed and the less well informed, who are interested in the country and in its constitutional experience. Because the Constitution is in hourly use as a benchmark and measuring stick for citizens and officials (some say it is the new *Dharmasastra*), touching lives in ways great and small, learning of its working truly opens a window into India.

This is a history, and not a law, book, although there is a good deal about the law in it, for laws make history and history makes laws. It is about politics and economics and conditions and culture, about politicians and civil servants and lawyers and judges and journalists and individuals, rich and desperately poor, and it is about success and failure and hope and despair and power and sacrifice and motivations, selfish and grand.

It is about those who acted upon the Constitution, how and why they did so, and about those the Constitution acted upon, or neglected. It is about Indians working their Constitution, for constitutions, however 'living', are inert. They do not work, they are worked.

It is a history about what human beings do ill and well while governing themselves.

We begin with the Constitution's inauguration in January 1950 and end, in the main, with Prime Minister Indira Gandhi's passing, late in 1984. Because constitutional developments neither began in 1950 nor ceased in 1985, the book looks back where background is needed and forward, briefly, at several major developments during 1985 and since that are related to matters discussed earlier in the book. It looks, for instance, at the Supreme Court's 1993 decision on the appointment and transfer of judges, and judicial 'activism' during the nineties; the implementation in 1990 of the Mandal Commission report on special consideration for the Other Backward Classes; and the failure in 1992 to use central government forces to protect the Babri mosque at Ayodhya. The desire was strong to bring the narrative closer to the present, but research and writing must stop if books are to be published.

For this account of the Constitution's working to be a window into India, Indians must be the ones speaking. This is their book, in their words; the author has attempted to keep his distance most of the time. But sometimes he enters the pages, more than he might have preferred, attempting to bring out the significance of certain developments and their growth into trends.

An outsider chronicling a people's history should tread warily. He must do so especially when, as a non-lawyer, he writes about the law. To prevent or reduce error, I have sought and received counsel from more than a few senior advocates and retired justices about the text. The errors that remain are, of course, my own. Other Indian friends and colleagues have commented upon, and improved, the text.

The 'objectivity' the outsider brings to his subject is generously exaggerated by his friends—whether in India or elsewhere. Yet, the disadvantage of lacking indigenous corpuscles is severe. One advantage for this outsider is that, having spent some years as a civil servant in the United States, I have been exposed to government processes very similar to India's.

Beginning with friendliness and sympathy, and seeking understanding through sympathy and friendliness, the outsider—or the insider— writes as close to the truth as he can. In this instance, the truth, the reality of and behind events, is sometimes elusive. Too few documentary sources are available, human memories are frail, and there are honest differences of recollection about happenings and of opinions about their meaning. So, despite using the sources evident in the footnotes and the bibliography, portions of this book are conjectural. Words like 'it seems', 'it appears', 'apparently', and 'probably' qualify more sentences than I would like. I have reconstructed events as best I could.

I have tackled this particular subject because of my affection and admiration for India, because of the subject's importance for all those interested in democratic governance, and because, although fascinating portions of this history have been treated in books and articles, the pieces have not been stitched together hitherto.

What should be included in this book and what omitted was often difficult to decide. Some readers will find the book too long and detailed and others too short, with telling details omitted. The subject deserves a multi-volume history of record to include every scrap of evidence and the relevant documents from several government ministries. But presently, even the files on constitutional amendments kept in the Law Ministry are hidden by a conspiracy of silence. I have included what I consider the maximum tolerable amount of evidence to support the narrative.

A few technical points: The spellings of individuals' names for, respectively, appointed and elected officials and judges, have been taken from the *Official Directory*, published by the Ministry of Home Affairs, the *Council of Ministers, 1974–1984*, published by the Lok Sabha Secretariat, and the *Judges of the Supreme Court and the High Courts*, published by the Department of Justice, Ministry of Law. In other instances, commonly accepted spellings have been used.

The word 'governance' is used frequently throughout the book. I have been informed that this is a fancy word unpleasing to some ears. In this book, 'governance' means what citizens do when governing themselves. Governance is the process, government is an object.

Before the Constitution was inaugurated, the country's major units were called 'provinces' and the leaders of their ministries were called 'premiers'. After 26 January 1950, the names changed to 'states' and to 'chief ministers'.

The terms 'the state' and 'elites' do not appear in the book because I find them more misleading than enlightening. And not liking acronyms, I have used them infrequently.

The terms 'council of ministers' and 'cabinet' are used interchangeably, although not all members of a council of ministers typically are included in the cabinet at any particular time. When the distinction is significant, it is made.

All the sources cited by name—whether documentary, written, or oral—are with permission. Names of all the individuals consulted appear in the bibliography and the acknowledgements.

PROLOGUE

The Constituent Assembly that drafted the world's longest democratic constitution began its work in New Delhi in December 1946. The people were eager for independence, the leaders ready. For decades, they had struggled to replace the British 'Raj' with self-rule, dedicating their lives to the goal. They knew what India needed, what they wanted the country to have: unity of peoples and purpose, representative democracy, and social-economic reform. While working to end British rule, they had absorbed the English language and British democracy and Common Law, each of which the British had imported in pieces over two hundred years. They had fought elections in 1937 under the limited self-rule of the 1935 Government of India Act and formed the ministries that governed many provinces. They had come to appreciate the principles and character of British-Indian administration, even when these put them in jail (where Jawaharlal Nehru, for example, spent nine years).

The school for freedom was the Congress Party. Formed in 1885 by an Englishman, its early purpose was Indian participation in the very limited popular government of the time. Under Mahatma Gandhi's leadership after World War I, the Congress grew to lead the independence movement—Congress men and women were not the only patriots—and to infuse it with the purposes of democratic government and social reform. Gandhi's dominance of Congress affairs somewhat paradoxically nurtured the development of able associates, and their strong personalities produced personal and ideological disputes that were resolved democratically, although not without acrimony. These men and women led the country in 1946, and no people gaining independence after World War II was so blessed with leaders of experience, talent, and personal character. Nor, it may be added, with so comparatively civilized a departing colonial power.

Events moved rapidly after the war. The transfer of power was around the corner; general elections, with a limited franchise, during the winter of 1945–6 produced provincial legislatures that would elect members of the Constituent Assembly. Disagreements between the Congress Party and the Muslim League thwarted Britain's belated attempts to hold

India together, and in the spring of 1947, the last Viceroy, Lord Louis Mountbatten, announced that India and Pakistan would become independent countries on 15 August.

With independence, the Constituent Assembly could move ahead with its work, having marked time since early in the year. By then, the Assembly had become essentially a Congress Party body (it had a few Communists and Independents), because most of its original Muslim League members had opted for Pakistan; Congress Muslims remained. The most important exceptions to this one-party complexion were a dozen persons prominent in law and public affairs who the Congress had arranged be elected so that their talents could contribute to constitution-making. Significant for the shaping of the Constitution was Assembly members' daily encounter with the problems of governing, for the Assembly wore two hats. As the Constituent Assembly, it drafted the Constitution during the afternoon, and in the morning, as the Constituent Assembly (Legislative), it was the Provisional, or Dominion, Parliament legislating for the new nation.

The framers drew for the Constitution's provisions from three sources. The Government of India Act, 1935, passed by Parliament in London was the foundation document. The Act established a parliamentary system (while keeping ultimate power in British hands), contained vast administrative detail for the structure of government, established a centralized federal system, and provided for elections to provincial legislatures. These, in 1937, brought the Congress Party to power in many provinces. It provided the basis for government, national and provincial, until the newly framed Constitution replaced it in 1950.

The framers also borrowed from other constitutions to include, particularly, fundamental rights and a body of social and economic desiderata called directive principles. The framers as a body—and especially the leadership of Jawaharlal Nehru, Vallabhbhai Patel, Rajendra Prasad, and Abul Kalam Azad—decided in favour of a long document in preference to rejecting the existing foundation and replacing it with a shorter constitution of general provisions. They sought continuity and stability, intending to entrench parliamentary democracy. Continuity came also from the Constitution's keeping in force all existing laws, unless and until the new national Parliament would repeal them.

The Constitution's spirit came from a third source: the Objectives Resolution adopted during the December 1946 Assembly session, which itself drew from Congress Party documents of two decades earlier. Nehru had drafted this resolution, which said that the Indian Union, whose integrity was to be maintained, derived its authority and power from the Indian people. It declared that there should be 'secured to all the people ... justice, social, economic and political; equality of status, of opportunity, and before the law; freedom of thought, expression, belief, faith, worship, vocation, association and action, subject to law and public morality'. The resolution also called for adequate safeguards for minorities, depressed and 'backward' classes, and underdeveloped and tribal areas.[1]

The Constitution embodied this philosophy in the lengthy and detailed provisions designed to fulfill it. It may be summarized as having three strands: protecting and enhancing national unity and integrity; establishing the institutions and spirit of democracy; and fostering a social revolution to better the lot of the mass of Indians. The framers believed, and Indians today agree, that the three strands are mutually dependent and inextricably intertwined. Social revolution could not be sought or gained at the expense of democracy. Nor could India be truly democratic unless the social revolution had established a just society. Without national unity, democracy would be endangered and there could be little progress toward social and economic reform. And without democracy and reform, the nation would not hold together. With these three strands, the framers had spun a seamless web. Undue strain on, or slackness in, any one strand would distort the web and risk its destruction and, with it, the destruction of the nation. Maintaining harmony between the strands predictably would present those who later would work the Constitution with great difficulties. The framers had undertaken an ambitious and noble enterprise. Their product pleased nearly everyone. Those disappointed thought it insufficiently 'Indian'. 'We wanted the music of [the] *veena* ... but here we have the music of an English band', lamented assembly member K. Hanumanthaiya.

It may help the reader navigate this account of the working of the Constitution to have a brief description of the document. Its more than 370 articles and ten schedules (eight in the original Constitution) fill 309 pages of the 1989 edition published by the Lok Sabha Secretariat. It is two constitutions in one: a constitution for the nation and the central government, and one uniform constitution for all the state governments. The two constitutions are consistent, for both are

---

[1] For the Objectives Resolution, see *Constituent Assembly Debates* (hereafter *CAD*), vol. 1, no. 5, p. 59. For the framing of the Constitution, see Austin, Granville, *The Indian Constitution: Cornerstone of a Nation*, Clarendon Press, Oxford, 1966, and subsequent reprints. See also Austin, Granville, 'The Constitution, Society, and Law', in Oldenburg, Phillip (ed.), *India Briefing 1993*, Asia Society, New York, NY, 1993.

parliamentary systems based on the Westminster Model. The President is the Head of State, and a presidentially appointed governor fills the analogous function in each state. The lower house of Parliament (Lok Sabha) is directly elected by adult suffrage, and the upper house (Rajya Sabha) is indirectly elected by state legislatures—apart from a few nominated members—and each state's delegation, contrary to that in the US Senate, is of a size proportional to its population. The authority of the central and state governments, and the relations between them, are laid down extensively in the Constitution's articles and schedules. One of the latter, the Seventh Schedule, contains three legislative lists— Union, State, and Concurrent—which define legislative jurisdictions. Part XVIII contains the 'Emergency Provisions', under which the central government may rule the country or one or more states in a unitary fashion, superseding the state government(s). The judicial system consists of subordinate courts, and there is a unified higher judiciary, ascending from high courts in (most) states (but which are not state courts) to the Supreme Court. This pleased most intellectuals, who disliked traditional, customary law, and also the common man, for whom it provided laws and a mechanism for adjudication of disputes outside society's repressive hierarchy. There are provisions relating to the national civil service, language, elections, finance, and trade and commerce. Citizenship is single and national; there is no state citizenship as in the United States.

The philosophy of the seamless web infuses the Constitution, and is especially apparent in certain provisions. Unity and integrity are mentioned in the Constitution's Preamble, which establishes India as a 'Union of States', and the Constitution's highly centralized federalism had unity and integrity as its purpose. The country shall be a 'sovereign democratic republic' says the Preamble, and the framers adopted adult suffrage because it would engage all in the common enterprise and, being democratic, it would help break the mould of traditional society. The essence of the democracy and social reform strands is to be found throughout the Constitution: in the democratic political institutions and processes of the parliamentary system, in adult suffrage, and in the independent judiciary; and in Parts III and IV of the Constitution, which lay down the 'Fundamental Rights' and the 'Directive Principles of State Policy', the latter taken from the Irish Constitution. The Rights contain the well-known negative rights of European and American origin and the rights to equality under the law and equal protection of the law. These were truly revolutionary provisions in a traditional and hierarchical society that did not recognize the principle of individual equality. The Directive Principles of State Policy were to be 'fundamental in the governance of the country'. They contain a mixture of social revolutionary—including classically socialist—and Hindu and Gandhian provisions (such as banning cow slaughter and instituting prohibition). Although not justiciable, unlike the Rights, they have become yardsticks for the measurement of governments' successes and failures in social policy.

Painstaking and prescient as the founding fathers and mothers were, those working the Constitution have found it inadequate to some needs and have amended it more than seventy-five times. Many amendments, made through the Constitution's flexible process, relate to administrative matters, the result of having adopted a constitution full of administrative details. The more significant amendments resulted from battles over how the country should live up to its ideals. Preserving a balance among the strands of the seamless web was central to several of these.

The changes to the Constitution, the functioning of constitutional and sub-constitutional institutions, the contexts of the times, and the roles of individuals are the subjects of this book. Its chronological narrative is divided into seven parts, each of which has chapters devoted to various topics according to their political prominence and constitutional significance both at the time and over time.

Part I covers the period from the Constitution's inauguration in 1950 until 1966. These were the Nehru years, for although Nehru died in 1964, his successor as Prime Minister, Lal Bahadur Shastri, who died in 1966, governed in the Nehru mode. The great constitutional themes dealt with in this book emerged during this period—and many continue lively today—as the government attempted to fulfill its promises and administer the country under the Constitution. Conflicts in power relationships had to be managed or resolved—among individuals and constitutional institutions, between government and the Congress Party, and between the central and state governments. The central and state governments and Parliament battled with the Supreme Court over fundamental rights issues: freedom of expression *vis-à-vis* national integrity; personal liberty *vis-à-vis* political stability; special treatment for some segments of society *vis-à-vis* equality for all; property rights *vis-à-vis* social revolutionary needs. The most fundamental struggle was between Parliament and the Supreme Court over custody of the Constitution, the central issue being whether Parliament's power of amendment was complete and unrestrained. Because these substantive themes and their treatment by rival constitutional institutions would persist over decades, their beginnings are treated in considerable detail, and this part is consequently rather longer than others.

Part II covers the period from 1966 to 1973, the beginning of Indira Gandhi's long years as Prime Minister. The relationship of the democracy and social revolutionary strands of the web—how much of either ought to be sacrificed for the other—was again an intense issue, accompanied by Mrs Gandhi's employment of the controversy in her personalization of power. The renewed battle—and such it was—over the fundamental issue of the separation of powers became bitter as the executive branch and Parliament on the one hand, and the Supreme Court on the other, claimed to be the final authority for constitutional interpretation.

Part III deals with twenty months during 1975–1977, the period of the internal emergency and unitary government that has come to be called Mrs Gandhi's Emergency. During this time, democracy was extinguished, personal liberty and the other fundamental rights suspended, legitimate political opponents kept under preventive detention, and the opportunity taken further to subvert democracy through amending the Constitution. Again, the judiciary and the government were in confrontation. With only a few exceptions, the courts lost—but they survived.

Part IV recounts the events of the twenty-seven months from the spring of 1977 to the summer of 1979. Indira Gandhi, for reasons still obscure, called elections in 1977 only to be defeated, and the country's first coalition government—the Janata Party, which was an amalgam of half a dozen parties—came to office riding a wave of revulsion against the Emergency. A victim of rampant factionalism and personality conflicts, the government fell, but not before it had restored democracy by amending the Constitution to repair the worst damage done to it during the Emergency. The coalition's lingering death raised the question, for the first time since 1950, of the President's power, as a constitutional head of state in a parliamentary system, to appoint a prime minister from among contenders.

Part V covers the years from 1980 to 1985, from Mrs Gandhi's return to office, upon winning the parliamentary elections of 1980, to Rajiv Gandhi becoming Prime Minister upon his mother's assassination. The principal motif of the period was how best to preserve national unity and integrity: groups within the states of Punjab and Jammu and Kashmir declared independence from India as their goal, and many state governments and non-Congress parties—resentful of Mrs Gandhi's over-centralization of authority—challenged the distribution of powers between the central government and the state governments, both as laid down in the Constitution and as practised. The belief grew among political practitioners and observers during this time that decentralization of authority would strengthen rather than weaken national unity.

Part VI is devoted to national unity and integrity and to the constitutional machinery for centre–state relations. Although the subject has been discussed in each part (centralization versus decentralization of authority will be seen to be a thread running from 1950 to 1985) it seems useful to gather together the major issues and themes from earlier chapters and augment them with fresh material in a section of the book dedicated to the subject, rather than discussing it in each part. This would become unduly repetitive.

Part VII contains the Conclusion.

This narrative account of the working of the Constitution ends in 1985, although mention is made of a few important constitutional developments thereafter. Indira Gandhi's departure from politics ushered in a new era. The Congress Party's dominance lasted only four more years, until Rajiv Gandhi was defeated as Prime Minister. Since then, a series of insecure governments have held office in New Delhi— and also in many states. But the institutions of the Constitution are stable and have continued to undergird national governance.

The Indian Constitution is a live document in a society rapidly changing and almost frenetically political. The touchstone for public, and many private, affairs, the Constitution is employed daily, if not hourly, by citizens in pursuit of their personal interests or in their desire to serve the public good. The working of the Constitution so fully expresses the essentialness of the seamless web and so completely reveals the society that adopted it that its study truly is a window into India.

Part I

THE GREAT CONSTITUTIONAL THEMES EMERGE, 1950–66

[India must have a] socio-economic revolution ... [to achieve] the real satisfaction of the fundamental needs of the common man ... (and) a fundamental change in the structure of Indian society.

Sarvepalli Radhakrishnan[1]

The Constitution ... [could be] both unitary as well as federal according to the requirements of time and circumstances.

B. R. Ambedkar[2]

(W)e have all derived from the British Parliament, and we still continue to derive inspiration from its proceedings, from its history ... (and) from its traditions.

Rajendra Prasad[3]

[Article 368 empowers Parliament to amend the Constitution] without any exception whatever.

Patanjali Sastri[4]

---

[1] *CAD*, vol. 2, no. 1, pp. 269–73.

[2] Ibid., vol. 7, no. 1, pp. 33–4.

[3] President Prasad to the Commonwealth Parliamentary Conference, New Delhi, December 1957. *Speeches of Dr Rajendra Prasad, 1957–1958,* Ministry of Information and Broadcasting, Government of India (hereafter GOI), New Delhi, p. 110.

[4] The Chief Justice of India giving the Supreme Court's decision in *Shankari Prasad Deo v Union of India* 1952 (3) SCR 106.

Chapter 1

SETTLING INTO HARNESS

'Hail Our Sovereign Republic... A Day of Fulfilment ... Good wishes from Far and Near ... Rejoicings All Over' said banner headlines in the *Hindustan Times* on 26 January 1950. Three years of debate and drafting had come to fulfilment with the Constitution's inauguration. 'Today India recovers her soul after centuries of serfdom and resumes her ancient name', enthused the newspaper's editorial. But there was a shadow. Two days later would be the second anniversary of the assassination of Mahatma Gandhi, the 'father of the nation'.

The festivities began mid-morning when Governor General C. Rajagopalachari (who had succeeded the last British Viceroy, Lord Mountbatten) actually announced the establishment of the republic. As '5,000 railway locomotives sent out shrieks of joy', Federal Court Chief Justice Harilal Kania administered the oath of office to Rajendra Prasad, who two days earlier the Dominion Parliament cum Constituent Assembly had elected President—nominated by Nehru and seconded by Sardar Vallabhbhai Patel. Then, Prasad, 'neatly dressed in a grey achkan, grey pyjama and a white Gandhi cap' received Jawaharlal Nehru's ' "loyalty and fealty to this Republic of which you are the head" ' as the first Prime Minister under the Constitution. Rajendra Prasad then administered the oath of office to the cabinet, to the Speaker of the Lok Sabha, to Harilal Kania, as Chief Justice of the new Supreme Court, and to his fellow justices. The country's new government was in place.[1]

Thus began the great enterprise of nationhood to which the Congress Party had so long been dedicated. The date had been chosen because on 26 January 1930 the party had adopted the 'Pledge Taken on Independence Day', dedicating itself to Indians' 'inalienable right ...

---

[1] Article 381 of the Constitution, which was repealed in 1956, provided that ministers in the Dominion (pre-constitutional) government should continue in office until any new ministers were appointed. With the Constitution in place, Nehru believed a new government should be constituted under Article 75, and he resigned on his own and his government's behalf and formed a new government, with some of the same ministers, in early May 1950.
The members of the Supreme Court were the judges of the just-defunct Federal Court.

to have freedom ... [and] complete independence'.[2] Although the
country had been independent since August 1947 and coping with
myriad difficulties, new constitutional institutions and tools now both
augmented and restricted government authority. Preserving the
seamless web necessarily involved the government in public affairs more
than previously, and citizens, by habit looked to government for
leadership. The Directive Principles of State Policy exhorted the
government, and other provisions of the Constitution imposed upon
it, the responsibility to pursue the social revolution and to protect
minorities. The Fundamental Rights enjoined government both to
protect rights and not to infringe them. State and central government
power to legislate and Parliament's power to amend the Constitution
now were subject to judicial review. The Supreme Court had become
the 'apex court'. No longer could appeals go to the Privy Council in
London as they might have from the Federal Court. The central
government had vast powers to intervene in state government affairs.
There was an entirely new institution, a constitutional head of state,
the President. Shortly, there would come into existence two vitally
important commissions, Finance and Planning. Government, including
the national civil service, now was responsible for economic development,
not merely for collecting taxes and maintaining order.

Self-governing and democratic, government and citizenry both were
confronted with the great issues arising from the Constitution's goals,
and that would persist over the years: How could authority be centralized enough to enhance national unity and to promote economic development without alienating subordinate levels of government and
stultifying local initiative? How, while applying the rule of law, would
social-economic reform be fostered and democratic institutions strengthened in a huge society in which religion and tradition sanctioned inequality and exploitation? How would government achieve these and
other national goals—indeed, how would it govern—when the law, the
courts, and administration failed to reach so many citizens effectively?
Under these general issues, Nehru and his ministers would be asked to
resolve concrete questions: How would the government further land
reform and the uplift of disadvantaged citizens when the Constitution's
fundamental rights to property and to equality before the law impeded
both? How would it protect national integrity and political stability from
seditious speech and subversive action while also protecting freedom

[2] For the full text of the pledge, see Nehru, Jawaharlal, *An Autobiography*, The Bodley
Head, London, 1958 (reprint), p. 612.

of speech and personal liberty? How would it pursue national development using the constitutional machinery of centre–state relations? How could the parliamentary system be made to work for the good of the poor as well as the rich? Playing their respective roles, the institutions of the Constitution cooperated and found themselves in conflict over these matters: the state governments versus the central government, executives versus legislatures, and, most especially, legislatures and executives in conflict with the judiciary. These momentous battles would shape the Constitution's working and the country's democracy.

This chapter briefly will provide the broad context for the early years as government and citizenry settled into harness. Then it will discuss the adjustments leaders and institutional centres of authority made in their respective powers as they tackled the problems confronting them. Subsequent chapters will describe major constitutional amendments, institutional conflicts, and the other issues and themes that would emerge during the Nehru years and bloom perennially on the national agenda.

The Broad Context

Prime Minister Nehru's new government was born into urgency. Twenty bills awaited attention in Parliament, and on 28 January 1950 the railway budget, second in importance only to the national budget, was to be considered. Problems of unity and integrity loomed large: Jana Sangh leader S. P. Mookerjee risked relations with Pakistan, if not war, by calling for the annulment of partition, and national integrity was threatened in the Northeast, the Punjab, and Kashmir. Issues of 'secularism', so important to the new democracy, attracted attention nationally. There were complaints that the Constitution was insufficiently 'Hindu' to suit the country's needs, and the Hindu Code Bill generated bitter controversy within and outside Parliament. National economic policy had to be set. The 1948 Industrial Policy Statement, foretelling increased government involvement, would be followed in 1950 by the formation of the Planning Commission and its drafting of the First Plan. The first linguistic state, Andhra Pradesh, would be established in 1953, and within a few years many state boundaries would be drawn along linguistic lines. Refugees streaming into West Bengal from East Pakistan, and those who had fled West Pakistan and still were encamped around New Delhi, strained food and shelter resources and were a constant reminder of partition's bloodbath. Famine existed in eight districts in Madras due to the failure of the northeast monsoon. Cloth prices had to be controlled, and sixt thousand sugar mill workers went on strike in Uttar Pradesh. Governments were unstable in several states, upsetting Home Minister Patel especially. Maintaining law and order figured regularly in internal government discussions.[3] Preparing for and holding the first general elections under the Constitution was an enormous task. House-to-house surveys registered 173 million adult voters on election rolls. Forty-six per cent of those registered voted in the election—held from October 1951 till March 1952—to give the Congress Party a massive victory in Parliament and the state legislatures. The Congress Party had passed its first test under the Constitution: winning an election by preparing electoral slates of attractive candidates.[4] The elections were conducted fairly, although Jayaprakash Narayan, the Gandhian socialist and erratic conscience-keeper of Indian politics, doubted they could or would be.[5]

The government's and the public's mood was a compound of elements: optimism and idealism about national renaissance; awe at the responsibilities assumed; hope that economic and social reforms would succeed quickly enough to preempt popular revolt; awareness that internal Congress fractiousness could hamper effective government, as it had when the party had governed in the provinces from 1937 to 1939; fears that democracy and (even centralized) federalism would

[3] For example, during the Conference of Governors on 18 March 1950 and annually in subsequent conferences. Proceedings, in the H. K. Mody and K. M. Munshi Papers, Nehru Memorial Museum and Library (hereafter NMML).

A bright spot was India's victory over a Commonwealth cricket team by seven wickets.

[4] Congress contested nearly all of the 489 seats in the Lok Sabha and gained 364 of them. The Communist Party of India won sixteen seats, the Socialist Party twelve, Acharya Kripalani's Kisan [Peasant] Mazdoor Praja Party nine, and nineteen smaller parties and a few independents the remainder. In the state legislatures, Congress won more than 2,200 of the more than 3,200 seats, allowing it to form governments in twenty-one states.

Election data from Butler, David, Lahiri, Ashoke, and Roy, Prannoy, *India Decides: Elections 1952–1991*, 2nd edn., Living Media Books, New Delhi, 1991, p. 74. See also *The Pilgrimage and After*, All India Congress Committee (hereafter AICC), New Delhi, 1952, and Kogekar, S. V., and Park, Richard L., *Reports on the Indian General Elections, 1951–52*, Popular Book Depot, Bombay, 1956, tables 1 and 3. There are small variations in the figures reported.

[5] He wrote to Nehru on 30 May 1950 that unless 'very special efforts' were made and 'strict measures adopted', the elections 'would never be fair'. There would be 'intimidation, violence and dishonesty of every kind'—all this 'considering the moral tone of the Congress organization and the Congress ministries ...'. It seems that the Election Commission will function 'merely as the secretary of a new department of government', he wrote. (The commission was part of the Law Ministry.) Narayan added that he was convening the representatives of the important opposition parties to make suggestions about election monitoring so the people might not lose faith in the honesty of the elections. Jayaprakash Narayan Papers, Jawaharlal Nehru File, NMML.

not prove viable in India's endless diversity. Congress Party general secretary Shankarrao Deo, for example, thought democracy a 'theoretical concept', for we are a 'politically immature people'. But he vowed to try to make it work.[6] Both leaders and the politically aware public understood that India was conducting its 'experiment with democracy' under the glare, the pressure, of international attention in the modern world of rapid communications and conflicting ideologies. On no account dared they fail.[7]

Circumstances also were propitious for the new Constitution. The trinity of a charismatic national leadership, a mass party, and effective civil services, plus the already functioning legislatures, executives, and courts, gave representative democracy a head start. The leaders in the states and New Delhi, forged by the independence movement, were believers in the seamless web: confirmed democrats, advocates of social and economic reform, and nationalists with broad perspective. Nehru, the English-educated, Brahmin patrician from Allahabad was the impatient democrat and national nanny. As Nehru was wont to quote Robert Frost, he had miles to go before he slept. Once he wrote, '"a little twist and Jawaharlal might turn into a dictator sweeping aside the paraphernalia of a slow moving democracy"',[8] but he did not, and the socialist Nath Pai described him as 'a great idealist whose faith in and loyalty to democracy are unimpeachable'.[9] Nehru had the Congress 1951 election manifesto say, 'The achievement of economic and social justice must proceed side-by-side with economic progress. Thus alone can social peace and democracy be preserved.'[10] Deputy Prime Minister and Home Minister Sardar Vallabhbhai Patel, from the Patidar caste of small peasants in Gujarat, like Nehru trained in the law in England, and, like Nehru and Rajendra Prasad, Gandhi's close associate, was a no-nonsense man, a political boss in the most constructive sense, whose staff was devoted to him because he encouraged their frank memoranda.

[6] From the draft of an article submitted for publication to the *Hindustan Times*, undated, but early fifties. Shankarrao Deo Papers, File S26, NMML.

[7] For an insightful account of these by a most felicitous writer about India, see Morris-Jones, W. H., *The Government and Politics of India*, Hutchinson University Library, London, 1964. For a different sort of excellent study, see Frankel, Francine R., *India's Political Economy 1947–1977*, Princeton University Press, Princeton, NJ, 1978.

[8] Nehru writing about himself in 1937 under the pseudonym Chanakaya. Cited in Mukherjee, Hiren, *The Gentle Colossus*, Oxford University Press, New Delhi, 1986 (1964), p. 222.

[9] Pai to an enquiring member of the British Parliament when visiting London. Nath Pai letter to Nehru dated 24 April 1956. Nath Pai Papers, Jawaharlal Nehru File, NMML.

[10] *Election Manifesto*, AICC, New Delhi, 1951, p. 6.

He believed in 'giving two *chappatis* to a peasant when he only had one'.[11] President Rajendra Prasad, a Kayastha from Bihar and sometime advocate of the Calcutta High Court, spoke of the 'silken bond' between British and Indian parliamentary democracy and the need to empower villagers by giving greater scope to panchayats.[12] Vice-President and later President, Sarvepalli Radhakrishnan, a Telugu Brahmin from Madras, wrote that adult suffrage 'is the most powerful instrument devised by man for breaking down social and economic injustice and destroying the walls that imprison men's minds'.[13] With rare exceptions, opposition political leaders and parties spoke for democracy. For them, it was both a philosophical belief and a tactical necessity if they were to have influence and to gain power. By 1956, even the Communist Party of India (CPI) had given up its 'open hostility to government ... bordering on open revolt' and declared that to 'play its rightful role as the builder and spearhead of the democratic movement ... it must act as a Party of Opposition in relation to the present government'.[14]

Inevitably, there were conflicts, over issues of great magnitude, among strong leaders, and among the Constitution's institutions. These were resolved through adjustments in power relationships, personal and institutional, and through establishing constitutional practices and adopting conventions from the Constitution's sources, especially from Britain and the United States.

Power Relations and Adjustments

Of the many sortings-out of power, themselves part of the context of the time, this chapter briefly will examine six, for they took place over

[11] H. V. R. Ienger, sometime Secretary of the Constituent Assembly and Home Secretary under Patel. Oral History Transcript, p. 167, NMML.

[12] Inaugural speech to the Commonwealth Parliamentary Conference, 2 December 1957. *Speeches of Dr Rajendra Prasad, 1957–1958*, pp. 110, 114.

[13] Radhakrishnan, 'Forward' in Shiva Rao, B., *The Framing of India's Constitution: A Study*, The Indian Institute of Public Administration/N. M. Tripathi Pvt. Ltd., Bombay, 1968. This volume is accompanied by four volumes of documents.

[14] 'Open hostility' from *Communist Violence in India*, Ministry of Home Affairs, GOI, New Delhi, 1949, p. 56. CPI 'rightful role' from 'Political Resolution', CPI 1956, cited in Overstreet, Gene D., and Windmiller, Marshall, *Communism in India*, University of California Press, Berkeley, CA, 1959, p. 322.

Nehru said that the government had no intention of opposing the preaching of any political or economic theory. He defended several young communist scientists in Calcutta from those opposing their freedom of expression. But the CPI sees liberty

the issues occupying these early years. Because neither the great issues nor the power relationships embroiled with them would be permanently resolved, we shall see more of them later in this book.

THE PRESIDENT AND THE COUNCIL OF MINISTERS

Here, the conflicts between the leader of the government, Prime Minister Jawaharlal Nehru, and the head of state, President Rajendra Prasad, went to the heart of India's Westminster Model Constitution. And they were at once substantive, institutional, and personal. Nehru would have preferred C. Rajagopalachari as the first President, but he nominated Prasad for the post in deference to party discipline. He would have preferred Radhakrishnan to a second term by Prasad in 1957.[15] Nehru thought Prasad intellectually inferior and an obscurantist on religious matters. They clashed over Prasad's objection, on astrological grounds, to 26 January as the date to inaugurate the Constitution, over the Hindu Code Bill (more below), and over Prasad's decision to inaugurate the rebuilt Somnath Temple in Gujarat.[16] Their official relations, however, were correct. Nehru briefed Prasad weekly, if not more often; they corresponded frequently and substantively. Nehru

---

as including the 'freedom to murder, maim, pillage and sabotage', he said, citing *Communist Violence*, p. 57.

[15] Patil, S. K., *My Years with Congress*, Parchure Prakashan Mandir, Bombay, 1991, pp. 76–7; and Gopal, Sarvepalli, *Jawaharlal Nehru*, 3 vols, Oxford University Press, New Delhi, 1979ff, vol. 2, p. 77. The Bombay tabloid *Blitz* reported in June 1949 the competition between Prasad and Rajagopalachari for the presidency, and during that autumn Nehru, Sardar Patel (who some believed also favoured Rajagopalachari), and Prasad exchanged letters full of irritation about the matter. Durga Das, *Sardar Patel's Correspondence, 1945–1950*, 10 vols, Navjivan Publishing House, Ahmedabad, 1973ff, vol. 8, pp. 195–227.

Nehru believed that Prasad would not desire a second term in office in 1957, for Prasad had expressed the wish, in 1955, to retire. Nehru had then dissuaded him. In 1957, Prasad was reluctant to leave office, and several Congress leaders, Maulana Azad especially, wanted him to be a candidate against Nehru's desire to have Radhakrishnan move from Vice-President to President. On 31 March 1957, the Congress Parliamentary Board settled on Prasad as the party's candidate for President, and Radhakrishnan, although miffed by the party's decision, agreed to a second term as Vice-President. One of his reasons, speculated his biographer, was that retirement might have meant 'joining the long line of extinct volcanoes in Madras'. Gopal, Sarvepalli, *Radhakrishnan*, Oxford University Press, New Delhi, 1989, p. 292. For his account of the 1957 presidential nomination, see pp. 287–92.

[16] Gopal, *Nehru*, pp. 77, 155. Nehru wrote to the chief ministers that the inauguration of the temple 'with pomp and ceremony' went against 'our protestations about the secular state'. Letter of 1 August 1951. Nehru, Jawaharlal, *Letters to Chief Ministers* (hereafter *NLTCM*), vol. 2, Oxford University Press, New Delhi, 1989 (reprint), p. 462.

leaned on Prasad for advice, according to Prasad's secretary, Vishwanath Verma.[17] But Prasad came 'to think that even his advice was not sought on many matters', recalled a cabinet minister of the time.[18]

Their sharp confrontations over the powers of their respective offices occurred because Prasad read the Constitution literally, attributing to the presidency greater authority than that of the nearly-powerless head of state under the Westminster Model.[19] He had shown this inclination even while the Constitution was being drafted by writing to the Constituent Assembly's 'Constitutional Advisor', B. N. Rau, that he did not find in the draft constitution a provision 'laying it down in so many terms' that the President would be bound to act upon the advice of his ministers.[20] Within two months of his becoming President, Prasad wrote a three-page paper entitled 'Questions relating to the powers of the President under the Constitution of India'. Among the questions were:

[17] Vishwanath Verma Oral History Transcript, p. 17, NMML.

[18] K. Santhanam, Oral History Transcript, p. 33, NMML.

[19] For the framing of the Constitution's provisions for the President and for the executive branch, see Austin, *Cornerstone*, ch. 5, especially pp. 132ff.

The President's powers are given in many articles in the Constitution of which several have been more controversial than others. Article 53 provides that the executive power of the Union and supreme command of the defence forces shall be vested in the President. Article 74 provides for a council of ministers headed by the Prime Minister 'to aid and advise the President in the exercise of his functions'; Article 75 says that the Prime Minister shall be appointed by the President and the other ministers by the President on the advice of the Prime Minister; Articles 76, 148, and 324 say that the President shall appoint the Attorney General, the Comptroller and Auditor General of India, and the Chief Election Commissioner and other commissioners. Articles 338 through 342 impose on him responsibilities for the welfare of the Scheduled Castes and Tribes and backward classes. Article 77 provides that all executive action by the government be taken in the name of the President. Article 79 establishes that Parliament includes the President and Article 80 that the President nominates twelve members of the upper house, the Council of States. The President summons Parliament and assents to bills it enacts. Articles 124 and 217 empower the President to appoint the justices of the Supreme Court and the high courts. Under Article 143, the President may request an advisory opinion from the Supreme Court. He appoints governors of the states under Article 155, the members of the Finance Commission under Article 280, and the Union Public Service Commission under Article 316. This is not all. Part XVIII of the Constitution bestows a variety of emergency powers on the President.

For early commentary on presidential powers, see Gledhill, Alan, *The Republic of India*, Stevens and Sons Ltd., London, 1951, and Alexandrowicz, Charles Henry, *Constitutional Developments in India*, Oxford University Press, London, 1957.

[20] Austin , *Cornerstone*, p. 135. Prasad was then President of the Constituent Assembly when it wore its constitution-making hat. The Speaker chaired the Constituent Assembly (Legislative) when functioning as the Provisional Parliament.

Does the Constitution contemplate any situation where the President 'has to act independently' of his ministers? What are the implications of the President being head of the armed forces in regard to appointments, discipline, and their use? Has the President any voice, apart from that of his ministers, in the appointment or the activities of many of the officers he appoints?[21] It is uncertain to whom Prasad sent his questions.[22] But his paper reached Attorney General Setalvad. Setalvad's 'Observations by M. C. Setalvad' responds point-by-point to Prasad's questions and clearly is directed to them. The essence of his six pages of observations was in his points two and three. 'The President has by virtue of Article 74, in the exercise of his functions—all functions whatsoever—to be aided and advised by a Council of Ministers,' read point two. Said point three, 'By the Constitution the President is required to act in all matters with the aid and advice of this Council ... The moment the President refuses to accept its aid or advice there will be a breakdown in the constitutional machinery.'[23] No doubt this paper reached the President and the Prime Minister and, most likely, other cabinet members.

[21] Paper dated 21 March 1950. Choudhary, Valmiki (ed.), *Dr Rajendra Prasad: Correspondence and Select Documents*, vol. 12, Allied Publishers Ltd., Bombay, 1984ff, pp. 278–80. Prasad also asked if the President, 'on his own account', could return a reserved bill to a state legislature or make suggestions about it. He asked if the President could be in direct contact with ministry secretaries. For reasons still obscure, the cabinet had asked Attorney General M. C. Setalvad on 14 February 1950 about the President's powers when assenting to state legislation, specifically a zamindari abolition act. (See ch. 3, footnote 63.) Coincidentally, Governor Asaf Ali in Orissa wrote to Nehru on 4 March 1950 asking if governors must act on the advice of their ministers even if the advice 'militates' against the Constitution. Ibid., p. 129.

[22] H. N. Pandit in his *The PM's President*, A. Chand and Co., New Delhi, 1974, appendix I, says it was a 'note' from Prasad to Nehru, but he provides no ground for asserting this.

[23] Paper dated 6 October 1950. Choudhary, *Prasad: Correspondence*, vol. 12, p. 281. Setalvad concluded his response by saying that the positions of the King in England and India's President were 'analogous' and that both the King and the President had 'a discretion in selecting the PM and in dissolving Parliament either at the instance of the PM or when he feels that there is a potent disharmony between the policy of the ministry and public opinion'. This would be 'an exceptional case and very unlikely to arise', wrote Setalvad. Ibid., pp. 285–6. The time lapse between Prasad's questions and Setalvad's response is strange and unexplained.

Setalvad strongly made the points again in the Hamlyn Lectures delivered at Lincoln's Inn in 1960, and he had held these views consistently. See Setalvad, M. C., *The Common Law in India*, N. M. Tripathi Pvt. Ltd., Bombay, 1970 (reprint).

Subhash C. Kashyap in his *History of the Parliament in India*, vol. 2, Shipra Publications, New Delhi, says that Prasad also sought Setalvad's views on 27 March 1950, but he does not indicate the source of this information or the substance of the President's enquiry (p. 46).

Prasad persisted. In August 1950, he wrote to Deputy Prime Minister and Home Minister Sardar Patel asserting that the President could advise ministers 'not on matters of detail but generally on matters of policy'. He wished, therefore, to have a senior staff person to inform him 'if there is any matter in which I should have a discussion with ministers'. Prasad also told Patel, as he had said in his 'Questions', that he read the Constitution as providing that the Comptroller and Auditor-General of Accounts and the Chief Election Commissioner reported directly to the President, who then submitted their reports to Parliament.[24] Twelve days after writing this letter, Prasad wrote to Nehru apparently questioning elements of the Bihar Zamindari Abolition Bill and expressing his reluctance to assent to it. The following year, Prasad, having received an information copy of a note for the cabinet about the First Amendment abolishing zamindaris, sent his own note of criticisms to the cabinet. When the enacted amendment went to him for assent in June 1951, Prasad expressed doubt regarding its constitutionality, and he asked the great constitutional authority Alladi Krishnaswami Ayyar if, so thinking, it was his duty to sign the bill. Ayyar informed him that he must sign. (This is discussed in detail in chapters 3 and 4.)

Confrontation over presidential powers flared again, in September 1951, over the Hindu Code Bill. In this omnibus measure, aspects of Hindu personal law—marriage, divorce, succession, inheritance, property and women's rights—were to be 'secularized', i.e. made part of the uniform civil code called for in the Directive Principles of State Policy. Three days after discussing the bill with Nehru, Prasad wrote him a letter in which he argued that a Parliament, elected to frame a constitution and to govern the country only until general elections were held, should not enact such a bill even though it was legally competent to do so; that the bill was 'highly discriminatory' in that it was confined to Hindu law and did not include Muslim law; and that Hindu law was evolving in ways making legislative changes unnecessary, whereas the Bill would force 'revolutionary changes' in Hindu life, thus creating conflict. Turning to his role as President, Prasad said that he would watch the Bill and send Parliament a message about

---

[24] Letter of 27 August 1950. Rajendra Prasad Collection, File 42, National Archives of India (hereafter NAI). The letter and note appear also in *Prasad: Correspondence*, vol. 14, pp. 104, 292–7. Sardar Patel's reply is not available.

Prasad's staff, one assumes on his instructions, drew up a list of 'Functions assigned to the President under the Constitution'. It was seven-and-a-half pages long. Ibid., vol. 12, pp. 415ff.

it if he thought this appropriate. Moreover, '(M)y right to examine it on its merits when it is passed by Parliament before giving assent to it is there.' He added that he might take action 'consistently with the dictates of my own conscience' so as to avoid embarrassment to the government.[25]

Nehru responded the same day to these 'serious matters of great constitutional importance'. He described the Bill as very moderate and said that the Speaker had ruled Parliament competent to pass it. Continuing, Nehru said, '(T)he President has no power or authority ... (in our view) to go against the will of Parliament in regard to a bill that has been well considered by it and passed ... . Otherwise the question would arise as to whether Parliament is the supreme legislative authority in this country or not.' Concluding, Nehru advised the President that in this session only those portions of the Bill dealing with marriage and divorce would be passed. Nevertheless, he would place the letter and note before the cabinet.[26] Although he was correct on the constitutional issue, Nehru's anti-religious 'secularism' prevented him from appreciating the Hindu values 'which were the essence of Prasad's character'.[27]

Meanwhile, Nehru had consulted Setalvad and Alladi Krishnaswamy Ayyar in Madras for their views. Setalvad responded that 'by Article 74(1), the President is required to act in all matters with the aid and advice of his Council of Ministers.'[28] Ayyar replied that it was 'perfectly clear' that the President's position is analogous to that of a 'constitutional monarch in England ... and there is no sphere of his functions in respect of which he can act without reference to the advice of his ministers.'[29]

---

[25] The letter, dated 15 September 1951, was classified 'Top Secret'. Nehru sent a copy of it and his reply to certain members of the cabinet with the request to keep the papers 'absolutely secret'. Hare Krushna Mahtab Papers, First Installment, Subject File 20, NMML. The letter appears in Choudhary, *Prasad: Correspondence*, vol. 14, pp. 104–6.

Kashyap in his *History of Parliament*, vol. 2, p. 46, says that Prasad wrote to Nehru on 18 September 1951 'armed with the Attorney General's opinion'. The President, it seems to the author, misread several of Setalvad's individual points (in his 'Observations') and found Setalvad's tone, overall, inaudible.

[26] Nehru's letter to Prasad of 15 September 1951. Choudhary, *Prasad: Correspondence*, vol. 14, pp. 104–6.

[27] Vishwanath Verma Oral History Transcript, p. 18, NMML.

[28] Letter dated 24 September 1951. A. K. Ayyar Papers—in the possession of K. M. Munshi when the author inspected them. This letter is cited in Austin, *Cornerstone*, p. 141.

[29] Letter dated 20 September 1951. A. K. Ayyar Papers, ibid. Ayyar followed this letter with another on 8 October 1951, expanding on the first letter. He said Article 74 was 'all-pervasive', and that the President 'seems to read every Article of the Constitution

Nehru conveyed these opinions to the cabinet, adding his own view that the President's [indirect] election 'makes no difference' in his powers compared to those of the hereditary monarch in Britain. Were the President to act contrary to the advice of his ministers, said Nehru, 'such action must inevitably lead to the resignation of the Council of Ministers who have the confidence of Parliament'. Nehru told the cabinet that he was sending the note for information, because the Hindu Code Bill was not likely to come up for decison 'in the near future'.[30] The issue did indeed become moot, for conservative resistance to the omnibus Bill delayed enactment until 1956, and by then it had been divided into several bills.[31] As for legal opinion rejecting his authority to deny assent to the Hindu Code Bill, the President 'lumped it'.[32]

Prasad set the presidential fox among the constitutional geese again, in 1960. Speaking at the laying of the foundation stone for the Indian Law Institute, New Delhi, on 28 November, he said he would like to have a study prepared examining 'the extent to which and the matters in respect of which, if any, the powers and functions of the President differ from those of the Sovereign of Great Britain'. Echoing his letter to B. N. Rau of twelve years earlier, he noted that the Constitution contained no provision 'which in so many words' laid down that the President was bound to act on his ministers' advice. Because Indian and British conditions varied, he said, 'it may not be desirable to treat

---

in which the word 'President' appears as conferring powers upon the President in his personal capacity without reference to the Cabinet'. Ibid., p. 142.

Ayyar also expressed the apprehension that if the President could act other than on the advice of his ministers, governors, also, might break loose from the conventions containing their powers. Both these opinions were later published by Alladi Krishnaswami's son in Ayyar, Alladi Kuppaswami, *A Statesman Among Jurists*, Bhartiya Vidya Bhavan, Bombay, 1993, pp. 307–17.

[30] The note is headed 'Prime Minister's Secretariat', signed 'J. Nehru', and dated 25 September 1951. Hare Krushna Mahtab Papers, NMML.

[31] B. R. Ambedkar, the Law Minister, resigned from the cabinet over what he considered Nehru's half-hearted efforts on behalf of the Bill. One of Nehru's chief supporters in the cabinet, N. Gopalaswami Ayyangar, Minister of Transport and Railways and formerly a distinguished member of the Constituent Assembly, favoured holding the Bill over until after the general elections. Nehru acceded to the wisdom of postponement. When pressed to act by Mrs Renuka Ray, long-time Congresswoman, member of the Constituent Assembly, and minister of the West Bengal government in the mid-fifties, Nehru asked if she trusted him to pick the time, for he wanted the Bill's passage as much as she. Mrs Ray agreed. Renuka Ray Oral History Transcript, pp. 35ff, NMML.

[32] H. V. R. Iengar Oral History Transcript, p. 157, NMML.

ourselves as strictly bound by the interpretations which have been given from time to time to expressions in England.[33]

Editorial reaction to the speech tended to favour Prasad's position. 'It would be unwise to accept mechanically any convention ... [established in Britain] without first exposing it to the test of reason and relevancy,' said the *Times of India*.[34] The 'general effect' of the Constitution was to vest in the President authority to 'enforce more mature deliberation of important questions of policy', said the *Hindustan Times*.[35] *Organiser*, the organ of the militantly Hindu Rashtriya Swayamsevak Sangh (RSS), called the speech a 'welcome bombshell' and expressed appreciation for Prasad's stand on the Hindu Code Bill.[36] The CPI weekly, *New Age*, however, thought the President's raising the issues 'very questionable' and said that the Prime Minister should tell the nation that the President's view of his powers was 'not consistent' with the Constitution.[37] Asked at a press conference two weeks later for his reaction to the speech and if it had been made with the advice of the cabinet, Nehru answered that 'we did not know anything about it until it was delivered.' He added that he doubted that 'the President himself attached much value to this point', for 'the President has always acted as a constitutional head.'[38]

Contention over presidential powers declined after May 1962, when Radhakrishnan was elected to succeed Prasad. A piquant exception came with the widespread clamour for the resignation of Krishna Menon, Minister of Defence and Nehru's close friend, who was blamed for India's defeat in the war with China in 1962. Nehru, personally devastated and politically weakened by the defeat, manoeuvred in a manner suggesting that he either wished to delay Menon's resignation or to transfer responsibility for it to Radhakrishnan. Radhakrishnan wrote to Nehru that ' "as you said" ' we have to accept Menon's resignation,

---

[33] *Speeches of Dr Rajendra Prasad, 1960–61*, GOI, New Delhi, 1962, pp. 164–6. One doubts that personal ambition lay behind Prasad's remarks. His presidency would end after two more years. Nehru was said to believe that Prasad had been advised by K. M. Munshi that the President was not bound by the advice of his ministers.

Munshi had been active in establishing the Indian Law Institute and, according to an authority, intended to have it serve as a 'think tank' for the newly formed Swatantra Party.

[34] Issue of 1 December 1960.

[35] Issue of 2 December 1960.

[36] Issue of 5 December 1960.

[37] Issue of 4 December 1960.

[38] *Jawaharlal Nehru's Speeches*, 5 vols, Ministry of Information and Broadcasting, GOI, New Delhi, 1949–68, vol. 4, pp. 100–1.

but the decisive pressure really had come from the President. 'Certainly the recognised procedure of the President acting on the advice of the Prime Minister was reversed,' wrote Radhakrishnan's biographer.[39] Tongue in cheek, Rajagopalachari, by this time leader of the opposition Swatantra Party, recommended that the Constitution be amended so that the Prime Minister should act on the advice of the President.[40]

WITHIN THE COUNCIL OF MINISTERS

Power relations within the executive branch, excluding the presidency, divide neatly into two periods: from the inauguration of the Constitution (indeed from independence) until Sardar Patel's death in December 1950, and from then until Nehru's passing. Close associates of Mahatma Gandhi (along with Rajendra Prasad) for some thirty years during the independence movement, Nehru's and Patel's personal relations ranged from near-rupture to cordiality and mutual admiration. Second in rank to Nehru as Deputy Prime Minister, but in reality co-equal, and one pledged (to Gandhi) to support Nehru,[41] Patel led the Home Ministry—which controlled central police forces

[39] Gopal, *Radhakrishnan*, p. 315.

[40] Ibid., p. 317. Bhupesh Gupta of the CPI, although friendly with Radhakrishnan, wrote to Nehru protesting the President's interference in policy-making. Nehru did not reply. Ibid.

Radhakrishnan stirred Delhi's rumour pot in 1963 with some remarks to the American Ambassador, Chester Bowles. which his biographer describes as joking, that upon Nehru's departure from office, the President might take temporary charge of government, set policy and administration right, and then step aside for a democratically chosen Prime Minister. Ibid., p. 328. The *New York Times* printed the rumour, and an aide-de-camp of the President during his first year in office gave credence to it in a book (Datta, C. L., *With Two Presidents*, Vikas Publishing House, New Delhi, 1971), which Radhakrishnan, in retirement, called a tissue of lies.

Presidential powers reappeared controversially several times during Indira Gandhi's terms as Prime Minister and once during the Janata interregnum. As will be seen in later chapters, the conventions of parliamentary government weakened, but did not disappear. Two amendments would write into the Constitution previously tacit conventions about presidential powers: one would require the President to assent to any constitutional amendment enacted by Parliament; the other that he 'shall' act on the advice of his ministers.

[41] Gopal, *Nehru*, vol. 2, p. 89. What predictably would have been a critical conflict within the cabinet, between the Prime Minister and Deputy Prime Minister, was avoided because Sardar Patel died in December 1950. In 1948, each had set out his view of the position of the Prime Minister. Briefly, Nehru held that ' "the PM should have full freedom to act when and how he chooses, though of course such action must not be an undue interference with local authorities who are immediately responsible ...".' Durga Das, *Patel's Correspondence*, vol. 6, pp. 18–19, as cited in L. P. Singh, *Office of Prime Minister; Retrospect*

and was the channel for the states' official communications with New Delhi. If Nehru was charismatic and determined and, it proved, politically skilled, Patel was iron-willed, a great administrator, and widely revered by the public and within the party. Their clashes took place largely over social revolutionary and administrative issues, as will be seen in greater detail in later chapters. On property rights, both favoured zamindari abolition, but Patel argued for relatively better compensation for expropriated property. He sympathized with the country's industrialists while Nehru, as a socialist, disparaged and distrusted them. Patel preferred to deal with the country's social structures as they were;[42] Nehru wished to overturn them. Patel feared that the rapid changes in society that Nehru desired would endanger political stability and perhaps national integrity.[43] After having enticed and pressured the princely states into a unified India, Patel was anxious that Nehru's tinkering with the princes' privy purses and privileges not queer the arrangements. On the issue, he and Nehru arrived at an agreement satisfactory to both.[44]

With Patel's death in December 1950, Nehru was freed from the restraint of the 'duumvirate'. But he still had to negotiate policies with talented and strong-minded colleagues. He had to persuade his prickly Finance Minister, C. D. Deshmukh, from resigning. Discipline was so imperfect that 'even where cabinet decisions have been reached, our cabinet colleagues or even Ministers of State (sometimes) do not feel bound by them.'[45] The strongest curb on the Prime Minister's arbitrary use of power came from Nehru himself. He both fought and yielded to 'the slow elephantine movements ... of democratic methods', recalled long-time peasant leader and Congressman N. G. Ranga.[46] He had to fight against 'the eagerness of his colleagues to leave all making of policy to him' and as the years passed against the increasing reality that the central government 'was basically a one-man show'.[47]

---

and Prospect, Centre for Policy Research, New Delhi, 1995, p. 4. Patel acknowledged the Prime Minister's 'pre-eminence' but thought ' "he has no overriding powers over his colleagues".' Ibid., p. 5.

[42] Shankardass, Rani Dhavan, *Vallabhbhai Patel,* Orient Longman Ltd., New Delhi, 1988, p. 12.

[43] K. M. Munshi Oral History Transcript, p. 22, NMML.

[44] For their exchange of letters, see Durga Das, *Patel's Correspondence,* vol. 8, pp. 597ff.

[45] Sardar Patel to the Minister of Works, Mines and Power, N. V. Gadgil, on 22 August 1949. Ibid., p. 606.

[46] A reminiscence in *Journal of Parliamentary Information* (hereafter *JPI*), Lok Sabha Secretariat, New Delhi, 1986, vol. 32, no. 2, p. 283.

[47] Gopal, *Nehru,* vol. 2, pp. 303–4.

Ambivalence toward power was part of Nehru's humanity. He enjoyed power, used it to pursue his vision of the national good, and could play rough to vanquish political opponents. Yet, lonely and anxious about affairs in the Congress and the constitutional issues of liberty and property (see chapter 2), he wrote in April 1951 to several 'old friends' seeking 'frank discussion' because 'whatever ... our present differences, [we] have functioned for many years in the Congress ... and ... [we] know each other well'. The talks were to be 'private and informal'.[48] Thrice, Nehru either contemplated resigning from the prime ministership or spoke of it openly. The first occasion came only four weeks after he took his oath under the Constitution. Worried about relations between government and the Congress Party and about India–Pakistan relations, especially 'in the Bengals', he wrote to Sardar Patel in February 1950, 'I am quite convinced that I could serve the cause of our country much better today in a private capacity than in the public office I hold.'[49] Patel responded the following day, saying that he could appreciate Nehru's sense of oppression, 'but we should do nothing which would make confusion worse compounded.'[50]

Nehru spoke again of resigning in the autumn of 1954, when he was both Prime Minister and Congress president (which he had been since 1951). This time, the context included constitutional amendment, Congress party in-fighting, and Minister of Education Maulana Azad's blocking of Krishna Menon's appointment to the cabinet, which greatly upset him.[51] He mentioned his physical and mental weariness to the Congress Parliamentary Party (CPP), to the chief ministers, and to the presidents of the Provincial Congress Committees (PCCs).[52] He turned for counsel to Lal Bahadur Shastri, the able diplomat of internal party affairs who would succeed him as Prime Minister, and to Morarji Desai, then Chief Minister of Bombay.[53]

---

[48] Quotation from the 13 April 1951 letter to Sampurnanand. Sampurnanand Collection, File A-75, NAI. Other recipients of the letter were Pandit G. B. Pant, B. C. Roy, B. G. Kher, Morarji Desai, Nabakrushna Chaudhuri, A. N. Sinha, S. K. Sinha, D. P. Mishra, H. K. Mahtab, G. L. Nanda, and Rafi Ahmed Kidwai. No record of the discussion, if one was kept, is available.

[49] Letter dated 20 February 1950. Durga Das, *Patel's Correspondence*, vol. 10, p. 5.

[50] Ibid., p. 6.

[51] Gopal, *Nehru*, vol. 1, p. 224.

[52] To the chief ministers in a letter of 1 October 1954. *NLTCM*, vol. 4, p. 55. To the PCC presidents in 'Dear Comrade' letter that he enclosed with his letter to chief ministers of 1 October 1954. Ibid., pp. 65–8.

[53] U. N. Dhebar Oral History Transcript, p. 67, NMML. Dhebar replaced Nehru as president of the Congress.

Close cabinet colleague and Minister of Commerce and Industry, T. T. Krishnamachari, wrote to Nehru that he recognized that Nehru no longer could share burdens with Patel and that Nehru's 'efforts to create an inner cabinet bore little fruit'. Lighten your burdens, Krishnamachari enjoined, but 'pray do not give in to your present mood,' for there was risk of government falling into 'unsuitable hands ... if you remove yourself from your present sphere of activities'.[54]

Nehru's final gesture toward leaving office came in his peculiar suggestion that he take a prime ministerial sabbatical. In April 1958, he informed the Parliamentary Party that he wished to leave the prime ministership temporarily to free himself to think ' "as an individual citizen of India and not as Prime Minister ... I am anxious to fit myself for the great tasks ahead, and I feel that it might help me to do so if I am away from the centre of activity and responsibility." '[55] The CPP resolved on 1 May that it could not accept the ' "severance" ', even temporary, ' "of the ties binding Nehru to the party and the government" '.[56] Again, cabinet colleagues wrote to Nehru, protesting that the country voted Congress into power 'because they wanted you to be Prime Minister'.[57]

[54] Letter dated 11 October 1954. T. T. Krishnamachari Papers, Jawaharlal Nehru File, 1954, NMML.

Ravi Shankar Shukla, then chief minister of Madhya Pradesh, wrote to Nehru from Nagpur on 5 November 1954 that, in view of the burdens on him, Nehru might 'appoint some senior statesman as Deputy Prime Minister who could assist you'. And Nehru might include 'younger persons with a fresh outlook and energy' to assist in administration. But 'the country can ill-afford to lose the benefit of your leadership and guidance even temporarily ...'. Jawaharlal Nehru Papers as received from M. O. Mathai, Ravi Shankar Shukla File, NMML.

[55] Nehru's written statement dated 29 April. *NLTCM*, vol. 5, p. 40, editor's footnote 3.

[56] Ibid. In the 'Points for Discussion' paper for the AICC meeting of 10–12 May 1958, Nehru said two things were troubling him: the 'fall in standards of public behaviour and job-hunting mentality ... At the base of these lie lust for power. We are not new to power. There is a natural love of power to do good ... [which] is different from the unnatural power clothed with a superfluous [sic] desire to be useful to society.' AICC Papers, Working Committee Proceedings, Item 3791, NMML. This document gives 3 May as the date Nehru decided against resigning.

[57] Personal and confidential letter from Minister of Scientific Research and Cultural Affairs Humayun Kabir, dated 2 May 1958. Humayun Kabir Papers, Indira Gandhi File, NMML.

B. Shiva Rao wrote to Nehru on 2 May opposing the temporary withdrawal. 'May I with all frankness suggest you withdraw completely and unconditionally to give your successor fullest freedom. If you want later to come back to active politics, this can be only as Prime Minister, and that place is yours the moment you feel the time is appropriate ...'. B. Shiva Rao Papers, Jawaharlal Nehru File, NMML.

Indira Gandhi's response to her father's whim is difficult to interpret. In a letter written after a conversation with him, she said, 'Having once suggested giving up the prime ministership is it wise to go back to the status quo? ... So much is rotten in our politics that everyone sees things through his own avaricious myopic eyes and is quite unable to understand nobility or greatness. There will therefore be a feeling that you ... were only bluffing.'[58]

It seems that Nehru threatened to resign three other times, but that these were tactical. Two were over controversies within the Congress Party: the Tandon affair in 1950 (see below) and when he threatened to resign from the Congress's Central Parliamentary Board over a state party matter in 1951. In 1950, he used the threat of his own resignation and that of his government to force President Prasad's assent to the Bihar Land Reforms Act (See chapter 3).[59]

THE COUNCIL OF MINISTERS AND PARLIAMENT

Parliament was Nehru's natural habitat, one whose health and strength he strove to secure. His personal popularity, his position as Prime Minister and leader of the Lok Sabha, and Congress's seventy-five per cent majority there made his dominance complete. Nevertheless, 'as soon as he entered the House, he brought grace and eloquence along with him'. Although 'impatient in his first reactions to any criticism ... not to his liking, ... he was always ... receptive to useful representation', remembered Hukum Singh, Deputy Speaker of the Lok Sabha from 1956 to 1962 and Speaker from 1962 to 1967.[60] In addition to his own instincts, Parliament's sense of its own significance and the spectrum of opinion within the CPP, which could deny him the votes to enact a measure, (witness his failure to push through the Hindu Code Bill), constrained him from riding roughshod over it. Moreover, in the Lok Sabha's first Speaker, G. V. Mavalankar, Nehru was dealing with an individual of strong character and great popularity, whose dedication to a strong Parliament matched his own. For instance, in November 1950 Mavalankar protested to Nehru about the government's 'inherently undemocratic' practice of promulgating ordinances instead of bringing

[58] Letter dated 1 May 1958. Gandhi, Sonia (ed.), *Two Alone, Two Together: Letters Between Indira Gandhi and Jawaharlal Nehru, 1940–1964*, 2 vols, Hodder & Stoughton, London, 1992, vol. 2, p. 623.

[59] Gopal, in his *Nehru*, vol. 2, p. 158, called resigning Nehru's 'favourite remedy' for political difficulties.

[60] Hukum Singh Oral History Transcript, pp. 121–5, NMML.

bills before Parliament.[61] Twenty-one ordinances had been promulgated that year, he wrote to Nehru, and, justifiable or not, a large number of ordinances gave the undesirable psychological impression that 'government is carried on by ordinances'. Parliament sensed it was being ignored, and the impression was created 'that it desired to commit the House to a particular legislation', Mavalankar said.[62] Nehru responded that all his colleagues would agree and that ordinances should be reserved for 'special and urgent occasions'. But Parliament's procedures were slow and 'important legislation is held up'.[63] Ordinances for executive convenience seem to have made their appearance, and a bad example set.

The imbalance in the power equation in Parliament between the Prime Minister and his ministers on the one hand, and opposition parties on the other, greatly concerned both sides, for all appreciated the importance of a healthy opposition to the proper functioning of a democracy. 'When one party remains always in power and dissent is dissipated among unorganized individuals and relatively insignificant groups, which do not and cannot coalesce, government will inevitably become totalitarian,' thought C. Rajagopalachari.[64] As the Praja Socialist

[61] Under Article 123 of the Constitution, the President may promulgate ordinances, which have the force of law, when either house of Parliament is not in session. An ordinance expires six weeks after Parliament resumes sitting, and often is replaced by an identical Act.

[62] Cited in *Presidential Ordinances 1950–1984*, Lok Sabha Secretariat, New Delhi, 1985, p. iv. Mavalankar had said to the presiding Officers' Conference in 1947 that it was wrong of the executive branch to promulgate ordinances merely 'for want of time, as inconvenient legislation might also be promulgated in that manner'. Ibid.

[63] Letter dated 13 December 1950. Ibid., p. v. Nehru and Mavalankar exchanged letters in 1954 in much the same terms. Ibid. Mavalankar's anxieties were well-founded, although the Nehru government's ordinances declined to ten in 1951 and never again rose above nine for the year, for future prime ministers would use the ordinance power heavily.

On 28 July 1954, Rajendra Prasad wrote to the Prime Minister saying that he had been told a cabinet-approved ordinance was coming to him for signature. However, if the matter could linger in ministries since May 1953, 'I think it could well have waited for another four weeks' until Parliament would be in session. '(R)ightly, objection is taken to recourse to ... [ordinances] where they can well be avoided'. Choudhary, *Prasad: Correspondence*, vol. 17, pp. 331–2.

[64] Rajagopalachari, C., *Our Democracy*, B. G. Paul & Co., Madras, 1957, p. 1.

K. M. Munshi, as Governor of Bombay, wrote to Seth Tulsidas Kilachand on 12 October 1952 that if you and Shyama Prasad Mookerjee will work together, 'it will lay the foundation of a responsible opposition which we badly need. At present, the distinction between those who want to destroy parliamentary government and those who constitute parliamentary opposition is being blurred. It is not a wholesome thing for the country.' Munshi Papers, File 130, p. 230, NMML.

Party (PSP) opened its election campaign in Patna in February 1957, Acharya Kripalani and Jayaprakash Narayan called for building a single opposition party. You can't ask the people to vote for the opposition if there isn't one, said Kripalani. Desiring a functioning opposition to strengthen parliamentary government, Nehru repeatedly 'cajoled' Narayan to enter Parliament and lead one.[65] Narayan repeatedly declined to do so. Later, as will be seen, he and Nehru corresponded about Narayan joining the government, but this would come to naught.

Yet, the opposition parties were not powerless, even as the Congress's legislative engine steamed ahead. They fulfilled an opposition's role as critic and, in combination with opposition to Nehru within the Congress, could act as a brake on legislation and government programmes. But, frustrated by the impotence brought on largely by their own personal and doctrinal fractiousness, they resorted to ritualistic charges of Congress 'corruption' and 'authoritarianism' and to employing 'extra-parliamentary' methods, turning the methods used to oppose imperial power against Indians' freely elected governments. 'In the interests of orderly progress, the people's right to civil disobedience must be recognised as much as the government's right to arrest and imprison under due process of law,' the Socialist Party asserted. Instead of the alternatives of parliamentary government or an exclusively insurrectionary path, the party ought to choose a balanced mix of constitutional actions and civil resistance where necessary, said its president.[66] The government reacted with righteous dismay that Indians would use tactics legitimate in the context of foreign rule against their own leaders.[67] By the mid-seventies, this behaviour would endanger the democracy it was intended to protect.

THE EXECUTIVE AND THE JUDICIARY

The relationship between these branches of government was at once mutually respectful and highly conflicted. The respect was between

---

[65] Nehru, B. K., *Nice Guys Finish Second*, Penguin Books, New Delhi, 1997, p. 516. B. K. Nehru is nephew of JN's cousin, and Indira's cousin.

[66] The quotation and the sentence following are from, respectively, 'Election Manifesto', Socialist Party, Hyderabad, 1957, p. 6; and the speech president Ram Manohar Lohia gave at the party's founding conference, 28 December 1955. *Hindu*, quoted in *AR*, 31 December 1955–6 January 1956, p. 609.

[67] K. M. Munshi, then Governor of Uttar Pradesh, wrote to the Chief Minister, G. B. Pant, on 12 November 1953 that the central government needed to enact legislation 'making hunger-strike a cognizable offence'. K. M. Munshi Papers, Microfilm Box 56, File 143, NMML.

the individuals involved and the institutions. The conflict was over the constitutionality of legislation and the Supreme Court's power of judicial review. (See forthcoming chapters, especially 2 and 4.) Nehru would rail at lawyers and stamp his foot at the courts; yet he did not denigrate the judiciary as a vital institution in a democracy, nor did he attempt to tamper with its independence. He supported it. Instead, he would lead Parliament to amend the Constitution to nullify the effect of Supreme Court interpretations. With Nehru's departure from the scene, the respect would disappear and the conflict intensify.

THE CENTRAL GOVERNMENT AND THE STATE GOVERNMENTS

From the outset, this was a power relationship between unequals. (We shall return to it often in later chapters and particularly in Part VI.) The central government held the purse strings and had powers bestowed by the Constitution's centralized federalism. Anxious, equally, to preserve the country's unity and integrity and to develop it economically and socially, central government leaders augmented the constitutional structure with sub-structures for national economic planning and development. Although there was considerable grumbling among the state governments at New Delhi's distribution of centrally collected revenues and its sometimes unwise uses of power, in general centralization of economic and political authority was accepted as necessary to national goals. The Congress Party's parallel federal structure provided channels for both enforcement of, and negotiations over, central government authority. Because state chief ministers and, somewhat less so, presidents of the Provincial Congress Committees had their own power bases, centre–state relations could be described by W. H. Morris-Jones as 'bargaining federalism'.

WHICH WILL GOVERN—THE CONGRESS PARTY OR THE GOVERNMENT?

One of the most important power struggles took place, constitutionally speaking, off-stage, between 'wings' of the Congress Party, i.e. between the government, or legislative, wing and its organizational wing. At issue was whether government in the country should be directed by constitutionally elected officials—the council of ministers and Parliament at the centre and, analagously, state ministries and legislatures—or from

---

For a thorough and insightful study of Parliament and the political culture in which it functioned, see Morris-Jones, W. H., *Parliament in India*, Longmans Green and Co., London, 1957.

behind the scenes by political functionaries and the party apparatus. Nehru, supported by the CPP and elements in the organizational wing, made sure that the legislative wing dominated the organizational wing. This was to serve the legislative wing, not the other way around. Nehru's election as president of the Congress Party in September 1951 while continuing as Prime Minister doubly assured legislative dominance. The chief minister's ascendancy over the PCC would become the pattern in the states, too, although in the Punjab, the Central Provinces, Madras, and Travancore–Cochin the struggle was prolonged.

The victory of the legislative wing in the 1950s strengthened the democracy and the social revolutionary strands of the seamless web. The socialists and secularists gained from it to the disadvantage of the cultural, social, and economic conservatives, although the fight between socialists and communists and the economic conservatives would continue for decades. Another result was that the party—to a limited degree—was nudged in the Gandhian direction of a social service organization, for the Working Committee and Nehru and U. N. Dhebar when party presidents, put their weight behind the party's 'Constructive Programme'. For many Congress members, however, politics and office-seeking proved to be more appealing than 'constructive work', to the dismay of the central leadership.[68]

The first power struggle between the party's 'wings' took place in 1947. Acharya J. B. Kripalani resigned from the party presidency complaining that the cabinet and the Congress Parliamentary Party does 'not feel that the government at the centre is a Congress government. After August 15 [1947] ... [it] seemed to make a distinction between Congress and the national government'.[69] Nehru had then explained, in a note to Kripalani and others, that the need for quick action and sometimes secrecy precluded consultation with the Working Committee as a customary procedure. It was a matter of the 'freedom of the government to shape policies and act up to them within the larger ambit of the general policy laid down in the Congress Resolutions', Nehru said.[70]

---

[68] Party documents often deplore the 'greed for office' among party members. The PCCs and the Constructive Programme Committee were 'to stimulate the initiative of the people themselves ... [and] to help the people in securing the advantages which a popular and representative government are bound to provide.' AICC Circular 27, dated 9 July 1947 to all PCCs and Constructive Organizations, Hare Krushna Mahtab Papers, File 7, NMML.

[69] In a letter to Rajendra Prasad dated 21 December 1947. Austin, *Cornerstone*, p. 16.

[70] Note dated 15 July 1947. Ibid.

The issue reappeared in 1950. In September that year, Purushot-tamdas Tandon, a conservative who differed from Nehru on econom-ic issues, the use of Hindi, and policy toward Muslims (whereas Kri-palani had shared Nehru's secular and socialist outlook) was elected Congress president. Nehru consented to join the Working Commit-tee, but he was affronted when Tandon appointed his own supporters as the other members, and he was infuriated by Sardar Patel's sup-port for Tandon. The party faced both an ideological and procedural schism, and the dispute simmered into the summer of 1951. Tandon wrote to Nehru that 'the Prime Minister and his cabinet are responsi-ble to the Congress and have to carry out policies laid down by the Congress from time to time.'[71] Nehru replied with his decision to resign from the Working Committee and the party's Central Election Committee. He wrote to the chief ministers that he had taken the step despite the obvious risks, hoping 'that ultimately it would bring some clarity in our thought and actions ... . The major problem has seemed to me ... how to bring about some kind of communion be-tween those in government or outside, who give the lead, and the masses of our people. That lead has to be realistic.'[72] Mediation of the dispute failed, and Tandon finally capitulated, resigning from the party presidency.[73] The AICC elected Nehru party president; he now had to play a dual role which he disliked on institutional grounds. Later in the autumn, the Congress Plenary Session passed resolutions embodying Nehru's economic and social policies, confirming 'the pre-eminent role of the Prime Minister and reinforced the boundaries of

[71] Letter of 6 August 1951. Kochanek, Stanley A. *The Congress Party in India,* Princeton University Press, Princeton, NJ, 1968, p. 45. For a detailed account of this affair, see ibid., ch. 2.

When Pattabhi Sitaramayya retired from the Congress Presidency in 1948, he wrote that the conception of the Congress as a parallel government had ceased to be relevant. Both the legislative and executive functions of the nation were now being performed by a popular government. Ibid., p. 24.

[72] Letter dated 19 August 1951. *NLTCM,* vol. 2, pp. 475–6.

[73] A. P. Jain, then Minister of State for Rehabilitation (of refugees from Pakistan), wrote to Nehru on 7 July 1951 that 'The suggestion that the parliamentary activities of the Congress should be divorced from the normal organizational activities and placed in your hands as the leader of the Parliamentary Party is well-worth considering.' A. P. Jain Papers, Subject File 1, NMML.

Biswanath Das, then president of the Utkal (Orissa) Provincial Congress Committee, urged that the Congress constitution be amended to allow the leader of the CPP to be the ex-officio president of the Congress, with parallel arrangements in the states, because power had passed from the Congress to the CPP. *Hindustan Standard,* 9 September 1951.

the office of Congress president, which had been revealed once more as limited strictly to organizational affairs with no special responsibility for policy-making'.[74]

The Nehru Years Reviewed

These were the years of creation, and much that occurred during them presaged developments to come. These tendencies, incipient trends, may be mentioned as we proceed into other chapters about the Nehru period, for they would gain significance under future prime ministers. Nehru, himself, set the tone. Nation- builder, reformer, ardent democrat, and flawed administrator, he and his colleagues tried to do everything at once. The very newness of national independence and the oldness of the country's needs created an atmosphere of impatience in which error and pettiness sometimes sullied the reigning humane and democratic spirit. The generation of men and women who had helped India attain independence had to make it work. Civic and social responsibility were the ideals, and making the legal–constitutional system function properly for its own health and for the common good was the rule rather than the exception. But in their earnestness for achievement, central government leaders would take on too much responsibility, overcentralizing and blunting local initiative.

The confrontations between the executive and Parliament on the one hand, and the courts on the other, over social reform legislation and other laws impinging on the Fundamental Rights, which were a distinguishing characteristic of the period, would result in restrictions on the courts' reach. Property began its career as the most divisive social

[74] Kochanek, *Congress Party*, p. 53. The Tandon affair is also described in Gopal, *Nehru*, vol. 2, ch. 8.

In the states, the tensions produced by PCC attempts to influence the ministries found no remedy but time. Congress president Pattabhi Sitaramayya suggested that the governments brief PCC leaders on their legislative programmes and that PCC presidents become *ex-officio*, non-voting members of legislative parties, but the chief ministers rejected the idea, and with it the PCC presidents' suggestion that ministers hold office on the PCCs' sufferance. Conference of PCC presidents and secretaries [with central party leaders], 17 May 1949. *Report of the General Secretaries, January 1949–September 1950*, Indian National Congress, New Delhi, 1950, pp. 60–6. When the same suggestion was made later, Nehru personally scotched it. By 1953, Nehru was hoping that conventions could be established for consultations between chief ministers and PCC presidents. Tensions were reduced, but relations between the PCCs and governments continued to range from uneasy to combative. See Kochanek, *Congress Party*, especially ch. 10 for his description of state-level affairs.

issue. Although conflict with the judiciary would be confined narrowly to areas of reform legislation, the example would be insidious. This tendency to amend the Constitution to limit judicial jurisdiction would develop into a predilection for undermining judicial powers broadly and even into attacks on the judiciary as an institution.

Good intentions thwarted by reality may become pretentions. These appeared in the Nehru years as the Congress realized it was not fulfilling its social revolutionary promises, and promissory rhetoric substituted for action. The faith that the central government could propose and dispose on economic affairs blinded the 'planners' to diversities of many kinds and to the necessity for monitoring implementation against intention. The faith in the efficacy of a centralized economy later would erode elements of the Constitution.

Trying to do what the nation needed, Nehru and his generation initially created tensions in the seamless web, many of which had subsided by the close of the period. It is difficult to imagine how it could have been otherwise. Citizens' expectations were high; their leaders' were higher. But the successes of the period were fundamental: power relationships were sorted out constitutionally; the parliamentary system became entrenched; democracy not only survived Nehru's charisma, popular participation strenghtened it; power was democratically transferred from one prime minister to another twice in sixteen years; one-party government combined internal party democracy and political variety with preserving national unity and integrity; the foundation was laid for an industrial economy and the social revolution set in motion. This was no golden age, but the Nehru years set standards against which others would be measured—and many fall short.

Chapter 2

FREE SPEECH, LIBERTY, AND PUBLIC ORDER

Soon after the Constitution's inauguration, India added its name to the long list of democracies whose constitutional ideals were tested against the government of the day's perception of national needs. The seamless web's three strands came under strain, and the cause seemed to be incompatibilities among them. To resolve these, was there genuine need to sacrifice one strand for the benefit of another? Nehru, his ministry, and the Parliament had their views; the judiciary had its interpretation of the Constitution, and the two branches disagreed sharply during the years of getting started. Protecting national integrity through preserving political stability was thought to be in conflict with the democratic rights to freedom of expression and personal liberty. The social revolutionary goals of the Directive Principles of State Policy were found to conflict with the right to property. Several provisions of the Fundamental Rights conflicted among themselves and with the Constitution's provisions for remedial treatment of disadvantaged citizens.

During the Nehru years, remedies for these conflicts were sought, in part, through the First, Fourth, Sixteenth, and Seventeenth Amendments to the Constitution. Each of these amendments was a multipurpose affair, and it will be less confusing to take them up not all at once in a group, which is how participants at the time reacted to them, but according to the subjects in their provisions. Hence, this chapter first will discuss freedom of speech and expression as treated in the First and Sixteenth Amendments. It will conclude with a burning issue of personal liberty covered by the Fundamental Rights, preventive detention, although instituting preventive detention did not involve constitutional amendment. Chapter 3 will open by giving the general background of property issues followed by their treatment in the First Amendment. It will conclude with the amendment's provisions that deal with remedial treatment for disadvantaged citizens, variously called positive discrimination and compensatory discrimination. Two more property amendments, the Fourth and the Seventeenth, are the subjects of chapter 4. Chapter 5 is devoted to the judiciary, whose rulings so often led to the amendments, and chapter 6 to the uses of the Constitution's provisions that deal with centre–state relations in the service of national unity and integrity.[1]

Although it will take us far ahead of the story, it may add clarity to sketch the course of the great confrontation that was now beginning between Parliament and the Supreme Court over guardianship of the Constitution. The issues were: which institution was supreme in interpreting the Constitution, in deciding what changes could be made to it, and what could lawfully be done under it. The government would learn the aptness of Chief Justice of India Harilal Kania's remark that 'different parts of the Constitution will act and react on each other and the Court will have to decide questions arising from such a situation'.[2] And it would be told, by his successor Patanjali Sastri, that when the courts exercised the power of judicial review of legislation they would not be tilting 'at legislative authority in a crusader's spirit, but in discharge of a duty plainly laid upon them by the Constitution'.[3]

Parliament under Nehru would revise laws in response to judicial decisions, and it would amend the Constitution to preclude judicial review of legislation, particularly legislation affecting property takings and compensation for them. This was constitutional, for Article 368 had given Parliament amending authority without specifying any

---

[1] The Constitution may be amended (Article 368) by passing a bill by a majority of the total members of each house and not less than two-thirds of those members present and voting. If the bill changes either Article 368 or other, in general, 'federal' provisions of the Constitution, it requires ratification by one-half the number of state legislatures. Assent by the President then completes the process. Strictly speaking, the two-thirds majority is necessary only at third reading, but 'by way of caution' this majority applies to all stages of the amending bill. Amending bills may be introduced in either house of Parliament, but government amendments are by convention introduced in the Lok Sabha. Kashyap, Subhash (ed.), *M. N. Kaul and S. L. Shakdher Practice and Procedure of Parliament,* Lok Sabha Secretariat/Metropolitan, New Delhi, 1991, p. 542.

Parliament may change the delineation of the country's states, which in fact alters part of the Constitution, but this is done by law and is not to be 'deemed' a constitutional amendment even though it is called such (Articles 3 and 4). For example, States Reorganization took effect through the Seventh Amendment (see ch. 6).

Only the amendments significantly affecting the Constitution or important institutions operating under it are discussed in this book. The many that are of a drafting character or whose content is largely administrative—some two-thirds of all amendments—will not be considered.

[2] Kania, inaugurating the Supreme Court on 26 January 1950. 1950 (1) *Supreme Court Reports* (hereafter SCR) 7.

[3] Sastri, giving the majority opinion on 31 March 1952 in *State of Madras v V. G. Row.* AIR 1952 SC 199.

limitation, and the Supreme Court in 1951 had upheld this position.[4]
Yet placing certain laws beyond judicial scrutiny (see chapters 3 and 4),
although understandable when keeping in view the web's social
revolutionary strand, diminished democracy by lessening the co-equal
status of the courts and started the country toward far more extensive
and dangerous efforts to quarantine the judiciary. By 1964, particularly
with regard to the Seventeenth Amendment (chapter 4), anxiety had
mounted that the CPP was playing fast and loose with judicial review.
Three years later fear prevailed, and the Supreme Court ruled that
Parliament's amending power *was* limited: the Fundamental Rights (Part
III of the Constitution) could not be touched (see chapter 8). This
decision also said that, from the beginning, Parliament had *not* had
unfettered power of amendment. Six years later, after Parliament had
attempted to restore, as its members saw it, its unlimited amending
power (the Twenty-fourth Amendment, chapter 10), the Supreme Court
again ruled the amending power limited: the Constitution's 'basic
structure' was not to be changed. Three years after this, during the
Emergency, Indira Gandhi's autocratic government amended the
Constitution to bar judicial review of amendments and much legislation
(chapter 17).

Freedom of Expression

Article 19(1)(a) in the original Constitution guaranteed the fundamental right to 'freedom of speech and expression' subject to the qualifiers
in clause 2: the government's authority to legislate concerning libel,
slander, defamation, contempt of court, any matter offending decency
and morality, 'or which undermines the security of or tends to overthrow, the State'.[5]

---

[4] In *Shankari Prasad Deo v Union of India.* 1952 (3) SCR 106. The court would uphold
this ruling in Sajjan Singh's case in 1964 (see ch. 4).

These positions were in accord with sentiment in the Constituent Assembly, where,
for example, Alladi Krishnaswami Ayyar had warned against a judiciary that would
'function as a kind of super-legislature or super-executive'. *CAD*, vol. 11, no. 9, col. 837.
He said that the judiciary's job was to 'interpret the Constitution' and its 'proper
functioning [depended] upon the cooperation of the other two [branches]'. Ibid.

[5] Other 'freedoms' protected by Article 19, with certain restrictions, were the freedom
to assemble peaceably and without arms, to form associations, to move freely within the
country, to reside anywhere in the country, to acquire and dispose of property, and to
practice any profession and carry on any business. More will be heard of these freedoms,
and the restrictions on them contained in other clauses of Article 19.

Early in 1950 three state governments invoked these qualifiers to curb freedom of expression. In Bihar, the government challenged a political pamphlet as inciting violence. In East Punjab, the government imposed pre-censorship on an English-language weekly in the name of maintaining public safety and order. In Madras, the government banned the entry into the state of the journal *Crossroads*. Each state took action under some version of a 'Public Safety Act', and each defendant turned for protection to the first clause of Article 19.

The Patna High Court rejected the Bihar government's contention that the pamphlet incited violence.[6] But, despite this, Patna's decision had a catalytic effect when it was found that Justice Sarjoo Prasad's ruling included his view that 'if a person were to go on inciting murder or other cognizable offences either through the press or by word of mouth, he would be free to do so with impunity' because he could claim freedom of speech and expression.[7] Nehru would use this assertion when defending the First Amendment in Parliament.

The East Punjab Public Safety Act, 1950, was struck down in the Supreme Court—by the same bench that decided the *Crossroads* case— on the ground that pre-censorship restricted liberty of the press.[8] The Madras incident in its effect proved the most significant of the three. *Crossroads* was, for all practical purposes, a communist publication, and Romesh Thapar, its publisher, and his wife, Raj, 'were known as communist party members, though we never held party cards'.[9] It first had been published in April 1949, the year the Madras government declared the Tamilnadu, Andhra, Kerala, and Karnataka communist parties unlawful organizations.[10] Thapar took the Madras government's action to the high court contending that his freedom of expression had been infringed. He then appealed to the Supreme Court under Article 32, which gives the Court original jurisdiction in fundamental

---

[6] The Supreme Court unanimously upheld the Patna High Court's judgement in *State of Bihar v Shailabala Devi* 1952 (3) SCR 654ff. The five-member bench comprised Mehr Chand Mahajan, Patanjali Sastri, Bijan Kumar Mukherjea, S. R. Das and Vivian Bose. The narrow issue was the constitutionality of the Indian Press Act (XXIII of 1931), which was upheld.

[7] 'In re Bharati Press' AIR 1951 Patna 21.

[8] In *Brij Bhushan v State of Delhi* AIR 1950 SC 129ff.

[9] Thapar, Raj, *All These Years*, Seminar Publications, New Delhi, 1991, p. 87.

[10] *Charge Sheet Against the Communists*, Director of Information and Publicity, Government of Madras, Madras, 1949, p. 1. This publication noted that the Second Congress of the CPI in 1948 adopted a revolutionary programme 'on the ground that the conditions in the country were ripe for staging a revolution'. Ibid.

rights disputes. On 26 May 1950, the court decided the *Crossroads* case by ruling the Madras Maintenance of Public Safety Act, 1949, unconstitutional. The majority ruling said that 'unless a law restricting freedom of speech and expression is directed solely against undermining the security of the State or the overthrow of it, such law cannot fall within the reservation of Clause 2 of Article 19'.[11] Although the Thapars were 'delirious with joy' that they had been vindicated by the Supreme Court and that the case 'went on the statute book ... establishing the freedom of expression in India',[12] it was far more significant that Home Minister Sardar Patel thought the *Crossroads* decision 'knocks the bottom out of most of our penal laws for the control and regulation of the press'.[13]

Himself upset by the court's decision on *Crossroads* and prodded into action by Patel, Nehru on 19 October wrote to the Law Minister, B. R. Ambedkar, who had chaired the Constituent Assembly's Drafting Committee, expressing the view that the Constitution's provisions pertaining to law and order and subversive activities needed to be amended. Reflecting the difficulties the government was having with the courts over other fundamental rights, Nehru added that the provisions affecting zamindari abolition and nationalization of road transport also needed amending. Two days later, a cabinet meeting directed the Law Ministry to examine the issues and to prepare draft amendments.[14]

---

[11] 1950 (1) SCR 602. In both courts, the case was listed as *Romesh Thapar v State of Madras*. Justice Patanjali Sastri delivered the opinion in the *Crossroads* case for himself and for Chief Justice Harilal Kania, Mehr Chand Mahajan, Bijan Kumar Mukherjea, and Sudhi Ranjan Das. Justice Saiyid Fazl Ali delivered a separate judgement.

For a commentary on the cases, see Seervai, H. M., *Constitutional Law of India*, 3rd edn., 3 vols, N. M. Tripathi Pvt. Ltd., Bombay, 1983, vol. 1, pp. 495ff, and Gajendragadkar, P. B., *The Indian Parliament and Fundamental Rights*, Eastern Law House, Calcutta, 1972, pp. 73ff.

For Justice M. C. Mahajan's thoughts on these cases, see his *Looking Back*, Asia Publishing House, New York, NY, 1963, pp. 198–201.

[12] Thapar, *All These Years*, p. 87. The Thapars had expected an adverse decision, especially from Mahajan.

[13] Patel–Nehru letter dated 3 July 1950. Durga Das, *Patel's Correspondence*, vol. 10, p. 358. Patel was explicit that the decision made it doubtful that the government could move against Shyama Prasad Mookerjee for his pronouncements about Kashmir and calling for the annulment of partition.

[14] Ministry of Law, File no. F34/51-C. Members present at the cabinet meeting included Nehru, Maulana Azad, C. Rajagopalachari, Baldev Singh, Jagjivan Ram, Rafi Ahmed Kidwai, Rajkumari Amrit Kaur, N. V. Gadgil, N. Gopalaswami Ayyangar, Hare Krushna Mahtab, K. M. Munshi, Sri Prakasa, C. D. Deshmukh, and Ambedkar.

Setting to work on the first part of the assignment, the ministry's Joint Secretary, S. N. Mukherjee, prepared a note summarizing Indian and United States cases bearing on freedom of expression and then presented his device for protecting legislation curbing freedom of expression from judicial review. Article 19 of the Constitution provided that the freedoms of assembly, association, and so on, could be subject to certain restrictions if these were 'reasonable'. No such qualification applied to the 'freedom of speech and expression'. Mukherjee recommended that 'reasonable' be removed as a qualification for restrictions on the other freedoms, apparently believing that if none of the 'freedoms' were so protected, consistency in the article would preclude judicial review of restrictions on speech.[15] Reacting to the note, Law Secretary K. V. K. Sundaram suggested rewording Article 19(2) so government could impose restrictions on speech and expression in the interest of the security of the state, public order, and decency and morality. The existing omission in the Constitution of 'reasonable' as qualifying freedom of expression was justifiable, he said. He agreed with the Joint Secretary's view that legislatures, not the courts, ought to be the final authority deciding the 'nature' of any restrictions on Fundamental Rights.[16]

Events moved on in February 1951. Nehru formed the Cabinet Committee on the Constitution (sometimes called the Cabinet Committee on Amendment) and requested his senior colleagues' opinions. Pandit G. B. Pant, then chief minister of Uttar Pradesh, responded at length. Freedom of expression, he said, had been 'wantonly abused … . Venomous and filthy attacks are being made … against the central and state governments … maliciously and in an extremely vulgar and indecent manner'. A remedy had to be devised, but he preferred appropriate legislation over constitutional amendment.[17] Hare Krushna Mahtab, Minister of Commerce and Industry, responded to Nehru in March with a note which said that placing 'rea-

---

[15] Note dated 6 January 1951. Ibid.

[16] Note dated 29 January 1951. Ibid.

[17] Letter of 5 March 1951. Ibid. Also to be found in G. B. Pant Collection, File 3, Pant–Nehru Correspondence, NAI.

Pant nevertheless appended a note prepared by an aide that suggested amending Article 19(2) to prohibit bringing 'the government of the state or the Union into contempt, scorn, contumely or disrepute'. He also enclosed a note analysing the problem. It referred to 'petty newspapers' being used by individuals and political parties for 'some personal gain' and said the basic question was 'whether the criticism of government not attended by violence can … be [deemed] an offence'.

sonable restrictions' on any of the freedoms of Article 19 left both the people and the legislatures uncertain of 'the framework within which they have to operate'.[18]

Law Minister B. R. Ambedkar sent Nehru a memorandum in reply. The rulings of the courts had not recognized any limitation on the Fundamental Rights where none was placed by the Constitution, and they had not recognized any further limitations where the Constitution had specified them, he said. He opposed deleting the existing limitations on the Rights to prevent the Supreme Court from interpreting them into Article 19 through the 'evil' of due process, which, he reminded Nehru, the Constituent Assembly had rejected. Reasonable restrictions could be placed on speech relating to libel, slander, and undermining the security of the state; laws placing such restrictions, he added, ought to be exempted from court intrusion.[19] Nehru, also agitated by Supreme Court decisions in property cases, as will be seen, replied the same day instructing Ambedkar to proceed 'with the utmost expedition' so as to get the necessary amendments through Parliament, then in session.[20] The Home Ministry recommended to the Cabinet Committee that public order and incitement to a crime should be included among the exceptions to the right to freedom of speech. It preferred dropping 'to overthrow' the state in favour of a wider formulation, 'in the interests of the security of the State'. And the note did not favour inserting 'reasonable' before restrictions on the freedom of expression in Article 19(2).[21]

The Cabinet Committee reported at the end of March that the Law Ministry was urging strongly that 'reasonable' be retained in all clauses in Article 19 where it existed and that it ought to be added before the

[18] Hare Krushna Mahtab Papers, File 21, NMML. Two years earlier, Mahtab had written to Nehru that 'I would strongly press for some legislation to prevent personal criticism of ministers ... [W]ild vulgar abuses are heaped upon you in public meetings ... Persistent vilification of this nature affects discipline in the services'. The central government had queried a number of state ministers about the subject. Letter of 1 September 1949, ibid., File 11.

[19] Memorandum dated 14 March 1951. Ministry of Law, File no. F34/51-C.

[20] Ibid.

[21] Ibid. The note concluded that Article 19(5) should be 'enlarged' so that the freedom of movement, residence, and to own property—originally subject to 'reasonable' restrictions in the interests of the general public or any Scheduled Tribe—be subject to martial law. The alternative to inserting 'martial law', the Ministry said, would be to proclaim an emergency, suspending the Fundamental Rights, which is a drastic remedy to deal with disturbance in a small area. A Law Ministry Note to the cabinet on 17 March seemed to concur with this, although it was contrary to Ambedkar's views.

restrictions on freedom of expression. Otherwise, the state would have the power 'altogether' to deny freedom of speech and expression. But the members of the committee disagreed with Ambedkar, the report said. They believed 'reasonable' ought not to qualify freedom of expression, although it was 'expedient' to leave the word in Article 19 where it was already.[22] Apparently they feared the political repercussions of taking away the protection that 'reasonable' accorded the other 'freedoms' in the article. But, they were so alarmed by the dangers to national security, friendly relations with foreign states, public order, etc., that they felt that possible curbs on free speech did not have to be 'reasonable'. Early in April, accounts of the amending process appeared in the press, and a continuing stream of newspaper editorials analysed and criticized the amendment's property and freedom of expression provisions which were thought to endanger freedom of the press. The *Hindustan Times* thought the changes 'animated ... by a desire to conserve and consolidate the power and patronage of the executive ... Particularly dangerous is the attempt to qualify freedom of speech'.[23]

President Prasad commented upon the draft amendment to the cabinet, in one of the occasions when some thought he was exceeding his powers. Raising substantive objections that would later be heard in Parliament and in the press, he said that, based on his reading of Supreme Court decisions, 'no case' for amending the Fundamental Rights had arisen. Amendment should come only if it was found impossible to bring the impugned provisions of law 'in conformity with the Constitution'. He doubted the wisdom of omitting the words—relating to speech— ' "tends to overthrow the State" ' and thought they might be added to the end of the language in the amendment 'by way of abundant caution'. Overall, Prasad opposed amending the Constitution at the 'fag-end of a long session'. Time should be given to all concerned to comment on the amendment, particularly because Parliament was a 'Provisional Parliament' acting under the 'transitory [sic] provisions of the Constitution until a Parliament having two houses comes into being'.[24]

[22] Ibid.

[23] Issue of 12 April 1951. At this time, the CPP established its own 'Constitutional Changes Committee' to consider the draft amendment. Members of this committee were reported to be Thakurdas Bhargava, Mohanlal Gautam, K. Hanumanthaiya, Mrs Renuka Ray, and Dr Punjabrao Deshmukh. *Hindustan Times*, 13 April 1951.

[24] Note dated 30 April 1951. Rajendra Prasad Collection, File 1, NAI. The President was commenting on the draft prepared by S. N. Mukherjee, Joint Secretary in the Legislative Department of the Law Ministry. This draft had gone earlier in April to the chief ministers for comment.

Prime Minister Nehru introduced the draft of the First Amendment in the Lok Sabha on 12 May and spoke extensively on it then and later. He found the argument that the Provisional Parliament was not competent to amend the Constitution 'curious' because the same restricted franchise had elected the Constituent Assembly, many of whose members sat before him. Was it sensible that the individuals who had framed the Constitution were not competent to amend it?[25] Besides, wide consultations with state governments and others had preceded the bill's introduction. He said that he had frequently expressed his appreciation for the press as 'one of the vital organs of modern life'. But was the 'press' responsible journals or 'some two-page news-sheet ... full of vulgarity, indecency and falsehood'? The amendment's language about friendly relations with foreign states was not 'meant to stifle criticism, but the international situation is delicate', and 'we cannot take any risks'. As to public order and 'incitement to an offence', Nehru continued, 'these words would have to be strictly examined in a piece of legislation'. A constitution should 'not limit the power of Parliament to face a situation'. It was an 'extraordinary state of affairs' that a high court had held 'that even murder or like offences can be preached'.[26] The 'concept of individual freedom has to be balanced with social freedom and the relations of the individual with the social group,' Nehru maintained.[27] Like democratic leaders before and since, Nehru deplored press scrutiny of his government even as he publicly praised freedom of the press. Yet, his dismay at the most inaccurate and scurrilous publications is understandable.[28]

[25] *Parliamentary Debates*, vol. 12, part 2, cols 8815–16, 16 May 1951. Further quotations are taken from columns 8817 to 8832. *Parliamentary Debates* was the designation for Lok Sabha debates during the 'Provisional Parliament'. The designation *Lok Sabha Debates* and a new series of volumes came into being during 1954 after election of the Parliament by the first general elections of 1952. During part of 1952, 1953, and a few months of 1954, the designation was 'Parliamentary Debates, House of the People'. Nehru's three speeches on the amending bill are given in full in *Nehru's Speeches*, vol. 2, pp. 486–538.

These debates were extensively reported in the English language press.

[26] 'Even Murder', *Nehru's Speeches*, vol. 2, p. 500.

[27] Ibid., p. 506. He also raised the matter of monopoly within the press community, an issue that his daughter would make much of as Prime Minister: 'When gigantic newspaper chains spring up and undermine the freedom of the independent newspapers, when the press in India is controlled by three or four groups of individuals, what kind of a press is that?'

[28] Nehru told members of the All India Newspaper Editors Conference at a meeting on 20 May 1951 that the amendment was not aimed at the press. Gopal, S. (ed.), *Selected Works of Jawaharlal Nehru*, 20 vols, Oxford University Press, New Delhi, 1995, vol. 1, part 1, p. 187. They were thinking of certain law and order situations in the country and of the international situation, he said.

Now it was the critics' turn. H. V. Kamath opposed rushing the bill through Parliament, favoured 'reasonable' as qualifying any restrictions on speech, and commented that in defending the bill Nehru seemed uneasy with his conscience.[29] Pandit Hriday Nath Kunzru, one of the distinguished non-Congressmen who the Congress had brought into the Constituent Assembly, declared that Article 19 was not being amended, but repealed. [30] Why are the current laws against offending decency and morality and undermining the security of the state not sufficient, asked Shyama Prasad Mookerjee of the Hindu Mahasabha, in what the *Times of India* called one of the 'two great orations' of the day—Nehru's having been the other. Who is to decide whether a criticism of foreign policy harms relations with other countries, asked Mookerjee. The Prime Minister believes that agitation to end partition is harmful to the country, but I think partition should be annulled. So why can we not each give our views and let the public decide, he said.[31]

Developments now took a surprising turn. Nehru, deeply concerned with the issue of freedom of speech, had overseen the deliberations of the Cabinet Committee on Amendment, and he surely had scrutinized the amending bill before approving its introduction in Parliament. Then, as chairman of the Select Committee reviewing the bill, he recommended to his cabinet that the draft bill be altered to insert the protecting word 'reasonable' to qualify the restrictions on the freedom of speech. He did not like the word 'reasonable', he wrote to T. T. Krishnamachari

---

[29] *Parliamentary Debates*, vol. 12, part 2, cols. 8913–24

[30] *Times of India*, 18 May 1951.

[31] *Parliamentary Debates*, vol. 12, part 2, col. 8846, for 'annul partition'.

Mookerjee shortly would become an officer of the All-India Civil Liberties Council, which had been formed in 1949. The Council was descended from the Indian Civil Liberties Union established in 1937, whose first president was the famed Bengali poet, Rabindranath Tagore. A general principle in the union's constitution had been that all thought on matters of public concern should be freely expressed. The Civil Liberties Council operated under the umbrella of the Servants of India Society based in Poona. After the passage of the First Amendment, the secretary of the Council, S. G. Vase, wrote to members that Roger Baldwin, then chairman of the International League for the Rights of Man, had been consulted about the amendment and he had replied that the introduction of the word 'reasonable' 'would provide a court review of the restrictions [on speech] ... [and] would probably mitigate the evil to a large extent'.

P. R. Das, then a lawyer prominent in civil liberties and zamindari abolition cases, became president of the Civil Liberties Council in 1950. Jayaprakash Narayan joined it in 1951 to become a leading figure in its activities. Narayan had been a member of the Indian Civil Liberties Union in the thirties. Jayaprakash Narayan Papers, First and Second Installments, File 365, NMML.

that evening after the meeting because it would be an invitation for each such case to go to the courts.[32] The cabinet accepted the recommendation at its meeting on 23 May 1951—in order to avoid a split in the cabinet and to ensure a two-thirds majority for the bill, according to the *Hindustan Times*[33]—and the Select Committee tabled its report two days later.[34] Delayed wisdom seems the best explanation for the Prime Minister's reversal of position.

The Select Committee's recommendations took two pages. Minutes of dissent filled sixteen, all by non-Congressmen. The dissenters frequently argued that, being 'provisional', Parliament should not pass the amendment, an opinion shared by the Federation of Indian Chambers of Commerce, and others. The All-India Newspaper Editors Conference called for the bill's withdrawal. Miss G. Durgabai and S. P. Mookerjee recommended that only Parliament, not state legislatures, should be empowered to pass legislation affecting the freedom of expression.[35] Naziruddin Ahmad thought the language about incitement to offence too broad and preferred the provision in the Indian Penal Code, where incitement was not an offence unless part of a conspiracy or followed by a criminal act.[36]

On 29 May, the Congress Parliamentary Party approved the amending bill, having rejected 'in no uncertain terms' a move to drop the Select Committee's recommendation to include the word 'reasonable'

[32] Gopal, *Selected Works of Jawaharlal Nehru*, vol. 1, part 1, p. 189.

[33] Issue of 25 May 1951.

[34] *The Constitution (First Amendment) Bill, 1951—Report of the Select Committee*, Parliament Library, New Delhi. The committee's other brief recommendations will be taken up subsequently. The freedom of speech issue had been the most vigorously debated, the committee reported, and it said that the only substantial change required in Article 19(2) was the one we have just seen.

Members of the committee were: Nehru, chairman, C. Rajagopalachari, B. R. Ambedkar, Miss G. Durgabai. H. N. Kunzru, M. Gautam, S. P. Mookerjee, Khandubhai Desai, Hukum Singh, K. T. Shah, L. K. Bharati, R. K. Sidhwa, Dev Kant Borooah, A. P. Sinha, M. C. Shah, T. R. Deogirikar, Raj Bahadur, Naziruddin Ahmad, K. Hanumanthaiya, and Satyanarayan Sinha. Minutes of dissent came from Durgabai, Kunzru, Mookerjee, Singh, Shah, and Ahmad.

Parliament had extended its session on 18 May to allow more time for debate on the bill.

[35] The cabinet took this idea seriously enough to consider it at its meeting on 30 May, but decided that it was not feasible because the subjects to which freedom of speech pertained were distributed among the legislative lists. Reserving bills affecting freedom of expression for the President's assent was also considered and rejected. Ministry of Law, File no. F35/51-C

[36] *Report of the Select Committee*, p. 16. Ahmad may have been referring to ch. V of the Code, on 'Abetment'.

as a protection of free expression.[37] Three days later, after a 'tumultuous and acrimonious' third reading, during which Nehru and Mookerjee traded accusations of bad faith, Parliament passed the bill by a vote of 228 to 20.[38] The First Amendment retroactively and prospectively empowered government to impose 'reasonable restrictions' on the freedom of expression 'in the interests of the security of the State [replacing the words "tends to overthrow the State"], friendly relations with foreign States, public order, decency or morality, or in relation to contempt of court, defamation, or incitement to an offence'. 'Defamation' replaced the words 'libel' and 'slander' of the original Constitution. '[I]ncitement to an offence' was directed at the Bihar and Punjab High Court decisions mentioned earlier.[39]

With the amendment enacted, Parliament passed The Press (Objectionable Matter) Act on 23 October 1951. 'Objectionable Matter' was defined as that inciting violence for the purpose of overthrowing the government; inciting the committing of murder, sabotage or offences involving violence; inciting interference with the supply of food or other essential commodities and essential services; seducing any member of the armed services from performance of his duties; promoting feelings of enmity among the 'sections' of society; and publishing matter which 'are grossly indecent, or are scurrilous or obscene or intended for blackmail'.[40] The Act also provided for securing and forfeiture of security deposits by newspapers and the seizure and destruction of unauthorized newssheets and newspapers. The Act was

[37] *Times of India*, 30 May 1951.

[38] *Times of India*, 3 June 1951. Among those who voted against the bill were Hukum Singh, Hussain Imam, Jaipal Singh, H. V. Kamath, Acharya Kripalani, Mrs Sucheta Kripalani, Kunzru, Mookerjee, Ahmad, S. L. Saksena, Damodar Swarup Seth, and K. T. Shah. To avoid ratification of the amendment by state legislatures, there were no amendments to the Legislative Lists, which had been contemplated several times.

Nehru justified the amendment in his 2 June and 15 June letters to chief ministers. He wrote that it was not government's intention to curb press freedom, and he did not want state governments to take advantage of the amendment to apply 'some obsolete law'. *NLTCM*, vol. 2, pp. 403–7, 417–9.

For a brief but useful analysis of legal issues involved at this time, see Blackshield, A. R., '"Fundamental Rights" and the Institutional Viability of the Indian Supreme Court', *Journal of the Indian Law Institute* (hereafter *JILI*), vol. 8, no. 2, 1966, pp. 203–5.

[39] For the text of the amendment, see *Constitution Amendment in India*, Lok Sabha Secretariat, New Delhi, 1986, pp. 179–84.

[40] Act No LVI of 1951. *Acts of Parliament*, Ministry of Law, GOI, New Delhi, 1952, pp. 389–402.

amended several times and repealed in 1957.[41]

This was a curious affair. The initial inclination of Nehru and the others had been to outlaw certain kinds of speech, and the amendment's language conceivably made prosecution easier. Yet providing that any limitations on free speech must be 'reasonable' strengthened the right through judicial review. Furthermore, much of the restrictive language in the amendment and the Objectionable Matter Act added little to government power under existing statutes.[42] And other means to intimidate publishers and editors could be employed.[43] Attempts to intimidate the press occurred from time to time, especially after the Nehru years, but, except during Indira Gandhi's Emergency, laws and practices to curb freedom of expression had more capacity to make mischief than was made. Remarkably, considering their strong wording, the various laws did not have a 'chilling effect' on the press during the Nehru years, according to members of the profession and lawyers. Scurrilous and fantastical reporting continued along with sober and responsible journalism.

Freedom of Expression—The Sixteenth Amendment

This 1963 amendment of Article 19 added that government might place restrictions on expression in the interests of 'the sovereignty and integrity of India', the qualifier 'reasonable' remaining in place. It also

[41] On 3 October 1952, the government established its first Press Commission which would report in 1954. Among other things, the commission was to examine freedom of the press and the repeal and amendment of laws not in consonance with it.

Individual examples of the desire to curb or protect the press occurred from time to time. Feroze Gandhi, a socialist member of Parliament and Indira Gandhi's husband, moved a private member's bill on 24 February 1956 to assure protection for the publication of defamatory language if the language had been first uttered in parliamentary debate.

Nehru wrote to K. N. Katju, then Home Minister, on 7 November 1954 that *Bulls Eye*, 'a new periodical of the worst type' had written a 'highly inflammatory' article about General Thimayya, the Chief of Staff. Nehru asked how one was to deal with 'these wretched rags' and noted that Thimayya wanted to horsewhip the editor, 'but I did not encourage him to do this'. Nehru Papers as received from M. O. Mathai, K. N. Katju File, NMML.

[42] For example, the Indian Penal Code, the Code of Criminal Procedure, the Industries (Development and Regulation) Act, and other laws. Passed in 1951, the latter authorized government investigation of industrial undertakings if managed in a manner highly detrimental to the public interest. A 1979 amendment to the Act exempted from it presses utilized mainly for printing newspapers.

[43] Withholding government advertisements was one. Restricting newsprint imports, controlling the prices of and the number of pages in newspapers were others. The latter two actions were struck down by the Supreme Court in *Sokal Papers (P) Ltd. v Union of*

included this formula in the oaths to be taken by candidates for, and members of, Parliament and the state legislatures, which oaths it placed in the Constitution's Third Schedule. The amendment also applied this new restriction to the rights in Article 19 to assemble and to form associations and unions.

A combination of panic, which from this distance seems to have been unwarranted, and rational concern produced the amendment. The Chinese incursions in the Northeast beginning in 1960 caused the former, although the threat reinforced, rather than weakened, the nation's sense of unity. Causing greater concern were Master Tara Singh's long fast for a Sikh state, Punjabi Suba, during mid-1961 and the Dravida Munnetra Kazhagam's (DMK) call for an entity separate from India called Dravidanad, comprising Madras, Mysore, Kerala, and Andhra.[44] Law Minister Asoke K. Sen, Home Minister Lal Bhadur Shastri, and his Home Secretary, L. P. Singh, especially, took Tamil separation seriously. Confronted by the Sikh agitation and aware of the DMK's inclinations, the Chief Ministers' Conference in August 1961 unanimously recommended that advocacy of secession be made a penal offence.[45] A National Integration Council was established. After its first meeting in

---

India, AIR 1962 SC 305, and *Bennett Coleman and Co. Ltd.* AIR 1973 SC 106 as cited in Singhvi, L. M., *Freedom on Trial*, Vikas Publishing House Pvt. Ltd., New Delhi, 1991, p. 73.

[44] This was stated in the DMK's election manifesto for the 1962 general elections, adopted in Coimbatore in December 1961. *AR*, 8–14 January 1962, p. 4363. The DMK had earlier called for Tamil secession from India. (See ch. 6.)

According to Robert L. Hardgrave, Jr., in late 1961 and early 1962, 'Dravidisthan, as an election issue, was shelved in favour of a concentration on the problem of rising prices in Madras ...'. See his *The Dravidian Movement*, Popular Prakashan, Bombay, 1965, p. 74. In 1960, the DMK leader, Annadurai, in response to a challenge from C. Subramaniam, then Finance Minister in the Madras government, that the DMK did not accept the Constitution, said the DMK 'seeks nothing more than "amendment of the Constitution through perfectly Constitutional methods"' to lessen central government domination of the states. Reported in *Link*, 27 December 1959 and 3 July 1960 and cited in ibid., p. 65.

Another American authority on India reported being informed that the DMK 'is not seriously demanding' the secession of Madras, Andhra Pradesh, Mysore, and Kerala. Talbot, Phillips, 'Raising a Cry for Secession', American Universities Field Staff Report, New York, August 1957, p. 1.

The terms Dravidisthan and Dravidanad, and Dravida Nadu were used by various individuals for the same concept of a body of Southern Indian states.

For Tara Singh and the Akali Dal, see Kapur, Rajiv A., *Sikh Separatism*, Vikas Publishing House Pvt. Ltd., New Delhi, 1987, pp. 212–6.

[45] *AR*, 10–16 September 1961, p. 4153. The chief ministers were giving their approval for a bill to amend the Indian Penal Code, which had been introduced on 10 August in

June 1962, one of the members of the council's Committee on National Integration and Regionalism, Lal Bahadur Shastri, began drafting the oath that would appear in the Sixteenth Amendment.[46] The committee's report went to Nehru on 5 November 1962, recommending that any 'demand for secession from the Centre be made unconstitutional'.[47]

Law Minister Sen introduced the amending bill in the Lok Sabha on 21 January 1963, saying that its purpose was to give 'appropriate powers ... to impose restrictions against those individuals or organizations who want to make secession from India or disintegration of India as political purposes for fighting elections'.[48] K. Manoharan, from Madras South constituency, called the amendment 'ill-advised', particularly in view of the DMK's 'unqualified' support of the war against China. The DMK's 'propaganda', he said, had always been made peacefully and legally, and its freedom of expression should not be denied.[49] Ravi Narayan Reddy from Andhra supported him, as did Gilbert Swell from the Assam Autonomous Districts. Putting forth an argument heard loudly in future years, Swell said that the root problem was over-centralization and unfair distribution of development among the states. Government policy fostered regionalism, he said.[50]

The amendment passed unanimously. It was counted a great achievement by many, especially when, later in the year, the DMK's senior figure, Dr Annadurai, 'unequivocally declared that the DMK once and for all gave up the demand for Dravida Nadu and henceforth solidly and sincerely stood for the sovereignty and unity of India'.[51] In the circumstances of the DMK threats of secession and Tara Singh's 'fast

---

the Lok Sabha. Passed on 31 August, the act was intended 'to deal effectively with communal and separatist tendencies'. *Statesman*, as quoted in ibid., 1–7 October 1961.

[46] Assisting Shastri were two ministry officials, the senior being L. P. Singh, and B. S. Raghavan. B. S. Raghavan, in an interview with the author.

The southern states' fears of imposition of Hindi by the north were re-emerging at this time, and Nehru's assurances that Hindi would not be imposed were incorporated in the Official Languages Act of 1963. See Srivastava, C. P., *Lal Bahadur Shastri: A Life of Truth in Politics*, Oxford University Press, Delhi, 1995, pp. 63–5.

[47] *AR*, 29 January–4 February 1963, p. 5017. The Southern Zonal Council unanimously supported this view at its meeting of 30 December 1962.

[48] *Lok Sabha Debates*, Third Series, vol. 12, no. 28, col. 5760.

[49] Ibid., cols 5797–802.

[50] Ibid., col. 5813. The bill went to the Joint Committee on 22 January 1963.

[51] This is either a quotation from, or a paraphrase of, a press statement by K. Karunanidhi, DMK spokesman. It was cited in a letter to the Chairman of the Rajya Sabha from T. K. Srinivasan, leader of the DMK Parliamentary Party. Jayaprakash Narayan Papers, Third Installment, File 12, 'Important Correspondence of JP', NMML.

unto death', the amendment with its oath may have injected sobriety into political discourse, although separatist talk by a few legislators can hardly have been a significant danger to national unity and integrity. The amendment is perhaps best understood as symptomatic of a mood in government of excessive fear for national integrity which also encouraged the enactment of undemocratic, intellectually wrong-headed legislation such as the Unlawful Activities (Prevention) Act, 1967. This made punishable any individual's or association's act or words intending or supporting 'the cession of any part of the territory of India or the secession' of the same. Good faith discussion was outlawed, and A. G. Noorani hoped the Supreme Court would strike down this 'repressive law', which 'spares the heretic only if he remains silent'.[52] Assuring national integrity by curbing freedom of expression may best have been characterized by the Bengali Communist MP, Hiren Mukerjee. Government ought to deal with the forces of disintegration differently, he said, and then quoted Alexander Pope: '"How small a part of that human hearts endure/The part that laws or kings can cause or cure."'[53]

Individual Liberty and Preventive Detention

As with other practices at the edge of democratic governance, the government of independent India was ambivalent about preventive detention, which, because it could be occasioned by or directed at actions or speech, affected the fundamental rights both to freedom of expression and personal liberty. Independent India had inherited the practice from the British, who had found it convenient to employ against those agitating for freedom.[54] Between 1937 and 1939, Congress Party governments in the provinces had repealed several preventive detention

[52] Noorani, A. G., *India's Constitution and Politics,* Jaico Publishing House, Bombay, 1970, p. 249.

[53] *Lok Sabha Debates,* Third Series, vol. 18, no. 57, col. 13418.

[54] As early as 1784, the East India Company Act allowed the detention of a person suspected of activities or carrying on correspondence prejudicial to the peace of British Settlements in India. The oldest preventive detention statute was the Bengal State Prisoners Regulation of 1818. The Defence of India Acts of 1915 and 1939, and the Restriction and Detention Ordinance of 1944, also authorized preventive detention. See Swaroop, V., *Law of Preventive Detention,* DLT Publications, Delhi, 1990, p. 15. For a helpful history of detention, see also Iqbal, Mohammed, *The Law of Preventive Detention in England, India and Pakistan,* Punjab Religious Book Society, Lahore, 1955.

Also Gledhill, *India,* p. 173; and Coupland, Reginald, *Indian Politics, 1936–1942: Report on the Constitutional Problem in India,* 3 vols, Oxford University Press, London, 1943, vol. 2, pp. 133–4, and ch. 12.

statutes, but from independence until the Constitution's inauguration, Congress ministries in some dozen provinces enacted 'Public Order' and 'Public Safety' laws. Most of these empowered government to regulate a person's actions or movements to prevent any act 'prejudicial to the public safety or maintenance of public order'; to impose restrictions on a person's freedom of expression; to extern him from or require him to reside in an area and to report his movements to government. Additionally, government had the broad power to 'regulate the conduct of the person in any manner otherwise than is covered by the above specific provisions'.[55]

There is little evidence that preventive detention either was used against a free press or was cruelly used during this period, but it certainly had the potential for use to curb speech as well as actions, incendiary or not.[56] And it was subject to overzealousness by possessive politicians' and to bureaucrats' ineptitude. For example, communists were detained in Calcutta in February 1949 to prevent a rail strike, but the lists of individuals proved defective. As a result several 'socialists' were arrested. Nehru saw the telegraphic messages on the matter and sent a note to the Home Ministry that 'in matters of this kind the fullest care should be taken,' and if the wrong persons had been arrested they should be released.[57] Preventive detention affected the Communist Party, the Hindu Mahasabha, and the RSS more than other parties, in part due to the latter two's alleged connections with Gandhi's assassination. The CPI attacked the government's 'grim' record on civil liberties, omitting acknowledgement of its own armed insurrection in South India in the late forties and its proclaimed goal of overthrowing the government. It charged that the Congress government had jailed fifty

[55] The act cited here is the Madhya Bharat Maintenance of Public Order Act, 1949.
Nehru saw the text of the Rajasthan Public Security Ordinance, 1949, and wrote to his secretary that it went far beyond any security order he had seen. A ' "prejudicial act" ' in the ordinance included bringing ' "into hatred or contempt or [exciting] disaffection" ' toward any government in the country and ' "any minister of such government" '. With ministers included, Nehru said, no criticism of governmental activity is permissible, which 'seems to me to go against the basic provisions of our [draft] Constitution ...'. He directed that the state ministry's attention be drawn to the ordinance. Gopal, *Selected, Works of Nehru*, vol. 15, part 1, 1993, p. 179.

[56] A. G. Noorani was to be detained several months in 1965 for his publication 'The Kashmir Question'.

[57] Note dated 25 February 1949. Below this, Home Secretary H. V. R. Iengar the next day wrote an explanation and returned the note to Nehru: the ministry's instructions 'made it quite clear that only ringleaders fomenting strike ... should be arrested and detained under Public Safety Acts'. Nehru Papers as received from M. O. Mathai, File 29, NMML.

thousand of its political opponents between 1947 and 1950.[58] Pandit Pant told Parliament that there were ten thousand detenus in India in 1950.[59]

Meanwhile, the Constituent Assembly was engaged in drafting an article authorizing preventive detention as a means to protect all the three strands of the seamless web. The Home Ministry under Sardar Patel wanted strong powers of detention; his view ultimately won the day; and, in a nice irony, the article was included among the Fundamental Rights.[60] Article 22 first provided that no person might be detained in custody without being informed of the grounds for his or her arrest or be denied counsel. Any such detained person had to be produced before a magistrate within twenty-four hours, and could not be detained longer without a magistrate's authority. Assembly members then provided that these general protections *did not apply* to individuals 'detained under any law providing for preventive detention'. Even the limited protection granted—that no law could authorize preventive detention longer than three months unless an Advisory Board (composed of persons qualified to be high court judges) held there was cause for further detention (Article 22(4)(a))—was not absolute. It did not apply to laws made by Parliament prescribing the circumstances and classes of cases under which a person might be detained for longer than three months 'without obtaining the opinion of an Advisory Board' (Article 22(7)(a)). Persons held under preventive detention laws were to be told the grounds for their detention and allowed to make representation against them unless the arresting authority decided that disclosing the facts would be 'against the public interest' (clause 6).

Governments and legislatures had been given a vast power virtually free from judicial restraint and the protection of the other fundamental rights. Although not always misused and, in certain circumstances, even a 'necessary evil', according to some, preventive detention would increasingly stain the country's democracy.

The central government put Article 22 to use immediately. With the coming into force of the Constitution on 26 January 1950, a number of existing laws providing for preventive detention lapsed or were vulnerable to overturning as violations of the Fundamental Rights. To keep such laws in effect, President Prasad that day issued the Preventive

---

[58] Ghosh, Ajoy, *Two Systems: A Balance Sheet*, CPI, New Delhi, 1956, p. 65.

[59] In a speech supporting the extension of the Preventive Detention Act. *AR*, 1–7 January 1961, p. 3717.

[60] For the history of the framing of the article, see Austin, *Cornerstone*, pp. 101–13.

Detention (Extension of Duration) Order.[61] Nevertheless, over the next month four high courts declared the order unconstitutional, and state detention laws were challenged in high courts.[62] And five hundred Communist detenus in Calcutta were due for release on 26 February because they then would have been held longer than three months without a review of their detentions by an Advisory Board. On 22 February, Home Secretary H. V. R. Iengar drafted a note for the cabinet in his own hand and sent a copy to Law Secretary K. V. K. Sundaram for review. Central legislation on preventive detention is urgently needed, Iengar wrote, because none of the states' laws that provided for detention, excepting Bengal's, had an advisory board. Moreover, state laws were under attack in the high courts and detenus were being released. He proposed that a preventive detention bill be enacted under items 9 and 3 of the Union and Concurrent lists.[63] On 24 February, the full cabinet, plus Attorney General M. C. Setalvad, approved the introduction of the bill. The next day—the day before the communists would have been released—Parliament, in a special Saturday session, passed it unanimously.[64]

Advocating the bill in Parliament, Patel and Nehru showed 'contri-

[61] The order was made under Article 373 of the Constitution, which provided that until Parliament passed a preventive detention bill under Article 22, or a year had expired, the President could make an order as though it were an act of Parliament.

[62] For much of what follows in these paragraphs, the author is indebted to Bayley, David H., *Preventive Detention in India*, Firma K. L. Mukhopadhyay, Calcutta, 1962, and to Swaroop, *Preventive Detention*.

The order was overturned in: the Bihar High Court (*Brameshwar Prasad v The State of Bihar*, AIR 1950 Patna 265); the Bengal High Court (*Sunil Kumar Bose v The West Bengal Government* AIR 1950 Calcutta 274); the Orissa High Court (*Prahalad Jena v State of Orissa* AIR 1950 Orissa 157); and the Hyderabad High Court (*Showkat-un-missa Begum v State of Hyderabad* AIR 1950 Hyderabad 20). Swaroop, *Preventive Detention*, p. 17.

[63] Ministry of Law, GOI, File F11-VI/50 L, NAI.

Item 9 of the Union List: 'Preventive detention for reasons connected with Defence, Foreign Affairs, or the security of India; persons subjected to such detention'. Item 3 of the Concurrent List reads: 'Preventive detention for reasons connected with the security of a State, the maintenance of public order, or the maintenance of supplies and services essential to the community; persons subjected to such detention'. These entries on the legislative lists are analogous to entries on the legislative lists in the 1935 Government of India Act.

[64] Ibid. At a meeting of Congress leaders at the time, T. T. Krishnamachari recalled that he had warned that certain clauses of the bill 'would be shot down by the Supreme Court'. Patel demurred, citing Setalvad's opinion. Krishnamachari responded, 'I am here as a Member of Parliament, and if you ask me, I think it will be shot down. It was very funny. Jawaharlal kept quiet.' T. T. Krishnamachari Oral History Transcript, p. 46, NMML.

tion' because it was 'repugnant to the ideal of a free and democratic government'.[65] Nehru just did not like the bill, recalled T. T. Krishnamachari.[66] Patel spoke of his sleepless nights before introducing the bill and defended it as necessary 'where the very basis of law is sought to be undermined and attempts are made to create a state of affairs in which ... "men would not be men and law would not be law"'. The bill was directed against no ideology or party, he said, but against those who 'make it impossible for normal government based on law to function'. Members should think of the 'liberties of the millions of persons threatened by the activities of the individuals whose liberties we have curtailed ...'.[67] Patel added, '"We want to protect and defend civil liberties, but I hate criminal liberties."'[68] One of the bill's critics, H. V. Kamath, advised that one of the bill's parts (section 14) probably would be ruled unconstitutional, for how could the courts determine whether a detention was unconstitutional if it could not examine the grounds for the detention. Parliament heard the Attorney General Setalvad's rebuttal, and Kamath's amendments to the section were voted down.[69]

The Act authorized detention of persons acting prejudicially toward the defence and security of India, relations with foreign powers, and the maintenance of public order and essential supplies and services. Detenus were to be given the grounds for the order, unless it was against the public interest to disclose them; they were allowed to make representation against them; and the grounds and any representations by

[65] Bayley, *Preventive Detention,* p. 12.

[66] T. T. Krishnamachari Oral History Transcript, p. 12.

Nehru several times in his letters enjoined the chief ministers to be careful in implementing preventive detention laws, making clear his view that they were directed at individuals causing disruption and not against ideology as such, including communist ideology. He also thought it 'very necessary that we should not mix up the labour questions with other questions of public order'. Illegal strikes and disrespect of law by labour unions might result from curtailment of liberties. He thought the 1947 Industrial Disputes Act contained sufficient safeguards 'to ensure that essential services function uninterruptedly'. Letter of 1 March 1950, *NLTCM,* vol. 2, p. 50.

Yet Nehru also agreed with the opinion of the chief ministers, in their August 1950 conference, that preventive detention could be used against persons interfering with the maintenance of essential services and supplies, including black marketeers and hoarders. Nehru thought using detention in such instances would act as 'a powerful deterrent'. Letters of 26 August and 14 September 1950, ibid., pp. 177-8, 193-4.

[67] *Parliamentary Debates* as cited in Bayley, *Preventive Detention,* p. 12.

[68] *Hindustan Times,* 26 February 1950.

[69] Bayley, *Preventive Detention,* pp. 16-17.

the detenu were to be placed before an advisory board (two high court judges or persons qualified to be such), which was to give its opinion whether there had been sufficient cause for the detention. *Except*, that for detentions relating to the defence and security of India, relations with foreign powers, the security of 'a state', and the maintenance of public order, persons could be detained for up to a year without obtaining an advisory board's view. Disclosure to a court of the grounds for the detention and any representation by a detenu was prohibited by section 14 of the bill.[70] The Act contained no language directing government to abide by an advisory board's decision. Whether an intentional or accidental omission, this was changed in the 1951 extension of the Act, something the government then hailed as a great improvement.

The Act was challenged in the celebrated Gopalan case of 1950, in which freedom of expression and personal liberty were joined in the first Fundamental Rights case to reach the Supreme Court. A Kerala native, member of the Congress Socialist Party in the thirties, and by 1951 president of the Communist Party's All-India Kisan Sabha, A. K. Gopalan had been in and out of jail since 1947, allegedly for threatening the police in a speech and otherwise speaking his mind. Each time the conviction had been set aside.[71] After having been detained again, Gopalan was detained further under the Preventive Detention Act of 1950. He appealed directly to the Supreme Court under Article 32 for a writ of habeas corpus, claiming that his fundamental rights to freedom of speech and expression and to travel freely in India (Article 19(1)(a), and (d)) had been violated; that he had been deprived of liberty other than by 'procedure established by law' (Article 21); and that his detention under Article 22 was in bad faith.[72]

[70] Preventive Detention Act, 1950, Bill No. 12 of 1950.

It was a punishable offence to disclose such information without state or central government assent.

[71] On one occasion, the future Chief Justice of India, K. Subba Rao, then with the Madras High Court, dismissed the case on the grounds that the magistrate had paid insufficient attention to the major question involved. *A. K. Gopalan v District Magistrate, Malabar* AIR 1949 Madras 596ff. Gopalan then had been detained under the Madras Maintenance of Public Order Act, 1947.

[72] *A. K. Gopalan v The State of Madras.* 1950 (1) SCR 88ff. Decision on 19 May 1950.

Each judge wrote a separate opinion. The majority of four consisted of Chief Justice Harilal Kania, Patanjali Sastri, B. K. Mukherjea, and S. R. Das. The two other judges were Saiyid Fazl Ali and M. C. Mahajan. M. K. Nambiyar defended Gopalan. The government's advocates were K. Rajah Aiyar, Advocate General of Madras. and M. C. Setalvad, Attorney General of India.

The Supreme Court declined to rule on the latter contention because it did not know the grounds for the detention because Gopalan had been denied them. Four judges of the six-judge bench upheld the detention, but, as H. V. Kamath had predicted, all six struck down section 14 of the Act. This, they said, contravened Article 22(5), which provided that the grounds for detention should be given to detenus. Justice Mahajan commented that Section 14 'is in the nature of an iron curtain around the acts of authority making the order of preventive detention'. The majority held that freedom of expression did not arise directly as an issue because no legislation restricting it was involved in the case, nor was it germane that punitive detention might result in the abridgement of the freedoms in Article 19.[73] Judges Fazl Ali and Mahajan held the detention illegal on the ground that Section 12 of the Act (under which a detenu could be held up to a year without an advisory board's review) and Section 14 were unconstitutional because they violated Article 22 itself. Article 22 had become, so to speak, a law unto itself, they said.[74]

The Act and the Supreme Court's ruling on it aroused apprehensions. The *Times of India* was concerned by the 'notes of hesitancy' in the opinions upholding the act.[75] The *Statesman* said that the public probably supported the legislation, but it ought not to be used 'merely to promote the convenience of officials'. The conduct of some detaining officials had been such that 'investigation by higher authority' was

---

For a brief analysis of the case, see Bayley, *Preventive Detention*, pp. 40–3, and Seervai, *Constitutional Law*, vol. 1, ch. 10.

[73] 1950 (1) SCR 89.

The majority also held that the freedom to move freely throughout India (Article 19(1) (d)) applied only to a free person and not to a person under detention. Justice Mukherjea, commenting on an issue that would appear in many future habeas corpus cases, said that the word 'law' in Article 21 meant state-made law and did not mean the principles of justice. Gopalan had argued that 'law' in this article included substantive due process and, at least, procedural due process, another contention the judges refused to accept.

[74] Within a few days of this ruling, the Court heard and reserved orders on seventeen other petitions from detenus who had challenged their detention on the basis of section 14 being struck down. But the Court upheld the detention of N. B. Khare, president of the Hindu Mahasabha, who had been externed from Punjab under the East Punjab Public Safety Act, on the ground that the Act gave a District Magistrate authority to pass such an order on his subjective satisfaction. *Times of India*, 27 May 1950.

[75] Issue of 28 May 1950. In this and in an editorial on 31 May, the paper regretted the absence of unanimity in the Court's decisions, which detracted from the court's authority and 'causes bewilderment and consternation in the public mind'.

urgent, and 'it is conceivable that a remedy for the grossest abuses might lie in a civil action for damages against the detaining authority'.[76] Homi Mody, then governor of Uttar Pradesh, wrote to President Prasad, quoting Justice Sen of the Calcutta High Court: ' "the judiciary is being converted into a legislature with limited powers and the executive is converted into a judiciary whose decisions were to be final." '[77]

On 19 February 1951, Parliament extended the act for another year.[78] Speaking on the bill, C. Rajagopalachari, who had become Home Minister upon Patel's death in December 1950, advocated the extension of the Act more vigorously than had his predecessor. ' "Stern and ruthless" ' action was needed, Rajagopalachari said, against ' "mischievous and violent elements, fanatical" ' communists, blackmarketeers, and communalists.[79] He admitted that the bill was ' "certainly an infringement of what may be called a normal principle of criminal justice" ', but in the preventive field ' "we cannot have the same amount of concreteness in evidence as we can demand when a prosecutor alleges overt acts in proving an attempt or an abetment of a specific crime." '[80]

---

[76] The *Statesman*. The *Hindustan Times* supported the legislation. Issue of 31 May 1950.

[77] Mody in his 'Fortnightly Letter' to the President, dated 8 April 1950. H. K. Mody Papers, File 20, NMML. Mody also wrote that in states where there was prohibition, ministers are talking of 'punitive police and collective fines' for offences, and one minister even talked of 'concentration camps'. He deplored this 'frame of mind' and wrote that it accorded ill with the principles of the Constitution.

The governors sent these letters quite regularly to the President, who often replied to them. President Prasad seems regularly to have passed on the letters to Nehru. (See ch. 6.)

[78] On the day the President gave his assent, 22 February, the Madras High Court released A. K. Gopalan, ruling his detention illegal on the grounds that the order was vague, indefinite, and did not specify the period of detention. The judges were Satyanarayana Rao and Raghava Rao. *Hindustan Times*, 23 February 1951. But no sooner had Gopalan's feet touched the courthouse steps than a policeman who had been waiting in the court detained him under the new Act. Worried about the case, Nehru wrote to Rajagopalachari on 25 February that Gopalan's arrest 'within a few yards of the high court building gives one a shock ... [and creates] a good deal of prejudice against us'. Gopal, *Selected Works of Nehru*, vol. 15, part 2, p. 156.

A year later, Gopalan was elected to the Lok Sabha from a Madras constituency, and he was re-elected in the second general election of 1957 from a constituency in Kerala. He was detained again in 1964 and 1965.

Soon thereafter, a little-known man, also wanted in Madras for communist-related activities, was arrested in Bombay. But the Supreme Court released Mohan Kumaramangalam on 5 April. Twenty years later he was one of the most important political figures in public life.

[79] *Hindustan Times*, 16 February 1951. For the entire two hundred pages of debate, see *Parliamentary Debates*, vol. 8, part 2, cols 2677ff.

[80] Ibid.

Again, the critics were heard but not heeded. Under this amended law, the grounds for a detention order and any representation made against it were to be given within six weeks to an Advisory Board, which might hear the detenu in person. If the Board found insufficient cause for the detention, it was explicitly provided that the person was to be released. If the detention were upheld, it could be continued 'for such period as it [the government] thinks fit'. The membership of advisory boards was raised from two to three, and decisions were to be by majority vote.[81] The Supreme Court upheld this Act, saying that it substantially satisfied the requirements of Article 22(4).[82]

Successive Preventive Detention Acts were passed in 1952, 1954, 1957, and 1960. The government repeated its by-now standard justifications but gave greater emphasis to protecting the web's social revolutionary strand. Public order comes first, said a Congress Parliamentary Party pamphlet, 'then all endeavours to promote social welfare ... are possible and practicable'.[83] Said Nehru during the 1952 debate, the detention power is necessary to combat 'anti-social activities ... [with] communal purposes' and 'jagirdari activities' in Rajasthan and Saurashtra. What would be the fate of 'that unhappy wretch' who testified against a jagirdar in open court, he asked. 'I doubt if ... Rule of Law ... concepts can apply *in vacuo* to any given situation in India.'[84] But he still was concerned about the law's abuses. He wrote to the chief ministers that some individuals had been in jail longer than they would have been had they been sentenced for a crime.[85] The bill is 'absolutely essential ... for the

---

[81] The Preventive Detention (Amendment) Act, 1951, no. IV of 1951.

[82] In *S. Krishnan v State of Madras* 1951 SCR 621. Swaroop, *Preventive Detention*, p. 69. Parliament had amended the February 1950 Act in August 1950, removing section 14.

[83] The pamphlet was intended 'to clarify the issues involved'. *Preventive Detention Act*, CPP, New Delhi, November 1952. The pamphlet had been prepared by the CPP's Bureau of Parliamentary Research and was pamphlet no. 6, the last, in a 'Talking Points Series'. '... [A]ll endeavours to promote ...' is from Home Minister K. N. Katju's Foreword to the pamphlet.

[84] *Parliamentary Debates, House of the People*, vol. 4, no. 4, especially cols 5198–9, 2 August 1952.

Jagirdars were landholders who, when divested of their lands under zamindari abolition laws, often terrorized peasants to regain possession. They also threatened to kill persons voting for Congress in the general elections, and, in some instances, made common cause with 'dacoits' (rural gangs of bandits) to enforce their will. Nehru devoted a large portion of his letter to chief ministers dated 25 July 1952 to this subject and referred to it again in his letter of 2 August 1952. *NLTCM*, vol. 3, pp. 54–64, 65.

[85] Nehru's concern was not unfounded. H. K. Mahtab soon thereafter wrote to Katju that he had definite information that tribunals had released detenus 'with the remarks that there has been gross abuse of power or the grounds shown are flimsy ... [The

suppression of communism', said Home Minister K. N. Katju, who had succeeded Rajagopalachari, adding that 'I am not talking of communists ... they are my great and dear friends.' Home Minister G. B. Pant in 1960, called the act necessary to ' "preserve democracy" ' when the country was faced with *satyagraha*, which led to ' "violence and disruption" ' whether so intended or not.[86]

The critics of all these laws attacked them as brutal, barbarous, and repugnant to democracy. They opposed the power to detain preventively being given to district magistrates, who were deemed to be untrustworthy.[87] The Act 'is a confession that the government in power cannot govern with rules of law ... but must have arbitary powers to imprison people on suspicion', said a statement issued by the All-India Civil Liberties Council.[88] Their suggestions that detention be limited to the defence of India or to parts of the country were rejected. Alterations in succeeding Acts made them slightly more favourable to detenus.

Preventive Detention Act] works as an engine of oppression in many cases. To suppress a few anti-social elements, a large number of anti-social persons are being created.' Letter of 27 May 1952. Hare Krushna Mahtab Papers, K. N. Katju File, NMML.

[86] *AR*, 1–7 January 1961, p. 3717. The renewal of the Act in 1957 had permitted Jammu and Kashmir to enact its own preventive detention law. Previous acts had explicitly exempted Jammu and Kashmir from their reach. State governments had all along been empowered to pass their own preventive detention laws under item 3 of the Concurrent List. But such laws were to contain at least the safeguards in the central act, thus giving some uniformity to state legislation and uniform protection—to the extent that the 'protections' were genuinely applied—to detenus throughout the country. Bayley, *Preventive Detention*, p. 22.

Parliament enacted legislation in 1955 that, although not strictly speaking authorizing preventive detention, nonetheless was drastic. The Armed Forces (Special Powers) Act, 1955, authorized governors to declare an area 'disturbed' and order the use of the armed forces 'in aid of civil power'. Once an area had been declared 'disturbed', commissioned and non-commissioned officers were authorized to warn and then shoot to kill, to arrest without warrant anyone committing or about to commit a cognizable offence, and to enter and search without a warrant. No legal proceeding against any officer involved could be instituted without central government sanction. The 1955 Act applied to Assam and Manipur and later was extended to other states as they were formed in the Northeast. This act was replicated in the Punjab and elsewhere in later years.

[87] It should be understood that arrest under a preventive detention law is an executive action, not one taken within the criminal justice system. The detenu does not come into contact with the judicial system until his case goes to the Advisory Board.

[88] *The Indian Civil Liberties Bulletin*, no. 35, August 1952, p. 152. Jayaprakash Narayan Papers, NMML. Both this *Bulletin* and that dated September were lengthy and carried legal analyses, reports of individual detention cases, reports of parliamentary debates, and descriptions of relevant law in other countries. The council's president was the prominent advocate P. R. Das who will be met again in forthcoming chapters.

Preventive Detention During An Emergency

The central and state government's existing powers of preventive detention paled compared with the massive authority to detain and otherwise to curtail liberty and the Fundamental Rights that came with the proclamation of India's first national emergency by President Radhakrishnan on 26 October 1962. Six days previously, newspapers had reported a 'massive attack' by Chinese troops across the MacMahon Line, India's northeast frontier with Tibet. Reports from the front grew steadily worse in ensuing days, creating near panic in New Delhi. The nation felt itself in crisis. Prime Minister Nehru, in a radio broadcast on 22 October, summoned the nation to ' "gird up its loins" ' to oppose ' "a powerful and unscrupulous opponent" '. The President followed his emergency proclamation (under Article 352) by promulgating The Defence of India Ordinance and a subsequent ordinance. Invoking Article 359 he suspended the right to move the courts for the enforcement of Fundamental Rights Articles 21 and 22, with the former's protections for life and liberty and the latter's limited protection for detenus. On 7 November, the government issued 156 'rules', named the Defence of India Rules (DIR), under the Defence of India Act (DIA) proclaimed by the first ordinance. On 11 November, the President suspended a third fundamental right, equality before, and equal protection of, the law (Article 14).[89]

These measures enormously strengthened the government's power to curtail civil liberties and to regulate citizens' affairs. The first of the two 1962 ordinances empowered the government to make rules for securing the defence of India, public safety, public order, the efficient conduct of military operations, and supplies and services essential to the life of the community. Under the Defence of India Rules, the government could arrest and try persons contravening them in order to prevent tampering with the loyalty of persons entering the service of

[89] The Constitution's 'Emergency Provisions' are in Part XVIII of the Constitution and empower the President to declare a state of emergency if satisfied that a 'grave emergency' exists that threatens 'the security of India' or any part of it from 'war or external aggression or internal disturbances' (Article 352). Such proclamations have to be endorsed by Parliament. Under an emergency, the central government and Parliament may govern the states directly, the freedoms of Article 19 shall not restrict government action, and the President may suspend, collectively or individually, the right to move the courts for enforcement of the Fundamental Rights. Two articles of the emergency provisions authorize the President to take over administration of a state. Called 'President's Rule', this will be discussed in later chapters along with the centralizing characteristics of the emergency provisions.

the government and spreading false reports 'likely to cause disaffection or alarm ... or hatred between different classes of the people of India', and to ensure the protection of ports, railways, and so on (48 items).[90]

The ordinance also continued in force the Official Secrets Act of 1923 and provided for the constituting of three-person tribunals to hear cases, which could 'take cognizance of offences without the accused being committed to it for trial'. An individual sentenced by a Special Tribunal to death or life imprisonment might appeal to the appropriate high court, but there could be no appeals on other grounds. Finally, no order made or power conferred by the ordinance could be questioned in any court and there could be no legal proceeding against any person for actions under the ordinance if done 'in good faith'.[91] The second, amending, ordinance empowered government to detain persons on any grounds it deemed reasonable to prevent them from the 'prejudicial' acts enumerated earlier and to make persons reside in, or refrain from residing in, geographical areas.[92] The 1955 Essential Commodities Act and the 1950 Preventive Detention Act (still in force, as renewed) further contributed to the assemblage of massive government authority. The two houses of Parliament unrestrainedly approved the proclamation of emergency on 13 and 14 November, and the Defence of India Act (DIA) replaced the two ordinances on 12 December.

Nationalistic response to the war was great. Women contributed their gold jewellery. The CPI said that Chinese withdrawal must precede negotiations on the border dispute.[93] Nehru formed the National Defence

[90] The first ordinance and the rules issued under it closely resembled the 1939 Defence of India Act, which the Governor General proclaimed on 19 September 1939, the 'British Empire [having] declared war against Germany' on 3 September, and Defence of India Rules which he issued under his power to promulgate ordinances with the force of legislative acts (see section 72 of the Government of India Act, 1935). Section 102 of this Act also empowered the Governor General to proclaim a state of emergency if 'a grave emergency exists whereby the security of India is threatened by war'.

For the text and analysis of the 1939 Act, see Kamat, A. N., *The Defence of India Act, 1939, and the Rules Made Thereunder*, Hindmata Printing House, Dharwar, 1944. Also, Prasad, S. and B. N. Mehrotra, Defence of India Laws and Rules, 4 vols, Law Publishers, Allahabad, 1963.

[91] Sections 32 and 34 of the ordinance.

[92] The Defence of India (Amendment) Ordinance, 1962, section 2, adding a new clause 13A after clause 13 of the first ordinance.

[93] Several communist leaders were detained for alleged pro-Chinese sympathies, and some of them became members of the China-leaning Communist Party of India (Marxist) when it split from the Communist Party of India in 1964. Hereafter the CPI (M), as it is typically referred to, will be designated the CPM.

Council to advise on the war effort and to reinforce the national will. President Radhakrishnan was patron and Indira Gandhi chairperson of the Citizens' Central Council, established to encourage and coordinate citizens' efforts.

With the unilateral withdrawal of Chinese forces on 21 December, patriotic spirit did not wane, but criticism of the suspension of civil liberties flared. Rajagopalachari, now a Swatantra Party leader, on 24 December 1962 said that the continuance of the emergency and the powers of the DIA in light of the withdrawal created a 'crisis of democracy'.[94] The Jana Sangh said the Congress slogan of ' "one nation, one party and one leader" smacked of fascist tendencies'.[95] By July 1963, the CPI was calling the emergency ' "an instrument of intimidation of the masses ... directed against the people's movement" '.[96] The Bar Association of India published a booklet, *Parliament: Emergency and Personal Freedom—Opinions of Jurists,* in which former Attorney General M. C. Setalvad, N. C. Chatterjee, and others argued that preventive detention infringed civil liberties.[97]

The government disagreed and in October 1963 extended the emergency for another three years.[98] Responding to loud criticism, the Home Minister asserted that government was not using preventive detention for political purposes and that since the emergency only 1,323 persons had been detained and only 282 of these remained in custody.[99] But the government continued to use the Defence of India Act and Rules in preference to the still-in-force Preventive Detention Act of 1950. Some seven hundred 'left communists' were detained at the end of 1964, supposedly because the government believed an uprising was imminent. During elections in Kerala in 1965, twenty-eight of these individuals

[94] *Times of India,* quoted in *AR,* 15–21 January 1963, p. 4991.

[95] *AR,* 29 January–4 February 1963, p. 5018.

[96] From a resolution passed at the meeting of the National Council in New Delhi, June 27–July 2. *AR,* 23–29 July 1963, p. 5320.

[97] Setalvad, M. C. et al., *Parliament: Emergency and Personal Freedom—Opinions of Jurists,* Bar Association of India, New Delhi, 1963.

The contributors were: M. C. Setalvad, A. V. Visvanatha Sastri, N. C. Chatterjee, M. K. Nambiyar, Sarjoo Prasad, A. S. R. Chari and C. B. Agarwala. See also Koppell, G. O., 'The Emergency, The Courts and Indian Democracy', in *JILI,* vol. 8, no. 3, 1966, pp. 287–337.

[98] *Statesman,* as reported in *AR,* 8–14 January 1964, p. 5608.

[99] Ibid. Dissatisfactions among members of Parliament caused the government to allow to lapse on 28 April 1964 the Constitution (Eighteenth Amendment) Bill, which Law Minister A. K. Sen had introduced on 24 April. This would have exempted the government from suits arising from the emergency. Ibid. For the legislative history of the bill and its text, see *Constitution Amendment in India,* pp. 170, 379.

(including A. K. Gopalan) won seats in the legislative assembly while detained. There were detentions under the DIA during the 1965 language riots in Madras. The war scare with Pakistan in the spring of 1965 and actual war that autumn caused government to employ the DIA yet again.

With the Tashkent Agreement of January 1966 having ended the war with Pakistan, Setalvad, Chatterjee, and members of Parliament renewed their campaign to revoke the DIA and the 1962 emergency proclamation They were joined by the CPI, the Jana Sangh, and the PSP. That March, thirty-four eminent individuals led by former Chief Justices of India M. C. Mahajan, S. R. Das, and B. P. Sinha sent an open letter to the President and Prime Minister saying that the moment was 'opportune' to 'restore to our democracy its true stature by making it possible for the citizen to exercise his basic rights'.[100] Making accusations that often would be heard in later years, the letter said that the DIR 'had been used ... not for the purpose of the defence of the country but for collateral purposes ... used ... in substitution of ordinary law ... used ... [against] ordinary criminals against whom conviction was difficult to obtain in ordinary criminal courts'.[101]

The government was undecided, first giving an assurance that preventive detention under the emergency powers would be used only in border areas,[102] then announcing that the emergency might end in July 1967, only to announce in June 1967 that it would be continued indefinitely ' "in the interests of national security and defence" '.[103] The emergency lapsed on 31 December 1967 when the government did not

[100] *President and Prime Minister Must Revoke Emergency, Restore Fundamental Rights: Appeal By All Former Chief Justices of India and Leading Citizens*, Communist Party Parliamentary Group, Communist Party of India, New Delhi, 1966, p. 5. Among those who signed the appeal, in addition to the former chief justices, were five former high court judges, eight editors of major newspapers, the vice-chancellors of five major universities, and public figures such as K. M. Munshi, H. N. Kunzru, Mulk Raj Anand, N. C. Chatterjee, and M. C. Setalvad.

[101] Ibid., pp. 2–3. The authors quoted a judge who said that detention orders would not have been ' "more arbitrary and oppressive ... [if] ours was a police state, and we had never heard of democracy and the rule of law" '.

[102] Home Minister G. L. Nanda's statement in Parliament. Nanda added ' "As some of these powers will not be available once the proclamation of Emergency is revoked, and since it is not possible under the Constitution to limit the operation of the proclamation to certain parts of the country, the proclamation should not be revoked for the present" '. *Hindustan Times*, 28 April 1966.

The Assam language riots of 1960 had also evoked talk of the need to change the Constitution to permit declaration of an emergency only in a part of the country. This was done through the Forty-second Amendment in 1976 (see ch. 17).

[103] *AR*, 23–29 July 1967, p. 7823. Y. B. Chavan was then Home Minister. He cited

seek its renewal, reportedly because of dissension within the Congress and doubts about having sufficient votes to assure its re-enactment.[104] The 1950 Preventive Detention Act would lapse in 1969, apparently for the same reasons, but, as will be seen in parts II and III, the country would not long be spared preventive detention or imposition of an emergency.

Preventive detention had had seductive charms for the executive branch, as the former chief justices' letter had pointed out. Although perhaps a 'necessary evil', as some believed, in certain political situations and when witness intimidation made impossible convictions of well-known criminals, it easily became a crutch whose over-use produced not only injustice to individuals but also atrophy in police investigatory and prosecutorial skills—hazards that would intensify over time. Another motivation for detention's over-use may be named 'executive convenience'. It is easier than the arduous, and chancy, process of trying to convict economic or political offenders. These former chief justices of India found themselves, as would many jurists and citizens after them, 'rudely disturbed' that the 'continuous exercise of the very wide powers ... is likely to make ... the ... authorities insensitive ... to the freedom of Indian citizens ... and pose a serious threat' to the country's democracy.[105]

---

disquieting conditions in the Northeast and said the emergency powers would not be exercised in the rest of the country.

[104] Meanwhile, however, the central government had enacted legislation giving it and several state governments extraordinary powers—although all of these did not provide for preventive detention—such as the Assam Disturbed Areas Act, the Armed Forces (Special Powers) Act, the Unlawful Activities (Prevention) Ordinance, and ordinances strengthening the Essential Commodities and Essential Services Acts.

[105] In *G. Sadanand v State of Kerala* 1996 (3) SCR 599. See also p. 595.

The danger to democracy and to individual liberty was all the greater because judges, jurists and lawyers were in a tangle over the citizen's right to habeas corpus during an emergency, as the Bar Association acknowledged in *Parliament: Emergency and Personal Freedom*. Under Article 359, the President may, during an emergency, suspend the right granted by Articles 32 and 226 to move the courts for a writ of habeas corpus. The issue would re-emerge a decade hence in the famous Habeas Corpus case (ch. 15).

Former Attorney General Setalvad, for example, argued that although the 'freedoms' under Article 19 were not suspended during an emergency, the right to move the courts for their enforcement was. Yet the suspension of the right to a writ did not suspend the writ itself, which would be 'issued as a matter of course', whereupon the court would decide 'whether the party applying is denied the right of proceeding any further with it'. *Parliament: Emergency*, p. 5.

As though this argument were not sufficiently opaque, Setalvad seemed to dilute his position further when he added that all governments during times of emergency have given 'even a strained construction to legislation' to uphold executive powers. Ibid., p. 9. Editorials in the *Indian Express* and in the *Times of India*, commenting on the opinions in the booklet, said that the Fundamental Rights of the Constitution should be treated as truly fundamental and their suspension was not warranted unless there were a genuine emergency, which, in the spring of 1963, there was not. Ibid., appendices II and III.

Judicial rulings clarified the matter only partially. Detenus had been released by the Allahabad High Court when granting pleas made on the same grounds as those found wanting by the Punjab and Bombay High Courts. The Supreme Court, when hearing the combined appeals of twenty-six detenus whose pleas had been rejected in the Punjab and Bombay High Courts, on 2 September 1963 upheld the government's authority to suspend enforcement of the Fundamental Rights. The case took its name, Makkan Singh's case, from one of Punjab's detenus. *Makkan Singh Tarsikka v State of Punjab* 1964 (4) *SCR* 797ff; also AIR 1964 SC 381ff. The bench consisted of Justices P. B. Gajendragadkar, A. K. Sarkar, K. Subba Rao, K. N. Wanchoo, M. Hidayatullah, K. C. Das Gupta and J. C. Shah. Gajendragadkar gave the majority opinion for himself and Judges Sarkar, Wanchoo, Hidayatullah, Das Gupta , and Shah. Subba Rao dissented.

The opinion said 'we will have to give effect to the plain words of Article 359 (1) and the Presidential Order issued under it,' because 'the democratic faith in the inviolable character of individual liberty and freedom and the majesty of the law which sustains it must ultimately be governed by the Constitution itself.' AIR 1964 SC 404. But this majority also ruled that there were avenues for challenging preventive detention. The Criminal Procedure Code both provided for preventive detention and that a high court could release a person illegally or improperly detained. (Section 491 (1) (b) in the 1923 version, then in force.) Thus a writ of habeas corpus was no longer 'a matter of common law' but 'a statutory right' existing outside the Constitution. AIR 1964 SC 896. An individual could challenge his detention on the ground that it was in bad faith, but he would have to prove this. A detenu could also claim that his detention 'suffers from the vice of excessive delegation'. Gajendragadkar's opinion, ibid., p. 400.

For the plaintiffs, M. C. Setalvad led a battery of some seventy lawyers including N. C. Chatterjee, Sarjoo Prasad, A. S. R. Chari, R. K. Garg, and Ashoke Desai. (R. K. Garg interview with the author.)

In two other cases, the Supreme Court enunciated principles supporting the right to habeas corpus. The order of the President 'does not form a bar to all applications for release from detention under the [Defense of India] Act or [the Defense of India] Rules', ruled Judge A. K. Sarkar in 1966. *Dr Ram Manohar Lohia v State of Bihar,* 1966 (1) *SCR* 709ff. Case decided on 7 September 1966. A detenu can urge statutory safeguards in his own support, and if the court is satisfied that the impugned order suffers from serious infirmities, then detention can be set aside, said Justice Gajendragadkar in *Sadanand v State of Kerala,* p. 590.

Chapter 3

THE SOCIAL REVOLUTION AND
THE FIRST AMENDMENT

Rajendra Prasad and Sarvepalli Radhakrishnan agreed. Said President Prasad, the government's aim is 'to end poverty ... to abolish distinction and exploitation'. Vice-President Radhakrishnan called 'for the removal of all social disabilities ... of man-made inequalities and injustices and [to] provide for all equality of opportunity'.[1] K. Santhanam brought together the strands of the seamless web in an article in the *Hindustan Times*. The meaning of the social revolution, he wrote, was to get India 'out of medievalism based on birth, religion, custom and community and reconstruct her social structure on modern foundations of law, individual merit, and secular education'.[2]

But conundrums lay in wait, as they did when provisions in the Fundamental Rights allowed personal conduct that seemed to endanger political stability and national unity and integrity. Demands of the social revolutionary strand of the seamless web would run head-on into other provisions in the Rights chapter with, additionally, critical implications for the democracy strand. The Supreme Court ruled unconstitutional government legislation and rules changing property relations and removing the 'man-made inequalities' of which Vice-President Radhakrishnan had spoken. Remedy again was sought in amending the Constitution.

At the heart of the confrontation were issues crucial in any democracy, and especially in India's, with its hierarchical social system, its predominantly agricultural economy, and its vital interest in the seamlessness of the web: individual interest against the national interest; one individual's rights against another's; government's role in reforming society; and conflicts between 'law' and 'justice'. What was to be the judiciary's share in '"ordering the life of a progressive people"'? (See

---

[1] For Prasad, see *CAD*, vol. 5, no. 1, p. 2. For Radhakrishnan, who then was Vice-President, see Radhakrishnan, *Occasional Speeches and Writings*, Ministry of Information and Broadcasting, GOI, New Delhi, 1956, p. 362.

[2] Issue dated 8 September 1946.

chapter 5.) Other than freedom of speech, the specific issues addressed in the First Amendment were the individual's right to enjoy his property versus government's authority to take it under its 'police power' or for social revolutionary purposes, and the subordinate issue of any compensation due for the taking; and one individual's constitutional right to protection against discrimination and to equality under the law versus another's right—because of his or her 'backward' status in society—to special opportunity in access to education and employment. This chapter will discuss the First Amendment's provisions relating to property, focusing on agricultural property and the nationalization of commercial and industrial property. The chapter concludes with the amendment's provisions relating to special treatment for disadvantaged citizens.

The Background

The Congress having been both the party of independence and of the social revolution, it was inevitable that constitutional government in India would be social revolutionary and socialist. Gandhi had made insistent efforts to end untouchability and other forms of discrimination. Sardar Patel and Rajendra Prasad had helped him lead *satyagrahas* for peasant rights. Nehru, whom Gandhi anointed his heir, was, as he said of himself in 1929, a '"socialist and a republican"'.[3] Such views were widely held. The party in its 1928 'Nehru Report' declared its dedication to the fundamental rights well known in England and the United States and added others such as protection of minority, language, and educational rights, and freedom of conscience and religion.[4] The content of the party's socialism became clear in its 1931 Karachi Resolution. Among other things, it said that 'key industries and services, mineral resources, railways, waterways [and] shipping' were to be government controlled, and the government was to safeguard the interests of 'industrial workers' and women and children.[5] The resolution called unspecifically

---

[3] Cited in Nanda, B. R., *Jawaharlal Nehru*, Oxford University Press, Delhi, 1995, p. 185.

[4] *Report of a Committee to Determine Principles of the Constitution for India*, All Parties Conference, 1928, pp. 89–90. This was the so-called Nehru Report, named after Motilal, Jawaharlal's father.

[5] 'Resolution on Fundamental Rights and Economic and Social Change', *Report of the 45th Indian National Congress*, AICC, Bombay, 1931, pp. 139–41.

for land tenure reform, treating the issue gingerly in line with Gandhi's policy of a unified effort against British rule unhindered by intra-party conflicts. Others in the party, like the Congress Socialists, were not so restrained. The Congress Socialist Party— formed in 1934, of which Nehru was a supportive non-member—had no such inhibitions. Among its objectives were the 'elimination of princes and landlords and all other classes of exploiters without compensation' and 'redistribution of land to peasants'.[6]

The social revolution was put at the top of the national agenda by the Constituent Assembly when it adopted the Objectives Resolution, which called for social, economic, and political justice, and equality of status, opportunity, and before the law for all people. The Directive Principles of State Policy would make explicit the 'socialist', as well as the social revolutionary, content of the Constitution.

The Planning Commission was established, with Nehru at its head, within a month of the Constitution's inauguration, to determine 'the machinery' for implementing the Directive Principles, and to assess national resources and plan for their effective and balanced use.[7] The government's Industrial Policy Resolution of 1948 said that 'the equitable distribution of wealth, not the distribution of poverty' should be the criterion for government participation in industry and for 'the conditions in which private enterprise should be allowed to operate'. Government would be 'exclusively responsible ... [for] new undertakings' in areas like coal and steel, it would plan for and regulate

[6] The Karachi Resolution limited itself to calling for rent reduction for tenants. The party's position in 1934 was that it did not contemplate confiscation of private property without cause or compensation. There was to be no '"class war"'. Bandyopadhyaya, J., *The Congress and Democratic Socialism*, Indian National Congress, New Delhi, 1968, p. 4. Congress provincial ministries formed in 1937 did not attempt zamindari abolition, although there was much talk of it, according to K. N. Katju, then Agriculture Minister in the United Provinces. K. N. Katju Oral History Transcript, NMML.

For the Congress Socialist agenda, see the *All India Congress Socialist Party Programme*, published by M. R. Masani for the party, Bombay, 1937. The quotes are from ibid., p. 7. Among the party's members who continued to be prominent after the Constitution was inaugurated were Jayaprakash Narayan, Masani, E. M. S. Namboodiripad, Sampuranand, Narenda Deva, Achyut Patwardhan, Ram Manohar Lohia, Ashoka Mehta, and Naba Krushna Choudhary.

[7] 'Resolution (Planning)', published by the Cabinet Secretariat in the *Gazette of India Extraordinary*, 15 March 1950. Text given in *Report: Commission on Centre-State Relations* (hereafter *Sarkaria Report*), 2 vols, Government of India Press, New Delhi, 1988, vol. 1, p. 391. For an invaluable source on the Planning Commission, see Frankel, *Political Economy*, throughout.

eighteen other items; and government had the right to acquire existing industrial undertakings.[8]

The predilection for socialism came to many in the national leadership from their personal backgrounds and from their belief in the indissoluble linkage between social revolution and democracy. Socialism was thought the antithesis of imperialism, at once its enemy and remedy. Nehru, among others, believed capitalism to be in decline, a victim of itself, exhausted by two world wars and therefore unfit to be a means to restructure India. Many Indian leaders had studied in England and been influenced by Harold Laski's view that 'political equality ... is never real unless it is accompanied by virtual economic equality'. Most of the upper class leaders of the independence movement looked down on industrialists and persons 'in trade', much as did their English class-conscious counterparts. Many leaders of the independence movement disdained the industrialists for their typically weak support for the independence movement and the merchants and shopkeepers for their reputations as exploiters—as moneylenders, manipulators of commodity prices, and food adulterers. None of them, and few members of government during the Nehru years, had personal experience in commerce or industry. The belief was common in society that wealth most likely was ill-gotten.[9] Zamindars and other large landholders had few friends even among those who espoused their right to greater compensation. Many of these owed their titles to property to the

[8] *Resolution on Industrial Policy,* Ministry of Information and Broadcasting, GOI, New Delhi, 6 April 1948. The Industries (Development and Control) Bill, 1949, gave the resolution legislative force. And the Indian Companies (Amendment) Bill, 1951, ensured government control over the composition of boards of directors of private companies, the selection of 'managing agents', and other company affairs.

The 1956 Industrial Policy Resolution went further. After reaffirming the 1948 resolution and the 1954 'socialist pattern of society' resolution, it divided industries into three categories, one of which comprised industries that were to be 'progressively State-owned'—in other words, nationalized.

[9] P. N. Haksar is instructive on this and related cultural aspects. See Haksar, P. N., *Premonitions,* Interpress, Bombay, 1979, p. 139.

Also, industrialists, the large commercial houses, and the banks were thought by the socialist-minded—with more than a little justification—to be monopolistic. 'The outstanding characteristic of our economy, as it has developed, is the control of industry in a few hands,' wrote Ashoka Mehta. Mehta, Ashoka *Who Owns India,* Chedana Prakashan Ltd., Hyderabad, 1950, p. 2.

Mehta then provides the data and describes the role of 'managing agents' who managed companies for owners, often with little regard for the economic health of the factories, mines, etc. under their control. During the late sixties and seventies, the 'managing agency system' would be severely attacked and weakened.

misguided British 'Permanent Settlement' and other arrangements. They commonly were seen as exploiters of tenants and agricultural labour, and many had supported British rule actively and been rewarded for this.[10] Finally, socialism in the form of a government-directed economy was thought necessary to mobilize national resources for development, to assure some balance in development among the country's regions, and because the private sector could muster neither the necessary capital nor the manpower to undertake huge enterprises like dams and steel plants.[11]

The Constituent Assembly laboured arduously for the social revolution when drafting the Fundamental Rights, Directive Principles of

[10] The *taluqdars* of Oudh—an area today included in Bihar and eastern Uttar Pradesh—had been consistently rewarded by the British for their loyalty since the late 1850s.

The zamindari system dated from the Mughal period and possibly earlier. Zamindars were 'tax farmers' or tax gatherers, who collected land revenue from the tillers of the land and sent it on to the seat of empire after having kept a percentage of the revenue for themselves as commission. They did not hold title to the lands for which they collected revenue. Having this power over tillers, they could also extract rents and other cesses for personal use. After the British had been in power for some time in Bengal, they assumed the power to collect land revenue for the Mughal emperor. In the 1793 'Permanent Settlement'—mistakenly equating zamindars with landowners in England—the British awarded zamindars rights and titles to land and made them, in effect, landlords. Thereupon, they paid a fixed land revenue to the government and extracted rents as they chose from their tenants. This land system prevailed in Bengal, Bihar and parts of Uttar Pradesh, Orissa, and Madhya Pradesh. There were variants of the system under other names. Zamindari was a North Indian phenomenon. Landlordism in other land tenure systems was prevalent throughout the country.

The zamindars and other such were also called 'intermediaries' between the government and the tillers, and the abolition of intermediaries was synonymous with the abolition of zamindari. Peasants who dealt directly with government regarding land revenue were called 'ryots' (or 'raiyats'), and variants of the ryotwari system prevailed in much of the rest of India. Some ryots had rent-paying tenants. Sharecropping was common in both systems, as was simple landless agricultural labour. For a brief description of land systems, see Anstey, Vera, *The Economic Development of India*, Longmans, Green and Co., London, 1957, pp. 97ff; also the excellent study, Merillat, H. C. L., *Land and the Constitution in India*, Columbia University Press, New York, 1970, p. 13.

[11] For very informative insights about this thinking, see R. C. Dutt's readable *Imperialism to Socialism: Memoirs of an Indian Civil Servant*, Milend Publications Pvt. Ltd., New Delhi, 1985. A member of the Socialist Society when at Cambridge University in the Thirties, where Mohan Kumaramangalam and Rajni Patel also were undergraduates, Dutt records that the Spanish civil war had a major effect on Indian students' thinking. 'I became convinced that the economic development of India ... would have to be on the socialist pattern.' Free enterprise could assure neither the 'desired pace of development nor, indeed, the equitable distribution of the fruits thereof'. Ibid., p. 41. Dutt joined the Indian Civil Service and would be an influential member of it until his retirement in 1972.

State Policy, and the provisions for the uplift of disadvantaged citizens. The Rights expressed not only prohibitions—what government must not do—but also conditions, such as equality before the law, that government should strive to bring about. Property relations presented the most difficult problem, involving as they did principles, the law, and money. Assembly members had been elected by members of provincial legislatures who, themselves, had campaigned under a manifesto that called for abolition of zamindaris in return for equitable compensation.[12] Even as the members were at work, the 1948 report of the party's Economic Programme Committee recommended eliminating all intermediaries between the tiller and the government,[13] and several provincial governments had begun to move on property issues. Legislators of the United Provinces, for example, passed a resolution in 1946 that endorsed zamindari abolition, appointed a zamindari abolition committee chaired by Premier G. B. Pant, and began drafting abolition legislation. The Bombay government established a land reform committee under Premier Morarji Desai.

These draft bills passed through Sardar Patel's Home Ministry—the official channel for centre–state communications—for vetting by the concerned central ministries. This process had the openness and vigour characteristic of Patel's own style and of the Nehru years. It was cabinet government at its best. Ministers expressed their views frankly, often exchanging notes several times daily. Staff analyses did not shy away from contentious issues, and communications between the central and state bureaucracies about the draft bills were forthright. The intricacies seemed infinite, the knottiest revolving around compensation. What did the word mean or imply: 'full' or 'just' or 'equitable' compensation, or simply what a legislature prescribed it to be?'How was compensation

---

[12] *Congress Election Manifesto,* AICC, New Delhi, 1945.

[13] It went further and introduced the subject of land 'ceilings' by saying 'the maximum size of holdings should be fixed'. *Report of the Economic Programme Committee,* AICC, New Delhi, January 1948, pp. 12, 14.

The committee had been established in 1938 with Nehru as chairman. Subcommittees for a variety of subjects were created, and several of these submitted reports before the war, when the British jailed Nehru and other members for civil disobedience. It resumed work after the war, again with Nehru as chair. See also *Crops: Planning and Production,* Report of the Sub-committee, National Planning Committee Series, Vora and Company Publishers Ltd., Bombay, 1949.

The Socialist Party called for the abolition of 'landlordism' and for government ownership of land. *Programme* (with a foreword by Jayaprakash Narayan), Socialist Party, Bombay, 1947, p. 20.

to be calculated—for example, as a percentage of the rents the zamindar received? How was compensation to be paid—cash, bonds, all at once or over time?[14] Could zamindaris be 'taken over' at once, but 'acquired' later, thus avoiding an immediate obligation to pay compensation? What of forests on and resources under a zamindar's land?—coal mines in Bihar were a major issue.[15] Finally, what zamindari abolition laws were likely to survive judicial review and how much could the central and state governments afford to pay?[16]

While central and state ministries were thus occupied, the zamindars were busy lobbying in Patna, Lucknow, and New Delhi. The Maharaja of Chota Nagpur wrote to Bihar Premier Shri Krishna Sinha that he hoped '"the wailing of the zamindars in their distress will touch your heart." '[17] While pleading their case with Patel and other ministers, the Biharis concentrated on President Rajendra Prasad, a fellow Bihari, telling him that the provincial government was 'bent' upon taking their rights, 'without compensation', contrary to promises.[18] Their leader, and perhaps the biggest zamindar of all, the Maharaja of Darbhanga, told Prasad that they did not oppose abolition but only wanted it done in a 'fair way'. Prasad seems to have acted in a constitutionally proper fashion on these occasions. He told the lobbyists that, 'as a constitutional

[14] When it once was asserted that 'compensation' meant cash paid at the time of takeover, Nehru wrote to Patel that this would mean no compensation because 'no government in the wide world can make payment in cash in such circumstances'. Letter from Paris, 27 October 1948. Durga Das, *Patel's Correspondence*, vol. 7, p. 672.

[15] Among the sources used for New Delhi's consideration of provincial bills are: Home Ministry Files 5/101/48 Judicial; File 5/74/48 Judicial; File 5/10/49 Judicial, vol. 1; File 43/3/50 Judicial; Law Ministry, Legislative Branch, File F 11/VI/I/48L vol. 1 and 2; Home Ministry File 17/92/50, vol. 1, Judicial (all at the NAI); the AICC and Mahtab Papers, NMML; Jannuzi, F. Thomasson, *Agrarian Crisis in India*, Sangam Books, New Delhi, 1974; Whitcombe, Elizabeth, 'Whatever Happened to the Zamindars?' in Sachs, I. Hobsbawm, E. J. *et al.*, *Peasants in History: Essays in Honour of Daniel Thorner*, Oxford University Press, Calcutta 1980; and interviews—including with L. P. Singh, who was Chief Secretary of Bihar during this period.

[16] Nehru wrote to the chief ministers on 15 July 1948 that large loans to finance compensation were unlikely because the central government's capacity to help was 'limited'. *NLTCM*, vol. 1, p. 158.

The Central Finance Ministry later warned the government of Orissa, and presumably other state governments, that it 'could not expect any financial assistance from the Centre by way of loans or otherwise' to pay compensation to zamindars. Cited in a letter from Orissa Chief Minister Naba Krushna Chaudhuri to Prime Minister Nehru, 26 June 1950. Hare Krushna Mahtab Papers, File 18, NMML.

[17] Jannuzi, *Agrarian Crisis*, p. 14.

[18] Ibid.

President', he was ordinarily guided by the advice of his ministers,[19] and he kept the cabinet informed of the deputations and their arguments.

The difficulties encountered in vetting provincial land bills directly affected the Constituent Assembly's drafting of the Fundamental Rights because of the dual functions performed by many of the individuals involved. Prasad was Assembly president. B. R. Ambedkar was both Law Minister in the government and chairman of the Assembly's drafting committee. Nehru and Patel, of course, were dominant in Assembly and government. Pandit Pant and other provincial premiers also sat in the Assembly.

Prasad, Nehru, and Patel were the dominant figures in the debate and agreed that zamindari must be abolished. Patel was no less adamant than Nehru. There was 'hardly any room for controversy on the merits' of abolition, Patel wrote to the Chief Minister of Orissa.[20] He wrote to Bihar Chief Minister S. K. Sinha that the Parliamentary Board had instructed him about 'taking immediate possession of zamindari' and that he should prepare a scheme and submit it to the Board.[21] The tensions among the three central leaders—shared by many others—arose over how much should be paid in compensation. Nehru preferred a minimal level, Prasad tilted toward the zamindars, and Patel, supported

[19] Home Ministry File 17/92/50 Judicial, NAI.

[20] To Naba Krushna Chaudhuri on 1 August 1950. Home Ministry File 17/5/50 Judicial, NAI.

[21] Letter of 8 May 1947. Durga Das, *Patel's Correspondence,* vol. 4, p. 103.

In mid-August, Sardar Patel wrote Nehru a most interesting letter about the compromise over the property article and zamindari abolition, which deserves quotation at length.

I have, therefore, told Munshi that the alternative draft which he brought would be adequate. There is still a certain amount of discrimination against the zamindari property, but that we could justify on the ground that this abolition of zamindari is either a fact already or is going to be a fact in the near future. It is necessary to ensure that whatever has been done is not undone on technical grounds. Apart from this, we can also contend that the zamindars are only intermediaries and all their rights in land flow from the recognition of their status as such by the State. *The land belongs to the State,* and therefore, the zamindars are not entitled to full rights of and compensation for ownership. I think, if put in this way, there will not be any difficulty in the party, particularly now, when lands other than zamindari are outside the scope of this discriminatory treatment.

Letter dated 16 August 1949. Ibid., vol. 8, p. 603. Emphasis added.

Additionally, court scrutiny was constitutionally prohibited on bills enacted less than nineteen months before the inauguration of the Constitution if the President had assented to them within three months after its inauguration—contravening the compensation clause of the article or Section 299 of the 1935 Government of India Act.

strongly by Finance Minister John Mathai, wanted compensation to be just and fair. Patel, however, intended to keep the qualification 'just' out of the Constitution to prevent abolition from being blocked, or slowed down, by court interpretation of the word.[22]

During August 1949, Assembly members reached the compromise that became Article 31 of the Constitution's Fundamental Rights. In essence, this said that no person could be deprived of his property except by authority of law, and no property (including anyone's interest in company, commercial, or industrial undertakings) could be acquired for public purposes unless the law provided for compensation and either fixed the amount of, or specified the principles upon which, the compensation would be determined. Such state bills were to have the President's assent; and any bill passed and assented to could not be questioned in court as contravening the compensation clause. The compromise satisfied Patel, and two of its architects commended its efficacy to the Assembly. K. M. Munshi said that if the principles of compensation laid down were genuine, the courts would ' "not substitute their own sense of fairness" ' and ' "they will not judge the adequacy of compensation ... unless the inadequacy is so gross as to be tantamount to a fraud on the fundamental right to own property" '.[23] Nehru told Assembly members that, eminent lawyers have told us that ' "on a proper construction of this clause (clause 2, the compensation clause) normally speaking, the judiciary should not and does not come in." ' Nehru also said that equity applied to the community as well as to the individual and that no individual could override the rights of the community at large.[24] How very wrong they were would be evident within a few months, and their chagrin may have had not a little to do with their subsequent antagonism toward the Supreme Court.

The Assembly already had adopted the property clauses of what would become the 'freedoms' article, Article 19, namely that citizens had the right to acquire, hold, and dispose of property, subject to 'reasonable

---

[22] See Austin, *Cornerstone*, pp. 87ff for the framing of the property provisions.

[23] Cited in ibid., p. 99.

[24] *CAD* vol. 9, no. 31, pp. 1192–5. The speech was given on 10 September 1949. It was reprinted in *Jawaharlal Nehru's Speeches, 1949–1953*, pp. 479–85.

This condensed version of Nehru's speech does not fully reveal its strong similarities to the ideas of Harold Laski, who said: '... the existing rights of property represent, after all, but a moment in historic time. They are not today what they were yesterday and tomorrow they will again be different. It cannot be affirmed that, whatever the changes in social institutions, the rights of property are to remain permanently inviolate. Property is a social fact, like any other, and it is the character of social facts to alter ...'. Laski, Harold, *A Grammar of Politics*, George Allen and Unwin, London, 1960, p. 126.

restrictions' in the interests of the general public or to protect the interests of a Scheduled Tribe. Citizens also had the right to practise any profession and to carry on any occupation, trade or business. All the Constitution's property provisions later would be at the centre of disputes between the government and the judiciary.

The Amendment and Agricultural Property

For months before 26 January 1950 there had been rumblings against zamindari abolition and other land reform legislation in Bihar by the Maharaja of Darbhanga and others. The Maharaja had challenged a Bihar act in a district court and in the Patna High Court. Hearings on the validity of several acts had begun in other high courts. Then, with the Constitution inaugurated, the courts dealt the social revolution a series of setbacks involving both property and special consideration for disadvantaged citizens. (And, it will be recalled from the previous chapter, government was sustaining reverses in the courts on freedom of expression.) On 11 May 1950, the Allahabad High Court ordered the state government to desist from nationalizing certain private motorbus operations in a case concerning the individual's right to own and operate a business. On 5 June, the Bihar High Court in Patna struck down as unconstitutional the Bihar Management of Estates and Tenures Act, 1949. The Act provided for 'taking over' zamindars' estates, including coal mines, managing them and sending profits to the zamindar, and eventually 'acquiring' them. The Act's purpose was to avoid paying compensation at the time of taking over. The Act originally had been assented to in 1949 by Governor General Rajagopalachari, but the cabinet reconsidered it, and President Prasad certified it again, partly as the result of Attorney General Setalvad's advice that he saw 'no legal objection to it'.[25] Chief Justice James Grieg Shearer in Patna did have objections. He ruled that it contravened Article 19(1) of the Constitution (which included the right to acquire, hold, and dispose

---

[25] Setalvad's 'Opinion' was dated 14 February 1950. Home Ministry File 43/3/50 Judicial, NAI. In this 'Opinion' Setalvad said that taking possession of the property and sending profits to the owner was not 'taking possession' under Article 31(2). Yet, he added, it could be charged that the owner's enjoyment of tne property was being taken for an indefinite period for no compensation.

The Secretary of the Ministry of Works, Mines and Power, B. G. Gokhale, earlier had given his view that the bill taking the estates, with its declaration that it could not be questioned in court, was subject to 'abuse ... too obvious to need any comment'. Letter dated 24 February 1949. Home Ministry File 5/10/49 Judicial, vol. 1, NAI.

of property) read with Article 31(2) and (6). Because it offended Article 19, it was invalid despite the President's assent. Moreover, the Act imposed far-reaching restrictions on the powers of landholders and peasants to deal with property, and the restrictions could not be said to be reasonable or in the public interest.[26]

Two days later, on 7 June, the judiciary reinforced the government's sense that its entire social revolutionary programme was endangered. As will be described presently, the Madras High Court, acting on a petition of a Miss Champaknam Dorairajan, a Brahmin, struck down as unconstitutional under Article 29(2) a local regulation giving preference to lower caste persons in entrance to medical schools.

Some weeks later, in August 1950, the substance of the challenge to the government's takeover of textile mills in Bombay produced further anxieties in New Delhi about the nationalization of industrial property—although the government won this particular case in the high court there. Under the Essential Supplies Emergency Power Act, 1946, the Bombay government had appointed a controller for the mills of the Sholapur Spinning and Weaving Company, which the owners had closed down that August. On 9 January 1950, by special ordinance under Section 42 of the 1935 Act (Governor General's Legislative Powers), the central government took over management of the mills, and the next day the Bombay government constituted a Board of Management for them. The owners challenged this 'taking' on the grounds that it violated their fundamental right to property because they received no compensation. New Delhi noted the argument even though the Bombay High Court rejected the petition, ruling in August 1950 that only when the government acquires or takes possession of a property is it obliged to pay compensation and that the right of management of a company is not property.[27] Adding to governmental anxieties, hearings had begun in the Calcutta High Court on two more property cases. One of these,

---

[26] *Sir Kameshwar Singh (Darbhanga) v The Province of Bihar* AIR 1950 Patna 392ff. In addition to Chief Justice Shearer, the judges were B. P. Sinha and S. K. Das. P. R. Das appeared for Darbhanga.

In a concurring opinion, Justice S. K. Das held the Act confiscatory, depriving the proprietor or tenure holder 'of his important rights of land' without providing for compensation.

[27] *Dwarkadas Srinivas v The Sholapur Spinning and Weaving Company Ltd.* AIR 1951 Bombay 86. Decision on 27 August 1950. The bench consisted of Chief Justice M. C. Chagla and P. B. Gajendragadkar, later Chief Justice of India. C. K. Daphtary was then Advocate General of Bombay. He was supported by Attorney General Setalvad. The Supreme Court would overrule this decision three years later, contributing to the passage of the Fourth Amendment.

which came to be known as the Bela Banerjee case, was a test of government 'police power' to take over property for another kind of public purpose—in this instance for housing refugees from East Pakistan—and the compensation due. Thus was the social revolution set back or in difficulty on three property issues: 'taking' under police power; nationalization of a trade or business, with obvious implications for government control of the economy; and abolition of zamindari—and on its policy of 'positive discrimination' for the disadvantaged.

Seeing that social-economic programmes were being slowed down and fearing they might be crippled, the Prime Minister, as seen in chapter 2, wrote to Law Minister Ambedkar on 19 October 1950 that the Constitution's provisions relating to zamindari abolition and nationalization of road transport needed amending—in addition to those relating to law and order and subversive activities. (Attention to positive discrimination would come later.) Joint Secretary S. N. Mukherjee's first internal paper expressed the view that 'compensation' had always been judicially understood to mean just or fair compensation, containing the idea of equivalent value. Also, it was a right inherent in every country to take or expropriate private property for public use, said Mukherjee, citing cases in the United States.[28] Three weeks later, on 25 January 1951, the Lucknow and Allahabad benches of the Uttar Pradesh High Court, acting on petitions filed by zamindars, issued restraining orders prohibiting the state government from issuing 'notifications' and from acquiring their property under its Zamindari and Land Reforms Act, which the UP legislature had passed on 16 January.[29] A week after the

[28] Note dated 6 January 1951. Law Ministry File F34/51-C.

[29] That day a deputation of 'taluqdars and zamindars' of UP met with Prasad to press their view that the Act was unconstitutional and to ask for time to obtain a stay. The government, the deputation said, 'should not embark upon a controversial measure likely to imperil National Solidarity ... . Extermination of the zamindars would not raise agricultural production.' Prasad's note recounting the meeting dated 16 January 1951, ibid.

On 20 January, a large number of zamindars had asked the state's chief and revenue secretaries not to take over their estates for three months because they intended to institute a suit against the Act. If the secretaries refused, the communication said, the zamindars would seek a mandamus writ under Article 226 of the Constitution directing the government not to take possession of their estates. *Indian News Chronicle*, 21 January 1951. The cabinet decided on 23 January 1951 that the Act should be sent immediately to the President. Prasad assented to the Act the next day and asked that there be a 'gap' of several days between publication of the Act and its subsequent 'notification' so the zamindars could have time to seek a stay of the Act's implementation. Prasad's paper was dated 24 January 1951, Law Ministry File F34/51-C. Carefully scrutinized in New Delhi, the bill had been thought a model compared with Bihar's fumbling.

court's action, Nehru wrote to the chief ministers that the judiciary's role was unchallengable, 'but if the Constitution itself comes in our way, then surely it is time to change that Constitution'.[30]

Two days before Nehru wrote that letter, Law Secretary K. V. K. Sundaram reacted to Mukherjee's note, making suggestions that were the genesis of the agricultural property provisions in the First Amendment. A new clause should be added to Article 31, he said, to exclude from its strictures legislation for the acquisition of, and compensation for, 'estates', which he defined as the rights of intermediaries between the cultivator and the state governments.[31] Additionally, Sundaram suggested wording that would protect three central and nine state laws from the fundamental right to property in Article 31, but without naming them. He may have got this idea of flatly excluding judicial review of zamindari legislation from Bihar Premier S. K. Sinha, who had written to Nehru the previous November that the contemplated constitutional amendment should provide that any tenure law that had received presidential assent under Article 31(4) 'shall not be called in question ... on any ground whatever'. This would stop legislation from being made 'ineffective by endless legal quibblings', Sinha wrote.[32]

Nehru discussed the prospective amendment with Chief Minister Pant while visiting Lucknow in mid-February 1951, and later in the month he reminded Pant of his desire for 'precise proposals'. Pant's response—the same letter in which he had suggested legislation instead of constitutional amendment to curb speech abuses—criticized the courts for not taking a 'broad view' of zamindari abolition, which 'can stifle all progressive legislation. Our experience of the past thirteen months has not been very happy,' Pant wrote. He joined the Sinha–Sundaram school of thought by recommending that any state bill 'relating to abolition of zamindari or land reforms', once assented to by the President, could not be questioned in court.[33]

The spring of 1951 was the 'Year of the Locust', said the *Times of India*, reporting the winged creatures swarming over Bengal. Nehru may have felt that he was fighting pests of another kind. First, on 12

[30] Letter dated 1 February 1951. *NLTCM*, vol. 2, p. 325.

[31] Note of 29 January 1951. Law Ministry File F34/51-C.

[32] Letter dated 24 November 1950. Ibid. Clauses 4 and 6 of Article 31 were designed to protect zamindari abolition laws from judicial review for a brief period only, and these clauses referred only to Clause 2 (compensation). Sinha's 'whatever' was broader than this.

[33] Letter dated 5 March 1951. G. B. Pant Papers, Microfilm Reel 1, Files 3, 8, 9, NAI; also, Law Ministry File F34/51-C. Nehru's reminder to Pant was dated 26 February 1951.

March, the Patna High Court struck down the Bihar Land Reforms Act (no. XXX of 1950), ruling it unconstitutional on the ground that the differing rates of compensation for different categories of zamindars violated Article 14, which guaranteed citizens equality before and equal protection of the law. Because of this, the court could examine the bill's compensation provisions despite the bar in Article 31(2). Moreover, according to the court, the word 'compensation' meant money value, and because the Act made no provision for raising the cash to pay compensation, the state intended 'no or inadequate compensation'.[34] Two days after this decision, Nehru instructed Ambedkar to proceed on the amendments 'with the utmost expedition'. A week later, he told the chief ministers that if the Congress's zamindari abolition policy were to fail, 'our entire social and economic policy fails' and millions of peasants can charge us 'with a grave breach of promise'.[35]

More damaging news was to come. Ten days later, on 22 March 1951, the Calcutta High Court ruled against the state government in the Bela Banerjee case. The state had acquired land under a 1948 law, took title to it, and gave it to a cooperative society for the building of shelter for refugees from East Pakistan. The court held that the owner's fundamental right under Article 31 had been violated because the compensation did not amount to a 'just equivalent' of the market value of the land. For the governments in Calcutta and New Delhi, this was another devastating blow both to policy and to the expectation that careful constitutional drafting would keep the judiciary away from compensation issues.[36]

---

[34] *Kameshwar Singh (Darbhanga) and Others v The State of Bihar* AIR 1951 Patna 91ff. On the bench were Chief Justice Shearer and Judges David Ezra Ruben, and Sudhanshu Kumar Das. 'No or inadequate compensation' was said by Judge Shearer. P. R. Das again represented the Maharaja. (For detailed reports of arguments, see *The Indian Nation* from 30 January 1951.) Sir S. M. Bose, formerly Advocate General of Bengal, who believed compensation should equal what had been taken away, also appeared for Darbhanga.

[35] Letter of 21 March 1951. *NLTCM*, vol. 2, p. 363.

[36] *The West Bengal Settlement Kanungoe Cooperative Society v Mrs Bela Banerjee and Others* AIR 1951 Calcutta 111.

The state government had indulged in a practice that seems unfair and which courts would deem so on subsequent occasions and which would cause it to strike down other acquisitions. It 'notified' the owner of the impending takeover in December 1946, but took over the land in March 1950; yet, it calculated the compensation as of the date of notification.

On the same day, the court also handed down its decision in *Subodh Gopal Bose v Bihari Lal Dolui and Others* AIR 1951 Calcutta 85ff. The case involved a landowner's right to evict tenants from land he had bought from the government. The case's importance

The striking down by the Patna High Court of the Bihar Land Reforms Act, 1950, must have been a particularly bitter pill in New Delhi because of the constitutional difficulties attending its enactment. These may be described briefly. First, drafts of the bill had shuttled between Patna and Delhi for months. After its passage by the state legislature, the zamindars during the summer of 1950 continued to press President Prasad not to give his assent to it. Prasad raised the question whether 'the President should not be satisfied that the provisions [of the bill] are fair and equitable before [he shuts] out the jurisdiction of the courts'.[37] The cabinet pondered this over several weeks and on 25 August 1950 decided that the compensation scheme in the bill was fair. Implicitly, at least, the ministers decided that the President should sign the bill.[38] But four days earlier, Prasad had solicited information personally from Patna and, using this, he wrote to Nehru on 8 September questioning certain wording in the bill. Having seen Prasad's note, Patel wrote to Nehru three days later asking him to delay the request for presidential assent until the Law and Home Ministries could consider Prasad's 'rather strong convictions on this problem'.[39] Prasad had said that he had asked the Attorney General's opinion, 'with special reference to Article 31'. He also was annoyed that he had learned of the bill only on 30 August, although it had been circulating in New Delhi since June. 'When I am asked to sign a document, I must satisfy myself and not sign blindly.'[40] Nehru responded to Patel, informing him that the cabinet—with all present save Patel, who was

---

in our context is the court's ruling that the law in question posed an unreasonable restriction on Bose's right to hold property under Article 19. See Merillat, *Land*, pp. 144–5. Both decisions were given by the same two-judge bench: Justices Arthur Trevor Harries and Sambhunath Banerjee.

[37] H. V. R. Iengar's summary note dated 24 July 1950 for the cabinet meeting of 1 August. Home Ministry File 17/92/50 Judicial, vol. 1, NAI.

[38] The cabinet subcommittee had heard Bihar ministers and officials at a meeting on 17 August. L. P. Singh, present as Bihar Chief Secretary, was repeatedly asked, ' "You are the civil servant, will it work?" ' 'The room had a cooler,' Singh later recalled, 'but I was sweating.' In an interview with the author Singh described the Indian Civil Service as 'pro-tenant in those days'.

[39] Letter dated 11 September 1950. Patel also said that the cabinet should avoid giving the impression that it had given Prasad's well-considered note summary treatment. Durga Das, *Patel's Correspondence*, vol. 9, p. 274. This letter also appears in Prasad's correspondence— demonstrating again the very open communication among leaders during this period.

The existence of Prasad's note is clear, but its text does not appear in Law Ministry File 17/92/50 Judicial, vol. 2 along with other documents of this time, apparently because it was too sensitive. (See footnote 41.)

[40] Prasad to Nehru, 11 September 1950. Rajendra Prasad Collection, File 42, 1950, NAI. See also Choudhary, *Prasad: Correspondence*, vol. 13, p. 77.

unwell in Bombay—had considered Prasad's note and decided that he should give his assent from both the constitutional and practical points of view.[41] Facing Prasad's delay, Nehru forced his hand by threatening his own and his ministry's resignation if presidential assent were not forthcoming.[42] The President returned the bill to Nehru with his assent on 11 September with a comment that he was doing so because of the urgency Nehru attached to the matter.[43]

Reacting to the Patna High Court's invalidation of the Bihar bill, Law Minister Ambedkar on 14 March 1951 sent the Cabinet Committee on the Constitution, the one Nehru had established in February, a lengthy note. He said that Article 31(2) should be amended so that nothing should prevent government from prescribing different principles for compensation for different classes of property, or should affect the validity of any existing law, or any law by which government would resume title to land, or laws regarding food supply. He suggested that the doctrine of government's 'police power' be made explicit by adding an article to the Constitution expressing the general doctrine, and that Articles 14 and 31 should not be subject to it. He added his opinion that the Supreme Court ought not to be invested with absolute power to determine which limitations on the Fundamental Rights were proper, for Parliament ought not to be placed in a position of having to undertake over time the inevitable task of constantly amending the Constitution. Finally, Ambedkar suggested redrafting Article 31 so that it would read that no person would be deprived of his property save by authority of law and for a public purpose. No property would be taken without compensation, but, he said, any law assented to by the President should not be questioned in court because it did not provide for compensation.[44]

---

[41] Nehru told Patel that the cabinet had agreed that Prasad's note should not be circulated 'to preserve secrecy'. Letter dated 12 September 1950. Durga Das, *Patel's Correspondence*, vol. 9, p. 275.

[42] Gopal, *Nehru*, vol. 2, p. 94. Patel had protested this. Ibid.

It may be recalled that this contretemps was taking place at the same time as that over Purushottam Das Tandon's presidency of the Congress, where Patel and Nehru were on opposite sides.

[43] Rajendra Prasad Collection, File 42, 1950, NAI.

[44] Note dated 14 March 1951. Law Ministry File F34/51-C, NAI. About this time, Hare Krushna Mahtab also attacked Article 14 as 'a legal impediment ... in the way of economic democracy'. Also, he wrote to Nehru, Article 13 had been a 'serious blunder', preventing land reform and petrifying 'the present deplorable condition of the common man'. Note undated but sent to Nehru under cover of a letter dated 23 March 1951. Hare Krushna Mahtab Papers, File 21, NMML. (Article 13 says that any law inconsistent with the Fundamental Rights is void.)

A personal letter dated that same day had a profound effect on the country's constitutional governance. Madras Advocate General V. K. T. Chari wrote to Law Secretary K. V. K. Sundaram suggesting that Sundaram's idea to name in Article 31 the tenure laws to be exempted from its reach be expanded to create a separate schedule to the Constitution that would contain acts certified by the President and deemed valid retrospectively and prospectively notwithstanding anything in the Constitution.[45] Thus the genie of the Ninth Schedule emerged from the bottle, for the schedule, a risky device in any event, would come to be used for other than land reform legislation. It prompted Chief Justice P. B. Gajendragadkar, according to judicial lore, to say that the Indian is the only constitution containing a provision providing for protection against itself. A Sundaram note to the cabinet a few days later said that the ministry assumed that, so far as compensation for acquiring or requisitioning property other than zamindari and jagirdari was concerned, there was no objection to Article 31 continuing to operate in such a manner as the Supreme Court may eventually construe it.[46] He seems to have been saying that compensation for property taken under the 'police power'—such as that for resettling refugees—might have to be 'fair' if the Supreme Court so ruled. In mid-April, the Cabinet Committee on the Constitution reported that, the main aim being to protect existing and future acts abolishing zamindari, a new Article 31A was to be added saying that nothing in the Fundamental Rights could be used to invalidate laws for the taking of estates or rights in them. Article 31 should be left as it stood.[47]

President Prasad received a copy of the Cabinet Committee's report and sent his comments about the projected amendment to the Prime Minister. His paper opened with several general points that may be recalled from chapter 2: it was deplorable that the Fundamental Rights, which stood 'above' other parts of the Constitution with their semi-entrenched character, should be 'the first [part] of the Constitution to

---

[45] Letter dated 14 March 1951. Law Ministry File F34/51-C, NAI.

[46] Note for cabinet dated 17 March 1951. Ibid.

[47] 'Cabinet Committee appointed by the Cabinet'. This is the name now given in the Law Ministry file to Nehru's earlier committee or to a new group.

The committee implicitly adopted the idea of naming the state acts to be protected; it did not think that the, already voided, Bihar Management of Estates and Tenures Act, 1949, and unsound portions of the Bihar Land Reform Act, 1950, should be brought within the purview of the new article. The committee also recommended that the President reserve the power to modify state acts before the legislation was accorded full protection from the judiciary.

be assailed'; the current Parliament was 'provisional' until a two-house Parliament could be elected; and, because this Parliament was about to conclude its session, members and the public would not have 'full time' to consider the amendment's implications. Turning to Article 31A, the President advised caution. The Bihar bill may have been invalidated in Patna, he said, but the Nagpur High Court had upheld another state's very similar bill, indicating 'not ... [that] there is anything wrong with the Constitution but ... the particular Act contains wrong provisions', which might be changed to make it conform to the Constitution.[48] Therefore, 'the first step should be to await the Supreme Court's verdict on the Bihar bill.' 'On the whole', Prasad concluded, '... the amendment will create more problems than it will solve.'[49] Likely, Nehru and many in the cabinet thought Prasad's intervention nagging. Yet, on this and some other occasions, he seems—in the British constitutional tradition as explained by Walter Bagehot—to have been exercising the head-of-state's right to be consulted, to encourage, and to warn.

By this time, critics outside government were objecting to the property dimensions of the amendment as well as to those affecting freedom of expression. A *Times of India* editorial entitled 'Fundamental Rights' said the changes seemed animated more by a desire to conserve the power of the executive than the rights of individuals.[50] Former member of the Constituent Assembly, and one of the few Indians to be made a member of the Judicial Committee of the Privy Council during the Raj, M. R. Jayakar, told a lawyers' conference in Bombay that it would be unwise to give the impression that the government was '"only too anxious to interfere with such ... guarantees ... [in the Constitution] as soon as these guarantees are found inconvenient"'.[51] The executive

---

[48] Paper dated 30 April 1951. Rajendra Prasad Collection, File 1, 1951, NAI. Published in Choudhary, *Prasad: Correspondence*, vol. 14, p. 274; the entire text, pp. 273–7.

[49] Choudhary, *Prasad: Correspondence*, p. 277. The President also disliked several of the Cabinet Committee's recommendations, which the cabinet subsequently rejected. He opposed the recommendation that the President might modify defective state legislation, and that the modifications were not to be justiciable. He doubted that a state's power could be so delegated and that either Parliament or the executive could transfer to themselves a state act upon which the state had exclusive jurisdiction. Moreover, were the amendment to have the effect of altering the Legislative Lists, it would need ratification by the states.

This incident points up how bad drafting of a law can embroil the legislature with the courts, causing the former to criticize the courts for its own carelessness and accusing the courts of abusing their function by 'making law'.

[50] *Times of India*, Bombay, 13 April 1951.

[51] Ibid., issue of 22 April 1951.

committee of the Federation of Indian Chambers of Commerce and Industry (FICCI) forwarded a long representation to Ambedkar saying that revision of such fundamental provisions as Articles 19 and 31 ' "is in effect a breach of faith not calculated to inculcate much respect either for the Constitution or for the authors of such amendments" '.[52]

The amending bill, introduced in Parliament on 12 May 1951 by Prime Minister Nehru, now contained the provisions regarding freedom of expression and agricultural and commercial/industrial property and most of its final content on special treatment for the disadvantaged. Two days earlier, the government had received the good news that the UP High Court had lifted the restraining orders of the previous January and had upheld the constitutionality of the state's zamindari abolition Act. It seems unlikely that the court's decision would have caused the government to change the amending bill even if it had come earlier.[53] Speaking on the bill, Nehru described it disarmingly as neither big nor complicated; yet without it the 'main purposes of the Constitution may be defeated or delayed'. Rebutting one of Prasad's points, he said that Parliament, having drafted the Constitution, was competent to amend it. Proceeding to the philosophy behind the amendment, he said that although the courts' decisions should be obeyed, 'it becomes our duty to see whether the Constitution so interpreted was rightly framed and whether it is desirable to change it ... to give effect to what really ... was intended *or should be intended*' (emphasis added). India, he explained, unlike the United States, had not had the time to develop judicial interpretations of its Constitution to overcome 'the extreme rigidity of the written word'. Perhaps the courts were right and in a generation things might stabilize, he continued. But we cannot wait, and if we do so, we may wait 'amidst upheavals'. As to any injustice of zamindari abolition, you have 'not just the justice of today but the justice of yesterday also ... [I]nevitably in big social changes some

[52] Ibid, issue of 30 April 1951.

[53] The UP High Court upheld the constitutionality of the UP Zamindar Abolition and Land Reform Bill, 1949, on 10 May 1951. Delivering the court's opinion, Chief Justice Bidhubbhusau Malik held that a law made for securing an aim declared in the Constitution (in the Directive Principles) 'is for a public purpose'. Compensation in the Act, although low, was not illusory. Article 14 did not apply because there was no inequality in taking over estates at different times nor in variations in the rehabilitation grants, which Malik said, in his own opinion, were not part of 'compensation'. *Raja Suryapal Singh and Others v The Government of Uttar Pradesh* AIR 1951 Allahabad 674ff.

The judges on the bench were Chief Justice Malik, Orbey Howell Mootham, Das Bulchand Chandiramani, Chandra Bhan Agarwala, and Piare Lal Bhargava. Attorney General Setalvad and the state's Advocate General appeared for the government. P. R. Das and G. S. Pathak represented the plaintiff.

people have to suffer.' It was a brilliant rephrasing of the well-known proposition that one person's exercise of his fundamental rights may not be at the expense of another's. Then Nehru made his oft-quoted statement, '[W]e have found this magnificent Constitution ... was later kidnapped and purloined by the lawyers.'[54] During a subsequent reading of the bill, Nehru would say that Parliament faced a 'peculiar tangle' if 'we cannot have equality because in trying to attain equality we come up against principles of equality'. 'We live in a haunted age,' Nehru said, perhaps reflecting personal turmoil.[55]

Criticizing the bill, S. P. Mookerjee spoke for many of its opponents. Why 'this indecent haste', he asked, when the Supreme Court had not considered the matter?—perhaps taking the words from the *Times of India* editorial of the previous day. The issue was not zamindari abolition, but that the Constitution was being treated as 'a scrap of paper'. Because the Prime Minister says we cannot wait, is the remedy to arm the executive with arbitrary powers?[56] Nehru reacted sharply. The whole object of the articles in the Constitution, which the amendment was intended to reinforce, he said, was 'to take away, and I say so deliberately, to take away the question of zamindari and land reform from the purview of the courts'.[57]

---

[54] *Parliamentary Debates*, vol. 12, part 2, col. 8832, 16 May 1951.

Nehru, in a letter dated that day, told Speaker G. V. Mavalankar that the country was on the eve 'of what might be called a revolutionary situation in rural areas'. *Selected Works of Jawaharlal Nehru*, vol. 16, part 1, p. 171. Mavalankar had written to Nehru objecting to the amendment because it deprived the individual of all his fundamental rights in regard to property. Ibid., editor's note.

[55] *Parliamentary Debates*, vol. 12, part 2, col. 9626, 29 May 1951.

It will be recalled from chapter 1 that six weeks earlier Nehru had written to Pandit Pant that he, himself, felt 'haunted' by conditions around him.

Several days earlier, on 17 May, Acharya Kripalani had left the Congress and formed the Praja Party. Nehru previously had tried to bring representatives of Kripalani's Congress Democratic Front, a reformist faction within the Congress, onto the party's Central Executive Committee, but he 'was powerless against the conservative majority on the Working Committee' (then headed by Purushottam Das Tandon). Frankel, *Political Economy*, p. 89.

[56] *Parliamentary Debates*, vol. 12, part 2, cols 8834–56, especially cols. 8837 and 8851. Mookerjee also charged that laws had been placed in the Ninth Schedule even if invalid and that Nehru had told Congress MPs to oppose any amendments to the bill. The latter was correct.

[57] *Parliamentary Debates*, vol. 12, no. 4, cols 19071, 19082.

Public reaction, in the main, continued to be critical. The Supreme Court Bar Association and various groups of advocates issued statements opposing the amendment. General elections were due within months. 'An air of indecent haste pervades' the amending process, said a second *Times of India* editorial. Bombay edition, 15 May 1951.

The Select Committee to which the bill had gone and where Nehru presided over twenty other members, reported on 25 May. It made two insubstantial amendments to the new Article 31A.[58] In the several lengthy minutes of dissent, S. P. Mookerjee reiterated the arguments he had made on the floor of the House, adding that the President should carefully scrutinize bills for their constitutionality before placing them in the Ninth Schedule.[59] K. T. Shah, Naziruddin Ahmad, and Hukum Singh, in their joint dissent, found it 'invidious' that bills relating to property were to be reserved for presidential assent, but not laws relating to freedom of speech.[60] Shah, in an individual dissent echoing Mookerjee's, objected to laws going into the Ninth Schedule as 'a dangerous precedent which should not be allowed'. Making a point that would be even more apposite with the Seventeenth Amendment thirteen years hence, he said that the Select Committee had not examined the twelve laws to be inserted by the amendment, although the Law Ministry said it had done so.[61] Ahmad, in his individual dissent, said that reserving bills no matter how 'they satisfy the crucial test of compensation ... [was] utterly expropriatory ... and would serve as a warning to owners of other properties and businesses of their approaching fate'.[62] When the bill passed on 2 June after four days of debate, 228 votes to 20, Nehru characterized it as a 'great gain' that presaged future actions. We must go beyond zamindari abolition, he wrote to the chief ministers, and pointed out that several states already had set a ceiling for holdings. Cooperative farming should be the next aim, he said.[63] But the great gain was in for difficulties, first from President Prasad and then from the zamindars.

Again raising the issue of the President's powers, Prasad objected to the bill after its enactment, but before it reached him formally for the

[58] *The Constitution (First Amendment) Bill, 1951: Report of the Select Committee*, p. 1. The English-language press reported the Select Committee report and the debates extensively.
[59] Ibid., p. 8. While the Select Committee was deliberating, several states requested Delhi to include their bills in the Schedule. Chief Minister B. C. Roy of Bengal wanted included the bill voided in the Bela Banerjee case. Nehru refused. Letter dated 25 May 1951. Law Ministry File F34/51-C, NAI.
When the bill was being debated on 1 June, two Hyderabad jagir abolition acts were added to the Ninth Schedule.
[60] *Report of the Select Committee*, p. 12.
[61] Ibid., pp. 14–15.
[62] Ibid., p. 17. Shah added that unless zamindari abolition were followed by 'simultaneous socialization of land' allowing collective or co-operative development of the land, no benefit would come from Article 31.
[63] Letter dated 2 June 1951. *NLTCM*, vol. 2, pp. 407 ̊

required assent. He wrote to Alladi Krishnaswamy Ayyar reiterating the points made in his 30 April note for the cabinet and seeking Ayyar's reaction to several contentions: that Parliament could not then amend the Constitution because it did not have two Houses as provided for in Article 368; that he could not assent to the bill under his power 'of removing difficulties' in Article 392; and that amending the Fundamental Rights would be unconstitutional because Article 13(2) said that Parliament could not make a 'law' abridging them. Prasad then asked Ayyar whether, assuming his points were correct and the amendment was unconstitutional, it was 'the duty of the President to assent to the bills even when he knows them to be *ultra vires,* particularly in view of Article 60'[64]—which contains the President's oath to 'preserve, protect and defend the Constitution'. Ayyar's response is not on record, but earlier, when Prasad had addressed him with such concerns, Ayyar had told him he must give his assent. Prasad assented to the amendment on 18 June.

Not silenced, the zamindars renewed their challenges. From Bihar, Uttar Pradesh, and Madhya Pradesh (where the zamindari abolition law had been upheld by the high court), they came to the Supreme Court to attack the amendment's constitutionality in what came to be known as the Shankari Prasad case. P. R. Das, N. C. Chatterjee (lawyer for Bela Banerjee), and others argued that the amendment was void because it had been passed by a unicameral parliament, and thus did not comply with the amending process described in Article 368; that a constitutional amendment could not abridge the Fundamental Rights because it was a law within the meaning of Article 13, an argument that would be at the heart of the famous Golak Nath case sixteen years later (Part II); and that the amendment having affected the jurisdiction of the high courts (Article 368(b)) should be declared void because it should have been ratified by one-half the states. Justice Patanjali Sastri, speaking for the majority, upheld the amendment on the ground that it had been enacted validly and that Parliament had unlimited power of amendment.[65] Later that month Nehru spoke at the 57th Congress

---

[64] Letter dated 14 June 1951. Choudhary, *Prasad: Correspondence,* vol. 14, pp. 69–70.

[65] *Shankari Prasad Singh Deo v The Union of India and the State of Bihar* 1952 (3) SCR 89ff. The decision came on 5 October 1951. On the bench were Chief Justice Harilal Kania, Patanjali Sastri, B. K. Mukerjea, S. R. Das, and Chandrasekhara Aiyar. Attorney General Setalvad and others represented the government. For a discussion of the case, see Merillat, *Land,* pp. 132, 237ff.

N. C. Chatterjee personally decried limitation on land holdings, believing that large holdings and mechanical farming were needed if food production were to be adequate—

Session of the need to 'put an end as rapidly as possible to all such rights in land which bear down upon people and come in the way of their growth'. He lamented the conflicts between 'reactionary and static elements and dynamic and progressive forces in the party'.[66]

The Maharaja of Darbhanga's suit against the Bihar Land Reform Act reached the Supreme Court in the spring of 1952 on the government's appeal against the Patna High Court's decision of 12 March 1951. Three judges of a five-judge bench upheld the high court verdict, ruling the Act invalid even though the First Amendment had placed the Act in the Ninth Schedule, supposedly beyond court scrutiny. To do this, the majority reached outside Article 31(2) and the other Fundamental Rights and based their ruling on the entry in the Concurrent List which provided that real principles for compensation had to be fixed, and Bihar had done this wrongly.[67] Justice S. R. Das dissented, holding that the First Amendment did protect the Act from judicial scrutiny. Coming so soon after enactment of the First Amendment, the decision 'was bound to seem an act of judicial defiance of the legislature sitting as a constituent body'.[68] On the same day, the same

---

even if something like collective farming should result. (Merillat Diaries, p. 40, generously made available to the author.)

The constitutionality of the Ninth Schedule was not separately challenged in *Shankari Prasad.*

[66] Cited in *Congress Revitalization and Reorganization: Nehru's Guidelines for the Congress,* Congress Forum for Socialist Action, New Delhi, 1968, pp. 23, 21.

Nehru had submitted to the AICC meeting in Bangalore on 6 July 1951 his *Report to the All India Congress Committee* (AICC, New Delhi, 1951). He wrote about conditions in the country, in general, and particularly about the party's and the government's economic programme. There was a 'large measure of unanimity' about this, despite public apathy, he claimed. He rejected as 'not feasible' a policy of *laissez-faire.* Zamindari abolition was but a first step; other agricultural reforms had to follow, such as 'cooperative cultivation with and the application of modern techniques'.

The Congress adopted its manifesto for the first general elections of 1952 at the Bangalore AICC meeting, although, according to some accounts, changes that Nehru wanted in it were made finally in October. As noted earlier in this chapter, this called for 'establishment ... by peaceful and legitimate means ... [of] a co-operative commonwealth based on equality of opportunity and of political, economic and social rights ...'. The manifesto called for the rapid completion of zamindari abolition, and that 'security of tenure and fair rents should be assured to tenants and tillers of the soil'.

[67] *State of Bihar v Maharajadhiraja Sir Kameshwar Singh of Darbhanga and Others* 1952 (3) SCR 889ff. Decision on 2 May 1952. The three judges were M. C. Mahajan, B. K. Mukherjea, and N. Chandrasekhara Aiyar. The other two judges on the bench were Das and Chief Justice Patanjali Sastri.

[68] Merillat, *Land,* pp. 133–5.

bench unanimously upheld the UP and Madhya Pradesh zamindari abolition acts.[69]

The Amendment and Non-Agricultural Property

When Nehru wrote to his Law Minister on 19 October 1950, citing the nationalization of road transport as one reason the Constitution needed amending, he seemed not fully aware of the implications of the so-called Moti Lal case for the government's socialist intentions. Law Secretary Sundaram and Joint Secretary Mukherjee, although aware of Moti Lal, barely mentioned non-agricultural property in their January 1951 papers, and Ambedkar was equally cursory in his 14 March memorandum. All eyes were focused on zamindari abolition. But Moti Lal would contribute to the passage of the First and Fourth Amendments.

During 1947 and after, the United Provinces government— where a future prime minister, Lal Bahadur Shastri, was Minister of Transport— began to operate public buses in competition with private transport companies and to accord its own bus operations special privileges. Large numbers of private owners, claiming unequal treatment under the law (Article 14) and that they were being deprived unreasonably of their right to carry on a trade or business (Article 19(6)), filed petitions in the Allahabad High Court and won. In the Moti Lal case, the high court on 11 May 1950 issued mandamus writs ordering the state to desist from certain practices. But it was the court's rationale whose import would finally motivate New Delhi.

A state government may own property and manage a business, said the court, 'so long as such activity does not encroach upon the rights of others or is not contrary to law.'[70] The court went on to say that

[69] As noted earlier, the UP Act was upheld in *The State of Uttar Pradesh and Another v Raja Suryapal Singh*. The MP Act was upheld in *Viseshwar Rao v The State of Madhya Pradesh* 1952 (3) SCR 1020ff. P. R. Das again represented the plaintiff, joined by B. R. Ambedkar, who by then had resigned as Law Minister.

Zamindari rights were formally vested in the UP government on 1 July. The Governor, K. M. Munshi, reported to President Prasad that all had gone smoothly, and he gave credit to Chief Minister Pant and to the ability and energy of the Revenue Minister, Charan Singh—who briefly would be Prime Minister in the late seventies. Munshi–Prasad 'Fortnightly Letter' dated 16 July 1952. K. M. Munshi Papers, Microfilm, File 354, NMML.

In his letter to the President on 15 January 1953, Munshi declared himself against the state's thirty acre ceiling on land holdings because it 'would retard the progress in intensive cultivation'. Ibid.

[70] *Moti Lal and Others v the State of UP and Others* AIR 1951 Allahabad 257ff. Quotation from the opinion by Chief Justice B. Malik, p. 266, for the full bench of Justices Mootham,

nationalization of any industry was impossible without legislation, which would have to be justified under Article 19(6). And for the state to carry on a business to the exclusion of others 'must be deemed to be an infringement on the rights of the citizen'.[71] The Law Ministry's note for the cabinet of 20 March did mention the Moti Lal case, but only in the context of Article 14, not mentioning Article 19(6), and said that Article 14 would not bar 'properly formed legislation'.[72] This complacency was due in part, also, to Chief Minister Pant's belief that the UP Road Transport Act, passed after the Moti Lal decision, had solved the problem the court had raised. He suggested to Nehru that a court pronouncement on the Act be awaited before drafting an amendment dealing with this particular issue.[73] Nevertheless, Pant in this letter told Nehru that there were differing opinions about the 'significance' of Article 19(6). Some persons thought the article 'does not authorise the state to enact laws for nationalizing industries or electricity or transport services'. We may hope, Pant added, that such legislation would be permitted ' "in the interest of the general public" '.[74]

An impetus now lost to memory finally awakened New Delhi to the broader implications of Article 19(6). The Cabinet Committee on

---

Sapru, K. N. Wanchoo, and Agarwala. Lawyers for the government included Alladi Krishnaswamy Ayyar; for the petitioners, one advocate was G. S. Pathak, a future Vice-President of India. The relevant law was the Motor Vehicle Act, 1939.

[71] Ibid., p. 267. Again, Chief Justice Malik.

[72] Law Ministry File F34/51-C. The ministry said that the state government had not appealed against the judgement and that the UP government was having no difficulty taking out permits and running transport services. Moreover, it said that full nationalization of transport services under a special law allowing for state monopoly would not be regarded as unconstitutional.

[73] Pant to Nehru letter dated 5 March 1951, responding to Nehru's request for his 'precise proposals'. Law Ministry File F34/51-C, and G. B. Pant Collection, NAI.

[74] Nationalization of financial institutions did not encounter constitutional difficulties during this early period. The (Congress's) 1948 *Report of the Economic Programme Committee* recommended unanimously that all resources available for investment 'should be subject to control and direction of the State', particularly so that credit might be available for agriculture. Ibid., p. 21. The Reserve Bank of India was nationalized in January 1949 by an act of Parliament, and the Imperial Bank in 1953, making it the State Bank of India. This gave the government control over some one-third of commercial banking in the country. Although banking practices were said to have been 'tamed' by the Banking Companies Act of 1949, this had had comparatively little to do with increasing the availability of credit. (See Part II for a detailed description of later bank nationalizations.) The government nationalized the life insurance businesses, with their large financial assets, in January 1956. Finance Minister C. D. Deshmukh had done the preparatory work in secrecy—to his own great satisfaction—and the actual nationalization was accomplished by ordinance to preserve surprise.

the Constitution, in its mid-April report, said that the impediment to nationalizations lay not in Article 14, but in Article 19. After rejecting the idea of deleting 'reasonable' as qualifying the various restrictions government might place on the several 'freedoms' in the article, the committee recommended amending clause 6 to the effect that the right to own property, carry on a business, and so on should not 'affect' the operation of any existing law for the carrying on by the government of any trade, business, industry, or service to the exclusion of citizens.[75] The draft amending bill contained wording very like this, and its Statement of Objects and Reasons explained the language as necessary to protect nationalization. The Parliament's Select Committee reported the bill with only a drafting change on this point, and it became law.[76] The scant attention given in the parliamentary debates to this portion of the amendment contrasts remarkably with its importance in subsequent litigation.[77]

Removing Man-Made Inequalities

During the weeks the government had been considering the shape of the First Amendment, the Supreme Court had been deliberating the Madras government's appeal of the Madras High Court's decision in Miss Dorairajan's case. On 7 June 1950, in the Madras High Court she had challenged a local regulation as discriminating against her, as a Brahmin, in regard to entrance to a medical school, citing Articles 15 and 29(2). On 27 July the court held invalid the local regulation as offending Article 29(2), thus undercutting another social revolutionary policy.

Apparently sensing which way the wind was blowing in the Supreme Court, the Law Ministry, in a note to the cabinet on 17 March, advocated changes in Article 15 of the Fundamental Rights. The Supreme Court's ruling on 9 April 1951 upholding the Madras High Court confirmed the wisdom of this course, because the decision struck at an essential

---

[75] 'Report of the Cabinet Committee on Amendments on 28 March 1951', Ministry of Law, File F34/51-C.

[76] The amendment also empowered government to legislate professional and technical qualifications for engaging in a profession or business, and it also made several procedural changes in other articles. The amendment left untouched the property rights of religious denominations in Article 26.

[77] See Part II when nationalizations were extensive. Also, see Singh, Mahendra P. (ed.), *V. N. Shukla's Constitution of India*, 9th edn., Eastern Book Company, Lucknow, 1994, pp. 137–50.

dimension of the social revolution. The government immediately sought to repair the damage through the First Amendment.

The Madras document at issue was the Communal General Order, commonly called the 'Communal G. O.'. This established a selection committee to fill places in Madras medical and engineering colleges according to the formula of six non-Brahmin Hindus, two backward class Hindus (read Harijans), two Brahmins, and so on, for each fourteen places available. This policy may be said to have had its roots in the formation of the South Indian Liberal Federation soon after World War I. With intellectual links to England and France, the group was anti-Brahmin from the beginning. Operating under its unofficial, popular name of the Justice Party, it negotiated the reservation of some twenty-five per cent of the seats in the Madras Legislative Council for non-Brahmins as part of the 1919 Montagu-Chelmsford Reforms.[78] After Congress eclipsed the Justice Party in the 1937 elections and later, it made 'compensatory discrimination' very much its own policy even while led by Tamil Brahmins like Rajagopalachari.

The Constitution has some two dozen articles providing for compensatory treatment for disadvantaged citizens or for protecting them against discrimination.[79] Although all these articles are relevant as expressing the spirit of the Constitution, three provisions are especially germane here, Articles 15 and 29 of the Fundamental Rights and Article 46 of the non-justiciable Directive Principles. The latter reads that the state 'shall promote with special care the educational and economic interests of the weaker sections of the people'. Article 15 prohibits discrimination broadly. It says the government may not discriminate against citizens on the grounds 'only' of religion, race, caste, sex, and so on. And on these same grounds no citizen can be subject to any restriction in regard to access to public places and to the use of other facilities if dedicated to public use or if supported by government funds. Article 29(2) says that no citizen shall be denied admission into any government-supported education institution on the grounds 'only of religion, race, caste, or language'.

---

[78] Hardgrave, *Dravidian Movement*, ch. 3.

[79] Part XVI, 'Special Provisions Relating to Certain Classes', contains thirteen articles providing for reservation of seats in legislatures for Scheduled Castes and Scheduled Tribes, and so on. Article 16 of the Fundamental Rights demands equality of opportunity for citizens, prohibits discrimination on the bases of caste, sex, etc. in government employment, and stipulates that nothing shall prevent government from reserving posts 'in favour of any backward class of citizens'. Article 17 abolishes ' "Untouchability" '. Other articles ban forced labour and child labour and permit special provisions for women and children.

(This and Articles 15 and 16 may, in theory, be read as prohibiting discrimination directed either upward or downward in the caste hierarchy.) Champaknam Dorairajan had challenged the Communal G. O. because she had come 'to know that despite her academic qualifications she would not be admitted [to medical school—to which she had not actually applied] ... as she belonged to the Brahmin community'.[80] The Madras High Court found that the Communal G. O. violated Article 29(2), and the government appealed to the Supreme Court. There, Madras Advocate General V. K.T. Chari argued that the government was seeking to protect the weaker sections of society under the Communal G. O. by reading Articles 29 and 46 together. Besides, he argued, Article 46 ought to override Article 29(2) even though the Directive Principles were not justiciable.[81] Justice Das, for the majority, said, 'We reject ... [these] contentions completely'. The Principles cannot override the Rights, he said, which are 'sacrosanct and not liable to be abridged by any legislative or executive act or order'. Therefore, Das concluded, the Communal G. O. is inconsistent with Article 29(2) and is void under Article 13, which says government may not make any law taking away the Rights.[82] The Supreme Court, in decisions related closely in substance and time to this ruling, also struck down other communal quotas—for instance in *Venkataramana v State of Madras* regarding quotas for government posts, which again were determined by a ratio such as that in Dorairajan.[83]

The potential danger presented by these decisions to many of the Constitution's 'special care' provisions convinced the Cabinet Committee on the Constitution that it needed to amend Article 15 along the lines of the Law Ministry's note of 17 March. The chief minister of Madras, P. S. Kumaraswami Raja, preferred amending the Constitution to retain the General Order '"in the interests of South India"'.[84] At its mid-April meeting the Cabinet Committee recommended that the Article read that

[80] Asserted in her affidavit to the Madras Court. Cited in *State of Madras v Shrimati Champaknam Dorairajan* AIR 1951 SC 227.

[81] Ibid., pp. 227–8.

[82] Ibid., p. 228. On the bench were Chief Justice H. L. Kania, Justices Fazl Ali, Patanjali Sastri, M. C. Mahajan, B. K. Mukherjea, S. R. Das, and Vivian Bose.

See Marc Galanter's excellent *Competing Equalities*, University of California Press, Berkeley, CA, 1984, pp. 164–7, 364–8, for his description of and comments on this case.

[83] The ratio this time was three-eighths for non-Brahmin Hindus, the same for Harijans and Muslims combined, one-eighth for Brahmins, and the remainder for others. For *Venkataramana v State of Madras*, see AIR 1951 SC 229ff.

[84] In a letter to Nehru. Gopal, *Selected Works of Jawaharlal Nehru*, vol. 16, part I, p. 153. Nehru responded on 11 April 1951, rejecting the suggestion and saying that the amendment

nothing in it should prevent the government from making special provision for promoting the educational and social interests of the backward classes. On 11 May, the day before the amending bill was introduced in Parliament, Alladi Krishnaswamy Ayyar advised K. V. K. Sundaram that Article 29(2) might be altered in the manner of Article 15.[85] At its meeting on 15 May the cabinet had before it a telegram from the chief minister of Madras saying that the amending bill's alteration of Article 15(3) was insufficient to protect the 'backwards', and hence a new clause(4) should be added to the article to the effect that nothing in the article or in Article 29(2) should prevent special provisions for the educational, economic, and social advancement of the backward classes.[86] The cabinet agreed to discuss this change with Parliament's Select Committee to which the bill was about to go. The committee first accepted this recommendation, and then, when it reported on 23 May, recommended that 'economically' be dropped. The cabinet agreed to this, leaving the language limited to 'socially and educationally backward' classes.[87] In Parliament, Nehru and Ambedkar forcefully supported the revised Article 15 against limited opposition, linking it to the Supreme Court's invalidation of the Communal G. O.

The First Amendment was consequential far beyond its immediately visible content. It established the precedent of amending the Constitution to overcome judicial judgements impeding fulfilment of the government's perceived responsibilities to the seamless web and to particular policies and programmes. A similar amendment devoted to property issues would follow in three years. Although this precedent would be long lived, the accompanying example of respecting the judiciary and protecting its independence even while disagreeing with it would not. The amendment's language giving it retrospective as well as prospective effect would be used by Nehru's daughter to render constitutional, actions that at the time of their commission had been both illegal and unconstitutional.[88]

---

would seek to make special treatment for the 'backward classes' consistent with the Constitution. Ibid., p. 154.

[85] Law Ministry File F34/51-C.

[86] Ibid.

[87] The *Times of India* reported on 26 May that 'economically' had been deleted due to 'fears' that it did not name.

The term in the First Amendment thus follows that in Article 340, which authorizes the President to form a commission to investigate 'the conditions of socially and educationally backward classes'.

[88] The amendment also added new Article 31-B, which established the Ninth Schedule

The Ninth Schedule was the amendment's most radical component. This constitutional vault into which legislation could be put, safeguarded from judicial review, the judges being denied the key, was distasteful to several of the cabinet members who voted to introduce the amendment in Parliament. Supreme Court Justice M. C. Mahajan thought it a 'lamentable departure' from Nehru's trust of the judiciary, although he also sought to absolve the Prime Minister of responsibility for it, attributing the schedule largely to pressure on Nehru from other ministers.[89] Neither Nehru nor others recognized the genie they had loosed: that the Schedule would be used for the protection of land laws regardless of their quality or legality (see chapter 4 for the Seventeenth Amendment); for laws other than land reform laws; for laws regulating business; and for laws to serve the personal interests of the powerful.[90] Although the Supreme Court had found a way around the Ninth Schedule when upholding Darbhanga's challenge to the Bihar Land Reforms Act, it took some thirty years, as will be seen, for the Supreme Court to master the keys to the Ninth Schedule and so protect the Constitution from those who might abuse it.

---

and said that no law placed in it 'shall be deemed to be void, or ever to have become void ...'. *Constitution Amendment in India*, p. 181.

[89] Mehr Chand Mahajan, 'A Pillar of Justice' in Zakaria, Rafiq (ed.), *A Study of Nehru*, 2nd revised edn., Times of India Publications, Bombay, 1960, p. 386. It may be recalled that Ambedkar had suggested that laws restricting speech dangerous to national security should be exempted from judicial review (see chapter 2).

[90] Interviews with, among others, Dharma Vira, K. V. K. Sundaram, and P. G. Gokhale, at the time a draftsman in the Law Ministry.

Chapter 4

THE RIGHTS AND THE REVOLUTION: MORE PROPERTY AMENDMENTS

Contrary to Prime Minister Nehru's hopes and expectations, the First Amendment resolved neither the fundamental rights issues surrounding property nor the contention between the government and the judiciary over them. The hoped-for one act play had become a many act drama. The next acts would be the Fourth Amendment—which is treated in the next section of this chapter—and, a decade later, the Seventeenth Amendment, which is discussed in a further section. Both exclusively concerned property. This chapter's final section will assess the results of the period's social revolutionary efforts.

Governmental and public frustration with unsuccessful efforts at keeping the social revolutionary and democracy strands of the seamless web in harmony marked this period. Tensions among the branches of government, in turn, raised doubts about the viability of elements of the Constitution. The Congress Party briefly contemplated a direct attack on the judiciary, and judges began to suspect executive branch designs on their independence. The Prime Minister and chief ministers were buffeted by factions in the Congress that said they were too socialist or not socialist enough. The electorate and the party rank and file think 'we are not moving fast enough and are too cautious and conservative,' Nehru wrote to the chief ministers.[1] Pressures came also from outside the party. Nehru's old colleague and dear friend, Jayaprakash Narayan, urged him to adopt a radical programme of fourteen points, which Nehru rejected for fear of alienating conservatives in the Congress. He told Narayan, 'we have to grow into things'.[2] The Praja Socialist Party

---

[1] Letter dated 15 March 1954. *NLTCM*, vol. 3, pp. 501–2.

[2] The fourteen points were appended to Narayan's letter to Nehru of 4 March 1953 and were published in Narayan, Jayaprakash, *Toward Total Revolution: Politics in India*, Popular Prakashan, Bombay, 1978, pp. 197ff. For the instructive Narayan–Nehru exchanges, see also Bhattacharjea, Ajit, *Jayaprakash Narayan: A Political Biography*, Vikas Publishing House Pvt. Ltd., New Delhi, 1975, and Singh, Hari Kishore, *A History of the Praja Socialist Party*, Narendra Prakashan, Lucknow, 1959.

(PSP) declared that non-violent class struggles such as *satyagraha* and strikes were a necessary method of democratic action. Nehru agreed with the PSP that land reform was 'bogged down'. There was a strange idea circulating 'of thinking private property sacrosanct', he wrote to K. N. Katju.[3]

Critical, above all, to social revolutionary progress—and giving impetus toward the remedial Fourth Amendment—were three Supreme Court decisions in December 1953. On 11 December, the Court upheld the Calcutta High Court judgement in the Bela Banerjee case (regarding the taking of land to be used for rehabilitation of refugees), ruling that 'compensation' meant 'a just equivalent of what the owner has been deprived of'.[4] Six days later, on 17 December 1953, the same judges in the Subodh Gopal Bose case (concerning the right to hold property under Article 19) asserted the court's authority to consider the rightness of compensation (although at the same time they upheld the Bengal government's stand against the judgement of the Calcutta court).[5] And the very next day, the court overturned the Bombay High Court's decision in the Sholapur Mills case, agreeing with an aggrieved shareholder that placing the company under government-appointed agents was a deprivation of property for which compensation under Article 31 was due, but for which he had not been paid. Taking over superintendence of the company was in substance taking over the company itself, said the court.[6] The previous month bus line operators, having lost in the Allahabad High Court their renewed challenge to the state government's nationalization of bus routes, had appealed the decision to the Supreme Court.[7] New Delhi was uneasy about the

---

[3] Letter dated 28 August 1953. Cited in Gopal, *Nehru*, vol. 2, p. 80.

[4] *State of West Bengal v Mrs Bela Banerjee and Others* AIR 1954 SC 170–2.

The bench consisted of Chief Justice Patanjali Sastri and Justices M. C. Mahajan, S. R. Das, Ghulam Hasan, and B. Jagannadha Das.

[5] See 1954 SCR 587ff for the Subodh Gopal Bose case.

[6] *Dwarkadas Srinivas v Sholapur Spinning and Weaving Co.* AIR 1954 SC 199. See also Merillat, *Land*, p. 144.

On the bench were Chief Justice Patanjali Sastri and Justices M. C. Mahajan, Sudhi Ranjan Das, (a close relative of the famed figure of the independence movement, C. R. Das), Vivian Bose, and Ghulam Hasan. The majority consisted of Sastri, Mahajan, Bose, and Hasan.

[7] *Saghir Ahmad v Government of the State of Uttar Pradesh and Others* AIR 1954 Allahabad 257ff. High Court decision on 17 November 1953.

On the bench were Justices Basudeva Mukerji and Misri Lal Chaturvedi. Among the lawyers for the bus operators were a future Vice-President of India, G.S. Pathak, and a future Chief Justice of India, R. S. Pathak, who were, respectively, father and son.

outcome, justifiably, it proved, because the bus operators would win the case a year later (see below). And memories still were fresh of the court's 1952 decision that upheld the Maharaja of Darbhanga's challange to the Bihar Land Reform Act.

The Fourth Amendment

The implications for the government's economic reform programme were clear. For Pandit Pant, the Sholapur Mills and Bela Banerjee decisions were grounds for amending Article 31.[8] For Law Secretary Sundaram, also, the Sholapur decision was the defining moment.[9] Beginning what would become a year-long process, the Congress Working Committee (CWC) on 4 April 1954 set up a subcommittee under Nehru's chairmanship to examine the working of the Constitution.[10] Additionally, the committee instructed Home Minister K. N. Katju to form a three-member commission on the judiciary—an interesting choice, the Home over the Law Ministry, perhaps reflecting the Home Minister's activism during the drafting of the First Amendment. A circular went out from the AICC on 9 April to Congress leaders in the states inviting them to set up expert committees to submit suggestions for constitutional change.

When the Working Committee met, on 22 May, it had before it the subcommittee's report. Among its suggestions were that further curbs on 'scurrilous propaganda and the Yellow Press' be added to Article 19, and that Article 31 be 'enlarged'. The intention was to permit 'temporarily taking over possession or control of any property' for its preservation or better management, while assuring that ' "the amount of compensation or the principles on which and the manner in which the compensation is determined" ' shall not be challenged before any court of law.

In a slashing attack on the authority of the judiciary to protect Fundamental Rights, it recommended that the courts' powers to issue 'directions' and the prerogative writs for the enforcement of Fundamental Rights be confined to failures of justice and serving the public interest. It also would have removed the high courts' authority

[8] At the 22 May 1954 Congress Working Committee meeting. *Report of the General Secretaries: January 1954–January 1955*, INC, New Delhi, 1955, p. 32.

[9] Sundaram in an interview with Inder Malhotra, then reporting on the Supreme Court. Malhotra interview with the author.

[10] Its members were Naba Krushna Chaudhury, Khandubhai Desai, G. B. Pant, Takhtmal Jain, Deokinandan Narayan, K. P. Madhavan Nair, U. S. Malliah, Balwantray Mehta, and S. N. Agarwal.

to issue the prerogative writs 'for any other purpose' (Article 226), and their powers of superintendence over tribunals was to be curtailed (Article 227).[11] These strictures revealed not only frustration with the judiciary's perceived interference with social-economic reform but also the tenuous hold separation-of-powers principles had on the minds of men who otherwise should not be thought radical.

Taking up the report at the Working Committee meeting, Nehru said the various changes should be made not singly, but in a 'bunch'. Naba Krushna Chaudhury said that the Fundamental Rights hindered the implemenation of the Directive Principles. Chief Minister B. C. Roy of Bengal commented that the Principles were vague and needed to be made clear. It was decided that proposals for amending Articles 31 and 226, among others, were to go to the Law and Home Ministries for examination and drafting.[12] At a meeting the following day, the Working Committee 'reiterated its earlier decision' that there should be ceilings on landholdings to be set according to the conditions in each state, and effective steps should be taken to stop eviction of tenants.[13] A second circular was sent asking central government ministers for their suggestions. This was, however, notably equivocal in tone. It said that it 'will not be desirable ... to take too much liberty with the Indian Constitution and to try to introduce too many amendments ... [Yet] it will not be proper to slow down the pace of social and economic progress ... simply because

[11] 'Proceedings of the Working Committee Meeting, 22 May [1954], at the residence of the Congress President', AICC Papers, Second Installment, File Circulars General, 1954, NMML.

In a possible precursor to the subcommittee's thoughts about changes in the Constitution, V. V. Giri—formerly a labour leader, then Minister of Labour, and later President of India—proposed that the Constitution be amended to abolish the power of the Supreme Court to issue writs in matters relating to industrial disputes, leaving all power in the hands of industrial tribunals. Letter to T. T. Krishnamachari, Minister of Commerce and Industry. Krishnamachari rejected the notion. Letters of 12 January and 17 and 18 February 1954. Krishnamachari Papers, Subject File 9, NMML.

The Congress was not the only party to think about its programme. Speeches and resolutions at the Thirty-first Session of the Hindu Mahasabha on 7 May 1954 made no mention of amending the Constitution, but President N. C. Chatterjee spoke of the party's 'full and complete economic programme', which included land to the tiller, nationalization of key industries, government ownership and management of 'certain credit institutions', insurance companies, iron and steel industries, mines and plantations, and heavy chemicals. Government corporations were to be managed by autonomous bodies due to lack of faith in the old bureaucracy. Chatterjee, N. C., *Presidential Address*, Hindu Mahasabha, New Delhi, no date, p. 17.

[12] *Report of the General Secretaries, January 1954–January 1955*, INC, p. 31–6.
[13] Ibid.

certain provisions in the Constitution tend to hamper such progress'.[14] Had Nehru—Prime Minister, Congress president, and chairman of the constitution subcommittee—come to think his colleagues had gone too far?

The Working Committee's subcommittee, having made its contribution, responsibility moved to the cabinet and a committee therein. The flow of notes and memoranda during the amendment's actual drafting revealed sharp philosophical divisions within the cabinet about property issues. The Ministry of Rehabilitation was concerned about validating laws taking land for the resettlement of refugees. In its note for the cabinet, it pointed out that West Bengal, Punjab, and UP laws for acquiring land for refugee resettlement had been struck down because, under the 'police power' fair compensation was due. Rehabilitation Minister A. P. Jain suggested that the compensation issue might be avoided by classifying the laws as emergency measures. The Law Ministry unsympathetically commented that the Calcutta High Court's decision in Bela Banerjee had been correct: legitimate increases in the market value of a property could not be ignored when determining the true equivalent value.[15] Minister of Commerce and Industry T. T. Krishnamachari took a long view of national economic development. Article 31 should be amended to protect land legislation and also to give government powers 'for the purpose of preventing abuse by those in possession or in management of ... [non-agricultural] properties', he wrote Nehru, but it would be wrong-headed 'to drop ... or radically vary ... [the clause calling for compensation] at this stage of our development'.[16] The cabinet committee met on 29 August and, apart from tactical decisions, took the view that neither deprivation of

[14] Circular letter dated 25 May 1954, signed by S. N. Agarwal, Congress General Secretary. T. T. Krishnamachari Papers, Jawaharlal Nehru File, 1954, NMML.

T. T. Krishnamachari asked Nehru if replies to the circular should go to the AICC or to the cabinet, whose collective views should go to the AICC. Nehru replied that letters should go to the cabinet and that the Working Committee had not finally considered the matter. Letters of 28 and 29 May, respectively. Ibid.

[15] Ministry of Rehabilitation, note for the cabinet, 12 August 1954. Law Ministry comments, date not given. Law Ministry File F53 (7)/54-C (c), collection no. II. Also see ch. 3, footnote 36.

The Court had identified a government practice that would result in the striking down of later acquisitions: compensation had been paid on the value of land when it was 'notified' for taking, although actual acquisition came much later, and the value of the property had increased in the interim.

[16] Letter dated 3 August 1954. T. T. Krishnamachari Papers, Jawaharlal Nehru File, 1954, NMML.

property nor reasonable restrictions on its use should by itself entitle persons to compensation and that Article 31(2) should not apply to land taken for relief of displaced persons. Cabinet meetings on 31 August and 1 and 2 September failed to move matters further. Yet, something said at the 2 September meeting upset T. T. Krishnamachari, for he wrote to Nehru that the discussion on Article 31 'has upset my programme for development of industries' and 'blasted' my hopes. I would not favour the capitalist class, Krishnamachari said, but investment is increasing and this could lead to 'reasonable size industrial expansion'. We have to move 'somewhat to the left' on agricultural land, he continued, but moving left in industry will prevent expansion. 'I agree generally,' penned Finance Minister C. D. Deshmukh, in reply to the copy of the letter Krishnamachari had sent him, but 'on the whole would let well alone ... We may yet hope for courts to show sense.'[17] After discussing the draft changes to Article 31 the cabinet sought the Working Committee's views.[18]

Shortly thereafter, the cabinet seems to have accepted K. N. Katju's view that a declaration of public purpose when taking land ought to put the matter outside the purview of courts. K. V. K. Sundaram disagreed, but thought the courts might be excluded from ruling on whether or not land was needed for a specified, declared purpose.[19] Making a declaration of public purpose non-justiciable was, however, the third of three optional draft amendments the Law Ministry submitted

[17] Letter from Krishnamachari dated 1 September 1954, with Deshmukh's handwritten note at the bottom, dated 2 September 1954. T. T. Krishnamachari Papers, Subject File 8A, NMML.

Krishnamachari was said by some to be opposed to his government's socialist policies. His own testimony and that of R. C. Dutt, among others, corrects this. Dutt says that in Prime Minister Shastri's time, Krishnamachari was the only one clinging to Nehru's socialist ideas. Dutt, R. C., *Retreat from Socialism in India*, Abhinav Publications, New Delhi, 1987, p. 45. Krishnamachari himself said '"I am not at all enamoured of private enterprise. We want progress if possible by state endeavour ... But with government resources ... extremely limited, greater emphasis on state enterprises merely leads to a dead end."' Tirumalai, R., *TTK, The Dynamic Innovator,* TT Maps and Publications Pvt. Ltd., Madras, 1988, p. 52. Krishnamachari wrote to Nehru that India had an extreme Left (communist or near-communist) and an extreme Right, similar to, but to the right of, the Swatantra Party. 'So, it is in our times we have to strengthen the progress toward a socialist democracy in an orderly way.' Letter dated 21 June 1963. T.T. Krishnamachari Papers, Jawaharlal Nehru File, 1963, NMML.

[18] AICC Papers, General Circulars, 1954, NMML.

[19] In a note for the cabinet dated 11 September 1954. Law Ministry File F53 (7)/ 54-C(c).

to the cabinet on 13 September. On 29 September, Katju again strongly expressed his views that the Supreme Court had not given effect to the Constituent Assembly's intentions and that all property ought to be in the same category and vulnerable to takeover. Pandit Pant that same day suggested rewording Article 31, clauses 1, 2, and 3 and adding a clause 3A. This would have made non-justiciable a law certified by the President that declared the acquisition was for promoting public welfare and securing social-economic justice.[20] K. V. K. Sundaram redrafted his earlier optional amendments, which the cabinet accepted on 1 October 1954. This version expanded Article 31A to include taking over industrial companies.[21] Despite the attention given to protecting legislation from judicial review through declarations of public purpose, the idea would not appear in the Fourth Amendment.

The concluding stages of preparing the Fourth Amendment brought a mixture of radicalism and restraint, in both of which Nehru was instrumental. The socialist views he expressed were in direct response to his difficulties with the courts, and he placed them in a paper that he circulated in the Working Committee, in the government, and sent to the chief ministers under a covering letter. To them he wrote that, to complete land reform government needed the power 'to modify, in some cases extinguish, the rights of owners of large agricultural holdings ... [to fix] maximum limits ... [on holdings and] to provide for the proper redistribution' of excess lands. Legislation requisitioning and acquiring property for refugee relief should be validated, grossly mismanaged companies should be taken over, and these should be above court challenge. But, Nehru said, 'it would not be wise to raise needless scares by taking more power than we actually require.'[22]

The paper Nehru circulated laid out a dozen changes to Article 31A (which had been added by the First Amendment) that would put an array of government actions beyond the courts' reach. He proposed specific protections for the temporary transference of commercial and industrial undertakings to government management (which often proved not to be 'temporary') and the extinguishing or modification of any rights of managing agents and directors of companies in order 'to secure the proper management of the undertaking'.[23] As though

[20] Ibid.

[21] Sundaram draft of 30 September 1954. Ibid.

[22] Letter dated 9 October 1954. *NLTCM*, vol. 4, pp. 56ff. Quotation from p. 59. The letter is also included in the K. M. Munshi Papers, Microfilm Box 119, File 359C, NMML.

[23] Nehru also recommended changes to the definitions of 'estate' and 'rights' when

timed to confirm Nehru's fears for the expansion of the public sector in commerce and industry and, by extension, for regulating the economy, the Supreme Court four days later ruled in the Saghir Ahmad case that the government of Uttar Pradesh could not, by nationalizing bus routes, deny citizens the right to carry on a business on public roads in the state. 'The property of a business may be both tangible and intangible,' said Justice Mukherjea in giving the bench's ruling—four of whose five members had ruled against the government in the Sholapur Mills case. The state government did deprive the operators 'of the business of running buses on hire on public roads', and the state was not to enforce the 1950 UP Road Transport Act.[24] It was between this letter to the chief ministers and the Supreme Court's decision in Saghir Ahmad that Nehru sent the letter to chief ministers and presidents of Provincial Congress Committees, mentioned in chapter 1, about his mental and physical tiredness and about unburdening himself 'of the high offices I hold'. This incident cannot have been unrelated to his anxieties for the social revolution and to the immediate situation in the Working Committee.

There, he had to overcome radical anti-judiciary sentiment, which he believed dangerous to the Constitution. This was a reversal of the situation in 1950–1, when the Working Committee under Purushottam Das Tandon had been conservative and Nehru the radical reformer. Now, Nehru scotched the suggestions of the spring to restrict freedom of expression further; to take away the courts' authority to issue prerogative writs expressly to protect the Fundamental Rights; and to remove from the Constitution entirely the high courts' authority to issue writs 'for any other purpose'. Also, in opposition to the majority in the cabinet and the Working Committee, he had had to 'tilt the scales' against K. N. Katju's desire to make compensation not justiciable, thus earning T. T. Krishnamachari's gratitude.[25] Nehru rejected striking

---

used in law; and he wished to place beyond judicial challenge the extinguishing or modification of the rights of lessors regarding minerals and oil and supplying power, light or water. This paper was not published with its covering letter to chief ministers in *NLTCM*, but is to be found in the Munshi Papers, as above.

[24] *Saghir Ahmad v The State of UP and Others* 1955 (1) SCR 707ff. Quotation from Justice Mukherjea, p. 730. Decision on 13 October 1954. The court also held that the UP Road Transport Act had been enacted before the First Amendment and therefore gained no protection from the amendment's changes to Article 19(6). The members of the bench were Chief Justice M. C. Mahajan and Justices B. K. Mukherjea, S. R. Das, Vivian Bose, and Ghulam Hasan.

[25] Krishnamachari–Nehru letter dated 24 November 1954. T. T. Krishnamachari Papers, Jawaharlal Nehru File, 1954, NMML.

at the judiciary's roots while curbing its reach on socialist issues, as he later explained to the Lok Sabha.

Accompanying the Fourth Amendment's drafting was the drafting of a resolution introduced and adopted in the Lok Sabha the day after the introduction of the amending bill. This named a 'socialistic pattern of society' as the nation's goal. Explaining it, Nehru said the resolution did not 'mean adherence to any rigid or doctrinaire pattern, but ... we are aiming at a particular type of society where there will be an approach to equality and where the state owns or controls the means of production ... not everything but ... all the strategic points.'[26]

Nehru introduced the amending bill on 20 December 1954. It represented the essence of the changes that he had circulated on 9 October without their extensive detail. The amendments to Article 31A protected from judicial challenge, as contravening the Fundamental Rights, the taking over of the management of any property or company and the extinguishing or modification of the rights of managing agents and directors. Those to Article 31 laid down that if ownership of property were not transferred to the government, it was not 'compulsory acquisition' even though it deprived a person of his property. A change in Article 305 made it clear that the government could have a monopoly in a trade despite the Constitution's provision that trade and commerce in the country should be free (Article 301). The bill also placed seven more laws in the Ninth Schedule, four of which dealt with non-agricultural property and three with business regulation. The four property laws were for acquiring land for refugee resettlement and rehabilitation—including the law in question in Bela Banerjee's case, the West Bengal Land Development and Planning Act, 1948.[27]

After debating the bill briefly, the Lok Sabha shelved it until 1955, apparently to allow public debate upon it—an intention for which several newspaper editorials gave the government credit. Predictably, reaction

[26] Letter dated 24 December 1954. *NLTCM*, vol. 4, p. 112.

Nehru moved a closely similar resolution on 21 January 1955 at the Avadi Session of the Congress. Speaking on this he said that in the socialist pattern the 'principal means of production are under social ownership or control, production is progressively speeded up and there is equitable distribution of the national wealth.' *Resolutions*, Indian National Congress, Sixtieth Session, AICC, New Delhi, 1955, p. 3. See also *Congress Bulletin*, INC, New Delhi, 1955, no. 2, p. 246.

[27] The bill's Statement of Objects and Reasons gave the Saghir Ahmad decision as one cause for the amendment, adding that the courts had ruled compensation due 'even where deprivation of property was caused by purely regulatory provisions of law and was not accompanied by an acquisition or taking possession'. *Constitution Amendment in India*, p. 18.

was mixed. More newspaper editorials were critical than favourable.[28] N. C. Chatterjee deplored the attitude of politicians who 'resent judicial review as an encroachment on parliamentary omnipotence'.[29] Former Chief Justice of India Patanjali Sastri thought it an error to consider social welfare incompatible with the protection of private property. He hoped that property rights in the country would not go out one by one 'like Diwali lights'.[30] The Federation of Indian Chambers of Commerce and Industry asked the government to drop the proposed Article 31A as striking at the fundamental right of property. Progress toward a welfare state, said the Federation, was possible only with an expanding industrial base.[31] H. M. Seervai attempted to 'rekindle' the 'inspiration' of the Rights. Saints may do without property, he reasoned, but constitutions are for 'frail humanity', and men 'who have the haunting fear of being deprived of their property are not the free Indians of our dreams'.[32]

Taking up the bill again on 14 March 1955, the Lok Sabha heard Nehru give an extensive rationale for the responsibilities of the branches of government in regard to the social revolution. A constitution must take cognizance of the dynamic nature of modern conditions, he said when moving that the bill go to a Joint Committee of members from both Houses of Parliament. Even an independent and powerful judiciary should 'not decide about high political, social or economic or other questions. It is for Parliament to decide ... [the] law we should have.' We are not by-passing the courts, whose interpretation we accept, said Nehru, but changing the Constitution. In normal land acquisition, said he, compensation would be paid, but in schemes of social engineering, we cannot give full compensation, for if this is done 'the "haves" remain the "haves" and the '"have-nots" the "have-nots"'. If the courts see a contradiction between the Fundamental Rights and the Directive Principles, he concluded, 'it is up to Parliament to remove the contradiction and make the Fundamental Rights subserve the Directive Principles of State Policy'.[33]

[28] *Statesman* and *Hindustan Times*, 22 December 1954.

[29] Speech on 29 December 1954 to the Ninth Madras State Lawyers Convention, which Chatterjee inaugurated along with Patanjali Sastri. Chatterjee, N. C., *Fundamental Rights in Peril*, Civil Liberties Union, New Delhi, undated, pp. 4–5.

[30] Speech given to the Convention. *Hindu*, 30 December 1954.

[31] *AR*, 5–11 March 1955, p. 114.

[32] Seervai, H. M., 'Fundamental Rights—A Basic Issue', part II, 'No Compensation for Shareholders', in *Times of India*, Bombay, 15 February 1955.

[33] *Lok Sabha Debates*, 1955, vol. 3, no. 16, cols. 1948, 1953, 1956, 14 March 1955. On 17 March 1955, the Planning Commission published its draft of recommendations for

The Joint Committee of forty-five members—which Nehru chaired, as he had the committee on the First Amendment—presented its report on 31 March. Along with technical changes, it recommended that Article 31(2) be altered so that the obligatory compensation could not be questioned in court, whether 'adequate or not', and such language was incorporated in the amendment. In his minute of dissent, N. C. Chatterjee recognized the need for social control for the rehabilitation of displaced persons and 'for temporarily managing big undertakings which are mismanaged by incompetent persons', but, he said, 'that is no reason for taking power to effect expropriation of any property' and leaving the citizen without redress.[34] Jaipal Singh, a representative of the Adivasis of Bihar and a member of the Constituent Assembly, wrote in his dissent that for the poor man's sake compensation must be justiciable, for the right to approach the courts 'is the most effective guarantee against executive tyranny'. Renu Chakravarty, a communist MP, K. K. Basu, and S. N. Mazumdar wanted all of Article 31 deleted excepting the clause allowing for the deprivation of property 'according to law'. The right to property 'should be restricted ... [to] men of small means', they said.[35]

During the concluding debates on the amending bill, perhaps the most revealing remark was Nehru's about personal property: 'In life's journey, one should be lightly laden,' he said.[36] A. K. Gopalan (of the

---

the Second Plan. This opened by describing the disquieting features of the economy and with the observation that 'the level of living is extremely low'. The Plan's objectives were: rapid growth of the economy; development of basic heavy industries for the manufacture of producer goods; development of factory production of consumer goods in a way not competitive with cottage industries; increasing purchasing power through investments in heavy industries in the public sector and through increasing expenditure on health, education and social services. As for agriculture, 'The fixation of ceilings and procedural arrangements for the redistribution of land to peasant cultivators must be decided at an early date in each state in accordance with general principles and standards settled on an all-India basis, and redistribution must be completed by 1958.' Mahalanobis, P. C., *Draft Recommendations for Formulation of the Second Five Year Plan, 1956–1961,* Planning Commission, GOI, New Delhi, 1955, pp. 3, 4 and 6.

[34] *The Constitution (Fourth Amendment) Bill, 1954: Report of the Joint Committee,* Lok Sabha Secretariat, New Delhi, 1955, pp. v–x. Although Chatterjee had represented the property interests of the Maharaja of Darbhanga, he disliked the Supreme Court's opinion in the Bela Banerjee case and said 'something should be done' about it.

[35] Ibid, x–xii.

[36] *Lok Sabha Debates,* 1955, vol. 3, no. 37, col. 4840, 11 April 1955. Nehru had written to the chief ministers on 4 April that the amendment bill, 'though criticised by certain sections outside, has had a remarkably easy career thus far in Parliament ... . It is not our policy to expropriate or to give what might be called nominal compensation. That does

Gopalan case) supported the bill on behalf of the Communist Party. Frank Anthony attacked the bill's placing the right to property in the hands 'of every crooked-backed and mountebank politician that you flash across the political scene'. Acharya Kripalani said the Fundamental Rights had become only directives. '[L]et us recognise that these amendments abrogate and *rightly abrogate* the rights of property.' (Emphasis added.)[37] After its passage in the Lok Sabha, Pandit Pant, who had become central Home Minister the previous January, defended it in the Rajya Sabha. The courts could rule on compensation only if it were illusory, he said. We are rehabilitating the Constitution, not tampering with it.[38] Despite the bill's broad support within the Congress Party, no chances were to be taken during the vote. The Parliamentary Party issued a three-line whip on 18 April demanding the presence of all party members throughout the sittings of the nineteenth and twentieth 'to participate on the voting'.[39] The bill passed 139 to 0 in the Rajya Sabha on 20 April 1955 and received the President's assent a week later.

The Seventeenth Amendment

The spark for this 1964 amendment came, as had the fourth's, from a Supreme Court decision, and it had several distinguishing characteristics. It was the last to be aimed directly at the abolition of zamindars and other 'intermediaries', although later amendments would add state land laws to the Ninth Schedule. It arose from a definitional dispute that got out of hand and raised storms of protest over its projected effect on the peasantry of South India. And it luridly revealed how central and state governments could abuse the Ninth Schedule. Accompanying the controversy were renewed emphasis on socialist goals and increasing recognition that the implementation of land reforms

---

not pay in the end even from the practical point of view. But we cannot allow all our social work to be hung up because a matter is taken repeatedly to the law courts, and we have to await their decision. This Constitution Amendment Bill is a good example of the conflict between the large mass of public opinion ... and some vested interests on the other side.' *NLTCM*, vol. 4, pp. 143–4.

[37] *Lok Sabha Debates*, 1955, vol. 3, no. 37, col. 4988.

[38] *Parliamentary Debates, Rajya Sabha*, vol. 9, no. 38, cols 5097–100, 5299.

[39] Whip 11/IX-55. Diwan Chaman Lall Papers, File 158, NMML.

Signed by S. N. Sinha, Chief Whip, the whip explained that the bill would have to be passed by a simple majority of the whole house and with a two-thirds majority of those present and voting.

had slowed badly, a subject that will be addressed at the end of this chapter.

On 5 December 1961, the Supreme Court had held that the taking of lands under the Kerala Agrarian Relations Act of 1961 was not protected from judicial scrutiny by Article 31A, despite the Fourth Amendment, because the lands did not come within that article's definition of 'estate'. The Court therefore could apply Article 14 (equality before and equal protection of the law). It did so and ruled the Act unconstitutional on the ground that the 'slab system'—smaller compensation for larger holdings, the same issue that had upset the Bihar Zamindari Abolition and Agrarian Reforms Act—was unfair.[40] With the variety of land tenure systems in the country, it was not surprising that nomenclature was a problem, but it may be asked if the court was splitting hairs. The Seventeenth Amendment was framed to overcome the definitional problem by broadening the definition of 'estate' to include tenure systems such as *inam, jagir,* land held under ryotwari settlement—the equivalents of 'estate' in 'local' law. The amending bill, as introduced in the Lok Sabha on 6 May 1963, also would have added 124 state land reform acts to the Ninth Schedule.

The bill was necessary, said Law Minister A. K. Sen, when in September moving that the bill go to a Joint Committee, to ensure that Article 31A's terms covered local land laws previously not covered. N. G. Ranga, the Andhra peasant leader, viewed the bill differently. It was the beginning of a 'long, dreary, black day for Indian peasants', particularly the ryots of Andhra, he said, for they were simply working farmers.[41] Not so, said Bibudhendra Misra, Deputy Minister in the Law Ministry, rebutting Ranga's assertion. In Andhra, Misra said, there were thousands of acres under ryotwari tenure 'where the owner does not cultivate. It has been settled with sharecroppers and tenants, and their

---

[40] *Karimbil Kunhikoman v The State of Kerala* 1962 *Supp.* (1) SCR 829ff. On the bench were P. B. Gajendragadkar, A. K. Sarkar, K. N. Wanchoo, K. C. Das Gupta, and N. Rajagopala Ayyangar. Attorney General Setalvad and K. K. Mathew, Advocate General of Kerala and later a Supreme Court judge, represented the government. M. K. Nambiar was among the petitioners' lawyers. See also Merillat, *Land,* pp. 139–40, 185–8, and 262–5. The Supreme Court invalidation of the Madras Land Reforms Act (no. 58 of 1961) in *Krishnaswami v State of Madras* also contributed to the amendment. *AIR* 1964 SC 1515ff.

[41] *Lok Sabha Debates,* Third Series, vol. 21, no. 27, cols. 6831–48, 18 September 1963. That Ranga's point about small peasants was not wholly ill-conceived was later borne out by the Praja Socialist Party. When it endorsed the amendment at its Seventh National Conference at Ramgarh, 17–20 May 1963, it suggested that small holdings should be excluded from the effects of this bill.

[the ryots'] position is that of an intermediary.'[42] The bill went on 21 September to a Joint Committee which reported to Parliament six months later, on 25 March 1964.

The Joint Committee said that the bill had aroused consternation. It reported receiving over one hundred thousand memoranda on the bill from individuals and groups in addition to the more than half that number Parliament had received before sending the bill to the committee. Opposition also had been heard during the extensive oral testimony it had taken, the committee said.[43] The committee then proceeded to rebuke the government sharply. It had 'carefully scrutinized' the 124 state land laws the government intended for placement in the Ninth Schedule and decided to delete eighty-eight of them from the bill.[44] The government had 'indiscriminately included all and sundry enactments ... [for the Ninth Schedule] showing shockingly insufficient regard for the Constitution,' said L. M. Singhvi, a rising young lawyer from Jodhpur, of the amendment's 'casual, ill-considered, half-baked and unscientific approach'. Indeed, the Schedule's very existence was 'improper' for it brought 'into existence a category of protected legislation the propriety or soundness of which we can scarcely vouchsafe', Singhvi said.[45]

The Joint Committee made a further change in the draft bill. Without giving its reasons or who among its number suggested it, the committee

---

[42] *Parliamentary Debates, Rajya Sabha*, vol. 44, no. 29, cols. 5246–7.

[43] N. G. Ranga personally and via the Swatantra Party organized opposition to the amending bill. He wrote to Nehru on 19 August 1963 asking him to suspend action on the bill, especially in regard to the national emergency in force from the war with China. He wrote to Swatantra colleagues on 3 October 1963 asking peasant organizers and local bar associations to flood the Joint Committee with memoranda opposing this 'obnoxious bill'. On 3 November 1963, he presided over the 'Andhra Pradesh State Convention on the Constitution 17th Amendment Bill', which urged the Congress to withdraw the bill. A month later he wrote to Nehru again enclosing a 'representation' from ninety members of the Congress Parliamentary Party asking that a ceiling be placed on agricultural incomes and, simultaneously, ceilings on urban, industrial, commercial, and professional incomes. N. G. Ranga Papers, Subject File 1, Constitutional Matters File, AICC File, J. Nehru File, Parliamentary Museum and Archives (hereafter PMA).

[44] *The Constitution (Seventeenth Amendment) Bill, 1963: Report of the Joint Committee*, Lok Sabha Secretariat, New Delhi, March 1964, p. vii. The laws deleted from the draft bill were listed on pp. 14–17.

Among the committee's diverse members were the communist A. K. Gopalan, former Food and Agriculture Minister Ajit Prasad Jain, Hare Krushna Mahtab, and Deputy Law Minister Bibudhendra Misra.

[45] Singhvi Minute of Dissent. Ibid, xviii–xxiii. A Law Ministry official, himself a legislative draftsman, later confirmed that badly drafted state laws were sometimes placed in the Ninth Schedule. S. K. Maitra, interview with the author.

recommended that the amendment add to Article 31A the proviso that compensation at market value should be paid for estate land taken by the government if the land were within the ceiling as allowed for an individual's 'personal cultivation'.[46] Because 'personal cultivation' was a term whose definition permitted zamindars and large landholders to retain large amounts of land, this language, on first inspection, could be interpreted as a device for enriching large landholders with full compensation for which they would otherwise not be entitled. Former officers of the Law Ministry do not support this interpretation. The provision was aimed at smallholders, for whom full compensation was thought to be justified, even by such stalwart communists on the Joint Committee as A. K. Gopalan and P. Ramamurthi. Nor, in the memory of law officers, has the provision been much used.[47]

The committee's report was to be taken into consideration on 28 April but then came a hitch in the proceedings. When the vote was due and the lobbies cleared, House Speaker Hukum Singh noted that a large number of members were upstairs voting on committee elections, but Minoo Masani—Swatantra now, but a member of the Congress Socialist Party in the thirties—insisted on an immediate vote. The vote was 206 ayes to 19 nays, barely short of allowing consideration of the bill as reported. Masani told the treasury benches to take the defeat sportingly. N. G. Ranga said government members could 'now accept the decision of God'.[48] Law Minister Sen and others challenged the vote. The Speaker upheld it, but he suggested that a special session could be convened to pass the bill quickly because Nehru was most anxious that this be done.[49]

Parliament having agreed to a special session, the government reintroduced the bill on 27 May 1964. P. K. Deo immediately challenged its introduction as contravening 'the very fundamentals of democracy': it was a 'carbon copy' of the Seventeenth Amendment Bill, which had been voted down by the 'collective wisdom' of the house.[50] Law Minister Sen rejoined, 'We are pledged in this House to bring about land reform ... and we shall overcome all obstacles, procedural or otherwise, if ...

[46] Joint Committee Report, p. vii.
[47] Interviews with the author.
[48] *Lok Sabha Debates*, Third Series, vol. 30, no. 60, col. 13217.

Frankel treats this as Congress MPs purposely failing to support the bill, subjecting Nehru to 'public humiliation'. *Political Economy*, p. 223.

[49] Hukum Singh Oral History Transcript, p. 126, NMML.

[50] *Lok Sabha Debates*, Third Series, vol. 32, no. 1, col. 95.

Under the Lok Sabha's rules, a bill closely resembling a defeated bill may be reintroduced after adoption of a resolution permitting this.

necessary, to achieve this objective.' The house divided; when the votes were counted, 318 favoured consideration of the bill and 31 opposed it. Ranga, some other Swatantra members, and L. M. Singhvi walked out. (Abstentions from voting are not recorded in the parlimentary debates.)

The Lok Sabha adjourned a few minutes later: C. Subramaniam announced that an era had ended. Nehru was dead. Deeply shaken by the Chinese attack in 1962, his health had declined. He had suffered a mild stroke at the Bhubaneshwar Congress session at the beginning of the year. Since then, his gait had been unsteady, his face puffy, and its alive expression missing. 'In its place was a tiredness and sadness and one sensed that he knew his end was near.'[51]

Debate on the amending bill resumed on 1 June 1964. Critics opposed it on procedural and substantive grounds. Government supporters offered rationales for the amendment startling for the bad light they cast over elements of it. Prime Minister G. L. Nanda rejected the objection, put forward by Masani, Kripalani and others, that the bill should not go forward because he led only a caretaker government, and there was a convention that caretaker governments ought not to take major policy decisions.[52] On property issues directly, Masani said the bill was a 'cold-blooded breach of faith' because Ambedkar, during the debate on the First Amendment, had said there was no intention to use Article 31A 'for the purpose of dispossessing ryotwari tenants'.[53] N. C. Chatterjee argued that the term 'ceiling' in the bill should not be defined as ' "any law for the time being in force" ' because state legislatures could then too easily alter established ceilings. He did, however, believe that property 'must be subjected to social control'.[54] A. K. Gopalan supported the bill while endorsing property ownership. 'A man who holds enough land, whether it is five acres or ten acres, which is considered enough for his livelihood—is not ... a class enemy,' he said.[55] The Praja Socialist Party also thought that small holdings should be excluded from

[51] Usha Bhagat Oral History Transcript, NMML. Mrs Bhagat became Indira Gandhi's secretary in 1953 and was an intimate member of the Nehru household on Teen Murti Marg.

[52] The CPP elected Lal Bahadur Shastri its leader on 2 June in an arrangement brokered by Congress president K. Kamaraj, and Shastri took the oath as Prime Minister on 9 June. Some observers thought Shastri not enamoured of the amending bill and that he supported it out of loyalty to Nehru. Even if true, it is unlikely that Shastri would have taken the drastic action of upsetting the applecart immediately upon assuming leadership.

[53] *Lok Sabha Debates*, Third Series, vol. 32, no. 3, col. 366, 1 June 1964.

[54] Ibid., col. 380.

[55] Ibid., col. 371.

the bill.[56] Thus, for both the communists and socialists, the heart of the property issue was not ownership or none, but, how much is enough?

Paradoxically, the most serious indictment of the amending bill came from two of its supporters. G. S. Pathak reaffirmed fears about the Ninth Schedule when he said it was needed 'because there may be some provisions [state laws] which are of doubtful validity or which may be open to attack. We want to immunize all these acts'.[57] Asoke Sen revealed the porousness of the new proviso to Article 31A (market-value compensation for lands taken if held within the ceiling and under personal cultivation), and of much land reform legislation, by giving his definition of the term 'personal cultivation': 'Personal cultivation', he said, 'not only includes cultivation by members of one's own family but also by servants and labourers hired or paid by a person so long as the cultivation is under his supervision.'[58] ('Supervision' was never precisely defined—the author.) The bill passed 177 to 9 on 5 June 1964 and received the President's assent two weeks later.

Soon challenged, the constitutionality of the amendment was upheld by the Supreme Court in the Sajjan Singh case.[59] The court's principal points were that Article 13(2) did not apply for there was a clear distinction between ordinary law and a constitutional amendment (see chapter 8 for a contrary ruling in the Golak Nath case three years later); that 'the power conferred by Article 368 includes the power to take away the Fundamental Rights guaranteed by Part III'; and that 'the expression "amendment of the Constitution" plainly and unambiguously means amendment of all provisions of the Constitution.'[60]

---

[56] At its Seventh National Conference, 17–20 May 1964 at Ramgarh. *General Secretary's Report*, PSP, p. 3; no place or date of publication given.

[57] *Parliamentary Debates, Rajya Sabha*, vol. 48, no. 6, col. 808.

[58] Ibid., col. 1026.

[59] *Sajjan Singh v State of Rajasthan* 1965 (1) SCR 933ff. Decision on 30 October 1964. On the bench were Chief Justice P. B. Gajendragadkar, K. N. Wanchoo, M. Hidayatullah, Raghubar Dayal and J. R. Mudholkar. Attorney General C.K. Daphtary and others represented the government.

[60] Gajendragadkar's ruling for the majority, ibid., pp. 946–7. The court also held that Parliament had no power to validate legislation invalidated by the courts.

Chief Justice Gajendragadkar, expressing a view often cited when the Constitution was being amended in the early seventies, wrote, 'The Constitution-makers must have anticipated that in dealing with socio-economic problems which legislatures may have to face from time to time, the concepts of public interest and other important considerations ... may change and even expand; and so, it is legitimate to assume that the Constitution-makers knew that Parliament should be competent to make amendments in these rights so as to meet the challenge of the problems which may arise in the cause of socio-economic progress and development of the country.' Ibid.

Democracy and Socialism: The Nehru Years in Retrospect

The Congress Party, and the Congress-controlled government, often had reiterated broadly reformist and socialist policies during the Nehru years. The Congress's socialist pattern of society resolution of 1955 will be recalled; the party adopted the democracy and socialism resolution, which envisaged 'fundamental changes in the social structure' in 1964; the Planning Commission in 1962 defined socialism's 'basic criterion ... [as] not ... private but social gain';[61] and the 1956 Industrial Policy Resolution intended 'to prevent private monopolies and the concentration of economic power'. On a grander scale was the 'Agrarian Organization Pattern' resolution of 1959. Famous as the Nagpur Resolution, this described agriculture's future as 'cooperative joint farming' in which those who worked the land 'would get a share of produce in proportion to the work put in'.[62] Nehru, who had edited and approved the Resolution[63] and who had been advocating cooperative farming for several years, was stunned when the move blew up in his face as critics condemned it as Soviet- and Chinese-style collective farming. The idea slipped into oblivion, but the shock waves were slow to

[61] *Second Five-Year Plan*, Planning Commission, New Delhi, 1956, pp. 22–3. See also Frankel, *Political Economy*, p. 130.

[62] *Report of the General Secretaries, January 1959–December 1959*, AICC, New Delhi, 1960, p. 13.

The Resolution endorsed the report of the Agricultural Production Subcommittee appointed earlier by the CWC. This apparently was the same committee as the Land Reform Committee set up at the Hyderabad Congress session of October 1958—with fifteen members, including U. N. Dhebar, G. B. Pant, and Morarji Desai—to examine the 'gap' that existed between existing land legislation and the Planning Commission's recommendations for the implementation of land reform. The committee had recommended the 'expansion of co-operative sector in agriculture by encouraging joint co-operative farming'. *NLTCM*, vol. 5, p. 181, editor's footnote. The idea of 'service co-operatives' to provide agricultural inputs and marketing assistance was older and more popular.

The AICC meeting held three weeks after the Nagpur session elected Indira Gandhi President of the Congress, her first official position in the party.

[63] Frankel, *Political Economy*, p. 162.

According to H. V. R. Iengar, Nehru 'Just announced it [co-operative farming] in the Nagpur session of the Congress and because he was in favour of co-operative farming, there was no one who would oppose him and therefore the resolution was passed ... . Indeed, he never consulted anybody about it. To him, as a Fabian socialist, it was just a concept which sounded good ... [H]e had ... not found out what were the pros and cons of the scheme ...'. Iengar Oral History Transcript, p. 237, NMML.

subside.[64] Among other things, they provided the impetus for the formation of the country's first anti-socialist, pro-property political party, the Swatantra (or Freedom) Party led by N. G. Ranga, C. Rajagopalachari, and Minoo Masani.[65]

Yet there were those in the party who, impatient with the slow pace of reform, agitated for more extensive measures. Krishna Menon and H. D. Malaviya called in 1964 for nationalization of banks and insurance and state trading in foodgrains. A 'group of Congress workers' formed the Congress Socialist Forum to 'rectify' the 'inert and obviously indifferent' attitude in the party toward building 'a socialist order democratically'.[66]

[64] Commenting on the 'ferocity' of the attack, Congress President U. N. Dhebar wondered how anyone in modern times could oppose co-operatives, especially as they were to be voluntary and to be preceded by 'service co-operatives'. But Dhebar committed the gaffe of saying that 'we would like the next step to be that of collective farming, with the ownership of the farmer remaining intact'. This elicited a 'Correction' slip from Nehru's private secretary, C. R. Srinivasan, to the recipients of Nehru's bi-weekly letters to chief ministers. This said that the words 'collective farming' should be changed to 'co-operative farming'. Dhebar letter to chief ministers dated 2 July 1959. U. N. Dhebar Papers, microfilm box 1, NMML.

Nehru defended his policy to the chief ministers, saying that co-operative farming had not suddenly been thrust upon the public, and he enclosed with the letter extracts from Congress election manifestos in 1945, 1951, and 1957 that supported co-operative farming. Letter dated 26 July 1959. *NLTCM*, vol. 5, pp. 271–81.

[65] The party's founding statement said: 'We hold that the guarantees specified in the original Constitution in respect of freedom of property, trade, employment and just compensation for any property acquired for public purposes should be restored.' *Birth of Swatantra (Freedom) Party*, Swatantra, Bangalore, 1959, p. 2.

Ranga wrote to Nehru that the Nagpur Resolution might come to be seen as 'the commencement of demotion of peasantry into a new depressed class of the socialist age'. It was too much like China, he said, and the justification for co-operative farming ended with its failure in the USSR. The letter of 16 September 1959 contained his resignation as the secretary of the Congress Party in Parliament so as to avoid embarrassing Nehru with any speech he might make against co-operative farming. N. G. Ranga Papers, Jawaharlal Nehru File, PMA.

The prominent Parsi industrialist J. R. D. Tata wrote to Nehru that his firm would be contributing to both Swatantra and the Congress. Nehru replied that Tata could give contributions to anyone he liked, but he was 'rather mistaken' if he thought Swatantra would become a viable opposition. Nehru to Krishnamachari, 28 August 1961. Krishnamachari Papers, Jawaharlal Nehru File, 1961, NMML.

Gunnar Myrdal told a group of members of Parliament in April 1958 that India was further from a socialist pattern of society than Western non-socialist countries. Social-economic reform, Myrdal said, was moving too slowly in India, not too fast. Myrdal, Gunnar, *Indian Economic Planning in its Broader Setting*, published by the Secretary of the Congress Party in Parliament, New Delhi, 1958.

[66] *Keep the Flame Alive*, A Thesis by a Group of Congress Workers, 1957, no publication

G. L. Nanda led the formation of the Congress Forum for Socialist Action to quicken 'the pace of planned development'.[67] Even Morarji Desai thought that if citizens ' "did not feel that their lot was improving every day, their faith in democracy would be shaken" '.[68]

But intentions are one thing, promises another, and performance yet another. The nobler the intention, the bigger the promise, the harder to honour either. The gap between promise and performance was widest in the land reform component of the social revolution. For in building public sector industry and constructing great dams, especially, and in nationalizing commerce and industry, the government had either an open playing field or weak opposition from industrialists.[69] When attempting land reform, however, the government confronted decades-old entrenched interests: landholders and landowners who had friends and supporters in the Congress, particularly in the states. For them, socialism was an urban-industrial-commercial doctrine, not a land-rural one. Yet the Constitution had been amended, its fundamental right to property diminished, other rights placed under a shadow, and the courts' powers of judicial review severely restricted especially to support land reform legislation. Into the bargain, judges and the judiciary as an institution of the Constitution had been cast as enemies of social-economic reform. All of which had produced limited results, according to government and Congress Party analyses. As the grandfather figure of the five-year plans, Tarlokh Singh, put it, Nehru's emphasis on land reform had been accepted, 'but, on account of weak-

---

information, pp. ii, iii. Those involved in the Socialist Forum included S. N. Mishra, Krishna Menon, G. L. Nanda and K. D. Malaviya.

At this time, Shriman Narayan, one of the more Gandhian socialists and then a general secretary of the Congress, wrote a pamphlet whose import is clear from its title, *A Plea for Ideological Clarity,* INC, New Delhi, 1957. In it, he said that Congress stood for the welfare of all, but 'it cannot continue to run with the hare and hunt with the hounds', p. 3.

[67] Nanda to Nehru, letter dated 15 May 1962, printed with other materials under the heading 'Congress Forum for Socialist Action' and dated 15 August 1962. AICC Papers, Second Installment, File OD 54, 1963, NMML. Nehru replied on 18 May that it was a good suggestion, but he hoped the group would not deteriorate into 'seeking personal preferment'. Ibid.

[68] Speech to Associated Chambers of Commerce, 5 December 1958. *AR,* 13–19 December 1958, p. 2405.

[69] Even so, a government report in 1964 said that despite ten years of planning and constant effort there still existed 'a considerable degree of inequality in the distribution of economic assets and consequent concentration of economic power in the hands of a numerically small section of the population'. Mahalanobis, P. C. *et al., Report of the Committee on Distribution of Income and Levels of Living,* Planning Commission, GOI, New Delhi, 1964.

ness in political organization and in administration, action lagged far behind'.[70] A Congress internal report put it less circumspectly: 'Nowhere has the gulf between promise and fulfilment been of more serious consequence to the material well- being of the common people than in the rural sector ... . And nowhere has this failure been so clearly a result of organizational weakness and inadequacies.'[71]

Where did the difficulties lie? The policy was sound. Intermediaries, tax farmers, zamindars, had to be eliminated for the governments' writ to run in the countryside. Social equity demanded an end to the zamindars' extortionate relationship with tenants, and tenants needed security of tenure to be productive. No leader disputed these principles. Equally, reduction in the size of large landholdings through land ceilings and the redistribution of these 'excess' lands to tenants and the landless was a sound policy if the goal was to produce a degree of levelling in society, to 'break up the old class structure of a society that is stagnant', as Nehru said.[72] For to be landless, particularly in rural areas, meant to be below the bottom rung of the social-economic ladder, without social status and political influence. Land redistribution was meant to serve democracy as well as the agricultural economy. At one level the policy, with the help of circumstances, succeeded. Land owning broadened among individuals and groups, began the creation of a powerful peasant stratum, a rural middle class that would change rural India. But an even broader band across the bottom of rural society—the sharecropper and the agricultural labourer—remained as deprived as ever.

---

[70] Singh, Tarlokh, 'Jawaharlal Nehru and the Five-Year Plans', *Yojana*, 7 June 1965, p. 8.

[71] *Report of the Subcommittee on Democracy and Socialism*, AICC, New Delhi, 1964, p. 2. This subcommittee—members U. N. Dhebar, C. Subramaniam, Sadiq Ali, S. N. Mishra, and Bali Ram Bhagat—had been set up to study and report on implementation of the 1964 Democracy and Socialism Resolution.

The agriculture minister in Uttar Pradesh, Charan Singh—who would emerge as a national figure during the Janata government (Part IV) and who was such a strong advocate of peasant proprietorship that his critics called him a 'kulak'—wrote a well-reasoned and excellently written book in 1964 entitled *India's Poverty and Its Solution*, Asia Publishing House, NewYork, 1964. Calling for peasant proprietorship and opposing the fragmentation of landholdings, Charan Singh said that the 'abolition of landlordism does not affect the farm, it powerfully affects the farmer'. Ibid., p. vi.

[72] See his thoughtful paper, 'The Basic Approach', first published in the *AICC Economic Review* on 15 August 1958. *Jawaharlal Nehru's Speeches*, vol. 4, p. 122.

'Agricultural production is the only foundation on which we can build,' Nehru wrote to the chief ministers on 30 July 1958. *NLTCM*, vol. 5, p. 106. A few months later, he wrote that 'delay in land reform is really a delay in the whole scheme of planning and progress'. Letter of 20 December 1958. Ibid., p. 181.

The failure of agricultural reform to improve the conditions of this huge layer of the rural population had all along rested more with the Congress Party and its state governments than with the courts. The legislation that survived judicial scrutiny contained loopholes ample enough to accommodate a tractor. Landholders could evict tenants, who then, not actually on the land, could not prove use and tenure—the land records being poor and often manipulated by landlords. Devices like 'personal cultivation', *sir* (pronounced seer), and *khudkasht* allowed great landholders to retain much land. Law Minister Asoke Sen, as just noted, had shown how 'personal' cultivation could be used to evade ceilings. The other terms could be used similarly. *Sir* was land that had been recorded as a landlord's, 'or which but for error or omission would have been so continuously recorded', and which had been cultivated for twelve years by the landlord with his own stock or by his servants or by hired labour.[73] *Khudkasht* was land other than *sir* (that is, not with the twelve year qualifier) that had been cultivated by a landlord or by his servants and hired labour.[74] Another commonly employed device was the *benami* transaction in which a landholder would register parcels of his landholdings in the names of family members and friends and, in the most outrageous cases, his farm animals, thereby keeping large areas under his control, although in law ownership had passed from him.

Nehru, in 1954, pointed out the malign uses of these terms—in the process revealing the extent to which he was out of touch on some matters.

> It comes as a shock to me that numbers of tenants are still being evicted. This is often done ... by land being declared *khudkasht* or reserved for personal cultivation. Many states place no limit to the quantity of land which could be retained as *khudkasht* ... . It is a fact that even now people hold many hundreds of acres of land, sometimes even a thousand acres or more. This result has not been what we had looked forward to.[75]

---

[73] George, P. T., *Terminology in Indian Land Reforms*, Gokhale Institute of Politics and Economics, Poona, Orient Longman Ltd., New Delhi, 1972, p. 97. This definition of *sir* applies particularly to Uttar Pradesh.

[74] Ibid., p. 49. With only slight variations in definition, this term was used in a half-dozen states.

[75] Letter to chief ministers dated 5 August 1954. *NLTCM*, vol. 4, p. 10.

Ten years later, this was continuing. Wolf Ladejinsky wrote that in the districts he had visited, tenants were still being ejected and denied tenure by other devices. Landlords were powerful and should be checked soon by giving tenants secure tenure, Ladejinsky said in a report for the central government, written while he was a consultant for the Ford Foundation. Ladejinsky, Wolf, *A Study of Tenurial Conditions in Package Districts*, Planning Commission, GOI, New Delhi, 1965.

Criticism of land reform implementation derived in part from the imprecision of terms and slogans. 'Zamindari abolition', the first stage, had a clear meaning, but it was accompanied by the slogan, used by all political parties, 'land to the tiller'. The image was the tenant, and possibly even the sharecropper, getting land to own, plots the government had divested from zamindars and redistributed. The actual results of zamindari abolition—with considerable variations by locality—were that zamindars as 'intermediaries' or tax farmers were abolished and portions of their lands taken by government for distribution. But not only was possession retained by the devices just described, in many cases the laws divested the ex-zamindar only of his uneconomic fragments. 'He retained the workable core of the estate while the fragments—hundreds of thousands of plots, many less than a *bigha* (about one-third of an acre)— were parted up [sic] amongst as many tenants as could prove legal claim.'[76] The result was that even the more fortunate tenants got only tiny pieces of land and that little land went to the 'landless', the sharecropper and the agricultural labourer.

Why state legislatures led by powerful chief ministers dedicated to zamindari abolition had enacted legislation so full of loopholes is a puzzle. Were they guilty of the original sin of drafting purposely porous laws? The simple explanations of ineptness or hypocrisy seem inadequate, although the Congress Working Committee's subcommittee for drafting the manifesto for the 1957 elections sounded hypocritical when it recommended that if the manifesto could 'say to all peasants [that] the land reforms would be completed within two years, the peasants' confidence in the government will become unshakable'.[77] Other explanations are that chief ministers like G. B. Pant, Morarji Desai, S. K. Sinha and Ravi Shankar Shukla were concentrating on breaking up the zamindari system and expected extensive land redistribution to follow via ceilings. Such intentions could have been accompanied by a willingness to let ex-zamindars retain considerable lands in order to gain passage of the laws, while harbouring the intention later to take away much of it. This would mean that the intention 'was not to extirpate zamindari but rather to cut it down to size'.[78] 'Zamindari, as a legal institution, was gone, but its abolition had produced no miraculous transformation of the agrarian scene two decades after passing of the

---

[76] Whitcombe, 'Whatever happened to the Zamindars', p. 179.

[77] At the meeting of the Election Manifesto subcommittee in November 1956. *Report of the General Secretaries, March–December 1956*, AICC, New Delhi, 1956, p. 26.

[78] Whitcombe, 'Whatever Happened to the Zamindars', p. 176.

Act' (the UP Zamindari Abolition and Land Reforms Act, 1951).[79] It appears, in the way of the world, that the poor had been forgotten.

Amending the Constitution to restrict the judiciary's reach over legislation affecting property rights produced an unintended consequence: the government could less use judges as whipping boys for its own failures in implementation—although civil servants still could be so used to a lesser degree. The Congress and its state governments thus were exposed as the principal impediments to the full implementation of land reform during the Nehru years, as they would be under his successors, Lal Bahadur Shastri and Indira Gandhi.

None of this resolved the conundrums, which had baffled party and government during the Nehru years, and which would confront governments to come. What degree of impatience is required to drive reform efforts, and how much patience with the realities of change is essential if constitutional norms are to be preserved? How are the Constitution's property rights to be understood, or measured from the standpoint of those holding property or those denied it because they lack social status and political influence? Is the retention of landholdings due to unimplemented land ceiling laws a crime in which landholder, politician, and civil official collaborate? If the resistance of landholders and recalcitrant politicians cannot be overcome in the country's democracy, what of those left without land and status? Both genuine reform and its absence will produce class tensions challenging the Constitution's seamless web. Where, then, will the politicians and the judges stand?

---

[79] Ibid., p. 157.

Chapter 5

THE JUDICIARY:
'QUITE UNTOUCHABLE'

The justices of the Supreme Court who took the oath on 26 January 1950 could not have imagined the controversies that awaited them, which have been described in previous chapters. But they knew that high-calibre judges and an independent judiciary were essential to the Constitution's preservation. The Court should interpret the Constitution '"with an enlightened liberality"' and administer the law with '"goodwill and sympathy for all"', said Chief Justice of India Harilal Kania after taking his oath from President Rajendra Prasad. To do this, Kania continued, it will '"be quite untouchable by the legislature or the executive authority in the performance of its duties"'.[1] Felicitating Kania, Attorney General M. C. Setalvad quoted Oliver Wendell Holmes on the '"organic living"' character of constitutions and advised that the Court's foremost task would be interpreting the Constitution as a '"means of ordering the life of a progressive people"'.[2] The Chief Justice also, if only by implication, had defined the position and the responsibilities of the entire judicial institution under the Constitution. During the years to come, philosophies of the law, as expressed by benches in decisions and by judges and jurists outside the courts, would vary over how best to preserve the seamless web. But an independent judiciary, and its related issue, judges' quality, would be a constant theme.

The original Supreme Court justices had long experience with judicial independence. These seven judges (four Brahmins, two non-Brahmin, and a Muslim) had been practising before the bar or on the bench for at least thirty years before becoming members of the Court. Their judicial careers had imbued them with the principle of judicial independence, for courts under the British had been independent and impartial, except where legal matters touched imperial

---

[1] For Justice Kania, see 1950 (1) SCR Journal 9, 13, 7. The *Hindustan Times* of 29 January 1950 reported the occasion.

[2] *SCR*, ibid., p. 3.

interests.[3] Those in the highest levels of government shared the ideal. Rajendra Prasad, who once practised in the Calcutta High Court, saw only one way for the courts: 'The course of justice, impartiality and honesty'.[4] Prime Minister Nehru believed that 'the independence of the judiciary has been emphasized in our Constitution and we must guard it as something precious'.[5] He rejected the idea of a packed court of individuals of the government's 'own liking for getting decisions in its own favour'. He wanted first-rate judges, not subservient courts.[6] Nevertheless, controversies over how to protect judicial independence soon arose. Comparatively mild during the Nehru period, they would become bitter and even threaten constitutional government during later years. This chapter will discuss the beginnings of these controversies in two sections and conclude briefly with a third section about issues of delivery of justice that emerged at this time.

Judicial Independence: Appointments

An independent judiciary begins with who appoints what calibre of judges. The Constitution established the bare process for appointments

[3] The other justices sworn in by Kania on 26 January were five puisne judges: Sudhi Ranjan Das, Mehr Chand Mahajan, Seyid Fazl Ali, M. Patanjali Sastri, and Brij Kumar Mukherjea. N. Chandrasekhara Aiyar joined the Court on 13 September 1950, bringing it to its full strength of seven.

All the men had their higher education in India. All but two had earned their law degrees in India. Fazl Ali had been called to the bar from the Middle Temple and S. R. Das from Lincoln's Inn. Cumulatively, they had served on six high courts, and two of them had been chief justices. All except S. R. Das had been judges on the Federal Court.

Kania had been made a permanent judge of the Bombay High Court in 1933, a member of the Federal Court in 1946, and he had been knighted in 1943. He never had become Chief Justice of the Bombay High Court, although he was in line to do so. He was superseded for the position because of his unhappy relations with the outgoing Chief Justice, Sir John Beaumont. Munshi, K. M., *The Bombay High Court: Half a Century of Reminiscences*, Bharatiya Vidya Bhavan, Bombay, 1963, p. 40.

For biographical information on Supreme Court judges, see the Law Ministry's series, *Judges of the Supreme Court and the High Courts;* Gadbois, George H. Jr., 'Indian Supreme Court Judges: A Portrait', *Law and Society Review*, vol. 3, Amherst, MA, 1968, pp. 317ff, ¬nd Gadbois, 'Selection, Background Characteristics, and Voting Behavior of Indian upreme Court Judges, 1950–59', in Schubert, Glendon and Danelski, David J. (eds), *mparative Judicial Behavior*, Oxford University Press, New York, 1969, pp. 221ff.

For an historical review of the evolution of the British-Indian legal system, see the classic, Ilbert, Courtney, *The Government of India*, Clarendon Press, Oxford, 1916.

[4] Speech at the Orissa High Court, 18 November 1951. *Speeches of Rajendra Prasad*, vol. 1, pp. 74ff.

[5] Letter to chief ministers dated 18 December 1950. *NLTCM*, vol. 2, p. 291.

[6] Sorabjee, Soli J., 'In Nehru's Judgement', *Times of India*, 30 April 1989.

to the Supreme Court and the high courts. The President appoints the judges of the Supreme Court after consultation with the Chief Justice of India (CJI) and other Supreme Court and high court judges as he may wish. He appoints high court judges after consultation with the CJI, the chief justice of the high court to which the individual is to be appointed, and the governor of the state. Whether the governor, when making his recommendations, may act in his discretion or only on the advice of the chief minister soon would become controversial. It became a convention that the President would consult the outgoing CJI about his successor, although this was largely a formality so long as the senior-most judge routinely became Chief Justice. All judges, therefore, are appointees of the government, which means of the Prime Minister and the cabinet, placing upon them primary responsibility for the quality and the independence of the judiciary.[7] This constitutional process left undecided the influence of the institutions and individuals participating in it; it could not do otherwise. The CJI during the Nehru period had virtually a veto over appointment decisions, a result of the conventions and practices of the time and the Chief Justices' strength of character.

As in all democracies, the issues of judicial independence and the calibre of judges were thought inseparable, and, at the risk of belabouring the obvious, an explanation about the Indian context seems worthwhile. At its most obvious, intellectually inferior judges were thought likely to produce bad law and poor justice. But judges of any ability could be affected by the 'extraneous influences' that Indians believed so prevalent in their society. These could come from a language or regional group, from family, caste, or clan. The public and the legal community during the Nehru years were more suspicious of such influences than of pressure on judges from government acting from its own ideological motivations, whether 'conservative' or 'socialist'. Executive influence would assume prominence after Indira Gandhi became Prime Minister (Part II).

Disputes about judicial appointments had begun before the Constitution was inaugurated. Kania, when Chief Justice of the Federal Court, wrote to Nehru about making permanent several acting judges of the Madras High Court. The things he said (the record is not available) about one of them, Bashir Ahmed, a Muslim, convinced Nehru that Kania was being 'unjudicial and indeed improper', and he wrote Patel that he doubted that Kania should (in three days) become Chief Justice of

---

[7] See the *Constitution*, Articles 124–7 and 214–7.

India.[8] Patel replied that he had told Home Secretary Iengar to go ahead with Ahmed's appointment, and he had told Kania that at this point any adverse action on Ahmed might be regarded as communal.[9]

Later that year, other appointments to the Madras High Court and to the Rajasthan High Court became controversial. In the former instance, the Chief Minister, P. S. Kumaraswami Raja, and the Chief Justice of the High Court, P. V. Rajamannar (of whom we shall hear more in Parts II and V) recommended to the government of India that one Koman of the Indian Civil Service (ICS) be appointed judge. Consulted, Kania expressed the view that Koman was not 'of requisite calibre' and offered another name. This so irritated the chief minister that he protested in an intemperate letter, which Patel declined to place in the file. Instead, Patel drafted a letter for Kumaraswami, to send back to him, reiterating his and the Madras chief justice's support for Koman.[10]

Also in 1950, the suggestion that K. N. Wanchoo go from a judge at the Allahabad High Court to become the chief justice in Rajasthan encountered a thicket of difficulties. The Acting Chief Justice in Rajasthan, Nawalkishore, wanted the position for himself, and was supported in this by Chief Justice Kania. Nawalkishore had also called upon Rajendra Prasad to importune his support. The chief justice in Allahabad did not wish to lose Wanchoo, so Patel asked his secretary, V. Shankar, to meet and discuss the matter with the Allahabad chief justice, whom he knew personally. Nehru, apparently ignorant of the affair and irritated by it, wrote to Patel, who replied that it was 'distressing' to have to defend finding such a good chief justice for Rajasthan.[11]

---

[8] Letter to Patel dated 23 January 1950. Durga Das, *Patel's Correspondence*, vol. 10, p. 378.

[9] Letter dated 23 January 1950. Ibid. Patel also wrote that some indiscretions by a chief justice have to be tolerated, 'but, on the whole, I think I have been able to manage him'. Kania's petty-mindedness 'is a trait not uncommon with some heads of the judiciary who feel that they have the sole monopoly of upholding its independence', Patel said. Ibid., p. 379.

[10] Kumaraswami Raja letter to Patel dated 12 November 1950. Patel to 'My Dear Raja' dated 20 November 1950. Patel, Manibehn and Nandurkar, G. M. (eds), *Sardar's Letters, Mostly Unknown*, vol. 3, Sardar Vallabhbhai Patel Smarak Bhavan, Ahmedabad, 1983 (1950), pp. 57–64.

The Governor of Madras State, the Maharaja of Bhavnagar, also supported Koman's appointment. Patel consulted C. Rajagopalachari about the matter and explained it fully to Nehru in a letter dated 3 December 1950. Durga Das, *Patel's Correspondence*, vol. 9, p. 305.

[11] Letters exchanged between Nehru and Patel, 21 November 1950, and 1 December 1950. Durga Das, *Patel's Correspondence*, vol. 9, pp. 502–8. The description of Nawalkishore's ambitions and his call on President Prasad appear in an unsigned, undated memorandum

The governor's involvement in the appointment of high court judges might or might not interfere with judicial independence. K. M. Munshi provides an example. During the months March–November 1953, when governor of Uttar Pradesh, Munshi exchanged letters with Chief Minister Pant about candidates and those that he, Pant, and the High Court's chief justice favoured or found unacceptable for the bench. They discussed the suitability of judges who were members of the British-formed Indian Civil Service (ICS) and Munshi's view that district judges often acquitted violent offenders too easily so as not to risk high court reversal of their decisions.[12] His activism introduced the constitutional issue of the governor's 'discretion', which President Prasad exacerbated by actions apparently taken without reference to the cabinet or the Prime Minister. In consultation with Home Minister Katju, Prasad decided 'that the governor ... has to express his own individual opinion when he is consulted about the appointment of a judge of the state high court as required by Article 217' (and not merely follow his chief minister's advice), although he need not write to the President directly.[13] The correspondence 'between the chief minister and the governor or *rajpramukh* should be in writing and ... copies of the correspondence should be forwarded along with the chief minister's recommendation ... [T]he authorities ... at this end will give due weight to both the views.'[14] Munshi—not one to underestimate his importance—interpreted

---

(but after 1956) entitled 'Procedure to be adopted in connection with the appointment of High Court Judges', Ibid., vol. 12, p. 296. Sardar Patel at the time of this exchange with Nehru was three weeks from his death.

[12] Munshi–Pant letters of 16 April, another undated, and 4 August 1953; Pant to Munshi of 20 November 1953, in which Pant also reports that he had been urging Home Minister Katju to make appointments speedily, but to no avail. K. M. Munshi Papers, Microfilm Box 56, File 143, NMML.

Munshi continued to involve himself closely with Pant's successor as chief minister, Sampurnanand, and with Pant after he become Home Minister in New Delhi. He wrote Sampurnanand favouring K. N. Wanchoo, who was by then chief justice of the Rajasthan Court, to return to the UP High Court as chief justice.

[13] Letter of 11 September 1954 from Shavax A. Lal, Secretary to the President, to Munshi. K. M. Munshi Papers, Microfilm Box 59, File 152, NMML..

[14] Prasad to the *Rajpramukh* of Mysore, 6 September 1954. This letter was attached to the Shavax Lal–Munshi letter. Ibid.

Prasad understood the appointments process thus: The proposal is first made by the high court chief justice to the government of the state, then to the governor, 'who makes his own recommendation on the basis of the high court's recommendation'. This is referred to the Chief Justice [of India] and his recommendation is considered by the home minister, who makes his own recommendation, which, if approved by the Prime Minister, comes 'to me'. Therefore, Prasad added, neither the cabinet nor any particular

this to mean that his opinions on appointments could go directly to the central government. Miffed when this proved not to be the case, he wrote to Pant, now Home Minister, that his letter about a new chief justice for the high court had gone to the chief minister and the chief justice and their comments on his letter had gone directly to Delhi. 'My views, only intended for the appointing authority,' wrote Munshi, 'were subjected to criticism ... without my knowing anything about it. ... This means that the opinion of the governor is subject to the chief justice's and defeats the principle of the governor being consulted as an *independent* person, in whom the general administration of the state is vested (emphasis added).'[15]

Another governor, Asaf Ali of Orissa, expressed concern that if a governor were compelled to accept the advice of his ministers, the judge will 'owe his appointment to the ministry and, therefore, I cannot conceive how we cannot expect certain members of the Bar not to seek to ingratiate themselves with the ministry in anticipation'.[16] Chief Justice B. P. Sinha recalled instances where governors who 'had been known to toe the line of the chief ministers', had tried to block judicial appointments for personal reasons by making false allegations about the candidate's communal bias, something chief ministers also had done. A state government, Sinha remembered in apparent amazement, even had the temerity to claim that it knew more about an individual's legal competence than the high court chief justice and the Chief Justice of India.[17]

---

minister has any initiative in high judicial appointments. Letter from Prasad to Girija Prasanna Sanyal of 17 April 1952, Rajendra Prasad Papers, File 6G/52, Miscellaneous Important Correspondence, NAI.

[15] Letter of 18 June 1956. Ibid. Munshi hoped to be excused for the 'frank manner' of his letter and referred to the 'humiliating position of my confidential opinion sent to the government being subject to the comments of the chief justice behind my back'. The chief justice in question was Orby Howell Mootham. When Mootham was to be sworn in as chief justice, a dispute arose as to whether the governor should swear him in at the high court, with other judges and lawyers present, or at Raj Bhavan, the governor's office and official residence. Munshi wrote to Prasad, saying that 'constitutional propriety' demanded a swearing-in at Raj Bhavan, which, with precedents in hand from other states, the President concurred it should be. K. M. Munshi Papers, Microfilm Box 67, File 188, NMML.

[16] Asaf Ali to Nehru, letter dated 4 March 1950. Chaudhary, *Prasad: Correspondence*, vol. 12, pp. 129ff.

[17] Sinha, B. P., *Reminiscences and Reflections of a Chief Justice*, B. R. Publishing Corporation, Delhi, 1985, pp. 93–8.

Individuals sometimes 'canvassed' for judgeships for themselves or their friends, Sinha said. For example, when he was a puisne judge on the Supreme Court, he had fought successfully to bring S. K. Das onto the court. Ibid., p. 75. V. V. Giri, when Indian high Commissioner in Colombo, wrote to Orissa Premier H. K. Mahtab recommending that 'my

The selection and appointment of judges attracted the close attention of the Law Commission. Established in August 1955 in response to widespread demands for reform of the legal system, its efforts were to encompass reform, both of laws and of the judicial system. Led by the Attorney General M. C. Setalvad, 'Mr Law' to his many admirers, it began work in May 1956.[18] The division working on law reform produced thirteen reports by autumn 1958. Setalvad chaired the division that sent the commission's famous Fourteenth Report on the reform of judicial administration to the Law Minister in September 1958. The division's terms of reference included examining speeding up the disposal of cases 'and making justice less expensive'; the organization of civil and criminal courts; the level of the bar and legal education; and the recruitment of the judiciary.

When researching the views of judges, lawyers, and political leaders, the commission discovered harsh criticism of the selection process, particularly for high court judges. Munshi, in his reply to the commission's questionnaire, said he believed that 'the High Court judiciary has deteriorated in recent years'. Among the causes were the chief ministers becoming 'a source of patronage' under the selection system of Article 217. Further, selection of high court judges from among senior district

---

friend Mr Jagannathdas' be recognized for his seniority on the court. Letter dated 16 July 1948, Hare Krushna Mahtab Papers, V. V. Giri File, NMML. This is the same as Bachu Jagannadha Das who joined the Orissa High Court in 1948 and became its Chief Justice on 30 October 1951, and was appointed to the Supreme Court in 1953. Mahtab tried unsuccessfully to gain appointment to the Supreme Court for retired Orissa High Court Chief Justice B. K. Ray, at Ray's urging. Mahtab, H. K., *While Serving My Nation*, Vidyapuri, Cuttack, 1986, p. 58.

[18] The other members of the commission were: M. C. Chagla, K. N. Wanchoo, respectively chief justices of the Bombay and Rajasthan High Courts; G. N. Das and P. Satyanarayana Rao, retired justices of, respectively, the Calcutta and Madras High Courts; V. K. T. Chari, Narasa Raju, and S. M. Sikri, Advocates General, of Madras, Andhra, and Punjab respectively; N. C. Sen Gupta, G. S. Pathak, and G. N. Joshi, advocates, respectively, in Calcutta, Allahabad, and Bombay. N. A. Palkhivala was appointed to the commission in October 1956 to work in the Statute Revision Section, particularly on income tax.

Nehru supported establishing the commission on a temporary basis, and thought the time not ripe for a permanent body. See Baxi, Upendra, *The Crisis in the Indian Legal System*, Vikas Publishing House Pvt. Ltd., New Delhi, 1983, p. 248. There had been discussion in Parliament in 1952 about forming a law commission, and Ambedkar, then Law Minister, had said that the government was considering whether such a body should be statutory and permanent. He did not favour an autonomous body and argued that it should become an arm of the Law Ministry, which it eventually became. The AICC resolved on 26 July 1954 that there should be a law commission, as in England, to revise laws that had been promulgated nearly a century previously, and to advise on current legislation from time to time. Ibid., p. 247. The work of the original two law commissions dated

judges was bringing in individuals 'who have little physical and judicial vigour left'.[19] Former Chief Justice Sastri also thought that there had 'been a marked deterioration ... in the standards [in high courts] ... due ... mainly to unsatisfactory methods of selection which are often influenced by political and other extraneous considerations'. Many of our politicians would apparently prefer to have a complaisant judiciary, Sastri said.[20] During visits to high court cities, the commission reported that it had heard 'bitter and revealing criticisms' of recent appointments from Supreme Court, high court, and retired judges, public prosecutors, bar associations, lawyers, and law school faculty. The 'almost universal chorus of comment' alleged that unsatisfactory selection had 'been induced by executive influence' reflecting 'political expediency or regional or communal sentiments'. This was the situation despite in most cases of concurrence in appointments by the chief justices of the high courts and the Chief Justice of India.[21] Critics expressed these sentiments other than to the commission. M. C. Mahajan wrote of his time as chief justice in 1954 that he 'was greatly pained ... [that] ... narrow parochial considerations were sought to be introduced in making these high legal appointments'. His suggested remedy was selection of judges from an all-India panel—an idea whose popularity would wax and wane for four decades.[22]

One wonders if the picture were as broadly black as painted. Disa-

---

from the Act of 1833. Thomas Babbington Macaulay was the first chairman. These commissions initiated the drafting of the Anglo-Indian Codes that would be placed in force throughout the remainder of the 19th century.

[19] Munshi, 'Replies' to the Law Commission questionnaire. K. M. Munshi Papers, Microfilm Box 67, File 188, NMML. Munshi also said that it was 'assumed too easily that the selection made by the chief justice [of the high court] is necessarily guided by considerations of merit', given the justices' close contacts with ministers. Also, several ministers have been known 'to have their favourite group of judges who exert considerable influence in favour of their proteges and where casteism is a consideration'. Ibid., p. 5.

[20] Patanjali Sastri, 'Answers to the Questionnaire' of the Law Commission, p. 2. Copy in the author's possession, kindness of Justice Sastri's daughter.

[21] *Fourteenth Report: Reform of the Judicial Administration*, 2 vols, Law Commission of India, vol. 1, 1958, pp. 69, 105. The chief justices of the country later expressed their apprehension that state governments might exert a baneful influence on the selection of judges. At a meeting during the mid-sixties, with the Chief Justice presiding, the justices 'resolved' that if the government did not agree to a name recommended by a high court chief justice, it might request he submit another name, 'but the State Government should not initiate and sponsor a new name of its own'. P. B. Gajendragadkar in a letter to Home Minister G. L. Nanda, dated 7 June 1966. P. B. Gajendragadkar Papers, G. L. Nanda File, NMML.

[22] Mahajan, *Looking Back*, p. 213. S. R. Das, CJI from 1956 to 1959, had complained about the 'political pollution' in the judiciary and aspirants 'canvassing' for judgeships, according to Frank Anthony in *Motherland*, 15 May 1973.

greements about the intellectual and legal qualifications of candidates for the bench may be rational. No one involved in the appointments process is immune from his own prejudice, error, and personality preferences. Finding hidden motives is a parlour game within the priesthood of the Indian legal community. Caution, therefore, seems advisable when considering the vigour of this criticism. Indeed, Mahajan himself also praised the appointment process. Nehru 'has always acted in accordance with the advice of the CJI', he recalled, except in rare circumstances, despite efforts by state politicians with 'considerable pull' to influence him.[23]

The Law Commission's assessment, given in an interim note for the cabinet, that the '"weight of testimony"' it had collected compelled it to conclude that some high court appointments had been made on considerations '"of political expediency or regional or communal sentiment"' caused consternation in the Home Ministry.[24] Home Minister Pant reacted to the note 'with bewilderment and concern' in a letter to Commission chairman M. C. Setalvad. He had been primarily responsible for appointments since 1955, Pant wrote, and every case 'has been processed in the Home Ministry and the recommendations made by me have as a rule been endorsed by the Prime Minister and accepted by the President'.[25] Pant enclosed a list of the forty-one judges appointed to high courts since he had become Home Minister in 1955. '[T]here was not a single case' among them where the final result did not 'follow the advice of the Chief Justice of India', he claimed. He enclosed a second list of five appointees to four high courts about whom there had been some

[23] Mehr Chand Mahajan, 'A Pillar of Justice', pp. 384–6.

A judge in the high courts of Punjab before and after Partition, Mahajan was recommended for appointment to the Federal Court in 1948, in preference to his former chief justice, Dewan Ram Lal. Ram Lal, being friendly with the Prime Minister, wanted Nehru to veto my appointment, Mahajan remembered. But Nehru (who had had strong differences with Mahajan over Kashmir, when he had been 'Prime Minister' there) 'advised the President to appoint me.'

In his autobiography, Mahajan recalled events somewhat differently. He wrote that Nehru preferred Ram Lal, but that Kania and Patel preferred him, so he was appointed, Nehru having acceded to advice. *Looking Back*, pp. 191–2.

[24] The original of the interim note is not available. These quotations from it appeared in the *Statesman*, 17 October 1957.

This note was also reported to have said the '"bitter and revealing"' criticism of appointments seem to express '"acute and well-founded"' public dissatisfaction.

[25] Pant to 'My dear Setalvad' dated 22 August 1957. Prasad papers, File 47, NAI. Pant had written to Setalvad on 16 August about the same subject, but the letter is not available.

disagreement, saying that the final decision in each instance followed the CJI's advice. Also, because four of the individuals came from the judicial services, there could have been no question of political bias.[26] Concluding his letter, Pant said that the idea of choosing judges from an all-India panel had been suggested in February 1955, but that the then Chief Justice B. K. Mukherjea did not favour it and the matter had been dropped.

Setalvad replied five days later. The analysis of the appointment process covered in the note began in 1950, he explained, and was not confined to 1955 and after. The information came from answers to the Law Commission's questionnaire and from oral testimony, some of which had been given in confidence. Setalvad quoted an answer from a former Chief Justice of India (who would seem to have been either B. K. Mukherjea or S. R. Das): '"In olden days"', this answer said, the chief justice (of the high court) had a '"preponderant voice"' and the governor could act in his individual discretion. Now, the governor had to be guided by his ministers and '"the chief minister thinks it is his privilege to distribute patronage and that his recommendation should be the determining factor."' This had brought about some demoralization among high court chief justices who, before making their recommendations, had tried to ascertain the chief minister's views so they would be spared the '"loss of prestige in having [their] nomination unceremoniously turned down"'. Setalvad told Pant that it was the commission's duty 'to find out why, in spite of constitutional procedures having been followed in most of the cases, satisfactory results have not been achieved'.[27]

The disagreement exploded publicly when a leaked account of the interim note appeared under the headline, 'Unsatisfactory Selection of Judges, Main Cause of Arrears'.[28] Pant wrote to a member of the commission, Satyanarayana Rao, Setalvad being abroad, that the leak would prove harmful to 'public confidence in the independence and efficiency of the judiciary'. Pant enclosed a list of high court appointments from

---

[26] Of the five, two were appointees to the Allahabad High Court: V. G. Oak and J. K. Tandon (who had apparently drafted several of the items Pant had sent to Nehru in 1951 about amending the Constitution (see chapter 2). The others were Panchkari Sarkar to the Calcutta High Court, Raj Kishore Prasad to the Patna High Court, and M. Sadasivyya to the Madras High Court. Pant to Setalvad, letter of 22 August 1957, footnote 25. The latter was not appointed to Madras, but was appointed to Mysore in 1957, where he retired as the chief justice in 1969.

[27] Setalvad to 'My dear Pantji,' 27 August 1957. Prasad Collection, File 47, NAI. Setalvad also told Pant that the 'inside information' about who agreed to the selection of particular candidates would not have been available if Pant had not provided it.

[28] *The Statesman,* 17 October 1957. See footnote 24.

6 March 1950 through 1954. He pointed out that, with two exceptions, all the seventy-five judges appointed during the period had been agreed to by the high court chief justice, the chief minister, the governor, and the Chief Justice of India.[29] Setalvad's evidence 'can hardly outweigh the manifest testimony of the indisputable facts given by me', Pant said. He found it difficult to conceive that a high court chief justice could be 'so lacking in the elementary sense of justice' that he would fear recommending an individual not in the chief minister's favour. Pant concluded by asking the commission, in light of his evidence, to delete the 'relevant portions' of the report and make other changes to remove any misunderstanding ... in the public mind on this score'.

Replying to this letter, upon his return to New Delhi, Setalvad regretted that the interim note had leaked, and acknowledged that, in view of Pant's evidence, the commission's statement about the selection process 'undoubtedly needs modification'. The fact remained, Setalvad said, that 'extremely responsible persons' held the view that unsatisfactory individuals had been selected due to extraneous considerations. Because there had been unsatisfactory appointments, 'the Commission will have to apply its mind to the devising of measures which may prevent such selections in future.'[30] As to Pant's request for deletions from the commission's report, no report had been sent to the cabinet, only an interim note by four commission members 'pursuant to your request'. The entire commission would go into all the evidence before making its recommendations. Setalvad added that he was including with his letter more evidence the commission had collected about appointments and that he would, 'if necessary', discuss the matter with Pant.[31]

Appointments to be chief justice of a high court or to be the Chief Justice of India were seldom controversial so long as the central government observed the convention of promotion by seniority.[32] The violation of the convention in 1973 would cause a national uproar

[29] Letter dated 17 October 1957. Prasad Collection File 47, NAI. The two exceptions were a judge appointed to the Andhra High Court despite the CJI's 'No' and a judge appointed to the Patna High Court where the chief justice of that court had agreed 'under protest'.

[30] Setalvad to Pant, 10 November 1957. Ibid. This letter and the previous correspondence had been sent to President Rajendra Prasad by Pant's private secretary. Letter of H. K. Tandon to C. S. Venkatachar, 13 November 1957. Ibid.

[31] *Fourteenth Report: Reform of the Judicial Administration*, vol. 1, pp. 34, 69–70, describes broad criticism about the appointment of judges heard by the commission.

[32] Only a dozen justices moved from a high court to the Supreme Court between 1950 and January 1958, selected, in general according to seniority in their own court.

(chapter 12); in this early period, there were rumoured instances of the 'supersession' (passing over) or intended supersession of a senior judge by a junior to be Chief Justice of India. The danger perceived in this, of course, was that judges might seek preferment by tilting their decisions to gain the government's favour. For example, B. P. Sinha 'was told' that when Chief Justice Kania died suddenly and prematurely, the government had been 'inclined to pass over' Justices Sastri, Mahajan, and Mukerjea—in order of their seniority—in favour of S. R. Das as Chief Justice of India. But an 'unwritten law' prevented this, Sinha recalled.[33] A persistent version of this rumour was that Nehru intended to supersede Patanjali Sastri in order to appoint a Muslim, Fazl Ali, to be Chief Justice. This canard may be set to rest. In the first place, Fazl Ali was the senior of the two, having been appointed to the Federal Court six months prior to Sastri.[34] Secondly, Ali had retired, at age sixty-five, some seven weeks before Kania died. It was Sastri who succeeded Kania—Fazl Ali became governor of Orissa with the backing of H. K. Mahtab.

Still heard in New Delhi is the tale that on Sastri's retirement, Nehru wished to supersede M. C. Mahajan in favour of B. K. Mukherjea. According to one version, this was because Nehru and Mahajan had had their differences over Kashmir, where Mahajan had been prime minister in 1947. Equally credible is the view that Nehru wished to bring in M. C. Chagla from the Bombay High Court. Supreme Court justices as a body resisted this, and 'I heard it from Justice Mukherjea's lips that someone on the Court told Nehru that if you want a Chief Justice other than Mahajan you might as well think of having a whole new Court.'[35] Nehru backed down and even, according to some reports, apologized to these judges orally and in a letter.[36]

Members of the Law Commission cannot have been unaware of these

---

The first of these was Vivian Bose from the Nagpur High Court and the last was K. Subha Rao from Andhra in 1958.

[33] Sinha, *Reminiscences*, p. 71.

[34] A Supreme Court judge's seniority was then, and is now, dated from his appointment to the Supreme Court, not from his first appointment to a high court or appointment as chief justice of a high court. For the date of Fazl Ali's appointment to the Federal Court, see Dhavan, Rajeev and Jacob, Alice, *Selection and Appointment of Supreme Court Judges*, N. M. Tripathi Pvt. Ltd., Bombay, 1978, p. 69.

[35] P. K. Chatterjee, since 1949 an advocate in the Supreme Court, in an interview with the author. The Chatterjee and Mukherjea families, both from Calcutta, were on friendly terms.

[36] See the chapters by Kuldip Nayar and Justice K. S. Hegde in Nayar, Kuldip (ed.), *Supersession of Judges*, Indian Book Company, New Delhi, 1973, pp. 12, 47. The letter of

whisperings while drafting their final recommendations about judicial appointments. Those to the Supreme Court should be on merit alone, without reference to 'communal and regional considerations', the commission said, and 'distinguished members' of the bar might be recruited directly to the Court. It then made a recommendation, sound in the context of the time, that would be invoked wrong-headedly in 1973. The Chief Justice of India, it said, should be chosen not merely on the basis of seniority, but should be the most suitable person, whether taken from the court, the bar, or the high courts.[37] The commission said also that Supreme Court judges, 'as lawyers and men of vision', should be superior to the body of high court judges so as to command respect. Appointments to high courts should be made solely on the basis of merit, and 'only' on the recommendation of the high court's chief justice and with the concurrence of the CJI. This latter recommendation should be embodied in the Constitution, the commission said.[38]

Judicial Independence: Other Risks, Other Protections

Other dangers to judicial independence were thought to exist and various protections against them were suggested. Transferring a judge from one high court to another, which the President could order, was suspect

---

apology is not to be found. Mahajan had been appointed to the Federal Court two weeks before Mukherjea, in 1948.

In 1942, the Viceroy, Lord Linlithgow, had not consulted the outgoing Chief Justice of the Federal Court, Sir Maurice Gwyer, about succeeding him with Sir Patrick Spens. Gwyer protested this, and Linlithgow sent him a letter of apology, saying that there had been 'a serious error of procedure' for which he took responsibility. Ibid., p. 18.

Spens later said that he disliked the 1950 Constitution's provision that judges would be appointed in consultation with the Chief Justice of India. He would have preferred 'with the consent' of the Chief Justice, and he hoped that the provision in the Constitution 'would remain sufficient to ensure that the independence of the Indian judiciary would survive'. Text of speech given to the Overseas League in London, 9 May 1950. K. M. Munshi Papers, Microfilm, File 118, p. 33, NMML.

There was a genuine 'supersession' in 1964. P. B. Gajendragadkar became CJI on 1 February 1964 superseding Justice S. Jaffer Imam. The action aroused no controversy because Imam had an illness that affected his mind. Retiring Chief Justice Sinha had alerted Nehru to this. Nehru visited Imam several times to make his own assessment, and then advised President Radhakrishnan to appoint Gajendragadkar to be Chief Justice. Gajendragadkar, P. B., *To the Best of My Memory*, Bharatiya Vidya Bhavan, Bombay, 1983, pp. 158–9. Imam retired from the Supreme Court on 1 April 1964.

[37] *Fourteenth Report: Reform of the Judicial Administration: Classified Recommendations*, p. 2. These classified recommendations were published separately from the two-volume report in a pamphlet of thirty-one pages.

[38] Ibid., pp. 2, 20.

as a means of executive retribution for ruling against the government, and the potential for transfer also was thought intimidating.[39] The clarity of the issue was muddied somewhat by the judiciary's initiation of transfers against its own on disciplinary grounds. During the Nehru years, the three branches of government addressed the propriety of transfers made by the executive or the judiciary and developed policies in regard to each. This did not dispel wariness, but it contained the issue until transfers became highly politicized during the seventies.

The Law Commission paid little attention to transfers, which were rare at the time, and confined itself to recommending that a high court chief justice might come 'even' from another high court in order to obtain the 'fittest person' for the post. But the transfer should be 'only' with the concurrence of the Chief Justice of India, a requirement that should be added to the Constitution, the commission said.[40] Transfers among high courts were subject to the convention that no judge should be transferred without his consent.[41] A recommendation from the States Reorganization Commission in 1955 would have altered this arrangement. One-third of all high court judges should come from out of state because this would enhance national unity, the commission said.[42] State chief ministers, at one of their periodic meetings, were 'not altogether favourable' to the recommendation.[43] But others, K. M. Munshi for example, believed that transfers could serve both justice and unity in parts of the country with great 'caste and provincial cleavages'.[44]

P. B. Gajendragadkar, when Chief Justice of India from February 1964

---

[39] Under Article 222, the President may transfer a judge after consultation with the CJI.

[40] *Classified Recommendations*, p. 2.

[41] Law Minister A. K. Sen in testimony to the parliamentary Joint Committee on the Constitution (Fifteenth Amendment) Bill, 1962. *Evidence*, Lok Sabha Secretariat, New Delhi, 1963, p. 6.

During the periods when Sardar Patel, Katju, Pant, Shastri, and Nanda were home ministers, they 'followed consistently' the advice of the CJI when transferring and appointing judges, recalled former Chief Justice B. P. Sinha. Sinha, *Reminiscences*, p. 98.

[42] *Summary of States Reorganization Commission Report*, Ministry of Home Affairs, 4 December 1955.

[43] The meeting was held on 22 and 23 October 1955. AICC Papers, Second Installment, File 11, 1955, NMML.

[44] Munshi, 'Replies' to the Law Commission questionnaire, paragraph 18. Munshi had made the same point vigorously in a letter to Pandit Pant of 11 October 1954. In his experience with high courts, Munshi said, he never had heard a complaint about transferred judges, who 'have been known to give every satisfaction'. K. M. Munshi Papers, Microfilm Box 67, File 188, NMML.

to March 1966, was willing to cooperate with transfers if the judge consented and if the transfer helped national integration without causing 'prejudice or damage' to an independent judiciary, he told Home Minister G. L. Nanda. But he thought several transfers the government was considering were 'ethically improper and ... would materially affect the independence of the judiciary'. Such transfers as Nanda was contemplating 'would create great bitterness' among high court judges and feelings of 'uneasiness' about the independence of the judiciary, wrote the CJI.[45]

Transfers of high court judges, other than to be a chief justice, did not always originate in the executive branch. Initiative might come from a high court chief justice or the Chief Justice of India. The justifications typically were that the judge was unduly susceptible to local 'extraneous influences' from which he would be free in another high court; that he had become corrupt, might be less so in another setting, and transferring him was simpler than attempted impeachment; or that his relations with the high court bar had become so strained that he could not function effectively on the bench. The latter could result from his being a poor judge or a good one, some bar associations being no better than they should be.[46] Although never undisputed and always serious affairs, the transfers of the Nehru years had little constitutional significance. The highly politicized and notorious transfers during the 1975–7 internal emergency and in the early eighties did have great constitutional significance, because they were perceived to be calculated attacks on judicial independence. Chief Justice Gajendragadkar in his memoirs describes several occasions when he had high court judges transferred, after himself investigating the accusations against them, without revealing either the accusations or the justices involved.[47]

A judge's independence might be swayed, the aware public and the legal profession believed, by inducements as well as by executive branch intimidation and local extraneous influences. Offers of government employment after retirement were thought to be one such inducement. Gajendragadkar, for example, saw this as a danger, for he told Prime Minister Shastri that 'it would strictly not be right' for him, when Chief Justice, to consider Shastri's idea that, after retirement, he go to London

[45] Letter to G. L. Nanda dated 12 February 1964. P. B. Gajendragadkar Papers, NMML.
Gajendragadkar was referring to Justices Harbans Singh and Hameedullah Beg, who apparently had been appointed high court judges after meeting the government's condition that they were willing to be transferred.

[46] Based on interviews with several dozen lawyers and justices.

[47] Gajendragadkar, *Best of My Memory*, pp. 165–72.

as High Commissioner.[48] The Socialist Party's 1957 election manifesto said there should not be such 'scope for patronage'. K. M. Munshi told the Law Commission, in his reply to its questionnaire, that 'the judge, anxious after retirement to get provided on some tribunal or committee, begins to develop close contacts with the ministers ... [and becomes] no better than other persons approaching the ministers for favours.'[49] The Law Commission recommended amending the Constitution to bar retired Supreme Court judges from government employment, except as *ad hoc* judges, and to bar retired high court judges from practising in any court except the Supreme Court and from government employment.[50]

K. Santhanam went to the heart of judicial independence issues when he wrote that true independence would be achieved 'only through the growth of traditions ... in which they [judicial officers] will refuse to be influenced by external factors ... [and the executive] will consider it altogether wrong to interfere with the independence of the judiciary'.[51]

The Quality of Justice

High calibre, untainted judges, it was recognized, were by no means the only requirement for providing the quality of justice necessary for society to be democratic and equitable. High quality justice demanded that bar as well as bench be intelligent, well educated, and able; that the judicial process be speedy and access to it both fair and affordable to the common man; and that judicial and executive functions in district government be separated. These issues confronted the institutions of the new Constitution from the first day. Seldom could remedies to weaknesses be found in constitutional change. Yet, the future of constitutional government would depend on strengthening the judicial system in all its aspects.[52] A thorough examination of these issues would

---

[48] Ibid., p. 184.

[49] Munshi, 'Replies', p. 5. K. M. Munshi Papers, Microfilm Box 67, File 188, NMML.

[50] *Classified Recommendations*, p. 20.

[51] Santhanam, K., *Union–State Relations in India*, Indian Institute of Public Administration/Asia Publishing House, London, 1960, pp. 27–8.

[52] The issues were considered widely. A high court arrears committee reported in 1951. A cabinet subcommittee reviewed various reform proposals. A reform bill was introduced and debated in Parliament, but was shelved pending a comprehensive study to be provided by the Law Commission. Nehru, cabinet ministers, and governors like Munshi corresponded actively about judicial reform, and an AICC resolution called for reform.

fill several volumes.[53] Here, we may review only the most prominent and persistent of them.

Improving the quality of individuals available to become judges concerned nearly everyone. President Prasad spoke often of the need for a strong bar, for 'if the bar is weak, the judiciary will be weak'.[54] The Law Commission in its *Fourteenth Report* recommended establishing an All-India Judicial Service along the lines of the Indian Administrative Service (IAS) to improve the quality of district and high court judges. K. M. Munshi, among others, favoured this, as did the Conference of Chief Justices at its annual meetings in 1961 and 1963.[55] The idea has reappeared several times, but has not been implemented. The Bar Council of India's Legal Education Committee in the mid-sixties established a basic curriculum for the country's law schools, and, in cooperation with universities, set the examinations, for the Bachelor of Law degree. But there are no bar examinations, and young graduates are unleashed on the courts, often ill-prepared to meet their responsibilities. The legal profession again began considering remedial measures in the mid-nineties.

Separating the executive from the judiciary had been a demand of the Congress Party and others from before independence. The same individual acting as prosecutor, judge, and jury—as did the 'Collector' (of revenue and as civil executive) and the Magistrate in district governments under the British—was unacceptable, a remnant of arbitrary, colonial rule. But the separation, called for in Article 50 in the Directive Principles, was implemented slowly. The government reported in 1960 that it had been completed in only six states.[56] Still incomplete in 1971, separation was made statutory in the 1973 revision of the Criminal Procedure Code (CrPC).

Speedy resolution of cases seemed to be beyond the capability of bench, bar, and court administrators. There were 164,000 cases in arrears, Nehru told the first Conference of Law Ministers in 1957. Home Minister

---

[53] For books wholly or in part dealing with the judicial system, see the writings by Upendra Baxi, Rajeev Dhavan, S. Sahay, and A. G. Noorani cited in the bibliography at the end of this book. See also publications by the Indian Law Institute, the Bar Council of India, and the journal sections of the law reports.

[54] Speech inaugurating the formation of the Bar Council of India, 2 April 1960. *Speeches of Rajendra Prasad, 1960–61,* pp. 43ff.

[55] For the Conference of Chief Justices, see *AR,* 7–13 May 1961, p. 3938, and 9–15 July 1963, p. 5297.

[56] Official statement of 23 July 1960. The laggards were Bihar, UP, Punjab, and Madhya Pradesh. *AR,* 6–12 August 1960, p. 3476.

Pant asked the ministers' assistance in resolving the problem which has ' "baffled all of us and which has proved intractable so far" '.[57] Not only was justice delayed justice denied, it was costly to litigant and taxpayer. The Congress called for speedier decisions because clogged courts excluded the teeming millions from justice, a demand supported by other parties.[58] Court delays were attributed to the greatly increased case load that arose from challenges to new legislation enacted under the Constitution—in areas such as fundamental rights, economic and industrial development, and appeals to the high courts from election tribunals—and to taking judges away from court duties by deputing them to special assignments. But the primary culprit, according to the Law Commission, was court indiscipline: judges' leisurely behaviour, the excessive length of lawyers' oral arguments, judges' ready granting of adjournments and 'stays', and the granting of special leave petitions (SLPs) by the Supreme Court, which could result in stays lasting years. Among other examples, the Law Commission cited one in Bihar, where a subordinate judicial officer was not required to explain a delay until a case was three years old.[59] For years, these failings would be ritually bemoaned by judicial personalities on appropriate occasions. The Law Commission's lasting contribution in 1958 was establishing a base-line analysis of judicial conditions and the requirements for their improvement.

[57] *Hindustan Times*, 19 September 1957.

[58] Hare Krushna Mahtab on 13 June 1952 wrote to the convenor of the CPP's Standing Committee on Law about the urgent necessity of simplifying legal procedures 'to help the common man who has not got the necessary means to take advantage of the machinery ... to secure remedies quickly and at minimum cost'. Hare Krushna Mahtab Papers, File 26, NMML.

[59] *Fourteenth Report*, vol. 1, p. 136.

Setalvad wrote a paper devoted to 'Backlog of Court Cases' in which he addressed the reasons and remedies for arrears. See Choudhary, *Prasad: Correspondence*, vol. 18, pp. 484–92.

The Law Commission recommended various devices to speed court process, the very simplicity of which constituted an indictment of existing practices. The recommendations included reviewing the adequacy of the strength of high courts every few years and appointing additional judges to clear up arrears. High court judges should sit in court at least five hours a day, work at least two hundred days a year, and 'observe strict punctuality on the bench'. *Classified Recommendations*, p. 29. A time limit ought to be fixed for the completion of arguments and delivery of the judgement, the commission said, and SLPs 'should not be given too freely'. Ibid., p. 21.

Justice Mahajan recalled that during his time as Chief Justice the court was 'flooded' with SLPs, some of which were 'so frivolous' that he could dispose of a dozen at a sitting. Mahajan, *Looking Back*, p. 196. What Mahajan did not say was that filing SLPs was, and is, a very lucrative practice for lawyers.

Seeking justice in court was expensive for the common man, often prohibitively so. Two reasons were the cost of a lawyer, and the existence of the fee system under which a litigant had to pay a fee to register his case. This had to be changed, the Law Commission said, pointing out that India was the only country under a modern system of government that 'deters a person who has been deprived of his property or whose legal rights have been infringed from seeking redress by imposing a tax on the remedy he seeks'.[60] Fees for petitioners acting under Articles 32 and 226 of the Constitution (moving the Supreme Court or a high court for relief) should be low if not nominal, the commission recommended, but it did not recommend stopping the practice altogether.[61] Fees computed according to the damages sought are still charged, with the exception of the fee of two hundred and fifty rupees charged for approaching the Supreme Court under Article 32—its original jurisdiction over the Fundamental Rights.

The Law Commission advocated legal aid so that the poor man could afford a lawyer. Citing the Preamble's pledges and Article 14's assurance of equality before and equal protection of the law, the commission said that, 'Insofar as a person is unable to obtain access to a court of law for having his wrongs redressed or for defending himself against a criminal charge, justice becomes unequal and laws meant for ... [the poor man's] protection have no meaning ...'.[62] Legal aid should be available for all and not be confined to those 'normally classed' as poor. Those unable to pay should get aid free; others would pay on a graduated scale.[63] With this recommendation, as with many others, the *Fourteenth Report* would be far ahead of its time—and consequently ignored. Legal aid became a statutory right in the 1990s, but the government-established legal aid agency is financially undernourished.

As the Constitution began its career, the judiciary—despite failings well known and confirmed so studiously by the Law Commission—was the most respected of the three branches of government. Its conduct,

---

[60] *Fourteenth Report*, vol. 1, p. 487. The British had brought the practice to Bengal in 1782.

[61] Ibid., pp. 509–10. Fees should be reduced and, if collected, money from them should be used to defray only the costs of the 'civil judicial establishment', with judicial officers' salaries being charged to the general taxpayer, the Law Commission said.

[62] Ibid., p. 587.

[63] Ibid., p. 591. In the commission's view, the government ought to pay the costs of legal aid, but not manage it. This should be left to the legal profession.

The commission also studied and made recommendations concerning legal education and the bar. The Advocates Act of 1961 embodied a number of its recommendations.

from the lowest court to the highest, would both increase and subtract from that respect as the years passed. During the Nehru years, the principles for the judicial system in the service of democracy and the social revolution had been firmly established.

Chapter 6

MAKING AND PRESERVING A NATION

India was not, and its peoples were not, one at the republic's beginning, which made the leaders anxious and focused their minds on achieving unity. The subcontinent's partition was only three years in the past, and its effects still reverberated. Some five hundred princely states had just been integrated into the union—one of them, Hyderabad, forcibly—after having been outside the 'British India' administrative system and not part of the 'federation' established by the 1935 Act.[1] Jammu and Kashmir continued tense in the aftermath of the Maharaja's accession under the pressure of an invasion by Pakistan-inspired guerrillas. The government's writ had to be made good in the distant Northeast, even more isolated by the way boundaries had been drawn at partition. Demands for redrawing state boundaries along language lines were thought by Nehru and some others to threaten unity. Then there was the country's famously diverse society: fourteen major languages (listed in the Eighth Schedule) and innumerable minor ones, regional and cultural loyalties, vast differences in economic conditions and potential for development, and the thousands of vertical and horizontal compartments of family, caste, clan, and class—each with strong, sometimes religiously prescribed, loyalties—all interacting in a multitude of ways. Underlying the anxieties generated by these factors was the fear that administration might break down under their burden, leaving government in the country helpless.

No wonder the Prime Minister, his colleagues, and the politically aware public were worried for national unity and integrity. Weakness in or failure of this third strand in the seamless web could doom the other two. Break-up or 'Balkanization' of the country would end the *national* democracy and create impossible conditions for social revolution. Conversely, without social revolution, what would become of unity? The web was indeed seamless. 'Fissiparous tendencies arise out of social

[1] See Menon, V. P., *The Integration of the Indian States,* Longmans Green and Co., London, 1956.

backwardness,' Nehru believed.[2] President Radhakrishnan warned the country that petty considerations, factions, and caste disputes raised "'doubts about the stability of a united, democratic India'".[3]

The leaders' anxieties hardly were groundless, but for two reasons it can be argued that they were overdrawn: the compartmentalization of society impeded national integration (in the 'melting-pot' sense), but did not endanger the country's unity and integrity, and the forces for unity operating in the country were stronger and more numerous than the forces against unity. In this chapter the unifying forces will be described first and, afterwards, the disruptive forces. The Constitution's part in fostering unity will be discussed as we go along. The machinery for unity, the Constitution's centre–state relations provisions, will be the subject of a third section.

Forces for Unity

History had dealt independent India unifying cards, a tendency towards unity and centralization.[4] Empires, ancient through the Mughal, had stretched broadly across the land through the force of arms and culture and were administered centrally to the extent they could be. Elements of a national culture existed in the form of a pantheon, later called Hinduism, whose individual deities descended from a trinity recognized countrywide. Sanctified locations were the object of region- and country-wide pilgrimages. The arrival of Islam brought a faith as uniting as divisive. To an extent, it became Hinduized; it and the 'Hindu' sub-sects came to share saints. The languages of the pre-Mughal Islamic and Mughal empires—Persian and, especially, Urdu—were used for diplomatic and commercial dealings throughout the land. With the British 'Raj' came an even more powerful unifying language, English, together with increasingly standardized administration, the nineteenth century's great 'Anglo-Indian Codes' and courts of law, the growth of representative bodies, and, above all, the centralizing force of the Viceroy representing the British Crown. Under the British also came

---

[2] Nehru to the AICC meeting at Madurai, October 1961. *Report of the General Secretaries, January 1961–December 1961*, Indian National Congress (INC), New Delhi, 1961 pp. 24–5.

[3] In his farewell speech as President, 25 January 1967. *AR*, 12–18 February 1967, pp. 7540ff.

[4] Of the many books on the subject, one of the most significant is Nehru, Jawaharlal, *The Unity of India*, 3rd impression, Lindsay Drummond, London, 1948 (1941). See also Nehru, Jawaharlal, *The Discovery of India*, 4th edn., Meridian Books Ltd., London, 1956 (1946).

unifying factors such as the telegraph and the railways, coastal shipping, an army drawn countrywide (although the units were organized by community), the growth of widespread commerical clans, English education, and the British democratic tradition—which captivated educated Indians even, or especially, when it was absent from India. Among the ordinary people, there was a proclivity to look to the *sarkar*, the government, for things both good and evil.

Building on these factors, the independence movement, under the leadership of the Congress Party, unified Indians further by testing their resolve. Although the Congress had championed Indians' rights since its founding in 1885 by an Englishman, it was under the influence of Mohandas Gandhi after 1915 that Congress became the party of independence. Although Gandhi advocated decentralized government based on village panchayats, the reality of his charisma, his tactical sense, and his rarely challenged leadership produced a highly centralized political campaign, as did his insistence that regional and other constituency interests be muted for the sake of unified resistance to British rule.[5] India's leaders at independence were the product of this atmosphere of common effort, of overcoming fractiousness from personality and strategy. Nehru, Patel, Prasad, Maulana Azad, and others on the national stage were joined by powerful chief ministers who combined local power bases with a national outlook—Pandit G. B. Pant in UP, B. C. Roy in Bengal, B. G. Kher and Morarji Desai in Bombay, Ravi Shankar Shukla in Madhya Pradesh, C. Rajagopalachari in Madras, and Pratap Singh Kairon in Punjab. All, putting national unity first, believed in a strong central government as well as strong states. The Congress even had practised centralized governance from 1937 to 1939 when it ruled eight provinces after winning elections under the 1935 Act—evolving mechanisms such as the Central Parliamentary Board (CPB) to direct the functioning of the provincial ministries—a mandate renewed by the Working Committee in 1948.[6]

---

[5] For an excellent account of Gandhi's leadership from among the many books about the Mahatma, see Brown, Judith M., *Gandhi: Prisoner of Hope*, Oxford University Press, Oxford, 1989.

[6] At the Congress session at Jaipur. Kochanek, *Congress Party*, p. 234.

Also in 1948 it established the Central Election Committee (CEC) to set the criteria for candidates for Parliament and state legislatures and to make the final distribution of tickets to those allowed to contest. During late 1961, for example, the committee met for four weeks to select candidates for 500 seats in the Lok Sabha and 2,800 aspirants for state legislatures. *Report of the General Secretaries, January 1961–December 1961*, AICC, p. 16.

State election committees, often with CEC intervention, prepared the state list to submit to the CEC.

Given this experience and the circumstances at independence, it was predictable that the leaders in the Constituent Assembly would draft a highly centralized Constitution, many of whose provisions were designed to contribute to unity: centralized administration, the federal government's extensive financial and legislative powers, a unified court system, single citizenship, and adult suffrage. This top-down federalism has been thus described: '[I]n India, the Union is not a federation of sovereign states .... This is an important distinction between the Indian Union and some other democratic federations where the federating units existed before the federal unions ... and could therefore insist on coming into those federations on their own terms.'[7]

Under the Constitution, the Congress had no greater goal than national unity, although individuals' 'greed for office' drew criticism in party publications. In unity lay its self-preservation, its power, its patronage, and its patriotic justification. In the central and most state governments, the party and government were Siamese twins, joined at head, hip, and toe. The Working Committee's authority was sometimes questioned but rarely disobeyed. Each of the Parliamentary Board's six members, drawn from the cabinet, from among the chief ministers, and chaired by the party president, was responsible for party affairs in several states. They arbitrated, mediated, and sometimes investigated internal party and party–state government disputes. Instructions to Provincial Congress Committee presidents and chief ministers could go down either the governmental or the party chain of command.[8] Several times after the 1962 elections, the CPB umpired who would be the chief minister and be included in his cabinet.[9] Yet, the combination

---

[7] *Report of the States Reorganization Commission*, Manager of Publications, GOI New Delhi, 1955, p. 165.

This commission was appointed to plan the reorganization of the states along linguistic lines, fulfilling Gandhi's promise of the twenties. The central government was empowered to do this under Article 3, which authorized Parliament to alter state boundaries and to create new states after the President ascertained the views of the state legislatures involved.

For an excellent, brief description of the federal system, see Hardgrave, Robert L. Jr. and Kochanek, Stanley, *India: Government and Politics in a Developing Nation*, 5th edn., Harcourt Brace Jovanovich College Publishers, New York, NY, 1993, ch. 4.

[8] Running parallel to Nehru's letters and government communications to chief ministers was a constant stream of letters and circulars from Congress headquarters to chief ministers, to state cabinet ministers and deputy ministers, to parliamentary secretaries, and to PCC presidents and District Congress Committee leaders. See Zaidi, A.M., *The Directives of the Congress High Command to Ministers and Chief Ministers*, Indian Institute of Applied Political Research, New Delhi, 1986.

[9] Hardgrave and Kochanek, *Government and Politics*, p. 261.

of the CPB, the Working Committee, and the Prime Minister did not make and unmake chief ministers with the frequency of later years. The average tenure of a chief minister (of a possible five years) was 3.9 years under Nehru and 2.6 years after him.[10]

This intimate party–government relationship constituted the pattern once the government wing of the party had vanquished the organizational wing in the Kripalani and Tandon affairs. Nehru's holding the offices of party president and prime minister reinforced it, and he arranged that party presidents from 1954 to 1964 had experience in government—in the main as chief ministers.[11] The Working Committee acted as an important forum for developing national policies on the broadest issues—e.g. on language and zamindari abolition. In several states, into the mid-fifties, Provincial Congress Committees attempted to control the chief minister and his government. The fullest expression of the Congress-government parallel-and-linked 'federalism' came late in 1963 with the so-called 'Kamaraj Plan'. K. Kamaraj, then Chief Minister of Tamil Nadu, had proposed that all chief and central government ministers resign from office 'and offer themselves for full-time organizational work.'[12] Nehru offered to resign, but the party invited him to stay as

---

Members of the Parliamentary Board during the Nehru years included Nehru, Maulana Azad, G.B. Pant, Jagjivan Ram, Morarji Desai, K. Kamaraj, Indira Gandhi, U.N. Dhebar, S.K. Patil, Y. B. Chavan, and Lal Bahadur Shastri.

The CPB could have wide responsibilities. For example, the committee chaired by UN Dhebar on the implementation of the 1964 Bhubaneshwar 'Democracy and Socialism' resolution recommended that state ministers be responsible to the CPB for failures in agricultural production. *AR*, 27 May–2 June 1964, p 5845.

[10] Guhan, S., 'Federalism and the New Political Economy in India,' in Arora, Balveer and Verney, Douglas V. (eds), *Multiple Identities in a Single State*, Konark Publishers Pvt. Ltd., New Delhi, 1995, p 264.

K. Santhanam doubted the 'rightness' of the party high command calling the tune for ministries. He thought there should be a convention that state ministers be sacked only by the chief minister and not by the Working Committee. Santhanam, K., *Planning and Plain Thinking*, Higginbothoms Pvt. Ltd., Madras, 1958, pp. 123–4.

The Working Committee, for example, forced Sampurnanand to resign as UP Chief Minister in 1960. *Report of the General Secretaries, January 1960–December 1960*, AICC.

[11] Hardgrave and Kochanek, *Government and Politics*, p. 60.

Even so, party presidents sometimes were thought to be little more than glorified office boys for the Congress government. Ibid., p 73.

[12] *Congress Bulletin*, INC, New Delhi, 1963, nos. 7–8, p 37. Cited in Kochanek, *Congress Party*, pp. 78–9. For an account of the origins and implementation of the Kamaraj Plan, also see Gopal, *Nehru*, vol. 3, pp. 244–6.

The plan's origins lay in the grave damage to national and party prestige from the defeat in war by the Chinese a year earlier and the party's defeat in three by-elections in

Prime Minister and to choose who would depart and who remain. Kamaraj became president of the Congress. Whatever Nehru's motives in backing the plan, it strengthened and invigorated the party and the top of its hierarchy.[13] When, in May 1964 and in January 1966, it became necessary to choose successors to Nehru and Lal Bahadur Shastri as prime ministers, the Working Committee and the party president played critical parts in the selection, which the Congress Party in Parliament ratified by electing first Shastri and then Indira Gandhi as its leader. Both successions took place decorously, although with a great deal more jockeying for position during the second than during the first. Constitutional government had passed two great tests.

Meanwhile, the already existing forces for unity outside the Constitution had strengthened. The army became a symbol of nationalism. It won a war with Pakistan in 1965, as it would in 1971. The economy became more national, including the market for consumer goods. Non-Congress parties were competing for national control. And the longer citizens proved themselves to themselves, the greater became their sense of common purpose.

The Congress Party's role as a force for cohesion had a less fortunate aspect. The more thoroughly its 'federalism' and command structure functioned, the more the Constitution's centre–state provisions fell into disuse. So long as Congress continued dominant in New Delhi and a large number of state capitals, party leaders and the public (but not opposition parties) paid this little attention. But as Congress Party dominance faded, the Congress government at the centre excessively used the centralizing features of the Constitution to compensate for its waning authority. This evoked the 'constitutional revolt' of the eighties (Part VI) in which state governments demanded decentralization of power either through changing the Constitution or changes in the way it was worked.

Forces Against Unity

These were both more apparent than real and very real. The former took two shapes. One, of which more will be seen throughout the book and especially in Part VI, was demands for 'autonomy' by state

---

May 1962—especially galling because they came at the hands of two former Congressmen, Acharya Kripalani and Minoo Masani (by then a leader in the Swatantra), and of the Nehru-hating socialist, Ram Manohar Lohia.

[13] Kochanek, *Congress Party*, p. 261.

governments or groups in areas within states. Although attacked as secessionist, typically these were cries to the national or relevant state capitals for sympathetic attention to genuine grievances. Unheeded, however, these could and sometimes did fester into violent crises that disrupted local stability and gravely strained relations between state governments and the centre. The second, more-apparent-than-real, threat to national integrity was more complex. Leaders, and many others, focused their fears on the four 'isms'—casteism, communalism (Hindu–Muslim friction, especially), linguism, and provincialism/regionalism, which often were lumped together as 'communalism'—for which the remedy was 'secularism'. A Congress Party resolution said every 'separatist tendency' must be removed, caste was separatist as well as anti-democratic, and 'provincialism' was a 'narrowing and disruptive factor'.[14] Nehru wrote of the necessity to build unity against 'disintegrating forces and destructive activities ... communalism, provincialism, and casteism'.[15] '[P]rovincial feeling, caste feeling, linguistic feeling should all be made subservient to the feeling of the country,' Rajendra Prasad told a Madras audience.[16]

He was correct. 'Indian' consciousness needed to be raised, although much existed. But the unrealistic image of the country's future as a homogenized society, of citizens without subordinate loyalties, as the *sine qua non* for national integrity generated unwarranted fears. The difficulties with which the leadership presented itself by confusing preserving national integrity with the concept of national integration will be revisited in Part VI, thus allowing the perspective of hindsight. For now, it may be said that, with few exceptions, regional, cultural, and linguistic loyalties would vie for recognition and status within the nation, not for existence outside it. The compartments of family, caste, clan, and language were incompatible with integration among themselves, but time would show that they cohabited successfully within the country. The genuineness and persistence of leadership fears is evident in the recurring appeals against schism in prime ministers' and presidents' speeches on Independence Day and Republic Day since 1950.

In their fears for national integrity and opposition to particularisms, Nehru and the Congress 'secularizers' had allies they disliked intensely.

---

[14] *Resolutions, Sixtieth Session*, INC, New Delhi, 1955, pp. 9–10.

[15] Letters to chief ministers dated 16 July and 1 August 1953. *NLTCM*, vol. 3, pp. 339–40, 350.

[16] Speech on Independence Day, 1960. *Speeches of Rajindra Prasad, 1960–61*, p. 136.

The Praja Socialist Party and other parties also inveighed against 'particularistic loyalties', for example at the PSP National Executive meeting in July 1961. *AR*, 16–22 July 1961, p. 4060.

The militant Hindu parties and bodies—the Hindu Mahasabha, the Jana Sangh, and the Rashtriya Swayamsevak Sangh (RSS)—would have ended articularisms through a sort of religion-based totalitarianism by scrapping the Constitution's distribution of powers to establish a unitary state. The Jana Sangh's election manifesto of 1957 said that the federal structure had created rivalries between the central and state governments that were an obstacle to national solidarity. The party would declare 'Bharat to be a Unitary State'.[17] Some years later, the party offered a plan to abolish the states and legislatures and to replace them with large administrative districts having no legislative functions, which would be reserved for Parliament.[18]

There were, however, serious threats to unity and integrity from groups with rampant language, cultural, or religious identities, which often overlapped. The explosive mixture of religion-based identity and language in Punjab oscillated between demands for autonomy, and secessionism. The Sikhs, having rejected an offer from the Muslim League to form a state confederated with Pakistan, expected India might similarly reward them.[19] When this did not happen, agitation began for 'Punjabi Suba', a

[17] *Election Manifesto, 1957*, Bharatiya Jana Sangh, New Delhi, 1956, p. 7

[18] Upadhyaya, Deen Dayal, *Principles and Policies*, presented at the Jana Sangh General Council meeting, Gwalior, 17 August 1964. *AR*, 9–15 September 1964, p. 6030.

In January 1961, the All-India Muslim Convention, with representatives from most political parties, recommended the abolition of the federal system because it interfered with economic planning *AR*, 9–15 July 1961, p. 4045. Convention held under the presidency of Congressman Dr Syed Mahmud.

Even former Chief Justice Mahajan espoused a unitary form of government to overcome the 'political disunity' in the country, despite its cultural unity. In a long letter to Prime Minister Nehru, with a copy to the President, Mahajan suggested doing away with 'the Federal Constitution and ... [making] it a unitary system of government ... [with] abolition of all State Legislatures and State Ministries, the States to be merely administrative units to be governed by Governors with the help of advisory bodies'. Mahajan, *Looking Back*, pp. 226–7.

Prasad responded that it was necessary to safeguard the Constitution as it exists. Some of us, he said, were anxious to have 'some unifying power but we could not do more to get the Provinces under the influence of the Centre'. Prasad wished that someone could think of a way 'the powers of the States could gradually be curtailed ... [to help] in creating a feeling of unity'. This letter, minus some personal items, was printed in *Looking Back*, pp. 229–30.

Rajagopalachari and V. V. Giri, the latter then a minister at the centre, wrote to Mahajan approvingly when he published his ideas in a newspaper in 1956.

[19] Many Sikhs to this day remember Nehru's saying that "'I see nothing wrong in an area and a set-up in the North wherein the Sikhs can also experience the glow of freedom." At a press conference in Calcutta as reported in the *Statesman*, 7 July 1946. Cited in Dhillon, G. S., *India Commits Suicide*, Singh and Singh Publishers, Chandigarh, 1992, p. 7

Punjabi-speaking state controlled by Sikhs. When this failed and the 1956 states reorganization also did not meet their demands, the Sikhs felt 'cheated', as some put it, and agitation recommenced, leading to fast-unto-death declarations by religious leaders. The Nehru government did not combat the danger to unity with emergency procedures such as President's Rule, but preventively detained one of the religious leaders, Master Tara Singh, and authorized the armed forces to use harsh measures against violence. Nehru's protestations that he was willing to do 'everything we can for the Punjabi language'[20] and the creation of a separate Punjab in 1966 by dividing Punjab into the states of Punjab and Haryana only dampened Sikh satisfactions for a time. Secessionism on the part of some Sikhs, sometimes fuelled by New Delhi's misguided policies in the Punjab, would plague India off and on for years (see also Parts V and VI). Particularly in the Punjab, as later in the Northeast, rivalry or warfare among local factions complicated any peace efforts the central government might attempt in co-operation with state government authorities.

Secession threatened briefly in Jammu and Kashmir. Islam, the religion of the majority of the individuals in the Vale of Kashmir was a vital issue to the governments of India and Pakistan, although far less so to the Muslim inhabitants of the Vale. The latter simply wanted to preserve their culture, while reaping New Delhi's largesse. This former princely state was given special status under the Constitution's Article 370 and allowed to frame its own constitution.[21] Sheikh Mohammad Abdullah, the state's 'Prime Minister' and leader of the Muslims in the Vale, found the inclusion of Article 370 in the 'Temporary and Transitional Provisions' of the Constitution's Part XXI unsettling. He wanted 'iron-clad guarantees of autonomy'.[22] Suspecting the state's

---

[20] Nehru's version of his correspondence with Tara Singh in 1961. *NLTCM*, vol. 5, p. 450. The Punjabi language, one of the many forms of Hindi or Hindustani spoken in North India, is spoken alike by Hindus, Muslims, and Sikhs in the Punjab, and before Partition typically was written in the Urdu script. It has come to be written most often in the Gurmukhi script.

For the Sikhs, Punjabi Suba was a code word for a state in which they would dominate politically. But the demand for Punjabi Suba, in essence, was not religion-based and anti-Hindu.

[21] Parliament's jurisdiction in Kashmir was limited to matters on the Union and Concurrent legislative lists 'which, in consultation with the government of the state, are declared by the President to correspond to matters specified in the Instrument of Accession'. Otherwise, the Kashmir legislature had jurisdiction. The Supreme Court's jurisdiction initially did not extend to Kashmir.

[22] See Bhattacharjea, Ajit, *Kashmir: The Wounded Valley*, UBS Publishers and Distributors Ltd., New Delhi, 1994. For 'ironclad guarantees', see p. 184.

special status might be lost, Abdallah advocated independence from India, causing New Delhi to dismiss his government in 1953 and place him under preventive detention. Enacted in November 1956, the state constitution said the state 'is and shall be an integral part of the Union of India'. Abdullah would claim this declaration invalid because, detained, he had not been a member of the assembly. New Delhi would become deeply and controversially involved in Kashmir affairs (sometimes to popular satisfaction as in extending the Supreme Court's jurisdiction to the state), but without altering the original text of Article 370. Kashmir was a vitally important issue for Nehru. Beyond his affection for the place as a Kashmiri, the inclusion of the valley's Muslims in India constituted for him evidence both of the country's secularism and of Pakistan's malevolent challenge to it.[23]

In the Northeast, the largely Christian Nagas in Assam, lightly governed by the British, began talking independence in the early 1950s under their leader, Angami Phizo, and the Naga National Council. Nehru could not tolerate independence, but he promised the Nagas considerable autonomy and enjoined the Assamese government to restrain the growth of Assamese influence in Naga areas. Not satisfied, Phizo renewed violent resistance to Assamese authority. When the Indian army was unable to suppress rebellion, the central government and the Naga People's Convention—a group more broadly representative of the Nagas than the National Council—found a constitutional solution. They agreed to the creation of a separate state within India, Nagaland, which was established in 1962 by the Thirteenth Amendment to the Constitution.[24]

In the South, the Dravida Munnetra Kazhagam (DMK—Dravidian Progressive Federation), threatened secession explicitly in 1957. ' "[E]ach state should have full freedom to secede from the Indian Union if it so desires and should be given full and equal representation in parliament so that the large states do not dominate the others," ' said the DMK's election manifesto.[25] This coming together of Dravidian cultural and

---

[23] For an account of the Kashmir 'issue' in 1947, see Gopal, *Nehru*, vol. 2, pp. 15–42. Indian society's pretensions to secularism were being shaken (in 1947) by communal killings from Bengal to the Punjab.

[24] With the President's assent in a new Article, 371A.

The amendment protected Naga religious and social practices, customary law, and ownership and transfer of land and resources by saying that no act of parliament would apply to the state of Nagaland unless the Naga legislative assembly agreed.

For a recounting of these events, see Gopal, *Nehru*, vol. 2, pp. 207–12. Also, Hazarika, Sanjoy, *Strangers in the Mist*, Penguin Books India, New Delhi, 1994.

[25] Hardgrave, *The Dravidian Movement*, p. 54.

Despite this language, Hardgrave was of the opinion that 'Dravidisthan, the symbol

Making and Preserving a Nation

Tamil language identities included strong anti-Hindi, anti-North India, anti-Brahmin, and pro-socialist sentiments. (Readers will recall the anti-Brahmin sentiment in the Champaknam case about positive discrimination in chapter 3.) The Tamil-speaking Congress Chief Minister of Madras, K. Kamaraj Nadar, denounced the manifesto as 'an affront to the unity and solidarity of the country.'[26] Nehru thought the Dravidian movement 'built up on communal hatred, narrow-minded bigotry and violence ... the worst type of communal organization'.[27]

Although the DMK split in 1959, with its largest faction calling not for secession but for decentralized government, New Delhi's anxieties persisted—perhaps not least from the DMK's legitimate electoral challenge to Congress power in Madras state. And in the panic accompanying the Chinese attack in 1962, as described in chapter 2, the Constitution was amended to make the freedoms of speech, assembly, and to form associations subject to laws made in the interests of 'the sovereignty and integrity of India'. Additionally, to qualify as a candidate for Parliament and state legislatures, to campaign if nominated, and to become a member of a legislature if elected, an individual had to take an oath to 'uphold the sovereignty and integrity of India'.[28]

---

of Tamil nationalist aspiration, was at the most a side issue, for the Manifesto implicitly accepted the existing Constitutional order.' Ibid.

In the 1957 election to the Madras legislative assembly, the DMK went from having no seats to fifteen. It did vastly better in local elections, at the Congress's expense.

The Dravidian peoples, probably originating in the eastern Mediterranean countries and the Iranian plateau, entered India prior to the Aryans, whose advent seems to have pushed them southwards from north-western and western India. See Mansingh, Surjit, *Historical Dictionary of India*, The Scarecrow Press Inc., Lanham, Maryland, 1996, pp. 126 ff.

[26] *The Dravidian Movement*, pp. 54–6.

[27] Letters to chief ministers of 17 October 1953 and 31 December 1957 *NLTCM*, vol. 3, p. 398 and vol. 4, p. 625.

[28] The Sixteenth Amendment added a proviso to the freedom of expression clause of Article 19, and the oaths were provided for in other articles and joined other oaths in the Third Schedule.

The oath emerged from the work of the National Integration Council, which first met in June 1962. C. P. Ramaswamy Aiyar, Home Minister Lal Bahadur Shastri, and his Home Secretary L.P. Singh are said to have been instrumental in its drafting. Sir C P Ramaswamy, when diwan of the princely state of Travancore, had opposed the integration of princely states into the Indian union.

The chief ministers' meeting of August 1961, with Nehru presiding, had recommended making advocacy of secession a penal offence. 'Summary of Previous Recommendations on National Integration', prepared by G. R. S. Rao for the National Committee for Gandhi Centenary at Patna, 1966, cyclostyled.

In the Indian Penal Code (Amendment) Act of 1961, Parliament already had made

Introducing the amending bill, Law Minister Asoke Sen, as will be recalled, told the Lok Sabha that its purpose was to give the government of India 'appropriate powers ... to impose restrictions against those individuals or organizations who want to make secession from India or disintegration of India as political purposes for fighting elections'.[29] Past Supreme Court opinions, Sen said, had made it clear that the term 'security of State' in Article 19 was a limited expression and did not of itself include the power to ban organizations or activities. He assumed that the amendment 'echoes the universal desire of this house' and the country to combat the 'evils' of disintegrating forces.[30] Following consideration by a Joint Committee, the bill was passed with little further debate on 2 May 1963. Sen had asked for, and the bill received, unanimous approval, showing, as Sen put it, 'the united will of the country'.[31] During debate, however, MPs from Assam, Andhra, and Madras criticized New Delhi for, in the words of Ravi Narayan Reddi of Andhra, the 'centralization of the entire administration that is going on at the cost of the states' and produces the talk of secession. The amendment seems to have contributed to ending the DMK's talk of secession, which simply disappeared—out of fashion, anyway, with the Chinese attack and contrary to the DMK's espousal of the national cause.[32]

Although rarely a source of secessionist sentiment, language was a disruptive issue broadly during the Nehru years. It had aroused such passions in the Constituent Assembly that there is no 'national' language specified in the Constitution, only an 'Official Language': Hindi, for official business conducted by the central government and among governments. And the 'imposition' of Hindi, as the other major language groups thought it, especially in the South, was so fiercely resisted that English has been the legislated substitute for or alternative to Hindi since 1950.[33]

---

punishable expressions that promoted feelings of enmity on the grounds of caste, language, religion, community, or that disturbed public tranquillity. This could apply to the DMK's anti-Brahminism, although it was aimed much more broadly.

[29] *Lok Sabha Debates*, Third Series, vol. 12, no. 28, col. 5760.

[30] Ibid., col. 5764.

[31] *Lok Sabha Debates*, Third Series, vol. 18, no. 57, cols. 13410–11.

[32] Hardgrave and Kochanek, *Government and Politics*, p. 152.

[33] The nine articles of Part XVII of the Constitution contain the compromise language formula arrived at by the Constituent Assembly. The Eighth Schedule listed fourteen 'Languages', and others have been added since. For the framing of the language provisions, see Austin, *Cornerstone*, ch. 12.

When, the Congress 'prime minister' of Madras state, C. Rajagopalachari, in 1937 instituted compulsory Hindi in the first three grades of the state's schools, the violent reaction set the example for the anti-Hindi riots that occurred nearly thirty years later, in 1965.

National leaders tried to calm fears of Hindi 'dominance' in education and civil service examinations with repeated assurances like President Rajendra Prasad's Independence Day speech in Madras in 1960, entitled 'No Imposition of Hindi: Plea for Unity and Understanding'. The central government propounded the three-language formula—education in one's mother tongue for linguistic minorities in primary schools, and teaching the regional language and English in secondary schools.[34] With the Official Languages Act of April 1963, Parliament made the first of a series of extensions of English, in addition to Hindi, for all official central government purposes and for business in Parliament, necessary under Article 343 to prevent the lapse of English.

Parliament amended this Act in December 1967, permitting the increased use of Hindi while calling for the development of all Indian languages. Language riots resulted in both the North and the South. A member of the pro-Hindi Jana Sangh burnt a copy of the bill on the floor of Parliament because it did not take Hindi far enough.[35] Language, as a nationally disruptive issue, has progressively disappeared, although sensitivities persist. Today, English is used widely and Hindi is spreading in states where once it was little known.

Accompanying this bitter debate for a time was a second one over the formation of 'linguistic provinces' along the internal organizational pattern that the Congress Party had adopted in 1920 at Gandhi's urging. Nehru, Patel, and others, thinking this might destroy unity, had prevented this during the Constituent Assembly. But proponents renewed the demand under the Constitution, and a death-by-fasting in late 1952 for a Telugu-speaking Andhra state broke Nehru's resistance.[36] The

---

[34] The National Integration Conference, chaired by Nehru, endorsed this. 'Statement Issued by the National Integration Conference, September–October 1961', pp. 7–8. Jayaprakash Narayan Papers, National Integration File, NMML.

The National Integration Council, meeting in June 1962, said that the replacement of English as the medium of instruction in universities was inevitable, but the transition should not jeopardize the quality of education. 'Proceedings of the First Meeting of the National Integration Council, 2 and 3 June, 1962', pp. 4–5. Ibid.

[35] Local disputes could be even more bloody. Bengali refugees from East Pakistan in Assam desired, in addition to land and economic opportunity, primary education in Bengali for their children. Riots over this issue in 1960 killed dozens and made thousands of Bengalis refugees again. Asked Nehru, 'How superficial is the covering of that we call "nationalism" which bursts open at the slightest irritation?' Speech to the Lok Sabha, 3 September 1960. *Jawaharlal Nehru's Speeches*, vol. 4, pp. 7–9.

[36] See Gopal, *Nehru*, vol. 2, ch. 12. Sometime Congress General Secretary Shankarrao Deo told Nehru that those aspiring to linguistic states 'do not even dream of opting out of the Indian Union'. Letter of 11 November 1953. Chaudhary, *Prasad: Correspondence*, vol. 16, pp. 215–16.

establishment of the States Reorganization Commission followed. Linguistic states came into being in 1956 with the Seventh Amendment under the Constitution's Article 3—which made no changes in the centre-state relations provisions. The commission predicted that reorganization would serve the country's 'unity and security', which it has.[37]

Constitutional and Sub-Constitutional Mechanisms for Unity

Faced with feared and real dangers to the country's unity and integrity, governments in New Delhi and the states had a variety of constitutional devices to hand, and they created others. The least spectacular, but most basic, of these were those already in Part XI of the Constitution, 'Relations Between the Union and the States', and elsewhere, under which daily affairs were conducted. These served the sensible assumption that constitutional governance, sound administration, and economic development—making the country run well—strengthened unity, indeed permitted the nation to survive. The mechanisms that were established under these provisions will be taken up shortly.

There were other provisions in the Constitution that were more immediately related to preserving unity and integrity. We considered in chapter 2 the prohibition of speech that was thought to undermine the security of the state. There also are the so-called 'Emergency Provisions' in Part XVIII. Of these, we shall consider those government and the public found most controversial.

THE 'UNITY' PROVISIONS

Article 352, as has been explained, changes the country from federal to unitary government and is to be invoked to protect 'the security of India' from threats from 'war or external aggression or internal disturbance'. An external emergency was proclaimed only once during the Nehru years, in 1962 at the time of the India–China war. Because this national emergency was still in force at the time of the India–Pakistan war of 1965, another emergency was not proclaimed. Already considered in its fundamental rights context in chapter 2, the emergency clearly could have affected the working of centre–state relations, but it seldom was criticized on these grounds. Rather, broader fears for federalism took the form of charges by opposition parties that the Congress was assuming dictatorial authority and using the emergency to strengthen its position at their expense. Only in theory does

---

[37] *Report of the States Reorganization Commission*, especially ch. 2.

federalism seem to have been a victim of the country's first emergency, although the government clearly found its continuance handy after its initial justification had passed.[38]

A unitary system may be put in place, also, for one state. According to Article 356 of the 'Emergency Provisions', this may be done by the President if, upon a report from the governor 'or otherwise', he is satisfied that the government of the state cannot be 'carried on in accordance with the provisions of this Constitution'. Therefore, 'President's Rule', as it is usually called, is only remotely concerned with national unity, nor would a national emergency be if proclaimed to meet an 'internal disturbance' (unless, perhaps, the disturbance threatened unity through, say, secession). Over the years, President's Rule became extremely controversial because it was thought often used to serve central government convenience or political party interests, not to protect constitutional governance and sound administration. Deplored as coercion, the device came to erode the sense of unity rather than confirming it. The central government imposed President's Rule nine times from 1950 through 1965, and two instances—Punjab in 1951 and Kerala in 1959— became symbols of its questionable use.[39]

In 1951, Nehru wrote to Punjab Chief Minister Gopichand Bhargava that the Congress was 'in a sense cracking up' due to the conflict between the state party and the state government. Also, the public was alienated from the government, there was Hindu–Sikh tension in rural areas, and the behaviour of a Sikh minister, Giani Kartar Singh, was considered

---

[38] To avoid declaring a national emergency, but to have emergency powers available for grave local crises, a parliamentary delegation to Assam (sent in 1960 after the language riots already mentioned) recommended authorizing the President 'to notify a state of emergency for any specified area ... [if] the security of India or any part thereof is threatened by internal disturbances'. *AR*, 17–23 September 1960, p. 3540. This recommendation was not acted upon, but such a provision would be added to the Constitution in 1976.

Article 355 says that it is the Union's duty to protect states against external aggression and internal disturbance and to ensure that government is according to the Constitution. Article 355 was not invoked during the Nehru years. See Part VI for a discussion of the implications of this article.

[39] In Punjab, June 1951–April 1952; the Patiala and East Punjab States Union (PEPSU), March 1953–March 1954; Andhra Pradesh, November 1954–March 1955; Travancore-Cochin, March 1956–November 1956; Kerala, November 1956–April 1957 and again from July 1959 till February 1960; Orissa, February 1961–June 1961; Kerala, September 1964– March 1965 and again from March 1965 till March 1967. *Sarkaria Report*, vol. 1, p. 184. See also *President's Rule in the States and Union Territories*, Lok Sabha Secretariat, New Delhi, 1987, throughout.

a grave liability to the government.[40] The Congress Parliamentary Board, in a 'stormy' meeting that Bhargava attended, issued him an ultimatum to conform to its wishes regarding the selection of his ministry. Nehru threatened to resign from the CPB if Bhargava persisted in defying its directives.[41] Bhargava fought this and the Board directed him on 13 June to resign, which he did, four days later, bringing to Delhi a letter from Governor C. M. Trivedi recommending the imposition of President's Rule.

President Prasad was unhappy with the situation. 'I intensely dislike suspending the normal working of the Constitution in the Punjab and assuming to myself the functions of the State government,' he wrote to Nehru. No emergency had arisen in the state and the chief minister said he had resigned 'in obedience to a directive of the Congress Parliamentary Board', not because he had lost the confidence of the legislature. 'I consider it wholly wrong,' Prasad continued, to permit a non-constitutional body [the CPB] to interfere with the normal working of the Constitution by producing an artificial emergency. 'My feeling is that we have created a very bad and a very wrong precedent ... [and] acted against the spirit of the Constitution, although the action may be justified as being in strict accordance with its letter.'[42]

Nehru replied that he understood Prasad's distaste, but no other avenue had been available. '[I]t is inevitable for ... [a] party to issue directives to its members'. As for the situation in the state, the ministry 'was losing all contacts with the public ... [and] was being controlled more and more by non-Congress elements'. Also, the worsening law and order and communal situation had to be controlled. Moreover, Bhargava was 'not acting in a straight manner'.[43] The central government revoked the proclamation on 17 April 1952 after elections had produced a Congress majority led by Bhim Sen Sachar.

---

[40] Nehru's letters to Gopichand Bhargava, 2 and 18 March 1951. Gopichand Bhargava Papers, Jawaharlal Nehru File, NMML.

[41] Kochanek, *Congress Party*, p. 257, citing a *Congress Bulletin* of May–June 1951 and the *Statesman* 13 June 1951. According to some observers of the scene, Bhargava was understood to have been a protégé of Sardar Patel, and his especial opponent within the Congress, Bhim Sen Sachar, a protégé of Nehru.

[42] Prasad to 'My dear Jawaharlalji' dated 18 June 1951. File 21, 1951, 'Correspondence with Prime Minister', Rajendra Prasad Collection, NAI.

[43] Nehru to 'My dear Mr President' dated 21 June 1951. Ibid. Nehru rejected Prasad's comparing the 'outside authority' in the Punjab case, the CPB, with Kripalani's resigning from the Congress presidency—when the central government had denied that the Congress Party had any authority over its policies or actions.

The imposition of President's Rule in Kerala on 31 July 1959 caused a greater stir. In the spring 1957 general elections, the Communist Party of India won 60 of the 126 seats in the Kerala legislature and formed a government with the backing of independents.[44] Chief Minister E. M. S. Namboodiripad (popularly referred to as EMS) vowed to allow all citizens to exercise 'the rights of freedom of speech, press, assembly or organization' in the Constitution and to 'adhere strictly to the limitations imposed on the state government by the Constitution'.[45] He initiated a major social reform programme that included land reform, banning eviction of tenants, providing legal aid to the poor, granting amnesty to political prisoners, and reserving 35 per cent of places in educational institutions and civil services for the backward classes. On 2 September 1957, the legislature passed the Kerala Education Bill, which gave the government a great deal of control over most schools in the state, many of them Christian. The governor reserved the bill for the assent of the President, who, on the Attorney General's recommendation, sent the bill in May 1958 to the Supreme Court for an advisory opinion. Prasad enquired specifically if the bill offended Article 14 (equality under and equal protection of the law); Article 30(1) (minorities right to establish and administer their own educational institutions); and Article 226 (the High Courts' power to issue writs for the enforcement of the Fundamental Rights). On 22 May 1958, the Court advised that portions of the bill violated the rights of minorities to establish and run their own schools, but it did not violate Article 14. The provision of the act barring judicial scrutiny of compensation paid for schools acquired by the state did not offend Article 226.[46] Responding to the opinion, the Kerala legislature

[44] Kerala had been under President's Rule in March 1956 when portions of Travancore became part of Kerala as a result of states reorganization. President's Rule was extended in Kerala in November 1956 and remained in force until the general elections that produced the Namboodiripad government in April 1957.

[45] Quotations, respectively, from *Problems and Possibilities*, CPI/New Age Printing Press, New Delhi, 1957, p. 49 and 'Statement of Policy' in *Prosperous Kerala: Government Policy Outlined*, Central Government (of Kerala) Press, Trivandrum, 1957, p. 5.

The CPI in West Bengal had also done well in the 1957 election, nearly doubling its percentage of the popular vote from 1952.

Namboodiripad may have harboured dreams or ambitions of Kerala being the beginning of the peaceful implantation of communism in India. Frankel, *Political Economy*, p. 158. S. Gopal expressed a similar opinion when he wrote that Namboodiripad considered gaining office in Kerala as a step in a 'war of position'. Gopal, *Nehru*, vol. 3, p. 54.

The following paragraphs about Kerala draw on Frankel, *Political Economy*, pp. 157–9, and heavily on Gopal, *Nehru*, vol. 3, ch. 3.

[46] *Statesman*, account as cited in *AR*, 24–30 May 1958, pp. 2066–8.

enacted a revised bill in April 1959, which the Roman Catholic bishops, among others, refused to accept.[47] A land ceilings law also contributed to the tenseness of the atmosphere, for under it lands in excess of the ceiling were to vest in the state and existing tenants could either lease land or buy portions at 55 per cent of market value. Proprietors of coconut and other 'plantations' and other landlords, who were to be compensated, attacked the bill on the ground that their holdings were not 'estates' and so were protected by Articles 14, 19, and 31.[48]

Nehru's attitude toward the Kerala government during this period went through several stages. Although he disliked communism, he was willing initially to give the government a chance and even was 'subconsciously almost proud' that Indian democracy had allowed the election of a communist government.[49] His view that the Kerala government should fall only from normal processes survived his visit to the state between 22 and 25 June 1959. Meanwhile, the Congress Party was speaking with three voices: 'the members in Kerala active in violent agitation, the central leadership permitting such activity without approving it, and Nehru disapproving of it but taking no action to curb it'.[50] The Congress

---

[47] Nehru's letter to chief ministers, dated 2 July 1959. *NLTCM*, vol. 5, pp. 270ff. See also Gopal, *Nehru*, vol. 3, pp. 57, 69.

[48] Merillat, *Land*, p. 184.

When the Agrarian Relations Bill passed, Governor B. Ramkrishna Rao reserved it, too, for the President's assent. In New Delhi, it was overtaken by the proclamation of President's Rule, and the bill lingered there until July 1960, when the President returned it to the freshly elected legislature with suggestions for changes. The now Congress-controlled legislature re-passed the bill on 15 October 1960, and the President gave his assent on 21 January 1961.

The Act was challenged in the Supreme Court in *Purushothaman Nambudri v The State of Kerala* at the time Bhuvaneshwar Prasad Sinha was Chief Justice. On the bench were P. B. Gajendragadkar, A. K. Sarkar, K. N. Wanchoo. K. C. Das Gupta, and N. Rajagopala Ayyangar. Lawyers for the state included M. C. Setalvad, still Attorney General, and K. K. Mathew, then Advocate General of Kerala and later a Supreme Court judge. In the leading opinion, given on 5 December 1961, Gajendragadkar rejected Nambudri's contention that the Act lapsed because the assembly was dissolved while the Act awaited presidential assent. Gajendragadkar then ruled that the Act was protected under Article 31A, that the petitioner's lands were an 'estate' within the meaning of the law, and that land ceiling legislation—with government acquisition of land above the stipulated ceiling—was the logical second step in land reform, after zamindari abolition. 1962 *Supp* (1) SCR 753ff.

[49] Gopal, *Nehru*, vol. 3, p. 54. Soviet policy toward Tito and the execution of Imre Nagy in Hungary reinforced Nehru's view that the communists used violent methods in India also. Home Minister Pant and the Kerala governor, B. R. Rao, took a more sceptical and conservative view of the Kerala government than did Nehru. Ibid, p. 54.

[50] Ibid., p. 66. Critics of the Kerala Congress's behaviour included Rajagopalachari and Patanjali Sastri. Said the former, they 'are laying the axe at the root of parliamentary

Parliamentary Board at a meeting on 29 June 1959, chaired by Indira Gandhi, as party president, adopted a resolution saying that elections would be the best way to resolve the situation and revealed what would be the government's rationale when it imposed President's Rule: 'It may be ... that the government has a majority in the state assembly, but nevertheless is unable to function satisfactorily because of widespread opposition from the public.'[51] The next day the CPB sent a 'Note of Instruction' marked 'Secret' to the Kerala Pradesh Congress Committee (KPCC) indicating the 'positive approach' it should take in the situation. The KPCC should demand elections as soon as feasible and join any discussions offered by the Kerala government, meanwhile preparing a 'chargesheet (to be finalised with the CPB) ... in the nature of a petition to the President' calling for early elections. The KPCC also should engage in token picketing, but not picketing of schools and transport vehicles.[52]

Near the end of July, the General Secretary of the CPI, Ajoy Ghosh, and CPI member of Parliament, A. K. Gopalan, visited Nehru to request central intervention to cancel the planned mammoth demonstration against the state government. When Nehru expressed his inability to do

democracy by what they are doing'. Said Sastri, agitating against a government to displace it means they are 'not really educated even in the fundamental concepts of democracy'. Sastri comments to the *Times of India* and other newspapers.

The Congress Party central organization's stance toward EMS from the beginning had been more critical and admonitory than Nehru's. See U.N. Dhebar's letter to Namboodiripad on AICC stationery, dated 6 August 1957. In this letter there also seems to be an implied threat. Said Dhebar, if your government takes the law into its own hands over property, all will find that the Communists 'are not the only persons who will be found adept in this art of taking law into their own hands'. T. T. Krishnamachari Papers, Jawaharlal Nehru File, 1957, NMML.

[51] 'Resolution and Note of Instruction, Kerala', AICC Papers, Second Installment, File 4313–20/1959 NMML.

The resolution also said that picketing as a method of political action is undesirable, but 'in order to give expression to public feeling, some form of peaceful token picketing may be admissible'. For Nehru, however, the kind of picketing Congress members and others in the opposition to the Kerala government were doing 'is not at all to my liking ... I am strongly opposed to picketing by boys and girls to prevent others from attending [schools] ... [and to] stopping transport vehicles by lying down in front of them. Indeed this is hardly picketing.' Letter to chief ministers of 2 July 1959. *NLTCM*, vol. 5, pp. 270–4.

[52] AICC Papers, File 4313–20/1959.

Indira Gandhi's part in this affair still is the subject of much speculation. She 'was not a negligible element' in the crisis, wrote Nehru's biographer. A leader of the Kerala Congress said in 1970 that 'but for Mrs Gandhi's influence they would not have been able to convert the central government to their way of thinking'. Two of Mrs Gandhi's

so, they told him "'the sooner you act [to dismiss the state government] the better.'"[53] The governor was asked to request the imposition of President's Rule, and Nehru wrote to Namboodiripad on 30 July that we have been 'most reluctant' to take the step, but matters could not be left to deteriorate further. Even from your government's viewpoint, Nehru continued, '"it is better for Central intervention to take place now.'" [54]

The governor's report calling for the imposition of President's Rule said of the situation, the spirit of give and take 'has been crushed' and the government cannot function in a 'normal way'. It barely mentioned the Education Bill and the Agrarian Relations Bill not at all.[55] Justifying presidential intervention, the governor—or, more likely, his New Delhi ghostwriters—propounded an utterly self-serving philosophy of government. It is not necessary that a no-confidence motion be passed 'in order to justify the change of government', the governor said. "'I am convinced that the government has lost the support of the majority of the people ... [S] ecuring ... a majority of seats in the Legislature ... cannot be pleaded as conferring a continuing right to claim the confidence of the majority.' The 'only solution' is to exercise the power under Article 356, he said.[56]

---

biographers believe that she pushed Nehru to his decision. Backed by 'a powerful combination of Congress conservatives, she now grew impatient and demanded that the Communists be sent packing without further delay'. Malhotra, Inder, *Indira Gandhi: A Personal and Political Biography*, Hodder and Stoughton, London, 1989, p. 64. 'Indira's views had prevailed with the Prime Minister and President's Rule had been imposed in Kerala,' wrote Pupul Jayakar. Jayakar, Pupul, *Indira Gandhi*, Penguin Books, New Delhi, 1992, p. 160.

[53] Gopal, *Nehru*, vol. 3, p. 71.

[54] Ibid., pp. 71–2. Nehru confirmed this when speaking to the Lok Sabha on 19 August 1959 about the imposition of President's Rule. Ghosh and Gopalan had visited him, he said; they 'did not in so many words ask us to intervene. But I say definitely that they left the impression upon me that nothing would be more welcome to them than intervention.' *Jawaharlal Nehru's Speeches*, vol. 4, p. 83.

[55] *The Summary by the Governor of Kerala of His Report to the President,* Home Ministry document, cyclostyled, date illegible, but presented in Parliament 17 August 1959. Papers Laid on the Table 1959, Lok Sabha Secretariat/LT 1541/59.

The report's litany of dissatisfactions with the government's policies included: death sentences of communists being commuted after the President had rejected mercy petitions; the government accusing the police of being 'anti-people'; discrimination against non-communist labour unions due to the expanded influence of the Communist, All-India Trades Union Congress (AITUC); and the government using its machinery 'for consolidating its own party at the expense of others'.

[56] Ibid. The Congress Party–central government connection, which had masterminded the whole affair, could have invoked Attorney General Setalvad's point—in his 1950 'Observations', see ch. 1—that the President, and, analogously, the governor, could dismiss

Perhaps it was true, as Nehru said in the Lok Sabha when defending the proclamation of President's Rule, that central government intervention averted a disaster.[57] But the Congress Party brought down the Kerala government with the very 'extra- parliamentary' tactics and violence it had castigated other parties for using. Moreover, many of the governor's accusations against the Kerala government could be levelled against Congress state governments, which the governor admitted—with apparent injured innocence—by acknowledging that 'isolated instances of irregularities and partialities can also be found in other states'. But he excused these as 'only the results of individual caprice, prejudice or even misconduct. They have no relation to the aggrandisement of the [Congress] party as such.'[58]

The Constitution's Emergency Provisions, if not greatly protecting national unity and integrity, might be said to have served national cohesion, but even here their use seems little to have served the nation.

The institution of the governor, having become prominent in so unfortunate a fashion, had dual functions: to be a unifying force, linking state governments with New Delhi, and to be the titular head of the state government, consonant with the parliamentary system. The governor was to be the central government's representative to, and eyes and ears in, the state government. The Constitution provided that the governor be appointed by the President and serve at his 'pleasure' meaning, of course, at the pleasure of the central ministry (Articles 155 and 156). Like the President, he was to reign, not rule, but local circumstances and New Delhi's uses of the position aroused criticism several times during the Nehru years and made it very controversial thereafter. Accusations would be heard that he was the central government's 'agent'. Beyond his role in impositions of President's Rule, there was the question of the extent of his 'discretionary' authority under the Constitution, particularly in appointing the chief minister when respective party strengths in the legislature were unclear. These matters will be explored in Part VI, and the paradox was that over the years the uses of the institution became detrimental to the

---

the legislature if he felt 'there is a potent disharmony between the policy of the Ministry and public opinion'. One may doubt that this truly was the situation in Kerala in 1959, and the truth never will be known.

[57] Speech of 19 August 1959. *Nehru Speeches,* vol. 4, pp. 82–92.

[58] *Summary by the Governor of Kerala,* pp. 14–15. President's Rule was revoked on 22 February 1960 after special elections had produced a new legislature in which the CPI held only 29 of the 130 seats. The Congress and the PSP formed a government with Pattom A. Thanu Pillai as chief minister.

sense of national unity: state political leaders believed that Delhi manipulated it.

SUB-CONSTITUTIONAL INSTITUTIONS AND MECHANISMS

The myriad tasks of government, explicit and implicit in the Constitution, needed for their fulfilment oversight and co-ordination. The Constitution specifically provided for several institutions and mechanisms; others were created according to perceived need. All would benefit initially from central government leadership and foster unity through a broader understanding of national problems. Central and state leaders, in the main, understood their respective needs as sides of the same coin. But many of these mechanisms, in the view of state participants especially, would come to suffer even in Nehru's time from uncooperativeness on the part of state governments and three central government vices: the assumption that it knew best, heavy-handedness, and its opposite, neglect.

The two pre-eminent coordinating institutions were the Finance Commission, provided for in Article 280, and the Planning Commission, not envisaged in the Constitution at all. Established in February 1950, this became the country's principal institution for economic development. It was closely linked to the cabinet: Nehru was its chairman, the Cabinet Secretary functioned as the commission's secretary, and the Finance Minister and the Statistical Advisor to the cabinet (for many years P. C. Mahalanobis) were directly involved with its work. Under the commission the National Development Council (NDC) was set up to allow the chief ministers to 'review and recommend social and economic policies'.[59] Nehru typically chaired NDC meetings and strongly influenced its decisions. Toward the end of this early period, the planning process drew criticism for being overly centralized and for applying a single development model to the country despite the great variety of conditions within the states. Chief ministers charged that the meetings rubber-stamped central government decisions more than contributing to them. For example, the NDC approved the draft Third Plan in September 1960 after it had been approved in Parliament.[60] Opposition

---

[59] Frankel, *Political Economy*, p. 113. President Prasad announced in Parliament in August 1951 that the NDC would be formed, and this was done in 1952.

The reader again is directed to Part VI.

[60] *AR*, 1–7 October 1960, p. 3560. Andhra Chief Minister Brahmananda Reddy in 1964 called for more state autonomy in development planning, to which Prime Minister Shastri responded that centre–state relations over development should not be portrayed as conflict because this created 'a good deal of confusion in the public mind'. *AR*, 25 November–1 December 1964, p. 6165.

parties, such as the Jana Sangh, said the planning apparatus risked 'over-centralization and totalitarianism'. The All-India Manufacturers Association found planning good, but thought dangerous to democracy the concentration of power in government hands.[61] Although the charge of 'totalitarianism' was ridiculous, the centralization of the planning process revealed disbelief in the state governments' and citizens' intellectual capacity for participation, and, therefore, was more than a little tinged with undemocratic attitudes. The potential for this concerned Nehru. He wrote to the Commission Deputy Chairman G. L. Nanda, troubled that the commission's 'manner of working ... becomes more and more officialized'. Talk with the chief ministers as colleagues, never order them about, Nehru advised. They are not subordinate in any way.[62] Nevertheless, the Planning Commission system made great contributions to national development.

The Finance Commission's responsibility for recommending the distribution between the central and state governments of centrally collected revenues, and the principles governing grants- in-aid from central funds to the states, makes its importance self-evident. The first Finance Commission report, December 1952, attempted to remedy early complaints that New Delhi was levying taxes that interfered with the states' own tax strategies.[63] For example, it recommended that a significant increase in the percentage of centrally collected income tax go to the states, partly on the basis of collection and partly on the basis of need, and a larger percentage of the excise duties on tobacco, matches, and vegetable products. The report also raised the amount of state subventions from the Centre.[64] The Second, Third, and Fourth Finance Commissions

[61] For the Jana Sangh view, see *AR*, 21–27 July 1956, p. 994. For the All-India Manufacturers Association, see *AR*, 14–20 April 1956, p. 786.

The Federation of Indian Chambers of Commerce and Industry shared many of the Manufacturers' Association's view.

Prime Minister Lal Bahadur Shastri opened up the planning process. He formed a National Planning Council of science and technology experts, with limited members from the Planning Commission, to advise on planning. He saw to it that the NDC could advise on Fourth Plan policy issues. In 1968, under Indira Gandhi as Prime Minister, money for development assistance projects in the states was 'untied' from centrally approved schemes, and central assistance came in the form of block loans and grants for state governments to use for their own development plans. Frankel, *Political Economy*, pp. 255ff, 311ff.

[62] *Selected Works of Jawaharlal Nehru*, vol. 20, p. 215. Letter dated 7 November 1952.

[63] See letters among Pant, Munshi, Rajagopalachari, B. C. Roy, and Sampurnanand during 1952. K. M. Munshi Papers, Microfilm Box 56, File 143, NMML, and Sampurnanand Papers, File 89, NAI.

[64] Generally speaking, the collection and distribution of revenues has been:

increased the amount of income tax revenue distributed to the states, a trend that would continue. Many other adjustments were made. For example, the states gave up sales taxes on textiles, tobacco, and sugar in return for larger central government subventions. The Finance Commission steadily gained importance as a forum for the resolution of money disputes between the centre and the states. Nevertheless, the distribution of revenues, and of capital development grants by the Planning Commission, would become contentious as the state governments would accuse New Delhi of inequitable distribution, while themselves incurring enormous overdrafts on the central treasury.

The zonal councils were a sub-constitutional mechanism with a different function. The States Reorganisation Act of 1956 set up five councils—the four points of the compass and a central zone—for centre–state and inter-state coordination. Each council comprised the chief ministers, the development ministers, and the chief secretaries of the relevant states, a member of the Planning Commission, and was chaired by the central Home Minister. Pandit Pant described the councils' function at the inaugural meeting of the Northern Zonal Council in April 1957: to attain the emotional integration of the country and to arrest acute regional consciousness; to help the central government and the states evolve uniform social and economic policies; to assist effective implementation of development projects; and to secure a degree of political equilibrium among the regions of the country.[65] Nehru hoped the councils would help settle day-to-day problems and help in economic planning, while not becoming 'a fifth wheel of the coach or ... coming in the way of close relations between the centre and

---

—Taxes levied, collected and retained by the central government: corporation tax, import/export duties, taxes on capital (other than on agricultural land).

—Taxes levied and collected by the Centre and shared with the states: income tax (other than agricultural income, which few states collect, although empowered to) and central excise duties.

—Taxes levied and collected by the Centre but turned over to the states: succession and estate duties, taxes on railway fares and freight, and terminal duties on goods and passengers.

—Taxes levied by the Centre but collected and retained by the states: stamp duties mentioned on the Union List. See M. M. Singhal, 'Devolution and Development of Indian Federal Finance' in the Special Number on Centre–State Relations in India, *Journal of Constitutional and Parliamentary Studies* (hereafter *JCPS*), vol. 20, nos. 1–4, 1986, pp. 146–7.

[65] K. A. Ramasubramaniam, 'Historical Development and Essential Features of the Federal System' in Mukarji, Nirmal and Arora, Balveer (eds), *Federalism in India: Origins and Development*, Centre for Policy Research, Vikas Publishing House Pvt. Ltd., New Delhi, 1992, p. 114

the states'.[66] K. M. Munshi was sceptical. He wrote in his fortnightly letter to President Prasad that the Uttar Pradesh government thought the councils would serve 'no useful purpose' and that a central government minister should not chair them.[67] Conversely, Sanjiva Reddy, when Congress president, later advocated giving the councils statutory administrative powers to combat provincialism.[68] The councils were by no means useless bodies, said a well-qualified observer, but 'they achieved at best a limited success'.[69]

Going beyond such mechanisms, Nehru launched endeavours bold in their paradox: the community development and *panchayati raj* programmes, whose purposes may be said to have been integration through decentralization and unity through participation, in addition to their obvious aims of economic development and social improvement in villages. These programmes were to be the ideal combination of the grand themes of unity, democracy, and social revolution. The idea was not original to Nehru, although he had a 'crusader's zeal' for community development.[70] Jayaprakash Narayan and the socialist parties shared the concept, and, as is well known, Mahatma Gandhi had been the great proponent of village development and empowerment. For Nehru, the community development projects were the beginning of a far-reaching social revolution that would ' "transform our country ... and promote a better order" '.[71] Congress President U. N. Dhebar advocated *panchayat* development as more than 'a decentralized form of administration', seeing it also as leading to 'emotional integration' and developing 'a conscious bond ... towards ... democracy ... the medium for the achievement of the Socialist Pattern of Society'. Nevertheless, Dhebar

---

[66] Letter of 16 January 1956. *NLTCM*, vol. 4, p. 336.

[67] Letter dated 16 April 1956. K. M. Munshi Papers, Microfilm Box 118, File 358, NMML.

[68] *AR*, 29 January–4 February 1961, p. 3756.

[69] Sarkar, R. C. S., *Union–State Relations in India*, National Publishing House, New Delhi, 1986, p. 76.

[70] Nehru's 'crusader's zeal' for the community development programme (Gopal, *Nehru*, vol. 1, p. 307) did not blind him to the factionalism in villages.

The democracy of the *panchayati raj* programme may release 'forces which do not exactly make for unity and cohesion', acknowledged Congress President Sanjiva Reddy. *Report of the General Secretaries, January 1961–December 1961*, AICC, pp. 2–9.

[71] In a speech in 1952 inaugurating the first fifty-five community development projects. Frankel, *Political Economy*, p. 109. See also a basic book, Dey, S. K., *Panchayati Raj*, Asia Publishing House, London, 1961. Nehru often promoted the two programmes in his letters to chief ministers.

Article 40 in the Directive Principles of State Policy enjoins the state to develop *panchayats* 'to enable them to function as units of self-government'.

was one of many who believed that 'the vote should not be allowed to divide the people' and, therefore, '[panchayat] elections on a party basis would be the worst service that we can render to the people in the villages'. Implicit in Dhebar's view was the fear that the dominant castes in a village would control the outcome of elections.[72] In 1957, Nehru was under the impression that community development had a fine organization and had spread 'to nearly half of rural India'.[73] But decentralization should not lead to weak government, Nehru said. ' "One of the big problems of modern life is to find a balance between the tendency toward concentration and the need for decentralization," ' he believed.[74]

Nehru was right, of course, but his predilections and those of many others in his government toward 'concentration' won out. A 1956 report issued by the Community Projects Administration found the programme strong in its theoretical approach and the practical experience of its officers. But it also found that villagers had changed 'more rapidly than have the concepts of some national leaders about villagers' and said 'it is impossible successfully to develop democracy at the bottom [of society] if feudalism exists at the top'.[75] Two reports of 1959 and 1960 said that the 'hierarchical growth of official machinery' had set back the Community Development Programme greatly and the programme had 'become more governmental than popular in character', with people hardly regarding it as their own programme.[76] But the difficulties did not lie entirely with the bureaucrats. State politicians resisted village power for fear of losing influence. And the 'segmented structures and primitive institutions' of rural society 'could not generate a responsive

---

[72] From the type-written text of the article. AICC Papers, Second Installment, File G-1 (17) Congress President, 1955, NMML.

Dhebar's assessment of village conditions, by no means inaccurate, also gave pause to those considering empowering judicial *panchayats*. K. M. Munshi, for one, feared that giving them authority could 'mean that justice might fall into the hands of village bullies'. *Proceedings of the Conference of Governors*, 4–5 February 1953, p. 15, K. M. Munshi Papers, Microfilm Box 63, File 176, NMML.

[73] Letter dated 23–24 January 1958. *NLTCM*, vol. 5, pp. 18–19.

[74] Speech to the All-India Manufacturers Association, 14 March 1959. *AR*, 4–10 April 1959, p. 2590.

[75] Taylor, Carl C., *A Critical Analysis of India's Community Development Programme*, The Community Projects Administration, GOI, New Delhi, 1956, p. 57. Taylor was a Ford Foundation consultant on community development.

[76] An article by Professor Rene Dumont of Paris, 'India's Agricultural Defeat' in the *New Statesman*, 19 December 1959. Cited in *NLTCM*, vol. 5, pp. 345–6. Also the Seventh Evaluation Report of the Planning Commission, 11 June 1960. Cited in ibid., pp. 379–80. Press accounts of the latter are quoted in *AR*, 25 June–1 July 1960, pp. 3405ff.

and creative leadership'.[77] The failures probably did not set back the cause of unity, but they did little to help it. These same factors would continue to inhibit the development of panchayats and community programmes for years to come. But Nehru's dream had taken root and would grow in the 1990s with a constitutional amendment mandating the establishment of panchayats and reserving a third of the positions in them for women.[78]

In addition to these more formal sub-constitutional institutions, there were many mechanisms for coordination and communication: the annual meetings of governors, presided over by the President; meetings of chief ministers, presided over by the Prime Minister; annual meetings of the Supreme Court and high court chief justices; and annual, or more frequent, meetings of state and central ministers of law, food and agriculture, housing, education, labour, community development, and irrigation and power. For legislators, there were annual meetings of presiding officers chaired by the Speaker of the Lok Sabha, and annual meetings of the chairs of estimates committees and chief whips (begun in the sixties), again presided over by the Speaker.[79] There also were meetings of *ad hoc* groups like those on food policy and inter-state river waters disputes.

Frequent communications served coordination and national 'education'. As seen, Nehru regularly wrote to the chief ministers and, less often, to PCC presidents. Governors wrote to the President fortnightly—a practice begun in 1948—with copies to the chief minister

---

[77] Haksar, *Premonitions*, p. 230.

[78] Others would have decentralized by revising the Constitution. The PSP believed that people in their local communities should 'make or mar their own fate as they wish ... [This] is surely the only way to rouse a lethargic people to action'. *Statement of Policy*, Praja Socialist Party, Bombay, 1954, p. 13. The Socialist Party said it would democratize the Constitution by replacing the two-pillar system of states and central government with a four pillar structure 'of the village, district, province and the Centre'. Police power would be transferred to district and village control; district and village councils would get 'a quarter share in all revenues and expenditures of the Republic'; and village councils would serve as sovereign agencies of legislation. *Election Manifesto*, Socialist Party 1957, Hyderabad, p. 5.

The Communist Party limited its prescriptions to abolishing the Constitution's emergency provisions, so the country could not be governed in a unitary fashion. And it called for the direct election of governors. *Election Manifesto*, Communist Party of India, New Delhi, 1961, cited in *AR*, 12–16 November 1961, p. 4281.

[79] The first Speaker, G. V. Mavalankar, used these forcefully to inculcate a democratic legislative spirit and to build up legislature secretariats the better to administer legislative business. For many examples of this, see Mavalankar, G. V., *Speeches and Writings*, Lok Sabha Secretariat, New Delhi, 1957.

and the Prime Minister, who sent extracts to relevant central ministers. In addition to the heavy bureaucratic traffic, there was a constant stream of communications from Congress Party headquarters to provincial and district Congress committees about national policy as well as on internal party issues—although local Congress units did not always acquiesce to central leadership direction.

If democracy is the worst form of government except for all the others, federalism is equally troublesome. The distribution of powers and resources is perpetually contentious. The efficacy of methods is always in dispute. And whether centralization or decentralization better serves national unity and the individual citizen, societies decide by the pendulum method—first one way, then the other. Indians would not be different, especially during the early years. Despite their difficulties, they made the Constitution's federal and related provisions work. Adult suffrage supported the parliamentary system nationally. The single judicial system functioned in both its original and appellate jurisdictions, even when rulings were unpopular. States reorganization had successfully rearranged boundaries to create linguistic states while strengthening unity, although the changes were marred locally by violence. Jammu and Kashmir had special status under Article 370. The Nagas were given a state. On this example, autonomous areas for tribal peoples were created in Assam in 1969 by the Twenty-second Amendment. Three actually or potentially secessionist crises were resolved, although the lessons of Kashmir and the Punjab were ill-learned. A sense for the national economy grew, and the states and the centre carried on the innumerable routine arrangements without which the nation would have failed. Above all, the country was more united and confident of itself in 1966 than in 1950. The third strand of the seamless web had been strengthened.

Part II

THE GREAT CONSTITUTIONAL CONFRONTATION: JUDICIAL *VERSUS* PARLIAMENTARY SUPREMACY, 1967–73

Our path is socialism. If we do not use the word, it does not mean we have forgotten it. We cannot wait for them [doubters], although we will try to take everyone with us.

Indira Gandhi[1]

Notwithstanding anything in this Constitution, Parliament may in exercise of its constituent power amend by way of addition, variation or repeal any provision of this Constitution ....

From the Twenty-fourth Amendment, 1971[2]

Article 368 does not enable Parliament to alter the basic structure or framework of the Constitution.

The Supreme Court in the Kesavananda Bharati case[3]

---

[1] Speaking to the AICC meeting, 3–4 April 1971. *Congress Marches Ahead IV*, AICC, New Delhi, 1971, p. 70.

[2] Clause 3 (b) (1).

[3] 1973 (4) Supreme Court Cases (hereafter SCC) 1007.

Chapter 7

INDIRA GANDHI: IN CONTEXT
AND IN POWER

The early hours of 11 January 1966 brought India two ends and a beginning. The life of Jawaharlal Nehru's successor, Prime Minister Lal Bahadur Shastri, ended that morning in Tashkent, where he had gone to sign an agreement with Pakistan ending the previous year's war between the two countries. Shastri's death also ended the Nehru years, for he had led the country in the Nehru tradition even while being his own man as Prime Minister. A new era, one that would be marked by confrontation over institutional and personal power, began with the arrival in the Prime Minister's office of Nehru's daughter, Mrs Indira Gandhi

The era may be divided into three periods: from 1967–73, the subject of this Part; from 1975–7, the period of Mrs Gandhi's Emergency, covered in Part III; and from 1980–5, the years from her resumption of power after the Janata interlude until her assassination, discussed in Part V. The confrontations of Mrs Gandhi's first period as Prime Minister occurred in a sequence of events described in this and the following five chapters: her consolidation of power in the Congress Party and as Prime Minister, leading to her centralization of centre–state relations and within the executive branch in New Delhi; the Supreme Court's rulings in three cases involving the right to property—Golak Nath, bank nationalization, and privy purses; Parliament's assertion of its power further to restrict the Fundamental Rights and to amend any part of the Constitution; the Supreme Court's reassertion of its power of judicial review; and Mrs Gandhi's long-brewing direct attack on the Court.

Self-evidently, essential issues of constitutional governance underlay her actions in these confrontations. Individual rights were pitted against the society's need for a social revolution, as they had been in Nehru's time. The increased central authority over the states ended the 'bargaining federalism' of the Nehru years, and the 'federal' structure of the Congress Party disappeared as many ministers became New Delhi's instruments and the Prime Minister gained control of the Congress Party machinery. In New Delhi, the distribution of powers among the three branches of government was gravely unsettled. Mrs Gandhi's grip on the Congress

Parliamentary Party exceeded the power typically enjoyed by prime ministers in parliamentary systems, where prime ministers heed as well as lead their followers. The executive branch came to dominate Parliament to such a degree that Parliament lost any effective identity of its own. And, authority within the executive became concentrated in the Prime Minister's office and then was exercised from Mrs Gandhi's residence, to the exclusion of all but a few. The two branches, if still they could be called that, attacked the third branch, the judiciary, intending to end its function as a co-equal branch of government.

These and related events strained two strands of the seamless web and somewhat strengthened the third. Mrs Gandhi's attack on judicial independence struck at democracy's heart as Parliament acquired a rash presumption of omnipotence. Her necessary consolidation of her position in the party and as Prime Minister progressively damaged, rather than strengthened, national unity and integrity. The seamless web's social revolutionary strand fared a bit better. For example, the Green Revolution increased grain production and spread the benefits associated with this, while making some agriculturalists particularly rich. Bank nationalization, despite its dubious origins, did broaden the availability of credit in the country for agriculture and small industry. And the attention given to the social-economic desiderata of the Directive Principles, even if largely rhetorical, did give prominence to an easily neglected portion of the Constitution.

This chapter provides the context for the constitutional developments that marked this period. Its principal topics are Mrs Gandhi's invocation of socialist themes to consolidate her authority; the rise to prominence of a new political generation; and the increasing migration of authority from a variety of institutions and individuals to the office and person of the Prime Minister.

A harbinger of new power relationships came in the inability of the 'Syndicate' of a few state party leaders (K. Kamaraj of Madras, Atulya Ghosh of Bengal, S. K. Patil of Bombay, S. Nijalingappa of Mysore and Sanjiva Reddy of Andhra) to arrange the succession from Lal Bahadur Shastri to a new prime minister, as they had arranged the succession from Nehru to Shastri in 1964. The organizational wing of the Congress then briefly had been dominant. In January 1966, the Syndicate could not produce a consensus candidate, nor could the Working Committee. Although eight chief ministers and Kamaraj finally declared themselves for Mrs Gandhi, the CPP made the ultimate decision, electing her leader in a secret ballot on 19 January 1966. She had defeated Morarji Desai because, according to the common assessment, he was personally unpopular, possessed of prodigious pride, and stubborn in office. Also, because Kamaraj and others believed they could control Mrs Gandhi.[1] Many in the party considered her a transitional prime minister until after the 1967 general elections. Thus, to survive politically, Mrs Gandhi faced the tasks that would confront any prime minister in similar circumstances. She had to assert her leadership within the government and lead the party to election victory.

She failed to do the latter, and it may be doubted that any leader could have overcome the Congress's self-destructive factionalism and other electoral handicaps of the moment. The 1967 general elections cut the Congress's majority in the Lok Sabha to twenty-five, lost it 264 seats in state assemblies and its majorities in eight states. This produced what reporter and editor Inder Malhotra described as a 'flourishing trade in political loyalties' as parties scrambled for enough adherents to allow formation of a government. Instead of ousting Mrs Gandhi, largely because the only viable alternative would have been Morarji Desai, the Congress compromised by renewing her leadership and by making Desai Deputy Prime Minister as well as Minister of Finance. It then turned to its staple fare, socialism.

In a 'post-mortem' on the elections, the Working Committee and, later, the AICC bemoaned its neglect of socialist programmes and the loss of its mass base by leaders consumed by competition for office.[2] Having attributed its election losses to unfulfilled promises, it then, in a pattern that had become familiar, made fresh, enlarged promises. The Working Committee on 12 May adopted a resolution containing a 'Ten-point Programme' that called for, among other things, 'social control' of banks, nationalization of general insurance, limits on urban incomes and property, and the removal of the princes' privileges.[3] Another resolution said that 'only by working the Constitution in letter and spirit is it possible to provide an orderly government ... and also preserve and promote the Fundamental Rights and the cherished principles and objectives enshrined in the Constitution ...'.[4]

---

[1] The commonly accepted picture of Desai seems overdrawn. Stiff-necked he was, but to two of his close subordinates, B. K. Nehru and Nirmal Mukarji, he was a responsive boss and had a sense of humour.

[2] For a detailed report on the post-mortem, see *Congress Bulletin,* June–July 1967, pp. 83–133.

[3] *Report of the General Secretaries, February 1966–January 1968,* AICC, New Delhi, 1968, p. 29. Subsequent chapters will return to the subjects of banks and princes.

[4] The Congress Forum for Socialist Action added its voice to the 'agonising reappraisal'. It called for a 'new Congress which would look like a real socialist party, the

Mrs Gandhi, 'Socialism', and Power

These sentiments gave the Prime Minister the justification for challenging the senior figures in the organizational wing of the party, who were critical of her leadership and still intent on controlling her. Younger, social-activist Congressmen would be her vanguard against the 'bosses', as they called them. As the *Statesman* put it, she intensified the battle over 'democratic socialism', between 'the Right and the Left'.[5] On the so-called 'Right' were party president S. Nijalingappa, other members of the Syndicate (some of whom were at least as socialist-minded as the Prime Minister), and Morarji Desai. C. Subramaniam, temporarily out of the ministry in New Delhi due to his defeat in recent elections and now president of the Tamil Nadu Provincial Congress Committee, led the 'Left', accompanied by the party's 'Young Turks' and others of whom more will be heard presently. The 'politics of commitment' appeared as the 'left's rallying cry'.[6] Mrs Gandhi told the Faridabad session of the All India Congress Committee that 'the party would neither abandon the goal of socialism nor allow itself to be pushed to the extreme left or right'.[7]

After these skirmishes at Faridabad, during which Nijalingappa had to defend himself by declaring, 'I am a socialist to the core,' the Prime Minister again attacked at the Working Committee meeting in Bangalore beginning 9 July.[8] The meeting opened that evening with Mrs Gandhi absent—apparently due to a tactical indisposition in Delhi. But one of her cabinet ministers, Fakhruddin Ali Ahmed, delivered her 'note' to

---

driving force of which would be provided by peasants, labourers and the working intelligentsia'. S. N. Mishra, *The Crisis, the Country, the Congress,* Congress Forum for Socialist Action, New Delhi, 1967. Later, the Forum took the lead in sending the Congress president and the Prime Minister a memorandum from 118 members of the Parliamentary Party urging implementation of the Ten-Point Programme.

Atulya Ghosh, hardly a 'socialist', in a pamphlet entitled *The Real Task* (AICC, New Delhi, 1967), harshly criticized the party's failure to fulfill its social revolutionary promises such as those on land reform and the abolition of untouchability. '[I] n practically no state have the relevant [land reform] laws been implemented in their totality' (p. 3). Policies must produce legislation and legislation must be implemented, he wrote.

[5] New Delhi edition, 26 April 1969.

[6] *Statesman*, 24 April 1969.

[7] *Hindustan Times,* 25 April 1969. Other vigorously contended issues at Faridabad included reorganization of the party structure in the wake of the 1967 election defeats and whether or not the Congress should form coalitions with other parties to fight the general elections due in 1972.

[8] 'To the core', *AR,* 28 May–3 June 1969, p. 8952.

the meeting. This she described as 'just some stray thoughts rather hurriedly dictated', aimed at setting to rest 'doubts ... with regard to our intentions and our willingness to take hard and difficult steps'.[9] The note's ten points included advocating 'nationalized financial institutions', more autonomy for public sector projects, appointment of a Monopolies Commission composed of 'persons of integrity', and banning big business from consumer industries. Yet, Mrs Gandhi did not commit herself entirely. In the note's narrative portion she confined herself to saying that 'perhaps we may review' the policy toward banks.

The 'Stray Thoughts Memorandum', as it has come to be called, was Mrs Gandhi's only in name. Her Principal Secretary, P. N. Haksar, had drafted it.[10] And it derived its shape and, frequently, its actual wording from a Congress Forum for Socialist Action document, 'A Note on National Economic Policies', which five CFSA members had submitted to the Working Committee before the Bangalore meeting. This note, itself, drew upon a speech CFSA leader Chandra Shekhar had given several months earlier in the hope that he could influence developments at the Faridabad Congress session.[11]

The Working Committee meeting gave the Prime Minister an empty victory. By adopting a resolution—drafted by Home Minister Y. B. Chavan

[9] For events at the Working Committee meeting, see 'Proceedings of the Working Committee Meetings Held in Bangalore,' AICC papers, Installment II, File OD 12, 1969, NMML. For the text of the Prime Minister's note, see *Revitalising Congress: Recent Speeches and Writings of Indira Gandhi*, Kalamkar Prakashan, New Delhi (undated, but 1969), pp. 7ff.

[10] According to I. K. Gujral and others, in interviews with the author. Gujral was a minister of state at the time and a member of Mrs Gandhi's 'kitchen cabinet', which he has described as 'comprised of her diverse personal friends ... [with] diverse groupings ... [among whom] she encouraged a low-voltage rivalry'. Gujral, I. K., 'Emergence of a Power Centre' in *Hindustan Times,* 14 August 1987.

The nomenclature for the Prime Minister's secretary had been changed by L. B. Shastri from Principal Private Secretary to Secretary to the Prime Minister.

[11] The speech was made in April 1969 in New Delhi to the 'Congressman's National Convention for the Implementation of Ten-Point Programme'. The burden of the speech was that the Ten-Point Programme was too 'modest' and that the struggle between 'reaction and progress has become more pronounced'.

For the texts of both the note on economic policies and the Chandra Shekhar speech, see *Young Indian,* Special Independence Number, 1972, pp. D153–55, and D145–51, respectively.

C. Subramaniam and Sadiq Ali, then a Congress General Secretary, joined Chandra Shekhar in submitting notes for the Bangalore meeting. Sadiq Ali interview with the author.

For the origins of the Congress Forum, see ch. 4.

and moved by Finance Minister Morarji Desai—giving its 'general approval' to the Stray Thoughts, it prevented the transformation of her struggle with party leaders from power to principle. She attempted to regain some ground in her address to the AICC meeting, held concurrently in Bangalore, where she proclaimed, 'The Congress may believe in socialism, but do we not have people amongst us who have decried socialism publicly and privately?'[12] Nationalizing banks might or might not be a good idea, she said, but it had become a slogan of 'radicalism', and 'it is not right to cling to slogans'. This was classic Indira Gandhi strategy: keeping her enemies on the run and her own options open.

After failing to vanquish the old guard, Mrs. Gandhi faced their counter-attack. The Presidency of India had become vacant upon the death in May 1969 of Zakir Hussain, and Vice-President V. V. Giri had become Acting President. Following the pattern since 1950, Giri would have been the Congress Party's nominee for President.[13] But Syndicate member Sanjiva Reddy, whose steadfastness to socialist values Mrs Gandhi had questioned at Faridabad, had also become a candidate. Mrs Gandhi favoured V. V. Giri, a former labour union leader she considered friendly. The Congress Parliamentary Board at Bangalore on 12 July nominated Reddy as the Congress's candidate by a vote of four to two. Syndicate members Kamaraj and Patil plus Morarji Desai voted for Reddy. Syndicate member and party president Nijalingappa abstained. For Mrs Gandhi, the bitterest pill was that her Home Minister, Chavan, voted for Reddy and her Agriculture Minister, Jagjivan Ram, abstained. Only Mrs Gandhi and F. A. Ahmed, who succeeded Giri as President of India, voted for Giri.

Furious, with Chavan in particular, Mrs Gandhi returned to Delhi bent on revenge. But, counselled during the following week by party insiders like D. P. Mishra and Uma Shankar Dikshit and by Haksar and younger activists like Mohan Kumaramangalam to give the confrontation the look of ideology and principle, she chose Morarji Desai instead of Chavan as her victim—as a symbol of the old guard who could be branded

---

12. *Revitalising Congress,* pp. 13–32.

13. The President is elected under Article 54 by an electoral college consisting of the elected members of both houses of Parliament and the elected members of state legislative assemblies using proportional representation with the single transferable vote, with the value of each assembly member's vote varying according to the population of the state.

Mrs Gandhi looked back on Zakir Hussain's election as a victory, for he had defeated K. Subba Rao, who, as Chief Justice of India, had ruled against the government in the Golak Nath case (ch. 9).

as pro-business and anti-poor. Chavan, although divested of the Home Ministry, otherwise was spared because he had a 'leftist image' plus a strong base in Maharashtra. She also picked bank nationalization as her weapon.[14] Yet it had to be used carefully. If she declared this her policy, Morarji Desai would acquiesce to nationalization. On the other hand, likely he would resign if divested of his finance portfolio. Desai received the letter relieving him of his portfolio as Finance Minister—a post Mrs Gandhi immediately assumed—soon after noon on 16 July 1969. The official announcement followed at 1:30 p.m. Desai resigned as Deputy Prime Minister on 19 July after calling upon Mrs Gandhi the day before. That evening of 19 July, Acting President V. V. Giri promulgated an ordinance nationalizing fourteen of the country's largest banks, accelerating progress toward constitutional crisis—a story told in chapter 9. In his resignation speech, Desai told members of the Lok Sabha that he had resigned so as not to be 'a silent spectator to methods that may endanger the basic principles of democracy on which our parliamentary system is established'.[15] A month later, V. V. Giri became President of India.[16]

As Mrs Gandhi continued her quest for job security, there ensued several months of virtually open warfare among individual Congressmen and factions, with marches and demarches and failed unity resolutions. Party leader Nijalingappa accused Mrs Gandhi of anti-party activities. Mrs Gandhi accused Nijalingappa of splitting the party. He told her, in your view 'all those who glorify you are progressives ... . Those ... loyal to the organization ... are reactionary and disloyal.'[17] Four

---

[14] This account is drawn from interviews with I. K. Gujral, Girish Mathur, K. C. Pant, B. N. Tandon, R. C. Dutt, Sheila Dikshit, and others.

Haksar at one point suggested that Mrs Gandhi take the finance portfolio upon Desai's departure. Seshan, N. K., *With Three Prime Ministers,* Wiley Eastern Ltd., New Delhi, 1993, pp. 98ff.

[15] The sequence of events from 16 July onwards is drawn from Desai's account of the affair to the Lok Sabha. *Lok Sabha Debates,* Fourth Series, vol. 30, no. 1, cols. 280ff.

[16] On 20–21 April 1970, Giri became the first sitting President to appear before the Supreme Court, where he testified against a petition challenging his election. The court, after hearing evidence, rejected the petition. See Part III for changes in the manner in which election petitions were to be settled.

[17] In a letter reported in *AR,* 3–9 December 1969, pp. 9264, 9267.

Mrs Gandhi's attacks on the old guard included charges that Prime Minister Shastri intended deviating from Nehru's socialism (in truth, Shastri wanted to review the government's economic policies for effectiveness) and that he had acted in a cowardly fashion during the 1965 India–Pakistan war, a calumny vehemently denied to the author by Shastri's close subordinate of the time, L. P. Singh. For a recent biography of Shastri, see Srivastava, *Lal Bahadur Shastri.* For Shastri's economic views, see especially pp. 108ff.

hundred and seven (of 703) AICC members, led by UP Congressman and party General Secretary H. N. Bahuguna, submitted a 'requisition' calling for an early AICC meeting to elect a new party president: the Prime Minister's 'enemy' had to go. On 12 November, the Working Committee under Nijalingappa removed Mrs Gandhi from primary membership in the Congress and from leadership of the Congress Parliamentary Party. The Prime Minister's faction responded with a statement saying that her removal from primary party membership was illegal, that the democratically elected parliamentary party elected its own leader, and that Indira Gandhi 'today represents the aspirations of millions of our countrymen'.[18] Eighty-four years after its birth, the Congress had split. Several days later, Mrs Gandhi's faction in Parliament—210 in the Lok Sabha and 104 in the Rajya Sabha—confirmed her leadership. But, short of a majority in both houses, she was to lead the country's first minority government, dependent upon the support of, and therefore constrained by, the CPI, DMK, and a few independents.[19]

The battle of protestations began anew. Each faction proclaimed itself to be the true Congress, supreme among the voters in its loyalty to socialism and in its ability to keep its promises. Mrs Gandhi opened her campaign by asserting that the party split was not a clash of personalities and 'certainly not a fight for power', but 'a conflict between those who are for socialism ... and those who are for the *status quo*, for conformism, and for less than full discussion inside the Congress'.[20] Newly elected faction president Jagjivan Ram's elegantly written speech at its plenary meeting in Bombay in December 1969 had a ring of sincerity—perhaps reflecting his Harijan background—as he characterized conditions in the country. 'Social tensions and the spirit of violence are on the increase,' he said. '[T]he poor half of the villages have little to

[18] *AR,* 17–23 December 1969, pp. 9285–8. For a detailed account of the Congress split, see Frankel, *Political Economy,* ch. 10.

[19] Ibid., p. 9291. The Nijalingappa faction, led in Parliament by Morarji Desai, held sixty-five seats in the Lok Sabha and forty-six in the Rajya Sabha.

CPI leader S. A. Dange remarked that his party was not satisfied with the 'mixed character' of Mrs Gandhi's ministry, but would support it as long as there was a 'rightist' threat.

[20] Dharia, Mohan and H.D. Malaviya (eds), 'Crisis in the Congress and Nation: PM's Letter to Party Members, *Souvenir—Requisitioned Meeting of AICC Members',* AICC, New Delhi, 22–3 November 1969. 'Democracy' inside the party was a major issue of the time, and Mrs Gandhi, after branding her opponents as against 'full discussion', herself opposed it.

thank anybody for ... [Z]amindars turned substantial farmers ... rule the villages ... [Congress] must pursue radical policies or disintegrate,' he said.[21]

But he offered few remedies, and none not heard before. He did sound a theme that would become familiar when he said that 'We need ... an apparatus with a purpose in mind. We need a service committed to the ideal of democracy, socialism, secularism.' A committed bureaucracy and judiciary would become the catch-phrases of the next decade. Curiously, Jagjivan Ram did not make the more common allegation against civil servants, that they were incompetent to administer economic development programmes or were actually hostile to them.

Utopian socialist rhetoric filled the Bombay session's economic policy resolution. Moved by Chavan, it said the party was 'pledged to the establishment of a casteless and classless society'. Land reform laws already enacted should be fully implemented during 1970–1 (this, in December 1969). All remaining intermediaries should be abolished by the end of 1970. Tenants should have security of tenure. Public sector enterprises were to be toned up. Licensing procedures should 'prevent the ... concentration of economic power and growth of monopolies'. Finally, three promises in the resolution that were kept: those to abolish the princes' privy purses, nationalize general insurance, and take over the wholesale trade in grains.[22]

---

[21] 'Presidential Address, by Shri Jagjivan Ram', *Indian National Congress, 73rd Plenary Session, Bombay, December 1969*, AICC, New Delhi, 1969.

During 1969, the Research and Policy Division, Ministry of Home Affairs, had prepared a paper, 'The Causes and Nature of Current Agrarian Tensions,' which Jagjivan Ram probably had seen. In twenty-nine pages it catalogued and analysed topics such as the 'serious social and economic inequalities in the rural areas ... [that have] given rise to tensions between different classes ... *satyagrahas* and forcible occupation of land' and other 'agitations' and 'widespread circumvention of the laws' by landholders. Copy in author's possession kindness of Professor Thomasson Januzzi.

[22] Policy resolution from *Indian National Congress 73rd Pleanary Session, Bombay, December 1969*, AICC, New Delhi.

The party split deprived Mrs Gandhi's faction—the Congress (R)—of the Congress's traditional offices at 7, Jantar Mantar Road, New Delhi, which the Desai faction, the Congress (O) (for 'Organization') kept for itself. The Prime Minister's party headquartered at 'Camp Office'at 15 Windsor Place. Proprietorship of the publications *Congress Bulletin* and *Reports of General Secretaries* series remained with the Congress (O). The Congress (R) (for 'Requisitionists') began a new series of publications, one of which, the *Congress Marches Ahead* series, contained extensive documentation. The first booklet in this series was entitled *From Bombay to Delhi*, AICC, New Delhi (Windsor Place), June 1970. The second was entitled *From Delhi to Patna*, AICC, New Delhi

As the Prime Minister used these promises to shore up her minority government's position, the activists in the Congress Forum for Socialist Action used her to promote their own political futures and the social revolution as they defined it. The alliance would not last, but while it did, the intentions of Mrs Gandhi and her supporters combined to produce profound changes in the Constitution affecting the integrity of the seamless web. These Congress activists especially merit our attention.

An Activist Political Generation

They were of several persuasions. Long-time Congressmen like Jagjivan Ram, Y. B. Chavan, C. Subramaniam, Dinesh Singh, Bhagwat Jha Azad, Uma Shankar Dikshit, F. A. Ahmed, and Jaisukhlal Hathi were Nehruvian socialists. Then there were those who called themselves socialists, former members of the Praja Socialist Party, who had joined the Congress in the 1960s after their party's decline—Ashoka Mehta, Ram Dhan, Chandra Shekar (later the Prime Minister), Mohan Dharia, and Krishan Kant (later Vice President). A third group consisted of those who Morarji Desai referred to as 'fellow travellers', who the socialists called 'the left' (thereby identifying themselves as in the mainstream), and who others, more precisely, named the 'ex-communists'. These included former CPI members and close sympathizers who had joined the Congress during the mid-sixties, like I. K. Gujral. Others joined the Congress much later, like Mohan Kumaramangalam in 1971, although he was close to Mrs Gandhi earlier. In between, there joined persons like Raghunatha Reddy, K. R. Ganesh, Chandrajit Yadav, Nandini Satpathy, Amrit Nahata, Nurul Hasan, and D. P. Dhar. The latter two groups and other individuals worked under the umbrella of the Congress Forum for Socialist Action.

In terms of ideology or philosophy, as much separated the three groups as united them, although all breathed the oxygen of India's political air, 'socialism'. The Nehruvians, whose life was the Congress, nourished some hopes that the social revolution could be advanced under Mrs Gandhi's leadership. In general, they did not share the

---

(Windsor Place), October 1970. *Congress Marches Ahead III* followed in April 1971, and this series ended with *Congress Marches Ahead 13* in October 1976.

The Congress (O) session, held at Gandhinagar near Ahmedabad earlier in December, was lacklustre by comparison with the Congress (R) session. Although Congress (O) leaders continued active in public life (for example, Desai became Prime Minister in 1977), the party's influence declined rapidly.

'socialists' socialism, and they thought the CFSA both pushy and too communist. The socialists had long looked to their roots in European socialism, and this made them democrats as well as believers in government control of, or very strong authority over, the means of production. A few were convinced Marxists.

The ex-communists were themselves not ideologically uniform. Although all were economic Marxists, some were also Marxist-Leninist in their admiration of the Soviet economic model, and one or two were Stalinists. For all, friendliness toward the USSR was central to their psychological and political identity, and with this went anti-Americanism. Their attitudes toward parliamentary democracy in India varied considerably. With few exceptions, they supported it, as did both Communist parties. The differences lay in the degree to which they were willing to erode constitutional practice and Indian political institutions in pursuit of their social-economic goals. The former communists, in Krishan Kant's view, would have given the Prime Minister unhindered power to implement social-economic reform. They had no love for the institution of democracy, thought Madhu Limaye. Democracy was not a way of life for them, said a journalist close to the communists. They accepted the democracy established in India, thought Sheila Dikshit, but wanted the Congress programme to be Marxism, not Gandhianism. They wanted to hold office, and they were more radical politically than the socialists, remembered I. K. Gujral.[23]

'[W]e left the CPI because Left elements in the Congress needed help ... . The Congress had become dominated by the rich, by feudalists, and by the landed,' said Chandrajit Yadav.[24] He and others were following the advice of their most prominent colleague and intellectual leader, Mohan Kumaramangalam, who would become one of the country's most influential politicians.[25] In Kumaramangalam's view, the CPI had made

---

[23] Kant, Limaye, Dikshit, and Gujral in interviews with the author.

[24] Interview with the author.

[25] S. Mohan Kumaramangalam was the son of P. Subbarayan, a Tamil Congressman prominent in the independence movement. Son Mohan was educated at the London School of Economics, where he became friendly with and charmed Indira Nehru, then briefly a student at Oxford. A 'dashing sort of person', according to a friend, he was a brilliant lawyer, and was noted for his integrity. Having been once underground and on the run as a communist, he resigned from the party when he became Advocate General of Madras state in 1966. (Some say the CPI expelled him.)

Kumaramangalam had been mentioned for appointment to the Madras High Court in 1960, but the then Chief Minister would not have a Communist on the court. Mrs Gandhi reportedly wanted him in her government in Delhi, but Morarji Desai successfully

a vast mistake in attempting to defeat the Congress, with its mass support, at the polls. That way the CPI would never be able to implement its social-economic programme. Instead, said he, the party should go to the polls as an ally of the Congress and offer to form 'National Governments' with it so that the CPI could benefit from the Congress's mass support and push the Congress toward genuine social and economic reform.[26] This was the so-called 'Kumaramangalam Thesis', and it was depicted by some as advocating the Congress's subversion. It certainly reflected Soviet tactics of the period, but given Kumaramangalam's reputation as 'an avowed Communist' (and the reputations of his associates), it was hardly a secret operation–even though the paper was circulated only privately within the CPI in 1964 and did not become public until 1973.[27] Rather than the plan of a would-be 'mole', the thesis 'reads like the strategy a liberal, non-doctrinaire communist thinker might advise his none-too-bright leaders to follow', wrote the well-known journalist, Ajit Bhattacharjea.[28] Nevertheless, the thesis was significant for the advice it offered and the fears it aroused.

Another individual of critical importance to constitutional developments was the Prime Minister's Principal Secretary, P. N. Haksar, whom we have met as the drafter of 'Stray Thoughts' and as one of those behind the defenestration of Morarji Desai. A Kashmiri from Nehru's home town, Allahabad, one-time student at the London School of

---

opposed this. Instead, the industrial magnate J. R. D. Tata made him chairman of Indian Airlines in 1969, an unpaid position. As chairman, he opposed buying Soviet passenger aircraft and supported buying American Boeings. Kumaramangalam acted as V. V. Giri's Senior Advocate when his election as President of India was challenged.

[26] Kumaramangalam, S. Mohan, *A Review of the Communist Party Policy from 1947*, Madras, 23 May 1964, pp. 18–19. (Original cyclostyled copy in the author's possession, kindness of his widow, Kalyani Kumaramangalam.) The full text of the paper purportedly was published in Singh, Satinder, *Communists in Congress: Kumaramangalam's Thesis*, D. K. Publishing House, New Delhi, 1973. But the text there is far from complete.

Kumaramangalam also wrote that he favoured a government of democratic unity because 'the class alliance to take India forward is the bourgeoisie, working class, petty-bourgeoisie, and peasantry. Congress is the political organization of the bourgeoisie; hence it must also have a place in the United Democratic Government.' *Review of Communist Party Policy*, p. 31.

[27] 'Avowed Communist': R. C. Dutt interview with the author.

Nor was Kumaramangalam's idea new. Members of the CPI joined the Congress Socialist Party in the 1930s on Soviet instructions to convert its members to the communist point of view and because they believed all socialists needed to stick together to influence the larger Congress. P. Sundarayya Oral History, pp. 83 ff, NMML.

[28] *Times of India*, 15 October 1973. Bhattacharjea was reviewing the Satinder Singh book. Bhattacharjea was at the time a close associate of Jayaprakash Narayan.

Economics, a junior colleague of Krishna Menon at the India League in London, and a lawyer, Haksar joined the Indian Foreign Service in the 1940s at Nehru's instance and in 1967 replaced L. K. Jha as Mrs Gandhi's Principal Secretary. Here he gained a much overdrawn reputation as the Prime Minister's evil genius, but powerful he was, as will be seen shortly. He contributed his views on administrative and economic issues, which were affected by 'his grounding in Marxian dialectics'.[29] Haksar became controversial particularly in regard to the slogan of 'commitment'. Likely to Mrs. Gandhi, and certainly to her detractors, 'commitment' meant loyalty to her, and only secondarily to the social goals she espoused. To the gentlemanly Haksar, the word meant commitment to the social revolutionary ideals of the Constitution, especially by his fellow civil servants, who should act with 'integrity and honesty, giving advice, not taking personal advantage and not caving in to politicians'. Bureaucrats who did not follow these precepts should be punished.[30] Haksar followed his own precepts in giving advice to the Prime Minister. 'I sometimes disagreed violently with Indira Gandhi', he remembered, and others recalled their 'shouting matches'. Indeed, she rusticated him to the Planning Commission in 1973 after he criticized Sanjay Gandhi's conduct in his Maruti automobile venture.

These individuals brought their ideas to power. Socialists by name or by viewpoint and former communists had been part of the Prime Minister's 'kitchen cabinet' (and also of what wags called her 'verandah cabinet') since 1966. Several had been ministers or risen to office in the Congress. But they vaulted to prominence and influence in 1971. The enabling event was the massive victory by Mrs Gandhi's Congress in the April parliamentary elections that year. General elections both

[29] For 'Marxian dialectics', see Sharada Prasad, H. Y., 'Vision and Warm Heart', in Sarkar, Bidyut (ed.), *P. N. Haksar, Our Times and the Man*, Allied Publishers Pvt. Ltd., New Delhi, 1989, p. 185. Sharada Prasad was the Prime Minister's information advisor. A cabinet minister of the time, C. Subramaniam, also recalls Haksar being 'a powerful factor' in economic affairs. Interview with the author. See also Awana, Ram Singh, *Pressure Politics in Congress Party*, Northern Book Centre, New Delhi, 1988, p. 78, and, especially, two books by P. N. Haksar, himself: *Premonitions* and *Reflections on Our Times*, Lancer Publications, New Delhi 1982.

[30] P. N. Haksar interview with the author. Haksar, in his fine book of thoughts and sentiments, *Premonitions*, said it was the nature of civil servants' commitment that required examination. It could not be the commitment of society to family, sub-caste, caste, community, or region. It had to be commitment to a 'new value system' marked by secularism, 'honesty, integrity and hard work as ethical compulsions', and national pride 'sustained by intellectual and spiritual self-reliance'. Ibid., pp. 201, 207.

to the Lok Sabha and state legislative assemblies had been held in 1952 and every five years thereafter under Articles 83 and 172. The next general election was due in 1972, but under the parliamentary system the legislatures or the Parliament could be dissolved sooner. Mrs Gandhi had 'delinked' elections to the Lok Sabha from those to the state legislatures in order to run by herself, in 1971, unencumbered by state issues and personalities. Her Congress(R) won 350 of the 520 seats in the Lok Sabha, gaining a two-thirds majority and leaving every other party far behind.[31] To become the acknowledged leader of the post-split Congress Party, she had campaigned on an election manifesto that promised to abolish poverty, *garibi hatao*; to amend the Constitution 'to overcome the impediments in the path of social justice'; to impose limitations on urban property; and to make the public sector dominant in industry.[32] Party officials greeted Mrs Gandhi's victory as 'a clear mandate ... to carry out the necessary constitutional amendments to narrow the gap between the haves and have nots'.[33]

The Year of the 'Socialists'

Mrs Gandhi rewarded her supporters for her solid majority in Parliament. Mohan Kumaramangalam became Minister of Steel and Heavy

[31] The Congress (O) won 16 seats, the CPM 25, the CPI and the DMK 23 each, and the Jana Sangh 22 seats. Elections were not delinked in Tamil Nadu, where Chief Minister Karunanidhi had the assembly dissolved and formed an electoral alliance with Mrs Gandhi to defeat Kamaraj.

Little noticed at the time, but later a burning political and legal issue, was the election petition charging that Mrs Gandhi had won her seat by using corrupt practices. This was filed by Raj Narain, the Samyukta Socialist Party candidate who Mrs Gandhi had defeated. (See ch. 15.)

[32] Mehta, Hemangini (ed.), *Election Manifestos, 1971*, Awake India Publications, New Delhi, 1971, ch. 7. The Congress manifesto also said that the 'lawless activities of the extreme Left and Right' were a threat to the country. The text of the manifesto is attributed to the efforts, among others, of H. D. and K. D. Malaviya, Mohan Dharia, and Chandrajit Yadav. Awana, *Pressure Politics*, p. 201. The slogan *garibi hatao* has been credited to Dev Kant Borooah (sometimes transliterated Barua), later Congress president and a fulsome praiser of Mrs Gandhi.

Socialism was the rhetoric of all (but two) of the other parties contesting the election: the Akali Dal. the two Communist parties, the Congress (O), the DMK, the PSP, and the Jana Sangh.

[33] H. N. Bahuguna, a Congress General Secretary, in the 'Foreword' of *People's Victory— An Analysis of 1971 Elections.* AICC, New Delhi, 1971. Inaugurating the new session of Parliament, President V. V. Giri also characterized the election results as 'a massive mandate for change'.

Engineering. S. S. Ray, not a socialist but eager to go along, became Minister of Education, with under him a 'left' Minister of State, Nurul Hasan. Chavan took Finance; Ahmed, Agriculture; Subramaniam (who was elected to the Lok Sabha in a subsequent by-election), Planning; and Bahuguna, Communications. A former Praja Socialist Party member and labour lawyer lately come to Congress, H. R. Gokhale, was given the Law Ministry. Eight of the twenty-two ministers of state were from the CFSA or associated with it.[34] D. P. Dhar served in the Ministry of External Affairs and as deputy chairman of the Planning Commission. More than a half-dozen fellow-thinkers held positions as secretaries of ministries or heads of semi-autonomous institutions.[35] In Parliament, there were some seventy staunch CFSA supporters (including Sashi Bhushan, Amrit Nahata, and K. P. Unnikrishnan); and Krishan Kant was secretary of the Congress Parliamentary Party.

A parallel pattern existed in the Congress Party. A Dozen of the twenty-one members of the Working Committee were CFSA members or close to them.[36] Shankar Dayal Sharma (later President of India), Yadav, and Chandra Shekhar were at some time party general secretaries. S. S. Ray, K. D. Malaviya, and Chandra Shekhar served on the Central Election Committee. In the states, CFSA members controlled, or were strong in, the Pradesh Congress committees in Mysore, Gujarat, Maharashtra, UP, Rajasthan, Bihar, Orissa, and Delhi.[37]

Secure in their power, the Prime Minister and her supporters set out to use it—they with at least her acquiescence. There began a period of radicalization of the Congress Party and of government policy. In the party, a constitution committee was formed to transform it into a cadre-based party.[38] Party workers were to receive intensive ideological

---

[34] These included Nandini Satpathy, Information and Broadcasting; K.R. Ganesh, Finance; I. K. Gujral, Works and Housing; Raghunatha Reddy, Company Affairs; Bhagwat Jha Azad, Labour; Mohan Dharia, Planning; and R. N. Mishra, Home Affairs.

[35] For example, Wadud Khan became chief of the Steel Authority of India. Others included R. C. Dutt, Ashok Mitra, P. S. Appu, Mantosh Sondhi, and T. S. Sankaran.

[36] A sampling of names: S. D. Sharma, Chavan, Ahmed, Chandra Shekhar, Chandrajit Yadav, Bahuguna, K. D. Malaviya, Satpathy, G. L. Nanda, Henry Austin, and Dinesh Singh. K. R. Ganesh had been on the committee earlier.

[37] For further information, see Frankel, *Political Economy*, pp. 462–75, Awana, *Pressure Politics*, and R. C. Dutt, *Retreat from Socialism*. The roles of the individuals named in these paragraphs have been corroborated during interviews.

[38] Yadav and R. C. Dutt interviews with the author.

At Working Committee meetings, the Prime Minister spoke in general terms of the need for 'cadres' and 'commitment' to policies that had 'received the seal of the entire nation'. *From Delhi to Patna*, AICC, New Delhi, October 1970, p. 106.

training, and a 'camp' was held at Narora with a syllabus prepared by
K. D. Malaviya, which a Youth Congress leader of the time described to
the author as 'pretty much Soviet stuff'. Rhetoric at odds with the party's
long-standing creed of 'not by class war' appeared in a draft Working
Committee resolution, which called for organizing agricultural workers
and poor peasants for 'enforcement' of agrarian reforms. The party
should mobilize the people and direct their 'justified discontent' into
'a powerful and creative weapon of social transformation'.[39] An AICC
resolution appealed to Provincial Congress Committees 'to mobilize ...
mass compulsions' to speed reform.[40]

Radicalization in government policy took several forms. Amendments
to the Constitution (to be discussed in forthcoming chapters) placed the
future of the Constitution and its Fundamental Rights in Parliament's
hands to the exclusion of the judiciary. Mohan Kumaramangalam provided the ideology and the energy for these amendments and for
large-scale nationalizations of commerce and industry.[41] Moscow-leaning
D. P. Dhar persuaded the government—against the advice of Kumara-

---

[39] Working Committee meeting of 7 October 1970. *Congress Marches Ahead III,* AICC,
New Delhi, 1971, pp. 13–14. Chandrajit Yadav was by this time a member of the Working
Committee. As a general secretary during 1972 and after, Yadav supervised the party's
'publications cell', which was staffed largely by CFSA members.

Socialist India, an organ of the CFSA edited by the radical (according to K. P.
Unnikrishnan) Iqbal Singh, appeared in May 1970.

[40] *Congress Marches Ahead IX,* AICC, New Delhi, 1973, p. 25.

[41] The government nationalized general insurance in May 1971. Between that August
and the end of 1974, some four hundred enterprises were nationalized—including shipping
and 'sick' textile concerns, steel plants, and coal and copper mines. However inefficient a
manager government would prove itself to be, many of the nationalizations were not
unreasonable in terms of the national interest in protecting the rational use of strategic
resources and the protection of industries and workers from the rapacity of managers
interested only in gains, and willing to ruin industries to get them, not in maintaining
healthy enterprises. The earlier nationalization of life insurance had been to protect citizens'
savings in a business that had become corrupt, according to P. B. Venkatasubramanian,
whereas the nationalization of general insurance was purely ideological. S. K. Maitra, of
the Law Ministry, drafted much of this nationalization legislation under Kumaramangalam—
who, he thought, was 'wedded' to Marxist theory and without business experience. Interview
with the author.

Kumaramangalam had made his views about property clear in a number of published
articles. In one, he asked if the Directive Principles could be achieved 'so long as property
remains a Fundamental Right ...'. This meant that property matters were in the hands of
judges, not Parliament. As to compensation for property taken by government, this 'is a
political and not a legal question; it cannot be assessed with reference to legal dogmas
but only to social needs'. Kumaramangalam, S. Mohan, 'Wrong to Treat Property as a
Fundamental Right', *Patriot,* 4 December 1969.

mangalam and civil servants in the Prime Minister's Secretariat—to take over the wholesale trade in wheat, only to drop the scheme a year later after it had resulted in disastrous shortages. Newspapers were to be made 'more responsive to the aspirations of the people' through a Press Bill, significantly initiated by Nandini Satpathy, Raghunatha Reddy, and R. C. Dutt. But premature publicity evoked an uproar before which Mrs. Gandhi retreated.[42] The Law Commission was 'reconstituted': one of its assignments was suggesting amendments to the Constitution that would enable government 'more effectively to implement the Directive Principles'.[43] Commission chairman, former Chief Justice of India P. B. Gajendragadkar, had been persuaded to take the job by Gokhale, Ray, and Kumaramangalam on the inducement that the government would 'informally consult me on all matters concerning constitutional amendments and the higher judiciary'.[44] Gajendragadkar was both a distinguished jurist and a believer in Parliament's authority to amend any part of the Constitution. Other members were V. R. Krishna Iyer, who had been Law Minister in the Communist government of Kerala between 1957 and 1959—and who was appointed at Kumaramangalam's instigation; and law professor P. K. Tripathi, who believed Gajendragadkar would make the commission 'an effective instrument for social change'.[45] But, as will be seen, these men would oppose one of the government's radical measures as unconstitutional.

[42] 'More responsive' was Information Minister Nandini Satpathy as quoted in the *Statesman*, 4 August 1971. At this time, Satpathy still was Minister of Information and Broadcasting and R. C. Dutt, Secretary in the ministry; Reddy was Minister of State for Company Affairs. According to I. K. Gujral, P. N. Haksar favoured the bill and was angry with Gujral when he, having replaced Satpathy as minister, opposed it because it would destroy the credibility of the Indian press. Interviews with R. C. Dutt and I. K. Gujral.

[43] Terms of Reference in P. B. Gajendragadkar Papers, NMML.

[44] Gajendragadkar letter to Indira Gandhi dated 24 August 1977. Ibid. He would leave the commission disappointed.

[45] P. K. Tripathi letter to Gajendragadkar dated 23 September 1971. Ibid.

As chairman, Gajendragadkar involved the commission in analysis of a wide variety of legal issues and championed the status, conditions of service, and independence of the judiciary with the Prime Minister. See his letter to Indira Gandhi of 4 February 1974, ibid.

Gajendragadkar wrote to the Prime Minister that he had met with his friends Kumaramangalam, Nurul Hasan, and H. R. Gokhale, and we 'are anxious to help you ... in the historic task which you have undertaken ... to create a new secular, social order in the light of the Directive Principles of our Constitution'. Letter dated 13 April 1972, ibid. At times, Gajendragadkar's tone with Mrs Gandhi seems fulsome. He wrote on 19 December 1971 of 'the inspired and superb lead you gave the nation ... . Your letter to President Nixon is a masterpiece,' etc. Ibid.

The Congress's victories in the state assembly elections in the spring of 1972—due to India's victory over Pakistan in December 1971, to Mrs Gandhi's brilliantly executed policy, and, again, to her rhetoric and charisma—added to her large majority in Parliament from the 1971 elections. Now, the Prime Minister no longer needed the Congress Forum to assure her dominance of both party and government.[46] And, sensing in it a competitor for power, she set out in May 1972 to cripple it. Loyalists like S. D. Sharma and Uma Shankar Dikshit let it be known that she favoured setting up a counter organization, which produced the Nehru Forum. It and the Congress Forum exchanged rhetorical arrows, giving the Working Committee justification for disbanding both.[47] Death dealt the activists their devastating setback: Mohan Kumaramangalam was killed in an air crash on 31 May 1973.

The Migration of Power

Indira Gandhi grew powerful, after her inauspicious first two years, from the authority inherent in the Prime Minister's office; from her political skills and her personality—both charismatic and steely; from propitious circumstances; and from these in combination. As Prime Minister, she chaired the Political Affairs and Economic Affairs Committees of the Cabinet and the Planning Commission. She reorganized the functions of the Cabinet Secretariat and the Prime Minister's Secretariat (PMS, later called the Prime Minister's Office, PMO) and the relationship between them. To the Cabinet Secretariat she moved external intelligence operations (the so-called Research and Analysis Wing, RAW) split off from the domestic intelligence organization, which was the Intelligence Bureau or IB. This remained in the Home Ministry. On the recommendation of the Administrative Reforms Commission, she transferred control of the civil service from its traditional location in the Home Ministry into a new Department of Personnel in the PMS, to which she also transferred responsibility for the Central Bureau of Investigation (CBI). A minister of state was placed in charge of the new department

---

[46] In the assembly elections the Congress won from 52 to 83 per cent of the seats in all but three small states and Tamil Nadu, where assembly elections had been held in 1971.

[47] The Congress Parliamentary Board, meeting on 3 April, and noting the 'controversy' between the two groups, decided that no forums were needed because the party was pursuing its policy of democratic socialism. *Report of the General Secretaries, June 1972–August 1973*, AICC, New Delhi, 1973, pp. 11–2.

Mrs Gandhi also let it be known that she regarded the CFSA 'as dominated by former Communists'. Dutt, *Retreat from Socialism*, p. 90.

under a cabinet minister, who happened to be Indira Gandhi. This gave her direct control over criminal investigations. The Central Bureau of Investigation remains under the Prime Minister's Office, after having been returned briefly to the Home Ministry under Janata. Revenue intelligence and the Directorate of Enforcement, both established under the Foreign Exchange Regulation Act, were transferred from the Finance Ministry to the PMS, according to one source, and to the Cabinet Secretariat, according to another.[48] Co-ordination of judicial appointments was moved in 1971 from the Home Ministry to a new Department of Justice in the Law Ministry—whose chief staff member nevertheless was the Home Secretary. The legal community seems to have approved at least the cosmetic degree of dissociation of judicial appointments from the Home Ministry, and, within it, from the Intelligence Bureau.'[49]

All in all, Mrs Gandhi's 'structural changes', in the view of L. P. Singh, 'ignored the salutory value of checks and balances within the system; the changes were designed to remove any internal constraints, however wisely conceived, on the exercise of the Prime Minister's will.'[50]

As Mrs Gandhi's Principal Secretary from 1967 to 1973, P. N. Haksar's oversight of governmental affairs was as extensive as it was demanding. Seen along with Mrs Gandhi as the embodiment of centralization, he was correspondingly reviled. To inject energy and efficiency into government and, as already mentioned, to bring 'commitment' to the social-economic goals of the Constitution, he 'took full charge of the Secretariat and made it the main focus of power ... . He was soon emerging as her main political adviser as well.'[51]

[48] To the Cabinet Secretariat: the *Hindustan Times*, 13 April 1977; to the PMS: Gujral, I. K., 'Emergence of a Power Centre' in *Hindustan Times*, 14 August 1987. Nirmal Mukarji, Cabinet Secretary in the Janata government says the two revenue offices were never moved at all. (Mukarji in a letter to the author.) It may be that the organizations were not moved but that the Prime Minister controlled their functioning.

[49] Perhaps making for increased centralization of the judicial appointments process under the rearrangement, a minister of state was said to report directly to the PMS about them. Panandiker, V. A. Pai and Mehra, Ajoy K., *The Indian Cabinet: A Study in Governance*, Centre for Policy Research, Konark Publishers Pvt. Ltd., New Delhi, 1996, p. 226. Given Mrs Gandhi's final decision on the appointment of judges, these may be subtleties with limited significance.

[50] Singh, L. P., *Office of Prime Minister, Retrospect and Prospect*, Centre for Policy Research, New Delhi, 1995, p. 9.

[51] Gujral, 'Emerging Power Centre'. Gujral notes that 'even when presiding over his all-powerful secretariat', Haksar kept his distance from the coterie around Sanjay Gandhi.
He 'alone held the key' and made a 'monumental contribution' to the Congress split, the Indo-Soviet Treaty, the birth of Bangladesh, and the Simla Agreement. K. Natwar Singh, 'Foreword' in Sarkar, *Haksar*, p. 19.

Haksar's and the PMS's authority relegated the Cabinet Secretariat and its Secretary to near obscurity, the former having taken over the latter's function as coordinator of cabinet business on its way to the Prime Minister. This also greatly reduced the Cabinet Secretary's responsibility—if not his authority as the senior-most civil servant and head of the civil service—for processing senior civil service appointments on their way to the cabinet. Because both the Cabinet Secretary and the Principal Secretary work directly for the Prime Minister, shifts of power between the two offices are not necessarily consequential. But the Cabinet Secretary has institutional, government-wide responsibilities not shared by the Principal Secretary. Downgrading the Cabinet Secretary's position was part of Mrs Gandhi's personalization of power.

The Prime Minister's Secretariat had become a 'power centre' that 'the politicians, bureaucrats and ... industrial barons courted ... for favours and patronage,' according to I.K. Gujral. It even decided about 'the composition of the party high command', he recalled.[52] 'The turning point' toward this concentration of communication and power in Mrs Gandhi's hands was 1967, according to all the individuals queried by Panandiker and Mehra in their study of the cabinet.[53] The 'watershed' was 1971, when the 'Cabinet Secretariat was completely relegated into insignificance and even ministers were subordinated to the PM's Secretariat'.[54]

With her aggrandizement of authority so thorough, the Prime Minister was hardly in a position to claim, although she often did so, that she was a mere bystander to governmental and Congress Party developments. In defence of Mrs Gandhi's centralization of power, Professor P. N. Dhar, who succeeded Haksar as her Principal Secretary in 1973, points out that 'the concept of the collegiate system of the cabinet' has been 'obsolete' even in England for more than a century. And he correctly points out, also, that some characteristics of Indian culture foster centralization of authority. (See chapter 31.) He adds that the Prime Minister and his or her establishment in the future will have to make 'a self-conscious effort' against the tendency toward centralization.[55]

[52] Gujral, 'Emergence of a Power Centre'.

[53] Panandiker and Mehra, *The Indian Cabinet*, p. 207.

[54] Ibid. This was the view of one respondent, according to the authors, but it has been confirmed directly to the author by many others in interviews. The study goes on to say that after 1971 'all established political institutions were undermined as she chose to function through small cliques'. Ibid., p. 223.

[55] Dhar, P. N., 'The Prime Minister's Office' in Sarkar, *Haksar, Our Times*, pp. 48–61. As Principal Secretary, Dhar was more the secretary and less the mover and shaker than Haksar.

During her first several years as Prime Minister Mrs Gandhi used her 'kitchen cabinet' as advisors in competition with her council of ministers. I. K. Gujral, a sometime member of the kitchen cabinet and of the council of ministers, says that official papers were routed through two kitchen cabinet members, himself and Dinesh Singh—a young acolyte of Mrs Gandhi assigned to the Foreign Ministry—to bypass her own secretariat.[56] By the end of 1970, the 'kitchen cabinet' had fallen from grace. Government was entering the period during which, according to a recent study, Sanjay Gandhi and his caucus 'had virtually hijacked the goverment' and real power shifted from the PMS to the 'PMH', the Prime Minister's house.[57]

Of Mrs Gandhi's circumstances, she was responsible for the three most propitious. She had led the Congress to the two great election victories of 1971 and 1972 and during the victory over Pakistan in December 1971. The success of her policy in the war (which included not invading West Pakistan after its December attacks on western India), had elevated Mrs Gandhi to the level of 'an omnipotent Mother Goddess—who had protected her people and liberated another from the forces of evil'.[58] But with India–Pakistan hostilities also had come the ultimate in constitutional centralization, the second national emergency, which her government continued in force for six years—long after the conditions for which it was imposed had disappeared. She already had reintroduced preventive detention in May 1971 with the Maintenance of Internal Security Act (MISA). Justifying this law, Minister of State for Home Affairs K. C. Pant said that security and integrity had to be protected against foreigners and other 'black sheep' in the country.[59] Opponents of the act thought it 'the beginning of a police raj' and 'the first step toward dictatorship'.[60]

---

[56] Gujral, 'Emergence of a Power Centre'.

[57] Panandiker and Mehra, *Indian Cabinet*, p. 227.

[58] Masani, Zareer, *Indira Gandhi, a Biography,* cited in Frankel, *Political Economy*, p. 461.

[59] The CPI (Marxist-Leninist), or CPI (ML), had been formed in April 1969 and was more Maoist than Leninist. Called 'Naxalites', from the region in Bengal where they originated, their tactics included killing villagers and government officials. The party was 'based on the theory of armed insurrection', according to the Parliament's Consultative Committee for the Ministry of Home Affairs. Brahmanand Papers, Subject File No. 40, 1969, NMML.

[60] A. B. Vajpayee of the Jana Sangh in *Motherland*, a paper backed by the party, 17 June 1971. The Swatantra Party and the CPM also damned the law.

The previous Preventive Detention Act had lapsed on 31 December 1969. Lacking the votes of opposition parties upon which her government depended, Mrs Gandhi then did not attempt to re-enact it. By 1973, the Home Ministry was urging chief ministers to

Although politically secure from 1971 onwards as she never had been, Mrs Gandhi moved away from constitutionalism toward absolutism. Aware of her people's adoration, she came to believe that she had the 'divine right of support'.[61] Suspicious of the courtiers in party and government who surrounded her, her attitude was 'if you oppose me, you are an enemy'.[62] As a result, ministers, chief ministers, and party officials did not assert themselves. Opposition parties and leaders were not political opponents, but anti-national forces. Feeling alone, power was her comfort, that and her two sons. '[T]here is hardly anybody to whom one can go to talk or to ask advice—ulterior motives are attributed even for a chance remark,' she wrote to T. T. Krishnamachari.[63] Her ruling style was to listen, keep her counsel, and act through others by hint and indirection. She preferred to lead from behind.

In combination, these factors led to the virtually one-person rule of 1971–7, during which her government first challenged and then subverted constitutional democracy. Owing their elections to her, chief ministers depended on her continuing favour. And she appeared to be 'deliberately manipulating Congress factionalism to prevent a healthy consolidation of power in the states'.[64] Congress Party officials were in a similar situation, and she had fulsome supporters Shankar Dayal Sharma and Dev Kanta Borooah elected party president at different times.

---

use the Maintenance of Internal Security Act against hoarders and other economic offenders.

[61] Ashoka Mehta Oral History Transcript, NMML, p. 205.

[62] Jagmohan in an interview with the author. Jagmohan's assessment, although not unusual, is particularly interesting because he continues to admire Indira and Sanjay Gandhi with whom he worked closely on Delhi development from1975–7. According to Jagmohan, Nehru forgave opposition, Indira Gandhi never did. 'She was not as temperamental as Nehru,' he said; 'she kept it inside.'

[63] Handwritten note dated 25 October 1965 in which she also thanks Krishnamachari for sending her an attache case. T. T. Krishnamachari Papers, File Indira Gandhi, NMML. Mrs Gandhi expressed a similar sentiment in a letter to Justice P. B. Gajendragadkar on 2 January 1977: 'The sort of life I have led since childhood has not allowed me to have what you call "a select circle of personal friends."' P. B. Gajendragadkar Papers, Subject File 1, NMML.

[64] Kochanek, Stanley A., 'Mrs Gandhi's Pyramid: the New Congress', in Hart, Henry C. (ed.), *Indira Gandhi's India*, Westview Press, Colorado, 1976, p. 111. The first quotation is Kochanek citing Romesh Thapar; the second is Kochanek, himself.

See also Seshan, *Three Prime Ministers*, ch. 31.

The critiques of the over centralization of the federal system that had appeared from time to time since 1950 were joined in 1971 by a serious study published by the Tamil Nadu government usually referred to as the Rajamannar Report. (See ch. 28 and other chapters in Part VI.)

Her domination of Congress members in Parliament, most of whom also owed their seats to her political skills, evolved to the point described by Sir Ivor Jennings: "'The flexibility of the cabinet system allows the Prime Minister to take upon himself a power not inferior to that of a dictator, provided always that the House of Commons will stand by him.'"[65] The Lok Sabha barely objected to her aggrandizement of power, and with her ministers subdued, constitutional power migrated from the voter to his legislator to the council of ministers and then to the Prime Minister. Mrs Gandhi had gone from vulnerability to the political system to mastery of it. The consequences progressively would become apparent.

---

[65] Jennings, Sir Ivor, *Cabinet Government*, 2nd edn., Cambridge University Press, Cambridge, 1951, p. 166. Jennings was quoting Lord Morley.

Chapter 8

THE GOLAK NATH INHERITANCE

Held in disgrace by his Kuleen Brahmin family for having converted to Christianity, Golak Nath Chatterji left Bengal in the mid-nineteenth century and walked across North India to the Punjab, where he joined the Scottish American Presbyterian Mission in Jalandhar. There, he became the first Indian in the country to be ordained as a Presbyterian minister, and he married a Kashmiri girl at the mission. Among their many children was Henry Golak Nath, who, after receiving his divinity degree in 1879 from Princeton Theological Seminary in the United States, returned to take his father's place as a minister. Expanding beyond the house and small plot of land given him by the mission, Henry, with his brother William, bought up some five hundred acres of farmland over the years. The dispute between the family and the Punjab government over the disposition of this property went to the Supreme Court to become the watershed Golak Nath case.[1]

Henry and William held the land jointly and, wanting to keep it in the family in the face of the 1953 Punjab Security of Land Tenures Act, deeded it to Henry's son and daughter, Inder C. and Indira Golak Nath and to Inder's four daughters. But this went awry. The Collector for Jalandhar held that Henry and his brother each could keep only thirty acres, a few acres would go to tenants, and the rest was 'surplus'. Years later, after Henry's death in 1962, aged 101, the Collector reversed his earlier decision, allotting thirty acres to each of the six heirs and declaring a smaller area to be surplus. His decision, in turn, was reversed by another Collector in 1963. In May 1965, the Punjab Financial Commissioner in Chandigarh, B. S. Grewal, restored an earlier decision, and declared 418 acres surplus. Inder Golak Nath and the other heirs, inheriting only thirty acres, to be shared among them, challenged Grewal's ruling in the Punjab High Court in October 1965. Failing there, they took their cause to the

---

[1] The author is grateful to sometime Punjab civil servant Prem Kathpalia, to Mrs Jaya Thadani, a descendant of the family, and to E. N. Mangat Rai, a family relative, for this and other background—a piece of which is that Henry Golak Nath wrote a book about his father entitled *Golak The Hero*.

Supreme Court.[2] They filed a petition under Article 32 challenging the 1953 Punjab Act on the ground that it denied them their constitutional rights to acquire and hold property and practice any profession (Articles 19(f) and (g)) and to equality before and equal protection of the law (Article 14). They also sought to have the Seventeenth Amendment—which had placed the Punjab Act in the Ninth Schedule—declared *ultra vires* and the First and Fourth Amendments as well. Inheriting a history of land reform legislation and judicial review of it going back to the Constitution's inauguration and to the property amendments of 1951 and 1954, the Golak Naths gave their name to a law case that raised a storm whose dust hung over the Constitution for six years.

Sowing the Wind

The Supreme Court, in its decision in the Golak Nath case on 27 February 1967, held that Parliament's power to amend the Constitution could not be used to abridge the Fundamental Rights, in part because an amendment was deemed to be a 'law' under Article 13 which prohibited Parliament from making any law abridging the Rights. Chief Justice Koka Subba Rao, in his opinion for the majority, also invoked the concept of implied limitations on the amending power. This precluded amendments that would destroy a constitution—about which more below. Justices Wanchoo, Bhargava, and Mitter dissented. They held that all parts of the Constitution are subject to amendment, and that an amendment is not a 'law' under Article 13. Delivering the opinion for himself and the other two, Wanchoo also rejected the contention that certain portions of a constitution could be too basic to be amended. Were this admitted, 'it would be only the courts which would have the power to decide what are the basic features of the Constitution,' and this would result in a 'harvest of legal wrangles'.[3]

---

[2] To this point, the account is drawn from interviews and from a document signed by B. S. Grewal ('R. O. R. No. 1181 of 1963–4—Sahan Singh, etc. v the Punjab State and I. C. Golak Nath, etc.'). A copy of this document was obtained for the author from Punjab state records by Prem Kathpalia. From here onward, the account is drawn from Merillat, *Land*, pp. 235–6.

[3] *I.C. Golak Nath and Others, Petitioners v State of Punjab and Another* 1967 (2) SCR 763ff. On the bench were K. Subba Rao, K. N. Wanchoo, M. Hidayatullah, J. C. Shah, S. M. Sikri, R. S. Bachawat, V. Ramaswami, J. M. Shelat, V. Bhargava, G. K. Mitter, and C. A. Vaidialingam. Concurring with Subba Rao were Justices Shah, Sikri, Shelat, and Vaidialingam. Justice Hidayatullah concurred on the operation of Article 13 to make up the majority. Chief Justice Subba Rao had been a Justice of Madras High Court and chief justice of the Andhra High Court

The Court's decision, which reversed precedents, was a masterpiece of unintentional timing, for it gave Mrs Gandhi a cause and an enemy in her quest for renewed power. Within several days of the decision, Congress would learn of its serious losses in the general election, and she would have to face election to continue as leader of the Congress Parliamentary Party. Socialism in danger was her central political refrain, and it would be her key to victory. Not only had the Supreme Court again, from her viewpoint, shown its true colours but also Congress's own devotion to socialism had been shown flawed by the Dhebar Committee's report on the implementation of the democracy and socialism resolution (chapter 4), by Prime Minister Shastri's allegedly anti-socialist reappraisal of the government's economic policy, and by the party's own post-mortem following the election defeats. The 'Ten Point Programme', announced after the post-mortem, set the government on a collision course with the judiciary, because its socialism could not be realized without modification in the right to property. All of this she could turn to her personal advantage as she out-manouvered the old guard by branding them anti-socialist. Thus the Golak Nath case began the great war, as distinct from earlier skirmishes, over parliamentary versus judicial supremacy. It gave fresh life to the issue of property and the Constitution, which had run, and would continue to run, insistently through decades of Indian politics.

Yet in a remarkable twist, the most significant element of the case constitutionally would prove to be not the majority decision, but the

---

The opinion given by Subba Rao also contained the strange assertion that Parliament's authority to amend the Constitution lay not in Article 368, which provided only the *mechanism* for amendment, but in those articles giving the power to make laws. Hidayatullah disagreed with Subba Rao on this remarkable interpretation of the Constitution and agreed with Wanchoo that the amending power lay in Article 368. Ibid., p. 836.

That an amendment should be considered a 'law' within the meaning of Article 13 seems strange to the author: an amendment and an ordinary law, constitutionally speaking, would seem to have superior and inferior status. N. A. Palkhivala argued strongly in Golak Nath that an amendment was a 'law'. When asked if this was merely a lawyerly argument, he responded that he never put forward an argument in which he did not believe. (Interview with the author.) That this issue—whether or not a constitutional amendment was a 'law' under Article 13—apparently remained undecided, a legacy of the Shankari Prasad and Sajjan Singh cases. In Shankari Prasad, though, the Court had rejected the contention that an amendment was a law. See Merillat, *Land,* p. 242.

Representing the government in the case was Additional Solicitor General Niren De, with assists from intervenors who included Mohan Kumaramangalam, then Advocate General of Madras. Other Advocates General participated from states where landholders had joined the Golak Naths in their suit. Lawyers for the Golak Naths were R. V. S. Mani and others assisted by prominent intervenors, including N. A. Palkhivala, M. K. Nambiar, A. K. Sen, and F. S. Nariman.

introduction in the hearings by the Golak Naths' advocates, principally M. K. Nambiar, of the 'basic structure' concept. Hoping to defend their property interests by attacking the Seventeenth Amendment, they asserted that the word 'amendment' implied an addition to the Constitution that improves or better carries out its purpose and 'cannot be so construed as to enable the Parliament to destroy the permanent character of the Constitution'.[4] Moreover, 'the fundamental rights are a part of the basic structure of the Constitution', and the amending power could be 'exercised only to preserve rather than destroy the essence of those rights'.[5]

The government of India argued from positions taken earlier, establishing even more firmly the foundations for its arguments in later great property cases. Constitutional amendments were made from 'political necessity', the government asserted, involving the exercise of power to improve the lot of the citizen. Not being judicial questions, they lay outside the court's jurisdiction. It was up to the petitioners, government contended, to show that the Constitution could not be amended in order to enforce the Directive Principles, something that had been done previously—a reference to the First, Fourth, and other amendments. No implied limitations to the amending power could be found in Article 368, 'and if the amending power is restricted by implied limitations, the Constitution itself might be destroyed by revolution. Indeed it [the amending power] is a safety valve and an alternative for a violent change by revolution,' the government contended. Moreover, all the Constitution's provisions are basic.[6]

The Chief Justice from the beginning had been very much at the centre of the Golak Nath case. Several senior advocates involved recalled that when a five-judge bench held a hearing on admitting the heirs' petition, he seized on it and said it should be heard by an eleven-judge bench. Five-judge benches in Shankari Prasad and Sajjan Singh had upheld Parliament's power to amend the Fundamental Rights. Subba Rao expressed his primary motivation in what came to be called 'the argument of fear'. For him, many of the freedoms in the Fundamental Rights had been taken away or abridged since 1950. He characterized the continuance in force of the national emergency of 1962—with its

---

[4] A. K. Sen, now helping to represent the Golak Naths, had piloted the Seventeenth Amendment in the Lok Sabha when he was the Law Minister.

[5] From Chief Justice Subba Rao's summary of the petitioners' positions. 1967 (2) SCR 781.

[6] Again, Chief Justice Subba Rao's summation, ibid., p. 783.

suspension of Fundamental Rights Articles 14, 19, 21, and 22—as 'constitutional despotism'. Commenting on an earlier Supreme Court decision that corporations were not legal 'citizens' and therefore were not protected by the Rights, he said that citizens have 'practically no right to property against legislative action ...'.[7] Subba Rao feared future damage to the Rights: without Nehru, the 'brute majority', a term he had been heard to use outside the Court, might change the quality of one-party rule.[8] Believing that a constitution is to be worked 'and not to be destroyed', Subba Rao wanted to bring government under greater judicial scrutiny, according to senior advocates familiar with his thinking. It was in this vein that he reversed the precedents in Shankari Prasad and Sajjan Singh—which, it will be recalled, upheld Parliament's authority to amend the constitution, including the Fundamental Rights.[9] Justice Hidayatullah shared some of Subba Rao's fears. 'I am apprehensive that the erosion of the right to property may be practised against other Fundamental Rights,' he said. 'Small inroads lead to larger inroads.'[10] Justice Wanchoo, on the other hand, found the 'argument of fear' a political argument, not a legal argument. There could be no limitation

[7] For this and other quotations here, see 'Freedoms in Free India', speech at Nagpur University College of Law, 23 September 1967. *AIR* (1968), Journal Section, p. 21.

[8] The Golak Nath decision was delivered just before the Congress lost its 'brute majority' in the 1967 general elections. Some have speculated that, had Congress losses been known, the Court might have ruled differently.

[9] *Shankar Prasad Deo v Union of India* (1952) *SCR* 3, pp. 89ff; *Sajjan Singh v State of Rajasthan* 1965 (1) SCR 933ff, as cited earlier. The five-judge bench in the former case unanimously had held that 'law' in Article 13 meant ordinary law.

Subba Rao's anxieties over the future of parliamentary democracy and the rule of law were also probably fuelled by two developments: by the government nationalizing the Metal Box Corporation by ordinance in September 1966, eight days after the Court had struck down an act nationalizing the corporation, and by the government's proposing to include, via the Seventeenth Amendment, over a hundred state land laws in the Ninth Schedule without members of Parliament having had the opportunity to read them.

Subba Rao further clarified his views several years later. The judiciary, he said, has to decide 'the permissible limits of the laws of social control'. And as to the government's relations with the judiciary, 'Autocratic power finds the judicial check irksome and seeks to explain away its incompetency or neglect of duty by posing an inflexible and irreconcilable conflict between the fundamental rights and directive principles.' Address to the Fundamental Rights Front on 30 August 1970. *Presidential Address and Other Papers for the Convention*, A. P. Jain, New Delhi, 1970, p. 13.

[10] This is according to Setalvad in *My Life, Law and Other Things*, N. M. Tripathi Pvt. Ltd., Bombay, p. 587. But Hidayatullah also thought the Court should recognize the social and economic needs of the hour. And he wondered if it had been a mistake to include property in the Fundamental Rights. Ibid.

on the power of amendment under Article 368 on the ground that the power might be abused.

Subba Rao explained at length in his opinion that there were limitations on the power of amendment in the Indian Constitution. Specifically, the Fundamental Rights were entrenched, having been 'given a transcendental position under our Constitution and are kept beyond the reach of Parliament'.[11] In support of this position, he cited the views of Motilal and Jawaharlal Nehru and a variety of American jurists.[12] He also was influenced, according to senior advocates in the case, by a German scholar, Dieter Conrad, who believed that written constitutions have in them implied limitations on amendment and judges should use these to protect the constitution. Conrad had given a lecture in India in 1965 on the 'Implied Limitations of the Amending Power', which M. K. Nambiar cited before the court.[13]

The Chief Justice's efforts to gain the majority he ultimately received were helped by circumstance as well as by his forceful argument. At the time, Justices Hidayatullah and Wanchoo were the only justices still on the Court who had been on the bench two years earlier when the Court had upheld the Seventeenth Amendment and Parliament's power to amend the Fundamental Rights in the Sajjan Singh case. Also, Justice Vaidialingam was newly come to the court, and he and Subba Rao had served in the same chambers as advocates before the Madras High Court. To these advantages may be added his 'enormous intellectual influence with his fellow judges'.[14] Indeed, Subba Rao's stature, plus the quality of the Golak Naths' advocates, aroused fears of defeat on the government side. Law Minister P. Govinda Menon dispatched Law Secretary R. S. Gae to ask M. C. Setalvad's counsel on the conduct of the case and to sound him out about taking over the government's brief. Setalvad refused, explaining that he never entered a case while it was in progress.[15]

---

[11] AIR 1967 SC 1656.

[12] He also cited the assessment of Austin, *Cornerstone*.

[13] Noorani, A. G., 'The Supreme Court and Constitutional Amendments' in Noorani, A. G. (ed.), *Public Law in India*, Vikas Publishing House Pvt. Ltd., New Delhi 1982, pp. 278–9.

Conrad had said that it is the 'duty of the jurist ... to anticipate extreme cases of conflict' between a legislature and a judiciary in which the judiciary would need to reject an amendment as destroying a constitution. What, Conrad asked, if a two-thirds majority of Parliament divided India into two states, Tamil Nadu and Hindustan? Ibid.

[14] The view of several judges on the bench as recalled by senior advocates.

[15] Setalvad, *My Life*, p. 583. Later, he would turn down a similar request from Mrs Gandhi, relayed to him by M. C. Chagla.

Subba Rao was aware that the position toward which the majority of justices was moving would shake the foundations of seventeen years of constitutional practice and call into question the validity of at least three constitutional amendments and the constitutionality of the sixty-odd state laws listed in the Ninth Schedule. So, rather than tossing out all this, which would produce a 'chaotic situation', Subba Rao decided to exercise 'judicial restraint'.[16] He found a saving device in 'prospective over-ruling': the relevant, existing laws and amendments were deemed valid on the basis of previous court decisions, but Parliament would have no power 'from the date of this decision to amend any of the provisions of Part III of the Constitution so as to take away or abridge the fundamental rights enshrined therein'.[17]

Reaping the Whirlwind

Subba Rao, it was said more often than not, had gone too far. In his determination to save the Constitution he had provoked what he intended to prevent: increased parliamentary authority to amend the Constitution and a Parliament strengthened at the expense of the Supreme Court. Five weeks after he had handed down the decision, Samyukta Socialist Party (SSP) member of Parliament Nath Pai introduced a private member's bill for easy amendment of the Constitution. Because of government caution, it ultimately failed to pass, but it was the foundation for the Twenty-fourth Amendment, which, depending on one's point of view, would give or restore to Parliament unfettered authority to amend the Constitution, including its repeal. Subba Rao further fuelled the reaction against the Golak Nath decision by resigning as Chief Justice on 11 April 1967 to run for president of India, evoking allegations that this proved his alliance with property interests, which Swatantra Party support for his candidacy did nothing to refute.[18]

[16] In his opinion in *Golak Nath. AIR* 1967 SC 1669.

[17] Ibid. Subba Rao attributed this 'doctrine' to American jurists. He cited Benjamin Cardozo and George F. Canfield among others. Canfield: "'A Court should recognize a duty to announce a new and better rule for future transactions whenever the court has reached the conviction that an old rule ... is unsound even though feeling compelled by *stare decisis* to apply the old and condemned rule to the instance case and to transactions which had already taken place."' Ibid., p. 1666.

[18] M. C. Setalvad spoke for many when he issued a statement to the press calling Subba Rao's joining politics a 'grave impropriety', particularly because he apparently had agreed to be the Opposition's candidate while still Chief Justice. Subba Rao lost to Zakir Hussain, who became President on 13 May. Setalvad, *My Life*, pp. 593–4. Justice Wanchoo became Chief Justice upon Subba Rao's resignation.

Nath Pai's bill said simply that Parliament could amend 'any provision' of the Constitution. He made his purpose clear in the formal 'Statement of Objects and Reasons' accompanying the bill and repeated this in his introductory speech. The amendment of the Fundamental Rights was an issue 'of cardinal importance to the supremacy of Parliament', especially due to the confusion created by the Golak Nath decision. Just as Parliament can extend these rights, 'it can in special circumstances also modify them. The bill seeks to assert this ...'.[19] The bill raised constitutional issues as elemental as the Supreme Court judgement. Parliament and the public debated them intensely and soberly during the following two years. Those favouring the bill thought it timely and necessary to permit forward movement on social-economic issues. Those opposing it thought it a 'disastrous' amendment because it 'tends to snuff out democracy'. The Swatantra Party did not wish even to be represented on the Joint Committee of both Houses that was formed to consider the bill, although Nath Pai wanted to have 'the benefit of their disagreements'. 'We do not want to have anything to do with it,' said Minoo Masani. The Jana Sangh also refused to join the committee, and its parliamentary leader, Atal Bihari Vajpayee (later Prime Minister of India), said the republic would be strengthened by the verdict of the Supreme Court.

The most vehement objections came from Nath Pai's parliamentary socialist colleagues, Rammanohar Lohia and Madhu Limaye. Lohia's were prescient, as time would tell. 'All the Nath Pai bill needs is "We hereby resolve that this Constitution be suspended and in its place ..."' he said, going on to cite Article 48 in the Weimar Constitution, which allowed for that constitution's suspension. Under this article, Hitler had the Reichstag

---

Editorial reaction in the press to Golak Nath was extensive and mixed. The common sentiment was that the Fundamental Rights were sacred, and thus the 'ruling party with the aid of a brute majority' could not ram through constitutional amendments (*Hindustan Times*, 1 March 1967) and that the decision introduced a 'rigidity in the Constitution' that might be unwise. *Statesman*, New Delhi, 1 March 1967.

[19] Speech of 9 June 1967. *Lok Sabha Debates* Fourth Series, vol. 4, no. 14, col. 4223. The Nath Pai Bill was No. 10 of 1967, dated 7 April 1967. A member of Parliament since 1957 and a sometime advocate in the Bombay High Court, Nath Pai had a lifetime's involvement in socialist issues. While studying in England, he had organized the Indian Socialist Group in 1950. Later, an active trade unionist, he supported adding 'the right to work' to the Fundamental Rights. Fellow socialist Prem Bhasin wrote of his 'bewitching smile', 'transparent sincerity', and 'undying faith in democratic socialism'. Bhasin, Prem, 'The Deathly Drama', *Janata*, Annual Number, 1971, pp. 5ff.

Several weeks earlier, MP Yashpal Singh introduced a private member's bill calling for ratification by the states of any amendment to the Fundamental Rights.

pass the so-called 'Enabling Law', or the 'Law for Removing the Distress of People and Reich', the constitutional foundation upon which he based his dictatorship.[20] The socialists and communists in India could suffer the 'catastrophe' of those in Germany, said Lohia, who had received his doctorate from Berlin University in 1933, and he asked Nath Pai to withdraw his bill. With equal fervour, Limaye asserted that 'no parliament or assembly in any country has the right to change the basic principles of the country and the Constitution because we all work within the ambit of the Constitution.' Parliament 'cannot snatch away the rights of the common people'. Both Lohia and Limaye favoured removing property from the Fundamental Rights in order to protect the other rights, and Limaye thought the Supreme Court had opened the door for this.[21]

The government liked Nath Pai's bill but treated it cautiously. Although it was not an official bill sponsored by the government, Law Minister Govinda Menon called it important and moved that it go to a Joint Select Committee to be considered in 'a very cool atmosphere'. The Supreme Court had ruled that Parliament could not amend the Fundamental Rights, Menon said, but it did not say that Parliament could not amend the amending article. The government would quietly support the bill over many months without finding a propitious moment to push it through. Deputy Prime Minister Morarji Desai told Madhu Limaye that ' "We would have liked to move such a bill ourselves, but Nath Pai got there first, and we decided to support it." '[22]

Public debate over first principles resulting from the linkage of the Golak Nath decision and the Nath Pai Bill was exemplified by the 'First

---

[20] *Lok Sabha Debates*, Fourth Series, vol. 7, no. 45, cols. 13795ff, 21 July 1967. After five widely spaced days of debate, the bill went to a Joint Committee of Parliament on 4 August 1967.

Lohia spoke on this occasion in Hindi, as he typically did. The translation was made for the author by Girdhar Rathi of the Centre for the Study of Developing Societies, New Delhi. This applies also to the speeches of Limaye and Vajpayee cited here. An English version of Lohia's speech appeared in *Mankind,* August–September 1971, pp. 49ff.

A year prior to the Nath Pai bill, the SSP resolved to seek an amendment 'to facilitate rapid social change [and] democratization of the political and economic structure ...'. Second Annual Conference in Kotah, 5 April 1966. *AR,* 14–20 May 1966, p. 7076.

Allan Bullock in his *Hitler: A Study in Tyranny* describes the enactment, and Hitler's subsequent use of, this law. Bantam Books, New York, 1958, pp. 114–17.

[21] Lohia would die in October 1967 while the Joint Committee was considering the bill. Limaye would continue to fight it. At this time, frustration with Congress rule again had created strange bedfellows. Nath Pai, Limaye, Minoo Masani of the Swatantra Party and CPI members A. K. Gopalan, Bhupesh Gupta, and H. N. Mukherjee signed an appeal for the election of Subba Rao as President.

[22] Limaye interview with the author.

Convention on the Constitution' held in August 1967. The topic was 'Fundamental Rights and Constitutional Amendment'. Nath Pai, himself, was among the panelists.[23] Opening the session, Justice Hidayatullah reviewed the findings in Golak Nath and repeated his earlier assertion that 'it was a mistake' to have property as a Fundamental Right. He also pointed out that Parliament's power to amend the Constitution was not utterly sovereign, for half the state legislatures must ratify certain classes of amendments.[24] M. C. Setalvad characterized 'prospective over-ruling' as the Court speaking 'with two voices'. And he employed arithmetic that others would adopt. He added the opinions of judges in a variety of earlier cases as to whether Article 368 contained a comprehensive power of amendment. He arrived at thirteen for comprehensive powers as against six who had held to the contrary. Later, others would use such a figuring to support bad law. Former Supreme Court Justice S. K. Das told the convention that he thought the Court should reconsider Golak Nath and measure future decisions against the intentions of the Preamble: would a ruling foster or impede the growth of the nation and secure social, economic, and political justice? Surely all rights are not fundamental in the same sense, Das said, nor is property 'an absolute right'.[25] Acharya Kripalani, member of the Constituent Assembly and sometime Congress president, concentrated on the 'moral aspect' of the situation. It was a fallacy, he said, to equate the people with Parliament and parliamentary government with majority government—Hitler had come to power on a majority vote. Property should not be in the Rights, but 'certain rights cannot be left at the mercy of the majority'.[26] Mohan Kumaramangalam put the matter in the context of the Fundamental Rights versus the Directive Principles, presaging his support for the Twenty-fifth Amendment four years later. The Directive Principles

[23] The author regrets that space limitations necessitate the omission of the details of these sober deliberations.

The Convention's proceedings were published as *Fundamental Rights and Constitutional Amendment*, Singhvi, L. M., general editor, Institute of Constitutional and Parliamentary Studies (ICPS), New Delhi, 1971. Citations here are from this volume. This work is not to be confused with a separate volume, referred to below, also published by ICPS and entitled, *Parliament and Constitutional Amendment*, Singhvi, L. M. (ed.), ICPS, 1970. It was published a year earlier, although recording an event that took place after the August 1967 convention. See footnote 34.

[24] Late in 1968, the press reported Hidayatullah as saying that property might be taken from the Fundamental Rights, but let us do it 'in a constitutional way'. *AR*, 22–8 January 1969, p. 8730.

[25] Singhvi, *Fundamental Rights*, pp. 190ff.

[26] Ibid., p. 196

cannot be implemented without taking away at least some of the Fundamental Rights, he said. Justice Subba Rao evades the issue when he says they can.[27]

N. C. Chatterjee, the eminent lawyer of property cases in the 1950s, civil rights leader, and in many ways conservative, supported the Nath Pai Bill. Referring to his defence of the West Bengal government's acquisition of land for the resettlement of refugees, which the Supreme Court had ruled unconstitutional in the Bela Banerjee case, Chatterjee quoted Thomas Paine and Nehru that no constitution can bind posterity for all time. Justice Subba Rao's 'basic error' was that he had ignored the distinction between constituent and legislative power. Chatterjee said that he recently had recommended to President Radhakrishnan that he seek an advisory opinion from the Supreme Court to obtain a 'final and authoritative clarification' of the issues raised in Golak Nath.[28] The President, however, never requested such an advisory opinion, one assumes because the government did not want the Court to reaffirm the position taken in Golak Nath.

Parliament's Joint Committee on the Constitution (Amendment) Bill, 1967 presented its report on Nath Pai's bill a year later, on 22 July 1968, after taking much testimony, fifteen meetings, and many deadlines postponed.[29] Its recommendations surprised many, and opposition views

---

[27] In a chapter, 'The Amending Power and Parts III and IV of the Constitution' in ibid., pp. 85–91.

[28] Chatterjee had earlier written to the President asking for a Supreme Court clarification on machinery for future amendment of the Rights. *Hindustan Times*, 4 March 1967.

The press also reported that K. M. Munshi praised the Golak Nath ruling, said that he would 'never have dreamt' when the Constituent Assembly adopted the Fundamental Rights that they could be 'at the mercy of Parliament'. *Hindustan Times*, 5 March 1967. C. Rajagopalachari wrote that the people of India should congratulate themselves on having a Supreme Court that protected their constitutional rights and for not giving the Congress a majority in the February elections, which 'would enable it to touch the Constitution in its vital part ...'. *Hindustan Times*, 3 August 1967.

[29] Testimony came from ten individuals, thirty-five memoranda were received from institutions and organizations such as high courts, state governments, chambers of commerce, and bar councils. Among the persons were K. Santhanam, K. M. Munshi, N. A. Palkhivala, who opposed the bill; H. M. Seervai, M. C. Setalvad, and S. Mohan Kumaramangalam, by then the ex-Advocate General of Madras, who supported it. Piloo Mody of the Swatantra Party and Acharya Kripalani later claimed that they were never called to appear before the Joint Committee, although they had requested the opportunity to do so.

The Committee published a volume of evidence in December 1967 and, in May 1968, a 'Statement Containing a Gist of Main Points Made by Witnesses in their Evidence before the committee'. Lok Sabha Secretariat, New Delhi, 1968.

made an impact in a Parliament shorn of Congress dominance. Committee members not only opposed Nath Pai's position but wished to give the Fundamental Rights fresh protections without being as rigid as the entrenchment envisaged in Golak Nath. They would have made amendments to the Rights subject to ratification by half the states, 'due to the importance of Fundamental Rights'. Additionally, the members overcame several of the oddities in Subba Rao's ruling by recommending the exclusion of amendments from the reach of Article 13 and by making it clear that Article 368 dealt with both the substantive and procedural aspects of amendment.[30]

The debate on the bill, which resumed on 15 November 1968, demonstrated that the Joint Committee's restrained position held sway in Parliament. Although the Prime Minister and the cabinet did not accept the Joint Select Committee report and held to Nath Pai's original position,[31] within the Congress Parliamentary Party opposition to the bill was growing in part because of a failure of communication between the cabinet and the CPP. There were threats to disobey a Whip, were one issued. The *Statesman* reported that S. N. Mishra, deputy leader of the Parliamentary Party, urged the government to refrain from pressing the bill. The combination of Congress dissenters, SSP, Swatantra, and Jana Sangh votes appeared unbeatable, and in December action on the bill was postponed.[32] '[I]t really beats me' why after a year we can't make up our mind, complained H. N. Mukherjee when the bill came up again in February 1969. Law Minister Govinda Menon responded that the government's position remained that 'Parliament should have the power to amend the Constitution including Part III thereof,' but the government wanted a second look at the bill due to the Joint Committee's report being 'materially different' from Nath Pai's original bill.[33] On 14 May 1969, the Speaker announced that it had been

---

[30] *Report of the Joint Committee of the Lok Sabha on The Constitution (Amendment) Bill 1967*, Lok Sabha Secretariat, New Delhi, p. vii.

[31] I. K. Gujral, then Minister of State for Parliamentary Affairs, in an interview with the author.

[32] Merillat, *Land*, pp. 282–6.

[33] Menon's caution was based also on a recent Supreme Court judgement. On 13 January 1969, the Court had held, in the Mangaldas case, that compensation for property acquired by the state could not be challenged 'on the indefinite plea' that it was not just or fair and that, since the enactment of the Fourth Amendment, compensation was not justiciable if the process determining the amount met the conditions of the law and the compensation was not 'illusory'. Many persons believed that the Supreme Court in Mangaldas had moved a considerable distance from Golak Nath, but, according to H. M. Seervai, this assessment shortly was nullified by the Court's decisions in the Bank Nationalization and Privy Purses cases (ch. 9).

proposed to hold the bill over until the next session. Perhaps they would then 'have a better atmosphere' in which to discuss it. The Minister for Parliamentary Affairs agreed and suggested that thought should be given to referring the bill to a 'fresh joint committee'. Nath Pai and others pressed for debate to begin at once. One member called recommittal of the bill an 'indecent' way to deal with the House; another said this flaunted 'all parliamentary proprieties'. Although the Lok Sabha was deeply divided, the government carried a vote to adjourn discussion 184 to 39.[34]

Many of those opposing recommittal of the bill apparently did so because—opposing its substance—they believed they could defeat it. Many among the parliamentary supremacists favoured recommittal, apparently hoping to keep the bill alive. Mrs Gandhi chose postponing further consideration of the bill because she wished neither to risk its defeat on the floor nor a reaffirmation of the Joint Committee's recommendations by another committee.[35] 'It was not from lack of desire that Mrs Gandhi did not back Nath Pai's bill. She wanted to curb the judiciary.'[36] Her opportunity to do so through unfettered parliamentary power of amendment would come after the Congress regained its majority in the 1971 elections.

On the bench were four justices who had been on the Golak Nath bench: Hidayatullah, by this time Chief Justice, Ramaswami, Mitter, and Shah. The fifth justice, A. N. Grover, appointed from the Punjab High Court, had been on the court for a year. *State of Gujarat v Shantilal Mangaldas* AIR 1969 SC 634.

[34] Golak Nath had been unpopular and parliamentary sovereignty popular in a 'Round Table' discussion on constitutional amendment and fundamental rights in March. However, none of those supporting Nath Pai quarrelled with the idea of amendments to the Fundamental Rights requiring ratification by half the states. Property as a fundamental right had few friends. There was some unrealistic talk of resorting to a referendum or a new constituent assembly if the mutual incompatibility of Golak Nath and 'Nath Pai' persisted.

The proceedings of the 'Round Table' were published in Singhvi, L. M. (ed.), *Parliament and Constitutional Amendment*, ICPS, New Delhi, 1970.

[35] The PSP attributed the bill's 'tortuous' history in Parliament to the 'divided mind' of the Congress. *General Secretary's Report* to the 10th National Conference of the Praja Socialist Party, PSP, Bombay, 1970.

[36] S. L. Shakdher, former Secretary General of the Lok Sabha, in an interview with the author.

Chapter 9

TWO CATALYTIC DEFEATS

Exercised though the Prime Minister and her government were over the Golak Nath decision and their inability to overcome it through the Nath Pai Bill, two subsequent Supreme Court decisions challenged the government even more sharply: the Bank Nationalization case (also called Cooper's case) and the Privy Purses case (also called the Princes case or Madhav Rao Scindia's case). Rights to property were at the heart of both. The government was also stung, in the privy purses matter, by the failure of its constitution-amending bill. These defeats, cumulative with Golak Nath, were the direct progenitors of three amendments. The government's framing of these amendments reveals much about its internal processes, including their constitutionality.

Social revolutionary aims and personal ambitions again were in collision with the distribution of powers in the Constitution. Nationalizing banks and ending the privy purses of rulers of the former princely states were populist tools in Indira Gandhi's battle for dominance and in young Congress activists' scramble for influence. Expanded rural credit also was a genuine issue for national economic development. For farmers, especially small farmers, to get loans, either the banks would have to change their policies or the government would have to take them over and carry out those changes. Whether policy was driven by personality or substance, relations among the branches of government and between the government and the Congress Party would be strained. This chapter will recount the history of the banks and privy purses issues. The following chapter will discuss the constitutional amendments they produced.

Bank Nationalization

Nationalizing banks was a desire with a long history. Legislation affecting banking dated from the Indian Companies Act of 1913. In 1934, the newly formed Congress Socialist Party called for the nationalization of certain industries and mentioned banking specifically. The Socialist Party did so in 1947. The most definitive early statement came in 1948 when the AICC's Economic Programme Committee, chaired by Nehru, said in its unanimous report that 'All resources available for investment should be subject to the control and direction of the State. The states should set up a Finance Corporation for financing industries. Banking and Insurance should be nationalised.'[1] Finance Minister Shanmukham Chetty wanted to nationalize the Imperial Bank that year, but dropped the idea when Sardar Patel persuaded him to do so upon the suggestion of C. D. Deshmukh, then the governor of the Reserve Bank.[2] The Reserve Bank itself was nationalized in January 1949—Deshmukh had begun drafting the papers in secret in August 1947. The Banking Companies Act of 1949 'tamed' the banks, in the word of one observer, but this had to do with certain bank practices and not with the wider extension of credit. A Socialist Party pamphlet of 1951 called for nationalization—as did Jayaprakash Narayan in his correspondence with Nehru in 1953, as part of the 'Fourteen Points'.

Parliament nationalized the Imperial Bank during its monsoon session of 1953, making it the State Bank of India, and thereby giving the government control of about one-third of commercial banking in the country. C. D. Deshmukh, prime mover in the nationalization, had thought the time 'ripe' for it because some 'socialist pattern measures' had already been enacted. He would later call the State Bank 'a lead bank in the world of India's nationalized banking'.[3] Nehru advocated insurance and bank nationalization again three years later, but cautiously. 'You may have to take them over,' he said, although 'when you nationalise, you have to pay compensation.'[4] P. B. Gajendragadkar, later to become

[1] *Report of the Economic Programme Committee*, AICC, 1948, p. 21. The same year, peasant leader N. G. Ranga recommended nationalization specifically to provide rural credit.

[2] Deshmukh, C. D., *The Course of My Life*, Orient Longman, New Delhi, 1974, p. 155.

[3] In 1972. Ibid., p. 215. T. T. Krishnamachari, Minister of Commerce and Industry and later Minister of Finance, had written to Deshmukh that he wished to see a 'shift' in the bank's management both to avoid 'straightforward nationalization' and to end the situation in which the bank 'has been deliberately used not merely to discriminate in favour of European companies but also to strangle Indian business all these years'. Letter from Krishnamachari to Deshmukh, 19 October 1952. T. T. Krishnamachari Papers, Subject File 7, pp. 2–7, NMML.

Prime Minister Nehru wrote to Krishnamachari in July 1953 that he had 'long been of the opinion' that insurance as well as banking should be made state concerns. He thought that progress toward nationalizing the Imperial Bank 'was rather slow'. Letter dated 24 July 1953. T. T. Krishnamachari Papers, Jawaharlal Nehru File, 1953.

The banks of former princely states such as Hyderabad, Mysore, and Travancore were nationalized during the next few years.

[4] Speech of 7 January 1956 to the Planning Commission. Raj Bahadur Papers, PMA.

Chief Justice of India, in his Foreword to the Bank Commission Award of the fifties, wrote that in the context of a socialistic pattern of society banks should recognize the necessity of affording credit to rural areas.[5]

More vigorous advocacy of bank nationalization came in Parliament in 1963 and at the Congress annual session in January 1964 at Bhubaneshwar, which adopted the famous 'Democracy and Socialism' resolution. Ms Subhadra Joshi and Raghunatha Reddy of the Congress Forum for Socialist Action spoke out. Joshi moved a motion in the Lok Sabha calling for bank nationalization 'in order to mobilize the national resources' in the aftermath of the India–China war. Reddy, moved a non-official resolution in the Rajya Sabha to nationalize fourteen banks. He based his case on Article 39 of the Directive Principles (the ownership and control of the material resources of the community should be distributed so as to serve the common good, and that the operation of the economic system should not detrimentally concentrate wealth and the means of production).[6] T. T. Krishnamachari, by then Finance Minister, opposed Joshi's resolution and it was voted down. Reddy's resolution evoked lengthier debate. The government spokeswoman, Deputy Minister of Finance Tarkeshwari Sinha, opposed it principally on the ground that the compensation necessary would be better used to stimulate the economy. Although Nehru agreed with the spirit of the resolution, he sought its withdrawal, fearing that he might not have enough votes in the Parliamentary Party to defeat it. He approached Arjun Arora, another CFSA member, who went to Reddy with the plea for withdrawal. Reddy agreed not to push his resolution, saying that voices had been raised stronger than the hands raised.[7] To the disappointment of Krishna Menon and K. D. Malaviya, the 'Democracy and Socialism' resolution did not mention bank nationalization. Menon protested, and Malaviya submitted his own five-page 'Democracy and

---

[5] Gajendragadkar, *The Best of My Memory*, p. 312.

[6] *Parliamentary Debates, Rajya Sabha*, vol. 45, no. 5, cols. 888–9.

Reddy quoted Franklin Roosevelt, ' "liberty ... is not safe if ... the growth of private power ... becomes stronger than the democratic state itself ...," ' and Harold Ickes, Roosevelt's Secretary of the Interior, that Jefferson had fought ' "the over-concentration of wealth and power in a few hands ...." '.

[7] For debates in Parliament, see *Parliamentary Debates, Rajya Sabha*, vol. 45, nos. 5, 15, and 16. *Lok Sabha Debates*, Third Series, vol. 16, no. 31, col. 7081; vol. 17, no. 41, cols. 9567–92; and vol. 20, no. 19, cols. 4905–21. The resolution to nationalize the banks was defeated on 6 September 1963.

The account of the Nehru–Reddy–Arora conversations is drawn from the author's interview with Reddy.

At this time, Krishnamachari favoured government control of banks, short of outrigh nationalization. P. B. Venkatasubramanian in a letter to the author.

Socialism' resolution, which claimed that the people demanded bank nationalization, greater government control of the 'commanding heights' of the economy, and state wholesale trading in foodgrains.[8]

The bank nationalization debate intensified from 1967. Some proponents put forth economic justifications; among these, a few focused on agricultural credit. Others seemed primarily moved by doctrine: government simply must control the economy. Among the nationalizers at the June 1967 AICC meeting in Delhi were Chavan, Syndicate members Atulya Ghosh and K. Kamaraj and K. D. Malaviya and several other CFSA members.[9]

Social control of banks was the Congress's official position, espoused at Delhi and at the Jabalpur AICC meeting in October by Morarji Desai and Mrs Gandhi, who assured the meeting that the banks would have only two years to improve their performance.[10] Desai's rationale consistently was that more credit could be made available through social control of all banks than by nationalizing six, as Kamaraj and others recommended. Government could control bank policies without having to pay some rupees eighty-five crore to acquire them, said Desai.[11] Late

---

[8] Malaviya, K. D., 'Democracy and Socialism: Draft Resolution for the 68th Session of the Indian National Congress at Bhubaneshwar'. No publication information.

The Maharashtra, Assam, and Punjab Pradesh Congress Committees, a District Congress Committee in Bombay, and minor members of the AICC also submitted memoranda supporting these views to the Bhubaneshwar session. Malaviya, K. D., *Socialist Ideology of Congress, a Study in Its Evolution,* A Socialist Congressman Publication, New Delhi, 1966.

[9] Malaviya later wrote, 'I think the basic expositions of Karl Marx are still relevant in India and would help us a lot in our search for a path to Socialism.' *Socialist India,* Independence Day Number, 1971, p. 20.

[10] The party's official policy had been expressed in the 'post-mortem's' Ten–Point Programme, as seen in ch. 7. In a circular letter dated 4 November 1967 to chief ministers, General Secretary Sadiq Ali said that bankers would have to accept 'the new social control' or face takeover by the government. Zaidi, *Directives of the Congress High Command,* p. 155.

I. K. Gujral drafted Mrs Gandhi's Jabalpur speech favouring social control over nationalization. (Gujral in an interview with the author.) For a description of the meetings, see *Report of the General Secretaries, February 1966–January 1968,* AICC, New Delhi.

Constituent Assembly member Renuka Ray, present at Jabalpur, said that eloquent speeches about bank nationalization reminded her of the early days, when it often was thought that enactment of legislation would bring about changes 'without further effort'. She wondered if 'mantra-like repetition ... [would] be sufficient to deliver the goods'. Her article for the Indian News and Features Alliance, 20 November 1967. Renuka Ray Papers, PMA.

[11] Desai, Morarji, 'Growing Faces of Disruption and Dictatorship' in *Souvenir AICC Session, Lucknow, 5–6 December 1970,* AICC (Congress–O), New Delhi, 1970. A young official in the Finance Ministry produced a memorandum that year saying that a policy should not be devised after the fact to justify nationalization, which, if it took place, should

in 1968, Desai took the concrete step of putting social control into law through the Banking Laws (Amendment) Act, 1968. This provided 'for the extension of social control over banks', in part by laying down that fifty-one per cent of a bank's directors should come from agriculture, the rural economy, and small-scale industry. The government might acquire a bank, after consultation with the Reserve Bank of India, if it did not follow certain policies, including the better provision of credit.[12] Commending the bill on the floor of the Lok Sabha, Morarji Desai— who had nationalized bus transportation in Bombay when Chief Minister there—spoke of the need to give 'small-scale industries, agriculture and other sectors of our economic life' more influence in credit decisions and of the need to snap 'the link between a few industrial houses and banks'.[13] As government policy, social control had a very short life. The Congress plenary session in Faridabad in the spring, followed by the AICC and Working Committee meetings in Bangalore—along with Mrs Gandhi's Stray Thoughts memorandum thereto—presaged its demise. It is uncertain exactly when after Bangalore Mrs Gandhi took the twin decisions to attack the old guard through Morarji Desai and to cloak his departure with a matter of economic policy. But as the decision to oust Desai was developing, schemes for bank nationalization orbited around the Prime Minister. Raghunatha Reddy submitted a paper reviving his plan to nationalize fourteen banks. Chandra Shekhar did likewise—the memorandum likely prepared by a young economist-follower, S. K. Goyal. P. N. Haksar had 'the whole thing prepared'.[14] The advice of various individuals was solicited: L. K. Jha, Reserve Bank governor and Mrs Gandhi's former Principal Secretary, summoned from Bombay; I. G. Patel,

---

follow an established policy and proper planning. At Desai's suggestion, he mentioned this to Mrs Gandhi, who seemed disinterested. The young official, V. A. Pai Panandiker, in an interview with the author.

[12] Section 21 of part IIC, the Banking Laws (Amendment) Act, 1968—No. 58 of 1968.

[13] 'Statement by the Deputy Prime Minister and Minister of Finance on Social Control Over Commercial Banks', 14 December 1968. *Statements Laid on the Table of Lok Sabha*, Parliament Library, New Delhi, 1968.

Haksar thought 'Morarji Desai's social control was meaningless', and he snorted at the 'vaporous ideologies', the lack of practical experience, and the 'bookish socialism' of Young Turks like Dharia and Kant. (Haksar's view in an interview with the author.)

[14] Pupul Jayakar interview with the author, based on her own interview with L. K. Jha. Chandra Shekar's paper from an interview with S. K. Goyal. Raghunatha Reddy's paper, sometimes described as a draft ordinace, from Reddy himself, and from R. C. Dutt in interviews with the author.

Haksar distinguished between 'rapacious and bucaneering' bankers and industrialists and brilliant, constructive industrialists like Tata, Godrej, Birla, and Kirloskar. Interview with the author.

formerly with the Reserve Bank and now Secretary of Economic Affairs; Pitambar Pant from the Planning Commission; T. A. Pai from the Syndicate Bank; and P. N. Dhar, from Delhi's Institute of Economic Growth, who, an eyewitness said, spent five hours with the Prime Minister. One of the questions directed at Dhar and Pai was whether nationalizing six banks was enough.[15]

On 17 July, bank nationalization was still up in the air, although Morarji Desai had been relieved of office the previous day. The Law Ministry issued a statement saying that ' "No proposal regarding nationalization of banks has been made to the ministry for consideration ... [H]ence ... promulgation of an ordinance ... does not arise for the present." '[16] But time was pressing. If there were to be an ordinance, it had to be promulgated within four days—before Parliament resumed sitting on 21 July.

Early in the evening of 18 July, the senior drafting officer in the Law Ministry's Legislative Department, S. K. Maitra, was summoned to the Prime Minister's Secretariat. When told he had an extremely secret assignment, to draft an ordinance nationalizing banks, he protested that he could not depart from normal procedures and act on oral instructions without the approval of his ministry. Thereafter, Law Minister P. Govinda Menon called Maitra to his home and told him to go to the Finance Ministry for instructions.[17] There, Maitra was shown into the presence of L. K. Jha, Deputy Reserve Bank Governor A. Bakshi, I. G. Patel, and D. N. Ghosh, Deputy Secretary in the Finance Ministry. Jha told Maitra to ask them for the information necessary for drafting the ordinance. What is the 'public purpose' of the takeover? Maitra asked, and I. G. Patel drafted a paragraph, which Maitra used. There followed questions and answers about which banks were to be taken over, how compensation would be calculated, and the like.

Maitra set to work. Ghosh rejected the first draft because no infrastructure existed for running the nationalized banks and the draft did not provide it. Maitra began another draft incorporating his own suggestion that the banks' existing management could act as custodians until new managements could be in place. This draft needed revision to comply with existing banking laws. At 6:30 a.m., Maitra took the draft to Law Minister Menon, who approved it. Maitra went home to breakfast only to

---

[15] T. A. Pai's involvement from S. L. Shakdher in an interview with the author.; that of L. K. Jha, I. G. Patel, and others from the *Hindustan Times*, 18 July, 1969, and the *Statesman*, 18 July 1969.

[16] *Hindustan Times*, 18 July 1969.

[17] This account is drawn from the author's interview with S. K. Maitra. Maitra disappeared and even his anxious wife did not know his whereabouts for a few hours.

be summoned to the Prime Minister's Secretariat, where the Prime Minister was reading the draft with the Law Minister. After a few minor modifications, the ordinance went to an afternoon cabinet meeting, where it was approved unopposed. No minister had seen the text before the meeting, and after it copies were retrieved to prevent leaks. Maitra and Ghosh took the ordinance to President V. V. Giri, who signed it 19 July as Acting President—the day before he resigned office to run for President. Desai had resigned as Deputy Prime Minister earlier that day.[18]

Mrs Gandhi announced the ordinance in a radio broadcast that evening. She said the banking system 'has necessarily to be inspired by a larger social purpose', traced the nationalization to Congress's 1954 'socialistic pattern of society' resolution, and proclaimed it would be a success.[19] Popular it certainly was. Even members of the Syndicate supported the principle, and the Jana Sangh said it was willing to give nationalization a chance. But Swatantra Party leaders such as Masani and Rajagopalachari opposed nationalization and criticized doing it by ordinance one day before Parliament was to reconvene.

The following day a shareholder in one of the nationalized banks, Rustom Cowasji Cooper, plus Minoo Masani, Balraj Madhok of the Jana Sangh, and others, filed petitions in the Supreme Court challenging the President's competence to promulgate the ordinance and claiming violation of their rights under Articles 14, 19, and 31. Despite Attorney General Niren De's argument that nationalization was a policy decision and therefore not subject to court scrutiny, an eight-judge bench on 22 July issued interim orders restraining the government from removing the chairmen of the banks and giving the banks directions under the Banking Companies Act of 1968. The Court scheduled its final decision for six months later.[20] On 4 August, in the face of objections that no bill could be enacted while the ordinance was *sub judice* and that nationalization would produce various economic and bureaucratic evils, Parliament passed a nationalization law replacing the ordinance.

[18] The unanimous approval of the cabinet is according to the *Sunday Standard,* 20 July 1969. Keeping nationalization ordinances secret was designed to prevent speculation.

The 'Banking Companies (Acquisition and Transfer of Undertakings) Ordinance, 1969' nationalized fourteen 'scheduled' banks with over rupees fifty crore in deposits. These banks contained 85 per cent of bank deposits in the country, according to Mrs Gandhi. The ordinance was a complicated document many pages long, a mammoth drafting job.

For more on the nationalization, see Frankel, *Political Economy,* pp. 417–21 and Malhotra, *Indira Gandhi,* pp. 117–19.

Chief Justice Hidayatullah became Acting President upon Giri's resignation.

[19] *Hindustan Times,* 20 July 1969.

[20] *Indian Express,* 23 July 1969.

An eleven-judge bench of the Supreme Court on 10 February 1970 decided the constitutionality of the Bank Nationalization Act.[21] The chief petitioner, Cooper, claimed violation of his fundamental rights: his right to equality before the law under Article 14 had been infringed because the nationalization of only certain banks was a denial of equality; his right to acquire, hold, and dispose of property under Article 19 (1)(f) was violated by the taking over of the banks; the taking-over of the banks by the state prevented them from engaging in non-banking business; and his right to property under Article 31 and to compensation for property taken had been violated because the compensation was inadequate.

Speaking for ten of the eleven judges, Justice J. C. Shah struck down the Act. He held that the 'principles' of compensation that a legislature could lay down for the taking of property were not beyond judicial scrutiny (for this could result in arbitrary parliamentary action); that where the restrictions imposed on carrying on a business were so strict that the business could not in reality be carried on, the restriction was unreasonable; that the principles upon which compensation for the banks was to be based omitted some of their assets, namely goodwill and the value of long-term leases; and that the declaration that banks had the right to continue to carry on non-banking businesses was an empty formality if the compensation was to be paid over time, as it denied the banks the funds to carry on other business activities.[22] One sentence of Justice Shah's opinion likely burned brighter in the government's eyes than all his others. In what appeared to be a reversion to the Bela Banerjee ruling of 1953, Shah said, 'The broad object underlying the principles of valua-

[21] *Rustom Cavajee (sic) Cooper v Union of India* 1970 (3) SCR 530ff.

Members of the bench were: Justices J. C. Shah, S. M. Sikri, J. M. Shelat, V. Bhargava, G. K. Mitter, C. A. Vaidialingam, K. S. Hegde, A.N. Grover, A. N. Ray, Jaganmohan Reddy, and I. D. Dua.

The senior-most judge on the Court, J. C. Shah, presided over the bench, Chief Justice Hidayatullah having recused himself from the case because he had assented to the Bank Nationalization Act when Acting President.

Acting for the parties had been a number of India's best known legal talents. On the government side were the Attorney General, Niren De, and the former attorneys general, M. C. Setalvad and C. K. Daphtary. Intervenors for the government included Krishna Menon, Mohan Kumaramangalam, and R. K. Garg. Appearing for Cooper and other petitioners were N. A. Palkhivala, the leading counsel, M. C. Chagla, J. B. Dadachanji, and others.

[22] 1970 (3) SCR 585–600, 610. An individual closely involved recalls that, in an attempt to reduce the amount of compensation payable, the provisions in the Act were changed from those in the ordinance. This change contributed to the court's striking down the Act and, before the matter was resolved, cost the government much more in compensation than it had originally expected.

tion is to award the owner the equivalent of his property with its existing advantages and potentialities.'[23]

The lone dissenter among the eleven judges was Justice A. N. Ray. Age 58, he had come to his August 1969 appointment to the Court via Presidency College, Calcutta, Oriel College, Oxford, Gray's Inn, and the Calcutta High Court. In his opinion he held that the principles for compensation fixed by a legislature cannot be questioned in court on the ground that the compensation paid on the basis of these principles is not just or fair compensation. Ray held that there was no infraction of Article 31 unless compensation was 'obviously and shockingly illusory'.[24] He held also that the non-banking businesses were part of the recognized business of a banking company and, as such, were part of the undertaking of the bank. He dismissed the 'goodwill' argument, and said the taking of the banks did not offend Article 14. Both Ray in his dissent and Shah in his majority judgement drew upon the Court's opinion in the Mangaldas case of thirteen months earlier. At the root of the differences between the dissenter and the majority were their philosophies about judicial review. For Shah and the majority, the power was extensive. For Ray, quoting Justice Mahajan, '"The legislature is the best judge of what is good for the community, by whose suffrage it comes into existence."'[25] In other words, it is a matter of 'legislative judgement', he said.

Of the little that is known about the internal workings of this bench, several things stand out. The bench as a group discussed the case more fully than was typical of benches on others cases. Several of the judges reacted adversely to the government's presentation because they thought the information about the assets of the banks and other data that the government submitted was inadequate to their need in determining the adequacy of compensation. This seems to have aroused the scepticism particularly of Justices Shah, Sikri, and Shelat, who had been on the bench in previous cases when judges had thought the government had submitted inadequate information—the Metal Box case for Shelat and the Madras Lignite case for Justices Shah and Sikri.[26] In these cases, according to a

[23] Ibid., p. 599.

[24] Ibid., p. 649.

[25] Ibid., p. 623. The analysis of the case is drawn from court reports and from: Gae, R. S., *The Bank Nationalization Case and the Constitution*, N. M. Tripathi Pvt. Ltd., Bombay, 1971; Merillat, *Land;* Singhvi, L. M., 'Preface' in Singhvi, *Parliament and Constitutional Amendment,* and newspaper reports and interviews.

[26] The account of dynamics within the bench is based upon the author's interviews. The decision in the Madras Lignite case was handed down on 3 March 1964. In the Supreme Court it was officially named *The State of Madras v D. Namasivaya Mudaliar and Others* 1964 (6) SCR 936.

well-informed civil servant, the government had played 'fast and loose' with the matter of compensation. In the Madras case, the government appraised the value of land acquired as of a date long before the land actually was taken, and in the Metal Box case it valued machinery in good condition—used and unused—at one hundred rupees.

Justices Shah, Sikri, Shelat, and Vaidialingam brought to Cooper's case memories of Golak Nath, where they had joined Subba Rao in his majority opinion. Other Golak Nath judges, V. Bhargava and G. K. Mitter, voted with the majority in the bank case, although they had dissented in Golak Nath. These two believers in the amendability of the Fundamental Rights, including the right of property, held that Cooper's fundamental right to property had been violated because his compensation was based on principles 'not relevant' to the determination of that compensation. Finally, all these men certainly were aware that, while their deliberations were proceeding, the government's Minister of State for Finance, R. K. Khadilkar, had said publicly that banks smaller than the fourteen also were to be nationalized; that Minister of Law Govinda Menon had said that general insurance would be nationalized by ordinance by 15 April; and that bills establishing an urban land ceiling and abolishing the princes' purses would be introduced in Parliament within months. Did the ten judges of the majority think that the time had come to show the government an orange light of caution regarding future takeovers?

The Court's decision in Cooper's case did nothing to dispel the confusion about what was law in cases of government acquisition of property. Constitution benches without uniform composition had produced inconsistent rulings on the First Amendment's provision regarding agricultural estates and on the Fourth Amendment's provision that the amount of compensation for property acquired by the government could not be challenged as inadequate if the amount or the principles underlying the amount were given. (See chapters 3 and 4.) Indeed, Shah in Mangaldas, the previous year, had held that if compensation were not illusory, it would not be justiciable.[27] For its part, the government had contributed to the Supreme Court's adverse rulings. Either from zealousness or carelessness, it had calculated compensation questionably low on several occasions, thus awakening suspicions of fraud among some judges. Also, the constitutional amendments had not

---

The Metal Box case was *Union of India v the Metal Corporation of India and Another* 1967 (1) SCR 255. It was decided on 5 September 1966.

[27] *State of Gujarat v Shri Shantilal Mangaldas* 1969 (3) SCR 341 ff.

See also Merillat, *Land*, especially chs. 7, 9, and 11; and M. C. Setalvad's 'Foreword' in Gae, *Bank Nationalization Case*.

removed the word 'compensation' from Article 31, inviting the judicial supposition that the government intended payment of the equivalent value for property taken. Above all, nationalizing the banks—leaving aside rational arguments for or against nationalization—had been a nakedly political gesture, botched from the start, inviting a punitive ruling by the court.[28]

The Prime Minister reacted to the Court's decision immediately. Four days after it, the President promulgated a new ordinance nationalizing the same fourteen banks, this time six days before Parliament was to reconvene. Two weeks later, her government introduced a bill to replace the ordinance. Revealing the government's continuing intention to reduce the Supreme Court's power, Mrs Gandhi told the Executive Committee of the Parliamentary Party that it should seriously consider passage of the Nath Pai Bill 'to get through progressive economic measures'.[29]

Others' reactions to the Supreme Court decision were mixed. The Swatantra welcomed it. The SSP and the PSP cried foul. The Congress (O) criticized the Prime Minister for a job badly done, while calling for a new ordinance. There were renewed demands for the removal of property from the Fundamental Rights. Former Supreme Court Justice S. K. Das expressed a widely held sentiment when he wrote that the country faced 'a real national problem', for social legislation would be impossible if 'we have always to pay one for one rupee'; just compensation, he said, should be understood as neither illusory nor full compensation. He hoped a confrontation between Parliament and the Supreme Court could be avoided through a 'harmonious construction' of Article 31.[30] Several

---

[28] The absence of staff work preceding the nationalization contrasts miserably with the intensive analyses and planning leading to the 1966 devaluation decision. See Denoon, David B. H., *Devaluation under Pressure: India, Indonesia, and Ghana*, MIT Press, Cambridge, 1986, entire and p. 46, especially.

[29] *Indian Express*, 28 February 1970.

[30] Das, S. K., 'Fundamental Rights and Supreme Court Decision on Nationalisation of Banks' in Singhvi, L. M. (ed.), *Bank Nationalization and the Supreme Court Judgement*, Institute of Constitutional and Parliamentary Studies/National Publishing House, New Delhi, 1971.

It is regrettable that there is not a more definitive answer to the cogent question, 'Given the significance of bank nationalization to the shape of the Constitution, did it produce the results its adherents intended?' However, there are partial answers. Banks took a greater interest in agricultural finance and introduced concessional lending at four per cent interest for the 'weaker sections'. *Report of the National Commission on Agriculture, Part I: Review and Progress*, Ministry of Agriculture and Irrigation, New Delhi, 1976, p. 165.' '[T] he banking system has spread phenomenally ... . Some 21,760 new bank offices have been opened between July 1969 and April 1979, of which 11, 200 are in unbanked areas. Total bank deposits have increased six-fold in the same period'. *Hindustan*

newspaper editorials blamed the government, attributing the Court's decision to poor drafting of the ordinance and the law replacing it.

The second nationalization ordinance and Act escaped successful challenge in the Supreme Court in part because of changes incorporated in it. The government dropped the provision forbidding the banks to continue in the banking business; it specified the actual amount of compensation each bank was to receive; and the banks could accept the compensation in cash or take it in whole or in part in interest-bearing securities.

The Princes and Their Purses

By the late 1960s, the former princes' 'privy purses' from the government of India and certain of their 'privileges' would have become a footnote to history had abolishing them not been adopted as a cause by Mrs Gandhi and the social-economic activists. For each it was a symbolic issue in their common and separate pursuits of power. Unexpectedly for both, the matter joined with bank nationalization to fuel the demands for unlimited parliamentary power of amendment and the clash with the judiciary that followed. Although the cause was ideologically clothed, it had party undertones, for a number of the ex-princes were anti-Congress or pro-Swatantra.

Under British Rule, as seen in Part I, India consisted of the provinces of 'British India', directly administered by the British, and the princely states (or Indian States), administered by Indian rulers under treaty arrangements that gave the British 'paramountcy' over their affairs—when the British needed it. The 'integration' of these states—several joined Pakistan—had been vital to the creation of India as a nation. This was largely accomplished by August 1947, and relevant provisions placed by the Constituent Assembly in the Constitution.[31] As part of

---

Times editorial, 24 July 1979. The fourteen nationalized banks increased the number of their offices, overall, between 1969 and June 1993 by 21, 898 and, in centres with under 10,000 population, by 12,226. The number of 'direct finance' agricultural accounts between June 1969 and March 1992 rose from 160 to 20,550. The amounts outstanding, in the same period, rose from 40.31 crore to 16, 944 crore. *Economic Survey*, Ministry of Finance, GOI, New Delhi, 1994, tables 4.5 and 4.6, respectively.

Since nationalization, 'the banking sector has been heavily politicized. Only such persons often are appointed who will help "political lending" at the bidding of ministers and politicians.' Panandiker, V. A. Pai, 'A Job Not Well Done', *Hindustan Times*, 1 January 1994.

[31] For descriptions of the integration of the princely states, see Menon, V.P., *Integration of the Indian States*. For the purses and privileges see pp. 159ff, and 476–83, especially. For constitutional provisions, Austin, *Cornerstone*, pp. 243–54.

the arrangements for 'accession' to India, the princes were granted certain privileges and privy purses—in effect, government allowances. They were 'a sort of *quid pro quo* for the surrender by them of their ruling powers and for the dissolution of their states'. Additionally, the princes could keep certain private properties and were guaranteed 'the personal rights, privileges and dignities which they had hitherto been enjoying'.[32] The arrangements made with the princes evoked little criticism at the time, for the unity of India was thought worth the price.

Nehru, egalitarian, anti-feudal, and a socialist, was ambivalent from the beginning. He wrote to Sardar Patel in 1949 that he was 'a little surprised and taken aback' that the purse payments were to be free of income tax and in perpetuity—this surprise despite the White Paper, draft covenants, and financial papers having been laid before the Constituent Assembly.[33] He shied away from placing the details of the settlement with the princes in the Constitution. Patel agreed that it would be sufficient to include in the Constitution a general article that the government would honour its obligations to the princes. But the government must place the details before the party, said Patel.[34] Nehru's distaste did not abate. 'Many of us feel these privy purses are too bloated,' he wrote to a cabinet minister who had spoken out against the purses. 'Nevertheless, we have committed ourselves to them and we cannot easily walk through our commitments.'[35] Some

[32] The States Ministry evolved a formula basing purses upon the annual average revenue of the ruler's state. In general, this was a purse of 130,000 rupees annually for each one-and-a-half million rupees of revenue, or approximately eight per cent. Of the 554 states dealt with, 'over 450 had an annual revenue of less than fifteen lakhs.' Generally speaking, a ceiling of rupees two lakh was placed on purses. There were eleven exceptions where the purses were much higher. Excluding these, there were ninety-one rulers with purses of this amount and above. These exceptions were to last only for the then ruling individual and not for his successors, where the ceiling would apply. Menon, *Integration of the Indian States*, pp. 477ff.

[33] Nehru to Patel, 11 August 1949. Durga Das, *Patel's Correspondence*, p. 601.

[34] Nehru–Patel letter, 11 August 1949 and Patel to Nehru, 16 August 1949. Ibid., pp. 601–3.

Nehru 'had strong reservations' about the arrangements with the princes, recalled Home Secretary H.V.R. Iengar, and his style often was to 'accept a decision, for the time being with strong mental reservations'. Nehru was not alone in his dislike of the deal with the princes. A number of Congress members of the Constituent Assembly tried to have them annulled. Patel met with them, said he would not "'rat on"' (go back on) the Cabinet's guarantees, and threatened to resign if this happened. H.V. R. Iengar Oral History Transcript, NMML.

[35] Letter from Nehru to H. K. Mahtab, Secret and Personal, 20 December 1951. Hare Krishna Mahtab Papers, File 20, NMML.

The Communist Party attacked the covenants in its manifesto for the 1951–2 general elections.

months later, Nehru wrote to the chief ministers that 'the present arrangements are completely illogical and difficult to justify. The idea of having *Rajpramukhs* for life and ... giving them a handsome privy purse and heavy allowances ... is something that does not fit at all with modern ideas ... . I have little doubt that this question will be raised more and more by the public and we shall have to face it.'[36]

Nehru expressed his dissatisfaction directly to the princes on 10 September 1953. 'Dear Friend', he began a lengthy letter to the 102 princes receiving a purse of more than a lakh of rupees. After praising their accession to India, he turned to implementing the Directive Principles and the 'glaring' disparities between rich and poor in the country. Shouldn't we reconsider purses and Rajpramukhs for life?, he asked. 'Political wisdom consists in anticipating events and guiding them'. He asked the princes to give consideration to what he had said, 'because events move ... . I am not making any positive suggestion in this matter ... I should like the princes themselves ... [to] suggest how best we can deal with this situation.'[37]

Ten months later, Nehru wrote the princes another Dear Friend letter, pointing out that only a few of them had acknowledged his first letter. Now it was time, he said, to come to 'close grips' with it. He had a 'moderate' suggestion: princes with purses of two to five lakhs should make a voluntary contribution of fifteen per cent of their purse to developmental schemes in their states and invest ten per cent in a national loan plan—and so on, according to the size of the purse.[38] The response again was uncooperative. There the matter rested for nearly nine years, excepting that in October 1961 the government began reducing the privy purses of the major recipients by as much as fifty per cent when a son succeeded to his father's 'titles'.

---

[36] Letter of 2 August 1952. *NLTCM,* vol. 3, p. 67. Late in the month Nehru wrote from Kashmir indicating that the issue kept churning in his mind.

Jayaprakash Narayan included abolition of the constitutional guarantees to the princes among his fourteen points sent to Nehru in 1953 as they were negotiating Narayan's possible return to the Congress Party.

[37] Nehru sent a copy of this Secret and Personal letter to K. Santhanam, the Lieutenant Governor of Vindhya Pradesh, on 11 September 1953, and, one assumes, to other governors. File 2, 'General Correspondence as Lt. Governor of Vindhya Pradesh', Santhanam Collection, NAI.

Although the ex-princes' privy purses were exempt from income tax, the princes were liable to tax on other income and on property excepting for one palace.

[38] Letter of 15 June 1954. Nehru sent a copy to C. D. Deshmukh. C. D. Deshmukh Papers, File 23, NMML. Nehru had sent a draft of this letter to President Prasad on 25 May, who responded on 4 June doubting the efficacy of the idea. Choudhary, *Prasad:*

The issue reemerged in 1963 when Kamaraj and Atulya Ghosh raised abolition of privileges and purses in the AICC. Nehru opposed them on the grounds that the government should keep its word, and that the cost of the purses was automatically going down.[39] Four non-official resolutions to abolish the purses were submitted at the Bhubaneshwar Congress a few months later, but the party's committee on non-official resolutions rejected them because they contravened the Constitution. Nevertheless, the committee recommended that the rate of purses be further decreased with each succession from father to son and the matter of privileges be re-examined.[40]

Pressures increased during 1967. In May, during the Congress's intensive election post-mortem, Atulya Ghosh introduced a note calling the purses 'incongruous to the concept and practice of democracy'. Morarji Desai thought this morally wrong and called it 'a breach of faith with the princes'.[41] The Ten-Point Programme included Ghosh's formulation, and the Young Turks engineered a surprise for the Prime Minister by passing a resolution at a late night AICC meeting after most members had gone to bed. This urged the government 'to examine the question of privy purses and privileges of the rulers ... and take steps to remove them.'[42] Mrs Gandhi objected to Dharia the following morning, saying his amendment to the resolution '"further added to the complications"'.[43] S. K. Patil called the move madness. Kamaraj and Atulya Ghosh supported the resolution, Ghosh openly and Kamaraj by remaining silent. A few days later, the princes, in the person of the Gaekwad of Baroda, one of the most distinguished princely families, attacked the Congress resolution. By late in the year the government

---

Correspondence, vol. 17, pp. 40–2. These letters and Nehru's being torn between his sense of economic justice 'and a government's honour' are discussed in Gopal, *Nehru*, vol. 2, p. 79.

[39] Sahgal, Nayantara, *Indira Gandhi: Her Road to Power*, MacDonald & Co., London, 1982, p. 59.

[40] *Report of the Sub-Committee on Non-Official Resolutions*, AICC, New Delhi, 7 April 1964.

[41] For this event, see Frankel, *Political Economy*, p. 397. For Desai, see Awana, *Pressure Politics*, p. 248.

[42] Cited in 'Note on "Privy Purses and Privileges of Rulers of Former Indian States" by Shri Y. B. Chavan, Union Home Minister'. AICC Papers, Installment II, File OD 11, 1969, NMML.

K. P. Unnikrishnan may have drafted the resolution. Mohan Dharia moved it, and Krishan Kant, Chandrashekhar, and Chandrajit Yadav were strong supporters. Y. B. Chavan was in the chair at the time, and it passed seventeen to four. From interviews. Also, Frankel, *Political Economy*, p. 398 and Awana, *Pressure Politics*, p. 149.

[43] Dharia, Mohan, *Fumes and the Fire*, S. Chand & Co. Pvt. Ltd., New Delhi, 1975, p. 4. The next day, the Prime Minister reportedly told one of her staff that this was 'Chavan sahib's mischief'.

had opened negotiations with the princes. Morarji Desai won agreement for a gradualist approach in the October AICC session at Jabalpur and promised unwisely to have the purses and privileges abolished in six months.[44] Charged with the actual conduct of the negotiations, Home Minister Y. B. Chavan met with the princes twice at the end of 1967, on the latter occasion telling the princes of the government's decision in principle to abolish purses and privileges.[45] Further inconclusive talks took place 29 May 1968, and the princes expressed the desire to send a formal note to the government. On 24 July 1968, Chavan told Parliament of the government's decision to abolish purses and privileges—but set no date for doing so—and that he had informed the princes of the 'basic decision'. During the month the heretofore separate groups of princes amalgamated into the purportedly one-voice 'Concord of States', and V. Shankar, formerly of the States Ministry under Sardar Patel, became one of its advisers. Little of note occurred during the remainder of 1968 and in 1969 in part due to Desai's departure from the cabinet.

Matters came to a head in 1970. The year opened with Chavan's conference with the princes on 8 January 1970. Here he reportedly reiterated the government's intention to implement the will of the people by abolishing purses and privileges. Reacting, the princes sent a 'memorial' to the President requesting that he seek an advisory opinion from the Supreme Court about the 'treaty regard question'.[46] The

---

[44] For Morarji Desai on negotiations, see Frankel, *Political Economy*, p. 399. For abolition in six months, see *Link*, August 1971, p. 12. See also *Report of the General Secretaries, February 1966–January 1968*, AICC, p. 34.

Opposition members of Parliament, who thought Desai was stalling, were provoked to move private members' bills calling for amendment to Article 291 of the Constitution and ending purses. During 1967, six such private members' bills were moved in the Lok Sabha and four in the Rajya Sabha.

[45] Chavan's Note. Also, *Lok Sabha Debates*, Fourth Series, vol. 18, no. 3, col. 1097.

[46] The memorial is referred to in a telegram sent by one of the princes' leaders and Swatantra Party member, Sriraj Dhrangadhra (from Saurashtra in Gujarat) to C. Rajagopalachari, the Swatantra leader. Rajagopalachari replied on 23 February that the President was entitled 'in his own right' to ask for an advisory opinion, but that he was 'afraid the president [V. V. Giri] holds a different view and believes he can do nothing unless advised to do so by the Government of the Union'. C. Rajagopalachari Papers, File 86, Microfilm, NMML. See also *Indian Express*, 13 February 1970.

Rajagopalachari had been the Governor General at the time of the princely states' integration and had participated in the negotiations with them. He then had thought the same Maharaja of Dhrangadhra remarkably poised and dignified for his age. (Menon, *Integration of the Indian States*, p. 179.)

One of the causes of the continuing stalemate, according to an individual then serving the Prime Minister, was that Desai had been willing to give the princes more compensation than the 'miserly amounts' offered by Chavan.

princes renewed this request in the spring. The President apparently never sought an advisory opinion. On 12 February, the 'Consultation of Rulers for India' (sic) issued a 'Convention Statement' recalling their contribution to 'the creation of a new national unity' by having parted 'with their powers and jurisdictions'. The princes saw 'no great difficulty in the gradual utilization of private wealth and income for public benefit' and therefore favoured 'the idea of setting up funds or trusts for social service and public benefit', which meant turning their purses to public purposes. But if the government 'persists in proceeding arbitrarily, thereby jeopardizing the honour and credit of our country', they would have to resist. The convention authorized the former rulers of Baroda, Bhopal, and Dhrangadhra to take 'whatever action that was necessary'.[47]

The government did move, very arbitrarily from the princes' viewpoint. On 18 May 1970, Chavan moved for leave to introduce the Twenty-fourth Amendment Bill in the Lok Sabha to delete from the Constitution two articles and a portion of a third providing for the Princes' purses and privileges.[48] P. K. Deo, of the Swatantra party and a member of a princely family, immediately challenged the bill on the ground that these covenants and agreements 'form the very basis of the Constitution, the foundations of the Constitution ... [and] it is not open to the legal, legislative competence of the House to challenge the foundations of the Constitution.'[49] Moreover, Deo averred, the purses were a property issue, which brought the Fundamental Rights into the picture. Balraj Madhok, a former activist with the militant Hindu RSS and a leader of the Jana Sangh party, supported Deo, although he wished the princes would voluntarily forego their privileges. Law Minister Menon responded by citing the President's speech opening Parliament in February in which he had said that rulership was '"incompatible with an egalitarian social order"'. After a voice vote allowed the bill to be

---

[47] *Indian Express*, 13 February 1970. Chavan's assessment of the princes' attitude, according to his biographer, was that 'For the princes, this was a matter of bread and butter ... . Even modern capitalists can perhaps give up their rights and privileges, but these people, entrenched so strongly in their own positions for centuries, would not like to lose them.' Kunhi Krishnan, T. V., *Chavan and The Troubled Decade*, Somaiya Publications Pvt. Ltd., Bombay 1971, p. 267.

[48] For the legislative history and text of the amending bill, see *Constitution Amendment in India*, pp. 171, 383.

Kunhi Krishnan, in his biography of Chavan, adds in a footnote that Mrs Gandhi suggested delaying introduction of the bill because she was negotiating secretly with the princes and a settlement was imminent in which the princes would forego fifty per cent of their purses. Kunhi Krishnan, *Chavan* p. 267.

[49] *Lok Sabha Debates*, Fourth Series, vol. 41, no. 6, col. 253.

introduced, the members shelved the bill until September. Negotiations between the government and the princes continued during the summer, but they came to naught, as the press occasionally reported.

At the end of August, just before Parliament would take up the bill again, its major opponents took a stand on the purses as a property and fundamental rights issue. They met as a Convention of the Fundamental Rights Front in Constitution Hall of Vithalbhai Patel House in New Delhi. N. A. Palkhivala and M. C. Chagla, advocates for the petitioners in the Bank Nationalization case and soon to represent the princes in their case, R. C. Cooper, the chief petitioner in the bank case, and former Chief Justice Subba Rao damned the bill. Delivering the presidential address, Subba Rao said that property is not an entrenched right but the weakest of the Fundamental Rights. It was up to the judiciary to decide 'the permissible limits of the laws of social control'.[50] Cooper and Chagla expressed their fear that there was an 'irresponsible majority' in Parliament.

On 1 September, Mrs Gandhi, having become Home Minister after shifting Chavan to Finance, moved that the Lok Sabha consider the bill. It was a bill historic 'in the further democratization of our society ... [representing] the momentum of social change in our country,' she said.[51] Morarji Desai responded that all Congressmen are committed to the abolition of the privy purses, but the bill 'is fraudulent and deceitful and is not consistent with the spirit of the Constitution'. He reiterated his claim that it would be a breach of faith not to honour commitments to the princes. Sriraj Dhrangadhra then spoke for the princes, saying that there was no greater hardship than dishonour, which the government was inflicting on the rulers. The glorious chapter written by the founding fathers is now 'brought to an inglorious end', he

---

[50] *Presidential Address and Other Papers for the National Convention*, Fundamental Rights Front/A. P. Jain, New Delhi, 1970, pp. 10–13.

[51] *Lok Sabha Debates*, Fourth Series, vol. 44, no. 26, col. 261. Moving consideration of the bill seems to have been a reversal of policy on the Prime Minister's part, for in a cabinet meeting in Parliament House on 27 August Mrs Gandhi said ' "there is no time for us to bring the bill relating to payments in this session." ' K. Hanumanthaiya Diary entry for 20 August 1970, p. 19, NMML.

A week prior to this, Hanumanthaiya—then Minister of Law and Social Welfare—had recorded his impressions of a meeting over tea with Chief Justice Hidayatullah and other Supreme Court justices at Justice Hegde's invitation. Expecting an 'elevating' discussion about judicial reforms, Hanumanthaiya was disappointed by the justices' talk of their being 'insidiously treated'. He wrote that 'the judges are in their own world of supremacy, the clients in their own world of misery, and the executive in its own world of indifference'. Diary entry for 20 August 1970, ibid., pp. 15–17.

said.[52] Chavan seemed to be trying to sugar-coat the pill when he said there could be transitional allowances. But these were not 'compensation' for 'certainly they [the purses] are not the property of the princes'.[53] Winding up the debate, Mrs Gandhi explained that the government's highest law officers believed the amending bill constitutional; hence it had not been sent to the Supreme Court for an advisory opinion. The agreements with the princes were not contracts, she said, but political agreements followed by the political act of presidential recognition of the princes. Thus the government could have discontinued the purses without an amendment, but it had moved an amending bill preferring 'to bring about a change by the democratic method of discussion'.[54] The Lok Sabha passed the bill with only eight votes more than the two-thirds majority required to pass a constitutional amendment. Among the 'noes' were many who would not qualify as conservatives, including Kamaraj, Acharya and Sucheta Kripalani, Ashoka Mehta, and N. G. Ranga.[55]

An Evening of Mystery

The bill met a decidedly different fate in the Rajya Sabha after a debate had re-emphasized the property/fundamental rights issues involved. Mohan Dharia, claiming paternity of the amendment, said that property being a fundamental right was 'the greatest possible impediment' to progress. Change must be brought about if the faith of the people in democracy was not to be lost.[56] Communist Party leader Bhupesh Gupta thought that the purses and privileges were not property and therefore the property provisions of the Constitution did not apply. Concluding the debate, the Prime Minister said that the purses were not property

[52] Ibid., col. 296

[53] *Lok Sabha Debates,* Fourth Series, vol. 44, no. 27, col. 225. Piloo Mody interrupted Chavan's speech, saying, 'My father ... advised the princes to compromise, to keep the purses and let Mr Chavan have the privy.'

[54] There had been discussion within the government about whether an amending bill was necessary, or whether the President could simply derecognize the princes. Law Minister Menon, who otherwise played a minor part in the affair, advised that a bill was needed. S. S. Ray interview with the author.

[55] After the vote, members of the opposition Congress, the Swatantra, and the Jana Sangh charged that there had been irregularities in the voting. They claimed that the government had received only 331 votes and therefore was defeated. *Indian Express,* 3 September 1970.

[56] *Parliamentary Debates, Rajya Sabha,* vol. 73, no. 28. col. 84. Three private members' bills abolishing the purses were pending at this time.

and no compensation would be paid. She invoked socialism as the justification for ending them. 'One section ... [of the party] wanted socialism ... major changes and ... [there was] another section which thought that independent India could grow and prosper within the old structure,' she said. 'It is not I who am showing a new light to the people; it is the people who are showing a new light to us.'[57]

Whatever the source of the light, it failed. The government's motion to consider the bill was defeated, 149 to 75. The Chairman of the Rajya Sabha, Vice President G. S. Pathak, had warned the government the previous afternoon that it might be difficult to calculate the fractions of votes. He was proved right when the vote did not 'satisfy' the Constitution's two-thirds requirement by one-third of a vote.[58] Many favouring abolition, but not liking the government's tactics, voted against the bill. Consternation and confusion. Mrs Gandhi departed furious— at Pathak and others—and a changed woman, according to some accounts.[59]

---

[57] *Parliamentary Debate, Rajya Sabha*, vol. 73, no. 29, col. 90.
Although there would be no compensation, Mrs Gandhi said, the 'human aspect' did call for transitional allowances.

M. N. Kaul, who had been Secretary of the Constituent Assembly (Legislative) while the princely states were being integrated and later was Secretary General of the Lok Sabha, recalled that Sardar Patel had never budged on the non-justiciability of the agreements with the princes. But 'nobody at the time thought that the payments were in perpetuity'.

[58] Immediately after the vote a call was made to the Law Ministry, where 'a few minutes of frenetic arithmetic' confirmed that the majority was insufficient. P. B. Venkatasubramanian in a letter to the author. The vote margin is more easily understood if the fractions two-thirds and one-third are reduced to decimals. A two-thirds majority would be .6666 per cent of the votes cast. But the aye votes totalled only .6651 per cent. This discrepancy has since been referred to as one-third of a vote.

[59] Mrs Gandhi was angry at Pathak for permitting the loss by such a narrow margin. I. K. Gujral interview with the author.

'After the vote, the Maharaja of Bikaner said to Mrs Gandhi, "You have saved us." Very upset, she responded, "We will execute you."' A senior member of the Prime Minister's staff in an interview.

The evening of September 3, sensing that the vote would be close, members of the cabinet met informally to discuss what to do should the bill fail. Views were expressed that the government need not resign over the issue and that a fresh bill would be needed. *Indian Express*, 4 September 1970.

The defeat was attributed variously: two members of Parliament missed the vote because they could not fly from Calcutta due to bad weather. (*Indian Express*, 6 September 1970.) A member of Parliament recalled that a DMK member absented himself at the moment of the vote. Another said a Congressman left for the toilet when the vote bell rang. Interviews with the author.

There is still no satisfactory published account of how events of the next ten hours resulted in what came to be referred to as the 'Midnight Order'. The government, in the person of Chavan, declined to give one to Parliament. No other official has offered a complete account. Mrs Gandhi may have taken the next step according to the government's Transaction of Business Rules, or she may have bent them. In either case, the Supreme Court would rule the step, itself, unconstitutional.[60] A meeting in Mrs Gandhi's Parliament House office of senior CPP members and a few others immediately following the bill's defeat discussed again the President's power to act in his discretion. Those present tipped toward the view that the President, having recognized the princes, could derecognize them. Meeting late that afternoon the cabinet's Political Affairs Committee—the Prime Minister, Fakhruddin Ali Ahmed, Jagjivan Ram, Y. B. Chavan, Swaran Singh, and Govinda Menon—decided on this course, having been informed by Attorney General Niren De that the process for the contemplated action could be taken within the Transaction of Business Rules. The Home Ministry prepared a note for the cabinet, which the Law Ministry cleared—but apparently without a formal process, including review by the Law Secretary—and the Home Secretary signed it. Several hours later the cabinet met and, without dissent, approved derecognition. An officer aboard an Air Force plane conveyed the note and the cabinet's decision to President Giri, who was in Hyderabad. The officer was instructed to inform Delhi by telephone or telegram when the President had assented to the decision.[61] It seems likely that Giri signed a broader derecognition order, for orders to individual princes concluded with 'By order and in the name of the President, L.P. Singh, Secretary to the Government of India'.[62] The deed was done. That

[60] These rules are classified by the Cabinet Secretariat. It seems to the author a flaw in Indian democracy that the public is denied knowledge of its government's routine rules of procedure. Description of the rules here was given to the author by a recently retired senior Home Ministry official.
This account of the events of 5 September is based on unusually sparse news dispatches and interviews with, among others, K. C. Pant, L. P. Singh, and B. N. Tandon.

[61] L. P. Singh in a letter to the author. B. N. Tandon recalled that Singh was cautious about mass derecognition, thinking it unethical and that the courts might strike it down. Interview with the author.

[62] One document read: 'No. 21/14/70–III Government of India Ministry of Home Affairs New Delhi the 6th September 1970, ORDER "In exercise of the power vested in him under Article 366(22) of the Constitution, the President hereby directs with effect from the date of this Order His Highness Maharajadhiraja Madhav Rao Jivaji Rao Scindia Gwalior do cease to be recognised as the Ruler of Gwalior"' followed by 'By order' etc., signed L. P. Singh. Singh remembers staying up all night signing the orders.

morning Mrs Gandhi departed for Lusaka and a meeting of the Non-Aligned Movement.[63]

In a statement to Parliament on 7 September, Chavan said that under the Constitution the President had 'the unquestioned power to de-recognize the Rulers'. Regrettably unable to get a constitutional amendment and fortified by its belief in the widespread support for 'putting an end to an antiquated system', said Chavan, the government acted to end 'uncertainties'.[64]

Madhav Rao Scindia and other princes immediately petitioned the Supreme Court under Article 32 to strike down the President's order as unconstitutional. They argued that the President had no power to withdraw the recognition of a ruler once he had been recognized; the order violated the constitutional mandates in Articles 291 and 362; and that derecognizing the rulers *en masse* was an arbitrary exercise of power for a collateral purpose—meaning that the government had attempted to do indirectly what it could not do directly. Claiming that his privy purse constituted property, Scindia said that deprivation of it violated his fundamental rights under Articles 19, 21, and 31.

The government argued that the petitions were not maintainable because the source of the right to receive a purse was 'a political agreement' and thus the purse was 'in the nature of a political pension'. In recognizing or derecognizing princes the President was exercising a political power that was sovereign, and the government could vary the rights and obligations 'in accordance with "State policy"'. The Indian government had inherited the concept of Paramountcy from the Crown;

---

[63] The *Hindustan Times* reported that President Giri's signature 'is understood to have been secured in Hyderabad last night before the Union cabinet took up the crucial decision in New Delhi.' Issue of 7 September 1970. The paper also reported that the aircraft bearing the document signed by the President returned to the capital at 1:34 a.m.

[64] 'Statement Laid by the Finance Minister on the Table of the Rajya Sabha, 7 September 1970.' Papers laid on the Table, LT 4167/70.

Chavan also thought that without the derecognition order 'the right reactionaries ... would have had the satisfaction of having thrown overboard a progressive measure'. Kunhi Krishnan, *Chavan*, p. 271.

Events may have occurred in somewhat different order. According to Chavan's account to Parliament, the cabinet met at 10:30 p.m., decided on derecognition in ten or fifteen minutes, and submitted its decision to President Giri between 11:00 and 11:30 p.m. Were this the case, the papers concerning derecognition—without the cabinet's decision—had been taken to Giri earlier by aircraft, and Giri received the Cabinet's decision by telephone. He then assented to derecognition on the basis of the preparatory materials he had in hand. This procedure is now acceptable, although unwritten, under the Transaction of Business Rules, according to the explanation given to the author by a senior official. Whether or not it was acceptable in September 1970, the author has been unable to discover.

therefore, recognition of 'Rulership' was a ' "gift of the Presidency" ', an act of state. Consequently, the government argued, the courts were excluded from enforcing agreements with the princes.

The Supreme Court struck down the derecognition order thirteen weeks later. Chief Justice Hidayatullah delivered a separate concurring judgement. Justice Shah and six judges of the eleven-judge bench delivered a judgement, with Justice Hegde concurring. Justices Ray and Mitter dissented.[65] Hidayatullah held: that the authority to recognize a ruler from among claimants to the 'throne', which the government had been exercising, was not an act of paramountcy. Therefore, Article 366(22) did not give the President the power to say there was no ruler of any state; that an 'act of state' was not available against a citizen; that the guarantees to the princes were part of the Constitution and therefore enforceable; and that the charging of the purses to the Consolidated Fund of India was 'to provide that this ... shall not be altered even by a vote of Parliament'. Finally, the majority held that the petitions were maintainable under Article 32 because the obligation to pay the privy purses was absolute.

Justices G. K. Mitter and A. N. Ray dissented. Although Mitter agreed in general with the majority, and found the order of the President 'unjustified', he did not think it subject to challenge under Article 363. Ray disagreed with the majority almost point by point. Accepting most of the government's submissions, he held that the agreements to pay privy purses 'were all political agreements born out of political bargains to achieve integration of the Indian states with the Dominion of India'. This political bargain was placed in Articles 291, 362, and 366, 'and the political character was preserved by inserting Article 363, which bar (sic) the jurisdiction of the court ...'.[66]

The decision capped a bad year for the Prime Minister. She just had

---

[65] Decision on 15 December 1970. The case was named *H. H. Maharajadhiraja Madhav Rao Jiwaji Rao Scindia Bahadur and Others v Union of India* 1971 (3) SCR 9ff. Members of the bench were: Chief Justice M. Hidayatullah and Justices J. C. Shah, C. A. Vaidialingam, K. S. Hegde, A. N. Grover, I. D. Dua, S. M. Sikri, J. M. Shelat, V. Bhargava, G. K. Mitter, and A. N. Ray.

Some legal authorities hold that, strictly speaking, paramountcy ended with India's independence.

[66] 1971 (3) SCR 229–30.

Article 363 says that neither the Supreme Court nor any court 'shall have jurisdiction in any dispute arising out of any provision of a treaty, agreement, covenant ... [etc.] which was entered into ... before the commencement of this Constitution by any Ruler of an Indian State ...'. The sole exception was reference to the Supreme Court for an advisory opinion.

been denied a populist plum she had thought ripe for the plucking—
first because she lacked the votes in Parliament, and then by the
Supreme Court. Her own party members' contribution to the defeat in
the Rajya Sabha must have been especially upsetting. She would have
expected no better from the Supreme Court, where the bench in the
Privy Purses case was nearly the same as the one that had ruled against
the government on bank nationalization.[67] And although she had
successfully nationalized the banks on the second try, the court had
caused the government to improve the compensation. Her government's
weakness in Parliament had prevented overcoming the Golak Nath
decision through enactment of the Nath Pai Bill. The old guard of the
Congress had formed the 'Grand Alliance' with Swatantra and the Jana
Sangh to fight the 1971 parliamentary elections and had stung her with
charges of being anti-democratic, while the Young Turks, the CFSA,
and the communists pressed her to fulfill her socialist promises.

Mrs Gandhi needed to gain control. Parliament was the place to
start. Nine days after the Supreme Court struck down derecognition,
she called upon the President and proposed that he dissolve the Lok
Sabha and call elections. He did so three days later, 27 December 1970,
on the cabinet's advice. That evening Mrs Gandhi told the nation in a
radio broadcast that the government could have remained in power
without an election. But, she said, we are concerned with using power to
satisfy our people's aspirations 'for a just social order'. The nationalization
of the banks, setting up the Monopolies Commission, and abolishing
the privy purses 'were welcomed by large masses of people throughout
the country ... [but] reactionary forces have not hesitated to obstruct ...
these urgent and vitally necessary measures'. The impatience of the
people was 'being exploited by political elements'. Time will not wait
for us, she said, so we have decided to go to our people.[68] Two days
later she told a news conference that when returned to power her party
would put through constitutional amendments to promote the interests
of the many against the few.[69] The twelve-point election manifesto

---

[67] The only differences were that Jaganmohan Reddy had retired after the bank
decision and Chief Justice Hidayatullah did not sit on that case.

[68] *AR*, 15–21 January 1971, p. 9958.

At a meeting of the Executive Committee of the Congress Parliamentary Party on 16
December, Mrs Gandhi reportedly rejected a suggestion by CFSA members that Parliament
be converted into a constituent assembly to amend the Constitution 'suitably'. *Indian
Express*, 17 and 19 December 1970.

[69] *AR*, 15–21 January 1971, p. 9960.

'"We are not in favour of curtailing all Fundamental Rights,"' the press quoted her as

published in January 1971 reiterated these themes, calling particularly for an 'end to anachronistic privileges such as privy purses etc'. To fulfill the manifesto's purposes one item in it said, 'such amendments of the Constitution [will be enacted] as may be necessary'.[70]

---

saying. '"We do not even want to take away the right to hold and enjoy property,"' but she went on 'to suggest', according to press reports, 'that her party would not in future treat property as a fundamental right'. Ibid.

[70] *People's Victory—An Analysis of 1971 Elections,* AICC, New Delhi, April 1971.

Chapter 10

RADICAL CONSTITUTIONAL AMENDMENTS

Amending the Constitution in pursuit of the social revolution was the domestic political motif of 1971.[1] Furious debate surrounded essential constitutional issues of personal liberty and the public good and constituent powers. Beliefs in the institutions and processes of representative government were tested. Not everyone, events would show, firmly believed in constitutional democracy. Four constitutional amendments, two of them radical, gave specific form to disputes simmering since the Constitution was inaugurated and bubbling since 1967. It was a vibrant time, for someone full of hope and expectation, for others full of anxiety for democracy and the integrity of the seamless web.

It was not only the Prime Minister's faction of the Congress Party that supported her programme of amendments—indeed, many of its members were more radical than she. The Congress(O) Working Committee and Morarji Desai strongly supported restoring to Parliament the power to amend the Constitution, including the Fundamental Rights, and they also supported abolition of privy purses.[2] The other political

[1] The principal international developments were the signing of the Indo-Soviet friendship treaty and the crisis next door in East Pakistan. Both affected domestic affairs, of which more will be heard. In East Pakistan, Sheikh Mujibur Rahman's popular movement for autonomy within Pakistan had culminated in an election victory in December 1970 which gave his Awami League a majority in the National Assembly, that entitled him to be prime minister of the whole country. Unable to accept this, West Pakistani political and military leaders in March 1971 arrested Rahman and began a period of atrocities against Pakistani Bengalis. Awami League leaders in India proclaimed an independent nation, Bangladesh. A combination of the continuing carnage in East Pakistan; the Indian government's awareness that the nation of Pakistan might be breaking up (with Indian help for Bengali guerrilla forces); the political and economic disruptions in West Bengal brought on by the arrival of nearly two million East Pakistani refugees; and, finally, an attack by Pakistani aircraft on western India on 3 December 1971 brought India and Pakistan into open war. Within several weeks, the Indian army defeated the Pakistani army in the East, a ceasefire would be announced for the West, and Mrs Gandhi declared in Parliament, 'Dacca is now the free capital of a free country.' Malhotra, *Indira Gandhi*, p. 140.

[2] *Congress Bulletin*, no. 3–5, April–June 1971, AICC, New Delhi, p. 114. Readers will recall that the *Congress Bulletin* stayed in the hands of the Congress (O) after the split of 1969.

parties sensed the political winds. Of ten election manifestos for the 1971 parliamentary elections, all but two called for some changes in the Constitution. The CPI wanted to 'restore' the supremacy of Parliament. So did the PSP and the SSP, and when they merged later in 1971 the new Socialist Party supported the amendments bestowing this supremacy. The Jana Sangh was cautious, calling for flexibility of amendment while ensuring that the Constitution's 'essential fabric ... is not tampered with levity (sic)'. The Communist Party Marxist went the furthest, proclaiming that the Constitution 'must go lock, stock and barrel and should be replaced by a new one enshrining the real sovereignty of the people'.[3] The Swatantra Party called for an 'unqualified guarantee' of the Fundamental Rights, while accusing others of 'systematic attempts ... to wreck the Constitution ... [and] destroy the liberty of the masses'.[4]

The *mantra* of 'socialism', like a tide, carried all but a few before it. 'Anything socialist was great,' recalled the Congress's Vasant Sathe. 'We thought property and capitalism absolutely bad.' There was a strong current in socialist directions, said ex-communist and Congress Forum member Chandrajit Yadav. The judiciary was seen as obstructive because of its decisions and for changing its mind, so there was wide support outside Parliament for amendment, remembered Madhu Limaye. The elections gave Mrs Gandhi a massive mandate to keep the courts away from amendments to the Constitution, thought a senior Law Ministry official, P. B. Venkatasubramanian.[5] The activists from the CFSA and a few others were influential as never again. When it came to asserting Parliament's authority, curbing the judiciary, and centralizing authority in the name of social revolution, Mrs Gandhi found herself pushing on an open door.

But her promises to amend the Constitution also awakened anxieties as 1971 began. Madhu Limaye continued to point out the danger to democracy of unbridled legislative power, despite his warnings being shrugged off as anti-Congressism. Chief Justice Sikri spoke to a bar association about the 'insidious efforts' to undermine the judiciary. The Constitution, not election returns, provided the only touchstone for

[3] CPM member of Parliament A. K. Gopalan repeated this during the debate on the Twenty-Fourth Amendment. *Lok Sabha Debates*, Fifth Series, vol. 7, no. 53, col. 159.

[4] Quotations are taken from the election manifestos in Mehta, *Election Manifestos, 1971.*

The two manifestos not calling for constitutional changes were those of the Tamil, socialist, Dravida Munnetra Kazhagam and the party of more-substantial peasants led by Charan Singh, the Bhartiya Kranti Dal or BKD.

[5] All in interviews with the author.

judges, he said, and asked, 'What kind of oath would a "committed judge" like to take?'[6] Former Chief Justice B. P. Sinha both defended the Supreme Court's power of judicial review and Parliament's authority to amend the Fundamental Rights.[7] K. Santhanam called the 'supremacy of Parliament' a 'specious slogan'. A written constitution and a powerful and impartial Supreme Court 'are indispensable for the protection of Indian federal democracy', he said.[8] Criticism would intensify as the amendments took shape.

But, her critics out-numbered, Mrs Gandhi was justified in interpreting the Congress's electoral showing and 350 seats in Parliament as a mandate for change. Likewise, it was a national vote of confidence in her, for in the 'delinked' election only seats in Parliament and her leadership of it were at issue. But what change? The citizenry had voted for Mrs Gandhi and *garibi hatao* in the hope that their lot might improve. But the Prime Minister's interest and that of many of her supporters was in political–economic theory, in constitutional change, and in the wielding of power— although they sincerely intended the constitutional changes to have immediate or trickle-down effects.

Framing the Amendments Begins

The returns from the 1–10 March 1971 elections were barely in when on 18 March Mrs Gandhi appointed H. R. Gokhale her Law Minister and the framing of the promised amendments began. Six ideas for carrying out the Congress's well-advertised intentions were afloat in the political and intellectual currents at the time.[9] One, parliamentary supremacy should be restored, along the lines of the Nath Pai Bill, to overcome the intrenchment of the Fundamental Rights by the Golak Nath decision. Two, the property articles (especially Article 31) should be amended to keep the courts away from property acquisitions and compensation issues. Three, 'property' should be taken entirely out of the Fundamental Rights. Four, the socialist promises of the Directive Principles of State Policy should be fulfilled by giving the Principles

[6] Speech to a conference of the bar of the Punjab and Haryana High Court. *Swarajya*, (a semi-official publication of the Swatantra Party), 27 March 1971. Sikri had become Chief Justice of India on 22 January, 1971.

[7] *Free Press Journal*, 23 January 1971.

[8] *Swarajya*, 30 January 1971. Acharya Kripalani admonished members of Parliament not to expect judges to represent public opinion. *Indian Express*, 30 January 1971.

[9] The following account is based upon interviews with more than a dozen individuals who then were participants or observers.

precedence over the Rights, even though the Constituent Assembly had made the Principles non-justiciable. Five, the princes' privileges and privy purses were to be abolished. Thought was given briefly to using legislation instead of constitutional amendment to abolish the princes' purses, but amendment won. And six, the perquisites of retirees from the 'Secretary of States Services' of the colonial period, the most prominent of which was the Indian Civil Service, were to be abolished.

Centrally engaged in sorting out ideas during the lengthy drafting process were Gokhale, Mohan Kumaramangalam, and S. S. Ray.[10] Gokhale, a convinced socialist, had been a trade union lawyer and a judge on the Bombay High Court—from which he resigned, complaining of the low pay. He had joined the Congress after the 1969 split, and after the 1971 elections, Kumaramangalam, Rajni Patel, and Ray, it is said, urged Mrs Gandhi to appoint him Law Minister, which helps to account for his reputation of being under their influence.[11] Ray was a long-time family friend of the Nehrus. He called Mrs Gandhi 'Indu' and he contributed loyalty, legal knowledge, and political 'savvy' unadulterated by democratic or ideological sensibilities. He provided many of the ideas for the Twenty-fourth Amendment, according to Sanjiva Reddy and others. Kumaramangalam, who was friendly with Mrs Gandhi, was the driving intellectual and ideological force of the trio (referred to by some as 'three musketeers'), and he made the most significant substantive contributions. Rajni Patel, once one of Bombay's 'whisky communists' and a Congress Party fund-raiser, and Dev Kanta Borooah, later Congress president, made contributions from their association with the Congress Forum for Socialist Action.[12] All functioned under Mrs Gandhi's instructions—if she gave them—and always under her watchful eyes.

The decision not to attempt to eliminate property from the Fundamental Rights and, instead, to pursue broader parliamentary authority, following the example of the Nath Pai Bill, seems to have been taken at the first cabinet meeting after the election. Mrs Gandhi

[10] In Mrs Gandhi's cabinet, announced on 2 May, were Kumaramangalam as Minister of Steel and Mines and Ray as Minister of Education (until he was sent off in March 1972 to be the Chief Minister of West Bengal and crack down on the Naxalites). Others included Chavan as Minister of Finance, Jagjivan Ram, Minister of Defence, and C. Subramaniam, Minister of Planning. The Prime Minister held the Home and several other portfolios.

[11] For the text of Gokhale's remarks when resigning from the High Court, see *Bombay Law Reporter*, Journal Section, vol. 68, 1966, p. 81. Gokhale joined the Congress at Rajni Patel's urging, according to a member of the Gokhale family. He ran for the Lok Sabha in 1971 at Kumaramangalam's urging, according to R. K. Garg and K. P. Unnikrishnan.

[12] From interviews with, among others, R. Venkataraman, S. S. Ray, Krishan Kant, N. K. Seshan, B. N. Tandon, K. C. Pant, S. K. Maitra, and P. B. Venkatasubramanian.

made this decision, reasoning, according to a person present, that the former course would arouse powerful resistance. As a result, Gokhale instructed the ministry through Law Secretary R. S. Gae late in March to 'get rid of the Golak Nath decision along the lines of Nath Pai', and the Twenty-fourth Amendment was born.[13] At the beginning of April, the AICC adopted a resolution calling for the necessary amendments, but, curiously, only after Mohan Dharia had moved such an addition to fill a lack in the original resolution.[14] In May and June came indications that there might be two amendments. One might address property, without removing it from the Rights, and another establish parliamentary sovereignty. The former was the germ of the first portion of the Twenty-fifth Amendment. Minister of State for Home Affairs R. N. Mishra told the press that the government was considering ways to deal with property rights because the Nath Pai model was inadequate.[15]

The by now highly influential Congress Forum, meeting in Bombay, adopted a resolution strongly favouring parliamentary sovereignty and attacking property. It advocated removing from the Constitution the article barring Parliament from making laws inconsistent with the Fundamental Rights—after which 'it would not be difficult to amend the Fundamental Rights' through ordinary legislation. The resolution also recommended amending Article 368 'to confer [sic] specifically the power of Parliament to amend Fundamental Rights'.[16] And the Forum suggested ending judicial review of laws 'in consonance' with the Directive Principles thus introducing an idea that would appear as the second portion of the Twenty-fifth Amendment. Raghunatha Reddy commented at the meeting that the Directive Principles 'should prevail' over the Rights were there a conflict between them.[17] The

---

[13] Gae instructions to P. B. Venkatasubramanian. R. V. S. Peri Sastri did the actual drafting. Venkatasubramanian interview with the author.

Some accounts of this cabinet meeting have Mrs Gandhi instructing Gokhale also to draft legislation—not a constitutional amendment—abolishing the princes' privileges and purses.

[14] *Congress Marches Ahead IV*, AICC, New Delhi, 1971, pp. 32–7. Y. B. Chavan had moved this 'Pledge to the People' resolution and accepted Dharia's addition. The common man, said Chavan, expected 'a new deal'; the Congress would 'serve ... [the people] and work for a better future'.

Concluding the session, Mrs Gandhi made her 'Our path is socialism' speech, used as a superscript for this part. Ibid., p. 70.

[15] *Statesman*, 1 May 1971.

[16] *Socialist India* (the CFSA journal), 8 May 1971, p. 19. Also, *Statesman*, New Delhi, 3 May 1971.

[17] *Socialist India*, p. 20.

Statesman reported early in June that in the property article Article 31(1) the word 'compensation' would be changed to 'amount' with the intent of ending judicial review of property legislation by denying the courts opportunity to apply qualifying adjectives—such as 'fair', 'just', 'adequate'—to 'compensation'.[18] The cabinet considered these drafts late in the month and early in July gave provisional approval to the Twenty-fourth Amendment's changes to Article 368.[19]

During June, unexpected language was added to the drafts of each amendment. To the Twenty-fourth was added a provision saying that the President 'shall give his assent' to a bill to amend the Constitution were one presented to him. This made explicit the convention of the Westminster Model—although, as mentioned earlier, Rajendra Prasad had questioned the convention. Accounts vary as to why the tacit now had been made formal. According to S. S. Ray, it was to establish the 'absolute supremacy of Parliament' by preventing a future President from refusing his assent.[20] It is doubtful that the provision was aimed at President Giri, known to be friendly with the Prime Minister. The ostensible, technical reason, according to a Law Ministry official, was to emphasize the distinction between presidential assent to ordinary legislation and to amendments, which were not 'law'.[21] Some others believed it was the CPI and the ex-communists in the CFSA who did not want 'their influence to be scuttled'. This supposition is supported by Rajni Patel's claim that he instigated inclusion of the provision.[22] The addition to the draft Twenty-fifth Amendment took to radical lengths the idea that the Directive Principles should have precedence over the Fundamental Rights. It inserted a new, two-part article into the Constitution (Article 31 C), the first part of which said that no law giving effect to certain of the Directive Principles should be void on the ground

---

More radically, the resolution recommended amending the articles providing for equality before and equal protection of the law so that the government could prescribe any land ceiling and take over lands in excess of the ceiling without compensation. Moving the resolution, Rajni Patel said the Constitution did not envisage the supremacy of the judiciary, rather that of Parliament, which 'represented the entire people of India'. Ibid., p. 19.

It was at this time, May, that the government nationalized general insurance by ordinance, and the Prime Minister 'restructured' the Planning Commission, ousting the highly respected economist, D. R. Gadgil, and appointing to it B. S. Minhas, Sukhamoy Chakravorty, and C. Subramaniam.

[18] *Statesman*, New Delhi. Editorial of 4 June 1971.

[19] *Hindustan Times*, 26 June 1971.

[20] Interview with the author.

[21] P. B. Venkatasubramanian in a letter to the author.

[22] Patel to Ram Panjwani, according to Panjwani in an interview with the author.

of inconsistency with several articles in the Fundamental Rights. More radically, the second part provided that no law declaring its intent to be fulfilment of the Principles could be questioned in court 'on the ground that it does not give effect to such policy'. Raghunatha Reddy, D. P. Singh, Chandra Shekhar, and Mohan Dharia drafted this article in Reddy's office when he was Minister of State for Company Affairs.[23]

After a meeting of its Political Affairs Committee on 15 July, the cabinet endorsed a Law Ministry note that laid out a strategy for three amendments: the first to establish parliamentary supremacy, another to modify the property article, and a third to end the princes' purses and privileges. The cabinet instructed Gokhale, Kumaramangalam, and Ray to make final revisions in the draft amendments. Finding the Twenty-fifth Amendment's new Article 31C controversial, the cabinet took it to a meeting of the Congress Parliamentary Party, where it was approved. The Law Ministry recommended that the amendment to Article 368 be enacted first to clear the way for the others. The amending bill on purses and privileges would be introduced in the session about to begin, but passage would be delayed until later.[24]

Two days before the 15 July cabinet meeting the Congress Forum had flexed its muscles publicly to complement its influence in the inner circles of government. On 13 July, 210 members of Parliament sent the Prime Minister a memorandum embodying the forum's positions and invoking the Congress election manifesto on constitutional amendments. The document contained the essence of the three amendments just described, and that of a fourth, one ending certain perquisites of the few surviving members of the ICS which would become the Twenty-eighth Amendment. A deputation of forty persons—including Krishan Kant,

---

[23] Raghunatha Reddy, in an interview with the author and confirmed by R. C. Dutt. K. P. Unnikrishnan recalled 'brainstorming' sessions in Reddy's home. Interview with the author.

The relevant Directive Principles were Article 39 (b) and (c): respectively, the State shall direct its policy towards securing that the ownership and control of the 'material resources of the community are so distributed as best to subserve the common good', and, the operation of the economic system 'does not result in the concentration of wealth and means of production to the common detriment'.

The Fundamental Rights that could not be invoked were Article 14 (equality before and equal protection of the law), Article 19 (the 'freedoms' article), and Article 31 (property). Article 31C clearly seems descended from the resolutions passed at the May CFSA meeting in Bombay.

[24] From reports in *Statesman* and *Hindustan Times*, 16 July 1971 and in *Socialist India*, 17 July 1971.

The Political Affairs Committee at this time consisted of Mrs Gandhi, F. A. Ahmed, Jagjivan Ram, Y. B. Chavan, and Sardar Swaran Singh.

Amrit Nahata, and D. P. Singh—delivered the memorandum to Mrs Gandhi, who responded that the government would consider it.[25] The initiative for the memorandum is disputed. According to some, the Forum conceived the idea in order to stiffen the Prime Minister's wavering resolve by demonstrating to her the strength of her support. Others think Mrs Gandhi instigated the affair—directly or by hint—to show the support she could muster for such radical measures. It was mutual, Krishan Kant recalled. 'Indira Gandhi understood the people's mind, but we were not sure she understood socialism.'[26]

Just ten days before the amendments would go to Parliament, the Forum again showed its strength by collaborating with the Congress Parliamentary Party—Krishan Kant, Secretary—to hold a seminar on 'Our Constitution and Social Transformation' whose declared purpose was to help jurists find a way out of the impasse created by Golak Nath.[27] Kant opened the seminar by saying that further social progress would be difficult if the Supreme Court's decisions were let stand, but there should be no antagonism between the Rights and the Principles. The Principles had been reduced to 'pious declarations', and to implement them 'it may become necessary to examine the basic needs of the Constitution,' Kant said.[28] The Attorney General, Niren De, told the meeting that the Constitution should be amended to ensure Indians' economic liberties, which were 'more fundamental than the Fundamental Rights'. He contended that 'an unamendable constitution is a contradiction in terms'.[29] Besides, asked De, what did the right to property amount to when ninety per cent of the population had none?

The report of the seminar, which was prepared by an 'Expert Committee' and sent to Mrs Gandhi by Krishan Kant, contained the full flavour of Congress Forum radicalism.[30] In its unanimously-agreed-to

[25] The *Times of India*, Bombay, 14 July 1971, described the MPs as belonging to the Congress Forum. The text of the memorandum appeared in *Socialist India*, 17 July 1971, pp. 5–6.

[26] Krishan Kant in an interview with the author. Interviews also with K. P. Unnikrishnan, R. C. Dutt, and S. L. Shakdher. There were rumours that D. P. Dhar had put the word about that the Prime Minister would welcome evidence of support.

The memorandum recommended that 'socialist' should be added to the Constitution's Preamble to define 'Republic'—a move whose time would come in 1976 with the Forty-second Amendment.

[27] *Statesman*, 13 July 1971. Former Chief Justice S. K. Das and Akbar Ali Khan, then Vice-Chairman of the Rajya Sabha, chaired the seminar.

[28] *Socialist India*, 24 July 1971.

[29] *Statesman*, 19 July 1971; *Socialist India*, 24 July 1971.

[30] Members of the committee were: M. Chalapathi Rau, editor of the pro-Nehru Lucknow newspaper, *National Herald;* V. A. Seyid Muhammad, Advocate General of Kerala,

narrative section, the report said that 'no provision of the Constitution is immutable ... the power of amendment ... is in the nature of a safety valve ... an unamendable Constitution is the worst possible tyranny ... [T]he word "compensation" should find no place' in the Fundamental Rights. The rights in Articles 14, 19, and 31 'must be withdrawn ... to reduce the concentration of wealth in the urban sector ... and monopolies in the industrial sector ... Without these changes our commitment to establish a socialist society shall remain a dead letter ... Parliament and legislatures must be free to exercise complete control over the ownership of the means of production and the property used for controlling others.' The report concluded with recommendations like those by the 210 members of Parliament.[31]

The public personalities who had so often criticized government policy reacted to these views negatively and sharply. Ashoka Mehta, N. A. Palkhivala, Subba Rao, and K. Santhanam challenged the seminar's 'propaganda' and its assumption that the Fundamental Rights obstructed social change.[32] For Subba Rao, the right to property and to do business 'is sought to be substituted ... by a totalitarian philosophy ... [enabling] the State ... to confiscate property directly or indirectly or nationalise any business ...'.[33] For Palkhivala, an attempt to abrogate the Fundamental Right to property 'would ... run counter to the eternal laws of human nature ... . "Property" has become a dirty word today, "Liberty" may ... tomorrow.'[34] Mehta wrote in the Sunday Statesman that excluding property from the Fundamental Rights could be 'looked into specifically'.

---

intervenor against the plaintiffs in the Golak Nath case, and later Minister of State for Law; Lotika Sarkar, professor of law at Delhi University; S. C. Aggarwal, advocate in the Supreme Court; and S. K. Goyal, the young economist close to the Young Turks.

[31] The report of the seminar was made under its second name, 'Parliamentarians' Seminar on Constitutional Amendments'. See Socialist India, 31 July and 7 August 1971.

Opinion at the seminar was unanimous that privy purses and privileges should be abolished. ICS privileges 'should be withdrawn forthwith'. The Expert Committee report also said, '[N] either the Union nor the States had treated them [the Directive Principles] with the respect they deserved ... . It was found necessary to amend the Constitution ... to compel the state to implement these directives under a duty to report to the President each year.' No law enacted to implement the Principles could be questioned 'on the ground of violation of any' of the Fundamental Rights (author's emphasis). Krishan Kant predicted '"bloody revolution"' if the government failed to bring about social changes, one newspaper reported.

[32] Swarajya, 31 July 1971.

[33] Subba Rao, K., 'Can Parliament Change' in Motherland, 26 July 1971.

[34] Palkhivala, N. A., 'Defend the Constitution and Protect the Common Man', Swarajya, Annual Number, 1971.

Otherwise, 'the Fundamental Rights determine the character of our polity
... [and] the Directive Principles ... will be robbed of their substance the
moment fundamental rights are made vulnerable.'[35]

Amendments in Parliament: The Twenty-Fourth

The stage had been set and the previews had revealed the play by the
time Law Minister H. R. Gokhale introduced the Twenty-fourth and
Twenty-fifth Amendments in the Lok Sabha 28 July 1971. They were
debated that day and for two days in August. The Rajya Sabha debated the former on 10 August and passed it on the eleventh, and the
President gave his assent to the bill on 5 November after ratification
by the states. The Twenty-fifth Amendment was not debated again
until 30 November, in part because the enactment of the Twenty-fourth
Amendment was to clear the way for it. The Twenty-sixth Amendment,
terminating the princes' purses and privileges, would be introduced
on 9 August. Debate on it was scheduled for early December, coincidental with debate on the Twenty-fifth Amendment.[36] The
Twenty-eighth Amendment, affecting ICS conditions of service, would
be introduced in May 1972.

In the midst of this activity, on 9 August came the signing of a
twenty-year Treaty of Peace, Friendship and Cooperation with the Soviet
Union. Arrived at, from the Indian side, because the government wanted
a deterrent to Chinese (or American) intervention should India have to
intervene to stop the blood-letting in East Pakistan, the signing greatly
enhanced the Prime Minister's domestic standing and seemed to be an
imprimatur for her radical constitutional policy. Congress Forum members
were 'electrified ... with joy', according to press reports.[37]

[35] Mehta, Ashoka, 'Fundamental Rights: Implications of Abridgement', *Sunday
Statesman*, 25 July 1971.

[36] At this time there had been introduced several private members' bills favouring
ending the princes' privileges and purses and ICS privileges, and there were eleven such
bills enabling Parliament to amend any part of the Constitution. Atal Bihari Vajpayee added
yet another private members' bill on 9 August calling for a national referendum on any
amendment of the Fundamental Rights. (From a study of private members' bills conducted
for the author by A. N. Kaul.) The Law Minister responded negatively in the Lok Sabha to
a suggestion from Morarji Desai that the government refer the issue of Parliament's power
to amend the Fundamental Rights to the Supreme Court for an advisory opinion.

[37] Negotiations for a treaty had languished since 1969 until P. N. Haksar and D. P.
Dhar urged the Prime Minister quickly to conclude an agreement. For the roles of Haksar
and Dhar, see Frankel, *Political Economy*, pp. 469–70. For the CFSA's delight, see Awana,
Pressure Politics, p. 223.

The Twenty-fourth Amendment went beyond Nath Pai's simple bill—that Parliament could amend any part of the Constitution. It excluded amendments from the reach of Article 13—Parliament could make no law infringing the Fundamental Rights. It empowered Parliament to amend any part of the Constitution 'by way of addition, variation or repeal', and it amended another clause in Article 368 to require that the President 'shall' give his assent to any constitutional amendment bill presented to him for assent.

The Twenty-fifth Amendment was devoted to the property article of the Fundamental Rights (Article 31) and the status of the Rights overall. The word 'amount' replaced 'compensation' for compulsorily acquired property, and the courts were barred from questioning the 'amount' on grounds that it was not adequate or paid other than in cash. It also inserted the new Article 31C, as already described, including the 'escape clause' (the author's term) that no law declaring its purpose to be fulfilling the Directive Principles in Article 39(b) and (c) could be challenged in court on the ground that it did not do so. The fundamental rights of equality before the law (Article 14), the 'freedoms' of Article 19, and the property terms of Article 31 were to be made subordinate to the two most classically socialist of the Directive Principles, and an entire category of legislation placed beyond judicial review.[38] These amendments now will be taken up individually.

With the Treasury Benches full following a three-line Whip, Gokhale moved consideration of the Twenty-fourth Amendment. The 'people are sovereign and Parliament, which is fully representative of the people, is supreme ... [elected] to remove impediments to the fulfilment of our socio-economic programmes,' he said.[39] He derided the 'argument of fear and nervousness' that the bill endangered fundamental rights like those of speech and assembly. Proclaiming the bill's innocence, he said it was merely an enabling amendment. Supporting him, S. S. Ray said that the Fundamental Rights are sacrosanct so long as the Right is fundamental and to be fundamental it has to be a Right. Life and liberty are natural rights, Ray said, inherent and innate. But civil rights, like property and freedom of contract are an outgrowth of civilization and, for Indians, did not pre-exist the Constitution. One assumes that he meant that the right to property could be taken away. Ray apparently was oblivious to this being criticism of the Twenty-fifth Amendment's Article 31C, which jeopardized the rights to life and liberty, the very rights he had categorized

[38] For the relevant Rights and Principles, footnote 23 also above.
[39] *Lok Sabha Debates*, Fifth Series, vol. 7, no. 53, col. 146.

as inherent and innate. He cited Franklin Roosevelt's desire for "'Justices who will not undertake to override the judgement of the Congress on legislative policy"'. He played down the Golak Nath decision: 'Excessive import should not be given to the single judgement of a narrowly divided court.' And he pointed out that in Shankari Prasad the court had ruled the Fundamental Rights amendable.[40]

Speaking later on the provision in the amendment compelling the President to assent to amending bills, Gokhale offered a seemingly contrived explanation. This really was 'the government depriving itself of its power to advise the President to withhold assent', he said. '[T]he power of the Council of Ministers is taken away by saying that the President shall give his assent, the reason being that in a matter where the Parliament has sat as a constituent body and exercised its sovereign power ... not even the government should have the power to advise the President to use the power of veto.'[41] An editorial in *Socialist India* came closer to the mark when it said that the provision 'would also eliminate the delaying power which the President could exercise by withholding assent temporarily under Article 111 and remitting any particular bill to Parliament for reconsideration'.[42]

Mrs Gandhi commended the bill as serving the common man. 'I see no reason in a denial of radical change .... Commitment is a good word and our commitments are [directed at] change in the lives of millions of people.' Returning to her father's arguments about 'compensation' during the First Amendment debate, she asked, 'Compensation for what ... compensation for land ... for a palace or big house? ... [W]hat about compensation for injustice?' We do not intend to abolish property, she added, but 'where property rights are in conflict with public purpose, the public purpose must hold sway'.[43] Congress Forum members predictably supported the bill. Kumaramangalam charged that every opponent of the bill was a man of property, and he attacked Supreme Court judges as coming from 'the class of men of money and property

[40] Ibid., cols 255, 258.
The Statement of Objects and Reasons accompanying the bill connected it directly to the Golak Nath decision, saying that the court reversed its earlier decisions 'upholding the power of Parliament to amend all parts of the Constitution' by a narrow majority. Therefore, it is necessary 'to provide expressly' that Parliament can amend any part of the Constitution.
[41] *Lok Sabha Debates*, Fifth Series, vol. 7, no. 54, cols 360–1.
[42] *Socialist India*, 31 July 1971. Writing in *Swarajya* on 7 August, K. Santhanam called the provisions 'a wholly unwarranted insult to the President'.
[43] *Lok Sabha Debates*, Fifth Series, vol. 7, no. 54, cols 267ff, especially col. 368.

... that undemocratic collection of very respected gentlemen'.[44] The Congress(O) decided on 2 August to give its support.

Opponents of the bill were impressive in argument, although not in the number of votes they could muster. Their pleas to protect civil liberty and the Constitution from outrage went unheeded. The Socialist Party, a recent merger of the PSP and SSP, said it supported the bill, but in essence it did not, for with 'support' came its reservation that Parliament had no right to amend any of the Fundamental Rights beyond property.[45] The several species of communists presented the curious spectacle of being more solicitous of the Fundamental Rights than the ex-communists and others of the Congress Forum. This perhaps is not curious: those out of power were more concerned about civil liberties than those in power. Hiren Mukerjee, the prestigious elder statesman of the CPI, spoke of 'our reservations ... misgivings ... suspicions' about how the government might use its massive majority.[46] The CPI offered an amendment to the amending bill exempting the freedoms of speech, assembly, association, and movement from abridgement by it— only to withdraw its amendment at Kumaramangalam's urging.[47] CPM members A. K. Gopalan, Somnath Chatterjee, and others, while supporting the amending bill, also favoured protecting rights like speech.[48] Swatantra member P. K. Deo, while being heckled loudly from the Treasury Benches, recalled Asoke Sen's characterization of the Nath Pai Bill as dangerous because a supreme and irresponsible Parliament with an irresponsible majority 'may sweep away the very basis of the Constitution'.[49] Vajpayee and his Jana Sangh party colleagues walked out when the Speaker refused to allow a full discussion of Deo's points. DMK member Era Sezhiyan pointed out that the Joint Committee on the Nath Pai Bill had recommended state ratification of amendments affecting the Fundamental Rights.

[44] Ibid, cols 219, 222ff.

[45] Karpoori Thakur to a press conference in Patna on August 20. *Hindustan Times*, 23 August 1971. Thakur, former Chief Minister of Bihar, had chaired the merger meeting of 9 August. The merger lasted nine months until it foundered due to a conflict between Madhu Dandavate and Raj Narain.

Opponent of the Nath Pai Bill and of Parliamentary authority to amend all the Fundamental Rights, Socialist Party leader Madhu Limaye was sticking to his guns. See *Janata*, Independence Day Number, 1971, p. 26.

[46] *Lok Sabha Debates*, Fifth Series, vol. 7, no. 54, col. 405.

[47] Noorani, A. G. 'The Constitutional Crisis', *Indian Express*, New Delhi, 15 December 1974.

[48] For Gopalan, see *Lok Sabha Debates*, Fifth Series, vol. 7, no. 53, col. 161.

[49] *Lok Sabha Debates*, Fifth Series, vol. 6, no. 48, col. 286.

All changes to the amending bill seeking to give extra protection to fundamental rights other than property were defeated. The bill passed 384 to 23 in the Lok Sabha with Congress members thumping their tables and shouting '"victory to the people"'.[50] Little of the debate in the Rajya Sabha, where the bill passed 177 to 3, distinguished it from that in the Lok Sabha.

The bill then went to the state legislatures for ratification—a course that would not have been taken but for the support for ratification given to the Law Minister by senior civil servants. The Secretary of the Law Ministry, R. S. Gae, had sent a memorandum in mid-July to Gokhale predicting that 'laws enacted in pursuance of the Article [368] as amended' would be ruled unconstitutional if the amending bill were not ratified.[51] Gae also suggested to Gokhale that M. C. Setalvad, as a former Attorney General, might be consulted. S. S. Ray and Kumaramangalam concurred, although they were thought by some to consider ratification needless. So, late in July, Gae travelled to the southern hill station of Ootacamund to meet 'Mr Law'. Within a few days, Setalvad sent a written opinion that the bill needed ratification.[52] His advice was rejected during further consultations in New Delhi. Gokhale told the Lok Sabha at the end of the second reading of the bill that ratification would not be sought because it was required only if an amendment affected federal issues.[53] Proponents of ratification persisted, and, at the last moment, the matter went to the Prime Minister, who decided in favour of ratification.[54] Only a few hours after saying the bill need not be ratified, an embarrassed Gokhale had to tell the Lok Sabha that it would be.[55]

Positive and Negative Reactions

A spate of reportage and commentary in the press greeted the three amendments when they were introduced. '24 Yes, 25 No' was the title of the lead editorial in the *Hindustan Times,* reflecting the mood of many. The flexibility of the pre-Golak Nath situation must be restored,

[50] *Hindu,* 5 August 1971.

[51] R. S. Gae in a letter to the author. Gae was supported by two of his senior officers, S. K. Maitra and P. B. Venkatasubramanian. (Their interviews with the author.)

[52] Gae letter to the author.

[53] *Lok Sabha Debates,* Fifth Series, vol. 7, no. 54, col. 359.

[54] S. L. Shakdher interview with the author.

[55] *Lok Sabha Debates,* Fifth Series, vol. 7, no. 54, col. 416. Many of those involved recalled that the Joint Committee on the Nath Pai Bill had recommended its ratification 'in view of the importance of the Fundamental Rights'. *Report of the Joint Committee,* p. vii.

the paper said, but Article 31C opened the door to 'arbitrary and vindictive political action against which the citizen has no redress'. The *Statesman* editorialized that the communists wanted the bills to enable them to impose any law on the ground that it was compatible with the Directive Principles. The *Indian Express* warned that the ruling party 'might not always be one that believes in orderly progress on democratic lines'. Loyal to Mrs Gandhi, the *National Herald* favoured both amendments and said 'nobody but monopolists and fascists can oppose' Article 31C. *Socialist India* said that the amendments should be welcomed by those who believed in 'major social change and redressing entrenched injustice through peaceful and democratic means'. M. C. Setalvad, who in the Rajya Sabha had favoured the Twenty-fourth Amendment for restoring the pre-Golak Nath situation, characterized the Twenty-fifth as an '"unwise step and a complete negation of the rule of law"'.[56] C. Rajagopalachari and V. M. Tarkunde also thought the amendment dangerous for democracy.

Unexpectedly, a startling critique came from a body within the Law Ministry, the Law Commission. The commission, as noted earlier, had been 'reconstituted' to make it more sympathetic to the government's views—in the same month that these amendments had been presented to Parliament. Initially, its members had not jarred expectations. For example, commission member Krishna Iyer, after the amendments had been presented to Parliament, wrote that he thought Article 31C had established a 'new harmony' between the Rights and the Principles. Talk of social justice is 'gibberish ... where inhuman poverty' is widespread and 'accumulated inequity wearing the armour of property rebuffs drastic restraints', he said.[57] Yet, the commission published an unsolicited report opposing portions of the Twenty-fifth Amendment a month before Parliament would take it up. Not all of the freedoms in Article 19 should be made secondary to implementation of the Directive Principles, the commission recommended, only clauses (1)(f) and (g)

[56] At a symposium at the Punjab University Law Department. *Motherland,* 8 November 1971.

[57] *Hindu,* 15 September 1971. Krishna Iyer quoted Lord Hailsham, then Lord Chancellor, that the law of one age may be the injustice of another, and that the courts were to say what the law is and Parliament was to make laws in the spirit of the day.

Commission chairman, former Chief Justice Gajendragadkar, had found it 'difficult to assume' that the framers thought the Fundamental Rights 'were immutable'. He thought that Parliament should be capable of amending the Rights to conform with the principles 'essential for the governance of the country'. Gajendragadkar, P. B., *The Constitution of India: Its Philosophy and Basic Postulates,* Oxford University Press, Nairobi, 1970, pp. 83–4. The Gandhi Memorial Lectures at University College, Nairobi, 1968.

of that article (the rights to property and to practice a profession or carry on an occupation or business) which the Supreme Court had used in striking down bank nationalization.[58] And the report 'strongly' advocated that the 'escape clause' of new Article 31C be omitted. It saw 'no justification for excluding judicial enquiry ... as to whether there is any rational nexus ... between the law passed ... and the objective intended to be achieved'.[59]

Gajendragadkar was sufficiently concerned about these elements of Article 31C to speak to the Prime Minister about them. At least ten days before the Law Commission would issue its report, he met her and expressed his 'serious misgivings' about the article. He then wrote to her on 18 October reminding her of his 'misgivings' and informing her that he had spoken about the amendment 'with my friends Ministers Gokhale, Mohan Kumaramangalam and Siddhartha Shankar Ray'. Because the Law Commission would soon make its report on the bill to the Law Ministry, Gajendragadkar continued, 'I am keen to meet you and give my views for your consideration before you take a final decision.'[60] If the requested meeting took place, Mrs Gandhi was not swayed.

Gokhale, also, had doubts about Article 31C, and, especially, about the 'escape clause'. He asked R. S. Gae to analyse it. Gae did so in a ten-page paper in which he advised that 'this provision in Article 31C be deleted'.[61] Gokhale's doubts, reinforced by Gae's and the Law Commission's views, seem to have caused him to attempt to soften the Twenty-fifth Amendment. Four days before the bill was to be considered he suggested three amendments to it. These allowed courts, with some restrictions, to review laws passed under Article 31C by Parliament and state legislatures;

---

[58] Law Commission of India, *Forty-sixth Report on the Constitution (Twenty-fifth Amendment) Bill, 1971,* Ministry of Law, GOI, New Delhi, undated (but report signed 28 October 1971), p. 10. The report quoted at some length Austin, *Cornerstone,* to the effect that the Indian Constitution is first and foremost a social document.

[59] Ibid., p. 11. As foundation for their views on the Twenty-fifth amendment, Commission members first discussed the Twenty-fourth, saying that it gave Parliament no power not originally held under Article 368. They believed it would not be challenged in court. Turning to the latter amendment, with whose object they were in 'full agreement', the members said that Parliament was taking the 'first major and significant step towards implementing two of the Directive Principles ... . So far as we are concerned, the days of *laissez faire* and the rule of the market are over ... [T]he Directive Principles ... must become a reality ... of national life.' Ibid., pp. 5, 10.

[60] Letter dated 18 October 1971. Gajendragadkar Papers, Subject File I, NMML.

Two weeks after the Commissin chairman had written this letter, Mrs Gandhi received an honourary doctorate in civil law from Oxford University.

[61] Note by R. S. Gae dated 12 November 1971. Ibid.

said that such laws must be passed by a two-thirds majority; and provide for market value compensation for takeover of property belonging to educational institutions run by religious and linguistic minorities. Raghunatha Reddy, Dharia, and others, opposed the changes. The government withdrew them and they were not moved in Parliament.[62] The Prime Minister had allowed her Law Minister to venture forth and then let others overrule him.

Amendments in Parliament: The Twenty-Fifth

When Parliament resumed consideration of the Twenty-fifth Amendment on 30 November, Gokhale acted the good soldier. He said that the government found it difficult to accept the Law Commission's recommendations in regard to Article 31C. All the freedoms in Article 19 must be excluded as a basis for judicial review of legislation declared to be for implementing the Directive Principles. The commission's recommendation that the 'escape clause' be deleted was not acceptable because if the courts could decide whether or not a law truly implements the Directive Principles, we would be 'dropping the judges ... into an arena which rightly belongs to the field of public life with which a judge ... is not concerned ... [T]he worst danger is that we enable them to infuse their own political philosophy in their judgements, which unfortunately has been the experience ... for the past ten years.'[63]

Mohan Kumaramangalam supported 'his' bill, arguing that there is nothing arbitrary or undemocratic about taking property for a public purpose and that judges should not decide political matters. 'We should not permit the courts ... to sit in judgement on issues which are really political.' It 'is for us to decide ... whether the laws would in reality implement the Directive Principles'. He quoted Morris Cohen that limiting the property rights of large landholders ' "may promote real freedom" '.[64] Soon we shall be taking over coal mines, Kumaramangalam

---

[62] Nakade, Shivraj, 'The Constitution (Twenty-Fifth) Amendment—A New Social Order', *JCPS*, vol. 6, no. 3, 1972, pp. 69–70.

[63] *Lok Sabha Debates*, Fifth Series, vol. 9, no. 12, col. 230.

Gokhale also defended the bill as part of a programme to restructure the 'entire socio-economic fabric' of the country, which would involve greater government 'intervention including nationalization'. Judges were to be protected from themselves and saved from the 'catastrophe' of public controversy. Ibid., cols 222, 225.

There was a more mundane reason for not removing Article 31C from the amending bill: it would have taken a cabinet decision to do so, reopening an issue more conveniently left closed.

[64] Ibid., cols 311, 317, 318.

said; should compensation include coal still underground? We say no, but it is a matter for Parliament to decide. Here in India some have property and 'vast millions ... have none or little'.[65] But V. K. Krishna Menon—socialist in outlook but at this time the Prime Minister's opponent—although supporting the bill as 'necessary', criticized the amendment's being 'rushed through'. He pointed out that legislation does not cure everything and called the amendment 'purely political claptrap and vote-catching'.[66] Piloo Mody agreed with two communist speakers that reactionaries were less obstacles to socialism than was the socialists' inability to live up to their preaching.[67]

Mrs Gandhi took the floor, to speak righteously of economic justice and the exercise of power. It was 'ridiculous to talk about arbitrary use of powers', she said, because the whole issue had been put before the people, who had spoken. What is market value?, she then asked. 'It is unacceptable to us that a few should skim the cream of social investments, defrauding society as a whole .... The whole idea of private profit at the cost of the common man is repugnant to me, to my party, and, I think, to the nation.' As to the judiciary, we do not wish to weaken it, but 'there is no decision in the world which is not political'.[68] Concluding this portion of the debate, the Law Minister wholly reversed the positions of the Principles and the Rights. '[T]he fundamental basis of all the structure that we provide for the governance of the country should be the Directive Principles and not the Fundamental Rights,' he said.[69] After the third reading, the Lok Sabha passed the bill 353 to 20.

In the Rajya Sabha, where debate began 7 December, attempts to delay the bill failed. The arguments made were familiar. For M. C. Setalvad, Article 31C destroyed the basis of the Constitution, 'judicial review in the rule of law'.[70] For M. C. Chagla, the Fundamental Rights were 'the essence of our Constitution', and the Directive Principles could be implemented without violating them. Parliament can change the Fundamental Rights only with a two-thirds majority, but a chief minister can 'wipe out' Articles 14, 19, and 31 by making a declaration

---

[65] Ibid., col. 316. Kumaramangalam mentioned favourably Salvador Allende's nationalization of Chile's copper mines. He cited T. H. Green and echoed an argument he attributed to Friedrich Engels: 'Since the enjoyment of property by the small narrow groups is dependent on the non-enjoyment by millions, it is "theft".'

[66] Ibid., no.13, cols 307, 313.

[67] Ibid., no. 12, col. 282.

[68] Ibid., no. 13, cols 337–46.

[69] Ibid., no. 13, col. 353.

[70] *Parliamentary Debates, Rajya Sabha,* 1971, vol. 78, no. 18, col. 46.

regarding a bill, Chagla pointed out correctly.[71] L. K. Advani said the Jana Sangh would support any bill earnestly seeking to implement the Directive Principles. But for twenty-five years the executive had failed to implement them. 'I regard this bill only as an attempt to make the judiciary and the Constitution a scapegoat for its own failures,' Advani said.[72] Again, the bill passed overwhelmingly.

The end for the princes' privileges and privy purses came in the Lok Sabha on 2 December when it debated and passed the Twenty-sixth Amendment in a single day—the day before the President declared a national emergency after Pakistan attacked India in the Punjab. The Rajya Sabha acted equally swiftly a week later. Introducing the amending bill in the Lok Sabha, the Prime Minister said that its principle had already been accepted 'with an overwhelming majority' in the Parliament. Its earlier failure to pass was 'a technical failure ... the will of the people was not in doubt'.[73] Chandra Shekhar expressed the views of the large number favouring the bill when he called the princes 'kings, remnants of feudalism, creating hurdles [to progress] in undivided India'.[74] The princes' spokesman, Fatesinghrao Gaekwad of Baroda, said the princes had been wronged by the government's 'unilateral and arbitrary decision' to abrogate 'sacred agreements'. All in all, it was not a pretty spectacle. Even supporters of the bill like Shyamnandan Mishra criticized the 'slovenly and improper manner' in which the issue had been handled.

In May 1972, after the Congress Party had won handsomely the March 'mini-General Elections' to state legislatures, Parliament passed the Twenty-eighth Amendment empowering itself to alter the pension and privileges of surviving members of the British-formed Indian Civil Service. The Amendment fell short of being a noble endeavour, and its economic significance was miniscule, for only eighty-one serving and retired officials were involved. Yet for the government, 'the concept of a class of officers with immutable conditions of service is incompatible with the changed social order,' said Minister of State for Home Affairs Ram Niwas Mirdha, introducing the bill for the two hours of debate allowed.[75] Attacking

---

[71] Ibid., no. 19, cols 3–11.

[72] Ibid., col. 185.

[73] *Lok Sabha Debates*, Fifth Series, vol. 9, no. 14, col. 139.

[74] The speech, in Hindi, was translated for the author by Giridar Rathi.

[75] *Lok Sabha Debates*, Fifth Series, vol. 16, no. 54, col. 275. Technically, the bill did not alter the pension and other privileges of retired and still-serving members of the civil service established by the British, which, once manned exclusively by them, by independence had admitted a large number of talented Indians. The bill only empowered Parliament to 'vary or revoke, whether prospectively or retrospectively', the terms of service. But it contained

these 'privileges' was not new. Private members' bills in this vein had been introduced in 1965, 1967, and 1970, and one was pending at this time. The brief debate permitted a number of members to criticize Indian Administrative Service officers (who replaced the ICS) as neither 'committed' to socialism and social revolutionary goals nor fitted by background or training to effectuate social and economic programmes in their districts. Although the bill passed 286 to 4 because it was seen as 'removing an anachronism', communist members deprecated it as 'another vote-catching slogan ... to divert the people's attention from the realities of the situation'.[76]

The Web's Seamlessness Forgotten

Among the varied beliefs and intentions of the Twenty-fourth and Twenty-fifth Amendments' proponents, several were commonly held: socialism, both as end and means, was unquestionably good; the Constitution's goal of social revolution had been ignored; Parliament had to be made supreme over a property-oriented and capricious judiciary. The amendments successfully cleared the way for large-scale nationalizations in industry and commerce that survived judicial scrutiny. Kumaramangalam had mentioned coal in this context while speaking in Parliament. In the months after the amendment passed, coal, coking coal, and copper mines were nationalized, along with steel plants, textile mills, and shipping lines—totalling hundreds of nationalizations. Kumaramangalam and his followers believed nationalization to be a 'good', even if efficiencies did not result, although Kumaramangalam strongly had advocated public sector efficiency.[77] Nationalization was

---

a provision that denied the Supreme Court or any other court jurisdiction over disputes arising from the amendment, a device that Mrs Gandhi would frequently employ in future amendments.

[76] Somnath Chatterjee. Ibid., col. 282. This was 29 May. The Rajya Sabha considered the bill on 30–31 May and the President assented to it 27 August 1972.

Most of the so-called privileges had become inoperative. The one thousand pounds annual pension had been reduced in the 1950s to a fixed sum of rupees. ICS officers recruited in London before 1924 were entitled to home leave every few years, an allowance paid in sterling. But in 1972, few such individuals were still alive. After the amendment's passage, the retirement age for ICS members was set at that for IAS members, age fifty-eight.

This did affect the few ICS members serving in the IAS.

[77] S. Guhan, who at the time served under C. Subramaniam in the Industry Ministry, in an interview with the author.

Kumaramangalam was not a man for subterfuge. He made his views clear in speeches and articles. One of his lesser known publications, published posthumously, is *Coal Industry*

attractive to less Marxist individuals because mine and mill owners and managers often exploited their properties shamelessly, placing profit above maintaining healthy enterprises. Land reform efforts were to be revived and strengthened, but the government and the Congress Party again would demonstrate that their socialism did not extend to the countryside.[78]

Kumaramangalam and the ex-communists in the Congress Forum held an extreme position in their willingness to sacrifice constitutional democracy and civil liberty to the social revolution. Some had never believed in the seamlessness of the web, others were willing to endanger it. And the Congress Party allowed Kumaramangalam's extreme position to stand as its own.[79] Explaining Article 31C, he said, 'The clear object of this amendment is to subordinate the rights of individuals to the urgent needs of society.' Defending the Article's 'escape clause', he claimed that the parliamentary 'declaration' it required 'would not protect a fraudulent exercise of this power ... [for] our courts will be more than vigilant enough to ensure that the power granted for a specific purpose ... will not be permitted to be used for any other purpose'.[80] Given the plain language of Article 31C, this argument is not believable

---

in India: Nationalization and Tasks Ahead, Oxford and IBH Publishing Co., New Delhi, 1973. Copy to the author kindness of Ram Panjwani.

[78] The Congress high command established a new land reforms committee in May 1972—which included Kumaramangalam, Gokhale, C. Subramaniam and F. A. Ahmed—which discussed redefining the terms 'personal cultivation' and 'family', the large diameter loopholes for avoiding agricultural land ceilings. Jagjivan Ram told an AICC meeting on 1–2 June what everyone knew, that there had been no proper implementation of land ceilings and village land records were unreliable. A circular letter was to be sent to PCC presidents to implement a 'crash programme' to collect information 'regarding records of real tillers of land' using trained cadres. The next sentence demonstrated that this was not sincerely intended, for it said that the collecting of 'real data' on land-holding should avoid 'any sort of tension or clash in villages'. Villagers, however, should sign the information to give it authenticity. *Congress Marches Ahead VI,* AICC, 1972, p. 163.

Although the unreliable quality of village land records was a genuine impediment to data gathering, the government and the Congress Party had long used it as a specious justification for inaction on land reform. As Jagjivan Ram put it, 'If Congressmen ... go into a village ... everybody knows what are the holdings of a particular farmer', within or beyond the ceiling, 'and if he possesses more than the ceiling limit, how he has managed to bifurcate it by ... not quite desirable transactions'. Zaidi, A. M. (ed.), *Not by Class War: A Study of Congress Policy on Land Reform During the Last 100 Years,* Indian Institute of Applied Political Research, New Delhi, 1985, p.79.

[79] Kumaramangalam, S. Mohan, *Constitutional Amendments: The Reasons Why,* AICC, New Delhi, November 1971. The pamphlet was allowed to stand publicly as the Congress's official position.

[80] Ibid., pp. 22–3.

and, were Parliament (or a state legislature) to misuse the provision, rectification of a citizen's denied civil liberties might never come from the clogged court system. It was romanticism, or craft, to claim, as these men did, that 'in the last analysis, there cannot be any limitation laid upon the sovereignty of the people', in part because the 'people's mandate' was renewed every five years and thus was a self-correcting mechanism—one apparently never to be sullied by manipulative leaders.

The communist parties were unwilling thus to relinquish liberty for the goal of social revolution. A theoretical approach might allow this, but there were the practicalities of their position. Although they, like the ex-communists, thought bourgeois democracy incapable of bringing about social revolution, and were willing to bend the Constitution to this need, they, being out of office, needed to preserve the liberties in the Constitution if they were to survive as a political opposition and to increase their influence. The ex-communists of the CFSA, in office and influential, apparently thought they needed liberty less. The Communist Party of India, but not the Communist Party Marxist, would lose interest in constitutional liberties when it thought it would share power with Mrs Gandhi under the Emergency she declared in June 1975—'the leftist coup turned rightist', as some named it.[81]

The socialists, Young Turks included, had lost their way, misled by their ardour. Although democrats by tradition, they had become so dismayed by the slow progress toward social revolution under Congress governments, coupled with their own political impotence, that they embraced a position that sacrificed the democracy strand of the seamless web for the strengthening—so they hoped—of the social revolutionary strand. They ignored the obvious risks, not pausing to think that where bad law exists, someone will use it. Parliament at this time, remembered Mohan Dharia, did not understand the argument of fear 'because the members had no intentions against freedom, liberty, and the democratic structure'.[82] The dangers from Article 31C to the freedoms in Article 19 went 'unheeded because of this atmosphere of enthusiasm', recalled R. C. Dutt.[83] The seamless web forgotten, Par-

---

[81] The CPI recanted in shame after the Emergency. The CPM sharply criticized the Emergency during it. See Parts III and IV.

[82] Mohan Dharia in an interview with the author.

[83] Dutt in an interview with the author. That no thought was given to the danger the amendment posed to democracy was confirmed by Vasant Sathe, K. C. Pant, and Krishan Kant, in interviews.

Article 31C was subjected to judicial scrutiny in the Kesavananda Bharati case in 1973, as will be seen. The article later was amended, and interpreted again in other Supreme

liament had given the country 'socialism minus democracy', said S. N. Mishra.[84]

Without the Prime Minister's favour, these amendments would not have been enacted, but one may only speculate about her thinking. She was 'tepid' on the privy purses issue, disinterested in banking, and otherwise 'ideologically neutral', according to K. P. Unnikrishnan. Many political participants and observers believe she welcomed the confrontation with the judiciary as a perceived obstacle to social progress, but more believe that she had it in her sights as a piece of governmental machinery beyond her control. Were mastery of the Supreme Court to be added to her mastery of Parliament, she would have virtually unchallengable control of the government and, nearly, of the country. Her motives are difficult to discern because it was her style to leave the initiative to others. Kumaramangalam, Ray, Gokhale, and their fellow-thinkers led the drive to amend the Constitution, but behind it was Mrs Gandhi, shadowy but omnipresent. Yet this was not the policy of 'drift' with which she has been charged. Although she seemed ambivalent at times, she could sense the direction of events and let them take her where she wished to go. She surely was aware that some of these activists believed they were using her, thinking that through her social-economic reform might be better pursued, their own personal power assured, or their undemocratic ends achieved. But she was confident that she could control them, and she pursued her own course, the strongest element of which continued to be her personal power and prestige.

Fifteen August 1972 was the twenty-fifth anniversary of independence. Suitable ceremonies had been planned for the 'stroke of midnight', when Nehru had told the Constituent Assembly that India had 'a tryst with destiny'. That day the Prime Minister presided over a mass pledge-taking by her ministers and members of Parliament. After homage to Mahatma Gandhi, members pledged

> Determined to uphold our gains, we resolve steadfastly to stand by our ideals of democracy, secularism and socialism in our domestic policies and peace, friendship and equality among nations in our international policies.

Court cases. Today, the extent to which the Fundamental Rights in Articles 14 and 19 may be over-ridden in pursuit of the Directive Principles remains unclear. For lengthy analysis of the law, see Seervai, *Constitutional Law*, and V. N. Shukla's *Constitution of India*.

[84] *Lok Sabha Debates*, Fifth Series, vol. 9, no. 13, col. 252.

We re-dedicate ourselves to the vision which Jawaharlal Nehru bequeathed to us of a nation liberated from poverty, injustice, disease and ignorance ... Poverty must go. Disparity must diminish. Injustice must end.

On this historic day, we pledge ourselves anew to work for an India which is united and strong, an India which lives up to her ancient and enduring ideals, yet is modern in thought and achievement ... .[85]

[85] *AR*, 26 August–1 September 1972, p. 10947.

Chapter 11

REDEEMING THE WEB:
THE KESAVANANDA BHARATI CASE

Eleven days before the pledge-taking, His Holiness Swami Kesavananda Bharati Sripadagalvaru lodged a case in the Supreme Court whose outcome would profoundly affect the country's democratic processes. The majority judgement—by seven judges of the thirteen-judge bench—overturned the anti-Parliament, anti-amendment rigidity of the Golak Nath decision; upheld the constitutionality of the Twenty-fourth and the Twenty-fifth Amendments (except for the 'escape clause' in the latter); but it also ruled that an amendment could not alter the basic structure of the Constitution. This 'basic structure doctrine' is fairly said to have become the bedrock of constitutional interpretation in India. Because the doctrine reduced the government's freedom to employ the two amendments, it treated the ruling as a defeat, despite the amendments having been upheld. The case's outcome confirmed for the government its distrust of the Court, whose decision in the case it had endeavoured energetically to influence.

The Kesavananda case embodied two issues critical in parliamentary, democratic governance, one substantive, one institutional. Substantively, the view that the Constitution had given Parliament unlimited constituent power—that is, unlimited power to amend the Constitution—confronted the view that the judiciary, with the Supreme Court at its head, was the Constitution's ultimate interpreter—and therefore protector. Institutionally, perforce, the confrontation took place, as in the past, between the Court and Parliament—and, because Mrs Gandhi led the Parliament at this time, the confrontation boiled down to one between Mrs Gandhi and the Court. In Kesavananda, the Court emerged victorious, in both confrontations, asserting its institutional role *vis-à-vis* Parliament in constitutional matters and strengthening its power of judicial review through the basic structure doctrine. Thereby the Court rescued the democracy strand of the seamless web from those who would have sacrificed it to genuine or pretended social revolutionary intentions.

The bench's glory was in its decision, not in the manner of arriving at it, which reflected ill on itself and on the judiciary as an institution.

The hearings consumed five months. The judges' deliberation process was bizarre. Their individual opinions were chaotically articulated. The relations of one or more judges with the executive branch during the case were thought to have been improper. As one judge understatedly put it, the case was 'full of excitement and unusual happenings'.[1] All the more remarkable, therefore, was the reasonable resolution of the tension between the democracy and social revolution strands of the seamless web provided by the outcome.

The case had originated in March 1970 when Swami Kesavananda, head of a monastery-like establishment in Kerala called a *muth*, challenged the Kerala government's attempts, under two state land reform acts, to impose restrictions on the management of church property. A local lawyer wrote to J. B. Dadachanji, advocate at the Supreme Court, about taking the case. Dadachanji shared the letter with N. A. Palkhivala, who said they should take the case, for it could be the basis for a major Supreme Court judgement.[2] Although the state government invoked its authority under Article 31, Dadachanji and Palkhivala convinced the Swami, who they never met, into fighting his petition under Article 29, concerning the right to manage religiously owned property without government interference. The grander issues of Parliament's power to amend the Constitution would arise as court proceedings evolved. For example, while the writ was pending, Parliament enacted the Twenty-fourth, Twenty-fifth, and Twenty-ninth Amendments—the latter placing the 1969 Kerala Land Reforms Act in the Ninth Schedule. The Swami believed that for his original petition to succeed he must challenge the constitutionality of the three amendments. A five-judge bench in August 1972 allowed this; and decided that thirteen judges should hear the case, making the bench superior to the bench of eleven that had heard Golak Nath.[3] The

---

[1] Justice Y. V. Chandrachud, *The Basics of Indian Constitution: Its Search for Social Justice and the Role of Judges*, Publications Division, GOI, New Delhi, 1989, p. 17.

[2] J. B. Dadachanji in an interview. He and Palkhivala were both Parsis. The laws concerned were the Kerala Land Reforms Act, 1963, and the Kerala Land Reforms Act, 1969, amending it.

[3] The members of this bench were Chief Justice Sikri and Justices A. N. Ray, Jaganmohan Reddy, K. K. Mathew, and M. H. Beg. About the decision on a thirteen-judge bench, and the idea of bringing on several additional justices to handle the daily workload during the Kesavananda hearings, see *Indian Express*, 11 August 1972.

At this time J. B. Dadachanji contended that the Twenty-fourth Amendment enabled Parliament to amend "'the most precious fundamental right'"—giving the case its second name, the Fundamental Rights case. *Hindustan Times*, 5 August 1972. Attorney General Niren De did not oppose registering the case because 'many aspects' of the constitutional issue remained to be decided.

following sections will describe the Kesavananda hearings, the Court's decision, confusing commentaries on it, and the 'unusual happenings' to which Justice Chandrachud referred.

Kesavananda: The Case

The hearings, which would be extensively reported in the English-language press, began 31 October 1972 and lasted until mid-March—some seventy working days at four and one-half hours daily.[4] The court gave its decision on 24 April 1973. Palkhivala began his thirty-three days of argument by saying that no one contended that the Constitution could not be amended, only that a creature of the Constitution cannot increase its own constituent power nor can it arrogate to itself the power to alter or destroy the Constitution's essential features—such as an institution like the Supreme Court.[5] Returning to arguments made in

[4] The case was *His Holiness Kesavananda Bharati Sripadagalvaru v State of Kerala and Another* 1973 (4) SCC 225ff. On the bench were Chief Justice S. M. Sikri and Justices J. M. Shelat, K. S. Hegde, A. N. Grover, A. N. Ray, P. Jaganmohan Reddy, D. G. Palekar, H. R. Khanna, K. K. Mathew, M. H. Beg, S. N. Dwivedi, A. K. Mukherjea, and Y. V. Chandrachud. Dwivedi and Mukherjea had been appointed to the Court on 14 August 1972 so that a constitution bench of adequate numbers might be constituted. They came from the Allahabad and Calcutta high courts, respectively. A. N. Alagiriswamy was appointed to the Court on 17 October 1972, but was not selected for this constitution bench. His task at the time—with the assistance of two ad hoc judges, retired from the Supreme Court, I. D. Dua and C. A. Vaidialingam—was to help handle court business while his colleagues wrestled with Kesavananda. Justices Sikri and Shelat were the only members of the bench who also sat on Golak Nath's case, when they were with the majority.

Distinguished advocates represented each side. On the government side were the Attorney and Solicitor Generals, Niren De and L. N. Sinha, respectively, and the Advocates General of fourteen states, among them L. M. Singhvi of Rajasthan and H. M. Seervai of Maharashtra—stars already well above the horizon and rising rapidly. Senior advocates appearing for those who had filed the six writ petitions (two former princes and two coal mining companies had joined Kesavananda in challenging the amendments) included N. A. Palkhivala, C. K. Daphtary, M. C. Chagla, Soli Sorabjee, and Anil Divan, along with J. B. Dadachanji.

A symptom of the judiciary–legislature friction of the time was an incident at the All India Whips Conference of 4 November 1972. 'Leftists' moved to have 'mutual respect' deleted from a resolution characterizing the relations between the legislature and the judiciary. *AR*, 25 November–1 December 1972, p. 11103.

[5] The accounts here of the oral arguments and written submissions of lawyers for the petitioners and the government are taken from the daily reports in *The Times of India*; from Surendra Malik (ed.), *The Fundamental Rights Case: The Critics Speak*, Eastern Book Company, Lucknow, 1975; from the summary of the case by the Chief Justice in 1973 (4) SSC 305ff; and from interviews with the participants.

Earlier in October, S. S. Ray and Kumaramangalam were reported to have attacked

Golak Nath, he said that Parliament in India operated under inherent and implied limitations, for it was the 'well-settled' meaning of 'amend' that it did not encompass altering or destroying constitutional fundamentals. In particular, Palkhivala continued, Parliament could not abridge or destroy basic human rights and fundamental freedoms 'which were reserved by the people for themselves when they gave to themselves the Constitution'.[6] Property was an essential feature of the Constitution because property was necessary for the meaningful exercise of other fundamental rights. Palkhivala pointed out that if Parliament could amend the Constitution at its own will, liberty could be lost, and an authoritarian government established. These were not the arguments of fear, but 'an argument of realism', he said. As to the Twenty-fifth Amendment, Palkhivala's principal target was Article 31C, which he described as giving a blank charter to Parliament and the state legislatures to defy the Constitution, thereby destroying its supremacy, which was one of its essential features. The article also abrogated the Fundamental Rights by making them subordinate to the Directive Principles.

Responding to questions from the bench, Palkhivala told Justice Hegde that Parliament could add to the Fundamental Rights, and it was inconceivable that the majority of the people would give them up. He told Justices Grover and Dwivedi that, yes, trying to identify the basic features of the Constitution would create doubt and uncertainty, but as

---

the Court at a gathering of lawyers in Ahmedabad. They described the Court as a '"coterie"' of persons '"accidentally elevated"' to the bench. They said Parliament should have the authority to set aside judicial rulings on constitutional matters. *Hindustan Times*, 11 October 1972; *Tribune* (of Chandigarh), 9 October 1972.

[6] Malik, *Fundamental Rights Case*, p. 17.

Since the Golak Nath decision's citation of Dieter Conrad's reasoning on implied limitations and constitutional basic features, Conrad also had published an article on the subject in 1970. Among other points, Conrad said that no amendment can make changes in a constitution amounting to 'a practical abrogation or a total review'. Nor can partial abrogations be so deep that 'the fundamental identity of the constitution is no longer apparent'. Conrad, Dieter, 'Limitation of Amendment Procedures and the Constituent Power', *The Indian Yearbook of International Affairs: 1966–67*, New Delhi, 1970, p. 420. Conrad addressed the subject again in the *Delhi Law Review*, vol. 6–7, 1977–8, pp. 1ff.

M. C. Setalvad's Hamlyn Lectures, delivered at Lincoln's Inn in 1960, were published in India in 1970. In the lectures, he said 'the basic fact [is] that the Constitution itself empowers ... judicial review, so that when the courts express their views as to the reasonableness of restrictions imposed on the fundamental rights ... they do so pursuant to powers vested in them by the Constitution ... [which is] not the supremacy of the courts but the supremacy of the Constitution.' Setalvad, *Common Law in India*, p. 197.

long as the human agency operated there would be uncertainty. Several judges asked if a monarchy could be established through amendment, to which Palkhivala responded affirmatively. Justice Mathew said there was no doubt the people are sovereign and not Parliament.

C. K. Daphtary, educated both at school and university in England and a former Attorney General, began his arguments for the petitioners when the Court resumed sitting on 9 January 1973, after the winter recess. He reiterated many of Palkhivala's points, adding that the Twenty-fifth Amendment endangered the rights of minorities and both it and the Twenty-fourth Amendment enabled the party in power to break the Constitution from within. Advocates Chagla and Sorabjee deplored as excessive Parliament's power under the amendments. For Chagla, Article 31C amounted to a parliamentary usurpation of the judicial function. Sorabjee argued that trusting Parliament or the executive not to act arbitrarily was misconceived, was inconsistent with the concept of limited government, and had been rejected in India.

H. M. Seervai opened the government's rebuttal on 18 January and took an important part in it thereafter.[7] '[H]ammering home his points', as Justice Chandrachud recalled, Seervai maintained that it would be gross irreverence to assume that Parliament would abuse its unlimited legislative power, and its unlimited amending power should not be understood as an abuse of power.[8] Article 368 carried with it *prima facie* the meaning of the power to amend any part of the Constitution. Seervai also resurrected the argument that the Fundamental Rights of the Constitution were not 'human rights', only social rights and thus did not belong to Indians before the inauguration of the Constitution. Although he acknowledged that the Constitution contained basic features (such as parliamentary democracy, federal structure, rule of law, judicial review), Seervai contended that the founding fathers had not meant them to be permanent because a self-governing government has unlimited constituent power. As to Article 31C, he said that it did not confer power to amend the Constitution, it only removed restrictions on legislative power placed by Articles 14, 19, and 31. Responding to a question from

[7] Seervai had been asked to do this by Law Minister Gokhale, in part because Attorney General Niren De, absent at a Commonwealth Lawyer's Conference, had been unkindly treated by judges during the bank nationalization and princes cases, which some in the government thought he had 'lost'. Interview with Seervai, who heard this from Kumaramangalam.

[8] Malik, *Fundamental Rights Case*, p. 35. This is from a summary of Seervai's arguments by V. G. Ramachandran. It was an intellectual formulation of the plea made by Congress leaders since the late 1960s especially in regard to Parliament, i.e. 'Trust us'.

Justice Shelat, Seervai told the court that a limb of the Constitution might have to be amputated so that the Constitution could survive.[9]

Attorney General De's turn came on 22 February. 'Augmenting his massive affidavits submitted to the Court earlier in [four] installments', reported the *Times of India,* De reiterated the position the government had taken in Golak Nath: in written constitutions there could be no inherent limitations on the amending power. '[N]o one would seek to improve or save a constitution by destroying it,' he said, but the purpose of the amending power would be defeated if it did not extend to the Constitution's fundamental features. He rejected as 'dialectical arguments' Justices Khanna's and Hegde's questions about whether the amendments would permit democracy to be taken away or rule to be vested in one person.[10] The power of amendment, De argued, extends to repeal, addition, variation, and substitution. The Fundamental Rights are subservient to the Directive Principles so long as the Principles advance the social and economic progress of the people.

Palkhivala then replied orally and also submitted written arguments. Principal among his arguments were that citizens need protection against their own representatives and that only those Directive Principles compatible with the Fundamental Rights had been included in the Constitution. Just before concluding, Palkhivala managed to add spice to the proceedings. He told the court that he wished to read views supporting his arguments expressed some years earlier by an eminent jurist. Was it not time 'we rekindled' the inspiration behind the Fundamental Rights, including 'just compensation' and the freedom to carry on a business and acquire property, this eminent individual had asked. There were 'grave consequences' to treating the Constitution 'as ordinary law to be changed at the will of the party in power'. If governments always could be trusted, Palkhivala's anonymous authority continued, there would have been no need for the Fundamental Rights. When Palkhivala revealed that his eminent authority was none other than H. M. Seervai, Seervai was furious, and the two, who had once served in the same chambers, did not speak for years.[11]

[9] *Times of India,* 23 February 1973. The first part of the Twenty-fifth Amendment's Article 31C, it will be recalled, changed the word 'compensation' to the word 'amount' in an attempt to end any judicial interpretation of 'compensation'.

[10] *Times of India,* 23 February 1973. According to Justice Reddy, De often made 'abrasive and even threatening' arguments. Reddy, P. Jaganmohan, *We Have a Republic: Can We Keep It?,* Department of Law, Sri Venkateswara University, Tirupati, 1984, p. 99. The rendition of Reddy's name varies from the title page of the book to the law reports; the latter is that used by the author.

[11] 'Furious,' Justice Chandrachud interview with the author.

A month after the hearings ended on 23 March the bench handed down its famous ruling in a remarkable fashion. That morning of 24 April 1973 in Chief Justice Sikri's courtroom the thirteen judges delivered eleven opinions and what came to be called a 'statement' by nine of them, which was published in the law reports after the last of the eleven opinions.[12] The 'statement' began, 'The view by the majority in these writ petitions is as follows.' It then specifically overruled Golak Nath, upheld the Twenty-fourth and Twenty-ninth Amendments, and struck down the 'escape clause' in the Twenty-fifth Amendment's Article 31C while upholding the remainder of the amendment. The essence of the statement of the nine judges was that 'Article 368 did not enable Parliament to alter the basic structure or framework of the Constitution.'[13]

Mrs Gandhi was silent about the decision. Unofficial reaction in the government was that it was '"an attack on Parliament and the Prime Minister"' by her ' "enemies"'.[14] She must have been dissatisfied by the performances of the five judges appointed since 1971 (excluding Alagiriswami, who was not on the Kesavananda bench) plus the two appointed especially for this bench. Only one of these (Dwivedi) found for the government, and three of the five signed the majority 'statement'.

Palkhivala was reading from Seervai, H. M., 'Fundamental Rights: A Basic Issue,' published in three installments in the *Times of India,* 14, 15, 16 February 1955. Texts kindly provided to the author by Anil Divan. Seervai was commenting on the Fourth Amendment, then being considered by a parliamentary committee.

He returned to these views to a considerable extent in subsequent years as a result of new legal interpretations and his own rethinking, inspired by the excesses of Mrs Gandhi's Emergency. Seervai became a defender of the basic structure doctrine, having concluded that 'the consequences of rejecting the doctrine ... would be so grave and so opposed to the objectives of the Constitution, that the consequence of uncertainty [in defining it] would be insignificant by comparison.' Seervai, *Constitutional Law,* vol. 2, p. 2692. And he implicitly rejected Article 31C, saying, '[O]nce it is realized that Directive Principles lack the character of a "law", and, therefore, of being a part of the supreme law, it is clear that primacy cannot be given to Directives over Fundamental Rights ...'. Ibid., Preface, p. vi. Without the Fundamental Rights, 'our country would have been in danger of being converted into a police State, as the experience of the Emergency ... clearly showed.' Seervai's change of view carried great weight in India's legal community because of his intellectual strength, forceful character, and reputation for honourableness.

[12] The judges' opinions consumed seventeen hundred cyclostyled pages and eight hundred when published.

There were eleven opinions because Justices Hegde and Mukherjea and Justices Shelat and Grover delivered joint opinions. The nine signatories to the 'statement' were Justices Sikri, Shelat, Hegde, Grover, Reddy, Palekar, Khanna, Mukherjea, and Chandrachud. Those not signing were Justices Ray, Dwivedi, Mathew, and Beg.

[13] Ibid., p. 1007.

[14] Malhotra, *Indira Gandhi,* p. 152.

This was not a pleasing score for a government increasingly bent on having its own way. 'Packing', had it been intended, had not worked. Press reaction was cautious. The *Hindustan Times* thought the decision removed 'obstacles to genuine as distinguished from pseudo-radicalism', but said Parliament's responsibility to exercise its powers with 'great circumspection' had increased enormously.[15]

A Confusing Decision

The 'view by the majority' is the law of India, clearly and emphatically expressed. Therefore, one need not go behind it. This is fortunate, because relying instead upon the eleven opinions by the thirteen judges accompanying it would have made it difficult to be precise about points of agreement and disagreement: what actually had been decided. This problem is mitigated slightly by the 'conclusions' with which the judges summarized their opinions. Adding to the confusion are discrepancies between what several justices said in their opinions and the points in the statement they signed. We may enter this curious terrain—thankful for the definitive 'statement'—by comparing the 'conclusions' of the nine judges who were also signatories of the statement.[16]

On the Twenty-fourth Amendment

All nine men declared that Golak Nath had been wrongly decided, that Article 368 contained both the power and the procedure for amending the Constitution, that the word 'law' in Article 13 (2) did not include constitutional amendments, and that the amendment was 'valid'. Eight said, variously, in their conclusions that Article 368 did not include the power to 'damage', 'abrogate', 'emasculate', 'destroy', or 'change or alter' the 'basic features/elements', 'fundamental features', or 'framework' of the Constitution. Justice Palekar was the exception. He held in his conclusion that there were no limitations on the amending power. (See below.)

On the Twenty-fifth Amendment

The nine justices held the second clause of the amendment valid (changing 'compensation' to 'amount', and so on). Agreeing with the

[15] Issue of 25 April 1973.

[16] For the 'conclusions' of the justices, see 1973 (4) SCC 593–4, Ray; p. 959, Dwivedi; pp. 897–8, Mathew; p. 919, Beg; p. 405, Sikri; pp. 462–3, Shelat and Grover; pp. 511–2, Hegde and Mukherjea; pp. 666–7, Reddy; pp. 823–5, Khanna; pp. 1005–6, Chandrachud; p. 726, Palekar.

view expressed in the Law Commission's report on the amendment, all the nine held that the third (or 'escape') clause in Article 31C was invalid. Justice Khanna also expressed doubt that property was a fundamental right. Chief Justice Sikri, in his conclusion, held Article 31C invalid in its entirety because it delegated the power of amendment to state legislatures. Justice Palekar, again the exception, accepted the amendment unreservedly. The nine judges signing the statement appear to have been able to uphold this amendment by ignoring the clear intent of Parliament when it removed 'compensation' from Article 31: The 'amount' of compensation, they said in their conclusions, could be reviewed if it appeared to be 'illusory'. Justices Shelat and Grover said in their opinion that the 'amount' paid for property taken should bear a 'reasonable relationship' to the value of the property.

On the Twenty-ninth Amendment

All signing the 'statement' held this to be valid with no qualifying language. But six of the nine majority judges—absent Justices Chandrachud, Khanna, and Palekar—held in the conclusions to their opinions that any legislative act for insertion into the Ninth Schedule could be examined by the courts to see if it abrogated any basic features of the Constitution. The other three of the nine, and the four minority judges, were silent on this point.

The four justices who did not sign the statement (the so-called 'minority' of Ray, Beg, Mathew, and Dwivedi) upheld the Twenty-fourth, Twenty-fifth, and Twenty-ninth Amendments, and they agreed in their conclusions that Golak Nath was wrongly decided. Ray, Beg, and Mathew said that amendments are not 'law' under Article 13; Dwivedi, however, was not specific. Only Palekar upheld the Twenty-fourth and Twenty-fifth Amendments without explanation or reservation. Beg, Ray, and Dwivedi held that there were no inherent or implied limitations to the power of amendment in Article 368. But Mathew and Ray also held that no amendment could utterly abrogate or repeal the Constitution 'without substituting a mechanism by which the State is constituted and organized', to use Mathew's phrase.[17] Ray said further that no distinction could be made between essential and inessential features of the Constitution; all were essential. While upholding the validity of the Twenty-fifth Amendment, Mathew, Dwivedi, and Beg qualified their opinions when they came to the

[17] 1973 (4) SCC 897.

'escape clause'. Mathew held that the declaration 'would not oust the jurisdiction of the Court to go into the question whether the law gives effect to the policy'. Justice Beg said the same thing in different words: despite the declaration, the courts could decide whether the declaration is really good or a mere pretence.[18]

These seem to be in direct contradiction to the wording of the declaration, which was, 'and no law containing a declaration that it is for giving effect to such policy shall be called in question in any court on the ground that it does not give effect to such policy'. Dwivedi's qualification, less clear, said that the declaration did not prevent the court from examining 'whether the impugned law has relevancy to the distribution of the ownership and control of the material resources of the community ...'.[19] Thus all three justices seem to have asserted the power of judicial review over parts of a constitutional amendment whose wording barred it entirely.

Justice Chandrachud's and Justice Palekar's conclusions put them at odds with the other seven signers of the statement. They had signed it, they said, to acknowledge that it was the view of the majority, namely, the other seven signers. They did this while themselves dissenting by upholding Parliament's unlimited amending power.[20] Yet their signing the statement, when the four 'minority judges' declined to recognize the seven to six vote by also signing the statement may indicate sympathy for the majority position. This is more probable in Justice Chandrachud's case because since writing this opinion, he at least twice, once publicly and once privately, has asserted that the 'statement' was correct.[21]

CONFUSION COMPOUNDED

Commentaries by eminent Indian legal thinkers about Kesavananda further muddied these waters. Examining ten of these expert opinions (four of which came from justices who had been on the Kesavananda

---

[18] Ibid., pp. 898, 919.

[19] Ibid., p. 959.

[20] For Palekar, see 1973 (4) SC 726. For Chandrachud, see ibid., p. 1005. In item 3 of his conclusion, Chandrachud said specifically that the Golak Nath decision was 'incorrect' when it said that 'Parliament had no power to amend the Constitution so as to abrogate or take away Fundamental Rights'.

[21] His public reaffirmation came in the Kesavananda Review hearings in 1975. Dhavan, Rajeev, *The Supreme Court of India*, N. M. Tripathi Pvt. Ltd., Bombay, 1977, p. 420. Privately, Justice Chandrachud told the author, 'The statement is not what each one of us decided, but what we as a court decided. This is the ratio of all thirteen judges. We summed up the result of the case.'

bench), one finds conflicting views on aspects of the decision.[22] For example, Justice Jaganmohan Reddy later wrote that eight judges had held that there are basic features in the Constitution.[23] According to Justice Khanna, the majority in the case numbered seven, and nine judges signed the statement indicating that this was the view of the majority—even though two had been in the minority in their individual opinions.[24] Palkhivala also used this arithmetic.[25] The statement of the nine judges, itself, was discredited by Seervai and Dhavan. Seervai believed that the four judges who had not signed it had refrained from doing so because 'there was a difference of opinion among the judges themselves as to what the majority had decided'. He submitted that 'the summary signed by nine judges has no legal effect at all'—this even in the revision of his book in which he accepted Kesavananda as law.[26] According to Dhavan, 'only a hard core of six judges ... really accepted the summary statement'. Justice Palekar had signed the statement by 'accident', and Chandrachud and Khanna really 'belong to the minority'.[27] Dhavan hoped that the 'summary statement' would be rejected as either too ambiguous or misleading. Upendra Baxi, on the other hand, asks how an understanding of the Court's conclusions

---

[22] The commentaries cited here and in the following paragraphs are: Reddy, P. Jaganmohan, *Social Justice and the Constitution*, Andhra University Press, Vishakhapatnam, 1976, and Reddy, *We have a Republic: Can We Keep It?;* Chandrachud, Y. V., *The Basics of Indian Constitution;* Dhavan, Rajeev, *The Supreme Court and Parliamentary Sovereignty*, Sterling Publishers Pvt. Ltd., New Delhi, 1976, and Dhavan, 'The Basic Structure Doctrine—A Footnote Comment' in Dhavan, Rajeev and Jacob, Alice (eds), *Indian Constitution: Trends and Issues*, Indian Law Institute, N. M. Tripathi Pvt. Ltd., Bombay, 1978; Tripathi, P. K., 'Kesavananda Bharati v The State of Kerala—Who Wins?' in Malik, *Fundamental Rights Case;* Upendra Baxi, 'The Constitutional Quicksands of *Kesavananda Bharati* and the Twenty-fifth Amendment' in ibid.; Khanna, H. R., *Neither Roses Nor Thorns,* Eastern Book Company, Lucknow, 1985; Seervai, *Constitutional Law;* Hegde, K. S., *Judiciary And The People,* A 'Friends of Democracy' Publication, New Delhi, 1973; Sathe S. P., 'Limitations on Constitutional Amendment: "Basic Structure" Principle Re-examined' in Dhavan and Jacob, *Indian Constitution: Trends and Issues;* and Noorani, *Public Law in India.*

Dhavan's *Supreme Court and Parliamentary Sovereignty* contains a useful examination of the legal views expressed at various times earlier by various members of the Kesavananda bench that may have shaped their opinions in the case.

[23] Reddy, *Social Justice and the Constitution,* p. 34.

[24] Justice Khanna in a letter to the author.

[25] Palkhivala, N. A., *Our Constitution, Defaced and Defiled,* Macmillan, New Delhi, 1975, pp. 147–9.

[26] Seervai, *Constitutional Law,* vol. 2, p. 2641.

[27] Dhavan, *Supreme Court and Parliamentary Sovereignty,* pp. 110, 154, and his 'The Basic Structure Doctrine', p 168.

is to be arrived at if the 'statement' of the nine judges is disregarded.[28] Justice Reddy many years later thought that the 'statement' was the operative part of the judgement.[29]

'Unusual Happenings' on the Bench

The composition of the Supreme Court at the time of Kesavananda provides a useful starting point for an examination of the 'unusual happenings' during the case to which Justice Chandrachud alluded. For Justice Reddy, these happenings had their origins well before the bench was formed. He thought Kumaramangalam, Ray, and Gokhale had begun 'packing' the court in 1971 in expectation of an attempt to overturn Golak Nath. As a result, Reddy believed that one judge was a Kumaramangalam nominee (probably Mathew), two were H. R. Gokhale nominees (probably Palekar and Chandrachud), two were nominees of S. S. Ray (possibly Beg and Mukherjea), and one was Sikri's (probably Khanna).[30] One of these judges (probably Dwivedi), told Justice Reddy that he had been interviewed by Gokhale, Kumaramangalam, and S. S. Ray before his appointment.[31] Madhu Limaye charged in the Lok Sabha that Justice Dwivedi came to the court with the declared purpose of

[28] Baxi also thought that these opinions generated 'many paradoxes', raised 'many varied and profound questions', and are 'likely to create an illiterate Bar in the country', because who would read the lengthy opinions in their entirety. Chandrachud thought the opinions an 'excessive indulgence' that could have been halved, the result of an 'each for himself' attitude among his colleagues. Seervai hoped India would never again see the likes of Kesavananda.

[29] Reddy, interview with the author.

[30] Reddy, *We have a Republic*, pp. 93–5. The names in parenthesis were not mentioned by Justice Reddy; they are the author's best guesses.

Justice Mathew, from Kerala, was known to be well thought of by Kumaramangalam and Mrs Gandhi. Beg, from UP, was a Nehru-family friend, and Dwivedi, also from UP is reported to have told the petitioners in the case that were they to agree to the removal of property from the Rights, 'he would see that Parliament did not touch other rights.' (Nayar, *Supersession of Judges*, p. 16.) Chandrachud, according to Delhi sources, had been brought to the court by Gokhale as a fellow Maharashtrian, as was Palekar, in preference to P. N. Bhagwati, a Gujarati, who Mrs Gandhi was said not to like. Khanna, like Sikri, came from the Punjab.

Of the pre-1971 judges, Hegde was said to be in the Prime Minister's black book due to a ruling he had made in her election case; A. N. Ray was considered pro-government because of his opinions in the bank nationalization and princes cases; Sikri was considered mildly conservative and a good judge; and neither Shelat nor Reddy had then projected a strong image. Grover, who thought himself a 'centrist' (interview with the author), was thought by others to be undistinguished.

[31] Reddy, *We have a Republic*, p. 93.

overturning Golak Nath—but many judges and lawyers disliked the Gokal Nath decision; this was not singular to Dwivedi. No matter the initial inspiration for these nominees, Mrs Gandhi was responsible for their appointments. And there is no evidence available that Chief Justice Sikri protested them, which he could have done.

The Kesavananda bench worked under continuous and sometimes intense pressures. The broadest of these was anxiety for the Court's viability and, by extension, of the judiciary as a co-equal branch of government. Several members of the bench felt this, and Justice Reddy referred in his opinion to 'the threat of the dire consequences which the Court would have to face if the judgement went against the Government'.[32] Perhaps Madhu Limaye had this in mind when he wrote that what 'weighed' with the judges was apprehension about the future of liberty and protecting the jurisdiction of the Court. A sense that the Court as an institution was threatened likely is why the nine signers of the 'statement' upheld with one hand the Twenty-fourth Amendment and most of the Twenty-fifth while strengthening judicial review with the other.

More intense pressure came directly from the government to assure a favourable ruling from the court. This took three forms, according to justices and advocates involved with and observing the proceedings: trying to discover the thinking of the judges; attempting to pre-determine the outcome of the case by influencing judges' opinions; and attempting to pre-determine its outcome by preventing a decision through prolonging the case beyond Sikri's retirement. The first two often took place together. Leaders actively seeking information from inside the bench were Law Minister Gokhale, Steel Minister Kumaramangalam, Law Commission Chairman Gajendragadkar, and S. S. Ray, now the Chief Minister of West Bengal.[33] In addition to information thus gleaned, drafts of some judges' opinions reached the government—and, perhaps, the Prime Minister. Justices Beg and Dwivedi were thought by many to be responsible for this. Beg did hand over drafts, Justice Grover and a close relation of one of the judges believed.[34] Justice Reddy, without naming a culprit, charged that drafts had reached the government, and he wrote that Mohan Kumaramangalam congratulated 'my colleagues a week before the judgement was pronounced ... [revealing the government's

---

[32] Ibid., p. 99. In his opinion, Reddy also said that 'We should free ourselves of any considerations which tend to create pressures on the mind.' 1973 (4) SCC 613.

[33] This account is based upon the author's interviews with advocates and judges in the case and well-informed journalists, plus several publications. Specific references appear in subsequent footnotes.

[34] Interviews with the author.

foreknowledge] that the three senior-most judges would ... be against the Government'.[35] It is not impossible that this happened, thought Palkhivala. 'You need not disbelieve' these accounts, Justice Chandrachud told the author.[36] On the morning the court delivered its judgement, the government had in its hands the texts of the favourable and unfavourable opinions, reported Kuldip Nayar.[37] H. M. Seervai doubted drafts and information were so passed. Chief Justice Sikri told the author that he had heard these rumours and had reacted (to whom is not specified): 'I'll send the drafts if the government wants. There is nothing secret about this.'[38]

The government also attempted to shape individual judges' opinions according to participants in and observers of the case. Gokhale, Kumaramangalam, and Ray tried to influence judges, recalled Justice Reddy, citing a lunch that S. S. Ray and his wife had with Justice and Mrs Mukherjea.[39] A senior member of the Prime Minister's staff recalled that there were attempts to influence the court. Pressures were 'unbelievable', Palkhivala remembered.[40] According to several accounts, Justice Chandrachud, then aged fifty-three and a junior member of the bench, discussed the case with Gokhale and Gajendragadkar. And Chandrachud's opinion, submitted at the last moment, had been influenced by Gokhale, who, the story went, had hinted to him that his eventually becoming Chief Justice might be affected if he ruled against the government.[41] Justice Chandrachud labelled the 'accusation' that the government of India tried to influence judges 'a myth'. 'No attempt was made to contact me or to affect my decision,' he said.[42]

[35] Reddy, *We Have a Republic*, p. 100. He added to this, 'the government [was] aware of what each one of us was going to decide quite some time before judgements were pronounced'. Ibid.

If Dwivedi had been involved, thought Reddy, the channel would have been H. N. Bahuguna, sometime chief minister of UP and related to Dwivedi by marriage. Justice Reddy in an interview with the author.

[36] In interviews with the author. Justice Chandrachud thought a Bahuguna connection possible.

[37] Nayar, *Supersession of Judges*, p. 14.

Nayar added, '[A]s and when some judges sent their judgements to their colleagues they found their way to the government. Even details of the informal discussions which the judges had among themselves had reached the government.' Sikri told Beg at a dinner party that copies of some judgements had reached the government before they were announced. Ibid.

[38] Sikri interview with the author.

[39] Reddy interview with the author.

[40] Palkhivala interview with the author.

[41] Fali Nariman, who had heard it from others, in an interview with the author.

[42] Chandrachud interview with the author.

The government intended to pre-empt an adverse ruling by another device, according to a suspicion wide-spread at the time and not forgotten. Chief Justice Sikri's retirement date was 26 April 1973. Were the case not decided by then, it would have to be dropped or re-heard. Did the government attempt to drag out the case with this in view? 'I knew that Seervai, De, and others demanded much time for oral argument to prolong the case and to get a new bench,' remembered Anil Divan. 'Palkhivala and I discussed this.'[43] This assessment did not, however, cause Palkhivala to shorten his own lengthy oral argument. What most aroused scepticism and suspicion was the illness suffered by a member of the bench. Was the government capitalizing on the illness to prolong the case? In the poisonous atmosphere that had come to surround the case, nothing else so set the lawyers on both sides and the judges against one another as suspicions about Justice Beg's illness.

Justice Mirza Hammeedullah Beg—from the Allahabad High Court, Trinity College, Cambridge, and later Chief Justice of India (1977–8)—went to the hospital on 4 or 5 March with a heart ailment.[44] Justice Reddy took him there, and Justice Grover and others visited him. Chief Justice Sikri went to the hospital to check on Beg's condition and obtained a certificate saying that Beg should rest a week and after two weeks could return to normal work.[45] Sikri had to decide what to do. His looming retirement and a two-week European trip that he was committed to begin on 26 March worsened the time pressure. Sikri recalled that he contemplated reconstituting the bench, but that Attorney General De asked him to wait—expecting Beg to side with the government.[46] Seervai and De wished to stop the hearings. Palkhivala wished them to continue. The judges, Justice Khanna remembered,

[43] Divan interview with the author.

[44] Three New Delhi newspapers reported on 6 March in very brief dispatches dated the previous day that the court would not sit because Beg was ill. The incident thereupon vanished from the newspapers.

[45] Justices Reddy and Grover in interviews with the author. Chief Justice to the hospital: H. M. Seervai in an interview with the author. Justice Sikri, who by this date had 'heard in a roundabout way that the government did not want a decision before I retired', confirmed the account of the certificate, something the Registrar of the Court usually would procure. Interview with the author.

'The illness was not fabricated,' Seervai flatly asserted. Beg had had a heart attack some years earlier, according to Seervai. Doubts about the genuineness of Beg's illness were fed by the impression that the government was trying to stall the case, according to Justice Grover, in an interview with the author.

[46] Sikri interview with the author. Law Minister Gokhale's personal staff expressed unhappiness at Beg's illness, fearing 'it might lead to the loss of a government vote'. P. B. Venkatasubramanian in a letter to the author.

were concerned that if Beg did not return before Sikri retired, all the effort would have been wasted.[47] Attempting to resolve the matter, the Chief Justice summoned his fellow-judges and both sides' advocates to a conference in his chambers. His announcement that he had decided to proceed without Beg evoked consternation and several reactions: Seervai responded that nothing in the hospital certificate said Beg could not render his opinion;[48] Palkhivala offered to submit written arguments that Beg might read without being in court; Sikri, himself, suggested that the hearings be tape-recorded for Beg's benefit.[49] Seervai and De rejected these suggestions, and De threatened to boycott the Court if the hearings continued without Beg. This evoked talk of citing De for contempt.[50] Justice Beg returned to his duties, and the affair ended with a legacy of hard feelings.[51]

As though there were not enough external pressures, the justices generated tensions within the bench. It seemed, recalled one the advocates involved, that the ill-feeling among the judges almost overwhelmed the substance of the case. Allowing judges to hand down multiple opinions and the circulation of them within the bench were sources of discord and confusion affecting both process and substance. Chief Justice Sikri and Justices Hegde and Mukherjea began writing their opinions while the hearings were going on, and Sikri circulated a draft before

[47] Khanna interview with the author.

[48] Seervai interview with the author.

Chandrachud recalled that he thought it useless to continue because a six–six vote was likely. Interview with the author.

[49] Nayar, *Supersession*, p. 27.

[50] Palkhivala and Dadachanji to Soli Sorabjee. Sorabjee interview with the author. Several judges and lawyers do not recall this meeting and apparently were not present.

Seervai recalled that he said at a subsequent meeting in the Law Ministry where Kumaramangalam was present, that if De were jailed for contempt, all us lawyers ought to go to jail with him.

[51] These accounts contain a puzzle. That the government rejected both (a) proceeding without Justice Beg and (b) devising ways to keep him 'in' the case, while not actually in court, supports the theory that the illness was either a plot by, or a splendid convenience for, the government to end the case inconclusively. Yet Beg's return to his duties, coupled with the common impression that he would side with the government, and that the government expected him to, argues against the plot theory. Or was the plot on the other foot? Once Beg was ill or 'ill', did anyone on the bench or at the bar, with the intention of getting a ruling against the government, decide to press ahead without him? Was this on Sikri's mind, because he did believe 'that the communists were out to break the Constitution'. Sikri interview with the author. There is no evidence that Sikri, or anyone else involved, had this intention. Nor did the four judges—Ray, Beg, Dwivedi, and Mathew—who did not sign the 'statement', and who were known to be close to each other and to the government ever allege it. History has its puzzles; this remains one of them.

departing for Europe on 26 March.[52] Justice Shelat asked Grover to draft an opinion incorporating their shared views and those of Sikri, Hegde, and Mukherjea—believing that 'one judgment by five judges ... would be weightier than five separate judgements'.[53] Justice Chandrachud produced the final version of his opinion on the morning the bench ruled, according to reports, and, it is alleged by some, after having been told by the Chief Justice to stay home and get it done.[54] Accounts conflict about the extent to which the various drafts were circulated. Justice Chandrachud went to the length of recording in his final opinion that he had seen only four of his fellow judges' drafts.[55] Justice Reddy believed Chandrachud had seen most drafts and Sikri thought he had seen all of them, these men told the author. Chandrachud, himself, later said that drafts were exchanged and changed, 'and some of us wondered why, and this caused disbelief in our colleagues to grow'.[56]

After Sikri returned from abroad on 10 April he decided to try to 'lessen the number of judgements' and to hear the 'tentative views' of others on the bench—an attempt at unity he might have begun earlier had he not been abroad. He decided to meet the judges in two groups and actually met with one. Justice Reddy recalls that about April 14 he received a telephone call from Sikri thanking him for a gift of grapes and inviting him to a meeting at Sikri's house the following morning. Arriving, Reddy found seven judges present and

---

[52] This attempt to recapture the workings inside the bench is based on interviews with Chief Justice Sikri, and Justices Grover, Reddy, Khanna, and Chandrachud, advocates Anil Divan, Soli Sorabjee, H. M. Seervai, Fali Nariman and N. A. Palkhivala; also from Nayar, *Supersession,* and Khanna, *Neither Roses Not Thorns.*

[53] Nayar, *Supersession, p. 26.*

[54] Many of the persons interviewed, including Justice Khanna, believed that one judge had so been told. But Khanna would not provide the justice's name, although others named Chandrachud.

[55] 1973 (4) SCC 1006. Chandrachud said that since the conclusion of the arguments (26 March) there 'has not been enough time' for a complete exchange of drafts.

It was the practice at the time for readers to return a draft to its author with notations such as 'Read' or 'Noted' or with comments or suggestions.

[56] Chandrachud interview with the author. One such change, as seen by Sikri, was in the evolution in Chandrachud's own thinking. He was 'harder for the Fundamental Rights' at the beginning than at the end. (Sikri interview with the author.) Another change was in Justice K. K. Mathew's views. Reddy and Sikri saw these as 'gymnastics'. 'Mathew was all for the right to property at the beginning and somehow came to another view,' recalled Sikri. 'Then in his judgement he seemed to favour property, but said it was not consequential.' Reddy and Sikri interviews with the author.

asked where the others were. Sikri replied that the others were committed to parliamentary supremacy, and there was no use talking with them. The other meeting never took place because several members of the bench thought that meetings of less than the entire bench were not proper.[57]

Sikri ultimately requested the entire bench to meet with him, but, after hearing the views of all, he could not persuade them 'to reduce the number of judgements'.[58] Nevertheless, Sikri was able to impose a little discipline on his twelve colleagues, these 'each for himself' judges, as Chandrachud called them. The 'Conclusions' each judge placed at the end of his opinion and the 'statement' of the nine were his initiatives. According to Justice Beg, the Chief Justice himself drafted the statement.[59] It likely was the Chief Justice who put the finishing touches on the statement, but the points made drew directly from Justice Khanna's fifteen point 'conclusion' to his opinion, as a comparison of the two indicates. Justice Khanna has confirmed this.[60] Without the statement, there would not have been a court 'decision' in any comprehensible sense. The basic structure doctrine would not have been clearly enunciated and would have stood on quicksand—with an effect on constitutional government in India that is both incalculable and fearsome.

The Court upheld the basic structure doctrine in the Indira Gandhi Election case in 1975, while A. N. Ray was Chief Justice, and in the Minerva Mills and Waman Rao cases in 1980 and 1981 (chapters 14 and 24). As Upendra Baxi wrote presciently, the judgement 'is, in some sense, the Indian Constitution of the future', and, he added, 'the truth is that all the Fundamental Rights together with the majority of the Directive

[57] Reddy in an interview with the author. Chandrachud confirmed that one group of judges was present, and perhaps only one had been invited.

Justice Grover recalled that there were half-a-dozen such meetings at Sikri's and other judges' houses and that those attending were not confined to those sharing Sikri's views. Chandrachud attended one or more meetings, said Grover, and then stopped coming. Interview with the author.

There seems to have been one, late, meeting of the entire bench, but no information about it is available. In their gatherings in the Chief Justice's chambers before each sitting, the judges did not discuss the case in depth.

[58] Kuldip Nayar, 'An Interview with Former Chief Justice Sikri' in Nayar, *Supersession*, pp. 132–3. Justice Hegde defended Sikri's method for avoiding multiple judgements.

[59] The statement 'was hastily drawn up by Chief Justice Sikri', Beg wrote a decade later. Beg, M. H., 'Our Legal System: Does it Need a Change?' in *Journal of the Bar Council of India*, vol. 9, no. 2, 1982, p. 332.

[60] See 1973 (4) SCC 823–4. The confirmation from Justice Khanna in a letter to the author.

Principles elucidate the constitutional conceptions of social justice for India ... values which cannot be fulfilled concurrently in an economy of scarcity.'[61]

The nine judges seem to have performed an act of statesmanship, even of legerdemain. Under self-inflicted handicaps and pressure that approached psychological warfare from a government in search of a favourable decision, the court mollified the government by over-ruling Golak Nath and upholding the three amendments—in effect, nearly returning to the Shankari Prasad case position—while preserving, indeed strengthening, its own power of judicial review. As Madhu Limaye put it, 'what weighed with them was both apprehension about the future of liberty as well as their own natural desire to save and protect their own power and jurisdiction.'[62] The Supreme Court had risen to the occasion, but what a bizarre fashion to save the Constitution.

Finally, in a piquant collaboration, the government, in enacting the Twenty-fourth and Twenty-fifth Amendments, and the Court by upholding them removed the Court as the Congress Party's whipping boy for its own failure to pass and to implement social revolutionary legislation. As Justice Reddy put it, after the Kesavananda majority had held 'that the right to property can be taken away ... the cry that the judgement ... obstructs legislatures and Parliament to enact [sic] social legislation ... has no validity.'[63]

These achievements could not obscure the confusion generated by eleven opinions—happily compensated for in the statement of the nine—in a demonstration of self-indulgence over self-discipline. A more instructive example of the dangers from multiple opinions to law and democracy in India would be difficult to find.[64]

The history of Golak Nath is a cautionary tale of unintended conse-

[61] Baxi, 'The Constitutional Quicksands of *Kesavananda*', in Malik, *Fundamental Rights Case*, pp. 130, 132.

[62] Limaye, Madhu, *Janata Party Experiment*, 2 vols, B. R.Publishing Corporation, New Delhi, 1994, vol. 1, p. 57.

In interviews with four Kesavananda judges, the author found opinions mixed about how many of their colleagues performed this jugglery consciously.

[63] Reddy, *Social Justice and the Constitution*, pp. 66–7. The Alladi Krishnaswamy Endowment Lectures, 1975.

[64] Chief Justice John Marshall, having decided that the judicial branch in the United States needed strengthening *vis-à-vis* the other branches, ended separate opinions so that the court would be heard speaking with one voice. Hall, Kermit L. (ed.), *The Oxford Companion to the Supreme Court of the United States*, Oxford University Press, New York, 1992, p. 708. Hall notes that since the mid-1940s the number of concurring and dissenting opinions has increased.

quences. The fears for civil liberty and for the institutions of the Constitution that fed that decision's rigid restrictions on amendment evoked amendments hazarding liberty and the Constitution—as their use during Mrs Gandhi's Emergency soon would demonstrate. The amendments, in their turn, produced Kesavananda, which entrenched the Fundamental Rights—as even the Constituent Assembly had not done—while strengthening the courts under the Constitution. But cause and effect had not run their course. Kesavananda also fortified the government's resolve to tame the Supreme Court, the subject of the next chapter.

Chapter 12

A 'GRIEVOUS BLOW':
THE SUPERSESSION OF JUDGES

On 25 April 1973, the day after the Kesavananda decision, within minutes of arriving home from attending a retirement party for Chief Justice Sikri, Justice Shelat received an urgent telephone call from Justice Hegde: All-India Radio's five o'clock news bulletin had announced that A. N. Ray had been appointed the new Chief Justice of India. The President had passed over Shelat, Hegde, and Grover, who, by the convention of seniority, were next in line for the position. Justice Ray had not mentioned this to Shelat as they rode from Sikri's party in Ray's car, 'carpooling' in each others chauffeur-driven Ambassadors on alternate days as had become their custom. Hegde also telephoned Justice Grover. They agreed to meet at Shelat's house. Just as Grover was departing, Sikri arrived, having been given the news at the Golf Club by the Supreme Court Registrar, and he joined the three others at their meeting. The four men decided to resign, Sikri even though he was to retire the following day, and they sent their handwritten resignations to the President the next day, 26 April, after Ray's swearing in. This news was broadcast at five o'clock.

Mrs Gandhi had struck a 'grievous blow to the independence of the judiciary', said Justice Khanna.[1] He might have added that the Prime Minister as well had struck a blow at democratic constitutionalism, for, by attempting to make the Court obedient to her government, she was unbalancing the power equation among the three branches of government and distorting the seamless web. It was an act of extreme centralization of power. The government's vigorously proclaimed motive for the supersession was furtherance of the social revolution, for which an accomodating Supreme Court was needed. No doubt, several members of the cabinet were so moved, but the Prime Minister's motive was personal. She and her closest associates intended to protect her personal political fortunes. The purposes of and the process for the event, still called the 'supersession of judges' are the subject of this chapter.

---

[1] Khanna, H. R., *Judiciary in India and Judicial Practice,* Ajoy Law House/S. C. Sarkar and Sons Pvt. Ltd., Calcutta, 1985, p. 22. The volume is Khanna's Tagore Law Lectures.

The Supersession

Between the 24 April decision of the Political Affairs Committee of the cabinet to appoint A. N. Ray, H. R. Gokhale's visit later in the day formally to offer him the position, and the news broadcast the next evening, Mrs Gandhi had to overcome President V. V. Giri's objections to the supersession. When she presented the papers for his signature on the morning of 25 April she discovered that Giri did not like the idea of appointing Ray. He was not confident of Ray's suitability for the responsibility, and he wanted particularly to avoid the adverse publicity he expected the supersession to generate. He suggested appointing Justice Shelat—whose term would end in two months with his mandatory retirement—while the government prepared public opinion for a possible supersession of Justice Hegde, who was next in seniority after Shelat. Law Minister Gokhale, who Mrs Gandhi summoned from an adjoining room, explained to the President that seniority in appointing Chief Justices was not the practice in other countries and that no provision in the Constitution required the President to consult a retiring Chief Justice about his successor. Despite this, the President advised that the appointment be reconsidered. The Political Affairs Committee did so that noon, and its reaffirmed decision was taken immediately to the President who, silenced if not convinced, assented to Ray's appointment. Additionally, Giri wished to respond to the four judges' resignation letters with personal letters of regret. Following Gokhale's and the Home Secretary's advice, he did not convey his personal regrets to the judges.[2]

The selection of A. N. Ray to be Chief Justice should be distinguished from the decision to supersede the other judges, and that decision should be distinguished from broader sentiment within the government and the Congress Party to alter the composition of the Supreme Court. The Kesavananda hearings seem clearly to have triggered the supersession,

---

[2] This account is drawn from Nayar, *Supersession*, pp. 9–15, and an interview with B. N. Tandon, one of the Prime Minister's secretaries at the time. *Supersession* is a very useful book because it contains Nayar's reportage on the event and articles about it by Justices Shelat, Hegde and Grover, and by Jayaprakash Narayan, Kumaramangalam, Gokhale, M. C. Chagla, and Nani Palkhivala.

The Constitution provides in Article 124 that the Chief Justice of India shall be consulted about the appointment to the court of 'a Judge other then the Chief Justice'. Although the Constitution is silent about consulting the Chief Justice about his successor, it had become a convention to do so—although this was somewhat symbolic so long as the second convention of appointing the next-senior judge was followed.

Members of the Political Affairs Committee were the Prime Minister, Jagjivan Ram, Y. B. Chavan, Fakruddin Ali Ahmed, and Swaran Singh.

although the assertion that the government decided upon it in a fit of 'peevishness' upon hearing the Court's decision may be rejected. Not only had the Political Affairs Committee meeting approved the selection of Ray hours before the Supreme Court ruled, the government had for weeks known that the decision would be close and that it well might receive an adverse ruling. The Political Affairs Committee probably was giving its *imprimatur* to two decisions Mrs Gandhi had made several weeks earlier: to change the composition of the court through supersession and to appoint A. N. Ray Chief Justice.[3] S. S. Ray probably sounded him out, likely in early April. 'He knew A. N. Ray better than any of us,' said K. C. Pant.[4] For Justice Ray's part, he seems neither to have coveted the position nor expected it to fall to him. Bewildered by his elevation, according to a high court justice who knew him, he saw it as '"God's Will"'.

Political and governmental sentiment in favour of a philosophical realignment within the Supreme Court predated the Kesavananda decision, and we heard in the preceding chapter Justice Jaganmohan Reddy's allegations about the government's attempts to pack the court after 1971. The Golak Nath ruling planted the seed, and the Court's decisions in the Princes and Bank Nationalization cases encouraged its growth, as Mrs Gandhi's pronouncements after 1970 made clear. At the Congress Forum for Socialist Action's 1971 meeting in Bombay, Rajni Patel said that if the Court invalidated any of the Forum's recommended constitutional amendments, Parliament had the right to increase the number of judges on the Court. Protesting too much, Patel claimed that 'this was not a question of packing the Supreme Court with judges committed to the Government.'[5] Mohan Kumaramangalam's enthusiasm

[3] In Justice Khanna's view, the supersession 'was by way of punishment or show of government's displeasure at their [the judges] not having towed [sic] the government line in the [Kesavananda] decision'. Khanna, *Judiciary in India*, p. 22.

[4] Pant interview with the author. Kumaramangalam accompanied S. S. Ray, according to an associate of the Prime Minister. The role of Ray, Gokhale, and Kumaramangalam is supported by Frankel, *Political Economy*, p. 487.

Another dimension of these events has been provided by an associate of Kumaramangalam. This was that Mrs Gandhi gave her assent to sounding out Justice Mathew, who was philosophically in tune with Kumaramangalam, about becoming Chief Justice before Ray was approached. She was said to be willing to supersede all judges senior to Mathew should Ray decline the appointment. Ram Panjwani interview with the author.

[5] *Statesman*, New Delhi, 3 May 1971. Also, *Socialist India*, 8 May 1971, p. 19.

Patel would write in 1973, soon after the supersession, that 'a threat to the independence of the judiciary exists in a capitalist society where preservation of property rights and vested interests are of primary concern to the courts and the lawyers.' Patel, Rajni, 'Law Must Subserve Social Justice' in Shrivastava S., and Kotare, D. (eds),

for a 'committed' judiciary and for supersession was well known. He spoke to R. C. Dutt in 1972 of supersession and placing on the court 'judges committed to basic principles'.[6] Kumaramangalam told Kuldip Nayar that he, S. S. Ray, and Gokhale had discussed supersession '"many a time"'.[7] 'Supersession had been brewing in the party and among Indira's advisers for a long time,' recalled Chandrajit Yadav, 'since the winter, at least. The judiciary was seen as creating hurdles to economic reforms needed expeditiously.'[8]

More immediate, and perhaps more important, was the scarcely hidden, far from philosophical, motive behind the supersession: the protection of Indira Gandhi's prime ministership. During the continuing Indira Gandhi Election case, resulting from Raj Narain's election petition alleging that she had indulged in corrupt practices during her 1971 parliamentary election campaign (chapter 14), Mrs Gandhi's counsel had appealed from the Allahabad High Court to the Supreme Court against the admission of certain evidence. The Supreme Court had ruled the evidence admissible. The judge who led the bench was Kawdoor Sadananda Hegde, a member of Parliament, judge on the Mysore High Court in 1957 and chief justice of the Delhi High Court before joining the Supreme Court in 1967. The Prime Minister and her advisers did not want Hegde on the Supreme Court if she brought an appeal to it from an adverse decision in the Allahabad High Court, which she intended to do if that court went against her. And the way to do this was to supersede Hegde in favour of a Chief Justice who would set a bench that did not include Hegde were her appeal to come to the Court. '"It was all her work,"' Hegde said, because '"I spoke for the Court"' in the Election case appeal.[9] This view might be treated as Hegde's injured pride were it not

---

Revolutionary Visionary: Dr Shankar Dayal Sharma Felicitation Volume, Dr Shankar Dayal Sharma Felicitation Volume Organizing Committee, Bhopal, 1973, p. 272.

A resolution adopted at the Forum meeting called for ending judicial review of any law 'in consonance' with the Directive Principles of State Policy.

[6] Dutt interview with the author.

[7] Nayar, *Supersession*, p. 15.

[8] Yadav interview with the author. As the event approached, certain senior advisers to the Prime Minister like Uma Shankar Dikshit took the temperature of the party because the action was certain to be debated in Parliament. Sheila Dikshit interview with the author.

I. K. Gujral recalled Kumaramangalam's frequent quotations of Franklin Roosevelt and the need for a tame judiciary. Gujral interview with the author.

[9] Hegde to Nayar. See *Supersession*, p. 11. A further motive for by-passing Hegde was said to be the influence he would have, as Chief Justice, over appointments to the many existing vacancies in the high courts.

Hegde later again ran for Parliament and was elected Speaker of the Lok Sabha in 1977.

for corroboration. Law Minister Gokhale confided, some years later, that the 'Prime Minister, Siddhartha [Ray], and Kumaramangalam were adamant. In fact the Prime Minister was scared of Hegde becoming Chief Justice ... [because] Hedge's decision was against the Prime Minister's interest.'[10] According to her personal secretary, N. K. Seshan, also, 'Indira Gandhi was bent on getting rid of Hegde. She was the moving force behind it.'[11] Shelat had to be superseded to get at Hegde. Next in seniority was Grover, but he did not have a pro-government record on the court, and Kumaramangalam considered him '"a lesser person"'.[12] Opposition to Hegde's becoming Chief Justice from Kumaramangalam, Gokhale, Rajni Patel, and S. S. Ray was predictable, for their political futures depended upon the Prime Minister's. Kumaramangalam also made clear his opposition to Hegde on ideological grounds, characterizing him as 'a brilliant judge though of a different philosophy', in touch with the Congress(O) and the Syndicate.[13]

Although Justice A. N. Ray was next in line after Grover, he was widely believed to have been selected for other reasons. As the lone dissenter, he had ruled for the government in the Bank Nationalization case and been one of two dissenters (with G. K. Mitter) in the Princes case. '"The boy who wrote the best essays got first prize,"' remarked former Attorney General C. K. Daphtary.[14] Asked, 'Why Ray?' by Inder Gujral, Mrs Gandhi replied, 'Jyoti Basu [a Bengali and leader of the Communist Party Marxist] said he's a reliable radical, and as a judge in Bengal he was a liberal.'[15] Gokhale, S. S. Ray, and Kumaramangalam recommended Ray, according to most accounts because he was expected to be 'pliable' as well as liberal. 'Mohan and Gokhale told Indira that A. N. Ray was the best,' said Sheila Dikshit.[16]

---

[10] Gokhale to B. N. Tandon, a friend and formerly on the Prime Minister's staff. Gokhale said he thought the supersession 'very wrong', and he was 'very unhappy' about it—feelings also reported to the author by members of his family. B. N. Tandon diary entry from 26 October 1980, kindness of Mr Tandon to the author.

[11] In an interview with the author. According to Inder Malhotra, Mrs Gandhi was 'egged on by her counsellors and confidants to bypass' the three judges. Malhotra, *Indira Gandhi*, p. 153.

[12] Kumaramangalam to Nayar. Nayar, *Supersession*, p. 15.

[13] Ibid.

[14] Quoted by Fali Nariman, in 'Chief Justice Sikri: A Good Judge, a Great Person', *Indian Express*, 19 October 1992.

Kumaramangalam joked to Seervai that Ray was 'rewarded' for his opinion in Kesavananda. Seervai interview with the author.

[15] Gujral interview with the author. Chandrajit Yadav recalled the widespread perception that A. N. Ray was 'liberal'. Interview with the author.

[16] Sheila Dikshit interview with the author.

When the Law Minister told Law Commission Chairman Gajendra-gadkar that the supersession would take place the next day, Gajendragadkar told him the action would be 'constitutionally unsound and politically unwise' and that Gokhale should convey his views to the Prime Minister.[17]

The Public Rationale

As Mohan Kumaramangalam was a driving force behind the supersession, he also was its most visible and articulate public defender. He prepared the brief for government hand-outs to the press. He defined the government's position in various speeches, in articles, and in a short book. He was the supersession's principal defender in Parliament—a decision made by Mrs Gandhi—in place of the logical spokesman, Law Minister Gokhale. In his writings, Kumaramangalam justified Ray's appointment with reference to other countries. He quoted persons ranging from Lincoln to Benjamin Cardozo to Franklin Roosevelt in support of his contention that it is vital 'to take into account, in Cardozo's words, the "philosophy", the "outlook" of a judge'.[18]

To the Lok Sabha, Kumaramangalam explained, 'we will take the forward-looking judge and not the backward-looking judge.' He enumerated his five criteria for the selection of the Chief Justice in a democracy. He rejected as requirements both seniority and 'innocence of political views and conviction'. He favoured discretionary appointment

[17] Gajendragadkar–Indira Gandhi letter dated 24 August 1977. (Gajendragadkar Papers, NMML.) This was the former Chief Justice's farewell letter to the Prime Minister as chairman of the Law Commission. In it he reminded her of this and other occasions and that he had been persuaded to chair the Law Commission so that he could be 'informally' consulted on constitutional matters.

[18] Kumaramangalam, S. Mohan, *Judicial Appointments*, Oxford and IBH Publishing Co., New Delhi, 1973 (May), p. 72. The research for this booklet was done by Kumaramangalam's lawyer–associate, Ram Panjwani, a jolly Marxist thoroughly in accord with Kumaramangalam's views. Panjwani used much of this material in a series of articles for the *National Herald*.

The exculpatory references in the book and by others to Roosevelt's 'packing' the American Supreme Court uniformly fail to mention that the Senate Judiciary Committee refused to approve these nominations. President Lincoln's attitude toward the US Supreme Court may be closer to Kumaramangalam's than Roosevelt's. See Jackson, Robert H., *The Struggle for Judicial Supremacy*, Vintage Books, paperback, New York, NY, 1941.

While writing the booklet, Kumaramangalam 'dashed' into C. Subramaniam's office asking, 'Can you think of a title?' Subramaniam's Special Assistant, S. Guhan, said, 'How about "*Chamcha CJ*"? Kumaramangalam was not amused: *Chamcha* means spoon and, in slang, 'flunkey'. Guhan interview with the author.

of the person the government found most suitable—an individual who should have knowledge 'of the larger things that move the minds and passions of millions' and who would give the Court its most important attribute: 'certainty and stability in relation to the major and vital questions of law'.[19] Many would ask if A. N. Ray met these criteria.

When the Law Minister spoke, he explained that the supersession was not intended to affect the independence of the judiciary. To say that judges 'have to have ... a special social philosophy' is nothing new. Justice Hegde, said Gokhale, thinks that a judge committed to the philosophy of bygone centuries is independent, whereas a judge 'wedded to social change ... is not independent'. Parliament reflects the will of the people, and the court must 'decide under the Constitution and not over it'. He praised Justice Ray as one 'who upholds the right of society in respect of property and ... who upholds personal liberties'.[20] The government also supported its case by referring to the Law Commission's *Fourteenth Report*. This, it may be recalled from chapter 5, recommended that the appointment of the Chief Justice of India 'should not be made merely on the basis of seniority' but must be the 'most

[19] The speech appears in Kumaramangalam, Mohan, 'Chief Justice of India: Criteria for Choice' in Nayar, *Supersession*, pp. 78–92. The quotation is from page 91. It appeared almost word for word in *Motherland*, 11 May 1973, under the title 'The Great Debate-I, New Congress, Jurisprudence'.

Kumaramangalam advocated this position too ardently for the Prime Minister's taste. Nayar reports that she told 'some newspapermen' that Kumaramangalam had '"overstated" the government's case'. Nayar, *Supersession*, p. 39. And there is a credible report that she sent S. S. Ray to get Kumaramangalam to moderate the tone if not the content of the speech.

The attitude toward the judiciary of the more Marxist individuals within the Congress was expressed less delicately while Parliament was debating the supersession. At the Southern Zone Conference of the AICC, held in Bangalore on 4–5 May 1973, D. P. Dhar castigated the '"black-robed gentlemen" who spoke about inroads into democracy and asked where were they when thousands of ordinary tenants and peasant cultivators were ejected by powerful landlords ... "Does democracy get hurt only if it affects the interests of the privileged? ... [if so] the sooner we get rid of such a democracy the better."' *Congress Marches Ahead VIiI*, AICC, New Delhi, 1973, p. 240.

[20] *Lok Sabha Debates*, Fifth Series, vol. 27, no. 50, cols 295–312. The speech was reprinted in Nayar, *Supersession*, pp. 93–112. The tone of Gokhale's speech was subdued compared with Kumaramangalam's, perhaps indicating Gokhale's unhappiness with the supersession.

Kumaramangalam's prominence as a Marxist alienated much public support for supersession. Malhotra, *Indira Gandhi*, p. 153. Whatever his role, Gokhale reaped the whirlwind: the Supreme Court Bar Association on 4 May issued show cause notices to Gokhale and Kumaramangalam as to why they should not be expelled from the organization.

suitable person' from the Court, the Bar, or the high courts.[21] Again, others would ask if Justice Ray met the Law Commission's requirements.

Public Reactions

Adverse reaction to the supersession from the legal community was immediate and vociferous. The day after the supersession, M. C. Setalvad, M. C. Chagla, former judge of the Bombay High Court V. M. Tarkunde, former Chief Justice J. C. Shah, former chief justice of the Gujarat High Court K. T. Desai, and Palkhivala sent a statement to the government saying that the supersession was 'a manifest attempt to undermine the Court's independence'.[22] Each of the members of the Law Commission accused the government of misinterpreting its *Fourteenth Report*. The same day, in a 'high pitch of excitement', the Supreme Court Bar Association adopted a resolution strongly condemning the 'purely political' action of the government as 'a blatant and outrageous attempt at undermining the independence and impartiality of the judiciary'.[23] Moving the resolution, Chagla called it a black day and said that 'what is left of democracy and the rule of law is fast disappearing from the country'.[24] When meeting-chairman and vice-president of the Bar Association, L. M. Singhvi, called for any amendments, emotions ran even higher. There was 'pandemonium' as Ram Panjwani and others attempted counter-resolutions. Protesting even the meeting, R. K. Garg ordered ice cream bars distributed to those present. This was greeted by shouts of 'ice cream will gain you nothing'.[25] Deafening applause was reported to have greeted the moving and seconding of the resolution.

---

[21] Quotation from the *Fourteenth Report's* 'Classified Recommendations', p. 2. The Law Commission, whose members it will be recalled, then were M. C. Setalvad, Sikri, Chagla, Palkhivala, G. S. Pathak, and K. N. Wanchoo, said in the body of the report that the criteria for selecting a Chief Justice 'are basically different from' those for appointment to the court of a justice. A Chief Justice must be a judge of 'ability and experience ... a competent administrator ... a shrewd judge of men ... and, above all, a person of sturdy independence and towering personality who would ... be a watchdog of the independence of the judiciary'. It may be that the senior-most puisne judge meets these paramount considerations, the report went on. If not, the 'healthy convention' should be established that the chief justiceship 'does not as a matter of course go to the senior-most puisne judge'. *Fourteenth Report*, vol. 1, pp. 39, 40.

[22] *Indian Express*, 27 April 1973.

[23] *Statesman*, New Delhi, 27 April 1973. Also, Nayar, *Supersession*, p. 28. The major English language newspapers reported the meeting and printed the resolution.

[24] *Indian Express*, 27 April 1973.

[25] *National Herald*, 27 April 1973.

Requested by Bar members to carry their protest to the Chief Justice, Singhvi approached Ray the next day in the presence of his fellow-judges and told him that the Association was upset by his appointment and its members would not attend his court that day.[26] The day A. N. Ray took the oath, over seven thousand lawyers practising in the Bombay High Court boycotted that court, while only fifty of their colleagues issued a statement welcoming Ray's appointment.[27] Three thousand lawyers boycotted the Madras High Court on 30 April.

Former Chief Justice Sikri and the immediate victims of the supersession made their objections public. Sikri told a press conference on 28 April that the words 'social philosophy' do not exist in the oath of a judge. Judges should go by the social philosophy laid down in the Preamble and the Rights and Principles of the Constitution, he said.[28] Justice Hegde in a press conference two days later said that Justice Ray's appointment could not be sustained on the Law Minister's criteria of merit, administrative experience, or length of experience.[29] Justice Shelat, speaking in Ahmedabad, predicted that the supersession would make judges suspicious of one another, including in the high courts as judges considered how their opinions might affect their advancement.[30] Justice Grover, speaking at a Rotary Club meeting in Bangalore, criticized Kumaramangalam's booklet, *Judicial Appointments,* for its misleading presentation of evidence about seniority in the appointment of judges in other countries.[31]

The supersession did have supporters outside New Delhi. A. R.

[26] Singhvi in an interview with the author.

[27] *Statesman,* 27 and 28 April 1973. M. C. Chagla in open court protested the supersession.

[28] *Indian Express,* 29 April 1973. For a fuller discussion of Sikri's views, see 'Consequences of Supersession', Nayar's interview with Sikri in Nayar, *Supersession,* pp. 130–6.

[29] *Statesman,* 2 May 1973. Hegde recommended that independent machinery be set up for the appointment and promotion of judges. For a full exposition of Hegde's views, see his 'A Dangerous Doctrine', in Nayar, *Supersession,* pp. 46–54. Hegde said that democracy was 'only a cover' for Kumaramangalam, who had entered the Congress Party 'to capture power from within'.

[30] *Statesman,* 3 May 1973. For a fuller exposition of Shelat's views, see his 'The Explanations' in Nayar, *Supersession,* pp. 42–5. Shelat attacked the notion that the social philosophy of a particular party should prevail on the ground that no party represented the majority of the electorate in Parliament.

[31] *Statesman,* 21 June 1973.
For a fuller exposition of Grover's views, see his 'Questions That Must Be Answered' in Nayar, *Supersession,* pp. 55–68. Grover indicated his preference for appointment of judges by an independent panel.

Antulay, sometime law minister of Maharashtra and its Congress chief minister in the 1980s, devoted 243 pages of a clever book entitled *Appointment of a Chief Justice* to challenging the arguments of the supersession's critics. Arguing that the Constitution as worked had neglected the needs of the common man, he said, 'To assert that the courts will uphold the philosophy of the Constitution and not of the ruling party is to defeat the process of constitutional progress and democratic and peaceful evolution, to disappoint and disillusion the people and ultimately to provoke them to take more violent methods.'[32] Antulay advised eminent lawyers and intellectuals to wake up and to 'catch the moving time by its forelock'.

In Parliament, where it was debated for seven hours on 3 May, the supersession and Kumaramangalam received strong criticism from socialists and communists of both parties. Old socialist N. G. Goray said Kumaramangalam had an ideology, 'call it the communist ideology or the Marxist ... there is nothing [in it] like independence of the judiciary'.[33] CPM leader A. K. Gopalan said Ray's appointment was made to intimidate the judiciary and make it 'toe the line of the executive'. Hiren Mukerjee, CPI, thought the supersession a preliminary 'weeding out' of the Court and suggested some method of associating Parliament with the selection of judges. His party colleague, Bhupesh Gupta, however, thought the supersession a 'good beginning', a return to the principles upon which Parliament had tried to build the country. Independent-minded Congressman P. G. Mavalankar said Kumaramangalam 'wants this country to go ... toward totalitarianism'.[34] Parliament's and Swatantra's ready wit, Piloo Mody, said the Prime Minister was being led by 'three Marx brothers'.[35] In a press conference Madhu Limaye released his letter to the President asking him 'to direct' Ray to resign.

Jayaprakash Narayan, already disenchanted with the Prime Minister, chose to make 'an earnest appeal' directly to Mrs Gandhi. Property 'must serve the social good as conceived of by the democratic will of the people ... [and thus] can be limited, regulated, and even extinguished if necessary', Narayan told the Prime Minister. But everyone should reject the 'fallacy' that citizens could be deprived of their freedoms 'in order to establish socialism. This is a slippery path ... [that] will end ... in dictatorial

---

[32] Antulay, A. R., *Appointment of a Chief Justice*, Popular Prakashan, Bombay, 1973, p. 184. The preface is dated 30 July 1973.

[33] *Parliamentary Debates, Rajya Sabha*, vol. 84, no. 3, col. 289.

[34] *Lok Sabha Debates*, Fifth Series, vol. 27, no. 50, col. 258.

[35] As reported in the *National Herald*, 4 May 1973.

communism'. Narayan added, 'I am merely pointing out the logic of unlimited power.'[36] Were the appointment of chief justices to remain entirely in the hands of prime ministers, said Narayan, 'then the highest judicial institution of this country cannot but become a creature of the government of the day'. He appealed to the Prime Minister to appoint an all-party parliamentary committee to make recommendations to Parliament about an appointing mechanism.

Replying to Narayan, Mrs Gandhi said there had been 'no question here of the executive subordinating the judiciary'. She welcomed the overturning of Golak Nath and supported supersession by pointing out that the court's pronouncements on property had been 'confusing'. The seniority principle had led to an unduly high turnover of chief justices, and it would be 'atrocious' to believe that freeing ourselves from the seniority convention had affected the judiciary's independence, she said.[37] Narayan responded that he saw 'little relevance' in her reply. If it were her considered response, he confessed 'to a sense of utter disappointment and deep distress'.[38]

Narayan was not the only person prompted to suggest a new appointment process. The Supreme Court Bar Association did so at an 'All-India Convention of Lawyers on the Independence of the Judiciary' in mid-August. Because the government is the most frequent litigant before the Supreme Court and high courts, it 'is clearly not the proper authority to assess the merits of a judge, including whether the judge is progressive or otherwise', said the convention's resolution. Therefore, a constitutional convention should be established that Supreme Court judges be appointed by a committee of the Court's five senior judges and two members of the bar. Government objections could be discussed, but the committee's recommendation 'should be accepted as a matter of course'. Chief justices of the Supreme Court (and of the high courts) should be the senior-most judge on that court except in cases of proven incapacity. A committee consisting of, among others, Setalvad, Chagla, Daphtary, Palkhivala, and Ram Jethmalani was to convey these recommendations to the President.[39] The method of appointing judges would be studied several times more over the next twenty-five years without definitive result.

---

[36] Narayan, Jayaprakash, 'Appointment of Chief Justice' in Nayar, *Supersession*, pp. 69–72. He sent a copy to the Prime Minister in mid-May 1973. Narayan released his 'appeal' to the press.

[37] Text of letter in ibid., pp. 73–4.

[38] Narayan's 'rejoinder', ibid., pp. 75–7.

[39] *Mankind*, July–September 1973, pp. 77–82. The text of the lawyer's convention resolution is given in Dhavan and Jacob, *Selection and Appointment of Supreme Court Judges*, Appendix VII, pp. 111–12.

News coverage about the supersession was extensive and editorial comment upon it hardly less so. *Patriot, Mainstream,* and *Blitz* were sympathetic to it. The intellectually socialist *Economic and Political Weekly* did not take sides. The *Statesman* saw the end of judicial independence, while the *Times of India* said the Prime Minister was trying to provide for orderly change, but might be making trouble for herself. The *National Herald* editorialized that if Hegde and his superseded fellows were correct, 'the divine right of judges alone can sustain the world. This is a wicked, undemocratic doctrine.'[40] *Motherland* was equally emphatic in the other direction: for her own personal reasons, its editorial said, 'Shrimati Gandhi seems to have acquiesced in the communist concept of class justice'.[41]

A Brief Assessment

That Indira Gandhi's first years as Prime Minister differed from her father's is hardly surprising. His were the foundation years, when government and citizenry were settling into harness under the democratic Constitution. The spirit from the independence movement was strong, and its leaders led the new republic. Despite the conflict, bitterness, uncertainties, and heartache inseparable from great affairs, it was a time of idealism, cooperativeness, and civility. Anxieties were more than counter-balanced by the conviction that a nation could be created and social transformation achieved democratically. The nation's business went as well as it did—not always not very well—in part because the established order of society was only beginning to change as self-governing institutions took hold. No age is golden, but this one shone.

The republic had moved ahead as it ended its second decade. Politics and society were opening, bringing new uncertainties and opportunities. The economy was expanding and its benefits spreading, if slowly. National unity was not in doubt. Democratic institutions were well accepted. These were conditions in which a successor prime minister and a younger political generation could have built on established foundations: moving the social revolution forward; strengthening the institutions of democracy—Parliament, cabinet government and collective responsibility, and the judiciary—and solidifying national unity through cooperative federalism in governance and national development. But motion took the opposite direction. The Congress decayed

[40] *National Herald,* 5 May 1973.
[41] *Motherland,* 4 May 1973.

as a mass party, following factionalism within it—a malady also afflicting the opposition parties. There was a quantum jump in the centralization of power in government and the ruling party. As Mrs Gandhi
tamed Parliament, power moved to the cabinet, thence from this timid
body to the Prime Minister and her secretariat, and ultimately to a small
coterie around Mrs Gandhi—producing conditions barely resembling
cabinet government and collective responsibility. The attacks on the
Supreme Court essentially were designed to reduce three branches of
government to two.[42] The already centralized federalism in government and the Congress Party grew tighter because of the dependence
of state government and state party leaders on Mrs Gandhi's favour.
(Chapters 25 and 26.)

The centralization of power was intended to enable great progress
in the social revolution to which the nation had dedicated itself in the
Constitution. The ambitions were no greater than those of the Nehru
years, and many of those involved pursued them equally sincerely under
Mrs Gandhi. But now, economic and social transformation were to be
sought at the expense of liberty and democracy. Surfeited with the
emptiness of earlier socialist rhetoric, members of the Congress Forum
for Socialist Action became mesmerized by their own. Highly unrealistic,
they believed that social revolutionary spirits not only could make policy
but also assure its implementation (which they intended to achieve
through radicalizing the Congress Party's organization, another
unrealistic notion) and that they had the Prime Minister's support for
their programme. Mrs Gandhi, herself a populist and a master political
strategist, let this movement appear to lead her while she used it to
solidify her personal power. Thus did a small group of determined

---

[42] The imbalance of constitutional institutions exceeded the expectations of the
architects of the supersession of judges. After becoming Chief Justice, A. N. Ray more
than shared the government's economic viewpoint—he developed an adulatory attitude
toward the Prime Minister, which was remarked upon by many observers and associates.
He made himself amenable to her influence by telephoning her frequently, using the
'RAX' telephone system directly connecting the most senior officials of government. He
would also ask her personal secretary's advice on simple matters, conveying the impression
that the Prime Minister's views might be heard concerning an ongoing case. The personal
secretary, N. K. Seshan, in an interview with the author. Seshan said that this was the only
time such a thing had happened during his long service with Prime Minister Nehru and
Indira Gandhi. There was a RAX telephone also in Seshan's office.

The author sent this information to Chief Justice Ray, in retirement in Calcutta, by
letter (Registered Mail, Return Receipt Requested—in India called 'Registered A.D.')
and asked for his comments. This letter was received at Ray's residence, but no reply was
forthcoming.

individuals, careless of democratic standards and employing a popular cause, come to dominate the politics of a large nation.

Unfortunately, the Prime Minister did not translate her virtually unchallengeable power, her popularity with the poor, and her tools, the constitutional amendments, into social revolutionary accomplishments. 'Power in the case of Mrs Gandhi has remained a potential except when used to safeguard her threatened position,' in J. D. Sethi's analysis. For her to consolidate her power through policy and programme, she would have to risk losing support within the Congress and replacing it through alliances with 'parties of the Left'. But, thought Sethi, she was shrewd enough not to attempt this for 'she has not got time, personnel, apparatus, resources ... to accomplish this task, hence this path must be ruled out'. Only 'appearances' remained, Sethi concluded.[43] Put another way, even if legislation facilitated by the Twenty-fourth and Twenty-fifth Amendments had been passed, its implementation— excepting the nationalizations—would have been unlikely. A deeper, less tactical consideration may also have lain at the root of the Prime Minister's reluctance to pursue the social revolution. 'In a country of India's size', she told an interviewer, 'you have to keep balancing as you go along. A violent revolution would uproot the foundation, which will take a long time to build anew. We certainly can't afford that.'[44] Was this a rationalization for not doing what she had never intended to do? If not, was the Prime Minister thinking of the landless, who, given some promise of land reform, would revolt to get more? Or, was she thinking of the landed violently resisting the implementation of reformist

---

[43] Sethi, J. D., *India's Static Power Structure*, Vikas Publications, New Delhi, 1969, pp. xxxii, xlvi.

Francine Frankel's analysis is similar. Mrs Gandhi's authority after the 1972 legislature elections seemed to offer favourable conditions for 'social transformation through democratic and constitutional methods', writes Frankel, but she 'appeared helpless against the organizational decay in her own party, but was unable to admit these internal limitations without exposing the hollowness of her promises'. Frankel, *Political Economy*, pp. 478, 483–4.

Among Mrs Gandhi's achievements of these years was to mediate the sons-of-the-soil dispute in Andhra Pradesh over employment between competing groups of citizens who had lived in Madras state before states' reorganization and those from the former princely state of Hyderabad, now thrown together in Andhra—the Mulki Rules affair. The agreement was incorporated in the Thirty-second Amendment, which received presidential assent in May 1974. See Weiner, Myron, *Sons of the Soil*, Princeton University Press, Princeton, NJ, 1978, pp. 217–59.

[44] Interview in Carras, Mary, *Indira Gandhi in the Crucible of Leadership*, Beacon Press, Boston, MA, 1979, p. 235.

legislation? Her 'balance', up to this time, largely had had the result of preserving the status quo in the countryside. In any case, it was the hollowness of the Prime Minister's promises that was seen. Democracy had been weakened without strengthening the social revolution.

These years had a bright side, and the light was not artificial. The Golak Nath and Kesavananda decisions and the reaction by bench and bar to the supersession demonstrated deep attachment to constitutionalism and, especially, devotion to the judicial system the country had inherited and then made its own. The latter was a remarkable display of support for judicial integrity even allowing for the instinct of self-preservation as lawyers and judges rose to protect their identity and livelihood. In Parliament, in the press, and among the politically aware public, the wariness of excessive power and its potential abuse evident in objections to the Twenty-fourth and Twenty-fifth Amendments and to the supersession demonstrated vigorous concern for constitutional democracy. The anti-democratic actions of a few aroused the constitutional sensibilities of the many.

Indians' steadfastness for democracy would continue to be tried over the months from the supersession of judges until mid-June 1975. Popular discontents, fuelled by largely unmet election promises and by poor economic and social conditions (for which the government was not always at fault) simmered and began to boil. The opposition political parties seized on these. Frustrated by two decades of near impotence, the more maddening because it was considerably due to their own fractiousness, and fearing that the constitutional rights upon which their political, if not personal, lives depended, they fought legitimate causes with counter-productive tactics. The Prime Minister refused to acknowledge the reasonableness of the causes and to negotiate with the protesters—even those within her own party. From the two sides' conduct developed a situation in which Mrs Gandhi could plausibly, if to her own advantage, claim that civil government was at risk.

Part III

DEMOCRACY RESCUED OR THE CONSTITUTION SUBVERTED?: THE EMERGENCY AND THE FORTY-SECOND AMENDMENT 1975–77

This action is totally within our constitutional framework and it was undertaken in order not to destroy the Constitution but to preserve the Constitution, to preserve and safeguard our democracy.

Prime Minister Indira Gandhi[1]

It is, therefore, proposed to amend the Constitution to spell out expressly the high ideals of socialism, secularism and the integrity of the nation.... . Parliament and the State Legislatures embody the will of the people and the essence of democracy is that the will of the people should prevail.

Statement of Objects and Reasons of the Forty-second Amendment[2]

Bhakti, or what may be called the path of devotion or hero worship, plays a part in its [India's] politics unequalled in magnitude by the part it plays in the politics of any other country in the world ... . [I]n politics, *Bhakti* is a sure road to degradation and to eventual dictatorship.

B. R. Ambedkar[3]

---

[1] To the Lok Sabha, 22 July 1975, in the debate preceding its approval of the Emergency. Speech reprinted in *Preserving Our Democratic Structure*, Division of Audio-Visual Publicity, GOI, New Delhi, 1975, p. 4.

[2] To be precise, the Statement of Objects and Reasons was of the Forty-fourth Amendment Bill, which would become the Forty-second Amendment.

[3] *CAD*, vol. 11, no. 11, p. 979.

Chapter 13

26 JUNE 1975

That morning, the Bombay edition of the *Times of India* printed the obituary of 'D'Ocracy—D. E. M., beloved husband of T. Ruth, loving father of L.I. Bertie, brother of Faith, Hope, Justice, expired on 26th June.'

A few hours later, Prime Minister Indira Gandhi told the nation in a radio broadcast that with Parliament not in session, the President had declared an emergency because of turmoil and incipient rebellion in the country. During the wee hours of the night just passed, Mrs Gandhi had been composing democracy's death notice. There had been mass arrests of opposition leaders and others in New Delhi and in many states. A government-ordered electricity cut off prevented Delhi's newpapers from publishing the news; a Home Ministry 'order' imposed censorship before noon on the 26th. The Constitution's Fundamental Rights were suspended, public gatherings and meetings of more than five persons banned, and preventive detention provisions made more stringent. A few days later, the Prime Minister announced the Twenty-Point Programme of social-economic reforms. Soon, talk of changing the Constitution began.

The government justified the Emergency as necessary not only to preserve order but also to save democracy, protect the social revolution, and preserve national integrity—in sum, to preserve the seamless web. The rebellion threatening the country, Mrs Gandhi said, was the manifestation 'of the deep and wide conspiracy ... brewing ... ever since I began to introduce certain progressive measures of benefit to the common man and woman of India'.[1]

The government's action was not utterly without justification. Opposition parties' frustration with Mrs Gandhi's imperturbability and their own powerlessness had boiled over. The two sides' behaviour had combined to stretch democracy until it snapped. Riots and civil disobedience during past months had brought the governments of Gujarat and Bihar to their knees. Claiming to have established parallel government in Bihar,

---

[1] *Prime Minister's Broadcast to the Nation on Proclamation of Emergency*, Division of Audio-Visual Publicity, GOI, New Delhi, 1975.

Jayaprakash Narayan was calling for a march on Delhi. Morarji Desai threatened to surround the Prime Minister's house if she did not leave office during the appeal against her conviction for election campaign fraud (chapter 14). The Prime Minister feared that the country was lapsing into chaos, and some reasonable persons shared this anxiety. Because conditions had become so unsettled, many citizens welcomed the Emergency for several months after it was declared. Calm was restored, bureaucrats became more responsive, food prices came down for a time. But, by winter, fear settled over the country like winter fog in New Delhi. The twentieth century was witnessing another example of the ease with which a ruthless government can subdue a democratic, but frightened, people.

The Emergency's purposes were shown to be not those claimed for it. It was not to preserve democracy, but to stop it in its tracks. It was proclaimed to protect the political office of one individual. It would neither protect nor further the social revolution, despite its now arbitrary authority to do so. It would not enhance national unity, although it did restore civil order and coherence in centre–state relations. But at the same time it bred hatred of over-centralized authority. Instead of protecting the seamless web, the Emergency distorted it beyond the imagination of the founding fathers. Self-governance in India ended. Would it return? And what damage might the country sustain before it did? '[M]any of us use the word democracy in order to try and defeat democracy, to weaken democracy,' Mrs Gandhi had said of her political opposition just five years earlier. In June 1975, the words perfectly described her own behaviour.[2]

This Part of the book addresses two broad topics: how democracy was extinguished during the Emergency's first phase, and how the executive branch and Parliament collaborated to overturn democracy, through a succession of amendments to the Constitution and attempts to subvert judicial independence. The present chapter sets the events in context and then describes the extinguishing of democracy. Chapter 14 takes up the denouement of the Indira Gandhi Election case and her government's enactments and constitutional amendments to preserve her prime ministry. Chapter 15 describes the government's pressures on judicial authority in two great cases—one an attempt to overturn the 'basic structure' doctrine—and through the punitive transfer of high court judges. The final two chapters are devoted to the origins

---

[2] Speech to the AICC meeting in New Delhi, June 1970, *From Delhi to Patna* (Congress Marches Ahead II), AICC, October 1970, p. 148.

and content of the Forty-second Amendment's destructive changes to the Constitution.

The Culmination of Trends

Although the Emergency, in the extensiveness of its evils, was an aberration in the history of Indian democracy, it also 'was the culmination of long tendencies'.[3] The centralization of authority grew from the Constitution and the central-command structure of the Congress Party. This was increased by the central direction inherent in socialist practice and by Nehru's towering presence. Centralization came into full flower with Indira Gandhi's arrogation of power within government and over the ailing body of the Congress organization, abetted by her over-zealous admirers. By 26 June 1975, power had shifted from Parliament through the ministry and the cabinet to the Prime Minister and it would then go to a coterie of individuals without constitutional office—led by her son, Sanjay. During this process, central and state governments rejected political compromise and came to rely on preventive detention for controlling social discontent. As this was going on, the shining ideal of the social revolution had dimmed. Property relations had pitted the executive and the legislature against the courts, resulting in bitter conflicts and major constitutional changes. Successive promises to the electorate exceeded each other in grandiosity.[4] For most parties and candidates, elections had become pursuits of power unrelated to gaining office for the genuine pursuit of programme. For the opposition parties 'extra-parliamentary' methods had become a way of political life; for the government high-handedness had become habitual.

The culmination of trends has been commented upon by several notable observers. B. K. Nehru, High Commissioner in London during the Emergency, Mrs Gandhi's cousin, and often her supporter, including during the early days of the Emergency, wrote that Jawaharlal Nehru and Shastri '"knew what a constitution was ... [its] checks and balances"'. But Indira Gandhi '"in the effort to have a populist image ... went on

[3] Shourie, Arun, *Institutions in the Janata Phase,* Popular Prakashan Pvt. Ltd., Bombay, 1980, p. xi.

[4] A Congress Working Committee meeting told itself in April 1977, after the government's defeat in elections, that the emergency was intended to effect long-neglected social reform, especially for '"poor farmers and Scheduled Castes and Scheduled Tribes"'. *AR,* 21–27 May 1977, p. 13746ff.

the concept of committed bureaucracy, committed judiciary"'.[5] Romesh Thapar, a sometime member of Mrs Gandhi's kitchen cabinet, thought that the suspension of democracy 'was the culmination of a process of manipulative politics set in motion many years earlier, and very often the handiwork of supposedly democratic men'.[6] P. N. Haksar, once Mrs Gandhi's Principal Secretary and her close adviser, thought it accurate that the Emergency was the handiwork of a small coterie surrounding the Prime Minister. But, he said, 'it is not the whole truth ... [M]ore fundamentally, the Emergency represented the maturing of the crisis in our entire social, economic, political, cultural and value system which became increasingly incapable of solving the structural problems of building a new India.'[7]

More Immediate Origins

The long-developing problems to which Haksar referred had worsened over the few preceding years.[8] The country manifestly was not doing well in the early 1970s. Inflation was growing, the prices of essential commodities were increasing, and there was a dearth of these commodities. Oil prices, as a result of the 1973 Arab–Israeli war, rose from US· $2.06 per barrel to US $11.45.[9] State trading in foodgrains—promoted

[5] B. K. Nehru writing in the *Sunday Mail*, 5 April 1992. Cited in Noorani, A. G., 'A Baleful Legacy', *Frontline*, 12 February 1993.

[6] Thapar, Romesh, 'The Real Meat of the Emergency', *Economic and Political Weekly*, 2 April 1977.

[7] Haksar, *Premonitions*, p. 228. Regarding the influence of Sanjay Gandhi's coterie, Haksar asked, did not cabinet, Parliament and executive 'endorse and carry out the behest of the coterie'? Ibid.

Madhu Limaye attributed the 'destruction of liberty ... encompassed on 26 June' to its 'slow death in the heart of intellectuals and other educated people when they allowed their conscience to go to sleep upon the achievement of freedom'. Thus the ruling party could achieve 'vast centralization and concentration of powers in their own hands'. Letter written in prison in September 1976 and published in Limaye, Madhu, *The New Constitutional Amendments: Death-Knell of Popular Liberties*, Allied Publishers Private Ltd., New Delhi, 1977, p. 3.

[8] These pages are drawn from Frankel, *Political Economy*, ch. 12; Hart, *Indira Gandhi's India*, especially chs 1 and 10; Hardgrave and Kochanek, *India, Government and Politics*, pp. 164–72; Malhotra, *Indira Gandhi*, especially ch. 10; and Nayar, Kuldip, *The Judgement*, Vikas Publishing House Pvt. Ltd., New Delhi, 1977. Also, from interviews and from political party literature.

[9] D. K. Borooah to the Rajya Sabha, 5 November 1976. The speech was later published as a pamphlet, *Shri D. K. Borooah on Constitution (Forty-Fourth Amendment) Bill*, AICC, New Delhi, no publication date but 1976, p. 8.

by Minister of Planning D. P. Dhar, but opposed as impractical by Mohan Kumaramangalam and by P. N. Haksar and P. N. Dhar in the Prime Minister's Secretariat—failed miserably, increasing food scarcity and hurting especially the poor. Heavily regulated private industry for years had not been producing enough jobs to absorb the rural unemployed. Awareness of government organizational inability to implement reform was spreading. A national railway strike called in May 1974 by union leader George Fernandes would have shut-down a country dependent on trains. His promised derailment of food trains could have brought starvation. Fernandes's detention and that of thousands of railway workers prevented this, while increasing class and political bitterness. Railways Minister L. N. Mishra was later assassinated.

To cope with rising disturbance and to combat economic decline, the government introduced several harsh measures. In September 1974 it expanded by ordinance the reach of the 1971 Maintenance of Internal Security Act (MISA), adding smuggling to the activities to which MISA pertained (originally national security), permitting preventive detention for up to one year before review by an Advisory Board, and permitting detentions of up to two years. Parliament enacted 'The Conservation of Foreign Exchange and Preventing of Smuggling Activities Act' (known widely by the acronym COFEPOSA, pronounced coffee-posa). It allowed detention for hoarding and smuggling, but persons could be arrested— and were arrested—months before a detention order, itself, was issued.[10] Later that year, the President issued an order under the still-existing emergency of 1971 suspending the right to move the courts for protection of certain Fundamental Rights so long as the emergency was in force. Another order suspended for persons detained under COFEPOSA the right to appeal to the courts for protection of rights.[11] The President also promulgated ordinances to combat inflation, including imposing forced savings on individuals.

The Prime Minister was criticized for personalizing government and riding rough-shod over her complaisant Parliament with its inner circle of her followers. Popular perceptions of government corruption, long a staple in the public's pantry of disaffections, grew. The business dealings of Mrs Gandhi's younger son, Sanjay, were especially suspect.

As mentioned above, dissatisfactions boiled over in Gujarat and Bihar. Riots by engineering students in Gujarat, who linked campus

---

[10] Swaroop, *Law of Preventive Detention*, pp. 278–447.
[11] These orders were respectively, G.ʿ.R., 659 (E) of 16 November 1974 and G.S.R., 694 (E) of 23 December 1974, issued by the Ministry of Law.

discontents to public ones over food scarcity and prices, spread over the state. The central government imposed President's Rule in February 1974 and suspended the legislature. Bihar—noted for its poverty, faction-ridden government, police excesses, and rule by ordinance as the executive by-passed the legislature—also was in a condition of upheaval.[12] Jayaprakash Narayan announced he would leave his retirement in Gandhian social work to return to politics and lead the students. He pressed for dismissal of the Bihar government as corrupt and for recall of the legislature and for electoral reform while vowing to establish a 'parallel government' for the state.[13] He advocated spreading the Bihar movement to other parts of India, and he began organizing for the parliamentary elections, due in the winter of 1976.

In the spring of 1975, Narayan led a 'People's March on Parliament'. He was increasingly being seen as a national alternative to Mrs Gandhi, who charged him with attempting to provoke class struggle, which Congress had always tried to avoid.[14] But Narayan failed to back up his advocacy of turmoil and resistance with an organizational alternative to Mrs Gandhi. Many regretted his acceptance of support from the revivalist and militant Hindu RSS and the Jana Sangh Party. A divisive contest arose within the Congress between those demanding that the Prime Minister stand firm against Narayan (a view supported by the CPI) and those who believed she should attempt accommodation with him. Young Turks Chandra Shekhar, Mohan Dharia, and Ram Dhan led this group, which the powerful Jagjivan Ram joined early in 1975. Mrs Gandhi sacked Dharia from her cabinet in March 1975 for advocating this view publicly.[15]

---

[12] In 1971 the number of ordinances promulgated in Bihar rose to 113 from sixteen in 1970. The number rose again to 185 in 1974 and 215 in 1975. See the meticulously documented study, Wadhwa, D. C., *Repromulgation of Ordinances: A Fraud on the Constitution of India*, Gokhale Institute of Politics and Economics, Pune, 1983, table 1.

The Congress Working Committee's reaction to the events of 1974 were insensitive. At a mid-July meeting, it called upon 'patriotic democratic and socialist forces ... to fight this menace ... of the anti-democratic and fascist forces ... [whose objective] is nothing less than the establishment of a dictatorship of the propertied classes, bolstered by communalism, regionalism and revivalism.' Circular to Congress chief ministers and PCC presidents dated 23 October 1974 and signed by Party President Dev Kant Borooah. Zaidi, *The Directives of the Congress High Command*, p. 247 and *Congress Marches Ahead* 10, AICC, New Delhi, 1975, p. 331ff.

[13] The concept and details Narayan later developed in Narayan, *Toward Total Revolution*.

[14] In an interview in *Blitz. AR*, 24–31 December 1974, p. 12362.

[15] A seminar, 'Emergency in the Constitution and Democracy', dedicated to ending the 1971 emergency was held in New Delhi on 15–16 March 1975. Among those present

Narayan and Morarji Desai, native of Gujarat and still leader of the Congress (O), by this time were making common cause against Mrs Gandhi's government. The suspended Gujarat legislature had later been dissolved under President's Rule and Mrs Gandhi twice had postponed fresh elections to it. Morarji Desai on 7 April announced an indefinite fast to force elections by May. The Prime Minister capitulated and set elections for 10 June. From the euphoria of 1971 and 1972 to this! Nearly in panic, Mrs Gandhi did not know how to cope.[16] In essence, neither side was acting democratically or responsibly. The opposition was using the unparliamentary, insurrectionary methods of widespread strikes and fast-unto-death. The Prime Minister possessed neither the desire to compromise nor the sensitivity to understand that her opponents both felt and had genuine grievances. Worse was to come.

Twelve June 1975 was a bad day for the Prime Minister. Her long-time associate D. P. Dhar died that morning. In the evening came news that the opposition had defeated the Congress in the Gujarat legislative election, reducing its seats from 140 to seventy-five, allowing the opposition to form the government. And the election case that had haunted her for years—and even forced her to testify in her own defence before the Allahabad High Court—resulted in the decision by Justice Jagmohan Lal Sinha that she was guilty of corrupt election practices. Were this decision to stand, her election to Parliament would be void, and she would be barred from holding elective office for six years.

The Prime Minister was not in her South Block office of the Central Secretariat when the decision came over the news ticker at 10:10 in the morning. Her Principal Secretary, P. N. Dhar, and her information Advisor Sharada Prasad took the news to her house where she would remain until the Emergency was declared. A drove of cabinet ministers and politicians assembled at her house where they agitatedly debated whether or not she should step down while she appealed to the Supreme Court Justice Sinha's verdict during the twenty-day stay of it he had granted. N. A. Palkhivala, who happened to be in New Delhi, was summoned. She invited

---

were Narayan, Acharya Kriplani, K. S. Hegde, A. N. Grover, L. K. Advani, S. N. Mishra, Madhu Limaye, and K. Subba Rao. Former Attorney General Daphtary told the group that 'There is no question that the tendency today is toward absolutism and despotism.' *Revoke Emergency,* published by the Deendayal Research Institute, New Delhi, no date (but March or April 1975), p. 37.

Commenting on the seminar, an *Indian Express* editorial of 18 March said, 'The continuance of the emergency when there is no justification for it proclaims lack of faith in democracy.'

[16] Nikhil Chakravarty interview with the author.

him—he who had argued the Bank Nationalization and Princes cases against the government—to plead her case before the Supreme Court. He agreed, and would appear before Justice Krishna Iyer, the papers for the court having been vetted by Additional Solicitor General Fali Nariman. Believing the evidence against her to be flimsy, Palkhivala advised Mrs Gandhi not to leave office.[17] Mrs Gandhi's personal secretary, N. K. Seshan, believed that for a few hours she genuinely considered stepping aside. There was another credible report that she intended to do so. But her indecision was brief, for son Sanjay convinced her that she should not, arguing that the probable stand-in prime ministers, Jagjivan Ram or H. N. Bahuguna, would be unlikely to return the baton if the Court exonerated her.[18] S. S. Ray, Rajni Patel, and D. K. Borooah needed no urging to importune her to hold on.

Massive organized demonstrations of support staged by Bansi Lal and Sanjay Gandhi began on 12 June and continued through 25 June. Some 1,700 public buses were commandeered by the Delhi Administration and police chiefs in neighbouring towns to bring demonstrators to her house at 1, Safdarjang Road (named after a man who was a successful Wazir under the Mughals). For a rally on 20 June special trains would bring supporters from as far away as Banares.[19]

Meanwhile, the *Hindustan Times* said Mrs Gandhi should step down during her appeal, the *Times of India* said Justice Sinha's judgement 'will ... detract from her moral authority', and the non-communist opposition parties called for her resignation. Important business organizations and the Communist Party of India supported her. The CPM tilted away. The Congress Parliamentary Party on 18 June resolved—450 to 44—

[17] Malhotra, *Indira Gandhi*, pp. 165–7.

[18] Inder Malhotra, N. K. Seshan, and a member of the Prime Minister's household in interviews with the author. The Intelligence Bureau reported to Mrs Gandhi that Jagjivan Ram and Bahuguna were conspiring against her. Also, she had for some time been wary of Jagjivan Ram. Mrs Gandhi would have been unlikely to choose either of these men as temporary prime minister, and Ram must have understood this.

[19] The demonstrations were to 'create an atmosphere' conducive to Mrs Gandhi's remaining in office despite the Allahabad verdict, according to testimony before the Shah Commission, which was extensively published in the *Hindustan Times*, 6–7 December 1977, and according to the commission's report. One surmises that Mrs Gandhi expected the rallies would not go unnoticed at the Supreme Court. See *Shah Commission of Enquiry, Interim Report I*, Controller of Publications, New Delhi, March 1978, pp. 17–32. Named after its chairman, retired Chief Justice J. C. Shah, the commission was appointed under the 1952 Commissions of Enquiry Act by the Janata government when it succeeded the Congress government in March 1977. The Shah Commission published two later reports, an *Interim Report II* in April 1978 and a *Third and Final Report* in August 1978. These will be referred to subsequently as *Shah Commission*, I, II, and III.

that Mrs Gandhi was 'indispensable to the nation.'[20] Either Sanjay Gandhi or Congress president Dev Kant Borooah is said to have coined the slogan, 'Indira is India, India is Indira'. On 20 June, there was a massive pro-Indira rally. On June 24, Supreme Court 'vacation judge' V. R. Krishna Iyer handed down his ruling on Mrs Gandhi's appeal of her conviction. He granted a conditional stay of Justice Sinha's decision, pending a decision by a larger bench, but denied her the right to speak or vote in Parliament. (See Indira Gandhi Election case in the next chapter.)

Accompanying the public uproar were sinister clandestine developments. As of 15 June, Sanjay Gandhi had begun developing "'some plans to set things right"', as he later reportedly said to a friend.[21] Working at the Prime Minister's house (the 'PMH'), he began to prepare arrest lists, along with Minister of State for Home Affairs Om Mehta and Haryana Chief Minister Bansi Lal, a chum of Sanjay's, and R. K. Dhawan, an additional private secretary to the Prime Minister.[22] Delhi Lt. Governor Krishan Chand testified to the Shah Commission that he had seen the lists at the Prime Minister's house and that R. K. Dhawan told him on 23 June that opposition leaders might have to be arrested the next day.[23] Significantly, on 22 June, S. L. Khurana, after being interviewed by Sanjay Gandhi, replaced Nirmal Mukarji as Home Secretary because the latter was thought to be 'too legalistic'.[24] Mrs Gandhi already had edged aside Home Minister Brahmananda Reddy, preferring the more pliant Om Mehta.

Although it seems clear that imposition of an emergency of some kind had been decided for some time, the veil of secrecy does not permit us to know when the stratagem of declaring a second, 'internal emergency' emerged, although R. K. Dhawan is reported to have said that it 'had not emerged as such even by the morning of 25 June'.[25] But the idea had been 'mooted' in January 1975 by S. S. Ray, and according to A. G. Noorani, Ray had discussed with P. N. Dhar in 1973 the idea of declaring an

---

[20] Intelligence Bureau reports about the alleged doings of Jagjivan Ram and H. N. Bahuguna—and the Young Turks and others—were sent to Mrs Gandhi on 17 June preparatory to this meeting, according to testimony of Intelligence Bureau Director Atma Jayaram before the Shah Commission. *Hindustan Times*, 6 December 1977.

[21] Nayar, *The Judgement*, pp. 24, 28.

[22] B. N. Tandon said he became aware of the lists on 22 June. N. K. Seshan asked Tandon if he knew 'some lists' were being prepared. Tandon interview with the author.

[23] *Hindustan Times*, 6 December 1977.

[24] Nayar, *The Judgement*, p. 31, newspaper dispatches, and the author's interviews with B. N. Tandon and Nirmal Mukarji.

[25] Vasudev, Uma, *Two Faces of Indira Gandhi*, Vikas Publishing House Pvt. Ltd., New Delhi, 1977, p. 90.

economic emergency. D. P. Dhar appears to have suggested an emergency directly to the Prime Minister once and possibly twice between January and June. D. P. Dhar wrote to Mrs Gandhi from Moscow in January 1975 saying he had heard that the Allahabad decision might go against her, and she should assemble a team of Haksar, S. S. Ray, and Borooah, who was personally close to Dhar, to decide what to do before and after the Allahabad decision.[26] During a visit to Delhi in May, accompanying the Soviet Defence Minister, Dhar visited the Prime Minister and probably recommended imposition of an emergency or its equivalent. In a conversation at the time with the well-known editor, Nikhil Chakravarty, Dhar said that "'Indira is facing a crisis in the Election case because her chances are only fifty-fifty. The President can suspend the Constitution and set it aside."' Chakravarty responded, "'That means martial law. Don't import the practices of Jammu and Kashmir"'—where Dhar had been the state's home minister in the mid-sixties. Dhar then said, "'After the Constitution is suspended, a new constitution can be imposed by turning Parliament into a constituent assembly."'[27]

With Mrs Gandhi's continuation in office having been assured by Justice Krishna Iyer's ruling until the Supreme Court could hear the case, the opposition parties led by Jayaprakash Narayan and Morarji Desai increased their efforts to force her from it. Narayan on the evening of 25 June told a massive audience at New Delhi's Ramlila Grounds that the Prime Minister was moving toward dictatorship and fascism. He announced a nation-wide *satyagraha* for her resignation and asked the army, police, and government employees not to obey 'illegal and immoral orders'. The man who organized this rally was a member of the RSS, Nanaji Deshmukh, which along with concurrent RSS activities among students, caused some senior Intelligence Bureau officers to fear an RSS coup against the government. A committee under Desai was to begin a national struggle the next day 'to overthrow, to force her to resign'.[28] There seems to be no evidence available that Mrs Gandhi's opponents had the faintest plans for what to do if they brought her down. The

[26] A member of the D. P. Dhar family in an interview with the author. A senior official in the Prime Minister's Office who should have been aware of this letter, recalls that he was not. For Noorani, see 'A Baleful Legacy,' p. 78.

[27] Chakravarty in an interview with the author. Dhar's advice to Mrs Gandhi 'well before the emergency' was to change the Constitution and 'even declare an emergency to do it', a journalist close to the Communist Party of India told the author.

Mrs Gandhi would have rejected any suggestion to use the military to quiet the 'bedlam' in the country, according to Inder Malhotra. She knew that once the military were 'in, you'd never get them out'. Malhotra interview with the author.

[28] Frankel, *Political Economy*, p. 544.

government, however, had already set in motion the machinery for what was to come. Certain chief ministers had been summoned to Delhi on Sanjay Gandhi's instructions, Om Mehta had issued arrest 'guidelines' for New Delhi and state capitals, and other measures were prepared for implementation that night.

Although it strains credibility, testimony before the Shah Commission and scanty other evidence indicates that the constitutional–legal justification for the drastic actions had not been decided upon by the afternoon of 25 June. According to S. S. Ray, then Chief Minister of West Bengal, the Prime Minister summoned him to her house that morning, described the drift 'toward chaos and anarchy', and said the country 'required a shock treatment'. Ray responded that he had handled similiar difficulties in Bengal using laws already on the statute books, and he agreed to look into the matter further. He returned at about five o'clock that afternoon and said she could impose an 'internal emergency' under Article 352.[29]

The Prime Minister immediately took Ray to call upon President Fakhruddin Ali Ahmed to explain the constitutional situation. She asked Ray if she could declare an emergency without consulting the cabinet, how to word her letter recommending one to the President, and how to word the proclamation itself. Ray explained (or claimed) that a category

---

At the Ramlila grounds during the autumn festival of Dusshera, huge effigies of the evil Ravana, abductor of Sita in the Ramayana, are burnt to vociferous acclaim. Did the audience that June interpret a connection between the burning of Ravana and the ousting of the Prime Minister?

Jayaprakash Narayan's reflection on these events was that a plan to paralyse the government was a 'figment of Mrs Gandhi's imagination'. If there had been a plan, it was 'a simple, innocent and short-time plan to continue until the Supreme Court decided your appeal', he wrote to Mrs Gandhi in a letter dated 21 July 1975. Narayan, *Prison Diary*, p. 104. The citizen has an inalienable right to civil disobedience 'when he finds that other channels of redress or reform have dried up', Narayan said. Ibid., p. 105. He described the activities he had inspired in the Bihar students as 'constructive' and said that they had attempted to settle disputes with the state government across the table.

[29] *Shah Commission*, I, pp. 23ff. Ray also testified that Mrs Gandhi had mentioned to him the need for shock treatment even before the Allahabad judgement and 'some sort of emergent (sic) power or drastic power was necessary'. Ibid. This may hint that D. P. Dhar's recommendation of May had taken root or, as several reports indicate, that Ray earlier in the year had discussed an emergency with Mrs Gandhi.

According to a member of the Prime Minister's household, she might not have declared an emergency 'if completely uninfluenced by others'. Shiv Shankar, a member of Mrs Gandhi's government in 1980 and her strong defender, said he believed her improbable assertion that she did not know about the emergency powers in the Constitution, and he said, 'S. S. Ray, Rajni Patel, and Dev Kant Borooah sat on her head and made her impose the emergency'. Interview with the author.

in the 'Government of India (Transaction of Business) Rules, 1961'—
Rule 12—allowed the Prime Minister to depart from the rules and thereby
take actions to be ratified by the cabinet subsequently. She chose this
course and wrote the President that if he were 'satisfied', as a result of
the explanations given him, a proclamation of emergency was necessary.
She recommended that a proclamation 'be issued tonight', to be made
public as early as possible thereafter. She would have liked to take the
matter to the cabinet, she wrote, but it was not possible 'tonight'. The
President signed the attached proclamation.[30] The Shah Commission
concluded in its report that 'it is not understood' how Rule 12 allowed
the Prime Minister to bypass other rules making it incumbent upon a
Prime Minister to take cases relating to proclamations of emergency to
the cabinet.[31] At ten o'clock that evening, the Prime Minister called her
information adviser, H. Y. Sharada Prasad, and P. N. Dhar to her office,
where they found Congress President D. K. Borooah and S. S. Ray present.
'"I have decided to declare an emergency. The President has agreed."'
Mrs Gandhi announced to Dhar and Sharada Prasad. '"I shall inform
the cabinet in the morning."' She then handed the two the draft declaration of emergency and asked them to prepare a draft broadcast to the
nation, which they did, working until one o'clock the next morning.[32]

Mrs Gandhi called a cabinet meeting at 6.00 a.m. on 26 June to
announce to her own ministers the actions that she, without consulting

[30] See *Shah Commission*, I, p. 25 for the Prime Minister's letter and the proclamation.
There are other, partial and hazy versions of the event. According to one, when Home
Minister Brahmananda Reddy was called to the Prime Minister's house at 10:30 that
evening and told that an internal emergency would be declared, he objected that a state
of emergency was already in force. Shortly thereafter, Reddy sent a letter to the President,
but its contents have not been disclosed. Ibid., p. 24.

A second version has it that one of the President's advisers told him that the matter of
his 'satisfaction' that an emergency needed to be declared was not relevant because he had
to act on the advice of the council of ministers, not on the advice of the Prime Minister
alone. Yet, the Prime Minister's letter to the President made it appear that he was acting on
his own 'satisfaction'. The President, 'apparently, saw the force of this argument' and
telephoned the Prime Minister. At this time, the assistant left the room for some ten minutes
and, when he returned, found that R. K. Dhawan had visited the President with a draft
proclamation, which the President signed and returned to Dhawan with the Prime Minister's
letter. The Shah Commission report hinted that a second version of the letter and the
proclamation existed. It then reproduced the Prime Minister's letter to the President and
his proclamation, dated 25 June, declaring 'a grave emergency exists whereby the security
of India is threatened by internal disturbance'. Ibid., pp. 24–5.

[31] *Shah Commission*, I, p. 29 contains the relevant texts and the commission's reasoning.
The commission's report noted that in 1971 the Proclamation of Emergency previously
had been approved at a cabinet meeting.

[32] Sharada Prasad to B. N. Tandon as recorded in Tandon's diary entry of 26 June 1975.

them, and thus probably unconstitutionally, had had the President take. During the meeting, Sardar Swaran Singh, Minister of Defence, is said to have wondered aloud if it were necessary to proclaim an emergency; others remained silent.[33] Swaran Singh did not pursue this, and Mrs Gandhi did not reply. The cabinet approved the Prime Minister's advice to the President.

The evidence seems conclusive that the Emergency was the doing of the Prime Minister and her son Sanjay, circled by her, and his, closest advisers of the moment: S. S. Ray, D. K. Borooah, Om Mehta, Bansi Lal—with Rajni Patel not central to the decision. It was implemented by them and a second circle of obedient chief ministers and officials. Neither her Principal Secretary, P. N. Dhar, nor Home Minister Reddy (until just before the proclamation was signed) nor Law Minister Gokhale nor the Director of the Intelligence Bureau knew of the plans.[34] The Cabinet Secretary, B. D. Pande, testified to the Shah Commission that the matter of declaring an emergency never came before the cabinet prior to the dawn meeting. The commission reported that, before the Emergency was declared, neither the governors' reports to the President nor the chief ministers' reports to the Home Ministry indicated that the law and order situation was out of hand. The Home Ministry, whose responsibility it was to monitor the internal situation, had not expressed concern to the Prime Minister.

Mrs Gandhi's justifications for her action were artful, and she may have believed them. Attacks 'ostensibly' on her, she said, really had been intended to subvert the government's progressive programmes and to dislodge it 'and capture power through extra-constitutional means'. Conditions in the country necessitated the Emergency; she had lost her case in the high court on a 'legal technicality'.[35] 'An extra-constitutional

[33] The Prime Minister the next day expounded to a meeting of some thirty top officials (Secretaries to government) her reasons for thinking the Emergency necessary. Her request for questions elicited one. Otherwise, 'there was pin-drop silence'. One of the Secretaries present, Ajit Mozoomdar, in an interview with the author.

The bureaucrats 'went along' with absolutism, as they customarily do in any country. Some probably approved of the firm hand. Others likely believed they could help the country by keeping absolutism and its excesses in check. More were frightened by the penalties expected from dissent. Most simply were accustomed to going to the office and hardly could contemplate doing otherwise. Few government servants in any society depart on principle.

[34] Gokhale testified that neither he nor his ministry were consulted before the proclamation. Nayar has it that Gokhale was called in to give the decision regarding the Emergency its 'legal form'. Nayar, *The Judgement*, p. 35. But this may be doubted, for S. S. Ray could have done the job.

[35] *Shah Commission*, I, pp. 26–9. This rationale came in a letter to the commission—before which she never testified—in which she attacked its enquiry as 'one-sided and

challenge ... was constitutionally met,' she later said.[36] The social revolutionary justification was often repeated after the Prime Minister's 26 June broadcast. '[T]he hardships of the poorer sections and the middle classes' must be 'alleviated' by increased production and employment and the better distribution of goods. The Twenty-Point Programme, she later said, was not the reason behind the Emergency, but it had created the right climate for its implementation.[37] Seven of the programme's points dealt with property issues. And, as a subsequent chapter will describe, property issues were central in the drafting of the Forty-second Amendment. The Bill's 'Statement of Objects and Reasons' said it was to remove difficulties to achieving a 'social-economic revolution which would end poverty and ... inequality of opportunity'.[38] And Mrs Gandhi later justified a year's postponement of the parliamentary elections due in February 1976 on the ground that they would 'put the 20-point programme in jeopardy. After it is implemented and the people have benefited we would certainly hold elections.'[39]

Many in India at the time, and later, did not see the Emergency in such public-spirited terms. Their sentiments are summed up in the assessment given to the author by a most senior elected official: 'the emergency was pure self-protection'. The popularity of this view is shown

---

politically motivated', particularly because it did not go into conditions in the country preceding the emergency.

[36] *The Sunday Times*, London, 13 July 1975. The Prime Minister told a Youth Congress delegation that 'in India democracy had given too much liberty to people ... and they were trying to misuse it and weaken the nation's confidence'. Press Trust of India dispatch in *Deccan Chronicle*, 3 July 1975.

[37] 'Hardships of the poorer sections': *Prime Minister's Broadcast to the Nation*.

The Twenty-Point Programme announced on 1 July 1975 was the centre- piece of 'a massive drive for the legitimation of the regime'. Baxi, Upendra, *The Indian Supreme Court and Politics*, Eastern Book Company, Lucknow, 1980, p. 32. (These were the Mehr Chand Mahajan Memorial Law Lectures delivered at Panjab University, 1979.) The programme's more striking goals were a rehash of past promises: compilation of land records, implementation of agricultural land ceilings and speedier distribution of surplus land, socialization of urban land, bonded labour to be declared illegal (already banned in Article 23 of the Constitution), a review of minimum agricultural wages, and new schemes for workers' association with industrial management. *AR*, 30 July–5 August 1975, p. 12711.

[38] 'Government Bills as Introduced in Lok Sabha, 1976', Parliament Library, New Delhi, 1976.

The 'property rights of individuals' were not to get in the way of the well-being of society, explained a Congress Party publication. *Congress and Constitutional Amendments*, Central Campaign Committee, AICC, New Delhi, p. 17. Undated but published in December 1976 or January 1977.

[39] *Hindustan Times*, 1 January 1976, cited in Hart, *Indira Gandhi's India*, p. 30.

by the capital 'E' bestowed upon the 1975–7 Emergency often called 'Indira Gandhi's Emergency'.

Democracy is Extinguished

With the sweep of her hand, Mrs Gandhi had snuffed out democracy. Repression would be piled upon repression. The government attacked liberty first, this being the most dangerous to itself. Detentions began during the early hours of 26 June 1975 even before the President's proclamation was published in the *The Gazette of India* later that day. Before dawn, Jayaprakash Narayan, Morarji Desai, and other opposition politicians, totalling 676, had been arrested.[40] Mrs Gandhi approved the list of those to be arrested in the pre-dawn sweep, according to Pupul Jayakar and several persons then near Mrs Gandhi.[41] By the Emergency's end, nearly 111,000 persons had been detained under MISA and the Defence of India Act/Defence of India Rules. Amendments to MISA made after the declaration of the Emergency 'completely metamorphosed the character of MISA ... [and] led directly to large scale abuse of authority'.[42] Of the some 35,000 persons detained under MISA alone during the Emergency, 13,000 allegedly were connected to political parties and banned (i.e. communal) organizations, and their detentions were based on the 'slightest suspicion', and for criticizing the Emergency in meetings at private homes.[43] The overall purpose of the detentions was 'to silence all opposition'.[44]

The suspension of constitutional protections enabled these violations of personal liberty. On 27 June, a presidential order suspended the right to move the courts for enforcement of the fundamental rights articles guaranteeing citizens equality before and equal protection of the law (Article 14), no deprivation of life or liberty except by procedure established by law (Article 21), and no detention without being informed of the grounds for it (Article 22). Meetings of five or more persons were banned, under Section 144 of the Criminal Procedure Code

[40] The official figure as reported in *Economic Times*, 27 June 1975. Cited in Hart, *Indira Gandhi's India*, p. 12.

[41] Jayakar and others in interviews with the author. Contrary to some reports, it seems that P. N. Haksar's name was not on the arrests list, although Sanjay Gandhi considered him an enemy. But Sanjay Gandhi shortly remedied the omission by arresting Haksar's uncle in a publicly humiliating manner. Haksar never was detained.

[42] *Shah Commission*, III, p. 41. Fewer persons were imprisoned under COFEPOSA. Habeas corpus had not been suspended under MISA, 1971.

[43] Ibid., pp. 42, 43.

[44] Ibid., p. 45.

(CrPC). Three days later an ordinance amended the Defence of India Act, adding 'internal emergency' to the Act's title and preamble, empowering government to make temporary amendments in other laws, and allowing the imposition of censorship under the Emergency proclamation and the President's order of 27 June. A Home Ministry order of 26 June had already instituted censorship.

On 29 June and thereafter, the government promulgated a series of ordinances amending MISA of 1971. The first of these barred the courts from applying the concept of 'natural justice' in detention cases; it said that detentions might be reviewed after four months (the inoperative Article 22 said three months), and that an individual could be detained without disclosing to him or her the grounds for detention or allowing representation against the detention.[45] The second, an ordinance of 15 July, said that no one, including a foreigner, detained under the Act 'shall have any right to personal liberty by virtue of natural law or common law, if any', and it allowed for attachment of the property of anyone who had 'absconded' rather than be detained. (The absconding provision had been appl; ·d to criminals under the Criminal Procedure Code.) The third ordinance came on 15 October, apparently as a result of the Delhi High Court's releasing the journalist, Kuldip Nayar, from detention on 13 September.[46] It added to MISA that the grounds for detention were confidential, and, because they were matters of state and thus against the public interest to disclose, should not be communicated to detenus and the courts.[47] The second and third ordinances were retroactive in effect to 29 June 1975.

Parliament amended the 1974 COFEPOSA on 5 August (replacing an ordinance of July) with brazen language providing that a detention was not void if the grounds for it were 'vague', 'non-existent' or 'not relevant', or 'invalid for any other reason whatsoever'.[48] In June 1976, an ordinance extended MISA for one year, but gave instructions to review detentions every three months. In that month an ordinance amending COFEPOSA permitted detention for two years—instead of the one in the presidential order of the previous June—without giving the grounds and allowed one year before a case had to be reviewed by an Advisory Board. Detentions could be made solely 'for dealing with the Emergency'.

[45] Ordinance no. 4 of 1975.

[46] V. M. Tarkunde in *The Statesman*, 4 February 1976.

[47] Ordinance no. 16 of 1975.

[48] 'The Conservation of Foreign Exchange and Prevention of Smuggling Activities (Amendment) Ordinance, 1975', *The Gazette of India*, part II, section 1, 1 July 1975.

Freedom of the press was extinguished, and freedom of speech to the extent that this could be done. This all began, as had the arrests, before the cabinet had approved the Prime Minister's solo venture and the Emergency was publicly proclaimed. The general manager of the Delhi Electric Supply Undertaking, while in the Lt. Governor's residence at 10:00 p.m. on 25 June, received orders sent in the name of the Prime Minister to cut off electricity to the presses at 2:00 a.m. on 26 June.[49] The Home Ministry issued an order later that day prohibiting the publication of news about detentions without prior 'authorised scrutiny'. Thereafter, censorship took hold, with instructions to editors from the Chief Censor about what might and might not be printed. This was desirable, the Prime Minister told the Indian Federation of Working Journalists, because 'freedom of the press has come to mean the freedom to attack Indira Gandhi and to dub as toadies anyone who supports her'.[50] A week later the Censor prohibited reporting the soon-to-begin session of Parliament and the Supreme Court's proceedings in the Indira Gandhi Election case.

The Prime Minister, Law Minister, Minister of Information and Broadcasting, and others held a series of high-level meetings in July and August to discuss methods of curbing the press—thus placing Mrs Gandhi at the centre of these efforts.[51] The first of three December 1975 ordinances repealed editors' and publishers' immunity from civil and criminal proceedings when publishing accounts of parliamentary proceedings. The second ordinance abolished the press's own watchdog group, the Press Council. And under the third, the 'Prevention of Objectionable Matter Ordinance', government could demand security from presses if they published any newspaper or book containing objectionable matter. The ordinance defined 'objectionable matter' broadly: material bringing into hatred or contempt the central or state governments; causing fear or alarm in the public; and defamatory of the President, the Vice-President, the Prime Minister, the Speaker of the Lok

---

[49] *Shah Commission*, I, p. 23.

[50] Speech on 4 July 1975. *Statesman*, 10 July 1975.

[51] *White Paper on Misuse of Mass Media During the Internal Emergency*, GOI, New Delhi, August 1977, appendix 1.

Like the Shah Commission reports, the *White Paper* was published by the Janata government. The Prime Minister told a meeting of the non-aligned powers in Colombo on 17 August 1976 that there was no pre-censorship in India. See Sorabjee, Soli J., *The Emergency, Censorship and the Press in India, 1975–77*, Central News Agency Pvt. Ltd., New Delhi, 1977, p. 18. Sorabjee also provides a partial list of the Censor's orders during the Emergency (pp. 26ff). He notes how publishers either bowed before the storm or actually supported the government, thus denying their editors and reporters support.

Sabha, and governors. The government said the ordinance should bring about high standards in journalism and avoid writings injurious to the moral and intellectual health of society.[52]

The government removed the most basic foundation of a free press when, on 8 January 1976, it suspended the right of citizens to move the courts for preservation of the freedom of speech and other 'freedoms' in the Constitution's Article 19. Within weeks thereafter, Parliament passed the Parliamentary Proceedings (Protection) Bill, prohibiting the publication of parliamentary proceedings. This was aimed, the government said, at 'checking the tendency of playing up malicious and politically motivated charges'.[53] A move was initiated to disband India's four news agencies and merge them into one, and although the government denied involvement, the Shah Commission said it supervized the news agency's operations. The 'pervasive atmosphere of fear in the media', reported by the Shah Commission, was reinforced by the 'disaccreditation' of senior Indian journalists and editors and the banning of entry into India and deportation of several foreign correspondents. The government also intimidated newspaper and magazine publishers in various ways.[54] A reputedly inefficient government achieved great effectiveness in managing the news of its doings.

The denial of civil liberties and the violation of human rights extended far beyond detentions and censorship. There were instances of torture— the most famous being that of Lawrence Fernandes, brother of railway union leader George Fernandes—and already poor jail conditions were greatly worsened by the overload from detentions. The demolition of *jhuggi-jopries* (shanty-towns) in and around Delhi devastated the poor. The rural and urban poor and lower middle class were subjected to the terror of a forcible sterilization programme organized by Sanjay Gandhi— especially in North India. Sterilization targets were assigned to chief ministers, who, in their efforts to gain favour, were reported to have exceeded them—in the manner of American 'body-counts' during the war in Vietnam. Persons were arrested under the DIR for opposing the 'family planning' programme.[55]

---

[52] The *Statesman*, 9 December 1975. It will be recalled from Part I that a Press Objectionable Matter Act was passed in 1951 and repealed in 1957.

[53] *AR*, 26 February–3 March 1976, p. 13040.

[54] See *White Paper on Misuse of Mass Media*, and Nayar, Kuldip, 'How RNG (Ram Nath Goenka, owner of the *Indian Express*) Fought the Emergency,' *The Indian-American*, November 1991, pp. 24ff.

[55] Dr Karan Singh (PhD not MD), Minister of Health, sent a note to the Prime Minister on 10 October 1975 saying that the population problem 'is now so serious that there seems

The lesson to be learned from these activities, concluded the Shah Commission, was that

If the basic unity and territorial integrity of the country is to be emphasized, at the political level it is imperative to ensure that the officials at the decision-making levels are protected and immunized from threats or pressures so that they can function ... governed by one single consideration—the promotion of public well-being and the upholding of the fundamentals of the Constitution and the rule of law.[56]

Several persons around Mrs Gandhi advocated that she declare the end of the Emergency in her Independence Day speech from the Red Fort on 15 August 1975, recalled Nikhil Chakravarty, but with the Emergency still popular due to the drop in food prices and the arrival of political quiet and with so little resistance to it apparent, they decided to continue with it. The Prime Minister's Information Adviser believed the Emergency would have been withdrawn near time had Bangladesh's Prime Minister Mujibur Rahman not been assassinated, an event that shocked everyone, including Mrs Gandhi, and caused her to suspect conspiracies against herself.[57] Apparently sincere fears of conspiracies, heightened by purposely spread rumours of them, became a justification for maintaining the Emergency. It would be premature to conclude that 'dangers of internal and external subversion' have been surmounted, said a Congress Party resolution of January 1976. 'Forces of destabilization are still actively at work.' The Emergency must continue until 'these dangers have been effectively contained'.[58]

---

to be no alternative but to think ... [of introducing] some element of compulsion in the larger national interest ...'. *Shah Commission*, III, p. 153. It is doubtful that Karan Singh privately supported the excesses of Sanjay Gandhi's sterilization programme, but there is no evidence available that he opposed them.

[56] Ibid., p. 229. Mrs Gandhi's assumption of arbitrary authority may intriguingly be compared with the possibility that a President of India might become a 'dictator' by dissolving Parliament and the council of ministers, appointing lackeys to be ministers, ruling by ordinance, and declaring an emergency, 'which the courts would find difficult to hold invalid'. Gledhill, *The Republic of India*, pp. 107–9.

[57] Chakravarty and H. Y. Sharada Prasad in interviews with the author. The story had gone round that Mrs Gandhi intended to announce the Emergency's end in the Red Fort speech, but did not do so, having learned of Rahman's assassination soon before giving it. This was not the case, according to an impeccable source, she learned of his death only after delivering the speech.

[58] Resolution moved by S. S. Ray in the Subjects Committee meeting, Congress's Kamagata Maru Plenary Session 31 December 1975–1 January 1976. Zaidi, A. M., *Encyclopaedia of the Indian National Congress*, S. Chand and Company Ltd., New Delhi, 1984, vol. 23, p. 317.

Chapter 14

CLOSING THE CIRCLE

'The Emergency suddenly was in place, power was in their hands, and they wondered what to do with it,' remembered a Law Ministry official senior at the time. Months would elapse before long-term plans were completed. But the short-run need was clear to the Prime Minister and her associates: to protect her prime ministry and her Emergency proclamation from judicial challenge. The two goals overlapped as did the actions serving each. Closing a circle around Mrs Gandhi meant destroying representative government for the benefit of one official. Protecting her 1971 election to Parliament, the most pressing need, takes us back to the origins of the challenge to her.

The Indira Gandhi Election Case

Justice Jagmohan Lal Sinha's 12 June 1975 catalytic ruling in the Allahabad High Court, and Justice V. R. Krishna Iyer's temporary stay of that decision on 24 June came four years after the causative events. On 8 March 1971, Raj Narain organized a parade in his constituency town of Rae Bareli in Uttar Pradesh to celebrate his victory over Indira Gandhi in the parliamentary elections of the previous day. But he hadn't won. Indira Gandhi had, by a wide margin. Narain's Samyukta Socialist Party,'s suspicions of Mrs Gandhi, swollen by its enormous frustration from its inability to unseat her and the Congress Party, hardened into certainty that she had won through election rigging and corrupt practices. Narain decided to challenge the Prime Minister's election through an election petition, which he did on 24 April before the Allahabad High Court.[1] The petition charged that in her campaign the Prime Minister had violated the provisions of the Representation of the People Act, 1951 because the campaign had been assisted by a gazetted government official, the armed forces, and local police; had used government vehicles; had

[1] The following account of Mrs Gandhi's Election case draws heavily on Bhushan, Prashant, *The Case That Shook India*, Vikas Publishing House Pvt. Ltd., New Delhi, 1978. The author of this good book is the son of Raj Narain's counsel, Shanti Bhushan.

exceeded the prescribed limit for campaign expenses; and had distributed liquor and blankets among the voters to gain their votes.

Hearings began on 15 July 1971 before Justice B. N. Lokur. Later in the month, Raj Narain requested that the Prime Minister be called to testify in the court and, more critical to the case, that certain government documents be produced in court. Later in the year, Narain appealed to the Supreme Court the High Court's ruling upholding the government's position that certain allegations of corrupt practices could not now be admitted because they had not been listed in the original election petition.[2] In New Delhi, a bench of Justices K. S. Hegde, Jaganmohan Reddy, and K. K. Mathew heard the case, and on 15 March 1972 Hegde delivered the bench's decision upholding Narain's appeal. Evidence could now be introduced about whether the gazetted officer in question, Yashpal Kapoor, had been a government official or a private citizen when he assisted Mrs Gandhi's election campaign.[3]

The case dragged on through 1973 and 1974. On 5 April 1974 the Supreme Court granted leave for the third appeal during the hearings. This time it was Mrs Gandhi, claiming 'privilege' in not having to produce the 'Blue Book' in the high court. (The 'Blue Book': 'Rules and Instructions for the Protection of the Prime Minister When on Tour or Travel'.) On 24 January 1975, a Supreme Court bench of five—Chief Justice Ray, K. K. Mathew, N. L. Untwalia, R. S. Sarkaria, and A. Alagiriswami—quashed the high court's ruling commanding production of the Blue Book in court. But it directed Justice Jagmohan Lal Sinha, the third judge to preside over the case, to get an official affidavit about disclosure of the Blue Book, and then he could decide whether or not to admit portions of it in evidence.

Meanwhile, a decision in another election case had affected Mrs Gandhi's strategy in hers. On 3 October 1974, a Supreme Court bench

---

[2] See Section 86(5) of the Representation of the People Act as it then was.

[3] For the decision, see 1972 (3) SCC 850ff. Also, Bhushan, *The Case That Shook India*, p. 14.

The point at issue was narrow: did Kapoor's resignation from government service become 'official' when he made it orally to a superior, or only when he submitted it in writing?

As seen in ch. 12, Justice Hegde attributed his supersession for the chief justiceship in part to this ruling. 'I had reason to believe that Mrs Gandhi was greatly piqued by my decision in her election appeal.' 'Statement issued by Sri K. S. Hegde, former Judge of the Supreme Court of India, in reply to certain criticism made by some of the Congress leaders', dated 1 May 1973. Jayaprakash Narayan Papers, Third Installment, Subject File 455, NMML.

of Justices R. S. Sarkaria and P. N. Bhagwati ruled that an election
expense incurred by any person with the candidate's consent or of which
a candidate took advantage should be treated as an authorized expense
and had to be included in the candidate's report of election expenses
(author's emphasis).[4] Mrs Gandhi and the Law Ministry reacted, as they
would in 1975, by retrospectively altering the law upon which the
Bhagwati–Sarkaria decision had been based. On 19 October, the
President promulgated the Representation of the People (Amendment)
Ordinance, 1974 (replaced by an Act of Parliament on 21 December)
to add an 'Explanation' to Section 77 of the 1951 Act. This said that
'Notwithstanding any judgement ... of any court ... any expenditure
incurred or authorized in connection with the election of a candidate
... [by anyone other than the candidate or his election agent] shall not
be deemed to be and *shall not ever be deemed to have been* expenditure ...
authorized by the candidate ...' (author's emphasis). By making legal
what had been illegal, Mrs Gandhi had kicked one leg from under Raj
Narain's election petition. In other developments, Justice Sinha
admitted into evidence portions of the Blue Book; Raj Narain moved a
writ petition challenging the 1974 Act amending the Representation
of the People Act; and Justice Sinha admitted this petition as connected
to the case. On 18 March 1975 Mrs Gandhi became the first Prime
Minister of India to appear in person before a court.[5]

Arguments ended on 23 May. Justice Sinha went with his family
literally into hiding to write his judgement.[6] Delivering it in 238 pages
on 12 June, he voided the Prime Minister's election because she was
guilty of the 'corrupt practice' of using the services of state and central
government officers in her campaign. He rejected Raj Narain's challenge

---

[4] *Kanwar Lal Gupta v Amarnath Chawla and Others* 1975 (2) SCR 2599ff, called Amarnath
Chawla's case. See also, Bhushan, *The Case That Shook India*, p. 17.

[5] President V. V. Giri had been the first official of the highest rank to appear before
the Supreme Court when in April 1970 he defended himself against a petition challenging
his election as President.

[6] At the time, J. Vengal Rao of Andhra, one of the chief ministers summoned to
Delhi to help prepare for the Emergency's imposition, was purported to have said that
Justice Sinha had revealed his forthcoming decision to Jayaprakash Narayan. Rao
subsequently published the charge. In 1996, he tendered an unconditional apology to
the Allahabad High Court for the false allegation. *India Today*, 30 November 1996, p. 19.
During a conversation with Mrs Gandhi, perhaps on 15 May, D. P. Dhar warned her
that her case had been badly handled, but found her smug about the outcome. A senior
official in the Prime Minister's office—who had it from D. P. Dhar—in an interview with
the author. Probably at this meeting, also, Dhar advocated the stern measures to restore
order described in chapter 13.

to the constitutionality of the 1974 act amending the Representation of the People Act. During the ensuing uproar in the courtroom, Mrs Gandhi's counsel applied for a stay order, and Justice Sinha granted an unconditional stay for twenty days. He had been informed (it appears wrongly) that Narain's counsel had agreed to the stay.[7]

During the previous few weeks, there had been goings-on backstage in Allahabad. Agents of the Intelligence Bureau were trying to glean Justice Sinha's views from his staff or from tidbits of gossip in the court and the city.[8] A Joint Secretary in the central Home Ministry met the chief justice of the High Court and suggested that the Prime Minister might be spared embarrassment if Sinha deferred his ruling until she had returned from a trip abroad. So angered was Sinha when the chief justice told him this that he promptly set 12 June as judgement day.[9] Threats against Justice Sinha were rumoured, and a member of Parliament from Uttar Pradesh 'casually mentioned to Sinha whether he could do with Rs 500,000'.[10] Justice Sinha, himself, claimed that retired Chief Justice D. S. Mathur, formerly a colleague on the Allahabad Court, had said to him ' "It is settled that today you decide the case in favour of Smt Gandhi and tomorrow you go to the Supreme Court." '[11] Justice Mathur denied the allegation, saying that he and Sinha 'were talking of rumours in Delhi' conveyed to him over the telephone.[12] Responsible persons disagree about the Sinha–Mathur affair. N. K.

---

[7] The version of Raj Narain's counsel in Bhushan, *The Case That Shook India*, p. 97.

Seven years later, Justice Sinha wrote, '[I]f the members of the executive or the legislatures are allowed to move unrestrained in any direction they choose, it would be the death-knell of democracy.' Sinha, J. M. L., *The Constitution, the Judiciary and the People*, Popular Prakashan, Bombay, 1983, p. 15. This is the Jayaprakash Narayan Memorial Lecture of 1982.

[8] Information to the author from a relation of then IB director, Atma Jayaram; also, Nayar, *The Judgement*, p. 2.

[9] Nayar, *The Judgement*, pp. 1–2.

The visit by a Joint Secretary to Allahabad at this time has been confirmed to the author by an official then in the Prime Minister's office. This individual, no fan of Mrs Gandhi, says the visit to the city was unrelated to the case.

[10] Ibid., p. 1.

[11] Judge Sinha's letter to Home Minister Charan Singh dated 9 July 1977. Sinha wrote that the incident occurred about 23 May. From *Papers Laid on the Table, 1977*, Lok Sabha Secretariat, New Delhi.

Charan Singh had written to Justice Sinha on 8 July enquiring for all the facts, after pointing to a passage in Nayar's *The Judgement* referring to such an offer having been made. Ibid.

[12] D. S. Mathur letter to Charan Singh dated 15 July 1977. Charan Singh had written to Mathur on 11 July. Ibid. The correspondence among the three men is much more extensive than is indicated here.

Seshan and a senior communist journalist tend to believe Sinha. P. N. Haksar doubts Sinha's account, thinking he was 'just showing he had guts'.[13] The truth of the matter is uncertain, but, given Mrs Gandhi's stake in the case and the personalities around her, it is likely that attempts were made to foreordain Justice Sinha's decision.

Two days after Sinha's ruling, H. R. Gokhale approached N. A. Palkhivala about representing the Prime Minister. Palkhivala said he would examine the cases and, after doing so, agreed to take it. He told Gokhale to tell Mrs Gandhi that the evidence on record did not justify Justice Sinha's ruling.[14] On 20 June, Palkhivala sought an unconditional stay of Justice Sinha's decision pending final disposal of her appeal by the Supreme Court. Her petition said there would be 'grave hardship and irreparable loss to the appellant and the country at large' if an unconditional stay were not granted. The stay application had been read and corrected by Solicitor General Fali Nariman.

The Supreme Court's vacation judge, V. R. Krishna Iyer, heard the case on 23 June and the next day he granted a conditional stay ruling that the electoral disqualification 'stands eclipsed' during the stay. Prime Minister Gandhi could address Parliament, but she could neither participate nor vote in Lok Sabha debates nor draw remuneration as a member. Additionally, Krishna Iyer made remarks in his judgement that would echo long thereafter. The high court's ruling, he said, 'however ultimately weak it may prove ... does not involve the petitioner in any of the graver electoral vices set out in Section 123 of the [Representation of the People] Act'. He added, 'Draconian laws do not cease to be law in courts but must alert a wakeful and quick-acting legislature.'[15] Justice Krishna Iyer's critics claim that with these words he had virtually exonerated the Prime Minister and all but invited Parliament to amend the 'draconian' passages in the election law, which, as will be seen, Parliament did in the Election Laws Amendment Act and the Thirty-ninth Amendment. A kinder reaction to the stay order was, 'Perhaps, unbeknown to Justice Krishna Iyer, whose judicial integrity is beyond question, he offered advice to her which was not warranted in judicial discourse and in any case proved disastrous to the Court later on.'[16]

Then came the Emergency, its repressions, and its almost limitless powers. With many opposition members of Parliament detained and

---

[13] Seshan and P. N. Haksar interviews with the author.

[14] N. A. Palkhivala interview with the author.

[15] *Smt. Indira Nehru Gandhi v Shri Raj Narain* 1975 *Supp* SCC 1ff.

[16] Baxi, *The Indian Supreme Court*, p. 51. See his analysis of the conditional stay period, pp. 46–56.

others either fearing the Prime Minister or loyal to her, it was not difficult to enact constitutional amendments to protect her position.

The Protective Amendments

The government introduced the first of these, the Thirty-eighth Amendment, on 22 July 1975 and it received presidential assent ten days later. This barred judicial review of proclamations of emergency whether made to meet external, internal, or financial threats (Article 360 for the latter). The amendment also barred judicial review of overlapping emergency proclamations, of ordinances promulgated by the President or by governors, and of laws enacted during emergencies that contravened the Fundamental Rights.

The second amendment, the Thirty-ninth, protected Mrs Gandhi's prime ministry by preempting any Supreme Court action that might result from its hearings on her election case, which were to begin four days after the bill's introduction on 7 August. Testifying to the Prime Minister's control, the Lok Sabha passed the amendment the same day after two hours 'debate'. In the Rajya Sabha it received equally expeditious treatment the next day and two days later, the President assented to the bill, state legislatures very efficiently having ratified it in special Saturday sessions. It removed from the Supreme Court authority to adjudicate election petitions. It inserted a new Article in the Constitution (Article 329A) that, in a masterpiece of dense wording, laid down that elections of the Prime Minister and the Speaker of the Lok Sabha could be decided only by an 'authority' or 'body' established by Parliament by law, no longer by the Supreme Court. Furthermore, an election petition against a member of Parliament would 'abate' were that individual to become the Prime Minister or the Speaker. Also, no law about election petitions passed prior to the amendment was valid, and any judicial declarations voiding elections were invalid. Additionally, the amendment took from the Supreme Court and placed in a body to be established by Parliament the authority to resolve disputes concerning the elections of the President and the Vice-President.[17] Elections of the President, Vice-President, and Speaker were included in the amendment, along with the Prime Minister's, so 'it would not appear

---

[17] Explaining the amending bill, Law Minister Gokhale said that because the President and the Vice-President were not answerable for anything done in exercise of their office, it was 'appropriate' that their election should be beyond court jurisdiction, and this applied equally to the Prime Minister and Speaker. *Lok Sabha Debates*, Fifth Series, vol. 54, no. 14, col. 8.

too obvious' that it was to save Mrs Gandhi's election, wrote Kuldip Nayar.[18]

To make doubly sure that the Supreme Court could neither challenge nor embarrass the Prime Minister, the amendment placed in the Ninth Schedule, and beyond judicial review, three laws dealing with elections: the Representation of the People Acts of 1951 and 1974 and the Election Laws Amendment Act. This 5 August 1975 law altered the Representation of the People Act and the Indian Penal Code to read that anyone found guilty of a corrupt election practice could go 'to the President for determination ... whether such person should be disqualified and, if so, for what period'.[19]

Opposing the bill in Parliament, Mohan Dharia bravely called it 'a surrender of parliamentary democracy to the coming dictatorship'.[20] Mrs Gandhi's Orwellian electoral coup was complete. It was 'a very personalized amendment ... to protect one person's interests', wrote constitutional authority S. P. Sathe.[21]

These two amendments were mild when compared with the Fortyfirst Amendment Bill. Introduced in the Rajya Sabha by Law Minister Gokhale on 9 August 1975, this time two days before the Election case hearings were to begin, it amended Article 361 to say that no criminal proceedings 'whatsoever' could lie in court against a person who is or who had been the President, Prime Minister, or governor for acts 'done by him, whether before he entered upon his office or during his term

[18] Nayar, *The Judgement*, p. 80.

[19] The law also was directed at two specific issues in the Indira Gandhi Election case. It provided that a government official (read Yashpal Kapoor), if assisting a candidate while on official duty, 'shall not be deemed' to have assisted the candidate, and it changed the legally effective date for an official's resignation from government service (again Kapoor).

[20] *Lok Sabha Debates*, Fifth Series, vol. 54, no. 12, col. 10. Dharia later walked out of the Lok Sabha to protest the Thirty-ninth Amendment because it changed the Constitution to favour a 'particular person'—many opposition members joined him. 'I will not be coming again', he said. Passing 336 to 0, the amendment also placed some thirty-five property laws in the Ninth Schedule, along with MISA, 1971, and COFEPOSA. Law Minister Gokhale presented it as, in the main, a socialist measure. Presaging developments to come, Gokhale also told the House that the time had come to take 'a fresh look at the whole fundamental structure of the Constitution itself'. Ibid., col. 59.

Another amendment, the Fortieth, placed in the Ninth Schedule—directly relevant to the Emergency's denial of fundamental rights—the Prevention of Publication of Objectionable Matter Act, 1976, four other non-property laws, and fifty-eight property laws. The bill was introduced on 21 May 1976 and received the President's assent a week later.

[21] Sathe, S. P., *Constitutional Amendments, 1950–1988*, N. M. Tripathi Pvt. Ltd., Bombay 1989, p. 28.

of office'. No civil proceeding against persons holding these offices, the bil' continued, 'shall be instituted or continued during his term of office in any court in respect of any act done or purporting to be done by him in his personal capacity' before or after he entered office.[22] The Rajya Sabha passed the bill (which will be revisited below) the day it was introduced. It was placed on the table in the Lok Sabha in January 1976, where it lapsed upon the dissolution of the Lok Sabha in early 1977.

Momentum toward protective measures of some sort had begun within hours of the 12 June Allahabad judgement. Congress Forum for Socialist Action members like K. P. Unnikrishnan, Raghunatha Reddy, and Chandrajit Yadav, joined by Shashi Bhushan and the Minister of State for Industry, B. P. Maurya, met at D. K. Borooah's house to discuss strategy.[23] When the group met Mrs Gandhi, she said little and advised the men to discuss the issues with Borooah and her other advisors.[24] Meeting separately were S. S. Ray, Rajni Patel, Gokhale, and Y. B. Chavan, who said, 'What happens to Indira today happens to India tomorrow.'[25] The idea of enacting one or more laws directly aimed at nullifying the challenge to Mrs Gandhi's election seems to have been rejected, perhaps on S. S. Ray's urging, in favour of one big measure such as imposing an internal emergency and amending the Constitution. Young Turks like Chandra Shekar, Krishan Kant, and Ram Dhan, were said to be holding their own meetings, anxious that events might take an authoritarian and anti-constitutional turn. After the Emergency was proclaimed, Mrs Gandhi and many around her feared she might be attacked for imposing the Emergency and for jailing large numbers of persons. Rumours circulated that suits for wrongful arrest might be brought against her in high courts.[26]

---

[22] *Constitutional Amendment in India*, Lok Sabha Secretariat, pp. 173–4, 392–3. Article 361 already to a degree protected the President and governors against civil and criminal proceedings while they were in office.

[23] Unnikrishnan interview with the author. The composition and activities of this group was confirmed by a senior Law Ministry official. Maurya was remembered as having been noisily concerned that Mrs Gandhi might 'be dragged through the courts'. In an interview, Maurya was unwilling 'to discuss the activities of friends'.

[24] Ibid.

[25] Ibid. This meeting was on 14 June.

[26] P. N. Dhar and I used to discuss these rumours and discount them, V. Ramachandran, Dhar's immediate subordinate, told the author. The executive of the Congress Parliamentary Party believed that Indira needed protection, recalled V. N. Gadgil in an interview with the author. Others in interviews recalling such fears included Jagmohan, S. L. Shakdher, N. K. Seshan, and I. K. Gujral.

When Law Minister Gokhale brought drafts of the Thirty-eight and Thirty-ninth Amendments to the cabinet (Borooah, Ray, and Patel, not being members of the central government, were not present), there was little opposition to them. They had been designed and partially drafted by S. S. Ray, D. K. Borooah, and Gokhale at Mrs Gandhi's house, bypassing her secretariat, and secretly at the Law Ministry by Gokhale and the ministry's two Secretaries, P. G. Gokhale and K. K. Sundaram. The Prime Minister had already given her imprimatur to them because she 'was panicky about the Supreme Court's judgement'.[27] Cabinet members C. Subramaniam, Y. B. Chavan, Jagjivan Ram, and Swaran Singh were thought especially to have disliked the Thirty-ninth Amendment as 'going too far', not in the Congress tradition, and possibly leading to an autocratic prime minister in the future.[28] Sardar Swaran Singh's muted discontent with the amending bill is thought to have contributed to his later dismissal from the cabinet. Subramaniam, according to a cabinet minister, upon returning to New Delhi and learning of a draft of the Thirty-ninth Amendment, sought out Gokhale to protest it as unwise and possibly unconstitutional. When Gokhale responded that S. S. Ray wanted it, Subramaniam suggested they go to the Prime Minister. After hearing out Subramaniam, Mrs Gandhi is said to have closed the matter by repeating that S. S. Ray thought it was a good idea. Ray was 'the moving force' behind the Thirty-ninth Amendment, according to a senior cabinet minister at the time.[29]

The originators of the two amendments also produced the Forty-first Amendment bill, according to most knowledgeable persons. D. K. Borooah 'got it done', said Vasant Sathe.[30] A 'radical group' including V. C. Shukla, Om Mehta, Shashi Bhushan, Mohammed Yunus (a Gandhi-family friend), and others produced the idea, but Ray, Patel, and Borooah were 'always there', according to I. K. Gujral.[31] Others trace the bill's origin to Sanjay Gandhi and his mother. The offices of President, Vice-President, and Speaker were 'tacked on' to an early draft to indicate Mrs Gandhi was not being singled out for

---

[27] P. N. Haksar interview with the author. Although Haksar had been rusticated to the Planning Commission, he had a standing invitation to attend cabinet meetings.

[28] Sheila Dikshit interview with the author.

[29] The minister to S. Guhan. Guhan in an interview with the author.

In interviews with the author, Ray and Borooah declined to discuss the history of these measures, although the latter said that Ray 'may have been behind' the Thirty-ninth Amendment. 'He has a long view of his attainments,' Borooah said.

[30] Vasant Sathe interview with the author.

[31] I. K. Gujral interview with the author. Several others among those politically active at the time agreed.

attention.[32] The cabinet discussed the bill at meetings at which the Prime Minister apparently did not preside. 'Many in the cabinet did not oppose the bill, but many did not approve of it, either,' remembered Chandrajit Yadav.[33] Despite its nearly-automatic passage in the Rajya Sabha, the bill engendered 'vehement opposition' among members of the Lok Sabha, where, it was not formally debated.[34] The objections seem to have been utilitarian rather than constitutional or moral: international reaction to the bill's enactment would be damaging to the government and party and popular resentment would discredit the Emergency. The argument most persuasive to the Prime Minister, and attributable to Subramaniam and several others, seems to have been that the public might think Mrs Gandhi had skeletons in her cupboard and the bill was needed to shield her from them. Mrs Gandhi, and it could have been only she, decided the bill should die in the Lok Sabha. 'When Indira was convinced that the party was strongly against something, she could be very sensitive.'[35]

The Supreme Court opened its hearings on the Election case on 11 August only to adjourn them to allow Raj Narain to prepare his challenge to the Thirty-ninth Amendment. N. A. Palkhivala had left the case upon learning the Emergency had been declared, to be replaced by one-time Law Minister in Nehru's cabinet, Asoke Se.1.[36] When hearings resumed on 25 August, Narain's attorney, Shanti Bhushan, attacked the retrospective character both of the amendment and Election Laws Amendment Act as violating the basic structure doctrine. Sen argued for Mrs Gandhi that there was no case to try, given the revised election laws.

The five to four majority decision handed down by the judges in their separate opinions on 7 November validated Mrs Gandhi's 1971 election to Parliament, but it struck down part of the Thirty-ninth Amendment. The court accepted the concept that laws could be changed with retrospective effect to make legal actions that previously had been offences under law. Thus, it upheld the Prime Minister's election because she had violated no law. At least three of the judges must have swallowed hard to

[32] V. N. Gadgil interview with the author.

[33] Chandrajit Yadav, at the time Minister of Steel and Mines, in an interview with the author.

[34] S. L. Shakdher interview with the author.

[35] Margaret Alva interview with the author.

[36] Palkhivala had telephoned Mrs Gandhi from Bombay on 26 June. When he failed to reach her, he spoke with Gokhale and told him that he could not represent Mrs Gandhi because the Emergency was not justifiable. N. A. Palkhivala interview with the author. Solicitor General Fali Nariman resigned his office the following day.

do this. Justice Mathew said to Shanti Bhushan during the hearings, 'There is no doubt of the unfairness of retrospective laws about corrupt practices, but can you cite some legal authority to impugn their validity ...?'[37] Justice Khanna also said during the hearings that 'all retroactive legislation is repressive'.[38] 'We disliked retrospective effect,' recalled Justice Chandrachud. 'It is an absurd, loathsome, and dangerous precedent in constitutional law.'[39] Law Commission Chairman Gajendragadkar, adhering to his long-held view, took a contrary position. I hope the Court 'will hear the constitutional point', he wrote to Mrs Gandhi, 'and I have no doubt that it will uphold Parliament's absolute power to amend any and every article of the Constitution.'[40]

Striking down the Thirty-ninth Amendment's Clause 4, which inserted new Article 329A, with its special protection for the election of the Prime Minister and the Speaker, the five justices gave different reasons. The Chief Justice Ray held that validating the Prime Minister's election through Article 329A was not by applying law and therefore offended the rule of law. Khanna said the article violated the principle of free and fair elections, which, being essential in a democracy, were part of the basic structure. Mathew rejected the article saying that an essential feature of democracy is the resolution of election disputes by judicial power using law and the facts. Chandrachud said the article was destructive of equality and of the rule of law because it applied a different election law to the Prime Minister than to others.[41] Justice Beg dissented from the others by upholding the amendment in its entirety. The basic structure doctrine had passed its first post- Kesavananda test. Excepting Beg, the four judges had upheld it, although A. N. Ray did this by holding that it was not necessary to challenge the Kesavananda decision.

Raj Narain was a good fellow and a staunch Socialist to his party comrades. To his critics, he was weak, crude, loud-mouthed, and irascible. By bringing petty, even if legitimate, charges arising from the pent up frustration of an incompetent opposition, after an election he had

---

[37] Bhushan, *The Case That Shook India*, p. 193. The five-judge bench comprised Chief Justice A. N. Ray, and Justices H. R. Khanna, K. K. Mathew, Y. V. Chandrachud, and M. H. Beg.

[38] Baxi, *Supreme Court and Politics*, p. 70.

[39] Chandrachud interview with the author. He, along with many others, thought the charges against Mrs Gandhi petty and difficult to uphold.

[40] Letter dated 13 August 1975. Gajendragadkar Papers, NMML.

[41] 1975 *Supp* SCC 1ff. For reporting and analysis of the judgement, see press reports; Nayar, *The Judgement*, p. 93; Bhushan, *The Case That Shook India*, pp. 220–39; Baxi, *The Indian Supreme Court*, pp. 56–70.

genuinely lost, he sought to bring down a Prime Minister only to make her position impregnable.

Completing the Circle

Protected constitutionally by the outer ring of amendments, so her supporters expected, the Prime Minister was also to be encircled by the inner ring of her son Sanjay and his henchmen—who were referred to as the 'coterie' or 'caucus' and as the 'extra-constitutional authority'—often acting in her stead.[42] His advocacy of the Emergency and his role in preparing arrest lists before it has been described.

Although Mrs Gandhi never relinquished control over the executive branch and Parliament, 'she allowed Sanjay to have a team of his own, and this developed into a real caucus,' recalled Nikhil Chakravarty.[43] 'What Sanjay tells me to do, I do', said Minister of State for Home Affairs Om Mehta, aptly describing dynamics within the coterie.[44] Mrs Gandhi did not have a high opinion of Sanjay's 'intellectual capacity', said a member of her staff at the time, 'but she knew his ability to get things done'. 'No extra-constitutional centre of authority is possible without the encouragement and support of the Prime Minister,' said Jagjivan Ram, Minister of Agriculture during the Emergency. 'For all acts of omission and commission by Sanjay Gandhi, the Prime Minister, Mrs Gandhi, is to be blamed.'[45] A member of the Prime Minister's household could tell the insiders because they entered the Prime Minister's house by the side door and not by the main entrance.

The coterie's activities and Sanjay Gandhi's increasingly dictatorial authority cannot now be demonstrated from documentary sources. First-hand evidence, however, is available in personal experiences. Om Mehta has made clear Sanjay Gandhi's control over the Home Ministry. His control over the Health Ministry is clear from the 'family planning' programme of forced sterilizations—which more than anything else

---

[42] Among the henchmen were '"hoodlums and gangsters"' who had '"infiltrated"' the Youth Congress while Sanjay Gandhi was its president and he used them as his private brown shirts. See Ambika Soni, Youth Congress president in November 1975, in *Hindustan Times*, 7 May 1977.

[43] Nikhil Chakravarty interview with the author.

[44] Om Mehta in an interview with the author. Several persons, including D. K. Borooah, told the author that Mehta, although Sanjay Gandhi's toady and tool, was not a hard-hearted person and quietly helped several persons under detention.

[45] Singh, Satindra, syndicated columnist, 'Interview with Babu Jagjivan Ram', mimeograph, no date (but spring 1977). Satindra Singh Papers, National Institute of Panjab Studies, New Delhi.

during the Emergency blackened the government's name.[46] He dictated nearly everything in the Prime Minister's house, recalled one of her personal staff. He had de facto authority and access to all government files, without responsibility, said T. A. Pai.[47] He sacked I. K. Gujral as Minister of Information and Broadcasting after a 'tiff', reported the *Hindustan Times* and a police officer on duty with the Prime Minister witnessed the incident.[48]

Sanjay Gandhi's influence over his mother 'never ceased to be a subject of avid discussion in India ...'.[49] It extended to advocating actions and policies with which the Prime Minister cannot have been in sympathy. Examples of the former include the brutalities of forced sterilization and destroying slums—which in Old Delhi produced police firing and killing. He also took political initiatives such as the interview he gave to a magazine in which he castigated Mrs Gandhi's ally, the Communist Party of India, and denounced the public sector as inefficient while calling for the privatization of industry.[50] Sanjay Gandhi was the keynote speaker at the Youth Congress Conference that preceded the Guwahati Congress Party plenary in November 1976 and that nearly outshone the plenary. By now, the Prime Minister's sychophants were proclaiming 'that Sanjay was the true and legitimate successor of "Madam", as Indira was now called by one and all'.[51]

Among the Prime Minister's supporters there was concern that her son's power and behaviour could damage her, personally, and, was turning the Emergency into the personal, idiosyncratic dictatorship of

[46] The Health Minister of that time, Karan Singh, does not like to speak about this. But Sanjay Gandhi's control over the ministry was asserted to the author by Jagmohan, who, as an official of the Delhi government, worked closely with Sanjay Gandhi on issues of municipal development.

[47] *Hindustan Times*, 6 May 1977.

[48] *Hindustan Times*, 7 December 1977, and the police officer in an interview with the author.

Uma Vasudev devotes ch. 3, 'Sanjay's Action Brigade', of her *Two Faces of Indira Gandhi*, to reports of his influence and activities.

[49] Malhotra, *Indira Gandhi*, p. 180.

[50] For an account of this incident, see ibid., p. 194, and Vasudev, *Two Faces*, pp. 108ff and 193ff, where the entire text of the interview is reproduced.

B. K. Nehru learned on his visits to Delhi from London of excesses inspired by Sanjay Gandhi and how 'the rule of law was being replaced by the rule of Sanjay Gandhi'. Nehru discussed this with Sanjay Gandhi's elder brother, Rajiv, who told him that his mother 'had abdicated in favour of her son'. Nehru, B. K., *Nice Guys Finish Second*, Penguin Books, 1977, pp. 560, 564.

[51] Malhotra, *Indira Gandhi*, p. 185. For reportage of the doings at Guwahati, see *Times of India*, 20–5 November 1976.

this young man. K. P. Unnikrishnan remembers discussing the problem with S. S. Ray and Rajni Patel in the latter's suite in the Ashoka Hotel. 'We should strengthen the PM politically,' they agreed. But Sanjay was suspicious, Unnikrishnan added; 'he probably suspected a power grab and he pushed us out.'[52] It was a hopeless project from the start. Mrs Gandhi's faith in her son was unswerving. And the ascendant Sanjay thought Ray and Unnikrishnan were 'left', and he despised Patel as a Communist.

Indira Gandhi had used the processes of the Constitution, and the hunger of her courtiers, to seize power and to protect herself against the law. Within the concentric circles, she ruled alone, and could turn her attention to altering the Constitution further to suit her desires and to subverting the authority of the centre of power she did not control, the judiciary.

---

[52] K. P. Unnikrishnan interview with the author

Chapter 15

THE JUDICIARY UNDER PRESSURE

Prime Minister Gandhi's view of the judiciary was by now not in doubt, having become clear in the Bank Nationalization and Princes cases, during the Kesavananda hearings, in the supersession of judges, and, most immediately, in the events described in the preceding chapter. From the onset of the Emergency, according to Upendra Baxi, there was 'a diffuse and subtle ... feeling pressing upon the Court ... that its actions were being watched by the regime and there were hints that judicial power might be curbed in the days to come.'[1] An attempt to curb the Court soon came. Mrs Gandhi's government acted to curtail its power of judicial review by overturning the basic structure doctrine laid down in Kesavananda and upheld by four of the five judges ruling in her Election case. Later, she would transfer a dozen and a half high court judges to punish them for ruling against the government in preventive detention cases. This occurred in the context of the famous Habeas Corpus case which will be taken up later in this chapter. Meanwhile, as will be seen, Mrs Gandhi's associates floated their personal schemes for 'reforming' the judiciary.

Basic Structure Revisited: The Kesavananda Review Bench

Three days after the Supreme Court reaffirmed the basic structure doctrine in the Election case, Chief Justice A. N. Ray convened a thirteen-judge bench to overturn the doctrine. Although the reaffirmation no doubt added to the government's resolve to rid itself of the concept, the train of events had begun months earlier. The review bench would prove to be the government's most bootless attempt to curb judicial review and to increase the government's authority to work its will unhindered by democratic institutions.

The train of events had begun in August 1975 soon after passage of the Thirty-eighth and Thirty-ninth Amendments.[2] On 11 August, when

[1] Baxi, *The Supreme Court and Politics*, p. 34.

[2] This reconstruction of events is based upon press reports (flimsy due to censorship), interviews, and the following books: Reddy, *We have a Republic*, pp. 102–5; Baxi, *The Indian*

pleading the Election case, Attorney General Niren De said he would like a review of the Kesavananda decision because it was unclear. H. R. Gokhale in Parliament spoke of the need for a new constitutional framework. Mrs Gandhi had said and would say again, 'we do not accept the dogma of the basic structure'.[3] In a magazine interview at this time she spoke of reforming the judicial system. The first concrete move came on 1 September when De and the Tamil Nadu Advocate General made an application to the Supreme Court that it hear a number of writ petitions on 10 November. Petitions charging that laws applying in land ceiling cases violated the basic structure, were languishing in high courts, it was claimed.[4] On 20 October, the Chief Justice issued a written order that on 10 November the Court would hear arguments on two points: whether or not the basic structure doctrine restricted Parliament's power to amend the Constitution, and whether or not the Bank Nationalization case had been correctly decided. The Court ordered parties to submit arguments on these points only, and it directed the Attorney General and the state advocates general to attend the hearing.[5]

It has never been established, definitively, from whence initiative for the review came. Speculation has ranged from the bar to the Chief Justice to the government. A segment of the Supreme Court bar at this time ardently supported the Prime Minister's policies toward the judiciary. Likely, some of them urged their views on the government and the Chief Justice. Chief Justice Ray, claimed De, sought the review. Yet Ray, himself, may have been under 'some kind of direct pressure from the regime' to instigate the review, speculated Upendra Baxi. It did not make any sense unless 'he was responding to the government's request to do something about Kesavananda'.[6] Ray probably was a willing participant if not an equal partner in the move. He had sided with the government in Kesavananda, and the Bank Nationalization and Privy Purses cases. He 'had never reconciled himself to Kesavananda, scorning it in court. He may have elicited the initiative from the bar,' thought

---

Supreme Court, pp. 42–5, 70–6; Bhushan, *The Case That Shook India*, pp. 256–67; Dhavan, *The Supreme Court of India*, pp. 419–21; Seervai, *Constitutional Law of India*, vol. 2, pp. 1627–8; and Nayar, *The Judgement*, p. 93.

[3] Speech in Parliament, 27 October 1976. *Indira Gandhi: Selected Speeches and Writings*, vol. 3, p. 288.

[4] Reddy, *We Have a Republic*, p. 104.

[5] *The Hindu*, 1 November 1975. On the bench would be Chief Justice A. N. Ray and Justices H. R. Khanna, K. K. Mathew, M. H. Beg, Y. V. Chandrachud, P. N. Bhagwati, V. R. Krishna Iyer, P. K. Goswami, R. S. Sarkaria, A. C. Gupta, N. L. Untwalia, M. Fazl Ali, and P. M. Shingal.

[6] Baxi, *Supreme Court and Politics*, p. 42–3.

bench member Justice Chandrachud.[7] Ray, during the previous few months, was said to have been looking for individuals who believed Kesavananda should be overturned to fill the two vacancies on the court.[8] Whatever the case's origin, the government thought that with the Emergency in full swing 'it might not be difficult for the government to have a favourable decision'.[9] If the government had needed additional incentive to overturn Kesavananda, the Court's striking down part of the Thirty-ninth Amendment in addition to upholding the basic structure doctrine in Mrs Gandhi's Election case would have provided it. The Court's independence must be curbed.

Opening the hearings on 10 November Attorney General De argued that the concept of the basic structure of the Constitution being unamendable had created great difficulty and confusion. Laws were being questioned, and 'every constitutional amendment is being challenged in the high courts ... Everybody was giving a different interpretation to the decision ... [I]t is essential that the court clears up the issues'.[10] His government wanted to undertake large-scale measures of social-economic uplift, he said, but Parliament did not know what to do. Judge Khanna took the opportunity to expose 'this utter fallacy'. He told De that, in the Kesavananda ruling, he had expressly said that the right to property was not included within the basic structure of the Constitution.[11] He then asked, 'Has this theory of basic structure impeded or come in the way of legislating any socio-economic measure?' De answered in the negative and then confusingly: 'No, that is not the only question. You don't require the power for amending non-essential parts of the Constitution'.[12]

The following day N. A. Palkhivala, arguing petitions by a coal mining company that had been nationalized and an individual preventively detained, rose in a tense and expectant hush to give what some hearers

---

[7] Chandrachud in an interview with the author. Ray was not moved by motives of personal gain, thought Chandrachud; he was too innocent. Nor was he driven by ideology or socialist philosophy, thought Chandrachud.

[8] From a senior advocate who claimed to have been approached by Ray.

[9] A remark by another member of the review bench to Justice Khanna. Khanna, *Neither Roses Nor Thorns*, p. 73.

[10] Bhushan, *The Case That Shook India*, p. 265.

[11] Khanna, *Neither Roses Nor Thorns*, pp. 73–6; Bhushan, *The Case That Shook India*, p. 265. Apparently no verbatim transcript of the hearings was kept. Bhushan's account includes what appear to be verbatim passages of the arguments.

Khanna indeed had said this in Kesavananda, but the Court had not spoken to the point.

[12] Khanna, *Neither Roses Nor Thorns*, pp. 73–4. Khanna here cites as the source for his own words Seervai, *Constitutional Law*, vol. 2, p. 2657.

believe to have been the most eloquent speech delivered in the Chief Justice's courtroom. He argued, in essence, that the Court could not undertake a review of Kesavananda and that even if it could, it should not. He began with Khanna's point about the 'right to property not being a part of the basic structure', and added that Kesavananda 'ensures that tyranny and despotism shall not masquerade as constitutionalism. It is an astounding request from the government that such a judgement should be overruled.' The necessary criterion for reviewing Kesavananda, Palkhivala said, was that the decision was in '"manifest error"' and had had a '"baneful effect on the public"', neither of which was true. If any of Kesavananda were to be reconsidered, the whole of the decision should be reviewed. This could not be done fairly when even the reporting of the hearing was subject to the censor's approval.[13] (Several newspapers did report the hearing, including Palkhivala's arguments.) Palkhivala also cited the Forty-first Amendment Bill as an example of the danger inherent in overturning the basic structure doctrine. When we argued the Kesavananda case, he said, we were told that the misuse of power was hypothetical. 'Today the misuse of power is no longer a hypothetical possibility ... If this bill became law, a person can commit the most heinous crimes' and if he can get himself made governor of a state he can 'get away scot free'.[14] Palkhivala was so disturbed by the hearing that the day before it opened he wrote to the Prime Minister 'beseeching' her not to review Kesavananda. Among the points he made was that the country's free democracy would not survive overturning the basic structure doctrine.[15]

At this time, the hearings began to come down around the Chief Justice's ears. When Palkhivala argued that a review of Kesavananda could not be entertained as an 'oral request from the government', Ray responded that

[13] Points taken from 'Propositions submitted by Mr N. A. Palkhivala in support of the plea that if the first preliminary point is rejected, the Supreme Court should not exercise its discretion in favour of reconsidering Kesavananda's Case', dated 11 November 1975. Jayaprakash Narayan Papers, Third Installment, Subject File 320, NMML.

[14] Bhushan, *The Case That Shook India*, p. 260.

[15] Palkhivala's letter was dated 9 November. 'My dear Indiraji,' he had begun, 'I am most distressed' by the government's attempt to get Kesavananda overruled. He then asked her to consider nine points, among which were: the government already had 'optimum latitude' for economic legislation because the Supreme Court had upheld Article 31C; probably 'a free democracy and the unity and integrity of the country will vanish within a few years if the basic structure were overturned, and who, after you, will be able to hold the country together?'; the basic structure 'is the real safeguard of the minorities'; and 'it would look strange' if the court should overrule its election judgement in your favour. Palkhivala-Indira Gandhi letter, copy in the author's possession kindness of Mr Palkhivala.

the request for the review came 'from these petitioners. Even the Tamil Nadu government had asked for a review'. Here the Tamil Nadu Advocate General, Govind Swaminathan, 'jumped up' to say, 'We never even once asked for a review.' Ray answered, 'Well, you were all asking for some constitutional amendment to be struck down on the basic features'.[16] The Kashmir Law Minister, D. D. Thakur, on Sheikh Abdullah's direct instructions, also opposed reconsidering the Kesavananda decision, as did the Gujarat Advocate General.[17] These developments had a telling effect within the bench, according to lawyers and justices involved. For a start, the justification for the hearings appeared non-existent. 'We all asked, even Mathew, who disliked the basic structure, why are we here, where is the review petition?' De's arguments for the government seemed weak and Palkhivala's eloquent. The judges were making disparaging remarks about the hearings to each other. These dissatisfactions reached Ray, probably, although perhaps not exclusively, through Justice Mathew.[18] And the judges may have believed that if the hearings succeeded in overturning Kesavananda, 'strange things might happen to the Court and the Constitution'.[19]

When the judges assembled in the Chief Justice's chambers on the morning of 12 November before entering the courtroom to resume the hearings, Ray informed them that he had decided to dissolve the bench. Amid sighs of relief and agreement, the judges filed into the courtroom to hear Ray publicly announce his decision. The Court had protected, or at least not relinquished, its institutional power. Stung by her defeat, Mrs Gandhi threatened retaliation. Three days after the dissolution, one of her long-time supporters, Uma Shankar Dikshit, Minister of Transport, told a meeting of Congress workers in Kanpur that if the Supreme Court debarred the government from making

---

[16] Bhushan, *The Case That Shook India*, p. 258. 'Jumped up': Justice Khanna interview with the author. Swaminathan later participated in a public meeting opposing what would become the Forty-second Amendment.

[17] Khanna, *Neither Roses Nor Thorns*, p. 74. In his letter to Mrs Gandhi just cited, Palkhivala had warned that these three governments were going 'to oppose the attempt to arm Parliament with absolute power'. All three state governments were then in hands unfriendly to the Prime Minister.

Khanna, Jaganmohan Reddy, and several other judges believed that the review bench had been established wrongly. No smaller constitution bench had requested review by a larger bench.

[18] This account is based on sources already cited and interviews with Justices Khanna, Krishna Iyer, and Chandrachud of the review bench and senior advocates associated with the case, Fali Nariman, Anil Divan, and N. A. Palkhivala.

[19] Baxi, *Supreme Court and Politics*, p. 76.

changes in the Constitution, a new constituent assembly might have to be convened to rewrite the Constitution to guarantee 'social and economic justice'. The government, Dikshit said, was making every effort to run the country according to the Constitution, but if the Constitution became an obstacle to 'ensuring the basic needs of the people ... the government would not hesitate to make drastic changes' in it.[20]

An Anonymous Attack

A month after the Chief Justice's announcement and as the Court was about to hear appeals in the Habeas Corpus case, an anonymous paper appeared in Congress circles that proposed drastic changes for the high courts and the Supreme Court. Rumoured at the time to have been written by two Congressmen, and entitled 'A Fresh Look at Our Constitution—Some Suggestions', it advocated that all judges in the country should be appointed by the President in consultation with the councils of ministers of the central or of the state governments. A 'Superior Council of the Judiciary', chaired by the President with the Chief Justice of India and the Law Minister as vice-chairmen, should decide all 'administrative matters in the judicial field'. The council's members would include two judges from the Supreme Court and two from the high courts elected by secret ballot plus four persons elected by Parliament and four nominated by the President. In the circumstances of the Emergency, this would have given the executive branch control over the judiciary. This council should be 'the authority to interpret laws and the Constitution; as also to determine the validity of any legislation'.[21] In other words, the Supreme Court would no longer be supreme, and the executive and legislative branches, in conjunction under India's parliamentary system, would sit in judgement over themselves.[22] Within several months, as will be seen in the next chapter, this scheme and many of the other proposals in the document would be discarded, but several of its provisions reappeared in the Swaran Singh Committee's report. Attacks on the judiciary would continue.

[20] *Indian Express*, 16 November 1975.

[21] The author is indebted to Francine Frankel for a copy of 'A Fresh Look', which later was published by A. G. Noorani in *The Presidential System: The Indian Debate*, Sage Publications, New Delhi, 1989, pp. 105ff. Congressmen A. R. Antulay and Rajni Patel were associated with the document's drafting, as will be seen in a subsequent chapter.

[22] As N. A. Palkhivala put it, the courts would 'become mere appendages of the administration', only ' "mice squeaking under the Home Minister's chair" '. N. A. Palkhivala, 'Should We Alter Our Constitution' in *Illustrated Weekly*, 4 January 1976, p. 9.

The Habeas Corpus Case

The Habeas Corpus case captures the Emergency as nothing else: its authoritarian and geographical reach; its inefficiencies; its meanness and occasional magnanimity; its evocations of judicial philosophies and degrees of courage among judges and lawyers; its testing of officials' consciences and their willingness to submerge them in duty; its restraint compared with authoritarian regimes and periods of authoritarian rule in other countries. The Supreme Court opened hearing in the case on 15 December 1975 and handed down its decision in 28 April 1976.

The case originated with the many preventive detentions made around the country in the early hours of 26 June. That day, in the city of Bangalore, the Commissioner of Police ordered the arrest of A. B. Vajpayee, L. K. Advani, and Subramaniam Swamy of the Jana Sangh Party, S. N. Mishra of the Congress(O), and Socialist Party member Madhu Dandavate under the Maintenance of Internal Security Act. All were in the city on official business as members of a parliamentary delegation.[23] The police commissioner later said he had made the arrests 'after scrutinizing the material placed before me'. This seems not to have been true, for 'the grounds for detention' were collected from Delhi after the detentions by a special officer sent from Karnataka, and the commissioner made the arrests because the Chief Secretary of Delhi had telephoned the Chief Secretary of Karnataka and requested them, mentioning the Prime Minister's concurrence.[24] Additionally, detention orders under MISA were served on these members of Parliament only on the evening of 26 June, although they had been arrested in the morning.[25] In other words, a political 'sweep' was under way. The police in Bangalore made arrests only on New Delhi's orders, and with no 'application of mind' as required by law.

---

[23] Vajpayee had gone to Bangalore, according to the *Deccan Herald*, to press the opposition's claim that Mrs Gandhi should resign while appealing her election case and, should she not resign, the opposition would engage in *satyagraha* to remove the 'corrupt' Prime Minister. Issue of 25 June 1975.

This account of the case in Bangalore and elsewhere and in New Delhi is based upon material in Nayar, *The Judgement*, pp. 94ff; Seervai, *Constitutional Law*, vol. 2, and Seervai, H. M., *The Emergency, Future Safeguards and the Habeas Corpus Case*, N. M. Tripathi Pvt. Ltd., Bombay, 1978, ch. 2; Dhavan, *The Supreme Court of India*, pp. xv–xvii; Rama Jois, M., *Historic Legal Battle*, M. R. Vimala, Bangalore, 1977; (copy presented to the author by Mr Rama Jois); dispatches in the *Statesman*, January and February 1976; and interviews. In the latter, Santosh Hegde has been particularly helpful.

[24] *Shah Commission Report*, II, p. 33, and Shourie, Arun, *Symptoms of Fascism*, Vikas Publishing House Pvt. Ltd., New Delhi, 1978, p. 216.

[25] Rama Jois, *Historic Legal Battle*, p. 9.

The Karnataka bar and local attorneys reacted sharply. The bar passed a resolution calling for withdrawing the Emergency, for the release of those arrested, and for a boycott of the state's courts on 4 July. Bangalore lawyers N. Santosh Hegde and M. Rama Jois, joined by N. M. Ghatate from New Delhi, with the advice of K. S. Hegde, Santosh's father, drafted writ petitions for the detenus. These asked the Karnataka (Bangalore) High Court to quash the detentions on the ground that the continuance of the emergency of 1971—after the end of the India–Pakistan war and the Simla Pact in 1972—was unconstitutional as was the 25 June declaration of internal emergency. Advani subsequently added another ground for ruling the Emergency unconstitutional: the President had signed the proclamation before the cabinet had approved it and thus without the advice of his council of ministers.[26] The government would blunt this line of attack by having Parliament enact the Thirty-eighth Amendment, barring judicial review of proclamations of emergency and presidential ordinances. The High Court accepted the petitions on 11 July and posted the cases for a preliminary hearing on 14 July—so that parliamentarians might be free to attend Parliament's opening session on 21 July. After hearing the Karnataka government and the detenus, the High Court expressed the view *prima facie* that the detentions appeared to be invalid, admitted the petitions, and posted them for a hearing three days later. Appreciating the significance of this challenge to the Emergency, the Prime Minister sent Attorney General Niren De to defend the government.

Now, the Emergency unsheathed its claws and perpetrated what Rama Jois named 'The Great Betrayal'. Just before the hearing was to open on 17 July, the detenus were handed release orders only to be detained a few minutes later under an order dated the previous day. The authorities cited for this MISA as amended on 29 June which allowed for detention without disclosing the grounds to the detenu or the courts. The right to move the courts for protection of Fundamental Rights Articles 14, 21, and 22 already had been suspended on 27 June. In the hearing, De argued that the second detention order would necessitate fresh writ petitions. The court agreed and ordered the jail superintendent to facilitate conferences between the detenus and their lawyers for this purpose. But when Rama Jois visited the jail late that afternoon he found that Mishra, Advani, and Dandavate had been flown to Rohtak Jail in Haryana, not

---

[26] Ibid., p. 10. K. S. Hegde, it will be recalled, was one of the judges superseded in 1973. Rama Jois had been the senior Hegde's election agent when he ran for Parliament.

far from Delhi. Vajpayee was not moved because he was recuperating from an operation.

New Delhi may have thought it had resolved the matter, but the court and lawyers in Bangalore thought differently. Because the second detentions had been made in the city, and the fresh petitions for writs of habeas corpus submitted there, the High Court ordered the central government to return the detenus to Bangalore by 26 September for a hearing scheduled for 29 September. The central government acquiesced to the High Court's order, and the detenus were transported to Bangalore. By this time, the cases, despite censorship, had attracted great attention and a rising young advocate from Madras, K. K. Venugopal, and M. C. Chagla had joined Santosh Hegde and Rama Jois for the detenus. Chagla argued that the continuing 1971 emergency was a fraud on the Constitution; that Mrs Gandhi had misused constitutional powers and the state's machinery for perpetuating herself in office; and, consequently, that the orders the detenus were challenging should be set aside. Convinced, the High Court on 30 September rejected the Government of India's contention that the challenges to the Emergency and the habeas corpus petitions were not maintainable because of the Thirty-eighth Amendment and the President's 27 June order. Therefore, the court said, the proclamation of Emergency had legally been challenged.[27]

Months of legal wrangling over these cases followed while writs of habeas corpus were filling the dockets of other high courts. Many of these upheld habeas corpus petitions by rejecting the government's contention that the President's 27 June order had suspended this right. They ruled that the courts' jurisdiction included knowing the grounds for detention, and that the cases involved substantial questions of law that the Supreme Court should decide. One of these cases was *Shiv Kant Shukla v ADM (Additional District Magistrate) Jabalpur* in the Madhya Pradesh High Court. This High Court on 1 September 1975 ruled that 'Habeas Corpus as an instrument to protect against illegal imprisonment is written into the Constitution. Its use by the courts cannot, in our opinion, be constitutionally abridged by the executive or by Parliament except in the manner provided by Article 368 of the Constitution.'[28]

---

[27] This account is drawn from Rama Jois, *Historic Legal Battle*, pp. 34–9 and from interviews with him and with Santosh Hegde. The Chief Censor in New Delhi ordered the Karnataka government's Department of Information and Publicity to ensure that news of th hearings on he four writ petitions 'i. not published in any of the newspapers'. Text repro. uced in ibid., p. 35.

[28] *Jabalpur Law Journal*, 1975, vo 24, p. 794. On the bench were A. P. Sen and R. K. Tankha.

The Government of India appealed these rulings to the Supreme Court, where they were 'clubbed together' into one case thereafter referred to as 'Shiv Kant Shukla' or the 'Habeas Corpus case'.[29] Hearings began on 15 December.

To remind the reader, the orders and ordinances central to these habeas corpus cases, other than the Proclamation of Emergency, itself, were: the presidential order of 27 June 1975 suspending the right to move the courts for the protections of Article 14 (equality before and equal protection of the law), Article 21 (no deprivation of life or liberty except according to procedure established by law), and Article 22 (which provided for preventive detention and curbs against its abuses); the retrospective ordinances of 29 June and 15 July denying detenus information about the grounds for their detention and excluding the use of the concepts of 'natural justice' and 'natural or common law' in detention cases; and the ordinance of 15 October amending MISA to declare that the grounds for detention were matters of state and could be disclosed neither to detenus nor to the courts.

We may digress here briefly to consider related matters, for they illustrate the flexible and harsh aspects of the Emergency. The Bangalore High Court allowed L. K. Advani, even while under detention, to go to Ahmedabad to scrutinize the nomination papers of his opponent in a parliamentary by-election, which Advani won. The central government did not prevent this, and it acquiesced also in a court order that permitted student detenus to sit for their examinations, although it first appealed the order. M. Rama Jois was detained for thirteen months beginning December 1975, again apparently for his defence of the detenus, although his former connections with the Rashtriya Swayam Sevak Sangh were known. He became a judge of the Bangalore High Court in November 1977 and, later, chief justice of the Punjab and Haryana High Court.

Before Chief Justice Ray could hear the appeals from the ten high courts, he had to select a bench. Delhi's perennial crop of rumours had it that, having failed to overturn Kesavananda, he would select colleagues likely to hold for the government. Worried about the composition of the bench, members of the Supreme Court Bar Association, several of whom

[29] Swaroop, *Preventive Detention*, pp. 76–7.

'Up to 1976, it was held that an individual's right to move the Supreme Court survives even during such Emergency,' wrote constitutional authority Durga Das Basu, 'to enforce Fundamental Rights other than those included in the Orders under Article 359 or on *other* grounds (emphasis in original), e.g. *mala fides* or *ultra vires*'. Basu, Durga Das, *Shorter Constitution of India*, tenth edn., Prentice Hall of India Pvt. Ltd., New Delhi, 1988, p. 264.

would represent the detenus before the Court, took steps that became choice morsels of judicial lore. They arranged to have telegrams sent to the Chief Justice from around the country urging bench selection according to seniority. C. K. Daphtary, formerly Attorney General, called on Ray, told him of the rumours, and suggested he follow the seniority criterion. Annoyed by such temerity, Ray asked if there were precedent for this. As quick-witted as he was courageous, Daphtary replied that S. R. Das once had done so—knowing that Ray much admired the Chief Justice of the late fifties. Although this precedent is elusive, Ray did select the bench according to seniority: himself and Justices H. R. Khanna, M. H. Beg, Y. V. Chandrachud, and P. N. Bhagwati. Many advocates and others were relieved. Surely, they calculated, Justices Khanna, Bhagwati, and Chandrachud would protect civil liberty. Chief Justice Ray and Justice Beg were expected to side with the government.[30]

The hearings that began on 15 December 1975 lasted into February 1976 over thirty-seven working days. They were reported extensively, although not always fully, in the press, including even the arguments for the detenus. For the government, Attorney General De, Additional Solicitor General V. P. Raman, and the advocates general of Kerala and Maharashtra based their position on MISA, 1971, the 1975 amendments to it, and, when it became available on 8 January 1976, the President's order under Article 359(1) suspending the citizen's right to move the courts for the enforcement of the 'freedoms' in Article 19. Condensed, the government's position was that writs of habeas corpus under Article 226 were not maintainable in view of the MISA amendments; that in all countries in time of war personal liberty was restricted; and that during the Emergency the executive had overriding power and the rule of law was suspended. The detenus' arguments overlooked the Emergency and were only "'political and emotional'", the government's advocates said.[31] Asked by Justices Khanna and Chandrachud what an individual's redress might be if he or she were detained on false information or if a detention order were issued in bad faith or without application of mind, Raman responded that it could not be known if this were the case because the courts could not examine the grounds for detention. President Fakhruddin Ali Ahmed's 8 January order and the MISA amendments had totally shut out any judicial scrutiny of detention orders, said Raman.[32]

---

[30] Many senior advocates tell this story. The author heard it from Soli Sorabjee and Fali Nariman. Justice K. K. Mathew was senior to Khanna and Beg, but was not selected because he was due to retire in January 1976.

[31] *Times of India*, 20 February 1976.

[32] *Statesman*, 10 January 1976.

In his argument De contended that the rule of law existed only within the four corners of the Constitution; natural rights did not exist outside it.[33] Justice Khanna intervened at one point. 'I put it to De that Article 21 pertains not only to liberty but also to life. Supposing some policeman, for reasons of enmity, not of state, kills someone, would there be a remedy? De replied "consistent with my position, My Lord, not so long as the Emergency lasts". And he added, "it shocks my conscience, it may shock yours, but there is no remedy."'[34] De's vehemence 'really hurt the government's case', recalled Justice Chandrachud many years later. De's arguing 'by *reductio ad absurdum*' may have been purposeful, according to credible speculation by Justice Khanna and others: an attempt to lose the case because he abhorred the Emergency's harshness. If true, the action took courage, for during this time the Attorney General feared he and his foreign-born wife might be harassed if the government and the coterie became aware of his doubts about the Emergency and its constitutional amendments. His friends noticed his tension and heavy smoking.[35]

Senior advocates Shanti Bhushan, Soli Sorabjee, V. M. Tarkunde, Anil Divan, Ram Jethmalani, C. K. Daphtary, and others represented the individual detenus. Opening the detenus' defence, Bhushan told the five judges that the denials of liberty during the Emergency were '"appalling"', and that with the remedy of habeas corpus denied, the protection of life and liberty of citizens was '"dead"'.[36] Giving unlimited powers to the executive to take away life and liberty denied the judiciary its '"sentinel"' role, and thus violated one of the basic tenets of the Constitution. Responding to questions from Justices Khanna and Bhagwati, Bhushan asserted that with Article 21 suspended detentions were contrary not only to law but also to the Constitution. Life and liberty were common law rights that pre-existed British rule in India. Detentions could be questioned even if the courts were not to look into the grounds of them; the courts could not be prevented from examining the legality of an issue. Bhushan then asked, If a district magistrate through a telegram orders the detention of three hundred persons, could there have been any application of mind or satisfaction in making the detentions?

[33] *Statesman*, 19, 20, 24 February 1976.

[34] Justice Khanna's account of the interchange in an interview with the author.

[35] Shanti Bhushan and others in interviews with the author. In Parliament, when Prime Minister of the Janata government, in 1977, Morarji Desai referred to the De–Khanna exchange and to De's fears for his own and his family's life. *AR*, 27 August–2 September 1977, p. 13904.

[36] *Statesman*, 17 January 1976.

During his presentation, Soli Sorabjee took Bhushan's argument a step further, maintaining that the rule of law was a principle embedded in Indian soil and was part of the basic structure of the Constitution. The right to liberty also was independent of the Constitution. Sorabjee argued that the executive could not interfere with an individual's liberty unless it could support the legality of its argument in a court of law.[37] Tarkunde agreed, adding that the onus for proving the legality of a detention order shifted to the government once a habeas corpus petition was filed. This precedent had been established in Makhan Singh's case, contended Anil Divan, where the high court then involved and the Supreme Court both had ruled that a detenu could challenge his detention on the ground that it was illegal in terms of the Defence of India Act.[38] (The Habeas Corpus Bench would hold Makhan Singh not applicable in this case.) The arguments had reduced Indians to a state of '"almost total rightlessness"', making them '"slaves"', said Divan. The hearings concluded on 25 February and the bench reserved judgement.[39]

When the bench gave its decision on 28 April the detenus' lawyers found their calculations had gone awry. Two of the judges they hoped would find for the detenus, Justices Chandrachud and Bhagwati, did not. They, Beg, and Chief Justice Ray upheld the Government of India's position. Only Khanna dissented. Each judge wrote his own opinion. Although there was no single majority ruling, the four-judge majority held that no citizen had standing to move a writ of habeas corpus before a high court under Article 226 in light of the President's order of 27 June 1975 or to challenge a detention order as illegal, as factually or legally *mala fide*, or as based on extraneous considerations. Section 16A(9) of MISA (grounds for detention a matter of state and not to be revealed) was ruled constitutionally valid. And the four judges held that Article 21 was the sole repository of rights to life and personal liberty against the state.[40] In his opinion Justice Beg made one of the most quoted remarks, and certainly the most fatuous one, of the case. '[W]e understand', he wrote, 'that the care and concern bestowed by the state authorities upon

37 *Statesman,* 4 and 5 February 1976 and *Times of India,* 5 February 1976.

38 *Makhan Singh v Punjab* 1964 (4) SCR 797ff. See ch. 2.

39 A recitation of the detenus' arguments appears in G. C. Sachdeva (ed.), *The Unreported Judgements (Supreme Court),* vol. 8, published by G. C. Sachdeva, Jodhpur, 1976.

None of the detenus challenged the constitutionality of the proclamation of Emergency nor of placing MISA in the Ninth Schedule.

40 The decision as summarized in *SCR* (1976), Supplement, pp. 172ff. See also 1976 (2) SCC 521ff. In the Supreme Court, the case was listed as *A. D. M. Jabalpur v Shiv Kant Shukla.*

the welfare of detenus who are well-housed, well-fed, and well-treated, is almost maternal. Even parents have to take appropriate preventive action against those children who may threaten to burn down the house they live in.'[41]

Justice Khanna's dissent, delivered in what he felt was a chilly atmosphere, began, 'Law of preventive detention, of detention without trial is an anathema to all those who love personal liberty.'[42] After invoking support from authorities ranging from the *Magna Carta* through the legal philosopher Sir Edward Coke to the United States Constitution to precedent in his own Supreme Court, beginning with Gopalan's Case, Justice Khanna summarized his conclusions: Article 21 cannot be considered to be the sole repository of the right to life and personal liberty; rights created by statutes being not fundamental rights can be enforced during the period of Emergency despite the presidential order; Article 226 of the Constitution (empowering high courts to issue writs) is an integral part of the Constitution, and this power cannot be bypassed by the presidential order in question; and there is no antithesis between the power to detain a person under preventive detention and the power of the court to examine the legality of detentions. Justice Khanna then added that unanimity in court rulings was desirable, but not for the sake of formality at the expense of strong conflicting views.[43]

Except among those supporting the Emergency, the court's decision evoked sharp criticism. Jayaprakash Narayan—who, ill, had been released from detention on 12 November 1975—spoke for many when he said the decision 'has put out the last flickering candle of individual freedom. Mrs Gandhi's dictatorship both in its personalized and institutionalized forms is now almost complete.'[44] Distaste, or more, for the judgement came in reactions to Justice Khanna's dissent. Nehru's Attorney General and Indira Gandhi's lawyer before the Supreme Court in her Election case, Asoke Sen, called on Khanna to congratulate him.

[41] *SCR*, Supplement, p. 371.

[42] Ibid., p. 246. According to Seervai, *The Emergency, Future Safeguards*, p. viii, the censor banned Khanna's dissent from publication in newspapers.

[43] This account is drawn from *SCR*, Supplement, pp. 302–4.

[44] Statement issued 15 May 1976. Narayan Papers, Third Installment, Subject File 323, NMML.

S. P. Sathe, referring to the decision, later would write, 'Many crimes committed during the Emergency seemed to be [a] natural consequence of total self-negation by the judiciary'. Sathe, *Constitutional Amendments*, p. 61. Being somewhat more colourful, H. M. Seervai said the high courts rose to the occasion, but the 'Supreme Court sank'. Seervai, *Constitutional Law*, vol. 2, p. 2177.

Niren De took Khanna aside at a tea party ar. d said '"May I offer my congratulations for your great judgement"'—thus revealing the effect of his personal fears and devotion to duty on his constitutional sensibilities.[45] Justice Chandrachud may have hinted in his opinion that his own '"predisposition"' was not in the direction he ruled. No matter this, he later regretted his ruling in a public speech. Although we believed we were following the law, he said, '"I regret that I did not have the courage to lay down my office and tell the people, Well, this is the law."'[46] Even Justice Beg may have had second thoughts, for in a later case he said the Habeas Corpus ruling was '"perhaps misleading as it gave the impression that no petition at all would lie under either Article 32 or 226 to assert the right of personal liberty because the *locus standi* of the citizen were suspended."'[47]

Why had the four justices found as they did? Their reasons and motives seem to have been both collective and individual, substantive and self-protective. No doubt there were mixtures. They ruled as they did principally because they believed they were reading the law aright. A narrow interpretation of the law as available for protection of fundamental rights—after the declaration of the Emergency and subsequent ordinances and enactments—supports the court's decision. Fears of chaos and disintegration in the country should not be discounted as impelling the judges toward their opinions. Great disagreements arise over great issues.

But few observers then understood the court's behaviour—or have since—as based on legal reasoning. The common view has been that the four judges either were protecting the institution from an ill-intentioned government or protecting their personal futures or both. Since 26 June, Parliament and the Prime Minister had given the judges ample cause to be both suspicious and anxious. More immediately, during the court's hearings and deliberations, the 'A Fresh Look' paper, with its suggestion for a 'Superior Council of the Judiciary', was aimed at the court's jugular vein. On 30 January 1976, K. P. Unnikrishnan had moved a resolution in

[45] Sen's and De's reactions from Khanna in an interview with the author.

[46] Speech to Federation of Indian Chambers of Commerce and Industry on 22 April 1978. *Hindustan Times*, 23 April 1978. Chandrachud's hint at his predisposition may be found in Seervai, *The Emergency, Future Safeguards and the Habeas Corpus Case*, p. 8. Justice Chandrachud continued to hold to his belief that for Indians there was neither natural law nor pre-constitutional rights. If the freedoms in the Constitution are suspended, then they are suspended, he said. In the Habeas Corpus case, 'I should have gone against the law.' Interview with the author, 1994.

[47] Baxi, *The Indian Supreme Court*, p. 111, citing Beg in 'In re Sham Lal', 1978 (2) SCC 485.

the Lok Sabha recommending 'significant changes' in the Constitution. Speaking on it he had said the time had come 'to consider whether it can be left to the judiciary to interpret ... basic questions'.[48] The day after the hearings concluded, Congress president D. K. Borooah appointed a committee 'to have a look at the Constitution'. The committee's tentative proposals—circulated to members of the bar while the bench was deliberating—concerned 'the power of judicial review, the writ jurisdiction of the courts and the Parliament's power to amend the Constitution'.[49] Justice Chandrachud was not exaggerating when he described the mood as 'most unpleasant' and that the Court was hard-pressed to maintain its independence.[50] '[T]he apprehensions were real and tangible', in Upendra Baxi's assessment. Had the Court acted in certain ways, it 'might ... have imperilled the Court's existence ... [and] have accelerated the already powerful movement to have a new Constitution.'[51]

In cynics' eyes, three of the bench saw a relationship between their rulings and their prospects on the Court. Justices Beg, Chandrachud, and Bhagwati, aware that in the normal process of seniority they would become Chief Justice one day, held for the government to assure that this took place, according to this view. It seems not uncharitable to ask if the reactions to the perceived threat—by the judges on this bench, and more widely in the court—were not overdrawn. Individually, the judges might have feared harassment or arrest for handing down the 'wrong' opinion. But, ugly as the Emergency was, New Delhi in 1976 was not Berlin under Hitler. It is very doubtful if the justices, metaphorically speaking, would have been hanged separately if they had hung together. Ruling against the government would have given them, and the Supreme Court as an institution, stature in public eyes such as to give even Mrs Gandhi pause. Justice Khanna's dissent resulted in Mrs Gandhi's superseding him for Chief Justice of India in January 1977. But it also made him a hero, revered still for his courage.[52]

As for the detenus, they remained in jail.

[48] For the resolution, which Unnikrishnan withdrew on 2 April, see *Lok Sabha Debates*, Fifth Series, vol. 56, no. 17, cols 285, 286.

[49] From the committee's report, *Proposed Amendments to the Constitution of India by the Committee Appointed by the Congress President Shri D. K. Borooah on February 26, 1976*, AICC, New Delhi, 1976, pp. 1, 2. This was the Swaran Singh Committee report (see ch 16).

[50] Chandrachud interview with the author.

[51] Baxi, *Indian Supreme Court and Politics*, p. 40.

[52] That Khanna's supersession was due to his dissent is his view and that of countless others. See ch. 21.

The Transfer of Judges

The Supreme Court's decision was the conclusion of the first act of the Habeas Corpus case. The second act consisted of the transfer of high court judges who had ruled against the government in those and in other preventive detention cases. Sixteen judges were transferred from their 'home' high courts to others without their consent and, in several instances, over their objections. Within and outside the legal community the transfers were understood to be punitive.[53] Mrs Gandhi first acted directly against the courts on 12 January and 24 February 1976 when she refused the continuation of two judges on the Bombay and Delhi high courts, U. R. Lalit and R. N. Aggarwal, despite favourable recommendations from, among others, the chief justices of their respective high courts and her own Law Minister. The Shah Commission, after hearing H. R. Gokhale's testimony and learning of Mrs Gandhi's handwritten 'I do *not* approve ...' on the recommendation for Lalit's continuance, concluded that the Prime Minister's action regarding Lalit amounted to an 'abuse of authority and misuse of power'. The commission noted that Aggarwal had sat on the 'MISA bench' that had released Kuldip Nayar from detention on 13 September 1975—and which had done so on the ground that the right to personal liberty pre-dated the Constitution.[54]

The sixteen judges were transferred during May and June 1976. Among them were two involved in the Bangalore cases, D. M. Chandrashekhar and M. Sadanandaswamy, and one of the two Madhya Pradesh High Court judges in Shiv Kant Shukla, A. P. Sen. The Prime Minister announced that 'national integration' was the purpose of these transfers.[55] She and Sanjay Gandhi had drawn up the lists, he after talking with several chief ministers. They then were discussed in the Home and Law ministries and sent to Chief Justice Ray—who 'had to sign the transfers or resign', recalled a senior Law Ministry official friendly with Mrs Gandhi. Senior officials in the Law Ministry did not favour the transfers, but there was no higher-level dissent because the

---

[53] At least one individual in the Prime Minister's house apparently had it 'in for' the high courts from the beginning. An order was given on 25 June 1975 'to lock up the high courts'. Om Mehta reported hearing this to S. S. Ray, who reacted that this was not possible, and he would speak to Mrs Gandhi about it. He did, and the order was rescinded, but not before Sanjay Gandhi 'met him in a highly excited and infuriated state of mind and told him (Ray) quite rudely that he did not know how to rule the country'. Ray's testimony before the Shah Commission, *Shah Commission*, I, p. 24.

[54] Ibid., pp. 51–2, and 49–51, respectively.

[55] Nariman, Fali S., 'Removal and Transfer of Judges', *Indian Express*, 10 September 1981.

issue had already been decided, according to a member of the Prime Minister's staff.[56] 'The transfers were a threat: agree with us or else,' remembered B. J. Divan, retired chief justice of the Gujarat High Court, who was, himself, transferred to the Hyderabad court. 'They could be made because A. N. Ray was a pliant judge. I know of judges asking not to sit on a case because they feared transfer.'[57] Justice Rangarajan, the second judge sitting on Kuldip Nayar's case, and transferred from Delhi to the Guwahati High Court, agreed.[58] The transfer orders 'created a sense of fear and panic in the minds of judges', said Justice N. L. Untwalia in a Supreme Court opinion rendered after the Emergency. They 'had shaken the very foundation of the independence of the judiciary throughout the country'.[59] Law Commission Chairman Gajendragadkar told Morarji Desai after the Emergency that he believed that the transfers had 'led to an indescribable dissatisfaction in the minds of the judiciary, the lawyers, and the enlightened citizens', sentiments which 'I fully appreciate and share'.[60] And at the time he had argued 'passionately' to Mrs Gandhi against the transfers.[61]

Transferring high court judges under Article 222 of the Constitution was not new. Some twenty-five had been transferred with the Chief Justice of India's concurrence since 1950. Each judge personally had consented. This had evolved into the convention affirmed to Parliament in 1963.[62] The Chief Justices of India at their 1974 annual conference had recommended that the convention be preserved.

The government apparently had intended to transfer a much larger number of judges, anywhere from fifty-six to seventy, according to several accounts. But additional transfers did not take place, and several

[56] According to B. N. Tandon, the draft note supporting the transfers, prepared by a Joint Secretary in the Department of Justice, did not include then Law Minister Asoke Sen's assurance of 1963 to Parliament that high court judges would not be transferred without their consent (ch. 5). Tandon, who saw the draft note, in an interview with the author.

[57] B. J. Divan in an interview with the author.

[58] S. I. Rangarajan interview with the author. Symptomatic of the atmosphere of the time was Rangarajan's wife's request to him that he not take his morning stroll because he might be 'accidentally run over'.

[59] In *Union v S. H. Sheth (1978)*—'Sankalchand's Case' after Sheth's first name—1978 (1) SCR 423ff, as cited in Seervai, *Constitutional Law of India*, vol. 2, p. 2265. Seervai was Sankalchand Sheth's lawyer. The Untwalia quotation comes from SCR, p. 508.

[60] Gajendragadkar letter to Prime Minister Morarji Desai, 1 April 1977. P. B. Gajendragadkar Papers, Subject File 1, NMML.

[61] Letter to Indira Gandhi dated 13 November 1976. Ibid.

[62] *Lok Sabha Debates*, Third Series, vol. 18, no. 55, cols 13006–8. See footnote 56.

explanations for this have been offered. Law Commission Chairman Gajendragadkar believed he deserved some credit. He advised the Prime Minister against it, and this time he may have been heeded.[63] Justice S. H. Sheth's courage in protesting his 27 May 1976 notification of transfer from the Gujarat High Court—by filing a writ petition against the Union of India and the Chief Justice of India—is thought to have had considerable effect, because even with the Censor's order specifically forbidding reporting of the transfers, the case attracted attention.[64] H. M. Seervai informed the press that a second lot of transfers was impending, and he believed this caused persons around the Prime Minister to advise her to drop the plan.[65] Another explanation is that New Delhi was frightened off by the heart attack of a popular Bombay High Court judge, P. M. Mukhi, soon after receiving the order transferring him to the Calcutta High Court in thirty days. Informed of Mukhi's illness by his friends, H. R. Gokhale, himself once a judge on the Bombay Court, had the transfer order annulled. Mukhi recovered temporarily but died soon thereafter. Former Bombay High Court Chief Justice, M. C. Chagla, attributed Mukhi's death to the transfer order and said he had fallen victim to 'the most brutal and inglorious period of our history'.[66] As will

---

[63] Gajendragadkar to Morarji Desai, letter of 1 April 1977, and Gajendragadkar to Indira Gandhi, letter dated 13 November 1976. Gajendragadkar Papers, Subject File 1, NMML.

[64] After filing his writ petition in the Gujarat High Court, Justice Sheth complied with the order transferring him to Hyderabad. In his petition, he argued that under Article 222 transfers may only be in the public interest and cannot be used to punish and to inflict public and private injury on a judge. Also, transfers without consent violate judicial independence and the basic structure of the Constitution, he said. The government's affidavit to the court maintained only that the President had unfettered power to transfer judges. The Gujarat Court heard the case in August 1976, upheld Sheth, filed a writ ordering New Delhi not to implement the transfer, and allowed the government to appeal to the Supreme Court. *Gujarat Law Reports* as cited in Seervai, *Constitutional Law*, pp. 2265ff. On the bench were Justices J. B. Mehta, A. D. Desai, and D. A. Desai.

A five-judge bench of the Supreme Court disposed of the appeal on 26 August 1977 on the ground that the new Janata Party government found no justification for Sheth's transfer and proposed to transfer him back to Ahmedabad. Speaking for the majority, Justice Y. V. Chandrachud said that Sheth's transfer had been ordered 'without effective consultation with the Chief Justice of India'. The court divided on the constitutionality of transfers. Justices Chandrachud, Krishna Iyer, and Fazl Ali held that a judge might be transferred in the public interest without his consent. Bhagwati and Untwalia disagreed. The issue was unresolved and would continue to agitate the judiciary and the executive. H. M. Seervai represented Sheth in both courts. AIR 1977 SC 2333, 2347.

[65] H. M. Seervai interview with the author.

[66] M. C. Chagla, 'Memorial Lecture', delivered at Bombay House 15 December 1977,

be seen in Part IV, the Janata government would allow these judges to return to their original high courts.

Because there can be little doubt that the transfers were retribution for the justices's rulings, it may fairly be said that the Prime Minister again had shown her contempt for the judiciary. The legal community was justified in its revulsion, and it is understandable that a judge would look over his shoulder if ruling against the government. But that the prospect of transfer—acknowledging its inconvenience—could intimidate a judge indicates individual and the judiciary's collective honour were cheaply held.[67] Mrs Gandhi and her government were not finished with the judiciary. By the time of the transfers, the Swaran Singh Committee's recommendations for reducing the judiciary's authority had become public, and the Forty-second Amendment's provisions would go much further, as will be seen in the next two chapters.

---

mimeograph. The author is grateful to Senior Advocate J. M. Mukhi, P. M. Mukhi's brother, for the text of Chagla's remarks and other materials.

[67] Judges did stand up to the government. The Bombay High Court provides several examples. It ruled against the Censor to allow Minoo Masani to publish a certain work. Delivering the judgement for himself and Justice M. H. Kania, Justice Dinshaw P. Madon said that constructive criticism was permissible within Rule 48 of the Defence of India Rules and the Censor 'is appointed the nursemaid of democracy and not its "grave-digger".' *Binod Rao v Masani* (1976), *Bombay Law Reports*, as cited in Divan, Anil B. 'Courts and the Emergency under the Indian Constitution' in Noorani, *Public Law in India*, p. 225. Also *Statesman*, 23 February 1976. Coincidental with the Court's consideration of this case, when it seemed that Justice Madon might be appointed to the Supreme Court, a friend told him that Minister of Information and Broadcasting V. C. Shukla was interested in the case. (Justice Madon in an interview with the author.) The Bombay court also struck down a 1975 order of the city's police commissioner prohibiting the assembly of more than five persons and any assembly at all were the Emergency to be discussed. During the hearing, Justice V. D. Tulzapurkar told the city's attorney that under the order, a Muslim husband could not host his four wives at lunch. (Justice Tulzapurkar interview with the author.) The case was *N. P. Nathwani v Commissioner of Police* (1976), *Bombay Law Reports*, as cited in Anil Divan, 'Courts and the Emergency' in Noorani, *Public Law in India*.

Chapter 16

PREPARING FOR CONSTITUTIONAL CHANGE

The most important constitutional development of the Emergency, other than its very imposition, was the enactment of the Forty-second Amendment. Coming in November 1976, the amendment demonstrates the progression of the Prime Minister and her government from having near-absolute power without a coherent programme—other than the protection of her prime ministry—to power expressed through fundamental constitutional change. There is no evidence that any grand plan to 'reform' the Constitution existed before the Emergency or that it was proclaimed as a means to facilitate such change. Early utterances were merely rhetorical flexings. Law Minister H. R. Gokhale told the Lok Sabha in early August 1975 that it was time to consider fundamental changes in the constitutional framework. Mrs Gandhi remarked that 'we have adopted the Anglo-Saxon juridical system, which often equates liberty with property ... [inadequately providing] for the needs of the poor and the weak ....'[1] With the Emergency in place, however, half-digested schemes and ideas proliferated, and an influential set of recommendations emerged.

As the Emergency was the culmination of long-visible trends, so the thorough attack on democratic institutions in the Forty-second Amendment was the culmination of trends and of predilections allowed to flourish by the Emergency. The seamless web was stretched nearly to the breaking point. Democracy had been abolished indefinitely, possibly forever. Unity enforced by central government—and, eventually, by personal—fiat undermined state government's belief in the future for national unity preserved through the Constitution's co-operative federalism. Justifying the Emergency with spurious social revolutionary promises further mocked New Delhi's pretensions toward this strand of the web. The government's appetite seems to have grown with the

[1] Gokhale: *Statesman*, 8 August 1975. Mrs Gandhi: Interview with the *Saturday Review*, 1 August 1975. *Prime Minister Gandhi on Emergency in India*, Ministry of External Affairs, GOI. New Delhi, 1975, p. 22.

eating—with the easy enactment of self-serving legislation and constitutional amendments in the summer of 1975, with the easy cowing of the citizenry, and with the new-found power to act unrestricted by scrutiny and criticism. The several reverses the judiciary dealt the government no doubt strengthened its appetite—for example, and above all, the Allahabad High Court decision in Mrs Gandhi's Election case; the high courts' rulings on habeas corpus; the Supreme Court's striking down part of the Thirty-ninth Amendment and its unwillingness to overturn Kesavananda and the basic structure doctrine. There was a cause and effect relationship between the latter and the Forty-second Amendment. 'Failure of the review was discussed in the Swaran Singh Committee,' recalled Vasant Sathe, a committee member, for 'Kesavananda limited Parliament's constituent power'.[2] The atmosphere was affected further by the pronouncements of prominent citizens. Chairman of the Law Commission P. B. Gajendragadkar continued to express his dissatisfaction with the basic structure doctrine and his belief in parliamentary supremacy. Two Supreme Court justices, V. R. Krishna Iyer and P. N. Bhagwati, spoke, in Bhagwati's words, of a judicial system ill-suited to 'a country where the majority lived in villages and was ignorant of its legal rights'.[3] However well-intended the two judges' sentiments were, they would be used by others less interested in the integrity of the Constitution and the judiciary. B. K. Nehru wrote to Mrs Gandhi in the autumn of 1975 about changing the Constitution so as to combat instability, especially in the states.

Thus there existed, separate from the power-hungry intentions of the Prime Minister and her clique, genuine ideological sentiment to reform the Constitution. This, too, was a culmination: of the trend, described in Part II, beginning with the Golak Nath decision, gaining strength from the Bank Nationalization and Princes cases rulings, and resulting in the Twenty-fourth and Twenty-fifth Amendments. To this was added the Allahabad judgement and dismay that a single judge, relying on 'footling points', could upset a Prime Minister.

The first concrete movement toward what was called constitutional reform came at the end of the 1975. Beginning here, this chapter will describe these early stages of the progression toward the Forty-second Amendment, focusing on the formation, deliberation, and report of the

---

[2] Vasant Sathe in an interview with the author. Margaret Alva and others shared this view in interviews, citing the vigorous debate over the basic structure within the Congress Parliamentary Party in the autumn of 1975.

[3] Bhagwati in *Statesman*, 1 December 1975.

Swaran Singh Committee. The next chapter will discuss the Forty-second Amendment itself.

Change Takes Shape

The work of the Swaran Singh Committee was preceded by two formative events, the Congress Party's annual session at the end of 1975 and the appearance of an anonymous document entitled 'A Fresh Look at Our Constitution—Some Suggestions', referred to in the previous chapter in connection with the judiciary.

For its plenary that year, the Congress reached back sixty-one years to name it the Kamagata Maru Session. According to a party publication, in 1914 'Indian patriots settled in various countries of the world returned to India burning with desire to sacrifice their all for the liberation of the Motherland'. In September, British troops fired on them near Calcutta, a large number were killed or wounded, and a few marched to the Punjab 'to organise a great rebellion against the foreign government'.[4] It seems not to have been this way.[5]

The movement to amend the Constitution had its formal roots in the Kamagata Maru session's resolution on the political situation: 'If the misery of the poor and vulnerable sections of our society is to be alleviated, vast and far-reaching changes have to be effected in our socio-economic structure ... . The Congress ... urges that our Constitution be thoroughly re-examined in order to ascertain if the time has not come to make adequate alterations to it so that it may continue as a living document.'[6]

---

[4] *Congress Marches Ahead 13*, AICC, New Delhi, October 1976, p. 147.

[5] A man named Gurdit Singh in the spring of 1914 chartered the Japanese-owned *Kamagata Maru* in Hong Kong to carry some 375 would-be immigrants, largely Sikhs, from there and from Yokohama to Victoria and Vancouver. Canadian authorities allowed none but a few passengers' representatives to disembark. There were negotiations, brickbats were exchanged, food was delivered to the ship, and the Viceroy in Delhi warned Ottawa that the use of force could cause repercussions in the Punjab. After returning via Japan, the ship entered the mouth of the Hooghly on 22 September, where the British intended to disembark the passengers and to send them by train to the Punjab. Several hundred Sikhs managed to leave the ship, and they were met by police and troops as they walked the railway line toward Calcutta. Some dozen persons were killed in the firing, and many passengers ultimately reached the Punjab. Johnston, Hugh, *The Voyage of the Kamagata Maru, the Sikh Challenge to Canada's Colour Bar*, Oxford University Press, Delhi, 1979. Joining the ship in Japan on its return trip, according to Johnston's account, was Sohon Singh Bhakna, the first president of the Ghadar party, who smuggled aboard two hundred automatic pistols and considerable ammunition.

[6] *Congress Marches Ahead 13*, p. 10. The resolution was drafted by a committee appointed by party president Dev Kant Borooah and consisted of himself, Mrs Gandhi, Y.

Speeches played variations upon this theme. Mrs Gandhi said that discussion of constitutional changes should include whether or not India should opt for a different form of democracy. Law Minister Gokhale advised a Congress front, the National Forum of Lawyers, at a meeting in Chandigarh, to give serious thought to the obstruction of administration and of legislation by judicial decisions. He said that the Congress session would consider taking property out of the Fundamental Rights and putting the right to work in its place. Commenting on the Congress meeting, *Times of India* editor and influential columnist Girilal Jain wrote on 31 December that there were no ready-made solutions via constitutional changes. The presidential system might provide greater stability than the parliamentary system, but the haves wanted stability more than the have-nots, so adopting this system would not alleviate the miseries of the poor.

Jain's mention of a presidential system was a reference to the anonymous document the 'A Fresh Look' paper. This radical attack on the basic structure would have changed the country's system of government—which, it said, 'has not come up to the expectation of the common man'—from the Westminster Model to a hybrid presidential system, American and French, to achieve 'the unobstructed working of the executive'. All in all, it was redolent of authoritarianism.

The Prime Minister's cousin, B. K. Nehru, was the unwitting progenitor of the writing of the paper (which he thought mostly wrong-headed and badly written). He had written a letter to Mrs Gandhi advocating change to a presidential system. This was passed to Congress President Dev Kant Borooah, who gave it to Rajni Patel, who encouraged A. R. Antulay to write the paper.[7]

B. Chavan, C. Subramaniam, S. S. Ray, and P. V. Narasimha Rao. H. R. Gokhale had constituted an informal group within the Law Ministry in November 1975, headed by its legislative secretary, K. K. Sundaram, to consider changes in the Constitution. Little is known of its doings. *Statesman*, 28 November 1975.

[7] B. K. Nehru's letter and its passing to Borooah, according to P. N. Dhar in an interview wih the author. B. K. Nehru's opinion of Antulay's paper, in an interview with the author and repeated in his memoirs. A. R. Antulay's own account, in an interview with the author, is similar: Mrs Gandhi mentioned to Borooah that it would be useful to have a paper discussing the ideas for constitutional change that were circulating; Borooah mentioned this to Rajni Patel, who spoke with Antulay.

Antulay later acknowledged authorship in Antulay, A. R., *Democracy: Parliamentary or Presidential*, Directorate General of Information and Public Relations, Government of Maharashtra, Bombay, 1981, p. 132, published when he was Chief Minister of the state.

Antulay's account to the author that he sent the paper to several high court judges is borne out by the public comments of two of them after the Emergency. And he discussed

Completed in the summer of 1975, the paper reached Mrs Gandhi, who gave a copy to P. N. Dhar with instructions that four persons, only, should see it.[8] Nevertheless, Boroooah, deliberately and without the Prime Minister's knowledge, leaked the paper as a trial balloon. The fears and the criticism that the paper aroused indicated public sentiment as clearly as the paper's substance indicated the anti-democratic mindset of many around Mrs Gandhi.

A copy came into the hands of an advocate in Gujarat, C. T. Daru, a senior personality in Citizens for Democracy, a group founded by Jayaprakash Narayan. Daru circulated the paper on 9 December 1975 under a covering text that he entitled 'Appeal for Public Debate' and in which he summarized his impressions of the proposal. He wrote that it placed 'vast concentration of power' in the hands of the President; would result in 'virtual subordination' of the judiciary; would end the freedoms of Article 19 by deleting the word 'reasonable' before the qualifications on the freedoms enumerated; would 'end federalism'; and would legalize 'administrative absolutism' by deleting Articles 32 and 226, thus ending judicial review of administrative or legislative action.[9] Addressing himself to the presidential system, as described in 'A Fresh Look', but without naming it, former Constituent Assembly member K. Santhanam said that the scheme would weaken federalism, not strengthen it. He recommended that any constitutional changes first be considered by a high-level non-party committee.[10]

To rid herself of any association with the paper and speculation about changing to a presidential system, Mrs Gandhi had H. R. Gokhale announce that the Prime Minister has said the document is not authentic and 'was an inspired document circulated by mischievous people to create a scare'.[11]

---

his paper with several colleagues in Delhi, including Vasant Sathe, who also favoured switching to the presidential system. Vasant Sathe interview with the author.

[8] P. N. Dhar interview with the author. Both drafting and circulating were so 'hush-hush that the relevant notes were handwritten, with the authors taking care against premature leakage'. Legal affairs correspondent K. K. Katyal, *Hindu*, 29 December 1980.

[9] Jayaprakash Narayan Papers, Third Installment, File 320, NMML. The New Delhi newspaper *Patriot* reported on 24 November that a paper in circulation among legal experts advocated a presidential system, likely the paper to which Daru reacted. Citizens for Democracy also convened a 'Save the Constitution' convention in Ahmedabad on 1 January 1976 to discuss the paper. As a reward for giving the document currency and denouncing it, Daru 'was promptly arrested and detained'. Baxi, *Supreme Court and Politics*, p. 35.

[10] *Indian Express*, 30 December 1975.

[11] In mid-February 1976. Mirchandani, G. G. (ed.), *India Backgrounders*, published

The debate over the parliamentary *versus* a presidential system was not new. Although the Constituent Assembly had rejected a presidential system, the idea revived as politicians and intellectuals faced governing the country without Jawaharlal Nehru. A minister in the Tamil Nadu government who would later be President of India, R. Venkataraman, sent a draft resolution to the AICC in 1965 recommending constituting a committee to examine an executive 'directly elected by the people for a fixed term of years' to help combat 'dissidentism' and 'groupism' in the executive and legislative branches.[12] In 1967, the India International Centre convened a colloquium on the subject with contributions from Max Beloff, among others, and during the next few years J. R. D. Tata, G. D. Birla, Justice K. S. Hegde, and former Chief Justice of India B. P. Sinha advocated a fixed executive where, as Sinha put it, the 'head is not dependent on the vagaries of the legislators'.[13] Jayaprakash Narayan opposed a presidential system because 'temptation would be too great for a President, if he were strong, to usurp people's rights.'[14] The socialist and communist parties consistently opposed a presidential system. The debate over the comparative merits of the two systems, as will be seen, continues to this day.

The Swaran Singh Committee

Embarrassed by the fiasco of leaking 'A Fresh Look', emboldened by the tone at the Kamagata Maru Session, and with much talk of constitutional change in the air, Congress President Borooah on 26 February 1976 appointed a committee 'to study the question of amendment of the Constitution in the light of ... experience'. Commonly referred to as the Swaran Singh Committee after its chairman, the committee had two other, unannounced purposes: to manage the proliferating suggestions for amendment and to control the process for considering them, and, while doing this, to serve the Prime Minister's interests. These were that her position not be detrimentally affected and that her official decisions would

---

and printed by G. G. Mirchandani, New Delhi, 12 April 1976, p. 16. The 'backgrounders' frequently contain information unavailable elsewhere.

[12] Text of the resolution and Venkataraman's letter covering it appear in *Parliamentary versus Presidential System of Government*, India International Centre, New Delhi, 1966, pp. 60–2. The proposal went unpursued at Prime Minister Shastri's request.

[13] Noorani, *The Presidential System*, p. 14.

[14] During an 8 April 1968 speech in London, *AR*, 27 May–2 June 1968, p. 8340. At this time, Mrs Gandhi spoke against it, saying, 'The presidential system cannot by itself confer more maturity on the people.' Ibid.

not be overturned by Parliament or the President nor opposed by the judiciary, according to S. L. Shakdher, at the time Secretary General of the Lok Sabha.[15] P. N. Dhar analysed Mrs Gandhi's intentions similarly: she did not want the Allahabad judgement to affect her; she wished the President, the Vice-President, the Prime Minister, and the Speaker to be immune from prosecution; and she wanted the executive to be able to function without judicial interference.[16] The Prime Minister, herself, declared her aims to be strengthening democracy and achieving true justice and equality for the common people. 'Our basic fight', she said, 'is against entrenched privilege of a few ...'.[17] But much about the committee lies in shadow, particularly why did a report prepared in these carefully managed circumstances so ill-suit the desires of the government that it went far beyond its recommendations when drafting the Forty-second Amendment. We shall look at the committee's composition, at its recommendations, and then at the consequent puzzles.[18]

Mrs Gandhi approved the committee's membership from the suggestions proferred by Borooah, S. S. Ray, and Rajni Patel. The Congress Working Committee gave the list its imprimatur, and it was presented as a party committee even though ten of its twelve members were officials in the central ministry or Congress members of Parliament. The exceptions were Ray, who was chief minister of West Bengal, where he harshly put down the Naxalite Maoist rebellion, and Rajni Patel, President of the Bombay Provincial Congress Committee.[19] Seven of the members were lawyers and D. P. Singh and S. S. Ray had been members of London's Middle Temple. All were Hindus with the exception of A. R. Antulay and Seyid Muhammad who were Muslim, C. M. Stephen, a Christian, and Swaran Singh, a Sikh. From different parts of the country, the members provided the degree of regional

---

[15] S. L. Shakdher in an interview with the author.

[16] P. N. Dhar in an interview with the author.

[17] Speaking at the AICC session during its consideration of a Swaran Singh Committee draft report. *Congress Marches Ahead 13*, p. 54.

The committee report is named *Proposed Amendments to the Constitution of India by the Committee Appointed by Congress President D. K. Borooah on February 26, 1976* (hereafter called the *Swaran Singh Report*, AICC. New Delhi, 14 August 1976.

[18] The committee consisted of Sardar Swaran Singh, Chairman; A. R. Antulay, Member-Secretary, Members: S. S. Ray, Rajni Patel, H. R. Gokhale, V. A. Seyid Muhammad, V. N. Gadgil, C. M. Stephen, D. P. Singh, D. C. Goswamy, V. P. Sathe, and B. N. Banerjee.

[19] The characterizations of these individuals that follow are derived from interviews with several of them and with K. C. Pant, Usha Bhagat, Bakhul Patel, Govind Talwalkar, D. K. Borooah, Girish Mathur, Chandrajit Yadav, Sheila Dikshit, Margaret Alva, S. L. Shakdher, B. N. Tandon, and N. K. Seshan, among others.

balance Borooah and the Prime Minister desired. Borooah, Patel, D. P. Singh, Goswami—were considered 'progressives', that is, ex-communists of the Congress Forum variety or still close to the Communist Party of India. (Borooah, although not a committee member, is treated as one here because of his close relations with it.) Gadgil, Gokhale, and Stephen were Congress socialists. Sathe and Antulay were considered mavericks of the centre-right. S. S. Ray, particularly, was the protector of Mrs Gandhi's political interests. All the members qualified as 'leftist', in the view of Margarat Alva, a member of Borooah's staff who sometimes attended Swaran Singh Committee meetings for him. Their common features were 'communism, leftism, pro-Soviet, pro-Marx', said I. K. Gujral, a Minister of State at the time and once a Communist.[20] Yet, a senior journalist who knew all the members thought them 'an ideologically mixed group otherwise unlikely to sit in the same room for an hour'. What most united them was loyalty to Mrs Gandhi, which caused P. N. Haksar to describe the committee as 'packed'.[21]

Sardar Swaran Singh varied from the mould. Tall, gentlemanly and dignified, he had a reputation for moderation and as a good administrator, as someone who would reason with the Prime Minister, but oppose her only to a point. He accepted Borooah's invitation to chair the committee only after some thought and played little part in selecting its members, although he was present in the Working Committee meeting when its composition was discussed. Presiding over this congeries, Swaran Singh was to be 'a restraining influence', giving it 'the correct direction', which his 'stature' fitted him to do, said Margaret Alva and V. N. Gadgil.[22] 'We thought him old-fashioned; he would not go in for anything unacceptably radical,' said D. K. Borooah.[23]

The committee set to work immediately upon its formation, the Prime Minister desiring results in a few months. After limited consultations with associations and individuals deemed friendly to the government, it submitted 'tentative proposals' to Borooah on 3 April. These Borooah circulated among members of the Working Committee and leaders of

[20] I. K. Gujral in an interview with the author—including his previous membership in the Communist party.
[21] P. N. Haksar in an interview with the author.
[22] Margaret Alva and V. N. Gadgil in interviews with the author.
[23] Borooah interview with the author. Swaran Singh told Inder Malhotra that nothing radical would come from a committee he chaired. Malhotra interview with the author. Singh had voiced mild criticism of the imposition of the Emergency, to the Prime Minister's displeasure, and he was forced out of his position as Defence Minister in December 1975 after disagreements with Sanjay Gandhi over defence and Punjab affairs.

Congress state governments. Consultations continued with selected members of the Parliamentary Party, several high court judges, and bar associations while the committee digested reactions to its tentative proposals. Slightly altered, the proposals along with a 'Resolution on Amendment' went to the AICC, which considered them on 28–9 May 1976.[24] The government touted this process and that leading to the Forty-second Amendment, in general, as open. In reality, as H. M. Patel later would say in the Lok Sabha, it was 'a convenient monologue'.[25]

This approach was not to the liking of Law Commission Chairman Gajendragadkar. As early as August 1975, he had written to the Prime Minister that, although amendments to the Constitution were necessary to expedite the social-economic revolution, 'ad hocism is undesirable and adoption of extremist doctrinaire positions is irrelevant and inadvisable'. He advised her to appoint a high-powered committee 'wholly unofficial if you like' to research and discuss the problem in depth, a dedicated and comprehensive effort.[26]

THE COMMITTEE'S RECOMMENDATIONS

The committee's recommendations were changed little by the AICC from the form in which they were submitted and later published as the so-called Swaran Singh Report. Hence references hereafter will be to the original report, to the political views of committee members, and to the internal deliberations that produced its recommendations. After announcing that the Constitution 'has functioned without any serious impediment', the committee report turned to the subject it had 'hotly discussed', changing to a presidential system. The report declared the parliamentary system 'best suited' for the country because it 'ensures greater responsiveness to the voice of the

[24] The text of the resolution appears in *Congress Marches Ahead 13*, pp. 5ff, 94ff. This publication also contains the proposals for amendment, the earlier tentative proposals, the relevant speeches, and much else.

At this meeting, the Congress Working Committee also expelled Chandra Shekhar from the committee and from the Congress Party for ten years for 'the gross indiscipline ... with which he publicly denigrated the Congress ... and carried on a propaganda against the decisions of the Congress ...'. Zaidi, *The Encyclopaedia of the Indian National Congress*, vol. 24, p. 146.

[25] *Lok Sabha Debates*, Fifth Series, vol. 64, no. 16, col. 18.

[26] P. B. Gajendragadkar–Indira Gandhi letter dated 13 August 1975. Gajendragadkar Papers, NMML. Discerning that his advice was being ignored, Gajendragadkar wrote to the Prime Minister on 6 and 27 March 1976, met with her on 9 March, and later met, with Mrs Gandhi's blessing, Borooah and D. P. Singh to hammer at the need for the proper 'modality' of approaching amending the Constitution. Ibid.

people'.[27] Antulay and Vasant Sathe, perhaps joined by Stephen, had argued vigorously to the contrary and they had recently heard respectable outside support for the idea. In January 1976 N. A. Palkhivala had written that a presidential system providing for 'a fair balance of power between the executive, the legislature and the judiciary' would be preferable 'to the present system'.[28] The previous summer, B. K. Nehru, High Commissioner in London, while visiting Delhi had advocated change to a presidential system to Mrs Gandhi personally, following up an earlier letter to her from London.[29] The Prime Minister publicly rejected the idea during the visit of French Prime Minister Chirac in February 1976. '[P]ower should not be concentrated but be with the people,' she said.[30] Within the Swaran Singh Committee, most opposed changing the system, and Gokhale, Seyid Muhammad, and S. S. Ray did so actively. Swaran Singh was happy to let the opposition win. He told veteran journalist Kuldip Nayar that he had 'stalled' the move toward a presidential system (it re-emerged six months later and again in the eighties), and he told the author that older Congressmen had 'thanked me for saving the country'.

As support for a presidential system did not necessarily indicate authoritarian tendencies in an individual, so proclaimed loyalty to the parliamentary system did not necessarily denote strong democratic sensibilities. Committee member Rajni Patel provides an excellent example. For him, Mrs Gandhi's 'stern measures' had saved the country's 'weak democratic system' from being 'undermined by an organized minority'. But the time had come for a 'Prime Minister elected by the popular vote ... enabling him or her to exercise authority without the

---

[27] *Swaran Singh Report*, p. 3. 'Hotly discussed': Swaran Singh interview with the author.

[28] N. A. Palkhivala, 'Should We Alter Our Constitution?', *The Illustrated Weekly of India*, 4 January 1976.

[29] B. K. Nehru interview with the author. The general impression at this time, Nehru recalled, was that she wanted a presidential system to perpetuate her own rule. 'But when I discussed it with her she said, "No, absolutely not. I don't want it." If she had wanted it, we'd have got it,' Nehru said. Nevertheless, Mrs Gandhi allowed him to discuss the changeover with others and to circulate a paper if he made sure '"they knew I am against it."'

P. N. Dhar discussed this with B. K. Nehru and believes that Mrs Gandhi 'all along' was against changing to a presidential system. Interview with author. Nehru has said that Dhar was 'totally enthusiastic about my proposal'. Nehru, B. K., *Nice Guys Finish Second*, p. 558.

[30] To the French news agency AFP. See 'India Debates Constitutional Changes', *India Backgrounders*, 12 April 1976, p. 15. Because her admiration for France and De Gaulle was well known, her choice of this moment was thought especially significant. She later rejected a presidential system on federal grounds, saying that it might lead to 'similar systems' in all the states, resulting in 'confrontation with other states or with the Centre'. 'Latest Constitutional Changes', ibid., 6 September 1976, p. 227.

vexation of pulls and pressures' afflicting an indirectly elected prime minister.[31] This 'strengthened' parliamentary system seems a first cousin to a presidential system, which may be why many believed Patel favoured it. Patel apparently had an ally in Borooah, deducing from Borooah's views that Indians did not understand parliamentary government and that government must be made effective. At the time, Borooah was said to admire the strong government in the Soviet Union.[32] Borooah, Patel, D. P. Singh, and Goswami were eager to explore amendments to transform society radically, thought the cheery senior advocate and progressive, R. K. Garg. 'Destroying democratic institutions did not matter, because India has no democratic culture.'[33] Such sentiments typically were cloaked in the euphemisms of 'strong government' or a 'strong centre'— reasonable aims at first inspection. They fit well with the Prime Minister's desire for 'a stable parliamentary system', as Vasant Sathe put it, and with S. L. Shakdher's recollection that she wanted to strengthen the authority of her office so that its actions would be beyond the reach of Parliament, the President, and the judiciary.[34] In the analysis of Bombay

[31] From a paper Patel read to a seminar on 'Disciplined Democracy' organized by the Bombay Provincial Congress Committee in February 1976 and inaugurated by Prime Minister Gandhi. *Socialist India*, 27 March 1976, and reprinted in Zins, Max Jean, *Strains on Indian Democracy*, ABC Publishing House, New Delhi, 1988, p. 177ff. For the text of the Prime Minister's speech, see *Indira Gandhi, Selected Speeches*, vol. 3, p. 254.

Patel during this period was a favourite of the Prime Minister. A former communist, 'he mulcted the rich of Bombay in the name of Indira Gandhi and the Congress Party'. Singh, Khushwant, *Women and Men in My Life*, UBS Publishers and Distributors Ltd., New Delhi, 1995, p. 164.

[32] Borooah's admiration for the Soviet Constitution from V. N. Gadgil, in an interview with the author. Gadgil also described Patel as envisaging a constitution that would make the Congress virtually the only party, 'sort of along communist lines'. Borooah declared to the author in an interview in 1994 that he opposed a presidential system. 'If you get a bad one, you're stuck,' he said.

[33] R. K. Garg interview with the author.

[34] 'Reforms' of parliamentary procedures had already been made in the Lok Sabha during the first day of the session after the Emergency was declared. In the guise of speeding up the conduct of business (admittedly most legislatures could be more efficient), the Lok Sabha by a vote of 301 to 76 adopted a resolution that suspended its rules, prohibited the questioning of ministers, calling attention notices, and any business except government business. Former members of Parliament and journalists were denied entry to Parliament House. *Statesman*, 20 July 1975. A Congress Parliamentary Party subcommittee, chaired by C. M. Stephen, recommended reducing parliamentary sittings by one-third; transferring the second reading of bills (when substantive changes might be made) to committees; restricting the right to amend a bill to its mover; and limiting adjournment motions and short-notice discussions. *Hindustan Times*, 27 December 1975, and Zins, *Strains on Indian Democracy*, pp. 133–4. Little came of the Stephen committee's ideas 'because Parliament

editor Govind Talwalkar, 'The ex-communists and the communists thought the Emergency would be their coup, but it turned out to be a right-wing coup.'[35]

One of the prime minister's 'vexations' was judicial review, and the time had come in a disciplined democracy, Patel said, 'to restrict or do away with ... [it] as is the case in France and England'.[36] Committee members to a considerable extent agreed with this. Parliament was 'the most authentic and effective instrument ... [of] the sovereign will of the people', said the report,[37] which recommended that Article 368 be amended so that constitutional amendments 'shall not be called in question in any court on any ground'. Gokhale and Gadgil, in an echo of the 'A Fresh Look' paper, had advocated some sort of constitutional council for judicial review. S. S. Ray disliked the basic structure because, he felt, no one knew what it meant. Stephen thought the doctrine 'very dangerous.'[38] The constitutional validity of legislation might be challenged, the committee said, but central laws should be open to challenge only in the Supreme Court. Constitutional cases should be heard by no fewer than seven judges in the Supreme Court and five in high courts; decisions should be by two-thirds majority. Swaran Singh, among others, favoured this, disapprovingly pointing out in a speech that Golak Nath had been decided by only one vote.[39] He went further

---

was functioning efficiently', according to MP Chandrajit Yadav, in an interview with the author. The Lok Sabha twice would extend its life by a year (on 4 February 1976 and 5 November 1976—until March 1978), which was constitutional under Article 83. Further Lok Sabha 'reforms' would come in the Forty-second Amendment.

[35] Talwalkar interview with the author.

[36] From the 'Disciplined Democracy' seminar paper, footnote 30.

[37] *Swaran Singh Report*, p. 3.

[38] In a speech to the Indian Council of World Affairs. Reprinted in *Constitutional Reforms*, Division of Audio-Visual Publicity, GOI, New Delhi, October 1976, p. 15.

The committee's emphasis on parliamentary supremacy continued to have support from Gajendragadkar. In the Motilal Nehru Memorial Lecture in May 1976, he reiterated his view that Parliament's powers were plenary and no doctrine of basic features could limit its power under Article 368. Kagzi, *The June Emergency*, p. 29.

[39] Even Motilal C. Setalvad, perhaps the country's most distinguished Attorney General, said of Golak Nath that 'a decision involving such far-reaching consequences should not have been arrived at by so slender a majority'. Setalvad, *My Life, Law and Other Things*, p. 584.

The committee was also said to be reacting to the invalidation of Mrs Gandhi's election by a one-man bench in Allahabad. Of course, the possibility of a four-to-three split in a seven-judge bench did not eliminate one-vote majorities. Some argued that the two-thirds idea, because of the fraction of a vote involved, effectively placed decisions in the hands of the three-judge minority: a two thirds majority in a seven-judge bench would be five votes to two (to avoid a fraction of a vote) thus allowing three judges to defeat four.

and expressed an opinion with which no prudent citizen of any country would agree: 'It should be reasonably presumed that normally no legislature will over-step the limits laid down for it in the Constitution.'[40]

Focusing on the high courts, where Mrs Gandhi's transfer of judges had begun, the committee recommended leaving intact their authority to issue writs for protection of citizens' fundamental rights (Article 226), but removing their authority to issue prerogative writs for 'any other purpose'.[41] Antulay, Borooah, Patel, and Ray were said to favour the elimination of the entire article. Prominent lawyers outside the committee fought against this. R. K. Garg advised Swaran Singh to tell the Prime Minister that its elimination would deprive her of the courts' protection,[42] and Swaran Singh has been credited with the article's retention. Member of the Law Commission P. K. Tripathi told the committee that the high courts should retain authority to issue writs for any other purpose as a means to keep the bureaucracy 'within the limits of law'.[43] Mrs Gandhi, in a March 1976 address to the governors at their annual conference, had suggested they write the President their ideas about how the high courts' writ powers had come in the way of progressive steps.[44]

The committee's most radical move against the courts came in its recommendation that Article 31C be expanded so that legislation to implement *any* of the Directive Principles of State Policy could not be questioned in court as infringing the Fundamental Rights. The committee's 'progressives' had brought Moscow to New Delhi. The Dean of the Law Faculty at Delhi University, Upendra Baxi, thought that making the Rights subservient to the Principles was 'as it should be in a poor society with massive maldistribution of property, income and wealth'.[45] The committee isolated the courts further through its proposal

---

[40] In the Hanumanthaiya Endowment Lecture, 21 August 1976. It was published in abridged form, in *Constitutional Amendment,* by the Congress Party in October 1976.

[41] The committee's report recalled that the Congress Party's constitutional review committee chaired by Nehru in 1954 had recommended this, but it conveniently neglected to mention that the cabinet then had rejected the idea. See ch. 4.

[42] Garg interview with the author. Antulay's support for the article's deletion may be found in annexure 5 to his 'A Fresh Look' paper. Noorani, *The Presidential System*, p. 120.

In V. N. Gadgil's recollection, no one intended to delete the whole article, only to restrict use of the writs 'because they had become cheap'. Interview with the author.

[43] Tripathi's mid-May 1976 submission to the Swaran Singh Committee was published in 1976 (2) SCC Journal Section 29–44.

[44] Kagzi, *The June Emergency*, pp. 56, 72.

[45] A commentary on the committee's report, Baxi's paper was published in 1976 (2) SCC Journal Section 17–28. Baxi also praised the committee's 'solicitude for judicial review, fundamental rights and for the Supreme Court'. Ibid.

that all matters concerning 'the revenue'—e.g., land reform, ceiling on urban property, and procuring and distributing essential commodities—should go before tribunals, not to the courts. Compared to these provisions, placing 'socialism' in the Preamble was a mere gesture.[46] Setting up tribunals did have a more praiseworthy side, reduction of the large number of cases in arrears—an 'unexceptionable' move, in Palkhivala's view. It was the extensiveness of the subject matter over which tribunals would have jurisdiction, the exclusion of the Supreme and high courts' writ jurisdiction over those subjects, and removal of the tribunals from high court supervision that aroused anxieties.

The committee directly addressed neither the right to property nor freedom of expression in its report. Although Antulay and Borooah pressed for removing property from the Rights, Swaran Singh, Ray, Sathe, Gokhale, and Rajni Patel opposed this on the tactical ground that the move would be too radical for many in the Congress Party. In another version of this dispute, nearly all the members favoured removal, but the Prime Minister vetoed it on the ground that public opinion was not ready. 'Prudence kept property in the Rights,' recalled Borooah.[47]

Antulay and Stephen led strong sentiment in the committee for curbing freedom of expression, particularly press freedom, already outlawed by the Emergency. Eventually, in a strategy approved by Mrs Gandhi, it was decided that curbs on the press would be effected better through legislation than by constitutional amendment.[48] But Antulay's

---

CPI parliamentarian Bhupesh Gupta wrote that the 'platonic love for the Directive Principles' must give way to something more meaningful, and that the Kesavananda ruling 'must go'. Article in *New Age*, republished in Gupta, Bhupesh, *Some Comments on Constitutional Changes*, CPI, New Delhi, August 1976, pp. 44ff. A CPI meeting in Trivandrum suggested that judges should be impeached 'on the ground of disregard on their part of the Directive Principles'. *Proposals of the National Council for Amendments to the Constitution of India*, Communist Party of India, New Delhi, 1976.

[46] The Preamble would read that India was a 'Sovereign Democratic Secular Socialist Republic'. Antulay favoured inserting 'socialist', but gives Borooah credit for it, while claiming that inserting 'secular' was his idea. A. K. Antulay in an interview with the author. This is consistent with Antulay's concern, as a Muslim, for minority rights.

[47] Borooah in an interview with the author. Several members advocated replacing the right to property with the right to work. Gokhale, while on the committee, told an Ahmedabad audience that the right to property might by amendment be so defined that it could not serve as an instrument of exploitation of the many by the few.

The CPI called leaving property in the Rights a 'glaring omission', and derided it as 'self-contradictory' in light of the proposal to add 'socialist' to the Constitution's Preamble. 'Note Adopted by the Central Committee of the CPI', Madras, 21 June 1976, as cited in Gupta, *Some Comments*, pp. 44–59.

[48] S. S. Ray interview with the author. Mrs Gandhi, said Ray, was moved in part by the desire to avoid international criticism.

zeal for curbing liberty had enough support from his fellows, for the committee to recommend that Parliament be empowered to legislate against 'the misuse or abuse' of the freedoms in Article 19 'by individuals, groups or associations'.[49] This vine would bear bitter fruit in the Forty-second Amendment.

The committee made several other significant recommendations to the AICC. One was that a state of emergency could be declared, and lifted, in only a part of India. In another, it said that the central government should have the power to deploy police and similar forces 'under its own superintendence and control' when helping a state government preserve order. This was something state chief ministers had protested during the committee's consultations with them, preferring the existing arrangement in which federal forces came under state control once they entered the state (see chapter 29). Otherwise, centre–state relations were all but ignored in the committee's report, although several committee members believed the country needed 'a dose of federalism'. The committee 'played the music to her ears' of how much they needed Mrs Gandhi and a strong centre to protect the unity and integrity of the country, V. N. Gadgil recalled.

Turning to election issues, the committee proposed that a separate, nine-member body—with its members appointed equally from the Lok Sabha, the Rajya Sabha, and by the President—should adjudicate questions of disqualification of members of Parliament and the President and Vice-President, instead of leaving disputes to be resolved by a body established by Parliament, as the Thirty-ninth Amendment had provided in new Articles 329A and 71. All members of the committee, recalled Swaran Singh, were not in favour of the 'grant of immunity' given to the Prime Minister by Article 329A because it would apply to future prime ministers. 'But the majority did, and, as chairman, I had to express the will of the majority, although, looking back, immunity for the Prime Minister should not be there,' Singh said.[50]

---

[49] *Swaran Singh Report*, p. 14.

Antulay in 'A Fresh Look' had suggested that the word 'reasonable', as qualifying restrictions that might be placed on the freedoms, should be deleted from the Constitution and that no law restricting the freedoms could be questioned in the courts. Noorani, *Presidential System*, p. 118.

[50] Swaran Singh in an interview with the author. Readers will remember that the Thirty-ninth Amendment substituted a new Article 71 for the old and added new Article 329A. The former applied to the President and Vice-President and the latter to the Prime Minister and Speaker, as members of Parliament.

In two other recommendations, the committee reacted directly to Mrs Gandhi's Election case and also picked up a suggestion from the Parliamentary Party's 'reform'

At the All India Congress Committee meeting on 29 May 1976 Swaran Singh moved the lengthy 'Resolution on Amendment', laden with social revolutionary language, and spoke on it and the committee's recommendations. He devoted particular attention to two items: the desirability of the central government being able to move forces under its own control into states to preserve law and order, while assuring state governments that law and order remained their 'sole responsibility'; and the desirability of having larger judicial benches and two-thirds majorities to rule on constitutional questions. Faced with the crucial situation the country is in, he said, 'niceties of law are very pleasing to all the lawyers ... [but] at times weakness would be there'.[51] Speaking that afternoon, first in Hindi and then in English as had Singh, the Prime Minister said that 'it was not the Constitution which was coming in the way, it was the interpretation which some people had given ...'. She said that no basic or fundamental changes would be made in the Constitution; the only aim was to strengthen democracy and achieve true justice and equality for the common people.[52]

The AICC's debate on the resolution and the committee's proposals was inconsequential, with two exceptions. One was an amendment to the tentative proposals, which was adopted in the face of Swaran Singh's resistance, that agriculture remain on the State Legislative List.[53] The second exception was Swaran Singh's own amendment to the resolution, which he agreed under pressure to move: that his committee prepare a list of 'certain Fundamental Duties and obligations which every citizen owes to the nation' and incorporate it in the committee's report.[54]

---

efforts of the previous autumn. In one, it said that the government's Transaction of Business Rules might be subject to the 'internal orders of the Prime Minister'. In the other, the committee recommended that state legislatures and the houses of Parliament should make their own rules about a quorum, dispensing with the Constitution's provisions that a quorum should be one-tenth of the membership of the House. Governments should be able to act in legislatures without hindrance, the committee was saying.

There was some agitation within the committee to extend the term of Parliament to seven years. Swaran Singh consulted S. L. Shakdher on the matter, who advised him that the world trend was toward reducing, not augmenting, legislative terms. The purpose of the seven years, in Shakdher's opinion, was to give Prime Minister Gandhi longer tenure. S. L. Shakdher interview with the author.

[51] *Congress Marches Ahead 13*, pp. 36–43.

[52] Ibid., p. 54.

[53] The chief ministers had taken this position several weeks earlier. As a result, the AICC resolved only that there should be 'a co-ordinated and comprehensive approach to agriculture at the National level'.

[54] This had been decided at the meeting of the Working Committee held on 28 May, which approved the resolution and the tentative proposals before passing them on to

The committee met in New Delhi regularly during July to re-examine its recommendations, particularly the Fundamental Duties it had drafted, and to discuss their possible enforcement. Swaran Singh told a Delhi audience that summer that he 'would not mind' if the Duties were not added to the Constitution, and he opposed their legal enforcement.[55] The committee published its first report on 14 August. It would not meet again until 30 October, when it was called together to comment on the amending bill that had been introduced in Parliament on 1 September and that would become the Forty-second Amendment. The list of Fundamental Duties in the committee's report included: to respect the Constitution, to uphold the sovereignty of the nation, to respect democratic institutions, to abjure communalism and violence, to work for the implementation of the Directive Principles, and to pay taxes—a burdensome duty later omitted from the Forty-second Amendment. The report added that Parliament might by law provide for 'penalty or punishment' for refusal to comply with or observe the Duties. No such law was to be questioned in court on the ground that it infringed the Fundamental Rights or any other provision of the Constitution.[56]

The Committee as a Puzzle

Indira Gandhi had supported the formation of the Swaran Singh Committee, and she had sanctioned the committee's composition, in effect appointing it. Its members consisted of loyalists. She monitored

---

AICC. Present were members: D. K. Borooah, presiding, Mrs Indira Gandhi, Messrs Jagjivan Ram, Y. B. Chavan, Swaran Singh, C. Subramaniam, S. S. Ray, Kamalapati Tripathi, V. P. Naik, Syed Mir Qasim, P. C. Sethi, Vayalar Ravi, V. B. Raju, A. R. Antulay, Mrs Purabi Mukherjee, and Mrs M. Chandrasekhar. Special Invitees: Messrs Shankar Dayal Sharma, Chandrajit Yadav, K. D. Malaviya, B. C. Bhagwati, Rajni Patel, Kartik Oraon, Om Mehta, Bansi Lal, Giani Zail Singh, Henry Austin, Nawal Kishore Sharma, Tarun Gogoi, Radha Raman, Amarnath Chawla, Mrs Nandini Satpathy, Mrs Ambika Soni, and Mrs Margaret Alva.

Invited especially to discuss the Swaran Singh Committee proposals were J. Vengal Rao, Chief Minister of Andhra, and Banarsi Das Gupta, Chief Minister of Haryana, who had been two of the chief ministers brought into the secret of the Emergency before it was proclaimed, and D. Devraj Urs, Chief Minister of Karnataka. Zaidi, *The Encyclopaedia*, p. 143.

[55] Kazgi, *The June Emergency*, pp. 56, 72.

[56] Ibid., p. 4. Shriman Narayan Agarwal in his *Gandhian Constitution for a Free India*, Kitabistan, Allahabad, 1946, had included a chapter on fundamental rights and duties. Rajendra Prasad, when President, spoke a number of times about citizen duties. There should be a balance between rights and duties; rights can flow from duty well-performed; too much stress has been placed on rights; the call of duty is forgotten, Prasad said at various times. Citizen duties in some form appear in a dozen or more constitutions.

the committee's deliberations through occasional meetings with Swaran Singh, Borooah, and S. S. Ray. She participated in the Working Committee and AICC meetings that approved the draft report, and she strongly advocated the addition to it of the Fundamental Duties. Yet she 'didn't like the report', Dev Kant Borooah told V. N. Gadgil, and she read the committee's final report cursorily.[57] She knew that it had lost much of its relevance and that she had authorized (probably in May) the secret drafting of a constitutional amendment that would go far beyond the committee's recommendations.

The most likely solution to the puzzle is that Mrs Gandhi had no clear ideas about the committee at its inception and no particular outcome in mind and that her intentions for the committee were mixed: it would be a helpful device for managing the suggestions and the emotional drive for amending the Constitution; putting 'progressives' on it would please part of her constituency; something good, and little harm, might come from it; she could accept or reject what it produced; and the committee gave her 'breathing space', as a Law Ministry official friendly with her put it. This would be consistent with the Prime Minister's tendency to let events develop until a decisive moment arrived and her characteristic of listening extensively to counsel before making up her mind.

But when she realized at the May AICC meeting, or before, that the committee's report would not go far enough in protecting her interests, she allowed the parallel drafting of an amendment to see if it would suit her better. This two track strategy would have had another advantage. If Mrs Gandhi calculated that Swaran Singh's report would be acceptable to senior Congressmen like C. Subramaniam, Kamalapati Tripathi, Uma Shankar Dikshit, and others, but that the Working Committee would demur at even more radical changes to the Constitution, she had best have these prepared out of view. This possibility is supported by the willingness of many Congress members of Parliament under the Janata government to vote to repeal much of the Forty-second Amendment (Part IV).[58]

Individuals closely involved with Mrs Gandhi doubt that she was reacting to the advice of Sanjay Gandhi and his coterie—increasingly influential as 1976 progressed—because she did not rate his intellectual capacity highly. Whatever the answer, it seems a casual manner with which

---

[57] V. N. Gadgil in an interview with the author. Borooah said the same.

[58] Sceptics had had doubts about the committee from the first. In interviews, they variously recalled their assessments that Mrs Gandhi was undecided and hoped the committee would show the way; that any amendment would benefit from having been sanctified by the committee; and that she expected nothing from it.

to treat the Constitution. Yet a well-informed observer's description of the Swaran Singh Committee as a 'charade', ignores the many radical contributions the report did make to the Forty-second Amendment. If Sardar Swaran Singh did indeed exert a moderating influence on the committee, one shudders to speculate what it might have done without him.

The Critics

During the weeks the Swaran Singh Committee was at work, prominent citizens analysed its proposals and opposed many of them, critiques that the Emergency's censors allowed the press to publish. One group of prominent citizens, the National Committee for Review of the Constitution, established itself in mid-March in Bombay and published its comprehensive critique late in May. Its committee's basic position was that any amendments by the current Parliament would be a 'constitutional impropriety' because the Lok Sabha's regular five-year term had expired, and it had voted its own extension. Also, due to government restrictions on assembly and expression, 'there is no proper atmosphere ... for the necessary and purposeful national debate.'[59] The National Committee opposed parliamentary supremacy; the minimum number of judges on constitutional benches coupled with the two-thirds majority provision; the proposed deletion of 'for any other purpose', as applied to writs under Article 226; empowering a body other than the judiciary to decide upon disqualification of members; and making the Fundamental Rights subordinate to the Directive Principles. If there were to be tribunals, the National Committee said, only chief justices should appoint their members. It recommended removing the right to property from the Fundamental Rights so that it could not 'be used as an excuse for depriving the people of their civil liberties or for practising discrimination'. It believed that a declaration of emergency should be justiciable; that an emergency could be confined to one area of the country; and that the deployment of

[59] *Interim Report,* National Committee for Review of the Constitution, New Delhi, 25 May 1976, p. 2. Jayaprakash Narayan Papers, Third Installment, Subject File 323, NMML. The committee never published a final report, pleading an insufficient number of meetings due to government restriction. *Statement* by the committee, 1 August 1976, ibid., File 318, NMML.

Members of the committee included M. C. Chagla, K. Santhanam, Babubhai Patel, Shanti Bhushan, H. V. Kamath, V. M. Tarkunde, Aloo Dastur. Era Sezhiyan and Krishan Kant were its conveners. The first meeting was held 'in the presence' of Jayaprakash Narayan.

central police or other forces in a state should be only with the state's permission.[60]

Retired Supreme Court judge K. K. Mathew, in a public lecture, said that judicial review by the courts was implicit under a written constitution, for 'it is ... incompatible with the very idea of limited powers to vest this power in Parliament or a committee thereof'.[61] In two articles in the *Times of India* entitled 'Basic Rights of the Citizen', H. M. Seervai wrote that it was an unfounded assumption, based on the battles over the right to property, that the Directive Principles were to secure social justice and the Fundamental Rights were 'mere selfish individual rights'. Once it was understood that the Rights, along with the citations of liberty and equality of status in the Preamble, were designed to serve national objectives, 'the objection to judicial review loses its force'.[62] P. B. Mukharjee, retired chief justice of the Calcutta High Court, often a critic of the Constitution, declared that 'If Parliament represents the will of the people, then the Courts and the Judiciary represent the conscience of the people.'

In Madras, a civil liberties conference suggested a complex amending process where the basic features of the Constitution were involved. Amendments could be enacted only with a three-fourths majority of each House in Parliament, approval of the assemblies of at least fifteen states having two-thirds of the country's population and area, and approval by sixty per cent of adult voters in a referendum.[63] Among the basic features, the conference listed adult suffrage, responsible government, the Fundamental Rights, federation, and an independent judiciary. Speaking at this conference, K. Santhanam said there should

[60] At the beginning of May, a symposium held by the Bar Association of India with C. K. Daphtary presiding, had produced other suggestions. Shanti Bhushan agreed with the idea of seven-judge benches, but not a two-thirds majority vote, for deciding constitutional cases. Fali Nariman wished to preserve the 'any other purpose' language in the high courts' powers to issue writs, but he would accept an amendment that a writ would not lie where an efficacious remedy existed. Danial Latifi suggested amending the Criminal Procedure Code and other laws so that 'stays' would be valid for only forty-eight hours unless adequate reasons for a longer 'stay' had been given. *Statesman*, 3 May 1976.

[61] Mathew in his *Sir Tej Bahadur Sapru Memorial Lecture*, 26 March 1976, *India Backgrounders*, vol. 1, no. 2. This from the justice who at the time of the 1973 supersession of judges was thought by some as close to Mohan Kumaramangalam in his views.

[62] *Times of India*, 26–7 May 1976.

[63] 'Resolutions adopted at the Civil Liberties Conference Held at Rasika Ranjani Hall', Madras, 18 July 1976. (Jayaprakash Narayan Papers, 3rd Installment, Subject File 265, NMML.)

Shanti Bhushan chaired two other meetings in Madras, this time in September in the Town Hall.

be no internal emergency for the whole country and an emergency might be declared only in a state where law and order had broken down. A seminar in Bangalore by the State Citizens Committee opposed amending Articles 226 and 227, called for judicial review of judgements by tribunals, and agreed with the National Committee for Review of the Constitution that there should be no amendments until after an election at the end of the Emergency so the will of the people could be known.[64] Speaking in Parliament earlier, the Law Minister said that the very persons talking of democracy have 'been creating obstacles ... in the functioning of democracy ... [E]ven Satan quoted the Bible.'[65]

The cleverest and most biting assault on the Swaran Singh Committee proposals, and on the Emergency in general, came from the Communist Party Marxist.[66] The CPM pamphlet, after its ritual castigation of the Constitution and the system of government as anti-people and pro-capitalist, said that the parliamentary system's enemies came from the exploiting classes and that blaming the judiciary for the failure of social and economic reforms was the government's trick 'just to establish an alibi'. When Congress had a two-thirds majority in both houses it did not amend the Constitution because of 'its own solicitude' for vested interests. How had the freedom of speech interfered with implementing the Directive Principles, asked the tract. Judicial review and Article 226 served the common man, it said, and it warned of the executive subverting the people's freedoms and 'abrogating' the Constitution 'under the cover of supremacy of Parliament'.[67]

The striking differences in the positions taken by the CPM and the

---

[64] K. S. Hegde, present in Bangalore, also critiqued the Swaran Singh Committee report in a document circulated about this time. If carried out, he wrote, these suggested amendments 'would disturb ... the existing federal set up substantially' and might 'establish ... a dictatorship of the central executive, the constitutional garb notwithstanding'. K. S. Hegde, 'Proposed Constitutional Amendments—Background Paper', Jayaprakash Narayan Papers, Third Installment, Subject File 320, NMML.

[65] *Lok Sabha Debates*, Fifth Series, vol. 59, no. 19, col. 285. Gokhale was speaking on K. P. Unnikrishnan's resolution about changing the Constitution.

[66] *Communist Party of India (Marxist) on Constitutional Changes*, CPI(M), New Delhi, June 1976. The text of this pamphlet reproduced almost exactly an earlier one, *Left Parties on Constitutional Changes*, signed for the CPM by Jyoti Basu and representatives of six other parties, no date. The pamphlet was released by Basu at a press conference in Calcutta on 11 June. Brahmanand Papers, Subject File 50, NMML.

CPM member of Parliament Somnath Chatterjee on an earlier occasion said that the amending article of the Constitution was being used 'to put some persons above the law' *Lok Sabha Debates*, Fifth Series, vol. 59, no. 19, cols 301–8.

[67] Ibid. p. 6. The pamphlet has been attributed to no single author. It was cleared by party politburo before publication, according to Basavupanaiah, then a secretary general

CPI toward the Emergency and the government's intentions toward the Constitution may be explained by the realism of the one and the irrealism of the other. The CPM knew it would never come wholly or partially to power on Mrs Gandhi's 'saree tails'. The CPM held power in two states, and, if it had hopes of gaining national influence, democratic institutions and the freedoms of the Fundamental Rights were essential. The CPI believed that supporting Mrs Gandhi would bring the implementation of at least some of its social-economic policies and that it could warm itself in the glow of the Prime Minister's authoritarian fires without being burnt. Some CPI members began to appreciate their error when the Forty-second Amendment made its debut in Parliament. By the end of the Emergency, all but the blind had seen their mistake.

Soon-to-retire Law Commission Chairman Gajendragadkar rendered his verdict on the Swaran Singh Committee in a letter to Mrs Gandhi after she was out of office. Saying that he hoped she appreciated that he was not carping, and assuring her that he held her 'personally in high esteem', he reminded her of his advice that amendment of the fundamental law of the land should not have been left to a party committee and that the proper 'modality' would have been a committee of experts to hear all parties and persons, including interned leaders. The committee Borooah appointed, he said, had worked in a hurry, discussed issues in a casual manner, and 'based its recommendations mainly on political considerations'.[68]

---

of the party, in an interview with the author. In twenty-six recommendations, the CPM strongly defended the Fundamental Rights by calling for the removal from the Constitution of five threats to them: the portions of the Twenty-fourth and Twenty-fifth Amendments allowing amendment of the Constitution at the expense of the Fundamental Rights; Article 31C, because 'under it, all fundamental rights can be over-ridden'; automatic suspension of access to the courts for protection of the Rights under Article 19 during an emergency; government power of preventive detention under Article 22; and placing laws other than those for social-economic reforms in the Ninth Schedule.

In one of its more piquant aspects, agreeing with Justice Subba Rao, the CPM said that constitutional amendments should be considered 'law' under Article 13. The pamphlet also said that the Constitution specifically should provide for protection of its basic features, namely India as a parliamentary republic, adult franchise, accountability of the executive to the legislature, protection of the Fundamental Rights, and judicial review of legislation until any conflict between the Parliament and the executive could be resolved by referendum. Regarding centre–state relations, the pamphlet recommended that the President's emergency powers should be 'drastically amended' so that an emergency could be declared only if there were war or external aggression and Articles 356, 357, and 360 should be deleted to end presidential dissolution of state governments and presidential interference in a state government on the ground of financial instability.

[68] Letter dated 24 August 1977. P. B. Gajendragadkar Papers, NMML.

Chapter 17

THE FORTY-SECOND AMENDMENT: SACRIFICING DEMOCRACY TO POWER

'The process of amending the Constitution ... is becoming curiouser and curiouser,' wrote noted political scientist S. V. Kogekar. The recommendations of the Swaran Singh Committee had 'disappeared into some lobbies somewhere, into some rooms in the Secretariat', charged CPI leader Bhupesh Gupta, 'and there, the tampering with recommendations started by some officials and ... some others ... to smuggle in things ... absolutely unnecessary ... from the point of view of socio-economic changes'.[1]

The government thought differently. The Constitution was to be amended to strengthen the strands of the seamless web: 'to spell out expressly the high ideals of socialism, secularism and integrity of the nation ... and give ... [the Directive Principles] precedence over those Fundamental Rights that had frustrated the Principles' implementation', said the Forty-fourth Amendment Bill's 'Statement of Objects and Reasons'.[2] The Constitution 'to be living must be growing', it continued. For the Prime Minister, as she said, 'keenly conscious of the high significance' of the bill, its purpose was 'to remedy the anomalies that have been long noticed and to overcome obstacles put up by economic and political vested interests'. The Constitution must provide 'order and stability ... and law', Mrs Gandhi added. The bill 'is responsive to the aspirations of the people, and reflects the realities of the present time and the future'.[3]

---

[1] Kogekar, S. V., 'Constitution Amendment Bill', *Economic and Political Weekly*, vol. 11, no. 42, 16 October 1976. Gupta in *Parliamentary Debates, Rajya Sabha*, vol. 98, no. 5, col. 47, 9 November 1976. Gupta, a friend of Mrs Gandhi for many years, added in this speech that this 'tampering' had been 'behind [the back of] the AICC ... [and] the Congress Working Committee' to introduce twenty-seven new items 'not warranted' by the Swaran Singh Committee recommendations.

Indrajit Gupta, no relation, had expressed similar sentiments in the Lok Sabha.

[2] This bill became the Forty-second Amendment and will be referred to in this way. For the 'Statement of Objects and Reasons', see 'The Constitution (Forty-Fourth Amendment) Bill, 1976', in *Government Bills as Introduced in the Lok Sabha, 1976*, Parliament Secretariat, New Delhi, 1976.

[3] Speech in the Lok Sabha, 27 October 1976. *Lok Sabha Debates*, Fifth Series, vol. 65,

Strange things had happened on the way from Kamagata Maru to Parliament House, where on 1 September 1976 in the Lok Sabha H. R. Gokhale introduced the amending bill to cheers. Debate on the bill began on 25 October, it passed in the Rajya Sabha on 11 November, and the President assented to it on 18 December upon ratification by thirteen state legislatures. This chapter will summarize the essence of the Forty-second Amendment, the government's and critics' contention over it, and consider the puzzle of the amendment's drafting. It also will examine a strange event of the time: an apparent attempt to derail the amendment entirely and substitute a presidential for the parliamentary system.

The Amendment

Building on the Swaran Singh Committee proposals, the amendment's twenty pages of clauses had four main purposes: to further protect from legal challenges Mrs Gandhi's 1971 election to Parliament and future elections of her and her followers; to strengthen the central government *visà-vis* the state governments and its capability to rule the country as a unitary, not a federal, system; to give maximum protection from judicial chalenge to social revolutionary legislation—whether intended sincerely or to cloak authoritarian purpose; 'to trim' the judiciary, as one Congressman put it, so as to 'make it difficult for the Court to upset her policy in regard to many matters'.[4] The headsman's axe had not fallen definitively on liberty and democracy, but its edge was being honed. A few of the amendment's changes were aimed at bringing generally supported reforms, and would be retained by the votes of both Congress and Janata Party members of Parliament when other provisions in the amendment were repealed.

In the category protecting social revolutionary legislation from judicial challenge, the amendment—after adopting the Swaran Singh Commitee's expansion of Article 31C giving all the Directive Principles precedence over the Fundamental Rights and its assignment to tribunals

---

no. 3, cols.141–2. Speech reprinted under the title 'Parliament Has Unfettered Right' in *Indira Gandhi, Selected Speeches and Writings*, vol. 3, pp. 283–91.

H. R. Gokhale voiced an argument that became popular at the time when he said that easy amendment of the Constitution was a 'safety valve'. A rigid process could result in violence. Gokhale had retreaded the 'argument of fear' that Chief Justice Subba Rao had employed to protect the Constitution from depredations from one-party rule (ch. 8).

[4] For the text of the Forty-second Amendment, see *Constitution Amendment in India*, Lok Sabha Secretariat, pp. 290–320.

of tax, land reform etc. matters—added a replacement Article 226. The new article prohibited high courts from issuing stay orders relating to 'any work or project of public utility'. No court was to have any jurisdiction over tribunals, although the Supreme Court could accept appeals from them, and cases pending before a court could be transferred to a tribunal. A new Article 32A prohibited the Supreme Court from considering the constitutionality of a state law unless the validity of a central law was also at issue—thus cutting deeply into the citizen's recourse to Article 32 to protect his fundamental rights. High courts still could determine the constitutionality of state laws.

The Swaran Singh report's suggestion that Parliament be empowered to legislate against abuses of the 'freedoms' in Article 19 seems to have lain behind the amendment's Article 31D, prohibiting 'anti-national activities'. According to this potentially totalitarian provision, no law for this purpose was to be unconstitutional because inconsistent with Fundamental Rights Articles 14, 19, and 31. Among the activities defined as anti-national, in addition to advocating secession from the nation, were questioning the sovereignty and integrity of India, intending to create internal disturbance, and intending to 'disrupt harmony' among society's various groups. These understandable sentiments had been fed before and during the Emergency by the 'phobia we had created', in V. N. Gadgil's words, about external and internal conspiracies against the government. Sanjay Gandhi's enmity toward any political opposition likely contributed to the article's inclusion. 'There was full support in the party for banning anti-national activities,' Sheila Dikshit recollected; 'the problem was defining them.'[5]

The amendment entirely excluded the courts from election disputes. It failed to include the committee's recommendation that a nine-member body decide on disputed elections of the President, Vice-President, Prime Minister, and Speaker. The amendment placed the decision about disqualification for membership in Parliament and in a state legislature—had a person been found guilty of corrupt practices in an election—unrestrictedly in the hands of the President and the governor by providing that either had only to *consult* the Election Commission (new Articles 103 and 192). Under the original Constitution, the President and the governor on such occasions were *bound by* the advice of the Election Commission. In legislatures having Congress Party majorities with governors appointed by the central government, and with the President bound to act on the advice of the council of ministers, basically Indira

[5] In an interview with the author.

Gandhi would decide disputes relating to corrupt practices in elections nationwide. In an echo of Mrs Gandhi's Election case—going beyond the Thirty-ninth Amendment—the amendment provided that no court could require production before it of the government's Transaction of Business Rules.

The amendment strengthened New Delhi's power *vis-à-vis* the states in several ways. It incorporated the Swaran Singh Committee recommendation that federal forces operate under federal control when in a state to preserve order, making no mention, as had the committee, of consulting the state government concerned before sending the forces. Its changes to the 'Emergency Provisions' went far beyond the committee's recommendation by enabling Parliament to make laws for any state if the security of India were threatened by activities in that state *related to* (author's emphasis) those in the area under emergency (Articles 353 and 358). Similarly, a new proviso to Article 359 permitted laws to be made and executive action to be taken contravening the Fundamental Rights in states not under emergency.[6] Centre–state relations were altered also by denying high courts the authority to rule on the constitutionality of central laws (new Articles 226A and 228A).

Further 'trimming' the judiciary, the amendment incorporated the Swaran Singh Committee's recommendation that Supreme Court and high court benches that would rule on the constitutionality of state or central laws must have seven and five judges, respectively, and take decisions by two-thirds majorities (new Articles 144A and 228A). The government's epitaph for the Supreme Court's most fundamental function, the power to review constitutional amendments, came in its adoption of the Swaran Singh Committee's recommendations regarding Article 368. The Forty-second Amendment said that amendments could not be questioned 'in any court on any ground'; that amendments to the Fundamental Rights were beyond review; and that there shall be no limitation on Parliament's power to amend the Constitution 'by way of addition, variation or repeal'.

The shift in the balance of power within the new Constitution made it all but unrecognizable. The Supreme Court had been divested of much of its original jurisdiction. The high courts had been hobbled. Parliament

---

[6] Also, the amendment provided that any law made during an emergency would remain in force until repealed, whereas in the original Article 357, such laws would lapse after a year. It altered Article 356 so that a proclamation of President's Rule lapsed one year after Parliament initially approved it (unless it were renewed) instead of the six months originally laid down in the Constitution.

had unfettered power to preserve or destroy the Constitution. Parliament now sat in judgement over the elections of its own members and those of the President and Vice-President. The President had to assent to Parliament's enactments as presented by the council of ministers—an addition to Article 74 not among the Swaran Singh proposals, making rigid a convention hitherto minimally flexible. Neither the central nor state governments were restrained from acting in their respective legislatures by quorum requirements for the amendment abolished these. A single government supporter in an otherwise empty house could pass a bill. Parliament's and the legislatures' terms had been extended to six years from five. Finally, the council of ministers had extraordinary powers given by the amendment's final clause. This provided that if there were any difficulties in giving effect to the Constitution as amended, 'the President may, by order', for up to two years, adapt or modify the provision to remove the difficulty. The original Constitution contained such a 'removal-of-difficulties clause' to ease the transition from the 1935 Act. But for Hiren Mukherjee and others, the time of Prasad, Nehru, and Patel was not 1976. '[P]lease don't revive the Henry VIII memory,' said he. There should not be in the Constitution anything that 'even remotely smacks of any potentially authoritarian device'.[7]

Who Were Its Authors?

The Forty-second Amendment's drafters operated out of public view, as said in the previous chapter, and at two levels: the Prime Minister and several individuals around her established the policy content; Law Ministry officials did the actual drafting.[8] S. S. Ray was at the hub of the process, working—sometimes at the Prime Minister's house (the 'PMH', often at odds with the staff of the Prime Minister's Office, the PMO), or at other ministers' houses, or in Rajni Patel's Ashoka Hotel suite—so clandestinely that 'some days even the Intelligence Bureau didn't know where he was', recalled a senior officer in the Delhi police. Collaborating with him were D. K. Borooah and Rajni Patel, and, less important, A. R. Antulay. All thought the Swaran Singh Committee's report inadequate and wanted 'to beef it up', recollected a senior member of the Prime Minister's staff, himself excluded from the creation process.

---

[7] *Lok Sabha Debates*, Fifth Series, vol. 65, no. 2, cols 122–3.

[8] Absolute certainty in assigning the amendment's authorship is impossible due to the unavailability of government documents. But written sources, although sparse, extensive interviews with senior officials of the time and other knowledgeable individuals, and a certain amount of deduction allow the following reconstruction of the drafting process.

Chandrajit Yadav recalled that Ray, Borooah, and Patel—sometimes referred to as the 'three musketeers'—felt frustrated with the Swaran Singh Committee. For himself, Yadav said the Swaran Singh Committee did not achieve our goal, 'so we had to get another way.'[9] Borooah was 'most intensively involved' in the drafting, Mrs Gandhi said publicly in praise.[10] H. R. Gokhale as Law Minister, contributing less to substance, led the team of drafters—he was considered an excellent draftsman— and acted as the link with the drafting officers in his ministry. Minister of State for Home Affairs Om Mehta occasionally advised as Parliamentary Affairs Minister.

The axle around which the wheel turned was the Prime Minister. As Gokhale later explained, 'although the instructions for each amendment and modification were first given to him (Gokhale) either by Siddharth (S. S. Ray) or some aide of the Prime Minister, he always approached her for confirmation. Her reply was always somewhat as follows, "Yes, the members of the Party are pressing hard for it. The chief ministers are also asking for it. You are yourself seeing the situation in the country is serious. What is to be done, this has to be implemented."'[11]

Ray would consult Mrs Gandhi about notes he had made for constitutional changes, consulting from time to time with the others, who agreed with Ray about the new election provisions and the enhanced emergency powers, which increased the Prime Minister's reach. Ray acquiesced, at least for tactical purposes, in Borooah's and Rajni Patel's interest in including the social revolutionary provisions in the draft amendment, interest that was shared by other 'progressives'. 'Parliamentary supremacy', as the mantra of the time, was not contested within this small circle. Patel's influence is seen in the language that the President 'shall' act in accordance with ministerial advice—self-evidently intended doubly to ensure the Prime Minister's control even with an accommodating President like

[9] Yadav in an interview with author.

[10] In a speech on the amendment to the Rajya Sabha. *Indira Gandhi, Selected Speeches and Writings*, vol. 3, p. 292.

[11] Excerpt from B. N. Tandon's 'Diary' dated 26 October 1980, recording a conversation with Gokhale. Tandon and Gokhale had been friendly for some years. Excerpt from the 'Diary' kindly provided to the author by Mr Tandon.

At this time Gokhale told Tandon of his fears during the Emergency, which are otherwise widely spoken of among India's judicial community. Asked by Tandon why 'he did not opt out of the government', given his strong dislike of much that was happening, 'Gokhale admitted that he was scared to resign during the Emergency. He firmly believed that if he did so the Prime Minister would send him to jail.' '"Bishan, you might consider it my weakness or anything else, the fact is that I did not want to go to jail."' Ibid. Gokhale was a 'frightened man', according to another official, and was made miserable by his 'judicial conscience'.

Fakhruddin Ali Ahmed. Banning anti-national activities and organizations fitted the mood in government. Apparently the 'progressives' among the drafters foresaw no dangers in these provisions to themselves and to the Communist Party of India. Antulay's recommendation in his 'A Fresh Look' paper—which lay behind Article 31D—that 'communal and fascist anti-national and anti-social organizations must be banned' was from its use of Congress code words, aimed at opposition political parties and at the Hindu parties, especially.[12] The drafters concentrated on increasing the central government's and the Prime Minister's authority, willing to sacrifice democracy for this greater cause and using the amendment's social revolutionary provisions toward this end. 'Patel', as K. P. Unnikrishnan said, 'sought solutions in power'.[13] Mrs Gandhi, said V. N. Gadgil, wanted to 'consolidate the things she thought she had achieved by the Emergency'.[14]

With the policy path cleared and with the Prime Minister's agreement to proceed, Ray would have Gokhale summon the Secretary of the Law Ministry's Legislative Department, K. K. Sundaram, to Gokhale's or some other residence. Sundaram led the secret drafting process at the ministry, doing much of the work himself at night with day-time help from a subordinate officer, Mrs Ramadevi, and others. A ministry committee, officially chaired by Gokhale (but typically he was absent) seems to have discussed the various drafts of the amending bill, which would be sent to Ray, commented upon, and returned to Sundaram for drafting revisions.

Two lengthy cabinet meetings took up the draft on 21 and 23 August, perhaps following meetings of the Political Affairs Committee. The Law Ministry's note for the cabinet dated 20 August 1976, and the accompanying text of the amendment had reached the ministers on 20 August.[15] Several persons who attended the cabinet meetings, sometimes chaired by Y. B. Chavan in the Prime Minister's absence, remembered only general discussion in them and no dissent.[16] A week after the final cabinet meeting, the Law Minister introduced the amendment in Parliament. Consideration was scheduled to begin on 25 October.

[12] See text of paper, in Noorani, *Presidential System*, p. 112.

[13] K. P. Unnikrishnan in an interview with the author.

[14] V. N. Gadgil in an interview with the author.

[15] Nurul Hasan, Minister of Education, attending the meetings by invitation, because not a member of the Cabinet, to B. N. Tandon and Tandon in a letter to the author.

[16] Om Mehta was one of these individuals interviewed by the author. For an extensive description and analysis of the Swaran Singh Committee and the Forty-second Amendment see Dhavan, Rajeev, *The Amendment: Conspiracy or Revolution?*, Wheeler Publishing, Allahabad, 1978.

Four Mysterious Resolutions

Five days before consideration of the bill was to begin, resolutions of mysterious origin in four Congress-ruled states threatened its extinction. In Bihar on 20 October, Chief Minister Jagannath Mishra, legislators, and Pradesh Congress Committee (PCC) members resolved that the amendment be sent to parliamentary drafting committees for scrutiny, as had been done in the Constituent Assembly.[17] In Punjab, the Congress state legislature party unanimously voted for convening a constituent assembly to rewrite and recast the entire Constitution.[18] Chief Minister Zail Singh, Deputy Railway Minister in the central government, Buta Singh, and Sardar Swaran Singh were present. The latter did not speak, was reported to be surprised by the development, and had to hurry from Chandigarh to New Delhi to chair the last meeting of his own Swaran Singh Committee that afternoon. In Haryana, former Chief Minister and now Defence Minister Bansi Lal and the Chief Minister Banarasi Das Gupta plus members of the PCC and Congress Legislature Party resolved in favour of a new constituent assembly.[19] The vice-president of the Haryana PCC told a reporter that there had been no central direction involved; he had drafted the resolution in his car on the way from Delhi that morning.

Events in Uttar Pradesh were even more bizarre. In Lucknow, Congress party members of Parliament from the state, state legislators, PCC members, and presidents of Congress-controlled zilla parishads met to discuss two resolutions: one welcoming the Emergency and the achievements of the Twenty-Point Programme and the other to welcome amendments to the Constitution 'based on the recommendations of the Swaran Singh Committee'.[20] Instead, the meeting resolved that Parliament be converted into a constituent assembly with additional representatives from the states 'to draft a fundamental law for the country'.[21] Among the senior Congressmen present were Kamalapati Tripathi, Uma Shankar Dikshit, K. C. Pant (all three Indira Gandhi loyalists), K. D. Malaviya, and Chandrajit Yadav. Coming by aircraft to attend the meeting, Mrs Gandhi was met at the airport by K. C. Pant—at Tripathi's suggestion—to learn from him that the resolution already had been adopted. Speaking to the

[17] *Times of India,* 21 October 1976.
[18] Ibid.
[19] The resolution also rejected the basic structure doctrine. *Tribune,* Chandigarh, 22 October 1976.
[20] *Statesman,* New Delhi, 21 October 1976.
[21] Ibid.

group shortly later, the Prime Minister said she had suggested that PCC presidents meet to discuss the recommendations of the Swaran Singh Committee and the provisions of the amending bill (presumably to endorse them), and she expressed surprise that a resolution had been adopted so swiftly. Parliament was fully empowered to amend the Constitution, she said.[22] Adding to the mystery, a paper advocating change to a presidential system was circulating at this Lucknow meeting, and no one seemed to know whence it came. 'We were all totally taken aback,' by its appearance, recalled Chandrajit Yadav, and by the 'word going round that Indira wanted it'.[23] A fifth state, Rajasthan, was to have joined the four, but declined. Around 20 October at least four other PCCs met, apparently at the urging of Mrs Gandhi through party channels. The resolutions they passed were limited to praising and supporting the Forty-second Amendment.[24]

Various motives have been ascribed to the not-accidental coincidence of the four resolutions. They had the common theme of prolonging and increasing power for the Prime Minister and those nearest to her. But it was not immediately apparent whether the Prime Minister and those nearest her were acting in concert. The device for enhancing Mrs Gandhi's power was to be the introduction of a presidential system, which meant convening a constituent assembly and drafting a new constitution, according to the analysis of the Communist Party of India, Chandrajit Yadav, and L. K. Advani, among others. '[T]he motive seemed to be to concentrate power in the hands of an individual,' Advani later wrote. 'Democracy was a nuisance in the country ... it was desired to have a benevolent dictatorship, and the presidential system seemed a euphemism for benevolent dictatorship.'[25] Another motive for convening a

---

[22] *Times of India*, 22 October 1976.

[23] Interview with the author. This account of events in Lucknow is drawn, also, from the author's interviews with K. C. Pant and Sheila Dikshit.

[24] In addition to the sources cited, see *Consembly Move and Democratic Fightback*, Communist Party of India, New Delhi, November 1976; *India Backgrounder*, 20 December 1976; *AR*, 9–15 December 1976, p. 19488; and *Hindustan Times*, 21–2 October 1976.

The idea of a second constituent assembly was not new. The government had found it necessary to reject calls for one during debate on the Nath Pai Bill in 1967. Lohia socialists of the Samyukta Socialist Party called for one at their Jabalpur conference in 1969 and reiterated the demand in its 1971 election manifesto. Madhu Limaye had called for a new assembly in 1973. And in the summer and autumn of 1975 President Ahmed suggested a new assembly might be necessary and Uma Shankar Dikshit threatened one right after the dissolution of the Kesavananda Bharati Review bench. In general, over the years, the CPI had opposed convening a constituent assembly, and the CPM had favoured it.

[25] L. K. Advani, 'Antidote to Divisive Forces' in Sathe, Vasant, *Two Swords in One Scabbard*, NIB Publishers, New Delhi, 1989, pp. 137–8. Sathe's book is sub-titled *A Case for*

constituent assembly was simply to prolong the existing power situation. With Parliament converted into an assembly, as foreseen in the Lucknow resolution, there would be no elections—then due in March 1977 (the Lok Sabha had not yet extended its term by another year, which would be done on 4 November). Parliament's term would be extended *de facto*, and the Emergency would remain in place. There were two other, less popular, theories: that constituent assembly passage either of the Forty-second Amendment or of a new constitution would preempt the Supreme Court from using the 'basic structure' doctrine to strike the amendment down, and that the threat of a constituent assembly would induce the Supreme Court to uphold the amendment were it challenged.

Observers in New Delhi speculated energetically about the resolutions' origins. They could have come only from the Prime Minister or Sanjay Gandhi, many agreed. The questions were which one, and could Sanjay Gandhi have moved without his mother's knowledge? 'Indira Gandhi sponsored the resolutions directly or indirectly,' according to Chandrajit Yadav. 'Sanjay wanted this, there was a lot of presidential system talk in the CPP, and Mrs Gandhi called me in to take the temperature,' recalled Ambika Soni, then President of the Youth Congress and close to Sanjay Gandhi.[26] 'Probably Sanjay was behind it', thought K. P. Unnikrishnan. 'Indira must have known and waited to see the fall-out.' 'It must have come from Indira,' thought V. N. Gadgil, because she had been advised that elections could be postponed under this pretext, and 'you could kill two to three years'. 'It must have been inspired by the coterie, who wanted to appear democratic when they were not,' said P.N. Haksar. 'It was Sanjay's doing,' recalled a cabinet minister of the time.[27] 'Bansi Lal and others, who

---

Presidential Form of Parliamentary Democracy, again blurring the line between those who advocated a 'presidential system' and those wanting to 'strengthen' the parliamentary system by, say, having a directly elected prime minister.

The CPI charged that 'reactionary forces' intended to stall the elections with the 'ominous aim' of subverting parliamentary supremacy with the 'obnoxious idea' of a presidential system. CPI, *Consembly Move and Democratic Fightback*.

This description of motives and the speculation about individuals is drawn from two dozen interviews.

[26] Soni interview with the author. Soni told the Prime Minister the idea 'was alienating people'. P. B. Gajendragadkar told the Prime Minister that convening a constituent assembly would be unconstitutional. Among the then supporters of a presidential system, Soni listed Shashi Bhushan, a junior member of the coterie, Yashpal Kapoor, Rajni Patel, and, possibly Borooah.

Bansi Lal had commended a presidential system to Mrs Gandhi, she told K. C. Pant. Pant interview with the author.

[27] P. N. Haksar in an interview with the author.

did not want her to go to the polls, started campaigning for a new constituent assembly to draw up a new constitution,' wrote G. K. Reddy in *The Hindu*.[28] 'Maybe Bansi Lal or some state leaders put the idea in Sanjay's head,' thought H. Y. Sharada Prasad, the Prime Minister's Information Adviser, 'on the supposition that if the son propounds, mother will accept'.[29] Sanjay Gandhi's involvement with the Haryana and Punjab resolutions is supported by his close relationship with Bansi Lal and Zail Singh.

There were elements of truth and one major misapprehension in this speculation. According to the Prime Minister's Principal Secretary, Professor P. N. Dhar, initiative for the resolutions came from Bansi Lal, inspired by A. R. Antulay's 'Fresh Look' paper, who 'sold' the idea to Sanjay Gandhi. Together, they arranged the resolutions without the Prime Minister's knowledge. Their passage alarmed Mrs Gandhi.[30] Sanjay Gandhi and Bansi Lal intended damage to democratic government going far beyond that already done by the provisions of the Forty-second Amendment.[31]

Negative reaction to the resolutions was immediate and sharp. The National Committee for Review of the Constitution rejected both a new constituent assembly and Parliament's competence to amend the Constitution in the manner of the current bill. The CPI opposed a constituent assembly, in an official resolution calling it a 'sinister move'. The CPM, although calling for a constituent assembly and for withdrawing the amending bill, was of a different mind from the progenitors of the state resolutions. The new constituent assembly should be directly elected according to proportional representation and take at least six months to consider either drafting a new constitution or amending the current one.[32] The *National Herald*, still loyal to the Nehrus, called the resolutions 'futile' because Parliament's authority to amend any part of the Constitution was 'generally accepted'.[33] Mrs Gandhi told the Parliamentary

[28] Issue of 2 November 1980.

[29] In an interview with the author. Bansi Lal was strongly for prolonging the Emergency, according to Vasant Sathe (in an interview), accompanied by Sanjay Gandhi, V. C. Shukla, Om Mehta, and Borooah.

[30] P. N. Dhar interview with the author. The accuracy of Dhar's version is confirmed by H. Y. Sharada Prasad. Both held high positions on Mrs Gandhi's staff.

[31] During the Emergency, Bansi Lal said to B. K. Nehru, '[G] et rid of all this election nonsense ... [J] ust make our sister (Mrs Gandhi) President for life and there's no need to do anything else.' Nehru, *Nice Guys Finish Second*, p. 559.

[32] The CPM also called for lifting the Emergency and ending censorship.

[33] Editorial of 22 October 1976. The newspaper continued that any constituent assembly would follow general elections and not precede them, and an assembly 'would

Party on 23 October that Parliament had the power to amend the Constitution as it wished, and she told the Lok Sabha four days later that there was no need for a constituent assembly.[34]

The Amendment's Supporters and Opponents

H. R. Gokhale moved consideration of the bill at noon on 25 October. The cabinet had decided to proceed the previous evening particularly to offset publicity about a constituent assembly.[35] Minister of Parliamentary Affairs K. Raghuramaiah said only government business could be transacted during the special session, which opposition parties had boycotted, contending that Parliament, having outlived its five-year term, was not competent to amend the Constitution.[36] Gokhale told members that of the bill's fifty-nine clauses only seven or eight were substantive. These were 'primarily and pre-eminently' to remove obstacles to achieving the nation's social and economic objectives. He reiterated arguments, often made before: Parliament was supreme because it represented the people; Parliament now could give effect to the Directive Principles by law; the basic structure of the Constitution was unaltered ('all that is regarded as basic to a federal structure is there'); and the bill did not lessen the reach of the courts. '[I]f at all the powers have been to a certain extent widened,' he contended, and 'they are not taken away in all matters in which really judicial action is justified'.[37]

When it was his turn to speak, Swaran Singh characterized the amendments relating to the courts as 'comparatively moderate'. When reviewing constitutional amendments, he said, the courts 'transgressed

---

be justified' only if there were thoughts of changing to the French or American system of government.

[34] Mrs Gandhi to the CPP: *Statesman*, 24 October 1976. Mrs Gandhi to the Lok Sabha: *Lok Sabha Debates*, Fifth Series, vol. 65, no. 3, col. 141.

The idea 'is by no means dead' wrote Kuldip Nayar in the *Indian Express*, 17 November.

[35] *Consembly Move and Democratic Fightback*, p. 18. The pamphlet reported that one cabinet member, unnamed, favouring a constituent assembly, had dissented.

[36] Three hundred and seventy of the Lok Sabha membership of 545 attended this special session. The others had boycotted it or were in jail. Six hundred amendments to the amending bill had by this time been preferred, according to the news agency Samachar.

[37] *Lok Sabha Debates*, Fifth Series, vol. 65, no. 1 cols 49–65, and, for the last quotation, pp. 61–2.

A decision to appoint a state law commission to suggest judicial reforms, improvements in judicial administration, and whether or not new laws would be necessary to implement the Directive Principles was announced by Maharashtra Chief Minister S. B. Chavan, on 27 October. *Statesman*, 28 October 1976.

the limits prescribed for them'. Parliamentary supremacy was 'axiomatic'; it was 'chaotic and ... unacceptable to Parliament ... [that] a single judge sitting in a remote part of the country ... [could] declare [an Act] ultra vires'. And tribunals would effectively handle highly technical subjects such as taxes, distribution of foodgrains, and civil service matters because their members would have the 'requisite expertise', and be independent, thereby inspiring confidence.[38]

The Prime Minister spoke to the Lok Sabha again in terms of the seamless web. The amendment was 'to restore the health of our democracy ... [and was] responsive to the aspirations of the people', she said. Its incorporation of 'secular' and 'socialist' in the Preamble 'will provide the frame of reference to all'. The new anti-national activities provision was necessary to protect national unity and integrity. Congress would never liquidate opposition parties, she asserted, and 'the preaching of dismemberment of India ... inciting communal or provincial hatred and violence is anti-national ...'. She linked the article and her Emergency in the same breath, asking what was the agitation before the Emergency 'except to throw aside the Constitution?' In the light of this, the Opposition's criticism of the amending bill was 'not so plausible'.[39] In the Rajya Sabha, she declared that there was 'nothing radical or new in ... [the] amendments'. As was her wont, the best defence was a grain of truth in a good offence. The Prime Minister attacked the opposition parties' absence from the House as 'escaping responsibility'. It was the opposition's 'abuse of democracy' and obstruction of its 'legitimate functioning' that had caused all the difficulties in the first place, she alleged.[40]

Anti-judiciary sentiment was notably strong in both Houses during the debate. Leaders set a harsh tone. Gokhale damned judicial review as undemocratic because what is democratically done by elected representatives 'is set at naught by people who are not so elected ... We should

---

[38] *Lok Sabha Debates*, Fifth Series, vol. 65. no. 2, cols 22–43.

[39] Ibid., no. 3, cols 135–47.

[40] During the parliamentary debate, A. R. Antulay outdid himself in praise of the Prime Minister. She had 'driven out of the Congress' members who would not implement Nehru's socialist programmes. It had been left to Nehru's 'proud daughter, the daughter of the Indian Nation, the daughter of India, ancient, present and future' to bring into effect what Nehru 'had visualized at Bhubaneshwar'. *Parliamentary Debates, Rajya Sabha*, vol. 98, no. 1, col. 61.

Antulay thought differently in an interview in 1994. Indira Gandhi wanted to be a dictator, which is why in October 1976, she wanted a presidential system, Antulay said. But you can't be a dictator in a presidential system, he continued. I wanted such a system for its checks and balances and to protect minorities and secularism through direct election of a president.

follow it up (the amendment) by having a complete review and restructuring of the judicial system'.[41] Swaran Singh Committee member C. M. Stephen threatened more explicitly with Parliament's powers now 'without any limit', if the courts had the 'temerity ... to defy ... [this] it will be a bad day for the judiciary. The committee of the House is sitting with regard to the enquiry into the conduct of judges ... We have our methods, our machinery.'[42] If the law comes in the way of our doing things, said Gokhale, Parliament must see that the law conforms to the aspirations of the people. 'It is for that purpose that even the fundamental law is being amended to see that no one at any time can say that anything extra-constitutional was done, that something illegal was done.'[43] Using this definition of constitutionality, the law could again devour the law.

The Prime Minister, Borooah, and Antulay even had discovered a judicial conspiracy. Antulay: 'The conspiracy started in 1967 when the Chief Justice (K. Subba Rao) resigned to contest' for the presidency; and it continued through the intervening years in attempts to thwart Mrs Gandhi.[44] Borooah: 'It is not the political belief of the judges ... [I]t is the political ambition that entered by the portals of the Supreme Court and judicial restraint and discretion escaped by the window' when a chief justice campaigned for the presidency.[45] Mrs Gandhi: Justice Subha Rao's action 'was a blatant indication, not only of the political bias of some of the judiciary, but of their intention to be involved in and interfere in politics ... [I]t was symptomatic of the basic struggle ... against everything that the Congress Party ... had advocated and struggled for ...'.[46]

The amendment's critics had opened fire immediately upon the bill's introduction on 1 September. A *Statesman* editorial of 2 September said

[41] *Parliamentary Debates, Rajya Sabha*, vol. 98, no. 5, col. 15.

Gokhale was on sounder ground when he said, also, that there had been 'judicial somersaults' and 'sometimes it was very difficult to understand really what the law of the land is'. *Lok Sabha Debates*, Fifth Series, vol. 65, no. 1, cols 49–65.

A *Statesman* editorial on 12 November said that Gokhale 'has just confirmed the citizen's worst suspicions ... [by] talking of a basic restructuring of the judicial system and legal education rather than how socio-economic progress can be achieved'.

Congress President Borooah already had suggested that Gokhale examine restructuring the judicial system.

[42] *Lok Sabha Debates*, Fifth Series, vol. 65, no. 8, col. 149.

[43] *Parliamentary Debates, Rajya Sabha*, vol. 98, no. 2, col. 34.

[44] *Parliamentary Debates, Rajya Sabha*, vol. 98, no. 2, col. 63.

[45] Ibid., no. 3, col. 40.

[46] *Lok Sabha Debates* Fifth Series, vol. 65, no. 3, col. 138. The AICC later published a pamphlet containing Mrs Gandhi's speeches on the bill in the Lok Sabha and the Rajya Sabha.

'by one sure stroke the amendment tilts the constitutional balance in favour of Parliament ... further strengthens the Centre, disciplines parties, and circumscribes the judiciary'. Two days later, Krishan Kant wrote to Congress(O) President Ashoka Mehta inviting him to nominate members to a new group named the People's Union for Civil Liberties and Democratic Rights, formed several days earlier by V. M. Tarkunde and others 'to strive for the restoration and strengthening of civil liberties and democratic rights'.[47] Mehta obliged, and the People's Union held meetings and published statements. A similar organization, Citizens for Democracy, published a major pamphlet.[48] A delegation including former Attorney General and President of the Supreme Court Bar Association, C. K. Daphtary, and R. K. Garg told the Prime Minister and the Law Minister that the basic structure should be retained, although property could be removed from the Fundamental Rights, and the anti-national activities provision should be deleted because 'an authoritarian or unscrupulous regime could abuse it'.[49] 'Women Oppose Changes in Basic Law' headlined the *Statesman*, reporting a meeting attended by such prominent figures as Sardar Vallabhbhai Patel's daughter, Maniben Patel, Mrs A. K. Gopalan, and Mrs Madhu Limaye.[50] Krishan Kant convened a seminar sponsored by the National Committee for Review of the Constitution, which adopted the 'National Consensus Statement' demanding postponement of the bill and containing detailed criticisms of it.[51] The

---

[47] AICC (Congress (O)) letter to Working Committee members and others, including text of Kant's letter, 4 September 1976. Jayaprakash Narayan Papers, Third Installment, Subject File 318, NMML.

[48] *Democracy and Constitution*, Citizens for Democracy, Pune, 1976. The authors were S. P. Sathe, Principal of a Pune law college, V. M. Tarkunde, and V. A. Naik, both former judges of the Bombay High Court, E.M.S. Namboodiripad, and the chief editor of the *Indian Express*.

[49] *Statesman*, 13 October 1976.

[50] *Statesman*, 26 October 1976. Others present included Mrs K. Hingorani, Miss Rani Jethmalani, Mrs Danial Latifi, Mrs Sushma Swaraj, and Miss Lily Thomas.

[51] Present, among others, were Daphtary, Tarkunde, M. C. Chagla, H. V. Kamath, Sarvepalli Gopal (President Radhakrishnan's son), Romesh Thapar, Mulk Raj Anand, Nikhil Chakravarty, A. K. Gopalan, E. M. S. Namboodiripad, Charan Singh, Soli Sorabjee, S. L. Saxena, and Era Sezhian. The Consensus Statement was published in pamphlet form on 4 December: *Nation-wide Demand for Postponement of Constitution Amendment Bill*, National Book Centre, New Delhi, 1976. The pamphlet also included articles by several of the seminar's participants.

Mrs Gandhi's supporters organized a meeting, parallel to this seminar, named the 'Convention on Constitutional Amendments'. Inaugurating it, D. K. Borooah said that laws made by the people should not be scrutinized by the courts. *Statesman*, 17 October 1976.

Opposition presented a 'Statement by Intellectuals'—with five hundred signatures—to the President, Prime Minister, Speaker, and Chairman of the Rajya Sabha on 25 October. It, too, called for postponement of the bill on the ground that Parliament, having extended its own life, was morally barred from amending the Constitution.[52]

Critics attacked the bill's provisions individually. From jail, Madhu Limaye wrote that Article 31D 'will act as [the] grave-digger of freedom'.[53] Others said it would 'pave the way for virtual one-party rule'.[54] The expanded Article 31C 'practically repeals' the Fundamental Rights, said K. Santhanam. Unfettered parliamentary supremacy, he said, 'will make for constitutional instability which will be exploited by revolutionary extremists and even communal elements'.[55] The provision allowing the central government to send its forces unbidden into a state and control them while there was 'a gross encroachment' on the state's responsibility for law and order, said Tarkunde.[56] The 'removal of difficulties' provision shows that 'the central executive is also seeking to usurp Parliament's power to modify' the Constitution, said the *Nation-wide Demand*.[57] Critics agreed that creating tribunals was desirable for speeding up the judicial process, but feared that individuals appointed to them might be poorly qualified and politically biased. M. C. Chagla pointed out that appeals from tribunals to the high courts could be denied by legislation, forcing 'a man wronged by a tribunal' to go all the way to the Supreme Court in Delhi to seek relief.[58]

---

[52] For the text of the statement and its signatories, see *Nation-wide Demand*, pp. 51ff. Among the signatories were Daphtary, Sorabjee, Tarkunde, Raj Krishna, J. D. Sethi, Chakravarty, Thapar, B. G. Verghese, Shanti Bhushan, Ajit Bhattacharjea, and Mrs Lotika Sarkar.

Several days later, the Prime Minister's supporters presented her with their own petition, with five hundred signatures, saying the time to amend the Constitution was 'ripe'.

[53] Limaye, *The New Constitutional Amendments: Death-knell of Popular Liberties*, Allied Publishers Pvt. Ltd., New Delhi, 1977, p. 15. Limaye dated the text 8 September 1976.

[54] Respectively, 'Consensus Statement' in *Nation-wide Demand*, p. 3, and K. Santhanam, 'Comments on the Constitution 44th Amendment Bill', mimeograph, 7 September 1976, Jayaprakash Narayan Papers, Subject File 318, NMML.

[55] Santhanam, 'Comments', p. 6.

[56] In *Democracy and Constitution*, p. 37.

[57] *Nation-wide Demand*, p. 4. The *Statesman* called this clause 'extraordinary indeed'.

[58] Chagla also objected that the arithmetic of the seven-judge bench for constitutional cases would have an effect opposite to that intended. Said he, 'Every court gives a decision by majority, but under this Bill, by an odd quirk, the minority becomes the majority.' *Himmat* (a new magazine published in Bombay by Raj Mohan Gandhi, a grandson of Mahatma Gandhi), date unknown. Chagla was speaking at a meeting organized by Citizens for Democracy.

With the judiciary under such heavy fire, even Communist Party Marxist statesman E. M. S. Namboodiripad gave it grudging support. My party has never subscribed to the supremacy of the judiciary, he said, nor forgotten its class character and many reactionary judgements. 'But in a number of cases the judiciary has acted as a check on the arbitrary actions of executive authorities as well as in scrutinizing legislative enactment with a view to checking whether the rights of citizens are being curtailed.'[59]

The critics also offered positive suggestions for constitutional change, several of which would be incorporated in the Constitution under the Janata government. The National Seminar Consensus wanted the conditions for a declaration of emergency set forth in the Constitution and recommended prescribing the limits within which Fundamental Rights could be suspended during an Emergency. Citizens for Democracy proposed that emergency declarations and proclamations of President's Rule be justiciable; that suspension of the Fundamental Rights be 'confined to the purpose of the Emergency'; and that the suspension of the citizen's right to seek enforcement of his rights 'not have the effect of suspending the rule of law'. It also recommended that preventive detention be restricted to times when the country was 'at war and for purposes connected with the war ...'. Santhanam recommended abolishing President's Rule entirely, with elections to follow the fall of a state ministry. Regarding the amending power, Citizens for Democracy and the National Seminar Consensus focused on the basic structure issue. The latter wanted a proviso added to Article 368 that no amendment could alter the basic structure. The former said there should be no alteration of the basic structure without a referendum.[60]

S. P. Sathe, otherwise a critic of the bill, favoured this provision, saying it would act as a check on the 'excessive invalidation of laws by the courts'. Sathe, S. P. 'The Forty-Fourth Constitutional Amendment' (Bill), in Sathe, *et al.*, *Democracy and Constitution*, p. 23.

[59] E. M. S. Namboodiripad, 'Amendment—in What Direction', *Indian Express* 26 October 1976, later published in *Democracy and Constitution*, p. 53. Some years earlier, Namboodiripad had been prosecuted for contempt of court for referring to the class character of judges.

[60] For recommendations of the National Seminar Consensus and K. Santhanam, see, respectively, *Nation-wide Demand*, p. 6 and *Comments on the Constitution Amendment Bill*. For Citizens for Democracy recommendations, see 'On Amending the Constitution' of June 1976 recirculated on 11 September 1976. Jayaprakash Narayan Papers, Subject File 318, NMML.

The documents of all three called for an independent judiciary—free from executive patronage, said Citizens for Democracy. It and the National Seminar Consensus wanted an improved Election Commission, with impartiality to be achieved, said the latter, by

In Parliament, the critics had few voices with which to challenge the government. P. G. Mavalankar, gentlemanly, dignified, devotee of Shiva, and spiritedly independent throughout the Emergency, called the amendment a 'Constitution Alteration Exercise ... a dishonest move on the part of the government'.[61] Mavalankar also pointed out that the government was acting contrary to Gokhale's praise for the Constitution of just three years earlier. Then, Gokhale had said that the courts' use of the writ jurisdiction to protect fundamental rights had '"produced socially desirable consequences ... [keeping] a check on government ... [and demonstrating] to the conviction of the common man that he was under a government of law and not of men .... [T]he Constitution has stood the test of time remarkably well,"' Gokhale had said.[62]

Krishan Kant, who until then had boycotted the session, rose to give a stirring defence of democracy. Speaking, he said, on behalf of Congressmen for Democracy, the Congress(O), the Jana Sangh, and the Bharatiya Lok Dal, he attacked those who claimed there is no basic structure. They are declaring 'that they have no basic framework of values and objectives ... [A]ll principles, values, and institutions can be moulded or subverted to suit their interests'. Mrs Gandhi's claim of power for the parliamentary executive is a 'proposition to transform the Divine Right of Kings into the Divine Right of Parliament', he said. And 'those who ridicule the concepts of checks and balances are speaking the language of authoritarianism'. Finally, Kant attacked the government's 'propounding that the Fundamental Rights are not fundamental', and the 'sinister philosophy ... that as the interests of the society are superior to the interests of the individual, they are justified in taking away the fundamental rights of individuals ...'. The government was saying in clear language, he concluded, that the 'people's rights have no place when a dictator wants to take up a programme'.[63]

---

having members appointed by a threesome of the Prime Minister, the Chief Justice of India, and the leader of the Opposition in the Lok Sabha. Members of the commission should be enjoined from accepting government jobs after retirement. Citizens for Democracy recommended that governors be appointed by the same method.

[61] *Lok Sabha Debates*, Fifth Series, vol. 65, no. 3, col. 95.

[62] Gokhale's introduction, 'The Constitution in Operation', in *The Constitution of India: Commemorative Edition*, Lok Sabha Secretariat, New Delhi, 1 January 1973.

[63] *Parliamentary Debates, Rajya Sabha*, vol. 98, no. 2, cols 78–96. Final quotation from col. 88.

Congresswoman Purabi Mukherjee interrupted Kant, saying to the presiding officer look at the patience with which we are listening. 'This shows we are too democratic and his party is taking advantage of democratic institutions.'

It was no use. The Rajya Sabha passed the Forty-second Amendment on 11 November 190 votes to nil, with no changes to the version received from the Lok Sabha. There, all but eight of the over six hundred amendments to the amending bill had been dropped or defeated during the second reading. Most of the bill's clauses were adopted by votes of 360 to three, and the bill passed by 366 to four. After ratification by thirteen of twenty-two state legislatures, the President signed the amendment on 18 December 1976.

The previous month, on 5 November, the Lok Sabha again had extended its own term, until 18 March 1978. Law Minister Gokhale told the House this move is in the larger interests of the country and 'to protect that democracy which you want and which I want'.[64]

Ten weeks later the Prime Minister called elections—for reasons to be considered in the next chapter.

Conclusion

Contrary to many countries newly independent after World War II, which were born authoritarian or soon became so, Indian democracy flourished in its first twenty years, its roots from the pre-independence, nationalist movement growing ever stronger. This was so even while Nehru and others occasionally showed ambivalence about the effectiveness of a democratic constitution for fostering social revolution and preserving national integrity. By 1970, many of the 'tall poppies', as some longingly recalled them, had died, and the political influence of those remaining was withering. From 1970, impatience increased with the imperfections to which all democracies are subject, and with frustration and shame over slow implementation of social revolutionary programmes. The casualness toward democratic institutions that became popular within government— among those believing that social-economic reform should be pursued even at the expense of democracy—initially did little harm, but a tolerance toward authoritarianism developed, culminating in the events of 25–6 June 1975. The Emergency and the Forty-second Amendment, with Mrs Gandhi's justification of them in nationalist, unity–integrity,

---

[64] *Lok Sabha Debates*, Fifth Series, vol. 65, no. 11, col. 70.

The Prime Minister did not bring the extension before the cabinet, according to cabinet member Jagjivan Ram in an interview with columnist Satinder Singh. Satinder Singh Papers, National Institute of Panjab Studies, New Delhi.

The Congress Legislature Party in Andhra Pradesh, led by Mrs Gandhi's reliable chief minister, Vengal Rao, had called for an extension on 25 October. *Statesman*, New Delhi, 26 October 1976.

and social revolutionary terms joined classic examples in Italy and Germany of socialist-nationalist rhetoric put at the service of the authoritarian intentions of a few.

Yet there were peculiarly Indian twists to this dictatorship and its product. Without minimizing the dictatorial character of the Emergency, the popular fears it engendered, the jailing of over one hundred thousand 'enemies', the brutality of Sanjay Gandhi's sterilization and slum clearance programmes, and the terrorizing of Parliament into obedience, the Emergency had its limits. Considerable individual and political freedom existed within it, ideological purity was not demanded, opponents were not shot. And the Forty-second Amendment, with all the evils here described, did not abolish the Supreme Court; left the judiciary with considerable powers; did not end the elections and legislatures of representative government; and did not abolish the Fundamental Rights. Even under the amendment, there would have existed genuine potential for its electoral overturn. All sense of democratic restraint had not deserted its drafters, although it may have deserted Sanjay Gandhi and his coterie.

Unfortunately, there was no social-economic reform to compensate for the absence of democracy. Despite the enormous power the Prime Minister and her government had, 'it was unmistakable that Mrs Gandhi did not intend to use the new powers to usher in a social revolution.' '[T]he ruling party had become more than ever dependent upon the very local elites it was presumably committed to displace in order to carry out its "growth"-oriented policies.'[65]

The especially Indian twist was the country's return to democracy, the triumph of the national democratic ethos, indeed of the Congress Party ethos. For, as will be seen in Part IV, Congress members of Parliament voted with the Janata government to repeal much of the Forty-second and the other Emergency amendments. Already, in the autumn of 1976, some Congress members, in Parliament and outside, had doubts about the amendment and 'were going sour' on the Emergency's excesses and corruption—realizing that these could cause them difficulty when next they faced elections.[66]

---

[65] Frankel, *Political Economy*, respectively pp. 570 and 561.

[66] V. N. Gadgil and Margaret Alva in interviews with the author. Congress propagandists saw it differently. '"[T]he political landscape of India is aglow with the people's enthusiasm and determination to build a new world rid of poverty and backwardness,"' said the political resolution adopted at the Congress Plenary Session at Guwahati 21–2 November 1976. *AR*, 16–20 December 1976, p. 13499.

Thus India's flirtation with dictatorship mercifully was brief. In retrospect, the ugly experience may have been the saving of democracy in ways not thought of by the Prime Minister when she told Parliament that the Emergency was not to destroy the Constitution but 'to preserve and safeguard our democracy'. It taught Indians about the dangers to democracy that lurk anywhere: of demagoguery, of leaders uncaring of liberty, of hero-worship and placing power in the hands of a few, of the dangers from citizen abdication of responsibility. Like the 'McCarthy period' in the United States, it taught that vigilance would be the price of its not happening again.

Finally, there was a lesson about the seamless web. Congress governments' failures vigorously to pursue the social revolution—which let that strand of the web go slack—weakened the democracy strand and underlay the rationalization for the Emergency's negation of democracy. Opposition parties' long-standing inability effectively to perform their function in representative government also had weakened the democracy strand and had been a provocation for the Emergency. Similarly, democracy's sacrifice in the name of protecting the national unity and integrity strand damaged the web's other strands. Memories of the amendment's extension of New Delhi's emergency powers would help to fuel the 'constitutional revolt' of state governments in the 1980s after Congress's return to power (Part VI).

Mrs Gandhi's wrenching of the seamless web brought the repudiation of the Emergency, her government's downfall, and the repeal of the Forty-second Amendment. So was proved what the founding fathers knew: that the character of the country depended upon the integrity of the web, which depended on the health and strength of its individual strands.

Part IV

THE JANATA INTERLUDE: DEMOCRACY RESTORED

When a shirt is dirty, change it.

Village saying

The clouds of fear ... have lifted.

Prime Minister Morarji Desai[1]

[The government will enact a] comprehensive measure ... to amend the Constitution to restore the balance between the people and Parliament, Parliament and the Judiciary, the Judiciary and the Executive, the States and the Centre, the citizen and the government ... .

Acting President B.D. Jatti[2]

[1] In his first broadcast to the nation as Prime Minister, 4 April 1977. *AR*, 14–20 May 1977, pp. 1374–6.
[2] In his address inaugurating the new Parliament, 26 March 1977. Ibid., 23–9 April 1977, p. 13709.

Chapter 18

INDIRA GANDHI DEFEATED—
JANATA FORMS A GOVERNMENT

In Delhi, everyone knew. The *tonga-wallahs* clucking to gaunt horses knew. The autorickshaw drivers dodging through traffic knew. The push-cart sellers with their mounds of oranges knew. The stringers of marigold blossoms before the temples, and the men, haunches on heels, puffing their *bidis* knew. That is, everyone knew except the Prime Minister and her followers.

They knew that Indira Gandhi would be defeated in the elections called for March 1977 and that her son, his coterie, and his bullies would go with her. Their own feelings told them so and they sensed the loathing of the Emergency and its excesses that was rising like magma before a volcanic eruption.

The Prime Minister's defeat would usher in the country's first national coalition government, made up of five parties, four of which had formed the Janata Party. This coalition would restore the Constitution and much democratic practice under it, although in several instances acting unwisely on matters touching the Constitution. It would collapse within two years from savage internal strife that itself would test constitutional institutions. Janata succeeded in saving the nation while losing its soul. These matters are the subject of the following four chapters. This chapter will describe the elections and their background, consider why Mrs Gandhi called them, and describe the new government's formation in the context of the time.

The Prime Minister announced the elections to a surprised public on 18 January 1977, although Parliament's extension of its term the previous November made elections legally unnecessary. She had met the President twice that day, the second time, according to press reports, after an emergency meeting of the cabinet had approved dissolution of the Lok Sabha, which President Fakhruddin Ali Ahmed ordered the next day.[1]

---

[1] According to Jagjivan Ram, Mrs Gandhi informed the cabinet about calling the election, but members 'were never consulted' beforehand. Columnist Satinder Singh's interview with Ram, undated, but likely February 1977, Satinder Singh Papers, National Institute of Panjab Studies, New Delhi.

Parliamentary government, Mrs Gandhi said, '"must report to the people"' and seek sanction for its programmes and policies. She appealed to political parties to '"eschew and refrain from vilification and calumny"'.[2] The *Hindustan Times* editorial said the announcement 'vindicates, as nothing else could, her unswerving commitment to democratic principles'.[3]

Mrs Gandhi called the elections because she expected to win them. Yet it is doubtful that this was her only motivation and the whole truth continues hidden in the mystery that was the lady. She acted from a compound of motives and reasons, according to individuals associated with her and observers Indian and foreign. As to expecting to win, the Intelligence Bureau assured Mrs Gandhi that she would, and her courtiers, even had they had doubts, were unlikely to have been discouraging.[4] Many may have believed in victory, because they were not fully aware of the degree of popular alienation. 'Censorship defeated us, we did not know what was going on,' recalled Ambika Soni, a sentiment shared by A. R. Antulay.[5] It has been suggested that the Prime Minister acted from other motivations: a genuinely democratic attitude inculcated by her father; a desire to be viewed by history as having deep sensitivity to the wishes of the Indian people (which she certainly had); and a sense that her own 'legitimacy' and the 'gains' of her Emergency were being eroded by its excesses—which belatedly were coming to her attention. Also, persons of democratic sensibilities like P. N. Dhar, her Principal Secretary since 1971, and cousin B. K. Nehru were urging her to call elections. There have been hints that Mrs Gandhi ended the Emergency to rein in son Sanjay (to whom she remained devoted) and his coterie because their advocacy of continued authoritarian rule

---

[2] *AR*, 19–25 February 1977, p. 13597.

As late as 4 January, Mrs Gandhi had told a Bhubaneshwar meeting that it was not yet time to lift the Emergency. The previous day the Minister of State for Home Affairs, Om Mehta, had denied rumours that an election was in the offing. *Hindustan Times*, 4 January 1977. But that one was coming would seem to be evident from Sanjay Gandhi's telling a Congress Party meeting that members should not ask for tickets on the basis of caste. Ibid., 5 January 1977.

[3] Issue of 19 January 1977.

[4] Evidence from interviews with persons who had been on Mrs Gandhi's staff or were otherwise well informed indicate that at least two IB assessments predicted victory. One other assessment predicted she would lose, but this came at the last moment and may have been an IB attempt to have it both ways. The negative assessment is also reported in Jayakar, *Indira Gandhi*, p. 313. Reliable individuals in a position to know continue to disagree about what the IB was telling the Prime Minister.

[5] In interviews with the author.

threatened her personal political ascendency and the reputation of devoted democrat she hoped to preserve. All these calculations seem to have combined to produce the Prime Minister's decision that the time had come to renew her 'mandate'.[6]

The elections held between16 and 20 March dealt the Congress Party a massive defeat almost everywhere. It deprived the party of all its seats from Bihar and Uttar Pradesh and damaged it badly in Gujarat, Haryana, Himachal Pradesh, Jammu and Kashmir, Madhya Pradesh, Maharashtra, Kerala, Orissa, Punjab, Rajasthan, Tamil Nadu, West Bengal, and the union territory of Delhi. Congress fared well in Andhra Pradesh, Karnataka, Manipur, and Assam. Of the 542 seats in the Lok Sabha, the Janata Party won 270 and its closest ally, the Congress for Democracy, twenty-nine. The Congress won 153 seats.[7] The Prime Minister herself lost in Rae Bareilly by 55,000 votes—to none other than Raj Narain. Son Sanjay lost his bid for a Lok Sabha seat by over 75,000 votes. Thirty-four central government ministers were defeated, including H. R. Gokhale (by Ram Jethmalani), Swaran Singh, and Bansi Lal.[8] Acting President B. D. Jatti— President Ahmed had died of a heart attack (in his bathtub) on 11 February—accepted the resignation of the Congress government on 22 March and asked it to continue in office until the new government was formed. Mrs Gandhi accepted defeat graciously, saying the collective judgement of the people must be respected. Her last major official act was to have Jatti on 21 March revoke her Emergency.

Opposition Attempts at Unity

The Prime Minister's massive defeat was caused by more than a reaction to the authoritarian rule of the Emergency. Her political opposition had

[6] A senior official in the Prime Minister's office recalls that she had become anxious about the direction being taken by Bansi Lal and son Sanjay. Interview with the author. And B. K. Nehru has written that, in the context of the 20 October resolutions, Mrs Gandhi announced elections 'giving Sanjay no time for further manipulation'. Nehru, *Nice Guys Finish Second*, p. 365.

[7] Other parties' winning were: CPI, seven; CPM and AIADMK, twenty-two each; DMK, one; the Akali Dal, eight. The remaining seats were shared by other small parties and independents.

[8] *AR*, 23–29 April 1977, p. 13697. See also *India Backgrounder*, vol. 1, no. 52, 28 March 1977.

Defeated ministers of state included K. C. Pant, Pranab Mukherjee, V. N. Gadgil, V. C. Shukla, Chandrajit Yadav, and B. P. Maurya. Many deputy ministers lost their seats.

Among the members of Mrs Gandhi's government who survived were Brahmananda Reddy, Chavan, Subramaniam, T. A. Pai, Karan Singh, and Seyid Muhammad.

organized itself far more rapidly and effectively than she—and opposition politicians, themselves—expected. Her opponents began small steps toward resolving policy and organizational issues even during the late autumn of 1976. Striving for common cause were those released from detention early—Charan Singh, Piloo Mody, Surendra Mohan, Ashoka Mehta, Biju Patnaik, and Jayaprakash Narayan (released due to illness on 12 November 1975); those not imprisoned—several of whom were members of Parliament; and even those in jail, who communicated in open and smuggled letters and underground publications. Personality frictions and disagreements over ideology and tactics made these beginnings prickly. Particularly touchy was whether or not the other parties ought to have any truck with the militant Hindu RSS and its political arm, the Jana Sangh.[9]

Opposition unity seemed within reach in November 1976 and in December discussions had progressed to the point that H. M. Patel, of Charan Singh's Bharatiya Lok Dal Party (BLD), could announce that the BLD, the Samyukta Socialist Party, the CPM, and the Congress (O), led by Ashoka Mehta, had agreed on policies and programmes.[10] Mehta had written to Mrs Gandhi in October and November appealing to her to restore normal conditions—a move disliked by SSP members Madhu Limaye and George Fernandes, who opposed any dialogue with the Prime Minister. Her reply of 23 December brushed off Mehta's overture by blaming the imposition of the Emergency on the Opposition and saying that for there to be dialogue, the Opposition must give evidence of its "'genuine acceptance'" of the changes wrought during the Emergency.[11] Five days before this, the Forty-second Amendment to the Constitution had become law.

With the 18 January announcement of elections, events moved

[9] For an exhaustive, well-documented account of opposition unity efforts during the Emergency, see Limaye, Madhu, *Janata Party Experiment*, vol. 1, chs. 8–11, especially. For a description of a meeting of opposition figures in March 1976 and those attending, see ibid., p. 124.

See also Sharma, Dhirendra, *The Janata (People's) Struggle*, A Philosophy and Social Action Publication, New Delhi, 1977. This is a narrative account and contains documents and letters of the period. A number of the documents protest government actions taken during the Emergency.

On 16 January, two days before Mrs Gandhi announced elections, Charan Singh wrote to Narayan that we must accept dialogue with Indira and asking if they should contest any elections, which he doubted would be free and fair. Jayaprakash Narayan Papers, Third Installment, Charan Singh File, NMML.

[10] Limaye, *Janata Party Experiment*, vol. 1, p. 174.

[11] Ibid., pp. 185–6.

rapidly. That day, the government released L. K. Advani and A. B. Vajpayee of the Jana Sangh and Morarji Desai from the detentions begun eighteen months earlier. Desai, with no money and no transport, told an officer that he would not leave '"as long as the government did not provide transport to go to my residence in Delhi from where they had arrested ... me"'. The district magistrate provided a car.[12] Two days later, the government announced the 'relaxing' of the Emergency to allow 'normal' political activity. There were to be no detentions under the Maintenance of Internal Security Act and the Chief Censor was ordered to stop functioning.

Descended from the Janata Front, which, led by Morarji Desai and Jayaprakash Narayan, had challenged Mrs Gandhi during the months leading to the Emergency, the Janata Party declared itself formed on 23 January 1977. Morarji Desai was chairman, Charan Singh deputy chairman and the three general secretaries came from among the member parties, which were the Jana Sangh, the BLD, the Congress(O), the tiny 'rebel' Congress, and the Samyukta Socialist Party. The Swatantra Party said that it proposed to join, and the Congress for Democracy declared itself Janata's ally.[13] Narayan, as the party's spiritual leader, opened its election campaign, saying that the choice for voters was between 'democracy and dictatorship'. Narayan promised that Janata would revive the independent institutions of democracy and involve the people in decision making through decentralization. The Communist Party Marxist, which had not joined the Janata coalition but would support it, announced that it was the only left and democratic alternative to the Congress.

Critical to the outcome of the elections, and later to the formation of the new government, were breakaways from the Congress-veteran Jagjivan Ram's departure and formation of the Congress for Democracy (CFD) on 2 February being the most significant of these.[14] The day of his resignation Ram told a press conference that he could not remain with an 'establishment' that concentrated power 'in a coterie or even an indi-

---

[12] Desai's diary account in Gandhi, Arun, *The Morarji Papers*, Vision Books, New Delhi, 1983, p. 45. Congressmen Mohan Dharia and Chandra Shekhar (expelled from the party in 1975) had been released six days earlier. Raj Narain would not be released until 7 February.

[13] The three general secretaries of Janata were L. K. Advani of the Jana Sangh, Surendra Mohan of the Socialist Party, and Ram Dhan of the Congress (O). A national committee of nearly thirty members would take decisions. Among its members were Ashoka Mehta, A. B Vajpayee, Biju Patnaik, C. B. Gupta, Chandra Shekhar, H. M. Patel, Sanjiva Reddy, Nanaj Deshmukh, N. G. Goray, Karpoori Thakur, and Shanti Bhushan.

[14] Three days before this event, the Intelligence Bureau had passed to Om Mehta. still Minister of State for Home Affairs, a rumour that Ram might defect, but it was not taken seriously. Nayar, *The Judgement*, p. 165.

vidual', that wanted to perpetuate itself in power by extraordinary means, and in a party that 'had virtually ceased to be a democratic organization'. In terms of ideology he was still a Congressman, he said. He invited other Congress members to join him to end the "'totalitarian and authoritarian trends that have of late crept into the nation's politics'". Mrs Gandhi responded that she failed to understand how Ram could make 'wholesale allegations' against the government after having been 'actively and directly associated with every decision' in the government and the party[15]—including, she might have added, moving in the Lok Sabha the resolution approving the Emergency. Two former Congress chief ministers joined Ram: H. N. Bahuguna, of Uttar Pradesh, ousted by Mrs Gandhi in 1975, and Nandini Satpathy, ousted from Orissa the previous December. K. R. Ganesh, an ex-minister of state, and others also defected to Janata. The Prime Minister received a further jolt when her aunt and Nehru's sister, Madame Pandit, came out of retirement to campaign for ending "'the authoritarian trend which has grown to vast proportions'" and for putting the country "'back on the rails of democracy'".[16]

The day after Jagjivan Ram's departure from the Congress, President Ahmed promulgated an ordinance establishing the body that would hear any disputes arising from the parliamentary elections, including Mrs Gandhi's contest for re-election. Using the Thirty-ninth Amendment's new Article 329A, the body was to be that recommended by the Swaran Singh Committee: nine members, three elected by the Lok Sabha, three by the Rajya Sabha, and three nominated by the President. As pointed out earlier, this could put Mrs Gandhi in a position to adjudicate any challenge to her own or her party colleagues' elections. A Congress electoral majority would assure that the first six members of the body would be Congressmen. And, with the President having to act on the advice of his council of ministers, the final three also would be Congressmen. Even if one or two non-Congress members were elected, Mrs. Gandhi would be sure that she dominated this 'authority'.[17] Two days later,

---

[15] Mrs Gandhi's letter was dated the same day. See *AR*, 19–25 March, 1977, p. 13641. For Limaye's account of these events, see his *Janata Party Experiment*, vol. 1, pp. 217ff.

[16] *AR*, 19–25 March 1977, p. 13645.

[17] This was the Disputed Elections (Prime Minister and Speaker) Ordiance, 1977. The President promulgated a second ordinance that day, the Presidential and Vice-Presidential Election (Amendment) Ordinance, 1977, which established a similar authority to decide any dispute arising in the elections of these two officials. Of the nine members of this second body, three each were to be elected by the Lok Sabha and the Rajya Sabha, and there were to be three nominated members: the Chief Justice of India, or a retired chief justice, a second person, and a third person knowledgeable about election

the Election Commission issued a twenty-three point code of conduct, which said that election activities should not aggravate existing differences, create mutual hatred, or cause tension between castes and communities.

The various parties issued their election manifestos between 8 and 21 February with Mrs Gandhi's Congress firing first. The five thousand word text, after recapitulating Congress achievements over the decades, blamed opposition parties for the Emergency and said that "'with order and discipline restored, and dynamic and mutually reinforcing socioeconomic programmes ... being carried out'" elections could be held. The Forty-second Amendment had been enacted "'to overcome the various obstacles put by economic and political vested interests, and not for the purpose of increasing the power of the executive at the expense of the judiciary or the legislature'". The manifesto concluded with its slogan of the 1971 election: "'poverty must go, disparities must diminish and injustice must end.'"[18] As to the opposition's campaign speeches, Mrs Gandhi said that the "'votaries of the rule of the jungle'" were now parading themselves "'as the saviours of democracy in the country'".[19]

The Janata Party's manifesto of 10 February, double the length of Congress's, contained three 'charters': political, economic, and social. The former promised to release the people "'from the bondage of fear'" by lifting the Emergency proclamations of 1971 and 1975; to repeal MISA and the law preventing the publication of parliamentary proceedings; to rescind the "'anti- democratic Forty-second Amendment'"; to restore fundamental freedoms, including that of the press; and to release Emergency detenus. The thirteen-point economic charter promised to delete property from the Fundamental Rights, although leaving it as a statutory right; called for affirmation of the right to work and full employment and putting an end to destitution within ten years; and said

---

law. See *Times of India*, 4 February 1977, and Limaye, *Janata Party Experiment*, vol. 1, p. 223. Due to Mrs Gandhi's defeat and the election of a new Parliament, the ordinances lapsed and were not replaced by legislation.

[18] Zaidi, *Encyclopaedia of the Indian National Congress*, vol. 24, pp. 359–72.

In actions taken during the previous two months, which may have been intended to bolster Congress's support, were an election to be held, the government extended the ban on cow slaughter to much of the country; announced that worker participation in management—long a staple Congress promise—would be extended to the public sector; and announced that, for the first time in the history of elections in India, persons convicted of an 'untouchability offence' would be disqualified from contesting an election for six years. Also, Mrs Gandhi attacked the CPI for collaborating with the British in the 1940s and for attacking Sanjay Gandhi's five point programme.

[19] *Hindustan Times*, 1 March 1977.

agriculture would be given primacy. The fifteen-point social charter called for reform of education and the eradication of illiteracy.[20]

The Congress for Democracy's manifesto—it was contesting separately from the Janata Party coalition— was the last to appear. Released by H. N. Bahuguna, it promised judicial enquiries into the '"administrative excess"' of the Emergency and abolition of arbitrary and anti-democratic laws.[21] In other manifestos, the Dravida Munnetra Kazhagam (DMK) claimed to be the first party to oppose the Emergency openly. It demanded non-secessionist autonomy for the states. The Communist Party of India, inching its way toward its later confession of error for its support of the Emergency, said that after initial good deeds, the Emergency had been used against the working class and had fostered authoritarian trends and extra-constitutional methods. The Communist Party Marxist manifesto bitterly attacked the Emergency and reiterated its long-standing economic programme of further nationalization of industry, banning multinational corporations from entering India, including private foreign investment, and incorporating the right to work in the Fundamental Rights.[22] The party declared that it would support Janata to avoid dividing the opposition.

Creating One From Many

On 24 March 1977, two days after Mrs Gandhi's government had resigned and she had assumed a caretaker role, Morarji Desai took the oath as Prime Minister. At a later press conference with Jayaprakash Narayan beside him, he promised to accept Narayan's advice and said that Janata— one party now, he asserted, no longer a group of parties—would make the people fearless and preserve democracy. At dawn, newly elected members of the Lok Sabha took a pledge at Rajghat, Mahatma Gandhi's cremation ground, to uphold the rights of the people, to give the best to the weakest, to promote national unity and harmony, and '"to practice austerity and honesty in personal and public life"'.[23] The next day the Lok Sabha elected Neelam Sanjiva Reddy the Speaker. Congress members re-elected to the Lok Sabha, as they became the official Opposition, elected Y. B. Chavan their leader. On the occasion, he characterized Congress's defeat as not against the party, but directed at the harsh

[20] *AR,* 26 February–4 March 1977, p. 13614 and Limaye, *Janata Party Experiment,* vol. 1, pp. 295ff.

[21] *AR,* 19–25 March 1977, p. 13643.

[22] Ibid., pp. 13645ff.

[23] *AR,* 23–29 April 1977, pp. 13704ff.

implementation of its policies. Election of a President came in July, and Sanjiva Reddy moved to Rashtrapati Bhavan, to be succeeded as Speaker by K. S. Hegde, one of the superseded judges of 1973. Except for the matter of the governments in the states, many of which were still in Congress's hands, the Janata government was in place.

Creating a government had not been easy. Jayaprakash Narayan and Acharya J. B. Kripalani were asked to resolve the impasse over whom should be prime minister, selecting by consensus from among the competitors— Morarji Desai, Charan Singh, and Jagjivan Ram. They failed. The Young Turks and others supported Jagjivan Ram. The Congress(O) and Jana Sangh preferred Desai. The BLD and others supported the BLD leader, Charan Singh. With no candidate's supporters dominant, Jayaprakash Narayan settled on Desai, reportedy having persuaded Ram not to oppose Desai in return for a senior cabinet position. Ram was miffed. He had national stature and thought himself a worthy candidate, and he disliked Desai as much as Desai disliked him. But he was unrealistic in expecting that his having moved the Lok Sabha resolution endorsing the Emergency and having served in the Emergency cabinet would so readily be forgiven. Charan Singh was more than put out. Having expected to be Prime Minister, he wished to be Deputy Prime Minister, but Desai denied him this. Appointed Home Minister, Charan Singh—frustrated and bitter—eventually would unseat Desai. '[S]ome of [the] senior colleagues never reconciled with this decision ... from the very first day ... till the last day ... this discontent continued,' recalled Chandra Shekhar, later Janata Party president.[24]

Selecting a council of ministers was hardly easier. The coalition's constituent parties had to be satisfied, or at least placated, with positions. Because they would not submerge their conflicting interests and identities for the larger cause, quota system for portfolios was arranged even though this produced a ministry of ill-fitting personalities and political orientations. On economic issues, there was some kinship among Finance Minister, H. M. Patel, once a Swatantra Party member,

---

[24] Chandra Shekhar Oral History Transcript, p. 2, NMML.
One of the Janata Party's general secretaries, Ram Dhan, resigned over Desai's selection, asserting—in a letter to Desai, who at the time was still chairman of the Janata Party—that the process had been in the dictatorial manner of the Congress. *AR*, 23–29 April 1977, p. 13706. For Desai's refusal of Charan Singh as deputy prime minister, see Limaye, *Janata Party Experiment*, vol. 2, p. 66. For the formation of the government according to Limaye in his diary, see ibid., vol. 1., pp. 240–60, and Limaye, Madhu, *Cabinet Government in India*, Radiant Publishers, New Delhi, 1989, pp. 137ff. Also see *Hindustan Times* for the period and Nayar, *Judgement*, pp. 183ff.

and Minister of Information and Broadcasting L. K. Advani and External Affairs Minister A. B. Vajpayee—from the Jana Sangh with its constituency of shopkeepers, traders, money-lenders, and, to a lesser degree big businessmen. But facing them were the ardent trade unionist George Fernandes Minister at the Industry, socialist Madhu Dandavate at Railways, Young Turk Mohan Dharia at Commerce, and other ministers from the Congress (O) with socialist credentials. The government's 'Statement on Industrial Policy' did not depart significantly from the 1956 Industrial Policy statement, as Fernandes explained when he laid it before Parliament in December 1977, but Charan Singh gave government policy strong emphasis on developing villages, agriculture, and small, even 'tiny', industry.[25] Although Advani and Vajpayee were cooperative members of the government, the Hindu nationalism of the Jana Sangh and, more so, its connections with the militant RSS put them at odds with the other, secularist cabinet members.[26] Caste origins inflamed several relationships, with Charan Singh, a Jat from Meerut, referring privately to Jagjivan Ram as that 'Chamar'.[27] From the other parties' points of view, the government was unbalanced in favour of the *old* Congress, with its six ministers, including the three senior figures of Desai, Charan Singh, and Ram. Finally, almost the only glue holding these individuals and their parties together was a negative: antipathy for Indira Gandhi and her Emergency. Once democracy had been restored through amendments to the Constitution, this was not strong enough to withstand the differences among individuals and the factionalism the parties brought with them from their years in the political wilderness. They were unable to adjust from having had little power and no responsibility in the Opposition to, in office, having the heavy weight of both.

Once established, the Desai government declared its principal purpose to be to restore the health of the democracy and other strands of the seamless web. Two speeches set the tone. Inaugurating the new Parliament, Acting President B. D. Jatti said the election had demonstrated that democracy had struck deep roots in India, and the people had given

[25] Nirmal Mukarji, the Cabinet Secretary under the Janata Government, in an interview with the author. See chapter 4 for mention of Charan Singh's position on peasant land ownership.

[26] The issue was alive even when the Janata Party was moribund. Mohan Dharia tried at a party meeting in September 1979 to force the separation of the Jana Sangh from Janata, and resigned from the party when he failed. Later, the party constitution would be changed to exclude dual membership in Janata and communally oriented organizations.

[27] Gandhi, *Morarji Papers*, p. 213.

a verdict "'in favour of individual freedom, democracy and the rule of law and against ... a personality cult and extra-constitutional centres of power'". He promised that his government would thoroughly review the repressive laws of the Emergency and enact a '"comprehensive measure ... to amend the Constitution to restore the balance between the people and Parliament, Parliament and the Judiciary, the Judiciary and the Executive, the States and the Centre, the citizen and the government ..."'.[28] The following day the government revoked the state of external emergency proclaimed in 1971, Mrs Gandhi having revoked her Emergency a week earlier upon losing the election.

Prime Minister Morarji Desai in a broadcast to the nation on 4 April told his countrymen that '"the clouds of fear and uneasiness have lifted ... by a revolution of the people to restore democracy"'. He then demolished the social revolutionary rationale for the Emergency. We were told that the Emergency was necessary for discipline and economic progress, he said, but '"freedom and bread are not competitive even in a developing society."' Turning to the web's national unity and democracy strands, Desai called the centralized state a menace to democracy and said change must come in the villages. Echoing Narayan, Desai promised to restore democratic institutions and spoke in Gandhian terms of government's responsibility to serve the people. The Prime Minister concluded that Janata had pledged itself '"to present a united front to the problems that are the legacies of centuries"'.[29]

Providing evidence of its democratic intentions, the government, for the first time since independence, invited the leader of the parliamentary Opposition to broadcast to the nation over All-India Radio. Y. B. Chavan, who had become leader of the Congress Parliamentary Party, appealed for national reconciliation in a speech given several day after Desai's. The Congress, he said, had '"fully absorbed"' the lessons of the Emergency and would cooperate in building a new nation. '"The people of India have shown tremendous political maturity and wisdom ..."', Chavan said.[30] Later, the government would go further and grant the status of cabinet minister to the leader of the Opposition in both houses of Parliament, along with related allowances and privileges.

The Janata government's intentions were noble, its members able men and women, and its record a paradox. It had remarkable success in

[28] Speech delivered 26 March. *AR*, 23–29 April 1977, p. 13709—used as a superscript for this Part.

[29] *AR*, 14–20 May 1977, pp. 13734–6.

[30] Ibid., p. 13736.

repairing the Constitution from the Emergency's depredations, in reviving open parliamentary practice through its consultative style when repairing the Constitution, and in restoring the judiciary's independence.[31] But its failures were dismal. It did not meet a government's critical test of survival, remaining intact only for sixteen months (chapter 22). In large part because of this brief tenure, its social revolutionary accomplishments were minimal. The JPP claimed that seven of the thirteen pledges in the party's economic charter had been implemented and eight of the fifteen pledges in the social charter, but this was an overly-generous assessment.[32] National unity was strengthened by the restoration of democracy and co-operation with non-Janata regional parties, but the government's injudicious dismissal of nine Congress state governments and imposition of President's Rule—reminiscent of Congress's overcentralization—damaged the sense of cooperative unity, while providing an example Mrs Gandhi later would use against Janata (chapters 21 and 26). The party's promise of popular participation through decentralization did not materialize, in considerable part because Desai was a strong centralizer. Yet there was abundant participation during cabinet meetings, although, as will be seen in forthcoming chapters, there were disastrous instances of failure to communicate. The Prime Minister's style seemed to vary from accommodation with his colleagues if they spoke frankly with him to being 'unbending and in many matters quite inflexible ... [H]e got himself isolated ...'.[33] The government badly damaged itself by its attempted prosecution, which was both mean-spirited and inept, of Mrs Gandhi for the Emergency's excesses. And Morarji Desai injected a smaller, yet still significant irritant by allowing his son, Kanti Desai, to live in the Prime Minister's house while pursuing his own activities. This gave Charan Singh a stick with which to beat the Prime Minister, which he did by leaking to the press charges of a scandal against the son.[34] And it gave rise to Madhu

---

[31] The Janata Parliamentary Party (JPP) also instituted the practice, on H. V. Kamath's resolution, of allowing party members to abstain from voting with the government with the JPP leader's permission. The resolution also provided that the JPP leader (the Prime Minister) should be a member of the Lok Sabha, not of the Rajya Sabha. *AR*, 10–16 September 1977, p. 13921.

[32] *Promises: How Many Fulfilled?*, Janata Parliamentary Party, New Delhi, undated (but late 1978 or early 1979), especially pp. 3, 40.

[33] Chandra Shekhar Oral History Transcript, p. 6, NMML. As Cabinet Secretary, from this officer's accustomed seat at the Prime Minister's left, Nirmal Mukarji witnessed this process, and drafted bare bones accounts of cabinet meetings.

[34] Gandhi, *Morarji Papers*, pp. 214ff.

Limaye's great aphorism of Indian politics, "'Politician's progeny is a curse.'"[35]

In getting itself organized, the Janata Party fared no better than the government. The elections won, the organization established on 23 January needed to be regularized and a new president found, for Morarji Desai did not wish to hold both the prime ministry and the party post.[36] Chandra Shekhar was settled upon as president; three general secretaries were drawn from constituent parties—Madhu Limaye from the Socialist Party, Nanaji Deshmukh from Jana Sangh, and Rabi Ray, later to become Speaker, from the BLD. Chandra Shekhar selected forty-three members of the Working Committee—a process 'not free from heartburn', wrote Limaye. The 'organizational wing' of the party increasingly found itself at odds with and ignored by the 'government wing', much in the manner of the contention between the two Congress 'wings' in the late forties and early fifties. As then, the organizational wing attempted to 'exert its supremacy' over the government wing. Chandra Shekhar was to lead a watchdog committee to review government implementation of party programmes. Central ministers and state chief ministers were asked to discuss policies and problems with the party secretariat.[37] Little came of this. Overall, the party and the government suffered from a mutually reinforcing disfunctionalism. Additionally, rivalries varying from strong to unruly within and among the Janata parties in the states and between them and the party central command made uniformity of policy and its implementation difficult.

The Congress Party: Death and Reincarnation

As the Janata Party and government proceeded toward their destinies, the Congress Party was undergoing death and reincarnation under the masterful hand of Indira Gandhi, which would assist Janata's demise and her return to office. The process began within a week of the party's

[35] Limaye, quoting his own diary, in *Janata Party Experiment*, vol. 1, p. 253. The following sentence said, "'No politician who had a son or daughter ought to be allowed to become Prime Minister.'"

[36] Desai opposed any minister holding party office. For an account of the formation of the Janata Party during April and May 1977, see Limaye, *Janata Party Experiment*, vol. 1, pp. 323–59. See also *Janata Bulletin*, Janata Party, New Delhi, April 1978. This had a foreword by Ramakrishna Hegde and was to be published quarterly, but seems not to have been.

[37] Decided upon at a National Executive meeting, 20–22 April 1978. *AR*, 4–10 June 1978, p. 14346. One of the party's complaints was that it had not been consulted about the draft five-year plan.

defeat, with informal meetings of Congressmen, many of them former members of the Congress Forum for Socialist Action. The demands at these that heads should roll were heard at the Working Committee's agonizing introspection in mid-April 1977: D. K. Borooah resigned from the party presidency to be replaced provisionally by Sardar Swaran Singh—the first Sikh to hold the office; Bansi Lal and others were expelled from the party; V. C. Shukla was reprimanded; Sanjay Gandhi, who had resigned from the party on 30 March was not directly blamed, reportedly as a way of sparing his mother, but demands were made to disband his vehicle, the Youth Congress. Mrs Gandhi was not criticized. She 'continues to be our leader', said party general secretary Mrs Purabi Mukherjee.[38]

Within a month, building on her humble acceptance of responsibility for the election defeat,[39] Mrs Gandhi initiated her comeback strategy. At a 5–6 May AICC meeting, she tearfully thanked party men for standing by her in good times and bad; then had her candidate, Brahmananda Reddy, elected party president. Elections to ten seats on the Working Committee produced a majority of her supporters, and when ten others were nominated to the committee a few days later, she was among them. She also became a member of the Central Election Committee and the Central Parliamentary Board. S. S. Ray, who had failed in his bid to be party president and had declined an invitation to join the Working Committee, charged that in the AICC meeting he had seen 'no remorse ... no desire to apologize to the people for the undoubted atrocities committed ... The cult of personality still dominated the entire show. Authoritarianism was the order of the day.'[40]

Although holding offices, Mrs Gandhi played little part in party affairs until October 1977. But her public activities, were spectacular. They included a trip through floods by elephant to visit Belchi village, where Harijans had been burned to death by members of upper castes, a triumphal tour of Gujarat, a visit to Jayaprakash Narayan, and her comic opera arrest and release by the government (chapter 21). By mid-October, a rift with Brahmananda Reddy had developed, Mrs Gandhi was being mooted for the party presidency, and Reddy, Chavan, still Congress

[38] Mirchandani, G. G., *Reporting India 1977*, Abhinav Publications, New Delhi, 1978, p. 99. See also Mirchandani, G. G., *The People's Verdict*, Vikas Publishing House Pvt. Ltd., New Delhi, 1980, ch. 4, for an overview of the period.

[39] In a letter to Dev Kant Borooah, dated 12 April 1977, when he was still Congress president. Mirchandani, *Reporting India*, p. 100.

[40] Ibid., p. 104. Among Mrs Gandhi's supporters now on the Working Committee were C. Subramaniam, K. C. Pant, Shankar Dayal Sharma, Chandrajit Yadav, P. V. Narasimha Rao, C. M. Stephen, and A. P. Sharma—convenor of the Nehru Forum in 1973.

leader in the Lok Sabha, and others were holding unity talks with her supporters. Mrs Gandhi quietly was fuelling schism by criticizing Congress members of Parliament for consulting with the government about amending the Constitution (chapter 20). On 18 December, she pronounced the schisms irreparable and resigned from the Working Committee, saying that she would work as an ordinary party member with 'no ambition or design to hold the office of party presidentship or any other position'.[41] She exchanged challenges with Brahmananda Reddy and Chavan, and on 1 January 1978 a National Convention of Congressmen, 'representing the Indian National Congress', resolved that '"in order to provide effective national leadership to meet the challenges before the nation ... [it] unanimously elects Mrs Indira Gandhi as Congress President,"' thereby forming the Congress(I) (for Indira).[42] She got no pleasure out of splitting the Congress, Mrs Gandhi said in her concluding address, but it had become necessary '"to have a clear cut ideology"'; our slogan should be '"forward with socialism"'.[43]

The following day, the *other* Congress Working Committee noted with deep regret that Mrs Gandhi and her followers had 'carried out their long-standing intention of disrupting the unity of the party and setting up a new party'.[44] Each faction then began what one publication named the 'war of expulsions'. Mrs Gandhi's faction gained adherents over the next few months. Swaran Singh became president of the other faction of the Congress Party and resumed unity talks with the Congress(I). In November 1978, Mrs Gandhi was briefly returned to the Lok Sabha (chapter 21). Unity attempts continued only to be broken off in March 1979—because the Congress(I) would not accept collective leadership and intra-party democracy, according to Swaran Singh.

[41] Ibid., p. 117 and *AR*, 5–11 January 1978, pp. 14155ff.

[42] *AR*, 5–11 February 1978, pp. 14155. The convention claimed to represent both a majority of the AICC as well as other Congress members. The AICC members present numbered 347 of the total membership of 657. Mirchandani, *Reporting India*, p. 118 and Zaidi, A. M., *Aloud and Straight: Frank Talks at Party Meetings*, Indian Institute of Applied Political Research, New Delhi, 1984, p. 339.

Among early members of this Congress (I) Working Committee were Kamalapati Tripathi, Mir Qasim, A. P. Sharma, Buta Singh, and P. V. Narasimha Rao.

[43] Zaidi, *Aloud and Straight*, pp. 346ff.

At this time, Mrs Gandhi chose the 'hand' as the party's election symbol, remembering her visit to the Shankaracharya of Kamakoti Peeth in October 1977. As Mrs Gandhi was leaving, she asked the Shankaracharya what she should do, and he replied '"follow your *dharma*" and lifted the plam of his hand in a gesture of blessing'. Jayakar, *Indira Gandhi*, p. 348.

[44] Among those present at this meeting were Chavan, Subramaniam, Stephen, Yadav, Shankar Dayal Sharma, and K. C. Pant.

According to Chavan, Mrs Gandhi '"wanted only those who were prepared to prostrate before [her] in surrender ... who were prepared to be captives"'.[45] Indira Gandhi completed her political rehabilitation with help from a peculiar quarter, from Janata's Charan Singh. He ill-advisedly turned to her for support in July 1979 as he attempted to become Prime Minister in place of Moraji Desai. Mrs Gandhi had gained the leverage she would need to return to power the following year.[46] She never had accepted responsibility for declaring the Emergency, only 'sorrow for any hardship or harassment' that the people had endured during it.

In this recurrently stormy political weather, the Janata government went about the task discussed in the next chapter: restoring the Constitution.

---

[45] For Chavan, see *AR*, 30 April–6 May1979, p. 14862; for Swaran Singh, Mirchandani, *People's Verdict*, p. 85.

[46] Meanwhile, the CPI National Council admitted the 'serious mistake' of not calling for the Emergency's lifting once its 'negative features' were evident. It praised the outcome of the election as protest 'against the gross misuse of the emergency powers and violation of all democratic norms and rights ...'. And it was 'utterly revolted by ... the extra-constitutional personal power centre with Sanjay Gandhi as its focus'. *Lok Sabha Election: Resolution of the National Council of Communist Party of India, Held in Delhi from 3 to 6 April 1977*, Communist Party of India, New Delhi, April 1977, pp. 9, 4, and 5, respectively.

Had the Congress and Mrs Gandhi won, the CPI might have sung a different tune. On 7 February 1977, CPI Chairman S. A. Dange told a public meeting that, faced with a choice between Mrs Gandhi and Morarji Desai, the CPI would choose the former.

Sanjay Gandhi had followed his mother's attack on the CPI with one of his own in January 1977, in which he said its '"one-point programme" was to tell lies'. *India Backgrounder*, vol. 1, no. 47, 21 February 1977, p. 487.

Chapter 19

RESTORING DEMOCRATIC GOVERNANCE

The principal tasks of Morarji Desai's government were to repeal legislation damaging to the Fundamental Rights and to restore a democratic Constitution through a comprehensive amendment, Acting President B. D. Jatti told Parliament in his inaugural address in April 1977. These endeavours were to proceed in parallel. This chapter deals with restoring the Constitution, leaving other issues of democratic governance to chapter 20.

Amending the Constitution confronted the government with tactical as well as substantive issues. Effective parliamentary tactics were critical to reform, for the Janata had to garner enough votes to pass the restorative amendment—a two-thirds majority in each House, plus ratification by half the state assemblies. The Lok Sabha, with its large Janata majority, posed no problem. But in the Rajya Sabha, in May 1977, Congress members of various hues held 154 of the 244 seats. The Janata Party held only twenty-seven seats.[1] Clearly, Morarji Desai's government would need Congressmen's and others' votes to enact any amendment and even to pass some legislation.

The Rajya Sabha elections of 3 April 1978 would change the picture somewhat—and the crucial Forty-fourth Amendment would not be voted on until December 1978. Indira Gandhi's newly-formed faction the Congress(I) had sixty seats, the Congress(O) fifty-three, Janata sixty-nine, and various other parties, sixty-one.[2] Two-thirds of the membership

[1] The CPI held eleven, the CPM three, and the Tamil parties, independents, and others a total of thirty-two seats.

[2] The figures for the 1977 Rajya Sabha come from Butler, Lahiri, and Roy, *India Decides*, p. 68. The figures for the Rajya Sabha after the 1978 elections are from *AR*, 7–13 May 1978. The figures for the results of the 1978 elections in *India Decides*, p. 68, do not lend themselves to assigning seats to the Janata government of Morarji Desai.

Figures for Parliament in the spring of 1977 also may be found in Limaye, Madhu, *Janata Party Experiment*, vol. 1, p. 264. They are, for the Lok Sabha: 'Janata Party (including the CFD and those elected on the Congress(O) symbol in Tamil Nadu). 298; CPM, 22; AIADMK, 19; DMK, 1; Akali Dal, 9; People's War Party, 5; Revolutionary Socialist Party (RSP), 4; Forward Bloc, 3; Republican Party (Kamble), 1; Nagaland United Democratic Front, 1.' This produced a total of 363 in the Janata column in Limaye's table. In the

(assuming the seats vacant at the time would be filled) meant 162 votes plus a fraction. Thus, if Janata and Congress(O) members voted solidly for an amendment, Desai's government still would need at least forty votes from the other, smaller parties to pass it. The government dared not depend on this; it would need votes from Congress members loyal to Mrs Gandhi. How and why the government got the necessary votes—including an especially surprising 'aye'—will be seen.

The first great substantive issue was whether the Forty-second Amendment should be repealed entirely with one stroke of the pen, or its provisions repealed selectively. If it were not to be repealed by a 'one-line amendment', which of its provisions were to be saved? If repeal were to be selective, should some provisions receive priority? Which approach would combine the substance and tactics necessary to gain support from Congressmen and, after the January 1978 split, from members of the Congress(I)?

The government's first step was hasty. The Prime Minister, probably at Law Minister Shanti Bhushan's urging, agreed to introduce a partially restorative amendment after just two weeks in office.[3] Shanti Bhushan introduced the Forty-third Amendment Bill on 7 April in the Lok Sabha. Containing only seven clauses, it deleted the 'anti-national activities' provision of the Forty-second Amendment, re-established five year terms for Parliament and state legislatures, and deleted the Thirty-ninth Amendment's provision protecting Mrs Gandhi's—and successive prime ministers'—elections. Because premature, the bill became lost in other

---

Congress column of his table, for a total of 178 seats were: 'Congress (I), 154; CPI, 7; Muslim League, 2; Kerala Congress, 2; National Conference, 2; others, 3; independents, 8'. These figures were for 541 seats declared of the Lok Sabha complement of 542 seats.

In the Rajya Sabha, according to Limaye, 'the party position ... around the time the Janata Government was formed was roughly as follows: Janata Party, 26; CPM, 3; DMK, 2; AIADMK, 5' for a total of 36 in the Janata column. 'Congress, 170; CPI, 11; others, 6'. This produced a total of 187 in the Congress column. Limaye's use of the word 'roughly' well described a confusing analysis of election results.

[3] Indeed, Bhushan began planning amendments even before the elections. He set up a committee of himself, E. M. S. Namboodiripad, V. M. Tarkunde, and George Verghese to work on substantive changes to the Constitution. (Bhushan interview with the author.) Tarkunde had been a high court judge and was a noted civil liberties lawyer; he had been a prominent opponent of the Forty-second Amendment. Verghese was a senior journalist, who in the late 1960s had been information advisor to Prime Minister Gandhi. Bhushan not only had been Raj Narain's lawyer but also Advocate General of UP in the late 1960s, treasurer of the Congress (O), and privileged as a young man to attend the 'evening durbars' of the noted constitutionalist and jurist, Sir Tej Bahadur Sapru. Namboodiripad was the long-time CPM leader and Chief Minister of Kerala.

government business, and Morarji Desai would establish machinery for extensive preparation of another bill.[4] Nevertheless, Bhushan's provisions were an indicator of things to come.

Lengthy Amending Preparations Begin

First, in May 1977, Desai appointed a parliamentary affairs committee to be the forum for considering substantive changes.[5] Then, in August, he inexplicably established a cabinet subcommittee to deal with the same issues. Charan Singh was chairman and Bhushan and Advani were members of both committees. Ravindra Varma, Minister of Parliamentary Affairs and Labour , was the fourth member of the first committee and P. C. Chunder, Minister of Education, Culture and Social Welfare, the fourth member of the subcommittee.[6] The cabi-

---

[4] The bill lapsed months later, overtaken by the other amending bills. The *Hindustan Times* on 8 April 1977 reported that the Congress opposition had been consulted and was willing to co-operate as evidenced by Chavan's endorsement on the floor of the House. President Jatti's immediate assent was predicted. But no immediate action was to be taken because the session would adjourn that day. Another report in the same edition indicated that Congress might later oppose the bill, 'at the consideration stage', because returning the legislatures to five year terms was 'aimed at destabilizing state governments'. This concern was overtaken by Janata's dismissal of nine state governments (see next chapter). Perhaps sobered by the intricacies of amending the Constitution, the President omitted any mention of the subject in his Independence Day speech of August 1977.

For the text of the lapsed bill, see Lok Sabha Secretariat, *Constitution Amendment in India*, p. 174. Also see Lok Sabha Secretariat, Background Note, 'The Forty-Second Amendment and Recent Proposals for Changes in the Constitution', for use of members of Parliament, dated 25 February 1978, p. 23, unpublished. A copy was provided to the author by the Secretariat.

[5] The description here of the government's internal consultation processes and its consultations with the opposition parties in Parliament is based upon newspaper reports, secondary written sources, and upon interviews with Shanti Bhushan, P. B. Venkatasubramanian, Madhu Limaye, Mrs Sarojini Mahishi, Minister of State in the Law Ministry during the Emergency who remained in a senior position in the ministry for some time under the Janata government, and Mrs Margaret Alva, a member of the Rajya Sabha in the Janata period.

Attempting to reach consensus within Janata and particularly with the Congress opposition, so important to Bhushan and Desai, also had been advocated strongly by Gajendragadkar in a 'Prefatory Note' for Desai, of which more shortly.

[6] Attorney General S. V. Gupte, Solicitor General S. N. Kacker and Additional Solicitor General Soli Sorabjee had been in office for months, but had a peripheral role in drafting the amendments. From interviews with Bhushan and Sorabjee.

In May, Desai had appointed the cabinet's Political Affairs Committee: himself as chairman, and with Ram, Charan Singh, and Vajpayee as members.

net subcommittee, which bore most of the burden regarding constitutional issues, met first on 16 August and immediately took up the paper submitted to it by Law Minister Shanti Bhushan and prepared under his direction by the Secretary of the Ministry's Legal Department, R. V. S. Peri Sastri, and the Additional Secretary, P. B. Venkatasubramanian.

Bhushan earlier had sent the Janata election manifesto to his fellow ministers to elicit their ideas for an amendment and to remind them of promises to be kept. He then built his paper on contributions from them and from many individuals, including two weighty written submissions to Morarji Desai from Law Commission Chairman P. B. Gajendragadkar and Justice H. R. Khanna who had retired from the Supreme Court after Mrs Gandhi had superseded him for the Chief Justiceship of India just prior to the 1977 elections (chapter 21). The two men's submissions had originated from discussions Desai had had with them before he became Prime Minister. Desai had asked Gajendragadkar to draft a note for study. Gajendragadkar responded with a six-page letter on 1 April 1977, to be followed by other letters and, on 8 July, by a 'Prefatory Note' of twenty-nine pages. In keeping with his letters to Indira Gandhi during 1975 and 1976, Gajendragadkar urged Desai to set up a 'high-powered committee' for a dispassionate study of amendment. Khanna's response to Desai's request was a note on the 'Basic Structure of the Constitution', which concentrated on the Constitution's emergency provisions.[7] Khanna recommended that these should not to be dispensed with despite current sentiment, but retained with safeguards to meet 'real crisis'.[8] To 'prevent abuses', he recommended that proclamations of emergency should be valid for only six months

---

[7] The date of the Desai–Gajendragadkar meeting is uncertain, but the latter's April letter makes clear that it took place between 20 and 24 March.

The Gajendragadkar correspondence with Desai and the 'Prefatory Note' are in the Gajendragadkar Papers, Subject File 1, NMML. Gajendragadkar shared these documents with Shanti Bhushan.

At this time, Gajendragadkar was also concerned that the Law Commission, of which he was still chairman, should not be disbanded. Bhushan assured him that this would not be done. (Bhushan in an interview with the author.) Gajendragadkar's term as chairman of the commission was due to expire on 31 August 1977, after which he wrote Desai he intended to leave Delhi for good. Letter of 23 August 1977, P. B. Gajendragadkar Papers, Subject File 1, NMML.

The Khanna talk with Desai, selections from his note dated 13 April 1977, and the text of Desai's thankful reply of 30 April 1977, saying "'We shall make good use of it,'" are to be found in Khanna, *Neither Roses Nor Thorns*, pp. 91ff.

[8] Letter covering the note dated 13 July 1977, ibid.

after their approval by Parliament unless renewed by both Houses. Both the original proclamation and any renewal should be passed by 'a certain percentage of members', implying more than a simple majority. Consultations with Parliament before issuing a proclamation, in the manner of the French Constitution, might be considered. Khanna thought that declarations of emergency should not be subject to court review if made for a purpose within Article 352 and if the correct procedures had been followed.

Khanna also recommended that the Supreme Court's power to issue writs of habeas corpus should not to be curtailed during emergencies. Referring to the Emergency's Habeas Corpus case (where, it will be remembered, he had been the lone dissenter upholding this fundamental right), he wrote that suspending the right 'strikes at the very basis of the rule of law'. In future, such writs could be issued 'in case the courts find that the detention is not in accordance with the law relating to detention'.[9]

Of Justice Gajendragadkar's lengthy prefatory note to Desai, only its principal points may be summarized here and elsewhere in this chapter.[10] Regarding the Preamble, Gajendragadkar said that both 'secular' and 'socialist' were ambiguous and should be defined. He objected to the 'escape clause' in Article 31C and 'saw no justification' for making all the Directive Principles superior to the Fundamental Rights. Article 31D barring anti-national activities should be deleted as abhorrent in theory and dangerous in practice.[11] He favoured restoring the Supreme and high courts' powers to consider the validity of state and central laws, and he favoured deleting the Forty-second Amendment's provisions for larger benches and two-thirds votes in constitutional cases. The high-sounding, but 'innocuous', Fundamental Duties might be kept. The oft-disputed words 'for any other purpose' for issuing prerogative writs should be restored to Article 226 to enable citizens to gain relief 'for their legitimate grievances' through the writs.

[9] Ibid.

[10] In the note, Gajendragadkar pointed out that he had sent comments on the draft version of the Forty-second Amendment to Prime Minister Gandhi, that his comments then had been made in a hurry, and that now he had given deeper thought to the issues. He told Desai that he had consulted Mrs Gandhi about submitting to Desai much of the material he had submitted to her earlier and that she had no objection to his doing this.

In his earlier letters to Desai, Gajendragadkar had recommended selective repeal of the amendment and had advised great caution regarding removing property from the Fundamental Rights.

[11] 'Prefatory Note', P. B. Gajendragadkar Papers, Subject File 1, pp. 9–10, NMML.

Turning to the amending article, Article 368, Gajendragadkar found 'most objectionable' the Forty-second Amendment's prohibition of the courts questioning constitutional amendments. He could not understand, he wrote, how the actual exercise of the amending power under the article's provisions could be beyond court scrutiny.[12] On the other hand, he reiterated that, under Article 368, Parliament had constituent power; therefore he was 'unable to subscribe' to the basic structure doctrine. '[I]f the government feels that basic features should not be amendable', he wrote, 'then it should add a clause indicating what the basic features are' so the law would not 'remain vague and uncertain'.[13]

Justice Gajendragadkar's views of the administrative and other tribunals that were provided for in the Forty-second Amendment strengthened the Janata government's negative view of them. He opposed retaining tribunals unless appeals to the Supreme Court were provided for expressly and unless tribunal members were required to have the same qualifications as Supreme Court judges. Then, tribunals might be able to reduce arrears. A number of Law Ministry officials shared these views.[14] Bhushan and Janata members, broadly, wanted to remove tribunals entirely from the Constitution because they had the taint of the Emergency and seemed subject to executive branch manipulation.[15] As will be seen, retaining tribunals, although with added safeguards, was part of the price exacted by Congress in the Rajya Sabha for its support for the Forty-fourth Amendment.

Soon after considering the Law Minister's note on amendment, at its 16 August 1977 meeting, the cabinet subcommittee sent specific proposals to the Opposition. Chavan was said to be willing to consider

---

[12] Ibid , p. 20. He also recommended that Article 3 of the Constitution should be included in the proviso of Article 368 because 'Parliament alone should not be able to make a law affecting the boundaries ... of different constituent units'. Ibid. According to Article 3, such bills were to be sent to the state legislature concerned 'for expressing its views'.

[13] Ibid., p. 23.

[14] Ibid., pp. 16–18. Venkatasubramanian in an interview with the author. Gajendragadkar commented at length on the qualifications and method of appointment of Supreme Court judges. And he thought that the article empowering the President to transfer high court judges should be deleted or a provision added that no judge could be transferred without his permission, a position consistent with his earlier thinking.

[15] Bhushan and Venkatasubramanian in interviews with the author. Bhushan's view presently is that tribunals can serve a useful function and that the quality of their functioning depends especially upon the quality of their members. The Chief Justice of India should have a larger role in selecting members, he believes.

them with his colleague, V. A. Seyid Muhammad, and it quickly became clear that many Congressmen either had been intimidated into voting for an amendment they disliked or that they had had great changes of heart since they passed the Forty-second Amendment. Muhammad had written a note for the Congress Parliamentary Party, the *Hindustan Times* reported, saying that a majority of the Swaran Singh Committee, of which he had been a member, had opposed adding Article 31D to the Constitution. His note favoured the repeal of the article empowering the government to deploy police forces under its own command in a state without the state government's concurrence (Article 257A). This was an 'unjustified encroachment' on states' rights. Muhammad's note favoured the Constitution's providing for only two kinds of emergency: an external emergency or an internal one only in a part of the country— and, then, only in cases of insurgency or threatened secession. This would do away with the '"horrible consequences and excesses"' of the recent Emergency, he wrote. He favoured reverting to five-year terms for Parliament and legislatures and to one-tenth membership as constituting a quorum. Equally significantly, Muhammad recommended restoring the Supreme Court's jurisdiction and powers of judicial review by repealing the relevant four provisions in the Forty-second Amendment. At a Parliamentary Party meeting the previous day, Chavan was reported to have said that '"We will adopt a practical and cooperative attitude"' toward amending the Constitution and that draft amendments should be discussed in the AICC.[16]

Janata's cabinet subcommittee continued its work over the next seven weeks. It favoured fulfilling the party's election promise to remove property from the Fundamental Rights so as to protect the other Rights from further erosion, newspapers reported. But the delicacy of the issue caused the cabinet to order a fresh study of the legal and political implications of the move, and a few days later, after Bhushan and Attorney General Gupte had discussed the matter with Desai, decision was reported to have been postponed. News reports also said that the subcommittee favoured retaining the provision that the President 'shall' act on the advice of his ministers, even though it smacked of the Emergency's authoritarianism, but had 'softened' it to authorize him to send a measure back to the cabinet for reconsideration—but only 'once'. The government had been loath to change the amendment's language, fearing that to do so might be understood in the courts as allowing the President to act independently of ministerial advice.

[16] *Hindustan Times.* 10 September 1977.

The subcommittee was reported to have decided, also, that the President could declare an emergency only on the written advice of the council of ministers, that a two-thirds parliamentary majority must approve the proclamation within a month, and that a tenth of Lok Sabha members could call for a review of the proclamation. Freedom of speech was not to be suspended during an emergency (unless it were due to armed aggression) nor could any preventively detained or any other person be deprived of life or liberty 'under any circumstances' except according to law (Article 21).[17] Periods of President's Rule could last only a year. Detentions were to be reduced to two months unless an advisory board authorized further detention (Article 22). The Fundamental Duties, once thought acceptable, were to be removed because they served no purpose. The 'escape clause' of Article 31C was to go and only Articles 39(b) and (c) of the Directive Principles were to have precedence over the Fundamental Rights. The authority to settle election disputes was to be restored to the Supreme Court. The subcommittee also decided to give constitutional recognition to the right to publish parliamentary and legislative assembly proceedings, which had been banned during the Emergency.

The cabinet reviewed the subcommittee's proposals and approved them by consensus.[18] The Janata Parliamentary Party's executive reviewed the proposals for four days and accepted them on 24 October. They then went to the Parliament Member Consultative Committee attached to the Law Ministry, which, under Shanti Bhushan's chairmanship, discussed the proposals on 28 October 1977, and released them to the press.[19] In forty-seven clauses, these proposals came close to restoring the pre-Emergency Constitution, often reflecting criticisms of the Forty-second Amendment made during the Emergency, and embodied several other changes as well. Their more significant points not already known, and discussed above, were to amend the Preamble to define the word 'secular'; to delete the provision protecting the government's Transaction of Business Rules from court scrutiny; and to delete the section on tribunals from the Constitution, while enabling Parliament to establish tribunals relating to state civil service employees. A further proposal required a decision of the cabinet to precede a proclamation of emergency.[20]

---

[17] *Hindustan Times*, 24 October 1977.

[18] Limaye, *Cabinet Government in India*, p. 143. Limaye attributes this claim of consensus to Morarji Desai.

[19] 'Background Note', Lok Sabha Secretariat, p. 26.

[20] 'Background Note', Lok Sabha Secretariat, appendix III. By way of context, the

Meeting to consider the forty-seven proposals on 18 November, the Congress Parliamentary Party executive 'passed' twelve of them and 'accepted' others with modifications. It will be remembered that the Congress Party at this time had not split and Mrs Gandhi's Congress(I) had not come into existence. The CPP opposed internal emergencies on any ground '"whatsoever"'. It accepted that advice to the President to proclaim an emergency should be in writing, that the continuance of an emergency beyond six months required a parliamentary resolution, and that one-tenth of Lok Sabha members could request a sitting to consider ending or continuing a state of emergency.[21] The meeting discussed reviving judicial review of amendments and accepted Janata's reduction of preventive detention to two months unless an advisory board approved a longer detention. A Congress Working Committee meeting on 6 December 1977 accepted most of the Parliamentary Party's recommendations and went beyond them. It accepted restoring five-year terms for Parliament and state legislatures and agreed to restoring most of the courts' powers stripped by the Thirty-eighth, Thirty-ninth, and the Forty-second Amendments. The Working Committee opposed Janata's attempts to define 'secular' and 'socialist' in the Preamble, deleting the Fundamental Duties, and deleting the section on tribunals which the CPP earlier had accepted.

The Forty-third Amendment Emerges

Beginning about 11 November 1977 an earlier idea re-emerged and the government began informal consultations with other parties about embodying several of the forty-seven proposals in an amendment to be passed before the end of the year, leaving the bulk of them for enactment in a second amendment. Minister of Parliamentary Affairs Varma sent the proposed content of what would become the Forty-third amendment to the Opposition on this date so that formal discussions might begin. On 7 December Desai met opposition leaders and reached a large measure of agreement, the *Hindustan Times* reported. The brief amendment would delete Article 31D on anti-national activities, dispense with larger benches

---

government, in the autumn of 1977, was attempting to redress other excesses of the Emergency, to prosecute Mrs Gandhi and others for alleged illegal activities, and to manage national affairs such as the budget and taxes and the ever-capricious typhoon that killed an estimated fifteen thousand persons on the Andhra Coast—all the while dealing with increasing tensions within the Janata Party.

[21] The account of the meeting is from the *Hindustan Times*, 19 November 1977.

and special majorities in constitutional cases, and restore the high courts' powers to examine the constitutionality of central laws and the Supreme Court's authority to examine the constitutionality of state laws. The meeting agreed to retain the Fundamental Duties (harmless, Desai was said to believe). In these consultations, Desai, Jagjivan Ram, and the members of the Parliamentary Affairs Committee represented the government. Y. B. Chavan, Congress leader in Parliament, and Kamalapati Tripathi represented the Congress.[22] Chavan, Brahmananda Reddy, elected president of the Congress the previous May, and C. Subramaniam co-operated well with Janata, while Mrs Gandhi, out of Parliament and intent on her comeback strategy, criticized them for this.[23]

The government was to begin drafting the actual bill. At Desai's second meeting with the Opposition, 14 December, it was further agreed that Article 257A would be deleted so that the central government would not be able to send its armed forces into states 'in aid of civil power' without the state government's concurrence. It also was agreed to eliminate the Thirty-ninth Amendment's provisions regarding disputes concerning election of the President, Vice-President, Prime Minister, and Speaker, but this would await incorporation later in the Forty-fourth Amendment.[24]

Shanti Bhushan introduced the Forty-third Amendment (at that moment the Forty-fourth Amendment Bill) in the Lok Sabha on 16 December 1977. He expressed regret that a comprehensive bill could not have been introduced as promised. The government, however, was alive to the necessity of undoing the mischief of the Forty-second Amendment. The one-line bill had been rejected, Bhushan said, because some of the Forty-second Amendment's provisions were already in force and other provisions were worth keeping.[25] He might have added that it would not pass in the Rajya Sabha. Commending the bill's provisions,

[22] Representing other opposition parties were: P. Ramamurthi, CPM; Bhupesh Gupta and Mrs Parvathi Krishnan, CPI; Sulaiman Sait, Muslim League; and two others.

[23] V. N. Gadgil and Madhu Limaye in interviews with the author.

[24] *Hindustan Times,* 15 December 1977.

[25] Strong advocates of one-line repeal included Madhu Limaye, Ram Jethmalani, George Fernandes, and Soli Sorabjee—Sorabjee on the ground that the Forty-second Amendment 'had been conceived in sin'. (Sorabjee in an interview with the author.) Advani was said to favour this until Bhushan talked him out of it. Bhushan thought legal aid to the poor among the provisions in the Forty-second Amendment worth saving. Shanti Bhushan in an interview with the author.

[26] *Lok Sabha Debates,* Sixth Series, vol. 9, no. 24, col. 269–71.

Bhushan made this argument forcefully in the Rajya Sabha. *Parliamentary Debates, Rajya Sabha,* vol. 103, no. 27, col 124.

Bhushan said that Article 31D should be repealed because it infringed citizens' fundamental rights. Seven-judge benches needing two-thirds majorities for judicial review rulings would give judges deciding in favour of the government 'a larger voice', worth two votes to a minority judge's one.[26] Speaking to other provisions of the bill, he said the high courts' authority to scrutinize the constitutionality of central laws had been restored because the poor could not travel to Delhi to protect their rights.

During consideration of the bill the Congress made admissions startling both in their content and for their public character. We want 'to reassert and to uphold the fundamental values for which the Congress has always stood', said Seyid Muhammad, supporting the bill. He cited Article 31D as not a recommendation of the Swaran Singh Committee, but one of the 'extremely restrictive' measures some in the party had opposed at the time.[27] Congress member Jagannath Rao welcomed the bill and explained how he and others had spoken against much of the Forty-second Amendment, but, obeying the Whip, had voted for it.[28] Other Congressmen spoke along similar lines. After the third reading on 20 December, the bill passed 318 to one.

The Rajya Sabha considered the bill on 23 December and passed it the same day without a 'nay' vote—the result of 'mutual persuasion', said Bhushan. Ninety-one Congress members who had voted to enact the Forty-second Amendment voted in the Rajya Sabha for the Forty-third. In the Lok Sabha twenty-nine Congress members who voted to enact the Forty-second Amendment did likewise. (Due to election defeats, Congress representation in the Lok Sabha was much reduced.) All the members of the Swaran Singh Committee then in either house voted for the amending bill.[29] After ratification by state assemblies, the amendment received the President's assent on 13 April 1978.

Coincidental events must have given impetus to the amendment's passage. Testimony about the origins and excesses of the Emergency filled the newspapers during the autumn, largely from the hearings of

---

The logic here, it will be recalled, is that the minority judges could control a judicial review bench by preventing a two-thirds majority. For instance, a two-thirds majority within a seven-judge bench would be five votes to two—to avoid fractions of a vote—thus enabling three judges to frustrate the will of four. Justice Gajendragadkar was also of this view.

[27] *Lok Sabha Debates*, Sixth Series, vol. 9, no. 24, col. 284–6.

[28] Ibid., cols 322–3.

[29] Vasant Sathe, Seyid Muhammad, and C. M. Stephen in the Lok Sabha, and B. N. Banerjee and V. N. Gadgil in the Rajya Sabha.

the Shah Commission (chapter 21). In these, the Cabinet Secretary and the Home Secretary of Mrs Gandhi's government were quoted as having said that imposition of the Emergency was unnecessary. The head of the Intelligence Bureau, Atma Jayaram, testified that the imposition had been so secret he had not known about it. Witnesses told how the arrest lists had been prepared in the Prime Minister's house and that signed but otherwise blank arrest warrants had been issued. Newspapers carried accounts of the infamous 'Turkman Gate' incident in Old Delhi, when the police had killed squatters resisting removal from slums.

Drafting the Forty-fourth Amendment Continues

The day before the Rajya Sabha passed the Forty-third Amendment, Morarji Desai had the third of his consultative meetings with the Opposition to reach agreement over the undecided proposals that might be included in the follow-on amendment. The parties agreed that the rights to life and liberty were not to be suspended during an emergency, that Articles 358 and 359 should be amended accordingly, and that there should be restrictions on the suspension of the freedoms of Article 19. The Opposition agreed that MISA 1971, and other Emergency legislation would be repealed during the current session, including their removal from the Ninth Schedule. President's Rule was to be restricted to a year unless renewed. Congress wished to retain and Janata to delete the Thirty-eighth Amendment's provision that the President's 'satisfaction' when promulgating ordinances could not be questioned in court. Similarly, Congress wished there to be no judicial questioning of a President's proclamation of emergency. Janata seems about now to have suggested the idea of adding a referendum to the amending article to be invoked if the basic structure of the Constitution were to be altered.[30]

Shanti Bhushan did not wish to leave defining the basic structure entirely to the judiciary. He thought the Supreme Court 'under the guise of protecting the basic structure, could prevent a much-needed amendment'.[31] The remedy was to go to the people in a referendum if an amending bill would affect certain basic features—such as the secular

[30] *Hindustan Times*, 23 December 1977.

Janata was again represented by Desai, Ram, Charan Singh, and Bhushan; Congress by Chavan; and other parties by Bhupesh Gupta, Ramamurthy, and S. D. Somasundaram, AIADMK.

[31] Shanti Bhushan interview with the author.

and democratic character of the Constitution, the Fundamental Rights, free and fair elections, and compromising the independence of the judiciary.[32] Chavan was reported to have accepted the idea and to oppose court review of amendments. Yet, practical and conceptual problems with a referendum remained, and it would be the subject of intense bargaining between Congress and Janata as voting on the Forty-fourth Amendment approached.[33]

Throughout Delhi's rose-filled winter of 1978 and into hot weather, crafting the Forty-fourth Amendment continued. One issue remaining to be resolved was the constitutional status of property. The Janata Party's election manifesto had pledged to remove property from the Fundamental Rights while retaining it as a statutory right. Morarji Desai and Charan Singh, considered the leader of the 'big farmers' lobby, supported the idea, as had Shanti Bhushan in the committee he had formed before the election to consider constitutional changes. The press reported that he still did.[34] The principal rationale for the move was to protect the other Fundamental Rights in the Constitution. Both government and Opposition recalled when in the wake of the Golak Nath decision, Rammanohar Lohia and Madhu Limaye (now a Janata Party general secretary) had advocated removing property from the Rights as an alternative to the Nath Pai Bill's bestowal on Parliament of blanket power to amend any part of the Constitution. With these memories, making property only a statutory right was a preventive measure.

Over the years, Limaye had become more cautious. He now thought taking property from the Rights endangered the smallholder and smacked of populism.[35] Law Commission Chairman Gajendragadkar agreed with him and advised the Prime Minister that if property were not a right, it could be taken without compensation and 'there would be probably no remedy to the party aggrieved'. No wise legislature would do this, he added, but 'my faith in the wisdom of legislatures has been rudely

---

[32] From the Statement of Objects and Reasons in 'The Constitution (Forty-fifth Amendment) Bill, 1978', which would become the Forty-fourth Amendment, as published by the Lok Sabha Secretariat.

[33] Looking back on the bill, constitutional authority H. M. Seervai thought the referendum idea 'ill-advised and ill-conceived' and unconstitutional. The basic structure of the Constitution was not to be amended, the Kesavananda decision had established, and therefore it could not be amended even through a referendum. Seervai, *Constitutional Law of India*, 3rd edn., vol. 2, p. 2702.

[34] Shanti Bhushan interview with the author. Also in a speech in Calcutta in February 1978. *Hindustan Times*, 12 February 1978.

[35] Limaye's recollection in an interview with the author—in which he also said that he did not know who put the pledge in the election manifesto.

shaken'.[36] It has been alleged that Janata had agreed to take property from the Rights in trade for the support of the two Communist parties in the March 1977 elections. Ramakrishna Hegde and Shanti Bhushan have denied this.[37] Given the CPM's hatred of the Emergency, it probably needed no inducement to support Janata in the elections. The CPI at the moment of the elections was still enough in Mrs Gandhi's camp so that no inducement Janata offered was likely to cause it to change its loyalties. By the time the Forty-fourth Amendment was in its final stages, however, Janata members may well have used removing property from the Rights, which they supported on its merits, as an inducement for communist and other support.

Urged on by President Sanjiva Reddy to build bulwarks against use of '"the Constitution itself to negate and to subvert the basic principles of democracy"', and to remove the '"dark spots"' from it, Prime Minister Desai and his colleagues again met opposition leaders on 20 April.[38] The Opposition (the Congress(I), which had been recognized on 12 April as the main opposition party in the Lok Sabha) agreed with the government that a comprehensive amending bill should be introduced in the current session, but positions differed on sending the bill to a joint select committee of both Houses. Congress and Congress(I) favoured this, Janata and the CPI and CPM opposed it, and the bill did not go to the committee. When discussion turned to adding a referendum to the amending process, opinion again was divided sharply. C. M. Stephen, by now the Congress(I) leader in the Lok Sabha and possessing a more aggressive character than Chavan, said he could not agree with the idea because his party's working committee still was considering it. The CPM's Samar Mukherjee not only favoured the idea, but, fearing unitary government, wanted any change to the federal character of the Constitution added to the subjects that would demand a referendum. Bhushan,

[36] Gajendragadkar, 'Prefatory Note', P. B. Gajendragadkar Papers, Subject File 1, NMML, p. 9.

H. M. Seervai disagreed with the government's and Shanti Bhushan's position about removing property from the Rights. Bhushan's rationale that property should be removed because it had evoked many amendments was 'not sufficient reason' to do so, Seervai wrote. Moreover, Bhushan had not taken into account the close relationship of the right to property to other fundamental rights. Seervai, *Constitutional Law of India*, vol. 2, pp. 1073ff.

[37] Ramakrishna Hegde, who became a Janata Party general secretary in August 1977, and Shanti Bhushan in interviews with the author claimed there was no trade-off. Soli Sorabjee in an interview with the author recalled that Shanti Bhushan told him there had been a trade-off.

[38] Quotations from Sanjiva Reddy speech inaugurating the session of Parliament commencing on 20 February 1978. *Hindustan Times*, 21 February 1978.

while continuing to favour a referendum before changing the basic structure, opposed this, saying that the Constitution was not strictly federal.[39] The cabinet approved Bhushan's position on 25 April and the Janata Parliamentary Party did likewise the next day.[40]

On other matters, the government and Opposition agreed that there should be certain safeguards to property after its removal from the Fundamental Rights. No land within the ceiling could be taken without compensation at 'market value', and if property were taken from a minority educational institution, the amount of compensation should not interfere with the minority's constitutional right to establish educational institutions of its choice. Concerning the emergency provisions, both the Congress and the Congress(I) accepted the government's proposals for curtailing them. The CPI and CPM wanted to eliminate any opportunity for declaring an internal emergency by removing 'internal disturbance' as a justification for imposing one and they opposed retention of President's Rule. Both causes failed, but in the Forty-fourth Amendment the more precise term 'armed rebellion' replaced 'internal disturbance'— the wording of the Constitution's original Article 352—as a cause for declaring an emergency. The opposition parties also proposed that constitutional protection be given to the publication of parliamentary and legislative assembly proceedings, going beyond Janata's restoration of the older 'Feroze Gandhi Act' of the fifties, which gave only legislative protection.[41] This cooperation between the government and the Opposition was in sharp contrast to the lack of it within the Janata Party: the next day, 21 April, Chandra Shekhar threatened to resign as president, along with the general secretaries, over criticism that he had not called internal party elections.

Shortly after this and ten days before the amendment was introduced in the Lok Sabha, C. M. Stephen summed up the Congress(I)'s position. Of the numerous clauses in the draft amendment, the party opposed only ten and might be brought around on several of these. Its objections

---

[39] The account of this meeting is drawn from the *Hindustan Times*, 21 April 1978. Bhushan had advocated a referendum on television four days earlier. *Hindustan Times*, 17 April 1978.

[40] *Hindustan Times*, 26 April 1978.

[41] Bhushan, Charan Singh, Ram, Advani, and Varma were reported to have represented the government at the meeting; Desai did not attend. For the Opposition, Stephen represented the Congress (I), Seyid Muhammad the Congress, Samar Mukherjee and Somnath Chatterjee the CPM, Govindan Nair and Bhupesh Gupta the CPI, Chitta Basu the Forward Bloc, George Mathew the Kerala Congress, and Mohan Rangam and V. Arunachalam, the AIADMK.

were mainly to the referendum; to 'diluting the primacy of the Directive Principles' by re-amending Article 31C; and to including 'armed rebellion' as cause for declaring an emergency, although the party said it might eliminate provisions for internal emergencies. Mrs Gandhi's Congress (I) was prepared to overturn the Forty-second Amendment's placing exclusively in the hands of the President the authority to determine whether a member of Parliament had disqualified himself for office, Stephen said. But, apparently with Mrs Gandhi's experience in mind, it would oppose disqualification for elective office for corrupt election practice, '"however technical or nominal"'.[42] Assessing the tactical position, Stephen noted that the Congress(I) had sixty-five members in the Rajya Sabha, not enough to defeat the amending bill if the other Congress voted with the government. '"We cannot block the amendment by ourselves,"' he said. As we shall see, the two Congress parties joined forces to defeat only a few portions of the bill.[43]

The Forty-fourth Amendment in Parliament

Law Minister Shanti Bhushan introduced the Forty-fourth Amendment in the Lok Sabha on 15 May 1978. The bill's Statement of Objects and Reasons opened with the lines: 'Recent experience has shown that the fundamental rights, including those of life and liberty, granted to citizens by the Constitution are capable of being taken away by a transient majority. It is therefore necessary to provide adequate safeguards against the recurrence of such a contingency ...'.[44] The amendment had two principal purposes, the Statement went on: to restore the Constitution

---

[42] *Hindustan Times*, 5 May 1978. Stephen was asked about a referendum and Parliament representing the people: What if Parliament becomes captive of one person, as recently? The reader can decide if his response was a compliment or an insult to the 'people' and to Indira Gandhi: '"People get the government leader they deserve,"' Stephen reportedly said. Ibid.

[43] This co-operation had its limits. In a move that could be interpreted as an attempt to block any repeal of the Forty-second Amendment, but seems not to have signified this, the two Congress parties, the CPI, and the Muslim League on 10 May brought a no-confidence motion against the government. Nothing came of a five-hour debate over whether or not popular sentiment indicated that Janata could not govern.

[44] 'The Constitution (Forty-fifth Amendment) Bill, 1978', Lok Sabha Secretariat, p. 16. As was typical of bills, the bill as introduced included the Statement of Objects and Reasons, the text of the bill, and 'Notes on Clauses', which explained the content and purpose of each clause.

For a contemporary analysis of the amendment, see Dhavan, Rajeev, 'Amending the Amendment: The Constitution (Forty-fifth Amendment) Bill, 1978', *JILI*, vol. 20, no. 2, 1978, pp. 249–71.

to its condition before the Emergency amendments and to add safeguards to restrict the executive's emergency and analogous powers.

The amendment did as promised. To prevent abuse of the emergency provisions in the Constitution, the bill proposed that an emergency could be proclaimed only in case of war, external aggression, or armed rebellion. The President could proclaim an emergency only upon 'written advice ... by the cabinet', and such a proclamation would have to be approved by Parliament within one month by a majority of the members and two-thirds of those present and voting. An emergency could be continued more than six months only if Parliament voted to renew it. 'President's Rule' proclamations would be valid for six months 'in the first instance and ... cannot exceed one year ordinarily'.[45] The Fundamental Rights were to be protected by permitting their amendment only by a national referendum. The right of habeas corpus could be preserved even during emergencies. Protections were increased for those held under preventive detention. The media's right to report legislative debates was guaranteed.[46]

Although introduced in May, the bill was not taken up until 7 August, in the monsoon session. Then, speaking in its favour Bhushan expressed gratitude for the friendly spirit of the 'detailed dialogue' during its preparation.[47] He emphasized the importance of the restrictions added to the emergency provisions and explained that Article 257A (central forces in a state) had been deleted because it 'was not in accordance with the scheme of things ... laid down in the Constitution'. He said that the Janata government favoured specialized tribunals supervised by the high courts so the 'small man' would have recourse to an independent court 'in his own state', and he praised restoring the Supreme Court's role in deciding election disputes by deleting Article 329A.[48] Bhushan defended taking property out of the Fundamental Rights, arguing that because the 'vast majority' of Indians did not own extensive property 'to equate the right to property to the more important rights ... [had resulted in curbing] ... the other fundamental rights'.[49] Turning to amendment of the

---

[45] Taken from the Objects and Reasons, 'The Constitution (Forty-fifth Amendment) Bill, 1978'.

[46] Ibid.

[47] Bhushan had contributed to this atmosphere; and he continued to do so. Several days before the bill's introduction, he had hosted a dinner at his Race Course Road residence for Congress and Congress (I) leaders Stephen, Muhammad, and Kamalapati Tripathi (then in the Rajya Sabha) to urge their support for the amending bill—using the argument that this would preempt the government from using the Forty-second Amendment against them.

[48] *Lok Sabha Debates*, Sixth Series, vol. 17, no. 15, cols 295–302.

[49] Ibid., cols 307–8.

Constitution, Bhushan said that 'we must ... seek [the people's] ratification' to change provisions in which they are vitally interested. We can't operate 'behind their backs'.[50]

He rejected all but a handful of the four hundred amendments offered to the amending bill. To one providing that property could be taken by government only by due process of law, he said that would be making property a fundamental right 'by the back door', and he added that so much importance should not be given to property or 'our credibility will not be there among the poor people'.[51] He expressed understanding for Somnath Chatterjee's desire to eliminate internal emergencies, but said that without emergency powers 'neither democracy nor liberty can be safe'.[52] But he accepted a private member's amendment providing that Articles 20 and 21 in the Rights could not be suspended during an emergency. Respectively, these were the *ex post facto* provision and the article laying down that no one shall be deprived of life or liberty except according to procedure established by law.[53] The bill passed 355 to nil on 23 August and went to the Rajya Sabha.

There, beginning on 28 August, Congress members exacted their price for the amendment's passage. Without the necessary two-thirds majority, clause 8 of the bill failed passage, thus leaving the Fundamental Rights in Articles 14 and 19 subservient to all of the Directive Principles and retaining the 'escape clause' in Article 31C. As will be recalled, this meant that a law claiming to give effect to the Directive Principles could not be questioned in court on the ground that it did not do so. The clauses in the bill deleting tribunals from the Constitution failed passage, as did those clauses defining 'socialist' and 'secular' in the Preamble, and those returning 'education' to the State Legislative List.[54]

---

[50] Ibid., col. 310.

[51] Ibid., vol. 18, no. 35, col. 18.

[52] Ibid., col. 72.

[53] Ibid., col. 99. The private member's amendment came from Kanwar Lal Gupta, and had an interesting history. Members of the public had been writing the government about the amending bill, and Peri Sastri and Venkatasubramanian in the Law Ministry had been reading the letters. One of them from a retired district and sessions judge, living in Jammu, Mr Kaul, suggested not suspending Articles 20 and 21 during an emergency. Taken with the idea, the two convinced Bhushan that this suggestion ought to be accepted, and Gupta was asked to submit it in a bill under his own name instead of the government moving an amendment to its own bill—which would have been a more laborious procedure. The relevant language was placed in Article 359 of the Constitution. P. B. Venkatasubramanian in correspondence with the author.

[54] For the debates in the Rajya Sabha, see *Parliamentary Debates, Rajya Sabha*, vol. 106, no. 29, cols 42ff through no. 32.

K. V. Raghunatha Reddy, a minister in Mrs Gandhi's Emergency cabinet and former

Also unsuccessful was the move to add a referendum to the amending process. Relying on the device of a referendum to protect the Constitution's basic structure seems to have been a major miscalculation by the government. With this defeat, the Constitution remained vulnerable under Article 368 as altered by the Forty-second Amendment, namely that no amendment made under the article, including to the Fundamental Rights, could be questioned in court and that 'there shall be no limitation whatever on the constituent power of Parliament' even to repeal the Constitution (Article 368(5)). It was left to the Supreme Court in the 1980 Minerva Mills Case (chapter 25) to declare unconstitutional these clauses of Article 368, which returned Parliament's power to amend the Constitution to the language of the Twenty-fourth Amendment as interpreted in Kesavananda Bharati. The Rajya Sabha passed its version of the bill on 31 August 1978 by a vote of 182 to 1. Of the aye votes, some eighty were cast by Congress members who had voted in favour of the Forty-second Amendment and three who had been members of the Swaran Singh Committee.

The Lok Sabha greeted the Rajya Sabha's revised bill with dismay when it returned on 6 December, this being the first time that an amending bill passed by the Lok Sabha had been changed and returned by the Rajya Sabha. There ensued a lengthy discussion about the rules for reconsideration. Managing the bill (with Bhushan absent due to illness), P. C. Chunder deplored the idea of not accepting the Rajya Sabha's changes because half a loaf was 'better than no bread'. If the bill shuttled back and forth between the Houses, with both sides rejecting the other's changes, it might fail, he argued. P. G Mavalankar, noted for standing up to the Congress during the Emergency, seemed to be speaking for many when he said the members were in the position of either accepting the 'political humiliation' inflicted by the other House or 'the entire thing collapsing'. He recommended that the government accept the Rajya Sabha's changes and later bring new bills to 'undo the remaining evil still lurking' in the Forty-second Amendment.[55] That day and the next, the members passed the amended clauses with no more than forty negative votes on any, and the bill passed with only one 'nay'.

Among the 357 votes cast on 7 December 1978 to enact the Forty-fourth Amendment were those of two enemies: Morarji Desai and Indira

member of the Congress Forum for Socialist Action supported the referendum, saying that a party with a two-thirds majority, using the Three-line Whip, could change the Constitution in twenty-four hours.

[55] *Lok Sabha Debates*, Sixth Series, vol. 20, no. 13, cols 316–20.

Gandhi. Desai was no surprise. Mrs Gandhi, having being returned to Parliament in a November by-election in the South (only to be expelled shortly for breach of privilege), also voted to repeal the Forty-second Amendment, along with some forty other Congress members. According to one assessment she did so because she realized the public's dissatisfaction with the Emergency and wanted to show that she had not intended to destroy the Constitution.[56] This is possible, but it is unlikely that her vote indicates that she had seen the error of her way or that she had not understood the import of the Forty-second Amendment when it originally was presented to her. Probably she calculated that a reversal of her position was a small price to pay for her political comeback, which already was well under way.

Political self-preservation no doubt motivated other Congress members of Parliament.[57] Still active in politics, they had to take their constituents' views into account. 'They were telling the people we are for the democratic process,' thought Margaret Alva, a Congress general secretary in 1976.[58] 'They were showing their dissatisfaction with the Forty-second Amendment by voting for the Forty-fourth,' thought Om Mehta.[59] 'Prime Minister Desai's being in his heart still a Congressman and his giving them a constructive role in the process encouraged the Opposition's co-operation,' recalled an official of the Law Ministry under both Janata and Congress governments. Bhushan's sensitivity to Congress members' sentiments also helped, particularly his awareness that a swift, blanket repeal of the Forty-second Amendment would have branded Congressmen as wholly evil.[60] Finally, the Congress Party's state of 'complete demoralization' allowed the amendment's passage, thought Madhu Limaye—something that would not have been possible had Indira Gandhi led a united party.[61]

The apparent alacrity with which Congressmen changed their

[56] Jagmohan in an interview with the author. As head of the Delhi Development Authority during the Emergency, Jagmohan had worked closely with Sanjay Gandhi on slum clearance and other projects.

[57] The following analysis is based on more than a dozen interviews, most of them with members of the Congress Party at the time the Forty-second Amendment was passed.

[58] Margaret Alva in an interview with the author.

[59] Om Mehta in an interview with the author.

[60] Interviews with, among others, Bhushan and Venkatasubramanian. Bhushan's depiction of his own central role may appear self-serving, but other evidence bears him out.

[61] Madhu Limaye interview with the author.

positions raises questions about their having voted for the Forty-second Amendment in the first place. Obedience to party discipline is a possible justification. Governments can usually rely on their followers, Sir Ivor Jennings has told us. 'They can, within wide limits, force unpopular measures through a sullen House.'[62] Some members may have agreed with the substance of the amendment. Did the others vote for what they later rejected in fear of a tyrannical Prime Minister's retaliation? Had they voted against her, she could have done them little harm, especially in the autumn of 1976, the Emergency's waning days. The few individuals who did vote against the amendment suffered no retaliation. A final assessment is impossible because we cannot know the fate of either the Forty-second or Forty-fourth Amendments had *all* the Congressmen who voted for the former been present to vote on the latter. Nevertheless, it seems reasonable to conclude that many of the Congressmen who voted for the Forty-second Amendment did so out of fear and for the Forty-fourth Amendment out of conviction. Thus was the Constitution put in peril by tyranny and cravenness, and thus was it rescued by belief in democracy and its open process.

As for Janata, it is remarkable that a party in such disarray managed to enact the Forty-fourth Amendment. Seventeen days before the government introduced the draft bill in the Lok Sabha (May 1978) Charan Singh had resigned from the Janata National Executive and its Parliamentary Board, charging that those of low social origin were having no share in shaping the country's destiny.[63] He had resigned from the cabinet on 30 June 1978, five weeks before the bill would be considered, along with Health Minister Raj Narain and four ministers of state from the Bharatiya Lok Dal—only to withdraw his resignation twelve days later. The antagonisms within both party and government continued to fester all summer, to burst in December 1978 while the Lok Sabha was reconsidering the Forty-fourth Amendment as returned from the Rajya Sabha. Charan Singh was again out of the government, and the cabinet was riven by disagreements over issues such as the extent to which Mrs Gandhi should be punished either by prosecution in the courts or expulsion from Parliament. Nevertheless, the amendment was passed and, with ratification by legislative assemblies in fourteen states, the

[62] Jennings, Sir Ivor, *Parliament*, 2nd edn., Cambridge University Press, Cambridge, 1957, p. 138.

[63] *AR*, 25 June–1 July 1978, p. 14374. In contrast to this picture of enmity, two very senior civil servants under this government spoke to the author of a 'camaraderie remarkable in such a disparate group'.

President gave his assent to the amendment on 30 April 1979. Beginning mid-June, many of its provisions were 'notified' by the government, thus actually coming into force.[64] Two months later Morarji Desai's Janata government fell.

---

[64] For details, see *Gazettee of India Extraordinary,* Government of India Publications, Part II, Section 3 (i), 19 June 1979.

There was an important omission. Clause 3 of the amendment affecting Article 22— which said that no one could be detained under a preventive detention law for more than two months without the sanction of an Advisory Board and which otherwise provided detenus more protections—was not notified, nor had it been as of July 1993. See *V. N. Shukla Constitution of India,* p. 180, footnote 65. S. Balakrishnan, long-time senior adviser in the Law and Home ministries, wrote a long note protesting the absence of notification. Shanti Bhushan explained to the author that the government then had individuals detained under COFEPOSA who it would have been obliged to release had this article come into effect. 'We needed several months to enact provisions to keep these persons in jail, but the government fell before we could streamline laws regarding them', Bhushan said.

Chapter 20

GOVERNING UNDER THE CONSTITUTION

The government's programme to restore democracy, Acting President
B. D. Jatti told Parliament, included the '"urgent tasks"' of removing
curbs on the Fundamental Rights and restoring the rule of law.[1] Prime
Minister Morarji Desai, in his broadcast to the nation, promised remedial
'"restructuring and system changes"'.[2] Pursuing these aims, while
amending the Constitution, the Janata government would be confronted
by the responsibilities of office and the accompanying perplexities, which
caused it to perform well and less well. And because important ministers
had been Congressmen, much that the government did and did not do
had a familiar ring—displaying again the well-known continuities in
Indian governance.

This chapter will take up these topics in four sections. The first of
these, 'Fundamental Freedoms', describes the successful repealing of
legislation curbing the freedoms of speech, the press, and so on. The
government's encounter with that long-standing liberty issue, preventive
detention, proved embarrassing. The second section describes the
executive's protection of judicial independence, which on two occasions
had to be from assaults by several of its own supporters. As to national
unity and integrity and centre–state relations, taken up in the third section,
Janata failed to fulfill its promises of increased political participation
through decentralization toward the grassroots. The government's
dismissal of state governments in Congress's hands bordered on the
undemocratic, although strictly speaking they were constitutional. In the
final section of this chapter are described the appointment of several
commissions to assist socially and economically disadvantaged citizens.
The work of one of these later would become profoundly influential.
Janata's ability to govern was severely tested by demands to punish Indira
Gandhi and her close associates for alleged wrong-doing during the
Emergency. So important were the constitutional and immediate political
ramifications of this test that they are treated separately in the next chapter.

---

[1] Speech of 26 March 1977 while inaugurating the session. *Hindustan Times*, 29 March
1977. The newspaper praised the speech for its 'realism and lack of verbosity'.
[2] 4 April 1977. *AR*, 14–20 May 1977, pp. 13734–6.

Fundamental Freedoms

Three days after assuming office on 27 March 1977, the Desai government began its efforts, through ordinances and legislation, to overturn the Emergency's restrictions on the Fundamental Rights. It revoked the long-existing external emergency proclaimed on 12 December 1971 at the time of the Bangladesh war—thus also ending the applicability of the Defence of India Act and the Defence of India Rules. Mrs Gandhi's government had revoked the June 1975 Emergency on 21 March 1977 upon its defeat at the polls. Shortly thereafter, 'amidst cheers', the Lok Sabha repealed the Publication of Objectionable Matter Act and the Parliamentary Proceedings (Protection) Act, which also restored the Protection of Publication Act of 1956. The Statement of Objects and Reasons of the first bill, piloted by Information and Broadcasting Minister L. K. Advani, said that 'Freedom of the press is necessary for the successful functioning of democratic institutions.' The statement for the second bill said that it is 'of paramount importance that proceedings in Parliament should be communicated to the public', and that the mass media should be able to publish 'substantially true reports of proceedings ... without being exposed to any civil or criminal action'.[3] Later, the government lifted the ban on imported publications. Within a few days, the government took from the cabinet secretariat and the Prime Minister's secretariat various organizations and functions Mrs Gandhi had centralized there. Law Minister Bhushan followed these in June with a bill that repealed President Ahmed's 3 February ordinances setting up nine-member election 'authorities' and thus restored to the Supreme Court the power to decide disputes concerning elections of the President, Vice-President, Prime Minister, and Speaker.[4]

A considerably more demanding task was dealing with that tenacious liberty issue, preventive detention. During the election campaign, Janata had pledged itself to reduce the central government's resort to preventive detention, specifically by repealing the 1971 Maintenance of Internal Security Act. Although Acting President Jatti had reiterated the popular promise in his speech inaugurating the new Parliament, the government acted slowly and equivocally. The essence of the matter was that governments over the years had come to believe preventive

---

[3] *Government Bills, 1977*, Lok Sabha Secretariat. For an account of these events, see also Limaye, *Janata Party Experiment*, vol. 1, pp. 395ff.

[4] *AR*, 16–22 July 1977, p. 13839. The bill passed with little debate and with Congress support. Congressman Seyid Muhammed said at the time that in passing the Thirty-ninth Amendment, Congress had intended no disrespect for the judiciary.

detention a necessary—and convenient—tool for governing. 'The Congress governments had always leaned heavily on preventive detention,' and the Janata government 'was dominated by former Congressmen', explained Madhu Limaye.[5] Mohan Dharia, a genuine friend of liberty and the Minister for Commerce and Civil Supplies, faced this dilemma. 'I have no doubt ... that measures like MISA cannot be used against political activities or to scuttle the hard-won freedom of the press,' he wrote to the Prime Minister in July 1977. Within these limitations, however, 'it is necessary to have certain preventive actions against economic offenders and anti-social elements.... Preventive measures, scrupulously avoiding the name MISA, should be immediately introduced against economic offenders and anti-social elements.'[6] The government both pledged '"absolute and unconditional"' repeal of MISA and then, that summer of 1977, explained its failure to do so as due to its need to re-examine the need for preventive detention against economic offences and to protect national security.[7]

During November 1977, detention received a good deal of press attention because of developments in two states. In Jammu and Kashmir, Sheikh Abdullah's government had assumed wide powers for preventive detention and banning the press. Srinagar ignored New Delhi's suggested modifications to the ordinance it intended to proclaim and followed this in April 1978 by enacting a Public Safety Bill providing for detention without trial and for curbs on the press.[8] Also during November, Morarji Desai defended a preventive detention ordinance promulgated in

---

[5] Limaye, *Janata Party Experiment*, vol. 1, p. 301.

[6] But Dharia also recommended important safeguards against the use of detention for political purposes. For his position see his 'Dear Morarjibhai' letter dated 11 July 1977, Jayaprakash Narayan Papers, Third Installment, Subject File 345, NMML. His safeguards were that no individual preventively detained should be 'debarred from approaching the judiciary' and the advisory board 'should necessarily' have on it a representative of the major opposition party (both at the central and state levels) to safeguard the Constitution's freedoms.

Dharia thought it necessary to clarify his position to Jayaprakash Narayan, and he wrote to him on 2 August along the lines of the letter to Desai, but being more specific about using preventive detention 'against hoarders, smugglers, economic offenders' and elements 'which function against the larger interest of the common man'. Ibid.

[7] *Hindustan Times*, 25 August 1977. A few weeks later this newspaper proclaimed that the government was considering repealing MISA by ordinance in a few days. It did not happen.

[8] The Jammu and Kashmir ordinance was dated 6 November. Limaye and Rabi Ray, general secretaries of the Janata Party, strongly deplored it. New Delhi's suggestions were in the form of a letter from Charan Singh to Abdullah. *Hindustan Times*, 7 November 1977, and 8, 11, and 30 November 1977.

Madhya Pradesh in September and admitted that his government was feeling the need for a law to deal with persons bent on disturbing the peace and engaging in anti-social activities.[9]

The government revealed its intention to have it both ways on 23 December. It introduced in the Lok Sabha 'The Code of Criminal Procedure (Amendment) Bill, 1977', which both repealed MISA and would have added to the code a new chapter providing for preventive detention. The bill's Statement of Objects and Reasons, signed by Charan Singh, said that without the power of preventive detention the government was 'greatly handicapped' in dealing with problems of security, public order, and rising prices. But aware of the abuses of the Emergency, the statement continued, the government did not propose to take 'away the right of persons to move the courts for enforcement of Fundamental Rights' and there would be other safeguards to prevent 'the use of this law for political purposes'.[10]

This 'dirty trick, an attempt at deception', as Madhu Limaye thought it, created an uproar in the party for two reasons. One was the reintroduction of preventive detention as such. More significant was that the bill made detention without trial the law of the land, for the Criminal Procedure Code was a permanent statute. The various acts over the years providing for detention were understood to be temporary measures. Several had expired or been repealed, although others had been unduly prolonged, as has been seen. Government explanations and assurances failed to allay fears, and on 16 March 1978 members of the JPP opposed immediate passage of the bill and called for continued

---

[9] *Hindustan Times,* 20 November 1977. At this time, the governments of Andhra Pradesh, Uttar Pradesh, and Rajasthan retained their own preventive detention statutes dating from 1969 and 1971.

[10] See *Government Bills, 1977,* Lok Sabha Secretariat. The government seems not to have fully disclosed the content of the bill at a Janata Parliamentary Party meeting on 22 December.

The bill's safeguards included: orders authorizing officers to detain offenders would be valid for three months only, detenus had to be given the grounds for their detention within five days of it, and detenus were allowed to make representations to the government against the order. Advisory Board members were to be approved by the chief justice of the appropriate high court, and the chairman of the board was to be a high court judge. Within four weeks of the detention, the government had to send the case to the advisory board, which could request information and witnesses. Other safeguards from earlier preventive detention acts were included, and the maximum detention period was to be twelve months.

Actions that could lead to detention included those prejudicial to the defence or security of India and to the maintenance of essential supplies and services. Use of lethal weapons, propagating enmity based on religion and caste, and mischief toward public property could also result in detention.

debate on the matter. A week later, Charan Singh, 'amidst thunderous applause', announced that the bill would be withdrawn, adding that the true test of democracy was its responsiveness to public opinion.[11] A bill repealing MISA passed on 19 July. Yet the chief ministers two months later were reported to favour preventive detention for 'violent and heinous' crimes.[12] More than a year later the issue was back. On 5 October 1979, Charan Singh's caretaker government promulgated The Prevention of Black Marketing and Maintenance of Essential Commodities Ordinance, which included provision for preventive detention while restricting its use to preventing actions endangering supplies. There were safeguards along the lines of the earlier attempt to amend the Criminal Procedure Code.[13] President Sanjiva Reddy, many chief ministers, and several political parties, reportedly opposed the ordinance.[14] Mrs Gandhi's government, after her victory in the January 1980 parliamentary elections, replaced the ordinance with an Act of Parliament on 12 February 1980.[15]

Judicial Independence

The principle of judicial independence that from the beginning of the country's constitutional experience had had the status of holy writ—whether or not profaned in practice—was again tested during the Janata years.

Morarji Desai's proclaimed 'zealous regard' for principle was tested within a few days of the government's formation. Several Janata Party members of Parliament sought to rectify, as they saw it, Mrs Gandhi's final attack on the judiciary before leaving office. On 28 January 1977,

[11] *Hindustan Times*, 24 March 1978. The bill was actually withdrawn on 30 March.

[12] At the chief ministers meeting of 24 September 1978. *AR*, 5–11 November 1978, pp. 14587–8.

[13] The safeguards included that detentions could last a maximum of six months after approval by an advisory board, the grounds for detention had to be communicated to the detenu within five days and to the board within three weeks, and the board had to report within seven weeks of the detention. The detenu could make a personal representation and appear before the board, which was to consist of the chief justice of the high court and two others. Appeals to the Supreme Court could be made under Articles 32 and 226 of the Constitution.

[14] *AR*, 12–18 November 1979, p. 15170.

[15] Siwach, J. R., *Dynamics of Indian Government and Politics*, 2nd and enlarged edn., Sterling Publishers Pvt. Ltd., New Delhi, 1990, p. 524, footnote 13.

For a text and explanation of the ordinance of October 1979 and the Act that followed in February 1980, see Swaroop, *Law of Preventive Detention*, p. 450.

ten days after he had called elections, President Ahmed superseded Justice H. R. Khanna by appointing M. H. Beg Chief Justice of India to succeed A. N. Ray, who would retire on 29 January. Khanna immediately resigned from the Court. Prime Minister Gandhi had ordered the supersession against the advice of both her Law Minister and the Chairman of the Law Commission.[16] Khanna who was next senior to Ray on the Court believed that he was superseded because he had been with the majority against the government in the Kesavanananda Bharati case and had been the lone dissenter against the government in the Emergency's Habeas Corpus case.[17] Many agreed with him, and from this distance there can be little doubt that he was correct.

Janata supporters sought to right this wrong. Bitter over the Emergency, angry at the Supreme Court for upholding the legality of the Emergency's punitive character in the Habeas Corpus case, and infuriated by Mrs Gandhi's treatment of the hero of liberty in that case, Khanna, Janata Party members K. S. Hegde (of the 1973 supersession), Ram Jethmalani, and others tried to have Beg removed so that Khanna could replace him. Jethmalani, who had defeated Gokhale for a Lok Sabha seat from Bombay, made 'no secret his wish' that Beg should be asked to step down and that Khanna 'should take over as Chief Justice of India', recalled Khanna, who told the visiting persuaders that it would 'not be proper to do so'.[18] Soon thereafter Khanna told the Prime

---

[16] Gokhale told Kuldip Nayar that he had advised Mrs Gandhi against this supersession, but that she did not listen to him. Nayar, *The Judgement*, p. 169. Gajendragadkar had asked Om Mehta to convey to Mrs Gandhi 'my keen desire' that Khanna not be superseded. Gajendragadkar–Indira Gandhi letter dated 24 August 1977, P. B. Gajendragadkar Papers, NMML.

[17] Khanna interview with the author.

For a variety of press reports and commentary about the supersession, see Pillai, S. Devadas (ed.), *The Incredible Elections: 1977*, Popular Prakashan, Bombay, 1977, chapter 4, 'The Khanna Issue'.

Law Minister Gokhale explained that Beg's appointment was in keeping with the government's policy since 1973 that seniority should not be the sole criterion for elevation to the chief justiceship, and it also was due to the '"very brief tenure"' of six-plus months Khanna would have had before his compulsory retirement. It was '"no reflection"' on him. *Hindustan Times*, 29 January 1977. Khanna resigned from the Court in a letter of protest to the President and went on leave, actually retiring from the Court in mid-March. Justice Beg's tenure would be thirteen months.

[18] Khanna, *Neither Roses Nor Thorns*, p. 91.

The Hindustan Times of 25 March 1977 reported that Jethmalani was saying publicly that Beg should resign because the policy of a committed judiciary under which he had been appointed Chief Justice was no longer in vogue, but that Janata should not try to oust him.

Minister the same after Desai told him of rumoured attempts to get Beg to step down. Desai then told Khanna that the government had decided against such a move.[19] Khanna went on to become Chairman of the Law Commission that December, and of the three important reports published during his time, one concerned the appointment of judges.[20]

The government faced greater difficulties when it came to replacing Chief Justice Beg when he retired in February 1978, but it would stand firm on democratic principles while these clashed with rage lingering from the Emergency. The next two judges after Beg in order of seniority were Y. V. Chandrachud and P. N. Bhagwati, the former appointed to the Supreme Court in August 1972 and the latter in July 1973. Personally competitive, they had come from competitive high courts, Bombay and Gujarat, respectively. Jayaprakash Narayan as early as mid-July 1977 wrote to Shanti Bhushan about this succession. Said Narayan, it seems to me most unfortunate if either becomes Chief Justice on the ground of seniority. I recognize a matter of principle is involved, and that we did object to Mrs Gandhi's supersession. But this is different because nonpartisan: these men abdicated their duty when they found for the government in the Habeas Corpus case. No doubt the country would support you, Narayan concluded. Bhushan replied on 31 July that the Habeas Corpus judgement was 'unsupportable besides being unfortunate', but the matter was complex and needed the 'utmost care' in handling.[21] Bhushan later flew to Bombay to talk directly with Narayan and convinced him against another supersession by arguing that if the government 'handpicked' the new Chief Justice, it would lose credibility. Some months later, Narayan was reported to hold the view that only an acting chief justice should have been appointed until proper guidelines for the selection had been established, even if this involved amending the Constitution.[22]

[19] Khanna, *Neither Roses Nor Thorns*, p. 91.

L. K. Advani told the Lok Sabha that the rumour was baseless. Another version of these events has Morarji Desai less solicitous of judical independence; Jethmalani claimed that Desai orally asked Beg to step down. A senior law officer of the time believed this to be true.

[20] The report dealt almost exclusively with the appointment of high court judges; the selection of Chief Justice of India was not mentioned.

[21] The author has reconstructed Narayan's letter, in Bhushan's possession, from Bhushan's description. For Bhushan's letter to Narayan, see Jayaprakash Narayan Papers, Third Installment, Subject File 345, NMML. This account of the controversy, where it is not otherwise attributed, is based upon interviews with Bhushan, Soli Sorabjee, Nirmal Mukarji, P. B. Venkatasubramanian, M. Rama Jois, and Justice Y. V. Chandrachud.

[22] *Hindustan Times* 19 February 1978.

At the end of 1977, with Justice Beg's retirement in February approaching, succession partisans became vocal. Led by former Chief Justice of the Bombay High Court M. C. Chagla, a group within the Bombay bar released a statement to the press characterizing Chandrachud and Bhagwati as being committed judges and not being upholders of individual liberty—because they had ruled for the government in the Habeas Corpus case.[23] Conversely, some 120 Supreme Court advocates publicly supported the seniority principle. They rejected the contention that Chandrachud's Habeas Corpus case opinion disqualified him for the chief justiceship, much though they deplored that decision. Learning of this, Morarji Desai declared that the new Chief Justice would be appointed 'according to the Constitution'.[24] Desai and Bhushan held firm against supersession with support from Additional Solicitor General Soli Sorabjee and K. S. Hegde, Speaker of the Lok Sabha.[25]

[23] For a discussion of the so-called 'Bombay Memorandum', see Baxi, *The Indian Supreme Court and Politics*, pp. 191–8.

Chagla was rumoured to have been in touch with Nani Palkhivala, then Indian ambassador in Washington, to sound out his willingness to take the job. If true, perhaps this was an attempt to avoid the seniority issue by bringing in an individual from outside the court.

Chief Justice Beg was involved during the autumn of 1977 in what some labelled a 'supersession' but which was not. On Beg's advice, he having first consulted two senior judges on the Supreme Court, the government had appointed two judges to the Supreme Court, D. A. Desai from the Gujarat High Court, and V. D. Tulzapurkar from the Bombay High Court. Neither of the two was senior on his own court, but such seniority on a high court had not been a prerequisite for elevation to the Supreme Court. Nevertheless, 'political motivation' was alleged by some. M.C. Chagla protested, and the Gujarat High Court Advocates Association passed a resolution protesting Beg's having described Desai as the ' "ablest judge" ' on the Gujarat court. Shanti Bhushan defended his government and Justice Beg. The fray is described in Dhavan and Jacob, *Selection and Appointment of Supreme Court Judges*, pp. 13ff.

[24] *Hindustan Times*, 13 January 1978. S. N. Mishra, Deputy Leader of the Janata Parliamentary Party, Raj Narain, George Fernandes, Ram Jethmalani, and others opposed Chandrachud. Published accounts of the controversy did not mention who was next in seniority to become Chief Justice were both Chandrachud and Bhagwati to be superseded: V. R. Krishna Iyer, who some considered far more 'committed' than the two judges senior to him.

[25] Hegde to M. Rama Jois, according to Rama Jois, in an interview with the author. Rama Jois had been Hegde's election agent in the 1977 general election, and, as seen in chapter 15, had been closely involved in the Habeas Corpus case.

Justice Chandrachud thought that Morarji Desai had been favourably impressed by his 'not having lifted a finger' to gain the chief justiceship and that the Prime Minister did not believe his opinion in the Habeas Corpus case had been due to 'ulterior motives'. Y. V. Chandrachud interview with the author.

As Chief Justice, Chandrachud may have somewhat redeemed himself in the eyes of

Wishing to be sure of his ground, Shanti Bhushan wrote to each of the judges of the Supreme Court, to the chief justices of the high courts, and to several prominent lawyers asking their views about adhering to the seniority principle. The 'overwhelming opinion' of the responses favoured selection according to seniority.[26] Bhushan then prepared a comprehensive note on the basis of the replies and submitted it to the Cabinet Committee on Political Affairs at its meeting on 17 February 1978. After a lengthy discussion, the committee settled on Y. V. Chandrachud, and two days later President Sanjiva Reddy appointed him Chief Justice of India—to serve longer than any other before or since.[27]

The Desai government further supported judicial independence by reversing the transfers of high court judges Mrs Gandhi had made during the Emergency. Law Minister Bhushan announced this in the Lok Sabha on 5 April 1977, saying that judges wishing to return to their high courts could do so, but the government would not compel them to return.[28] The Supreme Court would later hold that a judge's consent was not a necessary condition for his transfer.[29]

Judicial independence was most significantly affected during this period by the Supreme Court, itself. In what amounted to a declaration

---

his detractors by, soon after his appointment, cancelling Sanjay Gandhi's anticipatory bail and ordering him taken into custody because he had abused his liberty by '"attempting to suborn prosecution witnesses"' in the *Kissa Kursi Ka* case (on 5 May 1978). Gandhi went to Tihar Jail on 5 May. *AR*, 16–22 July 1978, p. 14406. Also on this bench were Justices Fazl Ali and P. N. Singhal. The Supreme Court was hearing an appeal from the Delhi High Court.

[26] 'Overwhelming', according to the *AR*, 26 March–1 April 1978, p. 14231. 'Almost all' the responses favoured seniority, Bhushan said in an interview with the author.

[27] Two months later, the *Hindustan Times* reported that Chandrachud had recommended that the appointment of chief justices of India, as matters of national importance, should not be left to the government of the day. He was said to believe that there should be a national debate in the press and other forums on the 'merits and demerits of the judges who were in the run (sic)' for the highest judicial office.

[28] *Times of India*, as cited in *AR*, 14–20 May 1977 and *Hindustan Times*, 24 June 1977. See chapter 15 for an account of the original transfers. Shanti Bhushan had been touched personally by the Emergency transfer of judges when his brother-in-law could not become chief justice of the Allahabad High Court because a judge transferred from the Karnataka High Court had been made chief justice. The brother-in-law later did become chief justice in Allahabad when the transferred judge returned to Bangalore.

[29] This was Sankalchand's case, named for Justice Sankalchand H. Sheth who appealed his transfer from the Gujarat High Court, the only instance of a judge challenging his Emergency transfer. The bench hearing the appeal consisted of Justices Chandrachud, Krishna Iyer, and Fazl Ali. *Union of India v Sankalchand Himatlal Sheth* 1977 (4) SCC 193ff; also *Times of India*, 20 September 1977. See chapter 15 for the origin of the case.

of independence, the Court invented for India the concept of 'public interest litigation'.[30] Due to the presence of several activist judges—who perhaps subconsciously were compensating for the Court's record during the Emergency—the Court became an active, not just a reactive, protector of the Fundamental Rights and the social revolution. On 5 February 1979 the court, acting in response to a habeas corpus petition filed by private citizen and senior advocate, Mrs K. Hingorani, ordered the release on personal bonds of thirty-four prisoners held in Bihar jails. Imprisoned for periods of two to ten years, the men claimed that their detention was unlawful because they had been held without trial for longer than their sentences would have been had they been tried and convicted. The court also ordered the state government to provide it with information about 'undertrials' not mentioned in the petition. Two benches were involved. One consisted of Justices V. R. Krishna Iyer and O. Chinnappa Reddy, the second of Justices P. N. Bhagwati, R. S. Pathak, and A. D. Koshal.[31] Of the five men, Krishna Iyer, Chinnappa Reddy, and Bhagwati would come to be considered the trend-setters in public interest litigation. A month later, in a similar action, a bench consisting of Bhagwati and Justice D. A. Desai ordered prisoners to be released from Delhi's Tihar Jail.[32] Such detentions, the Court said, were illegal under Article 21, and a speedy trial was every citizen's right. Further, the court ordered the governments of Uttar Pradesh, Karnataka, West Bengal, Meghalaya, and Jammu and Kashmir to provide it with information about undertrials in their states.

Closer to what would become the model for future public interest

[30] 'Public interest litigation', also called PIL and 'social action litigation', in essence gives third parties 'standing' to bring before the courts issues in the name of the public interest, including complaints from individuals or groups that could not, themselves, bring their case to the courts. An element of this has been called 'epistolary jurisdiction', meaning that the Supreme Court may act on receipt of a letter (even a postcard) from a citizen requesting protection of his fundamental rights. Upon receipt of such a communication, the Court may decide to appoint its 'commissioner' to determine if the complaint is worthy of adjudication. If so advised, the Court may proceed from there.

[31] *Hindustan Times*, 6 February 1979. Mrs Hingorani had filed the petition after reading articles published in Delhi by K. Rustomji of the National Police Commission—appointed by Janata—about the number and conditions of undertrials.

For more about the development of PIL, see Part VII and Shourie, *Institutions in the Janata Phase*, pp. 123ff. See also Dhagamwar, Vasudha, *Criminal Justice or Chaos?*, Har-Anand Publications Pvt. Ltd., New Delhi, 1997, especially pp. 62ff.

[32] *Hindustan Times*, 6 March 1979.

Justices Bhagwati and Pathak later would become Chief Justices. Pathak, Reddy, and Koshal were appointed by the Janata government, Krishna Iyer by Mrs Gandhi in 1973. Justice Desai also was appointed by the Janata government, and the minor controversy over his appointment has been mentioned.

litigation was a September decision the same year, again by Justices Krishna Iyer and Chinnappa Reddy. The case originated with the citizens in Ratlam Municipality who, 'tormented by stench and stink' of open drains, moved a magistrate under Section 133 of the Criminal Procedure Code to do his duty to the public by remedying the situation. The magistrate ordered the municipality to offer a plan within six months. The sessions (criminal) court reversed the magistrate, and the citizens' appeal was upheld by the high court and again by the Supreme Court. Doing so, Krishna Iyer and Reddy ordered the municipality to build latrines and provide good water, and they instructed the local magistrate to prosecute municipal officers if they failed to comply. Procedural rules should infuse life into substantive rights, said Krishna Iyer in the decision. At issue were the 'problems of access to justice for the people beyond the blinkered rules of "standing" of British-Indian vintage'. The centre of gravity was shifting from the individualism of *locus standi* 'to the community orientation of public interest litigation ... to force public bodies ... to implement ... plans in response to public grievances', Krishna Iyer said. With the Directive Principles of State Policy having found statutory expression, continued Krishna Iyer, 'the court will not stand idly by and allow municipal government to become a statutory mockery'.[33] The number of public interest litigation cases grew for a time during the eighties, then declined, and have risen dramatically in the mid-nineties.

Federal Issues

Having come into office proclaiming the centralized state a menace to society and promising to promote national unity and harmony, the Janata government within days initiated a massive display of centralized power. Euphoric with the electorate's rejection of Mrs Gandhi, it dissolved the Congress-led governments and legislatures in nine states—those in which the election nearly had wiped out Congress's representation in the Lok Sabha—and imposed President's Rule until state elections could be held, which was seven weeks later. The Janata government claimed that the defeats in Lok Sabha elections by implication showed that the majorities the Congress retained in these states, dating from the 1972 elections, no longer represented the sentiments of the people. Thus they had lost their moral right to hold office. Moreover, the Janata government argued,

---

[33] *Municipal Council, Ratlam, Petitioner v Vardichand and Others, Respondents* 1980 (4) SCC 162. Quotation from page 174. Otherwise called Ratlam Municipality, the decision was handed down on 29 September 1979.

Parliament had extended the terms of the legislatures in these states by one year in March 1976, denying citizens the elections due when the legislatures' normal five-year terms would have ended in the spring of 1977.[34] In sum, the government's position was that democratic principles and the possibility of severe strains in centre–state relations justified the dissolutions and President's Rule. It just so happened that these principles favoured practical political considerations. These came down to votes in the Rajya Sabha (most of whose members are elected by state legislatures) when they would become necessary for repealing the Forty-second Amendment and when they would affect the election of a new President in July.[35]

Dissolving the assemblies had had strong proponents before the Janata Party formed the government. During the election campaign Jayaprakash Narayan advocated fresh state elections, calling them constitutional. He did so again on the day Janata knew it had won in a national broadcast.[36] The Prime Minister seemed opposed to this view at first, or at least undecided. At a press conference on 4 April, the day he took the oath of office, he was reported to have said, variously: the government will not topple the ministries in the states, but '"if they topple themselves, what can I do?"'; there should be fresh polls in the states where the Congress had lost heavily, but '"we should not do it in a manner that we repeat what the last government had done"'; and '"there is no question of dissolving legally constituted governments or assemblies."'[37]

[34] Parliament extended the legislatures' terms by one year on 18 March 1976 when it extended its own life by a year. The latter act was under Article 83 of the Constitution, and the former under Article 172, which says that, during an emergency, Parliament may, for one year at a time, extend legislature sessions by one year.

The nine states placed under President's Rule were West Bengal, Himachal Pradesh, Madhya Pradesh, Uttar Pradesh, Bihar, Haryana, Punjab, Rajasthan, and Orissa.

[35] The Constitution required this election six months after President Ahmed's death in office. An electoral college consisting of elected members of state legislative assemblies and both houses of Parliament elects the President.

[36] To reporters on 22 March 1977. Limaye, *Janata Party Experiment*, vol. 1, p. 311. Also see *Hindustan Times*, 3 and 14 April 1977.

This hardly was surprising, for Narayan had demanded the dissolution of the Bihar assembly during the winter of 1975. Early support for Narayan came from an unlikely source, long-time Congressman and former President V. V. Giri, according to dispatches in the *Hindustan Times* and *National Herald*. Issues of 23 March and 25 March 1977, respectively, as cited in Limaye, *Janata Party Experiment*, vol. 1, p. 311.

Giri took this position in part because he believed that the same political party should govern in New Delhi and the state capitals—a dangerous view and a negation of the federal principle, thought Limaye. Ibid., p. 313.

[37] Because the remarks seem contradictory, it may be well to quote each account. 'The Prime Minister made it clear that he was not going to topple Ministries in any State but

But the proponents of dissolution within his ministry argued strongly, led by Home Minister Charan Singh backed by Law Minister Bhushan, who 'sold the idea to the Janata Party'.[38] Janata leaders like Madhu Limaye and Ram Jethmalani were quoted as saying that the state governments, themselves, should resign where their terms had been extended '"fraudulently"' during the Emergency. The cabinet decided unanimously that the nine state governments should be dismissed, but its strategy was to have the state governemnts take the step.[39] The decision taken, Charan Singh on April 18 sent a letter, which Bhushan claims to have drafted, to nine Congress chief ministers saying that the government had given earnest consideration to the '"most unprecedented"' situation created by the national elections and was gravely concerned about '"the resultant climate of uncertainty ... [and] diffidence at different levels of administration ... [that] has already given rise to serious threats of law and order"'. The letter continued that eminent constitutional experts had long been of the opinion that when a legislature and the electorate are at variance, dissolution and obtaining a fresh mandate would be '"appropriate"'. Charan Singh suggested to the chief ministers that they advise their governors to dissolve the legislature and call for elections.[40] Shanti Bhushan gave an even clearer indication of the government's policy during an interview on All India Radio four days later. Democracy was the

---

asked: "If they topple themselves, what can I do?" It would not be proper to topple any Ministry as long as it enjoyed a majority in the House. About holding fresh elections in states where the Congress Party had lost heavily in the Lok Sabha elections, Mr Desai said there should be a fresh poll but added: "We should not do it in a manner that we repeat what the last Government had done."' *Hindustan Times*, 25 March 1977.

The *Statesman's* account of this press conference contained substantially the same quotation about toppling. It also said: 'In reply to a question, Mr Desai ruled out the holding of fresh elections to the assemblies of states where the Congress had been defeated in the recent Lok Sabha poll. "There is no question of dissolving legally constituted governments of assemblies," he observed.' *Statesman*, 25 March 1977.

[38] Charan Singh's role from P. B. Venkatasubramanian and Shanti Bhushan in interviews with the author.

[39] From the author's interview with Nirmal Mukarji, then the Cabinet Secretary.

At no time during this entire affair did members of the government think that dissolving the assemblies might come back to haunt them, as it would in 1980. 'They thought they would be in power forever,' remembered a senior official of the time.

[40] Quoted in Jacob, Alice and Dhavan, Rajeev, 'The Dissolution Case: Politics at the Bar of the Supreme Court', *JILI*, vol. 19, no. 4, 1977, pp. 355ff.

The same day, Charan Singh announced the formation of three commissions to investigate Emergency's excesses.

During the period Janata Party leaders were embroiled in a dispute over whom should be party president.

most important element of the Constitution's basic structure, he said, and if state governments continued in power 'after having lost the confidence of the people, they would be undemocratic governments'.[41] Governors had the authority to summon and dissolve assemblies, argued Bhushan, citing Article 174. Article 355 said that it was the duty of the union government to ensure that government in the states was conducted according to the Constitution. Were government not so conducted, he said, the central government had the authority under Article 356 to take over the state government and invoke President's Rule.

Six of the nine governments attempted to protect what they believed to be their constitutional rights by taking their predicament to the Supreme Court. On 25 April, it began hearing their applications praying that the court declare Charan Singh's letter *ultra vires* and not binding on the state governments and asking the court to issue an injunction against the Janata government's resorting to President's Rule.[42] With hearings underway, the Desai cabinet deferred further action.[43] The state governments contended that it was erroneous to argue that the Congress's election defeats were sufficient cause to dissolve the assemblies; using Article 356 under these conditions 'would be destructive of the federal structure' and, because outside the purposes and objectives of the article, would be *male fides*.[44] H. R. Gokhale and Niren De, out of office and representing the states, argued that the Home Minister's letter was a threat and that the President could not dissolve the assemblies until *after* both Houses of Parliament had approved the proclamation—a requirement not in the Constitution.

Representing the government, Additional Solicitor General Soli Sorabjee argued that grounds for invoking Article 356 were not justiciable and the freedom of action of the 'highest organs of the Union should not be impeded by judicial interference except on grounds of clearest

---

[41] *Hindustan Times*, 23 April 1977. The *Statesman's* account is substantially the same.

[42] The state governments were those of Rajasthan, Madhya Pradesh, Punjab, Bihar, Himachal Pradesh, and Orissa.

The case was *State of Rajasthan and Others v Union of India* 1978 (1) SCR 1ff. The seven-judge bench was headed by Chief Justice Beg, along with Justices Y. V. Chandrachud, P. N. Bhagwati, P. K. Goswami, A. C. Gupta, N. L. Untwalia, and S. Murtaza Fazl Ali. For a useful discussion of the case, see *V. N. Shukla's Constitution of India*.

Three Punjab legislators had also filed suits that the dissolution of their assembly would violate their personal rights, depriving them of their livelihood and causing them to suffer '"irreparable injury"'. *Hindustan Times*, 28 April 1977. Senior Advocate R. K Garg represented them. The court heard the various suits together.

[43] *Hindustan Times*, 26 April 1977.

[44] 1978 (1) SCR 2–3.

and gravest possible character'.[45] Congress's defeats of themselves would not be sufficient cause for dissolution, Sorabjee continued; it was the conditions resulting from the defeats that necessitated dissolution. Several judges asked the lawyers if the case were not 'political' and therefore a dispute the court should stay out of. This allowed Sorabjee to argue that it was a question whether or not the states could bring to the court '"a dispute of political character"'.[46]

'As widely expected', the Supreme Court dismissed all the suits on 29 April.[47] The seven judges gave their reasons in four opinions delivered on 6 May. The essence of Justice Beg's opinion was that use of Article 356 can be either curative or preventive and its use cannot be excluded if the central government thinks the state governments must seek a fresh mandate to prevent a bad law and order situation; questions of political wisdom or executive policy should not be subject to judicial control. Justice Chandrachud believed the Home Minister's letter to be a legal issue and therefore not outside the Court's jurisdiction under Article 131; whether or not Parliament eventually approves a proclamation under Article 356, it would be valid for two months, he held. Justice Bhagwati ruled that the 'satisfaction' of the President is subjective and not subject matter for the judiciary; the Home Minister's letter was advice, not a directive, and therefore cannot be unconstitutional; and where there has been a total rout of ruling party candidates 'it is proof of complete alienation between the government and the people'.[48] Looking back on the Court's decision and choosing his words carefully, Sorabjee commented, 'in the prevailing atmosphere, the court readily accepted my arguments'.[49]

---

[45] Ibid., p. 3.

[46] *Hindustan Times*, 27 April 1977. Near the end of the hearing, Sorabjee handed to the judges a paper containing three propositions: that the President's 'satisfaction' when declaring President's Rule was not justiciable and the courts could not go into the adequacy or relevancy of the information upon which his decision was based; if the President's action under Article 356 were absolutely absurd, perverse, *mala fide*, and there was no nexus between situation and action, then the President's action might be questioned; and even if it were assumed that the facts in the Charan Singh letter were justiciable, it could not be said that they were extraneous, absurd, or perverse. Ibid.

[47] *Hindustan Times*, 30 April 1977.

[48] 1978 (1) SCR 1–123. Bhagwati's views from pp. 77–81, 85. Chandrachud's views, pp. 60–61. Justice Goswami wrote an opinion concurring with Bhagwati, who had written for himself and Justice Gupta. Justice Beg also said in his opinion that healthy conventions should grow and Article 356 should be used only in 'critical situations' (p. 30). Justice Goswami hoped the government would act with great care, for the welfare of the people at large, and to strengthen the Constitution.

[49] Sorabjee interview with the author.

Without waiting for the Court's reasons for rejecting the states' suits, in what came to be called the Rajasthan case, and faced with the state governments' unwillingness to cooperate with its stratagems, the cabinet met at Morarji Desai's Dupleix Road residence on 29 April and made two decisions. It decided, after much discussion, but again unanimously, to dissolve the state governments and impose President's Rule 'otherwise' than upon a report from the governor.[50] And it instructed Home Minister Charan Singh to write a letter to Acting President B. D. Jatti recommending that he act under Article 356. Apparently, a draft proclamation was enclosed with the letter.[51]

Jatti declined to act upon the letter, telling his private secretary, Balchandra, to inform the Home Ministry that he needed time 'to think over the issue'. That afternoon, Jatti consulted Indira Gandhi (whose photograph in 1994 adorned a wall in his Bangalore office), H. R. Gokhale, Y. B. Chavan, the Congress chief ministers directly affected, and perhaps others.[52] Impatient, Morarji Desai called upon Jatti that

Could the judges have been aware of the importance of Rajya Sabha votes to overturning that anti-judiciary document, the Forty-second Amendment?

Jacob and Dhavan in 'The Dissolution Case', p. 359, argue that 'In one sense, the Supreme Court did not have a justiciable issue before it. All the union government had done was to advise the chief ministers'; it had not yet used its powers to impose President's Rule.

Baxi in *The Indian Supreme Court and Politics*, p. 131, asserts that the Court's reasoning in the case gives 'the first hint, in the post-emergency Court, of populism'. The message is clear and categorical, Baxi says, '"We care for you. We shall not let you down."' The Court's decision, Baxi concludes, 'all in all ... was good politics' (p. 135).

[50] Nirmal Mukarji interview with the author.

Members were 'hell bent' on dissolving the governments, according to a minister present. Ramakrishna Hegde, then a Janata general secretary, has a different version of the actors and their views. Desai, Bhushan, Ram, and H. M. Patel were not in favour of dissolving the assemblies, Hegde remembered, but Charan Singh was adamant, joined by H. N. Bahuguna and Patnaik. Accordingly, this was one of several examples of Desai yielding reluctantly to views among his cabinet colleagues, said Hegde. The government's decision to dissolve the assemblies was not discussed at the party level. But the general issue was discussed in the party, and hotly. Hegde interview with the author.

In the actual decision to dismiss the assemblies, Additional Solicitor General Soli Sorabjee was not consulted, according to Sorabjee in an interview with the author and the Attorney General, S. V. Gupte, probably was not consulted.

[51] This account of the affair is based upon reports in the *Hindustan Times*, 30 April–1 May 1977; Nayar, *The Judgement*, pp. 189–91; Jatti, B. D., *I Am My Own Model: An Autobiography*, Konark Publishers Pvt. Ltd., Delhi, 1993, pp. 107–9; Limaye, *Janata Party Experiment*, vol. 1, pp. 316ff; interviews; and, especially, the oral history transcript that Nirmal Mukarji is preparing for the Nehru Library—kindness of Mr Mukarji.

[52] According to Nayar, *The Judgement*, p. 190, Jatti earlier had been 'persuaded' to 'stall' dissolution, an idea attributed to Yashpal Kapoor, working through R. K. Dhawan, because Kapoor was not at this time welcome among Mrs Gandhi's associates. Jatti had discussed

evening and, when Jatti told him that he had not assented to the proclamation, Desai departed.[53] But the encounter—if it took place, and Nirmal Mukarji insists it did not—may not have been so perfunctory. According to Limaye, Desai gave Jatti 'a piece of his mind'.[54] It is also possible that it was at this meeting that Desai told Jatti—who claimed to be in accord with Desai on all issues but this one—that his refusal to give assent would lead to the resignation of the government and the calling of parliamentary elections. Individual ministers, among them Vajpayee and Fernandes, already were talking about resigning over the matter.

The next day, 30 April, a deeply concerned cabinet met at 11.00 a.m. What to do? Members resolved provisionally that if Jatti persisted in his refusal to accept their advice, they should advise dissolution of the Lok Sabha and go to the country on the basis of Jatti's unconstitutional position.[55] But first, an attempt should be made to bring the Acting President around. Three members—Charan Singh, Shanti Bhushan, and Finance Minister H. M. Patel—met Jatti, but were ineffective. During the conversation, Jatti remarked that, being an old Congressman himself, he would not find dissolving the state governments easy. The three ministers reported their failure to the cabinet at 2.00 p.m.

The cabinet then decided that a second letter should go, this time from the Prime Minister. Cabinet Secretary Mukarji, V. Shankar (Desai's secretary and formerly secretary to Sardar Patel), and Home Secretary Srinivasvaradan were tasked with drafting it. The Prime Minister signed it, although few, if any, cabinet members had seen it.

Desai, acting on Shankar's advice had Mukarji take this letter to Jatti early that evening. Their conversation was private because Mukarji

---

dissolution with Charan Singh at breakfast on 21 April when another guest, Chenna Reddy, governor of UP, had asked Charan Singh if the advice in his letter to the chief ministers was not illegal because unconstitutional. Jatti, B. D., *I Am My Own Model: An Autobiography,* pp. 107–8.

[53] Ibid., p. 108.

[54] Limaye, *Janata Party Experiment,* vol. 1, p. 316. Jatti had been a minister under Morarji Desai when Desai was chief minister of Bombay two decades earlier.

[55] Cabinet members' concern from Shanti Bhushan, in an interview with the author. Charan Singh at one point considered taking Jatti's refusal to the Supreme Court. Limaye, thinking this a poor idea, went to Attorney General S. V. Gupte, with whom he was friendly, and asked Gupte to talk Charan Singh out of it, which he did. Limaye, *Janata Party Experiment,* vol. 1, p. 316.

According to Kuldip Nayar, Jatti at one time had decided not to dissolve Parliament if the Janata government held to its strategy of resigning and calling for elections, but instead to call upon Chavan to form a government. Nayar, *The Judgement,* p. 191.

explained that he bore a sensitive message from the Prime Minister. Jatti was shaken to find in the letter mention of his reluctance, as an old Congressman, to dissolve Congress governments, and he admitted to Mukarji that he had said this. In response to Jatti's request for suggestions, Mukarji told him that he had no option but to accept the cabinet's advice. If he attempted delay, the correspondence likely would be laid before Parliament, demonstrating publicly that, although Acting President, Jatti had not been able to rise above party loyalties. Taking the point about his honour being besmirched, Jatti asked Mukarji to retain Desai's letter and requested that it never appear on the public record. He assured the Cabinet Secretary that he would sign and return the proclamations that evening, which he did.[56] Congress had been hoist on its own Forty-second Amendment.

The proclamation Jatti signed reproduced the government's reasoning during the affair: in a federal polity, there could be different issues and parties represented in the state assemblies and the Lok Sabha, but in this case national and state issues were "'indistinguishable'". The massive rejection of the Congress meant that it no longer enjoyed the confidence of the electorate. '"Only by obtaining a fresh verdict of the electorate could democracy be upheld in the states,"' the proclamation read.[57]

Prior to the constitutional crisis thus narrowly avoided, there occurred two related events. A Congress deputation had called upon the acting President on 24 April, and its members had argued—blushing becomingly, one hopes—that he should ignore his ministers' advice because a President was bound to act on the advice of his ministers only if it were constitutional, not extra-constitutional or illegal. They asked Jatti to seek an advisory opinion from the Supreme Court and to refrain from acting on ministerial advice pending its receipt.[58] More

---

[56] Nirmal Mukarji draft oral history transcript.

Even as the Cabinet Secretary was closeted with the Acting President, Shanti Bhushan told Desai that if Jatti continued to refuse to sign, Desai should go to the people on the radio that evening. Bhushan went to his office and began drafting the speech 'at the Prime Minister's request'. 'An hour into drafting, I was told that Jatti had signed.' Shanti Bhushan interview with the author.

[57] *Hindustan Times*, 1 May 1977.

[58] *Hindustan Times*, 24 and 25 April 1977; *Times of India*, 25 April 1977 as cited in Limaye, *Janata Party Experiment*, vol. 1, p. 315.

The deputation consisted of close supporters of Mrs Gandhi like D. K. Borooah, A. R. Antulay, Mrs Purabi Mukherjee, and D. P. Chattopadhyaya. Limaye characterizes the reaction of the 'Congress Opposition' as well as that of the affected chief ministers to the prospective dissolution as 'not surprisingly, violent'. (Ibid.) But several Congress members have told the author that Y. B. Chavan did not strongly resist the dissolution move. According to

piquantly, before his contretemps with the cabinet, Jatti had made an ill-advised or an ill-intentioned call on the Chief Justice of India. While giving his opinion in the dissolution case on 6 May, Supreme Court Justice P. K. Goswami revealed that Chief Justice Beg had informed members of the bench that Jatti had visited him while the Court was hearing the states' petition. Saying that he reported this with a 'cold shudder', Goswami added that he had done so 'hoping that the majesty of the High Office of the President, who should be beyond the high-water mark of any controversy, suffers not in future'.[59] The same day, Beg, in a statement issued by the Court, acknowledged that Jatti had made a personal and private visit to him after 25 April to invite him to a wedding. Not a word about the case had been said, according to Beg.[60]

Leaving aside the legal and constitutional aspects of Janata's dissolving the nine legislatures, the June election results bore out its claims of Congress Party unpopularity. In Bihar, Janata candidates won 214 seats to Congress's 56; in Haryana it was 75 to 5; in Uttar Pradesh, it was 351 to 46. Only in Tamil Nadu and West Bengal did Janata do poorly.[61]

In 1980, as will be seen, Mrs Gandhi proved that what is sauce for the goose is sauce for the gander when she dismissed Janata state governments, and the Supreme Court upheld her government on the precedent of the Rajasthan Case.

Nayar, Chavan initially did go along with the dissolution idea because he had not realized its implications. He later opposed the dissolution of all state assemblies, barring Bihar, 'where JP's movement had the largest impact'. Nayar, *The Judgement*, p. 189.

The nine Congress chief ministers by now had rejected Charan Singh's letter, and the Congress Working Committee had opposed it as unconstitutional, 'politically motivated', and aimed at the forthcoming presidential election. Unfortunately for the Congress, Janata's move against Congress state governments coincided with a moment of great disarray: the party's agonizing four-day reappraisal of the Emergency and of its subsequent election defeat.

Not only Congressmen opposed the dissolutions. The Communist Party of India called them an 'undemocratic act'.

[59] *State of Rajasthan v Union of India* 1977 (3) SCC 592ff. Quotation from p. 671.

[60] *Hindustan Times*, 7 May 1977. According to several senior advocates, presenting invitations was not an uncommon way for Jatti to arrange timely visits.

[61] In Tamil Nadu, which had not been placed under President's Rule, the AIADMK with 130 seats won a clear majority in the assembly, the DMK and the Congress came next, and Janata won ten seats. In West Bengal, the CPM won 178 seats to Janata's twenty-nine and Congress's twenty. *AR*, 2–8 July 1977, p. 13811.

In Jammu and Kashmir, Sheikh Abdullah was returned as Chief Minister, leading his National Conference Party—with forty-seven seats to Janata's thirteen. The central government's refraining from meddling in this election made a significant contribution to national unity and integrity. Some have called this election the fairest in the state's history.

Protecting Civil and Minority Rights

Janata's public commitment to further the social revolution was at once broad and specific. The 'Economic Charter' of its election manifesto was reiterated in a Lok Sabha resolution, which proclaimed that the government would seek '"socio-economic revolution illumined by democratic standards, vivified by socialist ideals and firmly founded on moral and spiritual values"'.[62] The first of the government's specific proposals came after two months in office. It announced that it would establish an autonomous civil rights commission 'competent to ensure that the minorities, Scheduled Castes and Tribes and other backward classes do not suffer from discrimination and inequality'.[63] Commissions to assist disadvantaged citizens would follow.

Little more was heard of the promise for six months. Then it was reported that the government was contemplating substituting two other commissions for the civil rights commission—one for minorities and another for Scheduled Castes and Tribes. Election pledges had come up against the problems of implementing them. Most chief ministers were reported to support the civil rights commission. The Jana Sangh contingent within the Janata Party was said to prefer this to a minorities commission, thinking that the latter might be too solicitous of Muslims, although Atal Bihari Vajpayee later would claim the Minorities Commission to be a Janata achievement.[64] Doubters feared that a civil rights commission would become bogged down by appeals from it to the Supreme Court and that it would diminish the authority of the 'special officers' (often called 'commissioners') already in place to protect the rights of linguistic minorities and the Scheduled Castes and Tribes.[65] Yet others believed a civil rights commission desirable because these special officers were not being effective: they could only report conditions and could not take remedial actions on their own initiative.[66] Prime Minister

---

[62] Resolution passed on 22 July 1977. *AR*, 13–19 August 1977, p. 13880.

[63] See *Hindustan Times*, 20 May 1977 for the announcement. The language closely resembled that in the Janata election manifesto.

[64] Limaye, *Janata Party Experiment*, vol. 2, p. 394.

[65] A Special Officer for Scheduled Castes and Scheduled Tribes was provided for in Article 338 of the Constitution as adopted in 1950. The Office of the Special Officer for Linguistic Minorities was added to the Constitution in Article 350B by the Seventh Amendment in 1956. This was occasioned by the reorganization of the states along linguistic lines that year.

[66] According to Galanter, the Commissioner of Scheduled Castes and Tribes was unable to 'serve as an independent critic of government' and was reduced to tasks of oversight and evaluation. The officer 'proved no match for the problems of resistance, low priority, poor

Desai and Charan Singh assured the contestants that constitutional safe-guards would be protected whatever course the government adopted.[67]

On 15 January 1978, the government announced the establishment of a minorities commission 'to provide institutional safeguards for minorities and ensure their effective implementation'. This would fulfill Janata's commitment to preserve the country's secular character.[68] A month later, Minoo Masani was appointed chairman of the commission, only to resign in May over differences regarding the status of and the facilities for the commission.[69] At the beginning of April, Charan Singh told the Lok Sabha that the government intended 'to give [it] constitutional backing'. He said the government also would establish a commission for Scheduled Castes and Tribes and give this commission constitutional status as well.[70]

The promised 'constitutional backing' took the form of the Forty-sixth Amendment Bill, which would have added articles to the Constitution establishing a Minorities Commission and a Commission for the Scheduled Castes and Tribes. But the bill failed to get a two-thirds majority in the Lok Sabha on 17 May 1979.[71] The result was that there were constitutionally mandated special officers for linguistic minorities and Scheduled Castes and Tribes as well as two executive commissions that had been denied constitutional status—one for minorities and another for Scheduled Castes and Tribes. Especially bizarre was that the Special Officer for the Scheduled Castes and Tribes and the head of the new commission for them 'both submitted separate reports for years and reduced the matter to a farce'.[72]

---

planning, and lack of co-ordination that beset these programmes'. And these were but a few of his difficulties. See Galanter, *Competing Equalities*, p. 70.

[67] *Hindustan Times,* 12 November 1977.

[68] *Hindustan Times,* 16 January 1978. The commission's terms of reference included that it should evaluate the working of constitutional safeguards and the protective laws in the states, review and make recommendations for their effective implementation, investigate specific complaints, and suggest legal and welfare measures to be undertaken by either the central or state governments.

[69] Limaye, *Janata Party Experiment,* vol. 2, p. 394. Other members of the commission were M. R. A. Ansari, retired chief justice of the Jammu and Kashmir High Court, and V. V. John, former vice-chancellor of Jodhpur University.

[70] *Hindustan Times,* 2 April 1978. The government established the commission on Scheduled Castes and Tribes on 21 July 1978. Bhola Paswan Shastri was appointed Chairman, and the members were Shisher Kumar, then Special Officer for Scheduled Castes and Tribes, A. Jayaraman, and Thakur Negi.

[71] For the legislative history and text of the amending bill, see *Constitution Amendment in India,* Lok Sabha Secretariat, pp. 174, 395–7.

[72] George Verghese in a letter to the author. At this time Verghese headed a

Quite another matter was Prime Minister Desai's appointment in December 1978 of the Backward Classes Commission. Its report would be the most social revolutionary document in decades and would evoke violent reactions when its implementation was announced in 1990, for its terms of reference not only repeated the shop-worn instruction to the First Backward Classes Commission (1953) to recommend steps for advancing the socially and educationally backward classes but also the instruction to determine the criteria for defining the socially and economically backward classes. The commission also was to examine the desirability of reserving jobs in public services for members of these classes inadequately represented there. The Mandal Commission (so called after its chairman, B. P. Mandal) reported to the President on 31 December 1980 after Indira Gandhi had resumed office. Only in 1982 was the report laid on the table in Parliament, where the Prime Minister spoke in praise of it. Thereupon, its two volumes went on the shelf. In 1990, Prime Minister V. P. Singh announced that he would implement the reports. The resulting firestorm, and the social, economic, and political implications of the report for India are subjects to be discussed subsequently.[73]

Janata committee on radio and television broadcasting to examine giving both 'BBC status'.

[73] The Mandal Commission actually came into being in February 1979. Other members of the commission were Dewan Mohan Lal, R. R. Bhole, K. Subramaniam, and Dina Bandhu Saha. See Limaye, *Janata Party Experiment*, vol. 2, pp. 392ff and Galanter, *Competing Equalities*, pp. 186–7.

Limaye thought that the commission was Desai's device for ignoring the party manifesto's promise directly to reserve 25 to 33 per cent of all appointments to government service for the backward classes as recommended by the Kaka Kalekar Commission (the first Backward Classes Commission, 1953–5, established in accordance with Article 340). Limaye also believed Desai disliked the rise of the other backard classes (OBCs). Limaye, *Janata Party Experiment*, vol. 2, p. 393.

See *Report of the Backward Classes Commission*, Controller of Publications, GOI, New Delhi, 1980.

A fifth commission, the National Police Commission, not concerned with investigation, was appointed on 15 November 1977. Under the chairmanship of the former ICS officer Dharma Vira, it submitted eight reports between 1979 and 1981. Along with the many studies and recommendations having to do with internal police administration were recommendations for increasing police accountability to the public. The first report was submitted to H. M. Patel, who had replaced Charan Singh as Home Minister. *Report of the National Police Commission*, Ministry of Home Affairs, GOI, New Delhi, 1979–81.

Chapter 21

THE PUNISHMENT THAT FAILED

It was to be expected that a reckoning would be demanded for the imposition of the Emergency in June 1975 and its attendant events and excesses. The nation had been terrorized and tens of thousands of citizens imprisoned, including many of those who became members of the Janata government. Yet neither the Janata government nor the country were agreed about the action to be taken. Prime Minister Desai said his government would not be 'vindictive', and he ruled out a ' "witch-hunt" '. Law Minister Bhushan joined him in this restraint. Home Minister Charan Singh said the wrongs of the Emergency should neither be forgiven nor forgotten and justified a trial on the ' "Nuremberg model" '.[1] Most in the cabinet favoured some degree of punishment, and in the Lok Sabha, 'amidst uproarious scenes' and a Congress walk-out, members passed H. V. Kamath's resolution deploring the subversion of democratic norms, ethical standards, and spiritual values ' "engineered by ... Mrs Gandhi and her gang" '.[2] Further afield, Acharya Kripalani said that in any other country Mrs Gandhi would have been imprisoned without trial, or hanged.[3]

Were there to be an accounting, followed by punishment, it would have to address what could and should be done about those recently in high office who nearly had brought about democracy's ruin. Had they violated the Constitution, or broken laws, or otherwise committed corrupt or other illegal acts? To find out, there would have to be investigations, whose results would have to be tested in the courts through prosecutions. Constitutional institutions and their practices, now in the hands of the Janata, would be involved—ranging from the council of ministers as the policy-making body, to Parliament, to the judiciary, to the executive branch's bureaucracy. The constitutional implications of all this would

[1] Desai quotation from *Hindustan Times*, 2 April 1977; Charan Singh from ibid., 4 October 1977. Charan Singh also said that Mrs Gandhi should be whipped for her actions during the Emergency, according to Shanti Bhushan in an interview with the author.

[2] *Hindustan Times*, 9 July 1977 and *Lok Sabha Debates*, Sixth Series, vol. 5, no. 36, cols 293ff.

[3] To a Calcutta audience, as reported in the *Hindustan Times*, 10 October 1977.

prove to be profound. The political implications for the Desai government would be disastrous. Before examining these matters, we may review developments as they occurred.

Investigation and prosecution of alleged perpetrators of Emergency wrongdoings took three forms: appointment of what came to be called the 'Shah Commission' (headed by former Chief Justice of India, J. C. Shah) 'to enquire into the facts and circumstances relating to specific instances of ... subversion of lawful processes ... misuse of powers' and so on; investigation by the Central Bureau of Investigation (essentially a police, criminal operation), leading to prosecution in ordinary courts—and later in 'special courts' temporarily established for the purpose; and the Lok Sabha's 'trial' of Mrs Gandhi for breach of privilege and contempt.[4] The latter, as will be seen, concerned events prior to the Emergency, but it was fuelled by angers aroused by the Emergency.

Although desire for some degree of retribution against Indira Gandhi animated each member of the government, Charan Singh's 'vindictiveness', as it was widely perceived, drove government policy. As Home Minister, he had the tools at hand, the Central Bureau of Investigation (CBI), newly removed from the prime minister's office to his ministry, and the Intelligence Bureau, to the extent it could be employed in this cause. Charan Singh first acted against Mrs Gandhi secretly, without the cabinet's knowledge or assent, in August 1977. Having obtained from Law Minister Bhushan affirmative advice on the narrow question of whether an individual could be arrested legally as soon as the 'First Information Report' (FIR) was registered against him or her,[5] Charan Singh

---

[4] *Shah Commission*, I, pp. 1–2. Charan Singh informed the Lok Sabha within two weeks of the government's formation that a commission would be established under the 1952 Commissions of Enquiry Act and on 18 April 1977 he announced that J. C. Shah would chair it. Its terms of reference included, in addition to those cited above, investigating maltreatment of persons arrested, use of force in the family planning programme, and unauthorized demolition of shops and houses. The commission also was to recommend measures to prevent the recurrence of abuses.

The commission was not tasked with developing evidence that might be used in judicial prosecution of Mrs Gandhi and others, although information it had gathered would later be so used.

Several other commissions were set up to enquire into special subjects or the activities of particular individuals.

The three volumes of the Shah Commission report are in the author's possession but are not officially available in India to this day. They are said to have been banned since Mrs Gandhi's return to office in 1980. Copies that had been sent to Indian embassies were recalled by Delhi, according to several Indian diplomats.

[5] An FIR is registered/recorded at a police station. Under the Criminal Procedure Code, a person if caught 'red-handed' also may be arrested before an FIR is registered.

had the CBI register an FIR against Mrs Gandhi as an accused in a corruption case. Warned of the impending arrest while attending a committee meeting, the Prime Minister told the cabinet secretary, who was accompanying him, to "'Stop it!'" The order was passed on to the home secretary—also ignorant of the affair—who saved the situation 'by inches'.[6] During August also, the CBI arrested Sanjay Gandhi confidante and former Defence Minister Bansi Lal, R. K. Dhawan, Yashpal Kapoor, and eight others for financial conspiracy and embezzlement. All were released on bail.

Charan Singh moved against Mrs Gandhi next on 3 October 1977. This time the cabinet had been informed, although poorly, about his plans. The CBI arrested her for alleged corruption and misuse of her political position in acquiring jeeps for Sanjay Gandhi's 1977 election campaign and for her involvement in a tangled affair concerning a contract with a French oil and gas firm. The event immediately and publicly was described as 'the longest arrest in Indian history' and a spectacle that 'not even Charlie Chaplin could have managed ... without elaborate rehearsal'. The police arrived at 12, Willingdon Crescent in the afternoon to find Mrs Gandhi smiling, holding a bunch of roses, and telling the previously alerted reporters that the arrest was to prevent her from "'going to the people'".[7] After being taken hither and thither by the confused police, Mrs Gandhi was kept in New Delhi Police Lines overnight, and, when presented before the additional chief metropolitan magistrate the next morning, she was released after prosecution counsel admitted that the FIR was faulty: ' "We have no evidence at present," ' he said.[8] Irony of ironies, the CBI, after having

---

In cases of so-called 'white collar crime', typically an FIR is registered, an investigation conducted, and then the individual is either arrested or invited to appear in court to hear the charges against him.

[6] This account, for which the author is indebted to Nirmal Mukarji, is drawn from the oral history transcript Mr Mukarji is preparing for the Nehru Library. A slip of paper giving the information was handed to Mukarji, who passed it to Desai, who returned it with the two-word instruction.

[7] 'Longest arrest': *Hindustan Times*, 4 October 1977. 'Charlie Chaplin': Bhattacharjea, Ajit, 'A Tragedy of Errors', *Indian Express*, 8 October 1977.

[8] Limaye, *Janata Party Experiment*, vol. 1, pp. 457ff. This brief version of events is drawn from a much more detailed one in Limaye, from the *Hindustan Times*, 4 October 1977, and from the memory of Delhites amused and appalled at the time by the goings-on. See also the description of the arrest in Malhotra, *Indira Gandhi*, pp. 205ff.

This time, the home minister did not intend the home secretary or the cabinet secretary to scotch his plan. He invited Nirmal Mukarji to his office on the pretext of discussing various matters and, similarly, the home secretary somewhat later. During

been transferred from the Prime Minister's Office to prevent its 'political' use, became again an instrument in a personal political vendetta.

This time, the Prime Minister knew beforehand of the intended arrest, yet he was ill-informed due to poor planning and coordination within the council of ministers. The CBI's prosecution unit had prepared a file for Mrs Gandhi's arrest, but it went neither to the Law Ministry nor to the Advocate General, who likely would have been called upon to prosecute such a high-level accused, or to the Solicitor General.[9] Shanti Bhushan, however, told Charan Singh the day before the planned arrest that it was a bad idea.[10] The two had met during a ceremony at Mahatma Gandhi's memorial. Desai gave his approval orally to Charan Singh unaware that his Law Minister had not seen the file.[11] When the file reached Bhushan after Mrs Gandhi's release, he wrote a note for Desai saying that the evidence presented for Mrs Gandhi's prosecution was

---

this time, he received many telephone calls, which led Mukarji to believe he was receiving a running account of the affair. (Mukarji draft oral history transcript.)

Arrested at the same time for alleged corrupt practices, and also released, were P. C. Sethi, K. D. Malaviya, D. P. Chattopadhyaya, and H. R. Gokhale. All were long-time Congress members and had been in Mrs Gandhi's ministries before and during the Emergency.

Criticism against Gokhale was particularly strong because he was a senior advocate at the Supreme Court bar, and, as Law Minister, had shepherded through Parliament the Emergency's constitutional amendments. At the time of this arrest, he had been suspended from the Supreme Court Bar Association and subjected to investigation by a six-member committee headed by C. K. Daphtary for, in the words of the resolution establishing the committee, corruption, nepotism, and ' "polluting of the fundamental law of the land" '. *Hindustan Times,* 31 April 1977. The enquiry committee released its report to the press on 30 December which among other things charged that Gokhale had helped Mrs Gandhi acquire dictatorial powers for herself and had prepared and got enacted amendments and legislation ' "to shut out the natural course of law and justice" '. Gokhale was invited to appear to defend himself. But by no means did all bar association members condemn Gokhale; he died a broken man on 2 February 1978.

The month following Mrs Gandhi's arrest, CBI Director Narasimhan was moved to a far less important position on the new Police Commission, and John Lobo, who had been Joint Director of the IB in charge of prime ministerial security, took his place.

[9] P. B. Venkatasubramanian letter to the author.

[10] Shanti Bhushan interview with the author.

[11] That the Prime Minister was unaware the author heard from Shanti Bhushan in an interview; Desai's assent from Nayar in an interview and from Limaye, *Cabinet Government,* p. 146. Limaye says both men confirmed this at the time. Later, however, in a letter to L. K. Advani, Desai blamed the 'muddle' entirely on Charan Singh. Ibid., p. 147, citing Gandhi, *Morarji Papers.*

Ramakrishna Hegde recalled that Charan Singh told Morarji Desai that the decision was his as Home Minister: The arrest is purely an administrative matter, and 'I know my business'. Hegde said he learned this from Desai during a conversation at the time of Mrs Gandhi's arrest. Hegde in an interview with the author.

'hopelessly flimsy and contrived'.[12] This momentous political action—it helped Mrs Gandhi regain office in 1980—had been undertaken without anyone having been 'given the job of working out the details step by step, especially the mechanics of explaining it to the people in India and abroad'.[13]

Mrs Gandhi was quick to capitalize upon the fiasco. Claiming that her arrest had been ' "obviously political" ', she told admirers in Surat on 5 October that she had begun her comeback, something that really had been apparent for weeks. For their part, Janata Party general secretaries were dismayed. Arresting Mrs Gandhi, they wrote to Desai, had been ' "most unsatisfactory ... [C]omments in the friendly newspapers have been adverse ... [and] now Congressmen have adopted an aggressive line" '.[14] They recommended setting up a small committee ' "to plan out the political strategy, both parliamentary as well as non-parliamentary" ' to avoid future ' "unplanned actions" '.

Meanwhile, the Shah Commission's hearings had started on 29 September 1977. Early witnesses T. A. Pai, who had been Minister of Industry during the Emergency, and H. R. Gokhale blamed Mrs Gandhi for the Emergency. Late in October, the former Prime Minister declined the commission's request to appear before it, charging that its appointment had been ' "politically motivated" ' and its processes led to ' "character assassination" '. Following her example Pranab Mukherjee and other members of her government would refuse to testify, and in November the Congress Working Committee directed party members not to appear.[15] Mrs Gandhi did appear before the commission on 11 January 1978, but refused to take an oath and to testify. She claimed that making a statement would ' "amount to a violation of my [ministerial] oath of secrecy" '. But she did read for thirty minutes a statement justifying her

---

[12] Bhushan interview with the author. P. B. Venkatasubramanian reports that some papers, not the whole file, reached the ministry after the release. Whereupon officials hastily drafted a revision order against the release so that it could be filed in the high court before it closed that evening. P. B. Venkatasubramanian in correspondence with the author.

[13] Ajit Bhattacharjea, 'A Tragedy of Errors', *Indian Express*, 8 October 1977.

[14] Limaye, *Janata Party Experiment*, vol. 1, pp. 464–5. Limaye recounts that he prepared the draft letter, and that party president Chandra Shekhar signed it after adding a sentence that it was written with the concurrence of Nanaji Deshmukh of the Jana Sangh, Limaye, Rabi Ray, and Ramakrishna Hegde. A copy of the letter went to Charan Singh. Hurt by the criticism, Charan Singh accepted responsibility in a resignation letter, which his colleagues dissuaded him from acting upon.

[15] The Shah Commission, under the Commissions of Enquiry Act, 1952, had the powers of a civil court, namely, the power to summon and enforce attendance of persons, to require the discovery and production of documents, etc. *Shah Commission*, I, p. 7.

actions regarding the Emergency, which Justice Shah characterized as
'a political speech'.[16] Commenting on Mrs Gandhi's refusal to testify,
Morarji Desai said that 'there is no secrecy above the public interest'.[17]
Justice Shah ordered a complaint filed before a magistrate against Mrs
Gandhi for failing to testify, but she delayed this process for ten months
by tying the legal system into knots, using processes and proprieties
against it. On 1 December that year, Justice T. P. S. Chawla of the Delhi
High Court ruled that Mrs Gandhi had not refused to take an oath
before Shah because she merely had said 'no' to the question '"Are you
willing to take an oath?"'[18] A year later Mrs Gandhi released a statement saying that the Shah and other investigative commissions '"have
found practically nothing against her (sic)"'.[19] Justice Chawla later was
made chief justice of the Delhi High Court.

Frustrated by the government's apparent inability to prosecute Mrs
Gandhi in the ordinary courts and by her successful 'stonewalling' of
the Shah Commission, the cabinet found itself in crisis during the spring
of 1978 over whether to prosecute her in special courts established
particularly for this purpose. The acrimonious dispute over special
courts resembled the earlier one about prosecuting Mrs Gandhi at all.
Bhushan and Desai were opposed to special courts, preferring to use
the ordinary courts were Mrs Gandhi to be prosecuted, and Vajpayee
was coming round to Bhushan's view.[20] Ram Jethmalani, the adamant
proponent of special courts for Mrs Gandhi, was not to be deterred .
He wrote to Morarji Desai advocating their swift establishment, to which
Desai responded that such 'emergency courts ... may well run into
difficulty on account of legal objections likely to be raised and the time
of the court wasted in the hearing of these objections'.[21] Desai proved

---

[16] *AR*, 26 February–4 March 1978, p. 14185.

[17] *Hindustan Times*, 23 January 1978.

[18] Shourie, Arun, 'Justice Chawla's *tour de force*' in Shourie, *Institutions in the Janata
Phase*, Popular Prakashan, Bombay, 1980, p. 63. A detailed chronology of the Gandhi–
Shah skirmishes during late 1977 and through 1978 appears in ibid., pp. 56–61.

[19] Ibid., p. 61. The Shah Commission's reports provide a wealth of documentation
concerning Emergency events and denials of democracy. But the commission did not
publish testimony taken before it. Newspapers printed extensive portions of the testimony,
which are at least as revealing as the commission's reports.

[20] Bhushan interview with the author. Whether or not to establish special courts for
particular purposes separate from the ordinary judicial hierarchy, was a controversy pre-
dating the Janata government and Mrs Gandhi. The view that establishing them was
wrong on principle contended with the belief that they were especially suited for hearing
cases concerned with corruption, communal riots, terrorist activities. and so on.

[21] Gandhi, *Morarji Papers*, p. 67. Desai's reply was dated 2 June. The establishment of
special courts was sufficiently in the wind at this time that the *Hindustan Times* reported on

himself a good prophet, for that very day, Indira Gandhi loyalists of the Congress (I)—including Kamalapati Tripathi, Uma Shankar Dikshit, P. V. Narasimha Rao, Vasant Sathe, and A. R. Antulay—sent him a memorandum protesting against special courts to try Mrs Gandhi because they would make ' "serious inroads into the rule of law" '.[22]

The rift in the cabinet widened during June. Charan Singh established a special wing in the CBI to follow up Shah Commission revelations about Mrs Gandhi—some of which the CBI itself had provided to the commission.[23] In a seeming attempt to control his home minister, the Prime Minister appointed a cabinet sub-committee comprising himself, Shanti Bhushan, and Charan Singh to co-ordinate the prosecution. Singh claimed that Desai had '"felt it below his dignity"' to consult him about this. Charan Singh's view was that if the government could not 'tackle' an individual, the people would lose faith that it could tackle the country's problems.[24] Charan Singh contended that the legal community favoured special courts, possibly because he had the backing of H. M. Seervai and Ram Jethmalani.[25] Conversely, Desai claimed that legal opinion was 'overwhelmingly' against it.[26] From Surajkund, near

---

1 June that a special court soon would be appointed. The dispatch said that the court would have the stature of a sessions court, that one or two officers would preside, and the court would be directly under the supervision of the Supreme Court. To do this, an ordinance under the Code of Criminal Procedure was likely, reported the newspaper.

Meanwhile, on 5 May, the Supreme Court had sent Sanjay Gandhi to Tihar Jail, after cancelling his bail in the Kissa Kursi Ka case, because he had abused his liberty by trying to suborn witnesses and to prevent him from tampering with witnesses in the future. *Hindustan Times*, 6 May 1978. Also see footnote 25 in ch. 20.

[22] *Hindustan Times*, 3 June 1978.

[23] *Hindustan Times*, 13 June 1978. Charan Singh placed Raj Deo Singh in charge of the new unit. The latter had been appointed Special Director of the CBI in May, and a colleague described him as a man who would not 'back off' from prosecuting a prominent personality. Raj Deo Singh went on to become Director of the CBI as of June 30, 1979, upon the retirement of John Lobo.

[24] *Hindustan Times*, 27 June 1978. Nirmal Mukarji doubts that such a sub-committee was formed.

[25] Seervai, according to Limaye, later approved the revised version of the bill that established the special courts. Limaye, *Cabinet Government*, p. 148.

[26] At a 17 June press conference, after returning from a trip to the United States, Desai said the government was considering prosecuting Mrs Gandhi in the light of the Shah Commission's report. But 'any action taken will be under the existing law and for specific offences. I do not believe in high-handed action'. He also said that he did not agree with E.M.S. Namboodiripad's demand for a Nuremberg trial; and that Mrs Gandhi had been punished by the people and would be punished in the future because no one was going to forget what she did during the Emergency. Excerpts given in Limaye, *Janata Party Experiment*, vol. 2, p. 138.

Delhi, where he was recuperating from hospitalization, Charan Singh issued a statement saying that the people saw the government as '"a bunch of impotent men"' and wanted Mrs Gandhi arrested under MISA. He was taking a strong stand, he said, without '"being extremely vindictive"'.[27]

Charan Singh's public criticism of the government—a thing not done under ministerial collective responsibility in the parliamentary system—coupled with controversies over the issues, produced a crisis. Desai met with various cabinet members, and External Affairs Minister Vajpayee even postponed a trip abroad. At an informal emergency meeting of the members, fifteen disagreed with Charan Singh's conduct. Several believed he should be asked to give an explanation rather than be sacked, but Desai requested Charan Singh to resign from the cabinet 'forthwith'.[28] In his letter, Desai asked Singh how he could complain that the government was not moving on the special courts when his ministry had submitted no proposal to establish them, and how, in light of collective responsibility, he could justify ridiculing the cabinet.[29] Desai assumed the Home portfolio until the rift was papered over and Charan Singh withdrew his resignation two weeks later.

The government might be at odds within itself over special courts, but Ram Jethmalani did not dally. With Charan Singh's quiet approval, he introduced a private member's bill in the Lok Sabha on 3 July 1978 to set up such courts. The bill's Statement of Objects and Reasons said that the Supreme Court in the past had upheld special courts and that they were needed to prevent the powerful accused from using ordinary courts to delay action against them. The true character of persons whose

[27] 'Bunch of impotent men': in Seervai, *Constitutional Law*, vol. 2, p. 2708. MISA was still in force and would not be repealed for another month.

[28] *Hindustan Times*, 30 June 1978. Charan Singh had already resigned on 28 April from the Janata National Executive and Parliamentary Board, charging that the government had done little with its social-economic agenda and that persons ' "with low social origins have no opportunity to exercise their right to shape or lend a hand in shaping the destiny of the country" '. *AR*, 25 June–1 July 1978, p. 14374.

At the same time, Desai asked Health Minister Raj Narain to resign because of a speech critical of the government that Narain had delivered in Simla. Narain did so on 30 June. This was not related to the special courts controversy. Janata general secretary Ramakrishna Hegde wrote to Jayaprakash Narayan on 23 June reminding him that the party National Executive had decided that 'mutual recrimination by party men in public ... had to be dealt with severely'. Jayaprakash Narayan Papers, NMML.

[29] *Hindustan Times*, 30 June 1978. The text of Desai's letter, drafted by Ravindra Varma, is given in Limaye, *Janata Party Experiment*, vol. 2, pp. 147–50. Chapter XXX in Limaye's volume 2 gives a detailed account of the Charan Singh and Raj Narain affairs, and the following chapter an account of preventing a split in the Janata Party, which threatened at the same time.

offences had been disclosed by investigating commissions must be made known to the electorate as soon as possible to preserve democracy, the statement said.[30]

In an apparent attempt to forestall Jethmalani's bill, the cabinet in mid-July decided to ask the Supreme Court to consider the constitutionality of special courts and on 1 August, President Reddy officially did so.[31] The Court held hearings in the autumn and ruled on 1 December that Parliament had the legislative competence to establish such courts. It recommended that Jethmalani's bill be altered so that a sitting (not a retired) high court judge should preside over a court and that he or she should be appointed with the concurrence of the Chief Justice of India.[32] Five days later the government approved a draft bill to replace Jethmalani's, but, as this leisurely process continued, it did not ask the Lok Sabha to consider the bill until the beginning of March 1979.

With amendments offered in the Rajya Sabha by the Congress and the Communist Party of India to incorporate the Supreme Court's observations and to widen its scope to include pre-Emergency as well as Emergency offences, the bill passed in the Lok Sabha on 8 May 1979. On the last day of the month, Justices M. S. Joshi and M. L. Jain of the Delhi High Court were appointed to head Special Court 1 and Special Court 2 and the government called for extra security for the courts due to the Congress(I)'s declaration that it would not allow them to function.[33] The Supreme Court upheld the Special Courts Act on 4

[30] This was 'The Emergency Courts Bill, 1978'.

[31] The texts of President Reddy's reference to the Court and that of the bill are to be found in *AR*, 24–30 September 1978, p. 14523.

This was the seventh time since 1950 that the Supreme Court had been asked to render an advisory opinion under Article 143. But it was the first time the Criminal Procedure Code, under which the courts were to be established, had been involved. The other occasions were: 23 May 1951, concerning Delhi, Ajmer-Merwara and Part C states; 22 May 1958, the Kerala Education Act; 14 March 1960, the exchanges of Berubari territories with Pakistan; 10 May 1963, Article 289 and a state's immunity from central taxation; 30 September 1964, the jurisdiction of the UP legislature *vis-à-vis* the Allahabad High Court; and 5 June 1974, regarding election to the office of President.

[32] Special Reference under Article 143 (1). 1979 (2) SCR 476ff. On the bench were Chief Justice Chandrachud and Justices Bhagwati, Krishna Iyer, R. S. Sarkaria, N. L. Untwalia, Fazl Ali, and P. N. Shingal. Chandrachud, Bhagwati, Sarkaria, and Fazl Ali gave the majority opinion. Krishna Iyer, in a separate concurring opinion, said that the bill 'hovers perilously near unconstitutionality (Article 14) in certain respects but is surely saved by application of pragmatic principles rooted in precedents'. Ibid, p. 450.

[33] *Hindustan Times*, 31 May 1979. This threat is clear evidence of the Congress (I)'s impression of its growing strength and Janata's increasing weakness. Sanjay Gandhi was reported to have led a rally of fifteen hundred Youth Congressmen on the first of the

December 1979 when hearing appeals by V. C. Shukla and Sanjay Gandhi against their conviction in the Kissa Kursi Ka case.[34]

Cases against Mrs Gandhi and others were tried before these courts during the remainder of 1979, but there were no convictions. The day following Mrs Gandhi's return to the prime ministership after the elections of 3–6 January 1980, Justice M. L. Jain ruled that the establishment of Special Court Number 2 was unconstitutional and that the cases before it should be returned to Delhi's chief metropolitan magistrate. His ground for the ruling was bureaucratic: that the Law Ministry and the Home Ministry had assigned prosecutions to the Special Courts before these ministries had been assigned responsibility for these courts by the Transaction of Business Rules.[35] P. Shiv Shankar, Law Minister since 14 January in the new Congress (I) government, told the Lok Sabha that the government "'considers that the previous government hit upon the device of the special courts to harass their political opponents"'[36].

---

month against the bill. The police responded to the mob's stoning with teargas, and arrested Sanjay Gandhi and others. *Hindustan Times*, 2 May 1979.

In response to the amendments, Kamalapati Tripathi led Congress (I) supporters in a walkout against the '"black bill"'. *Hindustan Times*, 22 March 1979.

[34] The case was *V. C. Shukla versus the State (Delhi Administration)* 1980 *Supp* SCC 249ff. On the bench were Fazl Ali, P. S. Kailasam and A. D. Khoshal; Fazl Ali delivered the opinion that the Act in question did not violate Fundamental Rights Articles 14 and 21, or any other constitutional provision.

On 27 February 1979, Sanjay Gandhi and V. C. Shukla had been sentenced to two years' rigorous imprisonment, plus fines, for their destruction of Amrit Nahata's film, *Kissa Kursi Ka* (The Story of the Seat of Power) which ridiculed the political functioning of the government. The sentencing judge, O. H. Vohra, stayed the operation of his order for one month and released the two men on bail.

A peculiar event took place on 5 July 1979. Justice T. K. Basu of the Calcutta High Court, on the basis of a writ petition from Mrs Gandhi, enjoined the special courts from functioning for a week. Her counsel argued that 'clubbing' pre-Emergency with Emergency offences was both a violation of Article 14 and went against the Supreme Court's upholding of the Special Courts for Emergency offences. Arguing for the government, Soli Sorabjee said that the special courts could not be challenged because the Supreme Court's advisory opinion was binding on the high courts, and, besides, the Calcutta Court had no jurisdiction over cases in Delhi. On 20 July, a Supreme Court bench of N. L. Untwalia and A. P. Sen stayed the Calcutta High Court order. *Hindustan Times*, 21 July 1979.

[35] *Times of India*, 16 January 1980. Jain also ruled that the subsequent amendment to the Transaction of Business Rules allocating the work to the ministries that had issued the 'notifications' could not validate the notifications because the amendment did not apply retroactively.

[36] *Hindustan Times*, 30 January 1980. Shiv Shankar also said that the government was not currently considering a proposal to abolish the courts and that cases before them should run their course.

Shankar told the author in an interview that the cases against Mrs Gandhi and the

A. G. Noorani, India's prestigious legal journalist, attacked Justice Jain's decision piece by piece. Noorani reminded his readers that 'It is a fundamental principle of jurisprudence that a tribunal cannot enquire into the legality of its own establishment.' He concluded by saying that the judge's 'reasoning ... is hypertechnical and in glaring conflict with the constitutional text—Article 77(2) .... It would be most unfortunate if such a judgement were to remain the last judicial pronouncement on the subject.'[37] The Law Ministry told the registrar of the special courts that they should cease to function on 31 March. The cases pending in them were dropped, as were more than one hundred cases pending in other courts as a result of the information developed by the Shah Commission.

In Parliament, at the end of 1978, Mrs Gandhi had not fared so well. Although her ever more successful political comeback had culminated with her re-election to the Lok Sabha in November from the Chikmagalur constituency in Karnataka, her stay was brief. The Privileges Committee—unimpressed that admirers mobbed her as she arrived for the parliamentary session—had reported its 'opinion' that Mrs Gandhi had 'committed a breach of privilege and contempt of the House' in 1974.[38] The affair had originated when Madhu Limaye had given notice of a parliamentary question about the affairs of the Maruti car factory and Sanjay Gandhi's involvement with it. The answers the government had provided hardly had been straightforward, and the committee cited Mrs Gandhi for breach of privilege for causing obstruction, intimidation, harassment, and institution of false cases against the officers preparing answers to the questions. The report also said Mrs Gandhi had been in contempt by 'her refusal to take oath/affirmation and depose before the committee', and she had compounded her contempt by casting aspersions on it.[39] Her punishment was left to the wisdom of the House.

---

others were flimsy, that the Janata government had been vindictive, and that the bureaucrats had been forced to aid the politicians.

[37] Noorani, A. G., *Indian Affairs: The Constitutional Dimension*, Konark Publishers Pvt. Ltd., Delhi 1990, pp. 323–7. The article originally appeared in the *Economic and Political Weekly* on 23 February 1980.

See also Shourie, Arun, *Mrs Gandhi's Second Reign*, Vikas Publishing House Pvt. Ltd., New Delhi 1984, paperback edition, pp. 381–6, chapter entitled 'Special Courts : An Obituary'.

[38] See *Hindustan Times*, 22 November 1978 and succeeding days. Limaye devotes chapter 32 to the events in *Janata Party Experiment*, vol. 2.

[39] Text in Limaye, *Janata Party Experiment*, p. 277. The Privileges Committee also found R. K. Dhawan and D. Sen, the former CBI director, in contempt of the House on identical grounds.

The Lok Sabha began its debate on 7 December while Mrs Gandhi watched—'wearing a chrome-yellow saree and twiddling her thumbs'. This time Morarji Desai was willing to punish Indira Gandhi, and twelve days later, by a vote of 279 to 138, with thirty-seven abstentions, the Lok Sabha adopted his motion to expel her and to sentence her to jail until the prorogation of Parliament—a week later.[40] Janata had given Mrs Gandhi 'the taste of jail' it long had thought she deserved. Congress members, even those not of her Congress(I) Party, opposed Desai's motion. The Election Commissioner, S. L. Shakdher, later ruled that she had lost her seat by being expelled, and Mrs Gandhi vowed to recontest from Chikmagalur. She had been in Parliament just long enough to vote for the Forty-fourth Amendment.

With this exception, the attempts to punish Mrs Gandhi and her associates had failed. The autonomous Shah Commission had done its work, but the government had not capitalized upon this, and its own investigations were ill-conducted and its prosecutions ill-prepared.[41] Within the cabinet, policy had not been coordinated even when its members were not warring over how to revenge themselves on Mrs Gandhi.[42] This record first raises simple and obvious questions. Did the prosecutions fail because there was insufficient evidence of wrongdoing? What laws were broken? Of what, precisely, was Indira Gandhi guilty? Then come constitutional questions of the most fundamental kind. Was the government on sound constitutional ground when it prosecuted individuals for alleged violations of the Constitution that might fairly be described as 'political' as distinct from being defined more precisely by the Constitution or by law? Was Indira Gandhi, as Prime Minister, responsible, constitutionally, for actions by the crew of the ship of state in the same manner as the captain of a ship is responsible if it is wrecked— even when he is neither at the wheel nor on the bridge? Was Mrs Gandhi on sound constitutional ground when she refused to cooperate with the legally established Shah Commission? Are inept investigations and prosecutions such a distortion of the justice system—so essential to a

---

[40] R. K. Dhawan and D. Sen also served this week in jail. For an account of Mrs Gandhi's speech in the Lok Sabha defending herself, other aspects of the affair, and of her time in jail, see Jayakar, *Indira Gandhi*, pp. 368–75.

[41] One of the few constructive products of the commission's work was a secret study to reform the working of the Intelligence Bureau and the Central Bureau of Investigation, which the government asked L. P. Singh to undertake.

[42] For H. M. Seervai's succinct description of the government's ineptitude, see his *Constitutional Law of India*, vol. 2, p. 2708.

democracy—that they, themselves, may fairly be characterized as non-democratic or anti-democratic?

The Janata government did not answer these questions, nor is this study competent to do more than to ask them. Yet there seems to be a broader answer that reaches their essence. This is that the country's constitutional system had not matured sufficiently to meet one of any democracy's severest tests: the capability to investigate and prosecute senior public figures through its democratic, constitutional processes. Such situations—a fractured ministry, judicial timorousness, and bureaucratic ineptness—are not limited to India, but under the Janata government they were pronounced. Mrs Gandhi and her associates nearly had ruined the country's democratic system, but the government could not bring them to book.

The government's wiser course, as Morarji Desai and Shanti Bhushan had preferred, would have been to let the punishment of Mrs Gandhi's election defeat suffice. Beyond that, relying on the cultural characteristic of forgiveness might have denied Mrs Gandhi both the martyrdom upon which she built her comeback and freed the government for more constructive endeavours. As it was, the image of vengeful ineptness from the failed prosecution and its stain on the government's claim to democratic functioning greatly hastened its downfall.

Chapter 22

A GOVERNMENT DIES

A problematical government from the beginning, the approaching end to Janata's career became painfully apparent in June 1979 as it bled from massive defections. The government fell in July, and the tortuous course of forming a new one began. Indira Gandhi returned as prime minister following the 1980 elections, having brought down Charan Singh's government by removing the support she had earlier given him. Meanwhile, President Sanjiva Reddy was required to use his discretion in finding a viable leader of the Lok Sabha to appoint as prime minister—the first time under the Constitution that this situation had to be faced.[1]

Fulfilling this delicate task, President Reddy found himself in a month-long political storm, and, by many accounts, he did not weather it well. He did receive conflicting advice from legal men few of whom, although prominent, were scholars of constitutional conventions. And the British conventions for the appointment of the Prime Minister in such situations are not perfectly tidy. Nevertheless, the conventions applicable in the situation Reddy faced were clear enough and it seems that he did not follow them. These are the topics for this chapter.

Briefly, before turning to a more detailed account of them, the sequence of events in this monsoon month were as follows:

First: the Morarji Desai government dies of internal wounds on 15 July 1979. Having lost his majority in the Lok Sabha, Desai sends two letters to the President: in one he resigns as Prime Minister, but does not advise dissolution of the House; in the other he advises the President to allow him to form an alternative government. President Reddy, instead, invites Y. B. Chavan, the official leader of the Opposition, to form a government; Chavan fails to do so; Reddy then invites Charan Singh to form a ministry, and on 28 July Singh forms a minority government with support from Mrs Gandhi's Congress(I).

Second: Mrs Gandhi withdraws her support from the Charan Singh government, and on 20 August Charan Singh resigns as Prime Minister

[1] Article 75 (1) of the Constitution reads, simply, 'The Prime Minister shall be appointed by the President ...'.

rather than face a vote of confidence in the Lok Sabha. He advises the President to dissolve the Lok Sabha and hold elections.

Third: Jagjivan Ram, having become leader of the Janata Parliamentary Party, on Morarji Desai's belated resignation from the office, argues to the President that he can form a government and that Charan Singh lacks the legitimacy to advise dissolution, having never faced a vote of confidence in the Lok Sabha. President Reddy rejects Ram's claim, dissolves the Lok Sabha on 22 August, and orders elections. Charan Singh heads a caretaker government until elections the following January.

The year 1979 had begun badly with another installment of the Desai–Charan Singh feud. It was resolved temporarily by the reinduction on 24 January of Singh into the cabinet as a Deputy Prime Minister and Minister of Finance—with Jagjivan Ram also appointed a Deputy Prime Minister. Fractures also had been widening in the Janata-controlled state governments since February.[2] And Raj Narain's resignation from the Janata Party on 23 June triggered massive defections, reducing the government's supporters to about two hundred in a house of five hundred thirty-nine occupied seats.[3]

When the monsoon session of Parliament opened on 9 July, Mrs Gandhi's Congress(I) and the Congress Party led by Y. B. Chavan gave notice of a no-confidence motion against the Desai government. Raj Narain had bolted from Janata on 23 June 1979 and announced the formation of the Janata(S) (for 'secular') Party to distinguish it from Janata, which he dubbed 'communal' because it still had as a component the Jana Sangh, with its RSS connections. The no-confidence motion was debated on 11 July. Janata President Chandra Shekhar failed to stem the tide of defections at party meetings on 13 and 14 July, when many among the assembled Janata chief ministers, cabinet ministers,

[2] For the period of Janata decline and fall from the beginning of 1979, there are major sources: the English-language press reported events in detail; the *Asian Recorder* not only condensed these well and reproduced texts of letters and statements but also printed useful chronologies of events. See *AR*, 20–26 August 1979, pp. 15039ff. Also Mirchandani, *The People's Verdict*, pp. 1–25; Gandhi, *The Morarji Papers;* Limaye, *Janata Party Experiment*, especially vol. 2, chs. 34, 35, 38, and 39; Reddy, N. Sanjiva, *Without Fear or Favour: Reminiscences and Reflections of a President*, Allied Publishers Ltd., New Delhi, 1989, ch. 6; and Jain, H. M., 'Presidential Prerogatives in a Situation of Multipartite Contest for Power—A Case Study', *JCPS*, vol. 16, nos. 1–2, 1982, pp. 91–122; Seervai, *Constitutional Law*, vol. 2, 'An Epilogue', pp. 2706–28, which includes discussion of the relevant constitutional conventions; and, finally, the author's interviews with participants and observers of the time.

[3] The situation at the time was highly fluid, with defections and re-defections. There are various 'head counts' by participants and observers of the time.

and general secretaries expressed the belief that Desai would be defeated on the no-confidence motion. The group debated whether Desai ought to resign to avoid this defeat, thereby preserving the possibility of being asked to form another government. Could the party find another leader? On 14 July, Jagjivan Ram had sent a letter to Desai purporting to support him, but criticizing his record.[4] George Fernandes resigned from the government after having strongly defended it during the no-confidence debate two days earlier.

A President's Discretion

July 15th, a day of 'hectic activity', dawned steamy and cloudy. Pressures mounted on Desai to resign—from Mohan Dharia, among others—as defections from the cabinet and in Parliament continued. That evening Morarji Desai took two letters to President Sanjiva Reddy. One tendered his government's resignation because it 'is no longer the case' that Janata had an absolute majority in the Lok Sabha, but the letter did not advise dissolution.[5] The second letter reminded the President that no party now held an absolute majority, that Janata remained the largest single party, and that, as such, it was entitled by constitutional practice to explore the possibility of forming an alternative ministry. ' "I would, therefore, advise that it may be enabled to do so. As the leader of the party, I shall report to you the results of my endeavours as soon as I can." '[6] Reddy thereupon told Desai that if he were confident of majority support, he could defeat the no-confidence motion and need not resign. With his resignation, the motion would lapse. 'I thought it would

---

[4] Arun Gandhi called this 'a letter of diabolical cleverness'. Gandhi, *Morarji Papers*, p. 234; and Limaye 'exactly the reverse of what can be called a defence of the government's performance'. Limaye, *Janata Party Experiment*, vol. 2, p. 466.

[5] Text in Gandhi, *Morarji Papers*, p. 238. According to Nirmal Mukarji, H. M. Patel, who had become Home Minister six months earlier, called upon him to draft this first letter. Sometime later, President Reddy asked Mukarji to prepare a draft of his response to Desai. See footnote 7.

Mukarji believes it probable that Law Minister Bhushan saw the draft of this first letter. Mukarji in an interview with the author.

[6] Quotation from Reddy, *Reminiscences*, p. 25. On 21 July, Desai explained his claim to form another ministry in a letter to Ram Jethmalani. His resignation had not been due ' "to any apprehension that we would be voted out of confidence, but because we had lost absolute majority and as such an occasion arose for restructuring the majority" '. In support of this, Desai cited the occasion in 1931 when Ramsay MacDonald had resigned as Prime Minister of Britain but ' "was commissioned by the King" ' to form another government, ' "which he did with the remnant of the Labour Party ... and the Liberals and the Conservatives" '. Gandhi, *Morarji Papers*, p. 246.

be inappropriate for me,' Reddy continued to Desai, 'to call upon a person who had just tendered his resignation instead of facing the no-confidence motion in the House to form the Government again'.[7] He asked Desai to stay on as Prime Minister while he worked out other arrangements.

On 16 July Parliament adjourned. Chandra Shekhar—perhaps remembering how Desai's government in June 1978 had relegated Janata Party officers, including himself as president, to only an outsider's role in government policy-making (chapter 19)—declared that Desai should step down as leader of the Janata Parliamentary Party. Desai would not relinquish the post for some days, thus denying Charan Singh and Jagjivan Ram a chance at the parliamentary party leadership and the accompanying votes to contend for the prime ministership. Charan Singh defected from the cabinet and the party to be elected leader of the Janata(S). He and Raj Narain then visited the President to stake Charan Singh's claim to forming a government with the help of other parties. All sides bombarded Reddy with political and constitutional advice, while, Reddy said, he 'bestowed a great deal of thought upon the matter'. He concluded that because Desai had lost his majority he would have lost the no-confidence motion, and, therefore, the leader of the opposition, Chavan, 'should be asked to try and form a government'.[8]

Reddy issued the invitation personally and by letter on the evening of 18 July telling Chavan that it was his 'moral duty' as mover of the motion that had brought down the government to try and form a new one.[9] Chavan told reporters that the President had given him three or four days in which to do so. Speaking for Mrs Gandhi's Congress(I), C. M. Stephen said the party would join no government and would oppose any government formed by the original Janata or that depended on the support of the Jana Sangh or the RSS. Mrs Gandhi called upon the President and said nothing publicly.

For the next several days, while the Delhi Administration dispensed chlorine pills to the citizenry (monsoon floods had polluted the drinking water), legal authorities dispensed conflicting constitutional assessments and prescriptions to the President. M. N. Kaul, former Secretary General of the Lok Sabha, and the editors of the *Hindustan Times* agreed that Reddy had acted with constitutional propriety.[10] But Kaul also was

---

[7] Reddy, *Reminiscences*, p. 25. One notes that Reddy quotes the Desai letter directly, but only paraphrases, and does not quote, his response.

[8] Ibid., pp. 25–6.

[9] Ibid., p. 27. At this time, Chavan's Congress Parliamentary Party held some 77 seats.

[10] *Hindustan Times*, 22 July 1979.

reported to believe that Reddy could call on Desai to form another government. Former Attorney General Daphtary shared this view. Senior advocate Fali Nariman and former Bombay High Court judges V. M. Tarkunde and M. C. Chagla were reported to believe that the President had the authority, himself, to call elections if no one could form a government.[11] Tarkunde thought also that Desai, as caretaker Prime Minister, could advise the President to call elections, although it was a '"ticklish question"'. Nariman disagreed. An article cited Sir Ivor Jennings's views (from his *Cabinet Government*) that the opposition that brings down a government has the responsibility for forming another one and that minority governments were possible.[12]

Chavan reported to the President on 22 July that he had been unable to form a government, but that '"a combination of parties"' able to provide viable government had emerged, and he hoped the President would consider the new situation '"in your wisdom"'.[13] He meant, among other things, that he had pledged his party's votes to support Charan Singh.[14]

The next day, both Charan Singh and Morarji Desai wrote to the President staking their claim to form a government. Charan Singh said that he, as leader of a new political alliance, could form a stable government and was willing immediately to prove his majority in Parliament.[15] Desai's hand had been strengthened earlier in the day by Jagjivan Ram's withdrawing from contention for the JPP leadership, and their agreement to attempt jointly to form a government. Mohan Dharia claimed that if Janata remained united and accepted Jagjivan Ram as its leader, it could muster 208 votes in support of a government.[16] Unclear who could command a majority, the President invited Singh and Desai 'in writing to send me lists of their supporters' within two days.[17] Desai

---

[11] Ibid.

[12] *Hindustan Times*, 19 July 1979. At other times Jennings was cited in support of Desai's claim, after resignation, to be asked to form another government.

[13] Reddy, *Reminiscences*, p. 28.

[14] Chavan's actual letter to Charan Singh was dated 23 July and said that the Congress Working Committee, after reviewing the situation in light of Chavan's inability to form a government, '"decided to support the alliance between the Congress and the Janata(S) Party. The Charan Singh Papers, as cited in Limaye, *Janata Party Experiment*, vol. 2, pp. 507–8.

[15] Mirchandani, *The People's Verdict*, pp. 3–4. Also Reddy, *Reminiscences*, p. 28. According to Reddy, Charan Singh told him he could form a government with the support of the Janata (S), the Congress, H. N. Bahuguna's group, a remnant of the Congress for Democracy, and a group of socialists. Ibid.

[16] Jain, 'Presidential Prerogatives', p. 97.

[17] Reddy, *Reminiscences*, p. 29.

thereupon visited Reddy and asked 'jocularly' to be allowed four days, claiming that Chavan had been given eight days and that some of those he needed to contact were out of Delhi. 'Very casually', in Desai's recollection, Reddy responded that Desai could take 'a day more if necessary'.[18] According to Reddy the 'understanding was' that the lists should be delivered by four o'clock on 25 July 'although I had not indicated the time in the letter'. Reddy recalled that on 24 and 25 July first Desai and then his secretary had telephoned the presidency to request more time, but were refused. In Reddy's view, he had not 'gone back on any assurance given earlier' to Desai.[19] At 4.05 on 25 July, Raj Narain presented Charan Singh's list to Reddy's secretary. Desai's list followed at 4.25 accompanied by his letter saying that he hoped to submit a supplementary list the next day. Charan Singh and Morarji Desai challenged each other's vote count.[20]

By now, Charan Singh's claim had been strengthened by the support of Mrs Gandhi's Congress(I). He had written to Mrs Gandhi on 23 July soliciting her support, according to A. R. Antulay, an Indira Gandhi loyalist and a Congress(I) general secretary,[21] and had talked with her on the telephone. The next day, C. M. Stephen and Kamalapati Tripathi, Congress(I) leaders in the Lok Sabha and Rajya Sabha, respectively, handed to Charan Singh a copy of the letter they had that day sent to

[18] Gandhi, *Morarji Papers*, p. 241.

[19] Reddy, *Reminiscences*, p. 30. '[A]bout this time', Reddy recalled, he received a letter from 'the leader' of the Congress (I) (unnamed, but a man) saying that in England according to constitutional experts if the official opposition '"succeeds in defeating the Government and so causing its resignation, it is the duty of its leaders to form a new Government or to advise the Queen as to an alternative"'. The writer continued that it was incumbent upon Reddy to adopt the alternative that the leader of the opposition had recommended because the leader, himself, had been unable to form a government. Under no circumstances should Desai be given a chance to form a government, the Congress (I) letter said, 'as it would amount to sending back to Parliament as Prime Minister a person who had just been voted out of office'. Speaking on his own behalf, Reddy recorded his own views that although constitutional authorities might be cited 'to support one's predilections', there was nothing to show that the Opposition leader's alternative would produce a stable government. Hence Reddy believed that he could not make a decision without 'asking the two leaders to furnish detailed information ...'. Ibid., p. 29.

[20] Text of letter in Gandhi, *Morarji Papers*, pp. 242–3. The situation was enlivened at Rashtrapati Bhavan that afternoon, according to Arun Gandhi, by Raj Narain acting 'like a bull in a china shop browbeating everyone and watching the clock as though an Olympic race was on ... and his men raised hell [if Desai's late list were to be accepted] ... [and] virtually camping in the Rashtrapati Bhavan and threatening everyone with dire consequences if any leniency was shown to Morarji'. Ibid.

[21] Mirchandani, *People's Verdict*, p. 4.

Sanjiva Reddy informing the President that, at Singh's request, the Congress(I) Parliamentary Party had decided to support Singh '"for formation of a government under his leadership"'.[22] Commenting on this performance, senior *Statesman* correspondent S. Nihal Singh wrote, 'By a strange alchemy of politics, her sins seem to have been washed away; Mr Charan Singh, the man who most assiduously sought to punish her for her Emergency misdeeds, and bungled the process, is now wooing her to attain power'.[23] Charan Singh's position was even more craven if the conditions for Congress(I) support were, as they were reported to be, to end the Janata policy of 'vindictiveness' toward Mrs Gandhi and to withdraw all cases in the special courts against her, Sanjay Gandhi, and her other supporters.[24] If these were not Mrs Gandhi's terms at the moment, they soon would be, Charan Singh himself revealed.

Confronted by conflicting numbers, the President set his staff to counting. Although some names appeared on both lists, Reddy concluded that Singh's list showed a majority of twenty-four.[25] Acting according to his 'conscience', Reddy said, and taking an 'impartial view of the situation', he sent a letter to Charan Singh on 26 July inviting him to form a government. He suggested, 'in accordance with the highest democratic traditions', that Singh should seek a vote of confidence in the Lok Sabha by the third week of August.[26] On 27 July, Morarji Desai stepped down from the Janata Parliamentary Party leadership to be replaced by Jagjivan Ram. Desai apologized for the 'bungling' in the vote count submitted to the President and declared that he was retiring from active politics.

[22] Texts of letters in the Charan Singh Papers as quoted in Limaye, *Janata Party Experiment*, vol. 2, pp. 508–9.

In a letter to Mrs Gandhi that evening, Singh put a positive interpretation on this language, thanking her for Stephen's and Tripathi's '*"unconditional support* in my efforts at forming a stable Government"'. Ibid. p. 509, emphasis in Limaye's volume.

The *Hindustan Times* reported on 26 July that Ram Jethmalani was claiming that Charan Singh had met Mrs Gandhi at the Sagar Apartments on Tilak Marg in an apartment leased by Maneka Gandhi, Sanjay's wife, and that Raj Narain had met with Sanjay Gandhi. Charan Singh called the reports of his meetings with Mrs Gandhi lies. *Hindustan Times*, 28 July 1979. A senior official in a position to know confirms that Sanjay Gandhi conspired with Raj Narain against Morarji Desai.

[23] *Statesman*, 25 July 1979.

[24] *Hindustan Times*, 24 July 1979.

[25] Reddy, *Reminiscences*, p. 32. The next day, the *Hindustan Times* reported that Desai and Singh were 'level at 279', with the President's job made more difficult by the two lists totalling 558 votes when there were only 538 sitting Lok Sabha members and twenty-nine members were saying that they were neutral.

[26] Ibid., p. 35. The *Hindustan Times* reported Reddy's invitation to Singh as having been made on 27 July.

Reddy swore in Singh, Y. B. Chavan as Deputy Prime Minister and Home Minister, and others on 28 July. Three days later more members were added to the ministry, including H. R. Khanna as Law Minister, but Khanna, persuaded by friendly members of the bar, withdrew his participation on 2 August.[27] As advised by the council of ministers, President Reddy called on Parliament to assemble on 20 August when, it was expected, Charan Singh would have to prove his majority through a confidence vote. A *Hindustan Times* editorial congratulated Reddy on his 'correct and dignified manner' and his signal contribution to the exercise of presidential discretion.[28]

Charan Singh's foolish prime ministerial ambitions came to an end on 20 August, when Indira Gandhi pulled the rug from under him. Apparently calculating that she could bring about the elections that would return her to office, the Congress(I) Parliamentary Party, meeting at her house before Parliament convened, decided to vote against the confidence motion.[29] Upon learning this, Charan Singh's cabinet decided in emergency session not to face a vote, and Charan Singh drove to Rashtrapati Bhavan to tender the government's resignation passing Parliament House as the session was beginning. He advised the President to dissolve Parliament and call elections. In a public statement, Charan Singh said that the country would not have forgiven him had he agreed to Congress(I) conditions to withdraw the prosecutions against those guilty of atrocities during the Emergency. Nor would he have liked to continue in power after '"yielding to blackmail of this type"'.[30] The President was confronted with a knottier problem than before.

Jagjivan Ram's moment had arrived. Having become Janata Parliamentary Party leader, he called upon all right-thinking persons in early August to join him in bringing down the government of '"defectors and deserters"'. Were the government to fall, the President would have

---

[27] Khanna interview with the author. Khanna's letter is reproduced in *AR*, 20–26 August 1979, p. 15043. S. N. Kacker, who had been Solicitor General in the previous government, replaced Khanna. Chandra Shekhar continued as party president.

[28] *Hindustan Times*, 28 July 1979.

[29] That she would do this at some point as the culmination of her comeback strategy had been thought likely. She confided this intention to the President in mid-July, Sanjiva Reddy later told Madhu Limaye, according to the latter. Limaye, *Janata Party Experiment*, vol.2, p. 513.

[30] *Hindustan Times*, 21 August 1979. According to Limaye, Charan Singh had telephoned him early on the morning of the 20th and said that Biju Patnaik was urging him to contact Mrs Gandhi to ask for her support. Limaye told him not to, it would do no good, but to face the debate in the Lok Sabha. Limaye, *Janata Party Experiment*, vol. 2, p. 518.

to call upon him as the opposition leader to form the next government.[31]
Upon learning of Charan Singh's resignation, Ram called on the President and told him that without majority support in the Lok Sabha the Charan Singh government did not have the legitimacy to advise dissolution and that he could form a stable government.

From that morning, President Reddy recalled with some understatement, 'I had many visitors'.[32] Prime Minister Charan Singh, Law Minister S. N. Kacker, and Foreign Minister S. N. Mishra—followed by aides bearing red-bound legal volumes—told the President that he had no choice but to dissolve Parliament on the advice of his ministers, especially given the Forty-second Amendment's addition to Article 74 that the President 'shall' act according to the advice of his council of ministers, and given the Supreme Court's ruling in the Samsher Singh case,[33] Kacker told the President that 291 Lok Sabha members of the total of 532 desired dissolution and he visited the President the next day to reiterate these arguments.[34] Kacker later disclosed that he had mentioned requesting an advisory opinion from the Supreme Court to his cabinet colleagues, but they thought this superfluous given Article 74, and the idea apparently was not even mentioned to Reddy.[35]

Jagjivan Ram and Chandra Shekhar, accompanied by six Janata chief ministers, called on Sanjiva Reddy to urge him to invite Ram to form the government. They argued that because Charan Singh's government never had received the confidence of Parliament, it ' "was not at all competent" ' to advise dissolution. Later in the day Ram repeated this

---

[31] *Hindustan Times,* 6 August 1979. Also Limaye, *Janata Party Experiment,* vol. 2, p. 515. At this time, Jagjivan Ram was reported to have said that Janata would not mind Congress (I) support to form a government, but it is difficult to believe he said, or meant, this.

[32] This account of the following three days is drawn from the *Hindustan Times,* issues of 21–26 August 1979; *AR,* 24–30 September 1979, pp. 15089ff; Reddy, *Reminiscences,* pp. 36ff; Jain, 'President Prerogatives'; Limaye, *Janata Party Experiment,* vol. 2, pp. 391ff; Noorani, *Indian Affairs,* pp. 67–78; and from interviews.

[33] *Samsher Singh v State of Punjab,* 1974 (2) SCC 831ff. The case concerned the powers of governors. The judges ruled that a governor, in the country's parliamentary system, was bound to act according to the advice of his council of ministers. The ruling did not address whether the President could reject the advice of his ministers, although the court in other cases had held that he could not.

It will be recalled that the Forty-fourth Amendment, which had come into effect three-and-a-half months earlier, retained the 'shall' of the Forty-second Amendment while adding a proviso that the President could return a decision to the Cabinet for its reconsideration before the 'shall' came into effect. See *V. N. Shukla's Constitution of India,* p. 342, and Seervai, *Constitutional Law,* vol. 2, p. 2719.

[34] Reddy, *Reminiscences,* p. 38.

[35] For Kacker's disclosure, see *Hindustan Times,* 26 August 1979.

argument in a letter to Reddy, adding that he could form a stable government with ' "a clear majority of the Lok Sabha. The correct course, therefore, would be that I, as a leader of the Opposition, am invited" ' to explore forming a government; only if I failed to do so would the question of dissolution arise, said Ram.[36] Before the end of the day, Indira Gandhi called on Reddy and told him Ram could not form a stable government and that Charan Singh should not head a caretaker government. That evening, the President asked Charan Singh to 'satisfy him' that a coalition government that had not faced a confidence vote 'was entitled' to recommend dissolution.[37]

The following day advice flooded Rashtrapati Bhavan—in letters, through the press, and from the senior personalities admitted from the throngs outside its tall iron gates. The 'intellectuals' who at the beginning had been ardent Janata supporters—including Rajni Kothari, George Verghese, Bashiruddin Ahmad, and Romesh Thapar—issued a joint statement saying that Charan Singh's advice was no more than a personal opinion. Krishan Kant sent a letter signed by 102 Lok Sabha members urging Reddy to invite Jagjivan Ram, arguing that the President had invited Chavan when he had fewer votes than Ram, that a chance should be given to ' "one of ... [India's] tallest sons belonging to the Harijan community" ', and that Reddy should not heed ' "spurious arguments ... [which would be a] perversion of constitutional and democratic processes" '.[38] For his own part, Ram refused to give the President a list of his supporters, maintaining that his strength should be tested on the floor of the Lok Sabha, and he rejected Mrs Gandhi's conditional support in forming a government.[39] The five Left Front

---

[36] For the text of his letter, see *Hindustan Times*, 23 August 1979. Reddy describes, but does not quote, the letter in *Reminiscences*, p. 37.

Morarji Desai, L. K. Advani, and A. B. Vajpayee were reported to have advised the President to invite Ram to form the government.

[37] *Hindustan Times*, 21 August 1979.

[38] *Hindustan Times*, 22 August 1979. See also Reddy, *Reminiscences*, p. 38. The previous day's *Hindustan Times* editorial said that the President should invite Ram, rejecting 'without the slightest hesitation' advice from Charan Singh, who had 'ducked' the vote of confidence. *Hindustan Times*, 21 August 1979.

Acharya Kripalani, C. B. Gupta, and Nandini Satpathy also supported Jagjivan Ram.

[39] He also declined to form a caretaker government. P. G. Mavalankar, Mohan Dharia, and others also wrote to the President recommending that Jagjivan Ram be given the opportunity to form a government, with Dharia arguing that Ram had a strength of over two hundred in the Lok Sabha, whereas Chavan had had only about seventy-five sure votes, and that it would be important for the Scheduled Castes to have one of their own as Prime Minister. Reddy, *Reminiscences*, p. 37.

parties urged dissolution, and Limaye wrote to Reddy that he must abide by the advice of his ministers. Mrs Gandhi, Kamalapati Tripathi, and C. M. Stephen again urged dissolution on the President while the Congress(I) Parliamentary Board met in almost continuous session at Mrs Gandhi's house.

If the President opened New Delhi's major English language newspapers that morning of 21 August, he read articles by, and interviews reporting the opinions of senior advocates and others—most of whom favoured giving Ram the chance to form a government. Fali Nariman, Y. S. Chitale, and V. M. Tarkunde argued that in the current situation the President constitutionally could act in his discretion; only if he could not find a person commanding a majority should he dissolve Parliament. Senior advocate Ashok Desai, M. N. Kaul, and former Chief Election Commissioner S. P. Sen Verma said Ram should be given his opportunity. Kaul said that if someone could form a stable government, the advice of a ministry that had not gained Parliament's confidence could be ignored.[40]

August 22 was the critical day. First, the President received C. M. Stephen, who handed him a long letter again laying out Congress(I)'s arguments for dissolution and claiming that most members of Charan Singh's government supported this.[41] At 11.30 Ram and Chandra Shekhar met Reddy at his invitation to discuss the political situation 'informally'. Ram recaptured the meeting in a letter to Reddy that he wrote shortly after their meeting. The President, Ram recalled, had told them he thought it ' "unlikely" ' that Ram could muster the support of other parties. To this, Ram had responded, ' "I would be in a position to satisfy you as to the majority support I enjoyed and also that there were parties which would come forward to say that they would support me." ' Ram continued, ' "You were good enough to say that while you would like to have the matter settled quickly, you were in no hurry and would still take some time to consider the questions involved further. I took this to mean that you would be prepared to wait for a further communication from me giving details of my support." '[42] The men parted company before noon.

Ever helpful, Raj Narain threatened a 'peaceful agitation' if Reddy did not dissolve Parliament and later he made the threat in the press.

[40] *Hindustan Times*, 21 August 1979. In the same vein, Nariman argued separately that Articles 74 and 75 imply that a Prime Minister shall have the confidence of Parliament.

[41] See Reddy, *Reminiscences*, p. 39, for his description of the letter.

[42] The text of this letter was printed in the *Hindustan Times*, 23 August 1979.

'On 22 August, Janata leaders obtained pledges of support from enough MPs to

But Reddy already had decided against Ram and in favour of dissolution *before* this meeting. Supporting this conclusion is that an hour-and-a-half later he announced dissolution and preparations for this would not have been completed in that amount of time. They had been begun earlier as Reddy, himself, has indicated. 'Almost all political parties, except the Janata Party, were in favour of dissolution,' wrote Reddy in his *Reminiscences*, and in the circumstances the best way to end the impasse was dissolution. 'Accordingly', the President continued, 'on the morning of 22 August', the cabinet secretary, the Prime Minister's secretary, and my secretary met 'to prepare the necessary drafts for dissolution'.[43] These prepared, Rashtrapati Bhavan was in a position to issue the communique soon after Ram and Chandra Shekar had departed. The President had accepted the resignation of Charan Singh and his council of ministers, the communique said, and it asked them to continue in office pending other arrangements. The communique said that almost all the political parties had called for dissolution and that the President had consulted (unnamed) constitutional and legal experts.[44]

Ram immediately cried foul. Reddy had executed a '"planned scheme ... a well-planned conspiracy"' picking his own choice as prime minister. '"We had expected better of the President,"' Ram said. Chandra Shekhar talked of impeaching Reddy, and the next day he appointed a party committee of Shanti Bhushan, L. K. Advani, Ram Jethmalani, and Surendra Mohan—not all of whom were thought to favour impeachment—to examine the matter. In Bombay, M. C. Chagla called the move '"most unfortunate and erroneous"' and Nani Palkhivala thought it '"unjustified to the point of Constitutional impropriety"'.[45] Nariman, Bhushan, and S. V. Gupte, who had been Desai's Attorney General, said Ram should

---

assure that Ram would have a narrow majority' when the All-India Anna Dravida Munnetra Kazhagam (AIADMK) lent its backing, and they informed Reddy of this during that morning. Manor, James, 'The Prime Minister and the President' in Manor, *Nehru to the Nineties*, p. 131.

[43] Reddy, *Reminiscences*, p. 41.

[44] Text of the communique in ibid. The communique also said that the government would not take decisions during the caretaker period that would involve significant new spending or amount to major new administrative executive decisions.

[45] *Hindustan Times*, 23 August 1979. *AR*, 24–30 September 1979, p. 15902, citing the *Hindustan Times* and two other newspapers. Ram and Chandra Shekhar also laid out their position in 'An Appeal to the People' dated 23 August 1979, which is reprinted in *Steps Toward Dynamic Growth*, Janata Party, New Delhi, September 1979. (The party's office was then at 7, Jantar Mantar Road, for many years the Congress's office.) Yet another Janata pamphlet published in 1979, entitled *Paper on Conspiracy Against the People*, opened with an article entitled 'Darkness at Noon'.

have been given his chance. Predictably, the Congress(I), the Janata(S), and the Left Front parties welcomed the decision. The uproar continued the next day. Ram called on Charan Singh to step down and said that Mrs Gandhi had offered him her support if he would not appoint Jana Sangh members to his cabinet and would within three months call for an election. Mrs Gandhi partially confirmed this when she said that Ram would have had to appoint suitable persons to his cabinet to gain Congress(I) support. C. M. Stephen reiterated Mrs Gandhi's position that Charan Singh should step down in favour of a national, non-partisan government and that the special courts should suspend operations.[46]

President Reddy disagreed with Ram's version of their meeting. '"Your letter is not a correct record of our conversation," ' he wrote, ' "as you yourself are aware" '.[47] I told Chandra Shekhar as you were leaving, Reddy wrote, that there was 'no hurry [about coming to see me again] and that he was always welcome ... I only meant that he need not be in a hurry ... I had not implied at all that I was not in a hurry to come to a decision in regard to the prevailing political situation. Unfortunately, an unintended construction was put on my words'.[48] Ram replied that he did not appreciate the allegation that his letter was not accurate. Chandra Shekhar told the press that if Ram's version was not correct the President should give the correct one.[49] Reddy did not at the time, nor later in his *Reminiscences*, quote his own letter to Ram.

Chandra Shekhar's angry demand for President Reddy's impeachment died away. Like it or not, the President's decision could not be challenged in court, said senior advocates; he had acted within his constitutional discretion. But this did not preempt post-mortems. One of these, obviously, was President Reddy's own. Rejecting the analogy with his July invitation to Chavan to form a government, Reddy wrote in his memoirs, 'If Jagjivan Ram was invited to form a Government and if his Government too was found to lack a majority, what should be the next step? Would it again be necessary to try to form a Government with the

---

[46] *Hindustan Times*, 24 August 1979. On 24 August Stephen and Kamalapati Tripathi sent Reddy a memorandum calling on him to remove Charan Singh's government as a caretaker government and to appoint a new government.

[47] Reddy letter was dated 24 August. Only this much of the letter is quoted in the *Hindustan Times*, 26 August 1979.

[48] Reddy's *Reminiscences*, p. 42. Reddy also recounted that Ram had promised to submit a list of his supporters once called upon to form a government. 'I pointed out that this was not the method I had earlier adopted', apparently meaning that he had demanded lists from others *before* inviting them to form a government. Had Ram retreated slightly?

[49] *Hindustan Times*, 26 August 1979. Ram's letter was dated 25 August, the day he said he received Reddy's letter. Text of the letter in *AR*, 24–30 September 1979, p. 15093.

help of whosoever was the Leader of the Opposition at the time? Clearly such a process would be unending'.[50]

A. G. Noorani thought that 'President Reddy has in one fell blow violated ... a whole set of established conventions of parliamentary democracy.' H. M. Seervai found nothing good or acceptable in Reddy's performance. Seervai's principal points were that the President should have announced Desai's resignation, but refused to accept it—on the ground that there was no alternative government in sight and the Head of State should not be without ministers; that when Chavan had failed to form a government, Reddy should have turned to Desai—as leader of the largest party in the Lok Sabha; that Reddy's acceptance of Charan Singh's claim to form a stable government with Mrs Gandhi's support was odd—given that 'every intelligent schoolboy' knew what her support was worth; that 'no rational reason' had been given for not inviting Ram—especially given the desire to avoid an interim election; that allowing Charan Singh three weeks to secure a majority was 'hostile discrimination', and that in light of Charan Singh's never having commanded a majority in the Lok Sabha, Reddy was not bound to accept his advice to dissolve it, nor should he have named him caretaker Prime Minister.[51] More emotionally, Rajya Sabha member Krishna Kripalani wrote that the 'ordinary person like me is revolted at the sordid spectacle of blatant opportunism and shameless self-righteousness that are the conspicuous features of our present political scene'.[52]

President Reddy's actions continue to be controversial. Neither logic nor a thought-out scheme can be discerned. Without firm evidence one concludes that the President acted from personal caprice in opposing Jagjivan Ram for Prime Minister. It will be recalled that Reddy and Ram had competed to be the Congress Party's candidate for the presidency in 1969. And it is possible that Jagjivan Ram's scheduled caste background did not please Reddy. Also, Reddy may not have wished to be matched against such a wily politician and able administrator as Ram. A former Home Secretary offered the thought that Reddy had been mulling over

[50] Reddy, *Reminiscences*, p. 40.

[51] See Seervai 'Epilogue', in his *Constitutional Law*, vol. 2, especially pp. 2710–11, 2716, and 2718–9. Seervai cited as his sources Jennings, Halsbury, Dicey, and Hood Phillips.
The President's action is even more puzzling in light of the mutual antipathy he and Mrs Gandhi had shared since the late 1960s.

[52] Letter dated 5 August 1979. Jayaprakash Narayan Papers, Third Installment, File 345, NMML.
As Charan Singh's 'defector government' tottered on through the autumn, there was no dearth of analyses explaining what had gone wrong with the Janata government. One of the most interesting of these is Chandra Shekhar's Oral History Transcript in the NMML.

his rejection of Ram for some time; only the actual decision came at the last moment.[53]

The constitutionality of the President's actions is open to question. To demand that Charan Singh and Jagjivan Ram present him with lists of supporters was undignified for the contestants. Such a method invited inaccuracy because of the volatility from defections and re-defections and from the fudging of numbers that occurred. And it was not constitutional because, as Ram and many others pointed out, a majority could be demonstrated only in the Lok Sabha. Moreover, Sanjiva Reddy previously had taken a position seemingly contrary to his actions as President. When himself Speaker of the Lok Sabha in 1968, he told the Presiding Officers' Conference that 'it is not the governor who should decide from day to day whether or not a majority or a coalition of parties has a majority in the Assembly, particularly when defections are unhappily the order of the day. The proper place to decide the issue is the floor of the House'.[54] Reddy's claim that inviting Ram to form a government would have risked a never-ending search process seems a straw man, because had Ram been unable to form a government he would have been as likely as Charan Singh to advise elections.

Five days before Charan Singh's government resigned, Reddy had delivered the President's annual Independence Day speech. In addition to addressing wider national issues and after pointing out that the Constitution could not provide for every contingency, he said we will have to evolve ' "healthy conventions based on sound and lasting principles of public basic values" '. These had been treated with contempt, Reddy continued, without providing examples, and the time had come to '"review the provisions of the Constitution in the light of our experience of working it over the last three decades"'.[55] If the President was referring to the immediate situation and his being the first President forced to decide among contenders for prime minister, he seemed to be ignoring well-known British conventions, the view predominating in many of the country's best legal minds, and, into the bargain, common sense. If he wished healthy conventions established to meet the situation in which he found himself, he could have contributed to the process

[53] James Manor describes the speculation about the President's motives in his *Nehru to the Nineties*, pp. 131–2.

[54] *Journal of Parliamentary Information*, vol. 14, no. 1, Lok Sabha Secretariat, New Delhi, April 1968, p. 3. A. G. Noorani cited a portion of this speech in his 'Implications of President's Action' in *Will of Lok Sabha was Flouted*, Janata Party, New Delhi, September 1979, p. 1.

[55] *AR*, 10–16 September 1979, p. 15068.

instead of setting a regrettable example. And if he believed that alterations in the Constitution would reform human character and the nation's politics, he understood neither constitutions nor his fellow-men.

Coalition governments typically are uneasy affairs, and Janata's was more so than most. It achieved wondrously and failed miserably. With two amendments, Janata saved the Constitution and representative democracy for their countrymen and women. For this it is owed eternal gratitude. Also, it established the Mandal Commission, whose report would forever change representation in government, and the Verghese Commission, to take broadcasting from under government control; it appointed the first Muslim as a service chief—air force; and it increased outlays for agricultural development. Yet, the members of the government and the constituent parties of the Janata Party, many of whom for long had been unfriendly personally or been policy opponents, exemplified the factionalism, mutual suspicion, and casteism so endemic in India's national culture and politics (chapter 31). Extreme ambition and pettiness curdled this mixture further, and Morarji Desai—upright in character but difficult of personality—could not silence the caterwauling his open style of leadership permitted nor keep his colleagues focused on national issues. The government's end was particularly ignominious. Factionalism brought down Desai, and Charan Singh's desperate bargain bought him defeat. The conduct of Jagjivan Ram and several others stands out in contrast.

Withal, praise for the Constitution and, somewhat less, for Janata's political actors is due. The President's requests and decisions, popular or not, were obeyed. No one resorted to force to gain his ends—perhaps excepting Raj Narain's ill-mannered rowdyism. In the end, the issue was taken where it belonged: to the people in elections. Voters rebuked those who, despite having saved the Constitution, otherwise had failed to govern responsibly.

Part V

INDIRA GANDHI RETURNS

The Indian National Congress(I) is the only party and Mrs Indira Gandhi is the only leader who can save the country after its recent traumatic experience.

Congress(I) Election Manifesto[1]

You can't take the curl out of a dog's tail.

Village saying

[1] Released by Mrs Gandhi on 1 December 1979. *AR*, 24–31 December 1979, p. 15235.

Chapter 23

GHOSTS OF GOVERNMENTS PAST

Indira Gandhi's Congress(I) roundly defeated the Janata Party in the elections of 3–6 January 1980, but the approximately five years of her 'second reign' would not be happy ones for the country. Neither Mrs Gandhi nor her critics could shake loose from the past, and they had bitter memories of each other. These years would bring renewed attention to constitutional issues such as the independence of the judiciary and the calibre of judges and changing from a parliamentary to a presidential system—with its obvious implications for the relationship between the legislative and the executive branches of government. They would see a reaffirmation of the basic structure doctrine. The shape of center–state relations would be challenged more fundamentally than in a dozen years as state governments demanded reforms.[1] The social revolution strand of the seamless web received routinely rhetorical attention, but the government slightly loosened its grip on economic activity. The democracy and the national unity and integrity strands dominated public debate. These years would bring the Prime Minister great personal sorrow, and they would end with her death. That her sixteen years as Prime Minister should end with assassination was horrible enough. That they should end in a terrible paradox made the event worse. Her misguided policy in the Punjab had invited retribution from Sikh extremists. Yet, her genuine secularism had caused her to reject advice that she dismiss her Sikh security guards, two of whom killed her.

Mrs Gandhi had won her own Lok Sabha seat by two hundred thousand votes, campaigning on the assertion that the Congress(I) could ' "set the country once again on the path of dynamic, meaningful and orderly social change ... [while] ensuring stability" '. Sanjay Gandhi won Amethi constituency. The Congress(I) overall won 353 seats. Janata was reduced to thirty-one seats, the two communist parties to fifty-seven, and the DMK to sixteen.[2] State legislative elections held in May affirmed

---

[1] The 'constitutional revolt' of the eighties will be described in chapter 27, and the working of federalism since 1950 is reviewed in Part VI.

[2] Quotation from the Congress Election Manifesto. *AR*, 24–31 December 1979.

The tally of each party's seats is from Butler, Lahiri, and Roy, *India Decides*, p. 86. Elections

Mrs Gandhi's parliamentary victory, for the Congress(I) won a two-thirds majority in five of the nine states where Janata governments had been dismissed (chapter 27) and a simple majority in three. Tamil parties maintained their ascendancy in Tamil Nadu.

The Prime Minister's personal ascendancy was unchallenged: her cabinet was dependent upon her for of the nine principal ministers six were serving as such for the first time; three previously had been closely associated with her as central ministers. Later additions would follow this pattern.[3] In a national broadcast after taking the oath of office on 14 January, Mrs Gandhi proclaimed that her government had 'only one adversary—social and economic injustice'. She added, 'Our commitment to democracy, socialism and secularism is a matter of faith.'[4]

Mrs Gandhi's mood in this favourable situation has been described variously. Her election victory 'lifted at a stroke ... all her burdens' wrote a biographer.[5] She was supremely confident, the undisputed leader of a party, with ministers who 'had come up only because of her like Zail Singh', said a former minister.[6] 'There were no men of the calibre of

---

were not held in twelve constituencies in Assam and one in Meghalaya. Prominent among other winners were Janata president Chandra Shekhar, Indrajit Gupta, Somnath Chatterjee, V. C. Shukla, Jagjivan Ram, Y. B. Chavan, and Biju Patnaik. Among the defeated were S. N. Mishra, T. A. Pai, N. G. Goray, Mohan Dharia, Dinesh Singh, P. G. Mavalankar, Raj Narain, and Madhu Limaye.

[3] Mrs Gandhi's three long-time followers were Pranab Mukherjee, Minister of Commerce who became Congress(I) leader in the Rajya Sabha, P. C. Sethi, Minister of Works and Housing, and Kamalapati Tripathi, Minister of Railways. The newcomers to the government were C.M. Stephen (Communications), R. Venkataraman (Finance), Zail Singh (Home), Narasimha Rao (External Affairs), Vasant Sathe (Information and Broadcasting), and P. Shiv Shankar (Law). In June 1980, V. C. Shukla, previously a minister, rejoined as Minister of Civil Supplies, and N. D. Tiwari, a first-timer, became Minister of Planning—and, as such, Deputy Chairman of the Planning Commission. The inner group of the cabinet, the Political Affairs Committee, consisted of the Prime Minister, Narasimha Rao, Zail Singh, Kamalapati Tripathi, and R. Venkataraman.

As time went on, several who had left Mrs Gandhi rejoined her, for instance Dinesh Singh and Sardar Swaran Singh. The Congress(I) regained its majority in the Rajya Sabha in July 1981.

[4] *Indira Gandhi, Selected Speeches and Writings,* vol. 4, pp. 3–4.

[5] Jayakar, *Indira Gandhi,* p. 394.

[6] Except where printed sources are cited, descriptions of Mrs Gandhi are based on some two dozen interviews with persons associated with her at the time. The assessment just quoted was shared by Sanjiva Reddy, President when Indira Gandhi returned to office, in an interview with the author.

Reddy's critical view of Mrs Gandhi, is described by her Principal Secretary of the time, P. C. Alexander, in Alexander, P. C., *My Years with Indira Gandhi,* Vision Books, New Delhi, 1991, pp. 124ff.

Chavan or Subramaniam to challenge her,' recalled Madhu Limaye. So she acted as a 'semi-monarchist with power shared between the "monarch" and the Crown Prince and his coterie'.[7] To others, Mrs Gandhi's scars from her years 'in the wilderness' had made her—and son Sanjay—suspicious, hesitant, and cautious, 'more wary and less certain how to move'. At times, remembered an associate, she seemed fearful, and biographers have pointed out her taking solace in religion—including from the company of a 'godman' of dubious reputation, Dhirendra Brahmachari.

Whichever of these descriptions in more accurate, the tendencies toward both hesitancy and arbitrariness in national affairs seem to have been increased by the cataclysm that befell Mrs Gandhi on 23 June 1980. That day a mother lost a cherished son and the Prime Minister an adviser upon whom, by all accounts, she had become increasingly dependent. Sanjay Gandhi was killed in the crash of a light airplane, following warnings that for several weeks he had been piloting it recklessly.[8] His death 'broke her', according to Pupul Jayakar and others. In her black-bordered letter acknowledging condolences, Mrs Gandhi wrote of the public admiration for Sanjay's dignity in the face of 'the baseless propaganda and the concerted campaign of calumny [against him] ... [He] had come to symbolise the heroic spirit, promising new direction, reaching out to the future ...'.[9] She wrote to her American friend, Dorothy Norman, 'Sanjay's going has affected me profoundly.'[10]

Despite this trauma and the apparent swings in the Prime Minister's moods, all might have gone well for the country. But recrimination and the odour of discredited patterns of government and politics tainted the air. Neither the Prime Minister nor the Opposition seem to have

[7] Limaye interview with the author. See also Limaye, *Contemporary Politics*, p. 284.

[8] Jayakar, *Indira Gandhi*, p. 411 and Shourie, *Mrs Gandhi's Second Reign*, p. 3.

[9] Letter addressed to Ramavatar Shastri on the Prime Minister's stationery, dated 8 August 1980. Ramavatar Shastri Papers, Indira Gandhi File, PMA, New Delhi.

[10] In a letter dated 21 February 1981. Norman, Dorothy (ed.), *Indira Gandhi: Letters to an American Friend, 1950–1984*, Harcourt Brace Jovanovich, New York, 1985, p. 154. On 3 August 1980, Mrs Gandhi had written to Norman about the sustained campaign of calumny against Sanjay. Ibid., p. 152.

An AICC resolution praised Sanjay in extravagant terms.

Mrs Gandhi revealed somewhat more of herself during an interview with the French publication, *Madam Figaro* in October 1981. I think sorrow can enrich the personality, she is quoted as saying. 'It is something you absorb. You see, in the West you try to fight all the time, you fight sorrow, you fight death, that is why you get so tense.' She added that she gladly would have died in Sanjay's place. *Indira Gandhi, Speeches and Writings*, vol. 4, pp. 592–593.

learned from experience. The Janata Party, which split again in April 1980, frustrated in defeat and at its inability to remain in office, gave the Prime Minister neither credit nor the benefit of doubt. Mrs Gandhi accused Janata of 'continuing to flog the dead horse of the Emergency'. She called the special courts 'kangaroo courts' and said the atmosphere under Janata 'reminded one of mediaeval Britain'—this, although the Supreme Court had upheld the Special Courts Act and high court judges presided over them.[11] Her positive message consisted largely of the socialist rhetoric long associated with her. In an 'updated' 'New 20-Point Economic Programme: The Pathway to Progress', the government made its customary promises.[12]

Of all the ghosts from governments past that haunted the opening years of the decade, that of 'authoritarianism' was pervasive. Into this word Mrs Gandhi's critics packed their discontents with themselves (without acknowledging them as such) and with her governments' actions since she had become Prime Minister in 1966. Few matters of public policy or government action were free from the miasma of suspicion. For her critics, she was in the grip of behaviour patterns she was unwilling or unable to break. For her part, Mrs Gandhi called her critics ungrateful for her achievements and unwilling to acknowledge how well she had governed the country. Thus, the areas of contention were familiar. Mrs Gandhi's 'authoritarianism' was incorrectly and unfairly seen in the government's challenge to the basic structure doctrine in the Minerva Mills case; in the Law Minister's advocacy of the transfer of high court judges; in the enactment of new laws for preventive detention; in the government's perceived manipulation of state government affairs; and in the Prime Minister's dismissal of the critics' concerns as frivolous. All was yellow to Mrs Gandhi's and her critics' jaundiced eyes.

[11] Speech in the Lok Sabha, 30 January 1980. *Indira Gandhi: Speeches and Writings*, vol. 4, pp. 5–7. 'Kangaroo courts': in a message to the India League in London in November 1980, ibid., p. 119. And she told Parliament in a March 1983 speech that Janata had 'completely scuttled the family planning programme through vicious and false propaganda', never mentioning Sanjay Gandhi's forced sterilization programme.

[12] See, for example, Indian National Trade Union Congress's National Convention on the 20-Point Programme in October 1982. Convention programme published by INTUC, New Delhi, 1982.

But there was to be a change in emphasis toward 'private initiative for the greatest good of our society'. 'In socialist countries', Mrs Gandhi had told the National Development Council in February 1981, 'there is now not only greater but visible emphases on giving up controls and rigid regulations in favour of ... individual incentives and market forces'. *Indira Gandhi: Speeches and Writings*, vol. 4, pp. 236–7.

The language Mrs Gandhi and her supporters used reinforced impressions that their sentiments were anti-democratic. Mrs Gandhi's intolerance of the opposition parties as not understanding 'that they too have an obligation to preserve the system' was matched by her claim that the Opposition functioned responsibly only when 'we, in the Congress, constituted the Opposition'—ignoring that this was when Y. B. Chavan was leading Congressmen to cooperate with the Janata government to repeal the Forty-second Amendment.[13] A. R. Antulay said that the Opposition opposed a presidential system, 'because ... [were there to be one] her tremendous mass popularity ... [would make] Smt Indira Gandhi ... unbeatable'.[14]

Authoritarianism, Dynasty, and the Presidential System

Even more than in the areas mentioned above, fears of Mrs Gandhi's 'authoritarianism' centred on her perceived intention to establish a 'dynasty' by arranging that the prime ministry would go to the younger of her two sons, Sanjay.[15] Closely linked to this view was fear that she, and he, and many of their supporters intended to exchange the parliamentary for a presidential system of government so as to strengthen their grasp on power. This fear exacerbated existing anxieties that the government had sinister designs on judicial independence, state government power, and personal liberty.

Sanjay Gandhi's influence with his mother had grown—even beyond that he had enjoyed during the Emergency—as he stood by her during the years out of office. For example, he became instrumental in picking candidates for Congress(I) electoral slates, and Mrs Gandhi, as her responses to his death showed, saw him as the driving force for social and economic reform. His long-suspected ambitions became evident

[13] Quotation from her inaugural address to the All-India Conference of Lawyers in October 1980. Ibid., pp. 106–7.

[14] 'Who Should We Have: A Prime Minister or a President?', interview with Antulay in *Times of India*, 16 November 1980. Reproduced in Antulay, *Democracy: Parliamentary or Presidential*, Directorate General of Information and Public Relations, Government of Maharashtra, Bombay 1981, pp. 27–41.

In Antulay's presidential system, the president 'should not be allowed to be voted down by a Senate or a Congress'. Ibid.

[15] The belief that Mrs Gandhi intended a 'dynastic succession' was and is still very widespread among the politically aware in India. That Mrs Gandhi harboured such intentions appears in Jayakar, *Indira Gandhi*, pp. 400–20, is discussed throughout this chapter, and was told to the author by many persons interviewed, including Madhu Limaye, Margaret Alva, Ajit Bhattacharjea, and C. Subramaniam.

late in May 1980. The Congress(I) Legislature Party in Uttar Pradesh over two days made 'a determined bid' to have New Delhi select him as its leader, and therefore chief minister. There can be little doubt that he had engineered the affair, perhaps as a stepping stone to greater things, but his mother said no. It was '"out of the question"', she told a UP Youth Congress delegation. Sanjay Gandhi had to console himself with a job as national party general secretary.[16]

But other avenues were not closed. Sanjay Gandhi's great ambitions and his mother's interest in 'dynastic succession' seem to have come more clearly together a few days later. Andhra Pradesh Chief Minister Chenna Reddy, while releasing the Telugu version of the Constitution in Hyderabad in the presence of Law Minister Shiv Shankar, advocated the convening of a new constituent assembly to change to the presidential form of government.[17] He repeated the sentiment a few days later in New Delhi. Chenna Reddy had been close enough to Sanjay Gandhi and the Prime Minister to have been privy to the imposition of the Emergency the evening before the proclamation was signed, and astute observer A. G. Noorani thought it 'inconceivable' that Reddy would have so spoken 'unless he had the ground to believe that the idea was, to put it mildly, not disfavoured by the establishment'.[18] To another senior observer, Chenna Reddy's views were not to be lightly dismissed, for he was not an ordinary member of Congress. Shiv Shankar found it necessary to deny in the Rajya Sabha that the government had any such intentions. But many were not reassured. A *Statesman* editorial said that Shiv Shankar hardly had quieted misgivings because he failed to give an '"exact and precise"' statement and because he had said, as he would later often repeat, that the government did not subscribe to the basic structure doctrine.[19]

---

[16] *AR*, 22–28 July 1980, p. 15565. See also the account in Jayakar, *Indira Gandhi*, p. 410. A *Times of India* editorial of 5 June urged Mrs Gandhi seriously to consider the legislators' wishes, for Sanjay Gandhi had much power and Uttar Pradesh needed a strong man. See also *Indian Express* of 3 and 6 June and *Hindustan Times* issue of 8 June. V. P. Singh became UP chief minister.

[17] *Statesman*, and the *Hindustan Times*, both 11 June 1980. Also, K. K. Katyal in the *Hindu*, 24 June 1980; A. G. Noorani in *Indian Express*, 3 July 1980; *Hindu*, 4 June 1980.

Coincidentally, the *Statesman*'s front page on 11 June carried reports of rioting in Tripura, which left three hundred dead and many thousands homeless. President's Rule had been imposed and there was a massive airlift of troops to quell the violence between tribal and non-tribal peoples.

[18] Noorani, A. G., 'The Presidential System', *Indian Express*, 3 July 1980.

[19] *Statesman* editorial, 11 June 1980. The reference was to Shiv Shankar's opposition to the doctrine as recently upheld by the Supreme Court in the Minerva Mills case.

Sanjay Gandhi's intentions came to an end with the plane crash on 23 June 1980. His future course, had he lived, is speculative. Pupul Jayakar thought him 'determined to free himself from her shadow'.[20] A sometime senior minister once close to the Prime Minister thought Sanjay Gandhi would have sidelined his mother and ruled as a dictator, 'and that he did have the qualities of leadership and controlled his *goondas*'.

The idea of a presidential system, nevertheless, did not disappear. It would resurface in the autumn and be linked to 'dynasty' after elder son Rajiv Gandhi entered politics—reportedly against his will—to be elected to Parliament in June 1981. (Later in the year he would come, like his younger brother, to head the Youth Congress.) Mrs Gandhi on 25 October 1980 told the All-India Conference of Lawyers that she welcomed its debate 'on systems of government' to make the public 'knowledgeable'.[21] But prominent journalists believed that 'like-thinking lawyers' had organized the conference to push through a resolution for a presidential system— with 'the open or tacit consent of the Prime Minister', who was keeping 'her options open'.[22] A call for a presidential system 'coming from these cadres', thought Prem Shankar Jha, 'is nothing more than a thinly disguised call for dictatorship'.[23] Looking farther ahead, respected *Hindu* columnist G. K. Reddy linked Mrs Gandhi and the presidency. He envisaged the Congress(I) having a two-thirds majority in both houses of Parliament after the Rajya Sabha elections of 1982 and thus able to change to a presidential system. Also, in July 1982, President Sanjiva Reddy's term would expire and 'the question is', asked Reddy, whether the quality of government would be improved or Mrs Gandhi's authority enhanced 'by installing Mrs Gandhi in Rashtrapati Bhavan'.[24]

[20] Jayakar, *Indira Gandhi*, p. 409.

[21] *Indira Gandhi: Speeches and Writings*, vol. 4, p. 108.

[22] S. Sahay in the *Hindu*, 11 December 1980; Shourie, *Second Reign*, pp. 217ff, 223, 227; *Indian Express*, 28 October 1980; editorial in the *Amrita Bazar Patrika*, 31 October 1980; Prem Shankar Jha, *Financial Express*, 2 November 1980. An *Indian Express* editorial on 28 October called the conference a 'command performance' and 'a search for alibis by a party which is unable to deliver the goods in spite of enjoying absolute powers'.

Kuldip Nayar wondered why the idea of a presidential system was being 'hawked about' now and said it appeared that whenever the Congress(I) was confronted with a deepening economic crisis it talked of strong government to suggest that Parliament stood in the way of its performance.

[23] Jha, Prem Shankar, 'Authoritarianism on the Right', *Financial Times*, 3 November 1980.

[24] Reddy, G. K., 'It's Quality, Not Form of Govt., That Matters', *Hindu*, 2 November 1980.

Not all went according to plan at the lawyers' conference, for those present failed to reach consensus on change to a presidential system. Questioned later about the conference, Mrs Gandhi said, 'I did not initiate the debate .... Recently, some people came to me and suggested we should let our people know more about different forms of government .... Any objection to ... [a debate] is a sign of irrationality'.[25] Shiv Shankar again was asked to dampen the fires. '"As a spokesman for the Prime Minister"', he told the Rajya Sabha, there is '"no thinking"' on the part of the central government to change to a presidential system. He then cast doubt on the allegedly independent composition of the lawyers' conference by saying that if the government had wanted a resolution favouring a presidential system, '"we could have done it unanimously"'.[26]

But anxieties were not easily quenched. A six-party 'left and democratic front' presented a memorandum to President Reddy on 17 November 1980 expressing shock at moves to change to a presidential system and urged the President to protect the Constitution.[27] A resolution of the CPI-oriented All-India Kisan Sabha castigated the government's 'preparing the ground' to change to the presidential form 'in order to impose the [sic] authoritarian regime in the country'.[28] For A. B. Vajpayee, talk of a presidential system indicated a 'deep conspiracy aimed at perpetuating the hold on the state acquired by the present rulers'.[29]

Reawakened Fears for the Judiciary

As the public outcry linked change to a presidential system with authoritarianism, so both were thought to lead to the infringement

---

[25] In an interview with The *Times of India*, New Delhi, 29 December 1980. *Indira Gandhi: Speeches and Writings*, vol. 4, pp. 144–5.

[26] *Hindu*, 22 November 1980.

[27] *AR*, 23–31 December 1980, p. 15809. Signing the memorandum were Charan Singh, Chandrajit Yadav, Devi Lal, M. P. Sethi, Y. B. Chavan, and from the Bharatiya Janata Party (BJP), L. K. Advani, A. B. Vajpayee, Ram Jethmalani, and S. S. Bhandari.

[28] *New Peasant Upsurge*, All India Kisan Sabha, New Delhi, 1981, p. 59—documents and resolutions of the AIKS meeting at Trichur.

Antulay thought these 'mushroom fellows' opposed the presidential system because they 'will have no future in the set-up of the country ... [T]hey can make agitations, launch demonstrations ... and one day there will be chaos and these chaps can ... ride the crest of that chaos, and come in power ... [T]he Indian people will never vote for them ... so they want a system which can breed chaos.' Antulay, *Democracy*, p. 72.

[29] *AR*, 29 January–4 February 1981, p. 15863. This was at the first national convention of the BJP in Bombay, 28 December 1980. An official resolution referred to the '"sinister designs"' to push India under an '"authoritarian yoke"'.

of individual liberty and damage to the judiciary. The Kisan Sabha resolution accused the government of wanting a presidential system so it could impose 'draconian measures' like preventive detention. The six-party memorandum to President Reddy included a strong protest against the recently promulgated National Security Ordinance, especially against its preventive detention provisions. A National Convention of Lawyers for Democracy, which was inaugurated by former Chief Justice of India J. C. Shah (of the Shah Commission), opposed a presidential system while condemning the government for its attempt to weaken the judiciary through reversing the Kesavananda decision and its basic structure doctrine.[30] The policy advocated by the Law Ministry regarding transfer of judges was interpreted as an attack on the judiciary.

Antagonism toward the judiciary is clear in many of the pronouncements favouring a presidential system. With his call for a new constituent assembly, Chenna Reddy had accused the judiciary of not helping the government to implement social-economic reforms. A. R. Antulay. chief minister of Maharashtra after June 1980, along with proposing a presidential system, deplored the Supreme Court's power of judicial review.[31] G. K. Reddy wrote that those around the Prime Minister wanted to 'return to a pliable judiciary, a supine bureaucracy, and a conditioned public opinion'.[32] A. B. Vajpayee said that the fools and knaves advocating a presidential system also wanted an elected judiciary to perpetuate the present rulers in power.[33] Soli Sorabjee believed that the current debate started 'with an intention to attack the judiciary, particularly the Supreme Court'.[34] Superseded and retired Supreme Court Justice H. R. Khanna thought it particularly dangerous to change systems when spokesmen for a party with an absolute

[30] *Hindu,* 29 December 1980. The meeting had been held on 27 December and among those present were M. C. Chagla, Shanti Bhushan, A. B. Vajpayee, Mrs Vijayaraje Scindia, Ram Jethmalani, and Soli Sorabjee. In New Delhi, the Congress (I)'s legal cell described this convention as ' "a side show staged by a group of frustrated persons who were the mouthpiece of the Janata and Lok Dal governments" '. Ibid.

[31] Antulay, *Democracy,* p. 139. He had earlier expressed the view in columns in the *Indian Express,* 26 and 28 January 1981.

[32] Reddy, 'It's Quality, Not Form of Govt., that Matters', *Hindu,* 2 November 1980. Reddy added that the protagonists of the presidential system 'are doing immense harm by projecting her more as an ambitious builder of a power base than as a hard-nosed head of Government' dedicated to improving the lot of her people.

[33] *AR,* 29 January–4 February 1981, p. 15863.

[34] Speech to the National Convention of Lawyers for Democracy, *Hindu,* 29 December 1980.

majority in Parliament 'have made no secret of their aversion to the concept of judicial review and their desire to clip the courts of their powers ...'.[35]

Mrs Gandhi reiterated her position in Calcutta in January 1981. '"There is no proposal to change the present system. What we want is to make the system more efficient ... to bring in the system responsive to the people."'[36] Those who were not reassured became further alarmed late in the year. With a presidential election due in July 1982, rumours were abroad that Mrs Gandhi might herself seek the post, intending that Rajiv Gandhi then become Prime Minister. The Bharatiya Janata Party foresaw a presidential system by June 1982. '"Plans are seriously afoot to foist a dynastic quasi-authoritarian rule on the country under the garb of a presidential system of government,"' said a party resolution.[37] The Communist Party of India thought Mrs Gandhi was seeking the presidential system to give her 'absolute power'.[38] Senior journalist S. Nihal Singh wrote that Rajiv Gandhi was being readied for the succession. The presidency offered 'an ideal setting to break in the heir apparent as Prime Minister while she would remain above the din of battle directing policy as the elder stateswoman'.[39]

---

[35] Khanna, H. R., 'Shall We Toss for a President?', *Times of India*, 19 April 1981.

Senior Advocate Fali Nariman thought some Indians 'impatient of constitutional government ... because of the cult of hero worship' and the 'passionate attachment' of individuals to high office. Nariman, Fali, 'Why Flog a Dead Horse?', *Indian Express*, 31 January 1981.

Acharya Kripalani, long the Prime Minister's detractor, also joined the fray. Saying that the Constituent Assembly was more representative of India than any parliament since, he added there was no use reviving the debate over the system of government. Today's 'morass', he wrote, is due to 'self-centred politicians at the top'. Kripalani, J. B., 'Presidential Form of Government', *Hindu*, 5 January 1981.

[36] *Times of India*, Bombay, 4 January 1981.

[37] *AR*, 15–21 January 1982, p. 16411. According to the BJP analysis in this National Executive resolution of 5 December 1981, the government was chary of declaring its intentions because a sitting President, Sanjiva Reddy, and the Supreme Court's basic structure doctrine stood in the way; and the government lacked the requisite two-thirds majority in the Rajya Sabha to amend the Constitution. By June the BJP thought the government would have its majority and the basic structure doctrine would be no more. Ibid.

[38] 'Review of Political Developments and Party Activities Since Eleventh Party Congress', New Age Printing Press, New Delhi, April 1982, p. 22.

[39] Singh, S. Nihal, 'Towards Presidency', *Indian Express*, 10 June 1981. Singh also said that the Prime Minister wanted to consolidate her immense powers and 'has converted the present system into a presidential one in practice'. Ibid. This was a point also made by other observers.

All this might be attributed to that suspicion and conspiracy-mindedness so characteristic of Delhi had not Mrs Gandhi had these very ideas in mind in May 1982. According to her Principal Secretary: ' "Haven't I done enough for the Party and shouldn't I now hand over the burden to others?," she asked me once in great mental agony ... She said she wanted some time for rest and writing, which the Rashtrapati Bhavan could provide, and her advice to a new government would still be available in her capacity as President. I knew she was talking seriously,' wrote P. C. Alexander.[40] He recalled further that the mood lasted for two weeks 'as she seriously considered the pros and cons of this proposition', but then she turned her mind to whom might be a suitable candidate for the Congress(I) to nominate for the presidency.[41] This turned out to be Giani Zail Singh, then the Home Minister. (See chapter 27.)

It appears unlikely that she had abandoned the idea completely. In a press interview in 1984, Mrs Gandhi made the points she had made years earlier—that both parliamentary and presidential systems have advantages and disadvantages. Whatever India had must suit its needs and '"we all want the system to work"', she said.[42] Madhu Limaye considered this 'a deliberately ambivalent stand'.[43] A. R. Antulay and Vasant Sathe continued to advocate a presidential system. Although Romesh Thapar called them 'merely the puppets of 1 Safdarjang Road',[44] they may have been riding their own hobby horses and not fronting for the Prime Minister. On 12 April and 4 May 1984, Sathe wrote to Rajiv Gandhi, still in Parliament and now also a general secretary of the AICC(I), proposing to convert the Parliament into a constituent assembly '"to suggest suitable modifications and/or amendments to the Constitution"'—modifications, Sathe had made clear in his lectures and articles of the time, that would provide for the direct election of the President by universal franchise to strengthen the unity of the country.[45]

[40] Alexander, P.C., *My Years with Indira Gandhi*, p. 62. Alexander had become the Prime Minister's Principal Secretary in May 1981.

[41] Ibid., p. 132. Alexander also wrote that Mrs Gandhi was 'deeply disturbed' at the time by affairs in her party.

[42] Interview with *Blitz*, 2 June 1984, cited in Limaye, *Contemporary Indian Politics*, p. 55.

[43] Ibid., p. 64.

[44] Thapar, Romesh, 'The Constitutional Fixers', *Economic and Political Weekly*, 15 September 1984.

[45] See lecture to the Delhi Study Group, 20 July 1984, which later appeared as an article in *Mainstream*, Annual Issue, 1984, and his address at the Press Club of Calcutta,

496 *Working a Democratic Constitution*

Predictably, adherents of the presidential system proposed it again after Rajiv Gandhi succeeded his mother as Prime Minister. They acted presumably from a mixture of belief in the concept, their own self-interest, and feelings of loyalty toward the Gandhi family. Even the BJP would consider the idea. L. K. Advani in 1987 suggested setting up a commission on the Constitution that would, among other things, examine 'the suitability of the presidential system',[46] although he later said he was not a convert to the idea. Other fanciers continued to write about it into the 1990s,[47] but attention to the idea declined after Rajiv Gandhi's death— thereby again demonstrating the link between it and 'dynasty'.

Advocates of a presidential system for India frequently look to the American system and often possess a rosy and flawed understanding of its efficiency and effectiveness. N. A. Palkhivala and B. K. Nehru held similar views about the presidential system. Palkhivala thought it had four advantages. It enabled the President to have a cabinet of '"outstanding competence and integrity"'; unelected cabinet ministers '"are not so motivated to adopt cheap populist measures ... [and it permits them] to be absorbed in the job of government"'; and '"it would stop defections and desertions on the part of legislators"', who in most cases are '"motivated purely by ... hunger for office"'.[48] The *Hindustan Times* added that the presidential system 'tends, on balance, to work more effectively in a vast or heterogenous country'. And it enables the chief executive to administer 'without having to look over his shoulder as to which group of his followers is trying to bring him down'.[49] Such expectations reveal, as much as anything else, the expectation, or the hope, that a change in political–institutional arrangements would

---

27 October 1984. The texts are given in Noorani, *Presidential System*, appendices II and IV. The text of the letter to Rajiv Gandhi appears in ibid., appendix III.

A scattering of others during this period suggested the direct election of the Prime Minister.

[46] Advani, L. K., 'Presidential Address' at the 9th National Council Session, Bharatiya Janata Party, New Delhi, 1987, p. 6. The session took place at Vijayawada, 2–4 January 1987.

[47] For example, see Sathe, *Two Swords in One Scabbard;* two articles by others in Kashyap, Subhash (ed.), *Perspectives on the Constitution*, India International Centre/Shipra Publications, New Delhi, 1993; Jain, C. K. (ed.), *Constitution of India: In Precept and Practice,* Lok Sabha Secretariat, New Delhi, 1992; and Nehru, B. K., 'Fresh Look at the Constitution' in Kashyap, Subhash (ed.), *Reforming the Constitution*, UBS Publishers and Distributors, New Delhi, 1992.

[48] Palkhivala had written publicly on the subject since 1970. This quotation is taken from a speech made in 1979 in Madras. Noorani, *The Presidential System*, p. 35.

[49] *Hindustan Times*, 28 October 1980.

overcome human failings. As one newspaper editor put it, the demand
for change rested on 'the facile assumption that the system has failed
when the fault lay with those who run it'.[50] The controversy about
changing systems and the forces for change were far too serious to be
thought of as a tempest in a teapot. Yet, parliamentary government had
become so widely accepted that the likelihood of departure from it was
remote.

---

[50] Katyal, K. K., 'A Disconcerting Scenario—Current Controversies and Confronta-
tionist Trends', *Hindu*, 29 December 1980.

Chapter 24

THE CONSTITUTION STRENGTHENED AND WEAKENED

The Constitution and the ability of the judiciary to protect it gained and lost ground in the years of Mrs Gandhi's return. Scepticism greeted her government's policies affecting the judiciary, national security, and civil liberty—even when they may have been well intended. The Supreme Court's reaffirmation of the basic structure doctrine in the Minerva Mills case restored the balance between the judiciary and the legislature and definitively gave the Constitution the protection of judicial review. Yet during these years, the government's resort to preventive detention and its enactment of other repressive legislation diminished constitutional liberties and the courts' ability to protect them. The Prime Minister had not left all her authoritarian tendencies behind.

Parliamentary Supremacy Revisited: The Minerva Mills Case

On a main road behind the Bangalore railway station, near Sri Nagabhusana Rao Park and Gethsemane Lutheran Church, secluded by a steel-link fence and at the end of a long entrance road lined with poplars, stands the Minerva Mills, a unit of the National Textiles Corporation. Claiming that the privately-owned mills were ill-managed, the government assumed management of them in 1971 and then nationalized them under the Sick Textiles Undertakings (Nationalization) Act in 1974. Five years later, this gray structure became the focus of a renewed battle over parliamentary versus judicial supremacy when, in the first Minerva Mills case, the mills' previous owners challenged elements of the 1971 takeover and the 1974 nationalization and the constitutionality of portions of three constitutional amendments.

The case bridged two governments. It came to the Supreme Court in the autumn of 1979 when Charan Singh was caretaker Prime Minister, unbidden by his government. The Court's ruling in May 1980 confronted newly-elected Indira Gandhi with a reaffirmation of the basic structure doctrine. The mills' nationalization was a property matter, but counsel

N. A. Palkhivala's strategy was not to fight the nationalization on the basis of property rights, but to achieve the same result by framing the issue in terms of Parliament's power to amend the Constitution. (This strategy recalls that in the Golak Nath property case.) Although Palkhivala argued that the nationalization under the Act infringed his clients' fundamental right to carry on their business, he focused on clauses 4 and 55 of the Forty-second Amendment when hearings began in the Supreme Court in mid-October 1979. He posed the question "'whether the provisions of the Forty-second amendment ... which deprived the Fundamental Rights of their supremacy ... are *ultra vires* the amending power of Parliament'".[1] The Court allowed Palkhivala to pursue this reasoning against the contentions of Charan Singh's Attorney General, L. N. Sinha, and Additional Solicitor General K. K. Venugopal, who claimed that constitutional questions did not arise directly in the petitions. Moreover, the Forty-second Amendment had been passed after the Sick Textiles Undertakings (Nationalization) Act was in force, Sinha and Venugopal contended, and, therefore the mills' nationalization could be challenged only under Article 31C as it was written in 1974.[2]

In the hearings, Palkhivala described to the Court how Janata, in the Forty-fourth Amendment, had tried and failed to repeal elements of Articles 368 and 31C. He said that Article 31C, by prohibiting a chal-

---

[1] Hearing of 22 October as reported by the *Hindustan Times'* legal correspondent Krishan Mahajan. *Hindustan Times*, 23 October 1979; also 1981 (1) SCR 247.

The reader may need to be reminded that hearings in the Supreme Court were not (and are not) recorded verbatim by a court stenographer, nor are counsels' written submissions readily available from the court itself. The researcher must gain access to these from the counsel involved, and they, too, rarely are available. Counsel typically argue orally from notes. Lacking an official transcript of hearings, the researcher is forced to rely on newspaper accounts of them. Although this is most unfortunate, it need not be crippling, for the general reliability of the several legal correspondents' dispatches is indicated by their similar content. This account of the Minerva hearings is drawn from reports in the *Hindustan Times*, *Statesman*, and *Hindu*.

Clause 4 of the Forty-second Amendment Bill had expanded Article 31C to make the Fundamental Rights subservient to all the Directive Principles. Clause 55 had amended Article 368 to bar review of constitutional amendments by the courts. These two clauses, the mills' owners contended, were contrary to the basic structure doctrine established in Kesavananda Bharati.

Among Palkhivala's colleagues in the case were J. B. Dadachanji and Fali Nariman.

[2] For the thrust of Palkhivala's argument, see, in addition to press reports, Chief Justice Chandrachud's interpretation of it. 1981 (1) SCR 247ff, which is in *Minerva Mills Ltd and Others v Union of India and Others* 1981 (1) SCR 206ff.

The bench hearing the case consisted of Chief Justice Y. V. Chandrachud and Justices P. N. Bhagwati, A. C. Gupta, N. L. Untwalia, and P. S. Kailasam.

lenge to laws made under the Directive Principles, was constitutionally bad beyond issues of property, and that the Forty-second Amendment's changes to the amending power, by making Parliament's power boundless, overruled the Court's decisions establishing the basic structure doctrine in the Kesavananda and Indira Gandhi Election cases. These clauses, said Palkhivala, were '"the impertinence of those in power"' and the philosophy underlying Article 31C '"is the very quintessence of authoritarianism"'.[3] He contended that because the Directive Principles covered the 'whole spectrum' of governance, few laws were not in pursuance of them, and the article thus allowed establishment of a 'non-democratic state'. The version of the article in the Twenty-fifth Amendment and largely upheld by the Court in Kesavananda 'had been limited to specific subjects like land reforms and other issues like concentration of wealth', Palkhivala explained in response to questions from the bench. This was the Court's 'last chance', he warned, '... to choose between a free and an authoritarian society in India'.[4] Public appreciation of the case, judging from newspaper headlines, mirrored Palkhivala's. The Minerva Mills by name and the subject of property rights were not mentioned. A *Statesman* headline read '42nd Amendment An Arrogant Act' and one in the *Hindu* said 'Hearing Begins in Case Against 42nd Amendment'.[5] Continuing his presentation over a week's time, Palkhivala also pressed the point that it was baseless to claim that Parliament necessarily represented the will of the people. Article 31C violated the Preamble as well as the Fundamental Rights, he said, and the Constitution contained no power to frame a new constitution through a new constituent assembly—this in agreement with an interjection from Chief Justice Chandrachud.

Attorney General L. N. Sinha agreed that the Fundamental Rights were sacred, but argued that Article 31C did not abrogate them. The Court in Shankari Prasad had upheld Parliament's power to amend the Constitution affecting the Rights. Articles 31A, B, and C must be presumed 'reasonable', he said, and the Court in Kesavananda had upheld them. Sinha's claim would seem to be accurate, allowing for the fact that Articles 31A and 31B had been upheld prior to Kesavananda, and Kesavananda had upheld Article 31C as it then was with the exception of the 'escape clause' (chapter 12). Reacting to Sinha's specific claim that the Kesavananda decision had upheld the First

---

[3] *Hindu,* 24 October 1979.

[4] Hearing on 23 October. *Hindustan Times,* 24 October 1979.

[5] Issues of 7 November 1979 and 23 October 1979, respectively.

Amendment as not violating the basic structure, the five judges displayed the uncertainty about the clarity of Supreme Court decisions that on occasion has marked the country' jurisprudence. These men could not agree on exactly what the Kesavananda bench had decided, and three of them wondered whether there had been 'any majority decision at all'.[6] Over the next several days, Sinha argued the social revolutionary position that the Directive Principles 'prevailed' over the Rights because they 'provided the goals without which the Rights would be meaningless'. The new Article 31C improved the Constitution, he said, and extended the basic structure by making social and economic justice available to all citizens instead of a few.

Palkhivala began his rebuttal on 13 November. The changes made by the Forty-second Amendment, he said, had been made specifically to 'overcome' the 'obstruction' caused by the basic structure test introduced in Kesavananda. The amendment's language made clear that if the ends are legitimate, the means employed 'become irrelevant and non-justiciable'. This case is a last-ditch battle for citizens to 'stop the rot in the Constitution', Palkhivala warned, for Article 31C did not provide that laws passed under it had to meet the tests of reasonableness and public interest.[7] The twenty days of hearings concluded on 16 November with arguments by K. K. Venugopal, who was also representing the state of Maharashtra in the Waman Rao case, which the Court would rule on coincidentally with Minerva. Speaking from the bench during the hearings, Justices Bhagwati, Chandrachud, and Untwalia expressed the view that since the Indira Gandhi Election case 'the doctrine of basic structure had become the acceptable ratio'.[8]

While the bench was deliberating during January 1980, Justice Bhagwati wrote a ' "Dear Indiraji" ' letter to the Prime Minister. This congratulated her on her re-election and praised her ' "iron will ... uncanny insight and dynamic vision, great administrative capacity and ... heart

[6] *Hindustan Times*, 8 November 1979.

[7] *Hindustan Times*, 16 November 1979. The newspaper on 14 November had reported that Chief Justice Chandrachud had told a packed courtroom that one Y. P. Sharma, a member of the Congress (I), had advised his secretary that he should exercise ' "greatest care" ' when coming to court that day. Chandrachud said that Sharma had visited his residence the same evening and had repeated the 'threat'. The Court that day was hearing arguments regarding the cancellation of Sanjay Gandhi's bail on the ground that he had been misusing his liberty by intimidating witnesses. The Court ruled that Gandhi must show cause why his bail should not be cancelled. This concerned the Kissa Kursi Ka case. (see ch 22). Sharma denied evil intentions, and Sanjay Gandhi said Sharma had nothing to do with the Congress(I).

[8] *Hindustan Times*, 17 November 1979.

which is identified with the misery of the poor and the weak"'. The justice
continued that ' "the judicial system in our country is in a state of utter
collapse ... . [W]e should have a fresh and uninhibited look at ... [it] and
consider what structural and jurisdictional changes are necessary ..." '.[9]
A senior columnist's reaction to the letter was that it 'would have done
credit to a mofussil politician's according a civic reception to the Prime
Minister'. Its 'net effect is disastrous ... criticizing an arrangement of which
he is very much a part and that too in a letter to the Prime Minister
hardly seems appropriate'.[10]

Nearly six months after the hearings ended, the court on 9 May
1980 handed down its 'first orders' in the Minerva Mills case. These
said that section 4 of the Forty-second Amendment was beyond the
amending power of Parliament 'since it damages the basic or essential
features of the Constitution and destroys its basic structure by the total
exclusion of challenge' to laws to implement the Directive Principles at
the expense of the Fundamental Rights in Articles 14 and 19. (The
'clauses' of a bill are called 'sections' once the bill becomes an act.)
Section 55 of that amendment also was ruled beyond the amending
power of Parliament 'since it removes all limitations on the power of
the Parliament to amend the Constitution and confers powers upon it
to amend the Constitution so as to damage or destroy its basic or essential
features or its basic structure'.[11] Judges Chandrachud, Gupta, Untwalia,

[9] Letter dated 15 January 1980. The *Indian Express* published the text of the letter in
its Delhi edition of 23 March 1980.

Justice Bhagwati would expand emphatically on his theme of the judiciary in crisis in
his Law Day speech of 26 November 1985. In this he said that 'the judicial system in the
country is almost on the verge of collapse'.

[10] S. Sahay in the *Statesman*, New Delhi, 3 April 1980.

The executive council of the Supreme Court Bar Association scheduled a meeting
on 2 April to discuss the 'propriety' of the letter, following up a statement by some fifty of
its members taking 'strong exception' to it. *Indian Express*, 23 March 1980.

[11] 1981 (1) SCR 263–4. Orders read out by Chief Justice Chandrachud. See also 1980
(2) SCC 591–3.

Also on 9 May another bench handed down its decision, in the Waman Rao case, a
case involving agricultural property. On this bench were Chief Justice Chandrachud and
Justices Bhagwati, V. R. Krishna Iyer, A. P. Sen, and V. D. Tulzapurkar. *Waman Rao and
Others v the Union of India and Others* involved the 1961 Maharashtra Agricultural Lands
(Ceilings on Holdings) Act and amendments to it. Ruling on an appeal from the Nagpur
Bench of the Bombay High Court, the bench upheld the First and Fourth Amendments
and Article 31C as it stood prior to the change wrought by the Forty-second Amendment
and to the extent its constitutionality had been upheld in Kesavananda. Chandrachud
gave the ruling for himself and the others, excepting Bhagwati, who reiterated his opinion
in the Minerva ruling of that day. For Waman Rao, see 1981 (2) SCR 1ff.

and Kailasam joined in issuing the order and said they would give their detailed reasoning later, a delay that was not unprecedented. Justice Bhagwati did not join the others in passing the orders, explaining that, 'the issues being so momentous, he could not do so 'without a reasoned judgement' (seeming to imply that his colleagues 'orders' were not 'reasoned'). He would provide his judgement when the court reconvened after the summer vacation.

The *Hindu* in an editorial thought the ruling 'a blow struck in favour of judicial review as well as the basic structure'. To have done otherwise, the paper said, 'would have been to leave temptation in the way of Parliament to repeat what happened under pressure during the Emergency'. Columnist K. K. Katyal noted that the Court did what Janata had been unable to get through the Rajya Sabha in 1978.[12] The *Hindustan Times* said the ruling was inevitable given the Kesavananda decision and 'the Prime Minister would do well to accept the new situation'.[13] Both newspapers reported that the government might seek a review of the ruling. Law Minister P. Shiv Shankar, just returned from a trip abroad, was quoted as saying that he personally felt that a larger bench should go into such vital issues, and '"I always thought that Directive Principles are what the Constitution ordains the States (sic) to do in the interests of society. I feel individual interests must yield to the interests of society"'.[14]

Chief Justice Chandrachud gave the detailed rationale behind the May orders for himself and the three others on 31 July. Justice Bhagwati gave a separate opinion. The majority had held unconstitutional the Forty-second Amendment's provision (Section 55) that 'there shall be no limitation whatever on the constituent power of Parliament' on the ground that the power to amend is not the power to destroy; Parliament could not convert a limited power to an unlimited one. This section's other change to Article 368, which said that no amendment made before or after the Forty-second could be questioned in court, also was held unconstitutional for the reason that it deprived the courts of power to question an amendment even if it destroyed the basic structure. These changes in Article 368, therefore, permitted violation of civil liberties. Turning to the amendment's expansion of Article 31C, the Court said that the Directive Principles were vitally important, but to destroy the Fundamental Rights purportedly to achieve the Principles was to subvert

[12] *Hindu,* 12 May 1980.
[13] *Hindustan Times,* 12 May 1980.
[14] *Hindustan Times,* 11 May 1980. The *Hindu* on the same day, but without the direct quotations from Shiv Shankar.

the Constitution. Section 4 of the Forty-second Amendment abrogated Articles 14, 19, and 21 and the Court could not allow the balance between the Rights and the Principles to be destroyed.[15] The decision could not repeal Article 31C as expanded by the Forty-second Amendment nor delete it from the Constitution. It remains in the Constitution today, technically unrepealed, but 'all the cases under it are being decided as it was before that amendment'.[16]

Justice Bhagwati, writing one opinion for both the Minerva and Waman Rao cases, agreed with the others that the changes in the Article 368 made by the Forty-second Amendment were unconstitutional because after Kesavananda and the Indira Gandhi Election case 'there was no doubt at all that the amendatory power of Parliament was limited and it was not competent to alter the basic structure of the Constitution'.[17] But, referring to the amendment's section 4, he believed that 'the amended Article 31C ... [was] constitutionally valid ... [because it] does not damage or destroy the basic structure ... and is within the amending power of Parliament'.[18] The Constitution is first and foremost a social document, Bhagwati said, and therefore 'a law enacted ... genuinely for giving effect to a Directive Principle ... should not be invalid because it infringes a Fundamental Right'. The Rights are precious, he continued, but they 'have absolutely no meaning for the poor, downtrodden and economically backward classes' who constitute the bulk of the people.[19] He held that the government's takeover of Minerva Mills was valid. Bhagwati's sentiments were consistent with those expressed in his 15 January letter to Mrs Gandhi: Our judicial system 'has proved inadequate to meet the needs of ... [the] vast socio-economic developments taking place in the country', he had said.

Both in the text of his opinion and orally in court, Justice Bhagwati took a jab at his Chief Justice. In court, according to a press report, he 'deplored that the highest court in the land had violated the principle of judicial collectivity and of not giving orders without reasons unless there was an urgency to do so'. Momentous issues required collective deliberation, Bhagwati said, and this would have been possible if the Chief Justice had seen to it that draft opinions were circulated, fol-

[15] 1981 (1) SCR 206–13.
[16] *V. N. Shukla's Constitution of India*, p. 277. Official editions of the Constitution published after the Minerva Mills decision carry a footnote that in Kesavananda the Supreme Court held the 'escape clause' invalid.
[17] 1981 (1) SCR 288.
[18] Ibid., p. 342.
[19] Ibid., p. 333.

lowed by a judicial conference. Absence of this process 'introduced a chaotic situation'.[20] In his written opinion, Justice Bhagwati expressed the same regret at Chandrachud's failure to arrange a 'free and frank exchange of thoughts', during which 'I would either be able to share the views of my colleagues or ... to persuade them ... with my point of view'. He likened his situation to that Justice Chandrachud had said he faced during the Kesavananda Bharati case (chapter 12).[21] But Bhagwati would violate his own strictures within a year in the Judges case.

The government seized upon Bhagwati's charge in partial support of the review petition it filed on 5 September challenging the Minerva ruling. Bhagwati, asserted the government, had declared that the decision '"was not a judgement of the court at all"'. The Court's decision was '"merely"' the opinion of each judge, argued Miss A. Subhashini, representing the Law Ministry.[22] Additionally, the government contended that Article 38 (of the Directive Principles, which said that the state should strive to promote the welfare of the people by minimizing inequalities of income, and other inequalities) was also part of the Constitution's basic structure. The government did not pursue the review, and the matter was still 'hanging fire' when Shiv Shankar left the Law Ministry to become Minister of Petroleum in early January 1982.[23]

---

[20] *Hindustan Times*, 2 August 1980. Bhagwati also said in court, according to the newspaper, that it was only on 8 May, the day before the orders, that Chandrachud told him that four judges intended to strike down those provisions and give their reasons later. That there was no urgency in the case, Bhagwati said, was demonstrated by the many months between the end of the hearings and the 9 May orders. One of Bhagwati's colleagues on the bench, in an interview with the author, recalled that the judges frequently discussed the case while arriving at their opinions, but could not recall if draft opinions had been circulated.

[21] 1981 (1) SCR 270. Bench conferences and the circulation of draft opinions typically have been irregular, and would continue to be so.

[22] *Hindustan Times*, 6 September 1980. Accounts in the *Statesman* and *Times of India* confirm this.

An article in the *Hindustan Times* four days earlier had reported that the government was considering filing a review petition and must do so within the 'stipulated 30 days' after the decision. Shiv Shankar had told Parliament that the timing of the government's decision whether or not to file for review was a matter of 'strategy'. Normally, the newspaper article explained, a review petition was heard by the same bench as had heard the case in question, but this was impossible, for Untwalia had already retired, and Kailasam was due to retire on 12 September.

[23] Shiv Shankar interview with the author.

In a December 1982 decision, the Supreme Court upheld Article 31C as it was originally in the Twenty-fifth Amendment. Giving the decision, Justice Chinnappa Reddy

The Minerva Mills case was at once highly significant and peculiar. In upholding the basic structure (as it did also in the parallel Waman Rao case), the Supreme Court ensured that it would remain the foundation of the country's constitutionalism. The court had reaffirmed that the checks and balances of the Constitution were vital to the preservation of democracy and of the Fundamental Rights. Kesavananda had propounded the doctrine, the Indira Gandhi Election case had upheld it, and Minerva engraved it on stone. The peculiarities encompassed both context and substance. The hearings, begun while Charan Singh was the caretaker Prime Minister, produced a decision that the Charan Singh government would have welcomed. Yet delivered when Indira Gandhi was Prime Minister, the decision was unwelcome, and her government's first thought was to have the engraving erased through review.

Minerva was a nationalization, a property case. Yet the right to property was no longer in the Fundamental Rights—thanks to the recently passed Forty-fourth Amendment. And the precise issue of the mills' nationalization was not even mentioned in the court's 'order' of 9 May. Addressing the petitioners' challenge to the constitutionality of the Sick Textiles Act, Chief Justice Chandrachud wrote in his opinion, 'We are not concerned with the merits of that challenge at this stage'.[24] The case became a vehicle for N. A. Palkhivala and his fellow senior advocates to protect the Constitution from those provisions of the Forty-second Amendment that Congress in the Rajya Sabha had prevented the Janata government from repealing.

The government under Charan Singh's caretaker prime ministry seems to have been caught between millstones. Confronted with the Minerva Mills case, it wished to defend a public enterprise from de-nationalization. Yet, it had no love for the portions of the Forty-second Amendment that Janata had failed to get repealed. Could it separate the two issues? Could it win on keeping the mills public property while not minding a loss on the Forty-second Amendment—perhaps even hoping

---

made remarks, later considered *obiter dicta*, that the version of Article 31C as altered by the Forty-second Amendment was also constitutionally valid. Reddy's remarks have been criticized by Baxi, Upendra, *Courage, Craft and Contention: The Indian Supreme Court in the Eighties*, N. M. Tripathi Pvt. Ltd., New Delhi, 1985, p. 110 and in *V. N. Shukla's Constitution of India*, p. 902. Reddy is, nevertheless, a firm supporter of the 'basic structure' doctrine. (Reddy interview with the author.) The case in question was *Sanjeev Coke Manufacturing Co. v Bharat Coking Coal Ltd.* AIR 1983 (1) SC 239ff. The issue was the nationalization of mines.

[24] 1981 (1) SCR 236.

for it? Did such calculations lie behind the government's strategy to argue that the nationalization was defensible as a property issue, while leaving the constitutional issues to Palkhivala by claiming that constitutional issues did not arise? If this was the strategy, it succeeded brilliantly, for the Supreme Court did what the government had been unable to do in the Forty-fourth Amendment. 'Supremacy of Constitution' was the greeting the *Statesman* gave the Minerva orders in its editorial of 10 May.

For her part, Mrs Gandhi inherited a case whose outcome she was not in a position to affect. With the hearings concluded before she returned as Prime Minister, she and her government's law officers only could await the Supreme Court's decision. The government's resulting review petition lacked weight, and there seems to have been no energy expended in its pursuit.[25] Thus, one cannot accuse Mrs Gandhi during her second reign of direct attempts to overturn the basic structure doctrine, although it is unlikely that she had come to admire it. But when the Lawyers' Conference in the autumn of 1980 revived agitation for change to a presidential system, two months after the review petition had been filed, her critics, suspecting she favoured the conference, credited her with designs on the basic structure. The Prime Minister by this time may have lost interest in the issue.

Liberties Lost

As the Constitution was being saved in Minerva, liberties were being lost to repression at least as harsh as that during the Emergency, although less widespread. The pattern of the past had returned. From 1980, central and state governments enacted or re-enacted laws providing for preventive detention, banning strikes, and threatening freedom of speech. The justifications for such legislation typically were the public interest or protection of national security and integrity. Doubtless, stern measures were necessary against insurgents in, for example, the Punjab, as will be described more fully in chapter 27. But harsh laws were used harshly, and the conditions they were enacted to meet originated in no small part from Mrs Gandhi's misguided policies. Having sowed the wind, she reaped the whirlwind.

---

[25] As to its own immediate interests, Minerva Mills found it needed another try. In the *second* Minerva Mills case in 1986, the mills' owners challenged the original takeover of management in 1971 under the Industries Development and Regulation Act, only to have their challenge rejected by the Supreme Court. 1986 (3) SCR 718ff.

Justices Chinnappa Reddy and M. M. Dutt constituted the bench. Rohinton Nariman, Fali Nariman's son, represented Minerva Mills.

It was Charan Singh's caretaker government, however, that had re-instituted preventive detention after the Janata government had refrained from doing so. It promulgated an ordinance on 5 October 1979 providing for detention to prevent black-marketing and to ensure the maintenance of commodity supplies essential to the community. President Sanjiva Reddy took two days to sign the ordinance, reportedly because he did not share the Prime Minister's eagerness for it—any more than had a recently concluded conference of chief ministers, where all but two had 'bitterly' opposed it.[26] Making reference to the 1955 Essential Commodities Act, a well-known commentator on economic affairs wrote, 'This is not the first time that a government has armed itself with excessive power to deal with a problem ... [that] could have been tackled ... [under] existing laws'.[27] Sceptics said that Charan Singh thought the step would rescue his political position from the effects of sharply rising food prices.

Parliament, following an Opposition walk-out, replaced the ordinance with an act a month after Mrs Gandhi resumed power. Under this comparatively mild law, the advisory boards to be established to review detentions were to be constituted as prescribed by the Forty-fourth Amendment—i.e.according to the recommendations of the chief justice of the appropriate high court. The board chairman was to be a serving judge of the court, and its two or more other members should be serving or retired judges of any high court.[28] Within ten days the detenu was to be informed of the grounds for his detention and was allowed to make representations against them. But the government was not required to disclose facts considered 'against the public interest to disclose'. Within three weeks the government was to place its case before the advisory board, which could call for further information and hear the detenu. Within seven weeks from the date of detention the board either should uphold the detention or invalidate it. Detentions could last six months.

The terms of the National Security Act passed on 27 December 1980 presaged years of new repressive legislation. Detentions were sanctioned to prevent an individual from acting in a manner prejudicial 'to the

---

[26] *Hindustan Times.* 4 October 1979.

[27] Panandiker, V. A. Pai, 'The Preventive Detention Issue', *Hindustan Times*, 23 October 1979.

[28] The Prevention of Blackmarketing and Maintenance of Supplies of Essential Commodities Act, 1980. *Central Acts and Ordinances, 1980*, Parliament Library, New Delhi.
The provisions, themselves, of the Forty-fourth Amendment had not then and still have not been brought into force, but these principles were incorporated in the ordinance and the act replacing it. P. B. Venkatasubramanian letter to the author.

maintenance of public order', to the defence or security of India, to relations with foreign powers, to protect the maintenance of essential supplies and services. But the law's intent was far more inclusive. It was to combat ' "anti-social and anti-national elements including secessionist, communal and pro-caste elements" ' and elements affecting ' "the services essential to the community" '.[29] There were other significant differences from the Blackmarketing Act. Now the state government could appoint the advisory board without the high court chief justices's recommendations, and its members, except for the chairman, could either be high court judges or persons 'qualified' to be so, which included any advocate who had practised for ten years in a high court. An individual might be detained for a year and then detained again, without prior release, if ' "fresh facts had arisen" '.[30] A senior advocate feared abuse of such 'tyrannical laws' and said the Constitution did not contemplate detention on such wide grounds. Another commentator noted that there had been no arrests of 'big' smugglers and blackmarketeers, and cited highly questionable political detentions.[31] The Supreme Court upheld the Act's constitutionality at the end of December 1981.[32]

More egregious laws were to come. The President in April and June 1984, promulgated two ordinances amending the National Security Act—both these ordinances were later replaced by Acts of Parliament. The first ordinance allowed a detention order to be submitted to an advisory board four months and two weeks *after* the detention and allowed the board to take five months and three weeks to give its opinion—that is, ten months in jail on executive whim. Individuals might be detained

---

[29] From the bill's Statement of Objects and Reasons as quoted in Swaroop, *Preventive Detention*, p. 105.

[30] The National Security Act, 1980. Ibid. This replaced an ordinance of the same name promulgated in September.

This act did not have to comply with the Forty-fourth amendment because this section of the amendment had not come into force, not having been 'notified' in the Official Gazette. See ch. 19.

[31] Respectively, Nariman, Fali, 'Need for Judicial Vigilance', *Indian Express*, 14 November 1980; Shourie, Arun, 'All for the Nation's Security' in Shourie, *Mrs Gandhi's Second Reign*, pp. 235ff.

The *Economic and Political Weekly* found 'shoddiness' in the implementation of 'repressive legislation', with labour leaders detained 'without going through the necessary paperwork'. *EPW*, vol. 17, no. 7, 13 February 1982.

[32] Decision on 28 December 1981 in *A. K. Roy v Union of India* 1982 (1) SCC 271ff. On the bench were Chief Justice Chandrachud and Justices Bhagwati, A. C. Gupta, V. D. Tulzapurkar, and D. A. Desai. Chandrachud gave the opinion of the court for himself, Bhagwati, and Desai.

for two years. The second ordinance outdid this. It said that before or after its promulgation a person detained on two or more grounds, each ground qualifying as a separate detention, could not have his detention rendered invalid if 'one or some' of the grounds were 'vague, non-existent, not relevant, not connected or not proximately connected with such person, or invalid for any other reasons whatsoever'.[33] This 'lawless law' was explained as necessary to deal with the '"extraordinary situation"' in parts of the country and as needed '"to deal stringently with anti-national, extremist and terrorist elements ... in the larger interests of India"'.[34] The extraordinary situations included the Punjab, where, in July, the army invaded and occupied the Sikhs' Golden Temple and remained into October. Late that month, two Sikhs of Indira Gandhi's security guard murdered her. Locally, as it had nationally during Mrs Gandhi's Emergency, democracy had failed.

The Terrorist and Disruptive Activities Act (TADA), which followed on 20 May 1985 when Rajiv Gandhi had become Prime Minister, surpassed even the egregiousness of the amended National Security Act. It empowered the government to make rules as necessary and 'expedient' for 'prevention of and coping with terrorist acts and disruptive activities'; to prevent the spread of reports 'likely to prejudice maintenance of peaceful conditions'; to regulate 'the conduct of persons in respect of areas the control of which is considered necessary'; and to require persons 'to comply with any scheme for the prevention, or coping with, terrorist acts and preventive activities'.[35] The law, wrote Fali Nariman, defined terrorist and disruptive activities so broadly 'as to encompass even peaceful expression of views about sovereignty and territorial integrity'; permitted detention for up to six months without charge; provided for trials before designated courts 'in camera and adopting procedures at variance with the Criminal Procedure Code'; and said that if the person detained came from an area the government had declared to

---

[33] Text of the National Security (Second Amendment) Ordinance, 1984. *Black Laws, 1984–1985*, People's Union for Civil Liberties, New Delhi, June 1985, pp. 44ff. The content of the ordinance is analysed by V. M. Tarkunde in ibid., p 29ff. The laws replacing the ordinances had been enacted in May and August 1984, respectively.

[34] From the Statement of Objects and Reasons cited in Swaroop, *Preventive Detention*, p. 106.

[35] 'The Terrorist and Disruptive Activities (Prevention) Act, 1985', *Central Acts and Ordinances, 1985*, Parliament Library, New Delhi. Text also in *Black Laws, 1984–85*, pp. 11ff.

In July 1984, the President had promulgated an ordinance empowering the central government to establish special courts for ' "speedy trial of scheduled offences" ', which meant wanton killing, violence intended to put the public in fear, adversely affect social harmony, etc.

be a terrorist affected area 'the burden of proving that he has not committed a terrorist act in on him'.[36] Common law had been reversed: you were guilty until you proved yourself innocent.

Meanwhile, various state legislatures had passed their own preventive detention laws paralleling the centre's, as they often had since 1950. Or, they had enacted particularistic preventive detention laws: for the broad control of crimes (Bihar 1980–1); against communal and dangerous activities (Maharashtra 1981, Tamil Nadu 1982, Andhra Pradesh 1986); and anti-social activities (Gujarat 1985).[37] Parliament had passed, with many states following suit, laws banning strikes and allowing arrests without a warrant and providing for summary trials (the 'essential services' acts).[38] Mrs. Gandhi had said she wanted 'to assure workers that this ordinance is not against them ... [W]e will never do anything to suppress them or create difficulties ... . But it is necessary that the public services are kept going.'[39] Attempting to deal with the situation in Punjab, Parliament passed laws other than those already mentioned— such as those establishing special courts for disturbed areas, the Armed Forces (Punjab and Chandigarh) Special Powers Act, and the Fifty-ninth and Sixty-third Amendments to the Constitution (in 1988 and 1989, respectively), which gave the central government special emergency

[36] Analysis of the act by Nariman, Fali, 'The President's Page' in *The Indian Advocate*, Journal of the Bar Association of India, vol. 25, 1993, pp. 1ff.

The Supreme Court characterized TADA as harsh and drastic but upheld it unanimously in *Kartar Singh v Punjab* 1994 (3) SCC 569. Also see *Supreme Court Almunac (SCALE)*, a private commercial publication, 1994, Supplement. On the bench were S. Ratnavel Pandian, M. M. Punchhi, K. Ramaswamy, S. C. Agrawal, and R. M. Sahai.

There were other acts providing for preventive detention. On 27 August 1987, the government amended the 1974 Conservation of Foreign Exchange and Prevention of Smuggling Activities Act (which already provided for preventive detention). On 6 September 1988, it enacted the Prevention of Illicit Traffic in Narcotic Drugs and Psychotropic Substances Act. In general, the provisions of this act followed the model of detention acts just preceding it and allowed detentions for up to two years.

[37] For the texts of several of these state laws, see Swaroop, *Law of Preventive Detention*, appendices.

[38] Summary trials are a foreshortened process to achieve speedy disposal of cases. Witnesses need not be called, nor a charge framed. See Code of Criminal Procedure, chapter 21.

[39] Independence Day speech from the Red Fort, 15 August 1981. *Indira Gandhi: Speeches and Writings*, vol. 4, p. 179.

Two months later, the Prime Minister denied collective responsibility for legislation banning strikes. An interviewer asked 'when you say you are going to ban strikes ... Prime Minister: "Only in essential services. But it was not my decision. It came to the cabinet from the concerned ministry (Industry). It did not emanate from me at all."' Interview with the French newspaper *Madam Figaro* on 12 October 1981. Ibid., p. 583.

powers in Punjab. In particular, the latter said that during a Punjab emergency, there was no protection from Article 21—no person can be deprived of life or liberty except according to procedure established by law. A commentator captured the reaction of many to these ordinances and laws when he referred to the 'gay abandon' of the central government in 'accumulating extraordinary powers ... [which] makes one wonder whether in the not too distant future anything will be left of the normal law of the land'.[40]

Oppressiveness being infectious, it spread to other civil liberties such as freedom of speech. The legislatures of Bihar and Tamil Nadu in 1982 passed laws restricting press freedom. The Bihar Act, reportedly passed in five minutes, provided for fines and imprisonment for possessing, selling, or publishing pictures, advertisments, or reports that are ' "grossly indecent or ... [are] scurrilous or intended for blackmail" '. Publication was permissible if the material was expressed ' "in good faith" '. One would assume that Mrs. Gandhi's government previously had cleared these bills, given customary practice, namely that a state government consults the central government before enacting legislation dealing with an item on the Concurrent List.[41] Bihar Chief Minister Jagannath Mishra said the bill was not meant to intimidate the press.[42] To the accompaniment of an immediate and loud press and public uproar, both bills were withdrawn.

During 1986 and 1988, the central government ventured, itself, into curbing the press and civil liberty other than through preventive detention. On 11 November 1986 Rajiv Gandhi's government introduced in the Lok Sabha what came to be known as the Postal Bill. With its passage by the Rajya Sabha on 10 December, the central and state governments were empowered to direct that in the interests of public safety or tranquility, the security of India, or on the occurrence of any public emergency, any postal article or class of postal articles 'shall be intercepted or detained or shall be disposed of' as authority may direct. Public opposition again was vehement, although some knew that a

---

[40] Sahay, S., 'More and More Extraordinary Powers', in Sahay, *A Close Look*, Allied Publishers Pvt. Ltd., New Delhi, 1987, pp. 219ff. See also Desai, A. R. (ed.), *Violation of Democratic Rights in India*, Popular Prakashan, Bombay, 1986, vol. 1.

[41] 'Newspapers, books and printing presses' is Item 39 on the Concurrent List.

[42] *AR*, 10–16 September 1982, pp. 16785–8.

The Prime Minister told the Lok Sabha on 16 August 1982 that 'we stand committed to a free press', but the press has to be 'responsible' and no one is entitled to use his freedom of speech to injure another's reputation. *Indira Gandhi: Speeches and Writings*, vol. 5, p. 24.

certain amount of legal and 'informal' mail interception (by postal employees co-operating with the Intelligence Bureau and the CBI) had been going on for years.

The bill went to President Giani Zail Singh on 19 December for his assent, and the issue of presidential powers arose. Singh refused to sign the bill on 15 January 1987 and then sat on it, apparently without consulting anyone about his decision to do so. This was the first 'pocket veto', a thing not envisaged in the Constitution. By this time, the President's relations with Prime Minister Rajiv Gandhi had become bitter, and informed opinion was divided about whether the President was acting on principle, from pique at his treatment by the government (he and Rajiv Gandhi were oil and water), or from resentment at government policies in the Punjab.[43] R. Venkataraman became President on 25 July 1987 with the Postal Bill still lying at Rashtrapati Bhavan. The new President never understood his predecessor's mind on the issue, but himself disliked much of the bill.[44] He returned it to Rajiv Gandhi on 7 January 1990 with the recommendation that it go to the Law Ministry for reconsideration, having himself declined to suggest changes when the Prime Minister requested him to do so. The bill actually was returned

[43] In his memoirs, Zail Singh says that he received the bill on 22 November 1986. Thinking that it 'undermined' the Constitution's 'fundamental freedoms', he twice made suggestions for changes in it to the government, whose responses did not satisfy him. He records that he did not return the bill to Parliament for reconsideration, because he would have had to assent were it returned to him after re-passage. Singh did 'anticipate', he says, that his successor would be 'reluctant to endorse such a measure'. Singh, Zail, *Memoirs of Giani Zail Singh: The Seventh President of India*, Har-Anand Publications Pvt. Ltd., New Delhi, 1997, pp 276ff.

Constitutional and personal elements had strained relations between the Prime Minister and the President. Zail Singh complained, apparently accurately, that Rajiv Gandhi was not keeping him informed of government activities—a 'duty' prescribed for the Prime Minister in Article 78. Personally, the two men reportedly looked upon each other with distaste. Singh–Rajiv Gandhi relations would worsen to the point of constitutional crisis, and the President even researched his authority to dismiss a prime minister.

Zail Singh, elected President on 15 July 1982, had risen from Chief Minister of the Punjab to be a cabinet minister during Mrs Gandhi's second prime ministership. He was thought to be deeply in her political debt, and his election was challenged on the grounds that he was unfit for office. The Supreme Court dismissed the charges as false and frivolous and said that an election could not be challenged because the official was believed unsuitable. Some political observers feared that Zail Singh would stand up to Mrs Gandhi no more than had President Ahmed should she return to authoritarianism. Such apprehensions rested in part on Zail Singh's having 'blurted out', '"I am prepared to pick up a broom and sweep any place if Mrs Gandhi asks me to do so"'. Singh, Satinder, 'Giani the Great', *The Sunday Free Press Journal*, 26 July 1987.

[44] Interview with a person privy to Venkataraman's views.

to the Rajya Sabha, where it was tabled on 3 March 1990, and where it was still pending in 1994.[45]

The Rajiv Gandhi government again attacked the Fundamental Rights, at least in the view of an unusually united national press, when in August 1988 it attempted passage of the so-called 'Defamation Bill'. Allegations of corruption against the Prime Minister (regarding weapons purchased for the army), his close associates, and other ministers had been current for months. Parliamentary elections were due in a year, and the bill was, said a newsmagazine, 'an act of desperation'.[46] The bill's Statement of Objects and Reasons said it proposed to make an offence 'the publication of imputations falsely alleging commission of offences by any person'. Freedom of speech must not 'degenerate into licence', said the Statement. The 'draconian character' of the bill was exemplified, said the *Times of India* in its putting 'the onus of proof that no defamation was caused upon the accused'.[47]

The government rammed the bill through the Lok Sabha on 30 August after an acrimonious debate over substance. The opposition charged that, in the process, Parliament's rules of procedure had been violated. The uproar caused Rajiv Gandhi to announce that the bill would not be introduced in the Rajya Sabha. The Defamation Bill thus achieved the dubious distinction of being the first bill since independence to be withdrawn by a government after passage in the Lok Sabha.[48]

This attention to government policies affecting civil liberty should be understood in context. In several areas of the country state governments were unable to cope with internecine conflicts between

---

[45] For the legislative history of the bill's actual return to the Rajya Sabha, the author is indebted to M. K. Singh, Assistant Director of Research for the Rajya Sabha.

    For an analysis of the Postal Bill affair, see Limaye, Madhu, *President versus Prime Minister,* Janata Party, Bombay, 1987.

[46] *India Today*, 30 September 1988, p. 12.

[47] Editorial of 31 August 1988.

[48] Among the bill's active opponents was Dinesh Goswami, a member of the Swaran Singh Committee.

    At this time the government also was reported to favour amending the Official Secrets Act.

    The government already had taken a major step to prevent embarrassing information from becoming public. In May 1986, it promulgated an ordinance (replaced by an act of Parliament on 6 August) amending the 1952 Commissions of Enquiry Act so that the government could withhold reports of commissions from the public on grounds of the security of the state and public interest. One of the first reports subsequently withheld was the Thakkar Commission's report about Mrs Gandhi's assassination.

local factions or with insurrectionary violence. They came to depend on central government forces to contain or subdue the violence and preserve a measure of government authority. Yet, although the Terrorist and Disruptive Activities Act extended nationally, in much of the country it was not extensively employed. Only in several states did repression under the act result in the virtual extinction of democracy—notably, Jammu and Kashmir, the Punjab, Assam, and elsewhere in the Northeast. Rajiv Gandhi's government inherited both the ugly conditions in these areas and his mother's failed policies in the Punjab and Kashmir, which he attempted to redress. That the responsibility for these conditions rested both with local militants—secular and religious—and with New Delhi for its divide-and-rule meddling in state affairs did not lessen their precariousness. Nevertheless, repression became a substitute for reform. Authoritarian methods were the easy way out, demanding less intelligence, less political effort, and no recognition that your opponent might have a point. Repression was power without perspective, an imperium, not the statesmanship the country needed.

Chapter 25

JUDICIAL REFORM OR HARASSMENT?

Appointments and Transfers of Judges

Given Mrs Gandhi's past policies toward the judiciary, it was small wonder that after 1980 the ever-simmering issue of judicial independence boiled again. Nor was the principal sub-topic new: the appointment and transfer of high court judges. Indeed, the tenacity of both the broad and specific issues testified to their importance and to their unresolvable character: perfect independence of the judiciary was impossible. Were it claimed to exist, few would believe it, and others would be inclined to tamper with it. The most that might be achieved would be some approximation of independence resulting from an improved process and, most of all, from greater trust among those involved with judicial matters. But this was absent. The executive and the judicial branches again were battling. Senior Advocate Anil Divan's diagnosis was that 'powerful politicians want to be above the law ... to sit in court by proxy through a pliant and submissive judiciary'.[1]

Contained within the issues of independence of the judiciary and judicial appointments as they agitated the eighties were the sub-topics endemic to the judicial enterprise in the country: whether or not considerations of caste figured in the appointments of judges or in their behaviour on the bench; the susceptibility of high court judges to influences from local parties, private or governmental, including actual bribery; the intrusion of family relationships into a court's functioning, especially the matter of a judge's close kin practising as advocates in his high court; long unfilled vacancies on high courts, often believed to be an executive branch technique for diminishing the courts' capabilities; and the manipulation of appointments by executive branches in New Delhi and the state capitals with the intention of influencing judicial decision-making.

Mrs Gandhi, her critics believed, came to the renewal of these issues with hands unclean from, especially, the 1973 supersession of judges, the transfer of judges during the Emergency, and the supersession of

[1] Divan, Anil, 'The Government vs. The Supreme Court' *Statesman*, New Delhi, 28 June 1981.

Justice Khanna. Few were inclined to believe that the poacher had turned gamekeeper even when a measure her government proposed might be construed as a genuine attempt at reform and found approval from the Law Commission and among individuals ordinarily not her supporters. Lawyers, judges, and the aware public reacted less to the actual substance of a government statement or proposal than with suspicions about the motives assumed to lie behind it. Receptivity to the Prime Minister's policies regarding the judiciary—or perceptions of what they meant—could not have been enhanced by Law Minister Shiv Shankar's order, within weeks of the government's taking office, closing down the special courts and, coincidentally with this, his remark that ' "the judiciary continued to be a vestige of British imperialism and it should be reorganized" '.[2] Government actions regarding the transfer and appointments of several judges also fuelled the controversy, which culminated in the famous Judges case, also called the S. P. Gupta case, in the Supreme Court. But the court's decision produced questions as well as answers, and it would be a dozen more years before a potentially durable policy on these two issues would be found.[3]

Appointments and Transfers

The train of events began in mid-1980 with the rumour that the government intended to appoint the chief justice of each high court from outside its jurisdiction. Law Minister Shiv Shankar tended to confirm this when he told the Lok Sabha that, although the government had no such policy, it believed 'the proposal merits favourable consideration in the interests of sound judicial administration and also the independence of the judiciary'.[4] Government officials at this time also were thinking

[2] Cited in ibid.

[3] Article 222 of the Constitution provides that the President, after consultation with the Chief Justice of India, may transfer a judge from one high court to another. The Fifteenth Amendment (1963) provided that a transferred judge should receive certain compensatory allowances. Anxieties about transfers at that time evoked an assurance in Parliament by the Law Minister, Asoke Sen, that judges would not be transferred without their consent. Subsequently, this came to be regarded widely as a constitutional convention (chapters 5 and 15). It will be recalled that in Sankalchand's case, the Supreme Court ruled that a judge's consent to his transfer was not a necessary precondition for it (chs 20). The Seventh Amendment (1956) provided that the President could appoint for terms of up to two years additional high court judges if this were desirable because of 'any temporary increase in the business of a High Court or by reason of arrears of work therein'.

[4] 'Law Minister's Statement on Appointment of Chief Justices of High Courts', Press Information Bureau, GOI, 24 July 1980. Also, *Lok Sabha Debates*, Seventh Series, vol. 7, no. 35, cols 200–4.

in terms of one-third of all judges on a high court coming from outside of the state, although this would emerge as policy only in the summer of 1981. The Parliament's Consultative Committee for the Law Ministry favoured both courses of action, according to a then senior Department of Justice official. Judges could come from out of state by initial appointment as well as by transfer. Mrs Gandhi believed that many people thought 'that there should be greater movement of judges because if they stay in one place they get involved with something or somebody'.[5]

Two events now stirred the pot. First came a messy affair in which an additional judge of the Allahabad High Court resigned, declaring himself opposed to a transfer of judges policy '"aimed at creating fear and a sense of instability"' in the minds of judges, and protesting that the extension of his own tenure as an additional judge for only four months was due to political considerations, particularly his alleged connections with Mrs Gandhi's enemy, Raj Narain.[6] The governor of Uttar Pradesh had written to the Law Ministry that Justice Srivastava's extension was not desirable because he '"might be susceptible to political bias and pressure"'.[7] Doing this, the governor had bypassed the normal procedure of consulting the court's chief justice.[8] Shiv Shankar denied in the Rajya Sabha that questions had been asked about Srivastava's party connections. He said on this occasion that regional and caste considerations affected recommendations for judicial appointments; that the judicial system might break down if 'extraneous considerations' continued to play 'a vital role' in appointments; and that if the members were serious about

---

There were sixty-five high court judgeships vacant at this time, only thirty-one names had been recommended to fill them; five high courts had only acting chief justices; and arrears in the high courts had risen to over 600,000 cases at the end of 1979. Ibid., col. 202. Also *Indian Express*, 24 July 1980.

[5] Answer given on 26 July 1980 to a question from the American scholar Francine Frankel. *Indira Gandhi: Speeches and Writings*, vol. 4, pp. 66–7.

[6] Judge R. C. Srivastava's resignation letter to President Sanjiva Reddy was published in the *Hindustan Times*, 26 July 1980.

Srivastava thought the short renewal of his tenure was due to his having been Raj Narain's counsel during the Indira Gandhi Election case. He wrote this to President Reddy in his resignation letter and added that he did not like the government enquiring through the Chief Justice '"whether I was a member of the Socialist Party"', whether he had received telephone calls from Raj Narain, and whether he had worked in the January Lok Sabha elections—where, he claimed, he had not even voted.

The *Hindustan Times* commented that additional judges had 'invariably' been confirmed as puisne judges, excepting in two cases during the Emergency. *Hindustan Times*, 27 July 1980.

[7] *Hindustan Times*, 28 July 1980. The letter had been sent the previous March.

[8] Sahay, S., 'Appointment and Terms of Judges', *Statesman*, New Delhi, 31 July 1980.

judicial independence, they should consider having one-third of a high court's judges from outside the state.[9]

Shiv Shankar, himself, provided the second event. He wrote in August 1980 to chief ministers and high court chief justices that more individuals from the Scheduled Castes and Tribes should be considered for judgeships. Although this was a constructive suggestion, it nevertheless strengthened perceptions that the government had designs on judicial independence.[10]

Public reactions, particularly to talk of transferring judges, ranged from approval to dire predictions. The Bar Council of India opposed one-third the number of judges coming from out of state as potentially dangerous to judicial independence. The *Indian Express* agreed, saying that 'the public would not trust the executive with unrestricted powers to transfer High Court judges against their wishes'.[11] S. Sahay thought 'pernicious' the doctrine that a judge could not become chief justice in his own high court.[12] Experience with the executive's power of appointment 'so far has not been happy' thought K. K. Katyal. The recommendations emanating from chief ministers, he wrote, give rise 'to suspicions of extraneous considerations' and, therefore, 'additional safeguards are needed'.[13] A. G. Noorani thought the process suggested by the Law Minister would 'undermine the independence of the judiciary and outweigh any other merit the scheme might possess'.[14]

[9] *Hindustan Times*, 31 July 1980. Also, *Parliamentary Debates, Rajya Sabha*, vol. 115, no. 6, col. 199.

[10] Shiv Shankar informed Parliament of the letter. *Lok Sabha Debates* Seventh Series, vol. 7, no. 42, col. 292. Shiv Shankar also said he regretted that there were only five scheduled caste high court judges. Apparently, some caste considerations in judicial appointments are more acceptable than others.

[11] Editorial, issue of 25 July 1980.

[12] Sahay, 'Appointment and Terms of Judges'. Sahay referred to the Law Commission's recent suggestion (footnote 16) that the senior-most judge of a high court should become the chief justice unless found unsuitable (*Report*, p. 34) and that one-third of judges be from out of state. He pointed out the commission's recommendation that this normally should be achieved through initial appointment rather than through transfers—a recommendation that the government typically sidestepped in its citations of the commission's report.

Sahay also mentioned the renewed suggestions from the Law Minister to form an All-India Judicial Service and said that in the current context the idea needed to be reviewed to prevent harm to judicial independence.

[13] *Hindu*, 4 August 1980.

[14] Noorani, A. G., 'Transfer of High Court Judges', *Economic and Political Weekly*, 20 September 1980. Noorani pointed out that Shanti Bhushan, when Law Minister, had told the Rajya Sabha that no judge would be transferred without his consent.

The *Hindu*, on the other hand, thought such anxieties 'entirely misplaced'. The policy of having judges from out of the state would promote national integration, and they would not be swayed by local considerations or 'regional passions', the newspaper said.[15] Those favouring transfers, generally speaking, agreed with the *Hindu*'s points. Those opposed believed an outside chief justice, even more than puisne judges, would be hampered by ignorance of the local language and of local personalities and conditions. Several of the appointment and transfer policies to which the critics objected had been recommended by the respected H. R. Khanna, then Chairman of the Law Commission, in the commission's *Eightieth Report*. Khanna also had recommended devices for protecting judicial independence.[16]

The Bar Council of India in a 'National Seminar' in the autumn expressed a more favourable view of transfers than it had earlier and suggested a mechanism for high court appointments. The initiative for the appointment of judges should come from a collegium of 'three senior-most judges of the High Courts and two leading advocates nominated by the Bar'. The chief minister could discuss with the collegium any objections to its recommendation, but its recommendation would be final. If the chief minister unduly delayed forwarding the nomination to the governor for transmittal to the President, the recommendation could go to the President through the Chief Justice of India. High court chief justices should be selected by a collegium composed of the Chief

---

See also Noorani's views about Mrs Gandhi's and Shiv Shankar's alleged transgressions against the judiciary in his 'The Prime Minister and the Judiciary' in Manor, *Nehru to the Nineties*, pp. 94–114.

[15] Editorial of 26 July 1980.

[16] This thorough report, entitled *The Eightieth Report on the Method and Appointment of Judges*, dated 10 August 1979, was prepared by Justice Khanna, and it made detailed recommendations. Among these were that 'there should be a convention according to which one-third of judges in each High Court should be from another state. This would normally be done through initial appointment and not by transfer. The process will have to be gradual: it would take some years before the proportion is reached'. *Eightieth Report*, p. 33. The report also said that no judge should be transferred without his consent unless a panel of the Chief Justice of India and his four senior-most colleagues found sufficient cause—which was not defined—for the transfer. Ibid., pp. 34–5. And, 'In regard to the appointment of the Chief Justice, normally the senior-most judge of the high court should be appointed'. Ibid., p. 33.

Justice Khanna recommended that the Chief Justice of India, when making his recommendations to fill a high court vacancy, should consult with the chief minister concerned and the chief justice of the high court. If his two senior-most colleagues on the Supreme Court concurred with his choice, normally it should be accepted. Action to fill a vacancy should be initiated at least six months before it was to occur. Ibid., p. 32.

Justice of India, two of his senior colleagues, two chief justices of high courts, and two senior members of the bar. 'Ordinarily the group's recommendation must be accepted by the Executive', the seminar said. And the power of transfer 'remains only with the judiciary'.[17]

Everyone had a point. As Shiv Shankar was saying, one-third of judges and chief justices from out of state might protect judicial independence by helping judges resist pressures from local groups, but local or government manipulation of sitting judges (and their initial placement on the bench) still could mock these goals. The Bar Council's and the Law Commission's recommendations would have served the same purpose while greatly reducing opportunities for executive branch mischief. The Bar Council's involvement of local lawyers in the selection of judges would have provided an antidote to judicial self-centredness, but risked increasing the effect of bar politics on selections. All in all, the Law Commission seemed to have the better scheme. Arguably, judges from out of state might contribute to national integration through fostering uniformity in the judicial process.

Transfers Go To Court

Actual transfers now increased both the temperature of the controversy and the demand for an impartial appointment and transfer process. On 5 January 1981, Chief Justice of India Chandrachud telephoned K. B. N. Singh, the chief justice of the Bihar High Court in Patna, to tell him he was to become chief justice of the Madras High Court. To make room for him, the then chief justice in Madras, M. M. Ismail, was notified he was being transferred to the Kerala High Court. The transfers had been initiated the previous December in correspondence between Chandrachud and Shiv Shankar. The Chief Justice then had declared himself 'opposed to the wholesale transfers of Chief Justices', but said that transfers might be made for 'strictly objective reasons'.[18] Ismail

---

[17] *Summary of Proceedings of the National Seminar on Judicial Appointments and Transfers,* New Delhi, 1980, Bar Council of India, pp. 5–7.

Although this scheme was not unlike the Law Commission's, a *Hindustan Times* editorial called it 'impractical' and not surprising coming from lawyers. The editorial preferred Justice Khanna's recommendations. It added, 'Governments have tended to exhibit political bias in making judicial appointments and the trend has become more marked in recent years. As a result, a large number of second-raters have been elevated to the ... different High Courts'. *Hindustan Times,* 27 October 1980.

[18] The letter quoted from was dated 7 December 1980. Excerpts from this correspondence appeared in the Supreme Court's ruling in the S. P. Gupta case and also were

resigned in protest in a letter to the President; the Tamil Nadu Chief Minister, M. G. Ramachandran, protested sending a judge from Patna who did not know Tamil; and two advocates filed petitions challenging Ismail's and K. B. N. Singh's transfers. A Supreme Court bench of Justices Bhagwati and Baharul Islam, acting on the petition challenging Ismail's transfer, on 3 February ordered that the status quo be maintained: Ismail was free to remain in Madras or go to Kerala; Singh should continue as chief justice in Patna.[19]

These transfers were opposed outside the courts as well. A two-day All-India Lawyers Conference, under the auspices of the Supreme Court Bar Association, adopted a so-called 'Declaration of Delhi' urging the creation of independent machinery ' "with security of tenure and with a constitutional status ... to ensure the independence of the judiciary" '. At the conference, former Attorney General C. K. Daphtary called the transfers punitive and N. A. Palkhivala characterized the conflict as between the Constitution and ' "those who refuse to accept the discipline of the Constitution" '.[20] Senior advocate Fali Nariman, regretted that the Janata government had been unwilling to give up the transfer power—retaining it, Nariman said, because sometimes it was easier to transfer a judge 'to save him from undesirable environmental influence'

published by Baxi, *Courage, Craft and Contention*, appendix C. The letters were edited and the names of most of the individuals were deleted.

In his letter, Chandrachud referred to discussions with Shiv Shankar of the previous day, and there appear to have been earlier discussions. On 14 November, the *Indian Express* published a dispatch by Kuldip Nayar saying that Shankar, backed by Indira Gandhi, had insisted to Chandrachud that transfers were the prerogative of the executive. Nayar reported Chandrachud willing to consider specific transfer cases, but as believing that transfers as a matter of policy would result in their being influenced by the government's 'considerations'. The Chief Justice, Nayar reported, had recently held a meeting of his fellow judges and got their unanimous support for his position. Nayar continued that the government's 'legal experts' believed that a transfer amounted to changing a judge's service conditions and therefore consultations with the Chief Justice were necessary.

In what would have been an explosive development, had it eventuated, the government was considering a constitutional amendment meant to 'obviate' consultations with the CJI about transfers, Nayar reported. *Indian Express*, 14 November 1980.

[19] Hindustan Times, 24 January 1981.

The Madras High Court previously had had two chief justices from elsewhere: Chandra Reddy from Andhra Pradesh and Govindan Nair from Kerala.

An editorial in the *Hindustan Times* two days later said that at stake in transfers for purposes of national integrity was whether the government 'has any right to misuse this as a stratagem to push around judges not politically acceptable to it'.

[20] *Hindu*, 2 February 1981. Other speakers included L. M. Singhvi, president of the Supreme Court Bar Association, Chief Justice Chandrachud, H. R. Khanna, and V. M. Tarkunde.

than to impeach him. A judge transferred because of a complaint from the bar 'is virtually damned', wrote Nariman.[21]

Disputes regarding tenure were added to the transfer controversies. In February and March 1981, additional judges in four high courts whose two-year terms were to expire were given tenure extensions of several months instead of either being given longer extensions (to help cope with arrears in these courts) or being made permanent puisne judges. Writ petitions resulted and an advocate of the Allahabad High Court, S. P. Gupta, filed a writ petition concerning permanent appointments for three additional judges of that high court.[22] Several of these petitions also challenged a circular sent by Law Minister Shankar to all the chief ministers (excepting those in the northeastern states) and to the governor of Punjab. This threw kerosene on existing flames when it became public knowledge in mid-April that the circular asked the recipients to obtain from the additional judges in the state's high court 'their consent to be appointed permanent judges in any other high court' (they might indicate three courts in order of preference) and to obtain from potential judges 'their consent to be appointed to any other high court in the country'.[23] The written consents and preferences were to be sent to Shiv Shankar within two weeks.

In the Lok Sabha, the Law Minister dodged criticism of his circular. He seemed to confirm that he had sent it without consulting the Chief Justice—and that Chandrachud had protested this. Shankar asked if the independence of the judiciary meant ' "touch-me-not" '.[24] The Prime Minister commented that there was 'subtle and deliberate propaganda'

[21] Nariman article in *Indian Express*, 10 March 1981. Nariman believed that the Chief Justice of India should have available to him the service records of high court judges to enable him to investigate any allegations against them, thus lessening his dependency for information on the Department of Justice, with its close links to the Home Ministry (the Home Secretary is Secretary of the Department of Justice) and the Intelligence Bureau. A sometime Law Ministry official has told the author that service records are available to the CJI, but contain little that is helpful for deciding about transfers.

[22] A considerable amount of the correspondence between the Law Minister, the Chief Justice of India and Chief Justice Prakash Narain of the Delhi High Court, was published in Baxi, *Courage, Craft and Contention*, appendix B.

[23] The text of the circular, dated 18 March became part of the record of the Judges case and was published in ibid., appendix A. A copy of the circular went to the chief justices of the high courts concerned.

The government desired the information, the circular explained, because 'several bodies and forums' had suggested that one-third of judges be from out of state 'to further national integration and to combat narrow parochial tendencies bred by caste, kinship, and other local links and affiliations'.

[24] *Lok Sabha Debates*, Seventh Series, vol. 26, no. 42, col. 239.

against the democratic credentials of her party: 'any confrontation with the judiciary was far from her thoughts'. During thirty years of Congress rule ' "we never injected politics in appointments" ', she said.[25] S. Sahay thought the Law Minister had a 'grand design ...to dilute the independence of the judiciary and thereby make it more amenable to the wishes or hints of the ruling party'.[26] This was in part a reaction to the government's defeat in the Minerva Mills case, Sahay believed.

Nine of the petitions concerning judges' transfers or the continuations in service of additional judges were grouped together to be heard as the S. P. Gupta, or the Judges, case by a seven-judge bench of the Supreme Court between 4 August and 19 November 1981. The hearings, extensively reported in the English-language press, covered the substantive issues, re-emphasized the bitterness of the disagreements, and displayed the seamier side of politics in the judicial community.[27]

Opening the hearings, arguing the petition against Shiv Shankar's circular, H. M. Seervai said that transfers even in the public interest

[25] *Hindustan Times*, 17 March 1981.

[26] Sahay, S., 'Shiv Shankar's Grand Design', *Statesman*, New Delhi, 11 April 1981. Sahay supported his point by explaining that most high court judges do not begin as permanent judges, but as acting or additional judges. Data for 1980 showed for example, he wrote, that the Andhra Pradesh High Court had a strength of eighteen judges, ten of whom 'had to undergo an apprenticeship period'. In Allahabad, as many as thirty-three out of a strength of forty-four had first functioned as acting or additional judges. In Calcutta, the figures were thirty-two out of thirty-two, and in Bombay twenty-seven out of twenty-seven, Sahay claimed.

[27] The case officially was *S. P. Gupta v Union of India.* Chief Justice Chandrachud constituted the bench, and excused himself because he had been involved with the transfers. On the bench were P. N. Bhagwati, A. C. Gupta, S. Murtaza Fazl Ali, V. D. Tulzapurkar, D. A. Desai, R. S. Pathak, and E. S. Venkataramiah. Chandrachud set the bench according to seniority, with the first six members easily identified. To reach the seventh, he had to go to the tenth . judge in line, Venkataramiah; the three intervening judges—Chinnappa Reddy, A. D. Koshal, and A. P. Sen—declined to sit because each had been transferred during the Emergency.

L. N. Sinha, the Attorney General, Solicitor General K. Parasaran, P. R. Mridul, and others represented the government. The petitioners were represented by, among others, Soli Sorabjee, P. H. Parekh, H. M. Seervai, L. M. Singhvi, R. K. Garg, and P. G. Gokhale, a former Secretary in of the Department of Legal Affairs in the Law Ministry.

Several days before the hearings began, Kuldip Nayar wrote that since the Prime Minister's return to power she 'has wanted the executive to exercise the power (of transfers) without reference to the Chief Justice of India'. (Mrs Gandhi may or may not have desired this power, but she would have had to change Articles 217 and 222 to get it.) Nayar said that Shiv Shankar, in issuing the circular, has 'evidently acted only after consulting Mrs Gandhi at every step and getting her approval'. The question is not whether judges should be transferred, Nayar wrote, but who should decide on transfers. Nayar, Kuldip, 'Unfortunate Confrontation', *Tribune*, (Chandigarh), 30 July 1981.

were a punishment and the judge was 'branded' as incompetent in his own court. A judge could be transferred only for 'cogent reasons' and with his consent, argued Seervai, even though in the Sankalchand case the Supreme Court had held otherwise. No provision or convention empowered the government to ask for a judge's advance consent to transfer, as in the circular. This put individuals in fear, said Seervai.[28] Soli Sorabjee, representing Additional Justices Vohra and Kumar of the Delhi High Court, continued Seervai's arguments, contending that an additional judge's services could be 'non-continued' only if they were not needed at the end of his two year term, that is if the court had no arrears of cases. A judge's competence was to be determined only at the time of his original appointment.[29] Representing Justice K. B. N. Singh, who had been notified of his transfer from the Patna (Bihar) High Court by Chief Justice Chandrachud, L. M. Singhvi maintained that transfer without a judge's consent was unconstitutional because the Constitution required that a judge could be removed only on the ground of misbehaviour and by impeachment.[30]

[28] *Hindustan Times*, 5, 6, 7 and 12 August.

[29] *Hindustan Times*, 19, 20, 21, 26, 27 and 28 August.

Sorabjee said that the allegation that Additional Justice Vohra's term was not extended because of his conviction of Sanjay Gandhi in the Kissa Kursi Ka case could not be termed 'unfounded'. (In an interview with the author.) A. G. Noorani, 'The Prime Minister and the Judiciary' in Manor, *Nehru to the Nineties*, p. 109, cited H. M. Seervai that 'beyond doubt' Vohra was not reappointed for this reason.

During the hearing on 4 August, Soli Sorabjee called upon the government to produce the relevant documents on the various petitions concerning the Delhi High Court judges, and the bench ordered the government to prepare these. Sorabjee later would contend that the government could not claim privilege for these documents unless disclosure meant '"serious injury readily apparent in the national interest"'. Hearing on 26 August, *Hindustan Times*, 27 August 1981. This was in response to a government affidavit that there had been full consultation between the Chief Justice of India and Chief Justice Prakash Narain of the Delhi High Court, and the President had 'preferred' Narain's view, which was not favourable to Justice Kumar.

On 29 September, the bench ruled that it had the right to inspect documents regarding the appointment of Justice Vohra and would rule the next day on whether or not they could be revealed in the public interest. On 16 October, six of the judges (Fazl Ali dissented) ruled that the government should release to the petitioners the documents regarding Justice Kumar for this would not harm the public interest. The court called for other documents and these, too, were released. Quotations from many of these appear in the Supreme Court's decision in the case and in Baxi, *Courage, Craft and Contention*, appendix B.

While presiding, Justice Bhagwati said in open court that consultation by the President with the Chief Justice of India, the governor, and the chief justice of the high court could not be a basic feature of the Constitution and beyond amendment by Parliament. *Hindustan Times*, 14 August 1981.

[30] *Hindustan Times*, 17 September 1981.

Defending the government's position, Attorney General L. N. Sinha contended that additional judges were appointed because of a temporary increase in court business and at the end of a judge's term 'a positive assessment of his fitness' was a condition that had to be met before reappointment. Not to be reappointed had no stigma attached because it was an executive, not a judicial, decision, and a second appointment was not a continuation of the first. An additional judge had no legal right to move the court for reappointment after his two-year term expired even if reappointment were denied him by fraudulent means. The issue of judicial independence 'arises only after the appointment of a judge', Sinha said. Turning to the Law Minister's circular, Sinha argued that the government had no legal obligation to consult the Chief Justice when formulating a policy for appointment of high court judges—although it would have been 'tactful' to do so.[31]

During the hearings of the next several days, there were several interesting colloquies between the bench and the government's law officers. Justice Bhagwati said that a judge could not be transferred merely because the bar had made allegations against him. This would directly affect the independence of the judiciary. To this L. N. Sinha replied, what is the independence ' "if there is no more confidence in him" '? The next day, all seven judges of the bench were reported to have agreed that the Chief Justice of India must consult the chief justice of a high court whose transfer was being contemplated. Sinha disagreed. No consent was necessary, and the Court had no right to look into the correspondence regarding reappointment of judges. Four days later, the bench ruled against him.[32] When Solicitor General K. Parasaran said that transfers might be needed to remove a judge from a polluted environment, Justice Desai asked why transfer and punish a judge for the deeds of advocates?[33] The hearings concluded on 19 November and the bench reserved judgement.[34]

[31] Ibid., 21 September 1981.
[32] Ibid., 25 and 26 September 1981.
[33] Ibid., 1 October 1981.
[34] Arguing on behalf of the government, P. R. Mridul awakened memories of Mohan Kumaramangalam by arguing that the Constitution permitted the government to '"value pack"' courts as part of its power to appoint judges. The Constitution did 'not permit an "elitist non-elective body" like the judiciary to have any share in the government's power to formulate and implement policies', Mridul said, except for judicial review and protection of the Fundamental Rights. Bizarrely, Mridul contended in both his written and oral submissions that the President had discretion in appointing judges. He had previously said that the President and the Chief Justice had '"co-equal power"'. This performance hardly can have reassured those sceptical of the government's attitude toward the judiciary.

The Court's decision, given on 30 December 1981, in the main upheld the government's positions. Each of the seven judges wrote an opinion, somewhat clouding the resulting law. A majority of Justices Bhagwati, Fazl Ali, Desai, and Venkataramiah held that a judge's consent was not necessary for his transfer. But transfers were to be in the public interest and not punitive. These four also ruled that the Chief Justice of India does not have 'primacy' over other constitutional functionaries regarding judges' appointments and transfers (an executive branch function, the judges said), and, therefore, his advice is not binding on the President. 'Consultation' in the Constitution was not to mean the Chief Justice's 'concurrence' in appointments.[35] The other three judges—Untwalia, Gupta, and Pathak—believed the Chief Justice had primacy, but no veto. The bench ruled that an additional judge had no enforceable right to be reappointed, but he was entitled to 'weightage' in acknowledgement of the twenty-five year old convention that 'normally' an additional judge would be appointed permanent judge at the end of his two-year term. On significant other points, the Court decided that lawyers had standing in such matters and could express it by way of public interest litigation. Also, the government could not claim 'privilege'—i.e., immunity—from disclosure of documents bearing on the appointment and transfer of judges (the cabinet's advice to the President excepted).[36] Finally, the court held that Shiv Shankar's 'circular' was not unconstitutional because it had no 'legal force' in the first place.

The bench's delivery of its judgement was as indicative of its individualistic process as were its seven opinions. According to a member of the bench, the judges did not circulate draft opinions among themselves under Justice Bhagwati's guidance, as leader of the bench, despite Bhagwati's discontent with the absence of coordination in Minerva Mills. On 30 December, during the Supreme Court's winter recess, Justice Bhagwati convened the bench and its ruling was handed down.

These discrepancies were pointed out by Krishan Mahajan in the *Hindustan Times*, 20 October 1981.

[35] Justice Bhagwati would be singled out for criticism by many for strengthening the government's hand in appointments by saying in his opinion 'consultation [with the Chief Justice of India] cannot be equated with [gaining his] concurrence'. 1981 *Supp* SCC 227.

[36] This summary has been drawn from the judges' opinions and the headnotes in AIR 1982 SC 149ff, and 1981 *Supp* SCC 87ff.

The bench upheld the transfer of K. B. N. Singh to the Madras High Court and the non-extension of S. N. Kumar as an additional judge on the Delhi High Court.

The Battle of the Affidavits

Within and outside the bench, conduct of the case was marred by behaviour that some named 'the battle of the affidavits' and others, among them several judges on the bench, an attempt to embarrass the Chief Justice.[37] Regarding affairs in the Bihar High Court, the government there filed an affidavit with the Supreme Court claiming that Chandrachud had initiated K. B. N. Singh's transfer.[38] Singh protested his transfer in an affidavit, claiming that he had never consented to it and that the grounds for it had never been given to him. Chief Justice Chandrachud responded in an affidavit denying that the transfer was made without proper consultation with Singh and with the government. Singh then filed a counter-affidavit, and the Patna advocate protesting the transfer filed a long affidavit.[39] On the Delhi scene, additional judge S. N. Kumar of the high court filed an affidavit with the Supreme Court criticizing Chandrachud's consultations with him, and the government filed a counter-affidavit.[40] The chief justice of the Delhi High Court, Prakash Narain, wrote in a letter to Shiv Shankar that Kumar was susceptible to bribery. He requested Shiv Shankar to keep the letter secret from Chandrachud because the Chief Justice might reveal it to Kumar.[41] Chandrachud wrote to Shiv Shankar that his researches found no substance in the charges against Kumar, to which Shankar responded in a note dated 27 May that he preferred Narain's opinion and would not extend Kumar's term.[42]

[37] In interviews with the author.

[38] *Hindustan Times*, 26 September 1981.

[39] Texts published in Baxi, *Courage, Craft and Contention*, pp. 132ff, 140ff, and 144ff.

[40] *Hindustan Times*, 27 August 1981.

[41] Shiv Shankar asserted that Narain made this request in a telephone conversation with him—note recorded by the Law Minister on 19 May 1981. Shankar repeated this in a letter to Prakash Narain dated 29 May 1981. Texts in Baxi, *Courage, Craft and Contention* pp. 121–2, and 129.

[42] Texts in Baxi, *Courage, Craft and Contention*, pp. 121ff, 126ff. See also *Hindustan Times*, 4 November 1981 for further information about developments between December 1980 and November 1981.

The allegations against K. B. N. Singh included that his brother-in-law had pleaded cases, often bail petitions, before a judge friendly to Singh, and that this had been done against Chandrachud's recommendations. A second judge stopped hearing these cases. The allegations against Justice Ismail (transferred from Madras to Kerala) included frequently granting bail petitions for low sums, but he also was thought to be upright and honest. Interviews with justices on or close to the case.

The making of allegations against high court judges has raised many questions about prejudices against particular judges within the bars of the various courts and, also, about

Chief Justice Chandrachud's affidavit excited great interest. Defending himself in it he rebutted the Patna chief justice's criticisms of the transfer process, saying that the transfer was based upon a dispassionate assessment of 'the relevant facts' and was in the 'public interest'.[43] The central question, according to many observers, was whether Chandrachud should have filed the affidavit at all. A fellow judge on the bench believed he had to, for silence would have been interpreted as assenting to K. B. N. Singh's version of events. For one senior advocate close to the case it was a 'great mistake' because it lowered him to the level of others. But Justice Bhagwati had demanded from Chandrachud personally that he file an affidavit, according to Chandrachud[44]—an assertion believed also by a bench colleague. Justice Bhagwati, in his Judges case opinion, characterized Chandrachud's affidavit as 'delightfully vague'.[45] The final indignity for Chandrachud—and perhaps for the bench and the Supreme Court as an institution—was the vote within the bench on whether to accept or to reject the Chief Justice's affidavit. Justice Bhagwati led Justices Fazl Ali and D. A. Desai in favour of rejection. The majority of four voted acceptance, with Justices Tulzapurkar and Venkataramiah said particularly to support Chandrachud. The belief persists widely that the Bhagwati–Chandrachud confrontation derived primarily from the former's long-held 'grouse' against the latter's having been made a Supreme Court justice before him,[46] but other personality differences were said also to have played a part.

---

the role of the Intelligence Bureau as a gatherer and forwarder of unsupported and unevaluated information to central ministry officials about judges and candidates for the bench.

Other letters from Chandrachud to the Law Minister showed the former changing his mind several times about who should be transferred where.

[43] Text in Baxi, *Courage, Craft and Contention*, pp. 140–3.

[44] Y. V. Chandrachud interview with the author.

[45] Cited by Palkhivala in Palkhivala, N. A., ' The Supreme Court's Judgement in the Judges' Case', *Journal of the Bar Council of India*, vol. 9, no. 2, 1982, p. 207. Chandrachud had used the same words to describe Chief Justice Narain's description of Justice Kumar's alleged failings.

[46] Interviews with judges on and off the Judges case bench, former law officers of the Government of India, senior advocates, and others.

Bhagwati had been senior to Chandrachud in the sense that he had been chief justice of the Gujarat High Court and believed that he, therefore, should have been elevated to the Supreme Court before Chandrachud, who had been a puisne judge of the Bombay High Court when elevated to the Supreme Court. Taking judges on to the Supreme Court from high courts had not always been based on judges' seniority in their own high court. Chandrachud and H. R. Gokhale, Law Minister at the time of Chandrachud's elevation, both were Maharashtrians. Bhagwati was a Gujarati.

'[N]either the image nor the stature of the Supreme Court or of the judiciary as a whole' has been improved by the judgement, commented S. Sahay in the *Journal of the Bar Council of India*. The editorial for this issue of the journal said the case 'ended up with ... a sadly divided court embroiled in personal rivalries'.[47] Much that came to light during the case, said the *Indian Express*, was 'disquieting if not ominous'. The positions of the government counsel 'could only be construed as ... taking on the judiciary'.[48]

The Law Minister's motives during this period continue to be a subject for speculation. Acting on the Prime Minister's behalf, he intended to reduce judicial independence, according to one school of thought. And there should be little doubt that Shiv Shankar carefully avoided recommending for appointment judges unfriendly to Mrs Gandhi. Another body of opinion holds that his circular was not intended to intimidate judges into ruling in favour of the government. More likely, Shiv Shankar was not averse to 'shaking up' judges partly to caution them when considering the government's interest, but his principal motivation seems to have lain in class and caste consciousness. To him, judges were intellectuals or Brahmins or from the newly strong economic castes and classes—the upper reaches of the Other Backward Classes—whose 'monopoly had to be broken' so that lower-ranking members of the OBCs and Scheduled Castes and Tribes could 'thrive' as advocates and find their way to the bench.[49] He had spoken in the Rajya Sabha earlier about the dangers of caste (meaning higher caste) and other 'extraneous considerations' to the working of the judiciary. And he had written to chief ministers and high court chief justices recommending that low-caste individuals be made judges. Chief justices of high courts, Shankar believed, showed caste preferences in selecting colleagues and in deciding cases, and transfers might ameliorate this because outside judges would have no local roots.

A personal element also motivated him, according to some observers. A self-made man from the Kapu community in his home state of Andhra

---

[47] Sahay, S, 'A Judiciary in Executive's Image,' *Journal of the Bar Council of India*, vol. 9, no. 2, 1982, p. 230; editorial signed by N. Madhava Menon, p. iii.

[48] Issue of 31 December 1981. For further commentary, see other articles in this number of the Bar Council's *Journal*; also see Noorani, A. G., 'The Twilight of the Judiciary' in Noorani, *Indian Affairs: The Constitutional Dimension*, pp. 260ff; Baxi, *Courage, Craft and Contention*, entire; Deshpande, V. S., 'High Court Judges: Appointment and Transfer', *JILI*, vol. 27, no. 2, 1985, pp 179ff; and Seervai, *Constitutional Law*, vol. 2, pp. 2264ff, 2275ff, 2290ff, and elsewhere.

[49] Shiv Shankar in an interview with the author.

Pradesh (a large community of agriculturists at the lower rungs of the OBCs), he thought the Reddy community dominated the high court there, and he had resigned from the high court when he thought a Reddy judge had denied him the chief justiceship.[50] Whatever, Shiv Shankar seems not always to have been scrupulous in his methods nor temperate in speech. He once described the Supreme Court as a '"haven"' for '"anti-social elements, FERA (Foreign Exchange Regulation Act) violaters, bride-burners and a whole horde of reactionaries"'.[51] He considered himself to have been an influential supporter of Indira Gandhi—and kept a portrait of Sanjay Gandhi on his office wall even after his death. [52]

The government announced the first element of its transfer policy in January 1983. High court chief justices would be drawn from out of state, and seniority within his or her own court and suitability were to be the criteria.[53] Within a week, Chief Justice Chandrachud called a meeting of high court chief justices to discuss the policy, and he was reported to have seen Mrs Gandhi about it. Editorial reaction was predominantly negative. For the *Statesman*, Shiv Shankar's original proposals 'were born in original sin'; the S. P. Gupta decision 'handed to the government, on a platter as it were, the final powers in judicial appointments'. Now the government was 'relentlessly' trying to change the judiciary.[54] The Law Minister, now Jagan Nath Kaushal, formally

[50] From interviews in Hyderabad and New Delhi.

[51] *The Hindustan Times* (Legal Correspondent), 8 January 1988. The occasion was a speech to the Hyderabad High Court Bar Council (Andhra Pradesh) on 28 November 1987.

The Supreme Court did not cite Shankar for contempt, contrary to its citation of E. M. S. Namboodiripad for contempt in 1971 for saying that judges were dominated by caste and class prejudices and favoured the rich against the poor.

[52] Shiv Shankar interview with the author.

[53] Announcement on 28 January 1983. A chief justice with only one year until retirement would not be subject to transfer, and a senior puisne judge with only one year until retirement might become chief justice in his own court. *Statesman*, 29 January 1983.

[54] Editorial, *Statesman*, New Delhi, 1 February 1983. It also said that judges were partly to blame because of persistent reports of judges' relatives and friends receiving favoured treatment in their courts.

S. Sahay expressed his view of events in the title of his column, 'The Taming of the Judiciary', ibid., 10 February 1983. In another article, Sahay discussed the threesome he perceived of Shiv Shankar and Justices Bhagwati and D. A. Desai. They had a 'great insidious design' to socialize the judicial system. He deduced this from their looking for models to the German Democratic Republic and the Soviet Union in three seminars in recent years. Sahay quoted Desai as saying at the German seminar, '"Which other socialist country in a span of a quarter of a century has successfully devised and implemented the socialist legal system with results for all to observe and appreciate"' Sahay, S., 'What "Forces of Change" Are Up To', ibid., 29 January 1983.

provided Parliament with the guidelines of the new policy in August. He announced that the government had 'recently' accepted the Law Commission's recommendation that one-third of high court judges should come from out of the state. This was to be achieved both through initial appointments and transfers and 'in accordance with the constitutional provisions which provide for an elaborate procedure of consultation'.[55] An uneasy truce over transfers lasted a decade.

Mrs Gandhi's years as prime minister ended with glory neither for the executive's policies toward the judiciary, nor the judiciary's treatment of itself.

The basic issues reappeared in the nineties: writ petitions from Supreme Court lawyers that worked their way up to a special bench of nine judges. The most basic issue of all was the rampant suspicion with which the judicial and the executive branches regarded each other. This time, for a time, the Court prevailed. In the 'selection and appointment of judges to the Supreme Court and the high courts as well as transfer of judges from one high court to another high court ... the opinion of the Chief Justice of India ... is entitled to have the right of primacy', ruled the majority in the lead judgement by Justice J. S. Verma. Judicial review of transfers was to be limited to whether or not there was adequate participation by the Chief Justice of India.[56] Some weeks later, in December 1993, Prime Minister P. V. Narasimha Rao chaired a meeting of chief justices and the Chief Justice of India, which

---

[55] *Lok Sabha Debates,* Seventh Series, vol. 40, no. 16, cols 35–6. During the following five years, the government transferred thirty high court chief justices.

[56] See 'Judicial Appointments to The Higher Judiciary', SCALE (1993), *Supplement. S.C.A.O.R.A. (Supreme Court Advocates-On-Record Association) v Union of India,* para 215 of the judgement. This issue of SCALE is particularly useful because it contains the written submissions of the lawyers in the case, both private and governmental, and other background documents.

It is important to note that the judgement also said that the primacy of the Chief Justice's opinion 'is, in effect, primacy ... formed collectively ... after taking into account the views of his senior colleagues who are required to be consulted by him for the formation of his opinion'. Ibid., para 456. As to transfers of high court judges, 'the initiation of the proposal for the transfer of a judge/chief justice should be made by the Chief Justice of India alone'. Ibid., para 471. The Chief Justice was to follow 'suitable norms' in the matter of transfers, including those specified in the ruling. Ibid., para 475.

Delivering the judgement on 6 October 1993 was a bench consisting of S. Ratnavel Pandian, who presided, and Justices A. M. Ahmadi, Kuldip Singh, J. S. Verma, M. M. Punchhi, Yogeshwar Dayal, G. N. Ray, A. S. Anand, and S. P. Bharucha. Siding with Pandian were Justices Verma, Dayal, Ray, Anand, and Bharucha. Justice Punchhi held that the Chief Justice's role was 'primal' but participatory. Ahmadi held that there could be no such primacy unless the Constitution were amended. Kuldip Singh expressed no view on this issue.

decided that one-sixth of high court chief justices and one-third of judges be from out of state. As a result, Chief Justice of India M. N. Venkatachaliah set up a 'peer committee' of two Supreme Court judges, two high court chief justices, and the chief justice of the high court concerned with the transfer from his court 'to finalise norms' for transfers.[57] On 13 April 1994, the President, Shankar Dayal Sharma, announced the transfer of fifty high court judges. Criticism came from a few bar associations, but many associations and most editorial comments welcomed the transfers under the new procedures, for, as the *Hindu* headlined, hopefully, arbitrariness had been 'ruled out'.[58]

Who shall judge us? is a question for which few peoples have found a permanently satisfactory answer. The appointment of judges (and transfers may be treated as such)—involving as it does what sort of individual should be chosen and who should do the choosing—would bring forth the play of personal and group interests and perceptions existing in the most homogeneous society. More so in India's vertically and horizontally compartmented society, with its enormous gaps between economic classes, which nurtures suspiciousness and where the clash of interests, political and personal, makes judges' selection often seem a zero-sum affair to those concerned.[59] The constitutional implications become secondary in importance. All in all, the wonder is not that appointments have been messy on occasion, but that the society may have found a more satisfactory appointment process.[60]

---

[57] Bal Krishna, 'Putting an End to "Kin Syndrome"', *Hindustan Times*, 15 April 1994.

[58] Issue of 17 April 1994.

[59] For a discussion of the economic conditions that make India's a survival society, see ch. 31.

[60] Since this was written, criticism of the Chief Justice of India's 'primacy' has been heard, and suggestions have been revived for the formation of a 'judicial commission', or some similar arrangement, for the appointment of judges.

Chapter 26

TURBULENCE IN FEDERAL RELATIONS

Matters of national unity and integrity and the character of centre–state relations dominated the country's political affairs between 1980 and 1985, giving prominence to this strand of the web greater than it had had since partition and the years of getting started. Rebellious groups threatened national integrity in the border states of Jammu and Kashmir and the Punjab. In Assam, and more broadly in the Northeast, too, violence continued to be the rule rather than the exception—seeming to provide justification for the harsh laws already described. Governments in other states were reconsidering seriously the manner in which centre–state relations had been worked. They questioned the fairness and efficacy of the Constitution's distribution of powers, and called upon New Delhi to join them in making adjustments. This culminated in the states' constitutional revolt of 1983 and after, led by governments in opposition parties' hands, which had unadvertized sympathy from several Congress chief ministers.

Because the distribution of powers and New Delhi's exercise of authority had long been controversial, and because state governments and political groups had not always acted responsibly (and some irresponsibly), the difficulties should not be laid exclusively at Indira Gandhi's door. Yet, as the Prime Minister for most of the years since 1966, and as the architect of the over-centralization of power in the Congress Party and in the institutions of governance to ensure her personal ascendancy, she bore great responsibility for the developments described in this chapter. Her response to the states' soberly expressed concerns with federalism's structure and working was to deflect and temporize, not to seek reform. Her response to the violence in the border states—truly very difficult situations—in the main was to manipulate and to use force.

Alarmism about threats to the nation's unity and integrity, the Prime Minister seemed to think, served her political needs. Preserving the nation joined social revolutionary promises as the reasons citizens should support her and her government against enemies foreign and domestic. The anti-national forces of regionalism, linguism, and communalism were cited by President Sanjiva Reddy in his speech inaugurating Parliament on 23 January 1980—a speech, in the parliamentary tradition, prepared in the cabinet. The Prime Minister spoke to the revived National Integration Council of 'unjust social stratification' as a cause of tensions.[1] In a letter to voters just prior to 1981 by-elections in Uttar Pradesh, Bihar, and Karnataka, she warned of forces opposing India's progress and of opposition parties' rejection of her appeal to build a strong and self-reliant India.[2] '"[D]estabilization [by outside powers] is an insidious policy"' by domestic ideologies resulting from '"our insistence on our independence in policy and action"', Mrs Gandhi told the Congress(I) Plenary in 1983.[3]

Opposition parties adopted this theme for partisan purposes. The Communist Party Marxist said that secessionist and divisive forces were gaining because of the government's 'class policies'. The CPI castigated the Hindu parties for challenging constitutional secularism, and 'imperialism' for using conditions to destabilize the country.[4] The Bharatiya Janata Party praised the Constitution's establishment of a strong centre, but claimed the Congress had 'increasingly reduced [the states] to glorified municipalities'.[5]

Fears that some 'foreign hand' was 'destabilizing' the country were genuine, originating in the national cultural traits of suspicion and conspiracy-mindedness. But playing on fears had an exculpatory character, especially when the government employed them to provide a distant scapegoat for conditions whose origins were domestic. Mrs Gandhi's calls for 'a strong central government', citing genuine conditions

[1] Speech delivered on 12 November 1980. *Indira Gandhi: Speeches and Writings*, vol. 4, pp. 114ff. She was the council's chairwoman.

The council meeting recommended, in language reminiscent of its earlier incarnations, that urgent steps be taken '"to end socio-economic exploitation, regional disparities and secessionist trends and that the educational system should be so overhauled as to promote communal harmony and national integration"'. *Hindustan Times*, 13 November 1980.

The 35-member council appointed a standing committee to monitor implementation of the resolution, but then did not meet again until March 1984.

[2] *Hindustan Times*, 5 June 1981.

[3] *AR*, 29 January–4 February 1984, p. 17578.

Picking up the refrain, the plenary's political resolution spoke of the 'external forces ... posing a serious threat to our country' and called for 'a strong central government ... to meet the threat to the country's unity and integrity ... . If the Centre is weakened, the forces of disunity will become strong.' *Resolutions Adopted at the Calcutta Plenary*, AICC, New Delhi, 1984, pp. 5, 13.

[4] *Reports of CPI(M) and its Various Frontal Activities (1982–1985)*, West Bengal State Committee, CPM, Calcutta, 1985, p. 26; *Communist Party of India and Fight Against Communalism*, CPI, New Delhi, 1985, p. 13.

[5] BJP election manifesto, *Towards a New Polity*, BJP, New Delhi, no date, but 1984.

and imagined threats, supported her resumption of personalization of power.[6]

Taking retribution against Janata for its dismissal of Congress state governments, Mrs Gandhi slandered Janata state governments as enemies of a strong India. And her first action regarding centre–state relations was to dissolve nine Janata-led state legislatures and place those states under President's Rule.

The Dissolution of State Assemblies

Applying the maxim that what is sauce for the goose is sauce for the gander must have given the Prime Minister understandable satisfaction, and even more so the ease with which on 17 February 1980 she hoist Janata on its own dissolutions of Congress governments. The cabinet unanimously took the decision to dissolve the legislative assemblies at an urgent meeting, after which Home Minister Zail Singh, draft proclamations in hand, called on President Reddy to get his signature on them.[7] Reddy signed with little hesitation, he remembered: 'Given the precedent, how could I say no? But I told Indira that Morarji had been wrong in principle and to dissolve again was still wrong.'[8] The Supreme Court's 1977 decision in the Rajasthan case had provided the clear precedent, and officials in the Law Ministry were not asked for advice about the dissolutions' legality, but only about its modalities.

Although the proclamations gave no reasons for the dissolutions, Law Minister Shiv Shankar justified them by citing the opposition parties' '"obsession"' with continuing in power after losing the confidence of the electorate; their '"negative attitude"' to the President's address to Parliament; and their alleged obstruction—particularly in Uttar Pradesh and Maharashtra—of the ratification of the Forty-fifth Amendment.[9] The

[6] There can be little doubt, however, that Pakistan was fuelling the fires in the Punjab, Jammu and Kashmir, and in the northeastern states. But the origins of the problems in these areas were indigenous to them, often abetted by New Delhi's policies. Other nations' foreign policies, when distasteful to New Delhi, were not described as disagreements, but often were said to have as their purpose 'destabilizing' India. The popular definition of 'destabilizing' contributed to the confusion.

[7] 'Unanimously': Shiv Shankar interview with the author. According to a senior official, Mrs Gandhi was very keen on dissolution and no one could oppose her at this time.

The legislative assemblies dissolved were in the states of Uttar Pradesh, Madhya Pradesh, Bihar, Rajasthan, Punjab, Gujarat, Maharashtra (where President's Rule was imposed for the first time since independence), Orissa, and Tamil Nadu.

[8] Sanjiva Reddy interview with the author.

[9] *AR*, 18–24 March 1980, p. 15367.

amendment extended for ten more years reserved seats for Scheduled Castes and Tribes in Parliament and state legislatures and, similarly, representation by nomination for Anglo-Indians. Obstructionism on this amendment seems a spurious rationale for the dissolutions 'because all parties were agreed on' the extension of reservations, thought Madhu Limaye.[10] 'Politically, it suited us. But I was not happy with the dissolutions, personally,' Shiv Shankar later said. 'The people had elected their representatives for five years and dissolution with two years remaining in their terms was not in the spirit of Article 356.' [11]

Reactions to the dissolutions varied. For the Janata leadership, they were a threat to democracy. M. C. Chagla was '"shocked to hear the news ... . She wants a monolithic set-up, with the states subservient to the Centre."' Madhu Dandavate thought it wrong to compare these dissolutions with those of 1977, when the legislatures' terms were nearly over.[12] A *Times of India* editorial said the dissolutions were necessary to enforce discipline after the 'drift' of the past three years. The *Hindustan Times* reported that 'industry' generally approved.[13] The voters' reaction ratified the action: Mrs Gandhi triumphed in the state legislature elections held 28–31 May. Congress(I) won a two-thirds majority in five of the nine assemblies and a majority in three. No other party came close. Janata had been repudiated as thoroughly as had the Congress after the Emergency. The Congress(I) Party was Indira Gandhi's creation, and, with its state leaders dependent upon her favour, personalization increased as she set about selecting new chief ministers.[14]

Background to the Constitutional Revolt of 1983

Many elements contributed to the debate over centre–state relations during 1980–5. Thinking in the country about preserving national unity

[10] Limaye, *Janata Party Experiment*, vol. 2, p. 521. Parliament enacted the amendment on 25 January 1980; the President assented to it on 14 April 1980 after ratification.

[11] Shiv Shankar interview with the author.

[12] All reactions from *Times of India*, Bombay, 18 February 1980.

[13] Issues of 19 February 1980 for both newspapers. The *Times of India* also pointed out that Congress majorities in legislatures would be necessary for it to regain a majority in the Rajya Sabha.

[14] The Janata Party, already badly damaged by the divisions of autumn 1979, subsequently fell apart. Jagjivan Ram resigned from the party in late February 1980. The Jana Sangh left the coalition in early April and reconstituted itself as the Bharatiya Janata Party (BJP). The Janata Parliamentary Board on 12 March decided that no party functionary or legislator should take part in day-to-day activities of the RSS. *AR*, 20–26 May 1980, pp. 15467ff.

and the character of federal relations was changing. Many intellectuals and politicians, once strong centralizers, were becoming advocates of decentralization—believing that clamping the pieces of India together actually was forcing them apart. For example, President Sanjiva Reddy said that although local authorities might be 'swayed by unhealthy extraneous considerations ... [a] central authority cannot claim greater competence, wisdom and objectivity or greater immunity from extraneous influence' than states 'governed by popularly elected ministries'.[15] The strength of non-Congress, state-based and regional political parties had grown, partly an unforeseen result of Mrs Gandhi's 1971 delinking of parliamentary and state legislature elections. Also, Janata, when in office, had supported the development of such parties to increase its strength against the Congress.

By 1983 five major states were governed by opposition parties, and Punjab would join them in 1985.[16] Dissident Congressmen were increasingly outspoken. The chief ministers of all parties were discontented because of unfulfilled promises to establish policy and implement programmes through constitutional and sub-constitutional institutions such like the zonal councils, the Finance Commissions, the National Development Council, and the Planning Commission. Institutions such as the presidentially appointed governor increasingly were criticized. (All of which will be discussed in detail in Part VI.) Imposed twenty-three times from 1980 to 1986, President's Rule was bitterly attacked. All the while, accompanying issues such as the transfer of judges and the central government's rejection of the basic structure doctrine fed suspicions about its intentions toward federal issues.

The situations in Punjab, Jammu and Kashmir, and Assam contributed convincingly to the view that the working of centre–state relations urgently needed fixing and that perhaps the Constitution's distribution of powers should be changed throughout the country.[17] The states'

[15] Lecture on 'Sardar Patel and National Integration' on 31 October 1981 to the Sardar Patel Jayanti Samaroh, New Delhi. *Speeches of President Sanjiva Reddy,* Publications Division, GOI, New Delhi, 1983, pp. 36–7.

[16] The states and parties were: Punjab, Akali Dal; Jammu and Kashmir, National Conference; Bengal, CPM; Tamil Nadu, AIADMK; Andhra Pradesh, Telugu Desam; and Karnataka, Janata.

[17] The narrative in these paragraphs has been drawn in part from the following sources: Dua, 'India: Federal Leadership and Secessionist Movements on the Periphery', in Roy, Ramashray and Sission, Richard (eds), *Diversity and Dominance in Indian Politics,* vol. 2, Sage Publications, New Delhi, 1990; Arora, Balveer, 'India's Federal System and the Demands of Pluralism: Crisis and Reform in the Eighties', in Chaudhurie, Joyotpaul,

location on India's frontiers put them in a category of their own, making it vital that the Government of India, as the successor to British sovereignty, should be seen to be in control. All three had been profoundly affected by the Partition, including actual division of Punjab and Jammu and Kashmir and massive transfers of population in Assam and the Punjab. All had been affected by wars: the India–China war of 1962, and the India–Pakistan wars of 1965 and 1971. All were rife with internal factions, each drawing nourishment from religious, linguistic, tribal, economic, and sub-national differences. These interest and identity groups conflicted with each other, with the state governments, with neighbouring states, and with New Delhi. They also involved other countries. Sikh extremists in the Punjab and Muslim extremists in Kashmir looked to Pakistan for support, and Islamabad was not loath to capitalize on India's internal troubles. Tribals in the Northeast looked to China and, to a lesser degree, toward Burma.[18]

(ed.), *India's Beleaguered Federalism: The Pluralist Challenge,* Center For Asian Studies, Arizona State University, 1992; Mukarji and Arora, *Federalism in India;* Weiner, *Sons of the Soil;* Kapur, *Sikh Separatism;* Bhattacharjea, *Kashmir;* and Hazarika, *Strangers in the Mist.*

[18] The complex, if not tortured, history of these states must here, regrettably, be reduced to a footnote. Assam at independence had been the only state in the northeast, its neighbour, the Northeast Frontier Agency, being a tribal area directly administered by the Government of India. This in 1971 became the state of Arunachal Pradesh. Assam was divided into Assam, Nagaland (1960 to 1962, Article 371A), and later the states of Mizoram and Meghalaya. The influx into these areas of Bangladeshis, other Indians, and the consequent disputes over agricultural land and the use of the Bengali and Assamese languages led to riots and killing.

In Jammu and Kashmir, the Hindu Maharaja, with his predominantly Muslim subjects in the Kashmir Valley, had 'acceded' to India under threat from Muslim tribesmen sent by Pakistan. The Maharaja was supported by the popular leader, Sheikh Mohammed Abdullah. Article 370 allowed the state to frame its own constitution, but the central government over the years whittled away its special status. Sheikh Abdullah was preventively detained in 1953 for resisting this. He later returned to politics.

In Punjab, the Sikhs, accustomed to a comparatively privileged position under the British and led by Master Tara Singh, had called in 1948 for a Sikh province—language and religion being the justifications. After largely non-violent agitation, but threats of fasts unto death, the state was divided in 1966 into the states of Punjab and Haryana. The faction-bedevilled Sikh party, the Akali Dal, in October 1973 adopted the Anandpur Sahib Resolution, whose elements included limiting central 'intervention' in the state's affairs to defence, foreign affairs, railways, and several other items. 'Anandpur Sahib Resolution', pamphlet by the Indian Council for Sikh Affairs, New Delhi, 1985.

The text of the resolution became the subject of debate and confusion due to the factionalism, and in 1982 the Akali Dal president, Harcharan Singh Longowal, issued an authenticated version. Kapur, *Sikh Separatism,* p. 219.

The Anandpur Sahib Resolution also called for safeguarding the interests of Sikhs

New Delhi's involvement in the affairs of these states had ranged from attempts to preserve order and foster the economic development that might ease local discontents, to arranging compromises and reconciliations, to manipulating their internal affairs for the intended advantage of the central government and the Congress Party. Efforts to preserve order frequently aroused as much violence as they quelled. These elements would become increasingly evident during 1980 and the years following, contributing to the conviction in opposition—and other—states that New Delhi's overcentralization of power menaced their governments.

It was in the Punjab with Mrs Gandhi's return that central government actions produced their most harmful effects. The dismissal of the nine state governments included the one in the Punjab, which had established a degree of stability and communal harmony there, the Akali–Janata coalition led by Chief Minister Prakash Singh Badal. Mrs Gandhi, acting through son Sanjay and Giani Zail Singh already had become engaged in an even more dangerous tactic, abetting the rise of the religious extremist Jarnail Singh Bhindranwale in an attempt to rule the Punjab by setting its factions against each other.[19] Murder of Hindus and Sikhs became rampant as Sikh factions outbid each other with demands on the centre to implement the Anandpur Sahib Resolution or more separatist arrangements. Two and one-half years of off again, on again negotiations began.[20]

In Kashmir, having won the 1977 elections (described by some as the fairest in the state's history), Sheikh Abdullah fought the rise of extremist Islam fostered by events in Iran and accused New Delhi of provoking confrontation with his government. He died in September 1982 to be

---

outside Punjab; made the promise that the Akali Dal would 'also try that the Indian Constitution becomes federal in the real sense and all states are equally represented at the Centre'.

   [19] Malhotra, *Indira Gandhi,* p. 257; Jayakar, *Indira Gandhi,* pp. 461ff. Zail Singh goes to some lengths to rebut this charge without ever denying it clearly. Singh, Zail, *Memoirs,* pp. 289ff. Before becoming Home Minister under Mrs Gandhi in 1980, Zail Singh, an adherent of Mrs Gandhi since the Congress split in 1969, had been president of the Punjab PCC and chief minister of the state from 1972–77. He later became the President of India.

   Singh characterizes Sanjay Gandhi as shrewd and intelligent, 'but over-ambitious', helpful to those he liked, 'but if angry, he would know no limits of harm he could inflict on his adversaries'. Ibid., p. 134.

   'Giani' is an honorific title given to an individual able to teach about Sikhism and to expound on the Sikhs' holy book, the *Granth Sahib.*

   [20] It would be 'unfair' to blame Mrs Gandhi for allowing the Punjab to burn in order to serve her own interests, believed Inder Malhotra, but 'she was slow to negotiate' and her handling of the crisis 'was doubtless inept'. Malhotra, *Indira Gandhi,* p. 260.

replaced as chief minister and leader of the National Conference Party by his son, Farooq Abdullah. When, a year after his father's death, Farooq joined other chief ministers in urging review of the conduct of centre–state relations, the Prime Minister set about removing him from office. (See section of this chapter beginning below.)

In Assam, the All Assam Students Union declared and later withdrew 'direct action' over the 'foreigners' issue in response to Mrs Gandhi's negotiations and her release of detenus. The February 1983 elections there brought the Congress(I) a two-thirds majority in the legislature but at the price of pre-election violence that killed some one thousand persons and left ten times that number homeless. Assamese Hindu peasants killed Muslim immigrants and tribals, the Muslims reciprocated, and Bodo tribals killed both Hindus and Muslims. Luhang tribals hacked to death women and children in the village of Nellie. The Intelligence Bureau had warned the Prime Minister of likely violence, but she refused to heed the advice in the wake of Congress election defeats in the South.[21]

The Constitutional Revolt

The election defeats that had so upset the Prime Minister took place in Andhra and Karnataka on 5 January 1983. In Andhra Pradesh, her Congress lost control of the assembly to the Telugu Desam Party and its leader, N. T. Rama Rao. In Karnataka, Congress lost control of the assembly—for the first time since 1950—to the Janata Party led by Ramakrishna Hegde. These losses particularly hurt Mrs Gandhi because she had placed election strategy and tactics in the hands of Rajiv Gandhi and a young Rajya Sabha member, Arun Nehru—'"political illiterates"', senior journalist Prem Bhatia called them.[22]

It did not take long for the southern election victories further to annoy New Delhi. Ramakrishna Hegde inspired a meeting in Bangalore of four southern chief ministers that initiated a process during which both the conduct of centre–state relations under the Constitution and the distribution of powers in the Constitution, itself, would be challenged.

---

[21] Jayakar, *Indira Gandhi*, p. 449. The Election Commission, under Commissioner S. L. Shakdher, 'had clearly told the government on many occasions that the situation in Assam was not ideal' for holding elections and it was conducting them 'only because the state administration insisted that polling could be organized'. *AR*, 18–24 June 1983, p. 17229.

[22] Cited in Jayakar, *Indira Gandhi*, p. 446. Adding insult to injury, the Congress(I) candidate in an Uttar Pradesh by-election was defeated by one backed by Maneka Gandhi, Sanjay Gandhi's widow, now estranged from her mother-in-law. Malhotra, *Indira Gandhi*,). 298.

Attending the meeting on 20 March 1983 were Hegde, M. G. Ramachandran of Tamil Nadu, Rama Rao of Andhra, and D. Ramachandran, chief minister of the union territory of Pondicherry. K. Karunakaran, Congress chief minister of Kerala, was absent and was reported to have labelled the meeting seditious.[23] Hegde announced that the intention of the meeting was not confrontational, but was designed to strengthen the centre and unity. '"It is not a conspiracy against anyone."'[24] Hegde hoped that all chief ministers would join a council, so that they could settle their problems at their own level.[25] The four chief ministers unanimously decided to form a council of southern chief ministers which was not intended to be a forum to confront the centre and which would lessen the centre's burdens.[26] Mrs Gandhi almost certainly was affronted by the chief ministers' temerity in meeting and by their recommendations. These included the formation of a commission, with adequate state representation, to review fiscal relations between New Delhi and the states and to recommend remedial legislation and constitutional changes—possibly including an increase of the states' share of excise duties and monies from a surcharge to be placed on income tax revenues (both of which were collected by the central government).[27] Taking defensive action, Mrs Gandhi four days later announced that a commission on centre–state relations would be established.

This was the Sarkaria Commission, so called after its chairman, Justice Ranjit Singh Sarkaria.[28] Mrs Gandhi had invited Justice Sarkaria—the first Sikh to serve on the Supreme Court—from his retirement in Chandigarh and told him in 'a bolt out of the blue' that she wanted a study of centre–state relations and would he assume the task. At their meeting, she handed Justice Sarkaria a note about such a commission prepared by her staff and told him that she had to make a statement 'tomorrow in Parliament'.[29] Finding that the note said that the study was to be conducted 'within the Constitution', Sarkaria objected that this would be seen as 'insincere, as desiring that nothing happen'. The study must be able to touch the 'framework' of the Constitution, he added.

[23] *Economic and Political Weekly*, vol. 7, no. 13, 26 March 1983, p. 478.

[24] *Deccan Herald*, 20 March 1983.

[25] *AR*, 14–20 May 1983, p. 17171.

[26] Ibid.

[27] Ibid.

[28] Its official name was the Commission on Centre–State Relations. It submitted its two-volume report, published by the Government of India Press in January 1988. See Part VI.

[29] Justice R. S. Sarkaria in an interview with the author.

Mrs Gandhi responded that the note did not constitute the commission's terms of reference, which he could help draft. Sarkaria also said that he wanted five other members for the commission, some from the South, others with specialities in finance and administration. Mrs. Gandhi agreed,[30] and announced the commission and Sarkaria's chairmanship of it to Parliament. Nothing more happened for two months. The official 'Notification' of the commission was issued on 9 June, but the government made the terms of reference public only on 7 July. The commission was cut to three, and Sarkaria's two colleagues were inducted that day: B. Sivaraman, a former cabinet secretary and member of the Indian Civil Service, and S. R. Sen, an historian and economist, earlier member of the Planning Commission, and sometime official of the World Bank. Sarkaria later failed to gain the services of the long-time member-secretary of the Law Commission, P. M. Bakshi.

What was not said during the Prime Minister's meeting with Sarkaria was as important as what was said. The southern chief ministers—beyond their complaints about centre–state relations—represented the increasing importance of regional political parties. They challenged Mrs Gandhi and her party's power, which may have awakened memories of attempts by earlier southern chief ministers, those within the Syndicate, to control her.[31] The Sarkaria Commission was set up to contain their challenge.[32] Mrs Gandhi also seems to have hoped that the commission's formation, and especially Sarkaria's chairmanship of it, would bolster her position in the Punjab. But when the Akalis did not channel their complaints about centre–state relations to the commission, the Prime Minister 'maybe thought of backing off the commission'.[33] Her lack of enthusiasm for the commission was evident from its start-up difficulties—work began in February 1984, ten months after her announcement of the commission— and in the reluctance of Congress state governments to cooperate with it.

Two months after Mrs Gandhi announced the formation of the Sarkaria Commission, on 28 May, fourteen opposition parties assembled at Vijayawada. Chief Minister N. T. Rama Rao read the meeting's statement, which said that a new '"political brotherhood"' was needed to preserve national unity from '"the failure of the ruling party at the Centre

[30] Ibid.
[31] B. Sivaraman in an interview with the author. Three of the Syndicate were southerners: Kamaraj, Sanjiva Reddy, and S. Nijalingappa. S. K. Patil was from Bombay and Atulya Ghosh was from Bengal. None were from the North.
[32] Margaret Alva in an interview with the author.
[33] R. S. Sarkaria in an interview with the author.

to find timely and acceptable solutions"' to the urgent problems of the country and its different areas.[34] The statement also demanded the establishment of a fiscal commission, and said that the Congress(I) was undermining democratic institutions. The *Deccan Herald* reporter thought this a 'tame finale', indicating a failure to reach consensus in what had been billed as an 'unprecedented meeting'.[35]

A week after this, the National Conference, led by Farooq Abdullah, won forty-six seats to Congress's twenty-six in Jammu and Kashmir's seventy-six seat legislative assembly.[36] But Farooq challenged the Prime Minister further. Not only had he attended the Vijayawada meeting, he hosted the next meeting of non-Congress chief ministers in Srinagar between 5 and 7 October to discuss centre–state relations. The group's statement, among other things, said that the 'unitary features [of the Constitution] have increasingly come to overshadow its federal features', and it recommended amending or deleting many of the Constitution's federal articles.[37]

Apparently in response, the AICC at its meeting two weeks later accused Farooq's National Conference of '"manipulating the polls"' and of '"befriending ... communal and secessionist forces"'.[38] The AICC's Political Resolution went on to speak of the threat to the country from external forces and the need for a strong central government. Beyond deploring the situations in Kashmir, Assam, and the Punjab, the resolution did not mention centre–state relations. Later in the year, Kashmir Governor, B. K. Nehru, the Prime Minister's cousin, resisted her strategem of arranging defections from the National Conference so Farooq would lose his majority and could be replaced by someone more to her liking. But in February 1984, Nehru was transferred to Gujarat as governor. He was replaced by Jagmohan, and on 2 July Farooq was dismissed from office on the ground that he had lost his majority in the legislature.[39]

---

[34] *Times of India*, Bombay, 29 May 1983.

[35] Issue of 29 May 1983. Those present were not the Prime Minister's friends. Among them were Jagjivan Ram, L. K. Advani, H. N. Bahuguna, Maneka Gandhi, S. S. Barnala, S. S. Khera, Sharad Pawar, K. P. Unnikrishnan, and Basavupunaiah.

[36] *AR*, 9–15 July 1983, pp. 17258–9.

[37] 'Statement on Centre–State Relations released at Srinagar on 8 October 1983'. A pamphlet with this title published by Government of West Bengal, Calcutta, no date, pp. 3ff. The CPM Chief Minister Jyoti Basu, who long had opposed Mrs Gandhi's centralization of power, wrote the foreword to the pamphlet.

[38] *AR*, 19–25 November 1983, p. 17467. Mrs Gandhi later told George Verghese, once her press adviser, and Inder Malhotra that Farooq had allowed '"anti-national forces"' to be encouraged to an extent that was intolerable. Malhotra, *Indira Gandhi*, p. 295.

[39] Malhotra, *Indira Gandhi*, pp. 295–6; Jayakar, *Indira Gandhi*, p. 459.

Two chief ministers, Ramakrishna Hegde of Karnataka and Jyoti Basu of West Bengal, were the driving intellectual, as well as political, force behind the opposition leaders' reassessments. At the Bangalore and Vijayawada meetings, the positions were couched generally, directed at New Delhi's encroachment on the states' powers and mentioning, particularly, the need for the National Development Council and the Planning Commission to work co-operatively with the states instead of operating largely by central direction. The meetings called for establishing a fiscal commission and a thorough review of centre–state economic and fiscal relations.

By the time of the Srinagar meeting in October 1983, the discontents and recommendations were phrased quite specifically. Some ten articles of the Constitution were targetted for revision or deletion: President's Rule was to be curbed; the states' powers *vis-à-vis* the State Legislative List were to be supreme; residual powers were to be for the states not the Centre; central power to take over a state government in time of financial instability (Article 360 in the Emergency Provisions) was to be removed; and the content of the legislative lists should be reviewed. The meeting placed great emphasis on forming an Interstate Council (Article 263). Economic and fiscal issues were treated in detail. And, the meeting's 'Statement' said that there should be no central armed force deployed in a state nor should a state be declared a 'disturbed area' without the state government's prior concurrence.[40] The recommendations generated during the 'revolt' wrought no immediate changes in the conduct of centre–state relations, but they strongly influenced the conclusions of the Sarkaria Commission.[41]

[40] 'Statement on Centre–State Relations Released at Srinagar on 8 October 1983'. See footnote 37 above. The statement appeared in other publications.

[41] The Srinagar statement drew heavily on the work of a seminar composed of professionals—retired senior civil servants, academics, and legal and political commentators—that Hegde had convened on his own initiative at Bangalore the previous August. Its recommendations included establishing the Interstate Council; making more precise the conditions under which President's Rule might be proclaimed, and restricting the centre's powers under Articles 256 and 257 (which made the authority of state executive branches subordinate to central authority); curbing the powers of governors; freeing the electronic media from central government control; and building grassroots participation, in part by inserting in the Constitution a provision 'to ensure ... elections to local bodies'. *Seminar on Centre–State Relations, Bangalore, August 5–7, 1983: Papers, Group Reports and Conclusions*, Government of Karnataka, Bangalore, 1984; quotation from p. 314.

In addition to Hegde, the seminar was attended, among others, by V. K. R. V. Rao, Raja Chelliah, S. Guhan, Nirmal Mukarji, A. G. Noorani, N. A. Palkhivala, and H. K. Paranjpe. Hegde later delivered before the Karnataka Assembly his 'White Paper on the Office

Pathway to Death

Nineteen eighty-four was a year for George Orwell's imagination, marked by more manipulative politics, catastrophic military action, and murder. Mrs Gandhi and the Constitution became progressively separated. In Kashmir on 2 July, Governor Jagmohan, who was a tough administrator closely associated with Sanjay Gandhi's 'clean-up' of Delhi during the Emergency, invited Ghulam Mohammad Shah to form a government. Jagmohan rejected both Farooq's demand to be allowed to test his strength in the legislature and his advice to call elections—the latter on the ground that Farooq, having lost his majority, could not advise the calling of elections. Farooq characterized this as undemocratic and reminiscent of events in 1953, when his father had been dismissed.[42] The chief ministers of Andhra, Karnataka, West Bengal, and Tripura walked out of a 12 July chief ministers' meeting to protest Farooq's dismissal. Several publications strongly criticized Jagmohan's actions. He had 'flouted gubernatorial convention and the state's Constitution in his anxiety to further the centre's political objectives', said the *Statesman*. The 'defections' from the National Conference could not serve as a 'fig-leaf' for the 'scenario worked out during Jagmohan's visit to Delhi last week', wrote the *Economic and Political Weekly*. The *Indian Express* saw 'dubious propriety' undermining 'federal relationships'; Jagmohan's actions had elevated 'the governor to the position of a viceroy', said the paper.[43]

---

of Governor', which was published under that title by the government of Karnataka in September or October 1983. A. G. Noorani was said to have had a hand in drafting the White Paper.

[42] For details, see Bhattacharjea, *Kashmir*, pp. 246–9 and *AR* 26 August–1 September 1984, pp. 17906ff.

On 28 July the Jammu and Kashmir government released a White Paper on the events. Three days earlier Home Minister P. V. Narasimha Rao told the Rajya Sabha that in Kashmir '"certain elements had been indulging in anti-national secessionist activities since the latter half of 1983"'. Ibid., p. 17910. Mrs Gandhi had wanted Farooq 'to be sent packing for a long time'. Malhotra, *Indira Gandhi*, p. 295.

For a chilling account of intrigue in Srinagar and of Mrs Gandhi's campaign against Farooq (including a rebuttal of the charges that Farooq was secessionist), see Nehru, *Nice Guys Finish Second*, pp. 611ff. Nehru was the governor of Jammu and Kashmir at the time.

[43] Cited in Bhattacharjea, *Kashmir*, p. 299. See also Sorabjee et al., *The Governor: Sage or Saboteur*, Roli Books International, New Delhi, 1985, pp. 131ff for an account of the Farooq–Shah–Jagmohan affair.

Jagmohan viewed the situation differently: Jagmohan, *My Frozen Turbulence in Kashmir*, Allied Publishers, New Delhi, 1991, ch. VII, especially.

The government of India intervened in the affairs of Andhra Pradesh that August in an even clumsier fashion. While one of the leaders at opposition meetings, the popular Chief Minister N. T. Rama Rao, was in the United States for medical treatment, efforts to remove him began. Governor Ram Lal dismissed him two days after his return to Hyderabad and swore in as chief minister N. Bhaskara Rao, who had defected from the Congress to Rama Rao's Telugu Desam Party and then re-defected to the Congress(I). Negative reaction was immediate and widespread. Mrs Gandhi said she had not heard of the dismissal beforehand (and there is some evidence that Arun Nehru arranged the affair without her knowledge), but she was not believed. Rama Rao offered to prove his majority in the legislature, was ordered arrested by the governor, along with his supporters, only to be freed a few days later. He then flew to New Delhi with 161 assembly members—of the 294-member assembly—and called on President Zail Singh with them to demonstrate his majority. Shortly thereafter, he was reinstated as chief minister and somewhat later Ram Lal was relieved as governor.[44]

Meanwhile, Punjab became exceedingly tense as the killings of civilians—both Sikhs and Hindus—continued. The Akali Dal began a new agitation, including against Article 25 of the Constitution, which included Sikhs as Hindus in matters of freedom of religion.[45] Negotiations between the government and the Akalis resumed, with the government unwilling to meet Sikh demands, which, as presented by various factions, greatly varied. The President promulgated on 5 April the ordinance strengthening the National Security Act, as mentioned earlier, with its provisions that the maximum period of preventive detention could be two years and that detention without the decision of an advisory board

[44] For accounts of this affair, see Malhotra, *Indira Gandhi*, pp. 299ff; Jayakar, *Indira Gandhi*, p. 460; and Sorabjee et al., *Sage or Saboteur*, pp. 106ff. For a detailed chronicle of events, with supporting information, see 'White Paper on the Toppling of State Governments', Janata Party, New Delhi, September 1984, pp. 29–40.

The affair attracted comment outside India. The *Economist* wrote that Mrs Gandhi ' "has always viewed India's opposition as an unnecessary evil ... but ... even a fragmented opposition evidently posed an unacceptable risk ... so ... she set out to smite all centres of opposition power" ', starting with Sikkim and moving on to Punjab, Kashmir, and Andhra Pradesh. Cited in Jayakar, *Indira Gandhi*, p. 460.

[45] Article 25 says that subject to public order, morality, etc., the practice of religion is free. But government may regulate the economic and other secular activities associated with religious practice and may provide for social welfare and reform and for opening Hindu religious institutions to all classes and sections of Hindus. Sikhs (and Jains and Buddhists) are, for the purposes of this article, classed as Hindus. The article also provides that the wearing of *kirpans* is to be included 'in the profession of the Sikh religion'.

could extend for six months.[46] Amid plentiful signs that drastic action was imminent, the Government of India on 2 June used the army to seal off the Punjab from the rest of the country and to deploy tanks around the Golden Temple in Amritsar, which Jarnail Singh Bhindranwale had been fortifying and using as a safe-haven for Sikh extremists. Speaking that evening on radio and television, Mrs Gandhi said her heart had 'been heavy with sorrow' at developments, at the fruitless attempts to negotiate, and at the escalating demands and violence on the part of the Akalis.[47]

On 5 June, in Operation Bluestar, the army, led by Sikh and Hindu officers, entered the temple. Bhindranwale was killed, and 'substantial quantities' of arms, ammunition, and a grenade factory were discovered there.[48] Sikhs throughout the country were outraged at the sacrilege. Their honour had been demeaned and their identity attacked. The Golden Temple was their holiest place—their Kaba, Western Wall, Church of the Holy Sepulcre. They felt the attack and damage to the temple 'a deliberate attempt to humiliate their community', rather than as necessary to curb violence, which few Sikhs publicly condemned. Moreover, Sikhs, and many others, believed that 'Bhindranwale had initially risen to prominence through the support of the ruling Congress Party'.[49] In August, the Lok Sabha, in the Fifty-ninth Amendment to the Constitution, extended President's Rule in the state for one year beyond the forthcoming expiration date of 5 October. In late September, the army handed back control of the Golden Temple to the Shiromani Gurdwara Prabhandak Committee.

Speaking in Parliament on the government's 'White Paper on the Punjab' at the end of July 1984, Mrs Gandhi asked why 'powerful forces in the world' are attacking me? Concluding a lengthy description of her government's policies, she said that 'we have ... to remove the cause for grievances ... The battle for secularism, the battle for unity ... must be [won] in the hearts and minds of our people'.[50]

---

[46] This was promulgated while the Lok Sabha was in session, with the justification that because the Rajya Sabha was not in session, Parliament as a whole was not in session—the condition necessary for the promulgation of ordinances. Law Minister Jagannath Kaushal justified this as necessary given the urgent situation in the Punjab.

[47] Speech over All-India Radio and the government-controlled television network Doordarshan on 2 June 1984. *Indira Gandhi: Speeches and Writings*, vol. 5, pp. 74ff.

[48] Kapur, *Sikh Separatism*, p. 230. Extremists also had used other gurdwaras as secure bases.

[49] Ibid. p. 235. By this time, the head priest had excommunicated President Zail Singh and several other prominent Sikhs.

[50] Nineteen page speech to the Rajya Sabha on 24 July during discussion of the

Proceeding on the path leading from her home to her office on 31 October for an interview with a foreign journalist, the Prime Minister was shot to death by two of her security guards, sub-inspector Beant Singh, a member of her bodyguard for nine years, and constable Satwant Singh, both Sikhs. Beant Singh was killed a few minutes after the assassination, reportedly during a scuffle as he tried to escape. Satwant Singh, although wounded, survived, to be tried and then hanged in January 1989. Practising the secularism she preached, Indira Gandhi had refused to exchange her Sikh police security guards for non-Sikhs or for security provided by the army despite the advice of Defence Minister R. Venkataraman. The army in a democracy, she told him, 'should be kept "well out of such matters"'.[51]

That evening, President Giani Zail Singh swore in son Rajiv Gandhi as Prime Minister without waiting for the Congress Parliamentary Party to elect him its leader, an unprecedented action.[52] For three days thereafter, anti-Sikh riots in New Delhi, particularly, allegedly abetted by members of the Congress(I) Party, killed at least two thousand Sikhs and made some ten thousand homeless.

With Rajiv Gandhi presiding, the All-India Congress Committee adopted a resolution of homage to Mrs Gandhi, 'this great maker of History'. The resolution recalled her defences of India's 'honour and integrity', of 'democracy and secularism'. It praised her strengthening the nation's 'economic fibre' and her grand strategy 'for the alleviation of rural and urban poverty'. For her, the resolution said, 'victory and defeat were unimportant'; what had mattered was functioning 'according to the great principles and values of our organization'. From each crisis, she led the party 'as a better instrument for social transformation'. Concluding, the resolution said, 'she filled our lives with joy and beauty and dignity'.[53]

---

government's 'White Paper on Punjab'. *Indira Gandhi: Speeches and Writings*, vol. 5, pp. 78, 97.

[51] Among the many descriptions of the scene, see Jayakar, *Indira Gandhi*, pp. 485–6. For Venkataraman's advice, see Malhotra, *Indira Gandhi*, p. 303.

[52] In the parliamentary elections held between 24–28 December 1984, the Congress (I), led by Rajiv Gandhi, won 401 of the 495 seats contested. The party coming nearest to this was the CPM with twenty-two seats. Maneka Gandhi, Sanjay Gandhi's widow, lost her deposit, and Shiv Shankar and other Congressmen lost.

[53] Zaidi, *The Encyclopaedia of the Indian National Congress*, vol. 26, pp. 103ff. Resolution adopted 7 May 1985 in New Delhi.

Prime Minister Rajiv Gandhi resumed negotiations with the Akalis during 1985 and, even as Sikh terrorism resumed, reached an agreement in secret meetings with Sant Harcharan Singh Longowal, who had become head of the Akali Dal in May. On 24 July,

No explanation can erase the dastardliness of Indira Gandhi's murder. It was a catastrophe for family and nation. Yet she died for deeper reasons than two Sikhs' vengeance and bullets. In the Punjab, the Prime Minister and her party had been dealing with Sikh desires that were a mixture of the reasonable, difficult to satisfy under the best of circumstances, utterly unrealistic, and absurdly conflicting—the products of factions' and leaders' competing for dominance within their community. The most sensitive and accommodating government in New Delhi would have been bemused by these. The central government and the Congress were not bemused. They took the opportunity to manipulate Punjab politics, intending to rule by using and encouraging factions. Mrs Gandhi had the President in 1980 dismiss the Akali Dal–Janata coalition government, under which a degree of calm had returned to the state. She, her Home Minister, and son Sanjay then supported Bhindranwale until, like the sorcerer in the tale, they lost control of their apprentice. In Jammu and Kashmir, Congress had meddled in affairs long before dismissing Farooq on spurious charges. There and in Andhra Pradesh, party and central government had smeared the chief minister as anti-national, when it was they whose actions were both anti-democratic and damaging to national integrity.

These were but the most recent actions in a series, which originated soon after she took office in 1966, indicating that Mrs Gandhi believed the prime ministry and the leadership of the Congress Party to be her personal right. As has been seen, she split the Congress Party in 1969 and 1979 to preserve her control over it. She superseded three Supreme Court judges in 1973—so that Hegde, who had ruled against her in her election case, would not rise to the chief justiceship—and another judge in 1977. She amended the Constitution twice—the Thirty-ninth and Forty-second Amendments—to protect herself against prosecution for election campaign offences. The same purpose caused her to intimidate President Fakhruddin Ali Ahmad into declaring her Emergency in June 1975. To prevent challenges to her authority, between 1971 and 1977 and 1980 and 1984 she reduced to serfdom all but a few democratic stalwarts in Parliament and party. Her style in government, according to ministers

---

Rajiv Gandhi announced to Parliament that they had signed a memorandum of settlement, bringing, in his words, an end to '"confrontation"' and ushering in '"an era of amity, goodwill and co-operation ... [to] promote and strengthen the unity and integrity of India"'. *AR*, 13–19 August 1985, p. 18458. The text of the 'Gandhi–Longowal Memorandum' is given on this and succeeding pages of *AR*.

Three weeks later, on 20 August, two Sikh youths assassinated Longowal. Much of the Punjab remained a battleground for eight more years.

and officials working with her, typically was arbitrary and secretive.

A degree of ruthlessness is necessary for a political leader to be great, an ability to instill fear as well as respect and admiration in ministers, officials, and members of the legislature. Otherwise, the leader is apt to be led. But in a great leader, these characteristics will be accompanied by sensitivity to the national ethos, to the aspirations and rules laid down in the country's foundation document. Had Mrs Gandhi understood this, she neither would have imposed her Emergency in the first place nor called the elections of 1977 in the expectation that her transgressions against democracy would be rewarded by victory. She allowed Parliament to give the non-justiciable Directive Principles primacy over the justiciable Fundamental Rights, and she several times told associates—including S. S. Ray in June 1975—that she knew nothing of the Constitution. She was insensitive to the leaders and peoples of the constituent units of the country who wished to share in governance, to row their own boat in collaboration with the centre. In sum, she lacked awareness of the federal and democratic principles given life through accommodation. Her, and the Congress Party's, use of President's Rule for party purposes is the most unconstitutional example of this.

By the mid-eighties, the politician fabled for astute political manoeuvring among allies and opponents and skilled at associating herself with the people's longings for a better life seemed to have lost touch with reality. If for a decade and a half you are surrounded by courtiers who tell you that India is you and you are India; if you are brilliantly victorious in politics and in war (as in 1971); if you then succeed in making Parliament your creature; if you manipulate your own council of ministers and the nation by imposing a state of emergency, ostensibly to protect national unity and advance social reform, but actually to retain your office; and if, after ruling autocratically, you can return to office, acclaimed by the very voters who had rejected you, then your hubris can be understood. If you then plan for your sons, one of them devotedly contemptuous of civil liberty, to follow you as prime minister, then your hubris is confirmed.

Mrs Gandhi had asked in the Lok Sabha why 'powerful forces' in the world were attacking her. She did not understand, apparently, that her hand was turned against herself. Although she told close associates during the eighties that she had thought about her death, she behaved with exalted indifference—or like one who believed herself fated to die martyred in the nation's service.

These were at once the causes and the symptoms of government and politics for oneself. Mrs Gandhi was killed horribly, but she died from the personalization of power.

Part VI

THE INSEPARABLE TWINS: NATIONAL UNITY AND INTEGRITY AND THE MACHINERY OF FEDERAL RELATIONS

National integration cannot be built by brick and mortar, by chisel and hammer. It has to grow silently in the minds and hearts of men.

National Integration Conference[1]

We have a full and detailed Constitution ... [but] it depends ultimately on the people ... and more especially on those in positions of responsibility .... Thus, the element of co-operation, of seeking friendly counsel with each other and of ever keeping the larger end in view, are of paramount importance.

Jawaharlal Nehru[2]

[1] 'Statement Issued by the National Integration Conference', held between 28 September and 1 October 1961. Ministry of Information and Broadcasting, GOI, New Delhi, 1961, p. 4.

[2] Prime Minister Nehru's letter to the chief ministers on 15 April 1952. *NLTCM*, vol. 2, p. 578.

Chapter 27

TERMINOLOGY AND ITS PERILS

'Federalism' is an idea and a set of practices, the variety of which depends upon the goals of the citizenry and its leaders, the consequent definition of the term, and the conditions present in the would-be federation. This portion of the book gathers together the themes and issues on these topics from previous chapters to explore how ideas, intentions, and practices under the Constitution have combined in the working of the country's particular variety of federalism.

The three strands of the seamless web each were vital to the success over time of the Indian national enterprise. Grave inattention to, or excess in the pursuit of, any strand would risk the web's integrity. Having said this, it should be understood that the political leadership and aware citizens placed special emphasis on the national unity and integrity strand. Slow progress toward social revolution and more effective democracy could be tolerated for a time, but if national unity and integrity were lost all else would be lost. Aggravated relations between the central and state governments could lead to disunity. There would, or could, be no 'India'. On the other hand, greater unity and cohesion among the constituent political units and within society were likely to facilitate progress toward social revolution and greater democracy. As one of India's great figures, and at the time Home Minister, Pandit G. B. Pant, put it, 'the task before us is national unity and economic reconstruction'.[1]

Yet, favoured status for unity over the social revolution and democracy strands of the web, even if temporary, had a risky side. It could be diversionary, distracting attention from domestic woes, an excuse for exaggerated and unnecessary centralization of governmental and personal power. For all these reasons, no other issue has so greatly and persistently commanded public attention since 1950.

---

[1] In a speech to the Western Zonal Council meeting in 1957. *AR,* 21–27 September 1957, p. 1651.

Pant also believed that 'a catholicity of outlook has been the hallmark of Indian civilization'—in a speech to Allahabad University students in December 1955, published as *Be Good So That You May Be Great,* Indian National Congress, New Delhi, 1956, p. 7.

But how were the words 'unity and integrity' to be defined? Upon their interpretation depended one's assessment of the condition of the country at any particular moment. Appropriate policies should follow from the assessment, devised within the framework of the Constitution. But this would necessitate a second lot of definitions, this time of the 'federal' provisions of the Constitution, for the provisions of any great, basic document raise questions of interpretation—which rarely are permanently settled. Policies and their implementation at all levels of government, and the conduct of political parties and other political actors correspondingly would be affected, thus producing the 'federalism' as practised under the Constitution. This chapter will consider the definitions given to the words 'unity and integrity' and to 'federalism' and then proceed with an overview of the phases through which centre–state relations have gone during the period of this book. Succeeding chapters will deal in detail with the provisions of the Constitution that most agitated relations between New Delhi and state capitals and the problems of definition from which they arose. Readers kindly will tolerate what seems to be the desirable degree of repetition in this attempt to bring together earlier portions of this book.

Definitions and Their Uses

The words unity and integrity were susceptible to multiple interpretations. Did they mean preserving the frontiers as they were at independence, unbreached by external invasion or internally from secession by constituent states? Did the words mean preservation of the constituent states as they were in 1950? Or might they be constitutionally divided and reassembled—as they would be by the States Reorganization Act of 1956? 'Balkanization' into a number of countries or nations within the 1947 frontiers would be the opposite of this. Did the words allow for competition among the constituent states and between them and the central government over the management of and benefits from natural resources and over the collection and distribution of revenues? What if such economic and social revolutionary competition were clothed in regional and local identities such as language, culture, or religion? Did the words mean that citizens must feel a sense of 'Indianness', to the exclusion of any loyalties to region, language group, caste, or clan? In other words, did the various elements within society have to become homogenized—really melted in the melting pot—for unity and integrity to be thought, first, genuine, and then secure?

Indians have asked themselves each of these questions at one time or another and have given many answers. For some, true and viable unity and integrity equated with what may be called civic responsibility. President S. Radhakrishnan, for example, thought that unruly behaviour in legislatures, factions, caste disputes, political rivalries, and '"petty considerations"' raised '"doubts about the stability of a united, democratic India"'.[2] Others focused on 'sub-nationalisms'. The variety of the country's groupings, reported the Sarkaria Commission, 'promote[s] sub-nationalism in a manner that tends to strengthen divisive forces and weaken the unity and integrity of the country'.[3] L. K. Advani said that the founding fathers and he believed that India was one nation and that if the country's many 'ethnic' and 'linguistic' groupings were thought of as nations, the country's unity would not survive.[4]

For most persons, within and outside government, the gravest danger to unity and integrity came from four 'isms': casteism, communalism, linguism, and provincialism/regionalism. Frequently, these were treated as a compound named 'communalism'. The antidote to, and the cure for, communalism was yet a sixth 'ism', 'secularism'. This desirable condition of society was understood to mean a low level of consciousness of or partisanship in one's own 'community', and consequent tolerance of other 'communities'. Thus it was much broader than Hindu–Muslim amity, of which 'communalism', by another definition, was the antithesis.

For example, Prime Minister Nehru admonished the chief ministers in 1952 that 'the Congress by tradition and historic necessity stood for the unity of the country, anti-communalism and fought against disintegrating tendencies'.[5] He devoted six pages of a 'Dear Comrade' letter addressed to fellow Congress Party leaders to the forces 'which tend to disintegrate and weaken' our otherwise 'well-knit country'. The word 'secular', he wrote, meant more than the 'free play of all religions ...

[2] His farewell speech as President, in which he also was critical of the government's administrative performance, delivered on 25 January 1967. *AR*, 12–18 February 1967, pp. 7540ff.

[3] Sarkaria Report, vol. 1, p. 15. The commission added that these groups, initially based on linguistic and religious sentiments, gained strength from 'a blend of economic issues such as those relating to land, water and regional backwardness'.

[4] Text of a speech 'Antidote to Divisive Forces' delivered at a seminar on the presidential system of government in the eighties and published in Sathe, *Two Swords in One Scabbard*, pp. 139–40.

Language—in education, in civil service examinations, and for official use nationally—had been a most divisive issue, but was largely defused by the 1970s. By the nineties, if not before, it had ceased to pose a threat to national unity and integrity.

[5] Letter to chief ministers, 31 January 1952. *NLTCM*, vol. 2, p. 550.

[and] conveys the idea of social and political equality. Thus a caste-ridden society is not properly secular.' 'Communalism means the dominance of one religious community' and is thus 'a negation of nationalism'. This idea of linguistic states, Nehru continued, has some virtue and logic, but it 'may well become a curse if we do not restrain ourselves and do not keep in mind the unity of India'. He concluded: 'We must always keep the ideal of the unity of India and of the political and social equality of her people, to whatever group religion or province they might belong'.[6]

A resolution adopted by the Congress at its 1955 Avadi Session said that 'every separatist tendency' had to be removed. Caste was separatist as well as anti-democratic. 'Provincialism' was a 'narrowing and disruptive factor'.[7] Later leaders echoed these sentiments. Congress President U. N. Dhebar believed that ' "socialism and sectarianism cannot walk hand in hand" '.[8] Congress Party President Sanjiva Reddy said in 1961 that in his travels in the country he had found a 'subtle but strong thread of unity' among the people, but 'our mutual intolerances of each other ... reflected in such complexes as provincialism, linguism, communalism, etc., should be deemed anti-national forces'.[9]

Nehru's inclusive definitions of 'communalism', and of 'secularism' as its remedy, were widely shared, which made their semantic trap all the more insidious. They created more difficulties than they resolved. Going beyond government refraining from the sponsorship of religion (the church–state issue) and a sense of amity among religious faiths, 'secularism' posited a society without the four 'isms', one that, if not homogenous, was close to being freed from the subordinate loyalties that the 'isms' represented. A more accurate term for Nehru to have used would have been 'national integration', as in this part's first superscript, a term he used at the National Integration Council in 1961. Its connotations are those of a process toward the dying away of strong group identities in a society.[10] The reality of the compartmentalization

---

[6] Letter of 8 August 1954. AICC Papers, Second Installment, File Circulars General, 1954, NMML.

[7] Resolutions, Sixtieth Session, Indian National Congress, New Delhi, 1955, pp. 9–10.

[8] At the sixty-fourth party session at Nagpur, 9–11 January 1959. *AR*, 17–23 January 1959, p. 2452.

U. N. Dhebar wrote to Indira Gandhi in a 1951 letter that casteism was at the root of the problem of communalism. Dhebar Papers, Microfilm File 9, Box 1, NMML.

[9] Address to the Sixty-sixth Congress Session, Bhavnagar, 6 January 1961. Indian National Congress, New Delhi, 1961, p. 2.

[10] See Gopal Krishna's thoughtful 'National Integration—A Lost Cause?' in Ramakant (ed.), *Nation-Building in South Asia*, 2 vol., South Asian Publishers, New Delhi, 1991, vol. 1, pp. 109ff.

in Indian society, when set against the ideal of national unity (defined mistakenly as national integration), made anxieties for unity inevitable. An unrealistic definition evoked unwarranted fears. National unity and integrity existed, although national integration did not. The reality of the years since 1950 has been that the 'isms', with few exceptions, have co-habited successfully. They have not endangered the integrity of the nation,[11] although factionalism and riots, frequently based on the 'isms', have impaired the democratic process and progress in the social revolution. Carried to extreme lengths, factionalism and violence could bring the nation's functioning to a halt. A major product of fears for unity has been the over-centralization of authority to protect against forces thought to be disintegrating. A counter-intuitive remedy for the perceived threat to unity from the 'isms' came from former Chief Justice of India Mehr Chand Mahajan. As mentioned earlier, he believed that, because the Constitution had not contributed to the country's development 'into a single homogenous entity', a unitary form of government should replace the federal system.[12]

The origins of these anxieties about the assumed fragility of the country's unity are not far to seek. A heritage of doubt afflicted citizens and the leadership. Before 1950, India had never been united politically and administratively. The Mughal empire, India's most extensive, was not tightly united in the North and it did not cover the South. Other empires in the North and the South had been regional. Under the 'Raj', the country had been divided into 'British India' and the princely states. After independence, the latter had to be brought into the union. Psychologically, Indians had to overcome doubts that their diversities fitted them to become a nation. Was there a 'fundamental unity of India', as Radha Kumud Mookerji had claimed?[13] If so, what were its ingredients? Was it to be found in geography—one land from the Himalayas to the southern seas; in the Vedic past and the Sanskrit

---

[11] The author is flattered that P. N. Haksar agreed with this analysis.

[12] Mahajan, *Looking Back*, pp. 226–7. See also Mahajan, Mehr Chand, *Preserving Unity of India*, The Sulakhani Devi Mahajan Trust, New Delhi, 1970—publishing an article Mahajan had written in 1956. In this Mahajan wrote that he had only a 'negative answer' to his own question: Had the Constitution contributed to developing India 'into a single homogenous entity and of consolidating the people inhabiting the country into a single nation, swearing loyalty to Bharat and Bharat alone'? His answer was, 'The present Constitution may take us back to the age of separate kingdoms, persons therein owing their loyalty only to the states in which they live'. Ibid., pp. 2–3.

[13] Mookerji, Dr Radha Kumud, *The Fundamental Unity of India*, Bharatiya Vidya Bhavan, Bombay, 1960 (first published in 1914).

language; or 'in the common heritage ... of a composite culture', as suggested by the Sarkaria Commission?[14] Had the independence movement under Congress Party leadership brought lasting unity? Even the movement's great achievements could not erase memories of its factionalism and the evidence from Partition that many Indians had thought themselves a separate nation.[15] Jayaprakash Narayan put it succinctly and pessimistically when he wrote in 1961 that 'in the modern sense of the term, India was never a nation, nor is she a nation today, nor can she suddenly become one tomorrow'.[16] With these doubts and realities the founding fathers and their successors had to deal.

The Constitution's 'Federal' Provisions: Definitions and Uses

The founding fathers and mothers clearly had this history constantly in mind. They produced a constitution with a unitary tone and strong centralizing features—taking much from the British imperial model, the 1935 Government of India Act. There would be single citizenship, not dual, state and national, citizenships as in the United States. There would be a single system for the higher judiciary and single national civil and police services, although the states also would have their own services. The great 'Anglo-Indian Codes' of the nineteenth century, nation-wide in their reach, would be continued in force. The Fundamental Rights and the Directive Principles of State Policy would be national in reach, and the Rights were part of the original jurisdiction of the Supreme Court. The states would have a uniform constitution embodied in the nation's Constitution. The heads of government in the states, the governors, would be appointed by the President, i.e. by the Prime Minister and the council of ministers. Under the Constitution's 'Emergency Provisions' the central government could legislate for and administer governments in the states. Other provisions for centre–state relations clearly gave the central government strong influence or dominance.

With the Constitution inaugurated, the second set of definition issues arose. Interpretations of constitutional provisions had to be arrived at

---

[14] *Sarkaria Commission Report*, vol. 1, p. 5.

[15] Partition's effects linger today. Mukarji and Arora put it thus: '[T]he traumatic transfer of power engendered an obsessive concern for warding off further fragmentation and disintegration, which extended to viewing the political expressions of ethno-linguistic regional identities with suspicion and unease'. Mukarji and Arora, *Federalism*, p. 5.

[16] Jayaprakash Narayan, 'An Essential Requisite of National Integration', *India Quarterly*, vol. 17, no. 4, 1961, p. 323.

through political bargaining and in the courts of law, revealing the mindset of the definers. First, what degree of 'federal spirit' should mark the Constitution's functioning? Terms like 'quasi-federation', 'co-operative federalism', 'federal in form but unitary in substance', and 'centralized federalism' were used. Each term revealed an understanding of centre–state relations as, respectively, not quite 'federal' enough, just about right (with a hint of sceptical optimism), or too centralized. The president of the Constituent Assembly, Rajendra Prasad, had neatly avoided the definitional quicksand by telling its members that labels were unimportant. '[W]hether you call it a federal Constitution or a unitary Constitution or by any other name ... it makes no difference so long as the Constitution serves our purpose.'[17] More explanatory was K. Santhanam's analysis that India's was 'a Federation in which the paramountcy powers which the British Government had over the Indian [Princely] States have been taken over by the Union Government and applied to all its units ... . So, it will be appropriate to call our Federation a "Paramountcy Federation"'.[18]

Strong centralizers and decentralizers were at the ends of a philo-sophical continuum regarding the country's need. The decentralizers included former Congressman, Gandhi associate, Governor General, and Tamilian, C. Rajagopalachari, who thought that the solution to 'centrifugal interests' was to concede greater autonomy to the states. To centralize was 'both ridiculous and alarming'.[19] The Swaraj Party fifteen years later took the position that the federal principle was inex-tricably linked to democracy and 'the tendency to consider a strong Centre and a strong State [government] as antithetical to each other was mistaken'.[20] Swaraj members likely did not remember that Krishna Menon had supported this view in 1953. He favoured 'wider and wider degrees of decentralization simultaneously with increasing effective-ness and potency of central authority'. Without progressive decentrali-zation, Menon believed, government becomes 'increasingly alien to the people'.[21] The Praja Socialist Party had gone further only four years after the Constitution's inauguration. It then advocated replacing the

[17] *CAD*, vol. 11, no. 12, p. 987.

[18] Santhanam, *Union–State Relations*, p. 13.

[19] Rajagopalachari, *Our Democracy*, p. 4–5.

[20] 'The Federal Principle: How Best It Can Be Worked', *Swarajya*, 15 April 1972, p. 12. The party also believed that the Constitution need not be changed to achieve proper federalism. Ibid.

[21] Menon, V. K. Krishna, 'Desires without Deeds Breed Pestilence', *The Challenge to Democracy*, Publications Division, Delhi, 1953, p. 50.

current 'two pillar' system with one of 'four pillars', with power shared among village, district, province, and the centre to 'rouse a lethargic people to action'. The Communist Party Marxist thought the Constitution federal only in name, and truly federal government was the most suitable for a vast country like India.[22] Although such sentiments arose considerably from the Opposition's frustration with its inability to shake Congress's power, they should not be dismissed as frivolous. The central government's own Sarkaria Commission would deem many of them sensible.

Calls for generalized decentralization, or, occasionally, by individual states for 'autonomy', and in a few instances for secession, have alarmed prime ministers and central governments since 1950. The gravest threats to secede came in Tamil Nadu, Punjab, and from the Nagas. Although they did not materialize for lack of popular support and, in the Northeast, because New Delhi compromised, the threats shook the country. States' calls for decentralization and 'autonomy' have been a different matter. Based on genuine and perceived grievances against central government unfairness or neglect, they have been pleas for redress. A strong element of this underlay even the threats of secession. Similar demands have been directed at state capitals by discontented regional groups within states. Rarely have the latter discontents and demands threatened national unity and integrity—unless the violence and destruction that have sometimes accompanied them are defined as threats to more than stability. The central and state governments' unwillingness to heed pleas and to redress genuine grievances, and also to increase participation in governance through decentralization, have worsened many situations.

The centralizers were of two kinds. Parties like the Hindu Mahasabha and the Rashtriya Swayamsevak Sangh were strong centralizers, arguing that national unity and social and economic development had to be built upon the historical–cultural unity of Hinduism, which demanded scrapping the federal system in favour of unitary government. Joining them, as seen earlier, was former Chief Justice Mahajan. Also centralizers, but secular, were those exemplified by eminent political scientist Rajni Kothari, who said in 1966 (before the Congress Party's electoral defeats of several months later) that 'there is need to retain the authority of the dominant party ... [and] also need to restrain the powers of the states considerably ... [U]nless we devise an institutional system which ...

---

[22] For example, see CPM, Election Manifesto, 1971. Also former Chief Justice of India Subba Rao in *Swarajya Annual Number*, 1971, pp. 179ff.

establishes central authority without any doubt ... whatever else we have is not going to work'.[23]

The centralizers were supported by strong forces and tendencies. Two of these were connected directly to the seamless web. The Fundamental Rights and the protection of minorities and the weaker sections of society, both essential to democracy, ultimately were the responsibility of the central government and the Supreme Court. Similarly, the central government had the leading responsibility for the pursuit of the social revolution as embodied constitutionally in the Preamble and the Directive Principles of State Policy. The central government also had ultimate responsibility for the functioning of democratic government in the states (Articles 356 and 365). In the words of the States Reorganization Commission, this was '"the supervision by the larger democracy [of the Indian Union] over the smaller democracies [of the states] in respect of matters of national concern"'.[24] Socialism, the national economy planned and managed through the sub-constitutional Planning Commission, was inherently a centralizing force, the more so because the states lacked the wherewithal to fund their own economic development. Had some states possessed such resources, the central government still would have had to become involved to assure some measure of equitable development across the country.

Less tangible factors abetted centralization. Delhi, imperial capital under the Mughals and lesser early empires, and the British after 1911, was accustomed to dominance. Within it after independence, the imperial mannerisms of the Mughal Court lingered, limiting responsiveness to states' concerns.[25] The difficult struggle to build unity within the

---

[23] Kothari, who has since altered his views about centralization, was speaking in the context of India having a parliamentary as distinct from a presidential system, but his remarks apply equally to centre–state relations in politics and economics. *Parliamentary versus Presidential System of Government*, Proceedings of a Seminar, India International Centre, New Delhi, 1966, pp. 36–7.

[24] Quoted in this fashion in a letter from Madhya Pradesh Chief Minister Ravi Shankar Shukla to Congress President U. N. Dhebar, 9 February 1956. AICC Papers, Second Installment, File G-1(17), NMML.

The Reorganization Commission, when realigning state boundaries on a linguistic basis, did not address issues of relations between the states and the central government.

[25] The other side of this was southern resentment at the attempted imposition of Hindi as the national language and at the absence of prime ministers from the south— none until P. V. Narasimha Rao became Prime Minister in June 1991 after Rajiv Gandhi's assassination. What northerners—Punjabis especially, for Delhi is also a Punjabi city— saw as too many Tamil Brahmins in the Central Secretariat, did not allay southern

independence movement, and its centrally commanded engine, the Congress Party, created an instinct among party members for self-preservation: unity was necessary for the party to retain power, and, of course, it was good for the country! Although self-serving, this was also sensible, for the party could help hold the country together and resolve political and administrative problems. The AICC(I) recalled that under Prime Ministers Nehru and Shastri 'any dispute between the Centre and State[s] invariably used to be settled across the table at the party level and ... never came in the form of Centre–State problems'.[26]

The leaders of the early years were centralizers by personality. Nehru deeply felt his responsibility to lead and build the nation. Sardar Patel was a political boss and a stern administrator who tolerated no nonsense from state leaders and his ministerial colleagues to get things done. Mrs Gandhi and many of her ministers shared the belief that central dominance was essential to national progress and survival—this apart from any resulting personal benefits.

Finally, a characteristic of sub-continental culture has made political and administrative decentralization difficult. A respect, a reverence, for power and rank in a hierarchical society has supported the tendency among party and government officials to 'pass the buck' to higher levels of authority when confronted with difficult decisions and to defer unduly to the ideas of superiors. 'Let Panditji decide', and 'What is Madam's mood today?' were often heard during their years as Prime Minister. The pattern has persisted within parties and governments even as political rebelliousness has increased. The country's political parties are all central-command parties.

Which returns us to the history to which K. Santhanam referred. At independence power had been devolved from central authority, not, as in the United States, ceded to a new central government by colonies made independent by revolution. Centralized national government was foreordained in 1947. The future would produce the phases through which this centralization would go. These will be reviewed before discussing the details in the following three chapters.

---

dissatisfaction. As noted in Chapter 7, the central cabinet in 1954 decided that the President should spend some time in the South each year 'in the cause of the integration of the country'. Gopal, *Radhakrishnan*, p. 310.

[26] AICC (I) 'Memorandum' to the Sarkaria Commission. *Sarkaria Report*, vol. 2, pp. 662–3.

The AICC(I), unsurprisingly, believed that from the eighties onward central power should increase to deal with 'disruptionist forces' in the country.

Federalism's Phases

THE NEHRU YEARS

The Nehru years institutionalized centralization—as well as dedication to democracy and to the social revolution. His dominance as visionary, hero, and national nanny reinforced the factors already at work. The 'gentle colossus', the Communist Party statesman Hiren Mukerjee called him.[27] Under Nehru, government-to-government relations under the Constitution were developed and to a considerable degree became formalized. A political party operating as a two-way communications and command channel in parallel with constitutional federalism became an established pattern. This derived from the relationship between the Congress Working Committee and the Congress-led provincial governments after the 1937 elections.[28] A major government study a few years after Nehru's death described the Congress–government nexus, 'Where a single party has control over affairs at the Centre as well as in the states an alternative and extra-constitutional channel becomes available for the operation of centre–state relationships ... [T]his channel has been very active ... . In the process, the Constitution was not violated ... but was often bypassed'.[29] This arrangement allowed a degree of atrophy in the constitutional processes for centre–state relations by denying them strengthening exercise.

Yet all did not go New Delhi's way during this period. Powerful chief ministers both shared Nehru's national outlook and constituted counterweights to central power, acting as partial brakes on central authority

---

[27] Mukerjee, *The Gentle Colossus*, 1985, a reissue in paperback of the book published in 1964.

[28] For very useful treatments of this phase, see Sarkar, *Union–State Relations in India;* Bombwall, K. R., 'Federalism and National Unity in India', *JCPS*, vol. 1, no. 1, 1967, pp. 68ff; and Jacob, Alice, 'Centre–State Relations in the Indian Federal System', *JILI*, vol. 10, 1968, pp. 583ff. For a survey of the literature on centre–state relations, see Bhambri, C. P., 'Federal Politics: A Trend Report', *A Survey of Research in Political Science*, Allied Publishers Pvt. Ltd., New Delhi, 1981, vol. 2: *Political Process*, pp. 45ff.

[29] Administrative Reforms Commission (hereafter ARC), *Report of the Study Team: Centre–State Relationships*, Manager of Publications, GOI, New Delhi, 1968, pp. 1–2.

Continuing, the report said that, as a result of the above, 'constitutional provisions went into disuse and disputes were settled in the party rather than aired through open constitutional machinery. Party prestige and party discipline worked out party rather than governmental or constitutional solutions. A strong central leadership made such discipline possible. Ibid., p. 2.

As might be expected, this commission focused on administrative issues. Its major recommendations concerning individual constitutional provisions will be taken up in the following chapters.

in many administrative matters. They brokered the first and second prime ministerial successions. Indeed, chief ministers so often successfully defied the Congress high command that one party general secretary in the sixties expressed the fear that a situation might arise "'when state party chiefs would rule Parliament'".[30] Also, Nehru showed himself sensitive to state sensibilities. He apologized for a central minister visiting a state on official business without first informing that government, and said this should not be done.[31] When T. T. Krishnamachari spoke critically in Madras of the state government, Nehru admonished him: 'We have been trying to avoid public arguments and criticisms between ministers of the central government and the state governments because ... [they] only create conflict and ill-will'.[32] Nehru also initiated the Community Development and Panchayati Raj programmes, which could have led to a degree of political decentralization and empowerment in the villages.[33] Neither programme succeeded, but they were the progenitors of the movement toward a 'third tier' of government that gained momentum during the 1990s. (Part VII).[34]

During these years constitutional and sub-constitutional institutions began to play their part in centre–state relations. The Finance Commissions began allocating centrally collected revenues to the states and, in response to state pressures, increased these allocations. The Planning Commission commenced making capital development grants to the states, reinforcing New Delhi's political reach. Zonal councils were established. Three constitutional amendments—the Third, Sixth, and Seventh—increased central authority by extending Parliament's taxing power and New Delhi's authority over the production of and trade in foodstuffs and certain commodities. As an early chief minister of

---

[30] K. K. Shah in the *Hindustan Times*, 8 February 1963. Cited in Bombwall, 'Federalism and National Unity', p. 88.

[31] Letter to Madhya Pradesh Chief Minister Ravi Shankar Shukla dated 13 May 1951. H. K. Mahtab. Mahtab Papers, First Installment, Subject File 20, NMML.

[32] Letter dated 10 May 1953. Nehru sent a copy of the letter to C. D. Deshmukh the same day. C. D. Deshmukh Papers, File 23, NMML.

[33] Even if panchayats and village co-operatives made 'a mess of things ... they must learn how to rely upon themselves', the Prime Minister wrote the chief ministers on 12 November 1958. *NLTCM*, vol. 5, p. 157.

[34] Nehru also came to conclude that slackness and corruption at the lower grades of the civil service might be reduced by decentralization. Although it was easy to criticize 'such decentralization and devolution of powers', it appeared, that there was 'no other democratic way to deal with the multitude of problems that arise'. Letter to chief ministers dated 9 September 1958. Ibid., pp. 127–8.

Uttar Pradesh, Sampurnanand, saw it, 'there is a steady attempt on the part of central ministries to encroach on the jurisdiction of the component states'.[35]

The direct challenges to the nation's integrity and to central authority that the Nehru government faced help to account for the government's policies regarding unity. After the great shock of Partition came the problems of integrating the princely states, the communist insurrection in Telengana, and Master Tara Singh's separatist politics in the Punjab. Then came challenges from Phizo and the Nagas, from Tamil separatists, and, somewhat less so, from Sheikh Abdullah in Kashmir. Tamil separatism, coupled with hostilities with the Chinese, brought on the National Integration Conference and the Sixteenth Amendment's oaths to be taken by legislature candidates and elected representatives to uphold the sovereignty and integrity of India.[36] The creation of linguistic majority states by the States Reorganization Commission brought anxieties that their new senses of identity would, by strengthening the states' self-confidence, make New Delhi's dealings with them more difficult[37]—anxieties largely unfulfilled. Accusations by Nehru's critics that the country was being governed in a unitary fashion were unjustified, but centralization was a major motif of governance under him.[38]

Equal in importance to such developments was one that might have occurred but did not. No one challenged the compatibility of federalism and the parliamentary system, although some theoreticians outside India had done so. The ardent decentralizers of the eighties did not seek a change from, or change in, the country's parliamentary system because they thought it incompatible with the greater federalism they desired. Nor have those advocating change to a presidential system supported their cause by claiming it better suited to decentralization. Indeed, the principal proponents of a presidential system—A. R. Antulay, Vasant Sathe, and others—at the same time have favoured centralization of power in New Delhi. Indeed, Mrs Gandhi at one time rejected a presidential system as dangerously decentralizing. She explained that adopting one

---

[35] Sampurnanand, *Memories and Reflections*, Asia Publishing House, Bombay, 1962, p. 155.

[36] See ch. 2.

[37] The author is indebted to Ashis Banerjee for his insightful discussion of the subject in 'The Reconstruction of Federalism', unpublished. Manuscript from Mr Banerjee in the author's possession.

[38] For a fine study of Nehru's style and of decision-making in government, see Brecher, Michael, *Nehru: A Political Biography*, Oxford University Press, London, 1959, ch. 17, 'Democracy at Work'.

at the centre might lead to similar systems in the states, allowing the latter to pursue a 'policy of confrontation' both with the Centre and other states.[39]

THE INDIRA GANDHI YEARS

Federalism under Nehru's daughter may be said to have seen three phases: 1966–73; the Emergency years, 1975–7; and the years of her return to office, 1980–4. Mrs Gandhi's ascension to the prime ministry is commonly—one might say almost universally—seen as a watershed in centre–state relations, as in other aspects of governance. During the first phase, the Prime Minister progressed from vulnerability to pressures from chief ministers and state Congress leaders to ascendancy over them. The established patterns of 'federal' relationships within the Congress Party and between New Delhi and state capitals were increasingly centralized. The government's and the party's public utterances about the dangers to national unity and integrity and the need for strong central government, and the actual conduct of centre–state relations, seem to have been designed to serve the Prime Minister's personal, as much as the national, interest—although social and political fractiousness were genuine causes for concern.

Mrs Gandhi's election victories of 1971 and 1972 and her skills at manoeuvre concentrated in her hands authority in the Congress, in the central government, and in centre–state relations. Internal democracy in the party, always at risk from 'bossism', as it sometimes was called, ended. 'Even the chief ministers were appointed by the Centre. No one with a mass base was allowed to come up.' '[T]he states have become virtually the Zamindaris of the Centre ... and the Centre, too, has become the hand-maid of the Prime Minister.'[40]

Weakness in many state governments after the Congress's defeats in the 1967 elections contributed greatly to this condition. Defections and floor-crossings in state legislatures had become a 'chronic disease',

[39] See ch. 23.
  Douglas Verney has expressed doubt that 'federations like the Canadian or Indian can become federal systems through incremental change'. As a 'federal system' he has in mind the American, and he asks whether or not change to such a system is necessarily desirable. Verney notes that the British tradition of parliamentary cabinet government, came to India and Canada before their 'federations'. Verney, Douglas V., 'Are All Federations Federal? The United States, Canada and India' in Arora and Verney (eds), *Multiple Identities in a Single State*, pp. 19ff.

[40] Respectively, Justice R. S. Sarkaria in an interview with the author, and Mahtab, *While Serving My Nation*, p. 65.

according to party president S. Nijalingappa. He attacked Mrs Gandhi for her alleged contribution to these, for attempting to undermine ' "the foundations of democratic life in this country" '.[41] President's Rule was proclaimed twenty-two times during the years 1967–73.[42] Four instances involved non-Congress state governments. Several other instances involved states in which Congress was part of coalition governments. But relations between New Delhi and the state capitals where the Congress had lost its majority in the 1967 elections for the most part were carried on constitutionally. Mrs Gandhi's victory in the 1972 legislature elections left only three small states and Tamil Nadu with non-Congress majorities. After 1980, apart from her dismissal of the nine Janata ministries, Mrs Gandhi succeeded in bringing down one government, in Jammu and Kashmir, and attempted subversion of another, in Andhra Pradesh. Otherwise, constitutional federalism worked much the same whether Congress or opposition parties held state governments.

Increased centralization under Mrs Gandhi took bureaucratic forms. The nationalization of industries and mines extended central government control of the economy to the point where Mrs Gandhi's own secretary, L. K. Jha, would say that ' "the worst victim of the centralization psychosis which afflicts many government departments is the public sector" '.[43] Oversight of several ministerial functions was moved to the cabinet secretariat and the Prime Minister's secretariat. The Prime Minister's principal secretary and L. K. Jha's successor, P. N. Haksar, coordinated many government activities previously coordinated by the cabinet secretary. The high degree of centralization within the government, in the estimation of former home secretary and later governor, Govind Narain, resulted in direct government under the Prime Minister and the destruction of ministries' initiative.[44] The state governments' freedom of action became correspondingly narrowed.

Mrs Gandhi took centralization in more radical directions. Under her leadership, Parliament, in the Twenty-fourth Amendment, empowered itself to amend or repeal any provision of the Constitution. And it sacrificed in the Twenty-fifth the fundamental freedoms of Article 19 to major provisions of the Directive Principles. Civil liberties and

[41] At the Congress(O) Plenary on 21 December 1969 at Gandhinagar. *AR,* 22–28 January 1970, p. 9439.

[42] Dhavan, Rajeev, *President's Rule in the States,* Indian Law Institute/N. M. Tripathi Pvt. Ltd., Bombay, 1979, p. 70. At one time in 1972, President's Rule was in effect in seven states.

[43] Quoted by C. Rajagopalachari in his 'Dear Reader' column in *Swarajya,* 18 March 1967, p. 29.

[44] Govind Narain interview with the author.

the character of centre–state relations had been placed in the care of an obedient Parliament and persons dependent upon Mrs Gandhi's favour. Equally audacious was the 1973 attempt, in the supersession of judges (chapter 12), to reduce the Constitution's three branches of government to two by neutering the Supreme Court—again with great potential for affecting centre-state relations.[45]

The centralization of authority and Mrs Gandhi's contributions to it evoked critical reactions early in her prime ministry. In 1968, E. M. S. Namboodiripad told a Madras audience that a new constituent assembly should establish a truly federal system,[46] and the chief ministers of Andhra and Orissa called for '"real federalism"'.[47] The Praja Socialist Party rejected what it thought a trend toward unitary government and called for re-examination of the distribution of financial powers between the centre and the states. The most weighty critique appeared as the *Report of the Centre–State Relations Inquiry Committee* published by the government of Tamil Nadu in 1971. This addressed itself to 'the entire question regarding the relationship that should subsist between the Centre and the States in a federal set-up, with reference to the Constitution of India', and it would have shifted the balance in federal relations strongly toward the states.[48] (See subsequent chapters.)

Placing the country under unitary administration during the Emergency self-evidently was the apogee of centralization. Mrs Gandhi and a small circle around her largely succeeded in becoming government in India during this phase. As a Congress general secretary of the time put

[45] The Administrative Reforms Commission had reported that one of the attributes of 'federalism classicly' is the courts' authority to interpret the Constitution 'and to resolve conflicts ... between one unit and another and between a unit and the Union'. ARC, *Report of the Study Team*, p. 4.

A few years later, former Chief Justice Subba Rao said that the Supreme Court was 'the balance wheel of the Constitution'. *Swarajya Annual Number*, 1971, p. 184d.

[46] *AR*, 1–7 July 1968, p. 8400.

[47] *AR*, 12–18 February 1969, p. 8771.

[48] From the government order establishing the committee. *Report of the Centre–State Relations Inquiry Committee* (hereafter *Rajamannar Report*), Government of Tamil Nadu, Madras, 1971, p. 1.

Called the Rajamannar Committee after its chairman, P. V. Rajamannar, former Chief Justice of the Madras High Court and later chairman of the Fourth Finance Commission, the committee was established on the suggestion of Tamil Nadu Chief Minister A. N. Annadurai in 1968 to recommend a redistribution of powers because the 'strength of the Centre lay in the strength of the states'. *AR*, 5–11 August 1968, p. 8459.

The Rajamannar Committee recommended making the Rajya Sabha into a truly 'federal' Upper House with equal representation for each state, while continuing to support the parliamentary system. *Rajamannar Report*, p. 225.

it, 'The chief ministers became *subedars* of the Centre'[49]—whether they were members of the Congress or opposition parties. While she ruled largely outside the Constitution, altering the text of the Constitution's centre–state relations provisions proved to be another matter. The Swaran Singh Committee confined itself to recommending that the centre have authority to control its own police forces when operating in a state and that 'education' be moved from the State to the Concurrent Legislative List. Both recommendations were embodied in the Forty-second Amendment (chapters 16 and 17). The Prime Minister's refraining from pressing for changes in the Constitution's federal provisions may have been due to her wish not to reinforce the widespread perception that she intended her authoritarian grasp on the country to be permanent. Or, it may have been because the Emergency demonstrated that the centre's reach was extensive enough without altering the Constitution.

Federalism's final phase, in the period of this book, coincided with Mrs Gandhi's return to office in 1980. It saw relations between the central and state governments at their most tormented since independence—a condition that would endure into the 1990s. In general, her policies worsened instead of calming the difficult situations in the Punjab, Kashmir, and the Northeast. Her reaction to the 'constitutional revolt' of opposition party chief ministers was to 'sidetrack' it by appointing the Sarkaria Commission. The chairman of that commission thought Congress's dominance of centre–state relations over the years had been detrimental. 'This personalized style of functioning, which has been at its peak since 1969, inhibited the growth of a federal culture which is the *sine qua non* of the health and proper working of a two-tier democratic polity,' thought Justice R. S. Sarkaria.[50]

THE JANATA YEARS

The Janata phase of federalism was marked by the central government's unwise dismissal of Congress goverments in the states, by strengthened regional political parties, and most importantly by its primary mission, to redress the Emergency's excesses. In the Forty-third and Forty-fourth Amendments, Janata began curbing excesses in centre–state relations. With the help of Congress votes, it repealed the article permitting the central government to deploy its paramilitary forces in a state without the state government's permission, and it placed stringent restrictions

---

[49] A. R. Antulay interview with the author.
[50] From Justice R. S. Sarkaria's Preface for an unpublished book, sent to the author by Justice Sarkaria in 1995.

on the President's power to declare emergencies. President's Rule was limited to six months unless extended by Parliament. Relations between New Delhi and the states were comparatively untroubled during Janata's two years in office.

NEHRU AND MRS GANDHI COMPARED

Indira Gandhi's and Jawaharlal Nehru's different approaches to issues of national unity and integrity and to the machinery of centre–state relations arose from personality and situation. For each, situation initially was the more important. Nehru had national stature and authority and power when he became Prime Minister. Mrs Gandhi had to acquire them; an inherited mantle provided scanty covering. Nehru had opponents after 1951, but no competitors. When troubled and in doubt about national affairs, he had old colleagues to whom he could and did turn. Mrs Gandhi—with no close colleagues and surrounded by either competitors or persons intending to use her for their own purposes—had no such sources of support. She felt isolated and alone. Nehru's mistakes would be tolerated, if bemoaned. Mrs Gandhi's mistakes would be turned against her, threatening her hold on power. Therefore, Nehru could govern more openly and democratically, tolerant of dissent as a politician and as an administrator. For Mrs Gandhi, a closed style of operation, less democracy and more centralization—a tighter rein on power—were, she believed, necessary for her continuation in office. Nehru had inherited the centralized processes of the Congress Party, which he increased little, while increasing centralization in government, particularly through socialist developmental policies. Mrs Gandhi would build from this foundation.

Their personality differences, in essence, related to self-confidence and views of power. Nehru had abundant self-confidence, along with leavening self-doubt, and a lively sense of humour. Mrs Gandhi apparently had little self-confidence—and wit but little humour.[51] Persons or nations who cannot laugh at themselves will not bring perspective to their power. Nehru, then, could see his power as a means. For Mrs Gandhi, power might be a means; certainly it was an end—apparently an end in

[51] Sheila Dhar, wife of P. N. Dhar and a noted classical singer saw a different side of the Prime Minister. She 'had a puckish sense of humour which her own life wasn't very hospitable to .... . There was definitely a sporting and fun-loving person in her that did not often get a chance to emerge'. Dhar, Sheila, *Here's Someone I'd Like You to Meet*, Oxford University Press, New Delhi, 1995, p. 240. This memoir describes a number of persons of whom Mrs Gandhi is only one.

itself, for she seems seldom to have used power to pursue national achievement. Power was something she dared not lose. Nehru several times contemplated relinquishing it, to the consternation of his associates.

Combined, situation and personality translated into performance. While a centralizer for the purposes of policy and programme implementation, Nehru worked to strengthen the effectiveness of the country's centralized federalism and to establish the institutions and spirit of democracy. Although he could and did take undemocratic actions, he was a democrat by conviction and understood that at some point over-centralization crosses into authoritarianism. Conversely, Indira Gandhi removed collegiality from the central government's functioning, tamed Parliament and the Congress state governments, and drastically weakened whatever federal structure the Congress Party had—all in the name of the social revolution. She over-centralized for personal political survival, seemingly unconcerned with the effect this had on the institutions of democracy and federalism. She was unrepentant after the Emergency that her over-centralization had become authoritarianism. In contrast, the stature she had gained with her people, her firm grip on power, and her strength of character served the nation well in many domestic situations. This was true, above all, during the war with Pakistan in 1971. Her situation made her a brilliant political tactician, but by personality she was not a nation-builder, although her longevity in office and her wide popular appeal contributed to national consolidation.

Chapter 28

THE GOVERNOR'S 'ACUTELY CONTROVERSIAL' ROLE

The governor is the 'linchpin of the constitutional apparatus of the state', reported the Sarkaria Commission in 1988. His role 'has emerged as one of the key issues in Union–State relations', the commission continued, and he has been criticized for want of 'impartiality and sagacity' and for being used by the central government 'for its own political ends'.[1] Twenty years previously the Administrative Reforms Commission had expressed the view that the President's authority to appoint and remove governors departed from the federal principle.[2]

A number of former governors have criticized the institution. The highly respected L. P. Singh, formerly home secretary as well as a governor, wrote that the governor's office had 'undergone devaluation and even debasement'. Governors had been accused of political partisanship and for acting as 'agents of the Central government, and not as holders of an independent constitutional office', Singh said.[3] Former governor and cabinet minister C. Subramaniam believed that the governor had 'become a party appointment', serving the party rather than 'the interest of the nation'.[4] B. K. Nehru, as we have seen once

[1] *Sarkaria Report*, vol. 1, pp. 115, 120.
Article 155 provides for the governor's appointment by the President. Article 163 provides for his 'discretion' within the Constitution and for the state government's council of ministers to advise him, but the governor decides 'in his discretion' whether or not the Constitution requires him to act in his discretion.

[2] ARC, *Report of the Study Team*, p. 273. The report continued that governors chosen in such situations were 'as likely as not' to be chosen not for their ability but for other considerations, including 'his willingness to endure an abnegation of his role ... .' Therefore, the institution 'has languished from the incognizance it has suffered'. Ibid.

[3] Singh, L. P., 'Guide, Philosopher and Friend' in Sorabjee, et al., *Sage or Saboteur*, p. 37. Other contributors to this important book were Soli J. Sorabjee, Govind Narain, E. M. S. Namboodiripad, Sunanda K. Datta-Ray, Dharma Vira, P. Upendra, and Tavleen Singh.

[4] C. Subramaniam Oral History Transcript (1990 interview 'SL. No. 1, 'A', draft', p. 14) made by the Rajaji Institute for International and Public Affairs, Hyderabad. Copy to the author kindness of G. R. S. Rao.

governor of Kashmir and Gujarat, described governors as 'burnt out', as 'superannuated members of the ruling party for whom a governorship was a kind of luxurious retirement'.[5] The Bangalore Seminar of Experts reported in 1983 that, on more than one occasion, governors had been 'made to function as an agent of the Union Government'.[6]

The governors acting as a body have themselves expressed conflicting views. Meeting during the Nehru years, they agreed that in certain circumstances 'the governor can function as an agent of the government of India'.[7] Meeting during Mrs Gandhi's prime ministry, governors declared themselves innocent of acting as 'agents' of New Delhi. '[T]he Governor, as Head of State, has his functions laid down in the Constitution itself, and is in no sense an agent of the President .... In the framework of the Constitution as it is conceived, there is no power vested in any authority to issue any directions to the Governor or lay down any code of rules for his guidance,' said the report of the Committee of Governors.[8]

India's experience with 'governors' was millenia-old. Classical emperors from the Maurya period onward to the Mughals appointed 'governors', viceroys, and princes etc. to administer outlying districts and to collect revenues, manifesting a degree of imperial cohesion, if not more centrally controlled administration. With the consolidation of the British empire in India in the 1850s, governors became directly subordinate

---

Subramaniam went on to say that a convention was required to remedy this condition and that governors should have been out of 'active party politics' for three to five years, thus eliminating from contention any active politician who had been a central cabinet minister or a state chief minister or a person defeated in a parliamentary election—appointed governor because 'you want to [do] him some favour ...'. Ibid.

In the Constituent Assembly on 31 May 1949, piloting the debate on the *Draft Constitution* Article 131, T. T. Krishnamachari said we do not wish this or any other article in the constitution, 'to make the Governor of a Province an agent of the Centre at all'. CAD, vol. 8, no. 12, p. 460, Reprinted by the Lok Sabha Secretariat, New Delhi, no date. Its pagination will vary from the original edition of the *CAD*.

[5] B. K. Nehru, 'The Role of Governor Under the Indian Constitution' in *Silver Jubilee, Gauhati High Court,* Souvenir Committee, Guwahati, 1974, p. 56.

[6] Bangalore Seminar Report, *JCPS*, Special Number, 1984, p. 400.

[7] Proceedings of the Conference of Governors, 1956, p. 11. K. M. Munshi Papers, NMML.

[8] 'The Role of Governors', report of the Committee of Governors (hereafter *Governors' Report*), President's Secretariat, New Delhi, 1971, pp. 8–9.

President V. V. Giri suggested the formation of the committee to the November 1970 Conference of Governors, and six days later he ordered the committee established and appointed its members, all governors: Chairman Bhagwan Sahay, Jammu and Kashmir; B. Gopala Reddi, Uttar Pradesh; V. Vishwanathan, Kerala; S S. Dhavan, West Bengal; and Ali Yavar Jung, Maharashtra.

to the Governor-General, or Viceroy, but with arbitrary powers of their own that leaders of the independence movement often would find vexing.[9] As a result, members of the Constituent Assembly hotly debated the authority the new constitution should give governors as they weighed their goal of curbing executive power against the aim of protecting national unity by having a central government appointee at the head of the state government.[10] The result of their efforts was a governor appointed by the President and serving at his 'pleasure'. He was to act, like the President, as a constitutional sovereign, reigning but not ruling with the advice of the chief minister and the council of ministers. The governor also was given authority to act in his 'discretion', but these occasions largely were unspecified in the Constitution. In theory discretionary authority was subject to constitutional conventions; yet continuing controversies showed these still to be in formation. Here has lain the rub, and the topics of this chapter.

The Supreme Court twice has delivered rulings on the governor's constitutional status. The Constitution embodied the British parliamentary system, and the status of governors—and the President—corresponds to that of the monarch in the United Kingdom, the Court has said.[11] More definitively, it ruled unanimously in 1979 that because a governor is appointed by the President and holds office at the President's pleasure 'does not make the Government of India an employer of the Governor. The Governor is the head of the State and holds a high constitutional office which carries with it important constitutional functions and duties and he cannot, therefore, be regarded as an employee or servant of the Government of India.'[12]

Criticisms of governors' performances in office neglected to mention something the writers knew, that the Constitution had given the governor a clear responsibility as the central government's representative in and its link with the state government. One of his functions has

---

[9] 'There had been so much prejudice against the special powers of Governors who had all been appointed by the British crown and were representatives of the Viceroy ...'. H. V. R. Iengar, 'Vallabbhai Patel', a memorial lecture given at Surat, October 1973, p. 13, unpublished. Copy of the text given to the author kindness of Mr Iengar's son, H. V. R. Iengar.

[10] See Austin, *Cornerstone*, ch. 5.

[11] *Shamsher Singh v Punjab* 1975 (1) SCR 814.

[12] *Hargovind v Raghukul Tilak* AIR 1979 SC 1113. The Court elaborated saying that the governor 'is not amenable to the directions of the Government of India, nor is he accountable to them for the manner in which he carried out his functions and duties. His is an independent constitutional office which is not subject to the control of the Government of India.'

been to keep the President informed of local conditions and developments. From 1948 onwards, governors sent 'Fortnightly Letters' to the President—typically full, often frank, and sometimes critical assessments of the chief minister, the state government, and local conditions. Some governors shared their letters with the chief minister—Pandit Pant thanked Governor K.M. Munshi for doing so—and President Prasad and Radhakrishnan typically sent the letters on to Nehru, who sometimes sent them on to his cabinet ministers.[13] So the governor's relationship to the central government should be measured in degrees. To keep the governor functioning constitutionally, as defined by the Supreme Court, three approaches were recommended.

Gubernatorial Independence

The first of these approaches had to do with the appointment of the governor, the second with his security of tenure, and the third with prohibiting government-offered inducements that might prejudice the governor's behaviour in favour of the central government. The appointments approach had two aspects: the definition of the appropriate qualifications and the process that might produce more independent governors. For Prime Minister Nehru, 'merit' was the principal criterion, to which he added two others: 'appointment of a person from the same province should be avoided, the other is that a Governor should not have more than one full term of office'.[14] No one

---

[13] A number of these letters are in the private papers in the Nehru Memorial Library; H. K. Mahtab discussed them in his Oral History Transcript, NMML, p. 228.

B. K. Nehru thought that governors sharing the letters with chief ministers destroyed their utility; hence governors had resorted to reporting orally to the President and the Prime Minister during their visits to Delhi. Nehru, 'The Role of the Governor', p. 57.

When it came to reporting to New Delhi on the politics of and internal developments in the states, the Intelligence Bureau's wide network outreached the governor's. Leaving aside the ethical aspects of domestic political spying, the IB's 'intelligence' often was irrelevant to—and occasionally harmful to—sound governance.

[14] Letter to chief ministers dated 18 May 1952. *NLTCM*, vol. 2, p. 611. Nehru added that these 'should be made into firm conventions'. As 'constitutional head', the governor cannot 'override or interfere with the decisions of his Cabinet'. He should, however, be kept in full touch with the administration, see all important ministerial papers, and 'give his advice' whenever he thinks necessary, Nehru wrote. The governor should stay in touch with the people and pay special attention 'to the backward classes, tribal people etc ... . He is a symbol of the State ... [and] to dishonour him is to dishonour onself as part of the State'—which Nehru said with particular reference to the Opposition in Madras walking out of the assembly during the governor's address in 1952. Ibid., p. 612.

disagreed about merit, and the literature and utterances of the earlier years listed qualifications like 'eminence in some field', 'learned', 'impartial', 'of sound judgement', and 'above politics'.

There were many recommendations concerning process, especially during 1967 and after when governors had to deal with coalition and otherwise unstable governments resulting from the Congress defeats in the elections of that year. The Administrative Reforms Commission and K. Santhanam recommended strengthening the convention that the central and the state government should consult about appointments.[15] Consultation 'almost [as] a convention had been the early practice', according to Nehru's Law Minister, Asoke K. Sen.[16] The Rajamannar Committee, Soli Sorabjee, the BJP, Janata Party, and the Karnataka government would have made consultation mandatory.[17] Appointments from panels of nominees also was suggested. The Communist Party of India, the Srinagar meeting of opposition parties, the West Bengal government, and the Bharatiya Janata Party favoured appointment from a panel prepared by the state legislature, with the latter two advocating that actual selection be made by the Inter-State Council (for this council, see chapter 30).[18] Former Solicitor General Soli

---

[15] ARC, *Report of the Study Team*, p. 292. Santhanam cited in Narain and Sharma, 'The Emerging Issues', p. 181.

[16] Asoke K. Sen, 'Role of Governor in the Emerging Pattern of Centre–State Relations', *JCPS*, vol. 5, no. 3, 1971, p. 257.

The desirability of consultation with state chief ministers had been expressed in the Constituent Assembly—for example by T. T. Krishnamachari, who said on 31 May 1949 that the Prime Minister's nominee would be subject to the chief minister's preference. *CAD*, vol. 8, no. 12, p. 462.

[17] *Rajamannar Report*, p. 221; Sorabjee in Sorabjee, et al., *Sage or Saboteur*, p. 20; BJP *Election Manifesto (s)*, 1980, 1984. For Karnataka government see *Sarkaria Report*, vol. 2, p. 230. Karnataka called for amending Article 155 to require consultation.

[18] For the CPI, see 'The Programme of the Communist Party of India (1968)' in *CPI's Stand on Major Issues*, CPI, New Delhi, 1985, p. 137; Srinagar *Statement on Centre-State Relations*, cited in *JCPS*, Special Number, p. 410; Sorabjee, *Sage or Saboteur*, Tamil Nadu to Sarkaria Commission, in *Sarkaria Report*, vol. 2, p. 486; West Bengal to Sarkaria Commission, ibid, p. 600; the BJP's view in ibid., p. 620.

Both the Tamil Nadu and West Bengal memoranda to the Sarkaria Commission recommended abolition of the office of governor, and their other recommendations were fall-back positions in case abolition was not forthcoming. Others had recommended abolition of governors: the Praja Socialist Party in 1954, the CPI in 1962 and 1971, and the government of Andhra Pradesh in its memorandum to the Sarkaria Commission.

The Communist Party Marxist, in its critique of the Forty-second Amendment, had called for governors to be elected by state legislatures.

The *Governors' Report* (footnote 8), did not mention appointment of the governor

Sorabjee recommended panels of candidates chosen by a high-level body such as one composed of the Speaker of the Lok Sabha, the leader of the Opposition, and the Chairman of the Rajya Sabha. The Tamil Nadu government suggested a panel of four names be submitted to the President by the chief minister.

The Sarkaria Commission declared consultation with chief ministers about gubernatorial appointments unexceptionable and that 'effective consultation' between the Centre and chief ministers should be prescribed by amending Article 155.[19] But it believed that appointing governors from panels was not a 'workable' proposition.[20] It recommended that a governor be eminent, come from outside the state of his appointment, be 'not too intimately connected' with its politics, and not recently have 'taken too great a part in politics generally'. A politician of the party governing in New Delhi should not be appointed to a state governed by another party.

During the Nehru years, the governor's selection and functioning had been less controversial for several reasons: the generally higher calibre of the individuals selected, the comparatively harmonious condition of centre–state relations, and the stature of many of the chief ministers. Many of these, as 'national leaders of great prominence' rendered their governor a 'nullity'.[21] Also, during these years, governors

---

and the Bangalore *Seminar on Centre–State Relations* said only that the Inter-State Council should play a 'crucial role' in centre-state relations involving governors.

Although the Congress, as long the dominant party at the centre, attracted the bulk of the opprobrium, the Janata government when in power in New Delhi 'further reinforced ... the impression that Governors were political appointees ... when ... in 1977 ...[it] started filling in gubernatorial vacancies with former Congress(O) partymen'. Mody, Nawaz, 'Role of Governor Since 1967', *JCPS*, Special Number on Centre–State Relations, 1986, p. 97.

[19] *Sarkaria Report*, vol. 1, p. 124.

[20] Ibid., vol. 1, p.122.

If different parties governed in a state and at the centre, the commission explained, 'deadlock' over the nominee might result. Moreover, the basic principle of responsible government would be violated were 'the union cabinet ... made to share...[appointment] with a state functionary not answerable to Parliament for its action'. Ibid., p. 123.

[21] Nehru, B. K., 'The Role of the Governor', p. 54. The ARC study team concurred with this view. ARC, *Report of the Study Team*, p. 273.

As examples, B. K. Nehru cited the chief minister of Bihar in 1947 (then called premier) refusing to show the governor certain documents despite Sardar Patel's intervention, causing the governor to resign; and Pandit Pant as premier of Uttar Pradesh amending the Rules of Business to deprive the governor of all official sources of information. Ibid.

In the 1973 lecture cited in footnote 9, H. V. R. Iengar, who worked closely under

sometimes simply were by-passed as the central government or the Congress Working Committee communicated directly with the chief minister or to him through the president of the Provincial Congress Committee.

The governor's tenure came to assume importance as a 'federal' issue because it was believed widely that the central government used uncertainty of tenure, which included transfer to another state, to influence his decisions. (Throughout this discussion the reader will recognize the parallels with issues of judicial independence.) 'The exercise of the power to remove or transfer a governor must cause grave disquiet in the public mind,' thought H. M. Seervai.[22] L. P. Singh agreed, saying that 'functioning with the apprehension of dismissal or transfer ... without his willing consent' may make it difficult for the governor 'to function with complete impartiality and as an independent constitutional authority'.[23] Dharma Vira believed that governors should be removed from office only by a process of impeachment resembling that for Supreme Court judges to prevent their being 'completely at the mercy of the Centre'.[24]

The Sarkaria Commission recommended that the governor's five-year term 'should not be disturbed except very rarely and that too, for some extremely compelling reason'. Should a governor be transferred or his tenure terminated, the central government 'may' lay an explanatory statement before Parliament. The commission's analysis of the tenure issue was more telling than its recommendations: '[T]he ever-present possibility of the tenure being terminated before the full term of five years can create considerable insecurity in the mind of the governor and impair his capacity to withstand pressures, resist extraneous influences and act impartially in the discharge of his discretionary functions.'[25]

Patel and greatly admired him, refers to the Rules of Business incident. Patel wished to codify which papers should routinely be submitted to the governor, but because the governors could not enact the draft rules without the chief ministers' concurrence and because most, if not all, the chief ministers refused, 'the Governors continued to be figure heads'. Iengar, 'Vallabbhai Patel', p.13. When K. M. Munshi was UP governor, his relations with Pant were, in general, both cordial and effective. See Pant's friendly letter to Munshi dated 13 December 1954, when Pant left UP to become central home minister. K. M. Munshi Papers, Microfilm Box 56, file 143, NMML.

[22] Seervai, *Constitutional Law,* vol. 1, p. 1070.

[23] Singh in Sorabjee, et al., *Sage or Saboteur,* p. 42. The BJP would have barred transfers entirely.

[24] Dharma Vira, 'The Exercise of Discretion', ibid., p. 88.

[25] *Sarkaria Report,* vol. 1, p. 125.

The All-India Congress Committee(I), defending the record of Congress governments, thought that the governor's five-year term carried 'no legal or constitutional guarantee' and it was unnecessary to secure tenure. Since independence, exercise of the President's 'pleasure' in abridging terms had 'been used very ... rarely ... [and] where such power was exercised there were justifiable, valid and compelling reasons for the President so to act'.[26]

Contrary to the AICC(I)'s claim, analysis of the length of tenures tells a different story, although allowances must be made for illnesses and other factors not contemplated by the Constitution. According to the Sarkaria Commission, of the sixty-six gubernatorial tenures between 1947 and 31 March 1967 thirty-two lasted the full five-year term. Of the eighty-eight tenures, for the period from 1 April 1967 to 31 October 1986, only eighteen lasted for five years. The commission concluded that 'during the latter period, premature exits from office occurred at a much faster rate and relatively fewer governors completed their normal term of office compared to ... the former period'.[27]

As the central government was thought capable of influencing governors through pressures, it was thought, also, to use various inducements to affect their independence. These might be offers of post-governorship jobs in government, such as heading a commission, or support while seeking political office. To prevent this, the Administrative Reforms and Sarkaria Commissions recommended that an ex-governor should not 'take part in politics',[28] although the latter thought that a former governor might run for Vice-President or President.[29] The Tamil Nadu government and the Bharatiya Janata Party told the Sarkaria Commission that former governors should not again hold government office. The commission, itself, went to the heart of the matter—money—when it

---

[26] Ibid., vol. 2, p. 667.

[27] Ibid., vol.1, p. 125.

The author's own (crude) analysis of governorships from 1953 to 1985 indicates that some 167 individuals served as governors—not counting Manipur, Mizoram, and Meghalaya, which often shared a governor with Assam. Of these governors (again, the figures are approximate), two served ten years, seventeen served six to eight years, twenty-one served full five-year terms, and fifteen served for four years. Thus, about thirty-five per cent of governors remained in office three years or less, although a handful were transferred to governorships in other states. Twenty-five persons served for only a year. The states having had the most governors from 1953–4 to 1985 are: Andhra Pradesh, thirteen; Bombay/Maharashtra, fourteen; Orissa, eleven; and Punjab, twelve. In the case of Bombay/Maharashtra, this means governors lasted, on average, about two years.

[28] ARC, *Report of the Study Team*, pp. 292–3.

[29] *Sarkaria Report*, vol. 1, p. 135.

recommended that incumbent governors be promised 'reasonable retirement benefits' to strengthen their 'capacity to act with due objectivity and impartiality and independence'.[30]

Discretionary Authority of the Governor

The ramifications of the governor, as a constitutional head of state, having undelineated power to act in his discretion have been very troublesome. The Constitution defines the governor's discretionary authority only in regard to certain tribal matters in the five northeastern states and when his authority extends to an adjoining Union Territory.[31] Otherwise, if and when he acts in his discretion, the Constitution provides that only the governor shall be the judge of his discretionary action.[32] The Constitution thus left unanswered questions vitally important under a parliamentary system: who should the governor invite to form a government when no political party has a majority in the legislature?; under what circumstances may he summon, prorogue, or dismiss the legislature?; has he authority to dismiss a ministry and invite another person to form a government?; can he, in his discretion, reserve for the President's consideration a bill passed by the legislature?

Confronted with these questions, often in a political crisis, the governor had little in the way of guidance for answering them. He has been the advance guard in these constitutional skirmishes. The constitutional

[30] Ibid., p. 127.

[31] Articles 239, 371A, and the Sixth Schedule. Governors may act upon presidential orders according to portions of Articles 371B through 371D, and 371H—each dealing with the affairs of states in the Northeast. Additionally, under Articles 256, 257, and 258, the governor may not act on the advice of his ministers if it is contrary to directions given by the central government. See Sen 'Role of the Governor in the Emerging Pattern of Centre–State Relations', p.258. Nor, of course, may a state government act contrary to orders of the President under the Constitution's emergency provisions. There has been little controversy about the governor's discretion under these provisions.

Governors were also given 'special responsibility' for certain matters (such as dealing with tribal peoples and establishing separate 'development boards' for parts of Maharashtra and Gujarat Article 371). Yet, this is not to mean that 'the decision is to be that of the Governor to the exclusion of his Ministers'. It does mean 'a sphere of action in which it will be constitutionally proper for the Governor, after receiving ministerial advice, to signify his dissent from it and even to act in opposition to it if, in his own unfettered judgement, he is of the opinion that the circumstances of the case so require'. *Governors' Report*, p. 13.

[32] According to Article 163(2), if a question arises about whether or not a governor is required to act in his discretion 'the decision of the governor in his discretion shall be final' and his action 'shall not be called in question on the ground that he ought or ought not to have acted in his discretion'.

conventions of the British system were known only remotely,[33] and it is not certain that all governors were enamoured of them—nor, necessarily, were leaders in New Delhi. The few early occasions in the states when these questions arose were inadequate preparation for the unstable governments of 1967 and later. They would not arise for the President until 1979 and Janata's fall.[34] The governor's 'discretion' provided a large opportunity for the centre to work its will in a state, which was a recipe for confusion and ill-will.

The first controversial use of a governor's discretionary power came in Madras in 1952. In the first general elections, the Congress Party won 152 seats of the 375 in the legislature, but a United Front led by T. Prakasam gained 166 seats and claimed the right to form the government. The long-time Congressman and governor, Sri Prakasa, rejected Prakasam's claim, and invited C. Rajagopalachari to form a government. But Rajagopalachari had not even been elected to the legislature, so Prakasa nominated him to the Upper House, which elected him leader of the Congress Legislature Party, making him eligible to become chief minister. Rajagopalachari had the necessary majority after sixteen

[33] An Instrument of Instructions for governors—derived from the 1935 Act—was included in the 1948 *Draft Constitution of India*, but it did not address the issues described here and was not included in the 1950 Constitution.

[34] Instability in state governments was rife. During 1967–70, there were some 800 defections, of whom eighty-five per cent crossed the floor affecting government's majorities. 'A good number of these defections take place because of the promise of reward of office or other official patronage,' according to the *Governor's Report*. In an elaboration of this assessment, and seemingly in contradiction to it (although this may be accounted for by the inclusion of defections in the Lok Sabha), the committee said that an analysis of the names of 768 defections out of a total of 1,240, from March 1967 to August 1970, revealed that 155 had been rewarded 'with the office of Cabinet Minister or Minister of State or Deputy Minister or Parliament Secretary ... [and] apart from the reward of office, defections were being secured by other means not too honourable'. *Governor's Report*, pp. 24–5.

In an excellent study of defections and related matters (Kashyap, Subhash, and Kashyap, Savita, *The Politics of Power*, National Publishing House, Delhi, 1974, p.ix), the following figures are given. 'During 1967–73 some 45 State Governments were toppled in quick succession with as many as 2, 700 cases of defection by legislators. Over 60 per cent of legislators all over the country were involved in the game—many of them changing their affiliations more than once and some of them as many as four or five times within a year.'

Between the first and fourth general elections (1952–67), there were only 542 cases of defections. Sarkar, 'The Office of Governor', p. 20.

The Constitution (Thirty-second Amendment) Bill, intended to reduce defections, was introduced in the Lok Sabha in May 1973. Six months later it was referred to a Joint Committee, which was unable to report it out by the end of 1976, and it lapsed several months later at the end of the session. For the text of the bill, see *Politics of Power*, pp. 680 ff. The anti-defection Fifty-second Amendment became law in February 1985.

members of opposition parties crossed the floor, allegedly in response to inducements.

Prime Minister Nehru and President Rajendra Prasad opposed Rajagopalachari's becoming chief minister. Nehru wrote to Rajagopalachari that 'the one thing we must avoid is giving the impression that we stick to office and that we want to keep others out at all costs.'[35] Prakasa and Rajagopalachari justified their position on the ground that 'ideological democracy' was insufficient justification to 'leave patches of rebel areas [i.e, under the Communists in Telengana] and go into disorder'.[36] Unable to undo events, Nehru accepted them. K. M. Munshi, then governor of Uttar Pradesh, congratulated Prakasa. 'You have saved the country ... No one else could prevent the South from landsliding into Communism except our great and noble friend [Rajagopalachari] ... .'[37] Looking back, L. P. Singh disagreed: Prakasa's and Rajagopalachari's actions 'did not augur well for political or constitutional morality in the years to come', he said.[38]

With this as background, we may proceed to 'discretion' in West Bengal during 1967, with its emphatic demonstration of the need to establish conventions. A short chronology of the events will provide the setting for the constitutional issues they presented.

The Congress Party not having gained a majority in the 1967 general elections, a breakaway Congressman, Ajoy Mukherjee, formed the Bangla Congress and assembled a United Front (UF) and the governor, Padmaja Naidu, invited him to form a government. By July, a few defections, serious lawlessness over food supplies, and the beginning of the Naxalite-peasant-cum-tribal revolt rendered the government shaky. During the second half of September, the Congress Working Committee sent former Home Minister G. L. Nanda to reconnoitre. It was widely believed that

---

[35] Nehru to Rajagopalachari, 29 January 1952. Cited in Gopal, *Nehru,* vol. 2, p. 220.

Nehru told local Congressmen that the electoral loss was not a failure of the Constitution but the government's, due to incompetence.

This was the first time a nominated member of the legislature had been elected leader of the legislature party and subsequently become chief minister.

'Inviting a nominated member to form a Government is open to the ... criticism of being against the spirit of the parliamentary system... (for the member) has no electoral support and, therefore, no mandate from the electorate,' said the governors in their report. *Governor's Report,* p. 35.

[36] Ibid., p. 221.

[37] Letter dated 25 June 1952. K. M. Munshi Papers, Microfilm File 140, NMML.

[38] In Sorabjee, et al., *Sage or Saboteur,* p. 45.

Asoke Sen thought Prakasa was 'entitled to use' his discretion on the occasion. Sen, 'Role of the Governor', *JCPS,* vol. 5, no. 3, p. 267.

he was exploring toppling the UF government so that Congress could return to office in combination with Ajoy Mukherjee and his breakaway Bangla Congress.[39] Such did not happen, and Mukherjee denied collusion with the central government.

Soon thereafter, the UF government lost its majority in the legislature when cabinet minister and old Congressman P. C. Ghosh defected, taking seventeen others with him. On 6 November P. C Ghosh announced he was willing to form a government with the Congress. That day Dharma Vira, who had been governor since the summer, wrote to Chief Minister Mukherjee, saying that he doubted his majority and advising him either to resign or to summon the assembly as soon as possible—one report said by 30 November—to test his strength there. The next day, Mukherjee replied that his cabinet had ruled out a session before 18 December.[40] A week later Dharma Vira, after a consultation in Delhi, sent a letter to Mukherjee again urging the legislature's earliest summoning, a sentiment he conveyed personally two days later.

Two things happened on 17 November. The governor asked that the assembly be convened on 23 November, alleging that the proper functioning of the Constitution might be impaired by further delay. Mukherjee refused and sent a letter to the President requesting him to seek an advisory opinion from the Supreme Court on seven questions. The first two were: ' "Has the governor the authority to dismiss the Council of Ministers without taking the verdict of the Assembly ..." '? and, can the governor, on the basis of information available to him, ' "in his individual discretion, dismiss the Council of Ministers" '?[41] Three days later the President, on the advice of the cabinet's Political Affairs Committee,

[39] Kashyap, *Politics of Power*, p. 525. This description of events is drawn from Kashyap and from the *AR*, 10–16 and 17–23 December 1967; from Shiviah, 'The Governor in the Indian Political System', *JCPS*, vol. 2, no. 4, 1968, pp. 94ff; from Bhambri, C. P, 'Federal Politics: A Trend Report', in *A Survey of Research in Political Science*, vol. 2, *Political Process*, Indian Council of Social Science Research/Allied Publishers Pvt. Ltd., New Delhi, 1981, pp. 67ff; Nakade, Shivaj, 'Article 356 of the Constitution: Its Use and Misuse', *JCPS*, vol. 3, no. 4, 1969, pp. 102 ff; Dhavan, Rajeev, 'President's Rule in the States', p. 87; Dharma Vira Oral History Transcript, NMML; and Dharma Vira, 'The Exercise of Discretion', Sorabjee, et al., *Sage or Saboteur.*

[40] Before the cabinet took the decision, state Advocate General A. K. Datta was 'understood' to have advised Mukherjee that the governor could not constitutionally dismiss the govenment because of Ghosh's resignation and the reported defections, but the governor could legitimately dismiss the government if he thought it had lost its majority. Kashyap, *Politics of Power*, pp. 533–4.

[41] The text of the questions is given in *AR*, 10–16 December 1967, p. 8062, and in Kashyap, *Politics of Power*, pp. 536–7.

replied that the questions did not require reference to the Supreme Court.

The next day, 21 November, Dharma Vira issued a proclamation dismissing the UF government on the ground that it was constitutionally improper for the ministry to continue in office when it had lost its majority, and that night he swore in P. C. Ghosh as chief minister. On Ghosh's advice, the governor summoned the assembly to meet on 29 November. The United Front charged the governor with acting on the advice of the central government and committing '"rape on the Constitution"'.[42] In New Delhi, Home Minister Y. B. Chavan said that Ghosh's government was legitimate and that at no time did the central government give Dharma Vira instructions.[43] The Calcutta High Court on 6 February upheld the Mukherjee government's dismissal.[44] In Calcutta, riots followed Ghosh's oath-taking.

Remarkable developments continued when the assembly convened on 29 November. Dharma Vira addressed it briefly, 'amidst scenes of great disorder', he recalled. The Speaker adjourned the session *sine die*, declaring that Ghosh's ascendancy was illegal and therefore the summoning of the assembly on his advice was illegal. Only the assembly, could decide on the continuance of a ministry. Dharma Vira prorogued

[42] *AR*, 10–16 December 1967, p. 8061.

[43] *Hindu*, 28 November 1967.

K. Santhanam remarked that '"it is difficult to believe that he [the Governor] had to travel twice to New Delhi to make up his own mind"'. Quoted in Shiviah, 'The Governor', p 102. On the other hand, an individual so strong-minded as Dharma Vira, holding also such firm views about Ajoy Mukherjee's behaviour, may have needed little urging from New Delhi to act as he did.

In Dharma Vira's opinion, Mukherjee's 'delaying tactics ... [were] to postpone the summoning of the House till he was forced to do so under the provisions of Article 174 (1) of the Constitution'. In the meantime, 'every effort was made to browbeat the dissenters' to make them return to the fold or to keep them out of the assembly when it was convened. Dharma Vira, 'The Exercise of Discretion', in Sorabjee et al., *Sage or Saboteur*, p. 84.

In his Oral History Transcript, Dharma Vira confirmed this version and added that Ajoy Mukherjee intended to use the constitutional provision allowing six months between assembly sessions, which, 'to my mind, was not in accord with the spirit of the constitutional practice.. if that period is utilized for unsavoury practices in trying to win over members of the assembly by coercion, bribery or corruption of various types' (pp.124 ff). In this instance, a ministry that 'had prima facie lost its majority' was trying to remain in power and I had 'only two alternatives: to allow ... matters to go from bad to worse' or 'to exercise the discretionary powers vested by the Constitution in the Governor to withdraw the pleasure of the Governor from the ministry ... [I]t was becoming pretty obvious that if the calling of the Assembly was delayed for six weeks, there would be no verdict of the Assembly', for either the opposition would be prevented from voting or if they voted against the government 'there would be very unseemly incidents ...'. Ibid., pp. 126–7.

[44] *Mahabir Prasad Sharma v Profulla Chandra Ghosh* AIR 1969 Calcutta 198ff.

the assembly the next day. By the time it met again on 14 February 1968 P. C. Ghosh's majority was in question, and when the governor attempted his Address 'pandemonium and rowdyism' drove him out the back door. The following day, to the relief of all parties, he recommended the imposition of President's Rule—for the first time in the state since independence. Ajoy Mukherjee again became chief minister after the 1969 elections in which Congress lost badly, and shortly after this Dharma Vira was replaced.

These events, and those in several other states during 1967, raised the questions asked above and produced conflicting responses to them. In New Delhi, Home Minister Chavan said the governor had acted correctly: Mukherjee had lost his majority. The Law Ministry reportedly had advised the cabinet that 'the relative strength of the (state) government could be tested only on the floor of the House ... (and) the governor had no power to summon the State Legislature against the wishes of the Chief Minister'. Yet a Law Ministry spokesman also was reported to have said that the governor could dismiss a ministry 'on the basis of "any material or information available to him"'.[45]

Although the Supreme Court had held that the governor's power to appoint the chief minister, like the President's to appoint the Prime Minister, was 'unfettered',[46] what were the criteria for selection? The governor, like the Queen in England, thought M. C. Setalvad and M. C. Mahajan, should invite the '"most influential leader of the party or group commanding a majority in the House of Commons"'. In parallel with this, Setalvad continued, where the former governing party had lost its majority the governor should call upon the leader of the Opposition to form a government.[47] Mrs Gandhi's government concluded from the

[45] *AR*, 26 November–2 December 1967, p. 8037.

[46] When upholding Governor Dharma Vira's dismissal of the Mukherjee government and appointment of P. C. Ghosh as the Chief Minister in *Mahabir Prasad Sharma v Profulla Chandra Ghosh.*

[47] Setalvad emphasized the Queen's 'impartiality' when making her selection. He and Mahajan were responding to a request for advice that Home Minister Chavan had made because of a situation that had arisen in Rajasthan early in 1967. The two men, and also P. B. Gajendragadkar, A. K. Sarkar, and H. M. Seervai, had been asked for their views about what the governor should do when 'no party or pre-existing coalition of parties secures a clear majority'. The text of Chavan's letter, the replies to it, and the summary of them laid on the table in the Rajya Sabha on 13 May 1970 are reproduced in Kashyap, *The Politics of Power*, pp. 619ff. It is curious that these documents were laid on the table of the Lok Sabha three years after they were received. Setalvad was quoting O. Hood Phillips, *Constitutional and Administrative Law* and Ivor Jennings, *Cabinet Government.* He opposed the governor interviewing members of the Opposition to learn their loyalties.

opinions Setalvad, Mahajan, and others had submitted that the governor should invite to form a government the person 'found by him as a result of his soundings' to be the most likely to command a stable majority in the legislature.[48] Several years later, the Committee of Governors expressed the view that the governor should act upon his 'informed and objective appraisal' of who commanded a majority and that the largest party in the legislature had no 'absolute right' to be invited to form a government.[49] The AICC(I) reposed even greater faith in the governor—perhaps indicating its hope for continued Congress governments in New Delhi, which would appoint party sympathizers. The governor could 'verify' the majority 'by virtue of his experience'. That the power to select the chief minister 'has been vested in such a high dignitary is by itself a guarantee for the proper exercise thereof', the AICC(I) modestly said.[50]

As to dismissing a chief minister and his government, there was a good deal of agreement that the governor could dissolve the assembly only on the advice of the chief minister and that questions about a ministry's majority should be settled on the floor of the House 'and not by extra-legislative parleys'.[51] The Rajamannar Committee, the Bangalore Seminar, the Administrative Reforms and Sarkaria Commissions, and the Committee of Governors agreed.[52] The Conference of Presiding Officers of Legislatures resolved that a chief minister's loss of confidence '"shall, at all times, be decided in the assembly"'.[53]

But what if the chief minister refused to advise, or delayed, summoning the assembly to test his strength? In such a pass, the governor in his discretion may dismiss the ministry, said the Committee of Governors.[54]

---

[48] Kashyap, *The Politics of Power,* p. 619.

[49] *Governors' Report,* pp. 14, 28.

[50] Memorandum to the Sarkaria Commission. *Sarkaria Report,* vol. 2, p. 667.

[51] Sorabjee, 'The Constitution and the Governor', in Sorabjee et al., *Sage or Saboteur,* p.27.

[52] *Rajamannar Report,* p. 222; Bangalore Seminar, pp. 400–1; *Sarkaria Report,* vol. 1, pp. 135–6; ARC, *Report of the Study Team,* p. 281; *Governors Report,* p. 55.

The West Bengal government, citing the United Front government's dismissal, would deny the governor had authority to dismiss a ministry, and the Tamil Nadu government would vest all the governor's powers in the chief minister. *Sarkaria Report,* vol. 2. pp. 401, and 486, respectively.

[53] Resolution adopted 7 April 1968. Kashyap (ed.), *Kaul and Shakdher Practice and Procedure of Parliament,* p. 124.

But Asoke Sen held that if postponing the test of strength of a ministry that had 'manifestly' lost its majority would cause 'serious trouble and disturbances', then the governor could dismiss the ministry. Sen, 'Role of the Governor', p. 278.

[54] *Governors' Report,* pp. 38–9.

Dharma Vira would have amended the Constitution to empower the governor to summon the legislature without the otherwise constitutionally obligatory ministerial advice.[55] The Rajamannar Committee believed that the governor 'of his own motion' could summon the assembly, as did the Sarkaria Commission 'in the exigencies of certain situations'. The Committee of Governors, which might have been expected to think differently, said the legislature 'cannot be summoned without or against the advice of the chief minister ...'.[56] The Conference of Presiding Officers advocated a convention that, were there 'undue delay' in summoning the legislature, a majority of members wishing to discuss a no-confidence motion could request the chief minister to call a session, and he would be obliged to so advise the governor.[57]

Finally, there were the questions: had a governor to dissolve the assembly on the advice of a defeated chief minister, or one who had lost his majority? Could he dissolve the assembly, in his discretion, if the chief minister had lost his majority and no one else could command one? Again, there was uncertainty. Law Minister P. Govinda Menon said that a convention should establish whether a governor must dissolve a legislature on the advice of a defeated chief minister.[58] 'No definite answers' exist, according to Kaul and Shakdher's definitive *Practice and Procedure in Parliament*, as to whether a prime minister or a chief minister who has lost the confidence of the House or is in danger of doing so should advise dissolution, and, if he does so, should his advice be accepted.[59] Asoke Sen believed it would be 'very risky' to follow the British precedent that a defeated chief minister could advise dissolution and the calling of an election.[60]

The need to codify constitutional proprieties for governors, whether through law or by convention, should by now be evident. It is remarkable that governors, cast upon a sea of constitutional uncertainties when few had been near the water before, stayed afloat and that this juncture of the federal and parliamentary systems survived their flounderings without crippling damage. Suggestions for codification have been made

[55]Sorabjee, et al., *Sage or Saboteur*, p. 85.

[56] *Rajamannar Report*, p. 222; *Sarkaria Report*, vol. 1, pp. 135–6; *Governors' Report*, p. 45.
 In Asoke Sen's opinion, the governor may 'direct the calling of the Assembly' if the chief minister refuses to do so. Sen, 'Role of the Governor', pp. 277–8.

[57] Kashyap (ed.), *Kaul and Shakdher Practice and Procedure of Parliament*, p. 161.

[58] Law Ministry: *AR*, 26 November–2 December 1967, p. 8037; Govinda Menon, ibid., 3–9 September 1967, p. 7898.

[59] Kashyap (ed.), *Kaul and Shakdher Practice and Procedure*, pp. 172–3.

[60] Sen, 'Role of the Governor', p. 266.

from time to time. Asoke Sen suggested the central and state governments collaborate to devise a Code of Conduct. The Rajamannar Committee advocated amending the Constitution to enable the President to issue Instruments of Instructions to governors concerning their relations with the central government, and how they should act 'as head of the State', including in their 'exercise of discretionary powers'.[61] Such suggestions are not too late to follow, for the rules continue to be uncertain. The absence of a well-established understanding of the limits of the governor's role as a constitutional sovereign is an open invitation to personal prejudice and to central manipulation of a state's affairs—whether in more 'normal' parliamentary situations, as described in this chapter, or in instances of President's Rule, as described in the next. As the country moves toward more participative, decentralized governance, reformed practices are essential. Unless governors conduct themselves strictly as constitutional monarchs (whether by personal self-discipline, or as the result of constitutional requirements), the office is likely to prejudice cooperative centre–state relations and effective administration, and risk the viability of the democratic Constitution.

Reservation of Bills

The interlocked issues of gubernatorial discretion and central interference in state affairs also arose from a governor's constitutional authority to reserve a bill enacted by the state legislature 'for the consideration of the President'—whose assent then would be necessary for the bill to become law.[62] 'Reservation' of bills became an irritant in centre–state relations because of the principles involved and the volume of bills reserved over the years. The common perception that governors frequently reserved bills on New Delhi's instructions was an exaggeration, because chief ministers themselves sometimes advised reservation, and the Constitution provided that bills pertaining to items on the Concurrent List must be

---

[61] *Rajamannar Report*, p. 222.

[62] Article 200 provides that a bill passed by a state legislature shall go to the governor, who may then give or withhold his assent or 'reserve' the bill for the President. The governor may return a bill to the legislature with recommendations, but must assent to it if it is re-passed, with or without incorporating his recommendations. The governor is required to reserve a bill if, in his opinion, it would derogate from the powers of the high court.

Article 201 provides that if the President does not assent to the reserved bill he may return it to the governor; that the legislature shall reconsider the bill and the President's message concerning it; and that if the bill is re-passed, with or without change, it shall go again to the President for consideration.

cleared with the centre. Nevertheless, the governor did act in his 'discretion' often enough to be accused of interfering in the state's affairs. Resentment at the initial act of reservation was compounded by the often tedious process of gaining presidential assent, which was attributed to purposeful central 'foot-dragging', not solely to bureaucratic slowness. One and two years for action was not uncommon. Twelve years was not unknown.[63] A good deal of consultation between the central and state governments took place without reservation to avoid conflicts concerning items on the Concurrent List.[64]

Discontent over reservation of bills appeared early. In 1952 Morarji Desai, then chief minister of Bombay, complained that the governor's having sent the state's Essential Supplies Act to the President and then asking him to delay his assent 'was inappropriate ... very extraordinary and would set a very awkward precedent ...'.[65] President Rajendra Prasad commented unfavourably that during the years 1953–6, 1,114 of the 2,557 laws enacted by state legislatures had come to him for consideration.[66] From 1977 to November 1985, a similar number of bills was reserved for the President, and all but ninety received assent.[67] Presidential assent could benefit a state bill. For example, during the early 1950s, presidential assent was thought to strengthen the 'validity' of state zamindari abolition bills. Also, a state law having presidential assent might be more likely to survive court challenge, having received the Law Ministry's approval during consideration.[68]

[63] Mody, 'Role of Governor Since 1967', p. 109— citing a report in the *Indian Express*.

According to the newspaper *Sunday Mail*, in 1990 seventy-four bills were pending with the President. Fifty-eight had been pending for over one year, seven for three, two for five, three for six, and two for seven years. The newspaper reported that the Home Ministry recently had replied to the Karnataka government's query about the status of its Educational Bill, 1983, that the bill was '"under examination"'. Cited in Hegde, Ramakrishna, 'Plea for a "United States of India"', *Mainstream*, 8 June 1991, p. 11.

[64] Central laws prevail if there is such a conflict, according to Article 254.

[65] In a letter to a former chief minister, B. G. Kher, then Indian High Commissioner in London, dated 19 August 1952. B. G. Kher Papers, Part III, File 29, NMML.

[66] In his speech inaugurating the Indian Law Institute, of which he was Patron-in-Chief, in 1958. *JILI*, vol. 1, no. 1, p. 8.

Professor Alice Jacob estimated that in this early period some seventy-five per cent of the bills had dealt with items on the Concurrent List and had been reserved on the chief minister's advice. One hundred and sixteen bills were returned without assent. Jacob, Alice, 'Centre–State Governmental Relations in the Indian Federal System', *JILI*, vol. 10, 1968, p. 592.

[67] *Sarkaria Report*, vol. 1, p. 152. Fifty-five bills were pending when the report was published.

[68] Santhanam, *Union-State Relations in India*, pp. 22–3.

The governor's authority to reserve a bill in his 'discretion' was as generally conceded as it was widely disliked. A Law Ministry Note of 1969 for the cabinet argued that ' "the Governor could by and large act in his discretion" ',[69] and at various times H. M. Seervai, Durga Das Basu, Soli Sorabjee, Alice Jacob, and former President R. Venkataraman agreed.[70] Ever objective about Presidents with Congress backgrounds (and at the time it was Zail Singh), the AICC(I) said that gubernatorial discretion was to avoid state–central conflicts and that any delay in the President's decision would be 'neither wilful nor with any ulterior motive'.[71] K. Santhanam seems to have been one of the few who believed that the governor could not reserve a bill over the opposition of his ministers. He could only veto a bill he disliked.[72]

The perception in many state capitals that New Delhi was otherwise meddlesome reinforced the belief that reservation of bills often amounted to central interference in state affairs.[73] The Administrative Reforms Commission said that only in 'special circumstances' such as 'patent unconstitutionality' should the governor act in his discretion.[74] Criticism of reservation increased during and after the seventies. The Rajamannar Committee recommended omitting from the Constitution all provisions for reserving bills for the President.[75] The West Bengal government's submission to the Sarkaria Commission said that if reservation of bills continued to be provided for in the Constitution the

---

[69] Kashyap, Anibiran, *Governors' Role in Indian Constitution*, Lancers Books, New Delhi, 1993, p. 529—quoting the *Statesman* of 23 April 1969.

[70] Jacob, 'Centre–State Governmental Relations', p. 593. Her hypothetical example was if a communist-dominated Government of a state passed a bill 'which would undermine the democratic institutions therein', the governor can exercise his discretion in reserving it for the President. Ibid.

For Seervai, see his *Constitutional Law*, vol. 2, p. 1721; for Das Basu, see his *Shorter Constitution of India*, 10th edn. p. 462 ; for Sorabjee, see *Sage or Saboteur*, p. 24; and for Venkatraman, see his Rajaji Birthday Lecture, cyclostyled text, p. 9. Das Basu also said a governor could keep a bill pending 'indefinitely'.

[71] In its submission to the Sarkaria Commission, *Sarkaria Report*, vol. 2, p. 666.

[72] Santhanam, *Union–State Relations*, p. 24. Santhanam added that if a bill, like the Kerala Education Bill, creates great public controversy, and the central government tells the governor formally or informally to reserve it, the governor's position becomes 'difficult'. Ibid.

[73] For example, an Indian Law Institute Study of 1968 concluded that for the period 1956–67, ' "the centre does try to dictate its policies to the states" by attaching certain conditions to the President's assent'. Cited in *Sarkaria Report*, vol.1, p. 152.

Professor Alice Jacob conducted the study.

[74] ARC, *Report of the Study Team*, p. 277.

[75] *Rajamannar Report*, p. 217. The one exception to this the committee would allow was Article 288 (2), dealing with state imposition of taxes on water or electricity.

governor should have one month to 'make up his mind' and the President six months. If the President had not assented to a bill by then and the legislature re-enacted it, it would become law.[76] The 1983 Srinagar statement by opposition parties said that there should be no gubernatorial 'interference' excepting bills affecting the high court.[77] The Bharatiya Janata Party in a nice twist, said that before Parliament passed a bill dealing with an item on the Concurrent List, it must consult the state government.[78]

The Sarkaria Commission declared its view to be that Article 200 did 'not invest the Governor ... with a general discretion' in reserving bills. Only in 'extremely rare' cases should the governor reserve a bill in his discretion; and not 'merely because, personally, he does not like the policy embodied in the bill'.[79] To reduce delays in presidential decision-making, the commission advocated a series of 'streamlining procedures' such as presidential disposition of bills sent for consideration within four months of their receipt.[80]

Here, also, some guidelines for the governor's exercise of his discretion seem desirable.

---

[76] *Sarkaria Report*, vol. 2, p. 601.

[77] *Statement on Centre–States Relations*, p. 4.

[78] *Sarkaria Report*, vol. 2, p. 620.

[79] Ibid., vol. 1, p. 148.

[80] The commission recalled that in 1952 and 1978 the Home Ministry had issued instructions to other central ministries that bills sent to them for consideration 'should be very expeditiously considered' and returned to it 'within a few days'. In a splendid piece of understatement, the commission commented that these instructions were not being strictly followed. Ibid., p. 153.

Chapter 29

NEW DELHI'S LONG ARM

Central governments in all federations have means to make their will felt in the capitals of the country's constituent units. As has become apparent in earlier pages, these are unusually extensive in India. This has been true, as we also have seen, because of at least four factors: the country's initial top-down federalism, anxieties about national unity and integrity, the policies, strategies, and machinery for economic and social development, and the desires of political parties and individuals to exert power nationally. This chapter will review New Delhi's most far-reaching power, that exercised through the use of articles in the Constitution's Emergency Provisions (Part XVIII). These fundamentally alter the character of federal relations—in particular, the central government's authority to administer in a unitary fashion the entire country or a single state. The latter, President's Rule, placed the governor and the Congress Party's ambitions at the heart of controversy. Another article that has caused considerable anxiety in state governments, although seldom invoked, authorizes the central government to send its forces into a state to repel aggression, to protect it against internal disturbance, and to ensure that governance is carried on according to the Constitution. This authority and that to proclaim an emergency could be accompanied by further laws denying civil liberties. An article not among the Emergency Provisions authorizes the Centre to give the state 'directions' for the conduct of its affairs.[1] Abuse of this provision, too, has been feared.

---

[1] Under Articles 352, 353, 354, 358, 359, and 360, the President may declare and implement a nation-wide emergency that, in essence, gives the Parliament and the central executive authority to over-ride all state governments and govern the country from New Delhi. He also may declare what is in effect an emergency in a single state, called President's Rule (Articles 356, 357). President's Rule allows him to assume the powers of any authority in the state excepting the legislature, which would exercise its powers under the authority of Parliament. But Parliament may confer on the President the powers of the legislature, completing central control over the state. As an emergency changes the entire country to a unitary system of government, President's Rule is unitary government 'one on one', individual treatment, so to speak. Article 355 empowers the central government to dispatch central police and paramilitary forces into states to keep order. As will be seen below, a

National Emergencies

The central government's authority to proclaim national emergencies has been thought necessary, deprecated, and damned. The emergencies of 1962 and 1971 were accepted as necessary, or at least uncritically, because national integrity and security were thought to be in danger. In 1962, the Chinese moved deeper into the Northeast after the retreating Indian army (incursions there had begun a year or more earlier) and patrolled more actively in Ladakh (where in 1957 China had finished building a road across Aksai Chin from Tibet to Sinkiang). Public nationalist response to Chinese actions demonstrated immediately that the country's unity was not at risk. The 1971 emergency also was popular when declared, supported by public euphoria over Bangladesh's independence and Pakistan's defeat.

The criticisms of each emergency that swelled within a few years of its proclamation, made alike by prominent citizens and opposition parties, were directed less at the manner in which daily centre–state relations were conducted under the Constitution's distribution of powers—which changed little—than at one-party authoritarianism nationally. Critics suspected that these extraordinary powers were being continued for partisan purposes and might become permanent. Mrs Gandhi's eventual decision in 1968 to let lapse the 1962 state of emergency may have been aimed at bolstering the Congress's popularity in Parliament after the party's defeats in the 1967 elections. The Janata government revoked the December 1971 emergency in March 1977, three days after Morarji Desai became prime minister. Mrs Gandhi revoked her 1975 Emergency on 21 March 1977 after her election defeat had become clear and before she left office.

That the public, once convinced that neither national security nor

---

convention of uncertain durability required New Delhi to consult the state government before dispatching these civil forces. There were no such constitutional or conventional requirements for deployment of the army as such, but were army units used 'in aid of the civil power' the convention supposedly applied.

Under the closely related Articles 256 and 257, the central government may give a state 'directions' to ensure its compliance with laws made by Parliament and so that the state's executive does not 'prejudice the exercise' of the central government's executive power. Under Article 365 if a state fails to comply with any 'directions' received from the central government, the President may declare that its government cannot be carried on 'in accordance' with the provisions of the Constitution—the principal ground for a declaration of President's Rule. Under Article 360 of the Emergency Provisions, the President may declare that the financial stability or credit 'of India or any part' is threatened and then direct the state to observe the 'canons of financial propriety'.

integrity were threatened, directed its disapproval of the two emergencies' dangers to democracy and liberty showed how the seamlessness of the web had become accepted. The people were far more advanced as democrats than was their government—as often is the case in liberal democracies. The Bar Association of India and the Indian Civil Liberties Bulletin, among many other examples, strongly attacked the emergencies' enhanced powers of preventive detention and denials of other fundamental rights. While citizens demanded the revoking of the 1962 and 1971 emergencies, the central government continued them, apparently finding it convenient to have available their extraordinary powers, including those of the Defence of India Rules.[2]

Mrs Gandhi's Emergency was in its own category. Although briefly popular among the intelligentsia and the general public for stilling the political tumult extending from Bihar to Gujarat, it rapidly lost adherents once the evident was understood: no threat to national security, unity, or integrity existed within the country—as Home Ministry reports had informed the Prime Minister. Nor, the threat from the 'foreign hand' being imaginary, was there risk of 'destabilization' or aggression from abroad. Absent any constitutional justification, the Emergency's attacks on the institutions of democracy—Parliament, the judiciary, freedom of speech—and the widespread oppression through denial of personal liberty were so starkly self-serving and dictatorial that the Janata Parliament, and its unchained Congress Party members, amended the Constitution to prevent future abuse of the articles providing for the imposition of emergencies. As seen in Part IV, the Forty-fourth Amendment did away with 'internal disturbance' in Article 352 as justification for declaring an emergency in favour of the more specific term, 'armed rebellion', and it placed other restrictions on the President's power to declare an emergency and to suspend the Fundamental Rights during one. Justice H. R. Khanna convincingly had made to Prime Minister Morarji Desai the case for not doing away with the emergency power altogether, but the Janata government's revision of Article 352 and other articles in the Emergency Provisions so calmed fears of their abuse

---

[2] Anxieties about the potential for the emergency powers' misuse had been expressed before they first were used in 1962. The Praja Socialist Party in its 1955 'Lucknow Thesis' said that the emergency powers should be narrowly defined. The Communist Party of India called for their abolition in its 1962 election manifesto—months before the India–China war brought the declaration of emergency. The Rajamannar Committee said that Article 352 should be used only if there were 'war or aggression by a foreign power'. An 'internal disturbance' should not give cause for an emergency unless it were comparable to repelling external aggression. *Rajamannar Report*, p. 223.

that none of the major documents published during the constitutional revolt of the eighties or submitted to the Sarkaria Commission even mentioned them. 'In all the evidence before us', the commission reported, 'no concern has been expressed about the structure of Article 352 as it now stands ... [A]pprehensions of its possible misuse are no longer rife.'[3]

Perhaps the most significant aspect of Mrs Gandhi's Emergency was that it was not rooted in ideology and therefore totalitarian. Had it been, the country would have experienced centralization far more fundamental than existed in centre–state relations and far more extensive in its denial of personal liberty. This spoke of a non-ideological prime minister, which Mrs Gandhi was, by all accounts, and of an essentially non-ideological society. Its democracy and social revolution were ideals. Its 'socialism' was not doctrinaire. Only in the RSS, the Jana Sangh, and a few other militant Hindu groups, was there the germ of an ideology that might be employed to dominate the country. But neither the leaders of other parties nor citizens equated religious fervour with sound government. Mrs Gandhi's secularism prevented her from such use of religion. Citizens' loyalty to the Constitution, along with the very diversities of society that had been thought threatening to integrity, denied totalitarianism a hold until the Constitution's curative character could reassert itself.

Central Forces in a State

The central government has authority to bend state governments to the Constitution, or to its own will, beyond those to declare an emergency and to proclaim President's Rule (see below). Article 355 prescribes the centre's 'duty' to protect states 'against external aggression and internal disturbance' and to ensure that state government is carried on 'in accordance with the ... Constitution'. The related Article 257 provides that the state's executive power shall not impede the exercise of central executive power, and the centre may give 'directions' to the state to ensure this.[4] The bare working of the two articles leaves a grey area in which

---

[3] *Sarkaria Report,* vol. 1, p. 165.

[4] Items on the Seventh Schedule's legislative lists support these articles.

In the original Constitution, items 1 and 2 on the Union List reserved for the central government the power to make laws for the defence of India, the defence forces, and 'any other armed forces of the Union'. A third item 80 restricted to the centre the authority to extend 'the powers and jurisdiction' of a state police force 'to exercise powers and jurisdiction outside that State', but this is not to be done without the consent of the state to which the

political ambition and definitions and judgement can and do play a critical role. To this uncertainty we shall return shortly. But, first, the history.

The central government frequently has employed Article 355 as an enabling provision authorizing it to send the army and its own police and paramilitary forces and the police forces from other states into a state in the expectation of the need to preserve order, as well as actually to preserve order or to restore it—'in aid of the civil power', as it is called. On all but three occasions from 1950 to 1985, however, this was done with the receiving state's consent, according to the *Sarkaria Commission Report.* The first of these exceptions came in September 1968. Then, some two-and-a-half million central government employees throughout India threatened to strike. The government outlawed the strike with the Essential Services Maintenance Ordinance, and sent the state governments directives under Article 257 about dealing with the strike. Mrs Gandhi, unannounced, sent units of the Central Reserve Police Force (CRPF) into Kerala to protect central government properties. Outraged, Chief Minister E. M. S. Namboodiripad demanded the CRPF's withdrawal, only to be informed by New Delhi that under Article 355 it was not obliged either to consult with or get the concurrence of the state government before sending in its forces.[5] In West Bengal twice the following year,

---

police force is to be sent. No provision in the body of the Constitution or on the legislative lists obliges New Delhi to obtain a state government's concurrence before sending its own forces into a state. On the State List is public order, but not including the use of national defence forces 'or any other armed forces of the Union in aid of the civil power'. 'Police' is a state subject.

[5] The central government was fortified in this view by the opinion of the Administrative Reforms Commission the previous year. Cited in *Sarkaria Report,* vol. 1, pp. 196–8.

When Namboodiripad protested the central government's directive, saying he would give directions to the state's own police, New Delhi reminded him of Article 257, which says that the central government may give directions so that the state executive complies with laws made by Parliament. Namboodiripad retreated. Item 80 of the Union List was not referred to.

For accounts of this Kerala affair, see *Hindustan Times,* 1 September to 15 October 1968; Gehlot, N. S., 'Indian Federalism and the Problem of Law and Order', *JCPS,* vol. 14, no. 2, 1980, pp. 169–70; Gupta, D. C., *Indian Government and Politics,* 4th edn., Vikas Publishing House Pvt. Ltd., New Delhi 1978, pp. 45–8; Jain, M. P., *Indian Constitutional Law,* N. M. Tripathi Pvt. Ltd., Bombay, 1987, p. 356; and Narain, Iqbal, and Sharma, Arvind K., 'The Emergency Issues and Ideas in Indian Federalism', in Sarkar, *Union–State Relations in India,* pp. 185–8.

According to Jain, in November 1967 the central government sent a general letter to all state governments reminding them of their obligations under Articles 256 and 257. Should the states think they could not on their own ensure the proper functioning of central agencies, they should ask New Delhi for help, the letter advised. Ibid., p. 355.

there were analogous occasions involving the protection of central government property, using the CRPF and the Uttar Pradesh Provincial Armed Constabulary, the latter having been stationed outside Calcutta to protect a gun and shell factory. In this instance, New Delhi withdrew the UP constabulary at the Bengal state government's request.

The anxieties in state capitals so apparent in the 1980s about the uses of Articles 355 and 257 might never have become so strong were it not for other developments that had reinforced the states' apprehensions about New Delhi's potential for coercing them. One of these was the multiplication of central paramilitary and armed police forces. Formed in 1949 the CRPF was to be employed "'in any part of the Indian Union for the restoration and maintenance of law and order and for any other purpose as directed by the central government'".[6] Next came the formation of the Indo-Tibetan Border Police in 1962; the Border Security Force in 1965; the Central Industrial Security Force in 1969— formed under the 1956 Companies Act; and the Railway Protection Force (which became armed in 1985). Each of these organizations, no matter its name, at some time was employed on domestic law and order duties, typically at the request of the host state government. State armed police continued to be employed outside their states on central government orders. For example, the Punjab police was deployed in Kashmir. BSF troops were deployed to preserve law and order in Punjab, Jammu and Kashmir, Gujarat, and Delhi, and were used to apprehend smugglers. Six Indo-Tibetan Border Police battalions, of a total of twenty, did bank security duty in the Punjab during 1989–90.[7]

The increasing manpower of these forces also occasioned alarm. The CRPF grew from a modest early complement to 75,000 men in 1980, and to 150,000 in 1995.[8] The Industrial Security Force grew from its initial size of 2,000 to 17,000 in 1974 and 90,000 in 1995.[9] The BSF's

---

[6] The quotation is from the 1955 CRPF 'Rules'. Cited in Bhambri, C. P., 'Role of Paramilitary Forces in Centre-State Relations', in *Economic and Political Weekly*, vol. 13, no. 17, p. 736.

The precedent for creation of the CRPF and its use in the states, according to the Sarkaria Commission, was the Crown Representative's Police Force raised in 1939 as a reserve to aid the princely states in maintaining law and order in emergencies. *Sarkaria Report*, vol. 1, p. 200.

The Assam Rifles became a central force in 1941.

[7] *Home Ministry Annual Report, 1989–90*, Ministry of Home Affairs, GOI, New Delhi, p. 12.

[8] According to, respectively, Bhambri, 'Role of Paramilitary Forces', p. 736 and *India Today*, 15 April 1995, p. 97.

[9] Ibid.

strength was over 70,000 in 1974, and grew to 175,000 in 1995.[10] According to one authority, central police forces totalled some 800,000 in 1975, about three-fourths the size of the Indian army.[11] Although the army often has been called out in aid of the civil power, creating anxieties about the implications for civil governance and about the effect of such duties on army morale, this has figured less in debates about centre–state relations than police and paramilitary forces deployed by New Delhi.

A third source of apprehension among state governments and the public was the authority given to several of these forces to infringe civil liberty. The act establishing the Industrial Security Force, for example, empowered its members to arrest, without a warrant or orders from a magistrate, persons who might commit or had committed certain offences against public sector property.[12] The 1958 Armed Forces (Special Powers) Act—introduced initially in the Northeast and to appear subsequently in other states—provided for the designation of geographical areas in a state or the entire state as 'disturbed'. In these areas the armed forces— whether the army or other centrally controlled forces—had authority to arrest without a warrant and to fire to kill, and they might act in this fashion even before the area was officially declared to be 'disturbed'. Apprehensions on this account were greatly exacerbated by the dangerous internal security situations—during the eighties, especially—in the Punjab, Jammu and Kashmir, and the Northeast and the resulting opportunities for the excessive use of force and violation of civil liberties.

[10] Ibid.

[11] Hart, Henry C., 'Introduction', in Hart (ed.), *Indira Gandhi's India*, p. 18. The *Economic and Political Weekly* used the same figure in its issue of 1 June 1974, p. 846.

A figure of one million for the combined strength of paramilitary forces was given by Ganguly, Sumit, 'From the Defence of the Nation to Aid to the Civil: The Army in Contemporary India' in Kennedy, Charles H., and Louscher, David J.(eds), *Civil Military Interaction in Asia and Africa*, E. J. Brill, Leiden, 1991, p. 22. Ganguly reports that the army was called out four hundred seventy-five times from 1951 to 1970 and only one hundred fewer times from 1981 to 1984.

[12] Peoples Union for Democratic Rights, Delhi, 'Fewer Rights, More Bullets: The Central Industrial Security Force (Amendment) Bill' in Desai, *Violation of Democratic Rights in India*, p. 124.

V. C. Shukla, the Minister of State, Home Affairs argued in the Lok Sabha that a properly disciplined and trained force was needed due to the inadequacies in security at public sector undertakings and of local police forces. Ibid., p. 122.

A magistrate's authority was necessary for a state's ordinary police forces to open fire on civilians.

As though designed to impress upon the states their subservience to central power, the 1975 Emergency produced the Swaran Singh Committee's report followed by the Forty-second Amendment. The committee said that New Delhi should have authority to deploy its armed forces in states under its own superintendence and control, but it softened this with the recommendation that 'generally ... the Centre should consult the States, if possible, before exercising this power'.[13] Much harsher was the Forty-second Amendment's provision. A new Article 257A made it explicit that the central government 'may deploy any armed force of the Union' or any other force 'subject to ... [its] control' to deal with law and order situations and that they would not 'be subject to the superintendence or control of the State Government.'[14] Placing this provision following Article 257 rather then after Article 355 seems to have meant that New Delhi either foresaw state insurrections or was prepared to bully the states into implementing its policies. This promised to be overcentralization indeed. The Communist Party of India, the People's Union for Civil Liberties, and the National Committee for Review of the Constitution, among others, in reaction to the Swaran Singh Committee recommendation and to the draft article, demanded that central government forces either be deployed with a state's permission or operate under state government control after deployment. The article in the Forty-second Amendment was in effect only twenty-eight months because Janata repealed it in the Forty- fourth Amendment, only partly reassuring state governments and citizens' groups that the danger was past.[15]

The degree of apprehension about New Delhi's misuse of these articles was made clear during the constitutional revolt of 1983. As the Bangalore Seminar put it, President's Rule was enough to manage breakdowns of law and order.[16] Predictably, the AICC(I) disagreed. It told the Sarkaria

[13] *Swaran Singh Report*, p. 13.

[14] The amendment also added parallel entries to the Union and State Legislative Lists. One of these, entry 2A on the Union List, provided for 'deployment of any armed force of the Union' or any other force etc. 'in any State in aid of the civil power ...'. Obtaining the receiving state's consent was not mentioned. Item 80 of this list remained unchanged, with state consent required only for entering out-of-state police forces.

[15] Although the Forty-fourth Amendment repealed Article 257A, it left untouched the term 'internal disturbance' in Article 355 and did not replace it with 'armed rebellion', as it had in Article 352. Apparently this was to distinguish between levels of instability in a state.

[16] *Seminar on Centre–State Relations*, p. 179.

The Rajamannar Committee had recommended that the CRPF could not be deployed without a state's request or consent. *Rajamannar Report*, p. 226.

Commission that the Centre 'may be armed with more powers for protecting the unity and integrity of the nation and to prevent tendencies to secede including powers to deal with terrorism'.[17] Within this debate there were other apprehensions. These centred, first, around the definition of 'internal disturbance' as used in Article 355 and the judgemental decision about whether or not the disturbance jeopardized the state government's ability to govern according to the Constitution.

Additionally, the states' anxieties were reinforced by the commission's views that Article 355 'by necessary implication' empowered the centre to use force to do its 'duty', and that the entry on the Union List—(2A) bestowing the power to use central armed forces 'in aid of the civil power'—does 'not necessarily imply' that the centre can deploy its forces only at the request of the state government.[18] The commission's view that New Delhi could not deploy its armed forces, 'in contravention of the wishes of a State Government ... [in order] to deal with a relatively less serious public order problem ... which the state government is confident of tackling'[19] cheered state leaders somewhat while still leaving questions about the misuse of these provisions.

Understandable though anxieties in the states were, given the awesome forces controlled by the centre and given the over-centralization of central government authority taking place over more than a decade, there were other dimensions to the issue. State governments had requested the assistance of central forces to maintain their authority in the face of unrest far more often than New Delhi had pressured them into accepting central armed assistance, one suspects. And central intervention also had been arranged through negotiation. Moreover, it was legally established practice that central forces deployed in a state to aid the civil power—and equally police forces deployed from another state—could go into action to maintain public order only on the direction of officers of the state government, magistrates or senior police officers. 'It is the magistrate having jurisdiction who must authorize the

---

[17] *Sarkaria Report,* vol. 2, pp. 663, 665.

State government and political parties were not the only ones concerned about the swelling of federal forces. Parliament's Public Accounts Committee professed itself 'very much concerned over [the] large-scale and continuous increase in unproductive expenditure' of central forces and called for an 'urgent review' of them. Cited in *Seminar on Centre-State Relations,* Bangalore, 1983, p. 164. The expenditure rose from three crore in 1950–1 (a crore equals ten million) to 156.42 crore rupees in 1974–5.

[18] *Sarkaria Report,* vol. 1, p. 169.

[19] Ibid., p. 197.

See also Seervai, *Constitutional Law,* vol. 2, pp. 1565–66, 2212, 2620–29.

commanding officer of the unit to act,' said a senior Home Ministry official.[20]

No event better illustrates the complexities of applying Articles 355 and 257 and the confrontation that may arise between the central and a state government than the crisis at Ayodhya in Uttar Pradesh in November–December 1992. During the early months of that year, Hindu militant parties and their 'volunteers' had been agitating about, and making promises to, destroy the Babri Masjid (mosque), which allegedly had been built upon the mythical birthplace of Lord Ram, in order to erect in its place a temple dedicated to Ram.

The danger of violence on the spot and between Hindus and Muslims nationally, should attempts be made to realize these promises, was immense. The central government controlled by the Congress Party had committed itself to protecting the mosque. Yet the UP government was in the hands of one of the Hindu-militant parties (the Bharatiya Janata Party), whose willingness to protect the mosque with its own police forces was doubtful—despite its assurances that it would do so and its having filed an affidavit to this effect with the Supreme Court on 27 November. It seemed that New Delhi would have to use its own armed forces.

The UP government, however, refused to consent to the deployment of central forces in Ayodhya. In New Delhi the Political Affairs Committee of the cabinet and the cabinet contemplated placing the state under President's Rule and immediately thereafter moving its forces to prevent an attack on the mosque.[21] After dithering for days, Prime Minister P. V. Narasimha Rao on 24 November ordered the deployment of some twenty-thousand paramilitary forces (CRPF, CISF, and RPF—Railway Protection Force) at Faizabad—near, but not at, Ayodhya. As the state government continued to resist deploying these men at the mosque and as 'volunteers' filled the town, the Prime Minister continued to dither. On December 6, the militants attacked the mosque. Even during its destruction state officials for a time refused to request the forces to go into action against the mob. Ultimately, central forces captured the mosque-temple site. President's Rule was imposed in UP, followed by its imposition in three other BJP-governed states. (See footnote 50 below.)

[20] In a letter to the author.

Even under President's Rule, central forces deployed in aid of the civil power have to function under magistrates or, if the governor so directs, under the Director General of Police of the state. Ibid.

[21] For the following account of events and their analysis, the author has relied on Godbole, *Unfinished Innings*, pp. 361ff. Godbole, as home secretary, was at the centre of the events he describes.

The Sarkaria Commission was clear in its recommendations about the policy requirements of Article 355. The 'legally permissible' position under the article, it said, 'may not be politically proper'. '[P]ractical considerations make it imperative that the Union Government should invariably consult and seek the co-operation of the State Government if it proposes ... to deploy *suo motu* its armed forces in that State ... the constitutional position notwithstanding'.[22] The commission said that it would not make such consultation 'obligatory', but that federal forces should be used only as a 'last resort'. The commission also foresaw that 'it is conceivable' that a state government is both 'unable or unwilling' to suppress an internal disturbance and may refuse to seek the aid of central government armed forces. In such a pass, the commission continued, the centre 'cannot be a silent spectator when it finds the situation fast drifting toward anarchy ...'. Then, it 'may deploy its armed forces *suo motu* to ... restore public order.'[23] How apt these sentiments were: Ayodhya took place four years after the commission published its report.

Political Parties and President's Rule

The view commonly held throughout the Congress Party, and certainly by its leadership, that it deserved to govern the nation by virtue of its inherent capacity to do so and as its reward for having led the country to independence, gave the party an expansive view of its responsibility and the right to manage national affairs its way. Although the party had no monopoly on patriotism, talent and good ideas, there was considerable justification for this view throughout at least the Nehru years. The Congress had the rationale and, through its own federal structure, the means to exert its influence broadly and deeply throughout the country. But this dominance could lead even wise and moderate leaders to the pride that, sooner or later, precedes a fall.

---

[22] *Sarkaria Report*, vol. 1, pp. 170, 199.

The commission further conditioned the use of central armed forces by the manner in which it defined the term 'internal disturbance' as used in Article 355. The framers had intended to cover something more than 'domestic violence', the commission said. '[I]nternal disturbance' should be distinguished from 'ordinary problems relating to law and order ... [and] cannot be equated with mere breaches of public peace'. Internal disturbance is 'an aggravated form of public disorder which *endangers the security* (emphasis in original) of the State'. Ibid., p. 170.

The commission recommended that 'if large-scale public disorders are frequent ... the State Government should take on the social, economic and other fronts to prevent disorder. (Mere strengthening of Armed Police may not achieve the objective)'. Ibid., p. 204.

[23] Ibid., p. 197.

The party's Central Election Committee prepared the slates of candidates for the Lok Sabha and often for the state legislatures in the states it governed. The Working Committee, beginning in Nehru's time, heavily influenced who would become state ministers and chief ministers, especially in states where the party was weakly led. The Parliamentary Board, through diplomacy or pressure, worked to resolve disputes within state Congress parties and between them and state governments. Increasingly after Nehru, according to former central cabinet member and governor, C. Subramaniam, the Congress 'reduced the system almost to unitary government. The Congress central command selects candidates for assembly elections, selects the chief minister, and approves the members of his cabinet,' said Subramaniam, 'with the result that ministers owe their loyalty not to the chief minister but to the central leadership. This cannot be reconciled with independent state government.'[24] The Congress central command has changed the composition of state ministries both by having an individual dismissed and by bringing him or her into the government in New Delhi. An examination of the time chief ministers have spent in office—state legislature elections in general being held every five years—yields the following: an average Congress chief minister before 1967 spent fifty-four months in office, after 1967, thirty-five months in office.[25] Governors, as seen earlier, had a similarly tenuous grip on office. It is remarkable that, in such uncertainty, state governments have performed as well as they have. As leaders of the founding generation aged or died, and as the Congress Party looked to Mrs Gandhi's vote-getting prowess to win elections, state governments grew more dependent on her and the centre's favour.

The Congress and Janata when in power also had the constitutional device of President's Rule through which to decide the fate of state gov-

[24] C. Subramaniam in a 1994 interview with the author. He added that other parties had acquired these characteristics.

See also Kochanek, *Congress Party*, throughout. Also, 'Since 1980, many Congress chief ministers have been unseated between elections because Indira and Rajiv Gandhi were suspicious of strong state-level leaders and had the power to oust them when factional fighting (which the Gandhis often fomented) became too intense.' Manor, James, 'India's Chief Ministers and the Problem of Governability' in Oldenburg, *India Briefing, Staying the Course*, 1995, p. 67.

[25] Calculations for the author kindness of S. Guhan.

In some states, the turnover in chief ministers was particularly brisk. For example, in the thirty-one years between 1954 and 1985, Bihar had fifteen chief ministers, Uttar Pradesh seventeen, Orissa twelve; Andhra from 1954 to 1983 had ten chief ministers, with K. Brahmananda Reddy in office for eight years. Rajasthan from 1957 to 1985 saw eight chief ministers, with Mohan Lal Sukhadia in office for thirteen years.

ernments. The idea for this authority, but not its political uses, developed in August 1949, late in the life of the Constituent Assembly. The context of the time was concern for national security: the communist insurgency in Telengana, the demand for a Sikh state in the Punjab, protecting Kashmir, fears that Shyama Prasad Mookerjee's talk of annulling Partition might spark war with Pakistan, and so on. During the Assembly's early months, the governor was to be given authority in his discretion to declare an emergency in his province. Pandit G. B. Pant, then 'Premier' of Uttar Pradesh, and independent member H. N. Kunzru led opposition to this as dangerous to a province's management of its affairs. The cabinet thought it inadequate to possible need. Acting on a draft prepared by Sardar Patel's Home Ministry and Dr Ambedkar's Law Ministry, the cabinet decided that it was the duty of the central government to protect provinces from external aggression and internal disturbance and ensure that they were governed according to the Constitution. Such an 'obligation' should be placed on the centre, Ambedkar explained, with opaque reasoning, so that the centre would not commit a 'wanton invasion' (or, as the *Sarkaria Report* put it, an 'unprincipled invasion') of provincial affairs. The governor's discretionary power to proclaim an emergency was deleted, and the President empowered to assume the function of a provincial government with or without the governor's recommendation. Backbenchers opposed the provision, and Pandit Kunzru said it was aimed not at peace and tranquility, but at good government, giving the centre 'power to intervene to protect electors from themselves'. Kunzru continued to oppose the concept, and K. Santhanam and Ambedkar expressed the hope that before the President stepped in the centre would see that the state legislature was dissolved, fresh elections held, and the province given another chance. Ambedkar added to this that the President should warn the provincial government before acting, thus 'allowing the people of the province to settle matters for themselves'.[26]

The first use of President's Rule was a far cry from the Constituent Assembly's intentions, growing as it did from an internal Congress dispute. The government of the Punjab in 1951 held a majority in the legislature, and the governor's report to President Rajendra Prasad that the constitutional machinery had broken down was an official fiction. Additionally, the centre, and not the governor, had initiated the letter to the President. Leading the Congress Parliamentary Board, Prime

[26] *CAD*, vol. 9, p. 177, 4 August 1949, Lok Sabha Secretariat reprint. See also Austin, *Cornerstone*, pp. 211–15.

Minister Nehru, against Prasad's remonstrances, ordered Chief Minister Gopichand Bhargava to resign despite his having a majority. Nehru claimed that the law and order situation was worsening, but his arguments to Prasad that Bhargava was not acting 'straight' and that it was inevitable for parties to give directions to their members told a different story (chapter 6). The national mass party had blended its interests with questionable national needs to take over a state government. The office of governor for the first, but hardly the last, time had been mangled between the Congress Party and the Constitution to the detriment of even limited federalism and of representative democracy. It was widely acknowledged that Nehru had set the country a bad example.

The 'main consideration' in cases of President's Rule, wrote a careful observer, 'has always been the interest of the Congress Party at the Centre'.[27] 'More often than not, this power had been exercised for political purposes,' said former Law Secretary R. C. S. Sarkar.[28] Former Bengal governor Dharma Vira believed that governors 'generally' had functioned 'objectively', but 'they have been guided by the wishes of the powers-that-be at the Centre.' How, he asked, can governors act independently when they 'hold office at the pleasure of the Ministry in power at the Centre'?[29] After Kerala was placed under President's Rule in 1959 (as the result of the Congress Party's helping to bring the government down— see chapter 6), B. Shiva Rao suggested to then Congress President Indira Gandhi, that a 'Board of Advisers' might be constituted to 'greatly strengthen ... [the President's] position ... [so that] there should not be any impression in the public mind that in matters like this the President is guided by the party Cabinet in power at the Centre'.[30] Former Chief Justice of India K. Subba Rao wrote, 'It is said that in issuing the said proclamations the Governors and the President acted as the agents of the Central Ministry ... and ... the Congress Party ... manipulated the said proclamations in a bid to regain power in those states where it was defeated.' He added something he almost certainly did not believe: 'There may or may not be any justification for this criticism.'[31]

---

[27] Siwach, J. R., 'The President's Rule and the Politics of Suspending and Dissolving the State Assemblies', *JCPS*, vol. 11, no. 4, 1977.

[28] Sarkar, *Union-State Relations in India*, p. 68.

[29] In Sorabjee et al., *Sage or Saboteur*, p. 88.

[30] 'Dear Indiraji' letter dated 8 August 1959. Shiva Rao Papers, File Indira Gandhi, NMML. Shiva Rao had spoken with Nehru along the same lines before sending the letter to Mrs Gandhi.

[31] *Swarajya Annual Number*, 1971, p. 184. Subba Rao also said, '[E]very time such a proclamation is issued, it is a confession of the failure of democracy.' Ibid.

Evidence of central initiative came implicitly from the Sarkaria Commission. It divided the instances of President's Rule into six categories, three of which are most relevant here: instances when the ministry commanded a majority; when no chance to form a government was given to other claimants; and when it was 'inevitable'. Because it is highly improbable that a governor on his own initiative would dismiss a government enjoying a majority, and because it is unlikely that, in so many instances on his own initiative, he would deny other claimants their opportunity, it seems reasonable to conclude that he was acting on central instructions. Of fifty-seven instances of President's Rule from 1951 into 1987 (deducting from the seventy-five total the eighteen mass impositions in 1977 and 1980), the commission thought twenty-three had been inevitable, fifteen had been without allowing other claimants to test their strength, and thirteen had taken place when the ministry commanded a majority.[32] Accordingly, it seems that nearly fifty per cent had resulted from central government wishes. Of the twenty-five instances from 1967 to the spring of 1975, the Sarkaria Commission thought only nine inevitable.

Whatever the conditions in which President's Rule was proclaimed, the governor typically acted not on his own initiative but on central government instructions, sometime Home and Cabinet Secretary Nirmal Mukarji believes. He recalls it to have been normal practice, once the centre had decided upon imposition, for the Home Ministry to draft a letter which the governor was to use as the basis for his recommendation to the President.[33]

During Mrs Gandhi's Emergency, F. A. Ahmed proclaimed President's Rule four times. One of these the Sarkaria Commission found inevitable. The other three well illustrate the use of Article 356 for political purposes. In Uttar Pradesh (November 1975) and Orissa (December 1976), chief ministers H. N. Bahuguna and Nandini Satpathy resigned under instructions from the Congress in New Delhi.[34] In UP, President's Rule lasted only long enough for the Congress Legislature Party to elect a new leader. In Tamil Nadu, the Dravida Munnetra Kaghagam government under Chief Minister Karunanidhi was dismissed two

---

[32] *Sarkaria Report*, vol. 1, pp. 186–9.

[33] Nirmal Mukarji Draft Oral History Transcript. The imposition of President's Rule in Tamil Nadu in 1991 and in Madhya Pradesh, Himachal Pradesh, and Rajasthan in 1992 also resulted from central initiative. (See closing pages of this chapter.)

[34] Bahuguna reportedly did so because of Sanjay Gandhi's opposition to him. Satpathy had been weakened by factionalism in the state, and was unpopular with the Gandhis. Sanjay thought her a Communist.

months before the legislature's term was to expire in January 1976. Although Karunanidhi was accused of 'corruption, and misuse of power for achieving partisan ends',[35] closer to reality was the governor's charge that the ministry was guilty of 'deliberate attempts to thwart ... national policy ... [and] disregard of the instructions of the central government in relation to emergency'.[36] In other words, according to officials in Madras and New Delhi at the time, this was a 'coup' against Karunanidhi because he was not implementing Sanjay Gandhi's and V. C. Shukla's telephonic instructions. Central official P. K. Dave did not administer the state harshly under the governor, with the result that in the 1977 elections Congress did not fare so badly in Tamil Nadu as in many other states.[37]

The criticism of President's Rule that had grown to a crescendo by the mid-1980s developed slowly before 1967, partly because there were few instances of it, and these were primarily intra-Congress affairs. Only twice, in Punjab and Eastern Punjab States Union in 1953, and Kerala in 1959, were opposition parties significantly affected. The Praja Socialist Party in 1954 called for restrictions on the use of Article 356. The Communist Party of India's election manifesto of 1962 favoured annulling President's Rule if proclaimed when the government had a majority in the legislature. The Administrative Reforms Commission advised that the governor should report objectively the facts as he saw them, 'not as his ministers or the Centre interpret them'.[38] K. Santhanam said publicly that unless there was a grave breakdown of law and order, 'the imposition of President's Rule amounts to a grave repudiation of the democratic

---

[35] Summary of Governor K. K. Shah's report to the President. *President's Rule in the States and Union Territories,* Lok Sabha Secretariat, p. 52.

[36] Ibid.

[37] A few days after President's Rule was imposed, Justice R. S. Sarkaria, then on the Supreme Court, was appointed head of a commission to investigate Karunanidhi's alleged corruption. The Sarkaria Commission of Enquiry, 'Allegations Against the Erstwhile Chief Minister and Other Ministers of Tamil Nadu' (published as *Tamil Nadu, Sarkaria Commission of Enquiry,* 4 vols, Tamil Nadu Directorate of Stationery and Printing, Madras, 1978), found that many allegations of corruption—several of which dated to 1972—could not be proved without a reasonable doubt; found evidence to substantiate the allegation that he had abused his official position when awarding a contract; and found 'with a preponderance of probability' that the Chief Minister had received large amounts of cash in the matter of sugar supplies for the state (vol. 4, p. 117). It presented its findings on some twenty other allegations of misconduct.

[38] *ARC, Report of the Study Team,* pp. 276–7.

The Home Ministry's *Annual Report* for 1967–8 said that most state governments had worked well with the Centre during that year, and the Constitution was not made just for the party in power. *AR,* 15–21 April 1968, p. 8270

principles underlying the Constitution'.[39] The most ringing indictment of President's Rule came from Tamil Nadu where until then it had never been imposed, but whose citizens resented the Hindi-speaking states' domination of the Lok Sabha and their attempts to impose their language on the South. The Rajamannar Committee in 1971 recommended deletion of Articles 356 and 357 from the Constitution or, failing that, adding safeguards 'to secure the interests of the states against the arbitrary and unilateral action of a party commanding an overwhelming majority which happens to be in power at the Centre'.[40] The committee defined the only condition justifying President's Rule as 'complete breakdown of law and order ... when the state government is unable or unwilling to maintain the safety and security of the people and property'.[41]

The nineteen instances of President's Rule during the 1970s (several of which the *Sarkaria Report* considered 'inevitable'), the Emergency, and the changes made to Article 356 by the Forty-second Amendment, and not entirely repealed by Janata, lay behind the widespread criticism of the article heard in the 1980s.[42] The Bangalore Seminar opened the attacks, recommending that the 'only contingency' for the invocation of President's Rule should be 'one of complete breakdown of law and order'. The President should consult the Interstate Council (chapter 30) before making his decision and the Council's advice should be laid before

---

[39] The second Rajaji Birthday Lecture given under the auspices of the Gokhale Institute, Bangalore. Excerpts published in *Swarajya*, 25 March 1967, p. 15.

[40] *Rajamannar Report*, p. 223. In April 1974, Chief Minister M. Karunanidhi introduced in the legislature a government resolution calling on New Delhi to effect the Report's recommendations immediately. *Hindu*, 17 April 1974.

[41] *Hindu*, 17 April 1974. K. Santhanam greeted the recommendation as an attempt 'to restore the Constitution in its true spirit'. *Swarajya*, 19 June 1971, p. 4. Chief Justice Subba Rao reacted by saying that if no 'reasonable man' could conclude that a proclamation was necessary, the Supreme Court could set it aside as a 'fraud on power'. *Swarajya Annual Issue*, 1971, p. 184.

The governors, meeting in 1971, responded that the Rajamannar criticism emanated 'largely from a lack of appreciation of the situations which confront the Governors', namely the political instability 'and the politics of defection which has so much tarnished the political life of the country'. These developments demanded reactions not envisaged when the Constitution was written. Nevertheless, 'the norms of parliamentary government are best maintained by' political parties elected to office, the governors said. *Governors' Report*, pp. 67–8.

[42] The Forty-second Amendment extended the maximum length for a period of President's Rule from six to twelve months and said that any law made during the period would remain in force until repealed. Previously, such laws would expire automatically one year after the period of President's Rule had ended. The Forty-fourth Amendment restored the six-month period, but Janata left the rest of the earlier amendment intact.

Parliament.[43] In October, the Communist Party Marxist at the Srinagar meeting of opposition leaders again called for deleting Articles 356 and 357.[44] But the meeting's statement confined itself to calling for amending Article 356 so that failure to form a government would result in elections within six months. If violence made fair elections impossible, then the President might consult the Interstate Council and place its opinion before Parliament for its decision about imposing President's Rule.[45] The burden of the many submissions to the Sarkaria Commission was that Article 356 more often than not had been misused 'to promote the political interests of the party in power at the Union'.[46] Their recommendations would either have deleted the article entirely from the Constitution or severely curtailed the President's power. The major Congress-led states responded to Sarkaria's questionnaires and interviews cautiously, giving him the sense that Congress-led governments were looking over their shoulders toward New Delhi.[47]

In its memorandum to the commission, the All-India Congress Committee(I) predictably justified the use of President's Rule. In the some seventy-three times it had been used up to the end of 1984, the AICC(I) said, 'one can justifiably assert that the power was exercised in the larger public interest and national interest'. The memorandum advocated restoring Article 356 to the wording of the Forty-second Amendment. The 'Centre cannot be a spectator to Party defections, unstable ministries and widespread horse trading', said the AICC(I), but President's Rule should be the 'last resort'.[48]

The Sarkaria Commission recommended that Article 356 should be used only in extreme cases. An 'errant' state should be warned 'in specific terms' that it was not acting according to the Constitution, and the state's response considered, before the President acted. The governor's report to the President—precise, clear—should be given full and wide publicity,

[43] Bangalore *Seminar on Centre–State Relations*, p. 202.

[44] 'CPI(M)'s Proposals on the Question of Centre–State Relations', in *On Centre–State Relations*, Communist Party of India (Marxist), Calcutta, 1983, p. 17.

Also that August, the CPI proposed that Article 356 should be amended, deleting the 'wide powers of dissolution and suspension' of state ministries. If no ministry could be formed, elections should be held within four months. Resolution of August 9, 1983. *CPI's Stand on Major Issues*, p. 137.

[45] 'Statement on Centre–States Relations Released at Srinagar on October 8, 1983', p. 4. According to K. P. Unnikrishnan, he and Ashok Mitra (of West Bengal) drafted the Srinagar statement. Interview with the author.

[46] *Sarkaria Report*, vol. 1, p. 166.

[47] Justice Sarkaria interview with the author.

[48] *Sarkaria Report*, vol. 2, pp. 666–9.

said the commission. The 'material facts' should be made 'an integral part' of the proclamation so that judicial review on the ground of bad faith would be 'a little more meaningful'. And the constitution should be amended, the commission said, so that neither the governor nor the President could dissolve a state legislature before Parliament had considered the matter.[49]

The founding fathers' conviction that the Constitution should provide extraordinary means for coping with national emergencies was shared by their successors. The Congress government's use of Article 352 in 1962 and 1971 was followed by Janata's preserving this authority in the Forty-fourth Amendment, while protecting against its abuse, and by the *Sarkaria Report's* brief comment that (by 1988) the states evinced 'no concern' about the article after revision. It is not difficult to understand, however, that the commission devoted twenty-six pages to President's Rule. Emergencies were proclaimed nationally and placed states impersonally on the same footing. President's Rule was personal: the Prime Minister removing a chief minister, central ministers dismissing state colleagues—who would have remained in office during an emergency. Although the Congress government's prolongation of the two emergencies—apparently for its own convenience—drew harsh criticism, it lacked the partisan taint of many instances of President's Rule.

To nearly everyone, misuse of President's Rule seemed toying with the Constitution, amounting to an attack on participative governance within a state and between the state and the central government. Its misuse undermined the credibility of an office under the Constitution designed to serve national unity and effective federalism: the governor's. Joined with governors' unpopularity on other grounds, misuse of Article 356 dealt a double blow to the stature and viability of the Constitution.[50]

---

[49] *Sarkaria Report*, vol. 1, pp. 179–80. Ensuring the inclusion of 'material facts' in the proclamation would be done by amending Article 74(2).

[50] Two instances of President's Rule since the Sarkaria Commission's report was published deserve mention: its imposition in Tamil Nadu on 30 January 1991 and the 1992 dissolution of four state assemblies after the destruction of the Babri Masjid at Ayodhya. In 1991, the central government under Prime Minister Chandra Shekhar alleged that law and order had broken down in Tamil Nadu. But the Governor, S. S. Barnala, refused to submit a written or oral report to the President confirming this and recommending President's Rule. Barnala told a press conference after President's Rule had been imposed that he had made no '"adverse comments"' about the internal situation in Tamil Nadu in his Fortnightly Letters to the President. President R. Venkataraman nevertheless proclaimed President's Rule, and Barnala resigned his office. For an account of this affair, see Guhan, S., 'Constitutional Collapse: In Tamil Nadu or in Delhi?', *Frontline*, 16 February–1 March 1991, pp. 110ff.

The December 1992 dissolution by President Shankar Dayal Sharma of the legislatures of Uttar Pradesh, Madhya Pradesh, Rajasthan, and Himachal Pradesh on the advice of the P. V. Narasimha Rao government resulted from the destruction of the Babri mosque, the accompanying bloodshed, and the breakdown of law and order in UP. The BJP was in power in the four states. The official grounds for imposing President's Rule in the other three states was the actual or feared breakdown of order resulting from the mosque's destruction.

The actual situation in these states seems to have been quite different. Madhav Godbole reports that the law and order situation 'particularly in Rajasthan and Himachal Pradesh was quite satisfactory'. The communal situation in the Congress-governed states of Maharashra, Karnataka, and Gujarat conversely was 'very bad', said Godbole. For the tangled tale of the imposition of President's Rule in the three states, see Godbole, *Unfinished Innings*, pp. 397–401. The chief ministers of the BJP-governed states all were members of the RSS, and, because the central government had banned the RSS, they were subject to the provisions of the Unlawful Activities Prevention Act, 1997. No action was taken against them under this law. Ibid., p. 398.

The Madhya Pradesh Chief Minister, Sunderlal Patwa, challenged New Delhi's action with a petition in the Madhya Pradesh High Court to quash the proclamation and its dissolution of the state's legislature. The petition claimed that the proclamation was misconceived on the advice of the central government, and the governor's report was biased and in bad faith. The Indore Bench of the Madhya Pradesh High Court struck down the presidential proclamation, but the Supreme Court subsequently upheld it. See *Sunderlal Patwa v Union of India* AIR 1993 MP 214. In Indore a full bench of Chief Justice S. K. Jha and Justices K. M. Agarwal, and D. M. Dharmadhikari ruled in the case.

Chapter 30

COORDINATING MECHANISMS: HOW 'FEDERAL'?

While the more sensational issues discussed in the past three chapters were attracting attention, money and the distribution of powers—the bread and butter issues of federalism—were the steady fare of centre-state relations. They were the grist for a large number of formal and less formal institutions and bodies set up under the Constitution to coordinate policy-making and implementation. These institutions performed more and less well but none was devoid of achievement. Each, at one time or another, was accused of bias towards the centre, and several were the victims of overcentralization.

The institutions most important in financial relations were the Finance Commission and the Planning Commission. They will be treated briefly here as they broadly affected centre–state relations. Their technical, economic roles are described elsewhere in a generous and complex literature.

The Finance and Planning Commissions[1]

The Finance Commission sat at the heart of federal finance, charged under Article 280 to recommend to the President the distribution between the central and state governments of the net proceeds of taxes collected by the centre, the principles governing the grants-in-aid to

[1] From the wealth of literature on this topic and the others in this chapter, the following especially have been drawn upon: Sarkar, *Union–States Relations in India;* Indian Law Institute, *Constitutional Developments Since Independence;* Santhanam, *Union–State Relations in India;* Chand, Phul, and Sharma, J. P. (eds), *Federal Financial Relations in India,* Institute of Constitutional and Parliamentary Studies, New Delhi, 1974; Datta, Abhijit (ed.), *Union–State Relations: Selected Articles,* Indian Institute of Public Administration, New Delhi, 1984; Bhargava, R. N., *The Theory and Working of Union Finance in India,* George Allen Unwin, London, 1956; ARC, *Report of the Study Team; Centre–State Relationship; JCPS,* Special Number on Centre–State Relations in India; *Rajamannar Report; Sarkaria Report;* Chelliah, Raja, 'Towards a Decentralized Polity: Outlines of a Proposal', *Mainstream,* 25 May 1991; Bombwall, K. R., 'The Finance Commission and Union–State Relations in India', *Indian Journal of Public Administration,* vol. 10, no. 2 (1964); Bombwall, K. R., 'Federalism and

the states out of the Consolidated Fund of India, and advice on any other matter the President had referred to it.[2] The Constitution's framers intended the commission to be "'a quasi-arbitral body whose function is to do justice between the Centre and the states'".[3] The First Finance Commission was established on 30 November 1951 under the Finance Commission Act. The Planning Commission, although not called for in the Constitution, sat at the heart of the planned economy, at the heart of India's socialism, and therefore at the connection between democracy and the social revolution—the strands of the seamless web especially dear to its chairman, Jawaharlal Nehru. Congress's long- standing interest in planning lay behind it. The Planning Commission was established in March 1950 to assess the 'material, capital and human resources of the country' and how to augment them, to formulate a plan for their balanced use, and to determine 'the machinery' for effective planning.[4] Because the Planning Commission made capital development grants, it and the Finance Commission became the twin deities of centre–state financial relations.

An exchange of letters during 1952 proved the framers correct in foreseeing the need for the Finance Commission. K. M. Munshi and G. B. Pant, governor and chief minister of Uttar Pradesh, and C. Rajag-opalachari, the chief minister of Madras, were exercised about taxes. Parliament, acting according to entries in the Concurrent List, was

---

National Unity in India' and Bhattacharya, J. K., 'Development Planning, Its Impact on Union–State Financial Relations,' *JCPS*, vol. 6, no. 3, 1972; Jacob, Alice, 'Centre–State Governmental Relations in the Indian Federal System' in *JILI*, vol. 10; and Mozoomdar, Ajit, 'The Political Economy of Modern Federalism' in Arora and Verney, *Multiple Identities in a Single State*. Deserving special mention for its value is Frankel, *Political Economy*.

[2] The President appoints the chairman of the Finance Commission and four other members every five years.

Article 280 was amended in 1992 by the Seventy-third Amendment to include raising and allocating funds for the *panchayats* and other local governing institutions provided for in the amendment. Commissions were to be appointed no less than every five years; their recommendations were to be placed before both Houses of Parliament, along with a memorandum explaining actions taken upon them. Their recommendations, although not binding, usually have been followed.

[3] B. R. Ambedkar in the Constituent Assembly. Cited in Jacob, *Constitutional Developments Since Independence*, p. 318.

[4] From the resolution constituting the Planning Commission, 15 March 1950. Text in *Sarkaria Report*, vol. 1, p. 391.

The members of the original Planning Commission were Nehru, Gulzari Lal Nanda, V. T. Krishnamachari, C. D. Deshmukh, G. L. Mehta, and R. K. Patil. Its secretary was N. R. Pillai, and the deputy secretary was that giant figure in Indian planning, Tarlok Singh.

passing laws regulating sales taxes, which the men feared would reduce state revenues. In the exchange of letters, Pant wrote Rajagopalachari, 'the financial position in particular has to be reviewed ... [and] over-hauled and resources of the states may be augmented ... I hope that the [Finance] Commission will take a just and reasonable view, but unless the entire divisible pool (including income taxes) is reconstructed and enlarged even the minimum requirements of the states will not be met.'[5]

The First Finance Commission attempted to remedy such dissatisfac-tions by recommending that fifty-five per cent of the centrally-collected income tax go to the states as well as forty per cent of excise duties on certain products. Succeeding commissions increased the states' shares until the Seventh and Eighth Finance Commissions allocated eighty-five per cent of income tax and forty-five per cent of excise duties to the states. In return, the states agreed in the National Development Council in 1956 to refrain from collecting certain taxes.

The states' bargaining with the Finance Commission over the years and with the central government on financial matters otherwise, has been marked by their inability to act in concert *vis-à-vis* New Delhi. The state rabbits, as it were, never combined against the central wolf. As a result 'the Centre has reduced the States to utter dependence upon it, leading to accusations of political wire-pulling', according to a prominent newspaper columnist.[6] This picture was too bleak, according to another observer: 'The Finance Commissions ... have, by and large, been able to hold the balance between the Union and the States.'[7] Neither of these assessments, wrote a third observer, took into consideration the centre' increasing strength through both the central government's 'ownership

---

[5] Letter dated 21 July 1952. K. M. Munshi Papers, Microfilm Box 56, File 143, NMML

In this letter, Pant also complained that 'the entire field of finance is virtually governed by the Centre ... Whatever little has been assigned to us by the Constitution is now being tampered with.' He deplored the central government's marked tendency 'to interfere with the affairs of the States ...'.

Rajagopalachari replied to Pant on 24 July that the attempt to 'cut into' states' sale taxes 'is intolerable'. Pant wrote to Munshi about these issues on 30 July, saying that federal structure is based upon recognition of diversity and the 'necessity of maintaining their [the States'] autonomous character. If anything, there is need for greater decentra-zation and delegation of powers.' Ibid.

[6] Sahay, S., 'Centre-State Relations-II, The Financial Disequilibrium', *Statesman*, June 1973.

Notwithstanding the impartial Finance Commission, 'The States had to look to the Centre for money at every step,' wrote Ashis Banerjee, in 'The Reconstruction of Federalism unpublished, p. 35.

[7] Sarkar, *Union–State Relations*, pp. 128, 158.

of the almost entire gamut of financial intermediaries operating in the money and credit market' and the effect on the states 'of physical controls over economic activities, the most important of them being exchange control, licensing of industry and import control'.[8]

Yet the state governments' penury was partly their own doing. Their financial weakness was in part due to ' "inadequate expenditure control ... [and] mobilization of available resources" ', Finance Ccmmissions have pointed out. ' "[M]ost states do not levy tax on agricultural income." '[9] '[T]here is a lack of political will to tap these sources because the State governments are afraid they might lose the votes of the rural population.'[10] Partly as a consequence of this, the states have incurred enormous overdrafts at the centre. Several governments told the Fifth Finance Commission (1968) that this ' "extremely undesirable state of affairs" ' should end.[11] But the practice has continued, and in 1982 New Delhi converted overdrafts of two million crore rupees into loans.

In the critiques of centre–state relations that began with the Rajamannar Committee, the Finance Commission was treated comparatively lightly and often favourably. The committee advocated making the commission a permanent body and amending the Constitution so that the commission's recommendations would be binding on both central and state governments.[12] The Bangalore Seminar favoured establishing a 'National Expenditure Commission' to review expenditures at both levels of government and thus provide a basis for the division of resources between them.[13] The Srinagar 'Statement' only castigated the Centre for the 'over-centralization of economic powers and resources'

---

[8] Chelliah, 'Towards a Decentralised Polity', pp. 17–18. Chelliah 'granted' that the federal government should have powers 'to regulate the economy in key areas and to take adequate action to achieve macro-economic objectives' in the cause of economic unity, but 'any extension of its powers beyond these requirements must be held to erode the federal principle'. Ibid., p. 16.

[9] Cited in Jacob, *Developments*, p. 331.

[10] Sarkar, *Union–State Relations*, p. 98. But Sarkar also pointed out that the Centre 'has been given the resilient and expanding resources of revenue, while the States have been given the inelastic and even eroding sources of revenue'. Ibid., p. 96.

Justice Sarkaria thought likewise. The states have no major revenue source beyond sales tax, he said in an interview, and he had wished his commission to recommend the centre's sharing of corporation tax proceeds with the states, but New Delhi would not include this recommendation in the Sarkaria Commission report.

[11] Cited in *Sarkaria Report*, vol. 1, p. 313. The Sarkaria Commission's own opinion was that there could be no permanent solution to overdrafts unless the fundamental causes of the 'imbalance between resources and needs are dealt with imaginatively'. Ibid.

[12] *Rajamannar Report*, p. 219.

[13] *JCPS*, Special Number, p. 404.

618 *Working a Democratic Constitution*

that had produced 'the present economic imbalances and deprivation and backwardness of many states'.[14] The *Sarkaria Report* mentioned the high regard in which the commission was held, but it also registered the states' complaints that they were not allowed to participate in the selection of Finance Commission members, nor in setting its terms of reference, and that the central government had not implemented important recommendations made by several commissions.[15] Only four of Sarkaria's recommendations were directed at the Finance Commission and these concerned coordination with the Planning Commission.

Had the Finance Commission as a device not been provided for in the Constitution, it would have to have been invented. Without it, the distribution of revenues would have degenerated into something close to open warfare. Even the hypercritical Rajamannar Committee complimented the commission's 'independence and impartiality and its ability to hold the scales even as between competing claims'.[16]

The Planning Commission from its beginning was the more controversial institution of the two. Sardar Patel had opposed establishing it expecting it 'would become some sort of superbody over the cabinet'.[17] Instead, the government came to dominate the commission, but Patel was correct in sensing that the cabinet would be relegated to the fringe of national economic policy-making. Strong governmental coordination of economic activity was a necessary accompaniment to enormous infusions of central government money into development. But the degree of centralization bred in the planners an undue confidence in their ability to comprehend and manage diversity. Centralization excluded the skills and entrepreneurial spirit that state governments and private investors could have contributed to economic growth. Objections to centralization appeared early. The All India Manufacturers Association and the Federation of Indian Chambers of Commerce and Industry in 1956 expressed the view that planning, although a good thing, contained dangers to democracy due to the concentration of power in government hands.[18]

Nehru did attempt to bring the state governments into the planning process. In August 1952, at the Planning Commission's suggestion,

[14] Ibid., p. 413.

[15] *Sarkaria Report*, vol. 1, pp. 257, 282. It cited three recommendations that had not been implemented (p. 290) and commented that 'by and large' recommendations had been implemented.

[16] *Rajamannar Report*, p. 95.

[17] Hare Krushna Mahtab Oral History Transcript, p. 218, NMML. See also ch. 3.

[18] *AR*, 14–20 April 1956, p. 756.

the cabinet established the National Development Council (NDC), composed of the Prime Minister, central cabinet ministers, members of the Planning Commission, and the chief ministers of the states. At its twice-yearly meeting the council was to prescribe guidelines for the formation of national plans; consider the commission's plan and review its functioning; and consider important questions 'of social and economic policy affecting national development'.[19] But this institution, too, became overcentralized, according to chief ministers. They protested that the NDC had become a rubber-stamp for the Planning Commission.[20] Andhra Chief Minister Brahmananda Reddy called for greater state autonomy in planning.[21] Prime Minister Shastri acknowledged that centre–state conflicts regarding development created 'a good deal of confusion in the public mind',[22] and he arranged that the chief ministers advise on the formulation of the Fourth Plan. Indira Gandhi, on becoming Prime Minister in 1966, for a time loosened the reins a bit further.[23]

K. Santhanam offered a sober analysis of the issues. He had believed in planning for thirty years and supported the First and Second Plans, he said. But the Planning Commission, ignoring the country's immense diversities, had come to work on the basis that nationally 'there should be practical uniformity'. Seventy-five per cent of the First Plan and sixty-five per cent of the Second Plan, Santhanam continued, related to matters 'which have been exclusively assigned to the States ...'. Although this had been by agreement and consent, planning for economic development 'practically superseded the federal Constitution' with the result that it was 'functioning almost like a unitary system in many respects'.[24] Asok Chanda said that the Planning Commission's undefined position and

[19] From text of the resolution given in *Sarkaria Report*, vol. 1, p. 392. The President had announced to Parliament in August 1951 the government's intention to establish the NDC.

[20] *AR,* 1–7 July 1960, p. 3560. The chief ministers asserted that they had conferred on the Third Plan only after Parliament had approved it.

[21] *AR,* 25 November–1 December 1964, p. 6165.

[22] Ibid.

[23] Frankel, *Political Economy,* pp. 255ff and 311ff.

Writing in 1967, K. R. Bombwall reported that the 'steady deterioration of the financial position of most states' was evident in the states themselves raising sixty-five per cent of the revenues for their schemes under the First Plan, whereas they depended on the centre for the same percentage in grants during the Third Plan. Bombwall, 'Federalism and National Unity in India', p. 81.

S. Nijalingappa, then chief minister of Mysore, thought the picture of states' dependence on the centre overdrawn. Bombwall, 'Federalism', pp. 77–8.

[24] Santhanam, *Union–State Relations in India,* pp. 45, 47, and 56. Santhanam also said that the state governments originally had endorsed planning enthusiastically because 'they were not asked to decide first how much money they could find' for it. Ibid. p. 52. He

wide terms of reference had led to it becoming "'the Economic Cabinet, not merely for the Union but also for the States'".[25]

The ARC Study Team's review of planning sustained these views and caused it to recommend extensive decentralization. The centre has a 'vital role' in planning, it reported, but the states were not 'subordinate offices' of the central government. The planning capability of the states should be strengthened and all basic questions of planning policy should be placed 'squarely' before the NDC.[26] The ARC's final report went much further, and argued for dismantling 'most of the mechanisms of central control over allocation of investment outlays at the state level'. The Planning Commission should become an expert advisory body "'only for formulating the objectives, laying down the priorities, indicating sectoral outlays, fixing basic targets and approving main programmes'". Decision-making should be transferred from the centre to the states over Plan programmes on state subjects. The commission should not become involved in implementation.[27]

Although Prime Minister Gandhi acted on the ARC's recommendations, according to the American authority Francine Frankel, the Sarkaria Commission reported insufficient improvement in the situation. '[T]he emergence of planned development has concentrated all power' in the centre's hands, it said, 'with the Planning Commission acting as a limb of the Union government'. It recommended that only 'experts with established reputations for professional integrity' should be appointed to the commission and that the states should be 'fully involved' with centrally sponsored schemes, which should be 'kept to the minimum'.[28] But it opposed divorcing the commission from the central government. As for the NDC, the principle was sound, but not its functioning, the

---

returned to the theme of undue planning centralization in 1971. Santhanam, K., 'Federalism and Uniformity', *Swarajya*, 1 May 1971.

[25] Quoted by A. N. Jha in 'Planning, the Federal Principle and Parliamentary Democracy' (written in 1965), in Datta (ed.), *Union State Relations*, p. 7. Chanda had been a member of the Third Finance Commission (1960).

[26] ARC, *Report of the Study Team*, pp. 91, 93, 96–7, and 106–7.

[27] Frankel, *Political Economy*, pp. 310–11.

Professor Alice Jacob noted the 'severe criticism from many quarters including the states' that the original charter of the Planning Commission had been violated by the commission becoming involved in day-to-day administration. She attributed the ARC's attention to the planning process to this criticism. Jacob, 'Centre–State Governmental Relations', p. 616.

[28] *Sarkaria Report*, vol. 1, p. 387. The commission also commented that central licensing and the giving of permits gave 'undue power to a small coterie'. Ibid., p. 18. Also, Frankel, *Political Economy*.

Sarkaria Commission thought. It had met only at the initiative of the commission and meetings had been infrequent and inadequate—only thirty-nine meetings in the thirty- six years since 1952.[29] It should be reconstituted, renamed the National Economic and Development Council (NEDC), and set up by presidential order under Article 263 'so as to give it direct moorings in the Constitution'. The states should be involved in NEDC deliberations 'from the beginning'.[30] The NEDC has not been created, and the NDC 'has no influence today',[31] having fallen into disuse as the states lost faith in it as a means of furthering their own interests.

Coordination between the Planning and Finance Commissions has been described as complex, overlapping, and inadequate. State governments often submitted conflicting sets of figures to the two, and were wont to play one off against the other.[32] The rapid rise in the amounts of planning grants, it was argued, placed the Finance Commission in the shadow of the non-statutory Planning Commission. For example, the first three Finance Commissions were appointed after the formulation of successive five-year plans.[33] The Administrative Reforms Commission recommended that the appointment of the Finance Commission be timed so it would possess plan 'outlines'; that Finance Commissions be asked for their recommendations on the principles governing distribution of planning grants; and that a member of the Planning Commission be appointed to each Finance Commission.[34] One member has been common to both commissions since 1972. The Sarkaria Commission also favoured overlapping membership and called for synchronicity in the

[29] *Sarkaria Report,* vol. 1, pp. 380–1.

[30] Ibid., pp. 385–6.

As might be expected, debate over the role of the Planning Commission and the NDC did not end with the Sarkaria report. In 1991, for example, Ramakrishna Hegde advocated giving the commission constitutional status with state representatives on it. 'Plea for a "United States of India"', *Mainstream,* 15 June 1991, p. 12.

Sometime member of the Planning Commission Raja Chelliah expressed the opposing view the same year, writing that the commission should continue to be a 'quasi-autonomous body with no constitutional status'. It should be concerned with long-term planning and macroeconomic stability and preparing a macroeconomic framework for plans, acting as a forum for discussion and tendering 'technical advice' to the states about planning. Chelliah, 'Towards a Decentralized Polity', pp. 21–2.

[31] C. Subramaniam in an interview with the author in 1994. Other observers think the Planning Commission moribund.

[32] For conflicting figures, see Jacob, 'Centre–State Governmental Relations', pp. 627–8; for 'playing off', see ARC, *Report of the Study Team,* p. 27.

[33] Bombwall, 'The Finance Commissions and Union–State Relations', pp. 278ff.

[34] *JCPS,* 'Special Number', p. 373.

appointments of the two commissions.[35] The Third Finance Commission suggested that it disburse funds to the states for both budgetary assistance and to meet planning expenditures, but the central government rejected the idea.[36]

The excessive centralization characteristic of federal finance and national development planning resembled that affecting many other aspects of governance. The Finance Commission escaped its most crippling effects, and states' complaints in any federation about the distribution of central monies should be treated with caution. But a state contribution to the Finance Commission's formation and input to its functioning, in addition to testimony, would have given the states psychological reassurance while adding perspective to the commission's work. The Planning Commission had been founded with the best intentions and on the sensible conviction that the country's money and human and natural resources should not be expended thoughtlessly and that economic development should be as equitable as possible nationwide. But there were questionable premises as well. One of these in the 1970s grew to be dangerous to the federation, to economic progress and, potentially, to liberty: that the central government should occupy the 'commanding heights of the economy'. The second premise—that wise human beings could draw a national blueprint for the astounding diversity of the country—was intellectual centralization (as well as pride) that became political centralization as the NDC was marginalized—although state and central planning officials continued to meet. With, in recent times, sixty per cent of resource transfers to the states coming via the Planning Commission and central ministries,[37] and not via the Finance Commission, the opportunity for central intervention in the states' development programmes has increased. The point at which thinking for others becomes counter-productive seems at once obscure and quickly arrived at. And although its practioners in New Delhi were well intentioned, and their actions sometimes necessary, they were revealing their limited faith in democracy.

---

[35] *Sarkaria Report*, vol. 1, p. 284. As to overlapping membership between the two, it recommended that the member of the Planning Commission in charge of its Financial Resources Division be the person also serving on the Finance Commission.

[36] Jacob, 'Centre–State Governmental Relations', p. 631.

[37] Rao, M. Govinda, 'Indian Fiscal Federalism from a Comparative Perspective' in Arora and Verney, *Multiple Identities in a Single State*, pp. 284, 297. Rao adds that the NDC has attempted to resolve some of these issues, but 'there is no mechanism to enforce decisions taken by it'. Ibid.

Other Coordinating Mechanisms

The need to coordinate the affairs of the country 'has been recognized in many fields and various methods have been evolved to cope with it', reported the ARC's Study Team on centre–state relations.[38] Several dozen of these had been functioning from early-on. Their attempts were well intended, and their critics have not always given them their due. There were the so-called 'conferences'. The Conference of Governors, dating from British times and hosted by the President, was held annually for two days. The Prime Minister and other central ministers attended. Typical subjects were food policy, language issues, law and order, and minority rights.[39] The Chief Ministers' Conference, presided over by the Prime Minister, met annually with an extensive agenda. But the ARC reported that the meetings were called *ad hoc* by the Prime Minister, with no specific ministry having been 'given the function of organizing or coordinating their work', including 'follow-up action'.[40] The Conference of Chief Justices took up judicial matters in secret annual meetings, led by the Chief Justice of India. Then there were conferences of state ministers of food, finance, home affairs, and many more, usually held in New Delhi and presided over by the central minister holding that portfolio. The Conference of the Presiding Officers of Legislatures seems to have been more 'free-wheeling' than other meetings and included criticisms of executive branches in New Delhi and the states. Party whips from Parliament and the state legislatures also met. There were central–state 'councils' on food, national health policy, local government, and so on, and four regional sales tax councils.[41]

At these meetings, issues were aired, information and problems shared, and perspectives widened. Nevertheless, the ARC and the Sarkaria Commission found these subconstitutional arrangements wanting. The Conference of Finance Ministers, called at the will of the central finance minister, had not met between 1963 and 1967 and only

[38] ARC, *Report of the Study Team*, p. 295.

[39] Accounts of the meetings sometime quite detailed, were kept confidential, but minutes of them appear in private papers in the Nehru Library.

[40] Ibid., pp. 298–300. The study team added that, till lately, 'there was no procedure prescribed to keep even the Prime Minister informed of these conferences', and although Prime Minister Gandhi had 'asked her cabinet colleagues to consult her whenever they proposed to call such conferences, not enough systematic arrangement has been made'. Ibid., p. 299.

[41] Useful information about these activities will be found in Maheswari, Shriram. 'The Centre–State Consultative Machinery', in Datta, *Union–State Relations*, pp. 39ff. This article was written in 1970.

the centre suggested the topics for discussion, reported the ARC.[42] Among the Sarkaria Commission's findings was that many coordinating meetings, 'being *ad hoc* in nature ... [and having] no means of ensuring follow-up action', were of limited utility.[43] Both the Sarkaria Commission and the ARC recommended establishing the interstate council (see below) for better coordination.

The zonal councils created by the 1956 States Reorganization Act were to be coordinating mechanisms among the state governments included in each zone and between the zones and government in New Delhi. Originally, there were five of these: the points of the compass, and the Central Zone. (A council somewhat like a zonal council was established in the Northeast in 1971.) The zonal councils were chaired by the central Home Minister with, as members, the relevant chief ministers, two ministers appointed by the governors, the chief secretaries, and development ministers from each state plus a representative from the Planning Commission. The Northern Council was the first to meet, and it heard Home Minister Pandit Pant describe the councils' purposes: to attain the emotional integration of the country and arrest regional consciousness, to help the central government evolve uniform development policies and assist in their implementation, and to build political equilibrium among the country's regions.[44] For Prime Minister Nehru, the councils were designed to settle day to day problems among the states in the zone and to help in zonal economic planning. They were not to be 'a fifth wheel of the coach' or to interfere with each state's governance or close centre–state relations, he said.[45] K. M. Munshi, then governor of Uttar Pradesh, and others were not sanguine about the councils' prospects. Munshi wrote to President Rajendra Prasad that they would serve no useful purpose and, presaging opinions voiced in later years, he said that a central minister should not chair them.[46] Topics discussed at council meetings, according to press reports and other documents, included

---

The ARC Study Team published a list of items considered at 'selected meetings' of the chief ministers and of state ministers. ARC, *Report of the Study Team*, vol. 2, appendices, p. 145.

'Proceedings' of a number of the whips conferences have been published and may be obtained from the Department of Parliamentary Affairs in New Delhi.

[42] ARC, *Report of the Study Team*, vol. 1, p. 296.

[43] *Sarkaria Report*, vol. 1, p. 238.

[44] See also ch. 6. According to Pant, zonal councils were Nehru's idea. *Statesman*, 25 December 1955. This meeting took place in April 1957.

[45] Letter to chief ministers dated 16 January 1956. *NLTCM*, vol. 4, p. 336.

[46] Fortnightly Letter to the President dated 16 April 1956. K. M. Munshi Papers, Microfilm Box 118, File 358, NMML.

details of social and economic planning, protection of linguistic minorities, the role of the Central Reserve Police Force, power development, and financial issues.

The councils soon came to be criticized for irregular meetings and limited achievements. In 1961, Congress President Sanjiva Reddy advocated giving them statutory status and administrative powers so that they would become 'live institutions with authority and power to decide matters after discussion and also implement them'.[47] This did not happen, and the councils by 1983 had become such a non-issue that they did not figure in the constitutional revolt. First neglect and then overcentralization had crippled them. When Congress was dominant, central and state governments found it more convenient 'to sort out their problems through party channels', reported the Sarkaria Commission. Additionally, the individual secretariats of the zones had been centralized and the central secretariat 'has virtually become a part of the Ministry of Home Affairs'. Only after scrutiny by the Home Ministry were suggestions from central and state ministries put on agenda papers, and over the years there grew a tendency 'to exclude controversial and sensitive subjects from the agenda(s) of the Zonal Councils'. The commission therefore recommended that the councils be constituted afresh under Article 263 and 'be constitutional bodies functioning in their own right'.[48]

THE INTERSTATE COUNCIL

The Constitution's framers and successive central governments seemed to agree: some, but not too much, interstate and centre–state co-operation was desirable. Article 263 of the Constitution authorized the President to establish a 'council' to enquire into and to make recommendations to him about disputes between states and between the states and the centre for the purpose of 'better coordination of policy and action'. The Nehru government did not establish the council, and prior to 1967 it was rarely mentioned in political literature. Perhaps Nehru thought enough coordinating bodies had been formed or that it might give the states a constitutional platform to object to central policies. The article attracted the attention of the ARC's Study Team, which, after concluding that the 'existing system' of coordinating bodies had 'substantial defects', recommended establishing a body that would be

---

[47] *Report of the General Secretaries January 1961–December 1961*, p. 9.

[48] *Sarkaria Report*, vol. I, pp. 240–1. The commission also recommended that the centralized secretariat be located in a state capital and that the chief ministers of the states in the zone chair that council by rotation. The councils should 'provide the first level of discussion of most, if not all, of the regional and interstate issues.' Ibid., p. 241.

'wide-embracing and will provide a standing machinery for effecting consultations between the Centre and the states ... [on] all issues of national importance'.[49] The full Reforms Commission would not go so far. It recommended that the Interstate Council, as it had come to be called, be constituted for an initial two-year period and be limited to the advisory capacity laid down in Article 263.[50] Seemingly symptomatic of the central government's sentiments, a Law Ministry memorandum advised, perhaps correctly, that Article 263 did not envisage a council probing widely into centre–state relations.[51]

Opposition parties, apparently encouraged by the ARC reports, adopted the Interstate Council as their rallying point against excessive centralization. The Jana Sangh, Praja Socialist, and Swatantra Parties called for formation of the council several times from 1968 to 1972. The Rajamannar Committee said the Interstate Council should have wide powers, be constituted 'immediately', consist of the chief ministers, and be chaired by the Prime Minister unaccompanied by any other minister of the central government. It advocated referring all bills of national importance affecting the states to the council before introduction in Parliament; discussing all important national issues there; and making the council's recommendations binding, ordinarily.[52] With the reappraisal of center–state relations in the 1980s, the article drew much attention. The Bangalore Seminar of 1983 'could not understand' why, thirty years after the Constitution's inauguration, the article remained unused, and it recommended the council's formation—as did the election manifestos of the Janata and BJP in 1985 and 1987. The three would have given the council wide powers.

Opposition political parties and opposition-led state governments in their submissions to the Sarkaria Commission continued to advocate establishing the Interstate Council. It would provide 'a very healthy way out of all delicate problems', said the Andhra government, and far-reaching constitutional amendments should pass through it.[53] West

---

[49] ARC, *Report of the Study Team*, vol. 1, p. 302. The Study Team recommended, additionally, that the new council replace the NDC, the National Integration Council, the Chief Ministers' Conference, and the Conferences of Finance and Food Ministers. The council was not to involve itself in certain matters, like the appointment of governors.

[50] ARC, *Report on Centre–State Relations*, ch. 5.

The members were to be the Prime Minister and the Finance and Home Ministers, the leader of the Opposition, and a representative of each of the zonal councils. The proceedings 'must be secret'.

[51] Cited in Maheswari, 'The Centre–State Consultative Machinery', p. 51.

[52] *Rajamannar Report*, p. 215.

[53] *Sarkaria Report*, vol. 2, p. 49.

Bengal wanted the council to 'become the pivotal element in the structure of Centre–State Relations'. It should meet four times annually, with the Prime Minister as chairman and the vice-chairmanship rotating among the chief ministers.[54] The Congress government of Uttar Pradesh, in its memorandum to the Sarkaria Commission, broke ranks with other Congress governments by suggesting that the Council could serve 'a useful purpose' in sorting out differences, although it should not be a permanent body, but summoned only when necessary.[55] Other Congress chief ministers formally opposed the Interstate Council, but several told Justice Sarkaria 'confidentially' that it was 'vital' the council be established as soon as possible. They dared not advocate this openly because they had no firm base in their own legislature parties with which to fend off central retaliation should they deviate from the party line.[56]

Reflecting the central government's position, the AICC(I) claimed that in the Council the states would blow up their differences with the centre 'out of all proportion'. Were the centre out-voted in the council, it would be 'embarrassed', and the council would become 'a body more powerful than the Union Cabinet without responsibility to Parliament or the people'. Issues could be settled by dialogue, and the Prime Minister 'will always be willing to hear the Authorities of the States', the AICC(I) said.[57]

For itself, the Sarkaria Commission advocated establishing a permanent interstate council. Called the 'Inter-Governmental Council' (IGC), it would have a general body consisting of the Prime Minister, all chief ministers, and all central ministers dealing with subjects of common interest to the centre and the states. There would be a standing committee of the Prime Minister and six central ministers and a chief minister from each zone. The larger body would meet at least twice a year and the standing committee at least four times yearly. The IGC's activities were to be those mentioned in Article 263. The commission was unwilling to interpret into the article authority for the IGC to make more than recommendations.[58]

---

[54] Ibid., p. 602. Tamil Nadu would have deleted Article 263 and gave no explanation for its position—although it may have calculated that the extensive decentralization it otherwise recommended would make the council unnecessary.

[55] Ibid., p. 594.

[56] Justice R. S. Sarkaria in an interview with the author. Justice Sarkaria believed that the head of the Interstate Council should be an individual of great stature, like the Secretary–General of the United Nations, so that he or she would not be dependent on the Prime Minister.

[57] *Sarkaria Report*, vol. 2, p. 670.

[58] *Sarkaria Report*, vol. 1, p. 242. This apparatus should not operate in the public view, the commission said. The proceedings of both the general body and the standing

'Federalism' and the Seamless Web

The distribution of powers in the Constitution was designed to strengthen each strand of the seamless web. The Congress Party was to make the Constitution work: providing ministers for governments and reinforcing governing institutions through elder-brother supervision of state governments, using the party's own tight, 'federal' structure. During the Nehru years, this arrangement worked well, although not without difficulties while making adjustments. Passing time brought changes in context: leaders changed, the country gained experience with governance, and the economy and political and social awareness grew.

By the end of the second decade and thereafter, two conflicting trends increasingly became apparent: one toward much stronger centralization in government administration, economic management, and Congress Party internal politics; the other increasing assertiveness by opposition parties and some state governments for greater power-sharing with the central government—for, indeed, greater participation in their own and national affairs.

The greater centralization—in the name of the social revolution and preserving political stability and national unity—did little to assist social reform. It was dysfunctional in terms of strengthening democratic institutions, for weak chief ministers are not institution-builders. It damaged the spirit of unity by alienating citizens and leaders in the states. Mrs Gandhi's monopolization of power within the Congress destroyed its two-way communications, thus ending the party's value as an intermediary in federal relations. Centralization within an organization may provide increases in efficiency that outweigh in value decreases in its creativity, but this did not occur, and the increasing centralization revealed New Delhi's view that citizens and leaders beyond the capital were incompetent, unworthy, and politically unreliable.

---

committee should be *in camera* and be conducted along the lines of central cabinet meetings.

Additionally, the commission recommended that the National Development Council's separate identity should be maintained, but it should be given formal status under Article 263 and be renamed the National Economic and Development Council.

On 28 May 1990, President Venkataraman, acting on the advice of Prime Minister V. P. Singh, issued an order establishing the Interstate Council, which has a secretariat in New Delhi headed by an individual of Secretary rank. Until the end of 1995, the Council had met several times only, and neither the central nor the state governments have shown much interest in it—perhaps because the bargaining power of the states with New Delhi has so markedly increased.

Central government and Congress leaders seemed ignorant of, or oblivious to, how such policies were stunting democracy and stifling the private and state governmental initiative that could have furthered the social revolution. The 'bargaining federalism'— W. H. Morris-Jones's phrase—that had characterized the Nehru years had given way to politics where the centre was 'drunk with power'.[59]

The counter-trend of importunings by opposition political parties and some state governments for a redistribution of powers increasingly put the central leadership on the defensive. Although the states' and the opposition parties' motives should not be seen as entirely selfless, nor the centre's entirely blameworthy, the decentralizers believed they were strengthening the seamless web. Regarding the democracy and national unity strands, they were correct; their interest in the social revolutionary strand—except for the communist or socialist parties—was harder to detect. This counter-trend developed not only as a reaction to the centralization and overcentralization of the Nehru and Indira Gandhi years but also from more positive factors. With experience from time in office, state leaders had gained confidence in their ability to manage affairs. Governments in the states had acquired their own senses of identity with the resulting desire to act as they saw fit—even in ways not always savoury. Opposition parties had become firmer on their feet and more assertive in their ways, often capturing state governments.

Visible in election manifestos and public remarks by state leaders, the view that national unity and good government each would be best served by decentralization was nowhere more comprehensively expressed than in submissions to the Sarkaria Commission. Although one may disagree with the wisdom of specific recommendations, the thoughtfulness of the analyses and the sincerity of the sentiments should not be doubted. As Punjab's Memorandum to the Sarkaria Commission presciently put it, 'At present, the main threat to India's unity and integrity comes not from outside [the country] ... [T]he present relentless centralization drive ... may alienate millions ... An authoritarian and coercive approach ... will inevitably erode political democracy'.[60]

The reality depicted in the pages above should not obscure the existence of an accompanying reality: the actual conduct of centre-state relations has produced governance much better than adequate—

---

[59] Justice R. S. Sarkaria in an interview with the author. He was referring specifically to the working of the zonal councils after 1963.

[60] *Sarkaria Report*, vol. 2, p. 868. It seems noteworthy that the two Communist parties made constructive suggestions for reforming federal practices.

both despite, and in some ways because of, this highly criticized, overcentralized 'federalism'. The country is solidly unified politically, excepting a minority breakaway movement in the Punjab, deep popular discontent in the Vale of Kashmir over New Delhi's history of political meddling and armed repression there, and anarchic factionalism in the Northeast. Local and regional political parties contend on the national scene and, in coalition, even have captured the central government. The Sarkaria recommendations, the now constitutionally mandated *panchayats*, and the widespread advocacy of decentralization do not arouse, as once they would have, fears of 'Balkanization'. A national economy has developed, with the citizens of each state dependent on other states for goods and services, wholesale and retail. With mass communication, villagers gossip about events in New Delhi. The central and state governments' mutual need remains pervasive, undeterred by the displacement of the Congress Party in many states and in New Delhi. Overarching such specifics, a sense of 'Indianness' is strong.

Nevertheless, the good fortune in the second reality should not distract from the urgency of the first. The time has arrived for change in both the philosophy and administration of the distribution of powers between New Delhi and state capitals, whether or not this means altering the Constitution. National progress, the national future, depends upon preserving the seamlessness of the web.

Part VII

CONCLUSION

A Constitution is framed for ages to come, and is designed to approach immortality as nearly as human institutions can approach it. Its course cannot always be tranquil.

Chief Justice John Marshall.[1]

[1] *Cohens v Virginia*, February term 1821. Williams, Stephen K. (ed.), *Cases Argued and Decided in the Supreme Court of the United States*, The Lawyers Co-operative Publishing Company, Rochester, NY, 1926, Book 5.

Chapter 31

A NATION'S PROGRESS

During the brief fifty years that Indians have held the reins they have governed themselves successfully against awesome odds. The seamless web woven by the Constituent Assembly into the Constitution for the nation—establishing the institutions and spirit of democracy, pursuing a social revolution to better the lot of the mass of Indians, and preserving and enhancing the country's unity and integrity—is intact, having recovered from the terrible distortion of the Emergency. The interdependence of its strands is well-understood: none can continue to exist or prosper without the others. Particularly, neither democracy nor social revolution should be sought at the expense of the other. These were so interdependent as to be almost synonymous.

Distortions of the web—overzealous pursuit of one strand or laxness toward another—have been, and many continue to be, serious, produced by the country's conditions and culture and by human frailty. These appear on the country's list of things-to-do in the future. Still, it may accurately be said that representative democracy is popular and firmly established and that the Constitution has become, in the words of an authority, S. P. Sathe, 'the authentic reference scale for political behaviour'. The country is unified and pleased to be so—the situation in Kashmir being the exception. The social revolution has brought beneficial changes to many citizens, but it has gone nowhere near far enough. The meagre efforts by government and society's 'haves' to extend liberty and social-economic reform to the 'have-nots' should be cause for national shame—as should the use of elective and appointive office largely for personal advantage. Indians have discovered that their government, like others, is imperfect and that, like their fellow-humans everywhere, they can be inept at managing their affairs.[1]

A word of explanation and recapitulation before proceeding. Indians have expressed the idea of the seamless web in a variety of ways. One is

---

[1] The author believes that the virtues and vices in democratic governance are strongly similar among democratic countries and that those of India and the United States are particularly so.

the 'three Pillars' of 'socialism, secularism, and democracy'. Each term, as we have seen, has been given several definitions. But 'socialism' requires special attention due to its broader and narrower meanings. Broadly, it was used synonymously with 'social revolution', meaning national social-economic reform with an equitable society as its goal, and tacitly including such ideas as special treatment for disadvantaged citizens. In essence, it meant social egalitarianism and political equality. Narrowly, it had a more classical meaning: central government planning, the dominance of the state sector in the economy, and so on. It was urban rather than rural in connotation, and colloquially at least, it varied as to whether or not it encompassed land reform and zamindari abolition. Both leaders and citizens could use the terms interchangeably without making clear the sense in which they meant them. 'Socialism' gleamed in the heavens like a star, to be navigated by, or merely to be admired.

The Well-Shaped Cornerstone

Looking backward, the value of a written constitution for a society establishing fresh norms for itself has been proven. Positive and negative rights have been there for all citizens to claim as their own and to use as benchmarks for measuring their own and the government's performance. In a society where traditional forms of hierarchy and privilege have licensed exploitation, the Fundamental Rights and Directive Principles and the special provisions for the 'weaker sections' of society and for minorities have been especially important. Making the rules of representative, constitutional democracy specific has given them staying power. Questionable actions arising from the absence of firmly established constitutional conventions—for example, governors' and presidential powers—seem to be relics of the past. Constitutional institutions have become firmly established, surviving self-serving behaviour and containing within their framework the hurly-burly of politics. The Constitution's provisions for administration and the distribution of powers have made procedures and practices regular. If a number of these provisions and actions under them might now be altered, the Constitution has established clearly the basis from which change might proceed.

The bending of the twig that inclined the tree of India shift toward democracy, social revolution, and nationhood began in the second half of the nineteenth century. Its culmination, the 1935 Government of India Act, has been a durable foundation for an independent constitutional system used daily by citizens. Whatever the subcontinent might have developed into without the British presence, British imports started India from what it was to what it would become: imports such as a well-organized bureaucracy and representative governance; the concept of social-cultural traditions subject to laws established by non-religious and countrywide codes; the primacy of individual rights; and a national sense. The leaders of the Constituent Assembly believed that these elements, blended with others from their own traditions, would make the soundest foundation for the new republic. Citizens of India have taken this Constitution as the text—the scripture, even a new *Dharmasastra*—for public life. For if it seemed to fit their society ill, it suited them well, embodying the ideals for, and the constitutional means to, build a reformed society in which they would be free from traditional repressions.

The Constitution, above all, has been the source of the country's political stability and its open society. Stability in India should not be defined as decorum in legislatures, or factionless political parties, or as the absence of turmoil in state governments and caste–class violence in rural areas. These exist and predictably will continue to do so, for the latter are democratic, social revolutionary stirrings. Stability consists of continuity and a reasonable degree of predictability. It and the status quo cannot be equated, for the status quo is incompatible with reform. The stability deriving directly from the Constitution has been evident in the overall orderly conduct of the nation's business, in the stability of the system, even when governments have not been stable. Revenues are collected and distributed among the central government and the states. State and national legislative elections are regularly held. Transfers of power from one prime minister to another have been smooth—and, with few exceptions, between chief ministers as well. Commerce and industry go on routinely. The military establishment is professional and apolitical. Stability and the open society support each other reciprocally. Were public life not stable, it is unlikely that there would be freedom of expression, association, movement, and the protection of other fundamental rights. If governments were unstable, there would be repression and little movement toward reform. Conversely, a society is likely to be stable and not imperilled by explosions from repressed dissatisfactions if discontent with and criticism of government may be freely expressed and there are opportunities for upward mobility.[2]

---

[2] Existing along with the open society, in another of the country's paradoxes, is the government's conspiracy of silence. Derived from the imperial desire to keep information from the natives and a belief that information released is likely to be used against the government, this appears in many shapes, including the confidentiality of the Transaction of Business Rules and the files concerning amendments to the Constitution.

A Constitution, however 'living', is inert. It does not 'work', it is worked—worked by human beings whose conduct it may shape, whose energies it may canalize, but whose character it cannot improve, and whose tasks it cannot perform. The expectation that, by some magic, reform would spring from the Constitution, rather than from the efforts of those using it wisely, was but one of the notions of which many citizens and politicians had to disabuse themselves. The belief, shared by a number of prominent persons, that the country would govern itself better with a presidential system is an example of this—beliefs that a president would be free from political pressures when selecting experts as cabinet colleagues, that he could make policy without interference from the legislature, and thus assuredly be a strong leader of a strong government. As citizens and leaders worked the new Constitution, the self-evident became increasingly apparent to them: conditions and culture are the roots of politics. The politics of working the Constitution confronted Indians with two apparent incompatibilities: the first was between aspects of their culture and the pursuit of a democratic and reformed society; the second was among constitutional provisions carrying the strands of the seamless web. The goals of unity-integrity, democracy, and social revolution were not always in perfect harmony and on occasion seemed in competition. These difficulties had to be surmounted, circumvented, or accommodated in the conditions prevailing in the country. Leaders and citizens dared not be defeated by the great issues that emerged to challenge them immediately with independence, and, because truly great issues are seldom finally resolved, future generations also would have to face many of them. Our examination begins with a very brief review of conditions, and continues with culture in politics, after which we shall consider how difficulties were dealt with.

Conditions

The population that in 1950 was about 250 million has grown to nearly a billion persons, confined to an area of approximately the size of the United States east of the Mississippi river.[3] Compressed here are diversities and disparities without number. There are the vast disparities between higher castes and Scheduled Castes, between the rich and those living at the level of subsistence. Compressed here also are the diversities of the eighteen languages named in the Eighth Schedule (and many

---

[3] India's area is 1,270,000 square miles; the continental United States is 3,027,000 square miles.

nore minor ones), each of whose speakers represents a distinct culture centuries deep. And here are believers in major religions, each with its internal faiths, especially multi-faith Hinduism.

Analogous are the disparities between states—rich and poor, well watered and desert, natural resource full and resource empty, and commercial–industrial successes and laggards. For the citizen, this environment has been inescapable. With the land filled up since the latter part of the nineteenth century, the Indian was stuck where he was born, unless he moved to the city. There was no 'frontier', as in the United States, with greener pastures—literally or figuratively—to which he could escape. Unity, democracy, a reformed society had to be built with these materials. Fortunately, there were talented builders, but diversity, disparity, and compression breed conflict as well as cooperation, and the builders had to manage the shop, so to speak, while creating and developing the nation. The tasks were inseparable.

The Fourth Strand: Culture and the 'Survival Society'

The seamless web had a fourth strand, omnipresent, visible and invisible: culture. As used here, 'culture' does not include the variety of grandeurs in art, music, dance, theatre, literature, and scripture for which the country is justly famous, but, instead, refers to certain traits, viewpoints, and ingrained experiences and attitudes that are integral to the citizen. These traits, like the more tangible conditions just described, profoundly have affected politics, administration, and judicial processes—in short, governance. To venture into the territory called culture is exceedingly risky for someone not an Indian, the more so because it involves making generalities about complexities. Nevertheless, it should be attempted, for, to change the metaphor, 'culture' as meant here is the primer, the undercoat over which the top coats—glossy or flat—of the nation's daily affairs were painted.[4] A few old Congress members, like General Secretary Shankarrao Deo, believed that 'culture' in this sense made India's soil infertile for democracy (chapter 1). Time has shown the doubters in large part mistaken, but they may be forgiven for thinking so, for the fourth strand caused many difficulties for the democracy and social-revolution strands. Surprisingly, it has little affected national unity and integrity.

We may begin with the common man's view of government, shared

[4] The author's sources for the following are his own experiences living in India over a number of years, interviews and conversations with several score Indians, and the authorities cited in footnotes.

to some degree by the intelligentsia. Expressed as *Ma-Baap* (literally mother–father, but akin to a patron), government, 'the Sarkar', is parental, the source of good, of help, and of authority and oppression, of misfortune. As with the rest of life, there is no use protesting. '*Karma* made us listless and apathetic, accepting that we can't change things,' thought one-time Congress president S. Nijalingappa.[5] In the words of the authority on Hindu law, Duncan Derrett, 'Power in fact stemmed from a state of affairs produced in a caste society; the state was a symptom or function of such a state of affairs.'[6] Although the Constitution's concept of individual freedom is spreading to rival *karma's* determinism, the belief is millennia-old and is waning slowly, more slowly among the poorest, who need *karma's* solace. As citizens have looked up to government for whatever it dispensed, so government retains its inclination to look down on the people as objects whose affairs it is to manage—in short, paternalism, usually warm-hearted and well-intended even when misguided. This helps to explain, for example, centralization in government administration, in economic planning (and the states' limited role in it), and the unwillingness until recently to grant village *panchayats* enough powers to make them more than paper entities. As Nehru once said, decentralization was a sound policy even if villagers made a mess of things.

Of the characteristics of Indian society affecting governance, the most significant is hierarchy. Caste is its most visible and best known manifestation. Next come social oppression and economic deprivation derived from hierarchy. Hierarchy begins at home and surrounds the son even when he ventures outside it. Within the family, his father is autocratic, choosing his wife and his job, and he maintains a high degree of authority over the son even when he is adult. Loyalty to and responsibility for one's family, and secondarily, one's 'in-group' is central to the culture. To his father and figures in authority, in general, he owes unquestioning obedience, says G. Morris Carstairs, and he expects unquestioning subservience from all below him in rank and authority.[7] 'Domination' is the motif of society, according to Justice Jaganmohan

---

[5] S. Nijalingappa in an interview with the author. In P. N. Haksar's view, the belief that one deserved his condition in society has prevented massive revolt by the country's oppressed.

[6] Derrett, J. Duncan M., 'Social and Political Thoughts and Institutions' in Basham, A. L. (ed.), *A Cultural History of India*, 6th impression, Oxford University Press, New Delhi, 1989, p. 131.

[7] Carstairs, G. Morris, *The Twice-Born*, Indiana University Press, Bloomington, IN, 1967, pp. 159–60.

It is worth noting that Carstairs was a psychiatrist who spoke Hindustani from a childhood in Rajasthan.

Reddy.[8] This training produces the combination of arrogance, servility, and adulation that appear in hierarchical relationships, including among politicians and civil servants. Dharma Vira accused post-Shastri state and central legislators of 'blatant interference in administration', browbeating officials so that 'any officer having the courage to advise freely and fearlessly is now likely to get into serious trouble.'[9] Hierarchy determines a person's worth, Jagjivan Ram was pointing out when he said that a Brahmin beggar had higher status than a successful business-man from a lower caste. This, too, is changing as possession of money has begun to rival caste as a measure of status. But this is an urban more than a rural development, where possession of land continues to be the source of status and influence and where upper and, more re-cently, upper middle castes dominate landholding patterns. As N. A. Palkhivala has pointed out, possession of property is necessary for the Fundamental Rights to be meaningful (chapter 11). More money little improves the status of members of the Scheduled Castes in the coun-tryside and Scheduled Tribes, for they still are considered polluted. The Constituent Assembly laboured hard for equality, says Andre Beteille, the eminent Bengali student of society, but 'our practice continues to be permeated with inequality in every sphere.'[10]

The family experience has other effects. A child's break from the closest association with his mother to association primarily with his father amounts to deprivation, says Carstairs. 'His confidence is shattered and from now on he mistrusts everything that pretends to constancy.'[11] Whatever its origins, this mistrust, this suspicion, is almost universally evident in the individual's sense that conspiracies lurk in nearly every corner, that national politics and international affairs are characterized by plots. 'We live in a paranoid world suspicious that our neighbours are conspiring to do us in,' says Ashis Nandy.[12] The 'foreign hand' ever is

[8] In an interview with the author.
   See also Kakar, Sudhir, *The Inner World*, 2nd edn., Oxford University Press, New Delhi, 1982, and Spratt, P., *Hindu Culture and Personality*, Delhi Printers Prakashan, Delhi, 1977.
   [9] Vira, Dharma, 'The Administrator and the Politician', published by the Punjab, Haryana, and Delhi Chamber of Commerce, New Delhi, 1979, p. 9.
   Dharma Vira's ICS experience was showing. Things were not this bad throughout the country, but many legislators, including ministers, personalized government and expected officials to dance to their whim.
   [10] Beteille, Andre, *The Backward Classes in Contemporary India*, Oxford University Press, New Delhi, 1992, p. 2. The brevity of this book is matched by its excellence.
   [11] Carstairs, *Twice-Born*, p. 158.
   [12] As quoted in Bonner, Arthur, *Averting the Apocalypse*, Duke University Press, Durham, NC, 1990, p. 410.

attempting to 'destabilize' India. Prime Minister Gandhi saw in Mujibur Rahman's assassination in Dacca an omen for herself. Rajiv Gandhi believed that 'almost immediately' after the emergence of Bangladesh— 'and Indira Gandhi's historic role in it'—'began the collusion [in India] between external and internal forces of destabilization'.[13] 'The culture of India attributes much to conspiracy, despite some event or situation probably having arisen out of conditions,' says historian Gopal Krishna. 'Indian politics has been brought up in an age of distrust,'and because almost everyone thinks this way, 'it is a mark of a deeply divided society,' believes W. H. Morris Jones.[14] Such suspicion inhibits cooperative and constructive politics and administration. As pointed out earlier, the appointments and transfers of judges have been fraught with suspicions. Mrs Gandhi thought transfers a sound policy 'because if they stay in one place they get involved with something or somebody'. A Law Minister told the Rajya Sabha that the judicial system was in danger from appointments affected by 'extraneous considerations'.[15] In appointments, seldom was the individual's judicial philosophy at issue.

The uncertainty—social *and* economic—of the world around him focuses the individual's attention on survival for his own sake and for those for whom he is primarily responsible, his family. India's is a *survival society* from those at its top to those at the bottom of its vast disparity.[16] There is hardly a better example of this than the scramble for classification as an 'Other Backward Class' member within the Mandal Commission criteria in order to receive special consideration in employment. The poor quite literally are trying to have two *chappatis* where they have had one. Anyone who can is attempting to break out of 'the stoical patience of a people expecting nothing beyond subsistence and regarding prosperity as a temporary and delusory windfall'—out of a system where 'injustice is rooted in tradition and justified by popular religion'.[17] In these circumstances, wrote Charlotte Wiser, an empathetic participant in village life in Uttar Pradesh for some forty years:

---

[13] *Inaugural Speech by Congress President Shri Rajiv Gandhi and the Centenary Resolve,* at Bombay on 28 December 1985, AICC, New Delhi, 1985, p. 7.

[14] Morris-Jones, *Government and Politics,* p. 198.

[15] These examples are to be found in ch. 26. See also ch. 5.

On the golf course, according to an enthusiastic player, a player mistrusting his opponent may be preceded by his 'agee wallah' (man who goes ahead) to ensure that the opponent doesn't tamper with the lie of his ball.

[16] The author is gratified that M. N. Srinivas and others interviewed agree with his coining and definition of the term.

[17] Derrett, 'Social and Political Thoughts', p. 139. 'Injustice is rooted in tradition': Dutt, *Retreat from Socialism,* p. 159.

Each man feels himself directly responsible for his own family and its security ... . He has been taught this so firmly that he disregards the state of those outside his immediate family, be they of another caste or of his own. He is not disturbed if they go hungry while he has plenty, because he can never be sure that the next harvest will provide enough for his own family's needs.[18]

This orientation produces an indifference to the well-being of others and to the condition of society as a whole, particularly on the part of those in the urban middle class. Yet, paradoxical as it may seem, in rural areas, especially, a strong sense of community helpfulness may appear in times of difficulty and disaster. At all levels of society, joy often brightens the gloom of working to survive.

Among the better-off, survival society behaviour is no less prevalent. The wealthy try to protect what they have and 'try to increase their pile before they lose their connections', according to a man recently a central minister. For the several layers of the middle class, inching up the social-economic ladder preoccupies the man and, increasingly, his wife. Securing and bettering their own and their family's position is critical, for failure means poverty in a society lacking safety nets outside the family. 'The struggle for career advancement', said sometime Secretary to the Government of India R. C. Dutt, 'is greatly influenced by the surrounding moral atmosphere of the struggle for existence of different classes and groups in society ... . [This] has provided ample opportunities for corruption, and indeed for collective self-aggrandizement at the expense of the poor.'[19] P. N. Haksar thought 'our civil services ... are committed, first of all to themselves and their nuclear family ... [and beyond this to] making secure the future of our sons and daughters ... and, if possible ... the members of our subcaste, caste, community and region'.[20] For most above the poorest, nearly every aspect of life outside the home is 'politicized', sought to be based on kinship and 'connections': jobs, public and in the private sector; entry for one's children into a private school; better grades from connections with a university professor; student organizations promoting the causes of national political parties and politicians fostering campus factions, including using their own thugs to do so; appointments to head institutions such as libraries and government archives. Nothing is left to chance if it can be helped. The

[18] Wiser, William and Charlotte, *Behind Mud Walls, 1930–1960; With a Sequel: The Village in 1970*, University of California Press, Berkeley, CA, 1971, p. 261.

[19] Dutt, R. C., 'Indian Bureaucracy in Transition' in Sarkar (ed.), *P. N. Haksar, Our Times and the Man*, p. 40.

[20] Haksar, *Premonitions*, p. 201. Written in 1979.

University Grants Commission reported favouritism, not merit, in the selection of teachers and selection committees especially formed to favour the candidate. Administrators and teachers form their own groups 'for gaining and maintaining superior positions in the university', and some court politicians with the view of being appointed vice-chancellor.[21]

For those in government—from peon and clerk to civil servants and ministers, the survival society also assumes the form of the 'personalization of government'. Personalization is the attitude 'me first and not the country, which takes team-work', in the words of high court Justice H. G. Balakrishna. K. Santhanam made clear the shape of personalization in his 1976 'Code of Conduct for persons in power, authority or positions of trust in our country'—among whom he explicitly included ministers and members of Parliament and state legislatures. There should be no use of position for personal or family advantage, read his code; no action motivated by considerations of party, religion, region, caste, or community; no unofficial dealings with businessmen or hospitality or gifts accepted from them or other private persons.[22] The fourth century BCE master of statecraft, Kautilya, put it amusingly: the functionaries necessary to uphold *dharma* were suspected of corruption, for who can tell whether fish in water are drinking?[23] The rampant corruption of which elected and appointed officials are believed guilty by citizens should be understood in terms of the survival society—of the scriptural injunction to help one's own (this in a society where religious observance is common)—even while it is a clear threat to the credibility of democratic governance. It is startling to hear administrative and police officials readily admit, as the author has, that they seek posts where money is to be made on the side. Members of the Indian Civil Service (Indians as well as British) worked the administrative system for *its* own sake, according to senior advocate Rajeev Dhavan; whereas today's bureaucrats work it for *their* own sake.[24] 'Nepotism' as usually defined also should be under-

---

[21] Draft report of the UGC circulated in February 1967. Santhanam Papers, File no. 5, NMML. Included on the UGC Committee were Santhanam and B. Shiva Rao. The existence of such behaviour is less surprising—for C. P. Snow in his novel *The Masters* has shown us the childish and unsavoury aspects of academic politics—than its pervasiveness and shamelessness in the survival society.

[22] Santhanam, K., 'Code of Conduct', 30 July 1976. Jayaprakash Narayan Papers, Third Installment, Subject File 265, NMML.

Santhanam, who in 1964 had headed a government committee on the prevention of corruption, issued his code after attending a conference in Madras 18 July 1976 on the Swaran Singh Committee's report.

[23] As paraphrased by Derrett in 'Social and Political Thoughts', p. 131.

[24] Rajeev Dhavan in a conversation with the author.

stood thus. Indeed, there is a degree of approval—or at least of understanding—as well as opprobrium granted to minor 'corruption', because of one's responsibility for helping relations. The other form of personalization is the aggrandizement of power more for power's sake than for other forms of gain. This applies, for instance, to legislators bullying civil servants, as Dharma Vira described, and to Prime Minister Indira Gandhi—who also was looking out for her two sons.

The requirements of survival affect the civil servant's (and the politician's) job performance. To hold a job seems often to demand an unusual degree of deference to one's seniors in the workplace—which may be derived in part also from the cultural characteristic of acquiescence to the father's authority. (Undue deference to superiors, of course, is not exclusively Indian.) Thus, as Dharma Vira has already been quoted as saying, giving fearless and constructive advice may harm the adviser. As a result, according to him, bureaucrats are becoming 'supine and sychophantic ... [intent on] their own personal gains'.[25] '[A]n insecure leadership ... looks for conformism and is reassured by sychophancy,' said R. C. Dutt. 'The civil service finds sycophancy the easiest way of career advancement.'[26] It was to this and to civil servants' 'commitment' 'first of all to themselves and their nuclear family' and to their other in-groups that P. N. Haksar directed his homily on 'commitment': job performance should mean 'to protect, promote, advance ... [the] country's national interest'.[27] Deference exaggerated to adulation, as during Mrs Gandhi's tenure, resulted in that dangerous hero-worship about which Dr Ambedkar had warned.

Yet the civil servant clearly also is the victim—made vulnerable by his own economic position and by the survival society rapaciousness of officials higher on the food chain. Political executives 'consciously select pliable officers', writes former Home and Defence Secretary N. N. Vohra. '[T]he State cadres of all public services ... have been politicized and communalized with resultant inefficiency, indiscipline and unanswerability ... . Successive State Chief Ministers, even the better among them, have been running the administrative apparatus through patronage, rewarding pliant officers through attractive postings and

[25] Vira, Dharma, 'The Administrator and the Politician', p. 8.

[26] Dutt, R. C., 'Indian Bureaucracy in Transition', p. 40.

B. K. Nehru wrote of the Emergency period: 'The cult of sycophancy, which is endemic in societies used to being ruled by potentates exercising absolute power which Jawaharlal had laboured consciously to destroy ... returned with such vigour that that also seems now to be ineradicable'. Nehru, *Nice Guys Finish Second,* p. 561.

[27] Haksar, *Premonitions,* p. 202.

unmerited promotion for services rendered ... . The *quid pro quo* for such rewards is collection of funds for the politicians in power and keeping their supporters satisfied.'[28]

Related to these ingredients of culture (as they are related among themselves), but in a category of its own, is what may be called the rhetoric or the empty-promise syndrome. It would be superficial to attribute this merely to cynicism or hypocrisy, for it has deep cultural sources.

The phenomenon is well exemplified by Congress Party pronouncements about land reform, which follow a pattern clear in the party's publications. At a Working Committee or other high-level meeting, the failure to implement enunciated land reform programmes would be freely admitted, followed by self-castigation. The causes of the failure would be analysed—such as the party had lost touch with the masses and officials had been distracted by greed for office. After ardent pledges to do better in implementing socialism in general and land reform in particular, a new programme would be announced that exceeded in scope and ambition the goals whose non-fulfillment had just been admitted. As seen in earlier chapters, this pattern began in 1954 and was repeated cyclically through the years.[29] This 'rhetoric from the housetops but no implementation', as a Supreme Court justice put it, seems to come from a disjunction between word and deed, or from treating them as synonymous. 'The word is equivalent to action', says economist H. K. Paranjpe. There is 'a dichotomy between belief and practice', says poet Prem Kirpal.[30] A declaration of intent imposes no need or responsibility to ascertain that it actually has been carried out. Repetition of a promise unconsciously amounts to its fulfillment—the '*mantras*' to which Renuka Ray referred in an earlier chapter. Closely related to the word-equals-deed phenomenon is that of initiation equals completion: a programme is started, an institution established, but follow-up is ignored. A building is constructed, but not maintained. In a forestry scheme, saplings are planted, but not watered. H. K. Mahtab noted that irrigation works are built, but no provision is made for

---

[28] Vohra, N. N., 'The Rusting Steel Frame' in Narayanan, V. N. and Sabharwal, Jyoti (eds), *India at 50: Bliss of Hope, Burden of Reality*, Sterling Publishers Pvt. Ltd., New Delhi, 1997, pp. 163–5.

[29] In 1958, 1959, 1964, 1967, 1969, 1971, and so on. In December 1969, as mentioned in ch. 7, Indira Gandhi's Congress faction resolved that all 'intermediaries' would be abolished in a year and all land reform laws implemented in two years.

[30] Maurice Carstairs notes the disjunction between private cleanliness and public filth.

repairs.[31] Indians, Kirpal believes, don't like facts; 'there is the truth and the greater truth'. Psychiatrist Sudhir Kakar thinks that Indians are unsettled by differences between the real world and the 'inner world' which is 'the maternal cosmos of infancy'.[32] Dhirubhai Sheth's analysis is more down to earth. Goals are deliberately set that are known to be impractical, beyond the society's will to achieve, because they genuinely are worth cherishing and are consonant with ideology fashionable in the West.[33] Whatever its roots, the equating of word and deed often gives a make-believe air to public policy, is false to the social revolution, and discredits representative government.[34]

The cultural characteristics inimical to the working of constitutional democracy and pursuit of the social revolution rarely have received a worse tongue-lashing than from Prime Minister Rajiv Gandhi in a 1985 speech commemorating the Congress Party's one-hundredth anniversary. It is worth recalling at length. We see ourselves in regional, cultural, and—worse—in caste terms, Gandhi said. Government servants oppress the poor, and the police shield the guilty. There is no protection when

> the fence has started eating the crop.[There are] whole legions [of officials] whose only concern is their private welfare at the cost of society .... [O]ur private self crushes our social commitment ... . We obey no discipline ... follow no principle of public morality ... show no concern for the common weal ... . Flagrant contradiction between what we say and what we do have become our way of life.[35]

The Fourth Strand, Democracy, and Social Revolution

Although the relationship between culture and the working of the Constitution is inescapable, the connections are as often indirect and

[31] Mahtab in comments on Paul Appleby's second report on the Indian administrative system. Hare Krushna Mahtab Papers, File 16, NMML.

[32] Kakar, Sudhir, *The Inner World*, p. 185.

[33] Sheth comments to the author.

[34] This coin has another side. Legislation that infringes civil liberties often has a loud bark but much less bite through implementation.

The United States Congress provides an excellent example of the word-deed gap in its two-step appropriations process. Members can vote large sums in the authorization bill and trumpet their largesse to their constituents, and then keep silent about the money's absence in the appropriation bill.

[35] *Inaugural Speech by Congress President Shri Rajiv Gandhi and the Centenary Resolve*, AICC, 1985, pp. 13–14.

subtle as they are direct. Readers, and the author, should be wary of seeing direct linkages where they are not and of attributing exclusively to Indian culture political conduct commonly found in other societies.

One could be excused for expecting that these cultural characteristics would doom democratic processes and progress in the social revolution, but they have not, although they have limited the spread of democracy and social-economic reform, especially among the lowest castes and poorest citizens. Most important, cultural impediments have not denied the Constitution's gifts. Representative government and the vote have touched everyone and have become cherished for the empowerment they bring. Caste and community allegiances, while retaining their negative effects on democracy and social revolution (of which more below), have favoured democracy by becoming the focus for political mobilization at all levels of society and by being vehicles for the pursuit of power and group interests. Because caste politics operate horizontally in society, they do not pose a threat to national integrity, as might territorially-organized interest groups.[36] The personalization-of-government and survival-society complexes force open the political process as individuals scramble upwards on society's ladder—in addition to hampering democracy and retarding social justice.

The Constitution's provisions setting goals for the social revolution—such as the Directive Principles, the Fundamental Rights, the articles protecting minority rights, those assisting the weaker sections, and so on—somewhat have diminished the repressions of hierarchy and the effects of indifference among the upper castes to conditions among the lower. Reservations in education, in legislatures, and in government employment have brought into universities and the political process many individuals who otherwise would have entered neither, and they attest to the paradoxical erosion of the caste system as caste allegiance facilitates upward mobility.[37] The use of public interest (or social action)

---

[36] S. Guhan has provided an excellent brief sketch of caste. It both aggregates and divides, and thus is fertile soil for 'mobilizational' politics in a democracy. Caste reigns, he writes, and is not bereft of social utility, for intra-caste solidarity and inter-caste ties of kinship ameliorate class-based inequalities, induce *noblesse oblige* and mutual help and provide the bases for social capital and trust. Guhan, S., 'Three Pieces on Governance' unpublished paper prepared for 'Workshop on Governance Issues in South Asia', Yale University, November 1997. Copy to the author courtesy of Professor Guhan.

[37] Shah, Ghanshyam, 'Grassroots Mobilization in Indian Politics,' in Kohli (ed.), *India's Democracy*, p. 270.

Shah also says that the 'vast majority' of the lower backward castes do not have the assets to gain advantages from the Mandal Commission report as do other castes among the OBCs.

litigation (PIL/SAL) and the rapid growth of private organizations devoted to consumer and environmental protection, citizens' rights, and grassroots development have taken place despite the strictures of traditional society. The mandated establishment of village *panchayats* (under the Seventy-third Amendment of 1992) initially will serve the power of dominant castes in villages, but over time it almost certainly will empower lower castes and women—for whom seats on these *panchayats* now have been reserved, as have been seats for Scheduled Castes and Scheduled Tribes.

The Constitution's greatest gift to the social revolution and democracy has been an open society—if that is not a tautology. Open societies grow more open for all their citizens, although among them at varying rates. Speech and expression in India are free and communications widespread—although landlords still regularly arrange the detention of lower caste individuals or local activists, and a low caste villager who insults an upper caste member may find himself beaten or even be murdered. (Today, the reverse may happen.) Governments' constant reiteration of the social justice theme has fostered expectations. The idea that 'we have rights' has spread rapidly and citizens at all levels will not forever tolerate their absence. The visible failings of government officials, frequently made public by an acid-penned press, have reduced awe of officialdom. V. S. Naipaul's India of 'a million little mutinies' is the best evidence of the slow triumph of democracy and the social revolution over the strait-jacket of traditional society.[38] Yet, the framework of hierarchy, for the most part, has kept society orderly.

Polls in 1971 and 1996 reveal a good deal about the social-economic and political evolution in the country—some of it, as with all in-depth polls, not easy to understand. The proportion of persons responding that they were able to vote rose from seventy-eight to eighty-seven per cent from 1971 to 1996, while the percentage of those saying that they were not able to vote declined from twenty-two to thirteen. Those polled who believed it 'Not important to vote as your caste group does' rose from thirty to fifty per cent during the period. Responding to the question, 'Does your vote make a difference to how things run in the country?', the yesses rose from forty-eight to fifty-nine per cent from 1971 to 1996. Scheduled Caste/Scheduled Tribe members had a lower and upper castes a higher affirmative response. But this should be measured against respondents' assessment of personalities: fifty-eight per cent in 1971 and sixty-three per cent in 1996 said that the persons we elect don't

---

[38] Naipaul, V. S., *India: A Million Mutinies Now,* Penguin Books, London, 1992, p. 518.

care about us. In 1996, sixty-two per cent of respondents nationally believed caste relations had become more harmonious. Forty-three per cent in 1996 believed tensions between religious communities had decreased; twice as many thought this in Karnataka as in Uttar Pradesh. To the query, 'Do government development programmes go to the well-to-do or to the poor and needy?,' between fifty and fifty-five per cent in both Karnataka and UP believed they went to the former. The upper castes and the OBCs thought they went to the poor and needy about twice as often as did members of the Scheduled Castes and Tribes.[39]

Two other poll queries and responses may be significant. To the assertion that, 'What the country needs more than laws is strong leaders,' upper castes and OBCs responded most affirmatively, and Hindus over Muslims eighty-four to ten per cent. Hindus trusted the judiciary much more than Muslims and distrust was greatest among illiterates.

Economic development has been a powerful force against tradition, although it also has strengthened some caste distinctions and emphasized economic disparities among classes.[40] Modern seeds and machinery in the employ of the Indian's entrepreneurial spirit and the survival society's drive for self-betterment have shaken the traditional power structure and will continue to diminish its authority. Charlotte Wiser tells of a village untouchable having a *pukka* (brick) house, whereas twenty years earlier upper caste members of that village would not have permitted such rising above station. Others report that in cities money has come to rival caste as an indicator of status. 'No caste today has the moral authority to enforce on its middle class members any of its traditional sanctions,' writes Beteille, thus freeing these individuals 'to use [caste] instrumentally for economic and political advantage'.[41] The country now has a Scheduled Caste President and has had a Scheduled Caste lady as the chief minister of a still largely feudal state, Uttar Pradesh.

Accommodation, that characteristic of the society which allows apparently incompatible elements to exist in parallel—in contra-distinction

---

[39] The polls were conducted by the Centre for the Study of Developing Societies in New Delhi, the premier organization for the study of the country's society. The sample size was 9,614 in twenty states, and longitudinal research will be continued with three thousand of these individuals. The questions asked and the breakdown of responses by caste, religion, education, occupation, etc. is most inadequately represented in the paragraph here due to space constraints.

[40] The country's basic economy has brought the advantage of stability. Like a doll with weighted feet, a low-level economy is harder to knock over than a more technology-dependent one.

[41] Beteille, *The Backward Classes*, p. 50.

without contradiction (as President Radhakrishnan asked, why do things have to be this *or* that; why can't they be this *and* that?)—has allowed democracy and the social revolution to operate at one level while traditional norms operate at another. The ideal and the real in policy actions have coexisted because they partook of the disjunctions between word and deed, between rhetoric and implementation. In this fashion, many great constitutional issues—like zamindari abolition and the Twenty-fifth Amendment—were enacted in Parliament at an almost abstract level, their passage favoured by the cultural characteristic of the disjunction between promise and performance, of the word being equivalent to the deed. Implementation of such social revolutionary legislation by Congress state governments faltered or failed because of raw economic reasons and these cultural characteristics: the downward indifference of hierarchy, caste groups being uncaring about the well-being of groups below them (doubting even their worthiness), and the complex of ingredients composing the survival society.

Turning to the harmful effects of 'culture' on the social revolution and on democratic institutions and practices, one immediately thinks of government's laxness in addressing the vast disparity between the top and the bottom of society. The executive and legislative branches in New Delhi and the states, in reality as distinct from on paper, have neglected the social revolution as expressed in the Directive Principles, the Preamble, and in the Fundamental Rights provisions establishing equality before the law. Hierarchy, indifference or paternalism toward the lower orders, and the personalization of government at all levels have resulted in inadequate to poor administration, often-corrupt police, and neglect of national and local development directed at the poorest and low caste–citizens. Among the upper castes–classes, 'individual rights' and 'economic comfort' have meaning; among the bottom castes–classes, who constitute upwards of forty per cent of the population, they mean little or nothing. It must be acknowledged that conditions vary greatly throughout the country and from individual to individual. Typically, outside of North India, state governments are much more effective, and all but the lowest citizens better off. In India, unlike other societies, as Beteille points out, 'backwardness' is not an attribute of the individual, 'but of communities that are self-perpetuating'. Historically, a man's and a woman's social capacities were known from caste or lineage; no further test of capacity was needed.[42] In other words, they lacked the tools—and were 'known' to lack the tools—to fight the

---

42 Beteille, *The Backward Classes*, p. 2.

system óppressing them. In 1972–3, Mrs Gandhi told Parliament that of the rural poor in fourteen states, forty per cent or more were below the poverty line.[43] It would of course be ridiculous to expect that even the most energetic reform and development efforts since independence could remedy such conditions wholly. But ancient customs prevailed because the lower castes–classes and non-caste 'untouchables' (the Scheduled Castes), possessing little or no social–economic status and political influence, have been poorly equipped to fight back. They have had the vote, they have made electoral alliances with upper caste politicians wanting their votes, but only the beginnings of reform have been made.

Although the social revolution is evident in the shift of social-economic power in rural areas over the past three decades—from the castes in the top three *varnas*, the 'twice-born', to the so-called 'middle castes' or Other Backward Classes of the Shudra *varna* (like the Yadavs and Kurmis in the North and Nadars and Izhavas in the South)—this little has helped the lowest caste Shudras and the Scheduled Castes. Often the opposite. The Yadavs, who had been the upper castes' musclemen to keep lesser orders in line, now on their own behalf oppress those below them. But the shift has gradually introduced into state and national politics a layer of society whose dynamism is unquestionable and whose understanding that political prominence and office-holding are a public trust—not a private privilege—may increase with time. Presently, says Dhirubhai Sheth, these politicians tend to treat the vote 'as no more than an endorsement by the people in favour of the continuation of their rule'. Thus, officials, in what amounts to large-scale personalization of government,

> rely on manipulations of the power process rather than on building ...
> loyalties of the people through ensuring their participation in the
> decision-making processes ... [They] manipulate casteist and communal
> sentiments ... rather than ... improving performance on the economic
> front ... . There is no pro-poor programme; there are only pro-poor slo-
> gans.[44]

---

[43] *AR*, 6–12 May 1980, p. 15444. The percentage jumped to fifty in ten states and sixty in three, the Prime Minister said. Forty per cent or more of the urban poor were below the poverty line. The criteria were 2,400 calories a day in rural and 2,100 in urban areas. The Planning Commission's national figure in November 1980 was forty-eight per cent below the poverty line.

[44] Sheth, D. L., 'Social Basis of the Political Crisis', *Seminar,* January 1982. Nor, writes Beteille, have 'the new economic forces ... fully erased' conditions of caste, village community, and joint family 'but have ... added inequalities to those already in existence'. Beteille, *The Backward Classes*, p. 27. These forces have ameliorated conditions, however, at many levels in many locations, the author believes. For the already better-off, economic conditions have greatly improved.

A specific example of the indifference toward lower orders mentioned earlier has been government's avoidance of both the letter and the spirit of the Directive Principles—admirable goals admittedly difficult to reach in any society. For example, Article 45 charged government to endeavour to provide, within ten years, free and compulsory education for children through age fourteen.[45] But data tell that nearly one-third of the 105 million children age six to ten were not in school in 1993. Drop-out rates from the first to the fifth standard approach one-third of those who enroll. Learning achievement is low.[46] A conspiracy—except locally—to keep the poor uneducated or ill-educated is unlikely. But the higher castes seem to operate implicitly on the colonialist maxim that if you educate the natives they become restless; better that we don't equip them to challenge us.[47]

The Constitution Against Itself

As though the fourth strand did not present governing with enough complexities and obstacles, those working the Constitution have had to make adjustments among the web's three strands of unity–integrity, democracy, and social revolution. When they were in competition or conflict, decisions had to be made about whether, and if so how much, one should be sacrificed in favour of another. Several times, adjustments were made between one or more of the three strands and some element of the fourth. Having embraced the new Constitution, leaders confronted questions of essence inherent in it: Democracy for Whom?, Justice for Whom? What *is* Justice? What are the appropriate ways of employing the Constitution's 'means' among citizens and between them and their government? The framers foresaw some of this, which is why they insisted that neither the democracy nor the social revolution strand was to be

[45] 'Strenuous efforts should be made' toward early fulfilment of Article 45, said a 1968 central government policy statement. *National Policy on Education, 1968*, Ministry of Education, GOI, New Delhi, 1968, p. 2.

[46] *Primary Education in India*, The World Bank, Washington, DC, 1997. When researching this detailed report, bank staff worked closely with the National Centre for Education Research and Training in New Delhi. Sumi Krishna's research for the author corroborated these figures.

This state of affairs is partially the result of Nehru's policy, adhered to since, of giving priority to higher education. But primary education, with its contribution to better family health, lower fertility, and employment chances need not have been neglected. Ibid., p. 1.

[47] That this is a half-conscious strategy in the minds of some central and state government officials has been alleged to the author in some interviews and became apparent to him in others.

pursued at the expense of the other. Freedom and bread, said Morarji Desai, are not incompatible. Neither could they easily be sought together.

Equally formidable, it became apparent over the years, was the task of implementing the decisions taken. For this brought the three branches of government into confrontations that shook the entire structure and could have destroyed it. Parliament in the 1950s amended the Constitution to get around judicial rulings, acting on the premise that the Constitution had bestowed upon it constituent as well as legislative power. The Supreme Court, first in 1951 in the Shankari Prasad case, while exercising its own power of judicial review, upheld this view (chapter 3). But the Court later, as we have seen, most significantly in the Kesavananda Bharati case, ruled that Parliament's constituent power had limits. Fear had caused the change. Fear that Indira Gandhi intended to end the co-equality of the branches by eliminating judicial review of amendments—which Jawaharlal Nehru would not do—on the way to sacrificing democracy and its fundamental rights to authoritarian socialism. With the basic structure doctrine, a balance, if an uneasy one, had been reached between the responsibilities of Parliament and the Supreme Court for protecting the integrity of the seamless web.

It was the unexpected difficulties in keeping harmony among the strands that first startled Prime Minister Nehru and his government. The relationships between social revolution and democracy were the most problematic. On the democracy side, the Constitution's Funda mental Rights caused 'problems'. For example, the Congress Party': and the government's pledge, as Vice-President Radhakrishnan put it to remove 'social disabilities' and 'man-made inequalities', and the Constitution's two dozen articles providing for compensatory treatmen for disadvantaged citizens—the heart of the social revolution—cam into direct conflict with two Fundamental Rights articles. One of thes broadly prohibited discrimination; another said that no citizen shall b denied admission to a government-supported educational institutio: on the grounds of race, caste, and so on. A Ms Dorairajan, it will b recalled, a Brahmin in Madras, challenged as unconstitutional a loc; government order giving preference to non-Brahmins in admission t medical schools. The Supreme Court upheld the challenge (in th so-called Champaknam case), and Nehru's government got round th difficulty by changing the Constitution. The First Amendment provide that nothing in the Rights should prevent the enactment of speci laws for the educational and social advancement of backward ciasse An obstacle easily had been cleared.

Property issues brought the two strands into conflicts more diffict to overcome. The Constitution guaranteed the individual's right to own property and to be deprived of it only by a law fixing the amount of compensation or the principles for calculating it. But the Congress's social revolutionary promise to nationalize industry and much commerce and to implement land reform, giving 'land to the tiller', meant depriving some individuals of these rights in the cause of fairness. When the high courts struck down several state zamindari abolition laws—as in the Kameshwar Singh case—on the ground that they violated equal treatment under the law or that compensation was inadequate, Nehru was confronted by what he called a 'peculiar tangle': if 'we cannot have equality because in trying to attain equality we came up against principles of equality' (chapter 3). A major reform policy had brought the government and the judiciary face-to-face over the fundamental matters of constitutional interpretation and of 'law' as distinct from 'justice'—an eternal issue in any society that pretends to fairness. The central government's answer was to change the Constitution—again in the First Amendment—to bar judicial scrutiny of such land legislation. Also in this amendment were provisions to overcome a high court decision, so that government (in this case the Uttar Pradesh Government) could nationalize private property (namely bus lines), a step believed necessary to a socialist programme. A second tangle joined the dispute in the form of the President's role in policy-making. As Nehru was impatient to enact the amendment, President Prasad argued reasonably for patience. The President later went further and suggested to constitutional authorities that he could refuse to give his assent to the amending bill, but was told he must act according to the council of ministers' advice.

The collision between the means and goals of the two strands evoked in Nehru doubts about reconciling them within the Constitution. The 1951 Cabinet Committee on the Constitution, which he chaired (the first of some five constitutional reassessments over the years), developed the First Amendment's devices for pursuing social-economic reform unhindered by the courts. The first was quite evident, as we have just seen: amend the Constitution to get around Supreme Court interpretations of the Constitution obstructing the social revolution. As Nehru wrote the chief ministers, the judiciary's responsibilities were unchallengeable, but if the Constitution 'comes in the way ... it is time to change the Constitution' (chapter 3). Thus was initiated a precedent for amendment that drew praise for the Constitution's flexibility and criticism that the document had been reduced to a mere scrap of paper. The second device, even more obvious, was to revise laws to eliminate the portions the Court had found objectionable.

The third device was more than a device, for with it Nehru introduced two fundamental concepts. The first challenged historically-determined conditions as the proper measure, or basis, for justice. Was it fair, he asked, that the zamindar retain control of property, while they who had been deprived of it over the centuries, because of their position in the hierarchy, continued to be denied it? You have 'not just the justice of today, but the justice of yesterday', he said.[48] This also could be thought a new formulation of the long-standing proposition that one man's exercise of his fundamental rights should not deprive another of his rights. The supplementary concept, in support of Nehru's first, was to create a hierarchy for laws. In retrospect, Nehru and his ministers may have acted anti-constitutionally. At the top were laws *above* the Constitution, as the fundamental law of the land, because they had been placed in the newly-created Ninth Schedule, beyond judicial reach. This was irrespective of whether or not they were 'inconsistent with' the Fundamental Rights. The courts should 'not decide about high political, social or economic ... questions', Nehru said, proposing the amendment.[49] Implicit here was the radical reduction of the three branches of government to only two, Parliament and the executive, as far as land legislation was concerned. The next class of law in this new hierarchy was the Constitution itself. At the bottom, third tier, subject to the Constitution, came ordinary law. This example would assume a far more insidious character two decades later when the Twenty-fourth Amendment bestowed unlimited constituent powers on Parliament (or, according to another point of view, restored the constituent power intended by the framers). In 1951, the best and the brightest did not foresee the danger of this.

When Congress governments reviewed and amended the Constitution, in Nehru's time and later, they had strong majorities in Parliament, but not a majority of votes in the country. Although this was constitutional, one may ask if it was sound to change the nation's founding document without majority support in the country. Yet it may be argued equally that most of the amendments enacted—especially the social revolutionary ones and excepting those enacted during the Emergency— had the tacit support of the majority of the electorate. But the malign as well as the benign may invoke the silent majority. Nehru, in the employment of these concepts, did not compromise his belief in the essentiality of an able and independent judiciary.

[48] *Parliamentary Debates*, vol. 12, part 2, 16 May 1951, col. 8831.
[49] *Lok Sabha Debates*, vol 2, no. 1, cols 1945–6.

The collision between democratic rights and the social revolution sharply escalated between 1951 and 1954, and in the latter year produced a second reassessment of the Constitution. Propelled by two Supreme Court rulings against the government involving compensation,[50] a Congress Working Committee's sub-committee on the Constitution attacked the judiciary's power to issue prerogative writs to enforce the Fundamental Rights and would have taken from it jurisdiction over compensation disputes. The curbing of the courts' writ powers might have been included in the Fourth Amendment had Nehru not vetoed it. Nehru's propositions to ensure Parliament's and the executive's reach in property matters—including barring the courts from questioning the 'adequacy' of compensation—were placed in that amendment (chapter 4). Coincidentally with the amendment's passage, Parliament and the Congress Party adopted resolutions naming a 'socialistic pattern of society' as the national goal.

A sense that something needed to be done to protect national unity and integrity against perceived dangers to it from disruptive action and inflammatory spoken and written expression awakened in the government awareness of a new incompatability—this time between the Fundamental Rights and the web's unity–integrity strand. After two state laws curbing freedom of speech had been ruled unconstitutional by the Supreme Court,[51] Nehru instructed the Law Minister to reconsider the Constitution's provisions affecting law and order and subversive activities. Disagreements within the Cabinet Committee on the Constitution about how far to restrict free speech were resolved on the advice of the Select Committee in Parliament to which the First Amendment (actually, the amending bill) had been sent for scrutiny. The remarkable result was that although the amendment added to the Constitution areas in which speech might be restricted (national security, public order, and friendly relations with foreign countries), it also more fully protected free speech by adding the word 'reasonable' before restrictions that might be placed upon it. Speech and expression now had the protection of due process, a qualifier not present in the original Constitution. The explanation for this restraint seems to have been several unpalatable choices the government faced (chapter 2) and the strength in Parliament of constituencies for a free press. Peculiarly, Nehru explained it as the 'concept of individual freedom has to be balanced with social freedom ... and the relations of the individual with the social

[50] In December 1953, the Bela Banerjee and Sholapur Mills cases.
[51] Punjab and Madras laws in the Brij Bhushan and Crossroads cases (ch. 2).

group'.[52] Democracy, the Rights, and the courts had come out ahead in this dispute, after being bested by the social revolution in others. Fifteen years later, the Sixteenth Amendment, also as described in chapter 2, would provide for 'reasonable' restrictions on the freedom of expression in the interests of 'the sovereignty and integrity of India'.

Personal liberty did not fare so well as freedom of expression when it came to the government's perception of the dangers to unity and integrity. The preventive detention provisions in the Constitution were not strengthened by amendment, but legislation under Article 22 and during the national emergencies of 1962 and 1971 became progressively stringent. Judicial review of detention cases became excluded, in effect, by legislation and rules prohibiting informing the courts of the grounds for a detention. Executive branch consciences were soothed—sometimes justifiably, no doubt—by defending detention as a 'necessary evil'. But it remained an evil and a crutch, permitting persecution of social-economic activists and dulling government's investigatory and prosecutorial skills. Detention was used far more extensively against actions than against speech, although the line between the two could be fine, and in Gopalan's case—the first great detention case under the Constitution (chapter 2)—speech and action were both at issue. Concepts of law and justice were stretched especially thin by the use of preventive detention against economic offences like hoarding and black-marketeering, which, however reprehensible, endangered neither national security nor integrity.

The two strands of the web also collided when unrealistic definitions of what constituted dangers to unity and integrity, the 'isms', resulted in detentions. For example, language riots in Madras in 1965 against the 'imposition' of Hindi were met by detentions under the Defence of India Act. Some seven hundred 'left communists' were detained in Kerala to prevent a suspected uprising—twenty-eight of whom subsequently were elected to the legislative assembly in 1965 while detained. On too many occasions over the decades, when there seem to have been no incompatability between the unity and integrity and democracy strands, liberty was sacrificed for executive convenience and to protect the 'integrity' of a nation already strong.

The principles of democratic government also have been ill-served by partisan political and other unwise uses of President's Rule, justified as necessary to protect unity and integrity. These uses, along with the extreme overcentralization of emergencies and the absolutism of Mrs

---

[52] *Nehru's Speeches*, vol. 2, p. 506.

Gandhi's Emergency—proclaimed in the names both of unity and the social revolution—threatened faith in the Constitution. The Forty-fourth Amendment seems to have quieted anxieties about the misuse of the emergency power. Only time and New Delhi's restraint may wash the taint from President's Rule.

The demands of national development led logically to an interventionist central government. This did assist the social revolution, but the excessive centralization became counter-productive. It stifled state government initiatives dedicated to the common purpose, denied state leaders and citizens participation in policy decisions affecting them, and encouraged doubts about New Delhi's faith in democracy. Over-centralization unbalanced many of the Constitution's provisions for centre–state relations and set back the cause of unity. The central government's belief in its own infallibility and its jaundiced view of the abilities of state governments was partly derived from the cultural elements of hierarchy, authority, and suspicion of alternative centres of power.

The precedents established in Nehru's time during the collisions between the institutions of democracy and the goals of the social revolution were taken to their logical and extreme conclusion under his daughter's prime ministry. Democratic radicalism, as discussed above, was overtaken by socialist authoritarianism. Mohan Kumaramangalam declared that democratic methods were inadequate for bringing social revolution when he said that the 'clear object' of the Twenty-fifth Amendment 'is to subordinate the rights of individuals to the urgent needs of society'.[53] The extreme socialists had gone to the core of the social revolution, and, in so doing, sacrificed the Fundamental Rights to equality before and equal protection of the law (Article 14) and the 'freedoms' of Article 19. These justiciable provisions were made subservient to the non-justiciable Directive Principles that said that 'the ownership and control of the material resources of the community are so distributed as best to subserve the common good', and the principle saying that the operation of the economic system does not result 'in the concentration of wealth'.[54] The country now had 'socialism minus democracy', said S. N. Mishra, twice Deputy Minister of Planning under Nehru.[55] With this amendment in effect, laws could be put in Nehru's category of laws above the Constitution, out of reach of the judiciary, without having to place them in the Ninth Schedule. The Twenty-fourth

[53] Kumaramangalam, *Constitutional Amendments: The Reasons Why*, pp. 22–3. This was 1971. See ch. 10.

[54] Clauses (b) and (c) of Article 39.

[55] *Lok Sabha Debates*, Fifth Series, vol. 9, no. 13, col. 252.

Amendment's reiteration of Parliament's constituent powers, also enacted under the influence of the extreme socialists and in the name of the social revolution, placed the entire Constitution in the hands of Mrs Gandhi and her tame Parliament. The long-running battle over the custody of the Constitution was to have ended in victory for Parliament and defeat and banishment for the judiciary.

In June 1975, Mrs Gandhi again invoked social revolution—still her slogan, not her creed—to replace the country's democracy with her absolutist personalization of government. She denied the poor their freedom and brought them no bread. The Congress Party and Parliament for their fourth time reviewed the Constitution and produced the Forty-second Amendment. As we have seen, this contained provisions barring judicial review of amendments and placing further curbs on Parliament's enemy, the courts, and arranging, it was hoped, that Indira Gandhi would rule a unitary India as permanent Prime Minister. The amendment's sacrifice of democracy to social revolutionary pretensions by making equality before the law and the 'freedoms' of the Fundamental Rights subservient to *all* of the Directive Principles may have been its most appalling provision. Democracy hung by a thread. It still does: the provision has not been repealed, although it has fallen into disuse (chapter 24). Safeguarding the web continues to rest with the Supreme Court's basic structure doctrine, handed down in its ruling in the Kesavananda Bharati case, significantly known, also, as the Civil Rights case, and with law as defended by a participating public.

With the voters' decision in March 1977 and the Janata government's two amendments, the Constitution by 1980 had emerged from the valley of the shadow, strengthened by citizens' discovery of its value to them. But if the seamless web had been terribly distorted, rent almost beyond repair by the Emergency, earlier efforts—well-intentioned, if misguided— to strengthen one strand at the expense of others, already had strained it. The framers' prescription had been correct: great as the frustration in so governing might be, the web's strands were interdependent. They must prosper together, or they would not prosper at all.

Branches and Strands

Turning to the Constitution's branches of government, the executive, legislature, and judiciary, one sees that the web's strands affected their character and functioning just as they had their impact on democracy, social revolution, and national integrity. Here, also, much that began as tendency hardened into practice.

In the central executive, prime ministerial dominance and the centralization of policy were the motifs. Appearing with Jawaharlal Nehru, they strengthened throughout the period of this book—the Janata period being the exception. To the centralization inherent in the responsibilities of the central government, Nehru added his impatient pursuit of the social revolution through a centralized economy. Augmenting this were his powerful personality, his status as a Brahmin, and cultural acquiescence to authority. But Nehru's authority was constrained by his dedication to democracy, by his advocacy of the scientific mind over traditional behaviour, by his consequently open style of governing, and by the presence of independent-minded colleagues. Powerful chief ministers among these like C. Rajagopalachari, B. C. Roy, G. B. Pant, Morarji Desai, and others contributed to restraint in centre–state relations. In these conditions, the social revolution got off to a good start. So, too, did democratic governance, although this had dark spots in the use of preventive detention, and in Congress's partisan use of President's Rule, and had grey areas as power attracted power, reinforcing New Delhi's sense of infallibility. Chief ministers' powers in their own executives and legislatures did not fare so well. As prime ministerial dominance grew, their own authority declined proportionally.

Mrs Gandhi's dominance as prime minister produced a government as closed as her father's had been open. Authoritarian by predilection, 'Madam' worked with only a few associates, who rarely knew her mind. The extreme centralization within the central government, coupled with her domination of chief ministers and the Congress apparatus, damaged the structures for centre–state relations and evoked resentments endangering national unity even as they served her dominance. Her personalization of government drew its determination from her deep suspicions of conspiracies surrounding her at home and of the 'foreign hand' directed from abroad. Her letters—such as those to Dorothy Norman and T. T. Krishnamachari—reveal her loneliness and sense of isolation from the courtiers in her entourage, who she knew to be greatly motivated by interest in their own personal and political survival. Yet the atmosphere surrounding her was not exclusively of her making. That cabinet ministers 'behave like members of a feudal court towards the Prime Minister' was not surprising, wrote one of her Principal Secretaries, Professor P. N. Dhar, given that the 'pre-modern attitude toward society ... [being] based on hierarchical values'.[56] Dependence on her decision-making was greater than upon her father's, and 'only you can decide' and 'what is the PM's

[56] Dhar, P. N., 'The Prime Minister's Office' in Sarkar (ed.), *Haksar, Our Times and the*

mood today?' were phrases commonly heard—as earlier had been 'Let Panditji decide'. Dhar noted that 'after the first generation of post-colonial leadership hands over to the more indigenously rooted leadership' the governing style is 'apt to be more dogmatic and authoritarian'.[57] Nothing so well illustrated the timidity, if not the sycophancy, of ministers as their silence at the 6:00 a.m. cabinet meeting when Mrs Gandhi announced imposition of her internal Emergency—and the silence at the meetings of Secretaries to Government the following day. Despite this concentration of authority, the social revolution progressed little notwithstanding promises to abolish poverty, even as socialism in the doctrinaire sense increased during Mrs Gandhi's early years as prime minister with the many nationalizations arranged by Mohan Kumaramangalam.

Parliament has 'immense powers' and 'functions within the bounds of a written Constitution', says *Practice and Procedure of Parliament*, the Indian equivalent of Britain's T. E. May on Parliament. True at any time in theory, the assertion's accuracy as regards Parliament's service to the seamless web depended upon the time it was made. The first Speaker, G. V. Mavalankar, built Parliament 'as an independent institution not to be seen as an extension of government or of party'[58]—ideals running counter to a number of the nation's cultural traits. Nehru supported him. Congress Party dominance gave the body solidity, but its broad-spectrum composition also assured that a wide variety of views would be heard. The vocal, if weak, opposition parties, and the independent spirit in the Public Accounts and Estimates Committees contributed to this democratic functioning even under a dominant prime minister like Nehru. As important was Mavalankar's intention to foster a spirit of tolerance, for, he said, if we '"go merely by majority, we shall be fostering the seeds of fascism, violence and revolt"'.[59] Parliament under Nehru supported a powerful and independent judiciary even while working to prevent review of social revolutionary amendments and legislation.

Parliament's power as a branch of government increased as prime ministerial dominance declined between 1966 and 1971. But Mrs Gandhi's rousing election victory in the latter year ended Mavalankar's vision. The Prime Minister now dominated Parliament, reducing its

---

Man, p. 53. Dhar was not a career civil servant. Both before and after his period with Mrs Gandhi, he was a distinguished professor of economics at Delhi University.

[57] Ibid., p. 54.

[58] Morris-Jones, *Government and Politics*, pp. 198–9. See also his *Parliament in India*.

[59] Cited in *Kaul and Shakdher, Practice and Procedure*, p. iii. See also Mavalankar, G. V., *Speeches and Writings*.

representation in policy making.[60] Its voice became an echo of hers; it became an instrument in her centralization of power; and whatever legislation or amendments that were aimed at social-economic reform were undermined by the executive's inability or unwillingness to implement either. The timidity of all but a few members when voting to pass the Forty-second Amendment and other Emergency amendments and then—having recovered from their collective laryngitis—voting to repeal much of them under Janata again demonstrated the power of the traits of survival, subservience to authority, and indifference to the well-being of those around them.

Meanwhile, over the years alterations in Parliament's composition reflected social revolutionary changes in society. Although reliable data are wanting that would allow national comparisons over forty-six years (because neither the censuses nor Parliament and state legislatures record caste information), it is known that Brahmins constituted forty-five per cent of Constituent Assembly members in 1948 and that their percentage had dropped to fourteen in the Eighth Lok Sabha in 1984. In the Eighth Lok Sabha, the Shudra proprietary castes constituted fourteen per cent of the membership whereas there had been none in the Constituent Assembly, although there were seven Scheduled Caste members. Shudra, or Other Backward Class, membership had increased to one-third in the Lok Sabha in 1996. Correspondingly, representation of agriculturalists had risen from twenty-two to fifty-two per cent over the years.[61]

For several state legislative assemblies, better information indicating social revolutionary change is available. In Gujarat, for example, while Brahmin and Bania representation in the assembly dropped from thirty-one per cent to twenty-three per cent between 1960 and 1980, the representation of the agriculturalist-Kshatriya and *patidar* communities rose sharply, and the number of tribal representatives nearly doubled.

[60] Hart, Henry C., 'Political Leadership in India' in Kohli (ed.), *India's Democracy*, p. 48.

[61] See Rubinoff, Arthur G., 'The Changing Nature of India's Parliament' in Tremblay, Reeta Chowdhari, et al. (eds), *Indian/Pakistani/Canadian Reflections on the 50th Anniversary of India's Independence*, B. R. Publications, Delhi, 1998, pp. 251ff.

Education levels changed with the number of under-matriculates declining sharply and the number of graduates rising. The number of women in the Lok Sabha rose from twenty-two in the First Lok Sabha (1952) to twenty-eight in the Ninth (1989). Their representation in state legislatures, although still very low, doubled in most states between 1952 and 1996. *India Today*, 27 July 1998, p. 14.

In the North, especially in Uttar Pradesh and Bihar, the 'criminalization of politics' brought indicted criminals into the Lok Sabha—twenty-seven from UP in 1996. Rubinoff, 'Changing Nature of India's Parliament', p. 262.

Caste 'equations' have 'tilted in favour of the new social alliance of the lower and backward groups', wrote Pravin Sheth.[62] Among government ministers in Bihar from 1962 to 1985, upper caste representation was more or less level, but the upper backward castes tripled their presence and the lower backwards' representation rose from zero to twelve per cent. Scheduled Caste and Scheduled Tribe presence, however, was halved.[63] In Andhra Pradesh between 1957 and 1985, the percentage of Brahmin legislators dropped from twenty-three to five while the Reddy and Kamma agriculturalists remained roughly the same, as did the Scheduled Castes and Tribes. But the percentage of backward caste legislators rose from thirty-eight to fifty-nine.[64]

Changes in caste composition and the interests represented have increased factionalism and floor-crossing—especially in state legislatures after Congress's defeats in 1967. The appearance in Parliament and legislatures of many individuals unaccustomed to parliamentary manners—compounded by the survival society complex, personalization of government, and follow-the-leader attitude—has made politics even more unsavoury and unpredictable. The responsibilities of representative government have taken second place to personal rewards. Parliament attempted several times during the 1970s to pass anti-defection legislation, but only in 1985 was it able to do so in the Fifty-second Amendment.[65]

In a nation dedicated to the rule of law, the judiciary had great responsibilities and aroused great expectations. The country's resource of well-trained men—and, at the time, a few women—had been tasked with preserving the seamless web—'ordering the life of a progressive people', as Attorney General Setalvad had said in January 1950 (chapter 5). The judiciary has much of which to be proud. It has repelled attempted subversion and direct attacks from its constitutionally co-equal branches of government. It has struck down infringements of the Fundamental Rights and unwise changes in other constitutional provisions, notably using the 1973 basic structure doctrine and subsequent reaffirmations

[62] Sheth, Pravin, *Political Developments in Gujarat*, Karnavati Publications, Ahmedabad, 1998, pp. 60–1.

[63] Frankel, Francine R. and Rao, M. S. A. (eds), *Dominance and State Power*, 2 vols, Oxford University Press, Delhi, 1989, vol. 1, p. 118.

[64] Ibid., p. 305.

[65] This amendment recognized party splits only if the splinter group numbered one-third of the party's parliamentary or state legislature delegation. It provided for the disqualification of MPs and members of state legislatures if the person had given up membership in the party of which he had been a candidate, or voted contrary to his party's direction. The details of the amendment were included as the Tenth Schedule of the Constitution.

of it. Yet the judicial system (to include both the bar and the judges) has failed adequately to serve the democracy and social revolution strands of the web (the courts have had little to do with the national unity–integrity strand). First among these failures has been the system's denial of speedy access to justice through the dilatory and self-indulgent processes of which both judges and lawyers are guilty. Despite the Law Commission's concise catalogue of these in its *Fourteenth Report* in 1958, and frequent mention since in Chief Justices' Law Day speeches, there has been little reform.[66] Especially the poor suffer from delay. Low in the hierarchy, short of money, they often do not attract quality advocates, or motivated ones who can move their cases up the docket—and then pursue their cases diligently. In general, the judicial system, in addition to being genuinely overwhelmed by demands, simply does not care.[67] The Supreme Court did not until 1979 give 'standing' to third parties to enable them to assist the poor through public interest litigation. Only about this time did 'epistolary jurisdiction' permit the poor to address the Court directly. Lacking the constitutional mandates of the other two branches, the judiciary could not be in the vanguard of social revolution, but it has asserted only intermittently the reach it does have.[68]

Nor have the executive and Parliament assisted the judiciary in fulfilling its responsibilities. Vacancies on the bench have contributed to the slow disposal of cases. Legal aid was not thought about seriously until into the 1970s, and Parliament did not legislate a legal aid agency until 1987.[69] The executive has been lax in complying with court orders

[66] For example, the commission in this report recommended that judges should sit in court five hours a day and 200 days a year; time limits should be set for oral arguments and delivery of judgements. See ch. 5.

[67] Although the legal process remains glacial, the enormous backlog of cases in arrears in the Supreme Court has been dramatically reduced by better case management assisted by the use of computers. This reform has not yet reached the high courts.

[68] In 1985, Supreme Court Justice P. N. Bhagwati castigated "'legal institutions and legal actors [who] remain locked in stultifying patterns'" instead of using "'the law to provide justice for the most deprived and oppressed'". Cited in Galanter, *Law and Society in India*, p. 303.

See also Sharma, Mool Chand, *Justice P. N. Bhagwati: Court Constitution and Human Rights*, Universal Book Traders, Delhi, 1995.

In the considerable literature about the judicial system and the poor, see two books by Vasudha Dhagamwar, *Law, Power and Justice*, Sage Publications, New Delhi, 1992, and *Criminal Justice or Chaos?*, Har-Anand Publications Pvt. Ltd., New Delhi, 1997.

[69] This was the Legal Services Authorities Act, 1987. The agency's small budget is still unenthusiastically appropriated.

On legal aid, see *Processual Justice to the People* (Report of the Expert Committee on Legal Aid), Ministry of Law, Justice and Company Affairs, New Delhi, May 1973.

664 *Working a Democratic Constitution*

in Public Interest Litigation cases, and the courts have been loath to enforce them by using their contempt power. Nor has the bar played a constructive role. *Pro bono* practice was scarcely heard of in the early days, and it is uncommon today despite the recommendation by the Law Commission in its *Fourteenth Report* that members of the bar 'volunteer to represent in courts poor persons ... gratuitously' or for small fees and that bar associations should form legal aid committees for the same purpose. Important to social revolution though they are becoming, private voluntary organizations are able to assist only a few litigants. Government's and the judicial system's conduct toward the poor, despite protestations to the contrary, has its origins in the each-for-himself survival society and in indifference to the needs of those lower in society's hierarchy.

The higher judiciary and the subordinate systems in the states—bench and bar alike—and the executive branches at the centre and in the states share responsibility for the blackest blot on the nation's record: the lengthy incarceration of individuals awaiting trial. Some seventy per cent of jail inmates in the country—who number over 150,000 persons—are awaiting trial.[70] Today, as often in the past (chapter 20), many have been prisoners for periods longer than their sentences would have been had they been tried and convicted for the crimes of which they had been accused. The Indian Prisons Bill now awaiting Parliament's approval, illustrates how this evil continues, one might even say is condoned: undertrial prisoners jailed for more than half the maximum sentence for their offence may have their cases referred to the court.[71]

The report, whose language bears the imprint of the committee's chairman, V. R. Krishna Iyer, said that 'legal aid is an indispensable social function' whose 'spiritual essence ... consists in investing law with a human soul'. *Processual Justice*, pp. 1, 10. The government's enthusiasm for legal aid is revealed in Krishna Iyer's transmittal letter to Law Minister H. R. Gokhale, in which he detailed the absence of government support, 'including the absence of any special staff for the committee'. This was a common government treatment of commissions and committees of this kind: create, but do not assist to function. That the government should operate a legal system that 'promotes justice' and that it should arrange for 'free legal aid' was added to the Directive Principles (Article 39A) in 1976 by the Forty-second Amendment.

A follow-on to *Processual Justice* was the report on *National Judicare: Equal Justice, Social Justice* (Ministry of Law and Company Affairs, New Delhi, August 1977), prepared by Justices P. N. Bhagwati and V. R. Krishna Iyer with N. L. Vaidyanathan, as the secretary, and sent to Prime Minister Morarji Desai. If India is to be a true democracy, said this report, 'no government can deny or delay the planned organization and legislative execution of a comprehensive national project for law at the Service of the People' (p. 1).

[70] *India Today*, 17 August 1998, pp. 27ff.
[71] Ibid.

Speaking after taking the oath as Chief Justice of India in January 1950, Harilal Kania said the Court would 'be quite untouchable by the legislature or the executive authority in performance of its duties'. The next three-and-a-half decades would have disappointed him. He also would have been disappointed by the susceptibility of some judges in their personal and official lives to the cultural traits discussed earlier in this chapter and to the 'extraneous influences' that judges themselves have deplored. Judges have shown sensitivity to executive branch authority; to the desires of local groups; to considerations of caste and political correctness when making appointments in judicial administration; and to the survival society's interest in post-retirement government jobs, and in permitting close kin to practice in courts where they sit as judges. Lawyers have been criticized for many of the same susceptibilities. Bar associations, according to many senior advocates interviewed, have attempted to influence the selection of justices and chief justices and the transfer to another high court of unpopular judges—the 'politicization of practically everything' mentioned earlier.

Summing Up

'A constitution may indicate the direction in which we are to move, but the social structure will decide how far we are able to move and at what pace,' wrote André Beteille.[72] On the basis of this criterion, two thoughts are offered. First, the Constitution and its seamless web have met India's needs. The inadequacies in fulfilling its promise should be assigned to those working it and to conditions and circumstances that have defied greater economic and social reform during the short fifty years since Indians began governing themselves. The country has achieved greatly against greater odds. Second, the society and its hierarchical structure have shown themselves to be far more flexible and adaptable than might have been expected—due directly to incentives in the Constitution, and coincidentally from forces coming from within and outside society. The citizens initially disparaged—by many at home and abroad—as too backward intellectually, economically, and socially to participate successfully in representative democracy, have embraced the vote and turned it to their own account. Their influence is strongly felt in state legislatures and increasingly in Parliament. They have used the weapon of their oppression, their caste(s), as the focus for mobilization, the grain of sand around which to build the pearls of upward social and

[72] Beteille, *The Backward Classes*, p. 1

economic mobility and political influence. No system other than representative democracy would have served society so well and justified the framers' faith that adult suffrage would break the mould of traditional society. The many who society continues to disregard will come to be heard through their million mutinies. Time's pace is not only petty but inexorable.

As to outside forces, citizens low as well as high have been greatly—and continue to be increasingly—influenced by what M. N. Srinivas names 'Westernization'. He means the concepts of positive and negative rights; codes of law; humanitarianism and egalitarianism; land settlement and an end to local wars; and bureaucracy and police. He also classifies as Westernization the secularization of many daily practices, such as eating, which traditionally distinguish castes and families from one another.[73] One could add to this list the courts, public interest litigation, voluntary organizations as means to assist the poor in pursuit of their rights, and the spread of agricultural and industrial innovation in the country's society.

Srinivas's 'Westernization', economic development, and the Constitution's open door have combined to catalyze fundamental changes in the caste system. These, in their turn, are leading to opener society and governance. The sense of belonging to a high or a low status in the ritual hierarchy 'is gradually fading away', says Dhirubhai Sheth, along with the overlap of hereditary status and occupation. The ideology and organization of the traditional system has been 'vastly eroded', Sheth says. Affirmative action policies fostering modern education that have prepared individuals for non-traditional occupations have produced 'a new political leadership among backward castes'. New, broader caste-class groups are emerging, which, instead of being closed, as in traditional hierarchy, are relatively open-ended, Sheth observes. They represent 'a kind of fusion between the old status system and the new power system'.[74] The Constitution, for all its promise yet unfulfilled, has opened the door to national rebirth.

Society's adaptability also may be measured in terms of the seamless web. Society's disparities and diversities have been accommodated to the

[73] Srinivas, M. N., *Social Change in India*, Orient Longman, New Delhi. 1987, pp. 52–3. Srinivas credits the adoption of Westernization by the upper castes as critical to its spread. He says that upper castes' Westernization fuelled the determination of the lower castes to obtain education and Westernization's other fruits. Ibid., p. 91.

[74] This paragraph is based upon the thoughtfulness of Dhirubhai Sheth, 'Caste and Class: Social Reality and Political Representations' in Panandiker, V. A. Pai and Nandy, Ashis (eds), *Contemporary India*, Tata McGraw Hill, New Delhi. 1998.

point that the nation is united and its integrity assured. Overcentralization did not succeed in fragmenting the nation. Nehru's question—how shall we promote unity yet preserve the rich diversity of our inheritance?— has been answered, although not to the satisfaction of Hindu militants. Language issues, for example, so explosive during the Nehru years, have almost ceased to be an issue in relations between the Centre and the states and among and within states. Essential for national integrity, to use P. N. Haksar's succinct phrase, is understanding the concept of 'pluralism and transcendence'. Although the years of overcentralization may have passed, not least because of the advent of coalition governments in New Delhi, the deliberated decentralization so necessary for the country's future, has scarcely begun.

The social revolution has gained ground, although it has far to go. It has not taken half or more of the citizens to K. Santhanam's goal of a socialism of distribution, which the author interprets to mean fairer access to income and goods and services for all citizens. Paired with, and inseparable from, democracy, the revolution's inadequacy in assuring citizens their positive right of fulfilling their capacities has impaired progress in democracy. In an apparent paradox, socialism has impaired progress in the social revolution. But the retarding elements of socialism are on their way out. Yet government has not given firm evidence of understanding that in a survival society, without safety nets, redundant workers cannot be forgotten, and that economic liberalization needs to be accompanied by occupational safety and health, and other protections for workers in the private sector. Capitalism in India is in a very exploitative stage.

'Hindu apathy' nearly is a thing of the past. The oppressive effects of hierarchy are waning as the open society unwraps national talents. Awareness of rights is becoming unquenchable.[75] Nevertheless, as member of Parliament Jaswant Singh told an American audience several years ago, India should judge itself not by its gross domestic product, but by a domestic contentment index. Representative government and constitutional democracy are firmly established. Democratic breeze's are blowing everywhere, as proved, if disconcertingly to some, by the resulting turmoil and the million mutinies. Public dissatisfactions with

---

[75] '"[The low] are not in my control but are standing freely themselves ... *Bhagvan* [the Lord] has given us less power ... They are better than us now."' complained a Brahmin landlord in Uttar Pradesh to Susan Wadley. Wadley, Susan S., *Struggling with Destiny in Karimpur, 1925–1984*, University of California Press, Berkeley CA, 1994, p. 71. This is an extraordinarily informative book.

the current state of affairs are an affirmation of democracy's spread, not a denial of it. Politics, even when rough and tumble, are played within the bounds of the Constitution. The open society is a grand achievement even when sullied by personal selfishness and police-and class- perpetrated brutality. India is among that handful of modern democracies that has descended into absolutism and risen again to freedom, having learned the lesson of vigilance.

The country lost its maternal immunity late in the sixties with the decline of the founding generation. For the next two decades it had a difficult youth. Approaching maturity in the nineties, its most difficult times lie ahead. Conflict between the web's democracy and social revolution strands is inevitable. Absence of government efforts to bring about social-economic reform will engender conflict as the have-lesses, frustrated, struggle for opportunity; so, too, will government efforts at change result in conflict, for the have-mores will resist them as the have–lesses capitalize upon them. Efforts toward long-term harmony between the strands make short-term conflict inevitable. Yet a number of smaller explosions may be preferable to fewer, larger ones later. Changes underway in society will breed more change, and, as tradition loses strength, the citizen will be freer of both negative and positive restraints on his conduct—unless he has found a new faith, one that includes social consciousness. Democratic behaviour and social revolutionary aspirations are destined to conflict.

Governments then will be confronted by two conundrums. The first is how to stay in power through a reform programme tolerable to both have-mores and have-lesses—or to gain enough votes from the latter to do so. Nehru had the stature and the courage to attempt the former, and he succeeded only in part because the haves and their political allies thwarted him. Have-less votes brought Indira Gandhi to office in 1971, but she stayed there by not alienating the haves. The second conundrum will be how to avoid, or resolve, the apparently inevitable conflict between the executive and the judiciary. With or without government reform programmes, class violence in the countryside, especially, is predictable. Will government fulfill its responsibility to maintain law and order by siding with the haves, repressing the have-lesses, which long has been the rule more than the exception? If so, it will have violated its other responsibilities under the Constitution. Or will it side with the have-lesses by preventing retaliation by the haves against protesters? Either way, petitions against government actions will go to the Supreme Court, and the two branches will be in conflict over jurisdiction, power, and principle. Where, then, will the judges stand regarding democracy and social revolution? Article 14 of the Fundamental Rights says that 'The State shall not deny to any person equality before the law or equal protection of the laws within the territory of India.' The words in this article after the 'or' seem to place upon government the positive responsibility to give the have-lesses access to those rights they previously have been powerless to exercise. Government abstention from action will be leaving the have-lesses as they are now, at the mercy of the haves. Governments will be forced to decide between social intervention or none. The principle and purpose of such intervention would be quite the reverse of the dampening economic interventionism of 'licence, permit, quota *raj*'.

Rajni Kothari wrote that his society is 'involved in a democratic churning, which affects the social fabric, the institutions of the state ... and both political and economic as well as cultural and ethical ferment.'[76] The country's citizens will need patience and determination to preserve the gains they have made and the Constitution that made their attainment possible. But unless Kothari's 'churning' produces extensive social and economic reform, the society and its constitutional system will have failed the challenge in Mahatma Gandhi's 'talisman'.

[76] Kothari, Rajni, 'The Indian Enterprise Today', *Daedalus*, Fall 1989, p. 58.

BIBLIOGRAPHY

This book is based upon primary sources to the extent that they could be found and were accessible. Especially important among these are archival resources: the private papers and oral history transcripts of many of the principal actors in constitutional developments. The Nehru Memorial Museum and Library (housed in a building nearby Jawaharlal Nehru's official residence) has the best collections of both in the country, and an admirable effort to assemble them has been made. One hopes this effort will continue. The National Archives of India has very few post-independence private papers, indeed only fragments of collections, and the Parliament Museum and Archives has even fewer fragments, although there the will seems to exist to improve its collection. In these collections of papers, unpublished government documents are sometimes found. Otherwise, these rarely are available—due, primarily, to the disinterest in transferring ministry files to the National Archives of India, supported by the persisting imperial attitude that the public is not to know how its government is conducted.

Primary and unpublished sources, in the researching of this book, also have included a few documents in the Parliament Library (as distinct from the Museum and Archives), and others kindly given to the author by private persons. The author includes among primary sources interviews with individuals who actually participated in the developments described. Here, the kind, accommodating and sometimes confiding character of Indians is a blessing for the historian. Without the information and counsel provided by them, this book would be both emptier and fuller of error. Countless friends and acquaintances who have been involved closely with constitutional events have also provided information and guidance in their roles as secondary sources. Many are named in the acknowledgements and in the bibliography. Memoirs by persons historically prominent have been another source, and these are being published more frequently. But treasures of recollection are being lost because the tradition of writing memoirs is weak and the desire 'not to hurt someone's feelings' is strong.

Among published works, original sources are legion. There are government reports of many kinds, law reports, and the correspondence and speeches of presidents and prime ministers. The published correspondence of Sardar Patel, Rajendra Prasad and Jawaharlal Nehru are invaluable, as are the five volumes of Nehru's letters to the chief ministers. These collections are to be found in most serious libraries. Government reports, parliamentary debates, and much else of value, are to be found in the Parliament Library. Along with the Nehru Library these are the two finest in the country, and their staffs have been wonderfully helpful. The Lok Sabha Secretariat has published basic reference works : the 'Documentation Series' and several essential guides such as *President's Rule in the States and Union Territories, Council of Ministers,* and *Presidential Ordinances.* For law reports, other than those in the libraries of senior advocates, the source is the Indian Law Institute library, whose staff has for many years led the author to cases and through legal thickets.

Political party pamphlets are invaluable for the student of India, for the literature is extensive, rich, and often very frank about personalities, policy, and programmes. Philosophy, administrative detail, national and party goals, and propaganda mingle most informatively. The fullest collections of these are in the Nehru Library in New Delhi and in the Indian Institute Library in Oxford. The author maintains a useful collection. Fewer now are in the Library of Congress in Washington, but the library has collaborated with University Publications of America to produce a microfiche collection and a printed guide to it.

Newspapers occupy a space between primary and secondary published sources. Their dispatches are invaluable, for the country's senior journalists have been very well informed. Newspaper accounts of judicial hearings are a unique source, for the courts do not keep transcripts of hearings. Care here especially is advised, and the author hopes he has not gone astray when using them.

Finally, books and articles are the well-recognized published secondary sources. The latter, particularly as they appear in journals such as those of the Indian Law Institute and the Institute of Constitutional and Parliamentary Studies (both now sadly fallen on hard times), have contributed especially to the author's education.

Turning to the categories of sources listed below, several things may be said. The list of books used is self-explanatory, and this is confined to works cited in the text except for a very few heavily consulted but not cited. Countless more over the years have provided the foundation of the author's knowledge. This applies equally to articles, learned and otherwise.

Also, only the political party and other pamphlets cited in the book are listed here. It would be tedious to list the many hundreds the author absorbed in his effort to gain the flavour of the times. A selection of these is given in the University Publications of America guide mentioned above.

Archival Sources

COLLECTIONS OF PRIVATE PAPERS

Nehru Memorial Museum and Library

AICC Papers
Ambedkar, B. R.

Bhargava, Gopichand
Birla, G. D.
Brahmanand

Daulatram, Jairamdas
Deo, Shankarrao
Deshmukh, C. D.
Dharia, Mohan
Dhebar, U. N.

Gadgil, N. V.
Gajendragadkar, P. B.
Govind Das, Seth

Hanumanthaiya, K. (diary)

Iengar, H. V. R.

Jain, A. P.

Kabir, Humayun
Katju, K. N.
Kher, B. G.
Krishnamachari, T. T.

Lall, Diwan Chaman
Lohia, Rammanohar

Mahajan, Mehr Chand
Mahtab, Hare Krushna
Menon, P. Govinda
Mody, H. K.
Munshi, K. M.

Narayan, Jayaprakash
Nath Pai
Nehru, Jawaharlal (as received from M. O. Mathai)

Patil, S. K.

Rajagopalachari, C.

Saksena, Mohanlal
Santhanam, K.
Shiva Rao, B.

National Archives of India

Pant, G. B.
Prasad, Rajendra

Sampurnanand
Santhanam, K.

Parliament Museum and Archives

Bahadur, Raj
Shastri, Ramavatar
Ranga, N. G.
Ray, Renuka

National Institute of Panjab Studies

Singh, Satinder

UNPUBLISHED DOCUMENTS

Antulay, A. R., 'A Fresh Look at Our Constitution: Some Suggestions', mimeograph. (Later published.)

Banerjee, Ashis, 'The Reconstruction of Federalism'. In the author's possession kindness of Mr Banerjee.

'The Causes and Nature of Current Agrarian Tensions', Ministry of Home Affairs, Research and Policy Division, 1969, mimeograph.

'Proceedings of the First Integration Council—June 2 and 3, 1962', mimeograph.

Brass, Paul R., 'India's Domestic Political Developments'. Paper delivered at a conference on India and Pakistan, '50 Years of Independence: Progress, Problems, and Prospects', Woodrow Wilson International Centre for Scholars, Washington, DC, June 1997.

Chagla, M. C., 'Memorial Lecture', Bombay House, 1977, mimeograph. In the author's possession thanks to Advocate J. M. Mukhi.

Guhan, S., 'Three Pieces on Governance', paper prepared for 'Workshop on Governance Issues in South Asia', Yale University, November 1997. Copy to the author courtesy of Professor Guhan.

Iengar, H. V. R., 'Vallabhbhai Patel', Birthday Memorial Lecture, Surat, October 1973. Cyclostyle copy in author's possession kindness of his son, H. V. R. Iengar.

Jha, Prem Shankar, 'Indian Politics Since Independence: A Response to Paul Brass'. Paper delivered at a conference on India and Pakistan, Woodrow Wilson Centre, June 1997.

Kumaramangalam, S. Mohan, 'A Review of Communist Party Policy from 1947', Madras, 23 May 1964. Original cyclostyle copy in author's possession kindness of Mrs Kalyani Kumaramangalam.

Merillat, H. C. L., Diaries. Made available to the author kindness of Mr Merillat.

Rao, G. R. S., 'Summary of Previous Recommendations on National Integration'. National Committee for Gandhi Centenary at Patna, 1966.

Sastri, Patanjali, 'Answer to Questionnaire' of Law Commission, 1958. Copy in author's possession kindness of Justice Sastri's daughter.

Singh, Satindra, 'Interview with Babu Jagjivan Ram', mimeograph, no date but spring 1977. In Satinder Singh Papers, National Institute of Panjab Studies, New Delhi.

Sreedhar, Katherine and Desai, Sonalde, 'Growth and Inequity: Social Change in India', paper delivered at a seminar at the Woodrow Wilson International Center for Scholars, July 1997.

Tandon, B. N., Diary excerpts. Kindly provided to the author by Mr Tandon.

Venkataraman, R., Rajaji Birthday Lecture, cyclostyle.

ORAL HISTORY TRANSCRIPTS

Bhagat, Usha
Chandra Shekhar
Chavan, Y. B.
Deo, Shankarrao
Desai, C. C.
Deshmukh, C. D.
Dhebar, U. N.
Diwakar, R. R.

Durgabai, Mrs
Giri, V. V.
Iengar, H. V. R.
Jain, Ajit Prasad
Kamath, H. V.
Katju, K. N.
Kripalani, J. B.
Krishnamachari, T. T.
Lall, Diwan Chaman
Mahtab, Hare Krushna
Mehta, Ashoka
Mody, H. K.
Munshi, K. M.
Nambiar, A. C. N.
Narayan, Jayaprakash
Nehru, R. K.
Pant, Apa
Patel, H. M.

Ray, Renuka
Sachar, Bhim Sen
Sahgal, Nayantara
Sapru, P. N.
Sampurnanand
Santhanam, K.
Setalvad, M. C.
Shastri, Hiralal
Singh, Hukum
Singh, Ujjal
Subramaniam, C. (Rajaji Institute for International and Public Affairs, Hyderabad)
Sundarayya, P.
Thacker, M. S.
Verma, Vishwanath
Vira, Dharma
Yagnek, Indulal

INTERVIEWS AND WRITTEN COMMUNICATIONS

Aiyar, Mani Shankar
Alexander, P. C.
Ali, Sadiq
Alva, Margaret
Antulay, A. R.
Ayyar, Alladi Kuppaswami
Bakshi, P. M.
Balakrishna, H. G.
Balakrishnan, S.
Basavupanniah
Baxi, Upendra
Bhagat, Usha
Bhagwati, P. N.
Bhandare, M.
Bhandare, S.
Bhattacharjea, Ajit
Bhushan, Shanti
Borooah, D. K.
Chakravarty, Nikhil
Chandrachud, Y. V.
Chaudhari, P. A.
Chhibbar, Y. B.
Chopra, Pran
Desai, D. A.
Dhar, P. N.
Dhar, Vijay

Dharia, Mohan
Dhavan, Rajeev
Dikshit, Sheila
Divan, Anil
Divan, B. J.
Dutt, R. C.
Gadgil, V. N.
Gae, R. S.
Garg, R. K.
Gokhale, P. G.
Gokhale, Rajiv
Gopal, S.
Goray, N. G.
Grover, A. N.
Guhan, S.
Gujral, I. K.
Haksar, P. N.
Hegde, Ramakrishna
Hegde, Santosh
Jagmohan
Jain, Girilal
Jatti, B. D.
Jayakar, Pupul
Jethmalani, Ram
Kania, M. H.
Kant, Krishan

Khanna, H. R.
Kothari, Rajni
Kothari, Smitu
Krishna, Gopal
Krishna Iyer, V. R.
Kumaramangalam, Kalyani
Kumaramangalam, P. R.
Latifi, Danial
Limaye, Madhu
Madon, Dinshaw
Mahishi, Sarojini
Maitra, S. K.
Malhotra, Inder
Masani, Minoo
Mathur, Girish
Maurya, B. P.
Mavalankar, P. G.
Mehta, Om
Mishra, Brajesh
Mozoomdar, Ajit
Mukarji, Nirmal
Narain, Govind
Narain, Iqbal
Nariman, Fali
Nayar, Kuldip
Nehru, B. K.
Noorani, A. G.
Nijalingappa, S.
Palkhivala, N. A.
Panandiker, V. A. Pai
Panjwani, Ram
Pant, K. C.
Paranjpe, H. K.
Patel, Bakhul
Pathak, R. S.
Prasad, H. Y. Sharada
Raghavan, B. S.
Ram, N.
Rama Jois, M.
Ramachandran, V.
Rangarajan, S. J.
Ray, S. S.
Reddy, Jaganmohan
Reddy, N. Sanjiva
Reddy, O. Chinnappa

Reddy, Raghunatha
Sachar, Rajinder
Sahay, S.
Sarkar, Chanchal
Sarkaria, R. S.
Sathe, S. P.
Sathe, Vasant
Saxena, K. B.
Seervai, H. M.
Seshan, N. K.
Shah, Manubhai
Shakdher, S. L.
Shankar, Shiv
Sharma, Hari Dev
Sharma, Mool Chand
Sharma, Shankar Dayal
Sikri, S. M.
Silverman, Julius
Singh, Karan
Singh, L. P.
Singh, Sardar Swaran
Singhvi, L. M.
Sivaraman, B.
Soni, Ambika
Sorabjee, Soli
Subramaniam, C.
Subramaniam, K. S.
Sundaram, K. K.
Sundaram, K. V. K.
Talwalkar, Govind
Tandon, B. N.
Tarkunde, V. M.
Tonpe, V. Y.
Tripathi, Dwijendra
Tulzapurkar, V. D.
Unnikrishnan, K. P.
Varadarajan, A.
Venkataraman, R.
Venkataramiah, E. S.
Venkatasubramanian, P. B.
Venugopal, K. K.
Verghese, George
Vira, Dharma
Wadhwa, D. C.
Yadav, Chandrajit

POLITICAL PAMPHLETS

(All publications published in New Delhi unless otherwise noted.)

Congress

Report of a Committee to Determine Principles of the Constitution of India, All Parties Conference, 1928.

'Resolution on Fundamental Rights and Economic and Social Change', *Report of the 45th National Indian Congress,* AICC, 1931.

All-India Congress Socialist Party Programme, published by Minoo Masani for the Party, 1937.

Congress Election Manifesto, AICC, 1945.

Report of the Economic Programme Committee, AICC, 1948.

Report of the General Secretaries, January 1949–September 1950, Indian National Congress (INC).

Election Manifesto, AICC, 1951.

Report to the All-India Congress Committee, AICC, 1951 (Nehru's 'Report').

The Pilgrimage and After, AICC, 1952.

Preventive Detention Act, Congress Party in Parliament, 1952.

Report of the General Secretaries, January 1954–January 1955, INC.

Resolutions, INC, Sixtieth Session, AICC, 1955.

Congress Bulletin, INC, 1955.

Pant, Pandit G. B., *Be Good So That You May Be Great,* INC, 1956.

Report of the General Secretaries, March–December 1956, AICC.

Keep the Flame Alive, A Thesis by a Group of Congress Workers, no publication information, 1957.

Narayan, Shriman, *A Plea for Ideological Clarity,* INC, 1957.

Report of the General Secretaries, January 1959–December 1959, AICC.

Report of the General Secretaries, January 1960–December 1960, AICC.

Report of the General Secretaries, January 1961–December 1961, AICC.

Congress Bulletin, INC, 1963.

Report of the Sub-Committee on Democracy and Socialism, AICC, 1964.

Report of the Sub-Committee on Non-Official Resolutions, AICC, 1964.

Democracy and Socialism, Draft Resolution for the 68th Session of the Indian National Congress at Bhubaneshwar, Malaviya, K. D., no publication information, 1964.

Congress Bulletin, June–July, 1967.

Ghosh, Atulya, *The Real Task,* AICC, 1967.

Report of the General Secretaries, February 1966–January 1968, AICC.

Congress Revitalization and Reorganization: Nehru's Guidelines for the Congress, Congress Forum for Socialist Action, 1968.

Presidential Address by Shri Jagjivan Ram, 73rd Plenary Session, Bombay, AICC, 1969.

Dharia, Mohan and H. D. Malaviya (eds), 'Crisis in the Congress and Nation : PM's letter to Party Members', *Souvenir—Requisitioned Meeting of AICC Members,* AICC, 1969.

'Policy Resolution', *Indian National Congress, 73rd Plenary Session, Bombay, December 1969,* AICC, 1970.

From Delhi to Patna, AICC (Congress Marches Ahead II), 1970.

Desai, Morarji, 'Growing Faces of Disruption and Dictatorship', *Souvenir AICC Session, Lucknow*, 5–6 Dec, 1970, AICC, Congress(O), 1970.

Congress Marches Ahead IV, AICC, 1971.

People's Victory: An Analysis of 1971 Elections, AICC, 1971.

Kumaramangalam, S. Mohan, *Constitutional Amendments: The Reasons Why*, AICC, 1971.

Congress Bulletin, AICC, 1971.

Congress Marches Ahead VI, AICC, 1972.

Congress Marches Ahead VIII, AICC, 1972.

Report of the General Secretaries, June 1972–August 1973, AICC.

New 20-point Economic Programme: The Pathway to Progress, AICC, 1975.

Shri D. K. Borooah on Constitution (Forty-fourth Amendment) Bill, AICC, 1976.

Proposed Amendments to the Constitution of India by the Committee Appointed by the Congress President Shri D. K. Borooah on February 26, 1976, AICC, 1976 (the Swaran Singh Committee Report).

Congress Marches Ahead 13, AICC, 1976.

Congress and Constitutional Amendments, Central Campaign Committee, AICC, Dec. 1976 or Jan. 1977.

Resolutions Adopted at the Calcutta Plenary, AICC, 1984.

Inaugural Speech by Congress President Shri Rajiv Gandhi and the Centenary Resolve, AICC, 1985.

Socialist Party

Programme of the Socialist Party, Bombay, 1947.

Election Manifesto, Hyderabad, 1957.

Communist Parties

Ghosh, Ajoy, *Two Systems: A Balance Sheet*, Communist Party of India, 1956.

Problems and Possibilities, Communist Party of India/New Age Printing Press, 1957.

Election Manifesto, Communist Party of India, 1961.

President and Prime Minister Must Revoke Emergency, Restore Fundamental Rights, Appeal by All Former Chief Justices of India and Leading Citizens, Communist Party Parliamentary Group/CPI, 1966.

Election Manifesto, CPI, 1971.

Gupta, Bhupesh, *Some Comments on Constitutional Changes*, CPI, August 1976.

Communist Party of India (Marxist) on Constitutional Changes, CPM, June 1976.

Proposals of the National Council for Amendments to the Constitution of India, CPI, 1976.

Consembly Move and Democratic Fightback, CPI, November 1976.

Lok Sabha Election: Resolution of the National Council of the Communist Party of India Held in Delhi from 3 to 6 April 1977, CPI, April 1977.

New Peasant Upsurge, All India Kisan Sabha, 1981.

Review of Political Development and Party Activities Since Eleventh Party Congress, CPI,
New Age Printing Press, April 1982.
On Centre–State Relations, CPM, Calcutta, 1983.
CPI's Stand on Major Issues, CPI, 1985.
Reports of CPI(M) and its Various Frontal Activities (1982–1985), West Bengal State
Committee, CPM, Calcutta, 1985.
Communist Party of India and Fight Against Communalism, CPI, 1985.

Hindu Mahasabha

Chatterjee, N. C., *Presidential Address,* Hindu Mahasabha, no date.

Bharatiya Jana Sangh

Election Manifesto, 1957, Bharatiya Jana Sangh, 1956.
Upadhyaya, Deen Dayal, *Principles and Policies,* paper presented at Jana Sangh
General Council meeting, Gwalior, 17 August 1964.

Bharatiya Janata Party (BJP)

Election Manifesto (s), BJP, 1980, 1984.
Towards a New Polity, 1984.
Advani, L. K. 'Presidential Address', 9th National Council Session, BJP, 1987.

Praja Socialist Party (PSP)

Statement of Policy, Praja Socialist Party, Bombay, 1954.
General Secretary's Report: Seventh National Conference, 17–20 May, Ramgarh, PSP,
1964.
General Secretary's Report to the 10th National Conference of the Praja Socialist Party,
PSP, 1970.

Swatantra Party

Birth of Swatantra (Freedom) Party, Bangalore, 1959.

Janata Party

Election Manifesto, 1977, Janata Party, 1977.
Janata Bulletin, Janata Party, 1978.
Promises: How Many Fulfilled?, Janata Parliamentary Party, undated but 1979.
Steps Toward Dynamic Growth, September 1979.
Paper on Conspiracy Against the People, 1979.
Noorani, A. G., 'Implications of President's Action', *Will of Lok Sabha Was Flouted,*
Janata Party, 1979.
White Paper on the Toppling of State Governments, Janata Party, September 1984.
Limaye, Madhu, *President versus Prime Minister,* Janata Party, Bombay, 1987.

Miscellaneous

Setalvad, M. C., et al., *Parliament, Emergency and Personnal Freedom: Opinions of Jurists*, Bar Association of India, New Delhi, 1963.

Kumaramangalam, S. Mohan, *India's Language Crisis*, New Century Book House (P) Ltd., Madras, 1965.

————, *Democracy and Cult of Individual*, National Book Club, New Delhi, 1966.

————, *New Model for Governmental Administration of Industry*, A Mainstream Publication, New Delhi, 1973.

Parliamentary versus Presidential System of Government, Proceedings of a Seminar, India International Centre, New Delhi, 1966.

Presidential Address and Other Papers for the Convention, A. P. Jain, New Delhi, 1970.

Palkhivala, Nani, *The Mess We Are In*, Tata Press Ltd., Bombay, 1974.

————, *Centre–State Relations: A Broad Perspective*, Forum of Free Enterprise, Bombay, 1983.

Proceedings of the National Seminar on Judicial Appointments and Transfers, Bar Council of India, New Delhi, 1980.

'Anandpur Sahib Resolution', Indian Council of Sikh Affairs, New Delhi, 1985.

Government of India Publications
(All publications published in New Delhi unless otherwise noted.)

Constituent Assembly Debates

Annual Reports, Ministry of Home Affairs.

Judges of the Supreme Court and the High Courts (various editions), Department of Justice, Ministry of Law.

Resolution on Industrial Policy, Ministry of Information and Broadcasting, 6 April 1948.

Crops—Planning and Production, National Planning Committee Series, Bombay, 1949.

Communist Violence in India, Ministry of Home Affairs, 1949.

The Challenge to Democracy, Publications Division, 1953.

Acts of Parliament, 1952, Ministry of Law and Justice.

Report of the States Reorganization Commission, Manager of Publications, 1955.

Summary of States Reorganization Commission Report, Ministry of Home Affairs, 1955.

Mahalanobis, P. C., *Draft Recommendations for Formulation of the Second Five-Year Plan, 1956–1961*, Planning Commission, 1955.

Mahalanobis, P. C. et al., *Report of the Committee on Distribution of Income and Levels of Living*, Planning Commission, New Delhi, 1964.

Fourth Report: Proposal that High Court Should Sit in Benches at Different Places in a State, Law Commission, Ministry of Law, 1956.

Resolution on Industrial Policy, Ministry of Information and Broadcasting, 1956.

Second Five-Year Plan, Planning Commission, 1956.

Radhakrishnan, S., *Occasional Speeches and Writings: October 1952–January 1956*, Publications Division/Ministry of Information and Broadcasting, 1956.

Taylor, Carl C., *A Critical Analysis of India's Community Development Programme*, The Community Projects Administration, 1956.

Fourteenth Report: Reform of Judicial Administration, 2 vols with Classified Recommendations, Law Commission, Ministry of Law, 1958.

'Statement Issued by the National Integration Conference', Ministry of Information and Broadcasting, 1961.

Jawaharlal Nehru's Speeches, 1946–64, 5 vols, Publications Division.

Twenty-Seventh Report: Code of Civil Procedure, 1908, Law Commission, Ministry of Law, 1964.

Ladejinsky, Wolf, *A Study of Tenurial Conditions in Package Districts*, Planning Commission, 1965.

Twenty-Ninth Report: Proposal to Include Certain Social and Economic Offences in the Indian Penal Code, Law Commission, Ministry of Law, 1966.

National Policy on Education, 1968, Ministry of Education, 1968.

Report of the Study Team: Centre–State Relationships (Administrative Reforms Commission), Manager of Publications, 1968.

'The Role of Governors', Report of the Committee of Governors, President's Secretariat, 1971.

Forty-Sixth Report: Constitution (Twenty-Fifth Amendment) Bill, 1971, Law Commission, Ministry of Law, undated, but 1971.

Processual Justice to the People (Report of the Expert Committee on Legal Aid), Ministry of Law, Justice and Company Affairs, May 1973.

Speeches of President V. V. Giri, Publications Division/Ministry of Information and Broadcasting, 1974.

'The Conservation of Foreign Exchange and Prevention of Smuggling Activities (Amendment) Ordinance, 1975', *The Gazetteer of India*, July 1975.

Preserving Our Democratic Structure, Division of Audio-Visual Publicity, 1975 (Indira Gandhi speech reprinted).

Prime Minister's Broadcast to the Nation on Proclamation of Emergency, Division of Audio-Visual Publicity, 1975.

Prime Minister Gandhi on Emergency in India, Ministry of External Affairs, 1975.

Report of the National Commission on Agriculture, Part I: Review and Progress, Ministry of Agriculture and Irrigation, 1976.

Constitutional Reforms, Division of Audio-Visual Publicity, October 1976.

Speeches of Dr Rajendra Prasad–President of India, Publications Division/Ministry of Information and Broadcasting, 3 vols, 1952–77.

White Paper on Misuse of Mass Media During the Internal Emergency, August 1977.

Report on National Judicare: Equal Justice, Social Justice, Ministry of Law, Justice and Company Affairs, 1977.

Shah Commission of Enquiry, Interim Report I, March 1978, *Interim Report II*, April 1978, *Third and Final Report*, August 1978, Controller of Publications.

Eightieth Report: Method of Appointment of Judges, Law Commission, Ministry of Law, 1979.

Report of the Backward Classes Commission, Controller of Publications, 1980.

'Law Minister's Statement on Appointment of Chief Justices of High Courts', Press Information Bureau, 24 July 1980.

Report of the National Police Commission, Ministry of Home Affairs, 1979–81.

Speeches of President Sanjiva Reddy, Publications Division/Ministry of Information and Broadcasting, 1983.

Indira Gandhi, Selected Speeches and Writing, 1966–84, 5 vols, Publications Division.

Ninety-Fifth Report: Constitutional Division within the Supreme Court—A Proposal For, Law Commission, Ministry of Law, 1984.

One Hundred and Twenty-Fourth Report: The High Court Arrears—A Fresh Look, Law Commission, Ministry of Law, 1988.

One Hundred and Twenty-Fifth Report: The Supreme Court—A Fresh Look, Law Commission, Ministry of Law, 1988.

Report of the Commission on Centre–State Relations (the Sarkaria Commission), 2 vols, Government of India Press, Nasik, 1988.

Economic Survey, Ministry of Finance, 1994.

Rajya Sabha Secretariat

Parliamentary Debates, Rajya Sabha

Lok Sabha Secretariat Publications and Unpublished Documents

(All published in New Delhi.)

Parliamentary Debates (of the Lok Sabha pre–1952).

Lok Sabha Debates.

Journal of Parliamentary Information.

The Constitution (First Amendment) Bill, 1951: Report of the Select Committee, 1951.

The Constitution (Fourth Amendment) Bill, 1954: Report of the Joint Committee.

Speeches and Writings, G. V. Mavalankar, 1957.

Papers Laid on the Table, 1959.

Evidence, Joint Committee on the Constitution (Fifteenth Amendment) Bill, 1962.

The Constitution (Seventeenth Amendment) Bill, 1963: Report of the Joint Committee, 1964.

'Statement Containing a Gist of Main Points Made by Witnesses in their Evidence before the Committee', *Report of the Joint Committee on the Constitution* (Amendment i.e. Nath Pai) *Bill*, 1968.

'Government Bills as Introduced in the Lok Sabha, 1972', Parliament Library, 1972.

The Constitution of India: Commemorative Edition, 1 January 1973.

'Need for Constitutional Reforms', May 1976.

Papers Laid on the Table, 1977.

'Government Bills, Introduced in the Lok Sabha, 1977'.

Background Note, 'The Forty-Second Amendment and Recent Proposals for Changes in the Constitution', 25 February 1978.

'The Constitution (Forty-fifth Amendment) Bill, 1978'.

Central Acts and Ordinances, 1980.

'The Terrorist and Disruptive Activities (Prevention) Act, 1985', *Central Acts and Ordinances, 1985*, Parliament Library.

'The Summary by the Governor of Kerala of His Report to the President', Home Ministry document cyclostyled, undated. (Copy in Parliament Library.)

Presidential Ordinances, 1950–1984, 1985.

Constitution Amendment in India, 1986.

President's Rule in the States and Union Territories, 1987.

Council of Ministers, 1947–1984, and *Supplement, 1984–1987,* 1987.

The Constitution of India (as modified up to March, 1993).

State Government Publications

Government of West Bengal

'Statement on Centre–State Relations Released at Srinagar on October 8, 1983', Calcutta, no date, but 1983.

Government of Karnataka

'White Paper on the Office of Governor', Bangalore, 1983.

Seminar on Centre–State Relations, Bangalore, August 5–7, 1983: Papers, Group Reports and Conclusions, Bangalore, 1984.

Government of Kerala

'Statement of Policy', *Prosperous Kerala: Government Policy Outlined,* Central Government (of Kerala) Press, Trivandrum, 1957.

Public Opinion on the 'Direct Action' in Kerala, Directorate of Public Relations, Trivandrum, 1959.

Government of Tamil Nadu

Charge Sheet Against the Communists, Director of Information and Publicity, Government of Madras, Madras, 1949.

Report of the Centre–State Relations Inquiry Committee (the Rajamannar Report), Madras, 1971.

Law Reports

The Supreme Court Reports, Supreme Court of India/Manager of Publications, New Delhi.

The Supreme Court Cases, Eastern Book Company, Lucknow.

Supreme Court Almanac (SCALE), LIPS Publications Pvt. Ltd., New Delhi.
The All India Reporter (both Supreme Court and High Court reports), All India Reporter Ltd., Bombay.
G. C. Sachdeva (ed.), *The Unreported Judgements (Supreme Court),* published by G. C. Sachdeva, Jodhpur, 1976.

Books

Agarwal, J. C. and Chaudhry, H. K., *Elections in India,* Shipra Publications, Delhi, 1992.
Agarwal, Shriman Narayan, *Gandhian Constitution for a Free India,* Kitabistan, Allahabad, 1946.
Alexander, P. C., *My Years with Indira Gandhi,* Vision Books, New Delhi, 1991.
Alexandrowitz, Charles Henry, *Constitutional Developments in India,* Oxford University Press, London, 1957.
Anstey, Vera, *The Economic Development of India,* Longmans, Green and Co., London, 1957.
Antulay, A. R., *Appointment of a Chief Justice,* Popular Prakashan, Bombay, 1973.
——, *Democracy: Parliamentary or Presidential,* Directorate General of Information and Public Relations, Government of Maharashtra, Bombay, 1981.
Arora, Balveer and Verney, Douglas V. (eds), *Multiple Identities in a Single State,* Konark Publishers Pvt. Ltd., New Delhi, 1995.
Austin, Granville, *The Indian Constitution: Cornerstone of a Nation,* Clarendon Press, Oxford, 1966.
Awana, Ram Singh, *Pressure Politics in Congress Party,* Northern Book Centre, New Delhi 1988.
Ayyar, Alladi K., *A Statesman Among Jurists,* Bharatiya Vidya Bhavan, Bombay, 1993.
Bandyopadhyaya, J., *The Congress and Democratic Socialism,* Indian National Congress, New Delhi, 1968.
Basham, A. L., (ed.), *A Cultural History of India,* 6th impression, Oxford University Press, New Delhi, 1989.
Basu, Durga Das, *Introduction to the Constitution of India,* 13th edn., Prentice Hall of India Pvt. Ltd., New Delhi, 1987.
——, *Shorter Constitution of India,* 10th edn., Prentice Hall of India Pvt. Ltd., New Delhi, 1988.
Bayley, David H., *Preventive Detention in India,* Firma K. L. Mukhopadhyay, Calcutta, 1962.
Baxi, Upendra, *The Indian Supreme Court and Politics,* Eastern Book Company, Lucknow, 1980.
——, *The Crisis in the Indian Legal System,* Vikas Publishing House Pvt. Ltd., New Delhi, 1983.
——, *Courage, Craft and Contention: The Indian Supreme Court in the Eighties,* N. M. Tripathi Pvt. Ltd., Bombay, 1985.

————, *Toward a Sociology of Indian Law,* Satvahan, New Delhi, 1986.

Béteille, André, *The Backward Classes in Contemporary India,* Oxford University Press, New Delhi, 1992.

Bhargava, R. N., *The Theory and Working of Union Finance in India,* George Allen & Unwin, London, 1956.

Bhattacharjea, Ajit, *Jayaprakash Narayan: A Political Biography,* Vikas Publishing House Pvt. Ltd., New Delhi, 1975.

————, *Kashmir: The Wounded Valley,* UBS Publishers and Distributors Ltd., New Delhi, 1994.

Bhushan, Prashant, *The Case That Shook India,* Vikas Publishing House Pvt. Ltd., New Delhi, 1978.

Bonner, Arthur, *Averting the Apocalypse,* Duke University Press, Durham, NC, 1990.

Brass, Paul R., *The Politics of India Since Independence, The New Cambridge History of India,* vol. IV–1, Cambridge University Press/Orient Longman, Cambridge, 1990.

Brecher, Michael, *Nehru: A Political Biography,* Oxford University Press, London, 1959.

Brown, Judith M., *Gandhi: Prisoner of Hope,* Oxford University Press, Oxford, 1989 (paperback).

Bullock, Alan, *Hitler, A Study in Tyranny,* Bantam Books, New York, NY, 1958 (paperback).

Butler, David, Lahiri, Ashoke, and Roy, Prannoy, *India Decides: Elections, 1952–1991,* 2nd edn., Living Media Books, New Delhi, 1991.

Carras, Mary, *Indira Gandhi in the Crucible of Leadership,* Beacon Press, Boston, MA, 1979.

Carstairs, G. Morris, *The Twice-Born,* Indiana University Press, Bloomington, IN, 1967 (paperback).

Chand, Phul and Sharma, J. P. (eds), *Federal Financial Relations in India,* Institute of Constitutional and Parliamentary Studies, New Delhi, 1974.

Chandrachud, Y. V., *The Basics of Indian Constitution: Its Search for Social Justice and the Role of the Judges* (Sardar Patel Memorial Lectures, 1987), Publications Division, Government of India, New Delhi, 1989.

Chatterjee, N. C., *Fundamental Rights in Peril,* Civil Liberties Union, New Delhi, no date.

Chaudhary, Valmiki (ed.), *Dr. Rajendra Prasad: Correspondence and Select Documents,* 19 vols, Allied Publishers Ltd., Bombay, 1984.

Choudhurie, Joyotpaul (ed.), *India's Beleagured Federalism: The Pluralist Challenge,* Center for Asian Studies, Arizona State University, Arizona, 1992.

Coupland, Reginald, *Indian Politics, 1936–1942: Report on the Constitutional Problem in India,* Oxford University Press, London, 1943.

Datta, Abhijit (ed.), *Union–State Relations: Selected Articles,* Indian Institute of Public Administration, New Delhi, 1984.

Datta, C. L., *With Two Presidents,* Bell Books/Vikas Publishing House Pvt. Ltd., New Delhi, 1971.

Denoon, David B. H., *Devaluation under Pressure: India, Indonesia, and Ghana*, MIT Press, Cambridge, MA, 1986.

Desai, A. R. (ed.), *Violation of Democratic Rights in India*, Popular Prakashan, Bombay, 1986.

———, *Agrarian Struggles in India After Independence*, Oxford University Press, Delhi, 1986.

Deshmukh, C. D., *The Course of My Life*, Orient Longman, New Delhi, 1974.

Dey, S. K., *Panchayati Raj*, Asia Publishing House, London, 1961.

Dharia, Mohan, *Fumes and the Fire*, S. Chand and Company Pvt. Ltd., New Delhi, 1975.

Dhagamwar, Vasudha, *Law, Power and Justice*, Sage Publications, 2nd edn., New Delhi, 1992.

———, *Criminal Justice or Chaos?*, Har-Anand Publications, Pvt. Ltd., New Delhi, 1997.

Dhavan, Rajeev, *The Supreme Court and Parliamentary Sovereignty*, Sterling Publishers, Pvt. Ltd., New Delhi, 1976.

———, *The Supreme Court of India*, N. M. Tripathi Pvt. Ltd., New Delhi, 1977.

———, *The Amendment: Conspiracy or Revolution?*, Wheeler Publishing, Allahabad, 1978.

———, *President's Rule in the States*, Indian Law Institute/N. M. Tripathi Pvt. Ltd., Bombay, 1979.

———, *Justice on Trial: The Supreme Court Today*, Wheeler Publishing, Allahabad, 1980.

Dhavan, Rajeev and Jacob, Alice (eds), *Selection and Appointment of Supreme Court Judges*, N. M. Tripathi Pvt. Ltd., Bombay, 1978.

———(eds), *Indian Constitution: Trends and Issues*, Indian Law Institute/N. M. Tripathi Pvt. Ltd., Bombay, 1978.

Dhillon, G. S., *India Commits Suicide*, Singh and Singh Publishers, Chandigarh, 1992.

Durga Das, (ed.), *Sardar Patel's Correspondence 1945–1950*, 10 vols, Navajivan Publishing House, Ahmedabad, 1973ff.

Dutt, R. C., *Imperialism to Socialism: Memoirs of an Indian Civil Servant*, Milend Publishing Pvt. Ltd., New Delhi, 1985.

———, *Retreat from Socialism in India*, Abhinav Publications, New Delhi, 1987.

Embree, Ainslie. T., *India's Search for National Identity*, Chanakya Publications, New Delhi, 1980 (second revised edn.).

Frankel, Francine R., *India's Political Economy, 1947–1977: The Gradual Revolution*, Princeton University Press, Princeton, NJ, 1978.

Frankel, Francine R. and Rao, M. S. A., *Dominance and State Power in Modern India*, 2 vols, Oxford University Press, Delhi, 1989.

Gadgil, N. V., *Government from Inside*, Meenakshi Prakashan, Meerut, 1968.

Gae, R. S., *Bank Nationalisation Case and the Constitution*, N. M. Tripathi Pvt Ltd., Bombay, 1971.

Gajendragadkar, P. B., *The Constitution of India: Its Philosophy and Basic Postulates*, Oxford University Press, Nairobi, 1970.

————, *The Indian Parliament and Fundamental Rights,* Eastern Law House, Calcutta, 1972.

————, *To the Best of My Memory,* Bharatiya Vidya Bhavan, Bombay, 1983.

Galanter, Marc, *Competing Equalities,* University of California Press, Berkeley, CA, 1984.

————, *Law and Society in Modern India,* Oxford University Press, Delhi, 1989.

Gandhi, Arun, *The Morarji Papers,* Vision Books, New Delhi, 1983.

Gandhi, Indira, *Revitalizing Congress: Recent Speeches and Writings of Indira Gandhi,* Kalamkar Prakashan, New Delhi, (undated but 1969).

Gandhi, Sonia (ed.), *Two Alone, Two Together: Letters Between Indira Gandhi and Jawaharlal Nehru, 1940–1964,* 2 vols, Hodder & Stoughton, London, 1992, (vol. 1, *Freedom's Daughter,* contains letters from 1922–39).

George, P. T., *Terminology in Indian Land Reforms,* Gokhale Institute of Politics and Economics/Orient Longman Ltd., New Delhi, 1972.

Gledhill, Alan, *The Republic of India,* Stevens and Sons Ltd., London, 1951.

Godbole, Madhav, *Unfinished Innings,* Orient Longman, New Delhi, 1996.

Gopal, Sarvepalli, *Jawaharlal Nehru,* 3 vols, Oxford University Press, New Delhi, 1979ff.

————, *Radhakrishnan,* Oxford University Press, New Delhi, 1989.

——————(ed.), *Selected Works of Jawaharlal Nehru,* 20 vols, Oxford University Press, New Delhi.

Gould, Harold A., *Grassroots Politics in India,* South Asia Publications, Columbia, MO, 1994.

Gupta, D. C., *Indian Government and Politics,* 4th edn., Vikas Publishing House Pvt. Ltd., New Delhi, 1978.

Haksar, P. N., *Premonitions,* Interpress, Bombay, 1979.

————, *Reflections on Our Times,* Lancer Publications, New Delhi, 1982 (Sarojini Naidu Memorial Lecture at Jawaharlal Nehru University).

Hall, Kermit (ed.), *The Oxford Companion to the Supreme Court of the United States,* Oxford University Press, New York, NY, 1992.

Hardgrave, Robert L. Jr, *The Dravidian Movement,* Popular Prakashan, Bombay, 1965.

————and Kochanek, Stanley, *India: Government and Politics in a Developing Nation,* 5th edn., Harcourt Brace Jovanovich College Publishers, New York, NY, 1993 (and previous editions).

Hart, Henry C. (ed.), *Indira Gandhi's India: A Political System Reappraised,* Westview Press, Boulder, Colorado, 1976.

Hazarika, Sanjoy, *Strangers in the Mist,* Viking/Penguin Books India, New Delhi, 1994.

Hegde, K. S., *Judiciary and the People,* A 'Friends of Democracy' Publication, New Delhi, 1973.

Heginbotham, Stanley I., *Cultures in Conflict: The Four Faces of Indian Bureaucracy,* Columbia University Press, New York, NY, 1975.

Hood Phillips, O., *Constitutional and Administrative Law,* 5th edn., Sweet and Maxwell, London, 1973.

Ilbert, Courtenay, *The Government of India*, Clarendon Press, Oxford, 1916.

Iqbal, Mohammed, *The Law of Preventive Detention in England, India, and Pakistan*, Punjab Religious Book Society, Lahore, 1955.

Jackson, Robert H., *The Struggle For Judicial Supremacy*, Vintage Books, New York, 1941 (paperback.)

Jagmohan, *My Frozen Turbulence in Kashmir*, Allied Publishers, New Delhi, 1991.

Jain, C. K. (ed.), *Constitution of India: In Precept and Practice*, Lok Sabha Secretariat, New Delhi, 1992.

Jain, M. P., *Indian Constitutional Law*, N. M. Tripathi Pvt. Ltd., Bombay, 1987.

Jatti, B. D., *I am My Own Model: An Autobiography*, Konark Publishers Pvt. Ltd., Delhi, 1993.

Jannuzi, F. Thomasson, *Agrarian Crisis in India*, Sangam Books, New Delhi, 1974.

————, *India in Transition*, Westview Press, Boulder, CO, 1989.

Jayakar, Pupul, *Indira Gandhi*. Viking/Penguin Books, New Delhi, 1992.

Jennings, Sir Ivor, *Cabinet Government*, 2nd edn., Cambridge University Press, Cambridge, 1951.

————, *Parliament*, 2nd edn., Cambridge University Press, Cambridge, 1957.

Johnston, Hugh, *The Voyage of the Kamagata Maru, the Sikh Challenge to Canada's Colour Bar*, Oxford University Press, Delhi, 1979.

Kagzi, M. C. J., *The June Emergency and Constitutional Amendments*, Metropolitan Book Company Pvt. Ltd., New Delhi, 1977.

Kamat, A. N., *The Defence of India Act, 1939, and the Rules Made Thereunder*, Hindmata Printing House, Dharwar, 1944.

Kapur, Rajiv A., *Sikh Separatism*, Vikas Publishing House Pvt. Ltd., New Delhi, 1987.

Kakar, Sudhir, *The Inner World*, 2nd edn., Oxford University Press, New Delhi, 1982 (paperback).

Kashyap, Anibiran, *Governors' Role in the Indian Constitution*, Lancer Books, New Delhi, 1993.

Kashyap, Subhash and Kashyap, Savita, *The Politics of Power*, National Publishing House, Delhi, 1974.

Kashyap, Subhash (ed.), *N. M. Kaul, and S. L. Shakdhar: Practice and Procedure of Parliament*, Lok Sabha Secretariat/Metropolitan, New Delhi, 1991.

————, *Reforming the Constitution*, UBSPD Publications, New Delhi, 1992.

————(ed.), *Perspectives on the Constitution*, India International Centre/Shipra Publications, New Delhi, 1993.

————, *History of the Parliament in India*, Centre for Policy Research/Shipra Publications, New Delhi (two volumes published of six projected).

Kaul, Vimla, *India Since Independence: 1947–1977*, Sagar Publications, New Delhi 1978, vols 1–9.

Kennedy, Charles H. and Louscher, David J. (eds), *Civil Military Interaction in Asia and Africa*, E. J. Brill, Leiden, 1991.

Khanna. H. R., *Neither Roses Nor Thorns*, Eastern Book Company, Lucknow, 1985.

————, *Judiciary in India and Judicial Practice*, Ajoy Law House/S. C. Sarkar & Sons Pvt. Ltd., Calcutta, 1985.

Kochanek, Stanley A., *The Congress Party in India*, Princeton University Press, Princeton, NJ, 1968.

Kogekar, S. V. and Park, Richard L., *Reports on the Indian General Elections, 1951–52*, Popular Book Depot, Bombay, 1956.

Kohli, Atul (ed.), *India's Democracy*, Princeton University Press, Princeton, NJ, 1988.

————, *Democracy and Discontent*, Cambridge University Press, Cambridge, 1990.

Kothari, Rajni, *Politics in India*, Orient Longman Ltd., New Delhi, 1970.

Kumaramangalam, S. Mohan, *Judicial Appointments*, Oxford and IBH Publishing Co., New Delhi, 1973.

————, *Coal Industry in India: Nationalization and Tasks Ahead*, Oxford and IBH Publishing Co., New Delhi, 1973.

Kunhi Krishnan, T. V., *Chavan and the Troubled Decade*, Somaiya Publications Pvt. Ltd., Bombay, 1971.

Laski, Harold, *A Grammar of Politics*, George Allen and Unwin, London, 1960.

Limaye, Madhu, *The New Constitutional Amendments: Death-Knell of Popular Liberties*, Allied Publishers Pvt. Ltd., New Delhi, 1977.

————, *Contemporary Indian Politics*, Radiant Publishers, New Delhi, 1987.

————, *Cabinet Government in India*, Radiant Publishers, New Delhi, 1989.

————, *Janata Party Experiment*, 2 vols, B. R. Publishing Corporation, New Delhi, 1994.

Mahajan, Mehr Chand, *Looking Back*, Asia Publishing House, New York, NY, 1963.

————, *Preserving Unity of India*, The Sulakhani Devi Mahajan Trust, New Delhi, 1970.

Mahtab, H. K., *While Serving My Nation*, Vidyapuri, Cuttack, 1986.

Malaviya, H. D., *CIA: Its Real Face*, Rajkamal Prakashan, New Delhi, 1975.

Malaviya, K. D., *Socialist Ideology of Congress: A Study in its Evolution*, A Socialist Congressman Publication, New Delhi, 1966.

Malhotra, Inder, *Indira Gandhi: A Personal and Political Biography*, Hodder & Stoughton, London, 1989.

Malik, Surendra (ed.), *The Fundamental Rights Case: The Critics Speak*, Eastern Book Company, Lucknow, 1975.

Manor, James (ed.), *Nehru to the Nineties*, University of British Columbia Press, Vancouver, 1994 (paperback).

Mansingh, Surjeet, *Historical Dictionary of India*, The Scarecow Press, Inc., Lanham, MD, 1996.

Mehta, Ashoka, *Who Owns India?*, Chedana Prakashan Ltd., Hyderabad, 1950.

Mehta, Hemangini (ed.), *Election Manifestos, 1971*, Awake India Publications, New Delhi, 1971.

Menon, V. P, *The Integration of the Indian States*, Longmans Green and Co., London, 1956.

Merillat, H. C. L., *Land and the Constitution in India*, Columbia University Press, New York, 1970. (Published in India by N. M. Tripathi Pvt. Ltd., Bombay, 1970).

Mirchandani, G. G. (ed.), *India Backgrounders*, printed and published by G. G. Mirchandani, New Delhi, 1976ff.

———, *Reporting India, 1977*, Abhinav Publications, New Delhi.

———, *The People's Verdict*, Vikas Publishing House Pvt. Ltd., New Delhi, 1980.

Mishra, S. N., *The Crisis, the Country, the Congress*, Congress Forum for Socialist Action, New Delhi, 1967.

Mookerji, Radha Kumud, *The Fundamental Unity of India*, Bharatiya Vidya Bhavan, Bombay, 1960 (1914).

Morris-Jones, W. H., *Parliament in India*, Longmans Green and Co., London, 1957.

———, *The Government and Politics of India*, Hutchinson University Library, London, 1964.

———, *Politics, Mainly Indian*, Orient Longman, New Delhi, 1978.

Mukerjee, Hiren, *The Gentle Colossus*, Oxford University Press, New Delhi, 1986 (paperback).

Mukarji, Nirmal, and Arora, Balveer (eds), *Federalism in India: Origins and Development*, Centre for Policy Research/Vikas Publishing House Pvt. Ltd., New Delhi, 1992.

Mukarji, Nirmal and Banerjee, Ashis, *Democracy, Federalism and the Future of India's Unity*, Centre for Policy Research/Uppal Publishing House, New Delhi, 1987.

Munshi, K. M., *The Bombay High Court: Half a Century of Reminiscences*, Bharatiya Vidya Bhavan, Bombay, 1963.

Myrdal, Gunnar, *Indian Economic Planning in its Broader Setting*, Congress Party in Parliament, New Delhi, 1958.

Naipaul, V. S., *India: A Million Mutinies Now*, Penguin Books, London, 1992 (paperback).

Nanda, B. R., *Jawaharlal Nehru*, Oxford University Press, New Delhi, 1995.

———, *The Nehrus: Motilal and Jawaharlal*, George Allen and Unwin Ltd., London, 1962.

Narayan, Jayaprakash, *Toward Total Revolution: Politics in India*, Popular Prakashan, Bombay, 1978.

———, *Prison Diary*, Shah, A. B. (ed.), University of Washington Press, Seattle, WA, 1978.

Narayanan, V. N. and Sabharwal, Jyoti (eds), *India at 50: Bliss of Hope, Burden of Reality*, Sterling Publishers Pvt. Ltd., New Delhi, 1997.

Nayar, Kuldip, *The Judgement*, Vikas Publishing House Pvt. Ltd., New Delhi, 1977.

———(ed.), *Supersession of Judges*, Indian Book Company, New Delhi, 1973.

Nehru, B. K., *Nice Guys Finish Second*, Viking/Penguin Books, New Delhi, 1997.

———, *Thoughts on Our Present Discontents*, Allied Publishers Pvt. Ltd., New Delhi, 1986.

Nehru, Jawaharlal, *The Unity of India*, 3rd impression, Lindsay Drumond, London, 1948 (1941).

———, *The Discovery of India*, 4th edn., Meridian Books Ltd., London, 1956 (1946).

———, *An Autobiography*, The Bodley Head, London, 1958 (reprint).

————, *Letters to Chief Ministers*, Parthasarthi, G. (gen. ed.), 5 vols, Jawaharlal Nehru Memorial Fund/Oxford University Press, New Delhi, 1989 (reprint).

Noorani, A. G., *India's Constitution & Politics*, Jaico Publishing House, Bombay, 1970.

————, (ed.), *Public Law in India*, Vikas Publishing House Pvt. Ltd., New Delhi, 1982.

————, *The Presidential System: The Indian Debate*, Sage Publications, New Delhi, 1989.

————, *Indian Affairs: The Constitutional Dimension*, Konark Publishers Pvt. Ltd., Delhi, 1990.

————, *Indian Affairs: The Political Dimension*, Konark Publishers Pvt. Ltd., Delhi, 1990.

Norman, Dorothy (ed.), *Indira Gandhi: Letters to an American Friend, 1950–1984*, Harcourt Brace Jovanovitch, New York, NY, 1985.

Oldenburg, Philip (ed.), *India Briefing* (annual 1987–96), Asia Society/M. E. Sharpe, New York, NY.

Overstreet Gene D. and Windmiller, Marshall (eds), *Communism In India*, University of California Press, Berkeley, CA, 1959.

Palkhivala, N. A., *Our Constitution, Defaced and Defiled*, Macmillan, New Delhi, 1975.

————, *We, the Nation*, UBS Publishers and Distributors Ltd., New Delhi, 1994.

Panandiker, V. A. Pai and Nandy, Ashis (eds), *Contemporary India*, Tata/McGraw Hill, New Delhi, 1988.

Panandiker, V. A. Pai and Mehra, Ajoy K., *The Indian Cabinet: A Study in Governance*, Centre for Policy Research/Konark Publishers Pvt. Ltd., New Delhi, 1996.

Pandit, H. N., *The PM's President*, S. Chand and Co. Pvt. Ltd., New Delhi, 1974.

Patel, Manibehn, and Nandurkar, G. M. (eds), *Sardar's Letters, Mostly Unknown*, Sardar Vallabhbhai Patel Smarak Bhavan, Ahmedabad, 1983.

Patil, S. K., *My Years with Congress*, Parchure Prakashan Mandir, Bombay, 1991.

Pillai, S. Devadas (ed.), *The Incredible Elections: 1977*, Popular Prakashan, Bombay, 1977.

Prasad, S. and Mehrotra, B. N., *Defence of India Law and Rules*, 4 vols, Law Publishers, Allahabad, 1963.

Rajagopalachari, C., *Our Democracy*, B. G. Paul & Co., Madras, 1957.

Rama Jois, M., *Historic Legal Battle*, M. R. Vimala, Bangalore, 1977.

Ramakant (ed.), *Nation-building in South Asia*, 2 vols, University of Rajasthan/ South Asian Publishers, New Delhi, 1991.

Reddy, N. Sanjiva, *Without Fear or Favour: Reminiscences and Reflections of a President*, Allied Publishers Ltd., New Delhi, 1989.

Reddy, P. Jaganmohan, *Social Justice and the Constitution*, Andhra University Press, Vishakhapatnam, 1976.

————, *We Have a Republic: Can We Keep It*, Department of Law, Sri Venkateswara University, Tirupati, 1984.

Roy, Ramashray and Sisson, Richard (eds), *Diversity and Dominance in Indian Politics*, 2 vols, Sage Publications, New Delhi, 1990.

Rudolph, Lloyd I. and Rudolph, Suzanne Hoeber, *In Pursuit of Lakshmi*, University of Chicago Press, Chicago, IL, 1987.

Sachs, I., Hobsbawm, E. J. et al., *Peasants in History: Essays in Honour of Daniel Thorner*, Oxford University Press, Calcutta, 1980.

Sahay, S., *A Close Look*, Allied Publishers Pvt. Ltd., New Delhi, 1987.

Sahgal, Nayantara, *Indira Gandhi: Her Road to Power*, MacDonald & Co., London, 1982.

Sampurnanand, *Memories and Reflections*, Asia Publishing House, Bombay, 1962.

Santhanam, K., *Planning and Plain Thinking*, Higginbothoms Pvt. Ltd., Madras, 1958.

————, *Union-State Relations in India*, Indian Institute of Public Administration/ Asia Publishing House, London, 1960.

Sarkar, Bidyut (ed.), *P. N. Haksar, Our Times and the Man*, Allied Publishers, Pvt. Ltd., New Delhi, 1989.

Sarkar, R. C. S., *Union-State Relations in India*, Institute of Constitutional and Parliamentary Studies/National Publishing House, New Delhi, 1986.

Sathe, S. P., *Constitutional Amendments, 1950–1988*, N. M. Tripathi Pvt. Ltd., Bombay, 1989.

————et al., *Democracy and Constitution*, Citizens for Democracy, Pune, 1976.

Sathe, Vasant, *Two Swords in One Scabbard: A Case for Presidential Form of Parliamentary Democracy*, NIB Publishers, New Delhi, 1989.

Schubert, Glendon, and Danelski, David J. (eds), *Comparative Judicial Behaviour*, Oxford University Press, New York, 1969.

Seervai, H. M., *The Emergency, Future Safeguards and the Habeas Corpus Case*, N. M. Tripathi Pvt. Ltd., Bombay, 1978.

————, *Constitutional Law of India*, 3rd edn., 3 vols, N. M. Tripathi Pvt. Ltd., Bombay, 1983.

Seshan, N. K., *With Three Prime Ministers*, Wiley Eastern Ltd., New Delhi, 1993.

Setalvad, M. C., *The Common Law in India*, N. M. Tripathi Pvt. Ltd., Bombay, 1970 (reprint).

————, *My Life, Law and Other Things*, N. M. Tripathi Pvt. Ltd., 1971.

————et al., *Parliament: Emergency and Personal Freedom: Opinions of Jurists*, Bar Association of India, New Delhi, 1963.

Sethi, J. D., *India's Static Power Structure*, Vikas Publications Pvt. Ltd., New Delhi, 1969.

Shankardass, Rani Dhavan, *Vallabhbhai Patel*, Orient Longman Ltd., New Delhi, 1988.

Sharma, Dhirendra, *The Janata (People's) Struggle*, A Philosophy and Social Action Publication, New Delhi, 1977.

Sharma, Mool Chand, *Justice P. N. Bhagwati: Court Constitution and Human Rights*, Universal Book Traders, Delhi 1995.

Sheth, Pravin, *Political Developments in Gujarat*, Karnavati Publications, Ahmedabad, 1998.

Shiva Rao, B., *The Framing of India's Constitution*, 5 vols, The Indian Institute of Public Administration/N. M. Tripathi Pvt. Ltd., Bombay, 1968.

Shourie, Arun, *Symptoms of Fascism*, Vikas Publishing House Pvt. Ltd., New Delhi, 1978.

———, *Institutions in the Janata Phase*, Popular Prakashan Pvt. Ltd., Bombay, 1980.

———, *Mrs Gandhi's Second Reign*, Vikas Publishing House Pvt. Ltd., New Delhi, 1984.

Shrivastava, S. and Kotare, D. (eds), *Revolutionary Visionary: Dr Shankar Dayal Sharma Felicitation Volume*, Dr Shankar Dayal Sharma Felicitation Volume Organizing Committee, Bhopal, 1973.

Singh, Charan, *India's Poverty and Its Solution*, Asia Publishing House, New York, 1964.

Singh, Hari Kishore, *A History of the Praja Socialist Party*, Narendra Prakashan, Lucknow, 1959.

Singh, Khushwant, *Women and Men in My Life*, UBS Publishers Distributors Ltd., New Delhi, 1995.

Singh, L. P., *Office of Prime Minister, Retrospect and Prospect*, Centre for Policy Research, New Delhi, 1995.

Singh, Mahendra P. (ed.), *V. N. Shukla's Constitution of India*, 9th edn., Eastern Book Company, Lucknow, 1994.

Singh, Satinder, *Communists in Congress: Kumaramangalam's Thesis*, D. K. Publishing House, New Delhi, 1973.

Singh, Zail, *Memoirs of Giani Zail Singh: The Seventh President of India*, Har-Anand Publications Pvt. Ltd., New Delhi, 1997.

Singhvi, L. M., *Parliament and Constitutional Amendment*, Institute of Constitutional and Parliamentary Studies, 1970.

———, *Freedom on Trial*, Vikas Publishing House Pvt. Ltd., New Delhi, 1991.

———, (ed.), *Fundamental Rights and Constitutional Amendment*, Institute of Constitutional and Parliamentary Studies, New Delhi, 1971.

———, (ed.), *Bank Nationalization and the Supreme Court Judgement*, Institute of Constitutional and Parliamentary Studies, New Delhi, 1971.

Sinha, B. P., *Reminiscences and Reflections of a Chief Justice*, B. R. Publishing Corporation, Delhi, 1985.

Sinha, J. M. L., *The Constitution, the Judiciary and the People*, Popular Prakashan, Bombay, 1983.

Siwach, J. R., *Dynamics of Indian Governments and Politics*, 2nd enlarged edn., Sterling Publishers Pvt. Ltd., New Delhi, 1990.

Sorabjee, Soli J., *The Emergency, Censorship and The Press in India, 1975–77*, Central News Agency Pvt. Ltd., New Delhi, 1977.

———et al., *The Governor: Sage or Saboteur*, Roli Books International, New Delhi, 1985.

Spratt, P., *Hindu Culture and Personality*, Delhi Printers Prakashan, Delhi, 1977.

Srinivas, M. N., *Social Change in India*, Orient Longman, New Delhi, 1987 (paperback).

Srivastava, C. P., *Lal Bahadur Shastri: A Life of Truth in Politics*, Oxford University Press, New Delhi, 1995.

Subramaniam, C., *Hand of Destiny*, vol. 1, *Turning Point*, Bharatiya Vidya Bhavan, Bombay, 1993.

Swaroop, V., *Law of Preventive Detention*, D.L.T. Publications, Delhi, 1990.

Thapar, Raj, *All These Years*, Seminar Publications, New Delhi, 1991.

Tirumalai, R., *TTK. The Dynamic Innovator*, TT Maps and Publications Pvt. Ltd., Madras, 1988.

Vasudev, Uma, *Two Faces of Indira Gandhi*, Vikas Publishing House Pvt. Ltd., New Delhi, 1977.

Venkataramiah, V. (ed.), *Essays on Constitutional Law* (Alladi Krishnaswamy Aiyar Memorial Volume), Concept Publishing Company, New Delhi, 1986.

Wadhwa, D. C., *Repromulgation of Ordinances: A Fraud on the Constitution of India*, Gokhale Institute of Politics and Economics, Pune, 1983.

Wadley, Susan S., *Struggling with Destiny in Karimpur, 1925–1984*, University of California Press, Berkeley, CA, 1994.

Weiner, Myron, *Sons of the Soil*, Princeton University Press, Princeton, NJ, 1978.

Williams, Stephen K. (ed.), *Cases Argued and Decided in the Supreme Court of the United States*, The Lawyers Cooperative Publishing Company, Rochester, NY, 1926.

Wiser, William and Wiser, Charlotte, *Behind Mud Walls, 1930–1960, With a Sequel: The Village in 1970*, University of California Press, Berkeley, CA, 1971.

World Bank, *Primary Education in India*, World Bank, Washington, DC, 1997.

Zaidi, A. M., *Aloud and Straight: Frank Talks at Party Meetings*, Indian Institute of Applied Political Research, New Delhi, 1984.

————, *Not by Class War: A Study of Congress Policy on Land Reform During the Last 100 Years*, Indian Institute of Applied Political Research, New Delhi, 1985.

————, *The Directives of the Congress High Command to Ministers and Chief Ministers*, Indian Institute of Applied Political Research, New Delhi, 1986.

————, *Encyclopaedia of the Indian National Congress*, S. Chand and Company Ltd., New Delhi, vols 1–28 until 1994.

Zakaria, Rafiq (ed.), *A Study of Nehru*, Times of India Publications, Bombay, 2nd revised edn., 1960.

Zins, Max Jean, *Strains on Indian Democracy*, ABC Publishing House, New Delhi, 1988.

Articles

Austin, Granville, 'The Constitution, Society, and Law', in Oldenburg (1993).

Bal Krishna, 'Putting an End to "Kin Sindrome"', *Hindustan Times*, 15 April 1994.

Baxi, Upendra, 'The Constitutional Quicksands of *Kesavananda Bharati* and the Twenty-fifth Amendment', in Malik (1975).

Beg, M. H., 'Our Legal System: Does it need a Change?', *Journal of the Bar Council of India*, vol. 9, no. 2, 1982.

Bhambri, C. P., 'Role of Paramilitary Forces in Centre–State Relations', *Economic and Political Weekly*, vol. 13, no. 17.

————, 'Federal Politics: A Trend Report', *A Survey of Research in Political Science,* Allied Publishers Pvt. Ltd., New Delhi, 1981.

Bhasin, Prem, 'The Deathly Drama', *Janata,* Annual Number, 1971.

Bhattacharjea, Ajit, 'A Tragedy of Errors', *Indian Express,* 8 October 1977.

Bhattacharya, J. K., 'Development Planning and Its Impact on Union–State Relations', *Journal of Constitutional and Parliamentary Studies,* vol. 6, no. 3, 1972.

Blackshield, A. R., '"Fundamental Rights" and the Institutional Viability of the Indian Supreme Court', *Journal of the Indian Law Institute,* vol. 8, no. 2, 1966.

Bombwall, K. R., 'The Finance Commission and Union–State Relations in India', *Indian Journal of Public Administration,* vol. 10, no. 2, 1964.

————, 'Federalism and National Unity in India', *Journal of Constitutional and Parliamentary Studies,* vol. 1, no. 1, 1967.

Chelliah, Raja, 'Towards a Decentralized Polity: Outlines of a Proposal', *Mainstream,* 25 May 1991.

Conrad, Dieter, 'Limitation of Amendment Procedures and the Constituent Power', *The Indian Yearbook of International Affairs, 1966–1967,* New Delhi, 1970.

Derrett, J. Duncan M., 'Social and Political Thoughts and Institutions', in Basham (1989).

Deshpande, V. S., 'High Court Judges: Appointment and Transfer', *Journal of the Indian Law Institute,* vol. 27, no. 2, 1985.

Dhar, P. N., 'The Prime Minister's Office', in Sarkar (1989).

Dhavan, Rajeev, 'President's Rule in the States', *Journal of Constitutional and Parliamentary Studies,* vol. 3, no. 4, 1969.

————, 'The Basic Structure Doctrine—A Footnote Comment' in Dhavan and Jacob (1978).

————, 'The Government versus the Supreme Court', *Statesman* (New Delhi), 26 June 1981.

————, 'Amending the Amendment: The Constitution (Forty-fifth Amendment) Bill, 1978', *Journal of the Indian Law Institute,* vol. 20, no. 2, 1978.

Dumont, René, 'India's Agricultural Defeat', *New Statesman,* 19 December 1959.

Dutt, R. C, 'Indian Bureaucracy in Transition', in Sarkar (1989).

Gadbois, George H. Jr., 'Indian Supreme Court Judges: A Portrait', *Law and Society Review,* vol. 3, no. 2, 1968.

————, 'Selection, Background Characteristics and Voting Behaviour of Supreme Court Judges, 1950–59', in Schubert and Danelski (1969).

Ganguly, Sumit, 'From the Defence of the Nation to the Aid of the Civil: The Army in Contemporary India', in Kennedy and Louscher (1991).

Gehlot, N. S., 'Indian Federalism and the Problem of Law and Order', *Journal of Constitutional and Parliamentary Studies,* vol. 14, no. 2, 1980.

Guhan, S., 'Constitutional Collapse: In Tamil Nadu or in Delhi?', *Frontline,* 16 February–1 March, 1991.

————, 'Federalism and the New Political Economy in India', in Arora and Verney (1995).

Hart, Henry C., 'Political Leadership in India', in Kohli (1988).

Hegde, Ramakrishna, 'Plea for a United States of India', *Mainstream*, 15 June 1991.

Hewitt, Vernon, 'The Prime Minister and Parliament' in Manor (1994).

Jacob, Alice, 'Centre–State Governmental Relations in the Indian Federal System', *Journal of the Indian Law Institute*, vol. 10, 1968.

Jacob, Alice and Dhavan, Rajeev, 'The Dissolution Case: Politics at the Bar of the Supreme Court', *Journal of the Indian Law Institute*, vol. 19, no. 4, 1977.

Jain, H. M., 'Presidential Prerogatives in a Situation of Multipartite Contest for Power: A Case Study', *Journal of Constitutional and Parliamentary Studies*, vol. 16, nos. 1–2, 1982.

Jha, Prem Shankar, 'Authoritarianism on the Right', *Financial Times*, 3 November 1980.

Kashyap, Subhash C., 'The Ninth Lok Sabha: Socio-Economic Analysis of Membership', *Journal of Parliamentary Information*, March 1990.

Katyal, K. K., 'A Disconcerting Scenario: Current Controversies and Confrontationalist Trends', *Hindu*, 29 December 1980.

Khanna, H. R., 'Shall We Toss for a President?', *Times of India*, 19 April 1981.

Kochanek, Stanley, 'Mrs Gandhi's Pyramid: the New Congress', in Hart (1976).

Kogekar, S. V., 'Constitutional Amendment Bill', *Economic and Political Weekly*, vol. 9, no. 42, 16 October 1976.

Koppell, G. O., 'The Emergency, The Courts and Indian Democracy', *Journal of the Indian Law Institute*, vol. 8, no. 3, 1966.

Kothari, Rajni, 'The Indian Enterprise Today', *Daedalus*, Fall 1989.

Kothari, Smitu, 'Whose Independence? The Social Impact of Economic Reform in India', *Journal of International Affairs*, New York, vol. 51, no. 1, 1997.

Kripalani, J. B., 'Presidential Form of Government', *Hindu*, 5 January 1981.

Krishna, Gopal, 'National Integration: A Lost Cause?', in Ramakant (1981).

Kumaramangalam, S. Mohan, 'Wrong to Treat Property as a Fundamental Right', *Patriot*, 4 December 1969.

———, 'Chief Justice of India: Criteria for Choice', in Nayar (1973).

Mahajan, Mehr Chand, 'A Pillar of Justice', in Zakaria (1960).

Maheshwari, Shriram, 'The Centre–State Consultative Machinery', in Datta (1984).

Menon, V. K. Krishna, 'Desires Without Deeds Breed Pestilence', in *The Challenge to Democracy*, Publications Division, Delhi, 1953.

Mody, Nawaz, 'Role of Governor Since 1967', *Journal of Constitutional and Parliamentary Studies*, Special Number on Centre–State Relations, 1986.

Mozoomdar, Ajit, 'The Political Economy of Modern Federalism', in Arora and Verney (1995).

Nakade, Shivraj, 'The Constitution (Twenty-fifth) Amendment: A New Order', *Journal of Constitutional and Parliamentary Studies*, vol. 6, no. 3, 1972.

———, 'Article 356 of the Constitution: Its Uses and Misuses', in *Union-State Relations in India*, Institute of Constitutional and Parliamentary Studies, New Delhi, 1983 (reprint).

Nariman, Fali S., 'Why Flog a Dead Horse', *Indian Express*, 31 January 1981.

———, 'Removal and Transfer of Judges', *Indian Express*, 10 September 1981.

———, 'Chief Justice Sikri: A Good Judge, A Great Person', *Indian Express*, 19 October 1992.

———, 'The President's Page', *The Indian Advocate*, Journal of the Bar Association of India, vol. 25, 1993.

Narayan, Jayaprakash, 'An Essential Requisite of National Integration', *India Quarterly*, vol. 17, no. 4, 1961.

Nayar, Kuldip, 'Unfortunate Confrontation', *Tribune* (Chandigarh), 30 July 1981.

———, 'How RNG Fought the Emergency', *The Indian-American*, November 1991.

Nehru, B. K., 'The Role of Governor Under the Indian Constitution', *Silver Jubilee, Gauhati High Court*, Souvenir Committee, Gauhati, 1974.

Nehru, Jawaharlal, 'The Basic Approach', *AICC Economic Review*, 15 August 1958.

Noorani, A. G., 'The Constitutional Crisis', *Indian Express*, 13 December 1974.

———, 'The Presidential System', *Indian Express*, 3 July 1980.

———, 'Transfer of High Court Judges', *Economic and Political Weekly*, 20 September 1980.

———, 'The Supreme Court and Constitutional Amendments', in Noorani (1982).

———, 'A Baleful Legacy', *Frontline*, 12 February 1993.

Palkhivala, N.A., 'Should We Alter Our Constitution', *Illustrated Weekly of India*, 4 January 1976.

———, 'The Supreme Court's Judgement in the Judges' Case', *Journal of the Bar Council of India*, vol. 9, no. 2, 1982.

Panandiker, V. A. Pai, 'The Preventive Detention Issue', *Hindustan Times*, 23 October 1979.

———, 'A Job Not Well Done', *Hindustan Times*, 1 January 1994.

Ramasubramaniam, K. A., 'Historical Development and Essential Features of the Federal System', in Mukarji and Arora (1992).

Rao, M. Govinda, 'Indian Fiscal Federalism From a Comparative Perspective', in Arora and Verney (1995).

Reddy, G. K., 'It's Quality, Not Form of Government that Matters', *Hindu*, 2 November 1980.

Rubinoff, Arthur G., 'The Changing Nature of India's Parliament', in Chowdhari, Reeta Tremblay et al. (eds), *Indian/Pakistani/American Reflections on the 50th Anniversary of India's Independence*, B. R. Publications, Delhi 1998.

Sahay, S., 'The Financial Disequilibrium', *Statesman*, 13 June 1973.

———, 'Shiv Shankar's Great Design', *Statesman* (New Delhi), 11 April 1981.

———, 'A Judiciary in Executive's Image', *Journal of the Bar Council of India*, vol. 9, no. 2, 1982.

———, 'What "Forces of Change" Are up To', *Statesman*, 29 January 1983.

Santhanam, K., 'Federalism and Uniformity', *Swarajya*, 1 May 1971.

Sathe, S. P., 'Limitations on Constitutional Amendment: "Basic Structure" Principle Re-examined', in Dhavan and Jacob (1978).

Seervai, H. M., 'Fundamental Rights: A Basic Issue', in three parts, *Times of India* (Bombay), 14, 15, 16 February 1955.

Sen, Asoke K., 'Role of the Governor in the Emerging Pattern of Centre–State Relations', *Journal of Constitutional and Parliamentary Studies*, vol. 5, no. 3, 1971.

Setalvad, M.C., 'Backlog of Court Cases', in Chaudhary (1984).

Shah, Ghanshyam, 'Grassroots Mobilisation in Indian Politics' in Kohli (1988).

Sharada Prasad, H. Y., 'Vision and Warm Heart', in Sarkar (1989).

Sheth, D. L., 'Social Basis of the Political Crisis', *Seminar*, January, 1982.

———, 'Caste and Class: Social Reality and Political Representations', in Panandiker and Nandy (1998).

Shiviah, 'The Governor in the Indian Political System', *Journal of Constitutional and Parliamentary Studies*, vol. 2, no. 4, 1968.

Singh, S. Nihal, 'Toward Presidency', *Indian Express*, 10 June 1981.

Singh, Satinder, 'Giani the Great', *The Sunday Free Press Journal*, 26 July 1987.

Singh, Tarlokh, 'Jawaharlal Nehru and the Five-Year Plans', *Yojana*, 7 June 1965.

Singhal, M. M., 'Devolution and Development of Indian Federal Finance', Special Number on Centre–State Relations in India, *Journal of Constitutional and Parliamentary Studies*, 1986.

Siwach, J. R., 'The President's Rule and the Politics of Suspending and Dissolving the State Assemblies', *Journal of Constitutional and Parliamentary Studies*, vol. 11, no. 4, 1977.

Sorabjee, Soli J., 'In Nehru's Judgement', *Sunday Review Times of India*, 30 April 1989.

Talbot, Phillips, 'Raising a Cry for Secession', American Universities Field Staff Report, PT-8, New York, 1957.

Thapar, Romesh, 'The Real Meat of the Emergency', *Economic and Political Weekly*, 2 April 1977.

———, 'The Constitutional Fixers', *Economic and Political Weekly*, 15 September 1984.

Tripathi, P. K., 'Kesavananda Bharati v The State of Kerala—Who Wins', in Malik (1975).

Verney, Douglas V., 'Are All Federations Federal? The United States, Canada and India', in Arora and Verney (1995).

Vira, Dharma, 'The Administrator and the Politician', Punjab, Haryana and Delhi Chamber of Commerce, New Delhi, 1979.

Vohra, N. N., 'The Rusting Steel Frame', in Narayanan and Sabharwal (1997).

Whitecombe, Elizabeth, 'Whatever Happened to the Zamindars?', in Sachs and Hobsbawm (1980).

Newspapers and Periodicals Consulted and Cited

Amrita Bazaar Patrika

Asian Recorder

Blitz

Daedalus

Deccan Chronicle

Deccan Herald

Economic and Political Weekly
Economist
Economic Times
Financial Express
Financial Times
Free Press Journal
Frontline
Himmat
The Hindu
Hindustan Standard
The Hindustan Times
Illustrated Weekly
India Today
The Indian-American
Indian Express
The Indian Nation
Indian News and Features Alliance
Indian News Chronicle
Janata
Link
Madam Figaro
Mainstream
Mankind

Motherland
National Herald
New Age
New Statesman
The New York Times
Organiser
Patriot
The Pioneer
Samachar
Socialist India
The Statesman (New Delhi and Calcutta edns.)
Sunday Mail
The Sunday Free Press Journal
Sunday Standard
Sunday Statesman
The Sunday Times
Swarajya
The Times of India (New Delhi and Bombay edns.)
The Tribune (Chandigarh)
Young Indian

Journals Frequently Used

Annual Survey of Indian Law, vols 1–21.
Delhi Law Review
Journal of the Bar Council of India
Journal of the Bar Association of India
Journal of the Indian Law Institute
Journal of Constitutional and Parliamentary Studies.

INDEX